Holiday Symbols and Customs

4th Edition

J.Albert Adams
Academy Media Center

Holiday Symbols and Customs

A Guide to the Legend and Lore Behind the Traditions, Rituals, Foods, Games, Animals, and Other Symbols and Activities Associated with Holidays and Holy Days, Feasts and Fasts, and Other Celebrations, Covering Ancient, Calendar, Religious, Historic, Folkloric, National, Promotional, and Sporting Events, as Observed in the United States and Around the World

4th Edition

Edited by Helene Henderson

PO Box 31-1640 • Detroit, MI 48231-1640

Cherie D. Abbey, *Managing Editor*
Helene Henderson, *Editor*
Peggy Daniels, Tanya Gulevich, and Sue Ellen Thompson, *Writers*
Allison A. Beckett and Mary Butler, *Research Staff*

* * *

Peter E. Ruffner, *Publisher*
Matthew P. Barbour, *Senior Vice President*

* * *

Elizabeth Collins, *Research and Permissions Coordinator*
Kevin M. Hayes, *Operations Manager*
Cherry Stockdale, *Permissions Assistant*
Shirley Amore, Martha Johns, and Kirk Kauffman, *Administrative Staff*

Copyright © 2009 Omnigraphics, Inc.
ISBN 978-0-7808-0990-1

Library of Congress Cataloging-in-Publication Data

Holiday symbols and customs : a guide to the legend and lore behind the traditions, rituals, foods, games, animals, and other symbols and activities associated with holidays and holy days, feasts and fasts, and other celebrations, covering ancient, calendar, religious, historic, folkloric, national, promotional, and sporting events, as observed in the United States and around the world. -- 4th ed. / edited by Helene Henderson.
   p. cm.
   Rev. ed. of: Holiday symbols and customs / by Sue Ellen Thompson. 3rd ed.
   Includes bibliographical references and index.
   Summary: "Describes the origins of 323 holidays around the world. Explains where, when, and how each event is celebrated, with detailed information on the symbols and customs associated with the holiday. Includes contact information and web sites for related organizations"-- Provided by publisher.
   ISBN 978-0-7808-0990-1 (hardcover : alk. paper) 1. Holidays. 2. Festivals. 3. Fasts and feasts. I. Henderson, Helene, 1963- II. Thompson, Sue Ellen, 1948- Holiday symbols and customs.

GT3930.T48 2009
394.26--dc22   2008028403

The information in this publication was compiled from sources cited and from sources considered reliable. While every possible effort has been made to ensure reliability, the publisher will not assume liability for damages caused by inaccuracies in the data, and makes no warranty, express or implied, on the accuracy of the information contained herein.

This book is printed on acid-free paper meeting the ANSI Z39.48 Standard. The infinity symbol that appears above indicates that the paper in this book meets that standard.

Printed in the United States

Table of Contents

Preface

eople everywhere gather to celebrate many different types of holidays and festivals: religious holidays, such as Christmas and Ramadan; calendar/seasonal festivals, such as New Year's and the Summer Solstice; national holidays, such as Thanksgiving and Bastille Day; sporting events, such as the Daytona 500 and World Cup Soccer; promotional days, such as Earth Day and World AIDS Day; as well as ancient and folkloric days, such as May Day and Halloween. Holidays highlight the day-to-day lives of people of all cultures and reflect their history and identity. Through the ritual of commemoration, we honor the past, mark the present, and anticipate the future.

Symbols and customs associated with holidays emerge, migrate, undergo transformations, vary among different peoples and places, and sometimes fade away. *Holiday Symbols and Customs,* 4th Edition, provides an introduction to the myriad ways in which people celebrate and the meanings attached to these traditions. It also presents the background of 323 of these holidays and describes more than 1,000 symbols and customs associated with them.

Audience

Holiday Symbols and Customs can be used by students for class assignments, by general readers interested in holidays, and by teachers and librarians gathering information for units on holiday celebrations. The essays are written in a style designed to make them accessible to both school-age and adult readers. The book is organized in a way that makes information on specific holidays and customs easy to locate.

The Plan of the Work

Holiday Symbols and Customs includes entries that are arranged alphabetically by holiday name. Holiday entries begin with bold-faced headings that outline the following:

- **Name of Holiday,** including alternate names in parentheses, where appropriate
- **Type of Holiday,** identifying whether it is an ancient, calendar/seasonal, folkloric, historic, national, promotional, religious, or sporting holiday

- **Date of Observation,** giving both specific and movable dates, including any variants in different parts of the world

- **Where Celebrated,** outlining in which cities, states, or countries and for which religions a holiday is commemorated

- **Symbols and Customs,** listing the symbols and customs associated with each holiday

- **Colors,** noting those associated with the holiday, if any, as well as their symbolic meaning

- **Related Holidays,** showing other holidays in the book associated with this particular celebration

This first section is followed by a brief essay on the Origins of the holiday, including historic and folkloric information on the background of the commemoration. This is followed by a section on the Symbols and Customs attached to the holiday. Each Symbol or Custom is listed in alphabetical order, with detailed information on its origin and meaning. Each entry ends with suggestions for Further Reading and Web Sites, providing additional resources for those who want to attend an event or find out more about how it is celebrated.

Within the essays, cross-references to symbols and customs found in that specific holiday entry are set in small capital letters. Cross-references to holiday entries elsewhere in the book appear in bold-faced capital letters.

Because the study of holiday symbols and customs is in no way an "exact" science, the essays are based on the legend, lore, and history of what is known about each holiday. These include information about celebrations that have occurred since the dawn of humankind, such as those commemorating the seasons and the harvest, as well as events that are of more recent origin, such as the Finnish-American celebration of St. Urho's Day. Many of the essays trace how ancient celebrations have evolved in the modern era and how some have been absorbed into modern religious or national festivals. As such, the essays delve into how holiday symbols and customs reflect on the evolution of society itself.

New in This Edition

Expanded Coverage for Existing Entries

Existing entries—those from the previous edition—have been supplemented with updated material that provides background context on religions, cultures, and calendars, as well as additional information related to the holidays and festivals. In addition, contact information and web sites have been updated.

New Entries

Fifty new entries have been added to this edition, covering a wide range of topics. Some examples include the following:

- Academy Awards, which celebrates achievement in film by granting awards each year to actors, directors, screen writers, and others from the film world;

- Cinco de Mayo, which commemorates the Battle of Puebla, part of the fight for Mexican independence;

- Iditarod, which features teams of sled dogs racing through Alaska in what has been called "the last great race on earth";

- Mabon, which the ancient Celts used to honor the arrival of the fall season and the change in the balance of light and dark that occurs with the autumn equinox;

- Ridvan, which commemorates the events that occurred over the course of twelve days that the Baha'i prophet Baha'u'llah spent in a rose garden in Baghdad, Iraq;

- Seville Fair, which began as a springtime agricultural and livestock market in the nineteenth century and has since become a week-long, city-wide celebration throughout Seville; and

- Watch Night, which began as New Year's Eve services in Methodist and Moravian churches and is now also celebrated in African-American churches to mark Watch Night on December 31, 1862, when many waited to see if Abraham Lincoln would sign the Emancipation Proclamation and free the slaves.

The selection shown here demonstrates the breadth of coverage in the many new entries in this new edition.

New Appendices

Calendars Throughout History - This new appendix provides an overview of calendar systems around the world and explains various secular and religious calendars, including the Chinese, Hindu, Jain, Buddhist, Sikh, Mayan, Aztec, Babylonian and Egyptian, Zoroastrian, Julian, Jewish, Islamic, Gregorian, Christian, and Baha'i calendars.

Tourism Information Sources - Three new appendices list tourism organizations for the following: for North America, including all U.S. states, Canada, and Mexico; for countries around the world; and for individual festivals. Each listing provides full contact information, including names, addresses, phone and fax numbers, and web sites, where available.

Entries by Type - This new appendix lists the entries in *Holiday Symbols and Customs* by type of holiday. Some events may be listed under more than one category, as applicable. The holiday types are in this order:

> Ancient
> Calendar/Seasonal
> Folkloric
> Historic
> National
> Promotional
> Religious (organized alphabetically by entry name)
> Religious (organized alphabetically by religion)
> Sporting

Other Features

Bibliography - An extensive Bibliography lists all sources consulted in the preparation of this volume.

General Index - The volume ends with a general index to the subject terms, listing all countries, nationalities, names, symbols, customs, and other terms found in the text. The subject index includes:

- the names of holidays, festivals, and celebrations (the main form of the event name, as well as alternate names);

- people and organizations;

- place names (U.S. cities and states, as well as other nations);

- the names of houses of worship; monuments and historic sites;

- saints and deities;

- religious groups and denominations;

- titles of musical, cinematic, theatrical, and literary works;

- and more.

A Note on Terminology

To designate eras, this volume uses the terms B.C.E. (before the common era) and C.E. (of the common era). B.C.E. refers to the period of time before year 1 on the Gregorian calendar, which is used throughout the western world (see Appendix A, Calendars throughout History). C.E. refers to the period of time beginning with year 1 on the Gregorian calendar. These terms are preferred here because they have no religious significance and are thus more neutral than the alternate terms, B.C. (before Christ) and A.D. (*Anno Domino*, the year of our Lord).

Your Comments Are Welcome

We welcome your comments on *Holiday Symbols and Customs*, 4th Edition, including suggestions for topics that you would like to see covered in future editions. Please address correspondence to:

Editor, *Holiday Symbols and Customs*, 4th Edition
Omnigraphics, Inc.
P.O. Box 31-1640
Detroit, MI 48231-1640

Holiday Symbols and Customs

4th Edition

Aboakyer Festival
(Aboakyir)

Type of Holiday: Religious (Effutu)
Date of Observation: First Saturday in May
Where Celebrated: Ghana
Symbols and Customs: Asafo Companies, Deer Hunt

ORIGINS

The Aboakyer Festival has been celebrated by the Effutu people, who were among the earliest settlers of Ghana, for several hundred years. It originated when the Effutu left Western Sudan and migrated to what is now the town of Winneba in the Central Region of Ghana. They brought their god, known as Penkye Otu, with them.

The Effutu wanted to celebrate their arrival in a new land and were told by their priest, who had discussed the matter with the gods, that they would have to make an annual human sacrifice. This seemed too high a price to pay, so the people appealed to Otu and he relented, saying that he would accept a live wildcat instead. But when they tried to bring him a leopard, they discovered that leopards were extremely difficult and dangerous to bring back alive to be sacrificed. Eventually a bush buck, which resembles a deer, replaced the leopard, which is why the annual ceremony is often referred to as the Deer-Hunting Festival.

Before dawn on the first Saturday in May, members of the town's two ASAFO COMPANIES meet at the beach to participate in purification rituals. They proceed first to where Penkye Otu is housed and then to the village chief's palace, where they are

1

received by the royal family. Then they set out for the bush in opposite directions, and the first to return with a live deer is declared the winner. Each team performs rituals designed to undermine the other team's strength, but both Asafo companies want someone to win because failure to catch a deer is considered to be a very bad omen. The hunter who captures it carries it on his shoulder and returns in triumph with his group to the royal palace.

The Effutu chief kills the animal, and the meat is used to make a soup that is offered to Penkye Otu. This is followed by a night of drumming, singing, and dancing until dawn. The victorious hunters are treated like heroes for keeping Penkye Otu happy so that he will bring them a bountiful year.

SYMBOLS AND CUSTOMS

Asafo Companies

The word asafo means "war people." There are twenty-four states located along Ghana's Atlantic coast, and each state is governed by a "paramount chief" who rules over the lesser chiefs of towns and villages. There can be more than half a dozen Asafo companies in a single town, and rivalries among them are quite common.

The Asafo companies were at one time charged with defending the state, but their relationship to the Ghanaian government today is far from clear-cut. The traditional Effutu rulers use them to enforce their authority, and the companies often play a role when conflicts arise between the national militia and civilians. The Asafo elders play an important role in selecting new chiefs and act as advisers after a chief has been crowned. A chief who has the Asafo companies behind him rarely has to worry about challenges to his authority.

Deer Hunt

The traditional hunt to find a sacrificial deer lies at the heart of the Aboakyer Festival. At the time the festival was instituted, deer were plentiful in Ghana. But wildlife has been exploited here as it has in many other areas of the world, and capturing a live deer is no longer a simple matter. The deer population will probably continue to dwindle as long as people kill deer for food and those who ignore wildlife protection laws aren't punished.

FURTHER READING

MacDonald, Margaret R., ed.. *The Folklore of World Holidays*. Detroit: Gale Research, 1992.
Wyllie, Robert W. "Gods, Locals, and Strangers: The Effutu Aboakyer as Visitor Attaction." *Current Anthropology* 35, No. 1 (February 1994): 78-84.

Wyllie, Robert W. "Ritual and Social Change: A Ghanian Example." *American Anthropologist* (February 1968): 21-23.

WEB SITE

Ghana Home Page
www.ghanaweb.com/GhanaHomePage/tourism/aboakyer.php

Academy Awards
(The Oscars)

Type of Holiday: Promotional
Date of Observation: Late February or early March
Where Celebrated: Hollywood, California
Symbols and Customs: Gowns, Oscars, Red Carpet, Sealed Envelope

ORIGINS

Each year the Academy of Motion Picture Arts and Sciences grants awards to individuals of outstanding achievement in the world of film. Known as the Academy Awards, this glamorous awards ceremony gathers together hundreds of famous actors, actresses, directors, producers, writers, and film technicians. Although it is an invitation-only event, the ceremony is broadcast on television and reported all over the world. It takes place in late February or early March, with awards given for films released in the previous calendar year.

The Academy of Motion Picture Arts and Sciences is a professional organization composed of top-achieving individuals involved in the world of film-making. One of the organization's goals is to encourage high quality work in the motion picture industry. For that reason the Academy instituted its annual awards ceremony. When it was founded, the Academy of Motion Picture Arts and Sciences included just thirty-six members. These days the Academy boasts over 6,000 voting members. At the first Academy Awards ceremony, fifteen individuals were honored for their contributions to the world of film. The following year just seven awards were given: best actor, best actress, best picture, best director, best writer, best cinematographer, and best art director. Currently, the Academy bestows awards in up to twenty-five different categories of achievement. Academy members vote on who will win the Academy Award. Although all members may vote in such general categories as "best picture," voting in other categories is limited to members of that particular division. For example, only film editors may vote for the "best film editing" award.

The first Academy Awards ceremony occurred on May 16, 1929, with 270 people in attendance. The event took place in the banquet room of Hollywood's Roosevelt Hotel. The banquet and awards ceremony were presided over by the actor Douglas Fairbanks, who was at that time the president of the Academy. Winners were honored with a statuette that came to be known as an OSCAR, a tradition that has continued until this day.

In that first year, the names of the award recipients were announced in advance. The following year the names of the winners were given in advance to the newspapers, which were asked not to publish the information until the ceremony was over. In 1940, the *Los Angeles Times* ignored the Academy's request and broke the news before the start of the ceremony. As a result, the ceremony organizers devised a system whereby the results of the Academy's balloting was kept secret even from Academy members. The results were revealed only when the SEALED ENVELOPE containing the name of the winner was opened at the awards ceremony.

In 1930 the Academy Awards were the subject of a live radio broadcast. Radio coverage continued to provide the public with its only live access to the event until 1953, when the Academy Awards were broadcast on television for the first time. Today the Academy Awards broadcast is seen not only in the United States, but also in 100 different countries around the world.

Until 1942 the awards ceremony included a banquet for all the guests. This custom was discontinued the following year because each year the guest list grew longer and it simply became too difficult to combine the sumptuous meal with the awards ceremony. From 1943 on, the Academy Awards ceremony was held in theaters rather than in banquet halls. In the decades that followed, the event did not settle in a permanent home but instead shifted from theater to theater. In 2002 the Academy Awards ceremony was held at Hollywood's Kodak Theater, and the event has remained there since that time.

SYMBOLS AND CUSTOMS

Gowns

The media often pays as much attention to the gowns worn by the actresses who attend the Academy Awards ceremony as it does to the winning films and performances. For this reason top fashion designers compete with one another to convince

Other Film Awards and Festivals

hough the Academy Awards ceremony is perhaps the most popular awards event in film, other organizations also acknowledge achievement in film. They include:

Broadcast Film Critics Association has presented the Critics' Choice awards since 1996
www.bfca.org

Directors Guild of America has presented awards for directorial achievement since 1948
www.dga.org

Hollywood Foreign Press Association has presented the Golden Globe Awards since 1943
www.hfpa.org/goldenglobeawards/index.html

In addition, several film festivals worldwide provide an important outlet for recognizing film-making talent, including:

Berlinale, the Berlin International Film Festival inaugurated in 1951, takes place in Berlin, Germany, each February
www.berlinale.de/en/HomePage.html

Cannes Film Festival began in 1947 and is held in Cannes, France, each May
www.festival-cannes.fr/index.php/en

Sundance Film Festival in Park City, Utah, has highlighted independent films since 1984
festival.sundance.org

Toronto International Film Festival in Toronto, Canada, has been held since 1976
www.torontointernationalfilmfestival.ca

Venice Film Festival has taken place in Venice, Italy, since 1932
www.labiennale.org/en/cinema

famous actresses to wear their gowns to the Academy Awards. Actresses who are nominated for an award are especially sought after. In some newspapers, magazines, and broadcast media, these gowns and the looks of the actresses that wear them are subject to the same intense scrutiny and review as the movies themselves.

Oscars

Each winner receives a statuette whose official name is the "Academy Award of Merit." Better known as an "Oscar," these gold-plated statuettes are thirteen and a half inches tall and weigh eight and one half pounds. The figure is meant to represent a knight with a sword clasped in front of him, standing on a reel of film. No one knows exactly how the statuettes came to be known as Oscars. Some say that an early Academy librarian, Margaret Herrick—who later became president of the Academy—thought that the statuettes resembled her uncle Oscar. She started calling them by that name, and the Academy staff followed suit. This private name eventually spread throughout Hollywood. The Academy adopted "Oscar" as the nickname of its awards in 1939.

Red Carpet

When celebrities arrive at the Kodak Theater to attend the Academy Awards, they step out of their cars onto a red carpet. This carpet lines the path to the theater doors. Traditionally, red carpets have been spread in front of royalty or very high-ranking people. Certainly the famous actors, actresses, and directors who attend the awards ceremony may be viewed as Hollywood "royalty." Reporters and photographers line both sides of the red carpet, hoping to get a photo or a short interview with one of the movie stars. Celebrities often linger awhile on the red carpet, enjoying the free publicity.

Sealed Envelopes

The Academy mails nomination ballots to its membership in late December. These are collected and tallied in January, so that the final ballots can be mailed in early February. The members return the ballots to the professional services firm Price-WaterhouseCoopers, which completes the official count. This procedure ensures that even Academy members don't know the results of the voting until the winners are announced at the awards ceremony. PriceWaterhouseCoopers employees sworn to secrecy tally the votes and place the names of the winners in sealed envelopes. These sealed envelopes are delivered on the day of the event. The stars chosen to announce the award in each category list the names of the nominees, following a script whose last line reads, "and the Oscar goes to...." Then they break the seal of the envelope and announce to the world the winner of the most coveted award in the world of film.

FURTHER READING

Osborne, Robert. *75 Years of the Oscar.* New York: Abbeville Press, 2003.

WEB SITE

The Academy of Motion Picture Arts and Sciences
www.oscars.org

Advent

Type of Holiday: Religious (Christian)
Date of Observation: Sunday closest to November 30 through December 24 in the West; November 15 through December 24 in the East
Where Celebrated: United States, Great Britain, Europe, and by Christians throughout the world
Symbols and Customs: Advent Calendar, Advent Candle, Advent Letters, Advent Plays, Advent Wreath
Colors: Advent is associated with blue, the color of the Virgin Mary's cloak. The liturgical color is purple, a reminder of the fact that Advent was originally a time for fasting and penance.
Related Holidays: Christmas, Christmas Eve

ORIGINS

Advent is a Christian holiday. The word Christian refers to a follower of Christ, a title derived from the Greek word meaning Messiah or Anointed One. The Christ of Christianity is Jesus of Nazareth, a man born between 7 and 4 B.C.E. in the region of Palestine. According to Christian teaching, Jesus was killed by Roman authorities using a form of execution called crucifixion (a term meaning he was nailed to a cross and hung from it until he died) in about the year 30 C.E. After his death, he rose back to life. His death and resurrection provide a way by which people can be reconciled with God. In remembrance of Jesus' death and resurrection, the cross serves as a fundamental symbol in Christianity.

With nearly two billion believers in countries around the globe, Christianity is the largest of the world's religions. There is no one central authority for all of Christianity. The pope (the bishop of Rome) is the authority for the Roman Catholic

Church, but other sects look to other authorities. Orthodox communities look to patriarchs and emphasize doctrinal agreement and traditional practice. Protestant communities focus on individual conscience. The Roman Catholic and Protestant churches are often referred to as the Western Church, while the Orthodox churches may also be called the Eastern Church. All three main branches of Christianity acknowledge the authority of Christian scriptures, a compilation of writings assembled into a document called the Bible. Methods of biblical interpretation vary among the different Christian sects.

The name "Advent" comes from the Latin *adventus,* meaning "coming" or "arrival." Just as **LENT** is a period during which Christians prepare for **EASTER**, Advent is a period of preparation for **CHRISTMAS**. It was originally observed by Eastern and some Western churches as preparation for the feast of **EPIPHANY** (January 6), which at one time celebrated both the birth of Jesus Christ and his baptism. When Rome fixed December 25 as the commemoration of Jesus' birth in the fourth century, however, Advent underwent a shift not only in time but in mood as well. No longer a period of fasting and somber self-reflection, Advent became a time of joyous anticipation.

In 490 C.E. Bishop Perpetuus of Tours, France, established a period of penance and preparation for Christmas in his diocese. He advocated fasting on Mondays, Wednesdays, and Fridays for a forty-day period preceding Christmas. This fast period began on the day after **MARTINMAS,** November 11, thereby acquiring the name "St. Martin's Lent" or "The Forty Days' Fast of St. Martin." The observation of a period of penance in preparation for Christmas gradually spread throughout France and on to Spain and Germany. Later, the Advent fast was adoped in England as well.

Advent was observed in Rome beginning in the sixth century. Pope Gregory I (590-604 C.E.) developed much of the Roman Advent liturgy and shortened the period of observance from six to four weeks. The joyous, festive spirit with which Romans celebrated Advent clashed with the somber, penitential mood established in Gallic observances. For a number of centuries Advent celebrations throughout Europe varied in tone, length, and manner of observance. By the thirteenth century the observance of Advent in western Europe had stabilized. It combined the Roman tradition of a four-week observance, the Gallic custom of fasting, and a liturgy that mingled the themes of penance and joy. In recent centuries, the Roman Catholic church reduced and eventually eliminated fasting. In the West, Advent Sunday is the Sunday nearest the Feast of St. Andrew (November 30). The overall length of the Advent period may vary from twenty-two to twenty-eight days, but it always ends on **CHRISTMAS EVE**. The Orthodox (Eastern) Christian year begins on September 1, and Advent is observed beginning on November 15.

SYMBOLS AND CUSTOMS

Advent Calendar

The popular Advent calendar that parents give their children to help them count the days until Christmas originated in Germany, but quickly spread to other countries. It may consist of a "Christmas House" printed on cardboard with small cut-out windows that can be opened by folding them back, revealing a miniature picture or symbol associated with the feast of Christmas. The calendar is hung on a wall or window at the beginning of December, and one of the windows is opened each day. The last door or window is opened on Christmas Eve, and it shows the Nativity scene. Aside from this reference to the religious aspect of the season, however, Advent calendars are primarily a means of keeping children's minds occupied during the long wait for the arrival of Santa Claus.

Advent Candle

The Advent candle may be a single large candle located in a central place in the home or four separate candles set in a special holder. The candles are usually white and may be hand-dipped. One candle is lit on Advent Sunday and allowed to burn down a little way. On the second Sunday, both the first and the second candles are lit for a while—and so on, until all four candles are burning at different levels on the Sunday preceding Christmas Eve. Like the Advent calendar, these candles serve as a reminder that Christmas is coming soon.

At pre-Christmas church services in Germany, children hold a decorated orange in which a small candle has been inserted. Originated by the Moravian Brethren in eastern Germany, the candle is called the Christingle, which might have derived from either *Christ-kindl*, meaning "Christ Child," or *Christ-engel,* referring to the angel who brings gifts to children.

Advent Letters

A custom popular in Europe, Canada, and South America, Advent letters are notes addressed to Baby Jesus that children leave on their window sills when they go to bed on December 5, the eve of St. Nicholas' Day. The notes contain lists of Christmas presents the children hope to receive and are supposedly taken to heaven by angels or by St. Nicholas himself. In South America, children write their notes to "Little Jesus" between December 16 and 24, leaving them in front of the crèche for the angels to pick up.

This is very similar to the American custom of sending Christmas letters to Santa Claus at the North Pole. These letters are dropped in specially decorated red mailboxes that are put out every year a few weeks before Christmas.

Advent Plays

During Advent in Germany and Austria, the *Herbergsuchen* was a popular custom. People reenacted the Holy Family's fruitless search for shelter in Bethlehem on the night that Jesus was born. The performance usually ended with a "happy ending" tableau showing the Nativity scene.

A similar custom, **LAS POSADAS,** is popular in Central and South America, Mexico, and Hispanic communities in the U.S. Between December 16 and 24, several neighboring families gather in one house, where they prepare a shrine with a crib and traditional figures, but the manger itself is left empty. A procession moves through the house, pictures of Mary and Joseph are placed on the shrine, and a priest blesses everyone present. Sometimes a group of "pilgrims" will knock on the door and ask the owner of the house to let them in. This reenactment of Mary and Joseph's search for shelter (*posada* in Spanish) ends with a big party for the adults and an opportunity for the children to break a *piñata* filled with candy and suspended from the ceiling.

Frauentragen, or "woman carrying," is an old German Advent custom still practiced in some areas that closely resembles the Hispanic folk play **LAS POSADAS.** Children carry a picture or figurine representing the Virgin Mary to a neighborhood home. Once there they sing or enact a brief scene from the Nativity story, say a prayer, and place the picture or figurine near the family crucifix. The children return for the image the following evening and carry it to a new home. In this way, they act out Mary and Joseph's search for lodging in Bethlehem. On Christmas Eve, the children carry Mary back to the church, where she takes her place in the Nativity scene.

Advent Wreath

The Advent wreath is made of yew, fir, or laurel and is suspended from the ceiling or placed on a table. Four candles stand upright at equal distances around the circumference of the wreath, representing the four weeks of Advent. One candle is lit each Sunday during the Advent season. On the fourth Sunday, the family gathers in the evening to say prayers and sing Advent hymns, and all four candles glow.

Symbols for light played an important role in late November and early December, the season during which the pre-Christian festival of Yule was observed with the burning of torches and bonfires. When Christianity came along, many of these light and fire symbols were kept alive. By the sixteenth century, the custom of using candles as a religious symbol of Advent had been established in Germany and was spreading rapidly among Protestants and Catholics alike.

In some parts of Europe, it is traditional for someone named John or Joan to light the candles on the Advent wreath, because the Gospel of John refers to Christ as the "Light of the World." Another possible reason for this custom is that John the Baptist was the first one to see the light of divinity shining around Jesus when he was baptized in the River Jordan.

The wreath itself is an ancient symbol whose eternal circle stands as a reminder of new beginnings at a time of apparent endings. While Advent falls near the end of the calendar year, it marks the beginning of the Christian year. Because the wreath is made of evergreens, it also serves as a symbol of eternal life in Christian terms and the life that goes on in nature despite the cold winter weather.

FURTHER READING

Barz, Brigitte. *Festivals with Children*. Edinburgh: Floris Books, 1987.

Bellenir, Karen. *Religious Holidays and Calendars*. 3rd ed. Detroit: Omnigraphics, 2004.

Brewster, H. Pomeroy. *Saints and Festivals of the Christian Church*. 1904. Reprint. Detroit: Omnigraphics, 1990.

Christianson, Stephen G., and Jane M. Hatch. *The American Book of Days*. 4th ed. New York: H.W. Wilson, 2000.

Gulevich, Tanya. *Encyclopedia of Christmas & New Year's Celebrations*, 2nd ed. Detroit: Omnigraphics, 2003.

Harper, Howard V. *Days and Customs of All Faiths*. 1957. Reprint. Detroit: Omnigraphics, 1990.

Henderson, Helene, ed. *Holidays, Festivals, and Celebrations of the World Dictionary*. 3rd ed. Detroit: Omnigraphics, 2005.

MacDonald, Margaret R., ed. *The Folklore of World Holidays*. Detroit: Gale Research, 1992.

Metford, J.C.J. *The Christian Year*. New York: Crossroad, 1991.

Santino, Jack. *All Around the Year: Holidays and Celebrations in American Life*. Urbana: University of Illinois Press, 1994.

Spicer, Dorothy Gladys. *Festivals of Western Europe*. 1958. Reprint. Detroit: Omnigraphics, 1993.

Weiser, Franz Xaver. *Handbook of Christian Feasts and Customs*. New York: Harcourt, Brace, 1958.

WEB SITES

Christian Resource Institute
www.crivoice.org/cyadvent.html

New Advent Catholic Encyclopedia
www.newadvent.org/cathen/01165a.htm

Akwambo
(Akwanbo, Path-Clearing Festival)

Type of Holiday: Folkloric
Date of Observation: Varies
Where Celebrated: Central Region, Ghana
Symbols and Customs: Durbar, Offerings, Path Clearing

ORIGINS

Akwambo is observed annually, mainly in the Agona and Gomoa Districts in the Central Region of Ghana. The festival commemorates the journey and arrival of the founding settlers of the four towns of Gyinankoma, Ekrawfo, Atakwaa, and Otabenadze. Celebrations are held at various times of the year, usually lasting for several days, and can include different activities according to local custom. However, most Akwambo festivals share certain common customs such as the ritual PATH CLEARING, a public gathering known as a DURBAR, and family or community reunions. There may also be music and dance performances, soccer games, and parades. In some areas, young people hold an all-night party.

SYMBOLS AND CUSTOMS

Durbar

A durbar is usually held near the end of the Akwambo festival. Community leaders and chiefs are carried on covered litters in a procession of drummers, dancers, singers, musicians, and soldiers. A public reception follows, during which speeches are made by politicians and other dignitaries. Also at this time community members may bring forward any concerns or problems needing the leaders' attention.

Offerings

During Akwambo, communal offerings are made to honor the town's ancestors. It is believed that the ancestral spirits continue to interact with the living by providing protection, good fortune, and blessings in the form of rain and successful harvests. Offerings normally take the form of libations poured on the ground or food items scattered on the water.

Path Clearing

Perhaps the most important part of Akwambo is the ritual path clearing that is done in honor of the first settlers who established the town. Every member of the community is expected to participate in clearing the paths and roads leading to the town, as well as those that provide access to streams, rivers, farms, shrines, and communal spaces. Unpaved footpaths are weeded and maintained, while paved roads are ritually swept with branches, brooms, and fans made of leaves.

FURTHER READING

Henderson, Helene, ed. *Holidays, Festivals, and Celebrations of the World Dictionary*, 3rd ed. Detroit: Omnigraphics, 2005.

WEB SITES

Ghana Embassy in the United States
www.ghana-embassy.org

Ghana Ministry of Local Government, Rural Development and Environment
www.ghanadistricts.com

Ghana Ministry of Tourism and Diasporan Relations
www.touringghana.com

Ghana National Commission on Culture
www.ghanaculture.gov.gh

Alasitas Fair

Type of Holiday: Folkloric
Date of Observation: January 24
Where Celebrated: Bolivia
Symbols and Customs: Blessing Ceremony, Ekeko, Miniature Objects

ORIGINS

The Alasitas Fair is a festival of good luck. It is observed throughout Bolivia, but the largest celebration takes place in Bolivia's capital city, La Paz. The festival traces it roots back to the time before the Spanish conquered Latin America. In those days, a native American ethnic group called the Aymara lived in what is now Peru, Bolivia, Chile, and Argentina. They honored a number of gods, including a god of abundance called EKEKO. The Aymara were conquered by another group of Indian people, called the Incas, who were in turn conquered by the Spanish in the sixteenth century. The Aymara people survived all these battles, however, and so did elements of their culture and religion. During the Alasitas Fair, people make little offerings to Ekeko, hoping he in turn will bless them with money and material possessions.

The festival as we know it today got its start in the eighteenth century. At this time, the country was already under Spanish rule. A joint Spanish and Aymara festival that resembled the Alasitas Fair had already been established in La Paz. The local Catholic bishop, however, forbade the holiday, fearing the celebrations were taking on rowdy, sexual overtones. Although the Spanish had lived in Bolivia for two centuries, many native people still resented the foreign conquerors. In 1781, a group of Indians rebelled against the Spanish and set siege to the capital city of La Paz. During this time, the Spanish people living in La Paz flocked to church to pray to the Virgin Mary in the presence of a beautiful statue of her that was given to the city by the Spanish king Felipe II. Although the siege lasted for months, the Spanish eventually put down the rebellion. They credited the divine intercession of the Virgin of La Paz with ensuring their victory. In gratitude, they reinstituted the joint Spanish Aymara holiday, declaring it to be a feast day in honor of the Virgin Mary and moving it from October to January 24. Although special Roman Catholic religious observances were scheduled on this day, the native people preferred to continue their devotion to Ekeko. Over time, the Catholic observances diminished, and the activities surrounding Ekeko grew in importance. This event became known as the Alasitas Fair.

The name "Alasitas" comes from an Aymara word that may be translated as "buy me" or "come and buy." The name refers to the large markets that provide Bolivians with MINIATURE OBJECTS with which to adorn their Ekeko statuettes. In addition to the markets, the fair also features performances of Bolivian music and folk dancing.

SYMBOLS AND CUSTOMS

Blessing Ceremony

Many Bolivians believe that EKEKO is more likely to respond to their offerings if they take their Ekeko statuette, laden with its miniature possessions, to be blessed by a Yatiri. A Yatiri is a practitioner of traditional Aymara folk medicine. Yatiris use herbs as well as spiritual practices to heal. A yatiri will bless an Ekeko doll with prayers, the smoke of burning herbs, and incantations. In some places, people will take their Ekeko to a Roman Catholic priest to be blessed.

Ekeko

Archeologists have found statuettes of Ekeko that are more than 2,000 years old. Just as today, the ancient Aymara identified this god as the patron of good fortune and abundance. These days the Aymara people still create Ekeko statuettes. They usually fashion them out of clay, but other materials, such as wood, might also be used. Aymara artisans usually depict Ekeko as a short, round man with open arms, rosy cheeks, a big smile, and a mustache. He often wears items of clothing that identify him as an Indian, such as a poncho and the colorful knitted wool caps worn by mountain people. Historians believe that the Indians honored Ekeko with a festival before the arrival of the Spanish. Evidence suggests that it was celebrated on different dates in different locations.

During the Alasitas Fair, Bolivians adorn their Ekeko statuettes with miniature objects of all kinds. These objects represent the money and goods they hope to obtain in the year to come. The wide open arms of the Ekeko dolls provide ample space to load them up with goods. The Aymara hope that the miniature objects will please Ekeko and inspire him to bless them with the real thing.

Miniature Objects

The open air markets that spring up to meet the demand for miniature objects with which to adorn Ekeko are a highlight of the Alasitas Fair. Local artisans create an immense variety of the tiny trinkets, to suit each individual's needs and desires. Those who want to ensure a good food supply in the coming year will find tiny bags of sugar, cans of coffee, sacks of grain, and more. Farmers will find llamas, sheep, chickens, and all manner of agricultural animals. The tools of many trades are also represented. Those who are hoping to build a new house might purchase miniature bags of cement and wheelbarrows. Many people purchase household goods, such as washing machines, stoves, refrigerators, and computers, hoping that this will inspire Ekeko to improve their household appliances in the year to come. For those who believe that their fortune lies elsewhere, vendors offer tiny passports and plane tickets. Finally, many Bolivians feel that offering Ekeko a gift of cash is the best way to insure abundance in the year to come. To that end, Aymara craftspeople create paper money of all kinds. In addition to Bolivian currency they offer miniature American dollars, Euros, and even bills stamped "Bank of Fortune," or "Bank of Alasitas." Each year, many people equip their Ekeko doll with a small suitcase filled with a million of these "dollars."

FURTHER READING

Henderson, Helene, ed. *Holidays, Festivals, and Celebrations of the World Dictionary.* 3rd ed. Detroit: Omnigraphics, 2005.

Milne, Jean. *Fiesta Time in Latin America.* Los Angeles: Ward Ritchie Press, 1965.

WEB SITES

Aymara.org (in Spanish)
www.aymara.org/biblio/marina1.php

BBC
news.bbc.co.uk/1/shared/spl/hi/picture_gallery/07/americas_bolivia0s_
    popular_fairs/html/1.stm

Bolivia Embassy
www.boliviaweb.com/embassies.htm

Bolivia Travels
www.bolivia-travels.com/la_paz/alasitas.htm

Naya.org (in Spanish)
www.naya.org.ar/congreso2002/ponencias/fernando_caceres.htm

Alaska Day

Type of Holiday: Historic
Date of Observation: October 18
Where Celebrated: Alaska, primarily Sitka
Symbols and Customs: Costume Ball, Cultural Performances, Memorial, Parade,
    Sporting Events, Transfer Ceremony Reenactment

ORIGINS

Alaska Day commemorates the formal transfer of Alaska from Russia to the United States, which occurred on October 18, 1867. U.S. Secretary of State William Henry Seward had been pressing for the acquisition of Alaska as early as 1860, but negotiations took several years to complete. On March 29, 1867, Seward reached an agreement with the Russians by which the U.S. would purchase the territory of "Russian North America" for $7.2 million—about two cents per acre of land.

Many Americans criticized the idea, believing the purchase price to be too high for what was regarded as a frozen wasteland. Seward was publicly ridiculed, the Alaskan territory became known as "Seward's Icebox," and the proposed acquisition was referred to as "Seward's Folly." Nevertheless, the purchase was approved by the U.S. Congress, and the transfer was finalized in a ceremony held in Sitka,

Alaska. But even the harshest critics changed their opinion about the value of the land when gold was discovered in Alaska in 1896, bringing thousands of people to the region during the Klondike Gold Rush.

As a historic holiday, Alaska Day commemorates a significant historical event. People throughout the world remember significant events in their histories. Often, these are events that are important for an entire nation and become widely observed. The marking of such anniversaries serve not only to honor the values represented by the person or event commemorated, but also to strengthen and reinforce communal bonds of national, cultural, or ethnic identity. Victorious, joyful, and traumatic events are remembered through historic holidays. The commemorative expression reflects the original event through festive celebration or solemn ritual. Reenactments are common activities at historical holiday and festival gatherings, seeking to bring the past alive in the present.

Alaska Day was first observed in Sitka in 1949 with the unveiling of a two-ton commemorative bronze statue dedicated to early Alaskan pioneers. Alaska Day became an official state holiday in 1954. The largest celebration takes place each year in Sitka during a festival highlighting the culture and history of Alaska. Festival activities include a COSTUME BALL, SPORTING EVENTS, a PARADE, and various CULTURAL PERFORMANCES. A special proclamation from the mayor of Sitka encourages all men to grow beards and all women to dress in nineteenth century clothing for the duration of the festival.

SYMBOLS AND CUSTOMS

Costume Ball

Those who attend Sitka's Alaska Day Ball must dress in native regalia, nineteenth century styled clothing, or semi-formal wear. The ball festivities include a period costume promenade and native regalia display, with awards and prizes given to the best outfit in a number of different categories.

Cultural Performances

The diverse cultural heritage of the Alaskan region is showcased in a series of music and dance performances. Folk dancing in native and Russian traditions is generally presented along with performances by local musicians and dance groups.

Memorial

A military memorial service is held at the Sitka National Cemetery each year as part of the Alaska Day observance.

Parade

Sitka holds an annual Alaska Day parade including marching bands, military color guard and marching units, decorated vehicles, classic cars, living history reenactments, and other costumed participants. The parade concludes at the site of the transfer ceremony reenactment.

Sporting Events

Many competitive sporting events are held during the Alaska Day festival in Sitka. Races are held for runners, kayakers, and bicyclists, and a croquet tournament is also held. The annual biathlon draws participants from all over Alaska.

Transfer Ceremony Reenactment

A ceremony recreating the transfer of Alaska from Russia to the U.S. is conducted immediately after the Alaska Day parade. The reenactment takes place on Castle Hill in Sitka, the site of the original transfer. Military troops gather to fire a salute as the Russian flag is lowered. A second salute is fired as the U.S. flag is raised. The ceremony concludes with the reading of the original transfer proclamations.

FURTHER READING

Henderson, Helene, ed. *Holidays, Festivals, and Celebrations of the World Dictionary*, 3rd ed. Detroit: Omnigraphics, 2005.

WEB SITE

Official Alaska Day
www.cityofsitka.com/alaskaday

All Souls' Day

Type of Holiday: Religious (Christian)
Date of Observation: November 2 in the West (November 3 if November 2 falls on a Sunday); three Saturdays prior to Lent and the day before Pentecost in the East
Where Celebrated: United States, Britain, Europe, Mexico, Central and South America, and by Roman Catholics, Anglicans, and Orthodox Christians throughout the world. Some Protestants observe All Souls' Day.
Symbols and Customs: Candles, Graves, Soul Cakes
Colors: The liturgical color at all church services on November 2 is black. In parts of Europe, Roman Catholic services on this day are often referred to as "black vespers." In southern Europe, the churches are draped in black and worshippers wear black clothing.
Related Holidays: Día de los Muertos, Samhain

ORIGINS

Pope Gregory IV established All Saints' Day (November 1) in the ninth century as an attempt to Christianize the ancient Celtic festival of the dead, known as **SAMHAIN**. Near the turn of the eleventh century (998 C.E.), St. Odilo, the abbot of Cluny in France, proposed that the day after be set aside to pray for the souls of the departed—especially those who were still in purgatory. In the fourteenth century, Rome placed the day in the official calendar of the Western Church as November 2.

Many of the customs now associated with All Souls' Day—for example, laying out food for the dead, lighting candles on graves, and tolling the bells until midnight—can be traced back to the celebration of Samhain. Ancient Celts believed in pacifying the dead so they wouldn't haunt the living, while the Christian celebration of All Souls' Day is based on the belief that offering prayers for the dead will benefit the souls of the departed.

In Mexico, people celebrate **DÍA DE LOS MUERTOS** (Day of the Dead), which is related to All Souls' Day. **DÍA DE LOS MUERTOS** is a major celebration that blends European and Native American beliefs concerning the dead, whose spirits are believed to return to their families and communities at this time of year. The emphasis is on showing hospitality to these visiting spirits by giving them the opportunity to enjoy earthly pleasures. All Souls' Day is also observed by Native Americans on the Indian reservations of the western United States, particularly among those in the pueblos of New Mexico.

Now, All Souls' Day is a Christian holiday. The word Christian refers to a follower of Christ, a title derived from the Greek word meaning Messiah or Anointed One. The Christ of Christianity is Jesus of Nazareth, a man born between 7 and 4 B.C.E. in the region of Palestine. According to Christian teaching, Jesus was killed by Roman authorities using a form of execution called crucifixion (a term meaning he was nailed to a cross and hung from it until he died) in about the year 30 C.E. After his death, he rose back to life. His death and resurrection provide a way by which people can be reconciled with God. In remembrance of Jesus' death and resurrection, the cross serves as a fundamental symbol in Christianity.

With nearly two billion believers in countries around the globe, Christianity is the largest of the world's religions. There is no one central authority for all of Christianity. The pope (the bishop of Rome) is the authority for the Roman Catholic Church, but other sects look to other authorities. Orthodox communities look to patriarchs and emphasize doctrinal agreement and traditional practice. Protestant communities focus on individual conscience. The Roman Catholic and Protestant churches are often referred to as the Western Church, while the Orthodox churches may also be called the Eastern Church. All three main branches of Christianity acknowledge the authority of Christian scriptures, a compilation of writings assembled into a document called the Bible. Methods of biblical interpretation vary among the different Christian sects.

SYMBOLS AND CUSTOMS

Candles

Lighting candles is a symbolic attempt to illuminate the darkness for the returning souls of the dead. In Ireland, candles shine in the windows of Catholic homes on All Souls' Eve. In Belgium, a holy candle burns all night, and people walk in candlelight processions. In many Roman Catholic countries, the cemeteries are aglow with the candles that have been set on the graves, often protected by little glass lanterns, as symbols of the souls of the departed. The pueblo Indians of the southwestern United States place candles in their churches and houses in the belief that the dead will burn the fingertips of those who fail to light their way.

In Catholic sections of central Europe, it is the custom to ring church bells at the approach of dusk on November 1 to remind people to pray for the souls in purgatory. When they hear the bells, families gather in one room and extinguish all other lights except for the candle they have kept from the preceding **CANDLE-MAS** (February 2).

Graves

The cemetery is the focus of most All Souls' Day celebrations. The graves of the dead are thoroughly cleaned, raked, and weeded. Fresh flowers are set out, and other decorations—such as crosses, wreaths, and arrangements of silk or plastic flowers—are placed carefully on the grave.

The custom of decorating graves and praying in cemeteries on this day is widespread in Catholic Europe and America. In addition to flowers, candles or lanterns are often lit on the graves and left burning throughout the night on All Souls' Eve.

Soul Cakes

In the Middle Ages, the custom of "souling" was widespread in the British Isles. On All Souls' Eve (November 1), "soulers" went from house to house offering prayers for the dead and begging alms in return. Eventually the alms took the form of "soul cakes." According to an old superstition, for each cake consumed, a soul would be released from the torments of purgatory. This begging ritual, initially carried out by grown men, was eventually taken up by children who recited a rhyme or song requesting "mercy on all Christian souls for a soul cake."

Souling can be traced back to a winter custom in England known as "hodening." A man wearing a white sheet and a wooden horse's head whose jaws were hinged in such a way that they could snap ferociously would go around the village with a band of men and boys, leaping and prancing as people opened their doors. Hodening usually took place at **CHRISTMAS** and on All Souls' Day or Eve. The horse-man and his followers were given ale and other gifts.

The pagan custom of hodening—probably derived from the ancient fertility rites and horse sacrifices of the Romans and Norsemen—was either combined with or replaced by the Christian custom of souling. The soul cakes used today are left out on All Souls' Eve for the dead to eat when they revisit their homes. In Italy, *fave dei morti* or "beans of the dead"—actually bean-shaped cakes—are served on this day. In some sections of central Europe, the boys receive All Souls' cakes in the shape of a hare, while the girls are given cakes in the shape of a hen—an interesting way of combining symbols for fertility with a symbol for the souls of the dead.

Soul cakes can still be found in Great Britain, Belgium, southern Germany, and Austria. Some scholars think that the modern custom of begging for candy on **HALLOWEEN** is somehow linked to the medieval souling tradition.

FURTHER READING

Bellenir, Karen. *Religious Holidays and Calendars*. 3rd ed. Detroit: Omnigraphics, 2004.

Chambers, Robert. *The Book of Days*. 2 vols. 1862-64. Reprint. Detroit: Omnigraphics, 1990.

Christianson, Stephen G., and Jane M. Hatch. *The American Book of Days*. 4th ed. New York: H.W. Wilson, 2000.

Cirlot, J.E. *A Dictionary of Symbols.* New York: Philosophical Library, 1962.

Ferguson, George. *Signs and Symbols in Christian Art.* New York: Oxford University Press, 1954.

Henderson, Helene, ed. *Holidays, Festivals, and Celebrations of the World Dictionary.* 3rd ed. Detroit: Omnigraphics, 2005.

Hole, Christina. *English Custom & Usage.* 1941. Reprint. Detroit: Omnigraphics, 1990.

Hutton, Ronald. *The Pagan Religions of the Ancient British Isles: Their Nature and Legacy.* Oxford: Blackwell, 1991.

James, E.O. *Seasonal Feasts and Festivals.* 1961. Reprint. Detroit: Omnigraphics, 1993.

Jobes, Gertrude. *Dictionary of Mythology, Folklore, and Symbols.* New York: Scarecrow Press, 1962.

Miles, Clement A. *Christmas in Ritual and Tradition, Christian and Pagan.* 1912. Reprint. Detroit: Omnigraphics, 1990.

Pike, Royston. *Round the Year with the World's Religions.* 1950. Reprint. Detroit: Omnigraphics, 1992.

Santino, Jack. *All Around the Year: Holidays and Celebrations in American Life.* Urbana: University of Illinois Press, 1994.

Santino, Jack. *Halloween and Other Festivals of Death and Life.* Knoxville: University of Tennessee Press, 1994.

Urlin, Ethel L. *Festivals, Holy Days, and Saints' Days.* 1915. Reprint. Detroit: Omnigraphics, 1992.

Weiser, Franz Xaver. *Handbook of Christian Feasts and Customs.* New York: Harcourt, Brace, 1958.

WEB SITES

New Advent Catholic Encyclopedia
www.newadvent.org/cathen/01315b.htm

University of Kansas Diversity Calendar
www3.kumc.edu/diversity/ethnic_relig/allsouls.html

America's Cup

Type of Holiday: Sporting
Date of Observation: Varies; usually every three to four years
Where Celebrated: Location varies, depending upon who won the last race.
Symbols and Customs: The Cup

ORIGINS

The sailing race known as the America's Cup is the world's longest-running international sporting event. It was originally named The Hundred Guinea Cup by the Royal Yacht Squadron of Great Britain, which suggested that the Americans send a boat to compete in a race around the Isle of Wight to be held in conjunction with the International Exposition at London's Crystal Palace in 1851. John C. Stevens, Commodore of the New York Yacht Club, took up the challenge and formed a syndicate to finance the building of a new yacht that would be the fastest afloat.

Designed by George Steers and built by William H. Brown, the 100-foot schooner *America* got off to a slow start in the 53-mile course, but ended up so far ahead of her sixteen English competitors that the event triggered a now-legendary exchange between Queen Victoria and one of her attendants. "Who is first?" the queen asked when a solitary boat appeared on the horizon. When she was told that it was the schooner *America,* she asked who was second. "Your Majesty," came the reply, "there is no second."

America's victory marked the beginning of the longest winning streak in international sports history. For 132 years, American yachtsmen successfully defended the Cup against all challengers, first in schooners and later in sloops (single-masted boats). For nearly a decade (1930-37), the American defenders were all "J" boats, averaging 130 feet in overall length and with masts towering more than 155 feet above the water. But by the end of World War II (1939-45), it became evident that the size requirement for both challenger and defender would have to be reduced if the competition were to survive. The so-called "12-Meter" boats, sixty-five feet in length, raced from 1958 until 1987, although the passing of the "J" boats has always been mourned by yachting enthusiasts.

The structure of the races that make up the America's Cup is similar to that of major league baseball. Two leagues, consisting of the challengers and the defenders, compete against each other in the pre-season; but once the regular season begins, challengers only compete against other challengers and defenders against other defenders. The challenger who makes it to the final match faces the defending boat, which represents the country where THE CUP is currently held. For 132 years the New York Yacht Club successfully defended the Cup for America. But what had come to seem an invincible lock on the race ended in 1983, when the Royal Perth Yacht Club's *Australia II* defeated the New York Yacht Club's *Liberty* in the waters off Newport, Rhode Island, and brought the Cup home to Western Australia.

Australia II's victory led to an explosion of international interest in the race. While the number of challengers used to be quite limited, it is not uncommon nowadays for ten or more nations—including France, Great Britain, Italy, New Zealand, Australia, Sweden, and Japan—to mount a Cup challenge. The audience for the race has expanded as well, particularly after the sports television network ESPN started broadcasting the America's Cup races live on television in 1990. Over 2.7 billion spectators in more than 150 countries can now watch the competition unfold on their TV screens.

The International America's Cup Class (IACC) boats that compete in the race are built to a specific rule or mathematical formula that takes into consideration the boat's length, sail area, and displacement. It's the job of America's Cup designers to take this rule and produce the best boat possible, given the wind and sea conditions of wherever the next race is due to be held. The IACC boats introduced in 1991 are seventy-five feet in length, lightweight, and powered by huge sails that extend from the top of 100-foot masts. Announced in 2007, a new class of boat, measuring ninety feet in length and sailed by a crew of twenty, will debut in time for the thirty-third America's Cup, currently scheduled for 2009.

Perhaps no name is more closely associated with the America's Cup race than that of Sir Thomas Lipton, who was the only challenger from 1899 through 1930. Representing the Royal Ulster Yacht Club of Belfast, Northern Ireland, Lipton brought six different racing yachts (one of which was used only for trials), all named *Shamrock,* to the competition and lost every time. After his final defeat, in 1930, he was presented with a gold cup made by Tiffany & Company to commemorate his five courageous challenges. At eighty-two years old, he was dubbed the "Gamest Loser in the World of Sport."

SYMBOLS AND CUSTOMS

The Cup

The oldest trophy in international sport was commissioned in 1850 by the Royal Yacht Squadron of Cowes, England, which asked Garrard's of London to design a Victorian ewer (pitcher) from 134 ounces of silver. The result was 27 inches high, with an elaborate handle and extensive Victorian decoration.

RESULTS BY COUNTRY

COUNTRY	WINNER	RUNNER-UP
USA	28	2
New Zealand	2	2
Australia	1	7
Switzerland	1	0
England	0	11
Ireland	0	5
Canada	0	2
Italy	0	2
Scotland	0	1

For most of its life, the Cup rested in a case in the New York Yacht Club, but since Australia's successful challenge in 1983 it has moved from Perth, Australia, back to the United States (1987, 1988, and 1992) and then to New Zealand (1995). In March 1997, a Maori man attacked the Cup in its display case at the Royal New Zealand Yacht Squadron in Auckland, bashing it repeatedly with a sledgehammer and inflicting considerable damage on the trophy. The Maori, who make up fifteen percent of New Zealand's population, are among the poorest of its people and have a number of grievances with their country's government. Auckland, which boasts more yachts per capita than any city in the world, hosted New Zealand's defense of the Cup from October 1999 through March 2000.

FURTHER READING

Carrick, Robert W. *The Pictorial History of the America's Cup Races*. New York: Viking Press, 1964.

Christianson, Stephen G., and Jane M. Hatch. *The American Book of Days*. 4th ed. New York: H.W. Wilson, 2000.

WEB SITE

America's Cup Official Web Site
www.americascup.com

Annunciation of the Blessed Virgin Mary, Feast of the (Lady Day)

Type of Holiday: Religious (Christian)
Date of Observation: March 25
Where Celebrated: Britain, Europe, United States, and by Roman Catholics and Anglicans around the world
Symbols and Customs: Dove, Lady Day Cakes, Lily
Related Holidays: Assumption of the Blessed Virgin Mary, Feast of the

ORIGINS

The Feast of the Annunciation is celebrated by Christians worldwide. The word Christian refers to a follower of Christ, a title derived from the Greek word meaning Messiah or Anointed One. The Christ of Christianity is Jesus of Nazareth, a man born between 7 and 4 B.C.E. in the region of Palestine. According to Christian teaching, Jesus was killed by Roman authorities using a form of execution called crucifixion (a term meaning he was nailed to a cross and hung from it until he died) in about the year 30 C.E. After his death, he rose back to life. His death and resurrection provide a way by which people can be reconciled with God. In remembrance of Jesus' death and resurrection, the cross serves as a fundamental symbol in Christianity.

With nearly two billion believers in countries around the globe, Christianity is the largest of the world's religions. There is no one central authority for all of Christianity. The pope (the bishop of Rome) is the authority for the Roman Catholic Church, but other sects look to other authorities. Orthodox communities look to patriarchs and emphasize doctrinal agreement and traditional practice. Protestant communities focus on individual conscience. The Roman Catholic and Protestant churches are often referred to as the Western Church, while the Orthodox churches may also be called the Eastern Church. All three main branches of Christianity acknowledge the authority of Christian scriptures, a compilation of writings assembled into a document called the Bible. Methods of biblical interpretation vary among the different Christian sects.

The Feast of the Annunciation celebrates the appearance of the Archangel Gabriel to the Virgin Mary, announcing that she was going to be the mother of Jesus

Christ. Although the Christian church began commemorating this occasion early on, the exact date could not have been fixed until the date of **CHRISTMAS** was established in the late fourth century, since the two holidays obviously had to be nine months apart. Some scholars believe that the Feast of the Annunciation was established to curb the wild behavior associated with an ancient spring festival held in Rome around this same time of year.

According to tradition, Mary of Nazareth was living in her parents' home at the time. Although she had made a vow that she would never marry, Jewish custom decreed that she and her sister should marry young Jewish men so the family wealth could be handed down. Distressed by the thought that she might be forced into a marriage she did not want, Mary was overjoyed to discover what lay in store for her. Not only could she keep her vow, but it would not prevent her from fulfilling her role as the most important mother in all of Christianity.

The name of this feast has changed over the years. Roman Catholics now call it the "Annunciation of the Lord," while Orthodox Christians refer to it as the "Annunciation of the Mother of God." Anglicans call it the "Annunciation of Our Lord to the Blessed Virgin Mary." The English call March 25 "Lady Day of March," since there are four other feast days that qualify as Lady Days in the Christian calendar: The Purification of Mary (also known as **CANDLEMAS**), commemorating Mary's presentation of her son in the Temple at Jerusalem on February 2; the Visitation on July 2, commemorating Mary's visit to her cousin Elizabeth; the Nativity of Mary on September 8; and the Immaculate Conception on December 8. According to an old tradition, the crucifixion of Jesus took place on March 25, and as a result it was considered unlucky if **EASTER** and Lady Day coincided. The English had a rhyme that said, "If Our Lord falls in Our Lady's lap/England will meet with great mishap." Those who cling to this belief point to 1910, when the two holidays coincided and King Edward VII died soon after.

In many European countries, the Feast of the Annunciation is a day for weather predictions. In Belgium, for example, traditional beliefs hold that all seeds sown on this day are guaranteed to germinate. Although an Italian proverb says that frost on March 25 will do no harm, a French proverb says it will bring disaster to the fields. There is also a saying that rain on Lady Day will mean rain on all the other feast days dedicated to the Virgin Mary throughout the year.

SYMBOLS AND CUSTOMS

Dove

The white dove symbolizes purity, in part because of lore, which held that the devil could transform himself into any bird except the dove. After observing the traditional forty-day period of purification following the birth of Jesus, Mary brought her son to the Temple at Jerusalem, where two doves were offered as a sacrifice. In Christian art, a dove also appears sometimes on the top of Joseph's rod to show that he was chosen to be Mary's husband. Because Jesus instructed his followers to be "innocent as doves," the doves often seen on gravestones symbolize the innocence of the person buried there.

The most important use of the dove, however, is as a symbol of the Holy Spirit. In medieval paintings of the Annunciation, the Virgin Mary is usually shown kneeling or seated at a table, reading. The Holy Spirit is seen descending toward her in the form of a dove. The dove usually appears within a beam of light striking Mary's ear. The light is symbolic of God, who separated light from darkness on the first day of Creation. In medieval times, the ear was believed to house the memory.

Lady Day Cakes

In the English town of St. Albans, Lady Day is associated with the baking of special cakes. According to legend, a lady was traveling with her attendants when she lost her way near St. Albans. The lights from the monastery tower, located on a hill, guided her party to safety. To show her gratitude, she gave the monks of the abbey a sum of money to provide free cakes in the shape of ladies, to be distributed on March 25. The cakes were later called "Pope Ladies," a term that probably originated after the Reformation.

Lily

The lily has traditionally symbolized purity, innocence, and virginity, and for Christians it became both a symbol and attribute of the Virgin Mary. Together with the DOVE, the lily is associated with the Annunciation. In Christian art, Gabriel, the angel who appeared to Mary at the Annunciation, is usually shown holding a lily, as are Joseph and his parents, Anne and Joachim.

According to legend, the lily sprang from the tears of Eve when she was expelled from the Garden of Eden. The large white lily known as the Madonna Lily is sacred to the Virgin Mary and is said to have been yellow until she bent down to pick it.

FURTHER READING

Bellenir, Karen. *Religious Holidays and Calendars*. 3rd ed. Detroit: Omnigraphics, 2004.

Biedermann, Hans. *Dictionary of Symbolism: Cultural Icons and the Meanings Behind Them*. New York: Meridian Books, 1994.

Chambers, Robert. *The Book of Days*. 2 vols. 1862-64. Reprint. Detroit: Omnigraphics, 1990.

Cirlot, J.E. *A Dictionary of Symbols*. New York: Philosophical Library, 1962.

Ferguson, George. *Signs and Symbols in Christian Art*. New York: Oxford University Press, 1954.

Harper, Howard V. *Days and Customs of All Faiths*. 1957. Reprint. Detroit: Omnigraphics, 1990.

Henderson, Helene, ed. *Holidays, Festivals, and Celebrations of the World Dictionary*. 3rd ed. Detroit: Omnigraphics, 2005.

Hole, Christina. *English Custom & Usage*. 1941. Reprint. Detroit: Omnigraphics, 1990.

Leach, Maria, ed. *Funk & Wagnalls Standard Dictionary of Folklore, Mythology & Legend*. San Francisco: Harper & Row, 1984.

Olderr, Steven. *Symbolism: A Comprehensive Dictionary*. Jefferson, NC: McFarland, 1986.

Rest, Friedrich. *Our Christian Symbols*. New York: Pilgrim Press, 1954.

Urlin, Ethel L. *Festivals, Holy Days, and Saints' Days*. 1915. Reprint. Detroit: Omnigraphics, 1992.

WEB SITES

Gospel Communications International
www.biblegateway.com/passage/?search=Luke%201:26-55&version=31

New Advent Catholic Encyclopedia
www.newadvent.org/cathen/01542a.htm

Aoi Matsuri
(Hollyhock Festival)

Type of Holiday: Folkloric, Religious (Shinto)
Date of Observation: May 15
Where Celebrated: Kyoto, Japan
Symbols and Customs: Hollyhock

ORIGINS

Aoi Matsuri is a Shinto festival. Shinto is an ancient religion that originated in Japan. Most Shinto adherents live in Japan, but small communities also exist in Europe, Latin America, North America, and in the Pacific island nations.

The name Shinto was first employed during the sixth century C.E. to differentiate indigenous religions in Japan from faith systems that originated in mainland Asia (primarily Buddhism and Confucianism). The word is derived from two Chinese characters, *shen* (gods) and *tao* (way). Loosely translated, Shinto means "way of the gods." Its roots lie in an ancient nature-based religion. Some important concepts in Shinto include the value of tradition, the reverence of nature, cleanliness (ritual purity), and the veneration of spirits called *kami*. Strictly speaking, kami are not deities. The literal translation of the word kami is "that which is hidden."

Kami (which is both the singular and plural term) are honored, but do not assert their powers upon humans in the traditional manner of deities or gods in other religions. People may be descended from the kami, and kami may influence the course of nature and events. The kami can bestow blessings, but they are not all benign. Kami are present in natural things such as trees, mountains, rocks, and rivers. They are embodied in religious relics, especially mirrors and jewels. They also include spirits of ancestors, local deities, holy people, and even political or literary figures. The human role is to venerate the kami and make offerings. The ultimate goal of Shinto is to uphold the harmony among humans and between people and nature. In this regard, the principle of all kami is to protect and sustain life.

The central authorities in Shinto are the priests. Traditionally the duties of the priest were passed through heredity lines, but in modern times, priests are trained on the basis of recommendation. The priests' duties include communicating with the kami and ensuring that ceremonies are properly carried out. Shinto does not have a single collection of sacred texts analogous to the Christian Bible or Islamic Qur'an. Instead, several important books provide information and guidance: *Kojiki* (*Records of Ancient Events*), *Nihongi* (*Chronicles of Japan*), and *Engishiki* (*Chronicles of the Engi*).

One of the three major festivals of Kyoto, Japan, Aoi Matsuri dates back to the sixth century. It gets its name—the Hollyhock Festival—from the leaves used to decorate the headdresses worn by the participants. The festival takes place on May 15, when the cherry blossoms have fallen and the irises are not yet in flower. The heavy rains and gray skies that are common in Kyoto at this time of year are one reason, according to legend, that the festival was established. Flooding was so widespread during the sixth century that imperial messengers were sent to the Kyoto shrines of Shimogamo and Kamigamo to ask for the gods' help. When the floodwaters receded, the people held a celebration.

The festival, which was revived in 1884, consists of a recreation of the original procession to the shrines. The participants gather at the Imperial Palace in the morning to begin the long, circuitous route to the shrines. Spectators may purchase seats at the palace to watch the parade, or they can choose their own viewing place along the route. The highlight of the procession is the imperial messenger and his courtiers, who are dressed in elaborate kimonos and the high-backed black hats known as *eboshi*. They surround a large, lacquered *gissha* or oxcart draped with *fuji* or artificial wisteria flowers and pulled by a black ox who is drawn through the streets by ropes of orange silk. Other participants in Heian-period costumes carry huge ceremonial umbrellas covered with large, artificial flowers—usually peonies, symbolic of wealth and distinction. A lady carried on a litter represents a princess who has been chosen to lead the difficult life of a Shinto priestess. Traditional Japanese music with flutes, gongs, and drums accompanies the procession. Spectators often need a program to help them identify the various warriors, courtiers, and other dignitaries in the parade.

SYMBOLS AND CUSTOMS

Hollyhock

Aoi is usually translated to mean "hollyhock," but a different plant—probably a wild ginger—may originally have been used in the festival. When wild ginger became hard to find, other plants with heart-shaped leaves were substituted. At the end of the procession to the Kamigamo and Shimogamo shrines, the foliage is offered as a token of respect and appreciation to the gods.

The Japanese believed that hollyhocks could prevent storms and earthquakes. By bringing this plant with its heart-shaped leaves to the shrine, they are commemorating the heavy rains and flooding that plagued Kyoto during the sixth century.

FURTHER READING

Bauer, Helen, and Sherwin Carlquist. *Japanese Festivals*. Garden City, NY: Doubleday, 1965.

Bellenir, Karen. *Religious Holidays and Calendars*. 3rd ed. Detroit: Omnigraphics, 2004.

Henderson, Helene, ed. *Holidays, Festivals, and Celebrations of the World Dictionary*. 3rd ed. Detroit: Omnigraphics, 2005.

Shemanski, Frances. *A Guide to World Fairs and Festivals*. Westport, CT: Greenwood Press, 1985.

WEB SITES

Japan National Tourist Organization
www.jnto.go.jp/eng/indepth/history/traditionalevents/a24_fes_aoi.html

Kyoto Prefectural Government Tourism and Convention Office
www.pref.kyoto.jp/visitkyoto/en/info_required/traditional/kyoto_city/01

Apache Girls' Sunrise Ceremony

Type of Holiday: Religious (Apache)
Date of Observation: Four days in July
Where Celebrated: Arizona and New Mexico
Symbols and Customs: Abalone Shell, Blessing the Sick, Cane, Cattail Pollen, Ceremonial Dress, Crown Dancers, Molding, Running Ritual, Sponsor, Sunrise Dance, Symbolic Tipi

ORIGINS

The Apache Girls' Sunrise Ceremony is part of the Native American religious tradition. The history of this and other Native American cultures dates back thousands of years into prehistoric times. According to many scholars, the people who became the Native Americans migrated from Asia across a land bridge that may have once connected the territories presently occupied by Alaska and Russia. The migrations, believed to have begun between 60,000 and 30,000 B.C.E., continued until approximately 4,000 B.C.E. This speculation, however, conflicts with traditional stories asserting that the indigenous Americans have always lived in North America or that tribes moved up from the south.

The historical development of religious belief systems among Native Americans is not well known. Most of the information available was gathered by Europeans who arrived on the continent beginning in the sixteenth century C.E. The data they recorded was fragmentary and oftentimes of questionable accuracy because the Europeans did not understand the native cultures they were trying to describe and the Native Americans were reluctant to divulge details about themselves.

The Apache Indians, most of whom now live on reservations in New Mexico and Arizona, believe that their earliest ancestors emerged from the underworld by climbing up a cane stalk behind the Red Ants, also known as the First People. Changing Woman, also known as White-Painted Woman or White Clay Woman, was the first Apache. She appeared in the east as a beautiful young woman, moved to the west, and disappeared when she was old. Changing Woman is the primary deity in the Apache religion. She is embodied as the earth itself.

In July, ceremonies are held at both the Arizona and New Mexico reservations to celebrate the coming-of-age of young Apache girls. Although in the 1800s the U.S. government forbade the Apaches to congregate, in 1911 they were granted permission to get together on July 4th to celebrate the nation's birthday. They chose this date for one of their most important cultural rituals as an insult to their conquerors.

For the four days of the so-called "getting her ready" ceremony, the mythical power of Changing Woman is believed to enter these girls' bodies, giving them the power to heal those around them. Their faces are painted with white clay, and each girl is blessed with sacred CATTAIL POLLEN. They wear a piece of ABALONE SHELL above their foreheads and act out the role of their mythical female ancestor as they prepare for their lives as adult women.

The size of these ceremonies is one of their most distinctive traits: dozens of people may attend, and they must be fed for the four days that the ceremony lasts. In addition, singers, musicians, and dancers are hired, so the cost of the celebration is significant. Some families find it beyond their means, and this is one reason why the ritual is less common than it used to be. However, in many cases, the extended family will help underwrite the expense. Financial assistance may also come from the woman who serves as the initiate's SPONSOR. This figure is usually a mature friend of the family who aids the young woman throughout the ceremony and is somewhat similar to a godmother.

On the first day, a SYMBOLIC TIPI is constructed to house the ritual activities that will take place. Soon after, a medicine man blesses the CEREMONIAL DRESS that will be worn by the girl, a CANE, and various other sacred items used in the ceremony. On the morning of the second day, the SUNRISE DANCE is performed by the girl and her sponsor. It is during this dance that the girl is believed to take on the powers of Changing Woman, which she then uses in BLESSING THE SICK. The initiate also receives blessings, which take place when adult guests at the ceremony sprinkle CATTAIL POLLEN on her head.

Throughout the four days of the ceremony, the initiate must observe certain guidelines that are related to the sacred quality she is believed to possess. She can only drink through a straw, because if she touches water directly, it's believed that she will bring rain. If she scratches her skin with her fingernails, she will be scarred, so she is given a special scratching stick to prevent this from happening. She also must maintain a serious demeanor because if she laughs a great deal during the ceremony, she is said to become prematurely wrinkled.

Beginning on the second evening, four or more CROWN DANCERS perform a dramatic set of dances, representing the *Gaan* mountain spirits, who are thought to create good fortune for the girl and those attending the ceremony. The CROWN DANCERS and the girl dance on subsequent days as well, and the girl also completes a RUNNING RITUAL. When the ceremony concludes after four days, the initiate's supernatural powers come to an end, but she is then considered a woman and is eligible for marriage.

SYMBOLS AND CUSTOMS

Abalone Shell

The piece of abalone shell tied above the forehead of each girl participating in this ceremony represents the shell in which Changing Woman, according to Apache legend, survived a great flood to become the First Apache.

Blessing the Sick

When the initiate takes on the spirit of Changing Woman during the sunrise dance, she is believed to have the power to help those who are suffering from illness or otherwise need assistance. During the ceremony, they come before the girl, and she blesses them in hopes of giving them some of her qualities of longevity and strength. The girl will usually lay her hands on the person and then turn them to each of the four directions. In this way, the girl's coming of age becomes an event that also benefits the wider community.

Cane

Representing long life, the cane is made of wood and usually has bells, feathers, and ribbons attached to it. The initiate holds it during her dances, and it is also used in the running ritual.

Cattail Pollen

The Apache consider the pollen from the cattail plant to be a sacred substance that represents the life-giving quality of the earth. To invoke its power for the young woman, guests at the ceremony sprinkle the pollen on her head.

Ceremonial Dress

The girl undergoing the ceremony dons a bright yellow dress on the first day and wears it for the remainder of the ritual. Her sponsor sometimes wears one in a similar style. Traditionally, these were made of buckskin but now are often fashioned from cloth.

Crown Dancers

Wearing elaborate costumes that include enormous wooden headdresses and black hoods, the crown dancers are the most exciting element of the ritual. There are usually four of them along with a fifth clown-like figure, and they perform a long series of athletic dances around a huge bonfire, sometimes on their own and sometimes with the initiate. Impersonating the mountain spirits known as the Gaan, they are believed to have the power to drive away evil, and so are essential to making the ceremony an auspicious event. They wear fantastic headdresses, which tower above their black-hooded faces and painted bodies adorned with harness bells. As they dance around the fire, they resemble huge wooden marionettes as they swing their headdresses from side to side and brandish their wooden swords.

Molding

At one point during the ceremony, the girl lies on a piece of buckskin, and the sponsor massages her entire body. It is said that this causes the girl to be "molded" into the proper form so that she will have strength and good health.

Running Ritual

In this part of the ceremony, the girl's cane is stuck into the ground in specific places, and she runs to it and circles it, returning to her starting point. This symbolizes the different stages of life she will pass through. The girl then makes four additional runs to the four cardinal directions. Small children sometimes accompany the girl during the running.

Sponsor

As she enters adulthood, the girl has the assistance of an older female who helps her make the transition. In addition to molding the initiate and participating in the sunrise dance, the sponsor often contributes money to finance the ceremony.

Sunrise Dance

The central action on the part of the girl is the sunrise dance, which takes place early on the second day of the ceremony. Accompanied by the sponsor, the initiate faces east toward the rising sun and dances a specific program of songs, usually a total of thirty-two, with music provided by singers and drummers. The songs relate the story of Changing Woman, and in the course of this performance, the girl is believed to take on the holy powers of that figure.

Symbolic Tipi

The traditional house of the Apache people is the tipi. It is invoked in the ceremony, but rather than creating an actual tipi with walls, a ceremonial open-air structure is made, lashing together four spruce poles in a tipi shape. It provides a ceremonial enclosure, but the open design allows the guests to view the ritual.

FURTHER READING

Crim, Keith R. *The Perennial Dictionary of World Religions*. San Francisco: Harper & Row, 1989.

Eagle Walking Turtle. *Indian America: A Traveler's Companion*. Santa Fe: J. Muir Publications, 1989.

Fergusson, Erna. *Dancing Gods: Indian Ceremonials of New Mexico and Arizona*. New York: A.A. Knopf, 1931.

Ganteaume, Cécile R. "White Mountain Apache Dance: Expressions of Spirituality." In *Native American Dance: Ceremonies and Social Traditions*, edited by Charlotte Heth. Washington DC: National Museum of the American Indian, Smithsonian Institution, 1992.

Henderson, ed, Helene. *Holidays, Festivals, and Celebrations of the World Dictionary*. 3rd ed. Detroit: Omnigraphics, 2005.

Kavasch, E. Barrie. *Enduring Harvests: Native American Foods and Festivals for Every Season*. Old Saybrook, CT: Globe Pequot Press, 1995.

WEB SITE

Peabody Museum of Archaeology and Ethnology, Harvard University
www.peabody.harvard.edu/maria/Sunrisedance.html

April Fools' Day

Type of Holiday: Calendar/Seasonal, Folkloric
Date of Observation: April 1
Where Celebrated: England, France, Scotland, United States
Symbols and Customs: Fish, Pranks and Practical Jokes
Related Holidays: Feast of Fools

ORIGINS

Children have been shouting "April Fool!" since the 1600s in England, shortly before the custom was brought to America by the first English settlers. But there are a number of theories as to how it got started. One explanation points to Noah as the first "April Fool." It is said that on this day Noah mistakenly sent the dove out to find dry land after the flood began to recede. Another possibility is that it had something to do with the change to the New Style or Gregorian calendar.

The Gregorian calendar is named after Pope Gregory XIII, who in 1582 instituted a calendar that corrected time-keeping errors in Julius Caesar's Julian calendar, which had been in use since 45 B.C.E. In 1852 the Gregorian calendar subtracted ten days from the month of October so that October 6 was instead October 15. This shift brought the calendar more in line with the seasons. It also created Leap Year Day and established January 1 as the day of the new year throughout the Christian world. Catholic countries, such as Italy, France, Luxembourg, Spain, and Portugal, switched to the new calendar that year. Other European nations, predominantly Protestant or Orthodox, did not. Protestant Germany accepted the change in 1700, Orthodox Russia in 1706. Great Britain accepted the Gregorian calendar, and the New Year, on January 1, in 1752. By the twentieth century most of the world had accepted the Gregorian calendar for civic and business purposes.

Under the Old Style calendar, **NEW YEAR'S DAY** was celebrated around the time of the **VERNAL EQUINOX** in late March. Because this occasionally coincided with, or at least came close to, the celebration of **EASTER**, Church officials moved New Year's Day up to April 1. When the Gregorian calendar was officially adopted in 1582 and New Year's Day was shifted from April 1 to January 1, some people forgot about the change and continued to make their New Year visits on the old date. Others paid mock visits to friends and neighbors on April 1, shouting "April Fool!" at those who took them seriously.

April Fools' Day has been called by many other names—among them Huntigowk Day or Gowkie Day (in Scotland, where an April fool is called a "gowk"), All Fools' Day, and April Noddy Day (a fool in England is called a "noddie," "gob," or "gawby"). But all of these names echo that of the **FEAST OF FOOLS**, a popular medieval festival during which social roles were reversed and rules were deliberately flouted. The men would dress up as women, eat and gamble at the altar, burn old leather sandals in the censers, and engage in other activities that would normally be unthinkable. The Feast of Fools was especially popular in France, where April Fools' Day is widely observed.

SYMBOLS AND CUSTOMS

Fish

In France, the fish is the primary symbol of April Fools' Day. Chocolate candy shaped like fish is sold everywhere, and people often try to pin a paper fish on someone else's back without getting caught (for which the day is called Fooling the April Fish Day). The people known as "April fools" in English-speaking countries are called "April fish" (poisson d'Avril) in France. Since fish begin to run in the spring, it is likely that the April Fish is a symbol of rebirth and fertility.

Pranks and Practical Jokes

Some scholars theorize that the custom of pulling pranks and practical jokes on April 1 is a relic of the ancient Roman festival in honor of Ceres, the goddess whose daughter Proserpine was carried off to the underworld by Pluto to be his queen. Ceres' day-and-night search for her daughter was considered a "fool's errand" because Pluto was a very powerful god. A similar connection exists between April Fools' Day and the Hindu spring festival of **HOLI**. Although there is no historical evidence of a connection between the two, it is interesting to note that one of the principal Holi customs is playing practical jokes and sending people on fools' errands.

A more modern explanation for the custom is that it accompanied the shift from the Old Style (or Julian) calendar to the New Style (Gregorian) calendar. People in France who couldn't make the adjustment were often sent mock gifts and called "April Fish" (*see* FISH) or April fools. The custom of April fooling spread quickly throughout France and Europe. In England, the custom had already taken root in the early eighteenth century, even though the change in the calendar was not official until 1752.

In England, an April fool was called an April gob, gawby, or noddie. In Scotland, it was an April gowk or cuckoo. A favorite prank in Scotland was to send someone to deliver a letter. Upon receiving it, the recipient would tell the carrier that he or she was mistaken; the letter was meant for someone who lived farther down the road. Unbeknownst to the carrier, what the letter really said was, "It's the first of April. Hunt the gowk another mile." When the gullible person was sent back to where he or she started, everyone involved in the prank would gather around him or her and shout, "April gowk!"

Pranking was brought to America by British and French settlers. A classic April Fools' Day prank among children is to tell each other that their shoelaces are undone and then cry "April Fool!" when the victims glance at their feet. Sometimes the media get into the act, broadcasting fictitious news items designed to amuse or alarm the public. British television, for example, once showed Italian farmers "harvesting" spaghetti from trees. As other activities associated with the holiday—such as a Parade of Fools—have disappeared, pranking remains the only custom associated with this day.

FURTHER READING

Henderson, Helene, ed. *Holidays, Festivals, and Celebrations of the World Dictionary.* 3rd ed. Detroit: Omnigraphics, 2005.

Purdy, Susan. *Festivals for You to Celebrate.* Philadelphia: Lippincott, 1969.

Santino, Jack. *All Around the Year: Holidays and Celebrations in American Life.* Urbana: University of Illinois Press, 1994.

Urlin, Ethel L. *Festivals, Holy Days, and Saints' Days.* 1915. Reprint. Detroit: Omnigraphics, 1992.

WEB SITES

Library of Congress
www.americaslibrary.gov/cgi-bin/page.cgi/jb/modern/aprfool_1

University of Kansas Diversity Calendar
www3.kumc.edu/diversity/other/aprlfool.html

Arbor Day

Type of Holiday: Promotional
Date of Observation: Varied, but usually last Friday in April
Where Celebrated: Puerto Rico, United States, and many countries around the
  world
Symbols and Customs: Trees
Related Holidays: Earth Day, Tu Bishvat

ORIGINS

Known as the "Father of Arbor Day," Julius Sterling Morton settled on the treeless
plains of Nebraska in 1855, where he edited the *Nebraska City News* and developed a
lifelong interest in new agricultural methods. Believing that the prairie needed more
TREES to serve as windbreaks, to hold moisture in the soil, and to provide lumber for
housing, Morton began planting trees and urged his neighbors to do the same.
When he joined the State Board of Agriculture, he proposed that a specific day be set
aside for the planting of trees and that a prize be offered to the individual who planted the largest number of trees on that day. A million trees were planted in Nebraska
on April 10, 1872, and 350 million more were planted within the next sixteen years.
In 1895 Nebraska became known as the Tree Planter's State, although today it is
more commonly referred to as the Cornhusker State or the Beef State. Nebraskans
still honor Morton, who served as Secretary of Agriculture under President Grover
Cleveland from 1893 to 1897, on April 22, the anniversary of his birth.

The observation of what came to be known as Arbor Day was widespread
throughout the United States between the 1880s and World War II, when schools
and communities would routinely hold tree-planting ceremonies. All fifty states
still have an official Arbor Day—usually the last Friday in April. A few states call
it Arbor and Bird Day, emphasizing the planting of trees and shrubs that are
attractive to birds. And every year on this day the president or the first lady

Arbor Day Celebrations in Other Countries

 ustralia: National Tree Day has been promoted by Planet Ark, a non-profit organization based in Sydney, since 1996. It is observed each year on the last Sunday in July, when hundreds of thousands of volunteers around the nation plant trees and shrubs. Planet Ark also organizes School Tree Day on the last Friday of July to encourage school children to plant trees and shrubs at their schools.

China and Taiwan: Arbor Day is observed on or near March 12, the anniversary of the death of Sun Yat-sen (1866-1925), the first provisional president of the Republic of China. Each year tree-planting ceremonies and festivals are held throughout the country.

United Kingdom: The Tree Council, based in London, has organized National Tree Week since 1975. Each year during the last week in November, dozens of communities throughout England, Scotland, Wales, and Northern Ireland host events centered on tree planting.

plants a special tree on the grounds of the White House in Washington DC. But most of the activities associated with Arbor Day take place in the public schools, where there are pageants, music, poetry, bulletin board displays, and discussions about the importance of trees. Although Girl Scouts, Boy Scouts, civic organizations, conservation groups, and service clubs occasionally hold tree-planting ceremonies on Arbor Day, for the most part the importance of trees has been replaced by concern for the environment in general. In fact, since 1970, Arbor Day has been eclipsed in many parts of the United States by **EARTH DAY** observances on April 22. Still, many countries around the world have created their own Arbor Day celebrations.

SYMBOLS AND CUSTOMS

Trees

Trees are the original and most enduring symbol of Arbor Day. Although tree planting was widely associated with Johnny Appleseed, who planted thousands of apple seeds between 1801 and 1845 throughout Ohio and Indiana, there is no question that Julius Morton was the one who popularized the idea of planting trees and who established a special day for doing so.

Today, trees are symbolic of the conservation movement in general. On Arbor Day, trees are planted along roads and public highways, in parks and community forests, on the grounds of state capitols and school buildings, and on all types of public and private property for both ornamental and practical purposes. Trees have also been planted as memorials to outstanding Americans and in honor of various social causes, such as AIDS awareness. The National Arbor Day Foundation offers new members ten free trees if they join the organization.

FURTHER READING

Christianson, Stephen G., and Jane M. Hatch. *The American Book of Days*. 4th ed. New York: H.W. Wilson, 2000.

Cohen, Hennig, and Tristram Potter Coffin. *The Folklore of American Holidays*. 3rd ed. Detroit: Gale Research, 1999.

Henderson, Helene, ed. *Holidays, Festivals, and Celebrations of the World Dictionary*. 3rd ed. Detroit: Omnigraphics, 2005.

Ickis, Marguerite. *The Book of Festivals and Holidays the World Over*. New York: Dodd, Mead, 1970.

Schaun, George and Virginia, and David Wisniewski. *American Holidays and Special Days*. 3rd ed. Lanham: Maryland Historical Press, 2002.

Schmidt, Leigh Eric. *Consumer Rites: The Buying and Selling of American Holidays*. Princeton: Princeton University Press, 1995.

WEB SITES

National Arbor Day Foundation
www.arborday.org/arborday/index.cfm

Planet Ark (Australia)
www.planetark.com/campaignspage.cfm/newsid/3/story.htm

The Tree Council (United Kingdom)
www.treecouncil.org.uk

Arctic Winter Games

Type of Holiday: Sporting
Date of Observation: One week in March during even-numbered years
Where Celebrated: Canada, Greenland, Alaska (location varies)
Symbols and Customs: Bannock Making, Hodgson Trophy, Inuit Games, Three-Ring Logo
Related Holidays: Olympic Games, World Eskimo-Indian Olympics

ORIGINS

The Arctic Winter Games got their start in the late 1960s, when a Yukon businessman named Cal Miller and Stuart Hodgson, the commissioner of the Northwest Territories, found themselves at the Canada Winter Games in Quebec City, where they had come to support their local athletes. It disturbed both men to see how often the competitors from Canada's two northern territories were defeated by those from the southern Canadian provinces, who had the training facilities, sponsorship, and other forms of support that their northern counterparts lacked. The discussion that Hodgson and Miller had that evening led to the establishment of the Arctic Winter Games, which were held for the first time in Yellowknife, the capital of the Northwest Territories, in 1970.

At first, only athletes from the Northwest Territories, Yukon, and Alaska participated in the games, but they were soon joined by northern Quebec (which dropped out of the games a few years later), Greenland, and northern Alberta. Athletes from the nearby Russian provinces joined the competition in 1990, and since that time the games have been held every two years at varying locations in Yukon, northern Alberta, Alaska, and the Northwest Territories. Nearly 3,000 athletes—from Russia, Alaska, Yukon, Northern Alberta, Northwest Territories, Nunavit (Arctic Quebec), Nunavut, Greenland, and Sami—participated in the 2006 Games, which were hosted by the Kenai Peninsula in Alaska.

While the Arctic Games feature many of the same events as the **OLYMPIC GAMES**—including alpine and cross-country skiing, hockey, snowboarding, speed skating, curling, and the biathlon—there is a marked emphasis on traditional INUIT GAMES and on northern sports like dog mushing and snowshoeing. The Arctic Games also include other sports, including some that are associated elsewhere with summer—such as basketball, badminton, volleyball, soccer, and wrestling—because there is no real summer this far north and such games must be played indoors.

From their very inception, the emphasis of the Arctic Winter Games has been on getting as many athletes as possible to participate in the competition, rather than on attracting elite athletes, who have ample opportunity to compete elsewhere.

In addition to the sporting events, the games feature many cultural exhibits and activities. The 2006 Games, for example, included art exhibits, fireworks, traditional dance performances, and a pin-trading party.

SYMBOLS AND CUSTOMS

Bannock Making

Competitions and demonstrations that involve making bannock—a traditional round flour-water biscuit to which salt, lard, buttermilk, baking soda or powder, and other ingredients have since been added—are common at the Arctic Winter Games and at the smaller regional competitions leading up to the Arctic Games. Bannock making was often part of the "Good Woman Contest," a competition in which women competed against one another in such essential frontier skills as skinning seals and cutting up caribou meat—at one time the only part of the games in which women were allowed to participate. Nowadays women compete in almost all the events, but bannock making remains popular. Bannock resembles a large scone and is traditionally cooked in a cast iron frying pan over an open fire with lots of melted lard.

Hodgson Trophy

The Hodgson Trophy, named after Commissioner Stuart Hodgson of the Northwest Territories, one of the founders of the Arctic Winter Games, consists of a soapstone base and a narwhal tusk. There is a walrus carved into the base of the tusk and a bear near the top, symbolic of the athletes' striving to do their best. Although medals are awarded to individual athletes, the trophy is awarded to the team whose conduct best demonstrates "the ideals of fair play and team spirit."

Inuit Games

For most spectators, the highlight of the Arctic Winter Games is the traditional Inuit Games, which were developed by the aboriginal inhabitants of northern Canada, Greenland, Alaska, and northeastern Siberia as a way of amusing themselves and staying fit during the long, dark winter days. Most of these games fostered skills that were essential to survival, and they could be played with little or no equipment in the limited space of an igloo. Participation and self-improvement were stressed over competition, and it was unusual for someone to actually get hurt.

Today, both men and women participate in events that involve pulling, reaching, kicking, twisting, and sheer endurance. In the "mouth pull" and "ear pull," for

> ## Values of the Arctic Winter Games International Committee
>
> | | |
> |---|---|
> | Cultural Awareness and Understanding | Respect for Self and Others |
> | Fair Play | Partnerships |
> | Access and Equity | Personal Development |
> | Integrity | Community Development |

example, the object is to reach around behind the other person's head and grab his or her mouth or ear so that he or she is forced to turn his or her head to the side. In the "finger pull," two contestants face each other with their middle fingers locked, pulling until one of them is forced to straighten his or her finger. The "head pull" is similar, except that the competitors have a belt or piece of canvas webbing fastened around both their heads, against which they pull in an effort to throw the other off-balance. There is also an "arm pull" and a "hand pull" based on the same principle. The "knuckle hop" can be quite painful to watch, as the contestants get into a "push-up" position and then try to hop forward by balancing on their knuckles and toes.

Kicking events include the one-foot and two-foot high kicks. Both involve jumping up and kicking an object, typically a wad of sealskin, that is suspended at increasingly higher levels. The name of the event doesn't refer to the distance competitors must jump, however; it refers to how they land. In the one-foot high kick, they must take off on both feet, kick the target object with one foot, and then land on this same foot while not touching the floor with the other. In the two-foot high kick, they must jump with both feet, kick the object, and land on both feet. The "Alaskan high kick" involves so much strength, coordination, and balance that it defies description.

Most Inuit games require agility and extraordinary arm and hand strength—skills that were at one time needed for hunting and harpooning, for jumping from one ice floe to the next, and for outmaneuvering wild animals. In the "musk-ox fight," for example, women get down on their hands and knees, place their heads side by side, and push against one another's shoulders in much the same way the female musk-ox does in the wild.

Three-Ring Logo

The logo for the Arctic Winter Games consists of three interlocking rings symbolizing the three purposes for which the games are held: "athletic competition, cultural exhibition, and social interchange," according to the Arctic Winter Games International Committee.

WEB SITE

Arctic Winter Games Official Web Site
www.arcticwintergames.com

Ascension Day

Type of Holiday: Religious (Christian)
Date of Observation: Between April 30 and June 3; forty days after Easter
Where Celebrated: Britain, Europe, United States, and by Roman Catholics and Anglicans around the world
Symbols and Customs: Ascension Plays, Beating the Bounds, Birds, Chasing the Devil, Crickets, Well Dressing, Wheat
Related Holidays: Easter

ORIGINS

Ascension Day is a Christian holiday celebrated by Roman Catholics and Protestants. The word Christian refers to a follower of Christ, a title derived from the Greek word meaning Messiah or Anointed One. The Christ of Christianity is Jesus of Nazareth, a man born between 7 and 4 B.C.E. in the region of Palestine. According to Christian teaching, Jesus was killed by Roman authorities using a form of execution called crucifixion (a term meaning he was nailed to a cross and hung from it until he died) in about the year 30 C.E. After his death, he rose back to life. His death and resurrection provide a way by which people can be reconciled with God. In remembrance of Jesus' death and resurrection, the cross serves as a fundamental symbol in Christianity.

With nearly two billion believers in countries around the globe, Christianity is the largest of the world's religions. There is no one central authority for all of Christianity. The pope (the bishop of Rome) is the authority for the Roman Catholic Church, but other sects look to other authorities. Orthodox communities look to patriarchs and emphasize doctrinal agreement and traditional practice. Protestant communities focus on individual conscience. The Roman Catholic and Protestant

churches are often referred to as the Western Church, while the Orthodox churches may also be called the Eastern Church. All three main branches of Christianity acknowledge the authority of Christian scriptures, a compilation of writings assembled into a document called the Bible. Methods of biblical interpretation vary among the different Christian sects.

Christians believe that after Jesus Christ was resurrected from the tomb, he spent forty days with his disciples, instructing them on how to carry out his teachings. On the fortieth day, he took them to the Mount of Olives near Jerusalem. As they watched, he raised his hands and was carried up to heaven.

Ascension Day has been observed since 68 C.E Although the Bible specifically mentions what happened on the fortieth day after **EASTER**, the Ascension was not celebrated as a separate festival during the first three centuries following Jesus' birth but was included in the celebration of **PENTECOST**. By the end of the fourth century, however, it was universally observed throughout the Roman Empire.

From the very beginning, Ascension Day observances included a procession that went outside the city, and usually to the top of a hill, in imitation of Jesus leading the Apostles "out towards Bethany," as described in the Gospel according to Luke. In Jerusalem, the procession followed the path that Christ took to the summit of the Mount of Olives. Although such processions were widespread during the eighth and ninth centuries, they were eventually replaced by the pageants or ASCENSION PLAYS of the Middle Ages. But processions are still held after Mass on Ascension Day in some parts of Germany and central Europe, with worshippers following clergymen carrying candles.

Until 1970, Ascension Day was also the day on which the Paschal candle is extinguished (*see* **EASTER**). Since then, Roman Catholic doctrine instructs that the candle remain lit until **PENTECOST.**

SYMBOLS AND CUSTOMS

Ascension Plays

From the eleventh century onwards, the processions that usually took place on Ascension Day were replaced by pageants performed in churches. By the thirteenth century, it was common practice to reenact the Ascension by hoisting a statue of Christ aloft until it disappeared through an opening in the church ceiling. As the image moved slowly upward, people rose and stretched out their arms toward the Christ figure. Huge pieces of silk or cloth were sometimes hung from the ceiling to represent clouds, and angels with lighted candles would come down from "heaven" to meet the Lord and accompany him on His journey. A few minutes after he disappeared, a shower of roses, lilies, and other flowers would fall from the opening, symbolizing the gifts of the Holy Spirit.

Lutheran reformers attacked these plays for overdramatizing the story of the Ascension. But Martin Luther himself eventually decided that if such pageants were staged primarily as a way to teach schoolchildren about the life of Christ, they were permissible.

Beating the Bounds

The three days preceding Ascension Day, which always falls on a Thursday, were known in the Church of England as the **ROGATION DAYS** (from the Latin *rogare*, meaning "to pray" or "to ask"). The name refers to the ancient practice of having clergymen and members of the congregation walk around the boundaries of the parish and ask God's blessing on the fruits of the earth. Since maps were rare in those days, "beating the bounds" served a practical purpose as well: Greedy landlords often stole a corner of someone's property or made use of part of a neighbor's field without anyone noticing. At certain points in the procession, the people would stop. The clergyman would point out an example of God's goodness and lead them in singing a hymn of thanksgiving.

If a fence had been put up since the previous year, the processioners might take it down; if a canal had been cut across the boundary, someone had to strip off his clothes and dive in; if a house had been built on the boundary, the processioners would go in through a back door and out through a window. High walls had to be climbed, rivers and streams had to be crossed, and at the corners or boundary-crosses, small boys were whipped or bumped head downwards to help them remember the places better. The beating of young boys with willow switches was also a symbolic act designed to purify their souls.

The whole point of the Rogationtide ritual was to impress upon the younger generation the importance of keeping track of boundaries. It may have been a continuation of the ancient Roman festival known as the **TERMINALIA** (February 23), held in honor of Terminus, the god of boundary stones. Another theory is that it was a Christianization of the ancient Robigalia (April 25), held at the fifth milestone of the Via Claudi outside Rome to preserve the crops from mildew and other blights.

In many parts of England and Scotland, the custom of walking the parish boundaries is either still observed or has been revived after lapsing for many years. Choirboys and Boy Scouts are often stood on their heads at the most important places on the boundary, which in some cases has not changed since Anglo-Saxon times.

Birds

In imitation of the way in which Christ "flew" up to heaven, it was common in many European countries at one time for people to eat a bird on Ascension Day. Pigeons, partridges, and even crows were served for dinner. In western Germany, bakers made special pastries in the shapes of various birds. Throughout Europe, it was a day for mountain climbing and picnicking in high places.

In Sweden, people traditionally rise early in the morning on Ascension Day and go into the forest to hear the birds sing at sunrise. If a cuckoo is heard from the east or west, it means good luck. But it is a bad omen if the cuckoo is heard first from the north or south. According to an old Swedish saying, "Cuckoo in the west is the very best." After the sun rises, there is a picnic breakfast accompanied by music. These early morning outings are called *gök-otta* or "early cuckoo morning."

The cuckoo is a symbol of the future and of spring in particular. In modern Germany, the word for cuckoo (*kuckuck*) is a common euphemism for the devil.

Chasing the Devil

In some countries, a devil is chased through the streets on Ascension Day. When he is caught, he is dunked in a pond or burned in effigy—symbolic of Jesus' triumph over evil when he ascended to heaven.

In Munich, Germany, it was customary up until the end of the eighteenth century for a man disguised as a demon to be chased through the streets on Ascension Eve by people dressed as witches and wizards. When he was caught, he was dunked in puddles and rolled in dung. Upon reaching the royal palace, he took off his disguise and was given a good meal as a reward. The costume he had worn was stuffed with straw and taken to the church, where it was hung in a window in the tower all night. Before vespers on Ascension Day, it was thrown down to the crowd that had assembled outside the church, and a tremendous struggle ensued. The effigy was finally carried out of town and burned on a nearby hill—a ritual intended to drive evil away from the city.

Crickets

In Florence, Italy, people come to the Cascine Park on Ascension Sunday to pick up *grillos,* or crickets, and put them in decorated boxes or cages with fresh lettuce leaves. If the cricket chirps within three days, it is believed that the family will have good luck. But if the cricket dies, the family dreads whatever ill fortune may befall them.

The cricket is traditionally a symbol of approaching summer. It also represents courage, making it an apt symbol for Ascension Day, when the Apostles watched their Lord leave them and ascend to heaven.

Well Dressing

There are a number of links between water and Ascension Day. In England, the rain that falls on this day is considered to be a remedy for sore eyes, because it falls straight from the heaven that opened up to let Christ enter. The water that is drawn from certain "holy wells" on Ascension Day is also believed to have curative powers.

Well-dressing ceremonies, at one time popular throughout Great Britain, involved decorating the wells with flowers by building frames and trellises around them. After the morning church service, the priest and his congregation would form a procession and visit every well in the area, singing psalms and hymns as they went. The well-dressing ceremony at Tissington in Derbyshire dates back to 1615, when the town's wells continued to flow even during a terrible drought. People came from miles around to draw water, and the well-dressing celebration was instituted to commemorate the event. By the late twentieth century, this well dressing attracted about 50,000 visitors each year.

Some believe that well dressing is a Christian adaptation of the ancient Roman Fontanalia, a festival held in honor of the god of springs, streams, and fountains. Garlands were thrown into springs and placed around the tops of wells. But it was actually the **FLORALIA**—the festival in honor of Flora, goddess of flowers and gardens—that was held at this time of year.

Wheat

In Portugal, Ascension Day is known as "Ear of Wheat Thursday" because peasants make bouquets from olive branches and sheaves of wheat with poppies and daisies. The olive and the wheat are symbolic of an abundant harvest; the poppy stands for peace, and the daisy represents money. A bit of wheat—a traditional symbol of prosperity—is usually kept in the house throughout the coming year.

FURTHER READING

Bellenir, Karen. *Religious Holidays and Calendars*. 3rd ed. Detroit: Omnigraphics, 2004.

Biedermann, Hans. *Dictionary of Symbolism: Cultural Icons and the Meanings Behind Them*. New York: Meridian Books, 1994.

Brewster, H. Pomeroy. *Saints and Festivals of the Christian Church*. 1904. Reprint. Detroit: Omnigraphics, 1990.

Chambers, Robert. *The Book of Days*. 2 vols. 1862-64. Reprint. Detroit: Omnigraphics, 1990.

Ferguson, George. *Signs and Symbols in Christian Art*. New York: Oxford University Press, 1954.

Gulevich, Tanya. *Encyclopedia of Easter, Carnival, and Lent*. Detroit: Omnigraphics, 2002.

Harper, Howard V. *Days and Customs of All Faiths*. 1957. Reprint. Detroit: Omnigraphics, 1990.

Henderson, Helene, ed. *Holidays, Festivals, and Celebrations of the World Dictionary*. 3rd ed. Detroit: Omnigraphics, 2005.

James, E.O. *Seasonal Feasts and Festivals*. 1961. Reprint. Detroit: Omnigraphics, 1993.

MacDonald, Margaret R., ed. *The Folklore of World Holidays*. Detroit: Gale Research, 1992.

Olderr, Steven. *Symbolism: A Comprehensive Dictionary*. Jefferson, NC: McFarland, 1986.

Pike, Royston. *Round the Year with the World's Religions*. 1950. Reprint. Detroit: Omnigraphics, 1992.

Urlin, Ethel L. *Festivals, Holy Days, and Saints' Days*. 1915. Reprint. Detroit: Omnigraphics, 1992.

Weiser, Franz Xaver. *Handbook of Christian Feasts and Customs*. New York: Harcourt, Brace, 1958.

WEB SITES

Commission on Inter-Church Relations and Education Development
www.cired.org/faith/feast.html

Tissington Hall
www.tissington-hall.com

Ash Wednesday

Type of Holiday: Religious (Christian)
Date of Observation: Between February 4 and March 10
Where Celebrated: Britain, Europe, United States, and by Christians throughout the world
Symbols and Customs: Ashes, Jack-o-Lent
Colors: Violet or purple is the ecclesiastical color associated with this day.
Related Holidays: Burial of the Sardine, Easter, Lent, Palm Sunday, Shrove Tuesday

ORIGINS

Ash Wednesday is a significant holiday for Christians and marks the beginning of **LENT**. The word Christian refers to a follower of Christ, a title derived from the

Greek word meaning Messiah or Anointed One. The Christ of Christianity is Jesus of Nazareth, a man born between 7 and 4 B.C.E. in the region of Palestine. According to Christian teaching, Jesus was killed by Roman authorities using a form of execution called crucifixion (a term meaning he was nailed to a cross and hung from it until he died) in about the year 30 C.E. After his death, he rose back to life. His death and resurrection provide a way by which people can be reconciled with God. In remembrance of Jesus' death and resurrection, the cross serves as a fundamental symbol in Christianity.

With nearly two billion believers in countries around the globe, Christianity is the largest of the world's religions. There is no one central authority for all of Christianity. The pope (the bishop of Rome) is the authority for the Roman Catholic Church, but other sects look to other authorities. Orthodox communities look to patriarchs and emphasize doctrinal agreement and traditional practice. Protestant communities focus on individual conscience. The Roman Catholic and Protestant churches are often referred to as the Western Church, while the Orthodox churches may also be called the Eastern Church. All three main branches of Christianity acknowledge the authority of Christian scriptures, a compilation of writings assembled into a document called the Bible. Methods of biblical interpretation vary among the different Christian sects.

For Roman Catholic and some Protestant churches, Ash Wednesday marks the beginning of **LENT**, a forty-day period devoted to self-examination and penitence in preparation for **EASTER**. Lent originally began in the Western Church on a Sunday. But since Sundays were feast days, Pope Gregory I moved the beginning of Lent ahead four days in the latter part of the sixth century.

Gregory is also credited with having introduced the ceremony that gives this day its name. When penitents came to the church to ask forgiveness for their sins, the priest would take some ASHES and mark their foreheads with the sign of the cross while repeating what God said when He expelled Adam and Eve from the Garden of Eden: "Remember, man, dust thou art and to dust thou shalt return."

SYMBOLS AND CUSTOMS

Ashes

Ashes were a biblical symbol of repentance, based on the story of Job, who put on sackcloth and sat down in ashes to show how sorry he was that he had questioned the ways of God. According to the early medieval code of punishment, serious sinners who were ready to seek forgiveness had to come to the church barefoot on the first day of **LENT**. After they had expressed their sorrow, they had ashes sprinkled on their heads or were handed a sackcloth garment covered in ashes. As private confessions became more common, the practice of using sackcloth and ashes on individual sinners declined. Instead, ashes were distributed to the entire congregation.

Ashes are also a symbol of mortality and the shortness of earthly life. When churchgoers have ashes placed on their foreheads on Ash Wednesday, they are reminded of the penitential nature of the Lenten season and of their own human bodies, which will return to ashes when they die. The ashes used on this day are made by burning the palms used during the previous year's **PALM SUNDAY** celebration.

Jack-o-Lent

The English used to dress a straw figure in old clothes and carry it through the streets on Ash Wednesday. Afterward, the effigy—known as Jack-o-Lent—was hanged. The figure was supposed to represent Judas Iscariot, who betrayed Jesus by identifying Him to His enemies as He left the garden of Gethsemane. But it may originally have been a symbol of the dying winter, similar to the Shrovetide Bear (*see* **SHROVE TUESDAY**).

FURTHER READING

Bellenir, Karen. *Religious Holidays and Calendars*. 3rd ed. Detroit: Omnigraphics, 2004.

Ferguson, George. *Signs and Symbols in Christian Art*. New York: Oxford University Press, 1954.

Gulevich, Tanya. *Encyclopedia of Easter, Carnival, and Lent*. Detroit: Omnigraphics, 2002.

Henderson, Helene, ed. *Holidays, Festivals, and Celebrations of the World Dictionary*. 3rd ed. Detroit: Omnigraphics, 2005.

Hole, Christina. *English Custom & Usage*. 1941. Reprint. Detroit: Omnigraphics, 1990.

Metford, J.C.J. *The Christian Year*. New York: Crossroad, 1991.

Santino, Jack. *All Around the Year: Holidays and Celebrations in American Life*. Urbana: University of Illinois Press, 1994.

Tuleja, Tad. *Curious Customs: The Stories Behind 296 Popular American Rituals*. New York: Harmony, 1987.

WEB SITES

Catholic Online
www.catholic.org/clife/lent/ashwed.php

New Advent Catholic Encyclopedia
www.newadvent.org/cathen/01775b.htm

Ashura
(Husain Day, Hosay)

Type of Holiday: Religious (Shi'ite Muslim)
Date of Observation: First ten days of the Islamic lunar month of Muharram
Where Celebrated: India, Iraq, Jamaica, Trinidad, Turkey, West Africa, and by
Shi'ite Muslims throughout the world
Symbols and Customs: Ashura Pudding, Rawda-Khani, Self-flagellation, Sherbet,
Taziyah

ORIGINS

Ashura is a holiday in the religious tradition of Islam, one of the world's largest
religions. According to some estimates, there are more than one billion Muslims
worldwide, with major populations found in the Middle East, North and sub-Saharan Africa, Turkey, Central Asia, and Southeast Asia. In Europe and the United
States, Islam is the second largest religious group, with some seven million adherents in the United States. During the early years of Islam, the faith spread throughout the Arabian Peninsula into regions that are today occupied by Saudi Arabia,
Syria, Iraq, and Jordan. Contrary to popular opinion, however, Muslims are not just
Arabs. Muslims—followers of Islam—are found in many different ethnic groups all
over the globe. In fact, Arabs make up less than twenty percent of Muslims.

The word Islam is an Arabic word that means "surrender to God." Its other meanings
include peace, safety, and health. The central focus of Islam is a personal commitment
and surrender to Allah, the Arabic word for God. In Islam, the concept of Allah is universal and eternal. Allah is the same in every religion and throughout the history of
humankind. A person who follows Islam is called a Muslim, which means one who
surrenders or submits to Allah's will. But Islam is not just a religion of belief; it is a
religion of action. Five specific deeds are required of followers; these are called *The
Five Pillars of Islam*. They are 1) *Shahadah*—confession of faith; 2) *Salat*—prayer/wor-
ship; 3) *Zakat*—charity; 4) *Sawm*—fasting; 5) and *Hajj*—pilgrimage.

The message of Islam was brought by Muhammad (570-632 C.E.), who is considered
a prophet of Allah. The holy book of Islam is the *Qur'an* (also sometimes spelled
Koran or *Alcoran*). According to Islamic belief, the Qur'an was revealed to Muhammad by Allah over a period of twenty-three years. Authorship of the Qur'an is
attributed to Allah, and not to Muhammad; Muhammad merely received it. Muslims believe that because it originated with Allah, the Qur'an is infallible.

There are two main sects within Islam: Sunni and Shi'ite. Sunni Muslims are the majority (estimated at about eighty percent). They recognize the authority of the first four Caliphs, including Ali, and they believe that the Sunna (the example of the Prophet Muhammad) is interpreted through the consensus of the community. Shi'ite Muslims also look to special teachers, called imams. The imams are the direct descendants of Muhammad through Fatimah and Ali. These individuals are believed to be inspired and to possess secret knowledge. Shi'ites, however, do not recognize the same line of Islamic leaders acknowledged by the Sunnis. Shi'ites hold to a doctrine that accepts only leaders who are descended from Muhammad through his daughter Fatimah and her husband Ali. Many Shi'ite subsects believe that true imams are errorless and sinless. They receive instruction from these leaders rather than relying on the consensus of the community.

It is among the Shi'ites that the most important rituals associated with Ashura and the tenth of Muharram take place. Ashura is a holiday commemorating this day in the year 680 C.E. when Husain, the third imam and grandson of the prophet Muhammad, was killed in a skirmish between Sunnis and the small group of Shi'ite supporters with whom he was travelling to Iraq. He was buried on the battlefield where he fell in Karbala, now located in modern-day Iraq about sixty miles from Baghdad. Almost immediately, the site became a destination for Muslim pilgrimages. To this day, many Shi'ites come to Karbala to die or request that their bodies be brought there for burial. The town has become a devotional center for Shi'ite Muslims around the world and a vast burial ground.

Shi'ites begin the observation of Ashura, the commemoration of Husain's death, on the first day of Muharram, when they put on their mourning clothes and refrain from shaving or bathing. Black tents are pitched in the streets, adorned with draperies and candelabra. Wooden pulpits are erected, and speakers use them to tell the story of Husain's martyrdom with as much detail and elaboration as possible.

For the first nine days of the month, groups of men with their bodies dyed black or red roam the streets. Dragging chains and performing wild dances, they pull out their hair, inflict wounds on themselves with their swords, and occasionally engage in violent fights with Sunnis or other adversaries. On the tenth day there is a big funeral parade for Husain, featuring a coffin carried by eight men and accompanied by others holding banners. Horses and men march behind the coffin and sing battle songs.

While the tenth of Muharram procession has remained primarily a Shi'ite observance, the veneration of Husain has spread among Sunni Muslims as well. Modern-day Sunnis observe Ashura as an optional fast day, but in countries like Iraq they are not allowed to participate in the processions.

In Jamaica and Trinidad, the festival is called Hosay and is celebrated by Muslims and Hindus as a symbol of East Indian unity. In West Africa, the holy day is spent eating to ensure prosperity. In Senegal, Guinea, and Sierra Leone, the dried head and feet of the ram killed at **ID AL-ADHA** are cooked and served on this day. In addition to commemorating the death of Husain, the tenth of Muharram also celebrates the safe landing of Noah's ark (*see* ASHURA PUDDING).

SYMBOLS AND CUSTOMS

Ashura Pudding

According to legend, Noah was so happy to stand on dry ground at the end of the floods described in the Bible that he asked his wife to prepare a pudding so they could celebrate. She gathered dates, figs, nuts, and currants to make the largest pudding ever made and named it "Ashura."

In Turkey, the tenth day of Muharram is called Yevmi Ashurer, or the "day of sweet soup or porridge." It commemorates Noah's departure from the Ark onto Mount Ararat. Everyone makes *ashurer,* a pudding made from boiled wheat, dried currants, grain, and nuts, similar to that prepared by Noah's wife.

Rawda-Khani

One of the rituals associated with Ashura is the rawda-khani, or recital of the sufferings of the Imam Husain. An individual or a family will invite a group of friends to a private gathering, where a professional storyteller will recite the tale of Husain's martyrdom, playing upon the emotions of his listeners and often reducing them to tears or provoking them to cry out Husain's name. Sometimes these recitations take place in mosques, and they have been known to result in public frenzies where devout Shi'ites cut themselves with swords and knives or beat themselves with chains in imitation of the torments to which Husain was subjected.

Self-flagellation

The practice of self-flagellation, in which devout Shi'ite Muslims strike themselves with chains and knives while chanting the name of Husain, is symbolic of the pain and anger they feel about Husain's murder by Umayyad soldiers. It also serves as a ritual punishment, because many Shi'ites stayed home rather than march out to join Husain in fighting the Umayyad rulers. It is during Ashura that the Shi'ite community expresses its guilt and anguish over the death of one of its most beloved leaders.

Sherbet

Throughout the ten days of Ashura, Muslims eat a kind of sherbet in memory of the intense thirst that Husain experienced on the battlefield of Karbala. He was surrounded by an army of 4,000 soldiers near the Euphrates River, where they cut off his water supply for eight days. When he finally mounted his horse and rode into battle, he was so weakened by thirst that he was killed.

Taziyah

The *taziyah* or passion play performed during Ashura in Shi'ite communities is a detailed and emotional reenactment of Husain's martyrdom. The actors on stage portray not only the events surrounding the death of Husain but also the struggle of the Shi'ite community and its imams in their fight to overcome the Umayyad rulers. The play consists of forty or fifty scenes, some of which are highly realistic. Perhaps the most realistic of all is the portrayal of the attack on Husain and his infant son.

Throughout the performance of the taziyah, the audience is expected to participate. They shout their advice to the actors, laugh when the imams are doing well, and fall silent when events turn against the Shi'ite leaders. When the soldiers close in on Husain with their spears and swords, hacking away at his horse and finally beheading him, members of the audience have been known to weep out loud and hurl curses at the Umayyad soldiers. Sometimes they leap up on the stage to protect Husain and his family or to threaten the actor who plays Umar, the soldier who deals the fatal blow.

The word *ta-ziyah* means "solace" or "condolence," and the play's underlying message is the salvation that was achieved through Husain's sacrificial death. In India, *ta-ziyah* refers to small replicas of Husain's tomb, which are carried and buried in the local "Karbaela" grounds, named after the place where Husain was killed.

FURTHER READING

Bellenir, Karen. *Religious Holidays and Calendars*. 3rd ed. Detroit: Omnigraphics, 2004.

Glassé, Cyril. *The Concise Encyclopedia of Islam*. 2nd ed. San Francisco: Harper & Row, 1999.

Gordon, Matthew S. *Islam*. New York: Facts on File, 1991.

Gulevich, Tanya. *Understanding Islam and Muslim Traditions*. Detroit: Omnigraphics, 2004.

Henderson, Helene. ed. *Holidays, Festivals, and Celebrations of the World Dictionary*. 3rd ed. Detroit: Omnigraphics, 2005.

Smith, Huston. *The Illustrated World's Religions*. San Francisco: HarperSanFrancisco, 1994.

Von Grunebaum, Gustave E. *Muhammadan Festivals*. New York: Schuman, 1951.

WEB SITE

BBC (British Broadcasting Corporation)
news.bbc.co.uk/1/hi/world/middle_east/4274749.stm

Assumption of the Blessed Virgin Mary, Feast of the

Type of Holiday: Religious (Christian)
Date of Observation: August 15
Where Celebrated: Britain, Europe, United States, and by Roman Catholics, Anglicans, and Orthodox Christians around the world
Symbols and Customs: Assumption Plays, Bowing Procession, Fruits of the Harvest
Related Holidays: Annunciation of the Blessed Virgin Mary, Feast of the

ORIGINS

The Feast of the Assumption is celebrated by all branches of the Christian church. The word Christian refers to a follower of Christ, a title derived from the Greek word meaning Messiah or Anointed One. The Christ of Christianity is Jesus of Nazareth, a man born between 7 and 4 B.C.E. in the region of Palestine. According to Christian teaching, Jesus was killed by Roman authorities using a form of execution called crucifixion (a term meaning he was nailed to a cross and hung from it until he died) in about the year 30 C.E. After his death, he rose back to life. His death and resurrection provide a way by which people can be reconciled with God. In remembrance of Jesus' death and resurrection, the cross serves as a fundamental symbol in Christianity.

With nearly two billion believers in countries around the globe, Christianity is the largest of the world's religions. There is no one central authority for all of Christianity. The pope (the bishop of Rome) is the authority for the Roman Catholic Church, but other sects look to other authorities. Orthodox communities look to patriarchs and emphasize doctrinal agreement and traditional practice. Protestant communities focus on individual conscience. The Roman Catholic and Protestant churches are often referred to as the Western Church, while the Orthodox churches may also be called the Eastern Church. All three main branches of Christianity acknowledge the authority of Christian scriptures, a compilation of writings assembled into a document called the Bible. Methods of biblical interpretation vary among the different Christian sects.

The Feast of the Assumption represents a long tradition of speculation about how Mary died and what happened to her body. Legend says that after the Crucifixion of Jesus, Mary lived with the Apostle John in Jerusalem, revisiting many of the places associated with her son's life. Finally she became so lonely that she prayed for death. An angel visited her and promised that within three days, she would enter heaven, where Jesus awaited her. The angel presented her with a palm branch, which Mary in turned handed to St. John, requesting that it be carried before her at her burial.

Mary also requested that all the Apostles be present at her death, and the message reached them miraculously even though they were scattered all over the world. Only St. Thomas missed the final gathering at her deathbed. Arriving after the funeral was over, he was so filled with grief and regret that he asked to have the tomb reopened so that he might have one last look at her body. The tomb was empty—proof that rather than being subjected to the usual process of physical decay, her body had been "assumed" into heaven, where it was reunited with her soul. The commemoration of this event is called the Dormition of the Most Holy Mother of God in the Eastern Church, a reference to Mary's "falling asleep."

The choice of August 15 as the date of this event is significant, since it roughly coincided with the gathering of the harvest in southern Europe. There is some evidence that the date might have been chosen to replace an old harvest festival in honor of Diana, the Roman goddess of the hunt, on August 13 (*see* FRUITS OF THE HARVEST); in some parts of Europe, the feast is still called Our Lady of the Harvest. Farther north, where the harvest is delayed until autumn, the harvest rites dedicated to Mary were performed at the Feast of the Nativity on September 8.

Although belief in the Assumption was widespread by the fifth century and the feast was observed throughout Europe during the Middle Ages, it didn't become an official dogma of the Roman Catholic Church until Pope Pius XII ruled it so in 1950. The English suppressed the celebration of "Mary-Mass," as it was known in medieval times, because it took laborers away from their work in the middle of the harvest; but in Catholic countries, the Assumption became one of the most popular festivals of the year.

In Christian art, Mary's body is usually shown being carried up to heaven by angels—in contrast to the ascension of Christ, who rose up to heaven by his own power (*see* **ASCENSION DAY**).

SYMBOLS AND CUSTOMS

Assumption Plays

In the fourteenth century, miracle plays dramatizing the death, assumption, and coronation of the Virgin were common. They usually showed Mary as she summoned the Apostles to her deathbed from all parts of the world, and often reflected the legendary belief that St. Thomas was carried to her from India on a cloud. Similar plays in honor of the Dormition and the Coronation of Mary were a regular part of the popular play cycles performed in York, Towneley, and Chester, England at the time.

In France, a traditional pageant used to be performed in many places on Assumption Day. Figures of angels descended from the roof of the church to a flowery sepulcher or tomb and then reascended with the image of the Virgin Mary dressed in white. It was not uncommon for an image of the Virgin standing on a platform before the high altar to be drawn up through an opening in the roof—undoubtedly the same opening used to dramatize the Ascension of Christ in the spring (*see* ASCENSION PLAYS under **ASCENSION DAY**).

An assumption play is still performed at Elche in southern Spain, where the church is transformed into a theater for the annual event. A blue cloth is stretched across the dome to represent the sky, and there is a small trap door through which the angel makes his 60-yard descent on a golden pedestal called the *Ara Coeli*. The play, which is more like an operetta, concludes when Mary is raised from her tomb, and the Ara Coeli carries her to heaven.

Bowing Procession

In rural areas outside Rome, the Feast of the Assumption is celebrated with an annual Bowing Procession, known as *L'Inchinata*. A statue of Mary is carried through town, symbolizing her journey to heaven. She meets a statue of Christ under a gaily decorated arch of branches and flowers representing the gate of heaven. Both images are inclined toward each other three times, after which Christ accompanies his mother back to the parish church, symbolic of their joint ascent to heaven.

A similar procession in Sardinia, Italy, is called *Candelieri* because several huge candlesticks, each supporting a 100-pound candle, are carried to the Church of the Santa Maria. The candles are placed beside Mary's shrine, a tradition that dates back to 1580.

Fruits of the Harvest

The ancient Roman festival in honor of the goddess Diana held at this same time of year was known as the Nemoralia, after her temple on the shores of Lake Nemi outside of Rome. In addition to celebrating Diana's power, the Nemoralia was observed to protect the vines and fruit trees. Other symbolic rites designed to ensure good weather for the reaping of fall fruits were carried out between mid-August and mid-September as well. According to popular legend, this thirty-day period was a "blessed" time when animals and plants were believed to lose their harmful traits. Food produced during this period would remain fresh longer than at other times of year. The Christian Feast of the Assumption eventually incorporated the harvest-blessing element of this ancient festival, and many Assumption shrines show Mary wearing a robe covered in ears of grain. It is still common in the Orthodox Christian Church for worshippers to make offerings of new wheat, a symbol of prosperity and the bounty of the earth, on August 15.

Grapes are another harvest fruit associated with autumn. Along with wheat, they symbolize the consecrated bread and wine used in the celebration of the Eucharist. In Armenia, no one will taste the new crop of grapes until Assumption Day, when a trayful of grapes is blessed in the church. In Sicily, people traditionally abstain from eating fruit altogether during the first two weeks of August, in honor of the Virgin Mary. On the feast of her Assumption, they serve fruit that has been blessed in the church for dinner and present each other with baskets filled with a variety of fruits.

In Austria, Assumption Day is known as The Blessing of the Herbs. A statue of Mary is carried on a litter out to the fields, where four altars (representing the four Gospels) have been set up. Prayers are offered for good weather and crops, the Gospels are read, and the blessing is given. At one time in central Europe, the Feast of the Assumption was called Our Lady's Herb Day, based on the medieval belief that herbs picked in August had the power to heal.

In Latin countries, especially Portugal, where the primary "harvest" is fish, the ocean and fishing boats are blessed on Assumption Day. The Blessing of the Fleet also takes place in many coastal American towns on or around August 15.

FURTHER READING

Bellenir, Karen. *Religious Holidays and Calendars*. 3rd ed. Detroit: Omnigraphics, 2004.

"The Candelieri's Descent: Sassari's 'Great Celebration'." *The Island of Sardinia*, 2003. www.sarnow.com/sardinia/cand1.htm.

Ferguson, George. *Signs and Symbols in Christian Art*. New York: Oxford University Press, 1954.

Harper, Howard V. *Days and Customs of All Faiths*. 1957. Reprint. Detroit: Omnigraphics, 1990.

Henderson, Helene, ed. *Holidays, Festivals, and Celebrations of the World Dictionary*. 3rd ed. Detroit: Omnigraphics, 2005.

James, E.O. *Seasonal Feasts and Festivals*. 1961. Reprint. Detroit: Omnigraphics, 1993.

MacDonald, Margaret R., ed. *The Folklore of World Holidays*. Detroit: Gale Research, 1992.

Metford, J.C.J. *The Christian Year*. New York: Crossroad, 1991.

Monks, James L. *Great Catholic Festivals*. New York: Henry Schuman, 1951.

Weiser, Franz Xaver. *Handbook of Christian Feasts and Customs*. New York: Harcourt, Brace, 1958.

WEB SITES

Greek Orthodox Archdiocese of Australia
www.greekorthodox.net.au/pages/Theotokos.html

New Advent Catholic Encyclopedia
www.newadvent.org/cathen/02006b.htm

Women for Faith & Family
www.wf-f.org/Assumption.html

Athabascan Stickdance

Type of Holiday: Religious (Athabascan)
Date of Observation: One week in March
Where Celebrated: Kaltag and Nulato, Alaska
Symbols and Customs: Gifts, Potlatch, Ritual Songs, Spruce Pole

ORIGINS

The Athasbacan Stickdance is part of Native American religious tradition. The history of this and other Native American cultures dates back thousands of years into prehistoric times. According to many scholars, the people who became the Native Americans migrated from Asia across a land bridge that may have once connected the territories presently occupied by Alaska and Russia. The migrations, believed to have begun between 60,000 and 30,000 B.C.E., continued until approximately 4,000 B.C.E. This speculation, however, conflicts with traditional stories asserting that the indigenous Americans have always lived in North America or that tribes moved up from the south.

The historical development of religious belief systems among Native Americans is not well known. Most of the information available was gathered by Europeans who arrived on the continent beginning in the sixteenth century C.E. The data they recorded was fragmentary and oftentimes of questionable accuracy because the Europeans did not understand the native cultures they were trying to describe and the Native Americans were reluctant to divulge details about themselves.

The Athabascan Indians take their name from Lake Athabasca in Canada, which in turn takes its name from the Cree word for the way plants or grasses grow in the shallow end of a lake. The name of the tribe is spelled many different ways (Athapascan, Athapaskan, Athabaskan, etc.), but "Athabascan" is now the preferred spelling.

The stickdance—named after the SPRUCE POLE that is its central symbolic object—is a weeklong ceremony held by Alaska's Athabascan Indians to mourn for the male members of the tribe who have died and to provide comfort and support for their grieving families. Observed nowadays only at Nulato, in western central Alaska on the banks of the Yukon River, and at Kaltag, about thirty-five miles further downriver, the stickdance rotates each March between Nulato and Kaltag.

The widows of the deceased, with the help of other family members, sponsor the ceremony, which takes place in the tribe's community center. Starting on a Monday, people gather there for four consecutive evenings to participate in the ceremonial feast known as a POTLATCH or to share food in a less formal way. There is singing and dancing, and people get together in small groups to talk about their memories of the deceased. The stickdance itself takes place on Friday night, and because it can honor a number of male tribal members simultaneously, there may be hundreds of people in attendance.

The men put up a tall spruce pole in the center of the hall, while the family and friends of the deceased decorate it with their gifts. Then everyone joins in a slow, shuffling dance around the pole, chanting RITUAL SONGS repeatedly all night long and meditating privately about those who have died.

On Saturday morning the pole is taken down and carried past each house in the village before being broken up and thrown into the Yukon River, which is usually still frozen at this time of year but which will eventually melt and carry the pole's shattered remains to the sea. The rest of the weekend is devoted to rituals designed to help the living come to terms with their loss. Men who have been specially selected to represent the dead dress up in their clothes and bid a final farewell to their family and friends. Gifts that have been made or purchased by the family are distributed to every person attending the stickdance (*see* GIFTS) to show appreciation for their friendship and support, and there is more feasting on traditional foods.

Although a few years may elapse between the loss of a loved one and the stickdance that honors his memory, the Athabascan approach to dealing with grief and loss seems to be particularly effective. Surviving family members say that the opportunity to focus on their memories of the dead and to receive the support of the entire community is a valuable one, and that the stickdance does indeed make it easier for them to let go.

SYMBOLS AND CUSTOMS

Gifts

The sheer number of gifts that are distributed during the week of the stickdance is one of the primary reasons why it can take a family years to prepare for this event. Every single person who shows up receives a gift, and that means buying—or in most cases, making—hundreds of individual gifts. Merely gathering the furs, wood, and other materials needed to make the gifts can take the typical Athabascan family two or more years, which is why this event isn't held on an annual basis. It makes more sense to wait until several families are fully prepared and then hold a single stickdance for all of them.

Potlatch

The potlatch is perhaps the most important surviving religious practice among the Native people in Alaska and along the north Pacific coast in the aftermath of European arrival. This feast and gift-giving event is central to many important Athabascan ceremonies, including funeral rites. Hence it takes place not only on an annual basis but also throughout the year, at funerals and memorials. The first potlatch is held soon after death when the body of the deceased is burned, and then another potlatch is held during the stickdance or memorial service. Dishes served at the feast may include salmon, beaver, rabbit, and moose.

Ritual Songs

The ritual songs that are sung during a stickdance have been handed down from generation to generation by the Athabascan people. There were originally fourteen songs, but one has already been forgotten, and only the elder members of the tribe know all the words to the remaining thirteen. The stickdance is the only occasion at which these songs, known as *hi'o keleka*, may be chanted.

Spruce Pole

The pole from which the stickdance takes its name is a spruce tree from which all the branches have been stripped. Ribbons are wrapped around the rough wood, and furs and other gifts are often hung from the pole, making it resemble a Christmas tree. As the object around which the circular dance takes place, the spruce pole may be seen as a symbol for the dead and a focal point for the thoughts and memories of surviving friends and family members.

FURTHER READING

Hirschfelder, Arlene B., and Paulette Fairbanks Molin. "Stick Dance." *Encyclopedia of Native American Religions*. Updated ed. New York: Facts on File, 2000.

WEB SITE

"Athabascans of Interior Alaska," Alaska Native Knowledge Network, University of Alaska

www.ankn.uaf.edu/curriculum/Athabascan/Athabascans/appendix_a.html

Autumn Equinox

Type of Holiday: Calendar/Seasonal
Date of Observation: September 22 or 23
Where Celebrated: All over the world
Symbols and Customs: Balance of Light and Dark, Full Moon, Harvest Feasts
Related Holidays: Harvest Home, Higan, Mabon, Michaelmas, Mid-Autumn Festival

ORIGINS

The English word equinox comes from the Latin word equinoxium, meaning "time of equal days and nights." The word equinox refers to the two days of the year when night and day are equally long, the autumn equinox and the **VERNAL EQUINOX**. In the northern hemisphere, the autumn equinox occurs on September 22 or 23 and marks the beginning of the fall season. From this day forth the days will grow shorter and shorter until the time of **WINTER SOLSTICE**. After that time, the days will grow longer, but they will still be shorter than the nights until the arrival of the **VERNAL EQUINOX** on March 21 or March 22.

This BALANCE OF LIGHT AND DARK occurs only on the equinoxes. The equinoxes are also marked by other interesting celestial occurrences. Since ancient times, people who watched the sky have noticed that the sun's daily path across it varies throughout the year. The sun traces an arc that falls lower in the sky, or further south, in the fall and winter, and higher in the sky, or further north, in the spring and summer. Although the sun always rises in an easterly direction, and sets in a westerly direction, the equinoxes are the only days on which the sun rises due east and sets due west. Moreover, on the equinoxes, the sun passes directly overhead in the equatorial zones. In astronomical terms, this happens because the ecliptic intersects the celestial equator, an imaginary line in the heavens that represents a projection of the earth's equator onto the dome of the sky. The ecliptic is the name scientists have given to the plane in which the earth and the other planets of our solar system orbit the sun. When the ecliptic and the celestial equator meet, the sun crosses directly overhead in the equatorial zones.

In the northern hemisphere the autumn equinox marks the beginning of fall and the vernal equinox marks the beginning of spring. In the southern hemisphere, the September equinox kicks off the beginning of spring, and the March equinox the beginning of autumn. This difference in the seasons between the two hemispheres is caused by the fact that the earth does not rotate on an axis that runs perpendicular to the line joining the earth and sun. Instead, the earth's axis is tilted twenty-three degrees in one direction. As the earth moves through its yearly rotation around the sun, this tilt points the northern hemisphere towards the sun during one half of the year and the southern hemisphere towards the sun during the other half. The resulting difference in the exposure to the sun's light causes the differences in the length of days and nights. The equinoxes mark the two days of the year on which the earth's tilt results in equal exposure to sunlight and darkness all around the globe. As the earth moves past the September equinox, the northern hemisphere enters that half of the year when the earth's tilt points it away from the sun. Hence the days will be shorter than the nights.

The Autumn Equinox marks the changing of the seasons, which people in all parts of the world have honored since ancient times. Many cultures divided the year into two seasons, summer and winter, and marked these points of the year at or near the summer and winter solstices, during which light and warmth began to increase and decrease, respectively. In pre-industrial times, humans survived through hunting, gathering, and agricultural practices, which depend on the natural cycle of seasons, according to the climate in the region of the world in which they lived. Thus, they created rituals to help ensure enough rain and sun in the spring and summer so crops would grow to fruition at harvest time, which was, in turn, duly celebrated. Vestiges of many of these ancient practices are thought to have survived in festivals still celebrated around seasonal themes.

The earliest observation of the equinoxes can be traced back to ancient times. Archeologists have discovered that some of Great Britain and Ireland's prehistoric stone monuments are aligned in special ways with the equinoxes and solstices. These structures were built several thousand years before the time of Christ (between 4000 and 1500 B.C.E.). Halfway around the world in South America, the ancient Mayan peoples also built great rock structures aligned to the movements of the sun. The great pyramid of Chichen Itza, for example, located in Mexico, casts a striking serpent-shaped shadow on the day of the spring equinox. Other Mayan structures line up perfectly with the autumn equinox. Archeologists speculate about the importance of these dates to ancient astronomers and priests, but no one knows how they were observed or celebrated by ordinary people.

SYMBOLS AND CUSTOMS

Balance of Light and Dark

The balance of light and dark that occurs on the autumn equinox is a prominent feature of many celebrations. For example, the celebration of **MABON** calls attention to natural phenomena that characterize the fall, such as the growing darkness, cooler weather, and decline in nature's fertility.

The Christian observance of **MICHAELMAS** contains similar themes. This feast honors the archangel Michael, who strengthens the weak and protects the fearful. Old traditions recommend calling on Michael for aid in battle and for the power to resist the devil. His feast day, September 29, comes just as the nights are becoming longer than the days. This is the perfect time to remember Michael, who fights against the forces of darkness, inspires strength, and confers courage.

In Japan, some people observe a Buddhist ceremony known as **HIGAN** at the time of the autumn and spring equinoxes. The balance of light and dark on these dates is thought to represent the balance between this world and the next. In the ceremonies performed for this holiday, the living pay respects to the dead and clean family graves.

Full Moon

People the world over have noticed that the full moon that occurs around this time of year appears to be larger and rounder than other full moons. This appearance has generated much folklore and myth. Scientists today, however, know that the moon's apparent change in size is an optical illusion.

In the U.S. the full moon closest to the autumn equinox is known as the Harvest Moon. In past times, when farmers did not have a lot of machinery to rely upon, they often had to work late in the month of September to finish the harvest. Nature aided them by providing them with a special kind of full moon at that time of year. First, the full moon closest to the autumn equinox generally rises just as the light of sun is fading, permitting farmers to continue their work into the early evening. In addition, near the time of the autumn equinox, the time between each day's moonrise shortens considerably. This means that during the two days that follow the full moon, moonrise would also occur fairly early in the evening. The full moon closest to the September equinox was so handy to farmers that they dubbed it the Harvest Moon.

In many Asian countries, people celebrate a holiday known as the **MID-AUTUMN FESTIVAL** near the time of the autumn equinox. This holiday revolves around the celebration of the full moon that occurs at this time of year. People make time to go outside and enjoy the beauty of the moon and give thanks for the fall harvest.

Harvest Feasts

In the British Isles, an old folk holiday called **HARVEST HOME** took place around the time of the September equinox. In times gone by, when people harvested wheat, corn, and other crops by hand, the harvest occupied just about everyone in the village. So, when the villagers finished the last of the grain harvest, they celebrated with a communal feast. This traditional celebration continues today, though modern farm machinery has advanced the date of the holiday into August. The **HARVEST HOME** celebration is thought to have inspired both the American **THANKSGIVING** holiday and the Canadian Harvest Festival.

In addition to the continuing celebration of **HARVEST HOME**, some groups of people interested in reconnecting with ancient religions have revived the celebration of the equinox itself. Neopagans and Wiccans, people who follow a nature-oriented religion loosely linked to ancient pagan beliefs and inspired by old European folk practices, often celebrate the Autumn Equinox. Some of them call the holiday **MABON,** after an old Celtic legend that they associate with the day. Their celebrations often feature an autumn feast consisting of foods representing the late summer and early fall harvest.

FURTHER READING

Brennan, Martin. *The Stones of Time: Calendars, Sundials and Stone Chambers of Ancient Ireland*. Rochester, VT: Inner Traditions, 1994.

Cabot, Laurie. *Celebrate the Earth: A Year of Holidays in the Pagan Tradition*. New York: Delta, 1994.

Henderson, Helene, ed. *Holidays, Festivals and Celebrations of the World Dictionary*. 3rd ed. Detroit: Omnigraphics, 2005.

Krupp, E.C., ed. *In Search of Ancient Astronomies*. New York: Doubleday, 1978.

Urlin, Ethel. *Festivals, Holy Days, and Saints' Days*. 1915. Reprint. Detroit: Omnigraphics, 1990.

WEB SITES

NASA Science News Department
science.nasa.gov/headlines/y2000/ast11sep_2.htm

University of California at Berkeley's Center for Science Education
cse.ssl.berkeley.edu/lessons/indiv/beth/beth_intro.html

Awoojoh

Type of Holiday: Religious (Yoruba)
Date of Observation: Various
Where Celebrated: Sierra Leone
Symbols and Customs: Kola Nuts

ORIGINS

A thanksgiving feast observed in the west African nation of Sierra Leone, Awoojoh honors the spirits of the dead, who are believed to have influence over the fortunes of the living. It may be held at any time of the year, and the guests include not only friends and relatives but, in a small community, the entire village. The day begins with a family visit to the cemetery, where a libation (usually water or liquor) is poured over the relatives' graves, and the dead are invited to join in the thanksgiving celebration. Afterward, everyone returns home to share in a feast. All family quarrels must be settled before the feasting begins.

Preparations for the feast begin days ahead of time. Sheep and chickens are slaughtered, and supplies of rice, beans, plantains, onions, peppers, tomatoes, sweet potatoes, and other vegetables are gathered. The most popular dish is "Awoojoh beans," made by simmering cooked beans in fried onion and red palm oil, then adding plantains and sweet potatoes. The centerpiece of the meal, however, is an elaborate stew, one portion of which is set out for the dead ancestors or thrown to the vultures, who are believed to embody the souls of the departed.

Although the practice of holding a thanksgiving feast originated with the Yoruba, who came to Sierra Leone from Nigeria, Christian Creoles and Muslim Akus hold such feasts as well.

SYMBOLS AND CUSTOMS

Kola Nuts

Kola nuts symbolize the power exercised by the dead over the living. A popular custom on Awoojoh is to split in half two kola nuts, one red and one white, and then throw them up in the air over a dead relative's grave. The pattern in which they fall is believed to carry a message from the ancestors. For example, if two of the pieces fall with the hollow sides up and two with the hollow sides down, it is considered a very favorable message.

FURTHER READING

Henderson, Helene, ed. *Holidays, Festivals, and Celebrations of the World Dictionary*. 3rd ed. Detroit: Omnigraphics, 2005.

MacDonald, Margaret R., ed. *The Folklore of World Holidays*. Detroit: Gale Research, 1992.

Awuru Odo Festival

Type of Holiday: Religious (Igbo)
Date of Observation: Biennially in April
Where Celebrated: Nigeria
Symbols and Customs: Odo Play

ORIGINS

About fifteen million Igbo people live in Nigeria. The supreme god of the Igbo religion is Chukwu (also known as Chineke), who created the world and presides over people as well as spirits called *alusi*, who inhabit all of nature and may intervene in human affairs. Igbo religious practices include sacrifices of offerings such as food and animals, prayers, and healing rituals.

Among the Igbo people, the Odo are the spirits of the dead, who return to the earth to visit their families every two years. They arrive, in the form of costumed men wearing masks, sometime between September and November and depart in April. Before they leave, there is a big theatrical performance (*see* ODO PLAY) reenacting the story of their visit and the agony of their departure. The musical accompaniment featuring xylophones, drums, and rattles is known as *obilenu* music, meaning "that which lies above."

Preparations to receive the Odo are quite elaborate. Men prepare the shrines, surrounded by fences, where the returning spirits of the dead will worship. They also refurbish the masks that the Odo will wear or create new ones. All of these preparations must be conducted in secret, because women and non-initiates are not allowed to see what goes on. The women are primarily responsible for seeing that there is enough food to serve the Odo and any visitors who may come to watch the performance.

Although each family holds a welcoming ceremony for its particular Odo group, the big celebration in April features all of the Odo groups from all of the families.

Immediately after the performance is over, the Odo climb the Ukehe hills and make their way back to the land of the dead. With them they take the prayers of the living, who appeal to them for abundant crops and for many children. Women who have recently given birth often bring gifts of thanks.

SYMBOLS AND CUSTOMS

Odo Play

The Odo play, also known as the Awuru Odo performance, takes place in the Nwankwo market square in Ukehe, where the Odo shrine and the ritual stage are located. The performers include the Odo characters themselves and the people who accompany them. The characters are mostly concealed by masks, but sometimes their legs are visible. The elderly Odo are accompanied by middle-aged men who blow elephant tusks and horns, while the youthful Odo are accompanied by young men and the Odo children are either alone or in groups. The evil Odo, who were criminals when they were alive, wear black costumes and cover their bodies with thorns. The other performers wear costumes traditionally made from plant fiber, leaves, beads, and feathers, although more durable cloth costumes are becoming more common in contemporary Odo plays. The villagers serve as a chorus, with the women dressed in their most expensive clothing and jewelry and the men carrying long sticks, guns, and machetes.

The Odo play itself reenacts the end of the Odo's stay on earth. The story begins with their arrival, dramatizes their stay with the living, and finally portrays their agonizing journey away from their loved ones and back to the land of the dead. The spirits who await them there are anxious for their return and place many obstacles in their path to make them fall and be ashamed. But the Odo are very careful not to fall, knowing that it will bring bad luck to the living. When they have circled the marketplace successfully, there is great celebration and dancing.

FURTHER READING

Henderson, Helene, ed. *Holidays, Festivals, and Celebrations of the World Dictionary.* 3rd ed. Detroit: Omnigraphics, 2005.

MacDonald, Margaret R., ed. *The Folklore of World Holidays.* Detroit: Gale Research, 1992.

Aztec New Fire Ceremony

Type of Holiday: Calendar/Seasonal
Date of Observation: Every fifty-two years for twelve days
Where Celebrated: Mexico City, Mexico
Symbols and Customs: Blood Sacrifice, Calendar Stone, Fire, Hill of the Star, Ritual Bundle

ORIGINS

From the early fifteenth until the early sixteenth century, the Aztec Empire extended over much of what is known today as Mexico. Their capital, Tenochtitlán, stood where Mexico City now stands, and in its heyday it was the largest city in the world, with a huge temple—known as the Templo Mayor—at its center where important religious ceremonies were held.

The Aztecs used two different calendars. The first was the 365-day solar year, which they divided into eighteen months of twenty days each. The five days left over, known as *nemontemi,* were considered to be bad luck days. The second was a 260-day ritual calendar, consisting of thirteen months of twenty days each, which priests used to determine the most favorable days for planting seeds, building houses, launching attacks on enemies, and other important events. Once every fifty-two years, the last day of the solar year and the last day of the ritual year coincided. Because the Aztecs believed that the earth went through cycles of destruction and recreation, an offering had to be made to the gods at this time to ensure that they would allow another fifty-two-year cycle to begin. This was the reason for the twelve-day New Fire Ceremony.

During the last five days before the cycle's end, the fires in all temples and private homes were extinguished and business came to a halt. The people threw out or destroyed their dishes and cooking utensils along with their clothing, furniture, and religious statues. Everything was swept clean and people went into mourning. On the last of the five bad luck days that marked the end of the solar year, the priests went to the HILL OF THE STAR and waited for the Pleiades, a cluster of stars in the constellation Taurus, to appear in the night sky. If it did, this meant that the world would continue for another fifty-two years. A human BLOOD SACRIFICE was made, and the priests lit a fire on the victim's chest. Household and temple fires throughout the Valley of Mexico would then be lit by torches that had been dipped in this sacrificial fire, and people would spend the next twelve days celebrating, feasting, and putting their houses back in order. The New Fire Ceremony was an event that came along only once in the average Aztec's lifetime.

The Aztec Empire was destroyed after the Spanish conquest, but its highly evolved civilization continued to exert its influence on Mexican culture. Although the New Fire Ceremony is no longer held, many Mexicans living today are descended from the Aztecs, and more than a million of them speak the native Aztec language, known as Nahuatl.

SYMBOLS AND CUSTOMS

Blood Sacrifice

The Aztecs believed that their sun god, Tonatiuh, needed to be "fed" periodically with human blood. The highlight of the New Fire Ceremony, therefore, occurred when a sacrificial victim was taken from the Templo Mayor in a procession to the HILL OF THE STAR. At the very moment that the Pleiades reached its highest point in its journey across the night sky, the Aztec priests would take a sharp knife and cut out the victim's heart. They would lay kindling in its place and start a FIRE within the chest cavity, while frenzied spectators often cut themselves and let their blood mingle with the victim's.

Calendar Stone

The Aztec Calendar Stone, also known as the Sun Stone, was discovered by workmen who were digging up Mexico City's main plaza, El Zócalo, in 1790. It is huge—twelve feet wide and three feet thick, made from almost twenty-five tons of carved basalt—and in its center is the face of Tonatiuh, the sun god, with his tongue sticking out and a human heart clutched in either hand. There are also carvings that represent the days of the Aztec month and various religious symbols related to the sun god. Many archaeologists believe that Aztec priests placed the hearts of human sacrifices on this stone.

The Calendar Stone portrays the five ages or cycles of creation according to Aztec belief. At the time of the empire's demise, they were in the fifth and final age, the four previous ages having been destroyed by hurricanes, jaguars, fires, and floods. The Aztecs hoped to avoid a similar fate by feeding their god human blood, and they regarded a successful New Fire Ceremony as crucial to the survival of their civilization.

After it was discovered, the Calendar Stone was placed at the foot of the west tower of the city's cathedral. It remained there for a hundred years before being moved to the Museo Nacional de Antrolopogia (National Museum of Anthropology), where it can be seen today.

Fire

The fire that was kindled in the sacrificial victim's chest at the New Fire Ceremony symbolized the power of the sun god. If the fire didn't light, the Aztecs believed that the sun would perish and that darkness would overtake the empire.

After the new fire was kindled, couriers would line up to dip their torches into the flames and carry the fire to every house and temple in the empire, beginning with the Templo Mayor.

Hill of the Star

Located several miles from Mexico City, the Hill of the Star, or Cerro de la Estrella, was the site of a temple from which the entire dome of the heavens could be viewed. It was here that the Aztecs waited for a sign—the Pleiades crossing the zenith—indicating that the world had been saved and that life as they knew it would go on. The temple on the Hill of the Star was regarded as a physical representation of the body of the gods.

Ritual Bundle

The fifty-two-year cycle of the Aztec calendar was regarded as a "bundling" or "binding together" of the years. A bundle of fifty-two rods, usually made out of reed or wood, symbolized a completed cycle, and such bundles were commonly part of the designs found on Aztec pottery and murals. Because the New Fire Ceremony marked the start of a new cycle, the lighting of these ritual bundles symbolized not only the passage of time but the fire that would soon be kindled in the chest of a sacrificial victim and carried throughout the empire.

FURTHER READING

Bellenir, Karen. *Religious Holidays and Calendars*. 3rd ed. Detroit: Omnigraphics, 2004.

Leach, Maria, ed. *Funk & Wagnalls Standard Dictionary of Folklore, Mythology & Legend*. San Francisco: Harper & Row, 1984.

Miller, Mary, and Karl Taube. *An Illustrated Dictionary of the Gods and Symbols and Ancient Mexico and the Maya*. London: Thames and Hudson, 1997.

Parrinder, Geoffrey. *A Dictionary of Non-Christian Religions*. Philadelphia: Westminster Press, 1971.

Bastille Day

Type of Holiday: Historic, National
Date of Observation: July 14
Where Celebrated: France; New Caledonia, Tahiti, and other French territories
Symbols and Customs: Bastille, La Marseillaise
Related Holidays: Fourth of July

ORIGINS

Bastille Day in France is the equivalent of the **FOURTH OF JULY** in the United States. There is usually a parade down the Champs-Élysées, street dancing, fireworks, and free theatrical performances. It is the day on which the French celebrate their independence from the monarchy by commemorating the storming of Paris's Bastille prison on July 14, 1789—an event that marked the end of Louis XVI's rule and started the French Revolution. By freeing the political prisoners held there and dismantling the building stone by stone, the Parisians displayed their scorn for the Bourbon kings who had ruled France for so long. The Marquis de Lafayette, who had been named commander of the National Guard the day after the Bastille fell, later gave the key to the infamous prison to George Washington, under whom he had served during the American Revolution. It is still on display at Mount Vernon, Washington's home (*see also* **WASHINGTON'S BIRTHDAY**).

Americans were particularly happy to hear of the Parisians' revolutionary act, and they celebrated Bastille Day for a number of years, particularly in Philadelphia. But eventually the celebration diminished in the U.S. Bastille Day observances, however, still take place in New York City as well as Kaplan, Louisiana, an area

75

with many ties to French traditions. Bastille Day is also observed in a number of French territories in the Pacific with parades, fireworks, and dancing in the streets. In Tahiti and the rest of French Polynesia, it is called Tiurai, and the celebration goes on throughout most of the month of July.

In France, Bastille Day continues to be celebrated as the great national holiday. National holidays can be defined as those commemorations that a nation's government has deemed important enough to warrant inclusion in the list of official public holidays. They tend to honor a person or event that has been critical in the development of the nation and its identity. Such people and events usually reflect values and traditions shared by a large portion of the citizenry. Bastille Day has become one of the nation's most important shared celebrations.

SYMBOLS AND CUSTOMS

Bastille

Built around 1369 at the order of King Charles V, the prison-fortress known as the Bastille had eight towers and 100-foot-high walls. Beginning in the seventeenth century, it was used to house primarily political prisoners, including many famous people—such as the French writers Voltaire and the Marquis de Sade—who had displeased the court or were considered a threat to the monarchy.

Although it was razed to the ground two days after it was stormed by the angry Parisians, the Bastille remains a symbol to the French people of the oppression of the monarchy.

La Marseillaise

"La Marseillaise," the French National Anthem, was not even written when the Bastille was stormed in 1789, yet it has come to be associated with Bastille Day. The song was written by Rouget de Lisle, an army officer, during the night of April 25-26, 1792. It was taken up by volunteer soldiers and became the national song in 1795. Banned during the beginning of the nineteenth century, it was reinstated in 1830 and became the national anthem in 1879. Today, La Marseillaise is usually performed at official events and particularly on Bastille Day.

FURTHER READING

Chambers, Robert. *The Book of Days.* 2 vols. 1862-64. Reprint. Detroit: Omnigraphics, 1990.

Christianson, Stephen G., and Jane M. Hatch. *The American Book of Days.* 4th ed. New York: H.W. Wilson, 2000.

Dunkling, Leslie. *A Dictionary of Days.* New York: Facts on File, 1988.

Henderson, Helene, ed. *Holidays, Festivals, and Celebrations of the World Dictionary.* 3rd ed. Detroit: Omnigraphics, 2005.

MacDonald, Margaret R., ed. *The Folklore of World Holidays.* Detroit: Gale Research, 1992.

Van Straalen, Alice. *The Book of Holidays Around the World.* New York: Dutton, 1986.

WEB SITES

French Institute Alliance Française
www.fiaf.org and www.bastilledayusa.com

French Ministry of Foreign Affairs
www.diplomatie.gouv.fr/en

Bayou Classic

Type of Holiday: Sporting
Date of Observation: November; weekend after Thanksgiving
Where Celebrated: New Orleans, Louisiana
Symbols and Customs: Battle of the Bands, College Fair, Football Game, Greek Step Show, Job Fair

ORIGINS

Football Classics are a longstanding tradition among African-American collegiate teams. Although it is unclear when the first Football Classic game was played, Classics were being played as early as 1924. Since then, numerous Classics have been created and many traditions have formed around these events. Far more than just another college football game, the Classics give participating schools a chance to showcase the African-American college experience.

The Bayou Classic, officially known as the State Farm Bayou Classic, is one such Football Classic. This annual grudge match was first played in 1974 and grew out of the traditional football rivalry between Grambling State University and Southern University, both in Louisiana. The FOOTBALL GAME is the focal point of a weekend full of social, cultural, and educational activities. The popular BATTLE OF THE BANDS pits the rival schools' marching bands against each other in competition, while a GREEK STEP SHOW spotlights the talents of student fraternities and sororities. A JOB FAIR helps new graduates find employment, while a COLLEGE FAIR offers information to prospective students. Special luncheons and dinners are held throughout the weekend, along with pre-game tailgate parties and pep rallies. A gospel brunch closes the weekend's official festivities on Sunday.

SYMBOLS AND CUSTOMS

Battle of the Bands

Just as the football teams vie for a victory on game day, the marching bands of both schools participate in a series of competitions to determine which has the best showmanship and performance ability. Dynamic, complicated performance routines are executed by the bands as a whole, as well as by specific sections of the bands such as drum lines, horn lines, and flag corps. The winning band typically receives a grant to fund its continuing operation.

College Fair

The Bayou Classic College Fair allows interested high school students to collect information about historically black colleges and universities throughout the country.

Football Game

More than 70,000 fans attend the Bayou Classic football game each year, with an estimated total of 200,000 people traveling to New Orleans to take part in the weekend. The yearly competition on the field remains intense as each team vies for the win and the all-important bragging rights. Although Grambling State defeated Southern at the first Bayou Classic, Southern holds the record for the longest winning streak. The two teams are almost evenly matched, with the number of victories by each team closely divided in the series overall.

Greek Step Show

African-American fraternities and sororities typically create elaborate stepping routines, many of which are rooted in African and African-American dance traditions. Stepping involves intricate synchronized movements such as high steps, hand clapping, arm crossing, and shoulder tapping. Sometimes singing or chanting accompanies the routine. Step shows and competitions have become a popular part of many African-American festivals and celebrations in the U.S. and around the world.

Job Fair

The Bayou Classic Super Job Fair provides university graduates with opportunities to meet and network with prospective employers. More than 20,000 students and some 1,000 employers have participated in this job fair since 1989.

FURTHER READING

Gay, Kathlyn. *African-American Holidays, Festivals, and Celebrations.* Detroit: Omni-graphics, 2007.

Salzman, Jack, ed. *The African-American Experience: Selections from the Five-Volume Macmillan Encyclopedia of African-American Culture and History.* New York: Macmillan, 1998.

WEB SITE

State Farm Bayou Classic
www.statefarmbayouclassic.com

Bella Coola (Nuxalk) Midwinter Rites

Type of Holiday: Religious (Bella Coola), Calendar/Seasonal
Date of Observation: November-March
Where Celebrated: British Columbia, Canada
Symbols and Customs: Kusiut, Masks, Potlatch
Related Holidays: Kwakiutl Midwinter Ceremonies

ORIGINS

The Bella Coola (Nuxalk) Midwinter Rites is part of Native American religious tradition. The history of this and other Native American cultures dates back thousands of years into prehistoric times. According to many scholars, the people who became the Native Americans migrated from Asia across a land bridge that may have once connected the territories presently occupied by Alaska and Russia. The migrations, believed to have begun between 60,000 and 30,000 B.C.E., continued until approximately 4,000 B.C.E. This speculation, however, conflicts with traditional stories asserting that the indigenous Americans have always lived in North America or that tribes moved up from the south.

The historical development of religious belief systems among Native Americans is not well known. Most of the information available was gathered by Europeans who arrived on the continent beginning in the sixteenth century C.E. The data they recorded was fragmentary and oftentimes of questionable accuracy because the

Europeans did not understand the native cultures they were trying to describe and the Native Americans were reluctant to divulge details about themselves.

Midwinter ceremonials, one type of Native religious rite, are held by peoples throughout the north Pacific coast, including the Bella Coola (Nuxalk), Kwaikiutl, and others. The Bella Coola are a Native American people who flourished at one time along the northern banks of the Bella Coola River in British Columbia. A high point of the Bella Coola's ceremonial life came in the winter, a period devoted to honoring the spirits who walked the earth, often disguised as animals, during the cold weather months from November to March. Preparations, however, began as early as September, when they believed that the supernatural being known as Noäkxnim began his journey by canoe up the Bella Coola River, joined by other spirits along the way. It was also in September that members of the secret society known as KUSIUT, who organized the midwinter rites, began to prepare for the intricate and often terrifying dances they would perform.

These dances or dramatic performances formed the heart of the winter ceremonies. They used masked figures and what would nowadays be called "special effects." In the drowning dance and the beheading dance, for example, dancers would suddenly appear to lose their heads or drop out of sight through trap doors. There was also a burning dance and a stomach-cutting dance that used MASKS and trickery to achieve their illusions. POTLATCHES—gatherings at which gifts were handed out and individuals whose status in the tribe had changed were publicly recognized—were an important part of the Bella Coola rites.

Alcohol abuse and the diseases—particularly smallpox—brought by missionaries, trappers, and Scandinavian settlers had a devastating impact on the Bella Coola tribe by the end of the nineteenth century, and it currently has fewer than a thousand members. The power and mystique surrounding the Kusiut, too, have been undermined by the fact that membership is now no longer as exclusive as it once was. But POTLATCHES are still held and most of the remaining Bella Coola still reside in the same area of British Columbia on a reservation, which has been relocated to the river's south shore because of frequent severe flooding.

SYMBOLS AND CUSTOMS

Kusiut

The Bella Coola were one of several tribes along the British Columbian coast that offered membership in the masked dancing society known as Kusiut. Kusiut members were believed to have supernatural powers of their own, especially the ability to cure illness.

Only Kusiut members could participate in the dances performed during the Midwinter Rites, and young men were often forced to join and threatened with death if they should ever reveal the society's secrets. They went through elaborate initiation rites, in return for which they were taught the tricks used in the dances and received the protection of the society's guardian spirit. It was Kusiut members who made up the songs for the ceremonial dances and who created the MASKS, which were later burned so that new ones would have to be carved for the following year.

Nowadays membership in the Kusiut is open to all men, and as a result there are no longer enough spectators to make the Midwinter Rites the powerful spectacle they were hundreds of years ago.

Masks

The ceremonial masks used by the Bella Coola were among the most frightening of those created by the tribes of the Pacific Northwest. They usually resembled human faces on an inhuman scale, with huge eyes and thick-lipped mouths hanging open. Many of the masks featured moving parts and smaller masks that would suddenly be revealed within larger masks. A skilled dancer could manipulate his mask in such a way that it acted out an entire story.

The Thunder, Echo, and Laughter masks were among the most recognizable, and there was also one that resembled the supernatural bird known as the HokHokw. Today, surviving Bella Coola masks are regarded as rare and valuable works of art.

Potlatch

A potlatch—possibly from a Nootka word meaning "to give"—was a ceremonial distribution of property by North Pacific Coast tribal chiefs to other chiefs and high-ranking guests. Although feasting and dancing were an important part of the ceremony, the main purpose was to hand out gifts according to each guest's social status. The amount of prestige a chief enjoyed was reflected in how much of his wealth he gave away at this event. Although it might seem that such a custom would quickly lead to economic ruin, guests who attended a potlatch were then obligated to hold one of their own or risk social embarrassment. A chief who gave away all of his wealth, therefore, would probably get most of it back when he was invited to other potlatches.

The distribution of wealth was only part of the reason for potlatches, which were also held to announce publicly that the status of the individual hosting the ceremony (or that of a member of his family) had changed. For example, it was common to give a potlatch when a new chief was appointed, when ancestral names were assigned to his children, or when his daughter reached puberty. It made sense, therefore, to give a potlatch during the Midwinter Rites so that everyone would be aware that the supernatural beings were conferring the right to dance the sacred masked dances upon certain Kusiut members.

The potlatch is perhaps the most important surviving religious practice among the Native people in Alaska and along the north Pacific coast in the aftermath of European arrival. They take place not only on an annual basis but also throughout the year, at funerals and memorials.

FURTHER READING

Hirschfelder, Arlene B., and Paulette Fairbanks Molin. *Encyclopedia of Native American Religions*. Updated edition. New York: Facts on File, 2000.
Leach, Maria, ed. *Funk & Wagnalls Standard Dictionary of Folklore, Mythology & Legend*. San Francisco: Harper & Row, 1984.

WEB SITE

Blue Raven Co.
www.blueravenco.com/mythology2.html

Beltane (Beltine)

Type of Holiday: Ancient, Religious (Neopagan), Calendar/Seasonal
Date of Observation: April 30 or May 1
Where Celebrated: Brittany, Ireland, Isle of Man, Scotland, Wales
Symbols and Customs: Beltane Cake, Bonfires, Carline, Tree or Maypole
Related Holidays: Imbolc, Lughnasa, Mabon, May Day, Samhain, Summer Solstice, Winter Solstice, Vernal Equinox

ORIGINS

Celtic peoples lived in Ireland, Scotland, England, and northern France from around 500 B.C.E. until around 100 C.E., when the Romans conquered most of Celtic Europe. Little is definitely known about ancient Celtic religion. The Celts themselves left sparse written accounts. Julius Caesar, who led the Romans into

Celtic lands, wrote of his impressions of the people, as did other ancient Greco-Roman writers.

During the 1960s the modern Neopagan and Wiccan movements emerged in Great Britain, the United States, and other English-speaking countries. They follow a nature-oriented religion loosely linked to ancient Celtic and other beliefs and inspired by old European folk practices. They celebrate eight sabbats, known as the eight spokes of the wheel of the year, which include **SUMMER SOLSTICE**, **WINTER SOLSTICE**, **VERNAL EQUINOX**, **BELTANE**, **SAMHAIN**, **IMBOLC**, **LUGHNASA**, and **MABON**.

Along with **IMBOLC** (February 1), **LUGHNASA** (August 1), and **SAMHAIN** (November 1), Beltane was one of the four great Celtic festivals—the last to be celebrated before the Celtic year turned full circle back to midsummer and began all over again. It takes its name from the ancient god Bel, also known as Beli, Belin, or Belinus, and possibly associated with the Phoenician or Canaanite word *Ba'al*, which means "master." *Bellus* in Latin means "beautiful," and *tan* means "fire" in Cornish (*tine* in Irish or Gaelic), so it is not surprising that both the god Bel and the rituals associated with the festival involve fire.

Bel was the young sun god, counterpart of the older god Bran. His festival was the focal point of the second half of the Celtic year, just as the most important festival in the first half of the year was Lughnasa (Bran and Lugh were gods of the same type). Since the Celts believed that each day began with the setting of the sun the night before, Beltane was celebrated by lighting BONFIRES on the night of April 30 to honor the sun god. The fires were used for both purification and fertility rites, and a number of superstitions were attached to both flames and ashes.

Beltane is believed to be a survival of an even more ancient pastoral festival that accompanied the first turning of the herds out to wild pasture. It was a time of year when witches and fairies were said to be out in great numbers, and in Ireland it was said that whoever was foolish enough to join a fairy dance on Beltane Eve would not be set free until the following May 1. Beltane is still observed in Ireland, the Scottish highlands, Wales, Brittany, and the Isle of Man. In the United States, many of the customs originally associated with Beltane have survived in the modern observance of **MAY DAY**—including the making of flower garlands and dancing around a decorated MAYPOLE.

SYMBOLS AND CUSTOMS

Beltane Cake

A large oatmeal or barley cake called the Beltane cake was typically served at village feasts on Beltane. The person in charge of the feast would divide the cake and give everyone a piece. One particular piece was called the Beltane CARLINE, and whoever got it was threatened with being thrown into the BONFIRE or subjected to various mock tortures.

Sometimes the CARLINE piece was daubed with charcoal from the bonfire until it was completely black. Then all the pieces of cake were put in a bonnet, and everyone had to draw out their portion while wearing a blindfold. Whoever drew the black piece had to endure a mock sacrifice to Baal, whose good will was essential to a productive harvest. Instead of being thrown on the fire, the person would be allowed to leap three times through the flames.

In some areas of Scotland, oatmeal cakes were rolled down a hillside around noon on the first day of May. The superstition was that the person whose cake broke before reaching the bottom would die or have bad luck before the year was out. There is also some evidence that in rural areas, these Beltane cakes were kept for an entire year as a charm against spells that would ruin the cows' milk.

Bonfires

In ancient times, the bonfires that were lit with great ceremony on the night of April 30 in the central highlands of Scotland were often accompanied by human sacrifices, which is perhaps why Beltane fires were called "bone-fires." Eventually the human victims were spared, but people still regarded the fires as possessing magical powers. Since contact with the fire was symbolic of contact with the life-giving sun, people would leap through the flames to forestall bad luck and to cure barrenness. On the Isle of Man, branches or twigs from the rowan tree were carried three times around the fire in the direction of the sun (i.e., turning to the right) and then taken home to protect the family and animals from evil. Even today in Ireland the rowan branch is often hung over the hearth as a good-luck charm.

The Beltane fires were also associated with purification. Farmers would drive their livestock between two fires—a practice that required a good deal of prodding and prompting from the entire community—to purge them of disease as they emerged from the rigors of winter. Then they would be taken out to new pastures, often on higher ground, where they would have access to nutritious spring grasses. The custom of driving cattle through or between fires on **MAY DAY** or the evening before persisted in Ireland until fairly recent times. The Irish expression *idir dá teine lae Bealtaine* ('between two Beltane fires") can be loosely translated as "in a dilemma."

According to Welsh folklore, the bonfires that are lit in early May protected the fields from witchcraft so that good crops would follow. Even the ashes from the fire were considered a valuable charm against bad luck, infertility, and disease.

It was common at one time to cut a trench in the turf, forming a kind of bench for spectators, and then build a pile of wood or other fuel in the center. The fire would be lit with an elaborate and primitive system for producing sparks by friction, as evidenced by the Irish term *teine éigin* (fire from rubbing sticks), which is used to refer to the Beltane bonfire. Sometimes the villagers would sit around this table of turf eating custard and oatmeal cakes (*see* BELTANE CAKE) that had been toasted in the fire's embers.

Carline

The term *carline* refers to a hag or old woman. It was applied to the person who, after getting the blackened piece of the BELTANE CAKE, was routinely subjected to various mock tortures—including being nearly thrown in the BONFIRE or stretched out flat on the ground and "quartered." Once the carline had been through these torments, the rest of the villagers treated him as someone who was already dead. This treatment continued, not just for the duration of the celebration but for an entire year.

The whole idea of the Beltane carline probably goes back to ancient times, when human sacrifices were made on Beltane. The victim back then was usually a woman, perhaps indicating that the custom was part of a primitive female fertility cult.

Tree or Maypole

The idea of a central tree or pole at the axis of the cosmos is actually a very ancient one that can be found in many cultures. The custom of dancing around a decorated maypole may have been Celtic in origin and is believed to have been a part of the original Beltane celebration. It was obviously intended as a phallic symbol, as seen in the various fertility rituals involving young people and farm animals that were part of the festival (*see* BONFIRES). When the maypole came to America as part of the celebration of MAY DAY, however, its phallic associations so upset the Puritan authorities that they tried to outlaw the custom.

FURTHER READING

Bellenir, Karen. *Religious Holidays and Calendars*. 3rd ed. Detroit: Omnigraphics, 2004.

Frazer, Sir James G. *The Golden Bough: A Study in Magic and Religion*. New York: Macmillan, 1931.

Gulevich, Tanya. *Encyclopedia of Easter, Carnival, and Lent*. Detroit: Omnigraphics, 2002.

Heinberg, Richard. *Celebrate the Solstice: Honoring the Earth's Seasonal Rhythms through Festival and Ceremony*. Wheaton, IL: Quest Books, 1993.

Henderson, Helene, ed. *Holidays, Festivals, and Celebrations of the World Dictionary.* 3rd ed. Detroit: Omnigraphics, 2005.

Hutton, Ronald. *The Pagan Religions of the Ancient British Isles: Their Nature and Legacy.* Oxford: Blackwell, 1991.

King, John. *The Celtic Druids' Year: Seasonal Cycles of the Ancient Celts.* London: Blandford, 1995.

Leach, Maria, ed. *Funk & Wagnalls Standard Dictionary of Folklore, Mythology & Legend.* San Francisco: Harper & Row, 1984.

WEB SITE

Beltane Fire Society
www.beltane.org

Berber Bride Fair
(Moussem des Fiancailles)

Type of Holiday: Folkloric
Date of Observation: Late September
Where Celebrated: Near Imilchil, Morocco
Symbols and Customs: Folk Music and Dancing, Headdresses, Marriage Contracts, Silver Jewelry, White Turbans and Clothing

ORIGINS

For more than a thousand years, the Berber people of Morocco have lived in small communities spread throughout the rugged Atlas Mountains. People living in such tiny, remote communities had a hard time finding mates. The Berber Bride Fair addressed this problem. Each year, in late September, men and women looking for marriage partners converged on the shrine of a Muslim saint near the village of Imilchil. Once there they had three days to select a marriage partner from among the hundreds of other single, divorced, or widowed fair goers. The Berber Bride Fair continues till this day, providing Berbers both with an opportunity to find a mate and to stock up on necessary household wares at good prices.

No one knows exactly how and when the Berber Bride Fair began. A legend claims that once a boy and girl from warring tribes fell in love with each other. Due to the hostility between the two tribes, the couple was forbidden to marry. The boy and girl cried so many tears that two small lakes were created. After seeing the two lakes of tears the tribal rulers finally relented and allowed the couple to marry. They also created the Bride Fair, in order to give youngsters from different tribes a yearly opportunity to meet and marry.

The Berber Bride Fair is called a moussem, or pilgrimage, in French. Like other such events throughout the Muslim world, the pilgrimage takes as its destination the shrine of a Muslim holy person, or saint. The Berber Bride Fair takes place outside the shrine of Sidi Mohammed el Merheni, near the village of Imilchil. Although many people attend looking for mates, the moussem also includes an open-air market. Berber people from many remote locales attend the fair, looking to buy tea, sugar, jewelry, carpets, pots and pans, hardware, livestock, spices, and produce.

Until the eighth-century Arab invasion, Morocco was primarily populated by the Berber people. Although the Arabs successfully instilled their new religion, Islam, throughout the country, many Berber tribes remained intact. While Arab culture came to dominate Morocco's cities, Berber views and customs still have significant influence over Moroccan culture in rural areas. Unlike their Arab sisters, Berber women have traditionally had the right to arrange their own marriages. Moreover, compared to Arab women, their status has been closer to that of men. Among the Berbers divorce is common, and some prospective brides and grooms wandering around the Berber Bride Fair have been married seven or eight times.

At the Berber Bride Fair, women identify prospective grooms by their WHITE TURBANS. Grooms identify possible brides by their HEADDRESSES and SILVER JEWELRY. Courtship consists of meeting and chatting with one another in public. Holding hands signifies that a deal is in the making. If one person drops the other person's hand, then the deal is off and both members of the couple need to keep looking. When a woman decides to accept a man's offer, she declares, "You have captured my liver." In Morocco, the liver, rather than the heart, is believed to be the seat of emotion. If the couple roams the fair together holding hands, it is assumed by all that they are engaged.

The actual wedding ceremony does not take place at the fair. Only family members and friends may attend a traditional Berber wedding. In recent years, due to tourist interest, a typical Berber wedding is presented in a nearby village. The nearly week-long exchange of gifts and rituals is collapsed into a 90-minute scenario. Visitors often enjoy watching the bride's representative arrive at the groom's house and mock the gifts of clothing and jewelry that he had selected for her, compelling him to bring out more and finer goods. The show ends when the bride—riding on a mule and dressed in a red robe—arrives at the groom's house. She carries a lamb to symbolize prosperity. A child rides behind her on the mule, representing fertility.

SYMBOLS AND CUSTOMS

Folk Music and Dancing

The Berber Bride Fair is a joyous event, and the spirited music and sensual dancing reflect the crowd's excitement and happiness. These musical events are not scheduled, though they usually take place in the evenings. They occur spontaneously as musicians with drums and pipes gather and become inspired to play.

Headdresses

Berber men can tell which ladies have been married previously by examining the style of their headdress. Women who are divorced or widowed wear pointed or conical headdresses. First-time brides wear round, spangled headdresses. Some of them also veil their faces.

Marriage Contracts

Once a couple has become engaged, they await the last day of the fair when official marriage contracts are signed. A government official arrives on this day to record and notarize the couples' decisions. The men and women sit separately inside the officials' tent, waiting their turn to make these final arrangements. Sometimes couples who have been engaged for some time attend the Berber Bride Fair in order to take advantage of the reduced rates given on marriage documents at the fair.

Silver Jewelry

Prospective brides wander through the fair wearing silver and amber jewelry. Folk tradition teaches that silver jewelry brings them good luck. Merchants also sell silver and amber jewelry at the fair.

White Turbans and Clothing

Berber men who wish to find a bride at the fair often wear white djellabas, a garment that looks like a full-length white shirt. White turbans are another sign that men use to advertise their interest in finding a mate. By contrast, women looking for a husband usually wear colorful clothes.

FURTHER READING

Beckwith, Carol, and Angela Fisher. *African Ceremonies*. New York: Harry N. Abrams, 2002.

Covington, Richard. "Dreams in the Desert." *Smithsonian Magazine*. August 2002. www.smithsonianmagazine.com/issue/2002/august/dreams.htm

Dax, Peter. "Seven Brides for Seven Berbers." *New York Times*. September 3, 1989.

WEB SITE

Africa Travel Magazine
www.africa-ata.org/feature3.htm

Blessing of the Waters (Orthodox Epiphany)

Type of Holiday: Religious (Christian)
Date of Observation: January 6
Where Celebrated: Greece, United States, and by Orthodox Christians around the
world
Symbols and Customs: Basil, Cross, Dove
Related Holidays: Epiphany

ORIGINS

The Blessing of the Waters is a Christian holiday celebrated by Orthodox Christians. The word Christian refers to a follower of Christ, a title derived from the
Greek word meaning Messiah or Anointed One. The Christ of Christianity is Jesus
of Nazareth, a man born between 7 and 4 B.C.E. in the region of Palestine. According to Christian teaching, Jesus was killed by Roman authorities using a form of
execution called crucifixion (a term meaning he was nailed to a cross and hung
from it until he died) in about the year 30 C.E. After his death, he rose back to life.
His death and resurrection provide a way by which people can be reconciled with
God. In remembrance of Jesus' death and resurrection, the cross serves as a fundamental symbol in Christianity.

With nearly two billion believers in countries around the globe, Christianity is the
largest of the world's religions. There is no one central authority for all of Christianity. The pope (the bishop of Rome) is the authority for the Roman Catholic
Church, but other sects look to other authorities. Orthodox communities look to
patriarchs and emphasize doctrinal agreement and traditional practice. Protestant
communities focus on individual conscience. The Roman Catholic and Protestant
churches are often referred to as the Western Church, while the Orthodox churches
may also be called the Eastern Church. All three main branches of Christianity
acknowledge the authority of Christian scriptures, a compilation of writings

assembled into a document called the Bible. Methods of biblical interpretation vary among the different Christian sects.

While Roman Catholic and Protestant churches emphasize the visit of the Magi when they celebrate **EPIPHANY**, Orthodox Christian Churches celebrate the baptism of Jesus in the River Jordan on January 6. In honor of Jesus' baptism, when the Holy Spirit descended in the form of a DOVE and proclaimed Him the Son of God, the church's baptismal water is blessed, and small bottles of holy water are given to worshippers to take home. In many American cities, priests lead their congregations to a local river, which they bless. Many countries throughout the world mark the day with the immersion of a CROSS in the sea, a lake, or a river.

In Palestine, it was the River Jordan that received a blessing on Epiphany. Thousands of pilgrims would gather on its shores to step into the water after the rites were held, submerging themselves three times to obtain the maximum blessing. In Egypt, the Nile was blessed for many centuries. Christians and Muslims alike would plunge into the waters three times, then drive their domestic animals into the river. In Rome, the water that was blessed in the church and taken home on this day was believed to stay fresh throughout the year and even longer.

In Greece, the Blessing of the Waters is still one of the country's most important church days, especially in seaport towns. Back when Greek ships depended on the wind to get from one place to another, most seamen tried to be home before **CHRISTMAS**. Believing it wasn't a good idea to be at sea during the Twelve Days of Christmas, they cast anchor and waited for the priest to bless the waters before they set out on their next journey. Even today, Greek seamen try to be back in their home ports for Epiphany. When the CROSS is thrown into the water, the ships blow their whistles or fire cannons. Young men dive in to retrieve the cross, and the one who brings it to the surface has the privilege of carrying it around town and receiving gifts from the townspeople.

In the United States, the best-known Blessing of the Waters celebration takes place in Tarpon Springs, Florida. The community's Greek roots can be traced back to the early twentieth century, when sponge divers from Greece came there to take part in the growing sponge industry. The Epiphany Day ceremonies begin with a religious service, during which the water in the church is blessed with special prayers and rituals. A long and colorful procession through the streets follows, ending at the Spring Bayou. There a priest reads the story of Jesus' baptism from the New Testament and, at the stroke of noon, a white DOVE is released. The archbishop then throws a golden CROSS into the water and young men from the local Greek Orthodox churches compete in diving for it. The one who retrieves it receives a blessing from the archbishop and is supposed to have good luck for the entire year. Afterward, a Greek dinner is served, bouzouki music is played, and Greek folk dances are performed.

SYMBOLS AND CUSTOMS

Basil

In Greece, young girls sometimes sit up all night on Epiphany Eve to watch a pot of sweet basil, symbolic of good wishes, burst into flower when the heavens open up. They believe that wishes made on this night are more likely to be answered.

In Greek villages, the Blessing of the Waters often takes the form of having the local priest walk through the village after Mass and bless each home by sprinkling them with a sprig of basil dipped in holy water.

Cross

The cross that is thrown into the water on Epiphany is a symbol of Christ, who died on the cross. It is also a symbol of salvation and redemption through Christianity. Although the cross occupied a prominent place in other religions long before Christianity, it has come to be regarded as a uniquely Christian symbol.

Dove

In ancient and Christian art, the dove is a symbol of purity and peace. It also symbolizes the Holy Ghost, who appears in the story of Jesus' baptism as told in the New Testament: "And John bore record, saying, I saw the Spirit descending from heaven like a dove, and it abode upon him." (John 1:32)

FURTHER READING

Cirlot, J.E. *A Dictionary of Symbols*. New York: Philosophical Library, 1962.

Cohen, Hennig, and Tristram Potter Coffin. *The Folklore of American Holidays*. 3rd ed. Detroit: Gale Research, 1999.

Ferguson, George. *Signs and Symbols in Christian Art*. New York: Oxford University Press, 1954.

Gulevich, Tanya. *Encyclopedia of Christmas and New Year's Celebrations*. 2nd ed. Detroit: Omnigraphics, 2003.

Henderson, Helene, ed. *Holidays, Festivals, and Celebrations of the World Dictionary*. 3rd ed. Detroit: Omnigraphics, 2005.

Ickis, Marguerite. *The Book of Festivals and Holidays the World Over*. New York: Dodd, Mead, 1970.

Johnson, F. Ernest, ed. *Religious Symbolism*. New York: Institute for Religious and Social Studies, 1955.

MacDonald, Margaret R., ed. *The Folklore of World Holidays*. Detroit: Gale Research, 1992.

Olderr, Steven. *Symbolism: A Comprehensive Dictionary*. Jefferson, NC: McFarland, 1986.

Santino, Jack. *All Around the Year: Holidays and Celebrations in American Life*. Urbana: University of Illinois Press, 1994.

Weiser, Franz Xaver. *Handbook of Christian Feasts and Customs*. New York: Harcourt, Brace, 1958.

WEB SITE

GoGreece.com
www.gogreece.com/learn/epiphany.htm

Boston Marathon

Type of Holiday: Sporting
Date of Observation: Third Monday in April
Where Celebrated: Boston, Massachusetts
Symbols and Customs: Heartbreak Hill, Laurel Wreath, Unicorn
Related Holidays: Olympic Games

ORIGINS

The oldest footrace in the United States was first held on Patriots' Day, April 19, in 1897. Organized by members of the Boston Athletic Association (BAA), the race involved only fifteen runners. Nowadays the Boston Marathon, which has been held on the third Monday in April since 1969, draws more than 20,000 official starters, who must meet established qualifying times. Several thousand additional runners participate on an unofficial basis. To date, the record field size occurred in the 1996 centennial run, with 36,748 official starters and 35,868 runners finishing the race. In 1972, it became the first marathon to officially admit women runners.

The 26.2-mile course begins in Hopkinton and ends in front of downtown Boston's Prudential Center. It is based on the long-distance footrace first held at the revival of the **OLYMPIC GAMES** in 1896, which commemorated the legendary feat of a Greek soldier who is supposed to have run from Marathon to Athens, a distance of about twenty-five miles, to bring news of the Athenian victory over the Persians in

490 B.C.E. Appropriately, the first modern marathon winner in 1896 was a Greek, Spiros Louis.

The Olympic marathon distance was standardized at twenty-six miles, 385 yards in 1924. The extra 385 yards were added to accommodate the distance from Windsor Castle, where the 1908 Olympic race began, to the royal box in the stadium at London.

Runners from all over the world come to Boston to compete in the marathon, which is considered one of the most prestigious running events in the world. Well-known American winners include the "old" John Kelley, who won twice and continued to complete the race well into his eighties; the "young" John Kelley (no relation), who was the first American victor in the post-World War II era; "Tarzan" Brown, who in 1938 took a break at the nine-mile mark for a quick swim in Lake Cochichuate; and Bill Rodgers, who won three consecutive marathons in 1978-80. Among the women, Rosa Mota of Portugal was the first to win three official Boston Marathon titles. And few people will forget the infamous Rosie Ruiz in 1980, who many believed tried to defraud the BAA by showing up at the end of the race to capture the women's LAUREL WREATH without having actually run the full distance. This was later substantiated by television coverage of certain checkpoints. Jackie Gareau of Canada was later declared the women's winner, although Ruiz continued to insist that she'd run the race fairly.

BY 1988 the Boston Marathon became the **OLYMPIC GAMES** marathon trial for nine African countries, leading to what organizers called "the African running revolution." From 1988 to 2000, all but one winner in the men's division hailed from Africa, and every winner from 1991 to 2007 was from Kenya with the exception of two years, 2001 (winner was Korean) and 2005 (winner was from Ethiopia).

SYMBOLS AND CUSTOMS

Heartbreak Hill

Probably the best-known stretch of the course covered by the Boston Marathon is located at the twenty-first mile. It is a section of Commonwealth Avenue in Newton Centre known as "Heartbreak Hill," and it has literally been the downfall of many marathon competitors. Occurring as it does more than two-thirds of the way to the finish line, when many runners have expended most of their energy, the incline poses more of a challenge than non-runners can appreciate.

Laurel Wreath

The laurel wreath that is placed on the heads of the first male and female runners to cross the finish line in the Boston Marathon is a traditional symbol of victory that dates back to very ancient times. The laurel tree was sacred to Apollo, the ancient Greek and Roman god of light, healing, music, poetry, prophecy, and manly beauty. The leaves of the laurel were used to weave garlands and crowns for festivals, and the crowning of a poet, artist, or hero with laurel leaves signified that he had overcome many obstacles and negative influences—whether internal or external—to achieve his goal.

Unicorn

Chosen as the BAA's symbol ten years before the first Boston Marathon, the unicorn was selected as the marathon's logo as well. The unicorn appears on the marathon's medals and represents an unattainable goal for which competitors reach. In their pursuit, they cannot achieve perfection, but they can come close to excellence. This idea is central to the world of sports, where athletes are constantly striving to improve.

FURTHER READING

Christianson, Stephen G., and Jane M. Hatch. *The American Book of Days*. 4th ed. New York: H.W. Wilson, 2000.
Cirlot, J.E. *A Dictionary of Symbols*. New York: Philosophical Library, 1962.

WEB SITE

Boston Athletic Association, Boston Marathon's Official Web Site
www.bostonmarathon.org

Bouphonia

Type of Holiday: Ancient
Date of Observation: Late June or early July
Where Celebrated: Athens, Greece
Symbols and Customs: Ox

ORIGINS

The Greek religion flourished in the ancient Greek city-states and surrounding areas between the eighth and fourth centuries B.C.E. The city-state of Athens was the center of ancient Greek civilization and major ceremonies took place there. Within Athens, the Acropolis was the religious center, consisting of temples dedicated to the gods and goddesses. However, smaller sanctuaries to the gods and goddesses also existed throughout the region.

Ancient Greek religion pervaded every aspect of life, and there was no concept of a separation between sacred and secular observances. Thus, ancient Greek festivals were religious occasions conducted in honor of the deities in the pantheon. Ritual and sacrifice, athletic games, dramatic performances, and feasting were all elements of festivals.

The ancient Athenian ritual known as the "murder of the ox" or Bouphonia took place at the end of June or beginning of July, the time of year when the threshing of the grain was nearly over. According to legend, the custom of sacrificing an OX at the altar of Zeus on the Acropolis can be traced back to an incident in which a man named Sopatrus killed an ox who had eaten the grain he was offering as a sacrifice. He was so overcome by remorse afterward that he buried the animal and fled to Crete. But then a famine set in, and the people of Athens instituted the custom of sacrificing an ox to Zeus in the hope that it would bring the famine to an end.

The ritual that eventually became known as the Bouphonia has been described in great detail. Barley and wheat cakes were laid upon the altar of Zeus. Oxen were then driven around the altar, and the ox that went up and ate the offering was the one selected for sacrifice. The ax and the knife used to kill the beast were wetted with water, sharpened, and handed to butchers, one of whom struck the ox while the other cut its throat. As soon as the animal had been killed, both men dropped their weapons and fled. The ox was then skinned and everyone shared in eating its flesh. The ox-hide was later stuffed with straw and sewn up again, so that it stood upright and could be yoked to a plow—perhaps a means of bringing it "back to life."

After the ritual killing, a trial was held to assign responsibility for the murder of the ox. The young maidens who carried the water used to wet the weapons accused the men who had sharpened the ax and the knife, who in turn blamed the men who had handed the implements to the butchers. The butchers themselves laid the blame on the ax and the knife, which were accordingly found guilty, condemned, and cast into the sea.

SYMBOLS AND CUSTOMS

Ox

Because the ox is the domesticated (i.e., castrated) counterpart of the wild bull, it symbolizes patience and strength, representing all who bear their yoke while laboring in silence for the good of others. It was for this reason that the ox was popular as a sacrificial animal.

FURTHER READING

Biedermann, Hans. *Dictionary of Symbolism: Cultural Icons and the Meanings Behind Them.* New York: Meridian Books, 1994.

Ferguson, George. *Signs and Symbols in Christian Art.* New York: Oxford University Press, 1954.

Henderson, Helene, ed. *Holidays, Festivals, and Celebrations of the World Dictionary.* 3rd ed. Detroit: Omnigraphics, 2005.

Leach, Maria, ed. *Funk & Wagnalls Standard Dictionary of Folklore, Mythology & Legend.* San Francisco: Harper & Row, 1984.

Parke, H.W. *Festivals of the Athenians.* Ithaca, NY: Cornell University Press, 1977.

Braemar Highland Gathering

Type of Holiday: Sporting
Date of Observation: First Saturday in September
Where Celebrated: Braemar, Scotland
Symbols and Customs: Tartan, Tossing the Caber

ORIGINS

The Highland Games at Braemar date back to the eleventh century, when King Malcolm (1058-1093) held a gathering of the Scottish clans at the Braes (*brae* means hillside) of Mar to compete in running races. The fastest runners were then chosen to carry messages for the king throughout Scotland—a kind of primitive postal service. The first race was to the top of Craig Choinnich, a hill that overlooked Braemar.

For thousands of years, Braemar had been a gathering place; it was located in the heart of Scotland's largest deer forest and had always been a favorite among kings and nobles who enjoyed hunting. It was also a place of great strategic importance for the Scottish Highlands, which is what the hilly northern part of the country was called. The Highlanders formed clans that were widely regarded as primitive and violent, and their way of life was very different from that of the British-dominated regions to the south. Feuds between clans were common and often passed down from one generation to the next. In other words, competition among them was fierce, and they welcomed the opportunity to engage in contests that would show their superior strength and endurance.

These annual gatherings were formalized under the sponsorship of the Braemar Highland Society, founded in 1817. Although it had originated as a kind of trade union and social organization providing assistance to the sick and the elderly, by 1826 the society was also concerned with preserving the Highlands' unique form of dress, language, and culture. The society's annual gathering began to feature athletic contests, similar to those that had been held in King Malcolm's time, and the wearing of the kilt (*see* TARTAN). Several times during the latter half of the nineteenth century, Queen Victoria invited society members to hold their gatherings on her estate at Balmoral. The queen's patronage was reflected in the organization's name, which by 1866 had been changed to the Braemar Royal Highland Society.

By 1904, "Highland gatherings" or "Highland games" were being held in more than fifteen locations throughout Scotland, and Scottish emigrants to North America had established similar events throughout Canada and the United States. In fact, Highland games have taken place in Boston, New York, Philadelphia, and Newark, New Jersey, since the end of the nineteenth century. These gatherings typically feature dancing to traditional Scottish reels, bagpipe music, and such athletic events as throwing the hammer, putting (hurling) the stone, TOSSING THE CABER, and hill races.

SYMBOLS AND CUSTOMS

Tartan

Highlanders had a unique way of dressing as far back as the eighteenth century. They wore a mantle—a length of tartan (or plaid) cloth wrapped around the shoulders and tied around the waist to form a sort of skirt or "kilt" which made them look very wild and primitive. While the wearing of tartan originally symbolized a way of life known only to Highlanders, specific tartan colors and patterns eventually came to be associated with certain families or clans.

Today, many of these tartans have been reproduced and made into kilts, caps, shawls, and scarves. In fact, tartan has become a symbol for Scotland as a whole, and it can be seen on everything from whiskey bottles and tins of shortbread to Scottish tourist brochures. The typical Highlander no longer walks around in kilts, scarves, or other tartan clothing, although such costumes can occasionally be seen during the Highland Games.

Tossing the Caber

The event that is usually considered the highlight at Braemar and other Highland gatherings is called tossing the caber. It is one of the world's oldest sports, and it can be traced back to the eleventh century, when men hoisting beams to build houses often got bored and decided to see who could toss his the farthest. In the days when King Henry VIII of England practiced it, this sport was known as "Ye Casting of Ye Bar."

A typical caber is 19 feet long and weighs about 150 pounds. The thrower stands with his legs apart and the caber vertical, holding it near the bottom with clasped hands that have been coated with sticky resin. The actual lifting is done with the palms, and once the caber has been lifted waist-high, it is tilted slightly forward and the competitor begins to run. He must accelerate before planting his legs, or he'll never be able to toss the caber on the run. Ideally, it should turn end-over-end as it moves through the air, but in fact, this is a rare achievement. A "12 o'clock," which is similar to hitting a home run in baseball, occurs when the caber lands directly in front of the thrower, who is standing in the six o'clock position on the face of an imaginary clock.

Competitors always wear kilts, although the sport is increasingly popular among non-Scots. Tossing the caber has been an international event since the early 1980s; in recent years, famous caber tossers have come from Scandinavia, Australia, the United States, Canada, and even Nigeria.

FURTHER READING

Henderson, Helene, ed. *Holidays, Festivals, and Celebrations of the World Dictionary*. 3rd ed. Detroit: Omnigraphics, 2005.

Jarvie, Grant. *Highland Games: The Making of the Myth*. Edinburgh: Edinburgh University Press, 1991.

Trawicky, Bernard, and Ruth W. Gregory. *Anniversaries and Holidays*. 5th ed. Chicago: American Library Assocation, 2000.

Van Straalen, Alice. *The Book of Holidays Around the World*. New York: Dutton, 1986.

WEB SITE

Braemar Royal Highland Society
www.braemargathering.org

Burial of the Sardine
(Entierro de la Sardina)

Type of Holiday: Religious (Christian)
Date of Observation: Between February 4 and March 10; Ash Wednesday, the first day of Lent
Where Celebrated: Spain
Symbols and Customs: Sardine
Related Holidays: Ash Wednesday, Carnival, Easter, Lent

ORIGINS

Burial of the Sardine is a Christian holiday celebrated in Spain. The word Christian refers to a follower of Christ, a title derived from the Greek word meaning Messiah or Anointed One. The Christ of Christianity is Jesus of Nazareth, a man born between 7 and 4 B.C.E. in the region of Palestine. According to Christian teaching, Jesus was killed by Roman authorities using a form of execution called crucifixion (a term meaning he was nailed to a cross and hung from it until he died) in about the year 30 C.E. After his death, he rose back to life. His death and resurrection provide a way by which people can be reconciled with God. In remembrance of Jesus' death and resurrection, the cross serves as a fundamental symbol in Christianity.

With nearly two billion believers in countries around the globe, Christianity is the largest of the world's religions. There is no one central authority for all of Christianity. The pope (the bishop of Rome) is the authority for the Roman Catholic Church, but other sects look to other authorities. Orthodox communities look to patriarchs and emphasize doctrinal agreement and traditional practice. Protestant communities focus on individual conscience. The Roman Catholic and Protestant churches are often referred to as the Western Church, while the Orthodox churches may also be called the Eastern Church. All three main branches of Christianity acknowledge the authority of Christian scriptures, a compilation of writings assembled into a document called the Bible. Methods of biblical interpretation vary among the different Christian sects.

ASH WEDNESDAY is observed in Spain as Burial of the Sardine, with an event that pokes fun at Christian tradition. Ash Wednesday marks the end of **CARNIVAL** and the beginning of **LENT**, the forty-day period before **EASTER** during which the Roman Catholics Church prescribed fasting from meat. Thus, the mock funeral procession known as the Burial of the Sardine gives people a final chance to participate in the revelries of Carnival while displaying their true feelings about the church's "no meat" rule.

Although it is not certain when this event was first observed, the Spanish painter Goya saw it take place in Madrid in the early nineteenth century and used it as the subject for one of his paintings. It may be linked to a historical event—when a shipload of sardines sent to the court of King Carlos III (1716-1788) arrived spoiled, and the smell was so offensive that he said they should be buried immediately—or it may be a replacement for a much older custom, the burning or drowning of a straw effigy representing the spirit of Carnival. It clearly began as a way of mocking the church: People would dress up like priests and nuns and form a funeral procession, carrying ordinary household objects in place of the church's religious paraphernalia and burying a sardine (or a dummy holding one in its mouth) as a way of thumbing their noses at the fast.

Originally the funeral procession featured a real sardine, but nowadays it is usually made of wood, plastic, or papier-mâché. It sits in a coffin accompanied by mourners wearing black, many of whom engage in exaggerated displays of grief. The procession winds its way through the streets (with frequent stops at local taverns) and ends at a city square or a local beach. A man dressed up as a cardinal reads a make-believe "last will and testament," and then the sardine is set on fire, or sometimes thrown into the water or buried in the sand. There may be fireworks and music after the ceremony is over, and the mourners often dance over the burned remains of the sardine. Sometimes canned sardines are handed out to remind people what they should be eating during Lent. After the ceremony is over, people usually attend Ash Wednesday services at their local church, where the priest marks their foreheads with ashes as a symbol of penitence.

The fact that Lenten practices are no longer taken as seriously as they used to be has deprived this event of much of its original intention. It has survived primarily as an opportunity to participate in one last celebration before the more somber mood of Lent sets in.

SYMBOLS AND CUSTOMS

Sardine

The sardine or fish symbolizes the dietary restrictions of Lent. The burial of a fish was originally a protest against the Catholic tradition that fish be eaten instead of meat throughout the forty-day period. Nowadays, when meat is only forbidden on Fridays, it serves as a reminder that the worldly pleasures of Carnival must be put aside.

Sometimes a sausage link or a strip of pork is substituted for the sardine, which would seem to underscore its more recent use as a symbol of Lenten requirements (no meat on Fridays) rather than as a mockery or protest against these requirements.

FURTHER READING

Spicer, Dorothy Gladys. *The Book of Festivals*. 1937. Reprint. Detroit: Omnigraphics, 1990.

Urlin, Ethel L. *Festivals, Holy Days, and Saints' Days*. 1915. Reprint. Detroit: Omnigraphics, 1992.

WEB SITE

Tenerife Tourism Corporation
www.webtenerifeuk.co.uk/PortalTenerife/Home/Home.htm?Lang=en

Candlemas
(Groundhog Day)

Type of Holiday: Religious (Christian), Folkloric
Date of Observation: February 2
Where Celebrated: United States and throughout the Christian world
Symbols and Customs: Candles, Groundhog

ORIGINS

Candlemas is a Christian holiday marking forty days after the birth of Jesus Christ. The word Christian refers to a follower of Christ, a title derived from the Greek word meaning Messiah or Anointed One. The Christ of Christianity is Jesus of Nazareth, a man born between 7 and 4 B.C.E. in the region of Palestine. According to Christian teaching, Jesus was killed by Roman authorities using a form of execution called crucifixion (a term meaning he was nailed to a cross and hung from it until he died) in about the year 30 C.E. After his death, he rose back to life. His death and resurrection provide a way by which people can be reconciled with God. In remembrance of Jesus' death and resurrection, the cross serves as a fundamental symbol in Christianity.

With nearly two billion believers in countries around the globe, Christianity is the largest of the world's religions. There is no one central authority for all of Christianity. The pope (the bishop of Rome) is the authority for the Roman Catholic Church, but other sects look to other authorities. Orthodox communities look to patriarchs and emphasize doctrinal agreement and traditional practice. Protestant communities focus on individual conscience. The Roman Catholic and Protestant

churches are often referred to as the Western Church, while the Orthodox churches may also be called the Eastern Church. All three main branches of Christianity acknowledge the authority of Christian scriptures, a compilation of writings assembled into a document called the Bible. Methods of biblical interpretation vary among the different Christian sects.

According to the law of Moses, it was the parents' duty to bring their firstborn son to the church and make an offering to God on his behalf. This usually took place on the fortieth day following the child's birth. After observing the traditional forty-day period of purification following the baby's birth, therefore, Mary presented Jesus at the Temple in Jerusalem. An aged and devout Jew named Simeon held the baby in his arms and announced that he would be a "light to lighten the Gentiles" (Luke 2:32). This is why February 2 (which is forty days after **CHRIST-MAS**) came to be called Candlemas (Candelaria in Spanish-speaking countries) and has been celebrated by the blessing of CANDLES since the eleventh century. In the Eastern church, it is known as the Feast of the Presentation of Christ in the Temple, while in the Western church it is the Feast of the Purification of the Blessed Virgin Mary. But both festivals celebrate the same sequence of events and are characterized by the blessing of candles and candlelight processions.

Some think that the custom of forming a procession with lighted candles was not originally a Christian idea but was instead an attempt to create a Christian identity for an ancient Roman rite that took place in February and consisted of a procession around the city with lighted candles. Roman Christians borrowed the practice of using candles in religious services, and in 494 C.E. Pope Gelasius I established the Feast of the Purification of the Virgin Mary. The Feast of the Purification was also the time to kindle a "brand" left over from the Yule log at Christmas.

SYMBOLS AND CUSTOMS

Candles

Some researchers believe the candles custom of Candlemas derived from customs from pagan celebrations held at the same time of year. On February 1 the pagan Celts celebrated **IMBOLC**, a festival associated with the return of the spring goddess Bride (later St. Bridget). In some areas sacred fires and candles burned through the night in honor of Bride's return. In ancient Rome, people observed purification rites throughout the month of February, which included a procession throught the city with lit candles. In addition, they celebrated the return of the spring goddess Ceres on February 1. Pagans in other Mediterranean cultures also welcomed the return of a spring deity. Many of these observances featured fire rituals and torchlit processions, which some scholars see as the origin of the candlelight processions now associated with Candlemas.

In addition, lamps and candles are a traditional symbol of rejoicing. During the Middle Ages, Candlemas was the day on which the church blessed candles for the entire year. There was a procession of worshippers holding candles in their hands, and people believed that wherever these candles were used, they would chase away the devil. The unused candle stubs were often preserved as good-luck charms. In many Roman Catholic countries today, the candles blessed on Candlemas are still regarded as possessing special powers. In Brittany, France, for example, they are lit in times of storm or illness. In parts of Austria, they are lit at important family occasions such as christenings and funerals. In Sicily, the Candlemas candles are brought out when there is an earthquake or when someone is dying.

The candles that are "purified" or blessed in the church on February 2 are also used to bless people's throats on **ST. BLAISE'S DAY** (February 3), protecting them from colds and from fishbones getting stuck.

Groundhog

In the United States, February 2 is popularly known as Groundhog Day. There was a medieval superstition that all hibernating animals—not just groundhogs—came out of their caves and dens on Candlemas to check on the weather. If they could see their shadows, it meant that winter would go on for another six weeks and they could go back to sleep. A cloudy day meant that spring was just around the corner. Farmers in England, France, and Canada used to look for the stirring of the "Candlemas Bear" as a sign that spring was on its way; in Ireland, it was the hedgehog; and in Germany, it was the badger. The return of hibernating animals was one of several ways in which nature announced a change in the season, and those whose livelihood depended upon natural cycles were very attuned to such signs.

It was the early German settlers known as the Pennsylvania Dutch who brought this custom to the United States and chose the groundhog as their harbinger of spring. No one really knows why the weather on this day was believed to indicate the reverse of what was to come: Good weather meant prolonged winter, and cloudy weather meant an early spring. But the tradition took hold in America, giving rise to the legend of Punxsutawney Phil, a groundhog in Pennsylvania believed to be nearly a century old. There is a club in Punxsutawney whose members still trek up to Phil's burrow on February 2 and wait for him to emerge. Unfortunately, weather researchers have determined that the groundhog has been correct only 28 percent of the time.

If February 2 seems a little early to look for signs of spring, remember that before the adoption of the Gregorian calendar, Candlemas fell on February 14. Until recently, farmers in Mississippi and Arkansas observed Groundhog Day on the fourteenth because it was closer to the arrival of warm weather.

FURTHER READING

Crippen, T.G. *Christmas and Christmas Lore*. 1923. Reprint. Detroit: Omnigraphics, 1990.

Gulevich, Tanya. *Encyclopedia of Christmas and New Year's Celebrations*. 2nd ed. Detroit: Omnigraphics, 2003.

Henderson, Helene, ed. *Holidays, Festivals, and Celebrations of the World Dictionary*. 3rd ed. Detroit: Omnigraphics, 2005.

Ickis, Marguerite. *The Book of Festivals and Holidays the World Over*. New York: Dodd, Mead, 1970.

Miles, Clement A. *Christmas in Ritual and Tradition, Christian and Pagan*. 1912. Reprint. Detroit: Omnigraphics, 1990.

Santino, Jack. *All Around the Year: Holidays and Celebrations in American Life*. Urbana: University of Illinois Press, 1994.

Tuleja, Tad. *Curious Customs: The Stories Behind 296 Popular American Rituals*. New York: Harmony, 1987.

WEB SITES

New Advent Catholic Encyclopedia
www.newadvent.org/cathen/03245b.htm

Punxsutawney Groundhog Club
www.groundhog.org

Carnival (Mardi Gras)

Type of Holiday: Religious (Christian)

Date of Observation: Dates vary, between Epiphany and Shrove Tuesday (Ash Wednesday Eve)

Where Celebrated: Central America, Europe, South America, United States, Caribbean Islands, and throughout the Christian world

Symbols and Customs: Carnival King, Forty Hours' Devotion, Fried Dough, King Cakes, Krewes, Ox

Colors: Purple, green, and gold (*see* KING CAKES)

Related Holidays: Ash Wednesday, Lent, Maslenitsa, Shrove Tuesday

ORIGINS

Carnival is a time when Christians celebrate before the start of **LENT**. The word Christian refers to a follower of Christ, a title derived from the Greek word meaning Messiah or Anointed One. The Christ of Christianity is Jesus of Nazareth, a man born between 7 and 4 B.C.E. in the region of Palestine. According to Christian teaching, Jesus was killed by Roman authorities using a form of execution called crucifixion (a term meaning he was nailed to a cross and hung from it until he died) in about the year 30 C.E. After his death, he rose back to life. His death and resurrection provide a way by which people can be reconciled with God. In remembrance of Jesus' death and resurrection, the cross serves as a fundamental symbol in Christianity.

With nearly two billion believers in countries around the globe, Christianity is the largest of the world's religions. There is no one central authority for all of Christianity. The pope (the bishop of Rome) is the authority for the Roman Catholic Church, but other sects look to other authorities. Orthodox communities look to patriarchs and emphasize doctrinal agreement and traditional practice. Protestant communities focus on individual conscience. The Roman Catholic and Protestant churches are often referred to as the Western Church, while the Orthodox churches may also be called the Eastern Church. All three main branches of Christianity acknowledge the authority of Christian scriptures, a compilation of writings assembled into a document called the Bible. Methods of biblical interpretation vary among the different Christian sects.

The season known to Christians as Carnival actually extends all the way from **EPIPHANY** (January 6) to **SHROVE TUESDAY**, or the day before **LENT**. The Latin *carne vale* means "farewell to meat," but it could also be a broader reference to the pleasures that are forbidden during the forty days of Lent. Carnival in general is a time for feasting and self-indulgence, with the most intense period of celebration usually taking place the last three days before **ASH WEDNES-DAY** and particularly on Shrove Tuesday. It features masked balls, lavish costume parades, torchlight processions, dancing, fireworks, and of course feasting on all the foods that will have to be given up for Lent. It is interesting to note that processions, feasting, and masquerades were also popular activities among the pagans during their spring festivals, which were designed to ensure the health and growth of their crops. Most of the features of the modern Carnival celebration are firmly rooted in a tradition that can be traced back to the fourteenth century.

One of the most famous Carnival celebrations in the world takes place in Rio de Janeiro, Brazil. The parades, pageants, and costume balls go on for four days, but the highlight of the festival is the parade of the samba schools, which takes place on the Sunday and Monday preceding Ash Wednesday. The competition among these neighborhood groups is fierce, and people spend months beforehand making costumes and learning special dances for the parade.

The most flamboyant Carnival celebration in the United States takes place during the two weeks preceding Ash Wednesday in New Orleans, Louisiana. It was known among New Orleans' early French settlers as Mardi Gras ("Fat Tuesday") because the day before the start of Lent was traditionally a time to use up all the milk, butter, eggs, and animal fat left in the kitchen. This grand celebration culminates in a series of parades organized by groups known as KREWES. With marching jazz bands and elaborately decorated floats, the parades attract over a million spectators every year.

New Orleans' Mardi Gras has been cancelled only a few times in its 150 year history—during a 1979 police strike, the Civil War, and two World Wars. But it came very close to being cancelled again in February 2006. The previous year, on August 29, 2005, Hurricane Katrina ripped through New Orleans, damaging many critical levees, leaving eighty percent of the city underwater, claiming more than 1,600 lives, and decimating city infrastructure, schools, hospitals and libraries.

Many residents of New Orleans, still mourning the loss of family, friends, and neighbors, felt it was too soon and too painful to celebrate Mardi Gras. Others thought the city needed to proceed with its cherished tradition in order to demonstrate its resilience, provide a needed distraction, and to promote psychological healing and financial recovery. Ultimately, the 2006 Mardi Gras did take place with over half of New Orleans' pre-Katrina residents still missing from the city, a diminished crowd of visitors, fewer krewes, and parades shortened and re-routed to circumvent the most severely damaged sections of the city.

SYMBOLS AND CUSTOMS

Carnival King

Carnival is an especially important season for Roman Catholics. In Italy, Spain, France, and other European countries where the influence of Rome has been the strongest, a popular feature of Carnival celebrations is a burlesque figure, often made out of straw and known as the Carnival King. When his brief reign over the Carnival festivities is over, the king is usually shot in public, burned, drowned, or otherwise destroyed while the onlookers cheer openly. This may be a symbolic act designed to rid the spectators of their folly and sinfulness.

One theory about the origin of the Carnival King is that he is a direct descendant of the old King of the **SATURNALIA**, the ancient Roman festival held in December. This pagan king was a man chosen to impersonate the Roman agricultural god Saturn for the duration of the celebration; but at the end, he suffered a real death rather than a make-believe one. The brutal custom of putting a mock king to death eventually faded, but the idea of appointing someone to reign over the festivities appears to have survived in the figure of the Carnival King.

Forty Hours' Devotion

To encourage good Christians to compensate for the excessive behavior exhibited at Carnival time, Pope Benedict XIV in 1748 instituted a special devotion for the three days preceding Lent. Called the "Forty Hours of Carnival," it is still held in many American and European churches where carnival celebrations are a long-standing tradition. The Blessed Sacrament is exposed all day Monday and Tuesday, and devotions are held in the evening.

Fried Dough

Most Carnival and Mardi Gras celebrations throughout the world include the preparation of some form of fried dough. In New Orleans, for example, the *beignet* is a square doughnut without a hole, similar to a fritter. In some areas of Germany, where Carnival is called Fastnacht, fried dough is served in the form of *Fastnachtkuchen*. This raised doughnut was brought to the United States by the Germans who settled in Pennsylvania, and such fried cakes can still be found in other German-settled areas of the country.

Since it was customary on Mardi Gras, or "Fat Tuesday," to use up all the animal fat in the house before the start of Lent, food was often fried so the fat wouldn't go to waste.

King Cakes

The round or oval cakes known as King Cakes are one of the primary foods associated with the Carnival season. They are frosted with alternating bands of sugar in the three colors that have become associated with Mardi Gras: purple, symbolizing justice; green, symbolizing faith; and gold, symbolizing power. There are tiny dolls—or sometimes a bean—hidden in the cakes, and whoever is served the piece containing the doll or bean is crowned king for a day. In New Orleans, where the Carnival season begins with the *Bal du Roi* (King's Ball), a Parisian tradition, the person who gets the doll has to hold the next ball. These balls continue throughout the season, with the final one being held on Mardi Gras.

Krewes

The private clubs known as "krewes" that give parties, parades, and balls during the Mardi Gras celebration in New Orleans can be traced back to 1831 in Mobile,

Alabama. A man named Michael Krafft had been out celebrating New Year's Eve with his friends when they decided to break into a hardware store. They stole some cowbells and rakes, and paraded through the streets making as much noise as possible. This incident led to the establishment of the Cowbellion de Rakin Society, which organized a rowdy costume parade the following year featuring tableaux and dancing. In 1857, six men from Mobile who had been members of the society and who now lived in New Orleans decided to introduce a similar organization there, which they called the Mystick Krewe of Comus—a reference both to the masque (a dramatic entertainment featuring elaborate costumes, scenery, music, and dancing) *Comus,* written by English poet John Milton, and to the Greek and Roman god of revelry, feasting, and nocturnal entertainment. The word "krewe" is supposed to have come from the Anglo-Saxon spelling of "crew."

By 1988, there were approximately sixty other krewes in New Orleans, and today they parade through the streets for nearly three weeks before Mardi Gras. Comus remains the most traditional krewe, producing floats for the parade similar to those seen a hundred years ago. The other krewes—with names like Rex, Zulu, Proteus, and Momus—are also private clubs, often linked to old-line Protestant or Catholic social networks. In addition, there are "maverick" krewes whose membership is open to anyone who can pay the required fee. The floats designed by the krewes range from the most traditional—small, delicate floats with a great deal of ornamental sculpture and extensive use of gold and silver foil—to considerably less formal processions of decorated vans and trucks.

Some think that the krewes and their parades go back to the *reynages* of medieval France—make-believe kingdoms established as part of the Carnival celebration. It is also possible that the floats seen in today's Mardi Gras parades were derived from religious tableaux originally performed in churches but moved outside when they became too rowdy.

Ox

One theory regarding the origin of "Fat Tuesday" or Mardi Gras is that it was named after the practice of leading a fattened ox through the village streets before Lent. Afterward, it was slaughtered to provide the final meal before Lenten restrictions on meat and dairy products went into effect.

In many Carnival celebrations held in France today, a fattened ox plays a central role in the festivities. A child known as the "king of butchers" usually rides in a decorated car behind the ox, and people throw confetti or blow horns as the ox and the butcher pass by. In New Orleans, the Krewe of Rex (*see* KREWES) is credited with reintroducing the fattened ox to the Mardi Gras celebration by using it as the theme for a giant float.

FURTHER READING

Bellenir, Karen. *Religious Holidays and Calendars*. 3rd ed. Detroit: Omnigraphics, 2004.

Dobler, Lavinia G. *Customs and Holidays Around the World*. New York: Fleet Pub. Corp., 1962.

Frazer, Sir James G. *The Golden Bough: A Study in Magic and Religion*. New York: Macmillan, 1931.

Gulevich, Tanya. *Encyclopedia of Easter, Carnival, and Lent*. Detroit: Omnigraphics, 2002.

Henderson, Helene, ed. *Holidays, Festivals, and Celebrations of the World Dictionary*. 3rd ed. Detroit: Omnigraphics, 2005.

Purdy, Susan. *Festivals for You to Celebrate*. Philadelphia: Lippincott, 1969.

Santino, Jack. *All Around the Year: Holidays and Celebrations in American Life*. Urbana: University of Illinois Press, 1994.

Urlin, Ethel L. *Festivals, Holy Days, and Saints' Days*. 1915. Reprint. Detroit: Omnigraphics, 1992.

Weiser, Franz Xaver. *Handbook of Christian Feasts and Customs*. New York: Harcourt, Brace, 1958.

WEB SITES

Louisiana State Museum
lsm.crt.state.la.us/mgras/mardigras.htm

World Music Productions
www.afropop.org/multi/feature/ID/33

Chalma Pilgrimage

Type of Holiday: Religious
Date of Observation: Varies
Where Celebrated: Chalma, Mexico
Symbols and Customs: Blessing of Holy Images, Crosses, Dancing, Flowers, Miracles, Offerings, Sacred Spring

ORIGINS

Chalma is located in central Mexico and has been a sacred site for thousands of years. In the Pre-Columbian period, native people worshipped Ozteotl (alternately, Oxtoteotl), a deity believed to reside in a cave in the mountains near Chalma. Ozteotl sometimes took the form of a jaguar and was regarded as the god of human destiny, of the night, and of war, depending on various native traditions. Pilgrims commonly traveled long distances on foot through the mountains to reach the cave of Ozteotl, which contained a very large black cylindrical stone that represented the god and was thought to have healing powers. The ancient pilgrims would bathe in a spring just outside the cave and drink some of the water before making offerings to Ozteotl.

In the early sixteenth century, Spanish missionaries arrived in the area and discovered the cave of Ozteotl. Believing that the native people were offering human sacrifice to the god, the missionaries demanded the destruction of the black stone and an end to the worship of Ozteotl. A large crucifix took the place of the stone in Ozteotl's cave, and it is said that the native people transferred their worship to the new image. This is believed to have been the beginning of central Mexico's conversion to Christianity.

Pilgrims continued to visit the site after the replacement of Ozteotl's stone with the crucifix, believing that the Christ of Chalma could heal illness, grant fertility to women, and protect newborn babies. Over time the entrance to the cave was enlarged and a shrine to St. Michael was erected. In the late seventeenth century the crucifix was moved from the cave to the specially constructed Sanctuary of Chalma, a church officially known as the Royal Monastery and Sanctuary of Our Lord Jesus Christ and Saint Michael of the Caves of Chalma. In the eighteenth century, the original crucifix was destroyed by fire and a replacement was created using its remains.

Thousands of pilgrims known as *Chalmeros* continue to visit Chalma each year to bathe in the SACRED SPRING and make OFFERINGS at the sanctuary. It is customary to walk the last part of the journey at night by torch or candlelight. People make the pilgrimage throughout the year, but the most popular time for the journey is just before the beginning of Lent. The largest number of pilgrims arrives in Chalma for Ash Wednesday services. Chalma has become the second most visited pilgrimage site in Mexico, after the shrine to Our Lady of Guadalupe, the patron saint of Mexico.

SYMBOLS AND CUSTOMS

Blessing of Holy Images

Some pilgrims bring an image of their patron saint to Chalma in order to have it blessed. These images are usually covered with a blanket or cloth during the journey and only uncovered once inside the sanctuary, where the blessing is performed.

Crosses

The town of Chalma is surrounded by mountains and hills that have been covered over the years in crosses. Each cross is placed and maintained by one of the various groups of pilgrims who make annual visits to Chalma. During their yearly visit, the pilgrims repaint their cross and decorate it with flowers. A night is then spent dancing and singing around the cross.

Dancing

Many pilgrims who visit Chalma pray with dancing and music. This tradition can be traced back to the earliest Pre-Columbian people who visited the sacred site at Chalma and danced in honor of Ozteotl.

Flowers

People who make an annual pilgrimage to Chalma typically decorate their vehicles with flowers and often wear crowns of flowers in their hair. Flowers are also commonly left as offerings at the sanctuary and beside the sacred spring. This custom is an echo of the original offerings of flowers that were left by the early worshippers of Ozteotl.

Miracles

Chalma is a popular pilgrimage site because many people believe that miracles are granted to the faithful who visit the sanctuary. Healings, successful births, and the fulfillment of personal requests have all been credited to the completion of a pilgrimage and to offerings made at Chalma's sanctuary.

Offerings

Behind the Chalma monastery is an ancient tree known as the Ahuehuete, which grows over the mouth of the sacred spring. Pilgrims make offerings by hanging items on the tree branches and placing items along the wall beside the tree. Typical offerings include such items as paintings, photos, locks of hair, notes, and personal belongings. These are left in thanks for miracles that have been granted.

Sacred Spring

A spring flows from beneath the Ahuehuete tree and feeds a stream that runs behind the monastery. The water is regarded as holy and is believed to have healing powers of its own. Continuing the practice of the ancient worshippers of Ozteotl, pilgrims bathe in the stream, anoint themselves, or drink the water in order to be blessed or healed.

FURTHER READING

Davidson, Linda Kay. *Pilgrimage: From the Ganges to Graceland*. Santa Barbara, CA: ABC Clio, 2002.

Henderson, Helene, ed. *Holidays, Festivals, and Celebrations of the World Dictionary*. 3rd ed. Detroit: Omnigraphics, 2005.

WEB SITE

SacredSites.com
www.sacredsites.com/americas/mexico/chalma.html

Chinese New Year (Lunar New Year, Yuan Tan)

Type of Holiday: Calendar/Seasonal
Date of Observation: Between January 21 and February 19; first day of the first Chinese lunar month
Where Celebrated: China, and by Chinese communities in the United States and throughout the world
Symbols and Customs: Debt-paying, Firecrackers, Flowers, Gate Gods, Kitchen God, Lucky Phrases or Spring Couplets, New Year Prints, Nian Monster
Colors: The color red, associated with good luck, can be seen everywhere during the Chinese New Year celebration (*see* FIRECRACKERS, NIAN MONSTER). LUCKY PHRASES are printed on red paper, red luck candles are displayed in homes and offices, and at one time, doorways were painted red to frighten demons away.
Related Holidays: Lantern Festival, Li Ch'un, Sol, Tet

ORIGINS

The Chinese New Year celebration is actually a two-week sequence of events, beginning with the ascent of the KITCHEN GOD to heaven near the end of the twelfth lunar month and ending with the **LANTERN FESTIVAL** on the fifteenth day of the first month.

The Chinese lunisolar calendar is based on the oldest system of time measurement still in use. It is widely employed in Asian countries to set the dates of seasonal festivals. The Chinese New Year takes place on the new moon nearest to the point which is defined in the West as the fifteenth degree on the zodiacal sign of Aquarius. Each of twelve months in the Chinese year is twenty-nine or thirty days long and is divided into two parts, each of which is two weeks long. The Chinese calendar, like all lunisolar systems, requires periodic adjustment to keep the lunar and solar cycles integrated; therefore, an intercalary month is added when necessary.

The names of each of the twenty-four two-week periods sometimes correspond to seasonal festivals celebrated during the period. Beginning with the New Year, which takes place in late January or early February, these periods are known by the following names: Spring Begins (New Year and **LI CH'UN**), the Rain Water, the Excited Insects, the **VERNAL EQUINOX**, the Clear and Bright (**CHING MING**), the Grain Rains, the Summer Begins, the Grain Fills, the Grain in Ear, the **SUMMER SOLSTICE** (*see* **DOUBLE FIFTH**), the Slight Heat, the Great Heat, the Autumn Begins, the Limit of Heat, the White Dew (*see* **MID-AUTUMN FESTI-VAL**), the **AUTUMN EQUINOX,** the Cold Dew, the Hoar Frost Descends, the Winter Begins, the Little Snow, the Heavy Snow, the **WINTER SOLSTICE,** the Little Cold, and the Great Cold.

On New Year's Eve (Moon 12, Day 30) all the doors to the house are sealed with strips of paper and the head of the household performs three important ceremonies: the offering to the God of Heaven and Earth, the offering to the Household Gods, and the worship of the ancestral tablets, usually strips of wood with the names and dates of deceased family members in raised or gilded characters. Then the entire family, putting aside their quarrels with one another, sits down to a special reunion meal. At midnight, everyone presents New Year wishes to one another in a very formal ceremony known as *K'o T'ou* (or kowtow, meaning to touch the ground with the forehead), observing strict rules about who should bow to whom. Between 3:00 and 5:00 a.m., the head of the household breaks the seals on the front door and greets the returning Household Gods, led by Tsao Wang, the Kitchen God.

New Year's Day itself is spent paying respects to elders, setting off FIRECRACKERS, burning incense, and calling on friends and relatives. No knives or sharp instruments may be used on this day, for fear of "cutting" good fortune, and brooms aren't used because they might sweep good fortune away. The first five days of the New Year, known as the Beginning of the New Spring, are devoted to the worship of the God of Wealth. Married women visit their family homes and sweep out their houses to fend off poverty. Most people return to work after the fourth or fifth day of celebration, and by the thirteenth and fourteenth days, they're busy getting ready for the **LANTERN FESTIVAL**.

Telling fortunes based on the zodiac, an astrological diagram of the universe, is a popular New Year's custom in China. According to legend, the Chinese zodiac of twelve animals representing each year in succession came about in the sixth century B.C.E., when Buddha invited all the animals in creation to come to him. Only twelve responded: the tiger, rabbit, dragon, snake, horse, goat, monkey, rooster, dog, pig, rat, and ox. Buddha rewarded them by giving each one a year that would carry the animal's name as well as its traits: hence the "Year of the Rat," "Year of the Monkey," etc. By referring to the "eight characters" (which symbolize the hour, day, month, and year of a person's birth) and the twelve signs of the zodiac, fortunetellers can predict what events the coming year might hold.

New Year's Day is also a birthday celebration for all Chinese people, since birthdays are calculated according to the year in which a person is born rather than the day. Every new baby, in other words, is considered exactly a year old on New Year's Day. Some people, however, prefer to use the Western method of observing birthdays.

SYMBOLS AND CUSTOMS

Debt-paying

Anyone who has not paid his debts before New Year's Day loses face, which in China means that he is disgraced. Shops are open and customers line up, waiting to settle their accounts. Paying off debts is a symbolic as well as a practical act, enabling people to face the New Year with a "clean slate."

The Chinese have three traditional dates for settling their debts: New Year's Day, the **DOUBLE FIFTH** (Dragon Boat Festival), and the **MID-AUTUMN FESTIVAL**. In between times, many people live on credit. There is a great deal of scurrying around as the Lunar New Year approaches and people try to raise cash to pay their debts. If someone can't pay up, he may try to hide until New Year's morning. Then he is safe until the next settlement day—unless the person he owes goes searching for him with a lantern, indicating that it is still dark and that the debt may be collected without violating the New Year.

Poor debtors often find refuge in the courtyard in front of the temple of the City of God. Comedy troupes give free performances here, and creditors who spy their debtors in the crowd are usually hesitant to demand payment in front of other people.

Firecrackers

Firecrackers play an important role in many Chinese celebrations. Along with fire (or bright light) and the color red, loud noises are guaranteed to scare off evil spirits—particularly the NIAN MONSTER, a legendary beast who appears at this time of year.

Firecrackers are first set off when the KITCHEN GOD departs for heaven, several days before the New Year actually begins. The noise they make speeds him on his way and also keeps evil spirits out of the house until he returns. More firecrackers are set off during the **LANTERN FESTIVAL**, which concludes the New Year celebrations.

Flowers

Flowers can be seen everywhere during the celebration of the Lunar New Year, particularly in southern China. They are used to decorate houses and public places, and each flower has a symbolic meaning. The white narcissus, for example, stands for good fortune and prosperity; the camellia, springtime; the peony, wealth; the peach (or plum), longevity. The quince, traditionally a symbol of fertility, is often used by the Chinese community in San Francisco.

Any plant with red flowers is considered a symbol of good luck and happiness. Blossoms that open on New Year's Day signify an extra dose of good fortune.

Gate Gods

During the New Year celebration, the Chinese put up pictures of the Gate Gods, guardians of the home and protectors of mankind, on the panels of their front doors. These figures are often shown against a background of peach blossoms; according to legend, the Gate Gods were two brothers who lived under a peach tree so large that 5,000 men could not encircle it with their arms. Images of these traditional warriors have stood guard over Chinese households for thirteen centuries.

The earliest "New Year pictures" of the Gate Gods date from the late second century and show Shentu and Yulu, guardians of the underworld, who protected families by tying up threatening demons and throwing them to the tigers. They are dressed in full armor, and their faces are painted with the bright makeup of the Chinese opera.

The most popular Gate Gods today are the Tang dynasty (618-907) generals Qin Qiong (or Qin Shubao) and Yuchi Jingde (or Hu Jingde). Legend says that when the Tang emperor Tai Zong was kept awake all night by evil demons, two of his ministers offered to stand guard outside the palace gates, but they never saw a sign of ghosts or goblins. After letting them spend several nights like this, the emperor decided to have their portraits painted and hung up on either side of the gate. His sleep was never disturbed again.

Kitchen God

Tsao Wang, also known as the Kitchen God or Prince of the Oven, personifies the hearth or center of the home. He is one of the oldest gods worshipped in China, and he serves as a messenger between the inhabitants of the earth and the gods in heaven. Every Chinese kitchen has a shrine with a picture of Tsao Wang, usually in a small niche behind the cooking stove, which is considered the soul of the family and represents its fate. A good stove guarantees peace in the family, while a bad one brings strife.

The Kitchen God spends the entire year with the family, observing everything that goes on. Then, on the twenty-third day (twenty-fourth in the South of China) of the last month of the lunar year, he ascends to heaven to make his annual report on what he has seen and heard. Commonly called Little New Year, this occasion is marked with a farewell dinner given by the family and with offerings of sweet cakes and preserved fruits. Sometimes his picture is dipped in wine and his lips are smeared with honey so that he will be in a good mood when he reports on the family's behavior.

After the dinner is over, Tsao Wang's portrait is carried out into the courtyard and set up on an improvised altar with candles and incense. Prayers are offered, and the portrait is set on fire. The burning of the image releases Tsao Wang for his "ascent" to heaven. Paper spirit money (called *qianchang* or *yuanbao*) is thrown into the fire along with straw for the Kitchen God's horse. Peas and beans are tossed on the kitchen roof to imitate the clatter of the horse's hooves and to bring good luck in the coming year to the family's livestock.

The Kitchen God is usually shown sitting next to his wife. Sometimes a dog and a rooster, domestic symbols of a rural household, are shown with him. If the family is very poor and can't afford a woodblock print of Tsao Wang, his shrine may have nothing more than a plain sheet of red paper with his name written on it.

Lucky Phrases or Spring Couplets

On the last day of the twelfth lunar month, the gate posts and door panels of Chinese homes are decorated with images of the GATE GODS and "lucky phrases"—brief inscriptions printed on red paper (blue if the family is in mourning) with characters embossed in gold ink. Sometimes they are written in the form of "spring couplets" or two-line verses, and sometimes they consist of only a single character. "Fu," the character for good fortune, is often used because when it is printed upside down, it sounds the same as the word meaning "to arrive," thus implying that good fortune has arrived.

A popular custom for more than 1,000 years, lucky phrases are designed to bring good fortune of a particular kind. For example, a merchant might put up an inscription designed to attract success in his business; a farmer's lucky phrase might express the wish for a good harvest. In private households, lucky phrases usually concern wealth, longevity, the gift of sons, and official promotion—all traditional Chinese ideals.

The first spring couplets were composed to bring good fortune to the emperor Meng Zhang in the tenth century. It wasn't until the Ming dynasty (1368-1644) that the custom became a popular one. During the Qing dynasty (1644-1911), the composition of these brief verses was regarded as a means of measuring one's literary talent, education, and wit. They consist of two lines, called the "head" and the "tail," that correspond to and balance each other: for example, "By virtue united, heaven is strong;/Through compassion shared, earth is yielding." Many contemporary New Year couplets set political terminology against traditional descriptive elements. "Red flags," for example, might be paired with "fresh flowers." No longer composed by scholars, today's spring couplets are mass produced and can be purchased at stationery stores and magazine stands.

New Year Prints

Nianhua or New Year prints are posted at the same time as the GATE GODS and SPRING COUPLETS, providing visual images of the wishes that the couplets describe. The desire for many children might be accompanied by a picture of a pomegranate, a symbol of fertility. Wishes for wealth and honor are often represented by full-blossomed peonies. The bat is another popular subject; although associated with evil in European folklore, in China it is a common symbol for good luck and happiness. Plowing and weaving prints are popular, as are peaches (symbolizing longevity) and pictures of plump, healthy children holding pots of money (progeny and wealth). Some New Year prints portray scenes from historical novels and popular operas.

The subject matter of New Year prints has changed with the times. In the People's Republic of China, there was an increased demand for art with a socialist theme; prints often showed cooperative labor and bumper harvests. Since the Cultural Revolution (1966-76) ended, traditional New Year sentiments have been more acceptable. Some New Year prints try to combine both: for example, a picture of a communal fish pond may support the government's involvement in aquaculture, but it also symbolizes the traditional New Year wish for wealth. The word *yu*, meaning "fish," sounds the same in Chinese as the word meaning "affluence."

Like LUCKY PHRASES, New Year prints are purchased rather than created. Nianhua workshops throughout China produce more than 100 million of these prints each year.

Nian Monster

According to Chinese legend, there was a frightening creature called *nian* (which is the same as the word meaning "year") who appeared at the end of the year, attacking villagers and their livestock. Nothing could destroy the *nian*, but people eventually discovered that it had three weaknesses: It was frightened by loud noises, it disliked sunshine, and it was terrified of the color red. So they built a huge bonfire outside the village, set off firecrackers, and painted the doors of their houses red. The *nian* covered its head in fear and ran away.

FURTHER READING

Bredon, Juliet, and Igor Mitrophanow. *The Moon Year: A Record of Chinese Customs and Festivals*. Shanghai: Kelly & Walsh, 1927.

Frazer, Sir James G. *The Golden Bough: A Study in Magic and Religion*. New York: Macmillan, 1931.

Gaer, Joseph. *Holidays Around the World*. Boston: Little, Brown, 1953.

Henderson, Helene, ed. *Holidays, Festivals, and Celebrations of the World Dictionary*. 3rd ed. Detroit: Omnigraphics, 2005.

Purdy, Susan. *Festivals for You to Celebrate*. Philadelphia: Lippincott, 1969.

Santino, Jack. *All Around the Year: Holidays and Celebrations in American Life*. Urbana: University of Illinois Press, 1994.

Stepanchuk, Carol, and Charles Wong. *Mooncakes and Hungry Ghosts: Festivals of China*. San Francisco: China Books & Periodicals, 1991.

WEB SITE

Taiwan Government Information Office in Washington DC
www.gio.gov.tw/info/festival_c/spring_e/spring.htm

Ching Ming
(Pure and Bright Festival, Spring Festival)

Type of Holiday: Calendar/Seasonal
Date of Observation: April 5 or 6; fourth or fifth day of the third lunar month
Where Celebrated: China, and by Chinese communities in the United States and throughout the world
Symbols and Customs: Ancestral Graves, Cold Food, Kites, Willow
Related Holidays: Li Ch'un

ORIGINS

Ching Ming means "Pure and Bright," an apt name for a Chinese festival that takes place at the beginning of spring. Although **LI CH'UN** celebrates the first day of spring, it usually occurs in February when the weather is still cold and the nights are long. Ching Ming marks the *real* start of spring. It is always observed 106 days after the **WINTER SOLSTICE** and two weeks after the **VERNAL EQUINOX**.

The Chinese lunisolar calendar is based on the oldest system of time measurement still in use. It is widely employed in Asian countries to set the dates of seasonal festivals. The **CHINESE NEW YEAR** takes place on the new moon nearest to the point which is defined in the West as the fifteenth degree on the zodiacal sign of Aquarius. Each of twelve months in the Chinese year is twenty-nine or thirty days long and is divided into two parts, each of which is two weeks long. The Chinese calendar, like all lunisolar systems, requires periodic adjustment to keep the lunar and solar cycles integrated; therefore, an intercalary month is added when necessary.

The names of each of the twenty-four two-week periods sometimes correspond to seasonal festivals celebrated during the period. Beginning with the New Year, which takes place in late January or early February, these periods are known by the following names: Spring Begins (New Year and **LI CH'UN**), the Rain Water, the Excited Insects, the **VERNAL EQUINOX**, the Clear and Bright (**CHING MING**), the Grain Rains, the Summer Begins, the Grain Fills, the Grain in Ear, the **SUMMER SOLSTICE (DOUBLE FIFTH)**, the Slight Heat, the Great Heat, the Autumn Begins, the Limit of Heat, the White Dew (**MID-AUTUMN FESTIVAL**), the **AUTUMN EQUINOX**, the Cold Dew, the Hoar Frost Descends, the Winter Begins, the Little Snow, the Heavy Snow, the **WINTER SOLSTICE**, the Little Cold, and the Great Cold.

Ching Ming was originally a festival of life renewal celebrated with dancing, singing, and picnicking. Eggs would be boiled and colored, then broken to symbolize the opening and dispersal of life. The emperor would plant trees on the palace grounds; villagers would place pine branches, a symbol of longevity, in front of their doors and hang sprigs of WILLOW under the eaves of their houses to ward off the forces of evil. Much like **ARBOR DAY** in the United States, this holiday was also known as the Tree Planting Festival (Chih Shu Chieh).

Over a period of several centuries, the Spring Festival changed from a celebration of new life to a commemoration of dead ancestors, similar to **ALL SOULS' DAY** in Europe and elsewhere. This transition is less puzzling to the Chinese, who regard the dead as intimately connected with life because they are responsible for ensuring fertility in the family as well as the fields. Nowadays Ching Ming is observed with a ceremonial meal at the family tomb. Graves are cleaned and repaired, and offerings of food and "spirit money" are made to keep the ancestors happy and ensure a good harvest.

SYMBOLS AND CUSTOMS

Ancestral Graves

The Chinese believe that one of the several souls belonging to each person remains near the grave where it can stay in contact with family members. Because this spirit has the power to cause harm or promote good, it must be offered food, music, and burnt sacrifices so it will be favorably disposed toward the living.

Chinese families at one time had private burial grounds outside the city walls, often in the midst of cultivated fields. But the shortage of land has made public cemeteries more common. Early on the morning of Ching Ming, families carrying food, sticks of incense, and paper money tied up in cloth bundles go to visit their ancestral graves. They begin by cutting down any weeds that have grown up around the grave and sweeping away the dirt. The food is set out on stone altar-tables—with an emphasis on dishes the ancestor was fond of—and the paper money is usually left on the grave with a stone or lump of clay to hold it in place. After the spirits of the dead have been worshipped according to prescribed ritual, the family may dine near the graves or return home to feast on the food that was offered.

Those who can't visit their family graves at Ching Ming offer prayers to their ancestors and make an offering of paper bags decorated with two human figures in flowery robes. Between the figures there is a space where the names of those buried in the family graveyard can be listed. The bags are then filled with paper money, placed on an altar with fruit, sweets, and tea, and burned before sundown because the ancestors must return to their graves before the city gates close at nightfall. Most Chinese, however, make a special effort to be home in time for the Spring Festival.

It is considered essential to visit the family graves at least once a year, because an unswept grave is considered an indication that the family has died out. Neglected tombs, especially those located in fields, might be plowed under, or the land might be sold. The punishment for damaging or tampering with graves—as long as they're obviously being cared for—is harsh.

Cold Food

On the eve of Ching Ming, some Chinese observe the Han Shih (Cold Food) Festival. No fires are lit and nothing hot is eaten for twenty-four hours. This custom can be traced back to an ancient tribal rite whereby a new fire could only be kindled once a year. Han Shih, which originally lasted three days, marked the interval between the extinction of the old fire and the lighting of the new one by rubbing two WILLOW sticks together. Courtiers' children were performing this fire-kindling ceremony in the open space before the Imperial Palace as late as the Tang dynasty (seventh to tenth centuries). The first to set his or her sticks alight received a golden cup and three pieces of silk. This custom is believed to be a survival of an ancient sun-worship and purification ritual practiced by the nomads of the Zhou dynasty, who burned the fields in order to rid them of evil influences and clear the way for spring planting. It may also be linked to the Roman Catholic custom of letting the hearth fire go out on **Easter** Sunday and rekindling it on Easter Monday.

A myth has also been devised to explain the custom. It involves a faithful servant traveling with his lord who, when misfortune fell and food supplies ran out, cut off a piece of his own flesh to feed his master. Afterward, he fled to the mountains. The lord set fire to the underbrush to chase him out of hiding so he could be properly rewarded, but the hero preferred to burn alive. After his death, the lord proclaimed that people would honor his example by not lighting any fire in their homes for three days and eating cold food.

Observance of the Cold Food feast is dying out in Beijing, but it is still practiced elsewhere in China.

Kites

During the war between the states of Chu and Han in the third century B.C.E., a famous Han general by the name of Han Xin built a giant wooden kite for the great warrior Zhang Liang to ride in. The legend says that Zhang Liang flew above the Chu encampment singing traditional Chu songs, which made the enemy soldiers so homesick that they left their camp and were defeated. To this day Ching Ming is a popular day to fly kites. There are informal kite competitions and formal exhibitions of kites with participants from all over the world.

After people have visited their family graves and paid their respects to the ancestors, they often picnic, play games, and fly kites in a variety of shapes and designs. Some kites illustrate plots from Chinese folk tales or historical legends; others convey good luck wishes. Many are designed to make sounds in the wind or to create special visual effects. This is why the common word in China for kite is *fengzheng* or "wind zither."

Willow

Because it is the first tree to respond to the sun by putting out new leaves, the willow has always been an emblem of spring and erotic awakening. The Chinese phrase "willow feelings and flower wishes" refers to sexual desire. And the expression "looking for flowers and buying willows" means paying a visit to a prostitute. The willow is also a symbol of vitality because it is extremely hardy and will take root almost anywhere.

The origins of the willow's mystical connection to the Spring Festival are somewhat obscure, but according to a popular legend, a rebellious member of the Tang dynasty took the willow as his personal sign. Those willing to support him were asked to hang a willow branch outside their houses. When the signal for revolt was given on the day of the Ching Ming festival, those who had the branch on their houses escaped massacre. Their descendants continued the custom, and to this day, sprigs of willow are hung under the eaves of houses to keep demons away. In some parts of China, women wear willow sprigs in their hair at Ching Ming, and young people wear "willow dogs" (sprouts of willow) all day. There is a saying that "Those who wear no willow at the Ching Ming will be re-born as yellow dogs in future life"—a sufficient threat to ensure that willow is seen everywhere.

In addition to repelling demons, willow also has the ability to attract good. It can draw the spirits of ancestors back to their homes, which is why it is so often used for decorating graves.

FURTHER READING

Bredon, Juliet, and Igor Mitrophanow. *The Moon Year: A Record of Chinese Customs and Festivals*. Shanghai: Kelly & Walsh, 1927.

Eberhard, Wolfram. *A Dictionary of Chinese Symbols: Hidden Symbols in Chinese Life and Thought*. New York: Routledge & Kegan Paul, 1986.

Gaer, Joseph. *Holidays Around the World*. Boston: Little, Brown, 1953.

Henderson, Helene, ed. *Holidays, Festivals, and Celebrations of the World Dictionary*. 3rd ed. Detroit: Omnigraphics, 2005.

Hill, Jeff, and Peggy Daniels. *Life Events and Rites of Passage*. Detroit: Omnigraphics, 2008.

Stepanchuk, Carol, and Charles Wong. *Mooncakes and Hungry Ghosts: Festivals of China*. San Francisco: China Books & Periodicals, 1991.

WEB SITES

China Internet Information Center
www.china.org.cn/english/features/Festivals/78319.htm AND www.china.org.cn/english/2001/Apr/10256.htm

Global Volunteers
www.globalvolunteers.org/1main/holiday/Qingming.htm

Christmas

Type of Holiday: Religious (Christian)

Date of Observation: December 25

Where Celebrated: United States, Great Britain, Europe, and by Christians throughout the world

Symbols and Customs: Angels, Bells, Boar, Candy Cane, Christmas Card, Christmas Carols, Christmas Seals, Christmas Tree, Crèche, Farolitos, Father Christmas, Gifts, Holly, Mistletoe, Poinsettia, Wassail, Wreath (*see* **CHRISTMAS EVE** for Candles, Luminarias, Reindeer, Santa Claus, Yule Log)

Colors: Christmas is traditionally associated with the colors red and green.

Related Holidays: Advent, Christmas Eve, Epiphany, Ganna, St. Stephen's Day (Boxing Day)

ORIGINS

Christmas, which celebrates the birth of Jesus Christ, is one of the most important holidays for Christians. The word Christian refers to a follower of Christ, a title derived from the Greek word meaning Messiah or Anointed One. The Christ of Christianity is Jesus of Nazareth, a man born between 7 and 4 B.C.E. in the region of Palestine. According to Christian teaching, Jesus was killed by Roman authorities using a form of execution called crucifixion (a term meaning he was nailed to a cross and hung from it until he died) in about the year 30 C.E. After his death, he rose back to life. His death and resurrection provide a way by which people can be reconciled with God. In remembrance of Jesus' death and resurrection, the cross serves as a fundamental symbol in Christianity.

With nearly two billion believers in countries around the globe, Christianity is the largest of the world's religions. There is no one central authority for all of Christianity. The pope (the bishop of Rome) is the authority for the Roman Catholic Church, but other sects look to other authorities. Orthodox communities look to patriarchs and emphasize doctrinal agreement and traditional practice. Protestant communities focus on individual conscience. The Roman Catholic and Protestant churches are often referred to as the Western Church, while the Orthodox churches may also be called the Eastern Church. All three main branches of Christianity acknowledge the authority of Christian scriptures, a compilation of writings assembled into a document called the Bible. Methods of biblical interpretation vary among the different Christian sects.

The first celebration of the birth of Jesus Christ on December 25 took place in Rome about the middle of the fourth century, although the Eastern church was already observing January 6 as a joint commemoration of Jesus' birth and baptism. Since the exact date of the Nativity is not known, there are a number of theories as to why December 25 was chosen. One is that it was designed to replace the ancient Roman winter festival known as the **SATURNALIA**, which was held on December 17-23. Another is that it was a replacement for the Brumalia, or Birthday of the Unconquered Sun, which was observed on December 25 because it followed the **WINTER SOLSTICE**, when the days began to grow longer. Christmas also coincided, more or less, with the Jewish Feast of Lights or **HANUKKAH**, the Egyptian Birthday of the Sun-God, and the Anglo-Saxon Feast of Yule. Many of the symbols associated with Christmas still reflect its twin roots in Christianity and pagan seasonal lore.

Even in pre-Christian times, the period between December 25 and January 6 was considered a special time of year. Now widely referred to as "The Twelve Days of Christmas," this was a time when spirits roamed the earth and were apt to cause mischief if certain precautions weren't taken. A number of the superstitions associated with this period concerned spinning. In England, for example, it was said that if any flax were left on the distaff, the devil would come and cut it. In Denmark, it was believed that nothing characterized by a circular motion (such as a spinning wheel) should be used between Christmas and **NEW YEAR'S DAY**.

When the Gregorian calendar replaced the Julian calendar in 1582, eleven days were dropped to make up for the discrepancy that had accumulated over the centuries. Roman Catholic countries quickly accepted the new calendar, but in England and Scotland, people had trouble adjusting to the change. For almost 200 years, they continued to observe Christmas on what was now January 5. Even after the British adopted the Gregorian calendar in 1752, people living in rural areas continued to observe "Old Christmas Day" on January 5 (January 6 after 1800). The new calendar was never adopted by the Greek and other Eastern churches, where Christmas is still observed on January 6.

Xmas, the common abbreviation for Christmas, is regarded by many—especially those who are intent on preserving the holiday's religious roots and traditions—as an insult to Christ, if not a sacrilege. In fact, the abbreviation is entirely appropriate. The letter "X" (*chi*) is the first letter in the Greek word for Christ. According to the *Oxford English Dictionary*, there was an even longer abbreviation that came into use around 1550: *X-temmas*.

SYMBOLS AND CUSTOMS

Angels

Images of angels adorn Nativity scenes, CHRISTMAS CARDS, CHRISTMAS TREES, and other Christmas displays. These otherworldly beings take their name from the

Greek *angelos,* which means "messenger" or "herald." In the Gospel according to Luke's account of Jesus' birth, it is an angel named Gabriel who visits Mary to inform her that she will bear a child. Then, on the night of Jesus' birth, an angel appears to shepherds in a nearby field to announce the glorious event—followed by a "multitude" of angels who suddenly materialize behind the first angel, singing praises to God.

With so many angels involved in orchestrating the events surrounding Jesus' birth, it is no wonder that they became a symbol of the Christmas holiday. Today's Christmas angels frequently appear as winged human beings in flowing white robes with feminine faces and haloes. Some scholars believe that early Christian artists patterned the image of winged angels after the winged Greek goddess of victory, Nike. The disk of light, called a halo or nimbus, that appears behind their heads symbolizes purity, holiness, and spiritual power. Angels are also frequently shown with harps or other musical instruments, which signify what some consider to be their primary occupation: praising God.

Bells

The association between bells and Christmas can be traced back to the Middle Ages, when Church officials began to use bells for worship and celebration. Large bells were used to call parishioners to religious services, and they also chimed at certain points during the service so that those who were not inside the church could join in the prayers. Many churches had four or five bells; the more important the occasion, the more bells rang to honor it. A high mass, for example, warranted three bells. On the principal feast days, such as **EASTER** and Christmas, four or five bells pealed to celebrate the joyous occasion. In medieval England, Christmas bell-ringing began with a loud clang on the first Sunday in **ADVENT** to alert parishioners that the Advent season had begun.

Today, fewer churches carry out the old Christmas tradition of bell-ringing, and the folklore surrounding bells has been largely forgotten. Nevertheless, the public imagination still links bells with Christmas. A number of well-known Christmas poems and CHRISTMAS CAROLS mention pealing or jingling bells as emblems of the holiday. In addition, bells appear as symbols of the holiday on many Christmas decorations. And representatives of charitable organizations, such as the Salvation Army, who are seeking donations often announce their presence on street corners by ringing hand-held bells.

Boar

Perhaps because the ancient Celts supplied the rest of Europe with pork and bacon, the boar's association with the Yuletide feast goes back to prehistoric times. According to Norse folklore, boar was served in Valhalla, the mythical hall where

Odin received the souls of heroes who had fallen in battle. Pork was highly prized in Ireland and Wales, where many preferred it to beef and mutton.

In eleventh- and twelfth-century England, hunting the wild boar became a traditional Christmas sport. Its head would be carried into the dining hall afterward with a great flourish, often to the accompaniment of "The Boar's Head Carol," the oldest printed CHRISTMAS CAROL in existence (1521). Queen's College, Oxford, was at one time known for its traditional Christmas ceremony of ushering in the boar's head. According to legend, a student of the college was attacked by a wild boar while walking in the country. He was reading Aristotle as he walked, and was able to escape injury by shoving the book down the boar's throat.

In Scandinavia, it is customary to use the last sheaf of corn from the harvest to bake a loaf in the form of a boar or pig at Christmas time. Throughout the festival of Yule (*Jul*), the boar-shaped loaf remains on the table. It is often kept in the house until the crops are sown in the spring. Then part of it is mixed with seed-corn and part is given to the ploughman or his animals to eat. Scholars believe that the Yule boar represents the corn-spirit (a primitive deity who makes the crops grow) in pig form.

In Psalm 80, Satan is described as "the wild boar out of the wood" who has wasted the Lord's vineyards. Carrying the boar's head on a platter is symbolic of his final defeat by Jesus Christ, the newborn King.

Candy Cane

The very earliest Christmas trees were decorated with symbols associated with the birth of Jesus. Candles were used to symbolize Christ, the Light of the World, and the star placed on the topmost branch recalled the Star of Bethlehem that shone over the manger. The shepherd's crook represented the shepherds in the fields near Bethlehem, who were the first to receive the news that a Savior had been born.

In Europe, the most popular Christmas tree decorations were edible. Cookies and candy not only provided a treat for children but symbolically expressed Christians' gratitude for the "daily bread" that the Lord provided. The red-and-white striped candy canes that are hung on the branches of Christmas trees today were once a symbol of the shepherds who came to Bethlehem to worship the Christ Child.

Christmas Card

In ancient Rome, it was customary to exchange greetings and gifts on the first day of January. With the advent of Christianity, the giving and receiving of such tokens continued in some European countries, often taking the form of New Year cards. These contained no references to Christmas and were sent out after December 25 so they would arrive on **NEW YEAR'S DAY**. In England, however, seasonal greeting cards combined Christmas and the New Year—with the emphasis on Christmas. They were meant to be delivered on or before Christmas Day and to convey greetings for both holidays.

The invention of lithography at the end of the eighteenth century gave the production of New Year cards in Europe a real boost. But most stationery manufacturers looked upon these cards as a temporary fad that probably wouldn't last. People who didn't want to spend their money on manufactured cards often converted their printed calling cards for the purpose, decorating them with scraps of cloth or paper and adding a Christmas greeting.

The first printed Christmas card was produced in England in 1843. Designed by John Calcott Horsley, it sold for a shilling and looked like a postcard. It wasn't until the 1880s that cards became folders of four, eight, or more pages.

Cards became increasingly elaborate throughout the Victorian period, with "frosted" surfaces, fancy cut edges, layers of lace-paper, and other forms of decoration. Sometimes the top cover or flap was embossed, "jewelled" with sparkles, and edged with silk fringe or tassels.

Louis Prang started producing Christmas cards in the United States in 1875. His plant in Roxbury, Massachusetts, was the birthplace of what is now the American greeting card industry. The subject matter ranged from traditional midwinter and Nativity scenes to flowers, animals, birds, and insects; comic or serious illustrations of public figures or popular characters; and novelties—such as the bicycle and the telephone.

Christmas cards in America today are so much a part of the holiday tradition that people often regard sending them as a burden. And fear of offending the sensibilities of non-Christians has led many card manufacturers to omit the word "Christmas" altogether, substituting more secular messages focusing on world peace and understanding.

Christmas Carols

Although it is difficult to imagine the holiday season without Christmas carols, Christmas was observed for more than 800 years before the first real "carols" were written. The term originally referred to a ring-dance accompanied by singing, without any religious overtones. Eventually it came to mean a merry song with a tune that could be danced to.

The Italian friars who lived with St. Francis of Assisi were the first to compose simple, uplifting songs based on the stories of the Gospel (*see* **ST. FRANCIS OF ASSISI, FEAST OF**). Unlike hymns, the earliest carols treated religious subjects in a familiar, playful, or festive style. From Italy, the carol passed to Spain, France, and Germany, where it retained its cheerfulness, childish simplicity, and religious fervor. The earliest known English carol dates from about 1410 and describes the Virgin Mary singing a lullaby to her child.

Carols as they are known today typically describe scenes and events associated with the birth of Christ—for example, the shepherds watching over their flocks and seeing the Star of Bethlehem, the discovery of the infant Jesus in the stable, the journey of the Wise Men from the East, etc. The best-loved carols—including "Deck the Halls," "God Rest Ye Merry Gentlemen," and "Here We Come A-Wassailing"— were written before the Restoration (1660); those written later tend to lack the earlier carols' spontaneity and festive nature. The rise of Puritanism in England was nearly fatal to Christmas carols, and by 1800, the custom of singing carols had nearly died out. But people in rural areas kept the tradition alive, and a new generation of editors and publishers made sure that the best of the old carols survived.

Christmas caroling—the custom of singing carols in a group while moving from house to house—originally took place on **CHRISTMAS EVE** or early in the morning on Christmas Day. Today it is a popular Christmas Eve tradition. Since the nineteenth century, carols have been sung in place of hymns in most churches on Christmas Day. Although some very good carols have been written for holidays other than Christmas, no one ever seems to sing them.

Christmas Seals

Many people embellish the CHRISTMAS CARDS, letters, and packages they send during the holiday season with special decorative stamps called Christmas seals. Although the seals have no value as postage, the money collected in return for them supports various charitable causes. A Danish postmaster came up with the idea for Christmas seals in 1904, and since then the custom has spread to dozens of countries around the world. In 1919 the National Tuberculosis Association, which later became the American Lung Association, cornered the market on Christmas seals in the United States, becoming the sole issuers of the decorative stamps in this country. Today, the seals earn millions of dollars a year for the American Lung Association.

Christmas Tree

The decorated tree didn't really become a popular part of the Christmas celebration until the nineteenth century, but some scholars believe that the custom can be traced all the way back to ancient times. The Egyptians observed a midwinter festival in honor of the god Horus, son of Isis (goddess of motherhood and fertility). The symbol for this celebration was a palm tree with 12 shoots symbolizing the months of the year. The Romans decorated with candlelit trees during the **SATURNALIA** in December and brought laurel boughs and green trees into their houses at the kalends (first day) of January.

The Christmas tree as it is known today came to America from Germany in the early eighteenth century. The Germans had for some time been celebrating Christmas by setting up a wooden structure shaped like a pyramid and covering it with boughs of evergreen. The *Weihnachtspyramide* was probably derived from the "Paradise tree" used in medieval mystery plays. A fir tree decorated with apples and surrounded by candles, it symbolized the story of Adam and Eve. According to legend, when Adam left Paradise, he took with him a sprig (or seed) from the Tree of Knowledge. From this grew the tree that later provided wood for the cross on which Jesus Christ was crucified.

There is also a legend concerning the miraculous transformation of nature at the moment of Jesus' birth, when it is said that the rivers flowed with wine and the trees blossomed in the midst of ice and snow. The Christmas tree, which "blossoms" with light and ornaments at this time of year, may have been a symbolic representation of this legendary miracle.

Although Christmas trees can be seen everywhere in the United States—in homes, schools, office buildings, and shopping malls—they do not play the central role here that they do in the German celebration of Christmas. No one in Germany is too poor or too lonely to put up a tree. And unlike Americans, who tend to arrange their Christmas gifts around the base of the tree, the Germans consider their tree an object of wonder all by itself. It is decorated in secret behind closed doors and revealed to the assembled family and guests on Christmas Eve.

In the United States today a fir tree is traditionally placed at the highest point of a building under construction—even if it's a skyscraper. Just as Christmas celebrates the birth of Christ, the occupational symbol of the fir tree serves as a reminder of the work that goes into a new building and the people who make this modern "miracle" possible.

Crèche

The crèche, a display of a stable with figures representing the Nativity scene, is usually attributed to St. Francis of Assisi, who used real people and live animals to reconstruct the birth of Jesus in a cave near the Italian village of Greccio in 1224 (*see* **ST. FRANCIS OF ASSISI, FEAST OF**). The "living pantomime" became a popular Italian custom and eventually spread throughout the Christian world.

But the idea goes back even further, to fourth-century Rome. The early observance of the festival of Christmas included three Masses, one of which was referred to as *Ad Praesepe* (the Crib). The "Crib" was a shrine that had been built in the basilica of Santa Maria Maggiore from some of the boards believed to have been saved from the original stable in Bethlehem. The custom of saying a Mass over the manger seems to have inspired other churches in Italy and throughout Europe to set up their own "cribs." But it was St. Francis of Assisi who took the crèche out of the church and popularized it, giving rise to the practice of setting up crèches in public squares and private homes.

In Italy today, every home has its *Presepio* at Christmas. It includes not only the immediate scene—with Mary and Joseph, the Christ child, the shepherds, the Three Kings, and assorted farm animals and worshipping angels—but the surrounding countryside of Bethlehem with its hills and streams. South America is also known for its elaborate Nativity scenes. An entire room is often filled with a reconstructed landscape representing the mountains, plains, and valleys surrounding Bethlehem. The shepherds can be seen leading their sheep across the hills, while the Wise Men are crossing the desert on their camels. Sometimes there are water mills, grottos, and sailboats on the sea.

In fourteenth-century Germany, there was a very popular Christmas custom known as *Kindelwiegen* or "cradle-rocking." People danced around the cradle containing an image of the Christ child and then took turns rocking it with their own hands. Sometimes the participants would get carried away, rocking and fondling the Christ Child and leaping around the cradle. Because cradle-rocking so often got out of hand, the practice was eventually discontinued in most German churches.

There has been some controversy in the United States about erecting crèches in public places, such as town halls. State and local governments have been under pressure to make their displays non-denominational by adding other symbolic elements. Vandalism and theft of the figures in the crèche are becoming increasingly common, prompting some cities and towns to do away with outdoor Nativity scenes altogether.

Farolitos

In the American Southwest, glowing paper sacks decorate the outlines of buildings, patios, walkways, and plazas at night during the Christmas season. These ornamental lights are called *farolitos* (pronounced fah-roh-LEE-tohs), which means "little lanterns" in Spanish. They are made by filling brown paper lunch bags with a few inches of sand to weigh the bags down and to anchor the votive candles that sit inside. When the candles are lit, the light shining through the brown paper gives off a golden glow in the darkness.

Although farolitos came to the Southwest from Mexico, they are believed to have derived from Chinese paper lanterns, imported from the Philippines to Mexico by Spanish traders. When frontier settlers in the United States discovered that the delicate paper that surrounded the lantern frame would not hold up in rough winter weather, they started making their own lanterns with plain brown wrapping paper. The new farolitos not only proved more durable, but also cast an amber glow which favored the warm colors characteristic of the southwestern landscape. Today these beautiful lights constitute an important symbol of Christmas in the American Southwest.

In some areas of the Southwest, farolitos are known as *luminarias* (*see* **CHRIST-MAS EVE**), while in others the two customs remain distinct. In northern New Mexico, for example, the word "luminarias" refers to small Christmas season bonfires, while the decorative brown paper lanterns are known as farolitos.

Father Christmas

Father Christmas is an English folk figure who for centuries personified the Christmas season. Unlike Santa Claus (*see* **CHRISTMAS EVE**), Father Christmas did not distribute gifts. Instead, he represented the mirth, generosity, and abundance associated with the celebration of Christmas.

Father Christmas usually appeared as a large, robust man wearing a red or green robe with fur trim and a crown of HOLLY, ivy, or MISTLETOE. In Charles Dickens' famous story *A Christmas Carol*, the character who appears as "the Ghost of Christmas Present" bears a strong resemblance to Father Christmas. But sometimes he was a wizened old man—a robed and hooded figure who closely resembled conventional images of Father Time, although he did not carry a scythe. This association between Father Christmas and Father Time may well have sprung up because Christmas arrives just before the close of the old year and the beginning of the new.

During the nineteenth century, the American Santa Claus began to appear in England. Santa Claus was a gift-bringer rather than a personification of the Christmas season, but as his popularity increased in England, his identity began to merge with that of Father Christmas. Eventually Santa Claus all but erased the figure of Father Christmas, who retained his name but whose image and activities nearly mirrored those of Santa Claus.

Gifts

The custom of exchanging charms or small tokens of good luck at the end of the year goes back to very ancient times. The Egyptians used to give each other small, symbolic presents conveying good luck wishes on **NEW YEAR'S DAY**. When the tombs of the Pharoahs were unearthed, small blue-glazed bottles (probably scent flasks) with messages about the approaching New Year were found intact. The Romans, too, exchanged gifts and New Year's greetings on the Kalends (or first day) of January. Originally laurel or olive branches picked from the holy groves dedicated to Strenia, the goddess of health, these gifts or *strenae* became more elaborate, often consisting of symbolic objects such as lamps (symbol of light) or silver and gold (wealth). Giving people such gifts was supposed to bring them luck in the coming year. The Roman roots of the gift-giving custom can still be seen in the French word for New Year's presents: *étrennes*.

St. Nicholas, the Bishop of Myra, has also been linked to the gift-giving tradition. Because he was not only wealthy but modest, he liked to help people in need without drawing attention to himself. Poor families would often find a gold piece or a well-filled purse without knowing where it had come from. His American successor, Santa Claus, carried on the tradition by delivering gifts in his sleigh on **CHRISTMAS EVE**.

In Russia, it is Babuska (the Grandmother) who brings gifts at Christmas. According to legend, this is the old woman who deliberately misdirected the Three Wise Men when they stopped to ask directions on their way to Bethlehem. Another version of the story says that they urged her to come with them, but she said she was too busy spinning. In any case, she later repented and tried to make amends by going around the world on Christmas Eve distributing gifts to good children.

The growing commercialism surrounding Christmas, particularly in the United States, has placed so much emphasis on shopping for Christmas gifts that many people feel it has robbed the holiday of its religious significance. A popular slogan reminds busy American consumers to "Put the 'Christ' back in Christmas."

Holly

The *ilex* or holly oak is regarded as a symbol of the passion of Christ because its thorny leaves resemble the crown of thorns that Christ wore at His crucifixion. It is also said to have been the tree from which the cross was made. All the other trees, according to legend, agreed not to allow their wood to be used for this purpose. When touched by an axe, they splintered into a million pieces. Only the ilex remained whole and permitted itself to be felled.

Today holly is used to decorate homes and churches at Christmas. Like ivy and MISTLETOE, holly bears its fruit in the wintertime, which is why it is considered a symbol of eternal life. Other evergreens used for decorating at Christmas include the laurel (or bay), symbolic of triumph, and the yew or cypress, which is also symbolic of immortality because it stays green.

Mistletoe

The evergreen boughs and sprigs of holly, ivy, and mistletoe used to decorate homes during the Christmas holiday symbolize immortality because they retain their green color even after they've been cut. The custom of decorating indoors with evergreens dates back to the Roman **SATURNALIA**, where it may have been an offer of hospitality to the spirits that haunted the woods.

In ancient Britain, the Druids worshipped mistletoe, a semi-parasitic plant that draws its water and minerals from the tree on which it grows. According to legend, mistletoe was most likely to be found on trees that had been struck by lightning, particularly oaks. Although the Druids regarded mistletoe in general as a cure for almost any disease and a remedy against poisons, oak-mistletoe was considered the most powerful. It could heal ulcers or help a woman conceive; it was widely regarded as a cure for epilepsy (known as "the falling sickness") because it was rooted high in the branches of a tree and could not fall to the ground. Gathering it on the first day of the lunar month increased its power, and the Druids made sure that it was cut with a golden sickle and caught in a white cloth so it wouldn't touch the ground.

In Norse mythology Balder, the god of light and vegetation, dreamed that he was going to die. To protect him from every imaginable danger, the goddess Frigga made all of the beasts and birds, as well as the stones, the trees, fire, and water, swear an oath that they would not harm him. Once the other gods realized that Balder was invulnerable, they often amused themselves by shooting and throwing stones at him. But the mischievous Loki tricked Frigga into revealing that a plant called mistletoe had seemed too young at the time to participate in the oath. Loki gave a sprig of it to the blind god Hother and told him to shoot at Balder with the twig. The mistletoe struck Balder and he was killed.

Such legends contributed to mistletoe's reputation as a sacred and very powerful plant. The oak tree on which it grew became a Christian symbol when it was identified as the tree from which the Cross was made. Because of its solidity and endurance, it is also a symbol of the strength of the Christian faith. But because of its association with the ancient religion of the Druids, mistletoe is generally not allowed in church decorations.

The custom of hanging a sprig of mistletoe in a doorway at Christmas dates back to the ancient Scandinavian custom of having enemies who encountered each other under mistletoe in the forest lay down their arms and maintain a truce until the following day. Nowadays people who find themselves standing under the mistletoe in a doorway are expected to kiss each other—another way of making a pledge of peace and friendship.

In England, Christmas decorations were never simply thrown away; they were usually burned or allowed to stay up until **CANDLEMAS** (February 2). Mistletoe often stayed up until it was replaced by a new branch the following year.

Poinsettia

Native to Central America, the red and green poinsettia has been a symbol of Christmas in the United States since the 1820s, when it was first shipped to North

America by Joel Poinsett, the American minister to Mexico. The shape of the bright red petals has often been compared to the Star of Bethlehem.

Wassail

The term wassail comes from the Middle English *waes haeil*, which means "be in good health." Wassailing was the old English custom of toasting the holiday and each other's health. From the thirteenth century onward the term referred not only to the toasts that were exchanged during the Christmas season but to a traditional beverage—a mixture of ale, roasted apples, sugar, and spices, sometimes with eggs or cream added. It was served from giant "wassail bowls" and remained the favorite holiday drink until the early eighteenth century, when the growing popularity of spirits led to the invention of punch. Today, liquor-based punches and egg nog—a nineteenth-century invention—have replaced the original wassail. But the custom of offering toasts remains.

Wreath

The circular shape of the Christmas wreath makes it a symbol of eternity. Because the wreath remains green throughout the holiday season, it serves as a reminder that life is present even during the dead of winter.

The Christmas wreath is the logical continuation of the Advent wreath, an old Christian custom that originated with the Lutherans in Germany. It is a simple circle of greenery around which four candles, representing the four weeks of the **ADVENT** season, are equally spaced. One candle is lit the first Sunday and another is lit each week thereafter. Because of the burning candles, however, Advent wreaths were usually placed on a table or hung parallel to the floor. Christmas wreaths are traditionally hung on the doors, walls, or windows of homes and churches. Many people leave their wreaths up all winter. When the wreath is taken down, it is symbolic of winter's end.

FURTHER READING

Barz, Brigitte. *Festivals with Children*. Edinburgh: Floris Books, 1987.

Bellenir, Karen. *Religious Holidays and Calendars*. 3rd ed. Detroit: Omnigraphics, 2004.

Biedermann, Hans. *Dictionary of Symbolism: Cultural Icons and the Meanings Behind Them*. New York: Meridian Books, 1994.

Buday, George. *The History of the Christmas Card*. 1971. Reprint. Detroit: Omnigraphics, 1991.

Crippen, T.G. *Christmas and Christmas Lore*. 1923. Reprint. Detroit: Omnigraphics, 1990.

Dawson, W.F. *Christmas: Its Origin and Associations*. 1902. Reprint. Detroit: Omnigraphics, 1990.

Ferguson, George. *Signs and Symbols in Christian Art*. New York: Oxford University Press, 1954.

Frazer, Sir James G. *The Golden Bough: A Study in Magic and Religion*. New York: Macmillan, 1931.

Gulevich, Tanya. *Encyclopedia of Christmas*. Detroit: Omnigraphics, 2000.

Henderson, Helene, ed. *Holidays, Festivals, and Celebrations of the World Dictionary*. 3rd ed. Detroit: Omnigraphics, 2005.

Ickis, Marguerite. *The Book of Festivals and Holidays the World Over*. New York: Dodd, Mead, 1970.

Miles, Clement A. *Christmas in Ritual and Tradition, Christian and Pagan*. 1912. Reprint. Detroit: Omnigraphics, 1990.

Monks, James L. *Great Catholic Festivals*. New York: Henry Schuman, 1951.

Purdy, Susan. *Festivals for You to Celebrate*. Philadelphia: Lippincott, 1969.

Santino, Jack. *All Around the Year: Holidays and Celebrations in American Life*. Urbana: University of Illinois Press, 1994.

Tuleja, Tad. *Curious Customs: The Stories Behind 296 Popular American Rituals*. New York: Harmony, 1987.

WEB SITES

Library of Congress
www.americaslibrary.gov/cgi-bin/page.cgi/jb/modern/xmas_1

New Advent Catholic Encyclopedia
www.newadvent.org/cathen/03724b.htm

Christmas Eve

Type of Holiday: Religious (Christian)
Date of Observation: December 24
Where Celebrated: United States, Great Britain, Europe, and by Christians throughout the world
Symbols and Customs: Candles, Luminarias, Reindeer, Santa Claus, Yule Log
Colors: Christmas Eve is traditionally associated with the colors red and green.
Related Holidays: Advent, Christmas, Epiphany, St. Stephen's Day (Boxing Day)

ORIGINS

For Christians, Christmas Eve marks the night before the anniversary of the birth of Jesus Christ. The word Christian refers to a follower of Christ, a title derived from the Greek word meaning Messiah or Anointed One. The Christ of Christianity is Jesus of Nazareth, a man born between 7 and 4 B.C.E. in the region of Palestine. According to Christian teaching, Jesus was killed by Roman authorities using a form of execution called crucifixion (a term meaning he was nailed to a cross and hung from it until he died) in about the year 30 C.E. After his death, he rose back to life. His death and resurrection provide a way by which people can be reconciled with God. In remembrance of Jesus' death and resurrection, the cross serves as a fundamental symbol in Christianity.

With nearly two billion believers in countries around the globe, Christianity is the largest of the world's religions. There is no one central authority for all of Christianity. The pope (the bishop of Rome) is the authority for the Roman Catholic Church, but other sects look to other authorities. Orthodox communities look to patriarchs and emphasize doctrinal agreement and traditional practice. Protestant communities focus on individual conscience. The Roman Catholic and Protestant churches are often referred to as the Western Church, while the Orthodox churches may also be called the Eastern Church. All three main branches of Christianity acknowledge the authority of Christian scriptures, a compilation of writings assembled into a document called the Bible. Methods of biblical interpretation vary among the different Christian sects.

Christmas Eve marks the end of the **ADVENT** season, the period of preparation for **CHRISTMAS** that begins on November 30 (November 15 in the East). It was on this night that the shepherds keeping watch over their flocks outside Bethlehem saw the bright star in the sky that signaled the birth of Jesus Christ (*see* STAR OF BETHLEHEM under **EPIPHANY**).

Despite its Christian significance, there are a number of pagan and supernatural beliefs connected with Christmas Eve. In Scandinavian countries, it is believed that the dead revisit their former homes on Christmas Eve. People make sure that their parlors are tidy and that a good fire is burning before they go to bed. They often light candles, set the table, and leave out plenty of food for their ghostly visitors. They also make sure that the seats of their chairs have been dusted. When they get up in the morning, they wipe the chairs again with a clean white towel. If they find any dirt on the seat, it means that a relative fresh from the grave sat there during the night.

In many parts of Europe, people believe that at midnight on Christmas Eve, animals briefly possess the power of speech. It might have been the traditional association of the ox and the ass with the Nativity scene that gave rise to such superstitions, but the concept of talking animals is probably pagan in origin. A closely related belief, widespread in England and Europe, is that cattle rise in their stalls at midnight on Christmas Eve, or kneel to worship the Christ Child.

The midnight church service celebrating the birth of Jesus Christ is the main Christmas Eve tradition for Christians of all denominations and even for non-believers, many of whom come to hear Christmas music performed.

SYMBOLS AND CUSTOMS

Candles

Candles have always been symbolic of the sun's light and warmth, and in ancient times they were lit to dispel the darkness of winter at the time of the **WINTER SOLSTICE** (December 21 or 22). Early Christians preferred to see them as symbols of Jesus' "light," which replaced the darkness of paganism. Some scholars think that the custom of lighting candles on Christmas Eve came from the Jewish "Feast of Lights" or **HANUKKAH**, which was held around the same time of year and featured the lighting of candles or lamps.

Throughout the Middle Ages, it was customary to light one large candle on Christmas Eve, in both the church and the home, to commemorate the Star of Bethlehem. The candle may also have been symbolic of the Holy Child, whom Simeon called "A Light to lighten the Gentiles." These giant candles burned continuously throughout the Christmas season, right up until **TWELFTH NIGHT**. In Scandinavian countries, keeping the "Yule candle" burning was very important. Sometimes there were two candles representing the head of the house and his wife. If one of them went out first, it meant that the other partner would live longer. A similar belief prevailed in Scotland before the Reformation. If the Christmas candle was extinguished before midnight, it meant that a great disaster would befall the family. In Ireland, the Christmas Eve candle is often so big that a large turnip must be carved out to serve as a candlestick.

Luminarias

Luminarias (pronounced loo-mee-NAR-ee-yahs) means "lights" or "illuminations" in Spanish. The word also refers to the small bonfires that illuminate the dark nights of the Christmas season throughout the American Southwest. These bonfires are made from piñon pine logs that have been stacked in log-cabin fashion to form a box about three feet in height. Although one may spot luminarias throughout the Christmas season, they are most common on Christmas Eve, when the little bonfires blaze in front of churches, homes, and in public plazas.

Some believe that luminarias can be traced all the way back to the fires that warmed the shepherds to whom the birth of Jesus was announced. Others say the custom came from Native American traditions, which Spanish missionaries later incorporated into the celebration of Christmas. Still others think that Spanish missionaries brought the custom with them to Mexico. Whatever its origins, the earliest historical record of the practice in the New World dates back to the sixteenth century, when Spanish missionaries, sent to evangelize the native peoples of Mexico, wrote that on Christmas Eve the people celebrated by singing, drumming, and lighting bonfires on church patios and on the roofs of their flat-topped houses.

In some areas of the United States, luminarias are not bonfires but glowing paper bags filled with sand holding small candles. The custom of outlining buildings, patios, sidewalks, and public squares with these paper-bag lights on Christmas Eve started in the Southwest, where these lanterns are called *farolitos*, which is Spanish for "little lanterns" (*see* **CHRISTMAS**). It has since spread all the way to New England. In some areas the two customs—small bonfires and paper-bag lanterns—remain distinct, while in others both "luminarias" and "farolitos" refer to the homemade paper lanterns that line the streets on Christmas Eve

In Louisiana along the levees of the Mississippi River, bonfires built out of logs, cane reed, old tires, and bamboo are lit on Christmas Eve. Derived from the *feux de joie* (fires of joy) that burned in France on Epiphany Eve, the eve of **ASH WEDNESDAY**, and **NEW YEAR'S EVE**, these fires were brought to Louisiana after the Civil War by Marist priests. When Christmas became the predominant winter holiday, the bonfire tradition was shifted to December 24.

Reindeer

More than 600 years after St. Nicholas' death, Russians carried his legend back from Constantinople, and he became Russia's patron saint. From there, his story spread to Lapland, home of the reindeer, which may explain why the modern Santa Claus lives at the North Pole and gets around in a sleigh pulled by eight reindeer. In reality, of course, he often arrives by car or helicopter at the local shopping mall.

Clement Moore's poem "A Visit from St. Nicholas" popularized the names of Santa's reindeer: "Now Dasher! Now Dancer! Now Prancer and Vixen! On Comet! On Cupid! On Donder and Blitzen!" But to children everywhere, Rudolph is the most beloved. He first appeared in a complimentary Christmas store souvenir given out by Montgomery Ward during the holidays in 1939. The little book was written by Robert May, a Montgomery Ward ad man known for his light verse. It tells the story of Rudolph the Red-Nosed Reindeer, a variation on the ugly duckling motif. Illustrated by May's friend Denver Gillen, the story of Rudolph sold 2.4 million copies in Montgomery Ward stores that first year. The poem appeared in book form in 1947, and when the singing cowboy star Gene Autry recorded a musical version of the tale in 1949, it reached the top of the Hit Parade. What began as an advertising gimmick soon became a popular emblem of the modern American Christmas. Nowadays Rudolph can be seen on television, in store window displays, and on front lawns and rooftops everywhere.

Santa Claus

The original Santa Claus was Nicholas, the legendary saint who was bishop of Myra (Turkey) in the fourth century. He was usually shown wearing the fur-trimmed robes of a cleric, with a beehive (symbolizing industry) and a bulldog (fidelity) at his side. He was a gift-giver but also a disciplinarian, bringing switches and rods for children who misbehaved. December 6 was his feast day, and in many countries, it is on this day—not Christmas Eve—that St. Nicholas arrives to hand out his presents and punishments.

The Christian story of St. Nicholas was brought to Europe, where it got mixed up with the Germanic religion and its chief god, Woden (or Odin), who rode an eight-legged white horse. The Dutch *Sinter Klaas,* for example, wears bishop's robes and rides a white horse. In other northern European countries, St. Nicholas has been integrated with ancient gods to become a spirit of winter rather than a Christian saint.

Martin Luther substituted the Christ Child for St. Nicholas as a bearer of gifts, and moved the day of his arrival from December 6 to Christmas as part of an effort to remove the last vestiges of paganism from the Christian church. In some parts of Europe, it is still the Christ Child who brings gifts, which is why he is called Kriss Kringle (from the German *Christkindl*).

The American Santa Claus is actually a combination of three figures: (1) the English Father Christmas, a winter deity wearing a crown of holly who replaced St. Nicholas after the Reformation (*see* **CHRISTMAS**); (2) the German St. Nicholas, brought to the United States by German immigrants during the eighteenth and early nineteenth centuries; and (3) the Dutch Sinter Klaas, who was brought by Dutch settlers to New York. But it wasn't until the publication of Clement Moore's poem "A Visit from St. Nicholas" on December 23, 1823, that the American Santa Claus was transformed from a tall, thin bishop to a jolly, overweight, pipe-smoking figure wearing a fur-trimmed red suit. His elf-like image was reinforced by Thomas Nast, an editorial cartoonist who did numerous illustrations of Santa Claus based on Moore's poem. Washington Irving made his own contribution in *A History of New York,* when he described St. Nicholas as "laying a finger beside his nose" and dropping gifts down the chimney.

Most American children believe that Santa Claus comes down the chimney on Christmas Eve to fill the stockings they've left hanging on the mantle. This custom can be traced back to a folk legend in which three daughters decided to help their father escape poverty by selling themselves into prostitution. A wealthy man named Nicholas visited their house on three successive nights, and each time he tossed a ball of gold through an open window. The three gold balls, which landed in the stockings the girls had hung by the fire to dry, saved them from a life of sin.

Some scholars have traced this tradition back even farther, to the ancient Norsemen's winter solstice festival in honor of Herthe, goddess of the home. Before the holiday feast, a fire of fir boughs was laid on an altar of flat stones in the belief that Herthe would appear in the smoke to bring the family good fortune. The Norse altar stones became our modern hearth stones, and Santa's trip down the chimney was an updated version of Herthe's appearance in the smoke.

Yule Log

Traditionally burned on Christmas Eve and throughout the Christmas season, the Yule log gets its name from the pagan Norsemen, who observed a 12-day winter celebration called *Jól*, which means "wheel" and probably refers to the turning of the sun at the winter solstice. There is also an old English word, *geol*, which means "feast." In pre-Christian times, the entire month of December was known as *geola*, or "feast-month." The name was later attached to the Christmas feast known as Yule in England and Jul in Scandinavia.

It was common in ancient times to light bonfires at the winter solstice to scare off winter's demons and to brighten the darkest time of the year. But the Yule log, which appears to be a survival of this custom, is burned indoors and is more of a domestic than a public celebration. In its purest form, the Yule log is a whole trunk of a tree, selected and cut on **CANDLEMAS** (February 2) and dried throughout the year. The usual practice in England was to light the Yule log with a fragment of the previous year's log, which had been kept in the house throughout the year in the belief that it would offer protection against fire and especially lightning. Because it was usually an oak log, it's possible that this belief is a relic of the ancient Aryan religion, which associated the oak tree with the god of thunder.

The English Yule log is said to have come from the Druids, the ancient Celtic religious order. The Druid priests prayed that the oak or fruitwood log burned in their midwinter festival would flame, like the sun, forever. Both the log and its ashes were considered symbols of good luck and strength. Even in more recent times, bringing the Yule log into the house was often accompanied by great ceremony. The youngest child would pour wine on the log before it was thrown into the fire, and then a remnant of the log would be saved and used to kindle the new log on the following Christmas Eve. It was considered bad luck if the fire went out before New Year's Day.

Yule log ceremonies are most elaborate among the Serbs and Croats, where two or three young oaks are cut down for every house (sometimes one log for each male member of the family). As the logs are carried in, lighted candles are held on either side of the door, and as the father of the family crosses the threshold with the first log, someone throws corn at him or pours wine over the log. The log itself may be a symbol of the spirit of vegetation, and burning it may be symbolic of sunshine, whose influence is needed during the coming year. The corn and wine are probably symbols of the sun and rain the crops need to grow.

A number of superstitions surround the Yule log in Europe. In southern France, people put the log on the fire for the first time on Christmas Eve and then continue to burn it a little bit each day until **TWELFTH NIGHT** (January 5). If it is kept under the bed, it will protect the house from fire and thunder and will prevent those who live there from getting chilblains on their heels in winter. The unburned remains are also believed to cure cattle of many diseases and to help cows deliver their calves. If the ashes are scattered over the fields, it will save the wheat from mildew.

FURTHER READING

Bellenir, Karen. *Religious Holidays and Calendars*. 3rd ed. Detroit: Omnigraphics, 2004.

Crippen, T.G. *Christmas and Christmas Lore*. 1923. Reprint. Detroit: Omnigraphics, 1990.

Frazer, Sir James G. *The Golden Bough: A Study in Magic and Religion*. New York: Macmillan, 1931.

Gulevich, Tanya. *Encyclopedia of Christmas and New Year's Celebrations*. 2nd ed. Detroit: Omnigraphics, 2003.

Henderson, Helene, ed. *Holidays, Festivals, and Celebrations of the World Dictionary*. 3rd ed. Detroit: Omnigraphics, 2005.

Miles, Clement A. *Christmas in Ritual and Tradition, Christian and Pagan*. 1912. Reprint. Detroit: Omnigraphics, 1990.

Purdy, Susan. *Festivals for You to Celebrate*. Philadelphia: Lippincott, 1969.

Santino, Jack. *All Around the Year: Holidays and Celebrations in American Life*. Urbana: University of Illinois Press, 1994.

Schmidt, Leigh Eric. *Consumer Rites: The Buying and Selling of American Holidays*. Princeton: Princeton University Press, 1995.

Tuleja, Tad. *Curious Customs: The Stories Behind 296 Popular American Rituals*. New York: Harmony, 1987.

WEB SITES

Library of Congress
www.americaslibrary.gov/cgi-bin/page.cgi/jb/modern/xmas_1

New Advent Catholic Encyclopedia
www.newadvent.org/cathen/03724b.htm

Chrysanthemum Festival (Jugoya)

Type of Holiday: Calendar/Seasonal
Date of Observation: Ninth month of the Buddhist lunar calendar
Where Celebrated: Japan, Korea, Okinawa
Symbols and Customs: Chrysanthemum, Chrysanthemum Dolls, Mounting the Heights, Number Nine
Related Holidays: Chung Yeung

ORIGINS

The Chrysanthemum Festival was the last of the five sacred festivals of ancient Japan. It was observed throughout the ninth month and often into the tenth month of the Buddhist lunar calendar (September-October). The ninth day of the ninth moon, known as Chrysanthemum Day, was primarily an occasion for visiting one's superiors and expressing concern for their well-being during the cold months ahead. Chrysanthemums were planted in pots and gardens in anticipation of visitors.

For at least a thousand years, the Chrysanthemum Festival was basically a sun festival dedicated to assuring the health of the community by delaying the "decay" of the sun and of mankind's vital powers. Not only was the chrysanthemum an autumn-blooming flower, but its petals resembled the sun's rays. It wasn't until the late seventeenth century that this festival became a national holiday and a much more elaborate event. By that time feudal lords and other wealthy people had taken up the hobby of cultivating new varieties of the flower, especially very large ones. By the end of the Tokygawa period (seventeenth to eighteenth centuries), there were hundreds of varieties, and flower-viewing parties were popular. Depending upon the local climate, the festival might last a month or more.

Today, Chrysanthemum Day is observed in scattered locations throughout Japan, Korea, and Okinawa by eating chrysanthemum cakes (a dumpling made from yellow petals mixed with rice flower) and drinking chrysanthemum wine. Because the Double Ninth (ninth day of the ninth lunar month) is also associated with fear and death, it is considered by some to be a festival of the dead, a time to visit the graves of ancestors and tend their gravestones, similar to the **CHING MING** Festival in China.

SYMBOLS AND CUSTOMS

Chrysanthemum

The chrysanthemum was imported to Japan from China in 386 c.e., after which its popularity spread rapidly. Because it bloomed in the autumn, it was associated with melancholy thoughts, reminding people of winter and of their own approaching deaths. The chrysanthemum was also regarded as a symbol of the sun, which it resembled in color and shape. The traditional Japanese sun emblem became a stylized chrysanthemum on the personal badge of the late twelfth century Emperor Go-Toba, at a time when individual signs or badges were used among the nobility to identify their carriages and attendants. It remained as a badge in the Imperial family, and after 1868 it was reserved exclusively for the ruler and his relatives.

The chrysanthemum is known as the *kunshi* or "nobleman" of flowers. It is held in higher esteem than even the cherry or plum blossom, and its dignity has been compared to the upright character of a true gentleman. Its strong smell and taste make it a good plant for guarding against the evils of the approaching winter, and it is widely regarded as a symbol of longevity and good health. Buddhist temples often use chrysanthemums as an ornamental theme, shopkeepers may have a pot of chrysanthemums on their balconies, and wealthy families sometimes have a separate chrysanthemum enclosure in their gardens.

Chrysanthemum Dolls

In the latter part of the eighteenth century, the art of training small chrysanthemums to grow over a framework led to the popularity of *kiku ningyo* or chrysanthemum dolls. The plants were grown within a fragile network of woven bamboo or wire and trained so that the blossoms would only form on the surface, covering the entire structure with a smooth, velvety coat of flowers in varying sizes and colors. The frame was shaped and posed to resemble a human figure, with the head, hands, and feet made of wax or paste. The dolls were arranged in tableaux, with a background composed entirely of floral objects.

At one time, Edo (Tokyo) had more than 50 places where displays of *kiku ningyo* were held. Other large Japanese cities held such exhibitions in public parks. Eventually the cost of producing the figures became prohibitive, and by the early twentieth century such exhibitions had died out.

It is possible that these huge dolls descended from the primitive grass dolls known as *hammasama*. When thrown into a stream or swift-moving river, these ancient dolls were believed to carry the individual's sins with them as they floated away.

Mounting the Heights

Chrysanthemum Day is a popular time for "mounting the heights"—going to the nearest mountain or hill for a picnic. According to a Han dynasty legend, a famous soothsayer named Fei Changfang warned his friend, a scholar named Huan Jing, that a disaster was about to occur. Fei recommended that Huan pack up his family, some food, and a jug of chrysanthemum wine and seek the shelter of a high hill. Huan did as he was told, and when he descended later that day, he discovered that all of his livestock were dead. He realized that if he had not taken the soothsayer's advice, he would have been killed as well.

Hillside picnics and chrysanthemum wine remain a popular way of ushering in the autumn and commemorating Huan's good fortune.

Number Nine

The date of this festival—the ninth day of the ninth lunar month—was originally adopted from China (*see* **CHUNG YEUNG**), where the number nine was considered especially lucky. Since three is the universal "perfect number" and three times three equals nine, the "double ninth" can only bring the best possible fortune.

The ninth day of the ninth month is also a symbol of "yang," or the positive, masculine force in Chinese cosmology. According to the yin-yang theory, odd numbers are associated with the male principle, and the occurrence of two yang numerals, especially when they are both nine, is particularly advantageous.

FURTHER READING

Casal, U.A. *The Five Sacred Festivals of Ancient Japan*. Rutland, VA: Sophia University in cooperation with Tuttle, 1967.

Eberhard, Wolfram. *A Dictionary of Chinese Symbols: Hidden Symbols in Chinese Life and Thought*. New York: Routledge & Kegan Paul, 1986.

Henderson, Helene, ed. *Holidays, Festivals, and Celebrations of the World Dictionary*. 3rd ed. Detroit: Omnigraphics, 2005.

Stepanchuk, Carol, and Charles Wong. *Mooncakes and Hungry Ghosts: Festivals of China*. San Francisco: China Books & Periodicals, 1991.

Chung Yeung
(Chung Yang Chieh, Kite-Flying Festival, Festival of High Places)

Type of Holiday: Folkloric, Calendar/Seasonal
Date of Observation: Ninth day of the ninth Chinese lunar month
Where Celebrated: China
Symbols and Customs: Good-luck Charms, Kite Flying, Mounting the Heights, Têng Kao
Related Holidays: Chrysanthemum Festival

ORIGINS

The festival known as Chung Yeung in China has much in common with Japan's Chrysanthemum Day (*see* **CHRYSANTHEMUM FESTIVAL**). The ninth Chinese lunar month is known as the "Chrysanthemum Moon" because it marks the season when these flowers are in bloom. Chrysanthemum-viewing parties were at one time held by the Imperial Court in the grounds of the Forbidden City on this day. But now the "Double Ninth" is primarily an occasion for picnicking in the hills (*see* MOUNTING THE HEIGHTS) and KITE-FLYING. In southern China, it is a day for visiting the family graves and performing ceremonies in honor of dead ancestors. It is a public holiday in Hong Kong and Macau.

SYMBOLS AND CUSTOMS

Good-luck Charms

KITE-FLYING competitions are held throughout China on this day. It is primarily an activity involving boys and men; girls tend to watch from the sidelines, and the women are usually busy preparing the evening feast. Because maneuvering the kites, which are often quite large and elaborate, requires considerable skill, the kite-fliers come well prepared with their favorite good-luck amulet or charm. They may wear the claw of a tiger to make them brave, carry a peachstone to ward off misfortune, or wear a coffin nail tied to their ankle to protect them from accidents.

A jade amulet is considered the best good-luck charm of all. Jade is known as the "stone of the seven virtues," which include benevolence, knowledge, uprightness, power, purity, eternity, and moral principles. Best of all, it never wears out, no matter how often it is used. Before releasing their kites, the competitors rub the amulets in their hands. If they win the competition, they rub the charms again.

Kite Flying

Kite flying is such an important part of the Chung Yeung festival that huge crowds gather to watch the spectacle. The festival kites, made of silk or paper, are often so large that it takes four or five grown men to handle them. Shaped like butterflies (symbol of pleasure and a happy marriage), fish (health, wealth, and offspring), dragons (male vigor, fertility), and other symbolic creatures, some of the kites have movable eyes, limbs, and wings. As soon as they are in the air, the competition begins. Their operators try to cross each other's strings, pulling and vibrating their own string in such a way that it cuts the string of their opponent's kite. When someone's kite is downed, the spectators yell and cheer. The competition can be fierce, and sometimes the police are brought in to prevent fights. To add to the excitement, some kites have firecrackers attached, which are set to go off after the kite reaches a certain height.

Some of the kites give off eerie sounds as they flutter overhead. This is because they have tiny Aeolian harps (made from gourd-shaped frames of bamboo with slivers of the bamboo plant stretched across them to form "strings") attached. These "singing" kites are a reminder of the Han dynasty general who, when his army was trapped and about to be annihilated, frightened the enemy by flying kites overhead that had been fitted with metallic strings. They made such a strange noise that the enemy soldiers thought they were being attacked by supernatural powers and ran away.

Occasionally a kite flier will set his kite adrift in the hope that when it falls to earth, the evil lurking within the family will fall with it. Some believe that if the kite flies higher than the string allows, it will bring the family great honor.

Mounting the Heights

According to legend, the custom of climbing a nearby hill or mountain for a picnic on Chung Yeung goes back more than 2,000 years. A famous magician, Fei Chang-fang, warned his student, Huan Ching, to immediately take his family away from the valley where they lived and up the nearest mountain. Huan heeded the warning, leaving all of his possessions behind. When he returned, he discovered that his house, his cattle, and everything else he owned had been destroyed as Fei had predicted. The Chinese commemorate Huan's escape by going to the highest places they can find and flying their kites. Those who, like Huan, are scholars often spend the day sitting in picturesque mountain settings, composing poems and discussing classical texts.

148

There is another theory about why people mount the heights on this festival. Because it was observed at a time of year when the harvest had just been brought in, enemies felt free to make war on each other. Groups of men with provisions were sent up to the mountains as lookouts, so they could warn their people of any advancing armies. Long after the need for these expeditions passed, people continued to mount the heights with food and wine.

Têng Kao

Chung Yeung picnickers traditionally feast on chrysanthemum wine and special cakes called têng kao, made of glutinous rice, filled with meat, and steamed. The name of these cakes is a play on the Chinese words, which mean not only "cake" but "promotion." The individual who eats them is believed to secure his or her advancement in official life, just as the person who "climbs the heights" advances his or her scholarly knowledge.

FURTHER READING

Bredon, Juliet, and Igor Mitrophanow. *The Moon Year: A Record of Chinese Customs and Festivals*. Shanghai: Kelly & Walsh, 1927.

Gaer, Joseph. *Holidays Around the World*. Boston: Little, Brown, 1953.

Henderson, Helene, ed. *Holidays, Festivals, and Celebrations of the World Dictionary*. 3rd ed. Detroit: Omnigraphics, 2005.

MacDonald, Margaret R., ed. *The Folklore of World Holidays*. Detroit: Gale Research, 1992.

WEB SITE

Hong Kong Tourism Board in New York, New York
www.discoverhongkong.com/eng/heritage/festivals/he_fest_chun.jhtml

Chusok
(Chuseok, Ch'usok)

Type of Holiday: Folkloric, Calendar/Seasonal
Date of Observation: Late September-early October; fifteenth day of the eighth lunar month
Where Celebrated: Korea
Symbols and Customs: Hemp-Spinning, Merry-Go-Round, Moon Cakes, Tortoise Play
Related Holidays: Mid-Autumn Festival

ORIGINS

Also known as Chuseog or Gawi, Chusok is one of the great national holidays of the year in Korea. Because it is celebrated in late September or early October—for which reason it is sometimes referred to as Autumn Evening —the weather is usually very temperate and the crops ripe or newly harvested. Farmers in particular are eager to celebrate the end of the growing season, which they do by serving wine and other foods made from the season's new grain (*see* MOON CAKES). Farmers believe that if it rains on this day, the wheat crop will be poor the following year.

Since ancient times people in all parts of the world have honored the changing of the seasons. Many cultures divided the year into two seasons, summer and winter, and marked these points of the year at or near the summer and winter solstices, during which light and warmth began to increase and decrease, respectively. In pre-industrial times, humans survived through hunting, gathering, and agricultural practices, which depend on the natural cycle of seasons, according to the climate in the region of the world in which they lived. Thus, they created rituals to help ensure enough rain and sun in the spring and summer so crops would grow to fruition at harvest time, which was, in turn, duly celebrated. Vestiges of many of these ancient practices are thought to have survived in festivals still celebrated around seasonal themes.

In addition to being a harvest festival, Chusok is a day for honoring ancestors. Families get up early, change into new clothes, and arrange an offering of food for their ancestors and family god. After a brief ceremony at home, they visit their ancestors' graves, mowing the weeds and wild grasses that may have become tangled and overgrown. Other popular activities on this day include wrestling contests, tugs-of-war, and playing MERRY-GO-ROUND.

SYMBOLS AND CUSTOMS

Hemp-Spinning

According to an old Korean legend, King Yuri-wang of Silla in southeastern Korea had his princesses lead the ladies of his capital city in a hemp-weaving contest that went on for a full month, ending on the fifteenth day of the eighth moon. There were two groups of weavers, with the king himself serving as judge. The group that lost the contest had to prepare wine and food to entertain the winning group. At this victory celebration, one woman from the defeated group danced and sang a song lamenting her group's defeat. This melancholy but very beautiful melody soon became popular throughout the country, but unfortunately, it has not survived. The joint weaving of cloth from hemp, however, became a tradition that can still be seen in some of the customs associated with Chusok in the southern part of the country.

Merry-Go-Round

The festivities that are held on Chusok often include a singing folk play known as *Gang-gang-sullae,* in which women dressed in bright colors perform a circular dance to the accompaniment of a single vocalist. The song she sings can be traced back three centuries to the Japanese invasion of Korea. Women gathered in the hills along the coast and sang the song known as *Gang-gang-sullae* around bonfires to give the enemy the impression that the coast was well-guarded.

Gang-gang is a Korean dialect expression meaning "circumstances" or "round," and *sullae* is derived from *sulla,* which means "patrolling." Together, they imply looking out or around, which is exactly what the women were doing as they tried to protect their homeland. Sometimes the pronunciation of *sullae* is prolonged, sounding more like *suweol lae.* The custom of playing merry-go-round or *kang-kang-soo-wol-lae* under the full harvest moon at Chusok is undoubtedly related to this historical attempt to mislead the enemy.

Moon Cakes

The word sok in Chusok means "a moon-bright evening." It is popular during this harvest festival to eat rice cakes shaped like a moon or half-moon, stuffed with beans and flavored with pine needles. The round cakes are symbolic of family unity at a time of year when families honor their ancestors.

Tortoise Play

This play is performed by young men or boys on the evening of the fifteenth day of the eighth lunar month. A large tortoise shape is made with corn leaves, and two men (one in front and the other in the rear) get inside it and walk around, visiting farmers' homes and performing what is known as the tortoise play or the tortoise dance. At the end, the tortoise collapses on the ground as if exhausted by its efforts. The tortoise-driver then tells the head of the house or the farmer that the tortoise needs to be fed. Not surprisingly, the rice cakes, food, and fruit that are brought out revive the tortoise, who then stands up and plays his final scene before continuing on to the next house.

In Chinese mythology, the tortoise is a symbol of strength, endurance, and longevity that is particularly associated with winter. The Korean tortoise play may have originated from this association of the tortoise with long life and immunity from disease, and from the timing of this festival, which takes place in autumn before the arrival of winter.

FURTHER READING

Crim, Keith R. *The Perennial Dictionary of World Religions*. San Francisco: Harper & Row, 1989.

Henderson, Helene, ed. *Holidays, Festivals, and Celebrations of the World Dictionary*. 3rd ed. Detroit: Omnigraphics, 2005.

MacDonald, Margaret R., ed. *The Folklore of World Holidays*. Detroit: Gale Research, 1992.

Sang-su, Choe. *Annual Customs of Korea*. Seoul: Seomun-dang, 1983.

Trawicky, Bernard, and Ruth W. Gregory. *Anniversaries and Holidays*. 5th ed. Chicago: American Library Assocation, 2000.

WEB SITE

Cultural Spotlight
www.lifeinkorea.com/culture/festivals/festivals.cfm?Subject=Chuseok

Cinco de Mayo

Type of Holiday: Historic
Date of Observation: May 5
Where Celebrated: Mexico and the United States
Symbols and Customs: Ballet Folklórico, Battle Reenactments, Mariachi Music, Mexican Food, Parades

ORIGINS

Cinco de Mayo means "the fifth of May." It commemorates the Battle of Puebla, an important event in the fight for Mexican independence. In this battle, a badly out-numbered band of Mexicans fought off the French army, which at that time was one of the most highly trained armies in Europe. For Mexicans and Mexican Americans, Cinco de Mayo represents the courage, resourcefulness, and determination of the Mexican people. It also symbolizes the thrill of an underdog victory against a mighty enemy.

The Battle of Puebla took place on May 5,1862. Mexico had gained its independence from Spain about forty years earlier, but was not a strong country at that time. The Mexican government owed money to France, England, and Spain. The French, under Napoleon III, decided to invade Mexico and take over the government. Napoleon III wanted to re-establish a strong French presence in North America. Moreover, he reasoned that the United States wouldn't interfere, because it was embroiled in its own civil war at that time.

When the French troops reached the town of Puebla, they were met by a rag-tag Mexican army led by General Ignacio Zaragoza and Colonel Porfirio Díaz (who later became president of Mexico). The Mexicans numbered around 4,000 men. Their ranks included regular soldiers as well as Mexican farmers armed with farm tools, cowboys, and Zapotec and other Indians. The French army was much larger and consisted of well-trained, professional soldiers, both on horseback and on foot. As the battle began, the French were confident of victory.

General Zaragoza's clever battle plans turned the tide of battle in favor of the Mex-icans, however. He sent his cavalry (soldiers on horseback) to attack the French from the side. The French cavalry responded by abandoning the center of the bat-tle and moving to the side to engage the Mexican horsemen. This gave Zaragoza the moment he had been looking for. He released a stampeding herd of cattle right into the center of the French troops. The cattle scattered the French soldiers, thus conferring victory to the Mexican army.

Although the Mexicans won the battle, they did not win the war. Two years later, the French succeeded in taking over Mexico and in crowning Ferdinand Maximil-ian von Hapsburg emperor of Mexico. For the French, however, victory was short-lived. The Mexican people never accepted the new government and suc-ceeded in ousting Maximilian and his government in 1867. Throughout the time of French rule, the amazing victory at the Battle of Puebla inspired the Mexican people to resist the foreign occupation. People felt hope for the future and pride in their Mexican identity as they sang *corridos*, or folk songs, retelling the story of the Battle of Puebla.

As a historic holiday, Cinco de Mayo commemorates a significant historical event. People throughout the world remember significant events in their histories. Often, these are events that are important for an entire nation and become widely observed. The marking of such anniversaries serves not only to honor the values represented by the person or event commemorated, but also to strengthen and reinforce communal bonds of national, cultural, or ethnic identity. Victorious, joyful, and traumatic events are remembered through historic holidays. The commemorative expression reflects the original event through festive celebration or solemn ritual. Reenactments are common activities at historical holiday and festival gatherings, seeking to bring the past alive in the present.

Cinco de Mayo is widely celebrated in the United States—perhaps even more celebrated than in Mexico itself. Social commentators have proposed several reasons for this. Some suggest that because Mexican Americans are a minority within the United States, they feel more strongly aligned with the "clever underdog" theme of Cinco de Mayo than do the people living in Mexico. Historians also point out that Cinco de Mayo commemorations have a long history in the U.S. For example, the Mexican community in San Francisco held its first Cinco de Mayo celebration in 1863, a year after the battle took place. Although the date is honored throughout Mexico, Cinco de Mayo is most widely celebrated in the state of Puebla and in Mexico City. In the United States, Cinco de Mayo is celebrated throughout the southwestern states, where many Mexican Americans live, and in large cities that have significant populations of Mexican Americans. Many celebrations include BALLET FOLKLÓRICO, MEXICAN FOOD, MARIACHI MUSIC, and PARADES.

The strong nationalistic themes of the holiday have led some people to confuse Cinco de Mayo with Mexican Independence Day. In fact, Mexico celebrates its independence day on September 16. The fight for Mexican independence from Spain began on this day in 1810.

SYMBOLS AND CUSTOMS

Ballet Folklórico

Many Cinco de Mayo celebrations feature displays of Mexican folk-dancing, or ballet folklórico. Each state in Mexico preserves a style of dance and regional costume typical to the area. Mexican folk-dancing troupes preserve this diversity. Often adults pass on Mexican cultural heritage by teaching the young people in their community the dances of their forebearers. Dressed in the colorful traditional folk costume of their ancestral homeland, bands of young folk dancers perform these dances at Cinco de Mayo celebrations and other festive occasions.

Battle Reenactments

In Mexico, some towns celebrate by hosting large or small reenactments of the Battle of Puebla. The Mexican government plays a role in sponsoring certain large-scale reenactments.

Mariachi Music

In the United States, many Cinco de Mayo festivals feature performances of a popular kind of Mexican music called mariachi. A mariachi group usually includes at least five instruments: a violin, trumpet, vihuela (a five-stringed guitar), and a guitarrón (a large guitar-shaped string bass). Nevertheless, mariachi groups can be as small as three and as large as twenty. Mariachi groups sing songs about romantic love, home and country, and other universal themes.

Mariachi music developed in the nineteenth century, alongside Mexico's long fight for independence. This popular music has become a symbol of Mexican identity. It was first performed by wandering folk musicians dressed in simple peasant garb, such as ponchos, simple muslin pants, and sandals. Nowadays professional and semi-professional musicians dedicate themselves to this art form. When performing, Mariachi groups usually wear outfits referred to as a *traje charro*, or "cowboy suit." The cowboy suit consists of a broad-brimmed hat, tight-fitting trousers embellished with silver studs, a bolero jacket, and a scarf-like tie. This outfit represents the garb of a well-to-do horseman in Mexico in the late nineteenth and early twentieth centuries.

Mexican Food

Many U.S. towns and cities host street fairs for Cinco de Mayo. At these fairs street vendors sell typically Mexican foods, such as tacos, guacamole, salsa, churros, and tamales. At some fairs cooking or tasting contests take place. A number of different towns and cities hold jalapeño eating contests on Cinco de Mayo. Good-humored crowds gather to watch those who can gobble up the fiery hot peppers without wincing.

In Mexico, Cinco de Mayo celebrations often pay special tribute to the region of Puebla. Foods from Puebla, such as molé poblano, may be served in honor of the occasion. Molé is a thick sauce made from tomatoes, onions, spices, unsweetened chocolate, and ground nuts. It is usually served with meat or beans.

Parades

Parades often play an important role in Cinco de Mayo celebrations. Most feature marching bands or other forms of music. Some marchers wear military uniforms as a way of honoring those who lost their lives fighting for Mexican independence in the Battle of Puebla. Others wear traditional Mexican dress. Some marchers proudly carry Mexican flags. Patriotic parade watchers sometimes greet this spectacle with the cry, *"Viva Mexico,"* which means, "long live Mexico."

FURTHER READING

Gnojewski, Carol. *Cinco de Mayo.* Berkeley Heights, NJ: Enslow Publishers, 2002.

Henderson, Helene, ed. *Holidays, Festivals and Celebrations of the World Dictionary.* 3rd ed. Detroit: Omnigraphics, 2005.

"Mariachi Festivities … for Cinco de Mayo and Almost Anytime." *Sunset.* May, 1990.

Menard, Valerie. *The Latino Holiday Book.* New York: Marlow and Company, 2000.

WEB SITES

Inside Mexico
www.inside-mexico.com/featurecinco.htm

Mexico Connect
www.mexconnect.com/mex_/guadalajara/marhis.html

Mexico Tourism Board
www.visitmexico.com

Columbus Day

Type of Holiday: Historic, National
Date of Observation: Second Monday in October
Where Celebrated: Italy, Latin America, Mexico, United States, and most Spanish-speaking nations
Symbols and Customs: Parades, Reenactments

ORIGINS

Most educated Europeans in the fifteenth century believed that the earth was round, but even the best geographers thought that there were 10,000 miles of ocean between Europe and the East Indies, and few believed that a ship could successfully complete such a difficult journey. Christopher Columbus, a forty-six-year-old Italian explorer, was confident that it was barely a quarter of that distance, and his gross underestimation probably made him more courageous than he should have been when he set out on August 3, 1492, to find the so-called Spice Islands, also known as the Moluccas or East Indies. His famous voyage was financed by King Ferdinand and Queen Isabella of Spain, who hoped that he would bring back spices—in particular pepper, used in the days before refrigeration to preserve meats and to disguise unpleasant tastes.

Columbus not only underestimated the distance but failed to realize that another huge land mass lay between Europe and Asia. So when he arrived two months later on the island he named San Salvador, now believed to be Watling's Island in the Bahamas, he thought he had reached the East Indies. The "Indians" he encountered there were actually members of the Arawak tribe. They lacked spices, gold, or anything else worth bringing back, but they were peaceful and helpful, and they served as guides during the remainder of his voyage.

Columbus made three other voyages over a nine-year period, eventually visiting Dominica, Jamaica, Trinidad, and the mouth of the Orinoco River on the South American mainland. His fourth voyage took him down to the Isthmus of Panama, but he never found the westward passage that would take him home around the world, and he eventually returned to Spain for the last time in 1504. He lost his patron when Queen Isabella died a few weeks later, and Columbus himself died in 1506, poverty-stricken and with his achievements largely forgotten.

The celebration of Columbus's birthday is especially popular in Italy and among Italian-Americans in cities like New York and Philadelphia. Observances are also widespread in Spain, from which he launched his voyages, and in Mexico, where Columbus Day is part of the celebration of Día de la Raza, or Day of the Race. The first observance in the United States was held in New York City in 1792, the 300th anniversary of Columbus's first voyage. But another hundred years elapsed before a nationwide celebration was held in 1892. The Knights of Columbus, a Roman Catholic society for men founded in 1882, urged state legislatures repeatedly to declare October 12 a legal holiday, but it was not until 1901 that New York became the first state to do so. In 1968, President Lyndon Johnson signed a law designating the second Monday in October a national holiday. National holidays can be defined as those commemorations that a nation's government has deemed important enough to warrant inclusion in the list of official public holidays. They tend to honor a person or event that has been critical in the development of the nation and its identity. Such people and events usually reflect values and traditions shared by a large portion of the citizenry.

For Americans, the very act of celebrating notable occasions—like the Fourth of July, battle anniversaries, and others—nurtured patriotism and national identity. It was crucial for the new nation, which lacked a shared history and ancient local heroes, to invent traditions and mark important national occasions. The shared experience of celebrating common holidays created a bond of tradition and a sense of belonging to a relatively new homeland. As more and diverse peoples migrated to the United States, it became even more important to celebrate significant annual anniversaries.

But these celebrations can change over the years. In the late twentieth century, as the 500th anniversary of Columbus's first voyage approached, radical reassessments of Columbus and his effect on the New World appeared in the popular and academic press. The cultural and historical climate had changed. Many people questioned the validity of giving Columbus credit for "discovering" America.

In particular, the American Indian movement of the 1960s and 1970s did much to present a long-neglected side of the Columbus story—the perspectives of the peoples who lived on the continents for centuries before Europeans arrived. Thus, the 500th anniversary proved to be another instance when the actions of this pivotal figure from American history galvanized the interest of the public.

Today it remains a day of protest and mourning for some, commemoration of an ancestor for others. The Transform Columbus Day Alliance, a coalition of groups that participate in annual protests at Denver's Columbus Day Parade, the longest-running parade in America, urges the abolition of the Columbus Day holiday and instead "[advocates] a celebration that is much more inclusive and more accurately reflective of the cultural and racial richness of the Americas." In recent years, several U.S. cities and states, including Alabama, South Dakota, and Hawaii, have renamed Columbus Day to be more reflective of America's dawning cultural sensitivity.

SYMBOLS AND CUSTOMS

Parades

Probably the best-known celebration of Columbus Day is the huge parade that takes place in New York City, where more than 35,000 marchers and over one million spectators, including members of the Knights of Columbus and Italian-American groups, march up Fifth Avenue. Local, state, and national political leaders often participate in the parade or review the procession as it passes. Later in the day, they usually attend a Columbus Day dinner in one of the city's hotels.

The Columbus Day parade is also a big event in Boston, alternating between downtown in odd-numbered years and Revere/East Boston in even-numbered years. On the West Coast, the largest parades take place in Los Angeles and San Francisco. Although parades were not generally a part of the Anglo-American observance of Columbus Day until after 1892, in many ways they resemble Italian religious processions.

Reenactments

Reenactments of Columbus's first landing in the New World are held in various locations across the United States. In the seaside community of Asbury Park, New Jersey, there is a pageant depicting the landing of Columbus on the Sunday nearest October 12. A city employee portrays Christopher Columbus as he disembarks from the longboat that has just brought him to shore, while "Indians" emerge from a simulated village set up on the beach to welcome the explorer. After the mayor delivers a speech, a member of the local Sons of Italy lodge lays a wreath at the base of the explorer's statue.

In San Francisco, tepees are erected on the beach in Aquatic Park, and individuals wearing colorful Indian costumes walk among them. Queen Isabella, with her attendants, arrives on a float from the parade, and shortly afterward, three boats provided by the city's Italian fishermen enter the cove and drop their anchors. Christopher Columbus and a few of his men come ashore in a rowboat and proceed to the Indian village, where they smoke a peace pipe with the Indian chief. Then he walks over to the platform that represents the queen's court in Barcelona, and she listens while he recounts the highlights of his voyage.

The typical landing reenactment probably derives from the scene depicted in John Vanderlyn's painting, *The Landing of Columbus*, which was commissioned for the U.S. Capitol rotunda in 1839 and was later reproduced widely on U.S. postage stamps.

FURTHER READING

Christianson, Stephen G., and Jane M. Hatch. *The American Book of Days*. 4th ed. New York: H.W. Wilson, 2000.

Cohen, Hennig, and Tristram Potter Coffin. *The Folklore of American Holidays*. 3rd ed. Detroit: Gale Research, 1999.

Dunkling, Leslie. *A Dictionary of Days*. New York: Facts on File, 1988.

Harper, Howard V. *Days and Customs of All Faiths*. 1957. Reprint. Detroit: Omnigraphics, 1990.

Henderson, Helene, ed. *Holidays, Festivals, and Celebrations of the World Dictionary*. 3rd ed. Detroit: Omnigraphics, 2005.

Humphrey, Grace. *Stories of the World's Holidays*. 1923. Reprint. Detroit: Omnigraphics, 1990.

McSpadden, J. Walker. *The Book of Holidays*. New York: Crowell, 1958.

Schaun, George and Virginia, and David Wisniewski. *American Holidays and Special Days*. 3rd ed. Lanham: Maryland Historical Press, 2002.

Trawicky, Bernard, and Ruth W. Gregory. *Anniversaries and Holidays*. 5th ed. Chicago: American Library Assocation, 2000.

Van Straalen, Alice. *The Book of Holidays Around the World*. New York: Dutton, 1986.

WEB SITE

Library of Congress
memory.loc.gov/ammem/today/oct12.html

Compitalia

Type of Holiday: Ancient
Date of Observation: Early January
Where Celebrated: Rome
Symbols and Customs: Crossroads, Woolen Doll
Related Holidays: Plough Monday

ORIGINS

Scholars find the beginnings of ancient Roman religion in the sixth century B.C.E. Roman religion dominated Rome and influenced territories in its empire until Emperor Constantine's conversion to Christianity in the third century C.E.

Ancient Roman religion was heavily influenced by the older Greek religion. Roman festivals therefore had much in common with those of the ancient Greeks. Not only were their gods and goddesses mostly the same as those in the Greek pantheon (though the Romans renamed them), but their religious festivals were observed with similar activities: ritual sacrifice, theatrical performances, games, and feasts.

The Compitalia were moveable feasts, held between the **SATURNALIA** (December 17) and January 5, although in the later Roman Empire, they were traditionally held on January 3-5. The history of their celebration spans 1,000 years, beginning with the primitive agricultural villages of early Rome and ending with the late Empire.

The festivals were held in honor of the *Lares* or spirits of the household and family. They were instituted by Tarquin the Proud, the seventh and last king of Rome, after an oracle told him to make an offering of human heads to the Lares. After the brutal king and his family were finally expelled from Rome in 244 C.E., it was decided that the heads of poppies and human figures made out of straw were a sufficient offering. The sacrifices were held at special shrines that had been built at rural or town CROSSROADS, and the men who prepared these sacrifices had to be slaves from whom all signs of servitude had been removed. Slaves, in fact, were allowed to participate fully in the festivities, just as they were at the Saturnalia. They would often join their master in the feasting, dancing, and merrymaking that followed.

The purpose of the Compitalia may have been purification before beginning the year's work, or it might have been to seek the *numen* or mysterious power of the Lares. In any case, it provided a good excuse for neighbors to get together and celebrate the New Year. In the country, the celebration centered on neighboring farms; in the city, it meant games and dancing that spilled out into the streets. The spirit of this ancient festival survived in the rustic English holiday known as **PLOUGH MONDAY**, a time for farm workers to celebrate the completion of their plowing.

SYMBOLS AND CUSTOMS

Crossroads

The *compita* or crossroads were originally places where the paths of farms crossed each other or where country roads met. Shrines resembling small towers were built there, with small altars facing in all four directions so that the *Lares* or deities who protected each farm would have access to them. When the agricultural villages of early Rome developed into towns, the compita were the crossing-points of the *vici*, or residential streets. *Sacella* or shrines were erected there just as they were in the countryside, and fattened pigs were sacrificed to the Lares. The shrines served as a religious center for the area's inhabitants, including slaves.

The belief that crossroads are holy, sometimes haunted, places is widespread in folklore. They stood as symbols of the place where people crossed from one realm to another and were likely to need guidance. In ancient Rome, the meeting of two or more roads symbolized the "navel" of the world. Statues of the god who protected travelers were often placed there to give direction to those who were in doubt. Sometimes farmers would hang a broken plow on the shrine as a sign that their work had been completed.

Woolen Doll

On the night before the sacrifices were held at the crossroads shrines, woolen dolls or effigies of men and women—one for each member of the family, with a ball of wool for each slave—were hung on the doors of all the houses in Rome. The doll, of course, had a head, symbolic of a legal identity. The woolen balls representing slaves lacked heads, indicating that slaves were not considered full members of society.

Some scholars think that these effigies were substitutes for the original human victims sacrificed to the Lares. Given the fact that some Romans regarded the Lares as ghosts of the dead rather than benevolent deities of the house and farm, it might have been their hope that the ghosts would carry off the woolen dolls and spare the living.

FURTHER READING

Fowler, W. Warde. *The Roman Festivals of the Period of the Republic*. New York: Macmillan Co., 1925.

Frazer, Sir James G. *The Golden Bough: A Study in Magic and Religion*. New York: Macmillan, 1931.

Henderson, Helene, ed. *Holidays, Festivals, and Celebrations of the World Dictionary*. 3rd ed. Detroit: Omnigraphics, 2005.

Jobes, Gertrude. *Dictionary of Mythology, Folklore, and Symbols*. New York: Scarecrow Press, 1962.

Scullard, H.H. *Festivals and Ceremonies of the Roman Republic*. Ithaca, NY: Cornell University Press, 1981.

Confederate Memorial Day (Confederate Decoration Day, Confederate Heroes Day)

Type of Holiday: Historic
Date of Observation: Varies
Where Celebrated: Southern United States
Symbols and Customs: Confederate Constitution, Confederate Flag, Decoration of Graves, Reenactments
Related Holidays: Memorial Day

ORIGINS

During the U.S. Civil War (1861-1865), Union forces of the northern states battled the Confederate Army of the seceded southern states. The conflict divided the country in many ways beyond north vs. south—many states, towns, and even families had men fighting on both sides. More than three million men fought in the war, and by the time it was over more than 620,000 lives had been lost.

Confederate Memorial Day is observed in southern states to honor those who died fighting for the defeated Confederacy. Observance is thought to have originated with the organized grave-tending activities of women throughout the south immediately after the Civil War. In 1866, women's memorial societies formed in Atlanta and Columbus, Georgia, in part to push for the designation of a special day of honor for fallen Confederate soldiers. Their efforts were successful, and in 1874 the state of Georgia declared an official Confederate Memorial Day holiday on April 26.

In 1868 the U.S. designated a national **MEMORIAL DAY** holiday called Decoration Day, signifying the custom of decorating the graves of soldiers with flowers and flags. Many in the south believed Decoration Day was held specifically for Union soldiers, excluding those who had died serving the Confederacy. Consequently several southern states joined Georgia in observing Confederate Memorial Day, although on different dates and sometimes with different names for the holiday. States typically chose a date with historical significance that related to the Civil War, such as the date of that state's surrender to the Union army or the birth date of an important figure such as Confederate President Jefferson Davis (June 3), General Robert E. Lee (January 19), or General Stonewall Jackson (January 21). Confederate Memorial Day is observed in Alabama, Florida, Georgia, Kentucky, Louisiana, Mississippi, North Carolina, South Carolina, Tennessee, Texas, and Virginia. The day is known as Confederate Decoration Day in Tennessee and Confederate Heroes Day in Texas.

As a historic holiday, Confederate Memorial Day commemorates a significant historical event. People throughout the world remember significant events in their histories. Often, these are events that are important for an entire nation and become widely observed. The marking of such anniversaries serves not only to honor the values represented by the person or event commemorated, but also to strengthen and reinforce communal bonds of national, cultural, or ethnic identity. Victorious, joyful, and traumatic events are remembered through historic holidays. The commemorative expression reflects the original event through festive celebration or solemn ritual. Reenactments are common activities at historical holiday and festival gatherings, seeking to bring the past alive in the present.

Observances of Confederate Memorial Day vary widely, depending on local tradition and the time of year in which the day falls. Cemetery memorial services are customarily held to honor the dead, often including DECORATION OF GRAVES. In some areas parades, picnics, and living history REENACTMENTS are also held. The CONFEDERATE FLAG is often included in these observances. Where Confederate Memorial Day is an official state holiday, public government offices may be closed in observance of the day.

SYMBOLS AND CUSTOMS

Confederate Constitution

On March 11, 1861, the Confederate Constitution was formally adopted by representatives of the southern states that seceded from the U.S. As part of an annual Confederate Memorial Day observance, the original Confederate Constitution is placed on public display at the University of Georgia's Main Library in Athens, Georgia.

Confederate Flag

The flag of the Confederacy is an important part of Confederate Memorial Day observances. Also known as the Rebel Flag and sometimes as the Southern Cross, the flag's design features two rows of white stars on blue bands arranged diagonally to form an X on a red background. The Confederate flag is generally regarded by southerners as a symbol of pride in southern history, culture, and heritage. Some southern states fly the flag over public government buildings or have incorporated the design into their state flags. However, the Confederate flag has become controversial. Many Americans, as well as such organizations as the Anti-Defamation League and the Southern Poverty Law Center, consider the Confederate flag a symbol of racial oppression

Decoration of Graves

Memorial ceremonies are held at cemeteries throughout the south where Confederate soldiers are buried, and graves are often decorated with flowers, wreaths, and Confederate flags. These services sometimes include living history reenactors who represent Civil War era soldiers and civilians.

Reenactments

Many observances include living history exhibits of military encampments as well as demonstrations illustrating the everyday domestic life of civilians during the Civil War era. Reenactments typically include activities such as troop inspection and dress parade, military company and cavalry drills, storytelling, and theatrical portrayals of significant Civil War figures and events. A memorial and remembrance service may also be conducted to recreate the mourning customs of the Civil War era.

FURTHER READING

Henderson, Helene, ed. *Holidays, Festivals, and Celebrations of the World Dictionary,* 3rd ed. Detroit, MI: Omnigraphics, Inc., 2005.

WEB SITES

PBS
www.pbs.org/civilwar

University of Georgia's Carl Vinson Institute of Government
www.cviog.uga.edu/Projects/gainfo/confmem.htm

U.S. Department of Veterans Affairs
www1.va.gov/opa/speceven/memday/history.asp

Coptic New Year
(Enkutatash)

Type of Holiday: Calendar/Seasonal, Religious (Coptic Christian)
Date of Observation: September 11
Where Celebrated: Egypt, Ethiopia
Symbols and Customs: Dog Star, Flowers, Grass, Red Dates
Colors: The Coptic New Year is associated with the color red, symbolizing the blood of the martyrs in the Coptic Orthodox Church.

ORIGINS

The word "Copt" comes from *Hikaptah,* an early name for the ancient Egyptian capital Memphis. Christians in Egypt belong to the Coptic Church, which traces its legendary origins to the first century and St. Mark. When it comes to determining the dates for certain holidays, Coptic Christians follow the old Julian calendar, which was originally devised by the ancient Egyptians and is divided into twelve thirty-day months. The five extra days (six in a Leap Year) form a thirteenth month. This means that a Julian year is 365.25 days long—slightly longer than a solar year, which is only 365.242199 days long. Over the centuries this seemingly minor discrepancy has accumulated, and the Julian calendar is now seven years and eight months behind the Western or Gregorian calendar, which was adopted in 1582. As a result, New Year's Day in the Coptic Church falls on September 11 (September 12 in a Leap Year), at a time when Christians elsewhere are just beginning to anticipate the year's end.

The Coptic New Year is observed by Coptic Christians in both Egypt and Ethiopia, as well as by Egyptian communities elsewhere in the world. It honors the martyrs of the Coptic Church, whose blood is symbolized by the wearing of red vestments and the eating of RED DATES. In Egypt, this is the day when Sirius, the DOG STAR, can again be seen in the night sky, heralding the floods that prepare the ground for planting. In Ethiopia, it marks the end of the rainy season and is called *Enkutatash* (or Inqu-tatash), which means "gift of jewels"—a reference to the return of the Queen of Sheba after her visit to King Solomon in Jerusalem, when her chiefs presented her *enku* or jewels as a "welcome home" gift. Nowadays Ethiopian children wearing brand-new clothes dance through the streets, handing out bouquets of FLOWERS. Although there are celebrations in every village, larger observances take place in the city churches, where there are prayers, sermons, and colorful processions.

Although the Coptic New Year is observed only by those who belong to the Coptic Church, it is not primarily a religious holiday. It is more of a celebration of life returning to the earth and a time to exchange gifts, visits, and New Year's greetings.

SYMBOLS AND CUSTOMS

Dog Star

Sirius, commonly known as the Dog Star, is the brightest star in the sky and is part of the constellation known as Canis Major. Back when the pharaohs ruled Egypt, the Dog Star reappeared at the time of year when the Nile River would flood the plains so that farmers could sow their crops—an apt time to mark the beginning of a new year and a new planting season.

Flowers

It is a Coptic New Year tradition in Ethiopia to gather and hand out bouquets of wildflowers, a symbol of the rainy season's end. Because it is a time of year when the fields are filled with yellow daisies, children in rural areas gather bunches of them and bring them from house to house, singing. Flowers are also very much in evidence in the churches. In more sophisticated urban areas, New Year greeting cards have largely replaced the traditional bouquet of flowers.

Grass

Like flowers, grass symbolizes the return of life to the earth. In Ethiopia, young girls wearing white cotton dresses go from house to house carrying bunches of long green grass, and people in rural areas often spread freshly cut grass over the floors of their houses to celebrate the end of the rainy season.

Red Dates

Bags filled with dates are often given to young children in church during the observance of the Coptic New Year, and people traditionally serve dates at home.

The most popular are the red dates, because there is an old folk tale that says the Virgin Mary was sitting under a date palm one day when she took a bite out of a red date and broke a piece of her tooth off. Children consume one date after another in search of the Virgin Mary's missing tooth.

The color red is itself symbolic of the day, which is not only the first of the New Year but a day set aside in the Coptic Church to honor its martyrs. The white flesh inside the dates is considered symbolic of the martyrs' purity, and the hard pit represents the steadfastness of their faith.

FURTHER READING

Bellenir, Karen. *Religious Holidays and Calendars.* 3rd ed. Detroit: Omnigraphics, 2004.
Bowker, John, ed. *The Oxford Dictionary of World Religions.* New York: Oxford University Press, 1997.
MacDonald, Margaret R., ed. *The Folklore of World Holidays.* Detroit: Gale Research, 1992.

WEB SITE

Ethiopian Tourism Commission
tourismethiopia.org/pages/detail/detailfestival.asp

Corpus Christi, Feast of

Type of Holiday: Religious (Episcopalian, Roman Catholic)
Date of Observation: Between May 21 and June 24; Thursday after Trinity Sunday
Where Celebrated: Austria, Belgium, Canada, England, France, Germany, Hungary, Ireland, Italy, Mexico, Portugal, Spain, South America, Switzerland, United States, and by Roman Catholics all over the world
Symbols and Customs: Battles between Moors and Christians, Corpus Christi Plays, Flowers, Flying Pole Dance, Stations, Wreaths
Related Holidays: Easter, Maundy Thursday

ORIGINS

The Feast of Corpus Christi is a Christian holiday in honor of the Blessed Sacrament. Christianity is the largest of the world's religions, with nearly two billion believers in countries around the globe. The word Christian refers to a follower of Christ, a title derived from the Greek word meaning Messiah or Anointed One. The Christ of Christianity is Jesus of Nazareth, a man born between 7 and 4 B.C.E. in the region of Palestine. According to Christian teaching, Jesus was killed by Roman authorities using a form of execution called crucifixion (a term meaning he was nailed to a cross and hung from it until he died) in about the year 30 C.E. After his death, he rose back to life. His death and resurrection provide a way by which people can be reconciled with God. In remembrance of Jesus' death and resurrection, the cross serves as a fundamental symbol in Christianity.

There is no one central authority for all of Christianity. The pope (the bishop of Rome) is the authority for the Roman Catholic Church, but other sects look to other authorities. Orthodox communities look to patriarchs and emphasize doctrinal agreement and traditional practice. Protestant communities focus on individual conscience. The Roman Catholic and Protestant churches are often referred to as the Western Church, while the Orthodox churches may also be called the Eastern Church. All three main branches of Christianity acknowledge the authority of Christian scriptures, a compilation of writings assembled into a document called the Bible. Methods of biblical interpretation vary among the different Christian sects.

It was a thirteenth-century Belgian nun named Juliana who first suggested that a special feast be held in honor of the Blessed Sacrament on a day other than **MAUNDY THURSDAY**. Juliana had seen a vision repeatedly since the age of sixteen in which a full moon appeared, while part of it remained black. Finally, Jesus came to her and explained that the moon represented the ecclesiastical year, and the black spot indicated the lack of a festival in honor of the Blessed Sacrament. Although she was ridiculed when she spoke publicly about her vision, eventually the bishop of her diocese in Liège listened to her and instituted such a feast for the local churches in 1246.

One of the men who initially supported her efforts in Belgium later became Pope Urban IV. Six years after Juliana's death in 1258, he established a festival in honor of the Holy Eucharist for the whole church, to be celebrated on the Thursday after **PENTECOST** week. But the feast didn't really catch on until Pope Clement V renewed the decree in 1314, after which it spread quickly. Originally known as the Feast of the Most Holy Body of Christ, it commemorated the Last Supper, held on the day before Jesus' crucifixion. Worshippers received Holy Communion and, in some countries, the consecrated bread (or Host) was paraded through the streets, held by priests in a special receptacle known as a monstrance.

By the fourteenth century, the custom of carrying the Blessed Sacrament in a procession through the streets after Mass on Corpus Christi (which means "body of Christ" in Latin) was well established. Such processions were approved by the

Council of Trent (1545-63) and recommended as a way for Roman Catholics to publicly express their faith in the Holy Sacrament. During the later Middle Ages, these processions developed into elaborate pageants of devotion, and they are still held in France, Italy, Spain, Portugal, Austria, Belgium, Ireland, and the Catholic regions of Germany, Holland, Switzerland, Canada, the Slavic countries, and South America. Members of the royal family, presidents and ministers of state, members of trade and craft guilds, and honor guards from the military accompany the religious procession while church bells ring, bands play hymns, and spectators often fall to their knees and pray. In Spain and Provence (southern France), these processions can be spectacular, with saints and characters from the Bible following a path decorated with WREATHS and strewn with FLOWERS.

The Corpus Christi feast was brought to the United States by Catholic missionaries in Florida, California, Texas, New Mexico, the Great Lakes region, and what is now Canada. There is a town in Texas named after the feast, and it is located on Corpus Christi Bay, at the mouth of the Nueces River.

SYMBOLS AND CUSTOMS

Battles between Moors and Christians

In Mexico, Corpus Christi is often observed with symbolic battles between the Moors (Muslims) and Christians, particularly in the Sierras of Puebla and Veracruz. Although the costumes vary from one area to the next, the Moors can usually be distinguished by their turbans, while the Christians wear either elaborate plumed helmets with visors or derby hats with pink masks. The symbolic "battle" between the two groups can last four to five hours, at the end of which the Moors are defeated and their leader is symbolically buried.

Corpus Christi Plays

So-called Corpus Christi plays were an outgrowth of the Corpus Christi procession. At first the plays were simple tableaux of scenes from the Bible, but they gradually developed into little dramas enacted on platforms carried on men's shoulders during the procession. Eventually the dramas were held separately, usually in public squares or churches.

In Ireland during medieval times, roles in the Corpus Christi play would be assigned on the basis of membership in various trade guilds; for example, the fishermen might play the Twelve Apostles, while the butchers would play the part of executioners. The subject matter of these plays was usually a well-known legend or story from the Bible, such as St. George and the Dragon or the Passion of Christ.

Corpus Christi plays were especially popular in England, Germany, and Spain. One of the most famous was the *Autos Sacramentales* or "Plays of the Sacrament" by the Spanish priest and poet Pedro Calderón de la Barca, which is still performed today.

Flowers

Perhaps because Corpus Christi is a springtime feast in most countries, it is often associated with flowers. In Latin countries especially, it is customary to cover the streets with carpets of grass and flowers arranged into beautiful designs. On San Miguel in the Azores, the people make a flower-petal carpet almost three-quarters of a mile in length. Over this carpet passes a colorful procession of high-ranking clergy and red-robed priests, who are followed by young boys and girls who are about to receive Holy Communion for the first time. The high point of the ceremony comes when the bishop raises the silver monstrance and exposes the Blessed Sacrament or Body of Christ.

Flying Pole Dance

The Totonac Indians who live near Veracruz on Mexico's eastern coast perform a rain dance on Corpus Christi that dates back more than a thousand years. Four men climb a 90-foot ceremonial pole, wind ropes around its top, and attach the loose ends of the ropes to their ankles. On a signal, the dancers suddenly leap outward, head first, with arms outspread. The ropes quickly unwind and the men spin around the pole, swinging in wider and wider circles until they reach the ground. As they descend, which takes about two minutes, a Totonac priest on a platform at the top of the pole chants, "Mother Earth is everything, Mother Earth is life and death. Without rain, there is no life."

As he descends, each man makes 13 turns around the pole. Together, the four men make a total of 52 turns, one for each week in the year. Each dancer also represents a season—spring, summer, etc. The Indians say that the pole dance has never failed to bring rain, and the dancers themselves are symbolic of the rain that is certain to fall soon.

What the flying pole dance has to do with the feast of Corpus Christi is uncertain. The Spaniards brought Christianity to Mexico when Cortez first conquered the Aztecs in 1519, and the Indians appear to have mixed many of their ancient beliefs with those of Christianity. Other Central American Indian tribes perform a similar ritual, but associate it with other Christian holidays (*see* **ST. THOMAS THE APOSTLE'S DAY**).

Stations

The ancient Roman custom of setting up stations or stopping-points along the route is very common in Corpus Christi processions. It can be traced back to the

Stations of the Cross—the sites in Jerusalem and the surrounding area associated with various events in the crucifixion of Christ on **GOOD FRIDAY**.

In Corpus Christi processions, stops are made at various points, the Blessed Sacrament is placed on an altar table, and a passage of the Gospel is sung, followed by a hymn and a prayer asking for God's blessing. This ritual, approved by Pope Martin V in the mid-fifteenth century, is still observed in the Catholic regions of central European countries and in some Latin countries.

In Mexico, the *reposiar* is a small shrine or altar set up along the path of a Corpus Christi procession, covered with a lace-trimmed altar cloth and decorated with candles, flowers, and garlands. As the priest makes his rounds of the village, he stops at each of these shrines and gives his benediction, or blessing.

Wreaths

In central Europe and in France, Corpus Christi is also the "Day of Wreaths." Wreaths are attached to flags and banners, to houses, and to arches of green boughs that span the streets. Clergymen and altarboys wear little wreaths on their left arms in the Corpus Christi procession, while girls carry wreaths on their heads. Even the monstrance containing the Blessed Sacrament is decorated with a wreath of flowers. In Poland, these wreaths are blessed by the priest on the eve of the feast day and then used after the ceremonies to decorate private homes. People hang them on the walls of their houses or fix them to the doors and windows, much like **CHRISTMAS** wreaths. Others put them up in gardens, fields, and pastures, with a prayer for God's blessing upon the growing harvest.

FURTHER READING

Bellenir, Karen. *Religious Holidays and Calendars*. 3rd ed. Detroit: Omnigraphics, 2004.

Brewster, H. Pomeroy. *Saints and Festivals of the Christian Church*. 1904. Reprint. Detroit: Omnigraphics, 1990.

Chambers, Robert. *The Book of Days*. 2 vols. 1862-64. Reprint. Detroit: Omnigraphics, 1990.

Cohen, Hennig, and Tristram Potter Coffin. *The Folklore of American Holidays*. 3rd ed. Detroit: Gale Research, 1999.

Danaher, Kevin. *The Year in Ireland*. 4th ed. St. Paul, MN: Irish Books and Media, 1984.

Gwynne, Rev. Walker. *The Christian Year: Its Purpose and Its History*. 1917. Reprint. Detroit: Omnigraphics, 1990.

Harper, Howard V. *Days and Customs of All Faiths*. 1957. Reprint. Detroit: Omnigraphics, 1990.

Helfman, Elizabeth. *Celebrating Nature: Rites and Ceremonies Around the World*. New York: Seabury Press, 1969.

Henderson, Helene, ed. *Holidays, Festivals, and Celebrations of the World Dictionary*. 3rd ed. Detroit: Omnigraphics, 2005.

Ickis, Marguerite. *The Book of Festivals and Holidays the World Over*. New York: Dodd, Mead, 1970.

Leach, Maria, ed. *Funk & Wagnalls Standard Dictionary of Folklore, Mythology & Legend*. San Francisco: Harper & Row, 1984.

MacDonald, Margaret R., ed. *The Folklore of World Holidays*. Detroit: Gale Research, 1992.

Monks, James L. *Great Catholic Festivals*. New York: Henry Schuman, 1951.

Spicer, Dorothy Gladys. *Festivals of Western Europe*. 1958. Reprint. Detroit: Omnigraphics, 1993.

Spicer, Dorothy Gladys. *The Book of Festivals*. 1937. Reprint. Detroit: Omnigraphics, 1990.

Urlin, Ethel L. *Festivals, Holy Days, and Saints' Days*. 1915. Reprint. Detroit: Omnigraphics, 1992.

Weiser, Franz Xaver. *The Holyday Book*. New York: Harcourt, Brace, 1956.

WEB SITE

New Advent Catholic Encyclopedia
www.newadvent.org/cathen/04390b.htm

Crow Fair

Date of Observation: Third weekend in August
Where Celebrated: Crow Agency, Montana
Symbols and Customs: Crow Hop, Dance Arbor, Dancing Competitions, Grand Entry, Tepees

ORIGINS

The Crow Fair, considered to be the largest outdoor Indian powwow in the United States, dates back to 1904. S.C. Reynolds, a government Indian Affairs agent in Crow Agency, Montana, wanted to persuade the Crow Indians, who were traditionally nomads who wandered from place to place, to settle down and support themselves by farming. County fairs were very popular in the American Midwest at the time, so Reynolds organized a typical agricultural fair where Crow farmers could exhibit their livestock and produce and the women could show off their crafts and domestic skills. He even managed to sidestep the federal government's ban on tribal dancing, singing, and ceremonies. The event was a great success, and it soon expanded to include parades, a rodeo, horse and foot races, and reenactments of famous Crow battles. It gave the Crow an opportunity to keep their cultural traditions alive, and it also became a major tourist attraction for Crow Agency, which is located just a few miles from the site of Custer's Last Stand. The fair has been held every year since then, with brief interruptions during World Wars I (1914-18) and II (1939-45) and during the Great Depression of the 1930s.

Crow and other Native Americans start setting up their TEPEES a week before the event, and it is not uncommon to see 1,500 or more tepees erected on the shores of the Little Bighorn River. The fair begins with the GRAND ENTRY, an elaborate procession led by an honor guard of Native American war veterans and featuring Crow Indians on horseback in traditional dress, drumming groups, and representatives of the various dance groups who will compete at the powwow. The dancing itself takes place in a large open-air DANCE ARBOR, which is the focal point of the fair. Drum groups also compete for prizes, and both drummers and dancers are dressed in traditional and often elaborate Native American costumes that include bells, feathered headdresses, and beaded buckskin shirts and dresses. Hundreds of Native American cowboys compete in the all-Indian Championship Rodeo.

Approximately 7,500 Crow Indians live on or near the Montana reservation, but during the Crow Fair they are joined each day by more than 50,000 tourists from all over the world.

SYMBOLS AND CUSTOMS

Crow Hop

Although many traditional Native American dances are performed at the fair, none is more popular or more closely identified with the event than the dance known as the Crow Hop. Imitating the movements of the bird for which it is named, one style of Crow Hop involves stomping hard on the heel of the foot, while another combines skipping and hopping.

According to representatives of the tribe, the dance evolved around the same time that the Crow Fair began. Several groups of Crow Indians would establish separate encampments where the DANCE ARBOR is now located. They used the Crow Hop to make their way from one encampment to the next.

Dance Arbor

The arena known as the dance arbor is about 200 feet in diameter. It is where the GRAND ENTRY takes place and where all the drumming and DANCING COMPETITIONS are held. Although it is open to visitors day and night, there are certain rules of etiquette that must be observed. Using it as a shortcut to get from one part of the fairgrounds to another, for example, is discouraged.

Dancing Competitions

There are so many dancers who compete at the Crow Fair that they can't all fit in the arbor at once. There are male and female Fancy Dancers whose movements are quick and often breathtaking. There are Grass Dancers—named for the thick fringe of yarn decorating their shoulders, aprons, and pants—whose movements make the fringes shimmy and sway, and Jingle Dress Dancers whose costumes are stitched with rows of small tin cones made from the lids of tobacco cans. Other dances include the Fancy Shawl Dance and the Southern Cloth Dance. Drum groups accompany the dancers, who must stop exactly in time with the final drum beat or risk losing points in the competition. Some of the drummers have "trick songs" whose endings cannot always be anticipated, posing a special challenge for the dancers.

Grand Entry

The Grand Entry is an elaborate procession of fair participants, particularly the dancers. It is led by Native American veterans carrying Canadian, Mexican, and American flags, followed by the male and then the female dancers, with the older dancers preceding the younger. The men's Traditional, Fancy, and Grass Dancers file into the arbor first, followed by the women's Traditional, Fancy, and Jingle Dress Dancers in carefully prearranged order.

Many of the parade participants are on horseback—a reminder of how the Crow crossed the western plains hundreds of years ago—and the horses themselves wear traditional Crow saddles and handpainted saddlebags. There are floats, usually flatbed trucks with drummers and dancers, whose cabs are used to display Crow blankets, elk tooth dresses, and other traditional finery, leaving only a small area of the windshield clear so the driver can see where he's going. A highlight of the Grand Entry is the appearance of Miss Crow Fair, who is usually seated in an open Cadillac convertible, and her "princesses"—young beauty queens from other Native American powwows.

The Grand Entry is restaged several times, giving everyone who comes to the fair a chance to witness its most prominent spectacle.

Tepees

Visitors who drive to the fair can see tepees going up for several miles before they reach the fairgrounds, and it is for this reason that the Crow Fair is known as the "Tepee Capital of the World." Families tend to set up their teepees in the same place every year, and it's not uncommon for a particular campsite to be handed down from one generation to the next.

While the tepees that were originally erected at the fair were covered with sewn-together buffalo hides and decorated with paintings, today they are usually made of canvas—although it is still popular to decorate them with pictures representing the family's history.

FURTHER READING

Eagle Walking Turtle. *Indian America: A Traveler's Companion*. Santa Fe: J. Muir Publications, 1989.

Shemanski, Frances. *A Guide to Fairs and Festivals in the United States*. Westport, CT: Greenwood Press, 1984.

WEB SITES

Canku Ota
www.turtletrack.org/Issues00/Co08262000/CO_08262000_Crowfair.htm

Montana's Official State Travel Information Site
travel.state.mt.us/categories/moreinfo.asp?IDRRecordID=8832&SiteID=

Daytona 500

Type of Holiday: Sporting
Date of Observation: February
Where Celebrated: Daytona Beach, Florida
Symbols and Customs: Daytona Speedway
Related Holidays: Indianapolis 500

ORIGINS

Automobile racing in the United States began at the turn of the twentieth century, at a time when few of the nation's roads were paved and it was difficult for drivers to build up any speed. But there was a twenty-mile stretch of hard, flat sand between Ormond and Daytona Beach, a popular winter playground for the rich and famous—among them Ransom Olds and Alexander Winton, America's two most successful automobile manufacturers. Olds came up with the idea of running one of his cars (the precursor of the modern-day Oldsmobile) against one of Winton's right on the beach, and the first race was held in April of 1902. The two drivers were clocked at fifty-seven miles per hour, crossing the finish line in a tie.

The following year there were three competitors and 3,000 spectators, and what was known as the Speed Carnival became a regular event. From 1910 until 1936, drivers raced the world's most powerful cars on Daytona Beach, trying to break the land speed record. Among them was Sir Malcolm Campbell, a British race car driver who wanted to be the first to drive a car 300 miles per hour. The car he brought to the beach in 1935 was twenty-seven feet long and had an engine that had originally been designed for aircraft. Campbell discovered that minor bumps

Racing Flags

GREEN: track clear; proceed at speed; beginning of race and any restarts

YELLOW (CAUTION): track not clear; slow down; hold position behind pace car

RED: track unsafe; go to designated area and stop

WHITE: one lap remaining

CHECKERED: race has been won

BLACK: enter pits immediately for consultation

BLACK WITH WHITE CROSS: for cars refusing to acknowledge black flag

BLUE WITH YELLOW STRIPE: watch mirrors; faster car approaching from behind

YELLOW WITH RED VERTICAL STRIPES: debris or slippery conditions; used on road courses by corner workers

---

in the sand that posed no problem at fifty or sixty mph were a major problem at higher speeds, and he was forced to settle for a top speed of 276 mph.

In 1936 the first DAYTONA SPEEDWAY opened. It went down an old black-top highway for a mile and a half, made a turn in the sand and came back up the beach to another tight turn—around 3.2 miles in all. Because it was during the Depression and most Americans didn't have much money, the decision was made to let people race the same cars they used for everyday transportation, mostly Fords and Chevrolets, known as "stock cars." Stock car racing initially attracted bootleggers, who were already skilled at adapting regular cars to make them fast enough to haul illegal liquor.

After the slump during World War II (1939-45), stock car racing surged in popularity. A larger, improved speedway opened at Daytona in 1959, and the first 500-mile race for late-model stock cars was held in February of that year. The winner was Lee Petty, whose son, Richard, went on to win seven Daytona 500s—more than anyone else. The best-known woman to race at Daytona was Janet Guthrie, who finished twelfth in 1977.

Today, the Daytona 500 is the final race of the sixteen-day event known as Speed-weeks and the richest of the four biggest NASCAR (National Association for Stock Car Auto Racing) races, which include the Winston 500, the Coca-Cola 600, and the Southern 500. More than 150,000 spectators gather at the speedway, while tiny television cameras built into the racers' helmets enable millions of television viewers to watch the race from the driver's seat.

SYMBOLS AND CUSTOMS

Daytona Speedway

The Daytona International Speedway is a 2.5-mile oval, and racers must complete 200 laps (500 miles). It was the creation of William (Bill) France, a mechanic and racing enthusiast who moved to Daytona Beach in 1934, the heyday of beach racing. France founded NASCAR in 1948 and talked city officials into building a 3.2-mile oval track—half on the sand and half on the beach road next to it. But the cars got bogged down in the sand and created deep ruts in the turns. Although France managed to iron out most of these problems, he eventually persuaded the city to build the huge "tri-oval" track, capable of holding more than 100,000 people, that opened in 1959 and is still used today. France, who died in 1992, is widely known as the father of stock car racing.

Today, the Daytona Speedway hosts eight weeks of racing events, starting with the Sunbank 24, a twenty-four-hour endurance race similar to the French race known as Le Mans.

FURTHER READING

Henderson, Helene, ed. *Holidays, Festivals, and Celebrations of the World Dictionary.* 3rd ed. Detroit: Omnigraphics, 2005.
Neely, William. *Daytona, U.S.A.* Tucson: AXTEX Corp., 1979.

WEB SITES

Daytona International Speedway
www.daytona500.com

National Association for Stock Car Auto Racing
www.nascar.com

Dewali
(Divali, Deepavali, Festival of Lights)

Type of Holiday: Religious (Hindu)

Date of Observation: October-November; last two days of the Hindu lunar month of Asvina and first two days of Kartika

Where Celebrated: India, Malaysia, Mauritius, Nepal, and by Hindus throughout Asia

Symbols and Customs: Games of Chance, Good Luck Designs, Lamps

Related Holidays: Tihar

ORIGINS

Dewali is the most widely observed holiday in the Hindu tradition, which many scholars regard as the oldest living religion. The word Hindu is derived from the Sanskrit term *Sindhu* (or *Indus*), which meant river. It referred to people living in the Indus valley in the Indian subcontinent.

Hinduism has no founder, one universal reality (or god) known as Brahman, many gods and goddesses (sometimes referred to as devtas), and several scriptures. Hinduism also has no priesthood or hierarchical structure similar to that seen in some other religions, such as Christianity. Hindus acknowledge the authority of a wide variety of writings, but there is no single, uniform canon. The oldest of the Hindu writings are the *Vedas*. The word "veda" comes from the Sanskrit word for knowledge. The *Vedas*, which were compiled from ancient oral traditions, contain hymns, instructions, explanations, chants for sacrifices, magical formulas, and philosophy. Another set of sacred books includes the *Great Epics*, which illustrate Hindu faith in practice. The *Epics* include the *Ramayana*, the *Mahabharata*, and the *Bhagavad Gita*.

The Hindu pantheon includes approximately thirty-three million gods. Some of these are held in higher esteem than others. Over all the gods, Hindus believe in one absolute high god or universal concept. This is Brahman. Although he is above all the gods, he is not worshipped in popular ceremonies because he is detached from the day-to-day affairs of the people. Brahman is impersonal. Lesser gods and goddesses (devtas) serve him. Because these are more intimately involved in the affairs of people, they are venerated as gods. The most honored god in Hinduism varies among the different Hindu sects. Hindu adherents practice their faith differently and venerate different deities, but they share a similar view of reality and look back on a common history.

The word Dewali is a corruption of the Sanskrit word *Deepawali,* which means "a row of lights." Also known as the Festival of Lights, Dewali is observed primarily in honor of Lakshmi, the goddess of wealth and prosperity. In northern India, it is believed that this is the time of year when Lakshmi returns from her summer home in the country. The special oil LAMPS that line the rooftops and windowsills of Hindu homes during the four-day festival are put there to help her find her way.

Because it is the most widely observed Hindu holiday, a number of legends concerning its origin have clustered around Dewali, and Hindus everywhere can find something in it to celebrate. It marks the beginning of the New Year for Hindus in northern India, where people whitewash their houses and businesses, open new account books, and pray for success and prosperity in the coming year. Even the poor put on new clothes, and employers sometimes buy clothes for their workers. In other parts of India, Dewali celebrates the destruction of a demon named Naraka by the god Vishnu. This demon might originally have symbolized the monsoon that floods a good part of the country, and Dewali marks the end of the monsoon season. In any case, Dewali celebrations often include burning effigies of Naraka.

In Bengal, Dewali is dedicated to the worship of Kali, the goddess of strength. Spectacular images of the goddess are decorated and worshipped before being immersed in a river, sea, or sacred tank. In Maharashtra, Dewali is a festival to ward off King Bali, the ruler of the underworld. In the Punjab and Mauritius, Dewali celebrates the coronation of Rama (a manifestation of Vishnu) after his conquest of Ravana, the ruler of Sri Lanka who had stolen his wife. The Jains commemorate the death of their religion's founder, Mahavira, on Deva Dewali, the tenth day after the Hindu Dewali (*see* **MAHAVIRA JAYANTI**). The Sikhs—a Hindu religious sect —regard this holiday as a time to celebrate the freeing of their Guru Hargobind Sahib by the Mughal emperor. In Nepal, it is called **TIHAR**, a multiple holiday that celebrates the New Year and Lakshmi.

Dewali is as important to Hindus as **CHRISTMAS** is to Christians. In fact, there is a modern custom of sending greeting cards wishing friends and relatives a "Happy Dewali and a Prosperous New Year." It is a time for showing charity toward others and for making a fresh start at the beginning of the New Year.

SYMBOLS AND CUSTOMS

Games of Chance

Gambling on Dewali is a traditional activity, certain to bring good luck. According to Hindu legend, the god Shiva played a game of chance with his wife, Parvati, and lost everything. When his son, Kartik, saw how depressed his father was over his losses, he was determined to win back his father's money and reconcile his parents. He studied the art of throwing dice, went to his mother and challenged her to a game, and ended up regaining his father's lost wealth. Now it was his mother who became melancholy. She taught her other son, Ganesh, how to throw dice, and Ganesh defeated Kartik. Deciding that the entire business had gone far enough, Shiva sent Ganesh to bring his mother back home. Instead, Ganesh found her gambling with Narad and Ravana. Vishnu—who, along with Shiva, is one of the two most powerful Hindu gods—had taken the form of a pair of dice and caused Parvati to lose everything. She was about to curse Vishnu for cheating her when Ganesh intervened. Instead, she pronounced a blessing upon all those who play with dice on the first day of Kartika, assuring them that they will be successful in all of their dealings throughout the year.

Good Luck Designs

In some parts of India and Malaysia, families draw elaborate designs called alpanas on the floors of their homes near the front door to welcome Lakshmi. These good luck designs are made from a special rice flour, symbolic of abundance and welcome. The flour may be left white or mixed with dry pigments to form different colors. The design is usually abstract or incorporates a traditional folk motif like the paisley. Some cities hold competitions to see who can make the most beautiful alpana.

Lamps

The most outstanding feature of Dewali is the constant illumination by lamps, bonfires, and fireworks. People line their houses, courtyards, roofs, and gardens with oil-filled earthen lamps (called *dipas*), candles, or electric bulbs. Some buildings even use neon lights. But even where electric lights are used, it is customary to leave an open lamp of burnt clay filled with *ghee* or clarified butter burning throughout the night at the nearest place of worship so that Lakshmi will feel welcome and will be able to find her way home.

The custom of burning lamps originated with the Vaishnavas—those who worship Vishnu as the supreme god and who observe Dewali in honor of the coronation of Rama, the greatest of India's hero-kings and the seventh incarnation of Vishnu. On the night of the coronation, it is said that the entire countryside was illuminated by lights to symbolize Rama's role in leading the world from darkness to light.

In Bengal, Dewali lights take the form of lit torches held on long poles. Here it is believed that Dewali marks the beginning of the night of the *Pitris* (souls of the departed ancestors), and the torches are intended to guide them.

The best illuminations can be seen in Bombay and in Amritsar, where the famous Golden Temple is lit in the evening with thousands of glittering lamps placed along the steps of the huge tank or sacred pool.

FURTHER READING

Bellenir, Karen. *Religious Holidays and Calendars*. 3rd ed. Detroit: Omnigraphics, 2004.

Gupte, B.A. *Hindu Holidays and Ceremonials*. 2nd ed. Calcutta: Thacker, Spink & Co., 1919.

Henderson, Helene, ed. *Holidays, Festivals, and Celebrations of the World Dictionary*. 3rd ed. Detroit: Omnigraphics, 2005.

MacDonald, Margaret R., ed. *The Folklore of World Holidays*. Detroit: Gale Research, 1992.

Oki, Morihiro. *India: Fairs and Festivals*. Tokyo: Gakken Co., 1989.

Purdy, Susan. *Festivals for You to Celebrate*. Philadelphia: Lippincott, 1969.

Sanon, Arun. *Festive India*. New Delhi: Frank Bros., 1986.

Sharma, Brijendra Nath. *Festivals of India*. New Delhi: Abhinav Publications, 1978.

Sivananda, Swami. *Hindu Fasts and Festivals*. 8th ed. Shivanandanagar, India: Divine Life Society, 1997.

Thomas, Paul. *Festivals and Holidays in India*. Bombay: D.B. Taraporevala Sons, 1971.

WEB SITES

BBC (British Broadcasting Corporation)
www.bbc.co.uk/religion/religions/hinduism/holydays/diwali.shtml

Hindustan Times
www.hindustantimes.in/news/specials/diwali2006/index.shtml

Día de los Muertos
(Day of the Dead)

Type of Holiday: Religious (Aztec, Christian)
Date of Observation: November 2, or October 31-November 2
Where Celebrated: Mexico, United States
Customs and Symbols: Altars, Calaveras, Flowers, Food, Offerings, Parades, Skeletons and Skulls, Vigil, Visiting the Cemetery
Colors: The liturgical color at all church services on November 2 is black.
Related Holidays: All Souls' Day

ORIGINS

Día de los Muertos, or Day of the Dead, is an annual holiday observed primarily by Mexican Americans. It is a festive time of remembering and celebrating the lives of those who have died, whether in the preceding year or long ago. The origins of Día de los Muertos (pronounced *DEE-ah day los MWAIR-tose*) can be traced back nearly 3,000 years to the ancient Aztec people, who observed a month-long festival that included memorials for the deceased. When the Aztecs were conquered by Spain in the early 1500s, Aztec beliefs began to blend with those of Roman Catholicism. Día de los Muertos eventually overlapped with the Catholic All Saints Day and **ALL SOULS' DAY** (normally November 1 and 2, respectively). Although Spanish missionaries tried to stifle the Aztec culture and way of life, Día de los Muertos celebrations continued. Many of the old Aztec customs, such as decorating gravesites and making offerings to the dead, are still practiced by Mexican Americans today.

Observance of Día de los Muertos varies widely according to geographic location, community and family traditions, and individual preference. Parades are sometimes held, public or community altars are built, and there may be prayer ceremonies in the cemetery or other public space. Regardless of these differences, nearly all Día de los Muertos celebrations include these important elements: building an altar, making offerings, and, if possible, visiting the cemetery.

Even the dates for Día de los Muertos can vary. In some areas, Día de los Muertos is a three-day holiday beginning October 31 and ending November 2. Some celebrations last for a week or more, while others are held only on November 2. However, most observances occur on November 1 and 2, with preparations, such as the building of an altar, begun well in advance.

It is generally believed that the spirits of those who have died will return to visit their loved ones during Día de los Muertos. The exact day and time of a spirit's expected return varies according to the dates for observing the holiday. Those who observe Día de los Muertos only on November 2 believe that all spirits return home on that day. Those who observe Día de los Muertos over three days believe that spirits of deceased children (*los angelitos,* or little angels) return to their families beginning in the afternoon of October 31. This day is sometimes known as *Día de los Angelitos* (Day of the Little Angels) or *Día de los Niños* (Day of the Children). Adult spirits are then thought to return to their loved ones beginning in the afternoon of November 1. The night of November 1 is sometimes called *Noche de los Muertos* (Night of the Dead) while November 2 is sometimes known as *Día de los Difuntos* (Day of the Faithful Dead).

In anticipation of the spirits' return, families prepare special FOOD and OFFERINGS to welcome them. The evening of November 1 is a popular time for VISITING THE CEMETERY, and those who do this normally bring along offerings to place on the grave. Depending on geographic location and local custom, people may keep a VIGIL at the cemetery, waiting all night for the spirits of their loved ones to arrive. Some stay at the cemetery only until midnight, and some who leave may return to the gravesite before sunrise on November 2. Still others may keep a vigil at home. When spirits arrive at the gravesite or at the home altar, they may enjoy the offerings as well as the company of their loved ones for a short time. Visiting spirits are believed to return to their graves on November 3.

Día de los Muertos is publicly observed in areas with large Hispanic communities, particularly throughout the southwestern U.S. Many public events are held each year in the city of Phoenix, Arizona, with an annual calendar of festivities published by azcentral.com, a site sponsored jointly by the *Arizona Republic*, KPNX-TV, and *La Voz*. The Museum of Northern Arizona in Flagstaff also sponsors public events in observance of the day. The Mexic-Arte Museum in Austin, Texas, offers special programming for the day each year. The city of Albuquerque, New Mexico, also hosts many Día de los Muertos events, with an events calendar published each year by the *Albuquerque Tribune*.

CUSTOMS AND SYMBOLS

Altars

Most Día de los Muertos celebrants build at least one altar at home to honor deceased loved ones. Communities sometimes create public altars in remembrance of all those who have died in the past year, such as soldiers at war, police officers and fire fighters who died in the line of duty, or victims of natural disasters.

The domestic altar is central to the observance of Día de los Muertos. It is set up at home, in the church, or outside the cemetery and serves as a "threshold" providing access between heaven and earth. Home altars are usually made on a table, on top of another piece of furniture such as a chest of drawers, or on a shelf. Some elaborate altars are constructed with three tiers that represent heaven, earth, and purgatory (a place where it is believed that souls are purified before entrance into heaven; *see also* **ALL SOULS' DAY**). The altar is usually, but not always, covered with a white cloth, and offerings are then placed on the altar. Each altar is an intensely personal expression of its creator's memories of the deceased, and as a result, every altar is unique. Everything on the altar—flowers, candles, incense, and the dead person's favorite foods—is chosen because it will promote communication with the spirit world. The sights, smells, and colors are regarded as signals that will draw the spirit of the deceased ancestor home.

Calaveras

Another Mexican Day of the Dead tradition is the composition of short poems known as *calaveras* (*calavera* means "skull" or "corpse"). This tradition began in Mexico City in the nineteenth century and still continues there today. Aimed at mocking police, government officials, the police, and even priests, writing and publishing these poems is primarily an urban tradition. Even those who excel at *calaveras* find that their fame is short-lived: once the holiday is over, their taunts are usually forgotten. *Calaveras* are printed on large sheets of paper and are often illustrated with laughing skeletons dressed in fancy suits or gowns.

Flowers

Marigolds are the traditional flower of the dead and are used liberally in Día de los Muertos celebrations. They are woven into garlands and necklaces, placed on altars and gravesites, and thrown from floats in parades. Marigolds are also strewn on the ground to mark a path that guides spirits on their journey home. The particular scent of marigolds is thought to attract the spirits of the deceased.

Other flowers that are used during Día de los Muertos include cockscomb, white gypsophila, gladioli, and carnations. Decorative flowers are also made out of crepe paper or tissue paper and used to adorn altars and graves.

Food

Certain special foods are prepared and eaten only during Día de los Muertos, most notably *pan de muerto* (bread of the dead). Pan de muerto is sweet egg bread that is normally round and often baked with bits of dough placed on top to form skeletons or skulls and crossed bones. Pan de muerto can also be made in the shape of bones, people, or animals. Sometimes the loaves are decorated with colored sugar on top.

Sugar candies in the shape of skulls, skeletons, or tombstones are another popular food reserved for Día de los Muertos. These sweet treats are a particular favorite of children and are often included in offerings.

Other traditional Mexican holiday foods are also enjoyed during Día de los Muertos. These include *mole* (chicken or turkey in a sauce made with chocolate, chile peppers, and sesame seeds), *tamales* (corn dough stuffed with meat or vegetables and wrapped in corn husks), pumpkin candy, chocolate, and fruit. *Atole*, a thick beverage made of corn cooked with milk or water and spices, is sometimes also served.

Offerings (Ofrendas)

Offerings are gifts to the spirits that are placed on altars or at gravesites. (Some people use the term "offerings" to refer to the altar itself as well as the items on the altar.) Just as each altar is unique, offerings also vary according to the tastes, interests, and personality of the deceased. Offerings include anything that was loved and enjoyed by the deceased in life, such as music, toys, personal items, clothing, or jewelry. In addition, offerings usually include items that represent the deceased in some way—for example, symbols of a beloved hobby or occupation. Candles, flowers, incense, *papeles picados* (colored paper with elaborate designs cut out), favorite food and drinks, and photos of the deceased are common offerings.

Parades

Parades for Día de Los Muertos may be held in places with a large Mexican-American population. These parades include dancers, musicians, marchers carrying portable altars, floats displaying huge coffins or skeletons, and other images of the dead. People in the parade and also those watching often dress in costumes representing those they have lost in the past year. Parades may be a procession through town to the local cemetery, or they may lead to a public space where a communal altar has been constructed.

Skeletons and Skulls

Although the skeleton and the skull are clearly symbols of death, they appear in a very lively form at Mexican and Hispanic-American celebrations of All Souls' Day. The skeleton and the skull are perhaps the most widely recognized symbols of Día de Los Muertos, and they appear in every imaginable size and shape. There are dancing skeletons made with bouncing arms and legs, edible skulls made out of bread or sugar, life-sized and miniature skeletons, and skulls that can be worn as a mask. Especially popular are the handmade figurines called *calacas*, which are skeletons posed in activities such as taking a bath, riding a horse, playing a piano, performing surgery, typing, reading, and anything else that a living person might

The Meaning of Offerings

Some offerings have a particular meaning when included on an altar:

Candles provide light to guide spirits and heat to warm them when they arrive.

Empty chairs placed next to the altar welcome spirits.

Incense guides the spirits.

Pan de muerto or other food nourishes spirits.

Salt purifies the spirits.

Sugar skulls represent the sweetness of life and the sadness of death.

A washbasin or clean hand towel allow spirits to refresh themselves.

Water quenches the spirit's thirst and also cleanses the spirit.

A woven mat, or *patate*, gives spirits a place to rest.

A figure of a dog represents the belief that when a person dies, he or she is met at the edge of a river by a dog that dances with them, and then swims them across the river to the land of the dead.

do. Calacas are commonly used on altars and as gravesite decorations to represent the deceased.

Vigil

People waiting for the spiritual return of their loved ones often keep a vigil, meaning they stay up all night to watch for the spirit's arrival. Offerings are laid out to welcome the spirits. Flowers are sometimes strewn along a path to the home altar or gravesite in order to help the spirit find its way. Whether the vigil is held in the cemetery or at home, it is usually not a somber occasion. People normally use the time to share stories and memories of the deceased person. They may also choose to sing, dance, listen to music, play games, or engage in some activity that the deceased person enjoyed in life. Some people tell stories of events that occurred in the previous year, in order to keep the deceased informed of family news. A meal dedicated to the deceased is usually shared by those keeping watch, and special food is set out for the deceased to enjoy. It is believed that spirits consume only the "essence," or aroma, of the food. The actual food is either disposed of in a special ceremony or it is eaten later by the deceased person's loved ones.

Visiting the Cemetery

A visit to the gravesite is one of the most universal customs of Día de los Muertos. Family members tend to the gravesite by cleaning grave markers and making any necessary repairs. Weeds are removed and grass is cut if needed. The gravesite is then decorated with a variety of objects intended to please the deceased. These decorations might include streamers made of ribbons or colored paper, flags, flowers, candles, or artwork such as *papeles picados* (colored paper with elaborate designs cut out). Some people choose to paint grave markers or crypts in bright colors, usually some combination of blue, yellow, and pink. When the gravesite is sufficiently cleaned and decorated, offerings are placed on the grave. The amount of time spent at the gravesite varies according to geographic location, family tradition, and individual preference.

FURTHER READING

Barol, J.M. "Embracing One's Fears: Día de los Muertos Could Change Your Relationship with Death." *Albuquerque (NM) Tribune*, October 21, 2005.

Carmichael, Elizabeth, and Chloe Sayer. *The Skeleton at the Feast: The Day of the Dead in Mexico*. Austin: University of Texas Press, 1992.

"Halloween and Festivals of the Dead in Mexico." In *Junior Worldmark Encyclopedia of World Holidays*. Edited by Robert H. Griffin and Ann H. Shurgin. Vol. 2. Detroit: U*X*L, 2000.

Hill, Jeff, and Peggy Daniels. *Life Events and Rites of Passage*. Detroit: Omnigraphics, 2008.

Hoang, Vivi. "Spirits Live on Day of the Dead: Mexican Tradition of Dia de los Muertos Pays Respect to Deceased through Offerings, Communion." *Tennessean*, October 27, 2006.

Jacobs, Andrew. "As Joyous as It Is Macabre; A Mexican Holiday Ensures the Dead Have Their Day." *New York Times*, November 3, 1999.

Menard, Valerie. *The Latino Holiday Book: From Cinco de Mayo to Día de los Muertos— The Celebrations and Traditions of Hispanic-Americans*. New York: Marlowe and Co., 2004.

WEB SITES

Azcentral.com, sponsored jointly by the *Arizona Republic*, KPNX-TV, and *La Voz*
www.azcentral.com/ent/dead

Mexic-Arte Museum, Austin, Texas
www.mexic-artemuseum.org

Museum of Northern Arizona, Flagstaff
www.musnaz.org

*Dionysia
(Bacchanalia)*

Type of Holiday: Ancient
Date of Observation: Various
Where Celebrated: Greece
Symbols and Customs: Bull, Goat, Thyrsus, Winnowing Fan

ORIGINS

The Greek religion flourished in the ancient Greek city-states and surrounding areas between the eighth and fourth centuries B.C.E. The city-state of Athens was the center of ancient Greek civilization and major ceremonies took place there. Within Athens, the Acropolis was the religious center, consisting of temples dedicated to the gods and goddesses. However, smaller sanctuaries to the gods and goddesses also existed throughout the region.

Ancient Greek religion pervaded every aspect of life, and there was no concept of a separation between sacred and secular observances. Thus, ancient Greek festivals were religious occasions. Ritual and sacrifice, athletic games, dramatic performances, and feasting were all elements of festivals.

A series of festivals in ancient Greece were held in honor of Dionysus, the god of wine, fertility, and drama. In the fall there was the Oschophoria ("carrying of the grape cluster"), which included a footrace for young men. The rustic Dionysia was held in December or January at the first tasting of the new wine. The Lenaea, held in Athens in January or February (Dionysus was sometimes known as Lenaeus), included a procession of jesting citizens through the city. The Anthesteria, observed in February or March, celebrated the beginning of spring and the maturing of the wine stored during the previous year. Best known of all was the Great Dionysia, held in the spring (March-April) in Athens for five or six days. It featured the performance of new tragedies, comedies, and satiric dramas at the Theater of Dionysus on the side of the Acropolis.

According to mythology, Dionysus was the offspring of Zeus and Semele. When Semele died in the sixth or seventh month of her pregnancy, Zeus saved the infant by keeping him in his thigh until the full nine-month term was up. When the child was reborn from his father's thigh, he was given to Semele's sister, Ino, and her husband, Athamas, to rear. Hera, whose intense jealousy was originally responsible for Semele's death, drove Athamas mad, and the care of Dionysus was transferred to the nymphs on Mount Nysa. Roaming freely over the mountain, Dionysus tasted the wild vine and discovered how to extract its juice.

Like other vegetation gods, Dionysus was believed to have died a violent death. In one myth, he is attacked by the Titans with knives to punish him for mocking his father. He keeps changing form, appearing first as a young man, then a lion, a horse, and a serpent. It is finally in the form of a BULL that he is cut to pieces. In some versions of the myth, he is pieced together again, or rises from the dead and ascends to heaven. His resurrection was believed to ensure the regeneration of plants and the fertility of animals in springtime. At the festivals in his honor, Dionysus' death and resurrection were reenacted by killing a BULL (or GOAT) and then stuffing and setting up the slain animal, as was customary at the Athenian **BOUPHONIA**.

The Dionysia came to Greece by way of Egypt. Because the Greeks already had other fertility gods, the Dionysian rites there focused on wine and the exhilaration it produced. There were obscene songs and dances designed to magically stimulate plant growth, and sex orgies whose original purpose may have been to induce fertility in the fields. Peasants and shepherds dressed in animal skins and pretended they were Satyrs. The spring rituals in honor of Dionysus included a procession into the fields led by a maiden carrying a phallus and followed by the farmer, his wife, and his daughters, all of them singing bawdy songs. When the worship of Dionysus was introduced into Rome (where he was known as Bacchus, and his festival as the Bacchanalia), the debauchery eventually reached the point where it resulted in a wave of crime and immorality throughout Italy. The Roman authorities cracked down on such behavior and instituted a death penalty for anyone who failed to obey the new restrictions.

Just as wine could make people either high spirited or drunk and irresponsible, Dionysus was both a merry god who inspired great poetry and a cruel god. His festivals therefore combine elements of bloodshed and revelry. He is usually shown as an effeminate young man wearing a crown of vine and ivy and carrying a THYRSUS.

SYMBOLS AND CUSTOMS

Bull

Although Dionysus was a god of vegetation, he was often represented in animal form, especially that of a bull. One theory as to why he is associated with the bull is that he was the first to yoke oxen to the plow, which had formerly been dragged along by hand. But whatever the reason, images of Dionysus frequently show him wearing a bull's hide with the head, horns, and hoofs hanging down behind him. Sometimes he is shown as a calf-headed child with clusters of grapes around his brow and horns sprouting from his head.

The tearing apart of live bulls and calves was a regular feature of Dionysiac rites. According to Greek mythology, it was when he had assumed the form of a bull that Dionysus was torn to pieces by the Titans. When his worshippers killed a bull and ate it, therefore, they were symbolically killing the god and partaking of his flesh and blood, thus securing for themselves a portion of the god's life-giving and fertilizing influence.

Goat

To save him from the wrath of the jealous Hera, Zeus changed the youthful Dionysus into a kid. And when the gods fled to Egypt to escape the fury of Typhon, Dionysus was turned into a goat. But this is only part of the explanation for why worshippers of Dionysus often tore a live goat to pieces during his festival and ate its flesh raw. Although it may seem a strange practice to kill and eat an animal who embodies the god being worshipped, the custom of killing a deity in animal form can be traced back to a very primitive stage of human culture. Goats may also have been sacrificed during the Dionysia because they had a tendency to nibble away at grapevines, and Dionysus was the god who protected the vineyards.

Dionysus is closely associated with Pan, the Satyrs, and other minor deities who resemble goats. Pan is usually shown in painting and sculpture with the face and legs of a goat, while the Satyrs are depicted with pointed goat-ears, sprouting horns, and short tails. In early Greek drama, their parts were often played by men dressed in goatskins.

Whether it was a goat or a BULL that was sacrificed at the Dionysia, the purpose of eating the flesh raw was to physically ingest some of the positive force associated with the god of vegetation. Some worshippers carried pieces of goat home and buried them in their fields to convey to the earth some of the god's quickening influence.

Thyrsus

The thyrsus, a staff tipped with a pinecone and twined with ivy, is always associated with Dionysus, the Satyrs, and Dionysian revelers. In addition to being the god of the vine, Dionysus was also the god of trees in general, and cultivated trees in particular. Fruit farmers would often set up an image of him in the shape of a natural tree stump in their orchards.

Among the trees sacred to Dionysus was the pine tree. Like other evergreens, it was a symbol of immortality. Pinecones, because they contained so many seeds, symbolized fertility. So the thyrsus was not only a phallic symbol, in keeping with the wild sexual behavior that Dionysian revelers engaged in, but also an apt reminder of the fertility and regeneration in the natural world over which Dionysus was thought to have influence.

Winnowing Fan

A winnowing fan is a large, open, shovel-shaped basket. Until modern times, it was used by farmers to separate the grain from the chaff by tossing the corn in the air and allowing the chaff to blow away. Dionysus is said to have been placed at birth in a winnowing fan, and in paintings he is often shown as an infant cradled in such a basket.

FURTHER READING

Cirlot, J.E. *A Dictionary of Symbols*. New York: Philosophical Library, 1962.

Fowler, W. Warde. *The Roman Festivals of the Period of the Republic*. New York: Macmillan Co., 1925.

Frazer, Sir James G. *The Golden Bough: A Study in Magic and Religion*. New York: Macmillan, 1931.

Henderson, Helene, ed. *Holidays, Festivals, and Celebrations of the World Dictionary*. 3rd ed. Detroit: Omnigraphics, 2005.

Jobes, Gertrude. *Dictionary of Mythology, Folklore, and Symbols*. New York: Scarecrow Press, 1962.

Leach, Maria, ed. *Funk & Wagnalls Standard Dictionary of Folklore, Mythology & Legend*. San Francisco: Harper & Row, 1984.

Lemprière, John. *Lemprière's Classical Dictionary*. Rev. ed. London: Bracken, 1994.

Scullard, H.H. *Festivals and Ceremonies of the Roman Republic*. Ithaca, NY: Cornell University Press, 1981.

Whibley, Leonard. *A Companion of Greek Studies*. 3rd ed. Cambridge: University Press, 1916.

Distaff Day

Type of Holiday: Folkloric, Calendar/Seasonal
Date of Observation: January 7
Where Celebrated: England
Symbols and Customs: Distaff

ORIGINS

The DISTAFF and the spindle were used to spin flax or wool fibers before the invention of the spinning wheel in 1533. The flax was wound around a short staff known as the DISTAFF, which was fastened at the woman's waist by her girdle or tucked under her arm. The flax would be fed from the distaff through the woman's fingers to the spindle, which twisted it into yarn or thread. When women visited each other, they often carried their distaff and spindle with them to occupy them as they chatted. Sometimes the distaff was called the "rock"—from the German *rocken*, which described the spinning apparatus. When women gathered together to spin, it was often referred to as "rocking."

January 7 was traditionally the day on which women resumed their chores after the twelve-day **CHRISTMAS** celebration, which ended on **EPIPHANY**, or January 6. Because spinning was such a basic and essential female activity at one time, it made sense to call the day on which women returned to their normal routine Distaff Day or Rock Day. Some people called it St. Distaff's Day, although the name was a medieval joke. There never was a St. Distaff, nor was Distaff Day really a church festival. But it was widely observed at one time in England.

Men apparently didn't feel the same compulsion to get back to work after Christmas. They often made fun of the women by setting fire to their flax, in return for which they had pails of water dumped on their heads.

SYMBOLS AND CUSTOMS

Distaff

Because it was the women who did most of the spinning, the distaff became a symbol for the female sex. The "distaff side" was a legal term referring to the female branch of the family, while the "spear side" was the male branch. And a "spinster," of course, was an unmarried woman who had nothing better to do than spin all day.

The art of spinning was so essential and so completely identified with women that the Three Fates in Greek mythology were depicted as three women spinning the thread of human destiny.

FURTHER READING

Brewster, H. Pomeroy. *Saints and Festivals of the Christian Church*. 1904. Reprint. Detroit: Omnigraphics, 1990.

Chambers, Robert. *The Book of Days*. 2 vols. 1862-64. Reprint. Detroit: Omnigraphics, 1990.

Cirlot, J.E. *A Dictionary of Symbols*. New York: Philosophical Library, 1962.

Dunkling, Leslie. *A Dictionary of Days*. New York: Facts on File, 1988.

Harper, Howard V. *Days and Customs of All Faiths*. 1957. Reprint. Detroit: Omnigraphics, 1990.

Henderson, Helene, ed. *Holidays, Festivals, and Celebrations of the World Dictionary*. 3rd ed. Detroit: Omnigraphics, 2005.

Dosmoche

Type of Holiday: Calendar/Seasonal, Religious (Tibetan Buddhist)
Date of Observation: February; twenty-eighth day of the twelfth Tibetan lunar month
Where Celebrated: Tibet, northwestern India
Symbols and Customs: Black Hat Dancers, Butter Sculptures, Dosmo, Dumplings, Tsamba
Related Holidays: Losar

ORIGINS

Dosmoche, or the Feast of the Dying Year, is celebrated by Tibetan Buddhists in Tibet and northwestern India. Tibetan Buddhism is defined by Tibetan indigenous religious traditions and folk practices as well as by Buddhist teachings. Tibetans observe a form of Buddhism known as Lamaism, Lama Buddhism, or Tibetan Buddhism. It involves belief in evil spirits, magic, and the spirits of nature. The Dalai Lama is the spiritual leader of Tibetan Buddhists.

Buddhism, one of the four largest religious families in the world, is based on the teachings of Siddhartha Gautama (c. 563-483 B.C.E.) who came to be known as Buddha, or "The Enlightened One." The basic tenets of Buddhism can be summarized in the Four Noble Truths and the Eightfold Path. The Four Noble Truths are 1) the truth and reality of suffering; 2) suffering is caused by desire; 3) the way to end suffering is to end desire; and 4) the Eightfold Path shows the way to end suffering. The Eightfold Path consists of 1) right view or right understanding; 2) right thoughts and aspirations; 3) right speech; 4) right conduct and action; 5) right way of life; 6) right effort; 7) right mindfulness; and 8) right contemplation.

Tibetan Buddhists celebrate Dosmoche for five days just before **LOSAR**, the Tibetan New Year. The festival centers around the magical wooden pole known as the DOSMO, which is erected on the morning of the first day, and on various rituals designed to frighten away evil spirits that might cause harm during the coming year.

In preparation for the yearly festival, Tibetans plant barley seedlings in small dishes that they offer to Buddha in the hope that he'll bring them a bountiful harvest. They also put together the *droso chemar*, which is a grain dipper that has been decorated with flowers and ears of barley and then filled with a mixture of TSAMBA (barley flour), roasted wheat, butter, and ginseng to symbolize—much like Americans' **THANKSGIVING** cornucopia—the wish for a bountiful year. Preparations are particularly elaborate at the palace in Leh, capital of the region of Ladakh in northwestern India, where the traditions associated with Dosmoche originated many centuries ago. Lamas (Tibetan monks) from various monasteries congregate in the courtyard below the palace gates, and there is a festive procession featuring the well-known BLACK HAT DANCERS.

Sacrificial offerings play an important part in the celebration of Dosmoche. They include thread crosses made by the lamas and designed to catch evil spirits in their webs as well as cakes made from TSAMBA dough that are ceremonially burned or brought out to the desert as scapegoats and smashed. Because Tibetan Buddhists believe in magic and evil spirits, most of the activities associated with Dosmoche are aimed at scaring off or placating these spirits and ensuring that no disastrous events will take place in the coming year.

The festival reaches its climax on the fifth day, when the dosmo is torn down and burned. As the people participate in this abrupt end to the celebration, they feel they have done everything in their power to banish any hostile spirits who might wish to do them harm.

SYMBOLS AND CUSTOMS

Black Hat Dancers

The Black Hat Dancers, also known as Black Hat Magicians, who participate in the celebration of Dosmoche at Leh Palace take their name from the wide-brimmed black hats they wear. Their dance is designed to drive out evil spirits and purify the place where the festival is to be celebrated. It reenacts the story of Langdarma, a king known for persecuting Buddhists. Langdarma was assassinated by a ninth-century Tibetan monk named Pelkyi Dorje, who hid himself among a group of dancers performing for the king and, without warning, pulled out a bow that he had kept concealed in his costume. The Black Hat Dancers are therefore symbolic of the victory of good over evil.

Butter Sculptures

Tibetans celebrate Dosmoche by making figures out of yak butter. These sculptures range from free-standing figures 30 feet tall to the small flower-like discs that adorn the sacrificial tsamba cakes, and they are sometimes illuminated by special "butter lights." They're not designed to last very long —although the intense winter cold in the Himalayas means that melting isn't a great concern—and for this reason they are a symbol of one of Buddhism's most basic tenets: the transience of the physical world.

Tibetans who don't live in a cold climate make their butter sculptures out of ghee (a clarified liquid butter), wax, and fat. These sculptures are typically displayed as part of a family shrine or in monasteries.

Dosmo

The dosmo is a ceremonial pole decorated with streamers and religious emblems, including stars, crosses, and pentagrams. While such poles are used on other ceremonial occasions—for example, when a new building is dedicated—the one used at Dosmoche is usually higher and has much larger decorations. Like the BLACK HAT DANCERS and other ritual aspects of the holiday, the dosmo is designed to ward off evil spirits.

Dumplings

One of the most popular dishes served during Dosmoche is dumplings, each of which has a symbolic item hidden inside. As family members chew carefully to see what surprise awaits them, they may discover a pebble (symbolizing a hard heart), a small amount of chili (symbolizing the tendency to speak cruelly of others), or a twist of wool (symbolizing a kind heart).

Tsamba

Tsamba, or barley flour, is a staple of the Tibetan diet and plays an important role during Dosmoche. It is common for people to throw handfuls of tsamba at each other as a good-luck gesture, because white is considered an auspicious color.

Tsamba is also used to make special offering cakes shaped like cones or pyramids, which the lamas fling on the ground so they break into small pieces. They then invite the evil spirits to help themselves and, in exchange, to leave people alone during the coming year. Small lumps of tsamba—mixed with tea, butter, curds, and sugar—are a popular Tibetan snack.

FURTHER READING

MacDonald, Margaret R., ed. *The Folklore of World Holidays*. Detroit: Gale Research, 1992.

WEB SITE

Jammu and Kashmir Tourism Department
www.jktourism.org/cities/ladakh/festivals/cal1.htm

*Double Fifth
(Dragon Boat Festival)*

Type of Holiday: Historic, Folkloric, Calendar/Seasonal
Date of Observation: Fifth day of the fifth month of the Chinese lunar calendar
Where Celebrated: China, and by Chinese communities in the United States and throughout the world
Symbols and Customs: Dragon Boats, Five Poisonous Creatures, Hundred Grass Lotion, Mugwort, Red Threads, Rice Dumplings
Colors: Red, azure, yellow, white, black (*see* RED THREADS)

ORIGINS

The fifth moon of the Chinese lunar calendar is known as the Evil or Wicked Moon. The Chinese lunisolar calendar is based on the oldest system of time measurement still in use. It is widely employed in Asian countries to set the dates of seasonal festivals. The **CHINESE NEW YEAR** takes place on the new moon nearest to the point which is defined in the West as the fifteenth degree on the zodiacal sign of Aquarius. Each of twelve months in the Chinese year is twenty-nine or thirty days long and is divided into two parts, each of which is two weeks long. The Chinese calendar, like all lunisolar systems, requires periodic adjustment to keep the lunar and solar cycles integrated; therefore, an intercalary month is added when necessary.

The names of each of the twenty-four two-week periods sometimes correspond to seasonal festivals celebrated during the period. Beginning with the New Year, which takes place in late January or early February, these periods are known by the following names: Spring Begins (New Year and **LI CH'UN**), the Rain Water, the Excited Insects, the **VERNAL EQUINOX,** the Clear and Bright (**CHING MING**), the Grain Rains, the Summer Begins, the Grain Fills, the Grain in Ear, the **SUMMER SOL-STICE** (Double Fifth), the Slight Heat, the Great Heat, the Autumn Begins, the Limit of Heat, the White Dew (**MID-AUTUMN FESTIVAL**), the **AUTUMN EQUINOX**, the Cold Dew, the Hoar Frost Descends, the Winter Begins, the Little Snow, the Heavy Snow, the **WINTER SOLSTICE,** the Little Cold, and the Great Cold.

The fifth moon arrives at a time of year when dry winds and droughts give way to hot, humid weather, creating ideal conditions for the appearance of the FIVE POI-SONOUS CREATURES. To ward off these and other evil influences, people offer special prayers to Yao Wang, the King of Remedies, whose image can be seen in every village shrine. Yao Wang has the power to save people who are sick, particularly those suffering from fever. Since hot, steamy weather encourages the growth of insects and the spread of infectious diseases, Yao Wang and the other Gods of Medicine are especially worshipped on the "Dangerous Fifth."

The Feast of the Fifth Month dates back at least 2,000 years, when ceremonies were held around the time of the **SUMMER SOLSTICE** to ensure that there would be enough rain. In agricultural areas, these ceremonies were held right after the young rice plants had been transplanted and the torrential summer rains were about to begin. They included special rites in honor of the Dragon God, who controlled rivers and rainfall. Early summer was also a time when ancient people tried to please the alligators, who were believed to be possessed by the spirits of the people they'd eaten. If these spirits weren't satisfied, they might take their revenge by spoiling the crops or sending a plague. The Dragon God may have evolved from these earthly monsters.

The DRAGON BOATS that race on this day owe their origin not only to the Dragon God but to a more recent legend. A fourth-century statesman and poet named Ch'ü Yüan was an honest man who tried to expose the corruption of his government. When he realized there was nothing he could do to stop what was going on, he composed a poem cataloging his worries. Then, clutching a huge rock in his arms, he threw himself into the T'ung Ting Lake in Hunan Province. The people organized search parties to go out on the river and search for Ch'ü Yüan, decorating their boats and striking gongs to ward off the evil spirits. But his body was never recovered. In honor of his sacrifice, the people threw rice on the water every year to feed his ghost. Although Chinese officials have often tried to discourage the dragon boat races, hoping that people will forget the hero who chose to die rather than tolerate corruption, they have never been successful in stamping out this popular holiday.

SYMBOLS AND CUSTOMS

Dragon Boats

In ancient times, boats were believed to be guided by supernatural powers. The Romans raced boats at their **MIDSUMMER DAY** celebrations. In fact, water has played an important role in **SUMMER SOLSTICE** rituals all over the world. Paper or rush boats were often brought down to the beach or riverbank and set on fire so that their "ghosts" would carry off evil influences. The notion that sin, illness, and even death could be loaded on a vessel and sent away was both appealing and widely accepted.

The dragon boat races held throughout South and Central China, Hong Kong, and Taiwan on the Double Fifth may originally have been an attempt to appease the Dragon God so that he would send rain for the crops. People may also have hoped that their battles on the water would induce the dragons of the air to do battle, thus triggering rainstorms. The drums and gongs that were sounded during the races were meant to imitate the rumbling of thunder.

The boats used in these races are long and narrow, suggesting the hollowed-out tree trunks from which they were originally made. They are brightly painted with dragon-like scales and decorated with flags, with a high prow shaped like a dragon's head and a raised stern resembling a tail. A single boat can have as many as 80 rowers, depending on its length. One man stands in the bow, as if searching for the body of Ch'ü Yüan, and pretends to cast rice upon the water. Each boat is accompanied by a small band or a drummer who strikes the beat for the rowers to follow.

The earliest dragon boat races were violent struggles where at least one person had to drown as an offering to the river gods—a human sacrifice to ensure the fertility of the fields. Even as recently as the early 1900s, the annual dragon boat competition was outlawed for a period of time because of the large number of fights and fatal accidents that occurred. Today, dragon boat regattas are rare in Northern China but popular in the south, where rivers and lakes are more numerous. Accidents continue to occur, since the boats themselves are so unstable.

The dragon is one of China's most complex symbols. The Chinese believe that the kingdoms of the world are controlled by dragons whose spheres of influence are re-distributed each year at the beginning of summer. They sleep during the cold, dry season, begin to stir with the first warm weather, and then rise up to the clouds, where they gather in groups and challenge their rivals. These battles result in rain showers. In Chinese art, two dragons are often seen playing together in the clouds with a ball or a pearl, the symbol for thunder.

Five Poisonous Creatures

Many of the superstitions associated with the Double Fifth are designed to ward off the five poisonous creatures associated with this day and with midsummer in general: the snake, the scorpion, the lizard, the toad, and the centipede. Yellow paper charms with pictures of the five creatures are hung over doorways and windows, while young girls wear paper flowers in their hair with images of the creatures on each petal, or hang sachets filled with aromatic herbs (*see* MUGWORT) around their necks. Paper dolls representing each member of the family are burned in the hope that they will take away any misfortunes that might be coming their way. Sometimes a cloth boy doll is placed on the gatepost in front of the house as a way of warding off sickness.

Many Chinese burn realgar, a reddish mineral that gives off a yellow smoke and a foul odor that is believed to kill insects. In some areas, old women cut red paper into the shapes of the five creatures and place them, along with a cut-paper tiger, inside a gourd. The belief here is that by containing the poisonous creatures, they will not be able to cause any harm. Their evil influence can also be avoided by eating the cakes that are sold on this day—stamped, of course, with the image of the five poisonous animals. In fact, the *wudu* motif is so popular that it is embroidered on everything from vests and aprons to backpacks and shoulder bags.

It is interesting to note that the five creatures vary from one part of China to another, depending on the climate and which insects are considered the most bothersome. The spider, for example, often replaces the centipede or the scorpion.

Hundred Grass Lotion

It is a well-known custom in China on the Double Fifth to get up early and walk exactly 100 paces into a field. One hundred blades of grass are picked and brought back to the house, where they are boiled thoroughly in water. The water, which is now believed to possess all the virtues of the grass, is strained, boiled a second time, and stored in bottles as a remedy for headaches, wounds, and nervous diseases. It is called the *pai tsao kao* or "hundred grass lotion."

This special medicine loses its effectiveness if any part of the ritual involved in gathering and preparing it is not observed exactly as prescribed. And it must be done on the fifth day of the fifth moon, because this is the only day on which ordinary grass posseses *ling*—spiritual or health-giving properties.

Mugwort

According to legend, a famous Chinese rebel by the name of Huang Ch'ao gave orders to spare any family that hung mugwort (an aromatic plant whose scientific name is *artemisia vulgaris*) over its door. But the custom of hanging sprigs of garlic or other strong-smelling plants over doorways is an ancient method of repelling ghosts and demons. Leaves of sweet-flag, which are pointed and resemble swords, are also used to ward off summer odors and insects—a real problem in many Chinese cities lacking adequate drainage systems. Why are such odors considered so powerful? It's important to remember that Buddha himself was cured of sickness by the perfume of a lotus blossom.

The custom of hanging up fragrant herbs in midsummer is popular in the West as well. In Russia, Norway, Sweden, Belgium, and other European countries, artemisia is put up on houses and stables to protect them against evil on St. John's Day (June 24, *see* **MIDSUMMER DAY**). According to an old French belief, such herbs must be gathered on Midsummer Eve (June 23) if they are to be effective.

On their way back from casting RICE DUMPLINGS on the water in a symbolic search for Ch'ü Yüan, people bring with them branches of mugwort, banyan tree leaves, and sword grass. When stuffed in the cracks of the wooden doorposts, these branches are believed to preserve the household from summer illnesses.

Red Threads

Red is the color of the peach blossom, widely considered to be a powerful protector against demons. Red threads, symbolic of long life, are often tied to the wrists of young boys on the Double Fifth; girls wear these threads or silk ribbons in their hair. Sometimes threads of five colors are used, symbolizing the five elements: wood is azure, fire is red, earth is yellow, metal is white, and black stands for water. The five-colored threads also represent the FIVE POISONOUS CREATURES. The RICE DUMPLINGS thrown into the water in honor of Ch'ü Yüan were originally tied with five-colored threads.

Families give red or multicolored threads as gifts to each other's children. The mother ties them on, but takes them off again after noon on the Double Fifth—a symbolic gesture that represents "throwing away evil."

Rice Dumplings

Sticky rice dumplings known in China as zong zi are associated with the legend of Ch'ü Yüan, whose spirit was not satisfied by the rice being thrown into the river because the river dragon kept eating it. So people started to wrap the rice in palm leaves (zong is a homonym of the written character for "palm") and tie up the opening with multicolored silk thread (*see* RED THREADS). Another method was to stuff the rice into tubes of bamboo so the river dragon couldn't eat it before Ch'ü Yüan found it. Nowadays the dumplings are usually wrapped in bamboo leaves and tied with a special grass.

FURTHER READING

Bredon, Juliet, and Igor Mitrophanow. *The Moon Year: A Record of Chinese Customs and Festivals*. Shanghai: Kelly & Walsh, 1927.

Casal, U.A. *The Five Sacred Festivals of Ancient Japan*. Rutland, VA: Sophia University in cooperation with Tuttle, 1967.

Eberhard, Wolfram. *A Dictionary of Chinese Symbols: Hidden Symbols in Chinese Life and Thought*. New York: Routledge & Kegan Paul, 1986.

Gaer, Joseph. *Holidays Around the World*. Boston: Little, Brown, 1953.

Henderson, Helene, ed. *Holidays, Festivals, and Celebrations of the World Dictionary*. 3rd ed. Detroit: Omnigraphics, 2005.

MacDonald, Margaret R., ed. *The Folklore of World Holidays*. Detroit: Gale Research, 1992.

Stepanchuk, Carol, and Charles Wong. *Mooncakes and Hungry Ghosts: Festivals of China*. San Francisco: China Books & Periodicals, 1991.

WEB SITE

Hong Kong Tourism Board in New York, New York
www.discoverhongkong.com/eng/heritage/festivals/he_fest_drag.jhtml

Durga Puja
(Dussehra, Navaratri, Dasain)

Type of Holiday: Religious (Hindu)
Date of Observation: September-October; bright half of the Hindu lunar month of Asvina
Where Celebrated: India and Nepal
Symbols and Customs: Bathing in the Ganges, Durga Images, Ram Lila Pageant

ORIGINS

Durga Puja is a Hindu festival that honors the Divine Mother Durga. The word Hindu is derived from the Sanskrit term *Sindhu* (or *Indus*), which meant river. It referred to people living in the Indus valley in the Indian subcontinent. Many scholars regard Hinduism as the oldest living religion.

Hinduism has no founder, one universal reality (or god) known as Brahman, many gods and goddesses (sometimes referred to as devtas), and several scriptures. Hinduism also has no priesthood or hierarchical structure similar to that seen in some other religions, such as Christianity. Hindus acknowledge the authority of a wide variety of writings, but there is no single, uniform canon. The oldest of the Hindu writings are the *Vedas*. The word "veda" comes from the Sanskrit word for knowledge. The *Vedas*, which were compiled from ancient oral traditions, contain hymns, instructions, explanations, chants for sacrifices, magical formulas, and philosophy. Another set of sacred books includes the *Great Epics*, which illustrate Hindu faith in practice. The *Epics* include the *Ramayana*, the *Mahabharata*, and the *Bhagavad Gita*.

The Hindu pantheon includes approximately thirty-three million gods. Some of these are held in higher esteem than others. Over all the gods, Hindus believe in one absolute high god or universal concept. This is Brahman. Although he is above all the gods, he is not worshipped in popular ceremonies because he is detached from the day-to-day affairs of the people. Brahman is impersonal. Lesser gods and goddesses (devtas) serve him. Because these are more intimately involved in the affairs of people, they are venerated as gods. The most honored god in Hinduism varies among the different Hindu sects. Hindu adherents practice their faith differently and venerate different deities, but they share a similar view of reality and look back on a common history.

The festival Durga Puja honors the Divine Mother Durga, wife of Shiva and mother of the goddesses Sarasvati and Lakshmi. Since Durga has nine manifestations, the festival lasts for nine nights (ten days) during the month of Asvina (September-October). *Puja* means "worship," and the exact time to worship Durga is determined with great precision by Hindu astronomers. It is believed that her spirit lights upon her image for only as long "as a mustard seed can stand on the pointed edge of a cow's horn." This is the moment at which sacrifices must be made to Durga and worshipping must begin.

According to Hindu legend, Durga's mother longed to see her daughter, but Durga was only permitted by Shiva to visit her mother for nine days a year. The Durga Puja Festival commemorates this brief visit and ends with Vijaya Dasami Day, when the goddess Durga departs. In Bengal particularly, this is a time for reunions between mothers and their daughters or sons, similar to **MOTHER'S DAY** in the United States.

During the first three days of the festival, Hindus pray to Durga to destroy all their sins and vices. Once they've rid themselves of their bad habits, they spend the next three days trying to achieve a more spiritual personality by worshipping the goddess Lakshmi, who symbolizes purity. After the worshippers have acquired Lakshmi's pure, divine qualities, they are ready to attain wisdom. So during the final three days of the festival they worship Sarasvati, the Hindu goddess of divine knowledge. The tenth and final day of the festival, known as Vijaya Dasami, marks the soul's attainment of liberation.

In southern India, this festival is known as Navaratri, which means "nine nights." In addition to worshipping the goddesses Lakshmi and Sarasvati, Hindus in the south take advantage of the holiday to visit their friends and relatives. In other parts of India, the festival celebrates the victory of Lord Rama over Ravana and is known as Dussehra (*see* BATHING IN THE GANGES). During the ten days of the festival, scenes from the epic poem *Ramayana* are dramatized (*see* RAM LILA PAGEANT). In Nepal, where the festival is called Dasain (or Bada Dasain), the *Ramayana* story is modified to include the Goddess Durga's victory over the forces of evil represented by the demon Mahisasura. In the Katmandu Valley, there are masked dances and processions of priests carrying wooden swords, symbolic of the sword used to kill the buffalo-headed demon.

Durga is usually depicted as a very tall woman whose skin is tinged with the sacred color yellow. She has ten arms, each of which carries a weapon with which to destroy evil, and she rides on a sacred lion.

SYMBOLS AND CUSTOMS

Bathing in the Ganges

Every Hindu hopes to bathe in the Ganges River at least once before he or she dies. The water is believed to cure various diseases, to ease the agony of the dying, and to erase the sins of the living. The word "Dussehra," in fact, is an abbreviation of the Sanskrit phrase *Dasa-bidha pap hara*, "The destroyer of the ten kinds of sin." A dip in the sacred waters of the Ganges is therefore much more than a ritual bath; it is believed that merely uttering the name *Ganga* will purify a person from sin.

Men, women, and children come to the Ganges, which flows from the Himalaya Mountains to the Bay of Bengal, to take a dip. The tanks (or pools) of the river are particularly crowded with bathers during the Durga Puja festival. Those who can't get to the Ganges go to the nearest river, tank, pond, or sea, chanting "Hara Hara Gangey" as they immerse themselves.

Durga Images

During the holiday, Durga's image is everywhere, usually surrounded by images of her offspring. In Calcutta, craftsmen build huge clay figures of the goddess on her lion, slaying demons and engaging in other characteristic activities. Often ten feet tall, with straw-and-bamboo frames, these figures are used in tableaux throughout the city during the festival. On the fourth night, the images are taken down, placed on bamboo stretchers, and carried—accompanied by bagpipers and other musicians—to the banks of the Hooghly River. After being stripped of their clothes and valuable ornaments, the figures are thrown into the water. As they float toward the mouth of the River Ganges, they dissolve back into clay, straw, and bamboo.

Ram Lila Pageant

For two hours a day on each of the ten days of the Durga Puja festival, the Ram Lila Pageant is presented in every town, city, and village throughout northern India. The pageant portrays events described in the sacred Hindu epic *Ramayana*, based on the life of Rama, son of King Dasaratha. The story of Rama is as familiar to Hindus as the story of Jesus is to Christians, but the audience for this yearly spectacle respond as if they are watching the drama unfold for the very first time. Sometimes neighboring towns will compete with each other to see who can put on the most elaborate version of the pageant, which is also performed during the **RAM NAVAMI** festival.

Audience participation is central to the pageant. In between battle scenes, a chorus sings passages from the *Ramayana,* and the people respond to certain passages by shouting, "Victory to Rama! Death to Ravana!"—Ravana being the cruel demon with ten faces and twenty hands who threatened to conquer the earth until he was killed by Rama. The ten-day pageant ends with the death of Ravana, who is burned in effigy. An image of the demon made of bamboo and colored paper and stuffed with fireworks is placed on a platform and exploded in a great show of flames and noise.

FURTHER READING

Bellenir, Karen. *Religious Holidays and Calendars*. 3rd ed. Detroit: Omnigraphics, 2004.

Gaer, Joseph. *Holidays Around the World*. Boston: Little, Brown, 1953.

Henderson, Helene, ed. *Holidays, Festivals, and Celebrations of the World Dictionary*. 3rd ed. Detroit: Omnigraphics, 2005.

Oki, Morihiro. *India: Fairs and Festivals*. Tokyo: Gakken Co., 1989.

Sanon, Arun. *Festive India*. New Delhi: Frank Bros., 1986.

Sharma, Brijendra Nath. *Festivals of India*. New Delhi: Abhinav Publications, 1978.

Sivananda, Swami. *Hindu Fasts and Festivals*. 8th ed. Shivanandanagar, India: Divine Life Society, 1997.

Thomas, Paul. *Festivals and Holidays in India*. Bombay: D.B. Taraporevala Sons, 1971.

WEB SITES

Belur Math
rkmhq.org/durga_puja/article_on_durga_puja.htm

Society for the Confluence of Festivals in India
www.durga-puja.org

Eagle Dance

Type of Holiday: Religious (various Native American)
Date of Observation: Early spring
Where Celebrated: Jemez and Tesuque Reservations, New Mexico
Symbols and Customs: Eagle, Eagle Feathers

ORIGINS

For many Native Americans, the EAGLE is a sacred and symbolic bird because it is able to fly so high and thus move freely between heaven and earth. The eagle has always been regarded by Indians as having supernatural powers, particularly the power to control thunder and rain. Many Indian tribes—among them the Iroquois, Comanche, Iowa, and Midwestern Calumet—traditionally performed Eagle Dances on occasions that called for divine intervention, since eagles were regarded as capable of carrying messages to the gods. Today, the Eagle Dance is a popular feature of many Native American powwows and is particularly associated with the Jemez and Tesuque pueblos in New Mexico, where it is performed every spring.

The Eagle Dance varies from tribe to tribe, but it always portrays the life cycle of the eagle from birth to death, showing how it learns to walk and eventually to hunt and feed itself and its family. There is usually a chorus of male dancers, often wearing feathered war bonnets, who provide a singing and drumming accompaniment, and two central dancers who are dressed to resemble a male and a female eagle, with yellow paint on their lower legs, white on their upper legs, and dark blue bodies. Short white feathers are attached to their chests, which are also painted yellow, and they often wear wig-like caps with white feathers and a projecting yellow beak. Bands of EAGLE FEATHERS run the length of their arms, and they imitate the movements of the eagle with turning, flapping, and swaying motions.

It is believed that the Eagle Dance was originally part of a larger ceremony performed to bring rain at a time of year when crops were being planted and water was essential. But full details are not known, as is true with much of the information related to Native American history.

The Eagle Dance is part of several Native American traditions. The history of Native American cultures dates back thousands of years into prehistoric times. According to many scholars, the people who became the Native Americans migrated from Asia across a land bridge that may have once connected the territories presently occupied by Alaska and Russia. The migrations, believed to have begun between 60,000 and 30,000 B.C.E., continued until approximately 4,000 B.C.E. This speculation, however, conflicts with traditional stories asserting that the indigenous Americans have always lived in North America or that tribes moved up from the south.

The historical development of religious belief systems among Native Americans is not well known. Most of the information available was gathered by Europeans who arrived on the continent beginning in the sixteenth century C.E. The data they recorded was fragmentary and oftentimes of questionable accuracy because the Europeans did not understand the native cultures they were trying to describe and the Native Americans were reluctant to divulge details about themselves.

SYMBOLS AND CUSTOMS

Eagle

The eagle is revered by North American Indians because it can fly closer to the Great Spirit than any human can, thus making it a symbol of wisdom, power, and strength. Among some tribes, the eagle symbolizes the sun, its flight being compared to the sun's daily passage across the sky.

Eagle Feathers

Eagle feathers, especially from golden or bald eagles, are sacred to Native Americans and regarded as the means by which their prayers are carried to heaven. The wearing of eagle feathers is considered a great honor; boys are often given eagle feathers when they reach maturity. The proper handling of the feathers is crucial, especially during the Eagle Dance. They are never allowed to touch the ground, and if a dancer drops one, he is instructed not to pick it up but rather to allow a tribal elder, who has been chosen in advance, to do so. After it has been picked up, the dancer is supposed to thank the elder and show his appreciation with a gift.

Eagle feathers are also used to make ceremonial objects and ornaments, and they play a role in many Native American healing rituals.

Obtaining eagle feathers has never been easy. The Hopi Indians used to carry out special expeditions for the purpose of finding young eagles and removing them from their nests. They were fed and cared for until their feathers were needed, at which time they would be killed and placed in a special burial ground. When the Cheyenne Indians killed eagles for their feathers, they had to carry out a lengthy, complicated "apology" ritual beforehand to soothe the bird's spirit and then trick the eagle into coming close enough for them to grab it with their bare hands.

Today, Native Americans get the eagle feathers they need for special ceremonies like the Eagle Dance by applying to the government for a special permit. When dead eagles are found, government agencies such as the National Fish and Wildlife Service see to it that their feathers are given to Native Americans who need them.

FURTHER READING

Bellenir, Karen. *Religious Holidays and Calendars*. 3rd ed. Detroit: Omnigraphics, 2004.

Cirlot, J.E. *A Dictionary of Symbols*. New York: Philosophical Library, 1962.

Fergusson, Erna. *Dancing Gods: Indian Ceremonials of New Mexico and Arizona*. New York: A.A. Knopf, 1931.

Leach, Maria, ed. *Funk & Wagnalls Standard Dictionary of Folklore, Mythology & Legend*. San Francisco: Harper & Row, 1984.

Earth Day

Type of Holiday: Promotional
Date of Observation: April 22
Where Celebrated: In countries all over the world
Symbols and Customs: Environmental Activities
Related Holidays: Arbor Day

ORIGINS

Earth Day was first observed on April 22, 1970, at a time when concern for the environment was just emerging as a public issue. More than twenty million Americans took to the streets to demonstrate their concern for the environment, making it the largest demonstration in the nation's history. In Washington DC, more than 200,000 gathered on the Mall in front of the Capitol building to encourage government officials and their fellow citizens to preserve the wilderness and the earth's natural resources. Almost every politician in Washington was involved in the event, although, up to this point, most of them had assumed that environmental issues were relatively low on the average citizen's list of priorities.

The idea of preserving the environment was nothing new. Explorers, writers, and naturalists like John Muir, John J. Audubon, and Henry David Thoreau had already fought to save the American wilderness. Their efforts led to the establishment of the national park system and groups like the Sierra Club and the Wilderness Society. But it was Rachel Carson who brought the environmental message home to Americans with her 1962 book, *Silent Spring*. It warned people about the deadly effects of chemical pollution and led to the passage of federal laws banning DDT and other harmful agricultural chemicals.

It was Senator Gaylord Nelson of Wisconsin who came up with the idea for setting aside a day to honor the environment in which we live, and forty-two state legislatures passed Earth Day resolutions. Nelson's original idea was to hold an environmental "teach-in"—a day-long educational event that combined rallies, speeches, lectures, and other programs designed to raise public awareness of the hazards facing the environment. Nelson was also the first Congressman to introduce a bill banning DDT, and he sponsored a number of bills aimed at preserving the Appalachian Trail and other wild and scenic areas in the United States.

Activities that first year varied widely: Some cities lowered bus fares to encourage more people to leave their cars at home, while 200 demonstrators carried coffins into Boston's Logan Airport to protest its noise-polluting plans for expansion. Elsewhere, concerned citizens collected garbage and deposited it on the steps of their local courthouse or statehouse. Mayor John Lindsay of New York led a march that closed down part of the city's Fifth Avenue, one of the busiest commercial streets in the world. Altogether, more than 20 million people in 2,000 communities and on 12,000 high school and college campuses participated in ENVIRONMENTAL ACTIVITIES.

April 22 is also **ARBOR DAY**, which, with its emphasis on planting trees, has been largely replaced by Earth Day. Some people observe Earth Day on the **VERNAL EQUINOX**.

Although the observation of Earth Day has lost some of its initial excitement, it has become much more widespread over the past thirty years. In 1990, for example, more than 300,000 people gathered at the Capitol in Washington, while 200,000 gathered in Boston, 500,000 in New York City, 100,000 in Chicago, and 50,000 in San Francisco. It was estimated that somewhere around 200 million people in 136

Some Prominent Environmental Organizations in the U.S.

Environmental Defense Fund, founded in 1967 to create initiatives to
protect the environment
www.edf.org

National Wildlife Federation, founded in 1936 to protect wildlife
www.nwf.org

Nature Conservancy, founded in 1951 to protect natural resources
www.nature.org

Sierra Club, founded in 1892 by John Muir and others to foster appreciation and preservation of the environment
www.sierraclub.org

countries celebrated the twentieth anniversary of the event that helped spark the
modern environmental movement.

Ten years later, on April 22, 2000, hundreds of millions of people celebrated the
thirtieth anniversary of Earth Day, participating in scheduled events in 184 countries. In one of the largest events, held in Washington DC, hundreds of thousands
of people gathered on the National Mall with politicians, celebrities, and activists
to celebrate Earth Day 2000.

In addition to demonstrations, concrete action has been taken in support of Earth
Day, including the United Nations' work on the Kyoto Protocol. As part of a global
commitment to address the increasing problem of global warming, the U.N.
adoped the Kyoto Protocol as an amendment to the United Nations Framework
Convention on Climate Change (UNFCCC) on December 11, 1997, in Kyoto,
Japan. Whereas the UNFCCC, adopted in 1992, *encouraged* reduction of emissions
by developed nations, the Kyoto Protocol *required* participating nations to reduce
greenhouse gas emissions at least five percent (against 1990 levels) by 2012. For
the Protocol to become binding, at least fifty-five countries and industrialized
nations responsible for fifty-five percent of greenhouse gas emissions in 1990
needed to ratify the agreement.

On February 16, 2005, following the ratification by Russia, the Kyoto Protocol
became legally binding for over 141 countries. Developing nations such as China,

Brazil, and India have signed the protocol, but are not legally bound by it. Over 160 nations have committed to the agreement so far. But the largest global polluter, the United States, has not ratified the agreement. Instead, the U.S. has proposed its own climate change initiative, which calls for voluntary reduction in emissions.

SYMBOLS AND CUSTOMS

Environmental Activities

The most common way to observe Earth Day is by participating in activities designed to preserve the environment and our natural resources. These include collecting garbage for sorting and recycling, avoiding the use of gasoline-powered vehicles, picking up roadside trash, and planting trees. Schoolchildren often pack their lunches in recyclable containers, and families try to give up wasteful habits such as using paper towels and plastic garbage bags. Several major environmental groups have undertaken environmental activities aimed at stopping development, offshore drilling for oil, and the construction of new highways and nuclear power plants.

FURTHER READING

Henderson, Helene, ed. *Holidays, Festivals, and Celebrations of the World Dictionary.* 3rd ed. Detroit: Omnigraphics, 2005.

Mowrey, Marc, and Tim Redmond. *Not in Our Backyard: The People and Events That Shaped America's Modern Environmental Movement.* New York: W. Morrow, 1993.

Trawicky, Bernard, and Ruth W. Gregory. *Anniversaries and Holidays.* 5th ed. Chicago: American Library Assocation, 2000.

WEB SITE

Earth Day Network Official Web Site
www.earthday.net

Easter

Type of Holiday: Religious (Christian)

Date of Observation: Between March 22 and April 25 in the West; between April 4 and May 8 in the East; first Sunday after the first full moon on or following the vernal equinox

Where Celebrated: Worldwide, in over eighty nations

Symbols and Customs: Easter Bonnet, Easter Bunny, Easter Eggs, Easter Fires, Easter Lily, Paschal Candle, Paschal Lamb, Sunrise Service

Colors: The liturgical color for Easter is white or gold. White stands for joy and purity, and gold represents glory, exultation, and illumination. On Easter morning, the pope puts on his white vestments and lights a large white candle symbolizing the light of the world: the resurrected Christ. White is also the color of the EASTER LILY.

Related Holidays: Ash Wednesday, Carnival, Exaltation of the Cross, Forgiveness Sunday, Good Friday, Lent, Maundy Thursday, Yaqui Easter Ceremony

ORIGINS

Easter commemorates the resurrection of Jesus Christ. This holiday is considered the most important in the Christian year. The word Christian refers to a follower of Christ, a title derived from the Greek word meaning Messiah or Anointed One. The Christ of Christianity is Jesus of Nazareth, a man born between 7 and 4 B.C.E. in the region of Palestine. According to Christian teaching, Jesus was killed by Roman authorities using a form of execution called crucifixion (a term meaning he was nailed to a cross and hung from it until he died) in about the year 30 C.E. After his death, he rose back to life. His death and resurrection provide a way by which people can be reconciled with God. In remembrance of Jesus' death and resurrection, the cross serves as a fundamental symbol in Christianity.

With nearly two billion believers in countries around the globe, Christianity is the largest of the world's religions. There is no one central authority for all of Christianity. The pope (the bishop of Rome) is the authority for the Roman Catholic Church, but other sects look to other authorities. Orthodox communities look to patriarchs and emphasize doctrinal agreement and traditional practice. Protestant communities focus on individual conscience. The Roman Catholic and Protestant churches are often referred to as the Western Church, while the Orthodox churches may also be called the Eastern Church. All three main branches of Christianity acknowledge the authority of Christian scriptures, a compilation of writings assembled into a document called the Bible. Methods of biblical interpretation vary among the different Christian sects.

Easter marks the end of Holy Week. Holy Week in turn serves as the last week in **LENT**, a six-week period of spiritual preparation for the celebration of Jesus' resurrection. According to the Bible, some of Jesus' followers went to his tomb on the first Easter Sunday only to find it empty. In one biblical account, Jesus appears to Mary Magdalene as she wept outside his tomb and tells her of his resurrection. In others, the risen Jesus later appears to his disciples. Whatever happened had a profound effect on Jesus' followers, who thereafter believed in the possibility of salvation and new life through Jesus and his teachings.

It was common during the early days of Christianity to try to attract new converts by blending specifically Christian observances with existing pagan festivals. Just as the observation of Christmas was moved from January 6 to December 25, where it would coincide with the pagan celebration of the **WINTER SOLSTICE**, the crucifixion of Jesus Christ was traditionally identified with March 25, perhaps in the hope that it would supplant the ancient pagan festival in honor of the **VERNAL EQUINOX**.

Many of the symbols associated with Easter have their roots in the ancient rituals celebrating the arrival of spring. The name "Easter" may have come from the Anglo-Saxon goddess Eostre, whose feast was celebrated in the spring and who was associated with spring and fertility.

SYMBOLS AND CUSTOMS

Easter Bonnet

Wearing a new hat to church on Easter Sunday was a common practice in the United States during the years when hats themselves were in vogue. Well-known American songwriter Irving Berlin celebrated the custom in his song "Easter Parade," written in 1933. Now that women are less inclined to wear hats, the Easter bonnet is not the popular symbol it once was.

Wearing new clothes on Easter Sunday continues an ancient symbol of baptism and rebirth into a new life in Christ. In past times baptismal candidates put on new clothes right after the ceremony, as a sign of this new life. The early Christians usually baptized new members into the faith at Easter time, and some churches continue this practice today.

In some areas of the United States, the Easter bonnet has been transformed into a decoration for the home. Baskets of flowers, flower wreaths, and straw hats decorated with spring flowers can often be seen hanging on doors at this time of year.

Easter Bunny

Rabbits were common in pre-Christian fertility lore, where they symbolized the abundance of new life associated with spring. The ancient German goddess Ostara, for whom the German spring festival Ostern was named, was always accompanied by a hare, who may have been the precursor of the modern Easter Bunny. In any case, the association of the rabbit with Easter is probably the vestige of an ancient spring fertility rite.

Although rabbits and hares (their European cousins, with shorter ears and longer hind legs) have never had any connection to Christian religious symbolism, the Easter Bunny's role in the celebration of Easter is an important one, particularly for children. It is the Easter Bunny who lays the eggs that children hunt for on Easter morning, and who fills their Easter baskets with candy. Bunnies made out of pastry and sugar are popular in many European countries, while American children look forward to receiving chocolate or marshmallow rabbits.

The Easter Bunny came to America by way of the eighteenth-century German settlers, who referred to him as "Oschter Haws." Pennsylvania Dutch children prepared nests for this shy creature in a secluded corner or sheltered place in the garden or barn. On Easter Eve, the rabbit would lay his colored eggs in these nests, or in the caps and bonnets that children left out for him. The custom of leaving out an empty Easter basket didn't come along until later.

In Germany, the Easter Bunny lays red eggs on **MAUNDY THURSDAY** (the Thursday before Easter) and eggs of other colors on Easter Eve. In Panama, it's the *conejo* or "painted" rabbit who lays the eggs. He has smaller ears than his U.S. counterpart and is brown with white spots, similar to the markings of a fawn.

Some religious purists believe that the Easter Bunny has done to Easter what the cult of Santa Claus has done to **CHRISTMAS**. Others prefer to regard the rabbit emerging from his underground burrow as akin to Christ rising from His tomb on Easter morning. But no one has yet come up with a good explanation for why a rabbit would lay eggs.

Easter Eggs

As a symbol of fertility and immortality, the egg is an integral part of the mythology of all races, beginning with the ancient Egyptians and Hindus. Among Christians, the egg is associated with the rock tomb from which Christ emerged to begin his new life. Because the celebration of Easter is preceded by the forty days of **LENT**, during which eggs and other dairy products are forbidden among Orthodox Christians, it is traditional to begin the Easter meal in Russia and eastern Europe by cutting up an egg that has been blessed and distributing the pieces to each family member and guest.

The custom of dyeing Easter eggs, usually with vegetable colors, is practiced throughout the United States and in northern and eastern Europe. It has become an art form in Poland and the Ukraine, where *pysanki* (from *pysac*, meaning to write or design) are decorated with geometrical or abstract patterns etched in wax (so as not to absorb the color) and applied with a needle or a small metal tube. Russians often exchange eggs that have been colored red, in honor of Jesus' blood, on Easter Day. The elaborate jeweled Easter eggs created by Peter Carl Fabergé in St. Petersburg during the late nineteenth and early twentieth centuries were prized by the Russian royal family and other European aristocrats.

Games involving eggs are often played on Easter. In England, "Egg Saturday" marks the beginning of Shrovetide, or the last four days before **LENT**. Children used to go from door to door asking for eggs or meat and hurling broken crockery at the doors of those who refused—a custom known as Lent-crocking. Egg shackling, another English custom, involves placing eggs in a sieve and shaking them until all but one are cracked. The owner of the uncracked egg gets a prize. Pace-egging (a corruption of Pasch) refers to the custom of going from house to house asking for gifts of Easter eggs.

Egg-cracking, egg-rolling, egg races, and Easter egg hunts are also popular games at Easter time. In Greece, an egg is suspended on a string from the ceiling while the guests who sit around the table start it swinging by hitting it with their heads, then try to catch it in their mouths. Egg-tapping, where children strike their eggs against one another to see whose survives without damage, is popular in many parts of the world. Egg-rolling is believed to symbolize the rolling away of the stone from Jesus' tomb. Perhaps the most famous egg-rolling event takes place **EASTER MONDAY** in Washington DC, on the White House lawn.

Where do Easter eggs come from? According to German folklore, the Easter Bunny lays the eggs and hides them in the garden, although other creatures have also been given credit for the laying of Easter eggs. In France, children are told that the Easter eggs are dropped by the church bells on their way back from Rome.

Easter Fires

Primitive peoples believed that fire came from the sun and was capable of both giving life and destroying the forces of evil. It was a pagan custom to light bonfires around the time of the **VERNAL EQUINOX** to celebrate the re-emergence of the sun after the long, dark winter and to harness its life-giving powers. Torches, embers, or ashes taken from these fires were believed to be capable of stimulating the growth of crops and protecting the health of family members and farm animals.

When Christianity arrived, the tradition of setting bonfires at the beginning of spring was frowned upon by the Church. In Ireland, however, St. Patrick started the custom of lighting and blessing bonfires outside the churches on Holy Saturday night as a way of reinforcing the relationship between fire and Christ, the Light of the World. The Irish bishops and monks who came to the European continent in the sixth and seventh centuries brought the custom with them, and by the ninth century it had become so popular that it was eventually incorporated into the liturgy of Rome. The "blessing of the fire" has now become the opening rite of the Easter Vigil service.

In many Roman Catholic countries, people extinguish their fires and all other sources of light in their homes before the vigil service begins on Easter Eve. A bonfire is built in front of the church, where the priest lights it and blesses the fire. Glowing embers from the fire are then taken home and used to re-light the stoves and the lamps. Sometimes sticks charred in the Easter bonfire are laid on the hearth, where they offer protection from fire, lightning, and hail. Others are placed in the fields or gardens to preserve them from blight. Ashes from the Easter bonfire, often mixed together with ashes from the consecrated palms distributed on **PALM SUNDAY**, are sometimes mixed with the seed at sowing time, or sprinkled in with the cattle's drinking water to protect them from disease. The many superstitions associated with the Easter fires is strong evidence of their link to the old pagan fires of spring.

In Holland, Luxembourg, and several other European countries, worshippers carry wax candles to church on Easter Eve. One by one, they light their candles from the great PASCHAL CANDLE on the altar, until the entire church is illuminated by their flames.

Easter bonfires are still common in the Alpine regions of Austria, where they can be seen burning on the mountaintops after sunset on Holy Saturday, and where they are accompanied by children carrying lighted torches and bands of musicians playing sacred hymns. In western Sweden, the fires are usually built near the center of the village, where the singing, dancing, and merrymaking can last all night.

The alchemists of the Middle Ages regarded fire as an agent of transformation, since all things derived from and returned to fire. Among Christians, the light from the candles or fires lit on Easter Eve symbolizes Jesus' resurrection and rebirth.

Easter Lily

The flower commonly referred to as the Easter lily was brought to the United States in the 1880s from Bermuda. Although it was not originally associated with Easter, it was so named because it flowered around this time of year. Lilies in general were a symbol of purity in medieval iconography, and the Bible mentions them frequently as representative of beauty, perfection, and goodness.

Americans were quick to attribute symbolic value to the fact that this particular plant produced its impressive white flowers at a time that more or less coincided with the celebration of the resurrection of Christ. And because it grows from a bulb that is "buried" and then "reborn," it serves as a perfect emblem of the death and rebirth of the Savior. With their trumpet-shaped blooms suggesting the angel Gabriel's horn, lilies herald both the coming of spring and the celebration of the greatest Christian feast. They can be seen decorating homes and churches throughout the Easter season.

Paschal Candle

The earliest celebrations of Easter in Jerusalem featured a ceremony known as the "Illumination": the lighting of a candle at the beginning of the Easter Vigil or Night Watch on the eve of Easter Sunday. The blessing of the new fire (*see* EASTER FIRES) and the lighting of the Paschal candle is an adaptation of this ancient rite. As far back as the fourth century, a large candle decorated with five grains of incense (symbolizing the five wounds that Jesus received on the cross) was blessed on Easter Eve and lit with newly blessed fire to symbolize Christ and spiritual illumination.

In Roman Catholic and other Christian churches, the Paschal candle usually stands at the side of the altar during the Easter service. Placed there on Holy Saturday (the day before Easter), it is removed on **PENTECOST**.

In medieval times, parishes would compete with each other to see who could make the largest Paschal candle. One used at the altar in Salisbury, England, in 1517 measured more than 30 feet high. A giant candle made in 1558 for the altar at Westminster Abbey in London required 300 pounds of wax. After **PENTECOST**, the huge candles were usually melted down and made into narrow tapers for funerals of the poor.

Paschal Lamb

The name "Pasch," which means Easter, derives from the Hebrew *pesach* or **PASSOVER**, which commemorates the deliverance of the people of Israel the night before their departure from Egypt. The Angel of God killed the first-born sons of all the Egyptian families but passed over the houses of the Israelites, whose doors had been marked with the blood of a young lamb. That evening, the Israelite families roasted the lamb and ate it with unleavened bread and bitter herbs. Jews still repeat this rite every year on the night before Passover.

Jesus' death at the time of the Passover festival forged a strong link between the Jewish feast and the Christian observation of Easter. Christians mark his death on **GOOD FRIDAY**. The lamb sacrificed on the eve of Passover was later identified with the "Lamb of God, who takes away the sins of the world" (John 1:29). As a symbol that can be traced back to the Book of Enoch, the lamb signifies purity, innocence, and meekness as well as unwarranted sacrifice—qualities closely identified with Christ.

Christians all over the world traditionally serve lamb for Easter dinner. In parts of Greece, the master of the house selects the Paschal lamb from among his own flock, usually choosing the male with the whitest fleece. It is common in many European countries to serve a cake or an ice in the shape of a Paschal lamb, and the Paschal lamb candies made in Palermo, Italy, are among the most elaborate and artistic of Easter delicacies.

In past centuries, it was considered a lucky omen to meet a lamb, especially around Easter time. According to superstition, the devil could assume the form of any other animal but never the lamb, because of its deep religious significance.

Sunrise Service

Because Jesus' followers were recorded to have discovered his empty tomb at dawn, the early morning hours are a traditional time for Christians to gather for Easter Sunday worship. Centuries-old European folklore held that the sun danced for joy at dawn on Easter morning. In the United States, Moravian immigrants from Germany brought the early morning Easter service to American soil in the eighteenth century. Today many Protestant churches throughout the United States hold special sunrise services at dawn on Easter morning. Dawn services are also held at such locales as Grand Canyon National Park and some other national parks, the Hollywood Bowl in California, New York's Central Park, and the Tomb of the Unknown Soldier at Arlington National Cemetery.

FURTHER READING

Bellenir, Karen. *Religious Holidays and Calendars.* 3rd ed. Detroit: Omnigraphics, 2004.

Chambers, Robert. *The Book of Days.* 2 vols. 1862-64. Reprint. Detroit: Omnigraphics, 1990.

Cirlot, J.E. *A Dictionary of Symbols.* New York: Philosophical Library, 1962.

Crim, Keith R. *The Perennial Dictionary of World Religions.* San Francisco: Harper & Row, 1989.

Dobler, Lavinia G. *Customs and Holidays Around the World.* New York: Fleet Pub. Corp., 1962.

Frazer, Sir James G. *The Golden Bough: A Study in Magic and Religion.* New York: Macmillan, 1931.

Gulevich, Tanya. *Encyclopedia of Easter, Carnival, and Lent.* Detroit: Omnigraphics, 2002.

Hazeltine, Alice Isabel, and Elva Sophronia Smith. *The Easter Book of Legends and Stories.* 1947. Reprint. Detroit: Omnigraphics, 1992.

Henderson, Helene, ed. *Holidays, Festivals, and Celebrations of the World Dictionary.* 3rd ed. Detroit: Omnigraphics, 2005.

James, E.O. *Seasonal Feasts and Festivals*. 1961. Reprint. Detroit: Omnigraphics, 1993.

Lord, Priscilla Sawyer, and Daniel J. Foley. *Easter Garland*. 1963. Reprint. Detroit: Omnigraphics, 1999.

Lord, Priscilla Sawyer, and Daniel J. Foley. *Easter the World Over*. Philadelphia: Chilton Book Co., 1971.

Santino, Jack. *All Around the Year: Holidays and Celebrations in American Life*. Urbana: University of Illinois Press, 1994.

Weiser, Franz Xaver. *Handbook of Christian Feasts and Customs*. New York: Harcourt, Brace, 1958.

WEB SITES

Christian Resource Institute
www.cresourcei.org/cyeaster.html

Greek Orthodox Archdiocese of Australia
home.it.net.au/~jgrapsas/pages/orth_pascha.html

Polish American Journal
www.polamjournal.com/Library/Holidays/Easter/easter.html

Easter Monday

Type of Holiday: Religious (Christian)
Date of Observation: The day after Easter
Where Celebrated: Europe and many countries around the world
Symbols and Customs: Dousing, Egg Rolling, Emmaus Walk, Switching
Related Holidays: Easter

ORIGINS

Easter Monday is a holiday in more than eighty different countries. In these countries people relax and celebrate on the day after **EASTER**. Unlike Easter day celebrations, however, the customs associated with Easter Monday place less emphasis on religious themes and more emphasis on having a good time. In Central and Northern Europe people still enjoy a number of old folk customs—DOUSING, EGG ROLLING contests, EMMAUS WALKS, and SWITCHING—long associated with the holiday.

In the Middle Ages, people celebrated Easter for an entire week. Historical records show that King Alfred the Great of England (849-899) decreed that labor should cease in the weeks before and after Easter Sunday. While solemn religious devotions dominated the week before Easter, light-hearted festivities reigned during the week after Easter. This period of time, called Easter Week, ended on the Sunday after Easter, which is known in English-speaking countries as Low Sunday or White Sunday. During this week, people feasted, played games, relaxed, and attended parties. The newly baptized continued to wear white clothing in celebration of their initiation into the Christian religion. This period of feasting and merry-making broke the sober mood that had been established during the six weeks of **LENT**, during which many people fasted, examined their consciences, and took up additional spiritual practices. In the centuries that followed the Middle Ages, the period of post-Easter festivity gradually shortened. In many countries today, just one day of celebration remains, Easter Monday.

Some of the customs associated with Easter Monday, such as SWITCHING and DOUSING, seem to have little relationship to Easter or to Christian spirituality. In fact, some folklorists believe that these practices got their start as ancient European folk customs designed to confer the blessings of health or fertility. How they became associated with Easter is not known for sure, but it may be that people practiced these customs in the spring in order to celebrate the return of fertility and growth in nature. Over time they became associated with what became the main spring-time holiday in Europe: Easter.

EGG ROLLING games have a more logical link to Easter Monday, since Easter eggs are a symbol of the Easter holiday. The earliest records of egg rolling games in Europe date back to the sixteenth and seventeenth centuries. Christian folklore common to Orthodox and Protestant Christians views egg rolling as a symbol of the rolling away of the stone sealing Jesus in the tomb.

SYMBOLS AND CUSTOMS

Dousing

In Hungary and Poland, an old custom encourages boys to douse girls with water on Easter Monday. In fact, the Hungarian folk name for the holiday translates as "Dousing Day" or "Water Plunge Monday." Hungarian folk beliefs insisted that drenching women and girls with water on this day blessed them with good health, fertility, and the likelihood of being a good wife. Sometimes boisterous males dragged their female counterparts to nearby streams or ponds in order to confer these blessings on them. Folk tradition encouraged women to respond to this treatment by offering the men eggs, bread, or wine. Especially gracious women might offer all three. In some places these old Easter Monday customs continue today, with some modification. Nowadays men have adopted the more gentle-manly practice of sprinkling women with water or cologne.

In Poland young people often carry cans or buckets of water, in order to drench their targets. Indeed, the Poles call the holiday *Lany Poniedzialek* (Wet Monday), or *Swietgo Lejka* (St. Drencher's Day). As the water hits its mark, Polish youth cry out, *"Smigus!"* Hence, among Polish Americans the day is known as Smigus or Dyngus Day. In past times, boys sought to douse girls with water on Easter Monday. Girls were permitted to give the boys the same treatment on Easter Tuesday. These distinctions have blurred in recent times. Moreover, Polish youth have widened their targets of interest and often throw water at passersby, tourists, and neighbors.

Egg Rolling

Egg rolling is a traditional European folk game associated with Easter. Participants roll hard-boiled eggs down a hill or a slight incline. The person whose egg goes the farthest without cracking or gets down the hill first wins. In certain places, the goal consists of rolling the egg between two pegs in the ground. In some places uncracked eggs can be rolled again, and the person whose egg survives the most rolls intact wins the contest. In many countries, egg rolling contests traditionally take place on Easter Monday.

One very famous Easter Monday egg rolling contest takes place at the White House. This custom dates back to before the Civil War. In that era, bands of children who lived in Washington gathered at the Capitol Building on Easter Monday and set up their contests on the terraced lawns along the building's west front. By the 1870s, however, the nation's senators and congressmen had grown unhappy with the mess left behind by the egg rollers, as well as the toll the ever-growing number of participants took on the lawn. In 1876 Congress actually passed a law preventing anyone from using the grounds of the Capitol Building as a play area. President Rutherford B. Hayes (1877-1881) came to the rescue, permitting area youngsters to transfer their egg rolling contest to the White House lawn. The games have continued at the White House on Easter Monday since that time, with brief exceptions during World War I, World War II, and the White House remodeling that took place after the Second World War.

In the early days of the White House egg rolling contests, the children themselves organized the games. As the years went by, however, White House staff members became more involved in organizing the popular event. In recent years it has taken about 500 volunteers in addition to White House staff members to pull off this Easter extravaganza. These workers prepare by hard boiling between 5,000 and 10,000 eggs. On Easter Monday, about 30,000 people attend the event, including the young contest participants (children under the age of seven) and their family members. The free tickets given to the children specify the time at which they and their family members must arrive for their egg rolling heat. Contest participants are given a souvenir wooden egg to take home with them. In a twist of the rules governing many other events, all adults must be accompanied by children.

Emmaus Walk

The people of central Europe sometimes honor Easter Monday with an Emmaus Walk. These walks into the countryside for an outdoor meal symbolize the story of the first appearance of the risen Jesus as told in the Gospel According to Luke (Luke 24:13-35). In this account, Jesus appears to two of his former companions as the men journey on foot from Jerusalem to a small town called Emmaus. The three men talk about spiritual matters as they walk, and the stranger reveals heretofore hidden meanings in the scriptures to Jesus' followers. At the end of the journey, the men invite the inspiring stranger to spend the night and share a meal with them. When Jesus breaks bread with them, the men recognize the stranger as Jesus. In the same instant, Jesus disappears.

In past times, Emmaus Walks may have involved some religious activities. Today, however, they usually involve groups of friends and family members traveling together to a pretty spot in the countryside for a picnic, games, music, and other relaxing leisure activities. In some places, church congregations may organize events of these kinds.

Switching

In central and northern Europe, some people observe Easter Monday by striking one another lightly with birch or willow wands. Folklorists refer to this custom as switching. In past times, custom permitted the boys to switch the girls on Easter Monday. The girls returned the favor on the following day, Easter Tuesday. This distinction has been abandoned in most places however, and both boys and girls practice the custom on Easter Monday.

FURTHER READING

Gulevich, Tanya. *Encyclopedia of Easter, Carnival, and Lent*. Detroit: Omnigraphics, 2004.

Henderson, Helene, ed. *Holidays, Festivals, and Celebrations of the World Dictionary*. 3rd ed. Detroit: Omnigraphics, 2005.

Weiser, Francis X. *The Easter Book*. New York: Harcourt, Brace and Company, 1954.

WEB SITE

White House
www.whitehouse.gov/easter/2006

Ebisu Festival
(Toka Ebisu)

Type of Holiday: Religious (Shinto)
Date of Observation: January 9-11, or October 20
Where Celebrated: Japan
Symbols and Customs: Bamboo Branch, Fukumusume Girls, Sea Bream

ORIGINS

During Japan's Ebisu festival people seek the blessing of Ebisu, the Shinto god of good fortune, honest labor, and financial success. Shinto is an ancient Japanese religion that celebrates life and honors the sacred in the natural world. The name Shinto was first employed during the sixth century C.E. to differentiate indigenous religions in Japan from faith systems that originated in mainland Asia (primarily Buddhism and Confucianism). The word is derived from two Chinese characters, shen (gods) and tao (way). Loosely translated, Shinto means "way of the gods." Its roots lie in an ancient nature-based religion. Some important concepts in Shinto include the value of tradition, the reverence of nature, cleanliness (ritual purity), and the veneration of spirits called kami. Strictly speaking, kami are not deities. The literal translation of the word kami is "that which is hidden."

Kami (which is both the singular and plural term) are honored, but do not assert their powers upon humans in the traditional manner of deities or gods in other religions. People may be descended from the kami, and kami may influence the course of nature and events. The kami can bestow blessings, but they are not all benign. Kami are present in natural things such as trees, mountains, rocks, and rivers. They are embodied in religious relics, especially mirrors and jewels. They also include spirits of ancestors, local deities, holy people, and even political or literary figures. The human role is to venerate the kami and make offerings. The ultimate goal of Shinto is to uphold the harmony among humans and between people and nature. In this regard, the principle of all kami is to protect and sustain life.

Shinto believers have traditionally recognized many different spirits and gods. Ebisu is considered to be one of the Seven Gods of Luck, called the Shichifukujin in Japanese.

Some scholars believe that the Seven Gods of Luck may have originated in China in ancient times and later migrated to Japan. In addition to Ebisu, the other six gods are Benten, the goddess of music, arts, and beauty; Hotei, the god of happiness; Jurojin, the god of longevity; Fukurokujin, the god of wisdom; Bishamon, the god of spiritual enthusiasm; and Daikoku, the god of wealth. Artists often depict the Seven Gods of Luck traveling together on a ship, called the *takarabune,* or treasure ship.

The god Ebisu figures in one of the Japanese creation stories, in spite of his suspected Chinese origins. In one story the gods Izanagi and Izanami, the eighth pair of brother and sister gods to appear after the formation of heaven and earth out of chaos, gave birth to Ebisu. They called him Hiruko, or "leech child." Hiruko had no bones at birth, so his parents cast him adrift in a reed boat. He not only survived, but also healed, and become the god Ebisu. Artists usually create images of Ebisu that show him to be a short, fat, jolly man who carries a stick and a large fish, specifically, a SEA BREAM. One of his titles is "the laughing god." Ebisu may also appear with jellyfish, another symbol associated with the god. Japanese folklore teaches that Ebisu is somewhat deaf, and so he sometimes misses the summons to his own festival. Though Ebisu is associated with all the Seven Gods of Luck, he is most closely associated with Daikoku, the god of wealth. Often Ebisu, Daikoku, and Fukurokujin are pictured together as the "three gods of good fortune."

In coastal areas, Ebisu is understood to be a god of good luck for fisherman. In some towns, at the beginning of the fishing season fisherman dive blindfolded into the ocean and bring up stones from the bottom of the sea. They turn these rocks into shrines dedicated to Ebisu. Some fishermen call out his name as they cast their nets into the sea. In urban areas, people view Ebisu as the patron of merchants. Large urban shrines dedicated to Ebisu as a god of commerce can be traced back to the twelfth and thirteenth centuries. In farming zones, some people honor Ebisu as a god of agriculture.

The city of Osaka celebrates the Ebisu festival on January 9, 10, and 11, as do other towns in western Japan..This is one of the nation's most famous Ebisu celebrations. Osaka's Ebisu festival can be traced back to the Edo period in Japanese history (seventeenth through nineteenth centuries). January 9 is called "the eve of Ebisu." January 10 is the most important day of the festival, and the eleventh is called the "last helping of luck."

In Osaka Ebisu is known as the god of good luck in business. Over one million people visit Osaka's Imamiya Ebisu Shrine every year to pray for success in business and for happiness in life. Osaka's famous Ebisu bridge over the Dotonbori River was built to accommodate all the worshippers who come to pay their respects at Ebisu's shrine.

SYMBOLS AND CUSTOMS

Bamboo Branch

Local merchants sell bamboo branches decorated with lucky charms as festival souvenirs. Folklore suggests that these branches will help festival goers keep good luck with them. The lucky charms include such things as little replicas of sea bream, bales of rice, and old, gold coins. In addition to buying the branches, festival goers enjoy shouting out a common saying associated with the holiday, "business is thriving, fetch the bamboo branch!" People save these lucky bamboo branches and display them in their homes and shops when the festival is over.

Fukumusume Girls

The Fukumusume girls, or "daughters of happiness," parade through the streets on January 10. This event, called the "good luck palanquin parade," features around 600 participants, including celebrities, geishas, and fukumusume girls. Bearers carry the fukumusume on palanquins. The fukumusume ladies distribute good luck charms to the crowds. These charms include decorated bamboo branches and miniature sea bream tokens. In Osaka, more than 3,000 young ladies apply each year for around fifty positions as festival fukumusume. Those selected as fukumusume experience a big boost in their status, and many receive marriage proposals as a result of fulfilling this role.

Sea Bream

The sea bream is considered to be one of the symbols of the god Ebisu. In Osaka on January 10, there is a special market dedicated to the sale of sea bream. Sea bream is often served on special occasions in Japan and is one the nation's favorite fishes. The custom of celebrating with sea bream may have developed because the Japanese name for the fish, *mede-tai*, can also mean "celebratory," "admirable," or "lucky." Its association with Ebisu has also turned sea bream into a symbol of prosperity.

FURTHER READING

Bellenir, Karen. *Religious Holidays and Calendars*. 3rd ed. Detroit: Omnigraphics, 2004.

Henderson, Helene, ed. *Holidays, Festivals and Celebrations of the World Dictionary*. 3rd ed. Detroit: Omnigraphics, 2005.

WEB SITES

"Encyclopedia of Shinto," Kokugakuin University, Tokyo, Japan
eos.kokugakuin.ac.jp/modules/xwords/entry.php?entryID=206

Japan National Tourist Organization
www.jnto.go.jp/eng/indepth/history/traditionalevents/a04_fes_toka.html

National Museum of Ethnology, Osaka, Japan
www.kikoman.com/forum/099/ff009.html

Egungun Festival

Type of Holiday: Religious (Yoruba)
Date of Observation: June
Where Celebrated: Nigeria, Brazil
Symbols and Customs: Masks, Yam

ORIGINS

The Egungun Festival is part of the religious practices of the Yoruba people of Ede, Nigeria. The Yoruba religion is based on oral traditions. Beliefs and practices are preserved by passing history, customs, and traditions from one generation to the next. Authority for interpreting events and establishing proper conduct of ethics and morals rests with a bureaucratic structure of rulers who function in both religious and political realms.

According to traditional Yoruba belief, all power in the universe emanates from a supreme being, Olodumare. Olodumare, known as the owner of everlasting abundance, among many other praise names, holds all power and is the giver of all life. Olodumare is the mystical remote source of all things and is not identified by gender. All that exists, including supernatural divine realities and natural earth realities, are part of Olodumare.

As the supreme almighty source, Olodumare is directly involved in the affairs of the earth through a complex core of sub-divinities called orisa. The orisa are authoritative divine emissaries and serve as intermediaries between the people of earth and Olodumare. They are the major objects of veneration and ritual obligation. The names and number of orisa vary according to national and local custom, but they number in the hundreds. Some are more nationally known while others may be only venerated according to localized custom.

The Egungun is a secret society among the Yoruba people of Nigeria. A hereditary chief called the Alagba heads the society, which celebrates its most important festival in June. Members of the society come to the marketplace and perform dances for the Timi, or chief, wearing MASKS that represent the spirits of deceased ancestors. Which spirits are worshipped each year is decided by the Ifa oracle. A man who is instructed by the oracle to worship his ancestor has a special mask made for the dance. Although he himself doesn't participate in the dance, he is considered the owner of the mask. He takes it to the Alagba, along with appropriate gifts, and the Alagba secretly appoints a member of the Egungun society to wear it during the festival.

About thirty masqueraders in long, colorful robes gather in a grove not far from town and then arrive as a group to perform their dance in the marketplace. Some Egungun dance in one place, while others make sudden movements toward the surrounding spectators. When one leaps forward, the young men acting as guards lash out with their whips to prevent anyone from coming near the masked figure. The high point of the festival is the appearance of Andu, the most important and powerful mask. The other masqueraders clear a path for him, and the drums beat louder and faster as Andu rushes into the marketplace.

It is the Egungun who listen to the requests of the living and carry their messages back to the ancestral community in heaven. Women who are having difficulty conceiving, for example, frequently ask the masked figures to grant them children. The responses of the Egungun can be fierce as well as generous. They expect their descendants to uphold the highest moral standards and are quick to expose the evil thoughts that neighbors harbor against one another. Even though the annual appearance of the Egungun in the streets of Yoruba towns and villages inspires a certain amount of fear, it also assures the people of their continued guidance.

The word "Egungun" is sometimes translated literally as "bone" or "skeleton." This is probably the result of a misunderstanding of the correct tone, since Yoruba is a tonal language. When the word is pronounced with the correct tone, it means "masqueraders." Today there is a thriving community of Egungun worshippers in Salvador da Bahia, Brazil, where they wear the colorful costumes of their Nigerian counterparts.

SYMBOLS AND CUSTOMS

Masks

Some of the Egungun masks consist of colored cloth and leather that cover the entire body while the dancer looks out through a closely knitted net. Others are wooden masks worn in front of the face, and still others are carved heads worn on top of the dancer's own head. The mask-wearers are always accompanied by men holding sticks or whips who keep the crowd from getting too close. This is because it is considered extremely dangerous to approach the spirits of the deceased. According to an old Yoruban proverb, "Even a Prince cannot go near an Egungun with impunity." At one time, anyone who saw even part of the man who was wearing the mask could be put to death as a punishment.

Each mask represents the spirit of a particular ancestor. In reality, everyone knows that there is a human being beneath the mask. But it is believed that the spirit of the deceased may be persuaded to enter into the masquerader while he is dancing. At the height of the dance, every true Egungun enters into a trance-like state and speaks with a voice he has never used before.

Yam

The Yoruba honor the annual return of the ancestors to the world of the living during the season of the yam harvest. Their arrival not only brings a blessing upon the crops, but stands as a reminder that it was the ancestors who first cultivated Yoruba land.

When a Yoruba man dies, the Egungun are especially concerned about the separation of the dead from their former life. So after a certain amount of time has elapsed, the widow is led to a mound of earth that represents her husband. From this she takes a yam, which symbolizes the last gift she will receive from him. Then, a week or so later, one of the Egungun visits her house and calls to the dead person in a high-pitched or nasal voice. This is a signal for the dead person to leave the earth and his family behind.

FURTHER READING

Bellenir, Karen. *Religious Holidays and Calendars*. 3rd ed. Detroit: Omnigraphics, 2004.

Henderson, Helene, ed. *Holidays, Festivals, and Celebrations of the World Dictionary*. 3rd ed. Detroit: Omnigraphics, 2005.

King, Noel Q. *Religions of Africa: A Pilgrimage into Traditional Religions*. New York: Harper & Row, 1970.

MacDonald, Margaret R., ed. *The Folklore of World Holidays*. Detroit: Gale Research, 1992.

Murphy, Joseph M. *Santería: African Spirits in America*. Boston: Beacon Press, 1988.

WEB SITE

Egba-Egbado Descendants Association
www.egbaegbado.org/egba14.htm

Ember Days

Type of Holiday: Religious (Christian)
Date of Observation: Four times a year, in March, May/June, September, and December
Where Celebrated: England, France, Germany, Spain, United States, and by Christians all over the West; not observed in the Eastern Church
Symbols and Customs: Fasting, Ordination of Priests
Related Holidays: Ash Wednesday, Feast of the Exaltation of the Cross, Pentecost (Whitsunday), Rogation Days, St. Lucy's Day

ORIGINS

Ember Days is a Christian religious festival celebrated in the Western Church. The word Christian refers to a follower of Christ, a title derived from the Greek word meaning Messiah or Anointed One. The Christ of Christianity is Jesus of Nazareth, a man born between 7 and 4 B.C.E. in the region of Palestine. According to Christian teaching, Jesus was killed by Roman authorities using a form of execution called crucifixion (a term meaning he was nailed to a cross and hung from it until he died) in about the year 30 C.E. After his death, he rose back to life. His death and resurrection provide a way by which people can be reconciled with God. In remembrance of Jesus' death and resurrection, the cross serves as a fundamental symbol in Christianity.

With nearly two billion believers in countries around the globe, Christianity is the largest of the world's religions. There is no one central authority for all of Christianity. The pope (the bishop of Rome) is the authority for the Roman Catholic Church, but other sects look to other authorities. Orthodox communities look to patriarchs and emphasize doctrinal agreement and traditional practice. Protestant communities focus on individual conscience. The Roman Catholic and Protestant churches are often referred to as the Western Church, while the Orthodox churches may also be called the Eastern Church. All three main branches of Christianity acknowledge the authority of Christian scriptures, a compilation of writings assembled into a document called the Bible. Methods of biblical interpretation vary among the different Christian sects.

Ember Days didn't start out as a Christian event; instead, it was created by the early Romans. They were both pagans and farmers, and they wanted to make sure that the gods looked favorably upon them at certain crucial times of the year. They held a Feast of Sowing (*Feriae Sementivae*) between mid-November and the **WINTER SOLSTICE**, a Harvest Feast (*Feriae Messis*) in June or July for the grain harvest, and a Feast of Wine (*Vinalia*) in September before the **AUTUMN EQUINOX**.

When Christianity came to Rome, these pagan festivals fell out of favor, but the idea of praying for God's blessing at the beginning of the various agricultural seasons persisted. The early Christians decided to introduce their own seasonal prayer festivals, which roughly coincided with the dates of the earlier pagan festivals but involved FASTING rather than feasting. It was Pope Callistus I in the third century who first issued regulations concerning this celebration of the "Three Seasons." A fourth period of prayer, occurring in March, was added not long after, probably in the fourth century. The change seems to have been motivated by the mention of four fasting periods in the Old Testament (in the Book of Zechariah), and by the fact that the year contains four natural seasons.

By the early sixth century, the celebration of the so-called Ember Days was well established, at least in Rome. The only thing that had not been set was the exact dates. It was Pope Gregory VII who decided in 1095 that the Ember Days would be celebrated on the Wednesday, Friday, and Saturday of the weeks following the first Sunday in **LENT**, Whitsunday or **PENTECOST**, the Feast of the **EXALTATION OF THE CROSS** (September 14), and **ST. LUCY'S DAY** (December 13). The custom of setting aside these four periods of time for prayer and fasting eventually spread to other parts of Italy and from there to Spain, France, Germany, and elsewhere.

Why were they called the Ember Days? The word *ember* appears to have derived from the Anglo-Saxon *ymbren*, meaning "course" or "circuit," since the Ember Days marked the four quarters of the year and thus described the revolution of time. *Ember* is also an abbreviation of the German *Quatember*, which in turn is a corruption of the Latin *Quatuor Tempora*, or "Four Seasons." Another theory is that the name came from the early practice of sprinkling ashes on the head on fast days as a token of humility, and from the custom of eating only cakes baked upon embers, known as "emberbread."

The weeks in which these fast days occur are called "Ember Weeks," and the Friday in each of these four weeks is known as "Golden Friday."

SYMBOLS AND CUSTOMS

Fasting

Over the centuries, the Ember Days lost the festive character of the early pagan seasonal celebrations and became more somber, with an emphasis on penance and abstinence. The ancient Jewish custom of fasting two days each week, usually

Monday and Thursday, was changed by the early Christians to a Wednesday and Friday fast, since Christ had been betrayed by Judas on a Wednesday and had died on the cross on Friday. Saturday was added as one of the weekly fast days in Rome during the fourth century, probably because this was the day on which the Apostles fasted and mourned while Christ rested in his tomb.

The custom of fasting three days a week, which was at one time prescribed by law, was eventually confined to the four Ember Weeks by Pope Callistus I in the third century. By the ninth century, fasting during these periods was widespread throughout Europe. In 1966 the Roman Catholic Church eliminated the obligation to fast and turned the Ember Days into a period of prayer for various needs.

Ordination of Priests

In 494 Pope Gelasius I decided that deacons and priests would receive their holy orders on the four Ember Saturdays. Because candidates for the priesthood traditionally fasted and prayed for a few days before being ordained, it made sense to schedule the ordinations at the end of the four Ember Weeks, which were already established as periods of prayer and fasting.

In recent centuries, the Ember Weeks have been emphasized as a time for special prayer on the part of those who hope to become priests. But it is still traditional for priests in both the Roman Catholic Church and the Church of England to be ordained on an Ember Saturday.

FURTHER READING

Bellenir, Karen. *Religious Holidays and Calendars*. 3rd ed. Detroit: Omnigraphics, 2004.

Brewster, H. Pomeroy. *Saints and Festivals of the Christian Church*. 1904. Reprint. Detroit: Omnigraphics, 1990.

Chambers, Robert. *The Book of Days*. 2 vols. 1862-64. Reprint. Detroit: Omnigraphics, 1990.

Crim, Keith R. *The Perennial Dictionary of World Religions*. San Francisco: Harper & Row, 1989.

Dunkling, Leslie. *A Dictionary of Days*. New York: Facts on File, 1988.

Gwynne, Rev. Walker. *The Christian Year: Its Purpose and Its History*. 1917. Reprint. Detroit: Omnigraphics, 1990.

Harper, Howard V. *Days and Customs of All Faiths*. 1957. Reprint. Detroit: Omnigraphics, 1990.

Henderson, Helene, ed. *Holidays, Festivals, and Celebrations of the World Dictionary*. 3rd ed. Detroit: Omnigraphics, 2005.

Jobes, Gertrude. *Dictionary of Mythology, Folklore, and Symbols.* New York: Scarecrow Press, 1962.

Weiser, Franz Xaver. *Handbook of Christian Feasts and Customs.* New York: Harcourt, Brace, 1958.

WEB SITE

New Advent Catholic Encyclopedia
www.newadvent.org/cathen/05399b.htm

Epiphany, Feast of the (Twelfth Day, Three Kings' Day, Feast of Jordan)

Type of Holiday: Religious (Christian)
Date of Observation: January 6
Where Celebrated: Europe, Great Britain, Greece, South America, and throughout the Christian world
Symbols and Customs: Befana, Blessing of the Waters, Frankincense, Gold, Kings' Cake, Magi, Myrrh, Star Boys, Star of Bethlehem
Related Holidays: Christmas, Twelfth Night

ORIGINS

Epiphany is a Christian holiday related to the birth of Jesus Christ. The word Christian refers to a follower of Christ, a title derived from the Greek word meaning Messiah or Anointed One. The Christ of Christianity is Jesus of Nazareth, a man born between 7 and 4 B.C.E. in the region of Palestine. According to Christian teaching, Jesus was killed by Roman authorities using a form of execution called crucifixion (a term meaning he was nailed to a cross and hung from it until he died) in about the year 30 C.E. After his death, he rose back to life. His death and resurrection provide a way by which people can be reconciled with God. In remembrance of Jesus' death and resurrection, the cross serves as a fundamental symbol in Christianity.

With nearly two billion believers in countries around the globe, Christianity is the largest of the world's religions. There is no one central authority for all of Christianity. The pope (the bishop of Rome) is the authority for the Roman Catholic Church, but other sects look to other authorities. Orthodox communities look to patriarchs and emphasize doctrinal agreement and traditional practice. Protestant communities focus on individual conscience. The Roman Catholic and Protestant churches are often referred to as the Western Church, while the Orthodox churches may also be called the Eastern Church. All three main branches of Christianity acknowledge the authority of Christian scriptures, a compilation of writings assembled into a document called the Bible. Methods of biblical interpretation vary among the different Christian sects.

The word Epiphany means "manifestation" or "showing." In the ancient Greek and Roman world, the term *epiphaneia* referred to an occasion on which a king or emperor made an official state visit to a city, showing himself publicly to his people. Early Christians celebrated the birth of Jesus on this day—the day on which God manifested himself in human form. Nowadays Christians celebrate the Nativity on **CHRISTMAS**, December 25. But the original celebration took place on January 6, a date that coincided with an ancient Egyptian **WINTER SOLSTICE** festival held in honor of the sun god. As was often the case, early Church officials simply replaced this pagan festival with a Christian feast.

The feast of the Epiphany started out as a nativity celebration and stayed that way for more than 200 years. It came to Europe during the fourth century, at about the same time that the new feast of Christmas was being established in Rome. Once Christmas took hold, the purpose of Epiphany shifted. In the Western Church, it became a celebration of the adoration of the Magi—the day on which the three Wise Men reached the manger in Bethlehem and worshipped the Christ Child. In the East, it became a celebration of Jesus' baptism in the River Jordan, when the Holy Spirit descended in the form of a dove and proclaimed him the Son of God. For this reason, it is sometimes referred to as either Three Kings' Day or the Feast of Jordan. Both represent occasions on which the divinity of Jesus was manifested or revealed to humankind.

For most of the Christian world today, Epiphany marks the end of the "Twelve Days of Christmas"—an appropriate time to take down Christmas decorations and greenery. In some countries, it is the day on which the last gift of the holiday season is exchanged.

SYMBOLS AND CUSTOMS

Befana

According to an old Italian legend, Befana was sweeping her house when the Magi stopped by on their way to Bethlehem to bring gifts to the Christ Child. They invited her to come along with them, but she said she was too busy. She later regretted her decision and tried to catch up with them, but she got lost and never reached the manger. Every year she passes through Italy in her continuing search for the *Bambino*, hoping that each child to whom she brings gifts is the one she has been seeking.

The name Befana is actually a corruption of the Italian word for Epiphany. She is a cross between a witch and a fairy queen, and she plays much the same role in Italy as Santa Claus does in the United States. Children write letters to her, asking for specific presents. She slides down the chimney on Epiphany Eve and fills their socks and shoes with toys. If they misbehave, their parents threaten to tell La Befana to leave only pebbles, charcoal, or ashes. In most Italian cities and towns, young people gather in the streets on Epiphany to honor La Befana with trumpets, tambourines, drums, and tin horns—a survival, perhaps, of the pagan custom of scaring off demons with loud noises.

Blessing of the Waters

In the East, the custom of blessing the waters on Epiphany goes back to the holiday's origins as a commemoration of Jesus' baptism in the River Jordan. It is traditional there to bless both the baptismal water in the church and the waters of a nearby river or fountain. In Egypt, the Nile was blessed on this day for many centuries. The entire Christian population would plunge into its waters three times, then drive their cattle and other farm animals into the river. In Rome, the water that was blessed in the church on this day was believed to stay fresh all year.

The Blessing of the Waters remains an important symbolic act on Epiphany in all countries where the Greek Orthodox Church prevails. In Greece, the "Great Blessing" is an elaborate celebration in seaports and coastal towns, where people depend on the water for their livelihood. Sometimes a cross is thrown into the water and people dive after it, struggling to see who can bring it to the surface. After the cross has been recovered, the people take home some of the sanctified water to drink and to sprinkle around their homes and fields. The priest may bless a container of clean water before immersing a cross and raising it again, symbolizing the baptism of Christ. Holy water drawn on this day is used for baptisms and other sacraments throughout the year.

Some scholars believe that the practice of blessing the waters is actually a Christianized version of a primitive ritual designed to encourage rain by imitating a good drenching.

Frankincense

The sap of the frankincense tree dries into hard, yellowish-brown lumps of gum resin that in ancient times were burned as incense. The rising fumes may have offered worshippers a visual image of their prayers ascending to heaven, which would explain the widespread use of incense in churches. Frankincense is mentioned numerous times in the Old Testatment and was one of the four components of the sacred incense burned by the Jewish priests in the Sanctuary. Because of its close relationship with worship, the Magi's gift of frankincense has traditionally been interpreted as a recognition of Jesus' divinity. Because it was a luxury that was difficult to obtain and was affordable only by the rich, the Magi's gift of frankincense may also have signified their recognition of Jesus' great worth.

Gold

No other metal is named as frequently in the Bible as gold. It is most often referred to as a form of worldly wealth, but it also serves as a symbol of spiritual wealth. Gold was rarer in biblical times than it is today, and for the most part, only kings or the very wealthy possessed it. As one of the three gifts that the Magi offered to the baby Jesus, gold is most often interpreted as a symbol of Jesus' kingship or His spiritual authority.

Kings' Cake

Serving a cake in which a bean or charm has been hidden is an old Epiphany tradition that can be traced back to the large plum cake served at the ancient Roman **SATURNALIA**. Whoever found the bean hidden in his piece of plum cake was dubbed "King of the Bean" and ruled over the festivities for the next 12 days. The bean was considered a sacred vegetable in ancient times.

In France, where Epiphany is called *Le Jour des Rois* (Day of the Kings), the *Galette des Rois* or Kings' Cake is a puff pastry cake in which a bean (*fève*) has been concealed. Whoever finds it is crowned *Roi de la Fève*. If it's a girl, she becomes the Queen and must choose a King. It is customary to save a portion of the cake and set it aside for the Magi, a particular saint, or the Lord himself. This portion, called *la part du bon Dieu,* was usually given to the poor after the feast was over. The French Kings' Cake goes back at least as far as the thirteenth century, and similar customs can be found in Austria, Germany, Holland, England, and Canada. Sometimes a bean and a pea are hidden in the cake. The person who finds the pea is crowned Queen, with the bean going to the King. In Macedonia, a "St. Basil's Cake" is served on New Year's Eve, with a coin and a cross of green twigs baked inside. Whoever finds either one will prosper during the coming year.

The first Kings' Cakes were made of flour, honey, ginger, and pepper; some were ordinary plum cakes. By the end of the eighteenth century, however, they were elaborately decorated confections with brightly colored figures made of sugar or plaster. In England under the reign of King George IV, these very expensive cakes were displayed in every confectioner's shop in London.

Magi

The Three Kings or Magi who play such an important role in the story of Jesus' birth are largely fictitious creations. They are believed to have been wise men famous for their knowledge of astrology and astronomy. On the night of Jesus' birth, they noticed a star shining in the west, more brightly than any star they had ever seen before. They decided to follow it, and when it stood still over Bethlehem, they found the Christ Child in the manger (*see* STAR OF BETHLEHEM).

The Bible doesn't say anything about how many Wise Men there were, what they were named, or where they came from. The word "Magi" comes from the Latin meaning "magician" or "astrologer," and the earliest pictures of the Wise Men show them dressed quite differently from the kings' robes in which they began to appear from the tenth century onward. Their names—Caspar, Melchior, and Balthasar—were not standardized until the Middle Ages, and in early Christian paintings and mosaics there are often as many as 12 of them. But the Bible says that they offered three gifts to the Christ Child, which is probably why their number was eventually fixed at three.

Caspar, who is young and beardless with a ruddy complexion, is said to have been the king of Tarsus (southern Turkey), the land of MYRRH. Melchior, often depicted as an old man with white hair and a long beard, is said to have been the king of Arabia, the land of GOLD. Balthasar, of dark complexion with a heavy beard, came from Saba (near modern-day Yemen), a land where FRANKINCENSE flowed from the trees. Together the Three Kings symbolize the three races of humankind, descended from Noah's sons Ham, Shem, and Japheth.

Legend has it that many years after their trip to Bethlehem, the Magi were visited by St. Thomas, who instructed them in the ways of Christianity and baptized them. They were then ordained to the priesthood and later made bishops. At the end of their lives, the Star of Bethlehem appeared one more time, and they were reunited. Their relics were brought to Constantinople in the fifth century, transferred to Milan a hundred years later, and eventually deposited in Cologne, Germany. Their shrine there is a popular destination for pilgrimages.

In Italy and Spanish-speaking countries, toy store employees can often be seen dressed up as the Magi on Epiphany Day, delivering gifts to children. In Madrid, groups of people roam about on Epiphany Eve with bells and pots and pans, carrying torches and tall ladders to help them see whether the Three Kings are on their way.

Myrrh

The sap of the myrrh tree dries into hard, reddish-brown lumps of gum resin. Although unfamiliar to us today, in ancient times myrrh was a precious and much sought-after substance that was most commonly used as a medicine, particularly for treating sores in the mouth, infections, coughs, and worms. Shortly before his crucifixion, Jesus was offered a cup of wine mixed with myrrh (Mark 15:23), which suggests that it was also used as a painkiller. According to the Gospel of John, Jesus' body was treated with myrrh and aloe before being wrapped in cloth for burial (John 19:39).

Myrrh was highly valued as an ingredient in perfume and incense as well. Although it has a pleasant smell, it has a bitter taste; in fact, the English word "myrrh" comes from the Hebrew and Arabic terms for "bitter." The Hebrews made myrrh one of the primary ingredients of the holy oil with which they anointed their priests and the sacred objects in their temples. Like FRANKINCENSE, it came from Arabia and was considered a luxury affordable only by the wealthy.

Due to its bitterness, the gift of myrrh that the Magi brought to the infant Jesus has often been interpreted as a symbol of the hardships that He would suffer in His adult life. The fact that myrrh was used in embalming has led some to assert that myrrh represents Jesus' humanity. Another interpretation suggests that because it had so many medicinal uses, myrrh must represent Jesus' role as a healer of body and spirit. Finally, it might be argued that the gift of myrrh symbolizes Jesus' role as a Jewish religious leader, since it was a main ingredient in the holy oil used to anoint Jewish high priests.

Star Boys

In parts of central Europe and Scandinavia, troupes of costumed children, known as "star boys," entertain their neighbors with Christmas carols and dramas on Epiphany. One member of the group carries a long pole, from which a bright star, representing the STAR OF BETHLEHEM, dangles. Children dressed as the MAGI follow the star, sometimes accompanied by other figures associated with the Nativity. In some areas, a child dressed as Judas collects the coins that onlookers offer in return for the children's performances. In many areas, however, neighbors offer the group food and drink rather than money.

The yearly trek of the star boys reminds people of the journey of the Magi and their final arrival at the stable in Bethlehem on Epiphany. Researchers speculate that this custom evolved out of medieval Nativity plays reenacting the story of the Three Kings.

Star of Bethlehem

In the Gospel according to Matthew (2:2-14), we learn that an unusually bright star guided the MAGI to Bethlehem. The Three Kings interpreted this star as a sign that a great person was about to be born, and they followed it to the place directly above which it shone. There, in Bethlehem, they recognized Jesus as the newborn king whose birth the star foretold.

Did such a star really appear in the heavens at the time of Jesus' birth? Biblical scholars and astronomers have never been able to come up with a definitive answer to this question because the two most important pieces of information necessary to solve the mystery are themselves unclear. First, Matthew's account of the story provides only a vague mention of the star. Second, the exact year of Jesus' birth remains in doubt, making it difficult to scan astronomical records from the time and search for unusual happenings in the sky. Matthew might have been referring to a comet, although comets were generally thought to herald disaster in ancient times. The Magi might have been spurred into action by a conjunction—two or more planets appearing to draw very near each other in the sky—or they might have witnessed an exploding star, or nova. Many Christians feel that a scientific explanation for the Star of Bethlehem is not needed, since the story of the Star is a symbolic rather than a historical account—an attempt to convey spiritual truths rather than material facts.

Whatever truth there is to the story, the star is an important symbol of both **CHRISTMAS** and Epiphany. Stars often decorate the tops of Christmas trees and appear in other Christmas decorations. Old Christmas customs, such as the cavorting of the STAR BOYS, also make use of this symbol. Finally, it is common for modern planetariums to present special programs during the holiday season that explore the many theories about the Star of Bethlehem.

FURTHER READING

Bellenir, Karen. *Religious Holidays and Calendars*. 3rd ed. Detroit: Omnigraphics, 2004.

Crippen, T.G. *Christmas and Christmas Lore*. 1923. Reprint. Detroit: Omnigraphics, 1990.

Ferguson, George. *Signs and Symbols in Christian Art*. New York: Oxford University Press, 1954.

Gulevich, Tanya. *Encyclopedia of Christmas and New Year's Celebrations*. 2nd ed. Detroit: Omnigraphics, 2003.

Harper, Howard V. *Days and Customs of All Faiths*. 1957. Reprint. Detroit: Omnigraphics, 1990.

Henderson, Helene, ed. *Holidays, Festivals, and Celebrations of the World Dictionary*. 3rd ed. Detroit: Omnigraphics, 2005.

Ickis, Marguerite. *The Book of Festivals and Holidays the World Over*. New York: Dodd, Mead, 1970.

Ickis, Marguerite. *The Book of Religious Holidays and Celebrations*. New York: Dodd, Mead, 1966.

Leach, Maria, ed. *Funk & Wagnalls Standard Dictionary of Folklore, Mythology & Legend*. San Francisco: Harper & Row, 1984.

Metford, J.C.J. *The Christian Year*. New York: Crossroad, 1991.

Miles, Clement A. *Christmas in Ritual and Tradition, Christian and Pagan*. 1912. Reprint. Detroit: Omnigraphics, 1990.

Monks, James L. *Great Catholic Festivals*. New York: Henry Schuman, 1951.

Purdy, Susan. *Festivals for You to Celebrate*. Philadelphia: Lippincott, 1969.

Santino, Jack. *All Around the Year: Holidays and Celebrations in American Life*. Urbana: University of Illinois Press, 1994.

Spicer, Dorothy Gladys. *Festivals of Western Europe*. 1958. Reprint. Detroit: Omnigraphics, 1993.

Urlin, Ethel L. *Festivals, Holy Days, and Saints' Days*. 1915. Reprint. Detroit: Omnigraphics, 1992.

Weiser, Franz Xaver. *Handbook of Christian Feasts and Customs*. New York: Harcourt, Brace, 1958.

WEB SITES

Christian Resource Institute
www.cresourcei.org/cyepiph.html

New Advent Catholic Encyclopedia
www.newadvent.org/cathen/05504c.htm

Esala Perahera (Festival of the Sacred Tooth)

Type of Holiday: Religious (Buddhist, Hindu)
Date of Observation: Mid-June to mid-July for ten days
Where Celebrated: Kandy, Sri Lanka
Symbols and Customs: Raja the Tusker, Sacred Tooth, Water-Cutting Ceremony

ORIGINS

Observed annually in the city of Kandy, Sri Lanka (formerly Ceylon), this ten-day festival originally honored the Hindu gods Natha, Vishnu, Kataragama, and Pattini. Since 1775 it has also honored the SACRED TOOTH believed to have come from

Lord Buddha. Kandy, originally the capital of the independent kingdom of Kandy in the Sri Lankan highlands, is the site of the Dalada Maligava, or Temple of the Tooth, where the sacred relic is kept. The celebration originated in the fourth century, when the king of Kandy declared that the tooth be paraded annually through the city streets.

Although it appears that the roots of the festival were Hindu in origin, over the years the Buddhist celebration has merged with it. Today, it includes delegations from the four major Hindu temples as well as the Buddhist Temple of the Tooth. The highlight of the festival is a torchlight procession about a mile long, involving thousands of participants. Men snapping whips lead the parade, representing the whip-crackers who used to be special messengers to the king. They are followed by more than 200 elaborately decorated elephants, priests in flowing silver and gold robes, Kandyan dancers, flute players, and drummers. A huge elephant known as RAJA THE TUSKER carries the golden casket containing the sacred tooth, flanked on both sides by two other elephants. A canopy is held above the casket, and a white cloth is spread in the elephant's path as a symbol of respect. Spectators from Sri Lanka and other countries—not only Buddhists but Hindus, Muslims, and even some Christians—come to witness the spectacle. The procession is repeated every night for ten nights.

The largest and most important festival in Sri Lanka, the Esala Perahera is more of a nationalistic celebration than a religious one. The king, various government officials, and members of many different social castes in the community all participate in the Perahera or procession, which symbolizes the nation's victory over its enemies.

SYMBOLS AND CUSTOMS

Raja the Tusker

The Raja (or senior) tusker is the elephant chosen to carry the golden casket containing the sacred tooth of Buddha. Everyone admires the elephant's stately walk, which appears to keep time with the beating of the drums and the rhythm of the Kandyan dancers.

In 1959 there was an elephant stampede during the Esala Perahera. Raja the Tusker was nearly opposite the Queen's Hotel when word was received to turn back. Rather than joining the other elephants in the stampede, Raja went right back to the temple, where it is reported that he assisted the custodians of the sacred relic in returning it to safekeeping.

Sacred Tooth

The sacred tooth is supposed to have been brought to Ceylon in 311, concealed in the hair of an Indian princess, and kept in a temple at Anuradhapura. It was immediately recognized as the island's most precious possession, and the King of Lanka considered it the supreme symbol of his authority. It was stolen once or twice, but always recovered and put back in its shrine. Then in 1560 it was captured by the Portuguese and carried away in triumph to their stronghold of Goa on the western coast of India.

The tooth that belonged to Buddha was reportedly ground into powder, burned, and thrown into the sea by the Archbishop of Goa, a devoted Catholic who considered it a heathen idol. But many believe that it was only a copy of the tooth that was destroyed, and that the real tooth is still enshrined in the temple at Kandy. Those privileged enough to have seen the relic describe it as being nearly three inches high and about as thick as a man's little finger; if so, it could not have come from any human mouth. It is possible that the monks of Kandy found another tooth to replace the one they had lost.

The sacred tooth is housed in seven nesting caskets, carried on the back of RAJA THE TUSKER. When it is returned to the shrine at the end of the procession, a sacred dance is performed there.

Water-Cutting Ceremony

On the tenth and final day of the festival, the Esala Perahera procession is held in the daytime. It ends up on the banks of the Mahawali River just outside the city of Kandy. The tooth is carried down to the river and lowered into a special shelter or decorated boat. There, the priests of the four Hindu temples draw their swords and strike the water. Then they fill four clay bowls with the water and take them back to their temples, where they are kept until the following year's celebration. Sacred dances are then performed to ward off evil spirits and to seek the blessings of the gods.

The Kandy water-cutting ceremony symbolizes the return of the Sinhalese to Sri Lanka in the second century C.E. with 12,000 enemy captives from southern India. Nila, a Herculean soldier, divided the ocean with a blow of his sword, enabling the entire Sinhalese force to walk back to Sri Lanka.

FURTHER READING

Bellenir, Karen. *Religious Holidays and Calendars*. 3rd ed. Detroit: Omnigraphics, 2004.

Dobler, Lavinia G. *Customs and Holidays Around the World*. New York: Fleet Pub. Corp., 1962.

Henderson, Helene, ed. *Holidays, Festivals, and Celebrations of the World Dictionary*. 3rd ed. Detroit: Omnigraphics, 2005.

MacDonald, Margaret R., ed. *The Folklore of World Holidays*. Detroit: Gale Research, 1992.

Pike, Royston. *Round the Year with the World's Religions.* 1950. Reprint. Detroit: Omnigraphics, 1992.

Van Straalen, Alice. *The Book of Holidays Around the World.* New York: Dutton, 1986.

Welbon, Guy Richard, and Glenn E. Yocum. *Religious Festivals in South India and Sri Lanka.* New Delhi: Manohar Publications, 1982.

WEB SITE

City of Kandy
www.kandycity.org/festival.html

Exaltation of the Cross, Feast of the

Type of Holiday: Religious (Christian)
Date of Observation: September 14; formerly May 3 by Roman Catholics
Where Celebrated: Armenia, Dominican Republic, England, Ethiopia, Greece, Israel, Mexico, Philippines, Russia, Scotland, Sicily, South America, Spain, Syria, United States, and by Christians all over the world
Symbols and Customs: Bonfires, Elder Tree, Relics
Related Holidays: Maskal

ORIGINS

The Exaltation of the Cross is a Christian feast related to the crucifixion of Jesus Christ. The word Christian refers to a follower of Christ, a title derived from the Greek word meaning Messiah or Anointed One. The Christ of Christianity is Jesus of Nazareth, a man born between 7 and 4 B.C.E. in the region of Palestine. According to Christian teaching, Jesus was killed by Roman authorities using a form of execution called crucifixion (a term meaning he was nailed to a cross and hung from it until he died) in about the year 30 C.E. After his death, he rose back to life. His death and resurrection provide a way by which people can be reconciled with God. In remembrance of Jesus' death and resurrection, the cross serves as a fundamental symbol in Christianity.

With nearly two billion believers in countries around the globe, Christianity is the largest of the world's religions. There is no one central authority for all of Christianity. The pope (the bishop of Rome) is the authority for the Roman Catholic Church, but other sects look to other authorities. Orthodox communities look to

245

patriarchs and emphasize doctrinal agreement and traditional practice. Protestant communities focus on individual conscience. The Roman Catholic and Protestant churches are often referred to as the Western Church, while the Orthodox churches may also be called the Eastern Church. All three main branches of Christianity acknowledge the authority of Christian scriptures, a compilation of writings assembled into a document called the Bible. Methods of biblical interpretation vary among the different Christian sects.

What is known in the Eastern Church as the Feast of the Exaltation of the Cross is sometimes referred to as the Elevation, Recovery, or Adoration of the Cross. In the West, it is known as Holy Cross Day (Anglican), the Triumph of the cross (Roman Catholic), and sometimes the Invention of the Cross (from the Latin *invenire,* meaning "to find"). It commemorates three events: the finding of the cross on which Jesus was crucified, the dedication in 335 of the basilica built by Roman Emperor Constantine on the supposed site of Jesus' crucifixion, and the recovery in 629 by Emperor Heraclius of the relic of the cross that had been stolen by the Persians.

According to tradition, the Holy Sepulchre—the tomb where Jesus had been buried after the crucifixion—was later filled in with rubbish, and Emperor Hadrian (76-138 C.E.) built a temple to Venus on the site. Emperor Constantine (288-337 C.E.) wanted to build a Christian church there, and his mother Helena, although she was almost eighty, decided to visit the Holy Land herself and try to find the true cross. After a long search and many setbacks, Helena located three buried crosses. She was able to identify the one on which Christ had been crucified because a sick person touched it and was immediately healed. She brought back the fragments of what she believed was the true cross—although some people claim that over the centuries, enough "wood of the cross" has been found to build an entire ship.

After his mother returned from her successful journey, Constantine built two churches in Jerusalem: one on Mount Calvary, where the crucifixion took place, and the other over the Holy Sepulchre. They were dedicated on September 14, 335 C.E., the anniversary of the day on which the cross had been found. This September festival was initially confined to Jerusalem, where crowds of pilgrims came year after year to worship the sacred relic. In 614, Jerusalem was occupied by the Persians, and for thirteen years the relic remained in Persia. Christians were so overwhelmed with joy when the sacred relic was brought back to Constantinople in 629 by Emperor Heraclius that special coins were made to commemorate the event. The feast eventually spread through the East before being adopted in the West. Its celebration was widespread after Santa Croce in Gerusalemme (Basilica of the Holy Cross in Jerusalem) was built in Rome, where the major portion of the cross was enshrined.

Holy Cross Day is particularly popular in England, perhaps because Helena is believed to have been the daughter of a British king. Many English churches have

"Holy Cross" or "Holy Rood" in their names—*rood* referring to the wood of which the cross was made—and former names for this day include Holy Rood Day, Roodmas (Rood Mass), and Crouchmas (Cross Mass).

SYMBOLS AND CUSTOMS

Bonfires

The traditional harvest festival of the Incas—the early South American Indians whose empire at one time extended for more than 2,000 miles along the Pacific coast of South America and up into the Andes Mountains—was known as Aymuray. It was a nighttime festival in honor of the long winter nights to come and the life-giving powers sent from heaven to make the earth fertile. Today, in Peru and parts of neighboring countries where about five million descendants of the Incas still live, Aymuray has been replaced by the Christian Feast of the Invention of the Cross. The celebration is a curious mixture of Christian and Incan customs. All night long, bonfires burn along the highways and on mountaintops, where crosses have also been erected. In towns and villages, altars are set up with a lighted cross in the background hung with brightly-colored ornaments and flowers. The next day, crosses are carried in procession to the nearest church, where a Mass is said for them.

There are other links between this Christian feast and more ancient, pagan festivals. For example, in Syria, it is traditional to build fires on rooftops and then leap over the flames on September 14—a typically pagan custom that is probably a survival of an ancient fire festival.

Elder Tree

There have been many theories about the kind of wood from which the cross was made. People in some middle European countries believed that it was made from an elder tree, and this made the tree so repulsive to them that they would rather go without fuel to heat their homes and cook their food than resort to burning elder wood, which was often more plentiful than any other kind.

Another theory was that the cross was made from the wood of an aspen tree, and that the reason the leaves of the aspen appear to be in constant motion is that ever since the crucifixion, the aspen has trembled at the recollection of the role it played in this terrible event. Another explanation is that because the aspen was the only tree that did *not* tremble on the day that Christ was crucified, it was doomed to quiver forever thereafter.

Still another theory is that the cross was made from the wood of the mistletoe, which used to grow as a tall, sturdy tree but was punished for its part in the crucifixion by being reduced to the stunted, parasitic plant it is today.

Relics

In addition to the fragments of wood that St. Helena found, she also discovered the four nails that she believed had been hammered into Jesus' hands and feet, and the small plaque that hung above his body, which bore the sarcastic inscription "INRI" (for *Iesus Nazarenus Rex Iudaeorum*, Latin for "Jesus of Nazareth, King of the Jews"). Helena left some of the fragments of the cross at Jerusalem, where they were kept in a silver case and venerated every year on September 14. On her way home from Jerusalem, she gave some fragments to the city of Constantinople and then brought the major portion of the cross to Rome, where a basilica was built to enshrine it.

Helena is said to have thrown one of the nails into the Adriatic Sea when her ship was tossed by a storm—an act that brought an immediate halt to the turbulent weather. The other three nails were taken to Rome to Emperor Constantine: Two of them were placed in his crown, and the third was later brought to France by Charlemagne.

Is there any way to authenticate Helena's findings? Most of the relics currently enshrined in churches have been dated back to the fourth century, and the plaque, now preserved in Santa Croce in Gerusalemme, would seem to be the most difficult item to fake. But scholars have always admitted it was possible that Helena was somehow tricked, and that what she mistook for the remains of the cross were actually fragments of timber that had been part of a builder's waste pile long ago.

FURTHER READING

Bellenir, Karen. *Religious Holidays and Calendars*. 3rd ed. Detroit: Omnigraphics, 2004.

Brewster, H. Pomeroy. *Saints and Festivals of the Christian Church*. 1904. Reprint. Detroit: Omnigraphics, 1990.

Chambers, Robert. *The Book of Days*. 2 vols. 1862-64. Reprint. Detroit: Omnigraphics, 1990.

Cohen, Hennig, and Tristram Potter Coffin. *The Folklore of American Holidays*. 3rd ed. Detroit: Gale Research, 1999.

Coulson, John, ed. *The Saints: A Concise Biographical Dictionary*. New York: Hawthorn Books, 1958.

Harper, Howard V. *Days and Customs of All Faiths*. 1957. Reprint. Detroit: Omnigraphics, 1990.

Helfman, Elizabeth. *Celebrating Nature: Rites and Ceremonies Around the World*. New York: Seabury Press, 1969.

Henderson, Helene, ed. *Holidays, Festivals, and Celebrations of the World Dictionary*. 3rd ed. Detroit: Omnigraphics, 2005.

MacDonald, Margaret R., ed. *The Folklore of World Holidays*. Detroit: Gale Research, 1992.

Spicer, Dorothy Gladys. *The Book of Festivals*. 1937. Reprint. Detroit: Omnigraphics, 1990.

Urlin, Ethel L. *Festivals, Holy Days, and Saints' Days*. 1915. Reprint. Detroit: Omnigraphics, 1992.

Van Straalen, Alice. *The Book of Holidays Around the World*. New York: Dutton, 1986.

WEB SITE

Greek Orthodox Archdiocese of Australia
home.it.net.au/~jgrapsas/pages/elevation.htm

Father's Day

Type of Holiday: Promotional
Date of Observation: Third Sunday in June
Where Celebrated: United States
Symbols and Customs: Necktie, Rose
Related Holidays: Mother's Day

ORIGINS

The idea of setting aside a day especially for fathers was at least partially inspired by the success of **MOTHER'S DAY**, established in 1914. Sonora Smart Dodd from Spokane, Washington, was listening to a Mother's Day sermon in church and decided that the nation's fathers deserved a similar day of recognition. One of six children raised by her father after her mother's death in 1898, Dodd began working through Protestant churches and local groups in Spokane to promote the holiday. She circulated a petition suggesting the third Sunday in June as an appropriate time and urging people to wear a ROSE that day in honor of their fathers.

Because the petition was originally circulated among ministers and church organizations, the earliest observances took place in churches and modeled themselves on Mother's Day rituals. Father's Day was also seen as a good opportunity to underscore the "masculine" side of Christianity and to remind fathers of their obligation to look after their families' spiritual welfare.

Dodd formed a committee to promote the new celebration by getting political endorsements, answering inquiries from around the country, and staging local celebrations, but the idea was slow to catch on. By the 1920s Father's Day had more or less died out as a local event, and Dodd herself moved on to other projects. But after studying at the Art Institute of Chicago and working as a fashion designer in Hollywood, she returned to Spokane in the early 1930s and resumed her campaign, focusing on the holiday's 25th anniversary observance in 1935. This time she had more success, and Father's Day enjoyed a resurgence—at least in eastern Washington.

The rest of the country, however, regarded it as just another excuse for a holiday. What did fathers want with sentimental gifts and greeting cards? But then the Associated Men's Wear Retailers of New York City took up the cause, recognizing its commercial potential. They set up the National Council for the Promotion of Father's Day in 1938. The council coordinated the efforts of florists, tobacconists, stationers, and men's clothiers across the country to promote Father's Day. "Give Dad Something to Wear" was its slogan, and its goal was to boost sales by increasing the demand for Father's Day gifts.

President Calvin Coolidge had recommended that Father's Day become a nationwide observance as early as 1924. But it wasn't until 1972 that President Richard Nixon signed a proclamation to that effect. By the time Dodd died in 1978 at the age of 96, the Father's Day Council estimated the holiday to be worth more than $1 billion in retail sales.

SYMBOLS AND CUSTOMS

Necktie

What Mother's Day did for the florist industry, Father's Day did for the necktie industry. Along with tobacco, shirts, and other typically masculine gifts, neckties appeared on the earliest Father's Day greeting cards, and retailers wasted no time in turning the holiday to their advantage. Knowing that many people regarded Father's Day gifts as a joke, they designed ads showing fathers surrounded by ridiculous or tacky gifts, and then suggested the purchase of a classic silk necktie or pair of socks. Although their ploys were not difficult to see through, such advertising campaigns made it increasingly difficult to ignore Father's Day altogether.

As early as 1920 the custom of giving ties to fathers as a token of affection had already become a standing joke. The women who chose them often showed questionable taste. But the thought of giving flowers was even more laughable, and at least neckties were a more masculine, less sentimental gift. Along with socks, pipes, cigars, and shirts, neckties have somehow managed to retain their standing as the classic Father's Day gift.

Rose

Just as the carnation became a symbol for **MOTHER'S DAY,** the rose was suggested as the official Father's Day flower by Sonora Dodd in her 1910 petition to the

Father of the Year

The National Father's Day Committee, founded in 1942, promotes the observance of Father's Day, in part, by organizing annual Fathers of the Year awards. The Committee is part of the Father's Day/Mother's Day Council. In 2007 National Fathers of the Year ceremonies were held in more than twenty cities around the nation. Here are a few of the recent honorees:

2001: former boxer George Foreman, recording company entrepreneur Russell Simmons

2002: New York City Mayor Michael R. Bloomberg, basketball player Alonzo Mourning

2003: clothing designer Joseph Abboud, football player Steve Young

2004: jazz pianist Ellis Marsalis, NASCAR driver Richard Petty

2005: TV personality Larry King, business leader Donald Trump

2006: rapper LL Cool J (Todd Smith), actor Jack Klugman

2007: former Democratic presidential candidate John Edwards, basketball player Dwyane Wade

Spokane Ministerial Association. It would be appropriate, she thought, if people wore a white rose in remembrance of a father who had died and a red rose as a tribute to a living father. Although more than sixty years passed before the holiday was officially established, the rose never encountered any real competition as the symbolic flower of Father's Day.

FURTHER READING

Henderson, Helene, ed. *Holidays, Festivals, and Celebrations of the World Dictionary.* 3rd ed. Detroit: Omnigraphics, 2005.

Ickis, Marguerite. *The Book of Religious Holidays and Celebrations.* New York: Dodd, Mead, 1966.

Schmidt, Leigh Eric. *Consumer Rites: The Buying and Selling of American Holidays.* Princeton: Princeton University Press, 1995.

Tuleja, Tad. *Curious Customs: The Stories Behind 296 Popular American Rituals*. New York: Harmony, 1987.

WEB SITES

Father's Day/Mother's Day Council
www.momanddadday.com

National Center for Fathering
www.fathers.com

Feast of Fools

Type of Holiday: Religious (Christian)
Date of Observation: Late December or early January
Where Celebrated: France, Germany, and other European countries. Observed less widely in England.
Symbols and Customs: Archbishop of Fools, Ass
Related Holidays: Holy Innocents' Day, Saturnalia

ORIGINS

The Feast of Fools was a mock-religious Christian festival popular during the Middle Ages in Europe, particularly France. The word Christian refers to a follower of Christ, a title derived from the Greek word meaning Messiah or Anointed One. The Christ of Christianity is Jesus of Nazareth, a man born between 7 and 4 B.C.E. in the region of Palestine. According to Christian teaching, Jesus was killed by Roman authorities using a form of execution called crucifixion (a term meaning he was nailed to a cross and hung from it until he died) in about the year 30 C.E. After his death, he rose back to life. His death and resurrection provide a way by which people can be reconciled with God. In remembrance of Jesus' death and resurrection, the cross serves as a fundamental symbol in Christianity.

With nearly two billion believers in countries around the globe, Christianity is the largest of the world's religions. There is no one central authority for all of Christianity. The pope (the bishop of Rome) is the authority for the Roman Catholic Church, but other sects look to other authorities. Orthodox communities look to patriarchs and emphasize doctrinal agreement and traditional practice. Protestant communities focus on individual conscience. The Roman Catholic and Protestant churches are often referred to as the Western Church, while the Orthodox churches may also be called the Eastern Church. All three main branches of Christianity acknowledge the authority of Christian scriptures, a compilation of writings assembled into a document called the Bible. Methods of biblical interpretation vary among the different Christian sects.

The Feast of Fools had much in common with the ancient Roman **SATURNA-LIA**, observed in late December. Shortly after **CHRISTMAS**, various lower-level clergy and church officials held a series of revels. The deacons held their celebration on **ST. STEPHEN'S DAY** (December 26), the choirboys on **HOLY INNO-CENTS' DAY** (December 28), the priests on the Feast of the Circumcision (January 1), and the subdeacons on **EPIPHANY** (January 6). Collectively, these festivals came to be known as the Feast of Fools because they usually involved irreverent and disorderly behavior. The group to whom the day belonged would nominate a bishop or ARCHBISHOP OF FOOLS, who was then ordained in a mock ceremony and presented to the people. Wearing masks and dressed in women's clothing, the revelers would dance and sing obscene songs, play dice or eat black pudding at the altar while the Mass was being said, burn old shoes in the censers, and run around the church behaving in a way that would have been unthinkable under normal circumstances. The Feast of Fools eventually developed into a celebration for the poor and lower-class clergy in general, who undoubtedly had a great deal of fun mocking the sacred but tedious rites performed by their superiors.

The temporary reversal of authority associated with the Feast of Fools was characteristic of the ancient Roman observation of the *Kalends,* or first day of the month, as was the wearing of beast-like masks and dressing up in women's clothes. In fact, the Feast of Fools probably represents a combination of the Roman feast of the Kalends of January with other Celtic pagan festivals. The lower clergy usually belonged to the peasant or bourgeois class and were not well educated, which made them more inclined to cling to folk rituals. The whole idea of setting aside certain days for reveling and masquerading was probably designed to prevent them from misbehaving during Christmas week.

The Feast of Fools was most widely celebrated in France, although it was also observed in Germany and Bohemia, and to a lesser extent in England. During the twelfth to fifteenth centuries, Church reformers tried to crack down on some of the abuses and even to prohibit the celebration altogether, but it was too popular to be suppressed entirely. Even after it was expelled from the churches of France in the fifteenth century, its traditions continued to be observed outside the church, often at times other than the Christmas season. In the cathedral at Amiens, France, the Feast of Fools was still being observed as late as 1721.

SYMBOLS AND CUSTOMS

Archbishop of Fools

It was customary for a low-level clerk to preside over the services held throughout the Feast of Fools. He would be given the staff normally used by the official who directed the church's choral services and, dressed in the robes worn by his superiors, he would sit on the real bishop's throne, handing out benedictions and indulgences. He was referred to as the Archbishop (or sometimes cardinal or pope) of Fools.

Aside from being characteristic of the role reversal associated with the Kalends celebrations (*see* "Origins" above), the Archbishop of Fools may have been a survival of the tradition of crowning a mock king at the **SATURNALIA**.

Ass

The traditions associated with the Feast of Fools were continued by, and eventually blended with, the Feast of the Asses (or Feast of the Ass), which was also observed on January 1, the Feast of the Circumcision. This festival involved a crude reenactment of the flight of Mary, Joseph, and Jesus into Egypt to escape King Herod's order that all the young boys in Bethlehem and the surrounding area be slaughtered (*see* **HOLY INNOCENTS' DAY**). A young girl holding a baby would ride into the church on an ass, and at the close of the service the priest would bray like a donkey three times, and the congregation would respond in the same manner.

In France during the fifteenth century and later, when the Feast of Fools celebration moved outside the church after being condemned by church authorities as too blasphemous and irreverent, the popular figure of the ARCHBISHOP OF FOOLS was replaced by a *Prince des Sots* (Prince of Fools), whose distinctive costume included a hood with asses' ears. This is believed to be a relic of primitive times, when the heads of sacrificed animals were often worn by festival worshippers.

The ass is frequently portrayed in Renaissance paintings, particularly when the subject is the Nativity, the Flight into Egypt, or the Entry of Christ into Jerusalem. Because the ass represents the humblest of animals, its presence at such pivotal events in the life of Christ not only underscores his divine humility but also shows that even the lowliest beings of creation recognized him as the Son of God.

FURTHER READING

Ferguson, George. *Signs and Symbols in Christian Art*. New York: Oxford University Press, 1954.
Gulevich, Tanya. *Encyclopedia of Christmas and New Year's Celebrations*. 2nd ed. Detroit: Omnigraphics, 2003.

Henderson, Helene, ed. *Holidays, Festivals, and Celebrations of the World Dictionary.* 3rd ed. Detroit: Omnigraphics, 2005.

James, E.O. *Seasonal Feasts and Festivals.* 1961. Reprint. Detroit: Omnigraphics, 1993.

Jobes, Gertrude. *Dictionary of Mythology, Folklore, and Symbols.* New York: Scarecrow Press, 1962.

Leach, Maria, ed. *Funk & Wagnalls Standard Dictionary of Folklore, Mythology & Legend.* San Francisco: Harper & Row, 1984.

Miles, Clement A. *Christmas in Ritual and Tradition, Christian and Pagan.* 1912. Reprint. Detroit: Omnigraphics, 1990.

Urlin, Ethel L. *Festivals, Holy Days, and Saints' Days.* 1915. Reprint. Detroit: Omnigraphics, 1992.

Weiser, Franz Xaver. *Handbook of Christian Feasts and Customs.* New York: Harcourt, Brace, 1958.

WEB SITE

New Advent Catholic Encyclopedia
www.newadvent.org/cathen/06132a.htm

Feast of the Dead

Type of Holiday: Religious (various Native American)
Date of Observation: Every ten to twelve years
Where Celebrated: Northeastern United States and Canada
Symbols and Customs: Defleshing, Funeral Games

ORIGINS

The Feast of the Dead is part of several Native American religious traditions. The history of Native American cultures dates back thousands of years into prehistoric times. According to many scholars, the people who became the Native Americans migrated from Asia across a land bridge that may have once connected the territories presently occupied by Alaska and Russia. The migrations, believed to have begun between 60,000 and 30,000 B.C.E., continued until approximately 4,000 B.C.E. This speculation, however, conflicts with traditional stories asserting that the indigenous Americans have always lived in North America or that tribes moved up from the south.

The historical development of religious belief systems among Native Americans is not well known. Most of the information available was gathered by Europeans who arrived on the continent beginning in the sixteenth century C.E. The data they recorded was fragmentary and oftentimes of questionable accuracy because the Europeans did not understand the native cultures they were trying to describe and the Native Americans were reluctant to divulge details about themselves.

The burial ceremony known as the Feast of the Dead was held by various North American Indian tribes—particularly the Iroquois, Huron, Algonquin, and Ottawa. The ceremony was held on an irregular basis, usually every ten to twelve years when a field-rotation cycle ended and the people who had been living in a particular area or village were ready to move on. Rather than leave their dead behind, and as a way of making it possible for the spirits of the deceased to complete their journey to the afterlife, the surviving relatives would carry what remained of the corpses to a central location and bury them in a common grave.

Although it sounds like a gruesome event, several communities usually participated in the feast, which lasted for ten days and, like any other funeral, gave the survivors an opportunity to renew their family and social bonds. The bodies of the dead, which had sometimes been buried but more commonly placed in a temporary grave on a scaffold, were gathered up and laid out in a row. Then the family members removed the flesh (*see* DEFLESHING) from the bones and wrapped them with great care in animal skins and furs. The bodies of those who had died recently were left intact and wrapped in furs as well. Each family held a funeral feast at which speeches were made praising the deceased and gifts were presented in their honor.

The common burial ground was often many miles away, and families carried the corpses on litters and the bones in a bundle across their backs, wailing in imitation of the souls of the deceased as they marched. When they reached the burial ground, all the mourners would set up camp, light fires, and prepare for the ossuary ritual (an "ossuary" is a place for the bones of the dead). The younger men would engage in FUNERAL GAMES as entertainment, the women would prepare food, and the gifts that had been brought to accompany the dead on their journey would be laid out so that everyone could admire them. The huge open pit that would serve as a common grave was lined with beaver skins, ready to receive the remains.

When the time for the reburial arrived, people would line up around the edges of the pit and fling the bones and corpses in. A dozen or so Indians standing at the bottom would use long poles to arrange the heaps in an orderly manner. Families would cry out as the bodies of their loved ones toppled into the pit, and the level of noise and excitement was considerable. Then earth, logs, and stones were used to fill in the grave, and the shrieking and wailing subsided somewhat and became a funeral chant.

In addition to being the last step in the long process of saying good-bye to loved ones, the Feast of the Dead gave these Native Americans a chance to renew or repair their relationships with their neighbors. Although scholars believe that the last Feast of the Dead was held in 1695, construction workers excavating the ground for a housing development in Scarborough, Ontario, in the 1950s stumbled upon such an Iroquois burial site. Local Native Americans held a Feast of the Dead and reburied the bones in another location, where it is hoped they will remain undisturbed forever.

SYMBOLS AND CUSTOMS

Defleshing

The Native American tribes that practiced this ossuary ritual believed that when a person died, his or her spirit lingered for a period of time. Because flesh was what connected the body to earthly life, the soul or spirit could not depart until the body was free of it. The process of removing the flesh of a corpse from its bones, therefore, was symbolic of separating life from death, thus freeing the soul to continue its journey to the afterlife.

Funeral Games

The Feast of the Dead included sports activities. Young men (and frequently women) would have archery contests, and the mourners would award prizes for marksmanship in honor of their deceased family members. Another popular game was lacrosse, which was played by the tribes of the Iroquois Nation long before white settlers came to the New World. There was a spiritual aspect to the game back then, and it was often preceded by elaborate rituals and dances. Just as warriors played lacrosse to prepare themselves to endure the pains and injuries of battle, it may have been regarded as a symbolic preparation for the journey from this world to the afterlife.

FURTHER READING

Hirschfelder, Arlene B., and Paulette Fairbanks Molin. *Encyclopedia of Native American Religions*. Updated edition. New York: Facts on File, 2000.

WEB SITE

Wyandot Nation of Kansas
www.wyandot.org/burial2.htm

Fiesta de Santa Fe

Type of Holiday: Historic
Date of Observation: Weekend after Labor Day Weekend
Where Celebrated: Santa Fe, New Mexico
Symbols and Customs: Fiesta Ball, Historical Reenactments, Parades, Roman Catholic Masses and Procession, Zozobra

ORIGINS

The Spanish founded the city of Santa Fe, New Mexico, in 1610. In 1680, the local Pueblo Indian people revolted against the Spanish conquerors and drove them from the city. Spanish soldiers retook the city in 1692, led by General Don Diego de Vargas. De Vargas prayed before a statue of the Blessed Virgin Mary that the Spanish had rescued and taken with them before abandoning Santa Fe to the Indians. He implored the Blessed Virgin for aid in recapturing the city. When success crowned his efforts, he vowed to see the statue, dubbed "La Conquistadora" (the Conqueror), honored in Santa Fe. In 1712 the Spanish governor Marquez de la Penuela established the Fiesta de Santa Fe to commemorate the reoccupation of the city by the Spanish. This early starting date makes the Fiesta de Santa Fe one of the oldest civic festivals in the United States.

As a historic holiday, Fiesta de Santa Fe commemorates a significant historical event. People throughout the world remember significant events in their histories. Often, these are events that are important for an entire nation and become widely observed. The marking of such anniversaries serves not only to honor the values represented by the person or event commemorated, but also to strengthen and reinforce communal bonds of national, cultural, or ethnic identity. Victorious, joyful, and traumatic events are remembered through historic holidays. The commemorative expression reflects the original event through festive celebration or solemn ritual. Reenactments are common activities at historical holiday and festival gatherings, seeking to bring the past alive in the present.

Fiesta is a Spanish word meaning party or festival. In Spain and other Spanish-speaking countries, most towns and cities have a fiesta that celebrates the existence of the town and honors its patron saint. These fiestas usually include both religious ceremonies and secular celebrations featuring music, food, dancing, fireworks, and other fun activities. The Fiesta de Santa Fe is a good example of this kind of festival.

The earliest records of the Fiesta de Santa Fe indicate that it was mostly religious in nature, featuring special Roman Catholic masses and religious processions. In 1882 more elaborate celebrations took place to commemorate the 333rd year since Europeans arrived in New Mexico. The festivities included a reenactment of the return of the Spanish into the city, in which local people acted the roles of General de Vargas, Franciscan monks, soldiers, and noble ladies and gentleman. In addition to these characters, many other people marched in seventeenth-century costume, demonstrating the modes of transportation and occupations of that era. Similar HISTORICAL REENACTMENTS play an important role in today's festival.

In 1924 a local artist named Will Shuster added a new element to the Fiesta de Santa Fe. Shuster and his friends thought the festival had become too commercial and too somber in its tone. He constructed a large effigy of a bogey man out of wood, burlap, and paper, calling it ZOZOBRA, a Spanish word that locals have loosely translated as "Old Man Gloom." Shuster and his friends burned Zozobra at the start of the festival, as a symbolic means of casting out any sadness, gloom, and disappointment experienced during the past year. In developing the Zozobra burning event, Shuster was inspired by the Yaqui Indian Holy Week custom of burning an effigy of Judas that was filled with firecrackers. Shuster's innovation caught on with the people of Santa Fe and has been an important element of the festival ever since. Will Shuster continued to build Zozobra until 1964, when he turned over his plans for the construction of the effigy to the local Kiwanis Club. The Kiwanis have built Zozobra and managed the burning event since that time.

The Santa Fe Fiesta Council plans and manages the rest of the events that take place during the three-day festival. In addition to the special events that characterize the Fiesta de Santa Fe, food booths are set up in public gathering places and performances of mariachi and other kinds of music take place throughout the three-day festival.

SYMBOLS AND CUSTOMS

Fiesta Ball

The Fiesta Ball caps off the celebrations and provides participants with one more opportunity to celebrate the gloom-free period initiated by the burning of Zozobra. Organized by the Santa Fe Fiesta Council, the ball is held in a local hotel or convention center and features Mexican-style music.

Historical Reenactments

Each year a young man is chosen to represent General de Vargas and reenact his triumphant entrance into Santa Fe. Dressed in seventeenth-century Spanish garb, the young man and his retinue parade through the streets until they reach the central plaza in downtown Santa Fe. The retinue includes soldiers, Catholic monks and priests, and the Fiesta Queen and her princesses. The men ride horses while the young women walk, dressed in beautiful Spanish-style gowns of the period. When they arrive at the Plaza, they perform a small reenactment of the meeting between de Vargas and the leader of the Pueblo Indians. Speeches of welcome are made, and afterwards bands perform for free on the plaza.

The following day the Fiesta Queen, chosen yearly from among the civic-minded young women of Santa Fe, gives a royal audience at the Plaza.

Parades

The children's pet parade has been a favorite festival event for the past sixty years. Approximately 1,500 people and their pets have taken part in this parade in recent years. Dogs, cats, goats, lambs, roosters, rabbits, turtles, birds, rats, llamas, and guinea pigs have all participated in this popular event. The children and their pets wear clever costumes that could earn them a prize. The judges give awards in the following categories: most original, best historical, best hysterical, best child/pet look-alike, best message to other kids, best musical group, best family entry, best fiesta theme, and best story book character.

In addition, another, more adult-oriented parade also takes place during the fiesta. This parade features floats that satirize local politicians or depict local history.

Roman Catholic Masses and Procession

Roman Catholic masses are scheduled to open and close the festival weekend. What's more, La Conquistadora is still honored during the course of the fiesta. Dressed in rare fabrics, lace, and jewels, the statue is enshrined in a place of honor in St. Francis Cathedral. In recent years Roman Catholic officials have changed her name to Our Lady of Peace in order to shift her association with war and conquest to an association with peace and cooperation. In addition, Church officials have added a mass of reconciliation to the religious ceremonies that take place during the fiesta. This mass of reconciliation emphasizes the need for peaceful cooperation among people of different racial and ethnic backgrounds. A candlelit procession takes place to mark the close of the festival.

Zozobra

The burning of Zozobra kicks off the three-day festival. Members of the Santa Fe Kiwanis Club construct the 50-foot effigy in the three weeks preceding the festival. Approximately 3,500 volunteer hours are required to finish the project. The volunteers cover a wooden framework with chicken wire and muslin and stuff it with paper. The paper stuffing includes such things as completed loan and mortgage papers, police reports, and legal documents pertaining to divorces and other unpleasant events; these papers represent the sorrows that the people of Santa Fe want to leave behind them. Finally, the cloth covering is painted and decorated to look like a gloomy, glowering old man.

The burning of Zozobra takes place around sundown on the first evening of the festival. A small ceremony takes place before the burning in which a male dancer dressed in red, called the Fire Dancer or Fire Spirit, dances around Zozobra. The Fire Dancer taunts Zozobra with flames and wards off other dancers in white sheets, who are called "glooms." The assembled crowd yells "Burn him," until the Fire Dancer succeeds in setting the giant effigy alight. A fireworks display follows.

The burning of Zozobra attracts between 20,000 and 30,000 spectators. The Kiwanis Club charges admission to the event, and uses the money to send disabled kids to summer camp, to provide scholarships for teens graduating from Santa Fe high schools, and to fund its Children's Orthodontics programs.

FURTHER READING

Henderson, Helene, ed. *Holidays, Festivals and Celebrations of the World Dictionary.* 3rd ed. Detroit: Omnigraphics, 2005.

Nott, Robert. "Fiesta Forever, Dancing Our Troubles Away." *Free New Mexican.* September 1, 2006. www.freenewmexican.com/story_print.php?storyid=48639

WEB SITES

Library of Congress Local Legacies
lcweb2.loc.gov/cocoon/legacies/NM/200003356.html

Santa Fe Fiesta Council
www.santafefiesta.org

Santa Fe Kiwanis Club
www.zozobra.com

Flag Day

Type of Holiday: Historic
Date of Observation: June 14
Where Celebrated: United States
Symbols and Customs: American Flag, Betsy Ross
Colors: Red, white, and blue (*see* AMERICAN FLAG)
Related Holidays: Fourth of July, Memorial Day

ORIGINS

During the early battles of the American Revolution, the rebels fought under the flags of their individual colonies or local militia companies. The first "national" flag, often referred to as the Grand Union Flag, was first flown on New Year's Day in 1776 to celebrate the formation of the Continental Army. It had thirteen alternating red and white stripes, representing the thirteen colonies, and a canton, or square area, showing the crosses of St. George and St. Andrew, representing Great Britain. It served as a symbol of many Americans' hope that eventually the colonies could reconcile their differences with Britain.

The Continental Congress didn't adopt a design for an official national flag until June 14, 1777, almost a year after the Declaration of Independence was signed, and it was still two or three years before the new flag was widely used. Tradition generally credits BETSY ROSS with making the original thirteen-stars-and-thirteen-stripes banner, but there are several contradictory theories that attribute its creation to such individuals as John Paul Jones, the American naval hero, and Francis Hopkinson, a signer of the Declaration. When Kentucky and Vermont were admitted to the Union in 1794, the number of stars and stripes was increased to fifteen. But in 1818 Congress voted to restore the original thirteen stripes and to add a new star for each new state on the **FOURTH OF JULY** following its admission. Alaska and Hawaii were the forty-ninth and fiftieth stars, added in 1959.

Flag Day is a holiday that commemorates a significant historical event. Peoples throughout the world commemorate such significant events in their histories through holidays and festivals. Often, these are events that are important for an entire nation and become widely observed. The marking of such anniversaries serve not only to honor the values represented by the person or event commemorated, but also to strengthen and reinforce communal bonds of national, cultural, or ethnic identity. Victorious, joyful, and traumatic events are remembered through historic holidays. The commemorative expression reflects the original event through festive celebration or solemn ritual. Reenactments are common activities at historical holiday and festival gatherings, seeking to bring the past alive in the present.

The first Flag Day observance didn't take place until June 14, 1861, almost a century after the official adoption of the flag's design. William T. Kerr, who lived in Pittsburgh and later in Philadelphia, is recognized by many as the person responsible for promoting the observance of this day. He began his campaign when he was still a schoolboy, and his enthusiasm never waned. He lobbied government leaders and did everything he could to bring Flag Day to the attention of the American public.

It was President Woodrow Wilson who first issued a proclamation in 1916 establishing June 14 as Flag Day. President Calvin Coolidge issued a similar proclamation in 1927, but it didn't become an official holiday until Congress and President Harry Truman made it one in 1949. Only Pennsylvania observes this day as a legal holiday, but other states acknowledge its importance by displaying the AMERICAN FLAG on homes, businesses, and public buildings. Other popular ways of observing Flag Day include flag-raising ceremonies, the singing of "The Star-Spangled Banner," and the reciting of the Pledge of Allegiance, which was written by James B. Upham and Francis Bellamy in 1892. Schools and community centers often hold special programs designed to instill pride in the flag—especially after the way it was treated during American involvement in the Vietnam War (1964-75), when flag-burning and other acts of desecration were common as a means of expressing antiwar sentiments.

SYMBOLS AND CUSTOMS

American Flag

On June 14, 1777, the Continental Congress replaced the British symbols of the Grand Union flag with a new design featuring thirteen white stars in a circle on a field of blue and thirteen red and white stripes. Although it is not certain, this flag may have been made by Philadelphia seamstress BETSY ROSS. As the committee that had been formed to oversee the design of the new flag described it, the stars represented the constellation of the State rising in the West, and the blue background stood for the virtues of vigilance, perseverance, and justice. The circle formed by the stars symbolized the perpetuity of the Union, and the thirteen stripes stood for the original thirteen colonies. The red symbolized the newly formed country's defiance and daring, while the white symbolized purity or liberty.

The American flag, traditionally considered a symbol of patriotism and dedication to American ideals, is actually one of the oldest national emblems—even older than Great Britain's Union Jack. Its appearance has been changed 26 times, mostly to accommodate the admission of new states. The Easton Area Public Library in Pennsylvania has what it claims is the very first "Stars and Stripes," predating the Betsy Ross flag and others by almost a year. They say it was first displayed on July 8, 1776, during a public reading of the Declaration of Independence in Easton, and that it was made by the women of Easton. It is eight feet long and four feet wide.

Flag Day is also a time for the study of flag etiquette, which dictates that the flag should only be allowed to fly after sunrise and before sunset. When it is raised or lowered, it must not touch the ground or the deck of a ship, and it must be saluted by everyone present. When it is being placed at half-mast for the dead, it must be hoisted first to the top of the staff, then lowered into place. When it passes on parade, spectators should stand if they are seated, stop if they are walking, and uncover their heads, giving it their full attention. Nothing should ever be placed on the flag or attached to it, and it should never be used for decorative or advertising purposes.

Betsy Ross

Very little is actually known about the woman who is widely believed to have made the first AMERICAN FLAG. The only facts that have been substantiated are that she was an upholsterer living in Philadelphia during the American Revolution and that she had already made several Pennsylvania naval flags of unknown design, as well as flags for Revolutionary War troops. Her home at 239 Arch Street in Philadelphia is now a national shrine.

FURTHER READING

Christianson, Stephen G., and Jane M. Hatch. *The American Book of Days*. 4th ed. New York: H.W. Wilson, 2000.

Dunkling, Leslie. *A Dictionary of Days*. New York: Facts on File, 1988.

Henderson, Helene, ed. *Holidays, Festivals, and Celebrations of the World Dictionary*. 3rd ed. Detroit: Omnigraphics, 2005.

McSpadden, J. Walker. *The Book of Holidays*. New York: Crowell, 1958.

Schaun, George and Virginia, and David Wisniewski. *American Holidays and Special Days*. 3rd ed. Lanham: Maryland Historical Press, 2002.

Trawicky, Bernard, and Ruth W. Gregory. *Anniversaries and Holidays*. 5th ed. Chicago: American Library Assocation, 2000.

Van Straalen, Alice. *The Book of Holidays Around the World*. New York: Dutton, 1986.

WEB SITES

National Flag Day Foundation
www.flagday.org

Fort McHenry National Monument and Historic Shrine
U.S. National Park Service
www.nps.gov/fomc

Floralia

Type of Holiday: Ancient
Date of Observation: April 28-May 3
Where Celebrated: Rome, Italy
Symbols and Customs: Beans, Hares or Goats
Related Holidays: May Day

ORIGINS

Floralia was part of ancient Roman religion, which scholars date back to the sixth century B.C.E. Roman religion dominated Rome and influenced territories in its empire until Emperor Constantine's conversion to Christianity in the third century C.E.

Ancient Roman religion was heavily influenced by the older Greek religion. Roman festivals therefore had much in common with those of the ancient Greeks. Not only were their gods and goddesses mostly the same as those in the Greek pantheon (though the Romans renamed them), but their religious festivals were observed with similar activities: ritual sacrifice, theatrical performances, games, and feasts.

An ancient Roman festival held in honor of Flora, the goddess of flowers and gardens, the Floralia was instituted in 238 B.C.E. It was originally a movable feast whose date depended on the conditions of the crops and flowers in any particular year at the end of April and beginning of May. In 173 B.C.E., after severe storms had brought disaster to the cornfields and vineyards, the Roman Senate made it an annual festival extending for six days—from April 28, the anniversary of the founding of Flora's temple, through May 3.

The events of the festival included games, dances, and theatrical performances. From the very beginning, the Floralia was characterized by wild and often indecent behavior. Prostitutes claimed it as their feast day, and courtesans are said to have performed mimes and dances in the nude. The obscene nature of the festivities was probably due to their roots in early pagan fertility rites designed to promote the earth's fruitfulness. But when the festival was introduced into Rome, it became a good excuse for excessive drinking and carrying on.

The Floralia, which originally featured small statues of Flora that children would decorate with flowers, is believed to have been the precedent for the Christian **MAY DAY** celebrations and their dolls or images of the Virgin Mary.

SYMBOLS AND CUSTOMS

Beans

The temple dedicated to Flora was located on the lower slope of the Aventine, one of the seven hills of Rome, near the arena known as the Circus Maximus. Beans, lupines, and vetches were often scattered among the crowd that gathered there for the festival. It was a common practice at the time to throw all kinds of grain, including rice, peas, and beans, as part of the marriage rite and at the birth of children. Because legumes yield so many seeds, beans were a popular symbol of fertility and wealth. Given the fact that the Floralia was observed in April, the custom of throwing beans is probably a very ancient one rooted in beliefs about the fertility of the earth and of humans.

Hares or Goats

Hares and goats, which had a reputation for being very fertile animals, were let loose in the Circus Maximus during the celebration of the Floralia. The hare (or rabbit, which is not distinguished from it in terms of symbolism) was known for multiplying rapidly, making it a popular symbol of fertility and sexuality. Since Flora was the patroness of gardens and fields, not of forests and wild animals, the hare and the goat were appropriate symbols of fertility in a domestic setting.

FURTHER READING

Biedermann, Hans. *Dictionary of Symbolism: Cultural Icons and the Meanings Behind Them*. New York: Meridian Books, 1994.

Fowler, W. Warde. *The Roman Festivals of the Period of the Republic*. New York: Macmillan Co., 1925.

Henderson, Helene, ed. *Holidays, Festivals, and Celebrations of the World Dictionary*. 3rd ed. Detroit: Omnigraphics, 2005.

Scullard, H. H. *Festivals and Ceremonies of the Roman Republic*. Ithaca, NY: Cornell University Press, 1981.

Flute Ceremony

Type of Holiday: Religious (Hopi)
Date of Observation: Mid-August for nine days
Where Celebrated: Arizona
Symbols and Customs: Flute Altar, Sun Emblem, Tiponi
Related Holidays: Hopi Snake Dance

ORIGINS

The Flute Ceremony is part of the Hopi religious belief system. The historical development of this and other religious belief systems among Native Americans is largely unknown. Most of the information available was gathered by Europeans who arrived on the continent beginning in the sixteenth century C.E. The data they recorded was fragmentary and oftentimes of questionable accuracy because the Europeans did not understand the native cultures they were trying to describe and the Native Americans were reluctant to divulge details about themselves.

Native American cultures date back thousands of years into prehistoric times. According to many scholars, the people who became the Native Americans migrated from Asia across a land bridge that may have once connected the territories presently occupied by Alaska and Russia. The migrations, believed to have begun between 60,000 and 30,000 B.C.E., continued until approximately 4,000 B.C.E. This speculation, however, conflicts with traditional stories asserting that the indigenous Americans have always lived in North America or that tribes moved up from the south.

The Hopi observe a ceremonial calendar in which the year is divided into two parts. According to tradition, during one half of the year the kachinas (nature, ancestral, and guardian spirits) live in the village and reveal themselves to the people through ceremonial dances. During the other half of the year, the kachinas separate themselves from the village and return to live in their homes in the mountains. The Kachina season begins around the time of **WINTER SOLSTICE**, as people begin to prepare the ground for planting, and it closes in late July with the bringing in of the first harvest.

Like the **HOPI SNAKE DANCE**, the Flute Ceremony takes place over a nine-day period in the summer on the mesas of northeastern Arizona, where the Hopi Indians live. Although the Snake Dance attracts bigger crowds, the Flute Ceremony is just as central to the Hopi system of religion. Its purpose is to encourage rainfall and promote the growth of corn, the primary food of the Hopi nation.

Unlike other Hopi ceremonies, which are performed in the *kiva* or underground ceremonial room, this ceremony takes place in the ancestral rooms of the Flute clan. It begins with a procession into the pueblo led by the clan's chief, who is followed by the Flute boy, with a Flute girl on either side. Other members of the procession include men wrapped in white blankets, men carrying cornstalks, a warrior carrying a bullroarer (which makes a whizzing sound when swung in circles overhead), a man wearing a SUN EMBLEM on his back, a man carrying a rectangular "moisture tablet," and a number of small naked boys. The Flute girls each wear a feather in their hair and two white blankets, one of which serves as a skirt. The Flute boys wear white ceremonial kilts.

Once the procession has arrived at the pueblo, additional rites—which include ceremonial prayers for rain and corn, singing, and smoking—are conducted in the ancestral Flute room. Many of the rites involved in the Flute Ceremony are actually pantomimes of what the Hopis want their gods to do. For example, the priest may scatter meal on the ground or around the FLUTE ALTAR to imitate the falling rain. Pouring water into the medicine bowl that sits in front of the altar from the six cardinal directions of the world (north, south, east, west, up, down) shows the gods that he wants them to send rain from six different directions. Blowing clouds of smoke on the altar shows that he wants rain clouds to appear. And the bullroarer imitates the sound of thunder that often accompanies rain.

SYMBOLS AND CUSTOMS

Flute Altar

A special altar is constructed in the ancestral room for the Flute Ceremony. It includes a flat wooden arch, the upright members of which are carved or painted to represent rain clouds and falling rain. Ears of corn may be stacked up behind the altar. Other elements include rectangular tiles decorated with rain clouds and other symbols, and figurines representing the Flute Youth and the Flute Maid, the legendary ancestors of the Flute clan. These armless effigies are painted with symbolic representations of rain clouds and ears of corn. In front of them are short, thick, upright sticks rounded at the top and pierced with holes from which small wooden rods project like pins from a pincushion. These sticks, which are sometimes replaced by mounds of sand covered with cornmeal, symbolize the ancestral mounds of the underworld, and the wooden objects inserted in them represent flowers. There are also zigzag sticks (symbolic of lightning), cornstalks, and other symbolic objects arranged around the altar.

There is a zone of sand on the floor in front of the altar on which meal has been sprinkled. In the sand are placed roughly carved bird effigies and a medicine bowl from which one of the birds appears to be drinking. Other ceremonial items include rattles, a basket-tray of sacred meal, gourds of water, and a honey pot. Every element of the Flute altar symbolizes some aspect of the agricultural process, particularly the weather needed for corn to grow.

Sun Emblem

A man bearing a large feathered disk impersonates the sun during the procession into the pueblo that precedes the ceremonies in the ancestral rooms of the Flute clan. The central part of the sun emblem is about a foot in diameter and made of buckskin stretched over a hoop, with a border of braided corn husks. Eagle feathers and red-stained horsehair are inserted into the border of the disk to represent the sun's rays. The sun shield is attached to the back of the bearer by a cord tied across his shoulders. He carries a flute, which he plays to entice the Corn maids (Flute maids) into the pueblo, just as the Sun, or father of the gods, is said to have drawn the maids toward him in Hopi legend.

Tiponi

An important part of the Flute Ceremony is the unwrapping of the *tiponi*, which usually takes place on the sixth day. The tiponi is a wooden cup-shaped object in which an ear of corn has been inserted. The cup itself is divided into quadrants, each of which is decorated with symbols of corn and rain clouds. The corn that is safeguarded in the tiponi—either in the form of loose grains or on the ear—is a symbol of the seed that the early nomadic tribes carried with them during their migrations, when the danger of losing it might have meant starvation.

The tiponi, as well as the corn it holds, is called the "mother." It is unwrapped very carefully by the Flute priest in a ceremony that takes about an hour. After a new ear of corn is placed in the cup, the entire thing is rewrapped in cotton string and feathers and put away until the next year's ceremony. The old grains of corn are planted later.

FURTHER READING

Fewkes, Jesse Walter. *Tusayan Katcinas and Hopi Altars*. Albuquerque: Avanyu Pub., 1990.

Forgiveness Sunday

Type of Holiday: Religious (Christian)
Date of Observation: Seventh Sunday before Orthodox Easter
Where Celebrated: Worldwide
Symbols and Customs: Eggs, Fasting, Food, Forgiveness, Icon, Liturgy
Related Holidays: Easter, Lent

ORIGINS

Forgiveness Sunday is part of the Orthodox Christian religious tradition. The word Christian refers to a follower of Christ. Christ is a title derived from the Greek word meaning Messiah or Anointed One. The Christ of Christianity is Jesus of Nazareth, a man born between 7 and 4 B.C.E. in the region of Palestine. According to Christian teaching, Jesus was killed by Roman authorities using a form of execution called crucifixion (a term meaning he was nailed to a cross and hung from it until he died) in about the year 30 C.E. After his death, he rose back to life. His death and resurrection provide a way by which people can be reconciled with God. In remembrance of Jesus's death and resurrection, the cross serves as a fundamental symbol in Christianity.

With nearly two billion believers in countries around the globe, Christianity is the largest of the world's religions. There are three main branches of the Christian faith, but there is no one central authority for all of Christianity. The pope (the bishop of Rome) is the authority for the Roman Catholic Church, but other sects look to other authorities. Orthodox communities look to patriarchs and emphasize doctrinal agreement and traditional practice. Protestant communities focus on individual conscience. The Roman Catholic and Protestant churches are often referred to as the Western Church, while the Orthodox churches may also be called the Eastern Church. All three main branches of Christianity acknowledge the authority of Christian scriptures, a compilation of writings assembled into a document called the Bible. Methods of biblical interpretation vary among the different Christian sects.

A division between eastern and western forms of Christianity occurred over the course of several centuries in the early years of the church. During this time, Orthodoxy developed in Eastern Europe and the countries surrounding the eastern half of the Mediterranean Sea. Eventually spreading outside this geographic area, Orthodox Christianity is now practiced in many countries throughout the world.

Orthodox Christians follow a different church calendar than that commonly used by western Christians (Roman Catholics and Protestants). Orthodox Lent, also known as Great Lent, is observed earlier and for a longer period of time, and the preparations for **LENT** are also different than those observed by western Christians. The week before Orthodox Lent is known as Cheese Week or Dairy Week and concludes with Forgiveness Sunday, also known as Cheese Sunday or Cheesefare Sunday. Observances during this week anticipate the upcoming Lenten fast by encouraging indulgence in food and activities that are forbidden during Lent. In predominantly Orthodox countries such as Greece and Macedonia, people celebrate Cheese Week in much the same way as Mardi Gras and Carnival are observed in other parts of the world. The weeklong celebration includes parties and masquerades and culminates on Forgiveness Sunday, when people feast on the butter, EGGS, and cheese that are prohibited during the Lenten fast.

Cheese Week ends with the evening church services or vespers that are held at sunset on Forgiveness Sunday. These services focus on the need for forgiveness from God and others whom the faithful may have wronged during the past year. Orthodox Lent officially begins at the conclusion of Forgiveness Sunday services.

SYMBOLS AND CUSTOMS

Eggs

Hard-boiled eggs are traditionally the last food that is eaten by Orthodox Christians on Forgiveness Sunday. Some Orthodox Christians observe this tradition by announcing before the egg is eaten, "With an egg I close my mouth, with an egg I shall open it again." This is done to acknowledge that eggs are not permitted during the Lenten fast and will not be eaten again until Easter Sunday. The first food typically eaten on Easter is usually a hard-boiled egg.

In parts of Macedonia and Bulgaria another egg tradition is sometimes observed on Forgiveness Sunday. During the last festivities before evening vespers on that day, a boiled egg, piece of candy, or piece of cheese is suspended from the ceiling on a string. Those in attendance circle around it and knock it with their foreheads to get it swinging. Each member of the circle then tries to catch it with their mouths. The egg may also be suspended from the end of a stick held aloft by one of the participants.

Fasting

The full Lenten fast begins on Forgiveness Sunday, after the evening vespers service. During the period of Lent, Orthodox Christians are not permitted to consume any meat, fish, eggs, dairy products, olive oil, wine, or alcoholic beverages.

Food

Forgiveness Sunday is also known as Cheese Sunday or Cheesefare Sunday, so named because it is the last day that dairy products may be eaten before the Lenten fast. The full fast begins the following day on Clean Monday, the first day of the Orthodox Great Lent. Popular dishes enjoyed on Forgiveness Sunday are those that use up any remaining dairy products. For example, many enjoy dishes prepared with cheese or butter, as well as egg dishes such as custards. Russian Orthodox Christians typically prepare *blinis*, which are thin pancakes rolled around a rich filling such as sour cream, caviar, jam, salmon, honey, or a mixture of cheeses.

Forgiveness

On Forgiveness Sunday, Orthodox Christians hope to invite God's forgiveness and to begin Lent with the proper spirit of humility. Some Orthodox parishes follow a formal ritual of forgiveness after the Sunday evening services, in which members of the community bow to one another, request forgiveness from each other, and exchange mutual forgiveness for any offenses. One old Russian Orthodox folk tradition includes asking forgiveness from the dead as well.

Icon

An Orthodox Christian icon is a two-dimensional sacred image that is usually painted on a wood surface. Icons are regarded as holy objects and are used to focus prayer in a specific way to honor the subject of the icon. The icon for Forgiveness Sunday depicts the exile of Adam and Eve from the Garden of Eden, which illustrates the fall of humankind and represents the original sin that taints all humanity. Orthodox Christians believe that the disobedience of Adam and Eve resulted in the separation of humankind from God. By praying and reflecting on the Forgiveness Sunday Icon, Orthodox Christians hope to enter the proper spiritual state in which to repent and receive God's forgiveness.

Liturgy

Forgiveness Sunday concludes with church services held at sunset. This service includes the final preparations for the beginning of Lent, focusing on themes of repentance and forgiveness. During this liturgy, Orthodox Christians dedicate themselves to the worship, prayer, fasting, and solemnity of Lent.

FURTHER READING

Constantelos, Demetrios J. *Understanding the Greek Orthodox Church: Its Faith, History, and Practice.* New York: Seabury Press, 1982.

Gulevich, Tanya. *Encyclopedia of Easter, Carnival and Lent.* Detroit: Omnigraphics, 2002.

Henderson, Helene, ed. *Holidays, Festivals, and Celebrations of the World Dictionary*, 3rd ed. Detroit: Omnigraphics, 2005.

WEB SITES

Greek Orthodox Archdiocese of America
lent.goarch.org

Orthodox Christian Information Network
www.orthodoxinfo.com

Orthodox Church in America
www.oca.org/OCchapter.asp?SID=2&ID=65

Fourth of July
(Independence Day)

Type of Holiday: Historic, National
Date of Observation: July 4
Where Celebrated: United States
Symbols and Customs: American Flag, Eagle, Fireworks, Liberty Bell, Parades, Picnics, Uncle Sam, "Yankee Doodle"
Colors: Red, white, and blue (*see* AMERICAN FLAG)
Related Holidays: Flag Day, Memorial Day

ORIGINS

The chief festival of summer in the United States, the Fourth of July commemorates the day in 1776 when the Declaration of Independence was approved by the Continental Congress in Philadelphia. For more than two centuries, Americans have been celebrating this historic event with FIREWORKS, PARADES, and backyard barbecues. But it wasn't until 1941 that Congress officially established the Fourth of July as a legal holiday.

Independence Day is a national holiday in the United States. National holidays can be defined as those commemorations that a nation's government has deemed

275

important enough to warrant inclusion in the list of official public holidays. They tend to honor a person or event that has been critical in the development of the nation and its identity. Such people and events usually reflect values and traditions shared by a large portion of the citizenry.

In the United States, patiotism and identity were nurtured from the beginning of the nation by the very act of celebrating new events in holidays like the Fourth of July, battle anniversaries, and other notable occasions. This was even more important in the country's early years because the nation was composed of people from a variety of backgrounds and traditions. The invention of traditions and the marking of important occasions in the life of the new nation were crucial in creating a shared bond of tradition and a sense of common belonging to a relatively new homeland through the shared experience of celebrating common holidays. As more and diverse peoples migrated to the United States, it became even more important to celebrate significant annual anniversaries, and the Fourth of July has become one of the nation's most important shared celebrations.

The Fourth of July could just as well have been the Second of July, the day on which the Continental Congress approved a resolution for independence, or August 2, the day on which the members of Congress actually signed the document. But it was on July 4 that the final text of the Declaration, which had been drafted by Thomas Jefferson, was ratified. John Adams wrote to his wife that the event "ought to be solemnized with pomp and parade, with shows, games, sports, guns, bells, bonfires, and illuminations, from one end of this continent to the other." As it turned out, Adams managed to touch on almost every feature of the modern Fourth of July celebration.

The first celebration took place in 1777. Warships along the docks in Philadelphia fired a thirteen-gun salute in honor of the thirteen United States, and the soldiers who were stationed there paraded through the streets. By 1788, the Fourth of July commemorated the U.S. Constitution as well, which had recently been approved by ten states. The celebration that year featured a parade with horse-drawn floats, one of which was a huge EAGLE carrying the justices of the U.S. Supreme Court.

In 1790, Washington DC was chosen as the site of the nation's permanent capital. President Thomas Jefferson observed July 4, 1801, by opening the executive mansion to guests. This custom continued under subsequent presidents, but the burning of the White House by the British in 1814 put a damper on the practice. Other notable celebrations include the one held at the end of the Civil War in 1865 on the battlefield at Gettysburg, the procession of freed black slaves who paraded through the streets of Richmond, Virginia, in 1866, and the Bicentennial celebration in New York City on July 4, 1976.

Today, not every American greets the Fourth of July with enthusiasm. African Americans, many of whom celebrate **JUNETEENTH**—June 19, the day in 1865 when news that the slaves had been freed finally reached Galveston, Texas, by ship—have often felt that the freedom celebrated by white Americans on this day is not really theirs to share. In addition, many women's groups have pointed out that the phrase "All men are created equal" excludes half the country's population. Native Americans usually join in the celebration with dances and pow-wows, paying respect to their own ancestors rather than to the nation's founding fathers.

For most Americans, however, the Fourth of July is a day of national unification, a time when political, religious, and ethnic differences are put aside. In some parts of the United States—Maine, for example—the eve of the Fourth was at one time a popular occasion for pulling pranks, such as stealing outhouses and removing porch steps. Toasts were also popular on July 4, but the Temperance movement in the early 1900s discouraged public drinking. Today the Fourth is usually celebrated by tolling bells (*see* LIBERTY BELL), listening to patriotic prayers and speeches, igniting fireworks, saluting flags, and watching parades.

It is a striking coincidence that Thomas Jefferson, the author of the Declaration of Independence, died quietly at his Virginia home at noon on July 4, 1826—the fiftieth anniversary of the document's signing. John Adams of Massachusetts, another early supporter of independence and father of President John Quincy Adams, died just a few hours later on the same day.

SYMBOLS AND CUSTOMS

American Flag

The red, white, and blue American flag can be seen everywhere on the Fourth of July, and its colors carry their own symbolic meanings: Red stands for courage, white for liberty or purity, and blue for loyalty.

The first national flag was raised on a hill near Boston on January 4, 1776, by troops serving under General George Washington. It was called the Grand Union flag, and it had thirteen red and blue stripes. Instead of stars, it had the crosses of St. Andrew and St. George, the symbols of Great Britain. After the Declaration of Independence was signed, however, the American people wanted a new flag that would symbolize their independence from Britain. The Second Continental Congress appointed a committee (whose members included George Washington) to come up with an appropriate design. The committee asked Betsy Ross, an expert seamstress and upholsterer, to make them a sample. She looked at the sketch they gave her and suggested only one change: that the number of points on each star be reduced from six to five. The thirteen stars, representing the thirteen colonies that fought for freedom, were placed in a circle to signify that the Union would be without end.

Each time a new state was added to the Union, a new star and a new stripe had to be added to the flag. By 1792, it had fifteen stars and fifteen stripes. Congress soon realized that if this practice continued, the flag would just keep getting larger. So they decided in 1818 that the number of stripes would remain fixed at thirteen, and that only the number of stars would change.

Since Hawaii became the fiftieth state in 1960, the American flag has had seven red stripes and six white ones, with fifty white stars on a blue background. The flag's colors and design have inspired many nicknames, among them the "Stars and Stripes," the "Star-Spangled Banner," and the "Red, White, and Blue."

Eagle

The bald eagle is the national bird of the United States and one of the largest birds in the world. When the first English settlers in America saw the eagle they called it "bald" meaning "white"—not hairless.

Eagles have been a symbol of power since ancient times. One of the Egyptian pharoahs used the eagle as his emblem, and golden eagles were perched atop the banners that Roman armies carried into battle. In fact, many Americans felt that because it had represented kings and empires, the eagle wasn't an appropriate symbol for a young, democratic nation. Benjamin Franklin pointed out that the eagle was "a bird of bad moral character" because it was too lazy to fish for itself. He suggested the turkey, a true American native, as a better choice for the national bird.

America's eagle population dwindled as the popularity of hunting grew. In 1940 Congress passed a law forbidding the capture or killing of a bald eagle. Pesticides like DDT lowered the eagles' birth rate, but its use was banned in 1972. Since that time, biologists estimate that the eagle population of the United States has increased from 1,000 to over 9,700 breeding pairs in the lower forty-eight states.

The eagle appears on coins, postage stamps, dollar bills, and the Great Seal of the United States. On the Fourth of July it can be seen decorating banners, balloons, and Independence Day floats.

Fireworks

The term "fireworks" was first used in 1777 in connection with the first Fourth of July celebration; before that, they were called "rockets." After 1820, those that were made to be heard rather than seen were called "firecrackers." And in the 1880s, "sparklers" appeared—thin wands that sent off a shower of sparks and could be safely used by children.

During the Middle Ages in Europe, fireworks displays were used to celebrate military victories, religious festivals, and the crowning of kings or queens. These displays were created by experienced handlers called "firemasters," and their helpers were called "wild men" or "green men" because they wore caps made of green leaves. The green men would act like jesters, running through the crowds and telling stories, cracking jokes, and warning people to stand back. Then they would set off the fireworks with lighted sticks called fire clubs. Many green men were injured or killed when their firecrackers went off too soon or failed to rise high enough in the air. The largest and most elaborate fireworks displays today—like those set off in celebration of the country's Bicentennial in New York Harbor—are staged by experts who have much in common with the old firemasters.

When fireworks were brought to America, they were used for domestic as well as public celebrations. By the 1870s, American companies were marketing fireworks for private use with names like Roman Candles, Flying Dragons, Sun Wheels, and Prismatic Fountains. The popularity of "at-home" fireworks displays meant that, in many areas, the Fourth of July celebrations moved off the streets and into private back yards.

The danger involved in lighting fireworks led to restrictions on their purchase and use. They are legal for general use in only 35 of the 50 states today; even so, there are laws governing what kind of fireworks can be sold and when. Cherry bombs and other large firecrackers have been banned nationwide since 1966 due to the large number of injuries associated with them. The majority of the fireworks used in the United States today are imported from China, Japan, South Korea, and Taiwan.

Liberty Bell

The bell that originally stood on top of the State House in Philadelphia is known today as the Liberty Bell. When it arrived from England in 1752, it was placed on a temporary stand so its ring could be tested. The bell developed a crack. Some people thought it should be sent back to England for replacement, but it was finally decided to recast the bell in Philadelphia. The original bell was broken into small pieces so the metal could be melted down. A new mold was prepared, the metal was poured in, and the bell was recast. But the new bell had a dull, muffled-sounding ring. So it was melted down again, this time with success.

From 1753 until 1776, the State House bell was used to summon public officials to meetings. There is no record of its having been rung on the day the Declaration of Independence was adopted, but it did ring on July 8, 1776, when Colonel John Nixon, commander of the city guard, read the document in public for the first time. The bell was hastily removed from the State House in September of 1777 because the British army was approaching and people were afraid they would melt it down for ammunition. It was hidden in a church basement in Allentown and shipped back to Philadelphia after the British left the city in June of 1778. It was tolling for the funeral procession of John Marshall, chief justice of the Supreme Court, on July 8, 1835, when it suddenly cracked for the second time—exactly 59 years after it had summoned the people of Philadelphia to the first reading of the Declaration of Independence.

The bell remained silent until 1846. Then the edges of the crack were filed down so they wouldn't vibrate against each other. But when the bell was rung on George Washington's birthday that year, the crack spread. After that, it was never used again. It was put on display in the State House in 1852, the 100th anniversary of its arrival in the United States. It traveled to New Orleans in 1885, to Chicago in 1893, to Boston in 1903, and to St. Louis in 1904, riding on a flat, open railroad car surrounded by a protective railing. After a final trip to San Francisco in 1915, it was discovered that the crack had widened. The bell has remained in Philadelphia ever since, a symbol of the nation's independence.

At the Bicentennial celebration in 1976, the Liberty Bell was displayed in a modern pavilion on the grassy mall below Independence Hall. On July 4 that year, descendants of the original signers of the Declaration of Independence gathered at the Liberty Bell pavilion. Exactly at 2:00 p.m., they tapped the bell gently with rubber-tipped hammers.

Parades

The first Fourth of July parade took place on the Potomac River in Washington DC, when President John Quincy Adams (1825-29) and a group of American and foreign dignitaries boarded a steamboat and led a procession of barges and other boats up the river to the site of what is known today as the Tidal Basin. Transferring to smaller boats, the entourage floated up the old Washington Canal to the place that had been selected for the new Chesapeake and Ohio Canal. There President Adams turned the first spade of dirt for the waterway that for many years cut through the heart of Washington DC, between the Capitol Building and the Washington Monument.

Today, parades are held in almost every city, town, and village on the Fourth of July. Marching bands, fife and drum corps, and members of organizations such as the Boy Scouts and Girl Scouts participate in the parades. Local veterans usually march in formation or ride in specially decorated cars, and floats are used to illustrate various patriotic themes.

Picnics

Feasting has always been part of July Fourth celebrations. In 1777, grand banquets were held in Philadelphia and other cities to commemorate the first anniversary of the approval of the Declaration of Independence. Eventually the parties moved outdoors, and by the mid-nineteenth century, the Fourth of July picnic had become a national tradition. It usually included sports and games such as tug-of-war, potato sack races, watermelon-eating contests, and chasing after a greased pig. Favorite picnic foods included fried chicken, potato salad, lemonade, chocolate and angel food cakes, pickles, deviled eggs, and homemade ice cream.

By the late nineteenth century, it was customary for political campaigns to begin on the Fourth of July. Local politicians would often sponsor holiday picnics, offering free hotdogs, corn on the cob, and steamed clams to anyone willing to listen to long political speeches. Political campaigns today don't get under way until Labor Day, but families still pack picnic baskets on the Fourth of July and head to the nearest state park, picnic area, or beach. The games afterward are usually confined to softball, but in some places tugs of war, sack races, and watermelon-eating contests are still popular.

Uncle Sam

Uncle Sam—the gray-bearded man on stilts wearing a top hat, tailcoat, and striped trousers—is a popular symbol of the United States. But he is not entirely imaginary. The real Uncle Sam was Samuel Wilson, born in Arlington, Massachusetts, in 1766. He ran away from home at the age of fourteen to enlist in the army. After the Revolutionary War was over, he moved to Troy, New York, and started a meat-packing business.

Known for his honesty and common sense, Sam Wilson supplied meat to the U.S. Army during the War of 1812. When a group of officials visiting his meatpacking plant saw that all the barrels of beef were stamped with the initials "U.S.," they asked what it meant. A workman told them it stood for "Uncle Sam" Wilson. The story was picked up by the newspapers, and soon people were referring to everything supplied to the army as "Uncle Sam's." The soldiers themselves began saying that they were in "Uncle Sam's Army."

After the war was over, Uncle Sam began appearing as a political cartoon figure. In the 1830s he was portrayed as a young man with stars and stripes on his shirt but without the gray hair, chin whiskers, top hat, or tailcoat that later became his trademarks. Some say that the costume now associated with Uncle Sam was invented by Dan Rice, a clown in the 1840s. Rice also walked on stilts, to make Uncle Sam look taller.

Uncle Sam's appearance was actually derived from two earlier symbolic figures in American folklore: Brother Jonathan and Yankee Doodle. Both Uncle Sam and Brother Jonathan were used interchangeably to represent the United States by cartoonists from the early 1830s to 1861. The first political cartoonist to standardize the figure of Uncle Sam was Thomas Nast, beginning in the 1870s. It was Nast who gave Uncle Sam his chin whiskers. Perhaps the most famous portrait of this symbolic figure is the one used on an army recruiting poster painted by James Montgomery Flagg during World War I. Uncle Sam is looking straight out at the viewer with his finger pointed, saying, "I Want You."

In recent years, some people have criticized the use of Uncle Sam as a symbol for the United States because he no longer reflects the diversity of the American population. But in 1961 the U.S. Congress passed a special resolution recognizing "Uncle Sam" Wilson of Troy, New York, as the namesake of our national symbol. His birthday, September 13, has been proclaimed "Uncle Sam's Day" in New York State.

"Yankee Doodle"

As the unofficial anthem of the United States, the simple melody known as "Yankee Doodle" is played in almost every Fourth of July parade, usually by fife and drum corps. "Yankee" (*Janke*) is a familiar nickname for the Dutch name Jan, just as Johnny is a nickname for John. The Dutch who settled in New York used the term to describe the English settlers of Connecticut, who were regarded during colonial times as people who were more interested in making money than they were in behaving morally. A "doodle" was a simpleton or a foolish person.

Dr. Richard Shuckburg, a British army doctor who was serving in the American colonies, is believed to have written the lyrics for the popular tune. "Stuck a feather in his hat" is probably a mocking reference to the Yankees' attempts to appear stylish and European when they were actually quite uncivilized. "Macaroni" was symbolic of all things Italian, and was used in eighteenth-century England to mean a fop—someone who dressed as if he were Italian. The British loved to make fun of the poorly dressed, poorly educated Americans.

Some scholars think that "Yankee Doodle" derived from a children's play song—possibly a slave song—in Surinam on the coast of South America, whose lyrics went like this:

> Mama Nanni go to town,
> Buy a little pony.
> Stick a feather in a ring
> Calling Masra Ranni.

"Masra" is the equivalent of "Massa"—the way American slaves were taught to address their white "Masters." It is possible that British soldiers heard the children's song and thought it would be a good way of mocking the upstart Americans. But the Americans liked the song so much that they adopted it as their own and, during the Revolutionary War, whistled it as they marched into battle.

"Yankee Doodle" was sung at the first Independence Day celebration in Philadel-phia in 1777 and quickly became a July Fourth tradition. Other songs frequently played on this day include "Yankee Doodle Boy" (also known as "I'm a Yankee Doo-dle Dandy") by George M. Cohan, "America," and "The Star-Spangled Banner."

FURTHER READING

Christianson, Stephen G., and Jane M. Hatch. *The American Book of Days*. 4th ed. New York: H.W. Wilson, 2000.

Giblin, James Cross. *Fireworks, Picnics, and Flags: The Story of the Fourth of July Sym-bols*. New York: Clarion Books, 1983.

Henderson, Helene, ed. *Holidays, Festivals, and Celebrations of the World Dictionary*. 3rd ed. Detroit: Omnigraphics, 2005.

Hoig, Stan. *It's the Fourth of July!* New York: Cobblehill Books, 1995.

Ickis, Marguerite. *The Book of Patriotic Holidays*. New York: Dodd, Mead, 1962.

Santino, Jack. *All Around the Year: Holidays and Celebrations in American Life*. Urbana: University of Illinois Press, 1994.

Tuleja, Tad. *Curious Customs: The Stories Behind 296 Popular American Rituals*. New York: Harmony, 1987.

WEB SITES

American University Library
www.american.edu/heintze/fourth.htm

U.S. Government Printing Office
bensguide.gpo.gov/6-8/documents/declaration/index.html

Gai Jatra
(Cow Festival)

Type of Holiday: Religious (Hindu)
Date of Observation: August-September; Hindu month of Bhadra
Where Celebrated: Nepal
Symbols and Customs: Cow, Street Comedy

ORIGINS

Gai Jatra is a Hindu religious festival celebrated in Nepal. The word Hindu is derived from the Sanskrit term *Sindhu* (or *Indus*), which meant river. It referred to people living in the Indus valley in the Indian subcontinent. Many scholars regard Hinduism as the oldest living religion.

Hinduism has no founder, one universal reality (or god) known as Brahman, many gods and goddesses (sometimes referred to as devtas), and several scriptures. Hinduism also has no priesthood or hierarchical structure similar to that seen in some other religions, such as Christianity. Hindus acknowledge the authority of a wide variety of writings, but there is no single, uniform canon. The oldest of the Hindu writings are the *Vedas*. The word "veda" comes from the Sanskrit word for knowledge. The *Vedas*, which were compiled from ancient oral traditions, contain hymns, instructions, explanations, chants for sacrifices, magical formulas, and philosophy. Another set of sacred books includes the *Great Epics*, which illustrate Hindu faith in practice. The *Epics* include the *Ramayana*, the *Mahabharata*, and the *Bhagavad Gita*.

The Hindu pantheon includes approximately thirty-three million gods. Some of these are held in higher esteem than others. Over all the gods, Hindus believe in one absolute high god or universal concept. This is Brahman. Although he is above all the gods, he is not worshipped in popular ceremonies because he is detached from the day-to-day affairs of the people. Brahman is impersonal. Lesser gods and goddesses (devtas) serve him. Because these are more intimately involved in the affairs of people, they are venerated as gods. The most honored god in Hinduism varies among the different Hindu sects. Although Hindu adherents practice their faith differently and venerate different deities, they share a similar view of reality and look back on a common history.

The festival of Gai Jatra, a favorite among the Nepalese people, has its roots in ancient times, when Yama Raj was worshipped as the ruler of the kingdom of death, to which all mortal souls must journey after departing the physical world. All of the families who had experienced a death in the past calendar year would join together and form a procession that made its way through the capital city of Katmandu. Each family would have a cow on a leash, because the cow was revered by all Hindus as a sacred animal and thus the ideal companion for the deceased on his or her journey to the underworld. The day of the procession was the only day of the year on which the gates to this kingdom were opened.

One of the festival's most popular features, however, was instituted much later, during the seventeenth-century reign of King Pratap Malla. In a desperate attempt to cheer up his wife after the death of their son, the king offered a reward to anyone who could make his queen laugh. Street comedians, mimics, and satirists showed up in ridiculous costumes, poking fun at the social injustices and political institutions of the day until the queen could not help but laugh out loud.

Today, Gai Jatra combines humor and mockery with a solemn acknowledgment of loss. There are morning prayers for the dead, followed by family processions leading cows decorated with flower necklaces and paper fans —or, as a substitute, a young boy in a cow-face mask. Another young boy often accompanies the "cow"; this is the yogi or holy man, who wears a moustache and a yellow loincloth. Larger processions often feature huge artificial cows made from bamboo, paper, and cloth. In Bhaktapur, large bamboo cows with straw horns are carried through the streets, as are smaller clay statues of cows. In Katmandu, all the processions pass through Durbar Square, where crowds gather to watch. People here and in other Nepalese cities often stand at intersections to offer refreshments to the participants as they pass by.

After the processions are over, the mood changes quickly. The rest of the day is turned over to songs, jokes, satires, and every imaginable form of humor. Some young men dress up in women's clothing or animal costumes, while others roam around acting as if they've lost their minds—doing anything, in other words, to get a laugh. Magazines and newspapers put out special editions poking fun at local politicians, and people often play practical jokes on each other. The singing, dancing, and merrymaking continue for most of the night, spurred on by large quantities of beer.

Aside from giving the Nepalese people an opportunity to make fun of each other and their government officials, Gai Jatra serves a more significant purpose: Families who have lost someone can pay tribute to the deceased and, at the same time, engage in activities that are joyful and life-affirming.

SYMBOLS AND CUSTOMS

Cow

Among Hindus, the gai or cow is the holiest and most venerated of all domestic animals. She plays the important role of safely guiding the souls of the deceased on their journey to Lord Yama's kingdom, and she uses her horns to open the gates. So powerful is the cow as a symbol in Hindu societies that even a mask, image, or a person dressed up like one is considered an object of reverence.

Street Comedy

The practical jokes, political satires, and other forms of poking fun that are so prevalent during Gai Jatra are part of a long tradition in Nepal known as khyalaa or street comedy. It originated in the seventeenth century, and, as recently as the mid-1980s, dozens of khyalaa troupes were performing during the Gai Jatra celebration. The actors played the roles of doctors, lawyers, and other important citizens, and they put on satirical dramas that made fun of local and government officials.

Today, the role of street comedy during the Gai Jatra festival is no longer as prevalent or well-organized, perhaps because it is no longer the only channel open to Nepalese who want to ridicule their government. But the spirit of khyalaa remains strong in the mocking and satirical flavor of the humor that has become such a recognizable part of the celebration.

FURTHER READING

MacDonald, Margaret R., ed. *The Folklore of World Holidays*. Detroit: Gale Research, 1992.

WEB SITE

Nepal Home Page
www.info-nepal.com/society/festivals/gaijatra.html

Galungan
(Balinese New Year)

Type of Holiday: Calendar/Seasonal, Religious (Bali Hindu)
Date of Observation: Every 210 days
Where Celebrated: Bali
Symbols and Customs: Barong, Lamak, Penjor, Tri Datu
Colors: Galungan is associated with the *tri datu* or "three colors": red, white, and black (*see* TRI DATU).
Related Holidays: Nyepi

ORIGINS

When it comes to determining festival dates, the Balinese use an indigenous calendar known as the *wuku*, which is believed to have been linked to the cycle according to which the islanders traditionally planted and harvested their rice. Instead of having a standard-length week of seven days, the wuku calendar has weeks of ten different lengths that run simultaneously rather than sequentially. Certain weeks—particularly those with three, five, or seven days—are considered more auspicious than others, and the best days for festivals are those that occur when certain of these weeks conjoin. The wuku year is 210 days long, and the new year celebration known as Galungan is therefore observed about once every seven months according to the Western or Gregorian calendar.

The dominant religion of the island of Bali in Indonesia is known as Bali Hindu, or Agama Tirtha, the Religion of Holy Water. Claiming more than two million adherents in Bali, the faith is a blend of ancient indigenous Balinese beliefs and strong Hindu and Buddhist influences. The emergence of Bali Hindu as a distinct religion is thought to have occurred sometime between the fourteenth and nineteenth centuries.

Balinese Hindus believe that the gods and ancestral spirits return to their earthly homes at this time of year and must be entertained with ten days of feasting, dancing, prayers, and holiday visits. Preparations begin on the Sunday before the Wednesday on which Galungan is observed. This day is known as Panyekeban, and it is devoted to ripening green bananas, a key ingredient in Galungan offerings, by placing them in covered clay pots and heating them. The following day, known as Penyajaan, is also devoted to preparing offerings, this time rice dough cakes known as *jaja*. The day before the holiday, known as Penampahan, is spent slaughtering pigs and other animals for the holiday feast. Other preparations include erecting the PENJOR—a decorated bamboo pole—and the woven palm-leaf decoration known as the LAMAK at the gate of each home.

Galungan itself, which falls on a Wednesday, is a time for prayer, feasting, and family gatherings. The temples are decorated and their shrines are wrapped in cloth—symbolizing the presence of the visiting spirits. BARONG dancers and children playing traditional Balinese instruments go from house to house entertaining people and receiving gifts in return. On the last day of the festival, which is known as Kuningan and marks the end of the ancestral spirits' ten-day visit, a festive holiday dish known as *nasi kuning,* made from cooked yellow rice, spices, and coconut milk, is served.

In addition to marking the start of a new year, Galungan commemorates the victory of *dharma* (good) over *adharma* (evil). In fact, the name of the festival comes from a Javanese word meaning "win." This is because, according to legend, there was a time many centuries ago when Bali was ruled by an evil king named Mayadenawa, who did everything in his power to stamp out Hindu beliefs and celebrations—including the observance of Galungan. During his reign, there was famine, drought, and disease everywhere. Finally Indra, the Hindu god of weather and storms, came down and helped the people destroy the evil king, and his death became symbolic of the victory of good over evil. People started celebrating Galungan again, and suddenly the crops started growing, people and animals regained their health, and life returned to normal. By observing Galungan, the Balinese are reminded every 210 days how blessed they have been since that time.

SYMBOLS AND CUSTOMS

Barong

Balinese Hinduism mixes traditional Balinese folk beliefs with Hindu religious beliefs and practices. The Barong is a lion-like creature who, according to Balinese mythology, is widely believed to protect Balinese villages by fighting off evil in the form of a witch named Rangda. The Barong is visible throughout the ten days of Galungan, often wandering from door to door and scaring off evil spirits. Sometimes there are spontaneous performances at the temples by Barong dancers wearing shaggy lion puppet heads. During the dance, Rangda tries to get the Barong supporters to stab themselves with their knives, but they go into a trancelike state and the knives have no effect. Although the Barong symbolizes goodness in the battle between good and evil, he is also associated with fun and mischief.

Lamak

Lamaks are an ancient Balinese art form. They are made by weaving strips of palm leaf, bamboo, or other native plants together to form rosettes, treelike designs, or decorative borders. One of the earliest motifs in many lamak patterns is the figure of a shapely young girl known as a cili, whom scholars believe may represent an ancient fertility goddess. During Galungan, lamak banners several yards long can often be seen hanging from PENJOR or adorning the gates to private homes. Despite their beauty and complexity, however, lamaks are not made to last. By nightfall on Galungan day they have usually wilted.

Penjor

The long, curved bamboo poles known as penjor are used to decorate the entrances to family homes as well as village streets during the holiday period. They are elaborately decorated with sheaves of rice, woven coconut leaves, fruit, cereal grains, flowers, and often coins or a piece of ceremonial cloth. Penjor are erected not only in celebration of religious holidays such as Galungan but to mark special occasions such as marriages.

The arch formed by the penjor is said to symbolize Mount Agung, the sacred mountain where the Balinese Hindu gods live; the pole itself represents the river that flows from this mountain and provides drinking water; and the decorative items are the products of the harvest and the basic items people need to survive. The penjor is traditionally set up at the gate or entranceway to the family home, where it serves as a reminder of the things for which the Balinese must be thankful and whose existence they must protect.

Tri Datu

Tri Datu refers to the "three colors"—red, white, and black—representing the Hindu trinity of Brahma, Vishnu, and Shiva. The tri datu colors can be seen throughout Bali on temples, private homes, and other buildings, especially during the ceremony held to purge buildings of evil spirits; in fact, they are part of most Balinese ceremonies.

During the celebration of Galungan, the Tri Datu are most commonly seen in the colored threads that the Balinese wear on their wrists, ankles, and heads. The threads are believed to impart physical and mental strength while ridding the mind of negative or disturbing thoughts.

FURTHER READING

Bellenir, Karen. *Religious Holidays and Calendars*. 3rd ed. Detroit: Omnigraphics, 2004.
Merin, Jennifer, and Elizabeth B. Burdick. *International Directory of Theatre, Dance, and Folklore Festivals*. Westport, CT: Greenwood Press, 1979.

Shemanski, Frances. *A Guide to World Fairs and Festivals*. Westport, CT: Greenwood Press, 1985.

Trawicky, Bernard, and Ruth W. Gregory. *Anniversaries and Holidays*. 5th ed. Chicago: American Library Assocation, 2000.

Ganesh Chaturthi
(Ganesh Chathurthi)

Type of Holiday: Religious (Hindu)
Date of Observation: August-September; fourth day of the bright half of the Hindu month of Bhadrapada
Where Celebrated: India
Symbols and Customs: Elephant, Modakas, Moon, Mouse

ORIGINS

Ganesh Chaturthi is a religious festival that is part of Hinduism, which many scholars regard as the oldest living religion. The word Hindu is derived from the Sanskrit term *Sindhu* (or *Indus*), which meant river. It referred to people living in the Indus valley in the Indian subcontinent.

Hinduism has no founder, one universal reality (or god) known as Brahman, many gods and goddesses (sometimes referred to as devtas), and several scriptures. Hinduism also has no priesthood or hierarchical structure similar to that seen in some other religions, such as Christianity. Hindus acknowledge the authority of a wide variety of writings, but there is no single, uniform canon. The oldest of the Hindu writings are the *Vedas*. The word "veda" comes from the Sanskrit word for knowledge. The *Vedas*, which were compiled from ancient oral traditions, contain hymns, instructions, explanations, chants for sacrifices, magical formulas, and philosophy. Another set of sacred books includes the *Great Epics*, which illustrate Hindu faith in practice. The *Epics* include the *Ramayana*, the *Mahabharata*, and the *Bhagavad Gita*.

The Hindu pantheon includes approximately thirty-three million gods. Some of these are held in higher esteem than others. Over all the gods, Hindus believe in one absolute high god or universal concept. This is Brahman. Although he is above all the gods, he is not worshiped in popular ceremonies because he is detached from the day-to-day affairs of the people. Brahman is impersonal. Lesser gods and goddesses (devtas) serve him. Because these are more intimately involved in the affairs of people, they are venerated as gods. The most honored god in Hinduism varies among the different Hindu sects. Although Hindu adherents practice their faith differently and venerate different deities, they share a similar view of reality and look back on a common history.

Ganesh Chaturthi celebrates the birthday of Ganesha, the eldest son of the gods Shiva and Parvati and one of the five major Hindu deities. With his pot belly and ELEPHANT head, Ganesha is the god who removes all obstacles in the paths of those struggling to achieve both spiritual and worldly success. Almost every Hindu home has Ganesha's image over the doorway, and he is worshipped at the beginning of every important undertaking, whether it is the building of a new house, the beginning of a marriage, or the opening of a new account book.

After taking a bath on the morning of Ganesha's birthday, devoted Hindus go to the temple and say prayers in his honor, accompanied by offerings of coconut and sweet pudding (*see* MODAKAS). The worshippers ask Ganesha to help them overcome the obstacles they are likely to encounter on the road to spiritual wisdom. Beautifully decorated images of the god are carried through the streets and later immersed in the waters of the sea or a nearby river. MODAKAS or sweet-balls are served to everyone in the house.

Bombay is the center for Ganesh Chaturthi celebrations, and thousands of images of the god are made and sold there. Small images are used in the home, but life-size ones are often set up on temporary altars in the streets. These images are worshipped for three days, at the end of which they are carried in procession to the nearest body of water. In some parts of India, Ganesha is the god of the harvest, and after the immersion ceremony is over, sand or clay from the riverbed is brought back to the farm and scattered around the barns and storerooms.

SYMBOLS AND CUSTOMS

Elephant

According to Hindu legend, Parvati created her son out of clay and oil, and posted him outside her door to prevent anyone from entering the house while she was taking her bath. When Shiva himself was not allowed to enter, he became so angry he shattered the boy's head. Parvati was inconsolable when she discovered what had happened to the son she had created. His head was broken in so many pieces that no one could find them all. To make amends, Shiva set out in search of a suitable replacement head and came back with the head of an elephant. To this day, Ganesha is known as "the elephant-headed god."

Ganesha also represents *Om*, which is the chief mantra or chant-word among Hindus. The belief that nothing can be accomplished without uttering this sound explains why Ganesha is invoked before undertaking a project. The elephant head is significant because it is the only figure in nature that has the same form as the Sanskrit symbol for Om. Some scholars think that the elephant's head and snout are reminiscent of a farmer carrying a corn sheaf on his head, with the lowest ears swinging to and fro. This fits in well with Ganesha's reputation as the god of the harvest.

Modakas

Modakas or sweet-balls are symbolic of the sweet puddings that Ganesha was so fond of as a child. On one of his birthdays, he ate so many puddings that when the MOUSE on which he was riding was startled by a snake, Ganesha fell off and his stomach burst open. He stuffed all the puddings back in and tied the snake around his belly to hold it together. As the god of plenty, Ganesha is always shown with a round belly, symbolic of a good appetite and a plentiful harvest.

Modakas are made of rice flour, raw sugar, and the kernel of the coconut, all of which are in season in India during the month of Bhadrapada (August-September).

Moon

Hindus consider it bad luck to look at the moon on Ganesh Chaturthi because legend claims that the moon laughed when Ganesha fell off his MOUSE and his stomach burst open (*see* MODAKAS). The god cursed the moon, who was forced to hide himself in shame. After the moon apologized, Ganesha lifted the curse but declared that the moon would always be in disgrace on this day. Those who do look at the moon will earn a bad name or ruin their reputations. But if they do so inadvertently, they can forestall the consequences by making sure that their neighbors treat them badly, thus punishing them for their mistake.

Mouse

Ganesha is usually depicted riding on a mouse, a symbol of the conquest over egoism. Because he possesses the head of an elephant, the largest animal, and yet rides on a mouse, the smallest, Ganesha embodies the process of evolution—from small animals to large animals and finally to human beings.

Some scholars see the mouse as a field rat, the destroyer of crops, and Ganesha as its conqueror. The snake wrapped around the god's belly, which represents a barn full of harvested crops, is also capable of destroying the field rat. The root of the Sanskrit word for "rat" means "thief," which implies that Ganesha is riding over the thief of the field, or the field rat.

FURTHER READING

Gupte, B.A. *Hindu Holidays and Ceremonials.* 2nd ed. Calcutta: Thacker, Spink & Co., 1919.

Henderson, Helene, ed. *Holidays, Festivals, and Celebrations of the World Dictionary.* 3rd ed. Detroit: Omnigraphics, 2005.

Sanon, Arun. *Festive India.* New Delhi: Frank Bros., 1986.

Sharma, Brijendra Nath. *Festivals of India.* New Delhi: Abhinav Publications, 1978.

Sivananda, Swami. *Hindu Fasts and Festivals.* 8th ed. Shivanandanagar, India: Divine Life Society, 1997.

Thomas, Paul. *Festivals and Holidays in India.* Bombay: D.B. Taraporevala Sons, 1971.

WEB SITE

Maharashtra Tourism Guide
www.maharashtratourism.net/festivals/ganesh-chaturthi.html

Ganna (Leddat, Ethiopian Christmas)

Type of Holiday: Religious (Christian)
Date of Observation: January 7
Where Celebrated: Ethiopia
Symbols and Customs: Ganna, Gift-Giving, Sistrum
Related Holidays: Christmas, Epiphany, Timkat

ORIGINS

Christianity was established in Ethiopia in the fourth century, when a Christian from Syria named Frumentius traveled there and influenced the local ruler. At the time, Christianity in Syria was under the domain of the Orthodox Patriarch of Alexandria, Egypt. Thus, so was the new church in Ethiopia until 1959, when the Ethiopian Orthodox Church separated from the Coptic Church of Egypt.

The Ethiopian Orthodox Church still uses the Julian calendar. This means that they observe Ganna or **CHRISTMAS** on January 7, just twelve days before **TIMKAT** or **EPIPHANY** and at the end of a forty-day period of fasting. Unlike the celebration of Christmas in the West, however, Christmas in Ethiopia has remained primarily a religious holiday, untainted by commercialism and costly GIFT-GIVING. It is, however, the occasion for a spirited game of field hockey, the popularity of which has led to naming the holiday, which is officially called Led-dat, after the game, GANNA.

The day begins with a 3:00 a.m. church service. Everyone is given a candle upon entering the church, which is typically designed around a circular floor plan. After lighting their candles, people walk around the inside of the church three times before taking their places. Because Ethiopian churches do not have benches or chairs, everyone remains standing throughout the entire three-hour service. Priests dressed in robes and carrying SISTRUMS keep the beat of the religious dances that follow, which are also accompanied by the tapered drum known as the *kabaro*.

The traditional meal on Christmas is *injera,* a flat sourdough bread that has been cooked over an open fire, dipped in a spicy chicken stew. But the highlight of the day comes after the midday feast, when the game known as Ganna begins. It is similar to hockey, and it is usually the men and older boys who participate because it can get very rough. The game begins late in the afternoon and continues until it is too dark to see. This is the only day of the year on which it is played, and the winning team is honored afterward by going from house to house to receive gifts and refreshments.

SYMBOLS AND CUSTOMS

Ganna

According to legend, when the shepherds received the news of Jesus' birth, they were so overjoyed that they celebrated with a spontaneous game of field hockey, using their crooks for hockey sticks. The modern game of Ganna still uses curved sticks to drive a hard leather ball across the playing field toward a goal line.

Perhaps because it is only played on the Christmas holiday, there is a tendency for the game to get out of hand. Bloody cuts, bruises, and even broken bones are not uncommon, and the winning team often taunts the losers by shouting insulting limericks in their faces.

Gift-Giving

The giving of gifts at Ganna is nothing like what goes on during the Christmas season in the United States. It is only the children who receive gifts from their parents, and the gifts themselves are usually simple and inexpensive, such as clothing or a small toy.

Sistrum

The sistrum, known in Ethiopia as the sanasel or tsenatsel, is a ceremonial rattle that dates back to the third millennium B.C.E. It became popular during the time of the pharaohs in Egypt, where it was used to mark the cadence of religious processions and ceremonies and where it consisted of a handle with an enclosed drum or resonating chamber. As used today by Orthodox Christian priests in Ethiopia, the sistrum consists of a forked frame across which small metal disks or coins have been strung on wire, so that it rattles or jingles when shaken. During the church service held on Ganna, the priests use both the sistrum and the prayer stick—a t-shaped pole similar to a crutch—to keep the rhythm during the ceremonies and dances.

FURTHER READING

Ickis, Marguerite. *The Book of Festivals and Holidays the World Over*. New York: Dodd, Mead, 1970.

MacDonald, Margaret R., ed. *The Folklore of World Holidays*. Detroit: Gale Research, 1992.

Shemanski, Frances. *A Guide to World Fairs and Festivals*. Westport, CT: Greenwood Press, 1985.

Trawicky, Bernard, and Ruth W. Gregory. *Anniversaries and Holidays*. 5th ed. Chicago: American Library Assocation, 2000.

Van Straalen, Alice. *The Book of Holidays Around the World*. New York: Dutton, 1986.

WEB SITE

Ethiopian Ministry of Culture and Tourism
tourismethiopia.org/pages/detail/detailfestival.asp

Gauri Festival

Type of Holiday: Religious (Hindu)
Date of Observation: August-September; third day of Bhadrapada
Where Celebrated: Southern India
Symbols and Customs: Cradle, Number Two, Winnowing Fan
Colors: Red, yellow, white, and black. Yellow is the color of wealth, beauty, and good fortune. In this festival, it appears in the color of turmeric powder, bananas, and the sour rice dish that is served. Red, the color of blood and vitality, can be seen in the vermilion powder, betel nuts, and bright red saris worn in some parts of India. White, the color of purity and continuity, can be seen in the rice and milk that are served. Black is symbolic of death, difficulty, and danger. Hindu women are given black bangles to protect them from misfortune. These four colors define the basic forces with which married women must contend.

ORIGINS

The Gauri Festival is a religious celebration in Hinduism, which many scholars regard as the world's oldest living religion. The word Hindu is derived from the Sanskrit term *Sindhu* (or *Indus*), which meant river. It referred to people living in the Indus valley in the Indian subcontinent.

Hinduism has no founder, one universal reality (or god) known as Brahman, many gods and goddesses (sometimes referred to as devtas), and several scriptures. Hinduism also has no priesthood or hierarchical structure similar to that seen in some other religions, such as Christianity. Hindus acknowledge the authority of a wide variety of writings, but there is no single, uniform canon. The oldest of the Hindu writings are the *Vedas*. The word "veda" comes from the Sanskrit word for knowledge. The *Vedas*, which were compiled from ancient oral traditions, contain hymns, instructions, explanations, chants for sacrifices, magical formulas, and philosophy. Another set of sacred books includes the *Great Epics*, which illustrate Hindu faith in practice. The *Epics* include the *Ramayana*, the *Mahabharata*, and the *Bhagavad Gita*.

The Hindu pantheon includes approximately thirty-three million gods. Some of these are held in higher esteem than others. Over all the gods, Hindus believe in one absolute high god or universal concept. This is Brahman. Although he is above all the gods, he is not worshiped in popular ceremonies because he is detached from the day to day affairs of the people. Brahman is impersonal. Lesser gods and goddesses (devtas) serve him. Because these are more intimately involved in the affairs of people, they are venerated as gods. The most honored god in Hinduism varies among the different Hindu sects. Although Hindu adherents practice their faith differently and venerate different deities, they share a similar view of reality and look back on a common history.

Gauri is the Hindu goddess of married women as well as the goddess of daughters. She is a form of Parvati, the wife of Shiva, and is often described as "the golden one" because Brahma gave her a golden complexion when her husband complained that her skin was too dark. Her festival, which is celebrated by women throughout southern India, involves a series of rituals associated with welcoming, worshipping, and sending the goddess back to her home. These rituals are designed to reflect the typical experience of a Hindu woman, who is born into her family, lives in her parents' home until shortly after her marriage, and finally leaves her family to become part of her husband's household.

The celebration begins on the third day of the Hindu lunar month of Bhadrapada. Women wash their faces, bathe themselves and their children in oil, and decorate their floors with elaborate white line drawings. Then they dress in their best saris and prepare to summon Gauri from her home in the river.

Men are not entirely excluded from the festival. A group of them go to the river with a large wooden CRADLE suspended from a long pole. The ball of sand they put in the cradle represents Gauri, who is taken into the village for everyone to worship. The women bring their trays filled with offerings, each of which has a symbolic meaning or color (*see* "Colors" above). A comb, for example, symbolizes good grooming, which is closely linked to sexuality and the sexual discipline that women are supposed to exhibit. The feast that follows the principal welcoming ceremony has two required dishes: white yogurt rice (white symbolizing purity, duty, and discipline) and sour yellow rice (wealth, good fortune), which are eaten together, along with various side dishes.

There is a lull of a day or two after the welcoming celebration, during which the goddess's son Ganesha is said to arrive in the village to tell his mother that his father, Shiva, is lonely. Because it is taboo to send the goddess away on the second or fourth day of the month (even numbers being unlucky), the send-off ritual is performed on the third or fifth day. The sand ball representing the goddess is returned to the river, certain farewell rituals are carried out at the river's edge, and various foods and flowers are gathered to send with Gauri on her journey home.

The myth of Gauri symbolizes the transition a bride goes through when she leaves her family to live with her husband. The struggles that Gauri and Shiva go through before assuming their life as a married couple have many parallels in the marriage negotiations that take place between Hindu families and in the struggles a bride must endure in her effort to be accepted by her husband's family. The women of the village who get together to celebrate the Gauri Festival often take advantage of the opportunity to discuss their own problems and the concerns of women in general, such as infertility, poverty, and desertion. They regard Gauri as married in a permanent way that stands as a model of stability. Since the fear of widowhood is intense among Hindu women, the fortunate women whose husbands are still living do everything in their power to honor the goddess who can help them remain in that favorable state.

SYMBOLS AND CUSTOMS

Cradle

It is significant that Gauri is brought into the village in a cradle, not on a throne or some other conveyance befitting a goddess. The cradle is associated with pregnancy and childbearing, thus underscoring the festival's emphasis on a woman's experience.

Number Two

Hindus generally consider even numbers unlucky because they convey the idea of finality. An even amount of money, for example, suggests finality and "no future"; therefore, Hindus in southern India will often pay 101 rupees for an item that is officially priced at only 100 rupees.

The numbers one and two contradict this cultural rule. Perhaps because two equals one plus one and symbolizes non-solitude, it is considered lucky even though it is even. Similarly, the number one is considered unlucky even though it is odd. In the context of the Gauri Festival, the number two symbolizes the fruitful partnership of the married couple. Women celebrating the festival always bring gifts and offerings that come in pairs, such as palm-leaf earrings. Even WINNOWING FANS are never sold as single items, but only in pairs.

Winnowing Fan

The winnowing fan is used to separate grain from chaff, or useless husks. In India, it is used to produce clean, husked rice, which makes it a logical symbol of separation—the separation of the daughter from her family at marriage—and of purification. Used in the Gauri Festival to hold the gifts that women exchange with each other, the winnowing fans usually contain rice and other grains, salt, a cube of brown sugar, bananas, coconut, betel nuts, and turmeric root—everything that is needed for basic nutrition, with the exception of oil and spices. Such gifts are considered symbolic of nourishment and growth, and the women who exchange them are expressing the idea that each woman's wealth (symbolized by turmeric root, which is yellow) comes from another woman, both in the form of the dowry that is brought into a marriage and in the form of the gifts mothers give to their daughters.

Also known as "wealth-producing fans" or *bhagina mara,* the winnowing fans used in the festival are prepared in sets of four: a pair of fans is filled with gifts and covered with two more fans (*see* NUMBER TWO). A pair of doubled winnowing fans also rests in the CRADLE beside the ball of sand that represents the goddess Gauri.

FURTHER READING

Hanchett, Suzanne. *Coloured Rice: Symbolic Structure in Hindu Family Festivals.* Delhi: Hindustan Pub. Corp., 1988.
Henderson, Helene, ed. *Holidays, Festivals, and Celebrations of the World Dictionary.* 3rd ed. Detroit: Omnigraphics, 2005.

Gion Matsuri (Gion Festival)

Type of Holiday: Historic, Religious (Shinto)
Date of Observation: July 17
Where Celebrated: Kyoto and other cities in Japan
Symbols and Customs: Floats

ORIGINS

Gion Matsuri is a festival celebrated by practioners of Shinto, an ancient religion that originated in Japan. Most Shinto adherents live in Japan, but small communities also exist in Europe, Latin America, North America, and in the Pacific island nations.

The name Shinto was first employed during the sixth century C.E. to differentiate indigenous religions in Japan from faith systems that originated in mainland Asia (primarily Buddhism and Confucianism). The word is derived from two Chinese characters, *shen* (gods) and *tao* (way). Loosely translated, Shinto means "way of the gods." Its roots lie in an ancient nature-based religion. Some important concepts in Shinto include the value of tradition, the reverence of nature, cleanliness (ritual purity), and the veneration of spirits called *kami*. Strictly speaking, kami are not deities. The literal translation of the word kami is "that which is hidden."

Kami (which is both the singular and plural term) are honored, but do not assert their powers upon humans in the traditional manner of deities or gods in other religions. People may be descended from the kami, and kami may influence the course of nature and events. The kami can bestow blessings, but they are not all benign. Kami are present in natural things such as trees, mountains, rocks, and rivers. They are embodied in religious relics, especially mirrors and jewels. They also include spirits of ancestors, local deities, holy people, and even political or literary figures. The human role is to venerate the kami and make offerings. The ultimate goal of Shinto is to uphold the harmony among humans and between people and nature. In this regard, the principle of all kami is to protect and sustain life.

The central authorities in Shinto are the priests. Traditionally the duties of the priest were passed through heredity lines, but in modern times, priests are trained on the basis of recommendation. The priests' duties include communicating with the kami and ensuring that ceremonies are properly carried out. Shinto does not have a single collection of sacred texts analogous to the Christian Bible or Islamic Qur'an. Instead, several important books provide information and guidance: *Kojiki* (*Records of Ancient Events*), *Nihongi* (*Chronicles of Japan*), and *Engishiki* (*Chronicles of the Engi*).

One of the best-known festivals in Japan and the largest in the city of Kyoto, the Gion Matsuri (or Gion Festival) dates back to 869, when an epidemic swept through Kyoto and many of its citizens died. At the time, Kyoto was the capital city of Japan, and a brother of the Sun Goddess lived in the Gion (now called Yasaka) Shrine there. The head priest mounted sixty-six spears on a palanquin—a portable shrine, covered and elaborately decorated, that sits atop two poles resting on the shoulders of the men who carry it—and took it to the Emperor's garden. Miraculously, the plague ended immediately. In gratitude, the priest led a procession through the city's streets. Since that time, the Yasaka Shrine has been the site of a huge summer festival in which this procession is reenacted. The only interruption of this tradition was during the Onin War (1467-77), which largely destroyed the city.

On July 17 every year, huge FLOATS, some four stories high, are pulled through the streets of Kyoto. They are decorated with silks, gold ornaments, and treasures imported from Europe over the centuries. Sometimes people ride on top of the floats during the procession. The festival surrounding the procession lasts almost a month, but the parade is the event's highlight. Other towns in Japan, such as Hakata, Narita, and Takayama, have since imitated the Kyoto celebration and now have their own Gion festivals.

SYMBOLS AND CUSTOMS

Floats

There are twenty-nine *hoko* or "spear" floats and twenty-two smaller *yama* or "mountain" floats. The immense hoko weigh as much as ten tons and can be thirty feet tall; they look like very elaborate towers on wheels, decorated with Chinese and Japanese paintings and even French tapestries. Musicians play flutes and drums under the lacquered roofs, from which two men toss straw good-luck favors to the crowds as the floats are pulled slowly, on huge wooden wheels, through the streets with ropes.

The yama floats weigh only about a ton and are carried on long poles by teams of men. Life-sized dolls on platforms atop each float represent characters in the story that each float depicts.

FURTHER READING

Bellenir, Karen. *Religious Holidays and Calendars*. 3rd ed. Detroit: Omnigraphics, 2004.

Buell, Hal. *Festivals of Japan*. New York: Dodd, Mead, 1965.

Henderson, Helene, ed. *Holidays, Festivals, and Celebrations of the World Dictionary*. 3rd ed. Detroit: Omnigraphics, 2005.

Trawicky, Bernard, and Ruth W. Gregory. *Anniversaries and Holidays*. 5th ed. Chicago: American Library Assocation, 2000.

Van Straalen, Alice. *The Book of Holidays Around the World*. New York: Dutton, 1986.

WEB SITE

Yamasa Institute's Multimedia Studio
www.yamasa.org/japan/english/destinations/kyoto/gion_matsuri.html

Good Friday

Type of Holiday: Religious (Christian)
Date of Observation: Between March 20 and April 23; the Friday before Easter
Where Celebrated: Throughout the Christian world
Symbols and Customs: Cock, Cross, Crown of Thorns, Hot Cross Buns, Kite-flying, Stations of the Cross, Tre Ore, Veil
Colors: Good Friday is traditionally associated with the color black, a symbol of death, despair, sorrow, and mourning. In many countries, churches are darkened and draped with black on this day, and religious processions often feature black-robed penitents or statues of Christ and the Virgin Mary draped in black.
Related Holidays: Easter, Maundy Thursday, Palm Sunday

ORIGINS

Good Friday is a Christian holy day that commemorates the crucifixion of Jesus Christ. The word Christian refers to a follower of Christ, a title derived from the Greek word meaning Messiah or Anointed One. The Christ of Christianity is Jesus of Nazareth, a man born between 7 and 4 B.C.E. in the region of Palestine. According to Christian teaching, Jesus was killed by Roman authorities using a form of execution called crucifixion (a term meaning he was nailed to a cross and hung from it until he died) in about the year 30 C.E. After his death, he rose back to life. His death and resurrection provide a way by which people can be reconciled with God. In remembrance of Jesus' death and resurrection, the cross serves as a fundamental symbol in Christianity.

With nearly two billion believers in countries around the globe, Christianity is the largest of the world's religions. There is no one central authority for all of Christianity. The pope (the bishop of Rome) is the authority for the Roman Catholic Church, but other sects look to other authorities. Orthodox communities look to patriarchs and emphasize doctrinal agreement and traditional practice. Protestant communities focus on individual conscience. The Roman Catholic and Protestant churches are often referred to as the Western Church, while the Orthodox churches may also be called the Eastern Church. All three main branches of Christianity acknowledge the authority of Christian scriptures, a compilation of writings assembled into a document called the Bible. Methods of biblical interpretation vary among the different Christian sects.

Good Friday commemorates Jesus' journey to Calvary (*see* STATIONS OF THE CROSS) and his death on the CROSS, which took place on the Friday before **EASTER** Sunday. Christians have been observing Good Friday even longer than Easter, although there was a period when it was neglected by Protestant churches. Nowadays it is observed almost universally by Christians around the world, who devote this day to remembering Jesus' suffering and sacrifice.

There are several theories as to why the day commemorating Jesus' crucifixion is called "Good" Friday. Some scholars think it's a corruption of "God's Friday," while others take "good" to mean "observed as holy." Although it may seem paradoxical, Christians regard the death of Jesus as "good" in the sense that it opened the gates of everlasting life. Orthodox Christians call it Great Friday, but it's not surprising that the Friday before Easter is sometimes referred to as Black Friday or Sorrowful Friday.

SYMBOLS AND CUSTOMS

Cock

As the bird of dawn, the cock is a sun symbol and stands for vigilance and resurrection. It became an important Christian image during the Middle Ages, when it began to appear on weathervanes, cathedral towers, and domes.

In the context of Good Friday, the cock is symbolic of the denial of Peter, one of Jesus' disciples. After Jesus had been seized by the servants of the high priest Caiaphas as he was leaving the Garden of Gethsemane, he was brought to the palace, where the council tried to find people who would bear witness against him. Peter was there in the palace while Jesus was being accused. Some of the onlookers recognized him and accused him of being a follower of Christ. But just as Jesus had predicted would happen, Peter declared three times that he did not know the man who had been taken prisoner. When he heard the cock crow a second time, he remembered Jesus' words: "Verily, I say unto thee, That this day, even in this night, before the cock crows twice, thou shalt deny me thrice" (Mark 14:30). Peter wept when he realized that he had been unfaithful to his beloved Master.

Cross

Although the cross is even older than the Christian religion, the cross on which Christ died has become a symbol for salvation and redemption through Christianity. It can be seen in many different forms, but the so-called Latin cross (with a longer upright and shorter crossbar) is usually the symbol for the Passion of Christ. Five red marks or jewels are sometimes placed on the face of the cross to represent the five wounds Christ received when He was crucified. When the Latin cross stands on three steps—symbolizing faith, hope, and love (1 Cor. 13:13)—it is called the Calvary, or Graded, Cross. (*See also* Exaltation of the Cross.)

Crown of Thorns

The crown of thorns is an emblem of the Passion and the crucifixion of Christ. As described in the Gospel of Mark, chapter 15, verses 16-18, the soldiers into whose hands Jesus was delivered by Pontius Pilate dressed him in purple and placed a crown of thorns on his head. Then, saluting him with mock respect, they cried, "Hail, King of the Jews!" Christ is usually shown wearing the crown of thorns from this moment until he was taken down from the cross.

The way monks wear their hair—shaved on the top and with a short fringe all around—is designed to imitate Jesus' crown of thorns.

Hot Cross Buns

The pagans worshipped the goddess Eostre (after whom Easter was named) by serving tiny cakes, often decorated with a cross, at their annual spring festival. When archaeologists excavated the ancient city of Herculaneum in southwestern Italy, which had been buried under volcanic ash and lava since 79 C.E., they found two small loaves, each with a cross on it, among the ruins. The English word "bun" probably came from the Greek *boun,* which referred to a ceremonial cake of circular or crescent shape, made of flour and honey and offered to the gods.

Superstitions regarding bread that was baked on Good Friday date back to a very early period. In England particularly, people believed that bread baked on this day could be hardened in the oven and kept all year to protect the house from fire. Sailors took loaves of it on their voyages to prevent shipwreck, and a Good Friday loaf was often buried in a heap of corn to protect it from rats, mice, and weevils. Finely grated and mixed with water, it was sometimes used as a medicine.

In England nowadays, hot cross buns are served at breakfast on Good Friday morning. They are small, usually spiced buns whose sugary surface is marked with a cross. The English believe that hanging a hot cross bun in the house on this day offers protection from bad luck in the coming year. It's not unusual to see Good Friday buns or cakes hanging on a rack or in a wire basket for years, gathering dust and growing black with mold—although some people believe that if the ingredients are mixed, the dough prepared, and the buns baked on Good Friday itself, they will never get moldy.

Kite-flying

On the island of Bermuda, the custom of flying kites is synonymous with Good Friday. It dates back to the nineteenth century, when a teacher who was having trouble explaining to his students how Jesus ascended into heaven took them to the highest hill on the island and launched a kite bearing an image of Jesus. When he ran out of string, he cut the line and let the kite fly out of sight. Flying kites has been a Good Friday tradition ever since.

Stations of the Cross

Christ was crucified at Calvary, a place near Jerusalem also known as Golgotha, which means "skull." His journey there is usually divided into fourteen scenes or "Stations": (1) Jesus is condemned to death; (2) he receives his cross; (3) he falls the first time under his cross; (4) he meets his Mother; (5) Simon of Cyrene helps Jesus carry his cross; (6) Veronica wipes Jesus' face; (7) Jesus falls a second time; (8) he speaks to the women of Jerusalem; (9) he falls a third time; (10) he is stripped of his garments; (11) Jesus is nailed to the cross; (12) he dies on the cross; (13) he is taken down from the cross; and (14) he is laid in the Sepulchre. Although the number of stations was fixed at fourteen in the eighteenth century, five of them have no basis in the Bible's account of Jesus' Passion.

The original Stations of the Cross were the sites in Jerusalem and the surrounding area identified with these events. During the time of the Crusades, pilgrims to the Holy Land marked off these sites and, when they returned to their homes in Europe, they erected memorials of these stations in their churches and even their fields. Pictures of the Stations of the Cross can still be seen on the walls of Roman Catholic and Episcopal churches.

The form of worship that takes place at the Stations of the Cross has never been officially determined by any church authority. Sometimes groups of worshippers will pray together at each station and sing hymns as they pass from one station to the next. More often, individuals engage in private prayer and meditation.

Tre Ore

The Tre Ore or "Three Hours" service takes place in many Protestant and Catholic churches on Good Friday. The name refers to the last three hours that Jesus hung on the cross, and the service itself is based on the last seven things that Jesus said before he died (also known as the "Seven Last Words"):

1. Father, forgive them, for they know not what they do.
2. Today shalt thou be with me in paradise.
3. Woman, behold thy son!
4. My God, my God, why has thou forsaken me?
5. I thirst.
6. It is finished.
7. Father, into thy hands I commend my spirit.

The Tre Ore service is a devotional service that was first performed by Alonso Mexía, a Jesuit in Peru, after a devastating earthquake struck Lima in 1687. An Anglican priest named A.H. Mackonochie promoted it in England in the nineteenth century, and it eventually became the main Good Friday observance for many evangelical congregations. The words have been set to music by a number of composers, most notably Heinrich Schutz (c. 1645) and Charles François Gounod (1855). Brief speeches, hymns, and periods for meditation and prayer are usually interspersed throughout the musical score.

The Tre Ore service is held from noon until 3:00 p.m. to coincide with the period of time during which Jesus actually hung on the cross, which the Gospel of Matthew (chapter 27, verses 45-46) establishes as falling between the sixth and ninth hours of the day. In modern terms, this would be 12:00-3:00 p.m.

Veil

When Jesus was on his way to be crucified, according to legend, a woman in the crowd named Veronica took pity on him and wiped the sweat from his brow with her veil or handkerchief. Miraculously the cloth retained the likeness of Christ wearing his CROWN OF THORNS.

The veil passed through a series of adventures but finally ended up in Rome, where it has been kept for many centuries in St. Peter's Church.

FURTHER READING

Bellenir, Karen. *Religious Holidays and Calendars*. 3rd ed. Detroit: Omnigraphics, 2004.

Brewster, H. Pomeroy. *Saints and Festivals of the Christian Church*. 1904. Reprint. Detroit: Omnigraphics, 1990.

Chambers, Robert. *The Book of Days*. 2 vols. 1862-64. Reprint. Detroit: Omnigraphics, 1990.

Cirlot, J.E. *A Dictionary of Symbols*. New York: Philosophical Library, 1962.

Dobler, Lavinia G. *Customs and Holidays Around the World*. New York: Fleet Pub. Corp., 1962.

Ferguson, George. *Signs and Symbols in Christian Art*. New York: Oxford University Press, 1954.

Gulevich, Tanya. *Encyclopedia of Easter, Carnival, and Lent*. Detroit: Omnigraphics, 2002.

Harper, Howard V. *Days and Customs of All Faiths*. 1957. Reprint. Detroit: Omnigraphics, 1990.

Henderson, Helene, ed. *Holidays, Festivals, and Celebrations of the World Dictionary*. 3rd ed. Detroit: Omnigraphics, 2005.

Ickis, Marguerite. *The Book of Festivals and Holidays the World Over*. New York: Dodd, Mead, 1970.

Ickis, Marguerite. *The Book of Religious Holidays and Celebrations*. New York: Dodd, Mead, 1966.

Lord, Priscilla Sawyer, and Daniel J. Foley. *Easter the World Over*. Philadelphia: Chilton Book Co., 1971.

Metford, J.C.J. *The Christian Year*. New York: Crossroad, 1991.

Monks, James L. *Great Catholic Festivals*. New York: Henry Schuman, 1951.

Rest, Friedrich. *Our Christian Symbols*. New York: Pilgrim Press, 1954.

Urlin, Ethel L. *Festivals, Holy Days, and Saints' Days*. 1915. Reprint. Detroit: Omnigraphics, 1992.

WEB SITES

New Advent Catholic Encyclopedia
www.newadvent.org/cathen/06643a.htm

Orthodox Church in America
www.oca.org/OCchapter.asp?SID=2&ID=74

Great Elephant March

Type of Holiday: Religious (Hindu)
Date of Observation: January
Where Celebrated: Trichur, Kerala, India
Symbols and Customs: Festival, Pooram Reenactment
Related Holidays: Pooram

ORIGINS

The Great Elephant March takes place each year in Trichur, Kerala, a coastal village on the Arabian Sea in southwestern India. Elephants are an integral part of daily life for the people of Kerala, who have a long history and tradition as highly skilled elephant trainers. Keralans train elephants to perform routine and ceremonial tasks such as carrying or pulling heavy loads and bearing people as riders.

Also known as a *gajamela* (elephant pageant), the Great Elephant March is staged especially for tourists but is also attended by many Kerala citizens. More than 100 elephants are dressed in elaborate regalia made of gold and decorated with jewels. The elephants, each with riders carrying ornately decorated parasols, walk in a parade from Trichur to Thiruvananthapuram, Kerala's capital city. When the parade arrives in Thiruvananthapuram, the **POORAM** ritual is observed. This includes the POORAM REENACTMENT of the meeting of deities, followed by a FESTI-VAL. The word *pooram* means "meeting," and the original purpose of the event was for the gods and goddesses of neighboring provinces to meet ceremonially on an annual basis.

The Great Elephant March is part of the Hindu tradition, which many scholars regard as the oldest living religion. The word Hindu is derived from the Sanskrit term *Sindhu* (or *Indus*), which meant river. It referred to people living in the Indus valley in the Indian subcontinent.

Hinduism has no founder, one universal reality (or god) known as Brahman, many gods and goddesses (sometimes referred to as devtas), and several scriptures. Hinduism also has no priesthood or hierarchical structure similar to that seen in some other religions, such as Christianity. Hindus acknowledge the authority of a wide variety of writings, but there is no single, uniform canon. The oldest of the Hindu writings are the *Vedas*. The word "veda" comes from the Sanskrit word for knowledge. The *Vedas*, which were compiled from ancient oral traditions, contain hymns, instructions, explanations, chants for sacrifices, magical formulas, and philosophy. Another set of sacred books includes the *Great Epics*, which illustrate Hindu faith in practice. The *Epics* include the *Ramayana*, the *Mahabharata*, and the *Bhagavad Gita*.

The Hindu pantheon includes approximately thirty-three million gods. Some of these are held in higher esteem than others. Over all the gods, Hindus believe in one absolute high god or universal concept. This is Brahman. Although he is above all the gods, he is not worshipped in popular ceremonies because he is detached from the day-to-day affairs of the people. Brahman is impersonal. Lesser gods and goddesses (devtas) serve him. Because these are more intimately involved in the affairs of people, they are venerated as gods. The most honored god in Hinduism varies among the different Hindu sects. Hindu adherents practice their faith differently and venerate different deities, but they share a similar view of reality and look back on a common history.

SYMBOLS AND CUSTOMS

Festival

A festival begins after the **POORAM** reenactment is complete. Festival activities include elephant rides, elephant feeding, an elephant tug-of-war, boat races, folk dancing and music, martial arts demonstrations, and various cultural performances and exhibitions. The festival concludes with a fireworks display.

Pooram Reenactment

The Great Elephant March includes a reenactment of part of the **POORAM** observance held each year in Trichur. Upon arriving in Thiruvananthapuram, the elephants divide into two rows. The rows separate and circle around to meet in front of the local temple, with each elephant carrying Hindu priests. The central elephant in each row carries a figure representing a Hindu deity. When the elephant rows meet, the riders pass their parasols back and forth in a complex performance that is accompanied by lively music and intense drumming. The spectacular display of color, movement, and music is a highly anticipated event that draws a large crowd of observers.

FURTHER READING

Lamba, Abha Narain. *India*. New York: DK Publishing, 2002.

WEB SITES

Indian Government Ministry of Tourism
www.incredibleindia.org

Kerala Tourism Board
www.keralatourism.org

Green Corn Dance

Type of Holiday: Religious (various Native American), Calendar/Seasonal
Date of Observation: Various
Where Celebrated: Alabama, Florida, Mississippi, New Mexico, New York, and by Native American tribes throughout the United States
Symbols and Customs: Black Drink, Scratching

ORIGINS

The Green Corn Dance is a Native American religious rite. Not much is known about the historical development of this and other religious belief systems among Native Americans. Most of the information available was gathered by Europeans who arrived on the continent beginning in the sixteenth century C.E. The data they recorded was fragmentary and oftentimes of questionable accuracy because the Europeans did not understand the native cultures they were trying to describe and the Native Americans were reluctant to divulge details about themselves.

The history of Native American cultures dates back thousands of years into pre-historic times. According to many scholars, the people who became the Native Americans migrated from Asia across a land bridge that may have once connected the territories presently occupied by Alaska and Russia. The migrations, believed to have begun between 60,000 and 30,000 B.C.E., continued until approximately 4,000 B.C.E. This speculation, however, conflicts with traditional stories asserting that the indigenous Americans have always lived in North America or that tribes moved up from the south.

Most North American Indian tribes had three major corn ceremonies: a planting ceremony, a harvest ceremony, and most important of all, a green corn ceremony. Held several weeks before the main harvest, when the ears of corn were nearly ripe, it was an annual rite of purification and renewal involving ceremonial dances addressed to the god who controlled the growth of corn or maize. Up until the time the Green Corn Dance took place, it was considered a crime against the gods to eat or even touch the newly ripened corn. Among the southern American Indi-ans in the eighteenth century, it was a time for getting new clothes, new pots, and new household utensils. They would collect their worn-out clothing and, along with all the leftover grain and other provisions, make a huge pile and set it on fire.

Although the Green Corn Dance was at one time observed by the Indians of the Prairies and Southwest as well as by Eastern tribes, it has died out in many areas. Today it is usually associated with the Seminole Indians of Florida, who hold their Green Corn Dance in May. The Seminole dance is derived from the Creek ceremony known as the busk (from the Creek word *boskita,* meaning "to fast"), which marked the end of the old year and the beginning of the new year. Aside from its ceremoni-al purpose, the Green Corn Dance is the time when the Seminoles hold their annual council meetings. It is also a time when the sins of the old year are forgiven and members of the tribe repent for anything they've done wrong. Events that take place during the festival include ball games, stomp dances, and special rites for young male members of the tribe who have come of age during the preceding year.

Among the eastern Cherokee and Creek Indians, the Green Corn Dance has died out as a vegetation rite but survives as a curative ceremony. The Iroquois celebrate their Green Corn Dance for four days in early September, during which they per-form various thanksgiving rites including the Great Feather Dance and the Corn Dance itself. Almost every pueblo in New Mexico holds a corn dance on its saint's day, the most elaborate being the Santo Domingo Pueblo (New Mexico) Green

Corn Dance held on St. Dominic's Day in August. *Koshares* or holy clowns who represent the spirits of pueblo ancestors weave among the dancers, all of whom carry evergreens, symbolic of growth.

SYMBOLS AND CUSTOMS

Black Drink

Drinking an emetic or purgative, which induces vomiting, was a standard part of the rites that comprised the Green Corn Dance. It was usually cassine, from which a special tea was made, or *ilex vomitoria*, made from the holly shrub that was found along the coast of Carolina, Georgia, and northern Florida. The Indians believed that by drinking the so-called "Black Drink" on the evening of the festival's first day, they were purifying themselves physically and spiritually, emerging in a state of perfect innocence. The next day, they would eat the green corn, which they believed contained a divine spirit that must not be permitted to touch any common, unpurified food when it entered their stomachs. After fasting for an additional day, there would be a great feast.

There was a widespread belief that anyone who didn't take the Black Drink could not safely eat the new corn and would get sick during the year. The Indians also believed that the drink made them brave in war and cemented their bonds with one another.

Scratching

Ceremonial scratching was a common practice during the Green Corn Dance among the Cherokee, Creek, Seminole, Yuchi, and Catawba tribes. It took place just before the Feather Dance on the second day. Those participating in the ceremony would use various methods to inflict deep scratches on their bodies, particularly their backs. Among the Cherokees, a bamboo brier with stout thorns was used, while the Seminoles used snake fangs inserted into a wooden holder. Ceremonial scratching was a symbolic act believed to cleanse the body from impurities. At other times of the year, it was used to punish children and to relieve fatigue.

FURTHER READING

Bellenir, Karen. *Religious Holidays and Calendars*. 3rd ed. Detroit: Omnigraphics, 2004.

Cohen, Hennig, and Tristram Potter Coffin. *The Folklore of American Holidays*. 3rd ed. Detroit: Gale Research, 1999.

Dobler, Lavinia G. *Customs and Holidays Around the World*. New York: Fleet Pub. Corp., 1962.

Frazer, Sir James G. *The Golden Bough: A Study in Magic and Religion*. New York: Macmillan, 1931.

Henderson, Helene, ed. *Holidays, Festivals, and Celebrations of the World Dictionary*. 3rd ed. Detroit: Omnigraphics, 2005.

Leach, Maria, ed. *Funk & Wagnalls Standard Dictionary of Folklore, Mythology & Legend*. San Francisco: Harper & Row, 1984.

Penner, Lucille Recht. *The Thanksgiving Book*. New York: Hastings House, 1986.

WEB SITES

Oneida Nation of Wisconsin Museum
museum.oneidanation.org/education/greenCorn.htm

Seminole Tribe of Florida
www.seminoletribe.com/culture/dance.shtml

Guru Nanak's Birthday

Type of Holiday: Religious (Sikh)
Date of Observation: October-November; full moon day of Hindu month of Kartika
Where Celebrated: Great Britain, India, Pakistan, and by Sikhs all over the world
Symbols and Customs: Guru Granth Sahib
Related Holidays: Vaisakh

ORIGINS

Guru Nanak's Birthday is a celebration in Sikhism, an independent faith that developed during the fifteenth century in India. The word Sikh comes from the Sanskrit word shishya, which means disciple or student. Sikhs believe that God was the original guru (guru means divinely inspired prophet or teacher) and that he chose to reveal his message to Guru Nanak, the first Sikh guru. Sikhs believe that their gurus were prophets sent by God to lead people into truth. They emphasize equality among people of different castes, practice Kirat Karni (a doctrine of laboring), and follow the precepts of charity.

Sikhism resembles both Islam and Hinduism, but is not directly associated with either. Similar to Hindus, Sikhs believe that the human soul progresses through a series of births and rebirths and that its ultimate salvation occurs when it breaks free from the cycle. Sikhs, however, reject the Hindu pantheon and do not participate in bathing rituals. Instead they worship one God who they believe is the same God of all religions, including Allah of Islam. Unlike Muslims, however, they shun fasting and pilgrimages.

The Sikh holy scriptures are called the *Guru Granth Sahib* (*Guru* means divinely inspired teacher; *Granth* means book; *Sahib* means revered). A more ancient name is *Adi Granth*, which means first or original book. The Guru Granth Sahib was compiled by the fifth Sikh guru, Arjan, and revised by Gobind Singh, the tenth guru. It contains hymns composed by the gurus.

Sikhs do not have an established priesthood. Although individual gurdwaras may employ specially trained people to care for the Guru Granth Sahib, all Sikhs are free to read from their holy scriptures either in the temple or in their homes. In addition, there is no one person to whom all Sikhs look for guidance in religious matters. The Sikh community is called the Panth, and collective decisions may be made by the Panth for the entire community. The Shiromani Gurdwara Parbandhad Committee, whose members are elected, provides guidance for all the gurdwaras in the Punjab. Individual local gurdwaras elect their own committees to oversee local matters.

Guru Nanak was the founder of the Sikh religion. He was born in 1469 at Talwandi, a small village about forty miles from Lahore, now located in Pakistan. According to legend, his birth was accompanied by flowers falling from heaven and by musical instruments that started playing on their own.

Although he was born into a Hindu family, Nanak was influenced by Islamic teachings, particularly those of the Sufis, a mystical Islamic sect. His curiosity about spiritual matters was evident at a very young age, and by the time he was thirty, he had experienced a mystical encounter with God. Legend says that he was taken to God by the angels and that he stayed in God's presence for three days. His absence from the village triggered rumors that he had drowned in a stream where he was last seen bathing. After learning that he had been chosen as a prophet, Nanak reappeared on earth and set off on his mission to spread God's word. He went to Tibet, Ceylon (now Sri Lanka), Bangladesh, and Mecca, proclaiming his message to both Hindus and Muslims, whom he hoped to unite. He wanted to abolish caste distinctions and to promote more liberal social practices, encouraging his followers to work hard and pursue normal family relations. His teachings, in the form of poems and hymns, are preserved in the Holy Book known as the GURU GRANTH SAHIB. Those who followed him became known as Sikhs, from the Sanskrit word meaning "disciple."

When Guru Nanak died in 1539, a quarrel arose among his followers. Those who were Hindu wanted to cremate him, but his Muslim followers wanted to bury him. The next day, his body disappeared—Nanak's way of showing them that the way of God was neither Hindu nor Muslim, but included both. He was succeeded by nine other gurus who carried on his work. Sikhs believe that although these ten prophets were different individuals, they all shared the same spirit.

Nanak's birthday is by far the most important of the Sikh *gupurbs* or festivals to celebrate the birthdays of the gurus; it is comparable to the birthday of Jesus for Christians. The celebration frequently lasts for three days, during which every Sikh family visits its local *gurdwara* or temple. In the village where Nanak was born, now known as Nankana Sahib, there is a shrine and a holy tank where thousands of Sikhs congregate for a huge fair and festival. In India, there is a procession the day before Nanak's birthday, led by the Panj Pyare—five baptized Sikhs who represent the Khalsa, or spiritual/military brotherhood that is open to all baptized Sikhs (*see* **VAISAKH**). They carry ceremonial swords and the GURU GRANTH SAHIB on a covered litter, followed by schoolchildren, scouts, students, and adults singing hymns. The procession winds through the streets and ends outside the gurdwara. Other activities during the festival include prayers, lectures, the singing of hymns, and the distribution of free meals. In Great Britain, the celebration is a mixture of religious and social activities that includes fairs, games, and stalls offering foods and sweets.

SYMBOLS AND CUSTOMS

Guru Granth Sahib

The Guru Granth Sahib is the Sikhs' Holy Book. It is 1,430 pages long and includes all the hymns of Guru Nanak, other hymns and teachings added by Arjan (the fifth guru), and the final additions of Guru Gobind Singh (the tenth and last guru, who died in 1708). It was the latter who placed a volume of the Holy Book before a gathering of his followers, laid five coins and a coconut in front of it, and bowed his head, declaring that there would be no more human gurus; from now on, the Granth was to serve as their spiritual leader.

During the first two days of the festival surrounding Guru Nanak's birthday, a ceremony called an Akhand Path begins. This is a continuous, uninterrupted reading of the entire Guru Granth Sahib, timed so that it ends on the birthday anniversary.

Sikhs treat the Guru Granth Sahib with even more reverence than Christians show for the Bible, because it is not only a religious document but enjoys the same status as a guru. It is kept on a platform under a richly decorated canopy and covered with a special cloth. Sikhs must bow before the Guru Granth Sahib whenever they enter the prayer hall, and they must never turn their backs to it. All those who read it must wash their hands before touching it, and it is customary to place an offering of food or money in front of it. Next to the Granth Sahib is what is known as a *chaur*. Similar to a fly whisk or brush, it is waved over the Holy Book as a sign of respect.

FURTHER READING

Bellenir, Karen. *Religious Holidays and Calendars*. 3rd ed. Detroit: Omnigraphics, 2004.

Henderson, Helene, ed. *Holidays, Festivals, and Celebrations of the World Dictionary*. 3rd ed. Detroit: Omnigraphics, 2005.

Kapoor, Sukhbir Singh. *Sikh Festivals*. Vero Beach, FL: Rourke Enterprises, 1989.

WEB SITE

BBC (British Broadcasting Corporation)
www.bbc.co.uk/schools/religion/sikhism/gurunanak.shtml

Guy Fawkes Day (Bonfire Night)

Type of Holiday: Historic
Date of Observation: November 5
Where Celebrated: England, New Zealand, and other countries with historical ties to England
Symbols and Customs: Bonfires, Fireworks, "Guys"
Related Holidays: Halloween, Samhain, Winter Solstice

ORIGINS

This day commemorates the Gunpowder Plot of 1605, when a group of Roman Catholic dissidents tried to blow up King James I of England and his government officials, who had assembled for the opening of the Houses of Parliament. The reason for this bold attempt can be traced back to the persecution of English Catholics under Elizabeth I, James's predecessor. When James took the throne, the Catholics thought their problems would be resolved: He was, after all, the son of Mary, Queen of Scots, widely regarded by Catholics as a martyr, and the husband of Anne of Denmark, a Catholic convert. But James I failed to meet these expectations, and the persecution of Catholics continued.

Guy Fawkes was not the leader of the plot, but it was his job to light the train of gunpowder. He was found in the cellar beneath the Houses of Parliament on November 4, 1605, crouched in a corner amidst casks of explosives. He was arrested in the early morning hours of November 5 and taken to the Tower of London. The rest of the conspirators fled, but were eventually caught and made to stand trial. Fawkes, along with Robert Catesby, the leader of the plot, and several of the other conspirators were hanged and then drawn and quartered. The executions took place on January 30 and 31 in St. Paul's Churchyard, London.

A year later, November 5 was declared a day of public thanksgiving. Since that time, it has become a popular holiday on which people remember the Gunpowder Plot and confirm their faith in the Anglican Church. It is still a tradition on this day for the Royal Yeomen of the Guard to prowl through the vaults beneath London's Houses of Parliament in a mock search for explosives. They are dressed in their traditional "beefeater" costumes (so called because they used to wear these uniforms when they attended the King and Queen at state banquets) and carry lanterns so they can peer into dark corners.

Guy Fawkes Day is a holiday that commemorates a significant historical event. Peoples throughout the world commemorate such significant events in their histories through holidays and festivals. Often, these are events that are important for an entire nation and become widely observed. The marking of such anniversaries serves not only to honor the values represented by the person or event commemorated, but also to strengthen and reinforce communal bonds of national, cultural, or ethnic identity. Victorious, joyful, and traumatic events are remembered through historic holidays. The commemorative expression reflects the original event through festive celebration or solemn ritual. Reenactments are common activities at historical holiday and festival gatherings, seeking to bring the past alive in the present.

Guy Fawkes Day in England has been compared to **HALLOWEEN** in America. The begging, BONFIRES, and making of dummies (*see* "GUYS") are certainly similar to what goes on in the United States just a few days earlier. They also recall the ancient Celtic celebration of **SAMHAIN**. The celebration of Guy Fawkes Day was brought to America by British colonists, but it has since died out. As late as 1893, however, there were reports of its observation in the United States under the name of "Pope's Day."

SYMBOLS AND CUSTOMS

Bonfires

Another name for Guy Fawkes Day is "Bonfire Night." The bonfires that are lit throughout England after dark on November 5 are considered symbolic of Guy

Fawkes' execution, although he was not burned at the stake. They may also be a survival of the midwinter fires lit during pagan times to symbolize the sun's struggle to rise again in the sky after the **WINTER SOLSTICE**.

Fireworks

For children, Guy Fawkes Day comes as a welcome break from the long, dreary spell between the end of summer and **CHRISTMAS**. They are allowed to stay up late on this night to watch the grown-ups set off fireworks symbolizing the Gunpowder Plot that was foiled. Fireworks fill the skies throughout Britain on the night of November 5, and children spend most of the money they've collected (*see* "GUYS") on fireworks for the display.

"Guys"

Several days before Guy Fawkes Day, children in England build dummies referred to as "Guys." Sometimes these effigies are displayed on street corners, and children ask passersby for a "penny for the Guy." Then, on the night of November 5, the "Guys" are thrown on the BONFIRES and burned. It is ironic that these effigies represent a man whose only role in the plot was to make sure that the gunpowder was lit. The real leader, Robert Catesby, does not have a role in the celebration.

Burning effigies in BONFIRES was a popular folk custom throughout the British Isles. It is thought that these effigies originally represented the spirit of vegetation. By burning them in fires that symbolized the sun, people hoped to secure good weather and sunshine for their crops.

In the town of Ludlow in Shropshire, any well-known local man who has aroused the dislike or anger of the townspeople has his effigy substituted for (or added to) that of Guy Fawkes.

FURTHER READING

Chambers, Robert. *The Book of Days*. 2 vols. 1862-64. Reprint. Detroit: Omnigraphics, 1990.

Henderson, Helene, ed. *Holidays, Festivals, and Celebrations of the World Dictionary*. 3rd ed. Detroit: Omnigraphics, 2005.

Miles, Clement A. *Christmas in Ritual and Tradition, Christian and Pagan*. 1912. Reprint. Detroit: Omnigraphics, 1990.

Purdy, Susan. *Festivals for You to Celebrate*. Philadelphia: Lippincott, 1969.

Santino, Jack. *All Around the Year: Holidays and Celebrations in American Life*. Urbana: University of Illinois Press, 1994.

WEB SITES

Gunpowder Plot Society
www.gunpowder-plot.org

House of Commons Information Office
www.parliament.uk/documents/upload/g08.pdf

Hajj
(Pilgrimage to Mecca)

Type of Holiday: Religious (Muslim)
Date of Observation: Eighth to the thirteenth day of Dhul-Hijjah, the twelfth lunar
  month of the Islamic calendar
Where Celebrated: Mecca, Saudi Arabia
Symbols and Customs: Black Stone, Ihrâm (Pilgrim's Robe), Kaaba, Tawâf (Circumambulation), Ten Rites, Well of Zamzam
Colors: The Hajj is associated with white, the color of the IHRÂM or pilgrim's robe;
  with black, the color in which the walls of the KAABA are draped; and with green,
  the color of the scarf or turban worn by returning Muslims who have successfully completed the TEN RITES of the pilgrimage.
Related Holidays: Id al-Adha

ORIGINS

The Hajj is one of the central precepts in the Islamic religion, which is one of the
largest of the world's religions. According to some estimates, there are more than
one billion Muslims worldwide, with major populations found in the Middle East,
North and sub-Saharan Africa, Turkey, Central Asia, and Southeast Asia. In
Europe and the United States, Islam is the second largest religious group, with
some seven million adherents in the United States. During the early years of Islam,
the faith spread throughout the Arabian Peninsula into regions that are today
occupied by Saudi Arabia, Syria, Iraq, and Jordan. Contrary to popular opinion,
however, Muslims are not just Arabs. Muslims—followers of Islam—are found in

many different ethnic groups all over the globe. In fact, Arabs make up less than twenty percent of Muslims.

The word Islam is an Arabic word that means "surrender to God." Its other meanings include peace, safety, and health. The central focus of Islam is a personal commitment and surrender to Allah, the Arabic word for God. In Islam, the concept of Allah is universal and eternal. Allah is the same in every religion and throughout the history of humankind. A person who follows Islam is called a Muslim, which means one who surrenders or submits to Allah's will. But Islam is not just a religion of belief; it is a religion of action. Five specific deeds are required of followers; these are called *The Five Pillars of Islam*. They are 1) *Shahadah*—confession of faith; 2) *Salat*—prayer/worship; 3) *Zakat*—charity; 4) *Sawm*—fasting; and 5) *Hajj*—pilgrimage.

The message of Islam was brought by Muhammad (570-632 C.E.), who is considered a prophet of Allah. The holy book of Islam is the *Qur'an* (also sometimes spelled *Koran* or *Alcoran*). According to Islamic belief, the Qur'an was revealed to Muhammad by Allah over a period of twenty-three years. Authorship of the Qur'an is attributed to Allah, and not to Muhammad; Muhammad merely received it. Muslims believe that because it originated with Allah, the Qur'an is infallible.

There are two main sects within Islam: Sunni and Shi'ite. Sunni Muslims are the majority (estimated at about eighty percent). They recognize the authority of the first four Caliphs, including Ali, and they believe that the Sunna (the example of the Prophet Muhammad) is interpreted through the consensus of the community. Shi'ite Muslims also look to special teachers, called imams. The imams are the direct descendants of Muhammad through Fatimah and Ali. These individuals are believed to be inspired and to possess secret knowledge. Shi'ites, however, do not recognize the same line of Islamic leaders acknowledged by the Sunnis. Shi'ites hold to a doctrine that accepts only leaders who are descended from Muhammad through his daughter Fatimah and her husband Ali. Many Shi'ite subsects believe that true imams are errorless and sinless. They receive instruction from these leaders rather than relying on the consensus of the community.

Every year over two million Muslims complete the Hajj, the pilgrimage to Mecca, the city in Saudi Arabia where the Prophet Muhammad was born. Considered to be the religious center of the universe—the point at which heaven is nearest to the earth, and where prayers can therefore be more easily heard—Mecca is as sacred to Muslims as Rome is to Catholics and Jerusalem is to Orthodox Jews. Although Muslims may visit Mecca at any time of year, the Hajj may only be performed during the twelfth lunar month. Every pilgrim's goal is to reach Mecca by the seventh day of the month of Dhul-Hijja. Although the rituals associated with the Hajj do not begin until the eighth day, this is the day on which the pilgrims receive their instructions concerning the ceremonies in which they are about to take part.

Every Muslim capable of making the trip is expected to make a pilgrimage to Mecca at least once in his or her lifetime, although those who are too ill to travel or who simply cannot afford the expense are exempt from this requirement. The Hajj is considered one of the "five pillars" or fundamental duties of Islam, and the Qur'an (the sacred book of the Islamic religion) describes in great detail the rituals that must be followed when the pilgrim reaches the Holy City. Non-Muslims are forbidden not only to observe or participate in the pilgrimage but even to visit the city of Mecca. Any non-Muslim who is caught doing so faces the death penalty, although Westerners occasionally manage to sneak into the city disguised as Muslims.

Now that air travel is common, the journey to Mecca is not nearly the hardship it was for earlier pilgrims, who traveled on camels or horses—and sometimes barefoot across the burning desert sands—to fulfill their obligation. Because the Islamic calendar is lunar, the timing of the Hajj shifts back eleven days according to the Christian calendar each year. This means that sometimes it falls during the mild Saudi Arabian winter, but it also means that some pilgrims make their journey during the summer, when the heat can cause discomfort and serious health problems. The Saudi Arabian government does everything it can to keep the pilgrims comfortable, but the crowds can be so huge that simply moving about and getting sleep become a challenge. Pilgrims who arrive from the same country usually stay together and are looked after by a guide, who finds them accommodation and helps with their travel arrangements.

The custom of journeying to a sacred place to perform religious rites was common in pre-Islamic Arabia and among the Semitic peoples. But the real model for the Hajj comes from Muhammad's "farewell pilgrimage" from Medina, where he lived and ruled, to his birthplace several months before his death.

SYMBOLS AND CUSTOMS

Black Stone

Also known as the Ruby of Heaven, the Black Stone that is set into the eastern corner of the shrine in Mecca known as the KAABA is believed to have been brought by Adam from the Garden of Eden after he was banished. The stone itself is actually a dark reddish-brown. Because it was once split in a fire, it now consists of three large and several small pieces about twelve inches in diameter, held together by a silver band. As the pilgrims circumambulate the Kaaba (*see* TAWÂF), they are supposed to kiss the Black Stone or touch it with their fingers.

Ihrâm (Pilgrim's Robe)

Pilgrims must be in a state of purity when they enter Mecca, so it is customary for them to stop about six miles outside the city and begin the purification process.

After taking a ritual bath and reciting certain prayers, they put on a special garment known as the *ihrâm* or pilgrim's robe, which consists of two pieces of unsewn white cloth, usually linen or cotton. One piece is wrapped around the waist, and the other is flung over the left shoulder, leaving part of the right arm free. Although it is permissible to use an umbrella for protection from the hot sun, male pilgrims' heads must remain uncovered. Female pilgrims are covered from head to ankle, and their faces are often concealed by a mask that keeps the white fabric from touching their skin. Although bare feet are preferred, heelless slippers may be worn on the feet.

Uncomfortable as it must be when worn for several days in hot weather, the pilgrim's robe is rich in symbolism. It serves as a reminder that Muslims must be prepared to give up everything for Allah (God). When Muslims die, they leave all their clothes and belongings behind and are dressed for burial in simple pieces of cloth similar to those of the ihrâm. It is also symbolic of every Muslim's equality in Allah's eyes.

Most pilgrims put on their white robes several miles outside of Mecca at Miqat. Those arriving by air often change into the ihrâm on the plane so they don't arrive in Miqat wearing the wrong clothes.

Kaaba

The Kaaba is a fifteen-foot-high square granite shrine in Mecca that contains the BLACK STONE believed to have been brought by Adam from the Garden of Eden. According to legend, Adam was so miserable after leaving the garden that God set up a red tent on the spot where the Kaaba now stands, and this is where Adam spent the remainder of his life. The Black Stone that he brought with him was later set into the eastern corner of the shrine built by Abraham at Allah's command. Some say that the footprint of Abraham, from whom Muhammad is believed to have descended, can still be seen in the stone.

The shrine itself—Kaaba means "cube"—is made of reddish granite and has only one door, which leads into an unfurnished room and is only opened on special occasions. The walls are draped in black brocade curtains, which are replaced every year. The old ones are cut up in small pieces and sold to pilgrims as precious souvenirs.

Tawâf (Circumambulation)

As soon as possible after arriving in Mecca, the pilgrims enter the courtyard of the Great Mosque. They proceed toward the BLACK STONE, and with the KAABA on their left, they circle the shrine seven times. The first three circuits are done at a very fast pace, kissing or touching the Black Stone each time it is passed. Known as the *har-*

walah, this quickened step is symbolic of what the Prophet Muhammad did on his "farewell pilgrimage" to show that he wasn't tired after his long journey. The last four circuits are walked at a more leisurely pace. After the seventh circuit, the pilgrims press their bodies against the *multazam,* a space between the eastern corner of the shrine and the door, that is considered to be especially holy. In doing so they hope to absorb some of the *baraka*—the blessing of virtue—with which this holy building is endowed.

The root meaning of the word *hajj* is "to describe a circle." It is from this ritual circumambulation of the Kaaba, therefore, that the pilgrimage gets its name.

Ten Rites

There are ten rites or ceremonies that must be performed by each pilgrim during the Hajj:

1. Entrance through the Gate of Peace. There are nineteen gates leading to the courtyard of the Great Mosque of Mecca, which is 550 feet long and 360 feet wide. Pilgrims must enter through the Bab a-Salam or Gate of Peace.

2. Kissing of the Black Stone. The pilgrims make their way to the center of the courtyard, where the KAABA rises fifty feet into the air. They go directly to the BLACK STONE and kiss it with reverence.

3. Circumambulation. As described above (*see* TAWÂF), the pilgrims travel around the Kaaba seven times counterclockwise, always keeping the shrine on their left.

4. Prayer at the Mosque of Abraham. The next stop is the small, domed Mosque of Abraham, in which Ishmael (son of Abraham) and his mother Hagar are buried. Prayers are offered, and then the pilgrims walk over to drink from the sacred Well of Ishmael (*see* WELL OF ZAMZAM).

5. Ascent to Mount Safa and Mount Maret. Pilgrims leave the Mosque of Abraham with their left foot forward, going out of the courtyard through the Gate of Safa and following the road that leads from the hilltop of Safa to the top of Mount Maret (or Marwa), a distance of about one-seventh of a mile. The pilgrims must then run back and forth between these two points seven times, stopping at certain fixed points to offer prayers. This rite commemorates Hagar's search for water in the desert between the two mountains (*see* WELL OF ZAMZAM).

6. Journey to the Mountain of Mercy. The Hajj proper begins on the eighth day, as the pilgrims begin their long journey to Mount Arafat, also known as the Mountain of Mercy, several miles away. According to legend, exactly 700,000 pilgrims will reach Mount Arafat; if fewer than this number manage to do so, angels will come down and make up the difference.

7. Sermon on Arafat. Once they have gathered on Mount Arafat, the pilgrims listen to a sermon delivered by a religious leader, who addresses them while mounted on a camel.

8. Night in Muzdalifa. That evening, the pilgrims depart again for Mecca; but halfway between Arafat and the Holy City, they must spend a night in Muzdalifa. Huge crowds gather at the mosque there, and there is usually so much music and commotion that no one gets any sleep. Pilgrims also take advantage of this stop to gather the seventy pebbles they will need for the next day's rite.

9. Stoning of the Devils in Mina. On their way to Mecca the following day, the pilgrims stop in the village of Mina. Three pillars are there, and the pilgrims throw their pebbles at the pillars in a ceremony known as the Stoning of the Devils. This ritual is based on the story of how the devil tried three times to persuade Abraham to ignore God's command to sacrifice his son, Ishmael. Each time, Abraham threw pebbles at the devil in disgust and continued on his way. By throwing stones at the three pillars, the pilgrims are symbolically expressing their own ability to resist temptation. The stones that accumulate there are eventually taken to Mecca to be used as gravel on the floor of the Great Mosque. Animal sacrifices are also performed at Mina to commemorate God's provision of a ram to be sacrificed in Ishmael's place. The killing of so many animals has forced Saudi Arabian officials to explore new methods for freezing, preserving, and distributing the meat produced. After the sacrifice, male pilgrims' heads are shaved and women's hair is trimmed. The ihrâm is then taken off.

10. Visit to the Tomb of Muhammad. The pilgrims return to Mecca and try to get a bottle or tin of water from the WELL OF ZAMZAM, also known as the Well of Ishmael. They then go to Medina, the city where the Prophet lived and was buried, to visit Muhammad's tomb. Although the visit to Medina, 200 miles away, is not compulsory, it is regarded as an act of great merit.

Well of Zamzam

Also known as the Well of Ishmael, this sacred source of water is located just a few steps from the southeast corner of the KAABA beneath a domed building erected in 1661. The well itself is a shaft that goes down more than 100 feet and possesses the miraculous ability to maintain the same water level, no matter how much is drawn from it by pilgrims who believe in its curative powers. Some dip their robes in it or take some home to their relatives as gifts, to be used when someone is ill or to wash the body after death. Others drink as much of it as they possibly can.

Legend has it that when Hagar and Ishmael were abandoned in the desert near Mecca, they used up all the water in the goatskin that Abraham had given them. In a frantic search for more, Hagar ran back and forth between the two hills of Safa and Marwa seven times. God finally heard Ishmael's prayers, and the water gushed forth not far from where the KAABA now stands, making a sound like *zam-zam*.

Today the water is channeled to underground galleries that can be reached by a flight of stairs, where a number of faucets can supply many people at once. The well is fed by several springs and is visited by thousands of people daily.

FURTHER READING

Ahsan, M. M. *Muslim Festivals*. Vero Beach, FL: Rourke Enterprises, 1987.

Bellenir, Karen. *Religious Holidays and Calendars*. 3rd ed. Detroit: Omnigraphics, 2004.

Crim, Keith R. *The Perennial Dictionary of World Religions*. San Francisco: Harper & Row, 1989.

Gaer, Joseph. *Holidays Around the World*. Boston: Little, Brown, 1953.

Glassé, Cyril. *The Concise Encyclopedia of Islam*. 2nd ed. San Francisco: Harper & Row, 1999.

Gulevich, Tanya. *Understanding Islam and Muslim Traditions*. Detroit: Omnigraphics, 2004.

Henderson, Helene, ed. *Holidays, Festivals, and Celebrations of the World Dictionary*. 3rd ed. Detroit: Omnigraphics, 2005.

Pike, Royston. *Round the Year with the World's Religions*. 1950. Reprint. Detroit: Omnigraphics, 1992.

Von Grunebaum, Gustave E. *Muhammadan Festivals*. New York: Schuman, 1951.

WEB SITE

Kingdom of Saudi Arabia's Ministry of Hajj
www.hajinformation.com/main/f.htm

Halashashti

Type of Holiday: Religious (Hindu)
Date of Observation: August-September; sixth day of the waning half of the Hindu month of Bhadrapada
Where Celebrated: India
Symbols and Customs: Plough

ORIGINS

Halashashti is a religious festival in Hinduism, which many scholars regard as the oldest living religion. The word Hindu is derived from the Sanskrit term *Sindhu* (or *Indus*), which meant river. It referred to people living in the Indus valley in the Indian subcontinent.

Hinduism has no founder, one universal reality (or god) known as Brahman, many gods and goddesses (sometimes referred to as devtas), and several scriptures. Hinduism also has no priesthood or hierarchical structure similar to that seen in some other religions, such as Christianity. Hindus acknowledge the authority of a wide variety of writings, but there is no single, uniform canon. The oldest of the Hindu writings are the *Vedas*. The word "veda" comes from the Sanskrit word for knowledge. The *Vedas*, which were compiled from ancient oral traditions, contain hymns, instructions, explanations, chants for sacrifices, magical formulas, and philosophy. Another set of sacred books includes the *Great Epics*, which illustrate Hindu faith in practice. The *Epics* include the *Ramayana*, the *Mahabharata*, and the *Bhagavad Gita*.

The Hindu pantheon includes approximately thirty-three million gods. Some of these are held in higher esteem than others. Over all the gods, Hindus believe in one absolute high god or universal concept. This is Brahman. Although he is above all the gods, he is not worshipped in popular ceremonies because he is detached from the day to day affairs of the people. Brahman is impersonal. Lesser gods and goddesses (devtas) serve him. Because these are more intimately involved in the affairs of people, they are venerated as gods. The most honored god in Hinduism varies among the different Hindu sects. Although Hindu adherents practice their faith differently and venerate different deities, they share a similar view of reality and look back on a common history.

The Hindu festival Halashashti is often referred to as Balarama Shashti, after Krishna's older brother, Balarama, who was born on this day. According to the Hindu scriptures, Vishnu took two hairs, one white and one black, and these became Balarama and Krishna, the sons of Devaki. As soon as Balarama was born, he was taken to a safe place to preserve his life from the tyrant Kansa. He and Krishna grew up together, sharing many adventures, and Balarma's death while sitting under a banyan tree near Dwaraka was followed soon after by the death of his brother. Balarama's weapon was a PLOUGH, so this is also the day on which the farmers and peasants of India pay special tribute to the implement that helps them sow their crops.

Hindu women fast on this day, eating only buffalo milk and curds in the belief that it will ensure happiness, prosperity, and longevity for their sons. A fast may also be observed by farmers in rural areas, who hope that Lord Shiva will bless their families' welfare and send them better crops in the coming year. Everyone shares in a huge feast in the evening.

SYMBOLS AND CUSTOMS

Plough

The hala or plough that gives this festival its name is a symbol not only of Balarama but of farmers and farming in general. Hindu farmers show their reverence for the plough by applying powdered rice and turmeric to its iron blade and by decorating it with flowers.

FURTHER READING

Bellenir, Karen. *Religious Holidays and Calendars*. 3rd ed. Detroit: Omnigraphics, 2004.

Henderson, Helene, ed. *Holidays, Festivals, and Celebrations of the World Dictionary*. 3rd ed. Detroit: Omnigraphics, 2005.

MacDonald, Margaret R., ed. *The Folklore of World Holidays*. Detroit: Gale Research, 1992.

Halloween

Type of Holiday: Folkloric
Date of Observation: October 31
Where Celebrated: United States, British Isles
Symbols and Customs: Bat, Black Cat, Bonfires, Colcannon, Costumes, Goblins, Harvest Sheaves or Harvest Dummy, Jack-O-Lantern, Nuts or Apples, Trick-or-Treating, Witch
Colors: Black and orange. Orange, the color of the Jack-O-Lantern, is a symbol of strength and endurance. Along with gold and brown, it stands for autumn and the harvest. Black is primarily a symbol of death and darkness. The black of the witch's cloak and the black cat are a reminder that Halloween was once a festival of the dead.
Related Holidays: All Souls' Day, Guy Fawkes Day, Samhain

ORIGINS

Halloween can be traced directly back to **SAMHAIN**, the ancient Celtic harvest festival honoring the Lord of the Dead. Observed on November 1 in the British

Isles and parts of what is now France, Samhain also marked the beginning of the Celtic New Year, while Samhain Eve marked the end of the old year. The night was a time of transition between the old and the new, a time when the separation between the world of the living and the world of the dead was very thin. On Samhain Eve the boundary between this world and the netherworld of fairies, gods, spirits, and magic was at its thinnest. As a result, passage between the two dimensions was easier than at any other time. Visitations from the spirits of one's own departed ancestor, divine beings, or demons were believed to be possible—though not desirable.

The Celts believed that the souls of those who had died during the previous year gathered to travel together to the land of the dead. They lit BONFIRES and sacrificed fruits and vegetables, hoping to win the favor of the spirits of the deceased and to avoid their punishments. Sometimes the living disguised themselves in masks and COSTUMES so that the spirits of the dead wouldn't recognize them. Charms, spells, and predictions about the future seemed to carry special weight on the eve of Samhain (*see* NUTS OR APPLES).

By the fourth century, the Christian church was doing everything it could to stamp out pagan festivals like Samhain, but the Celts wouldn't give up their ancient rituals and symbols. So the Christian church gave them new names and meanings. November 1 became All Saints' Day (All Hallows' Day in England), a celebration of all the Christian saints. The night of October 31 became All Hallows' Eve (later Halloween). But its association with the supernatural persisted.

Halloween came to America with the Irish immigrants of the 1840s. Their folk customs and beliefs merged with existing agricultural traditions. The early American Halloween, therefore, was not only a time to foretell the future and dabble in the occult but to complete certain seasonal tasks associated with the fall harvest. Over the years the holiday's agricultural significance faded, and it became primarily a children's holiday—a time to dress up as the ghosts and GOBLINS their ancestors at one time feared.

SYMBOLS AND CUSTOMS

Bat

Both positive and negative symbolic meanings have been associated with bats over the centuries. On the one hand, they are eerie creatures, winged mammals who fly around like ghosts at night and sleep hanging upside down during the day. On the other, they are regarded as particularly intelligent. The bat is a symbol of good fortune in China, and in ancient times, placing drops of bat's blood under a woman's pillow was believed to guarantee that she would bear many children.

Early pictures of WITCHES show them worshipping a horned figure with the wings of a bat—most likely the devil. Before attending a Sabbath or witches' gathering, they would rub a special ointment containing bats' blood into their bodies. The wings and entrails of bats went into their brews. The fact that bats could fly around at night made it easy to believe that they possessed mysterious powers. And when they hung upside down to sleep, they draped their wings around their bodies like witches' cloaks.

Because of their association with witches, the black paper bats that can be seen in Halloween decorations today are symbols of evil and the supernatural.

Black Cat

Long before they were associated with Halloween, cats were believed to have magical powers. The ancient Egyptians worshipped a cat-goddess named Pasht and used cats as a motif in their furniture and jewelry designs. The Celts believed that cats were human beings who had been changed into animals by evil powers. During the ancient celebration of **SAMHAIN** (*see* "Origins" above), it was customary to throw cats into the fire.

Back when people feared WITCHES and accused one another of witchcraft, cats were believed to assist witches in carrying out their magic. Since all cats looked black at night, the witch's cat was always thought of as being black. People were especially wary of cats at Halloween, when witches were known to be out riding the skies on their broomsticks. The fact that cats could see in the dark and move without making any noise added to their reputation as animals that couldn't be trusted.

With their links to the ancient festival of Samhain and later to witches, cats found a permanent place in the folklore of Halloween. Typically shown with their backs arched and their yellow eyes glaring, the cat is symbolic of the spirit of evil.

Bonfires

Bonfires were an important part of the celebration of Samhain, the ancient festival from which Halloween derived. On a night when evil spirits were believed to be roaming about, a bonfire must have provided a reassuring source of light and comfort. Live animals and even men—usually criminals or prisoners of war—were often burned alive as sacrifices to Saman, the Lord of Death. Bonfires were also kindled on **MIDSUMMER DAY** and at other seasonal festivals to promote fertility, to protect the fields against thunder and lightning, and to ward off sickness.

Although not part of the American Halloween ritual, bonfires are still common in parts of Ireland on October 31. After the flames have subsided, young people often sit around the glowing embers and eat blackened potatoes that have been roasted on the coals.

Colcannon

Colcannon is a traditional dish made of mashed potatoes, parsnips, and onions that is still served on Halloween in Ireland. Just as tiny figures or beans were hidden in Kings' Cakes on **EPIPHANY** and **CARNIVAL**, small objects are often concealed in the colcannon. If someone finds a coin, it means that he or she will be very wealthy. A ring stands for marriage, a doll for children, and a thimble for spinsterhood.

Costumes

From ancient times, people have worn masks to frighten off demons and thus avoid droughts, epidemics, and other disasters. Even after the pagan festival of the dead known as **SAMHAIN** became the Christian All Hallows' Eve, the people of Europe continued to feel uneasy at this time of year. If they left their homes after dark, they often disguised themselves with masks and costumes so they wouldn't be recognized by the evil spirits who were out roaming the earth. It was only natural for them to dress up as the ghosts, witches, and GOBLINS they were most fearful of meeting.

Trick-or-treaters in the United States are still apt to dress up in costumes that reflect their culture's most prevalent obsessions. During the Great Depression, for example, children often disguised themselves as hobos, burglars, pirates, and Indians—in other words, as economic and social outcasts, symbolic of the troubles from which their parents were struggling to escape. In contrast, during the 1980s children were dressing up as television and movie heroes and characters from television commercials, such as E.T., Ninja Turtles, or California Raisins. Witches and skeletons have always been popular costumes, representing the fear of death and evil; but nowadays it is not unusual to see children dressed up as Freddie Krueger and other horror movie characters, ax murderers, or nuclear waste materials. Although they may not do so consciously, children who disguise themselves as the agents of death and destruction are actually helping themselves (and their parents) defuse their deepest fears.

Goblins

Goblins are symbolic of the evil spirits that were believed to emerge at **SAMHAIN** and roam the earth at Halloween. They were ugly, menacing creatures who lived underground or in dark places. The word "goblin" is actually the French name for these fairy folk, who resembled leprechauns and pixies.

Some scholars say that during the Stone Age a small, dark-skinned people lived in Northern Europe and the British Isles. They wore green clothing so they could conceal themselves in the forests and fields, and they lived in low huts with turf as their roofs. They waylaid travelers, kidnapped children, and sometimes committed murder. Over the centuries, these real dwarf people were absorbed into the Celtic population around them. But they survived on a mythical level as the elves, goblins, and other fairy folk who also lived in low, mound-like houses and wore green clothing. They were symbols of the danger and evil that were believed to threaten people at this time of year.

Harvest Sheaves or Harvest Dummy

Even in urban and suburban areas today, people tend to romanticize the tradition of the harvest and rural lifestyles by decorating their homes with sheaves of Indian corn, gourds, and pumpkins. Usually dried and attached to fence posts, outdoor lighting fixtures, or porch railings, these harvest decorations represent the approaching death of the natural world in the form of winter.

Dummies resembling scarecrows are often placed outside the house, sometimes in the midst of an arrangement that includes cornstalks and pumpkins, symbolizing the harvest that is being brought in from the garden or the fields. Unlike the scarecrow designed to protect the summer crops from hungry birds and animals, however, the Halloween dummy is usually placed near the house, perhaps to protect its inhabitants from the ravages of the approaching winter.

Jack-O-Lantern

In England and Ireland, people often saw a pale, eerie light moving over bogs and marshes that resembled a lantern held in someone's hand. They referred to the phenomenon as "Lantern Men," "Hob-O'-Lantern," "Jack-O'-Lantern," or "Will-O'-the-Wisp." Similarly, the ghostly lights that seemed to hover over graves dug in marshy places were called "Corpse Candles." It's possible that these strange lights were the result of the spontaneous combustion of methane or marsh gas given off by rotting plant and animal life. But some people thought Jack-O-Lanterns were the souls of sinners condemned to walk the earth, or the souls of men who had been lost at sea.

Jack-O-Lantern became a legendary folk figure in Great Britain. He was the spirit of a blacksmith named Jack who was too evil to get into heaven but who was not allowed into hell because he had outwitted the devil. Doomed to wander the earth forever, he scooped up a glowing ember with the vegetable he happened to be eating at the time and used it as a lantern to light his way.

Jack-O-Lanterns, as they are known today—hollowed-out pumpkins with carved faces and lit candles burning inside—were originally made from turnips in Scotland, potatoes in Ireland, and "punkies" or large beets known as mangel-wurzels in England. When the Scottish and Irish immigrants who settled in the United States discovered pumpkins, they immediately recognized them as the ideal shape and size for Jack-O-Lanterns. Uncarved, they serve as a symbol of the harvest and are often displayed on front porches right up until **THANKSGIVING**. Carved and illuminated by a candle, they are symbolic of death and the spirit world.

Nuts or Apples

The nuts and apples traditionally used to predict the future on Halloween in the British Isles were once symbols of the harvest. Nuts, symbolic of life and fertility, were so much a part of Halloween that in some parts of England, Scotland, and Ireland the night of October 31 was called "Nutcrack Night." Scottish young people put pairs of nuts named after certain couples into the fire. If the pair burned to ashes together, it meant that the couple could expect a happy life together. If they crackled or sprang apart, it meant that quarrels and separation were inevitable. In Wales, a brightly blazing nut meant prosperity, while one that smoldered or popped meant bad luck. Nuts may have taken the place of the live animal sacrifices performed during the ancient Celtic New Year celebration known as **SAMHAIN**.

Apples were also considered fertility symbols and were used to make predictions about love. At the first Halloween parties, people roasted apples and bobbed for them in tubs of water. If a boy came up with an apple in his teeth, it meant that the girl he loved wanted him as her boyfriend. In a traditional game known as Snap Apple, the boys took turns trying to bite an apple that was twirled on the end of a stick. The first to succeed would be the first to marry. For this reason, Halloween was sometimes referred to as Snap Apple Night.

Girls pared apples on Halloween, trying to keep the peel in a single unbroken strip. Then they would swing it three times around their head and throw it over their left shoulder. The fallen peel was supposed to form the initial of their future husband's name. Apple seeds were also used to foretell the identity of a girl's future mate. Seeds named for two different boys were stuck on the girl's eyelids. The seed that stayed on the longest was her true sweetheart—although skillful winking or twitching often gave one seed the advantage.

Trick-or-Treating

The Halloween custom known as trick-or-treating—going from house to house begging for candy and threatening to cause mischief for those who don't cooperate—seems to have originated in the British Isles. It was customary for the poor to go begging on **ALL SOULS' DAY** in England, and children eventually took over the custom. In Ireland, legend has it that farmers used to go from house to house asking for food for their Halloween festivities in the name of the ancient god, Muck Olla. Good luck and wealth were promised to those who contributed; those who were stingy were threatened with bad luck.

Many believe that trick-or-treating is a relic of the Celtic New Year celebration known as **SAMHAIN**. Since this was the time of year that the spirits of the dead returned to visit the living, people would unbolt their doors, keep their hearth fires burning, and set out gifts of food to appease these troublesome spirits. Later, they dressed up as spirits themselves (*see* COSTUMES) and demanded contributions from neighbors for communal feasts.

What "Trick or treat" really means is "Give me a treat or I'll play a trick on you." The phrase is American in origin, and it dates back to about the 1930s. It combines the food- and money-begging traditions of England and Ireland with the ancient belief in supernatural activity on this night. In fact, the "tricks" that are played on Halloween (or Mischief Night, October 30) often look as though supernatural forces were behind them. A favorite Halloween prank in rural areas, for example, involves disassembling a piece of farm equipment and reassembling it on a rooftop. Pranks characterized by a reversal of the usual order symbolize both the unpredictable weather at this time of year and the delicate balance between man and nature that can so easily be upset. In the nineteenth century, favorite Halloween pranks included "threshold tricks"—removing gates and fences, soaping or rattling windows, fixing bells so they rang constantly, and tying doors shut. The message behind these and other attacks on domestic security is the importance of exercising caution at a time of year when everyone is vulnerable to the forces of death and destruction. Just as **SAMHAIN** was the time for the pagans to secure their farms and animals against the winter weather, Halloween pranks serve as a reminder that nature will not be kind to those who fail to take the necessary precautions.

In the 1930s, people who offered candy to Halloween visitors were genuinely concerned with protecting their homes against pranksters. But the custom of playing tricks on Halloween declined in popularity over the years, and by the 1950s, most children had no idea what kind of "tricks" they were expected to perform; all they wanted was the candy. Trick-or-treating rituals underwent a major shift in the 1970s and 1980s, when stories of razor blades or pins concealed in candy and apples began to surface. Suddenly symbolic fears were transformed into real ones, and children's freedom to roam the streets after dark was curtailed in many areas. Rather than being invited indoors for homemade treats, children now typically wait on the porch or doorstep while the host or hostess hands them their goodies. Young children are usually accompanied by their parents, who check the candy carefully for signs of tampering before allowing their children to eat it. In some areas, trick-or-treating is discouraged altogether. Instead, children attend organized Halloween parties.

Witch

The witch is probably the most recognizable symbol of Halloween. The name comes from the Saxon word *wica,* meaning "wise one." Most witches were pagans, which explains why they fell out of favor as Christianity grew in popularity. Several times a year, witches from all over a certain region would gather in a sacred spot, such as the Hartz Mountains of Germany. Halloween was one of several dates on which these Witches' Sabbaths took place. They would perform marriages, initiate new witches, and participate in fertility dances. Sometimes the witches would gallop about on branches or broomsticks.

The early Americans' belief in witchcraft came from the European continent, particularly from Scottish and Irish immigrants. The GOBLINS and other evil spirits they feared at Halloween became identified with witches. Farmers in the Pennsylvania Dutch country painted hex signs on their barns to scare off witches. Iron and salt—two things that witches wouldn't touch—were often placed by the beds of newborn babies.

By the nineteenth century, few educated people took witchcraft very seriously. But those who were less educated, particularly those living in rural areas, went right on believing. Today, witches are usually depicted as old women with matted hair, black robes, and bony fingers, with BLACK CATS as their only companions. They are symbols of the evil spirits traditionally believed to be roaming the earth at Halloween.

FURTHER READING

Barth, Edna. *Witches, Pumpkins, and Grinning Ghosts: The Story of Halloween Symbols.* New York: Seabury Press, 1972.

Bellenir, Karen. *Religious Holidays and Calendars.* 3rd ed. Detroit: Omnigraphics, 2004.

Biedermann, Hans. *Dictionary of Symbolism: Cultural Icons and the Meanings Behind Them.* New York: Meridian Books, 1994.

Henderson, Helene, ed. *Holidays, Festivals, and Celebrations of the World Dictionary.* 3rd ed. Detroit: Omnigraphics, 2005.

Ickis, Marguerite. *The Book of Festivals and Holidays the World Over.* New York: Dodd, Mead, 1970.

Purdy, Susan. *Festivals for You to Celebrate.* Philadelphia: Lippincott, 1969.

Santino, Jack. *All Around the Year: Holidays and Celebrations in American Life.* Urbana: University of Illinois Press, 1994.

Santino, Jack. *Halloween and Other Festivals of Death and Life.* Knoxville: University of Tennessee Press, 1994.

Thompson, Sue Ellen. *Halloween Program Sourcebook.* Detroit: Omnigraphics, 2000.

Tuleja, Tad. *Curious Customs: The Stories Behind 296 Popular American Rituals.* New York: Harmony, 1987.

American Folklife Center of the Library of Congress
www.loc.gov/folklife/halloween.html

Hanami
(Cherry Blossom Festival)

Type of Holiday: Calendar/Seasonal
Date of Observation: March-April
Where Celebrated: Japan
Symbols and Customs: Cherry Blossom, Cherry Dance

ORIGINS

Hana means "flower" in Japanese, and *hanami* means "flower viewing." While the word for "cherry blossom" is *sakura*, the appreciation of the cherry blossom is so widespread in Japan that *hanami* has come to refer specifically to cherry blossoms. The pink-and-white blooms last for about two weeks in March-April, and during that time people swarm to Japan's public parks to picnic, play games, tell stories, and dance beneath the canopy of flowers. Companies even book certain places in advance so they can have hanami parties for their employees.

In Tokyo's Ueno Park—one of the most noted cherry blossom viewing places—the traditional way of viewing the cherry blossoms was an elaborate affair. Family groups would arrive in the morning and set up their quarters for the day, spreading mats and red blankets on the ground under the blossoming trees and hanging striped curtains bearing the family crest to screen off the area. Some of the groups stretched ropes from tree to tree and hung brightly colored kimonos over the line to serve as curtains. These closed-off areas served as a combination dining room and stage. After feasting, the groups visited with their neighbors or joined in the dancing and singing under the trees. Young girls would try to outdo each other by putting on their best holiday kimonos and parading around the park.

Today, people talk constantly during the brief blooming season about where the best cherry blossoms can be seen, the different varieties, and where trees of particular interest—because of their age, size, or number—can be found. Throughout the month of April, trains and buses are crowded with people on their way to see the cherry blossoms. While some prefer to see an isolated tree in a remote mountain setting, others want to see hundreds of trees blooming together in a public park. Blossoms can also be seen in temple gardens, in pastures, and along riverbanks. The most famous viewing place is Yoshinoyama near Nara in the west of Japan, where it is said that a thousand trees can be seen at a glance and where young children holding cherry blossoms walk in procession through the main streets.

Since ancient times people in all parts of the world have honored the changing of the seasons. Many cultures divided the year into two seasons, summer and winter, and marked these points of the year at or near the summer and winter solstices, during which light and warmth began to increase and decrease, respectively. In pre-industrial times, humans survived through hunting, gathering, and agricultural practices, which depend on the natural cycle of seasons, according to the climate in the region of the world in which they lived. Thus, they created rituals to help ensure enough rain and sun in the spring and summer so crops would grow to fruition at harvest time, which was, in turn, duly celebrated. Vestiges of many of these ancient practices are thought to have survived in festivals still celebrated around seasonal themes.

The cherry blossom viewing season usually starts at the end of March in Kyushu, in early April in the Tokyo area, and in late April in northern Japan.

SYMBOLS AND CUSTOMS

Cherry Blossom

The Japanese have always thought of the sakura or cherry blossom as a symbol for their nation. Poets and artists have celebrated it in their work, and it is the one flower that embodies perfection. Samurai warriors regarded the way the cherry blossom falls at the peak of its beauty as a symbol of grace in death and of the samurai way of life, since so many of them died young. Modern-day Japanese soldiers have often compared their few brief hours of glory in combat to those of the short-lived blossom. The cherry blossom is also an important symbol in the Buddhist faith, which stresses the impermanence of life.

Cherry Dance

The real name for this dance is the *Miyako Odori* or "Dance of the Capital," but because it is performed during the cherry blossom season, it has become known as the Cherry Dance outside Japan. In Tokyo, Osaka, and other places where there are *geisha*—women trained as dancers, singers, and companions for men—there is a Cherry Dance at this time of year.

The famous Cherry Dance in Kyoto is held during the month of April, and the best available artists and musicians take part in the performance. The opening scene, lit by lanterns, is especially beautiful, as are the geisha dances executed with a series of graceful movements done to the accompaniment of flutes and drums.

FURTHER READING

Bauer, Helen, and Sherwin Carlquist. *Japanese Festivals*. Garden City, NY: Double-day, 1965.

Henderson, Helene, ed. *Holidays, Festivals, and Celebrations of the World Dictionary*. 3rd ed. Detroit: Omnigraphics, 2005.

Ickis, Marguerite. *The Book of Festivals and Holidays the World Over*. New York: Dodd, Mead, 1970.

MacDonald, Margaret R., ed. *The Folklore of World Holidays*. Detroit: Gale Research, 1992.

Thurley, Elizabeth. *Through the Year in Japan*. London: Batsford Academic and Educational, 1985.

Trawicky, Bernard, and Ruth W. Gregory. *Anniversaries and Holidays*. 5th ed. Chicago: American Library Assocation, 2000.

WEB SITES

Japanzine
www.seekjapan.jp/article-1/912/Field+Guide+to+Japan:+Hanami+Fun+Facts!
www.seekjapan.jp/article-1/901/Hanami+Manners+101

Hanukkah
(Chanukah, Feast of Dedication,
Festival of Lights)

Type of Holiday: Religious (Jewish)
Date of Observation: Between November 25 and December 26; from 25 Kislev to 2 Tevet
Where Celebrated: Europe, Israel, United States, and by Jews all over the world
Symbols and Customs: Dreidel, Latkes, Menorah

ORIGINS

Hanukkah is a religious holiday in Judaism, one of the oldest continuously observed religions in the world. Its history extends back beyond the advent of the written word. Its people trace their roots to a common ancestor, Abraham, and then back even farther to the very moment of creation.

According to Jewish belief, the law given to the Jewish people by God contained everything they needed to live a holy life, including the ability to be reinterpreted in new historical situations. Judaism, therefore, is the expression of the Jewish people, attempting to live holy (set apart) lives in accordance with the instructions given by God.

Although obedience to the law is central to Judaism, there is no one central authority. Sources of divine authority are God, the Torah, interpretations of the Torah by respected teachers, and tradition. Religious observances and the study of Jewish law are conducted under the supervision of a teacher called a rabbi.

There are several sects within Judaism. Orthodox Judaism is characterized by an affirmation of the traditional Jewish faith, strict adherence to customs such as keeping the Sabbath, participation in ceremonies and rituals, and the observance of dietary regulations. Conservative Jewish congregations seek to retain many ancient traditions but without the accompanying demand for strict observance. Reform Judaism stresses modern biblical criticism and emphasizes ethical teachings more than ritualistic observance. Hasidism is a mystical sect of Judaism that teaches enthusiastic prayer as a means of communion with God. The Reconstructionist movement began early in the twentieth century in an effort to "reconstruct" Judaism with the community rather than the synagogue as its center.

Hanukkah commemorates the successful rebellion of the Jews against the Syrian-Greek King Antiochus, who was determined to impose the Greek religion on all of his subjects. He forbade the Jews to read from their holy books, to pray to their god, or to celebrate their holidays. When Matthias, a Jewish priest of Modin (near Jerusalem) and his five sons heard about the king's decrees, they decided to fight back. They ran to the hills and organized a small army led by one of the sons, Judah (also known as Judas Maccabeus). They fought the Syrians for three years and finally succeeded in forcing the Syrian army out of their land in 162 B.C.E.

After the battle was over, the Jewish victors went into their Temple to get rid of the pagan altar and the statues of Zeus and other Greek gods. They wanted to rededicate the Temple to their own god by relighting the holy candelabrum known as the MENORAH. According to the story, they could only find enough consecrated (pure) oil to burn for one day, and it would take eight days to get more. Miraculously, the menorah burned continuously for eight days on its small supply of oil. The rededication ceremony took place on the twenty-fifth day of the Jewish month of Kislev—the anniversary of the Temple's desecration by the Greeks three years earlier. For this reason, the festival is sometimes called the Feast of Dedication (Hanukkah means "dedication" in Hebrew) or the Festival of Lights.

What Hanukkah really celebrates is the survival of Judaism. The Maccabees' primary goal was to preserve their own Jewish identity. So the holiday is not so much a commemoration of a military success as a celebration of Jewish independence and of religious freedom in general. Interestingly, it is the only major Jewish festival that is not mentioned in the Bible.

SYMBOLS AND CUSTOMS

Dreidel

Known as a *sevivon* in Hebrew, the dreidel is a small, flat-sided top that spins on a central post or stem. Each of the four sides bears a Hebrew letter: Nun, Gimel, Hay, and Shin. Taken together, NGHS stands for the words *nes gadol hayeh sham*, which means "A great miracle happened there"—a reference to the miraculous burning of the MENORAH for eight days.

There is a theory that the game of dreidel was brought to Europe from India during the Middle Ages and eventually played by German Christians on **CHRISTMAS EVE**. The German letters H, G, H, and S stand for *Nichts* (nothing), *Ganz* (all), *Halb* (half), and *Stell ein* (put in). The Jews, according to this story, replaced the German letters with Hebrew ones that sounded similar, and made them into an acrostic of the Hebrew phrase, "A great miracle happened there."

The Hebrew letters found on the dreidel also carry numeric values: Nun=50, Gimel=3, Hay=5, and Shin=300. The players take turns spinning the dreidel and accumulating points. After an agreed-upon number of rounds, the person with the highest score wins. Sometimes small change, candy, or raisins and almonds are put in a pot. If the dreidel falls on Gimel, the player takes the entire pot; if Hay, the player takes half; if Nun, he or she takes nothing; and if it falls on Shin, he or she must put half of his or her pile in the pot. The game can be made more challenging by drawing a circle two feet in diameter and trying to keep the spinning dreidel inside the circle. The player whose spin travels outside the circle loses a turn.

The dreidel was often used in places where Jews were forbidden to practice their religion. They would meet, supposedly to play the dreidel, but in fact they would secretly pray together or study the Torah. Although early dreidels were carved from wood found in the forest, nowadays they can be purchased in many sizes, made from a variety of materials, including redwood, silver, and plastic. In addition to recalling the miracle of the burning menorah, the spin of the dreidel also symbolizes the spinning of the earth on its axis and the cyclical nature of both the seasons and the fortunes of the Jews.

Latkes

Latkes are potato pancakes served at Hanukkah in memory of the Maccabee women who cooked latkes for the Jewish soldiers when they were fighting the Syrians. Because they are fried in oil, latkes also symbolize the tiny jug of oil that miraculously lasted for eight days when the MENORAH in the Temple was first rekindled after the Syrians were driven out.

Menorah

The original menorahs were made out of clay and burned oil. The design of today's menorah, which stands on a base from which nine branches sprout like the fingers of a hand, dates back to the Middle Ages. The Hanukkah menorah is called the *hanukkiyyah.* It has eight places for separate candles and a ninth place for the *shammesh* or "servant" candle, which is used to light the others. The shammesh is usually set apart by being higher than the other candles.

The lighting of the Hanukkah candles, which stand for spirit, courage, justice, and hope, is the festival's most important ritual. Using the shammesh, the first candle is lit at sundown on the 24th day of Kislev. On the second night, two candles are lit. On each night thereafter, one more candle is added until, on the eighth night of the festival, all eight (along with the shammesh) are burning together. Because Hebrew is read and written from right to left, the candles are set each night from right to left. But they are lit from left to right. The candles are left burning for at least a half hour and are allowed to extinguish themselves. The lighting ritual is accompanied by a blessing and a brief statement in Hebrew about what is being commemorated. The 30th Psalm, a kind of anthem for the festival, is then recited.

The lights associated with Hanukkah are not even mentioned in the Book of the Maccabees, which has led many scholars to conclude that they had nothing to do with the festival originally, but were adapted from the popular pagan custom of lighting candles, torches, or bonfires at the time of the **WINTER SOLSTICE**. But for most Jews today, the lighting of the candles in the menorah is symbolic of the rekindling of the Temple candelabrum by Judah and his followers.

FURTHER READING

Bellenir, Karen. *Religious Holidays and Calendars.* 3rd ed. Detroit: Omnigraphics, 2004.

Cashman, Greer Fay. *Jewish Days and Holidays.* New York: SBS Pub., 1979.

Cuyler, Margery. *Jewish Holidays.* New York: Holt, Rinehart and Winston, 1978.

Drucker, Malka. *Hanukkah: Eight Nights, Eight Lights*. New York: Holiday House, 1980.

Gaer, Joseph. *Holidays Around the World*. Boston: Little, Brown, 1953.

Gaster, Theodor H. *Festivals of the Jewish Year*. New York: William Sloane Associates, 1953.

Henderson, Helene, ed. *Holidays, Festivals, and Celebrations of the World Dictionary*. 3rd ed. Detroit: Omnigraphics, 2005.

Ickis, Marguerite. *The Book of Festivals and Holidays the World Over*. New York: Dodd, Mead, 1970.

Purdy, Susan. *Festivals for You to Celebrate*. Philadelphia: Lippincott, 1969.

Renberg, Dalia Hardof. *The Complete Family Guide to Jewish Holidays*. New York: Adama Books, 1985.

Santino, Jack. *All Around the Year: Holidays and Celebrations in American Life*. Urbana: University of Illinois Press, 1994.

Trepp, Leo. *The Complete Book of Jewish Observance*. New York: Summit Books, 1980.

WEB SITE

Union of Orthodox Jewish Congregations of America
www.ou.org/chagim/chanukah/default.htm

Hari-Kuyo
(Service for Broken Needles)

Type of Holiday: Religious (Shinto)
Date of Observation: February 8 or December 8
Where Celebrated: Japan
Symbols and Customs: Konnyaku, Needles

ORIGINS

Hari-Kuyo is part of the Shinto religious tradition. Shinto is an ancient religion that originated in Japan. Most Shinto adherents live in Japan, but small communities also exist in Europe, Latin America, North America, and in the Pacific island nations.

The name Shinto was first employed during the sixth century C.E. to differentiate indigenous religions in Japan from faith systems that originated in mainland Asia (primarily Buddhism and Confucianism). The word is derived from two Chinese characters, *shen* (gods) and *tao* (way). Loosely translated, Shinto means "way of the gods." Its roots lie in an ancient nature-based religion. Some important concepts in Shinto include the value of tradition, the reverence of nature, cleanliness (ritual purity), and the veneration of spirits called *kami*. Strictly speaking, kami are not deities. The literal translation of the word kami is "that which is hidden."

Kami (which is both the singular and plural term) are honored, but do not assert their powers upon humans in the traditional manner of deities or gods in other religions. People may be descended from the kami, and kami may influence the course of nature and events. The kami can bestow blessings, but they are not all benign. Kami are present in natural things such as trees, mountains, rocks, and rivers. They are embodied in religious relics, especially mirrors and jewels. They also include spirits of ancestors, local deities, holy people, and even political or literary figures. The human role is to venerate the kami and make offerings. The ultimate goal of Shinto is to uphold the harmony among humans and between people and nature. In this regard, the principle of all kami is to protect and sustain life.

The central authorities in Shinto are the priests. Traditionally the duties of the priest were passed through heredity lines, but in modern times, priests are trained on the basis of recommendation. The priests' duties include communicating with the kami and ensuring that ceremonies are properly carried out. Shinto does not have a single collection of sacred texts analogous to the Christian Bible or Islamic Qur'an. Instead, several important books provide information and guidance: *Koji-ki* (*Records of Ancient Events*), *Nihongi* (*Chronicles of Japan*), and *Engishiki* (*Chronicles of the Engi*).

Central to Shinto is the belief that all things—living and nonliving—possess a spirit or *anima.* One of the reasons why Buddhism flourished when it came to Japan in the sixth century is that it was able to accommodate this and other Shinto traditions within its own, more formal religious structure. Today, evidence of the Shinto influence on Japanese Buddhism can be seen in the ritual event known as Hari-Kuyo, which pays tribute to the spirit that resides in ordinary sewing NEEDLES.

Also known as the Service for Broken Needles or Broken Needles Festival, Hari-Kuyo has been traced back to the Heian Period (794-1185 C.E.) and was at its most popular during the Edo Period (1603-1867). Today it is observed not only by those who sew for a living, such as tailors and kimono-makers, but by ordinary homemakers, home economics students, and anyone else who sews. While in America bent or broken needles are routinely discarded, in Japan they are carefully put aside and saved for this event, which can take place on either December 8 or February 8, depending on the location. People do not sew on this day but instead bring their worn-out needles to the local temple and stick them into cakes of tofu or KONNYAKU while reciting special prayers to give thanks for the work that the needles have performed. There is a brief Buddhist ceremony, after which the needles are collected in a mound and buried. Conducting what is essentially a memorial service for an inanimate object is not unusual in Japan, where tools and items essential to daily life are treated with the same respect accorded to human beings who have died.

One explanation for this practice lies in a custom practiced by fishermen in what is now the Wakayama Prefecture. Once a year they would take a day off fishing and, in an effort to win the respect and cooperation of the sea god, they would sink their broken fish hooks into the sand at the bottom of the sea.

SYMBOLS AND CUSTOMS

Konnyaku

There are many varieties of konnyaku, which comes from the root of the plant commonly known as devil's tongue. It is related to taro and yam, and it is found only in Japan's more temperate areas. Although many foreigners find konnyaku tasteless, the Japanese prize it as a fat-free, high-fiber snack.

As a typically Japanese food with a smooth, rubbery texture, konnyaku makes an appropriate resting place for the needles brought to the temple for Hari-Kuyo. Soy curd or tofu may also be used. Like konnyaku, they are mild, soothing foods that are believed to comfort and console the departing souls of the broken needles.

Needles

In Japan, needlework was at one time regarded as an essential skill that every young woman had to master if she wanted to marry and maintain a home. Although this is no longer the case, needles and needlework remain a symbol of love and marriage, and it is possible that some of the women who participate in the Service for Broken Needles do so in the hope that it will guarantee marital happiness.

FURTHER READING

Bellenir, Karen. *Religious Holidays and Calendars*. 3rd ed. Detroit: Omnigraphics, 2004.

MacDonald, Margaret R., ed. *The Folklore of World Holidays*. Detroit: Gale Research, 1992.

Trawicky, Bernard, and Ruth W. Gregory. *Anniversaries and Holidays*. 5th ed. Chicago: American Library Assocation, 2000.

WEB SITE

Pulse of the Planet
www.pulseplanet.com/archive/Feb98/1550.html

Harvest Home Festival

Type of Holiday: Calendar/Seasonal
Date of Observation: Autumn; around September 24
Where Celebrated: England, Ireland, Scotland
Symbols and Customs: Harvest Knot, Last Sheaf
Related Holidays: Autumn Equinox, Harvest Home, Lammas, Mabon, Samhain,
  Shavuot, Sukkot, Thanksgiving

ORIGINS

Harvest rituals date back to very ancient times. Many cultures divided the year into two seasons, summer and winter, and marked these points of the year at or near the summer and winter solstices, during which light and warmth began to increase and decrease, respectively. In pre-industrial times, humans survived through hunting, gathering, and agricultural practices, which depend on the natural cycle of seasons, according to the climate in the region of the world in which they lived. Thus, they created rituals to help ensure enough rain and sun in the spring and summer so crops would grow to fruition at harvest time, which was, in turn, duly celebrated. Vestiges of many of these ancient practices are thought to have survived in festivals still celebrated around seasonal themes.

The Celtic **SAMHAIN** (November 1) was partly a harvest festival, although it was also a festival of the dead. Similarly, **LAMMAS** (August 1) was the pagan celebration of the grain harvest. In England and Ireland, the festival that followed the "ingathering" of the crops became known as the Harvest Home Festival; in Scotland, it was called the Kirn (from the churn of cream that was presented on the occasion). Farmers would prepare a festive meal for their laborers, who usually danced and celebrated long into the night.

The reaper who cut the LAST SHEAF of grain was known as the lord of the harvest. As the final load of grain was pulled by huge draft horses in from the fields, the reapers and their friends or sweethearts would often ride on top or walk along-

346

side, carrying garlands of dahlias, marigolds, and other autumn flowers. In some parts of England, a harvest queen was chosen. She was decorated with the fruits of the harvest and paraded through the streets in a carriage drawn by white horses. The village church was also decorated with autumn flowers and vegetables, particularly potatoes, beets, onions, and pumpkins. A loaf of bread made from the newly harvested wheat was placed on the altar, just as loaves were brought to the Temple at the Hebrew festival of **SHAVUOT**, and people came to the church to give thanks to God for the harvest.

The Harvest Home supper took place after the grain had been safely stored. Although the earliest harvest suppers were held in the farmhouse kitchen or in the barn, the feast was eventually extended to include everyone in the parish, and it was served under a tent or out-of-doors. Traditional foods included roast beef and ale, accompanied by autumn vegetables. The LAST SHEAF of grain to be cut was displayed prominently at this feast; at the dance that followed, the girl who had tied the last sheaf was led out first by the farmer or his eldest son.

The Harvest Home Festival in England eventually gave rise to Canada's Harvest Festival and the American celebration known as **THANKSGIVING**. It is interesting to note that the invention of the mechanical harvester has not only simplified the farmer's work but has advanced the date of the harvest by almost a month. In England, it is often completed before the end of August, whereas it used to be finished in late September.

SYMBOLS AND CUSTOMS

Harvest Knot

Small ornamental twists of grain or knots of braided straw were made and worn as a sign that the harvest was over. There were two basic types: a more elaborate braid, with the heads of the grain still attached, was worn by the women, and a less elaborate twist, although made with equal skill, was worn by the men. The men typically wore their harvest knots in their buttonholes, while girls wore them in their hair. It was customary for young lovers to exchange knots as a token of love.

Last Sheaf

At one time, country people still believed in the Corn Mother, who was a direct descendant of Demeter, the Greek goddess of grain. They believed that the spirit of the Corn Mother was present in the last sheaf of grain left standing in the field, and they were often reluctant to "kill" her by cutting the sheaf. If they beat it with sticks instead, the seeds would be threshed out and the Corn Mother driven away. Sometimes cutting or threshing the last sheaf was more of a game than a serious threat. In parts of Scotland, a reaper would be blindfolded and spun around until he was dizzy. Then he stumbled about, trying to cut the last sheaf while the others laughed at his misguided swings with the scythe—not unlike a game of "Pin the Tail on the Donkey."

Once it was cut, the last sheaf was brought home and set up in the house or barn where the Harvest Home feast was to be held. In some parts of England, the last sheaf was made into a doll, dressed up in white, decorated with colored ribbons, and hoisted on a pole. Then it was carried to the harvest feast and set up in a prominent place. It was called the "Kern Baby" (corn baby), a descendant of the pagan Corn Spirit or Corn Mother.

How the sheaf was disposed of varied widely. Some people believed that it had curative powers and fed it to their sick animals or cows who were about to give birth; some set it on fire and used the ashes to make an ointment that would cure skin ailments. Sometimes the last sheaf would be left hanging in the house or barn until it was replaced the following year, ensuring that the spirit of the Corn Mother would stay with the reapers and bring a good harvest. If someone had drowned, it was believed that the body could be located by laying the last sheaf on the water with a lit candle at the place where the victim had fallen in and allowing it to drift with the current until it came to rest where the body could be found.

A particularly gruesome custom was the ceremony known in Ireland as "burying the sheaf." A last sheaf was stolen and named after someone the thief wanted to get rid of; then the sheaf was "killed," by stabbing or striking it, and buried. As it decayed in the earth, the victim for whom it had been named fell ill. The only way he or she could be saved from death was to find the sheaf, dig it up, and burn it.

FURTHER READING

Brewster, H. Pomeroy. *Saints and Festivals of the Christian Church*. 1904. Reprint. Detroit: Omnigraphics, 1990.

Chambers, Robert. *The Book of Days*. 2 vols. 1862-64. Reprint. Detroit: Omnigraphics, 1990.

Christianson, Stephen G., and Jane M. Hatch. *The American Book of Days*. 4th ed. New York: H.W. Wilson, 2000.

Danaher, Kevin. *The Year in Ireland*. 4th ed. St. Paul, MN: Irish Books and Media, 1984.

Helfman, Elizabeth. *Celebrating Nature: Rites and Ceremonies Around the World*. New York: Seabury Press, 1969.

Henderson, Helene, ed. *Holidays, Festivals, and Celebrations of the World Dictionary*. 3rd ed. Detroit: Omnigraphics, 2005.

Leach, Maria, ed. *Funk & Wagnalls Standard Dictionary of Folklore, Mythology & Legend*. San Francisco: Harper & Row, 1984.

Long, George. *The Folklore Calendar*. 1930. Reprint. Detroit: Omnigraphics, 1990.

Trawicky, Bernard, and Ruth W. Gregory. *Anniversaries and Holidays*. 5th ed. Chicago: American Library Assocation, 2000.

Hemis Festival

Type of Holiday: Historic, Religious (Buddhist)
Date of Observation: June or July
Where Celebrated: Ladakh, Jammu, and Kashmir (India)
Symbols and Customs: Cham, Masks, Thangka

ORIGINS

Buddhism, one of the four largest religious families in the world, is based on the teachings of Siddhartha Gautama (c. 563-483 B.C.E.) who came to be known as Buddha, or "The Enlightened One." The basic tenets of Buddhism can be summarized in the Four Noble Truths and the Eightfold Path. The Four Noble Truths are 1) the truth and reality of suffering; 2) suffering is caused by desire; 3) the way to end suffering is to end desire; and 4) the Eightfold Path shows the way to end suffering. The Eightfold Path consists of 1) right view or right understanding; 2) right thoughts and aspirations; 3) right speech; 4) right conduct and action; 5) right way of life; 6) right effort; 7) right mindfulness; and 8) right contemplation.

Tibetan Buddhism is defined not only by Buddhist teachings, but also by Tibetan indigenous religious traditions and folk practices. The Hemis Festival is related to these traditions. Tibetans observe a form of Buddhism known as Lamaism, Lama Buddhism, or Tibetan Buddhism. It involves belief in evil spirits, magic, and the spirits of nature. The Dalai Lama is the spiritual leader of Tibetan Buddhists.

The Hemis Festival is held every summer at the Hemis *gompa* (monastery) in Ladakh, a region in the northern state of Jammu and Kashmir, India (formerly Western Tibet), It celebrates the birth of Padmasambhava, also known as Guru Rimpoche, the eighth-century Indian Buddhist teacher who brought Buddhism to the Himalayas and completed the building of Tibet's first Buddhist monastery. Padmasambhava was a Tantric Buddhist—a member of a Buddhist sect that emphasized the attainment of magical powers through the performance of certain rituals—who was brought to Tibet when the construction of its first monastery had been halted due to the presence of earthquake-causing demons. Padmasambhava used his magical powers to get rid of the demons and complete the monastery in 749, establishing himself not only as a local hero but as the father of Tibetan Buddhism.

While Hemis is not the monastery Padmasambhava helped complete, it is the largest and probably the wealthiest in Ladakh. Built in the seventeenth century and located about twenty-six miles from the town of Leh, it features a courtyard where the masked dances known as CHAM (or *chaam*) are performed for two days in late June-early July. According to legend, Padmasambhava was able to get rid of the evil spirits who were interfering with the construction of the first monastery by using the so-called "Black Hat Dance," one of the *cham* dances that is still performed during the festival. These dances, therefore, reenact the victory of Buddhism over the shamanic beliefs that characterized religion in Tibet before Padmasambhava's arrival.

Hemis is also the home of the world's largest THANGKA, or Tibetan scroll painting. Once every twelve years during the Hemis Festival, this thangka is unrolled and hung from the second story of the monastery to the accompaniment of traditional Tibetan music played by yellow-robed monks. It was last displayed during the 2004 festival and will be shown again in 2016.

Although the Hemis Festival is named after the monastery with which it has been identified since the early eighteenth century, this is not the only location where Padmasambhava's birthday is celebrated. Monasteries throughout the Ladakh region hold their own dance-drama festivals at the same time, although none of these is quite as elaborate or as widely attended by spectators from all over the world.

SYMBOLS AND CUSTOMS

Cham

The cham dances originated as a ritual form of dance in pre-Buddhist Tibet, where people believed in evil spirits who could only be kept at bay by offering animal and human sacrifices. After Buddhism was introduced by Padmasambhava in the eighth century, these ritual dances were reinterpreted to show how Buddhist beliefs had triumphed over shamanism. The cham dances even managed to replace the barbarism of blood sacrifices with symbolic sacrifices involving the use of effigies that were beheaded or dismembered and spouted make-believe blood.

As seen at Hemis during the annual festival, the cham consists of a sequence of dances performed by elaborately costumed monks wearing MASKS and executing very slow movements. Each dance serves a specific purpose; for example, the Black Hat dancers—so named because of their wide-brimmed black hats—are supposed to define the outer limits of the area where the dances will be performed and to get rid of any evil spirits who may be lurking there. The next dance, performed by the Compassionate Dakinis, purifies the performance space in preparation for the arrival of the guru Padmasambhava, who wears a golden mask with a peaceful smile, and his attendants, who represent the guru's seven incarnations. Other dance groups include the Masters of the Graveyard, dressed like corpses with white masks, whose purpose is to bring about the destruction of any remaining evil spirits, and the Dharma-Protectors, who ensure the survival of goodness (dharma) by flourishing their weapons and performing movements that symbolically bind the evil spirits in chains.

Although the costumes worn by the cham dancers are often frightening, it is believed that through repeated exposure to these horrifying personifications of death and evil, Tibetan Buddhists will better understand the nature of their existence and come to accept it without fear. Because the cham dances symbolize the victory of good over evil and of belief over nonbelief, they also serve as a reminder of Buddhism's ability to overcome the fears that are common to more primitive forms of religion.

Masks

The masks worn by the CHAM dancers are more than a means of concealing the dancer's true identity. When a monk puts on the cham mask, he is believed to undergo a transformation from the human to the divine. Every movement he makes while wearing the mask is therefore no longer a human gesture but one that reveals the character of the divine or supernatural figure that he portrays.

The cham masks are designed to represent evil spirits, mythical creatures, and various Buddhist figures. Some look like skulls, grotesque monsters, and devils, while others are more benign and reassuring.

Thangka

The scroll paintings known as thangkas are usually painted on cotton or linen that has been treated with animal glue and talcum powder to make it less porous. They illustrate stories from the life of Buddha or other religious figures, and they range in size from very small rectangles just a few inches long to those covering many square yards.

The Hemis thangka, which portrays various Buddhist deities but is closely identified with Padmasambhava, is embroidered on silk using special patterned stitches to give the design three-dimensional texture and depth. So highly revered is the unnamed artist who produced this huge scroll painting that his hands have been mummified and preserved as a relic at the monastery.

FURTHER READING

Bechert, Heinz, and Richard Gombrich. *The World of Buddhism*. New York: Facts on File, 1984.

Bellenir, Karen. *Religious Holidays and Calendars*. 3rd ed. Detroit: Omnigraphics, 2004.

Leach, Maria, ed. *Funk & Wagnalls Standard Dictionary of Folklore, Mythology & Legend*. San Francisco: Harper & Row, 1984.

WEB SITE

Indira Ghandi National Centre for the Arts
ignca.nic.in/nl_01104.htm

Henley Royal Regatta

Type of Holiday: Sporting
Date of Observation: Five days in late June/early July
Where Celebrated: Henley-on-Thames, England
Symbols and Customs: Conservation, Grand Challenge Cup, Pimm's Cup No. 1, Stewards' Enclosure

ORIGINS

The international rowing competition known as the Henley Regatta was first held in 1839, inspired by the first Oxford and Cambridge Boat Race that had been run on the Thames River at Henley ten years earlier. The long, straight, nearly-two-mile stretch of river about thirty-five miles west of London made Henley an ideal location for oarsmen to compete—in fact, it was the site of the Olympic rowing competition in both 1908 and 1948, when London hosted the **OLYMPIC GAMES**. Prince Albert became the event's first royal patron in 1851, and thereafter it was known as the Henley Royal Regatta.

The five-day Regatta's many events include races for eight-oared, four-oared, and pair-oared boats as well as sculling races for quadruple, double, and single sculls. The course takes six to seven minutes to row, and there are often two races taking place simultaneously. During the early part of the Regatta, when as many as 100 elimination heats are held each day, officials start the races at intervals of precisely five minutes—whether or not all the competitors are ready. In fact, there's a popular saying that "If your watch says five minutes past the hour and there is no race starting at Henley, you'd better reset your watch."

The Henley Royal Regatta has been described as "the last bastion of Edwardian England," and it's true that the event has preserved many of the gentlemanly traditions of amateur athletic contests. It is not only a world class rowing competition for oarsmen from over a dozen countries and more than 400 crews, but a huge lawn party attended by nearly half a million spectators. The center of social activity during Regatta week is the STEWARDS' ENCLOSURE, a private spectators' area located near the end of the course. But parties also take place in tents called "chalets" set up along the banks of the river, as well as in the parking lot, where people serve elaborate buffet meals from their cars. The men traditionally dress in straw hats and rowing blazers and neckties, whose colors indicate what school, college, or club they once rowed for. The women put on their finest summer dresses and hats; short skirts, culottes, or slacks of any kind are forbidden. The racing pauses twice each day, for lunch and at 4:00 p.m. for afternoon tea.

After allowing only male oarsmen to compete for 154 years, an open women's event was introduced in 1993. The so-called "Women's Henley," held annually a few weeks before the Royal Regatta, has grown rapidly in popularity.

SYMBOLS AND CUSTOMS

Conservation

The Henley Royal Regatta has for many years been involved in conservation efforts along the Thames. The group plants trees in an area that has been designated a Site of Special Scientific Interest, upstream on the Buckinghamshire bank. There is no sign of the Regatta's presence in the area from September through March, as all of its land and river installations are erected only during racing season and taken down for the remainder of the year.

Grand Challenge Cup

The most prestigious award of the regatta is called the Grand Challenge Cup, and it is given to the best of the crews in eight-oared boats. Americans have competed at Henley for many years, but their presence was especially strong in 1985, when the crew from Harvard beat Princeton for the Grand Challenge Cup.

Nearly two-and-a-half feet tall, the Cup is the most famous trophy in the sport of rowing. It dates all the way back to the first Henley Regatta in 1839, although new bases were added in 1896 and 1954 to accommodate more winners' names. By 1964 the old cup had become fragile, so the 1914 Harvard crew gave the Regatta a reproduction of the original Grand Challenge Cup.

Pimm's Cup No. 1

Just as mint juleps are associated with the **KENTUCKY DERBY**, Pimm's Cup No. 1 is the traditional drink of the Henley Royal Regatta. It is an amber-colored, gin-based mixture of liqueurs, herbs, and citrus extracts invented in 1840 by James Pimm, the owner of a London oyster bar. Regatta-goers consume huge quantities of the tangy-sweet drink, which is often garnished with lemon, cucumber, and mint.

Stewards' Enclosure

Situated near the end of the course on the Berkshire side of the Thames, the grassy lawns of the so-called Stewards' Enclosure are accessible only through closely guarded checkpoints. It is only open to 6,500 members and their guests, and there is a waiting list of over 1,100 for membership. All of the members are men who are either connected with or interested in the sport of rowing, and preference is given to rowers who have competed at Henley in the past.

It is the Henley Stewards who organize, supervise, and manage the Regatta. They are appointed for life, and each one receives a solid silver badge in the shape of the Regatta's crest.

FURTHER READING

Deitz, Paula. "At Henley, Fast Boats and Straw Boaters." *New York Times,* June 28, 1987, Section 10, p. 19.

Kimbell, Lucy. "Boys and Boats—Oh, and Ladies, Too." *New Statesman & Society,* July 9, 1993, p. 12.

Lambert, Craig. "Sporting Spectacle, Sartorial Splendor." *Town & Country Monthly,* April 1988, p. 190.

Stewart, Lane. "Glory Glory Henleylujah." *Sports Illustrated,* July 5, 1982, p. 36.

WEB SITE

Henley Royal Regatta
www.hrr.co.uk

Hidrellez

Type of Holiday: Calendar/Seasonal, Folkloric, Religious (Muslim)
Date of Observaton: May 6
Where Celebrated: Turkey
Symbols and Customs: Folk Magic, House Cleaning, Nahil Tree, New Clothes
Colors: Green

ORIGINS

In Turkey, people celebrate the arrival of spring with a holiday called Hidrellez, which falls on May 6. In addition to marking the start of spring, the holiday also honors the mysterious folk figure called Hizir (Khidr in Arabic).

Turkish folk tradition divides the year into two halves. The warm half of the year begins on May 6. The cold half of the year begins on November 8. Thus Hidrellez is associated with the start of spring and summer. In fact, some people call the days from May 6 to November 8 "the days of Hizir."

A legend proposes that May 6 was the day on which Hizir met the Prophet Ilyas (Elijah). Together they set about awakening the earth with the warmth and fertility of spring. Hence Hidrellez is celebrated on May 6. In fact some folklorists believe that the word Hidrellez is a contraction of the names Hizir and Ilyas. The date May 6 has additional significance in Turkey. In the Middle Ages, before the Turks arrived in Anatolia, the land was populated by Orthodox Christians. They celebrated St. George's Day on April 23, according to the Julian calendar. This date corresponds to May 6 on the Gregorian calendar that is in use today. Thus, even before the arrival of the Turks, May 6 was an important holiday in Anatolia.

Turkish folk tradition suggests that Hizir was a Muslim saint or prophet. He achieved immortality by drinking the water of life and spends his days wandering about the world helping people in difficulty. He is thought to be especially active in the spring. Some historians have a different view, however. They believe that Hizir may have been a folk figure who was popular in Anatolia before the arrival of the Turks, or a folk figure from Central Asia, the ancestral home of the Turkish people.

According to Turkish folk belief, Hizir not only helps people in difficult situations, but he also grants wishes and performs miracles. He is especially attracted to kind and well-meaning people. Wherever he goes, health and wealth follow. Hizir can cause crops to flourish, animals to reproduce, and people to grow strong. He rights wrongs, brings solutions to problems, and bestows good fortune on all. Thus, he has become a symbol of good luck and abundance. Hizir often brings aid to people making journeys, and thus has become a patron saint of travelers. Finally, Hizir brings spiritual enlightenment to those who seek to understand the ways of God.

Hizir's Arabic name (Khidr) means "the green one." Green is a color strongly associated with the Prophet Muhammad and thus with Islam itself. To Muslims, green symbolizes peace, hope, spirituality, and paradise. Hizir is also associated with these things. He may have acquired his name in this way, or because he often appears in green places, such as fields, forests, or meadows.

SYMBOLS AND CUSTOMS

Folk Magic

There are many little charms and good luck formulas associated with Hidrellez. Since Hizir performs miracles of increase, on the evening before Hidrellez some people leave coin purses open on a table, open pantry doors, and set out uncovered bowls of food. They hope that Hizir will cause their money and food to increase as he passes by. Often a window is left open to help the saint gain entrance to the house. People also make little models of things they want Hizir to bring them. For example, they might craft a miniature house, garden, or car. Tradition suggests that the tiny models help Hizir to know what is desired, thus increasing one's chances of receiving these things. Another way of delivering one's request to the saint involves writing down one's desires on a piece of paper and throwing the paper into a river or stream. Hizir is sure to find the paper in his journeys to and fro across Turkey.

Women seeking husbands can also work Hidrellez magic. One such charm advises women to gather in a green place on the evening before Hidrellez. They must place some of their personal belongings, such as jewelry, in earthenware jars, and cover them with muslin. Then they must leave the jars underneath a rose tree. The next morning they approach the jars, drink coffee mixed with milk, and pray for peace and tranquility. Then they open the jars, reciting Qur'an verses or snippets of poetry.

House Cleaning

Hizir is especially attracted to clean dwelling places. In fact, Turkish folklore suggests that he will not even enter a home that is not clean. So, many people prepare for the holiday by cleaning their houses. Turkish folk tradition suggests that by doing so they increase the chances that Hizir will visit and bless them with good fortune.

Nahil Tree

A nahil tree is an artificial tree that is covered with ornaments. These ornaments usually consist of some combination of flowers, fruit, ribbons, human or animal figures made of wax, or miniature ships and other modern devices. In past times Turkish people celebrated weddings and circumcisions with nahil trees. These trees figure prominently in Hidrellez celebrations. On Hidrellez, people write down what they hope the saint will do for them and attach these slips of paper to the tree.

New Clothes

Hidrellez is a popular day on which to wear new clothes. The new clothes represent the cleanliness that attracts Hidrellez. They also symbolize the arrival of spring.

FURTHER READING

Gulevich, Tanya. *Understanding Islam and Muslim Traditions.* Detroit: Omnigraphics, 2004.

WEB SITES

Mymerhaba.com
www.mymerhaba.com/en/main/content.asp_Q_id_E1775

Turkish Ministry of Culture
kultur.gov.tr

Turkish Tourist Office
www.tourismturkey.org

Higan
(Spring and Autumn Equinoxes)

Type of Holiday: Calendar/Seasonal; Religious (Buddhist)
Date of Observation: Around March 20 or 21 and around September 23
Where Celebrated: Japan
Symbols and Customs: Higanbana, Memorial Tablets, Ohagi
Related Holidays: Autumn Equinox, Vernal Equinox

ORIGINS

Higan is part of the tradition of Buddhism, one of the four largest religious families in the world. Buddhism is based on the teachings of Siddhartha Gautama (c. 563-483 B.C.E.) who came to be known as Buddha, or "The Enlightened One." The basic tenets of Buddhism can be summarized in the Four Noble Truths and the Eightfold Path. The Four Noble Truths are 1) the truth and reality of suffering; 2) suffering is caused by desire; 3) the way to end suffering is to end desire; and 4) the Eightfold Path shows the way to end suffering. The Eightfold Path consists of 1) right view or right understanding; 2) right thoughts and aspirations; 3) right speech; 4) right conduct and action; 5) right way of life; 6) right effort; 7) right mindfulness; and 8) right contemplation.

The spring and autumn equinoxes are celebrated in Japan with a ceremony known as Higan, which means "the other shore" in Sanskrit and describes the state of bliss and enlightenment—known to Buddhists as Nirvana—that is attained after death. Because the equinoxes mark the times of year when day and night are of equal length, they represent a balance between light and darkness and are thus symbolic of the "Middle Way" or union between the spiritual and physical worlds that is so central to Buddhist belief.

For three days preceding and three days following the equinoxes in March and September, the Japanese pay their respects to their deceased ancestors —those who have already crossed the river that lies between earthly life and enlightenment and have thus reached "the other shore"—by visiting family gravesites and clearing them of dirt and debris. Then they offer fresh flowers, incense, and the sweet rice balls known as OHAGI to the ancestors, along with prayers for their souls. It is also common for people to visit their local temple for special memorial services during Higan and to ask their priest if he will read a *sutra* (a short verse or prayer) in honor of a deceased relative. Only the actual equinox day, which lies in the middle of the seven-day Higan observance, is considered a national holiday.

There is an old Japanese saying that neither the heat nor the cold last beyond Higan—a reference to the fact that the spring equinox marks the end of bitter winter weather and the autumn equinox marks the end of summer's heat and humidity. This twice-yearly celebration is therefore as much a seasonal observance as it is a Buddhist ceremony.

SYMBOLS AND CUSTOMS

Higanbana

It is customary to bring flowers to decorate the family graves at Higan. One of the most popular is the higanbana or higan flower, a type of red cluster amaryllis so named because it blooms during the week of the autumn equinox and is therefore identified with the Higan observance.

Memorial Tablets

Toba or memorial tablets are typically displayed in the home or at the family gravesite during Higan. These are usually made of wood and contain the names of the deceased ancestors. They remind those who are still living to pay their respects to family members who have already reached "the other side."

Ohagi

The glutinous rice balls covered in sweet bean paste that are offered at the gravesites and served during the autumn Higan take their name from the flower known as hagi, which is a Japanese bush clover and one of the seven plants traditionally associated with autumn in Japan. Similar rice balls covered in sweetened soybean powder and known as botamochi are served at the spring equinox. Both have been associated with the observation of the equinoxes since the Edo period in Japan (1603-1867).

FURTHER READING

Bauer, Helen, and Sherwin Carlquist. *Japanese Festivals*. Garden City, NY: Doubleday, 1965.

Bellenir, Karen. *Religious Holidays and Calendars*. 3rd ed. Detroit: Omnigraphics, 2004.

MacDonald, Margaret R., ed. *The Folklore of World Holidays*. Detroit: Gale Research, 1992.

Trawicky, Bernard, and Ruth W. Gregory. *Anniversaries and Holidays*. 5th ed. Chicago: American Library Assocation, 2000.

WEB SITE

Japan National Tourist Organization
www.jnto.go.jp/eng/indepth/history/experience/ab.html

Hina Matsuri
(Girls' Day, Dolls' Festival)

Type of Holiday: Folkloric
Date of Observation: March 3
Where Celebrated: Japan
Symbols and Customs: Dolls, Peach Blossom
Colors: The dolls associated with Hina Matsuri are displayed on shelves covered in red cloth. Symbolizing the sun, red is the color of vigor and good fortune.

ORIGINS

Sometimes referred to as Girls' Day, Hina Matsuri is observed by Japanese families with daughters by displaying sets of DOLLS, often with elaborate costumes and tiny utensils and furnishings, on elevated platforms. The practice originated 1,500 years ago during the reign of Emperor Kenso. On the third day of the third month, the Emperor's household and guests would seat themselves along the banks of a stream. Lacquer *sake* cups (*sake* being an alcoholic drink made from fermented rice) were set adrift upstream. By the time a floating cup reached one of the guests, he or she had to have composed a special poem. If successful in doing so, he or she could pick up the cup, fill it with sake, and drink it.

Purification rituals were also associated with this day. Small paper dolls were thrown into the river in the belief that they would carry away sin and unhappiness. This custom gave rise to *amagatsu,* which were dolls made from two pieces of bamboo or wood, crossed in the middle and covered with a kimono. Buddhist verses were written on paper and tied to the doll's waist. The dolls were placed near children's beds as a charm to ward off evil and illness. Although boys usually gave up these charms at the age of 15, girls would continue to use them until they were married. In rural areas, dolls made of straw were often hung in a doorway or at the entrance to a village to protect against sickness, disaster, and other evil influences.

Skilled doll makers soon began to produce more sophisticated dolls. In the early seventeenth century, Emperor Gomizuno-o's daughter became Empress Meisho on her seventh birthday. Her mother celebrated the occasion by displaying dolls for her in their Kyoto palace. Eventually other wealthy families adopted the practice, and additional dolls were added to the display, along with miniature tables, chests of drawers, and other doll furnishings. Some of these doll sets became family heirlooms, handed down from one generation to the next.

By 1770, Hina Matsuri was a national holiday in Japan. It remained so until 1874, when its holiday status was removed. But the custom of displaying dolls on elevated platforms regained its popularity, and today the celebration is observed throughout Japan. It is primarily an opportunity for young girls to socialize, inviting their friends over to see their doll displays and serving them diamond-shaped cakes, fruit-shaped candies, and tiny bowls of rice boiled with red beans. The "utensils" that accompany the dolls have become extremely elaborate and refined: gold lacquer writing-boxes; racks for airing kimonos; tiny picnic chests complete with miniature lacquer plates and sake bottles; illustrated books only an inch tall; and everything needed for a formal Japanese tea ceremony. After the festival is over, the dolls and furnishings are wrapped up carefully, boxed, and put away for safekeeping.

SYMBOLS AND CUSTOMS

Dolls

As described above, the earliest Japanese dolls were used as scapegoats. After the Japanese began to manufacture paper in the seventh century, paper dolls could be easily obtained from a priest. They were rubbed all over the body to absorb the person's evil thoughts and tendencies; then they were thrown into running water so the evil would be carried away. Later on, people got in the habit of placing these dolls on their *kamidana* or deity-shelf before using them. This may be where the custom of arranging the dolls on shelves or platforms originated.

Today the dolls displayed on Hina Matsuri are arranged on a *hinadan*, a five- to seven-tiered shelf covered with bright red fabric. The *Dairi-sama* (Court People) occupy the top shelf and consist of a male-female couple representing the Emperor and his Empress. On the second tier are three *Kanjo* (Ladies-in-Waiting) who represent the three stages of life: youth, middle age, and old age. The third tier is filled with five Court Musicians who play the *taiko* (drum), *okawa* (lap drum), *kotsutsumi* (shoulder drum), and *fue* (flute). The fifth musician is usually the *utai* or singer, but there may also be dolls playing the gong, mouth organ, oboe, or *kaen taiko* (large standing drum). The fourth tier consists of two *Yadaijin* (Ministers) who function as guards rather than statesmen. Three *Jicho* (Footmen) occupy the fifth tier: one with a laughing face, one crying, and one angry. Sometimes they are called *Sannin Jogo* (the Three Drunks) because each face reflects a mood associated with drinking. The remaining lower tiers are for the miniature furniture, utensils, and other articles belonging to the dolls.

The dolls that were originally used to cleanse children from sin and protect them from illness now serve a cultural and educational purpose: to teach Japanese girls how to behave like young ladies and how to take care of their valuable belongings.

Peach Blossom

Hina Matsuri originally took place a month later than it does now, after the warm spring weather had arrived. Sometimes it was called the Peach Blossom Festival (Momo-no-sekku), because it was a popular time for families to get out in the countryside and enjoy the blossoming trees. Part of the outdoor celebration was to cast crudely made paper dolls into the river and thus get rid of disease and misfortune.

The peach blossom remains a symbol for the traditionally feminine qualities of beauty, gentleness, and peacefulness that Japanese girls hope to acquire by the time they are married. It is customary to include a branch of peach blossoms, either real or artificial, as part of the doll display. Since the peach is also a symbol of fertility and happiness in marriage, a branch is often placed in each of two ritual sake bottles that stand between the Emperor and Empress on the top tier of the *hinadan* or doll stand.

FURTHER READING

Araki, Nancy K., and Jane M. Horii. *Matsuri Festival: Japanese-American Celebrations and Activities*. San Francisco: Heian International Pub. Co., 1978.

Bauer, Helen, and Sherwin Carlquist. *Japanese Festivals*. Garden City, NY: Doubleday, 1965.

Casal, U.A. *The Five Sacred Festivals of Ancient Japan*. Rutland, VA: Sophia University in cooperation with Tuttle, 1967.

Dobler, Lavinia G. *Customs and Holidays Around the World*. New York: Fleet Pub. Corp., 1962.

Henderson, Helene, ed. *Holidays, Festivals, and Celebrations of the World Dictionary*. 3rd ed. Detroit: Omnigraphics, 2005.

WEB SITE

Japan National Tourist Organization
www.jnto.go.jp/eng/indepth/history/traditionalevents/a70b_fes_hina.html

Hiroshima Peace Ceremony

Type of Holiday: Historic
Date of Observation: August 6
Where Celebrated: Japan
Symbols and Customs: Bell Ringing, Paper Cranes, Peace Declaration, Release of Doves, Silence

ORIGINS

The Hiroshima Peace Ceremony marks the use of the first atomic bomb in war. In the summer of 1945, World War II was drawing to a close. The people of the United States were weary after four years of warfare, and President Harry Truman was determined to end the war in the quickest way possible. Germany surrendered on May 8, but fierce battles were still fought in the Pacific against a Japanese military determined not to give an inch. In the meantime, scientists in the United States were perfecting a secret new weapon called the atomic bomb. This bomb was designed to be far more powerful that anything the world had ever seen before. On July 16, President Truman received word that the atomic bomb had been successfully tested in New Mexico. On July 17, at an event known as the Potsdam Conference, the United States gave Japan an ultimatum: surrender to the United States, or face complete destruction. Japan did not believe that the United States had a powerful new weapon and refused to surrender.

American military leaders had already drawn up plans for the invasion and conquest of Japan through the usual military measures. They calculated that about 40,000 American soldiers would die in the attempt, and 100,000 would be wounded. Many more Japanese troops would die and be wounded in defense of their homeland. Truman thought that too many American soldiers had already died fighting the Japanese. He gave orders to use atomic weapons against Japan.

On August 6, 1945, at exactly 8:15 a.m., the United States dropped an atomic bomb on the city of Hiroshima, Japan. Between 70,000 and 80,000 people died immediately, many of them incinerated to the point of leaving behind no recognizable remains. The blast also flattened four and half square miles of the city, wounded 70,000 people, and left 200,000 people homeless. Deaths from radiation sickness and cancer mounted in the years to come. Three days later, the U.S. dropped another atomic bomb, on the city of Nagasaki, Japan. On August 10, 1945, Japan surrendered to the United States, thus ending World War II.

In the U.S. in 1945, there was almost no opposition to the dropping of the atomic bomb on Hiroshima. A few scientists urged restraint, but most condoned military use of the bomb. As the years went on, people have debated whether it was really necessary to drop the atomic bombs on Hiroshima and Nagasaki. In addition, people have become more and more uneasy about the growing number of countries that stockpile atomic weapons. The anniversary of the atomic bomb blast in Hiroshima has become an occasion for many people around the world to think about nuclear disarmament and to take action on this issue.

In Hiroshima, the part of the city that was destroyed by the bomb blast has been made into an extensive memorial site called Peace Memorial Park. Monuments to the people, schools, neighborhoods, and buildings destroyed by the explosion are spread throughout the park. Museums and lecture halls have been built on the site as well. At the heart of the park sits a large cenotaph dedicated to all the victims of the bomb blast. Shaped like an upside-down "U," it was designed to represent a simple shelter from the elements. Its creator carved upon it the following words: "Let all the souls here rest in peace, for we shall not repeat the evil." Underneath the arch, a large stone chest contains a list of names that spans seventy-seven volumes. These are the names of all the people who died in the massive explosion and later as a result of the blast. The current death toll is 221,893.

Ever since 1947, the city of Hiroshima has held an annual Peace Ceremony on August 6 to commemorate the bombing and mourn the victims. The ceremony takes place in Peace Memorial Park. As survivors of the most devastating bomb blast in history, the people of Hiroshima dedicate their observance to those who died as a result of the explosion and to their hopes for lasting world peace. Many political dignitaries give speeches at the annual peace ceremony, including the Prime Minister of Japan and high-level officials from the United Nations.

SYMBOLS AND CUSTOMS

Bell Ringing

At exactly 8:15 a.m., the moment when the atom bomb exploded over Hiroshima, the Peace Bell is rung. Each year a child and a representative from a family who lost loved ones in the explosion are chosen to perform this task.

The Peace Bell was made especially for Peace Memorial Park by Masahiko Katori. Katori inscribed a world map without political borders on the surface of the bell, representing the hope that all people will come to see themselves as belonging to one world. The platform on which the bell sits reminds viewers of the shape of the radiation warning sign, a reminder to future generations to abolish nuclear weapons. A nearby mirror symbolically reveals the feelings in the hearts of those who ring the bell. Finally, lotus plants flourish in the pond alongside the Peace Bell platform. In the hours and days following the blast, survivors comforted bomb victims by placing lotus leaves on their burns, hoping to reduce their pain and comfort their spirits.

Paper Cranes

One little girl who died as a result of the atomic bomb has made the folded paper crane a symbol of the Peace Ceremony. The traditional Japanese art of making ornaments out of folded paper is called origami. Sadako Sasaki was two years old when the bomb exploded over Hiroshima. Although she survived the blast, she came down with leukemia ten years later. As Sadako grew sicker, one of her classmates told her about the legend of the thousand paper cranes. According to this legend, anyone who succeeds in folding 1,000 origami cranes will have their wish granted. Sadako's greatest wish was to live, so she began folding paper cranes. Sadly, Sadako died after folding only 644 cranes. Her schoolmates folded the remaining 356 cranes so that Sadako could be buried with her 1,000 paper cranes.

Devastated by her loss, Sadako's classmates started a national movement to memorialize Sadako and all the children who died as a result of the atomic bombs. As the movement grew, students from over 3,100 schools in Japan and nine other countries contributed money to build the Children's Peace Monument in Peace Memorial Park. The monument depicts a girl holding above her head a giant, gold-colored paper crane. On the base of the monument the following words are inscribed:

> This is our cry
> This is our prayer.
> For building peace in this world.

Sadako's story has spread around the world and continues to inspire children with sympathy for Sadako and hopes for peace. Till this day children from around the world fold paper cranes for Sadako and mail them to Hiroshima around the time of the annual Peace Ceremony.

Peace Declaration

Each year, on the anniversary of the Hiroshima bombing, the mayor of the city sends a peace declaration to the leaders of every country in the world. The document urges these leaders to abolish all nuclear weapons and to work to create peace in the world.

Release of Doves

At the climax of the Peace Ceremony the mayor of Hiroshima presides over the release of 1,000 white doves. The soaring white birds represent the city's hope for peace and opposition to warfare. In the symbolism of ancient Japan, a flying dove symbolized news of peace.

Silence

After the bell ringing announces that the exact moment of the bombing has arrived, everyone attending the peace ceremony keeps silent for one minute. The silence honors those who died in the blast. People also take this time to pray for lasting peace in the world. All across the nation, people at home, at school, and at work observe the minute of silence.

FURTHER READING

Coerr, Eleanor. *Sadako and the Thousand Paper Cranes.* New York: G.P. Putnam's Sons, 1977.

Henderson, Helene, ed. *Holidays, Festivals, and Celebrations of the World Dictionary.* 3rd ed. Detroit: Omnigraphics, 2005.

WEB SITES

City of Hiroshima, Japan
www.city.hiroshima.jp/shimin/shimin/shikiten/shikiten-e.html

Hiroshima Peace Memorial Museum
www.pcf.city.hiroshima.jp/index_e2.html

Hogmanay
(New Year's Eve in Scotland)

Type of Holiday: Calendar/Seasonal
Date of Observation: December 31
Where Celebrated: Scotland
Symbols and Customs: Coullin, First-Footing, Last Sheaf or New Year's Wisp, Noisemaking
Related Holidays: New Year's Eve

ORIGINS

There are a number of theories about where Hogmanay, the Scottish New Year's Eve celebration, got its name. One is that it came from the Greek *hagi mene* (Holy Month), but this is considered unlikely. Another, equally unlikely, is that it came from the ancient Scandinavian Yuletide celebration known as Huggunott ("Hogg-night" or "Slaughter Night," since it was customary to sacrifice or slaughter cattle at this time of year), combined with "Mennie," the cup that was drained at the Yule feast. A more likely explanation is that it came from an old French **EPIPHANY** carol that began, "L'Homme est né, Troi rois là" ("A Man is born, Three Kings are there") which became "Hogmanay, Troleray" in Scotland. Yet another is that it came from *hagg*, an old Yorkshire word for a wood or coppice. A "hagman" was a woodcutter, and "Hogmanay" was what he called out when he appealed to his customers for some kind of seasonal tip or remembrance.

Scottish children, often wearing a sheet doubled up in front to form a huge pocket, used to call at the homes of the wealthy on this day and ask for the traditional gift of an oatmeal cake. They would call out "Hogmanay!" and recite traditional rhymes or sing songs, in return for which they'd be given their cakes to take home.

Hogmanay was celebrated at a time of year when people needed some assurance that the crops would return in the spring. Just as **NEW YEAR'S EVE** was an occasion to look both backward and forward, it represented a threshold between death and life in the natural world. The customs associated with Hogmanay suggest a relationship among the seasonal cycle, the agricultural cycle, and the human life cycle.

SYMBOLS AND CUSTOMS

Coullin

In the ceremony known as *coullin* or *calluinn*, which was traditional in the Scottish Highlands as late as the nineteenth century, young men went from house to house carrying sticks with bits of rawhide attached. One of them wore a cow's hide on his back. Blowing a horn to announce their arrival, they would chase the man wearing the hide around the house three times, beating him on the back and making a sound like a drum. One of the men would then go into the house and pronounce a blessing upon it. Then each man would singe a small piece of the rawhide attached to his stick in the fire on the hearth and apply it to the nose of every person and animal living in the house. This was believed to protect them from diseases and other misfortunes, particularly witchcraft, during the coming year. They also gathered Hogmanay gifts, primarily food, in a bag made of animal skin.

Although it is not certain what the act of beating a cow's hide and making its wearer run around the house represented, many believe it symbolized the continuation of the past year's fertility into the next year. By always keeping the house on their right side as they circled it, the participants in the ceremony were believed to be imitating the course of the sun.

First-Footing

The first visitor of the New Year was an important omen of what the coming year would be like. Many Scottish people living in rural areas still observe the old custom of opening all the doors in the house a minute or two before midnight on December 31 and leaving them open until the clocks have struck the hour—a practice known as "Letting the old year out and the new year in." The first visitor to cross the threshold after the stroke of midnight was known as a "first-foot." It was considered good luck if this first-footer was male, dark-haired, and did not have flat feet.

The first-footer would usually arrive with his or her arms filled with cakes, bread, and cheese for his or her hosts. One of the traditional foods shared with the first-footer was Hogmanay shortbread. The shortbread was baked in the shape of the sun—perhaps a survival of pagan sun worship. Wisps of straw (*see* LAST SHEAF OR NEW YEAR'S WISP) were another common first-footing gift.

Last Sheaf or New Year's Wisp

Back when wheat, oats, and rye were harvested by hand using sickles, it was customary at the end of the harvest to keep a handful of stalks representing the last sheaf of the harvest. They were divided into three parts and braided, then fastened at the top. The result was often referred to as the *calliagh* (from the Gaelic meaning hag, old woman, or witch), the "hare" (an animal with supernatural associations, often believed to be an old woman in animal form), or the "churn." The witch or old woman "trapped" in the last sheaf may have represented a pre-Christian fertility goddess or corn spirit. Some clergymen were reluctant to allow these "corn dollies" or decorated calliaghs to be hung in the church as part of the harvest thanksgiving decorations.

At the end of the harvest, the last sheaf was brought back in triumph to the farmhouse and placed around the neck of the master or mistress of the house, who was then obligated to put on a feast. The worker who cut the last sheaf was the guest of honor at this harvest supper. Sometimes the calliagh was placed on the supper table, but more often it was hung over the hearth or door, or on the kitchen wall. If it was placed over the door, the first young woman to enter the house afterward could be kissed by the reapers in a custom similar to that associated with mistletoe at **CHRISTMAS**. Another superstition was that this young woman was destined to marry the man who had placed the last sheaf over the door.

Last sheaf traditions, which served as an important symbol linking agricultural life with the life of the community and the harvest with human fertility, were common at one time throughout the British Isles and Europe. Sometimes the sheaf would be fed to the livestock or mixed with seeds to be sown the following spring in a gesture designed to symbolize the continuity of life in the midst of winter. If the sheaf was kept in the house, it was considered a charm against bad luck or witchcraft. The use of a braided straw wisp as a typical New Year's gift in Scotland is regarded as a symbolic gesture linking the previous year's harvest to the next year's planting. A sheaf of oats—whether or not it is actually the last sheaf of the harvest—was a common FIRST-FOOTING gift.

Noisemaking

Blowing horns, beating drums, and firing shotguns is common on Hogmanay. The fact that these same noisemaking activities accompany weddings may indicate that they are related to an ancient fertility ritual. Noise was also believed to frighten off evil spirits, and New Year's Eve was a time when such spirits were believed to be very active.

FURTHER READING

Chambers, Robert. *The Book of Days*. 2 vols. 1862-64. Reprint. Detroit: Omnigraphics, 1990.

Crippen, T.G. *Christmas and Christmas Lore*. 1923. Reprint. Detroit: Omnigraphics, 1990.

Frazer, Sir James G. *The Golden Bough: A Study in Magic and Religion*. New York: Macmillan, 1931.

Henderson, Helene, ed. *Holidays, Festivals, and Celebrations of the World Dictionary*. 3rd ed. Detroit: Omnigraphics, 2005.

Hervey, Thomas K. *The Book of Christmas*. Boston: Roberts Brothers, 1888.

Santino, Jack. *Halloween and Other Festivals of Death and Life*. Knoxville: University of Tennessee Press, 1994.

WEB SITE

City of Edinburgh Council
www.edinburghshogmanay.org

Hola Mohalla

Type of Holiday: Religious (Sikh)
Date of Observation: February-March
Where Celebrated: Anandpur Sahib, India, and by Sikhs all over the world
Symbols and Customs: Nihangs, Sports Competitions
Related Holidays: Holi

ORIGINS

Hola Mohalla is a Sikh festival celebrated at Anandpur Sahib, in the Punjab region of India. Sikhism is an independent faith that developed during the fifteenth century in India. The word Sikh comes from the Sanskrit word shishya, which means disciple or student. Sikhs believe that God was the original guru (guru means divinely inspired prophet or teacher) and that he chose to reveal his message to Guru Nanak, the first Sikh guru. Sikhs believe that their gurus were prophets sent by God to lead people into truth. They emphasize equality among people of different castes, practice Kirat Karni (a doctrine of laboring), and follow the precepts of charity.

Sikhism resembles both Islam and Hinduism, but is not directly associated with either. Similar to Hindus, Sikhs believe that the human soul progresses through a series of births and rebirths and that its ultimate salvation occurs when it breaks free from the cycle. Sikhs, however, reject the Hindu pantheon and do not participate in bathing rituals. Instead they worship one God who they believe is the same God of all religions, including Allah of Islam. Unlike Muslims, however, they shun fasting and pilgrimages.

The Sikh holy scriptures are called the *Guru Granth Sahib* (*Guru* means divinely inspired teacher; *Granth* means book; *Sahib* means revered). A more ancient name is *Adi Granth*, which means first or original book. The Guru Granth Sahib was compiled by the fifth Sikh guru, Arjan, and revised by Gobind Singh, the tenth guru. It contains hymns composed by the gurus.

Sikhs do not have an established priesthood. Although individual gurdwaras may employ specially trained people to care for the Guru Granth Sahib, all Sikhs are free to read from their holy scriptures either in the temple or in their homes. In addition, there is no one person to whom all Sikhs look for guidance in religious matters. The Sikh community is called the Panth, and collective decisions may be made by the Panth for the entire community. The Shiromani Gurdwara Parbandhad Committee, whose members are elected, provides guidance for all the gurdwaras in the Punjab. Individual local gurdwaras elect their own committees to oversee local matters.

Hola Mohalla (which means "attack and counter-attack") is celebrated on the day after **HOLI**, the well-known Hindu springtime festival. It was in the Punjab that the Sikh religion was founded in the late fifteenth century, and it is here that the majority of the Sikhs still live.

Guru Gobind Singh, the tenth and last of the Sikhs' human gurus, established Hola Mohalla in 1680 as a substitute for the popular Hindu festival. He disapproved of Sikhs taking part in the Holi festivities and decided to provide an alternative gathering at Anandpur Sahib, where an important *gurdwara* or shrine was located. It was at Anandpur that Guru Gobind Singh had formed the order of the NIHANGS, a Sikh military force that fought against religious persecution at the hands of the Moguls. It seemed an appropriate place, therefore, to stage a festival designed to show off the Nihangs' skill in the martial arts.

Today, the three-day celebration features mock battles, SPORTS COMPETITIONS, and displays of martial arts using traditional weapons. It closes with a ceremonial procession through the streets of Anandpur. Outside the Punjab and especially in the West, Hola Mohalla celebrations are similar to those held in Anandpur. Military exercises are staged before the whole Sikh community, and there are games and tournaments organized by various Sikh institutions. On the last day, people go to the gurdwara (temple) to pray for their health and strength.

SYMBOLS AND CUSTOMS

Nihangs

The Nihangs' skill in various martial arts still play a central role in the celebration of Hola Mohalla at Anandpur. They continue to use the same weapons their predecessors used in medieval times, and their performances show the results of years of devoted practice.

The Nihangs traditionally wear long, bright blue tunics and elaborate turbans, sometimes huge in size, with bands of bright yellow. They are armed with bows and arrows, spears, swords and shields, muskets, or whatever other weapon they might choose to display their skills. They travel to Anandpur from all over India to participate in the celebration.

Sports Competitions

The most popular sports competitions held during Hola Mohalla involve swordsmanship and horsemanship, although children's games are an important part of the modern festival observance. Archery, fencing, tent-pegging, and the skillful handling of ancient weapons continue to be the focus of the festival at Anandpur.

FURTHER READING

Bellenir, Karen. *Religious Holidays and Calendars*. 3rd ed. Detroit: Omnigraphics, 2004.

Henderson, Helene, ed. *Holidays, Festivals, and Celebrations of the World Dictionary*. 3rd ed. Detroit: Omnigraphics, 2005.

Kapoor, Sukhbir Singh. *Sikh Festivals*. Vero Beach, FL: Rourke Enterprises, 1989.

Kennedy, Richard S. *The International Dictionary of Religion*. New York: Crossroad, 1984.

Sanon, Arun. *Festive India*. New Delhi: Frank Bros., 1986.

WEB SITE

Gateway to Sikhism
allaboutsikhs.com/index.php?option=com_content&task=view&id=1148

Holi

Type of Holiday: Religious (Hindu)
Date of Observation: February-March; full moon day of the Hindu month of Phalguna
Where Celebrated: India
Symbols and Customs: Bonfires, Colored Water, Swing
Colors: Holi is associated with red and yellow, as seen in the colored water and powder that people sprinkle over each other. Sometimes Holi is referred to as the Fire Festival because the saffron and crimson that people smear or sprinkle on each other are the colors of fire.
Related Holidays: April Fools' Day, Songkran, Valentine's Day, Vernal Equinox

ORIGINS

Holi is a festival in Hinduism, which many scholars regard as the oldest living religion. The word Hindu is derived from the Sanskrit term *Sindhu* (or *Indus*), which meant river. It referred to people living in the Indus valley in the Indian subcontinent.

Hinduism has no founder, one universal reality (or god) known as Brahman, many gods and goddesses (sometimes referred to as devtas), and several scriptures. Hinduism also has no priesthood or hierarchical structure similar to that seen in some other religions, such as Christianity. Hindus acknowledge the authority of a wide variety of writings but there is no single, uniform canon. The oldest of the Hindu writings are the *Vedas*. The word "veda" comes from the Sanskrit word for knowledge. The *Vedas*, which were compiled from ancient oral traditions, contain hymns, instructions, explanations, chants for sacrifices, magical formulas, and philosophy. Another set of sacred books includes the *Great Epics*, which illustrate Hindu faith in practice. The *Epics* include the *Ramayana*, the *Mahabharata*, and the *Bhagavad Gita*.

The Hindu pantheon includes approximately thirty-three million gods. Some of these are held in higher esteem than others. Over all the gods, Hindus believe in one absolute high god or universal concept. This is Brahman. Although he is above all the gods, he is not worshipped in popular ceremonies because he is detached from the day-to-day affairs of the people. Brahman is impersonal. Lesser gods and goddesses (devtas) serve him. Because these are more intimately involved in the affairs of people, they are venerated as gods. The most honored god in Hinduism varies among the different Hindu sects. Although Hindu adherents practice their faith differently and venerate different deities, they share a similar view of reality and look back on a common history.

Hindus celebrate Holi in a colorful spring festival that has much in common with both **VALENTINE'S DAY** and **APRIL FOOLS' DAY**. The spirit of the day is to make people look and feel ridiculous by spraying them with COLORED WATER and playing practical jokes on them. The presiding deity is Kama, the Hindu version of Cupid whose sugarcane bow is strung with a line of humming bees, and whose arrows are flower stems that have been tipped with passion to wound the heart. Kama is most active in the springtime, when he wanders through the woodlands looking for victims. In southern India, Holi is known as Kamadahana, the day on which Kama was burned by Lord Shiva.

Although Holi is a two-day festival in some parts of India, in others the celebration goes on for up to ten days. During this period people often overindulge in an intoxicating drink known as *Bhang*, use foul language, and show little respect for their elders and masters. The usual distinctions of caste, sex, and age are ignored as they smear each other with red and yellow powder and shower each other with COLORED WATER shot from bamboo blowpipes or water pistols. The streets, parks, and public squares are filled with merrymakers and people painted in bright colors.

Holi gets its name from the wicked Holika. In Hindu legend there was an evil king who declared himself to be a god and ordered his subjects to worship him. His son, Prahlad, refused to do so because he believed only in Rama, one of the incarnations of the Hindu god Vishnu. To punish the child, the king tried to kill him with fire, but Prahlad was able to save himself merely by uttering Vishnu's name. Finally the king's evil sister, Holika, who believed that she was immune to fire, took the child in her lap and sat in the flames with him. When the fire had subsided, Prahlad was found safe. But his aunt Holika had perished.

Another legend says that Holi commemorates the destruction of a female demon named Putana. When Krishna was a baby, Kansa, his enemy and king of the realm, ordered a general massacre of all children so that he would be destroyed. Putana, one of Kansa's agents, assumed human form and went about the country offering her poisoned nipples to every baby she could find. The infant Krishna, knowing exactly who she was and what she represented, sucked so hard that he drained Putana of her life.

For children living in India, Holi is as exciting as **HALLOWEEN** is to children living in the West. They roam the streets with bamboo blowpipes, looking for people to spray with liquid or powdered colors. In western India, Holi is also a celebration of the **VERNAL EQUINOX** and the wheat harvest. Festivities among the lower classes in particular can get very boisterous. No women in western India dare to leave their houses during this festival for fear of having obscenities shouted at them in the streets.

SYMBOLS AND CUSTOMS

Bonfires

Bonfires are a longstanding Holi tradition. Some light them to celebrate the cremation of Putana, who was eventually burned to death by the people whose children she'd poisoned. Others light bonfires in memory of the evil Holika, who was burned in the fire that Prahlad survived. Still another legend says that an old woman whose grandchild was about to be sacrificed to Holika gathered as many children as she could find and made them abuse Holika with foul language. Holika fell dead, and the children made a bonfire of her remains.

For a week before Holi, boys in India go from door to door collecting fuel for the bonfires—everything from wood shavings from the floor of a carpenter's shop to broken furniture and old barrel staves. When the moon is high on the night before the festival, bonfires are lit all over the country, accompanied by the blowing of horns and the beating of drums. People dance and sing songs around the fire. At dawn, the embers are doused with water and people dip their fingers into the warm ashes and make a mark on their forehead to bring luck in the coming year.

Fire is also a purifying agent. People often take a little fire from the Holi bonfire and bring it home to make their houses pure and free from disease.

Colored Water

According to legend, the small monkey god Hanuman managed to swallow the sun one day, plunging everyone into darkness. The other gods suggested that people squirt each other with colored water to make Hanuman laugh. The monkey god laughed so hard that the sun flew out of his mouth.

Because Holi falls just before the start of the wet season in India, water is an appropriate symbol of the coming rains. Hindus also regard water as protection against evil. At this and other festivals, they take ritual baths in the Ganges River or other sacred waters.

Swing

Holi is sometimes referred to as Dol Yatra or the Swing Festival. Based on the legend of how the infant Krishna sucked the life out of Putana, an image of the god as a baby is placed in a small swing-cradle and decorated with flowers and colored powder. In Bengal, dolas or swings are made for Krishna instead of preparing BONFIRES. In other places, the fire is built in front of the swing. Women often celebrate Holi by sitting on swings and swaying back and forth to the accompaniment of music.

FURTHER READING

Bellenir, Karen. *Religious Holidays and Calendars*. 3rd ed. Detroit: Omnigraphics, 2004.

Gaer, Joseph. *Holidays Around the World*. Boston: Little, Brown, 1953.

Gupte, B.A. *Hindu Holidays and Ceremonials*. 2nd ed. Calcutta: Thacker, Spink & Co., 1919.

Henderson, Helene, ed. *Holidays, Festivals, and Celebrations of the World Dictionary*. 3rd ed. Detroit: Omnigraphics, 2005.

Ickis, Marguerite. *The Book of Festivals and Holidays the World Over*. New York: Dodd, Mead, 1970.

MacDonald, Margaret R., ed. *The Folklore of World Holidays*. Detroit: Gale Research, 1992.

Santino, Jack. *All Around the Year: Holidays and Celebrations in American Life*. Urbana: University of Illinois Press, 1994.

Sharma, Brijendra Nath. *Festivals of India*. New Delhi: Abhinav Publications, 1978.

Sivananda, Swami. *Hindu Fasts and Festivals*. 8th ed. Shivanandanagar, India: Divine Life Society, 1997.

Thomas, Paul. *Festivals and Holidays in India*. Bombay: D.B. Taraporevala Sons, 1971.

WEB SITE

BBC (British Broadcasting Corporation)
www.bbc.co.uk/religion/religions/hinduism/holydays/holi_1.shtml

Society for the Confluence of Festivals in India
www.holifestival.org

Holy Innocents' Day (Childermas)

Type of Holiday: Religious (Christian)
Date of Observation: December 28
Where Celebrated: England, Germany, Ireland, Italy, Mexico, and throughout the Christian world
Symbols and Customs: Boy Bishop, Whipping
Colors: The liturgical color for Holy Innocents' Day is purple, the color of mourning, since the children commemorated on this day died without being baptized. But if this day falls on a Sunday, custom permits the use of red, an indication that the Innocents have been given their rightful place as martyrs "baptized in blood."
Related Holidays: Feast of Fools

ORIGINS

Holy Innocents' Day is a religious holiday related to Christianity, the largest of the world's religions, with nearly two billion believers in countries around the globe. The word Christian refers to a follower of Christ, a title derived from the Greek word meaning Messiah or Anointed One. The Christ of Christianity is Jesus of Nazareth, a man born between 7 and 4 B.C.E. in the region of Palestine. According to Christian teaching, Jesus was killed by Roman authorities using a form of execution called crucifixion (a term meaning he was nailed to a cross and hung from it until he died) in about the year 30 C.E. After his death, he rose back to life. His death and resurrection provide a way by which people can be reconciled with God. In remembrance of Jesus' death and resurrection, the cross serves as a fundamental symbol in Christianity.

There is no one central authority for all of Christianity. The pope (the bishop of Rome) is the authority for the Roman Catholic Church, but other sects look to other authorities. Orthodox communities look to patriarchs and emphasize doctrinal agreement and traditional practice. Protestant communities focus on individual conscience. The Roman Catholic and Protestant churches are often referred to as the Western Church, while the Orthodox churches may also be called the Eastern Church. All three main branches of Christianity acknowledge the authority of Christian scriptures, a compilation of writings assembled into a document called the Bible. Methods of biblical interpretation vary among the different Christian sects.

Holy Innocents' Day commemorates the children slaughtered by King Herod in his attempt to destroy the infant Jesus (Matthew 2:16). When Herod heard that a child had been born who would become King of the Jews, he had every male child under the age of two in Bethlehem destroyed. But an angel appeared to Joseph, Mary's husband, and warned him to take his family and flee. Portrayals of this event, known as the Flight into Egypt, usually show the Virgin Mary riding an ass with the Infant Jesus in her arms (*see* **FEAST OF FOOLS**).

How many young boys were actually killed? Although their number has been wildly exaggerated, what is now known about the population of Bethlehem at the time would seem to indicate that only about fifteen to twenty "Innocents" actually died. But in the Greek catalogues of saints' feasts, the number of Innocents is still officially recorded as 14,000.

The earliest recorded mention of this feast dates back to the end of the fourth century. Christians in Rome during the early celebrations of the feast were expected to observe it by abstaining from meat and from foods cooked in fat. In many religious communities, Holy Innocents' Day was the traditional feast of youth. Children were given the privilege of sitting at the head of the table, and in many convents and monasteries, the last one to have taken vows was allowed to act as superior for the day. The youngest member of the community was often given a holiday and served baby food at dinner.

In England, where Holy Innocents' Day was known as Childermas, the coronation of Edward IV was postponed because it fell on December 28.

Because the young martyrs died before they could be baptized, the day devoted to them was considered extremely unlucky. In Cornwall, no housewife would scour or scrub on Childermas, and in some areas it was considered unlucky to do any washing throughout the year on the day of the week on which the feast fell. In Ireland, it was known as "the cross day of the year," and any venture begun on this day was doomed to an unhappy ending. Despite the bad luck associated with Holy Innocents' Day, it was observed throughout the Middle Ages with extravagant festivities, similar to those of the Roman **SATURNALIA**.

SYMBOLS AND CUSTOMS

Boy Bishop

In England, France, and Germany, Holy Innocents' Day was also the Feast of the Boy Bishop, a celebration instituted by Pope Gregory IV in 844 when he declared March 12, the feast day of St. Gregory I, a holy day for all students and choirboys. One of the choirboys would dress in pontifical robes and impersonate St. Gregory. Sometimes he would preach a sermon or test his fellow students on their knowledge of religious doctrine. From the eleventh century onwards, the Feast of the Boy Bishop was moved to December 28, for by that time Holy Innocents' Day had become the official feast of students and choirboys. Unfortunately, it became identified with the **FEAST OF FOOLS** in some places, and for a long time it reflected the strange abuses of religious authority and decorum associated with this celebration. Choirboys would play at being bishops and call their self-appointed archbishop an "ass." Although the Feast of Fools was finally suppressed in the fifteenth century, the tradition of the boy bishop survived.

In England, the boy bishop's term of office extended from St. Nicholas' Day, December 6, until Holy Innocents' Day, when he would preach a sermon and be the guest of honor at a special dinner. If the boy bishop died during his term of office, he would be buried with full church honors. Although this cannot have been a very common event, in England's Salisbury Cathedral there is a small sarcophagus believed to have been made for a boy bishop who died between December 6 and 28.

Whipping

Although the custom of whipping children on Holy Innocents' Day is believed by some to be a means of underscoring the biblical account of Herod's slaughter of the Innocents, it is probably a survival of a pre-Christian custom. Similar ritual beating can be found in many countries at various seasons, and it was originally intended not as a punishment, but as a way of driving out harmful influences or evil spirits. In central Europe, Innocents' Day was one of the traditional "spanking days" observed by an ancient fertility cult. Groups of children would go from house to house with branches and twigs, gently stroking women and girls while reciting an old verse wishing them many children.

In south and central Germany, the custom of *pfeffern* ("peppering") was also common on St. John's Day (*see* **MIDSUMMER DAY**) and **ST. STEPHEN'S DAY**. In the Thuringian Forest, children would beat passers-by with birch boughs and be given apples, nuts, and other treats in return. In France, children who slept late on Innocents' Day were whipped by their parents. The practice even gave rise to a new verb: *innocenter*, meaning "to excuse or declare someone not guilty."

FURTHER READING

Bellenir, Karen. *Religious Holidays and Calendars*. 3rd ed. Detroit: Omnigraphics, 2004.

Chambers, Robert. *The Book of Days*. 2 vols. 1862-64. Reprint. Detroit: Omnigraphics, 1990.

Dunkling, Leslie. *A Dictionary of Days*. New York: Facts on File, 1988.

Ferguson, George. *Signs and Symbols in Christian Art*. New York: Oxford University Press, 1954.

Harper, Howard V. *Days and Customs of All Faiths*. 1957. Reprint. Detroit: Omnigraphics, 1990.

Henderson, Helene, ed. *Holidays, Festivals, and Celebrations of the World Dictionary*. 3rd ed. Detroit: Omnigraphics, 2005.

Leach, Maria, ed. *Funk & Wagnalls Standard Dictionary of Folklore, Mythology & Legend*. San Francisco: Harper & Row, 1984.

Miles, Clement A. *Christmas in Ritual and Tradition, Christian and Pagan*. 1912. Reprint. Detroit: Omnigraphics, 1990.

Urlin, Ethel L. *Festivals, Holy Days, and Saints' Days*. 1915. Reprint. Detroit: Omnigraphics, 1992.

Weiser, Franz Xaver. *Handbook of Christian Feasts and Customs*. New York: Harcourt, Brace, 1958.

WEB SITE

New Advent Catholic Encyclopedia
www.newadvent.org/cathen/07419a.htm

Homowo
(Hooting at Hunger Festival)

Type of Holiday: Calendar/Seasonal, Religious (Ga)
Date of Observation: August-September
Where Celebrated: Ghana
Symbols and Customs: Ban on Drumming, Homowo Dance, Kpekpei, Twins

ORIGINS

The Ga people of Ghana are part of a larger ethnic and religious group known as the Akan. The supreme god in the Akan religion is Nyame. The Ga also call him

Nyonmo. The Akan also believe in hundreds of lesser deities known as *abosom*—who inhabit natural objects—and *asuman*—who inhabit man-made objects. Akan religious practices include the honoring of ancestors and healing rituals.

Among the Ga people, who live along the coast of Ghana and account for about ten percent of the country's population, Homowo is a combination homecoming, harvest festival, and new year's celebration. The word *homowo* means "hooting [in the sense of jeering or making fun] at hunger," and the festival traces its origin to a legendary famine that befell the area surrounding Accra, now the capital of Ghana, hundreds of years ago. The people's prayers were finally answered with a record rainfall and an abundant harvest, for which the Ga hooted not only for joy but to mock the hunger that had so nearly destroyed them.

Since ancient times people in all parts of the world have honored the changing of the seasons. Many cultures divided the year into two seasons, summer and winter, and marked these points of the year at or near the summer and winter solstices, during which light and warmth began to increase and decrease, respectively. In pre-industrial times, humans survived through hunting, gathering, and agricultural practices, which depend on the natural cycle of seasons, according to the climate in the region of the world in which they lived. Thus, they created rituals to help ensure enough rain and sun in the spring and summer so crops would grow to fruition at harvest time, which was, in turn, duly celebrated. Vestiges of many of these ancient practices are thought to have survived in festivals still celebrated around seasonal themes.

The entire Homowo season lasts a few months, beginning with the opening of the fishing season and the planting of the millet crop in May and ending with the harvest in late September, but the day designated by the chief priests as Homowo Day is usually a Saturday in August (or a Tuesday in some of the smaller towns). Above all, Homowo is a time of homecoming for the Ga people, and the real celebration begins on the Thursday before Homowo Day, when thousands of Ga travel from all over the world to the Accra Plains to visit their families and their homeland. These pilgrims are known as *Soobii* or "Thursday People," and they bring with them the vegetables and other harvest products that will be used to make the traditional Homowo meal that is shared by both the living and the dead members of each family. Their arrival is celebrated by the crowds of people who gather to welcome them home, and it marks the beginning of a period of peace and harmony during which debts are forgiven, arguments are forgotten, and petty differences are put aside.

Friday is dedicated to honoring TWINS, whose mothers cover their bodies with whitish clay and dress them in white clothing before asking the priests to bless them. Friday night is Homowo Eve, and the firing of guns can often be heard, warning people to stay home because it is widely believed that this is the night when the spirits of the dead wander through the streets. Friday is also the day on which gift-giving takes place. On Saturday or Homowo Day, a traditional Ga dish known as KPEKPEI is prepared in anticipation of the ritual family feast. Local chiefs also sprinkle the kpekpei around doorsteps and other places where the spirits of the departed are likely to gather. People throw open the doors of their houses and let anyone who wants to visit come in, no matter what their social status, and the festival culminates with the boisterous HOMOWO DANCE. Sunday is known as Noowala Day, and it is usually spent making family visits and exchanging warm embraces and new year's greetings.

Although the Homowo celebration lasts a full four weeks in the capital city of Accra, it may last only a few days in some of the smaller towns. Homowo is also observed by Americans of African descent, especially in cities like New York, Houston, and Portland, Oregon.

SYMBOLS AND CUSTOMS

Ban on Drumming

Traditionally a monthlong ban on drumming, music, and other loud noise is imposed sometime in June, before the celebrations associated with Homowo begin. Nightclubs close down and even the playing of drums in church is forbidden, because it is believed that the gods need silence in order to do their work, and too much noise might frighten the spirits of the departed.

This ban on noise has triggered conflicts in recent years between Ga traditionalists and African Christians, for whom drumming is an integral part of worshipping their God. Many merchants and businesspeople, such as taxi drivers, have complained that the ban on noise and the closing of nightclubs and other establishments during this month triggers a serious drop in business. The ban is still strictly enforced in most areas, but tensions between the Ga and the Christians, particularly in the capital city of Accra, have run high in recent years.

Homowo Dance

The so-called Homowo Dance takes place after the family meal on Homowo Day. It often begins with Ga priests drumming on their knees—a symbolic act representing the "hooting at hunger" that took place many hundreds of years ago—and ends in a free-for-all dance where men and women wear whatever they want (including each other's clothes), bump into one another without fear of causing offense, and sing songs that make fun of otherwise prominent citizens and officials. The idea here is to get rid of all the normal social constraints and differences in status, to mock the very idea of hunger in the midst of abundance, and to show joy and gratitude for the gifts that the gods have bestowed on the Ga people.

Kpekpei

The traditional Ga food known as kpekpei or kpokpoi is made from steamed, fermented corn meal and palm oil, often with okra or smoked fish added, served with palm soup. It is traditional for everyone in a family to dip into the same bowl or pot of kpekpei at the same time as a symbolic reminder of the fact that distinctions of age, rank, and gender are overlooked during the Homowo celebration.

In addition to being served at the family feast, kpekpei is sprinkled by Ga priests around residential areas and cemeteries as a tribute to the dead ancestors and as a way of symbolically "nourishing" them. In private homes, the head of the family might sprinkle some kpekpei in places where the departed ancestors are likely to find it, especially around the doorways. After this ritual, the dancing, drumming, and hooting that lie at the heart of the Homowo celebration begin.

There is a theory that Homowo is rooted in the Jewish celebration of **PASSOVER**, and that kpekpei plays a role similar to that of matzoh or unleavened bread. The fact that the Ga often apply red or ochre clay to their doorposts during Homowo to keep evil spirits away, just as the Jews sprinkled blood on their doorways to keep the Angel of Death from harming their firstborn sons, would seem to support this theory.

Twins

The Ga regard all multiple births as a particularly blessed event. Because Homowo is a harvest celebration, twins and triplets, as a symbol of fertility, receive special treatment. After having white clay rubbed on their skin to emphasize their purity, young twins are given a special meal of eggs and yams. Their mothers ask the gods to bless these children and give thanks for the gift of their birth.

FURTHER READING

Freeman, Dave, et al. *100 Things to Do Before You Die: Travel Events You Just Can't Miss*. Dallas: Taylor Pub. Co., 1999.

Haven, Kendall. *New Year's to Kwanzaa: Original Stories of Celebration*. Golden, CO: Fulcrum Resources, 1999.

MacDonald, Margaret R., ed. *The Folklore of World Holidays*. Detroit: Gale Research, 1992.

Opoku, A.A. *Festivals of Ghana*. Accra, Ghana: Ghana Pub. Corp., 1970.

Van Straalen, Alice. *The Book of Holidays Around the World*. New York: Dutton, 1986.

WEB SITE

Homowo African Arts & Cultures
www.homowo.org/festival.html

Library of Congress Wise Guide
www.loc.gov/wiseguide/nov02/homowo.html

Hopi Snake Dance

Type of Holiday: Religious (Hopi)
Date of Observation: August (or early September) for sixteen days
Where Celebrated: Arizona
Symbols and Customs: Kisi, Kiva, Pahos (Prayer Sticks), Sand Painting, Snake Youth and Antelope Maid
Related Holidays: Flute Ceremony, Soyaluna

ORIGINS

The Hopi Snake Dance is a Native American religious ceremony. The history of this and other Native American cultures dates back thousands of years into prehistoric times. According to many scholars, the people who became the Native Americans migrated from Asia across a land bridge that may have once connected the territories presently occupied by Alaska and Russia. The migrations, believed to have begun between 60,000 and 30,000 B.C.E., continued until approximately 4,000 B.C.E. This speculation, however, conflicts with traditional stories asserting that the indigenous Americans have always lived in North America or that tribes moved up from the south.

The historical development of religious belief systems among Native Americans is not well known. Most of the information available was gathered by Europeans who arrived on the continent beginning in the sixteenth century C.E. The data they recorded was fragmentary and oftentimes of questionable accuracy because the Europeans did not understand the native cultures they were trying to describe and the Native Americans were reluctant to divulge details about themselves.

The Hopi observe a ceremonial calendar in which the year is divided into two parts. According to tradition, during one half of the year the kachinas (nature, ancestral, and guardian spirits) live in the village and reveal themselves to the people through ceremonial dances. During the other half of the year, the kachinas separate themselves from the village and return to live in their homes in the mountains. The Kachina season begins around the time of **WINTER SOLSTICE**, as people begin to prepare the ground for planting, and it closes in late July with the bringing in of the first harvest.

The Snake Dance held every two years by the Native American Hopi tribe dates back to the earliest era of human life in what is now the southwestern United States. Scholars believe that the dance was originally a water ceremony, because snakes were the traditional guardians of springs. Today it is primarily a rain ceremony, since the Hopis regard snakes as their "brothers" and rely on them to carry their prayers for rain to the underworld, where the gods and the spirits of the ancestors live. The tourists who flock to the Hopi villages to observe the ceremony, however, are usually more interested in the spectacle than they are in its power to influence the weather.

Performed by members of the Snake and Antelope clans on the three mesas in Arizona where the Hopis live, the dance represents the grand finale of a sixteen-day ceremony that begins a few days after the **NIMAN KACHINA FESTIVAL** or Going Away of the Gods. Preparations for the dance take place during the last nine days, and they include making the PAHOS or prayer sticks, designing the SAND PAINTING, and building an altar around the painting that includes bowls of water from a sacred spring, green cornstalks, and trailing vines of melons and beans—all symbolic of the rain that is needed for the survival of the Hopis and their crops.

During the last four days, the Snake priests leave their villages to gather snakes, often taking young boys with them. According to Hopi legend, boys of the Snake clan can capture and handle snakes without fear from the time they are born. They stroke the snakes with a feather to make them straighten out of their dangerous coils, then grab them behind the head. The priests are usually armed with a digging stick to dig the snakes out of their holes and a snake whip, which is a rod with two eagle feathers attached.

Foot races are held on the last two mornings. The runners streak across the plain and up the steep slope of the mesa just before sunrise in a symbolic gesture representing the rain-gods bringing water to the village. Although the runners at one time were naked, with their hair worn loose in imitation of the falling rain, nowadays they usually wear underwear and cut their hair short. The winner of the first race is given a ring and a prayer-plume, which he plants in his field to ensure a good harvest. The trophy for the second race is a jar of sacred water, also poured over the fields to bring rain.

On the day of the dance itself, the snakes are washed in a large jar filled with water and herbs and then thrown on a bed of clean sand. Young boys guard the snakes to keep them from slithering away, and they use their snake whips to prevent them from coiling. Finally the snakes are gathered up in a huge bag, carried to the village plaza, and placed in the KISI or snake-shrine.

The highlight of the ceremony occurs when the Snake priests reach into the kisi and grab a snake, carrying it first in their hands and then in their mouths. Each priest is accompanied by an attendant who uses the snake whip to prevent the reptile from coiling. As the pairs dance around the plaza, each is followed by a third man called the gatherer, whose job it is to make sure that when the time comes for the dancer to drop his snake, it doesn't wander into the crowd. At just the right moment, the gatherer touches the snake with his feathered wand, drops meal on it, and catches it behind the head. Then he lays it over his arm and goes after another one. As many as 50 or 60 small whip-snakes, long bull-snakes, and even rattlesnakes can often be seen curling around the gatherers' arms and necks.

When the bag of snakes is empty, one of the Snake priests makes a large circle of meal on the ground. The gatherers throw all of their snakes into the circle, while women and girls scatter meal on the wriggling pile. Then the Snake priests dash in, scooping up armfuls of snakes, and rush out of the plaza. They carry them off to special shrines, where they are released so they can carry the prayer for rain from the mouths of the priests to the underworld, where the rain-gods live. The dance concludes with the drinking of an emetic, which makes the dancers vomit and thus purges them of any dangerous snake-charms (*see* BLACK DRINK under **GREEN CORN DANCE**). With a little luck, dark clouds will gather later in the afternoon and the rains will come.

SYMBOLS AND CUSTOMS

Kisi

The kisi is a shrine built to hold the snakes used in the Hopi Snake Dance. It is supported on four sticks—usually fresh-cut cottonwood boughs—driven into the ground and tied together at the top to form a cone-shaped structure, open on one side and covered with a piece of canvas or animal skin. A hole about a foot deep is dug in front of this opening; a board is laid over the hole, and the ground around it is smoothed over until the board is barely visible. This is the *sipapu* or symbolic entrance to the underworld, where the spirits of the Hopi ancestors and the rain-gods dwell.

The kisi can be traced back to the ancient brush shelters in which the Hopis' ancestors, who were wandering tribes with no permanent homes, often lived. When they turned to agriculture and needed more permanent structures, they would dig a circular room into the ground, cover it with mud-daubed logs, and enter it from above by means of a ladder. Today such a structure serves as the KIVA or ceremonial lodge.

Kiva

The original kiva was an underground home that could only be entered by climbing down a ladder through a hole in the ceiling. When Native Americans first joined together to form villages, they maintained their blood relationships through ceremonies conducted in the kiva, thus establishing the clans (such as the Hopi Snake and the Antelope clans) that are the basic unit of pueblo organization to this day.

The modern-day kiva is a ceremonial room that serves as the center of a tribe's clan and religious life. Until recently, male tribe members were expected to sleep in the kiva until they were married. While modern kivas may be either round or square and built either above or below ground, most retain the basic features of the original: a windowless room entered by a ladder through a hole that serves as a smoke-vent with a fire in the center and a *sipapu* or hole in the floor that represents the gateway to the underworld. All important clan and pueblo business is conducted in the kiva, and the preliminary rituals for every dance—including the Hopi Snake Dance—take place there.

Pahos (Prayer Sticks)

Pahos or prayer sticks are usually no larger than a man's middle finger. One of the sticks has a flat side and is known as the "female" stick; the other is the "male" stick. Both have faces painted on one end.

At one time, according to Hopi legend, actual human sacrifices were part of the Snake Dance. But now it appears that the pahos serve as symbolic substitutes for human victims. The Aztecs used images made of dough as substitutes for human sacrifices to the gods, so there is good reason to assume that this practice was familiar to Native Americans.

Pahos are made by the Antelope priests and the Snake priests on the day before the Snake Dance. The male and female sticks are tied together in the middle along with a small bundle of herbs. Then the sticks are laid in front of the altar in the KIVA in tray-shaped baskets. Eventually they are used as offerings to the rain-gods, as rewards to the winner of the footraces, and in the arrangement of symbolic objects around the SAND PAINTING.

Sand Painting

In the center of the altar erected in the KIVA before the Snake Dance begins is an elaborate picture made of colored sand. The border is usually composed of four bands: yellow, green, red, and white. These bands are separated by black lines and represent the cardinal points of north, south, east, and west. The rectangular space they enclose, which can be as large as three by four feet, is filled with rows of semicircles arranged to look like fish scales. These represent rain clouds, and the short parallel lines on the border behind them represent the falling rain.

There are zigzag designs that represent lightning in the form of snakes, also colored yellow, green, red, and white with black outlines. Each of these lightning symbols has a triangular head with two dots for eyes, parallel bands around the "neck," and a single horn attached. The upright sticks set in clay holders and lined up on either side of the sand picture probably represent arrows or weapons of war, and there may be other symbolic items arranged around the border as well, such as cornstalks and gourds.

The sand painting is more than a work of art to the Hopis. It symbolizes the forces that bring rain to the fields and provide the crops so essential to the tribe's survival.

Snake Youth and Antelope Maid

A few days before the Snake Dance takes place, two children about fourteen years old are selected to represent the Snake Youth and the Antelope Maid. The girl is dressed in white robes, with her hair worn loose and a great deal of jewelry. She holds a ceremonial jar filled with trailing bean and melon vines—symbolic of the crops that need rain to flourish. The boy wears a white kirtle (tunic) and sash, and he holds the *tiponi*, which is a hollow cottonwood root containing snake rattles and tied with the feathers of eagles and other birds symbolizing the directions of the compass.

The two young people stand at the head of the SAND PAINTING while the priests blow ceremonial smoke wreaths, sprinkle meal and water over the painting, and recite the legend of the Snake Youth and the Antelope Maid—a process that can take several hours. Because the Snake Dance is actually a form of ancestor worship—not snake worship, as many believe—the Snake Youth and the Antelope Maid represent the ancestors of the Snake and Antelope clans.

FURTHER READING

Dobler, Lavinia G. *Customs and Holidays Around the World*. New York: Fleet Pub. Corp., 1962.

Fergusson, Erna. *Dancing Gods: Indian Ceremonials of New Mexico and Arizona*. New York: A.A. Knopf, 1931.

Fewkes, Jesse Walter. *Hopi Snake Ceremonies*. Revised ed. Albuquerque: Avanyu Pub., 2000.

Henderson, Helene, ed. *Holidays, Festivals, and Celebrations of the World Dictionary*. 3rd ed. Detroit: Omnigraphics, 2005.

WEB SITE

Hopi Tribe
www.hopi.nsn.us

Hungry Ghosts Festival

Type of Holiday: Religious (Buddhist, Taoist)
Date of Observation: August-September; fifteenth through the thirtieth day of the
seventh Chinese lunar month
Where Celebrated: China and throughout eastern Asia
Symbols and Customs: Ghost Money, Water Lanterns
Related Holidays: All Soul's Day, Ching Ming

ORIGINS

The Hungry Ghosts Festival forms part of the tradition of Buddhism. One of the
four largest religious families in the world, Buddhism is based on the teachings of
Siddhartha Gautama (c. 563-483 B.C.E.), who came to be known as Buddha, or "The
Enlightened One." The basic tenets of Buddhism can be summarized in the Four
Noble Truths and the Eightfold Path. The Four Noble Truths are 1) the truth and
reality of suffering; 2) suffering is caused by desire; 3) the way to end suffering is
to end desire; and 4) the Eightfold Path shows the way to end suffering. The Eightfold Path consists of 1) right view or right understanding; 2) right thoughts and
aspirations; 3) right speech; 4) right conduct and action; 5) right way of life; 6)
right effort; 7) right mindfulness; and 8) right contemplation.

Dating back to the sixth century and Confucius, the Hungry Ghosts Festival is similar to the Christian **ALL SOULS' DAY**—a time when the souls of the dead roam the
earth and, if they are not treated properly, cause trouble for the living. During the
last fifteen days of the seventh lunar month, therefore, families visit and repair
graves and make offerings of food, GHOST MONEY, and paper reproductions of such
useful items as cars, furniture, and clothing in the hope that when they are burned,
these items will be freed for the dead souls' use. Although the roots of this festival
can be traced to primitive spirit-worship, today it has become identified with the
popular Buddhist belief that for one whole month, the souls of the dead are
released from hell and permitted to enjoy earthly pleasures. According to the Buddhist calendar, the mouth of Hell opens on the last night of the sixth moon and clos-

es again on the last night of the seventh moon. But it is on the fifteenth day of the seventh month that a community-wide celebration is usually held.

While the original Buddhist rite was designed to placate the spirits of ancestors, today the Hungry Ghosts Festival is devoted to the unhappy spirits of those who died an unnatural death (by accident or murder, for example) and those who have no human descendants to care for them. These discontented souls suffer from hunger and thirst and, if no one attends to their needs, are most likely to haunt the living. On the fifteenth day of the month, Buddhist and Taoist priests chant prayers, perform rituals on outdoor altars, and make offerings to the ghosts who have not yet attained the status of stable, contented spirits. Lantern processions (*see* WATER LANTERNS) guide these souls to their final resting place. The ceremony comes to a climax when the priest tosses candy to the "hungry ghosts"—and children rush in to gather whatever falls on the ground.

SYMBOLS AND CUSTOMS

Ghost Money

People who live too far away to spend this holiday with their families and visit the local graveyard often fill paper bags with make-believe money. Each bag is labeled with a strip of red paper on which are written the name and death date of the individual for whom it is intended. The bags are laid on an improvised altar, a priest offers prayers, and then the bags are set on fire so that the "ghost money" will reach the spirits of those who died by accident or suicide, who died in childhood, or who died far away from home.

In addition to mock money, miniature paper reproductions of automobiles, horses, sedan-chairs, and other modes of travel may be burned so that the spirits of the dead can reach Heaven. Paper furniture, clothing, and other useful items are also burned for their benefit.

Water Lanterns

Boats are supposed to convey the souls of Buddhist and Taoist monks across the Heavenly River to save the souls of those who are suffering in hell. During the Hungry Ghosts Festival paper boats—some with paper crew members and the images of various gods on board—are carried in procession either to the temple or the banks of a nearby river, lake, or canal. Priests conduct special ceremonies to invoke the blessings of the gods, and then, illuminated by candles, the boats are launched. Eventually they burn and their frames collapse, but not until they have served the purpose of guiding the hungry ghosts to their final resting place.

Because it is considered bad luck to meddle with these water lanterns, fishermen spend the day on shore and other boats are left at their moorings.

FURTHER READING

Bellenir, Karen. *Religious Holidays and Calendars*. 3rd ed. Detroit: Omnigraphics, 2004.

Bredon, Juliet, and Igor Mitrophanow. *The Moon Year: A Record of Chinese Customs and Festivals*. Shanghai: Kelly & Walsh, 1927.

Henderson, Helene, ed. *Holidays, Festivals, and Celebrations of the World Dictionary*. 3rd ed. Detroit: Omnigraphics, 2005.

MacDonald, Margaret R., ed. *The Folklore of World Holidays*. Detroit: Gale Research, 1992.

Stepanchuk, Carol, and Charles Wong. *Mooncakes and Hungry Ghosts: Festivals of China*. San Francisco: China Books & Periodicals, 1991.

Id al-Adha
(Feast of Sacrifice)

Type of Holiday: Religious (Muslim)
Date of Observation: Tenth day of Dhu al-Hijjah, the twelfth Islamic month
Where Celebrated: Saudi Arabia, Turkey, Africa, and throughout the Muslim world
Symbols and Customs: Ram
Related Holidays: Hajj

ORIGINS

Id al-Adha is one of the traditions of Islam, one of the world's largest religions. According to some estimates, there are more than one billion Muslims worldwide, with major populations found in the Middle East, North and sub-Saharan Africa, Turkey, Central Asia, and Southeast Asia. In Europe and the United States, Islam is the second largest religious group, with some seven million adherents in the United States. During the early years of Islam, the faith spread throughout the Arabian Peninsula into regions that are today occupied by Saudi Arabia, Syria, Iraq, and Jordan. Contrary to popular opinion, however, Muslims are not just Arabs. Muslims—followers of Islam—are found in many different ethnic groups all over the globe. In fact, Arabs make up less than twenty percent of Muslims.

The word Islam is an Arabic word that means "surrender to God." Its other meanings include peace, safety, and health. The central focus of Islam is a personal commitment and surrender to Allah, the Arabic word for God. In Islam, the concept of Allah is universal and eternal. Allah is the same in every religion and throughout the history of humankind. A person who follows Islam is called a

391

Muslim, which means one who surrenders or submits to Allah's will. But Islam is not just a religion of belief; it is a religion of action. Five specific deeds are required of followers; these are called *The Five Pillars of Islam*. They are 1) *Shahadah*—confession of faith; 2) *Salat*—prayer/worship; 3) *Zakat*—charity; 4) *Sawm*—fasting; and 5) *Hajj*—pilgrimage.

The message of Islam was brought by Muhammad (570-632 C.E.), who is considered a prophet of Allah. The holy book of Islam is the *Qur'an* (also sometimes spelled *Koran* or *Alcoran*). According to Islamic belief, the Qur'an was revealed to Muhammad by Allah over a period of twenty-three years. Authorship of the Qur'an is attributed to Allah, and not to Muhammad; Muhammad merely received it. Muslims believe that because it originated with Allah, the Qur'an is infallible.

There are two main sects within Islam: Sunni and Shi'ite. Sunni Muslims are the majority (estimated at about eighty percent). They recognize the authority of the first four Caliphs, including Ali, and they believe that the Sunna (the example of the Prophet Muhammad) is interpreted through the consensus of the community. Shi'ite Muslims also look to special teachers, called imams. The imams are the direct descendants of Muhammad through Fatimah and Ali. These individuals are believed to be inspired and to possess secret knowledge. Shi'ites, however, do not recognize the same line of Islamic leaders acknowledged by the Sunnis. Shi'ites hold to a doctrine that accepts only leaders who are descended from Muhammad through his daughter Fatimah and her husband Ali. Many Shi'ite subsects believe that true imams are errorless and sinless. They receive instruction from these leaders rather than relying on the consensus of the community.

Just as Muslims celebrate the safe landing of Noah after the flood *(see* **ASHURA**), they also commemorate Abraham, Adam, Joseph, David, Moses, and many other great Jewish leaders and prophets. The three-day festival known as Id al-Adha is held in honor of Abraham, from whom they believe that the prophet Muhammad is descended. According to the Qur'an, Abraham had two wives, Hagar and Sarah. With Hagar, he had a son named Ishmael; with Sarah, he had a son named Isaac. The descendants of Isaac eventually became the people known as Jews. The children of Ishmael became the Arabs.

Also known as Id al-Kabir or "the Great Feast," this festival celebrates a particular event in Abraham's life. God told Abraham to sacrifice his beloved son Ishmael as proof of his faith. Abraham was fully prepared to comply with God's request, but just as he raised the ax over the boy's head, a voice from heaven told him to stop. He was permitted to sacrifice a RAM instead. Within moments a ram miraculously appeared, his horns tangled up in a bush. So Abraham sacrificed the ram and his son was spared.

In the Old Testament, it is Isaac who is nearly killed. Muslims explain this and other discrepancies between the Qur'an and the Bible by saying that some of the stories told in the Bible were corrupted as they were handed down over the years and translated into different languages. They believe that the Qur'an is the final and infallible revelation of God's will. In any case, Abraham's willingness to sacrifice his then only son revealed the extent of his obedience to God. The birth of his second son, Isaac, was his reward.

It is customary during the festival to tell children the story of Ishmael's childhood, particularly how he saved his mother in the desert by kicking at the sand with his foot so that a spring of fresh water gushed out and how he founded the sacred city of Mecca. In fact, the Id al-Adha is the concluding ceremony of the **HAJJ** or Pilgrimage to Mecca. Pilgrims stop in the village of Mina outside Mecca and sacrifice an animal to commemorate Abraham's show of faith. Those who are not participating in the pilgrimage also carry out an animal sacrifice, usually in their backyard or garden. In countries where there is a large Muslim population, schools, universities, and government offices are closed during the three days of the festival, and the air is filled with the smell of roasting meat.

Although the Id al-Adha is primarily a festive occasion, it is also a time for remembering the dead—similar to **MEMORIAL DAY** in the United States. Muslims visit burial grounds, decorate the graves with palms, and recite passages from the Qur'an. The women often spend an entire day and most of the night in the cemetery, although the men usually go home after the ceremonies are over.

SYMBOLS AND CUSTOMS

Ram

The ram—although it is sometimes a cow or a lamb—that is sacrificed at the Id al-Adha represents the story of Abraham and Ishmael. In commemorating the example set by Abraham, the ram also symbolizes Muslims' readiness to sacrifice their wealth and, if necessary, their lives for the cause of God.

The ram must be slaughtered according to Islamic rules, which means that the sacrifice is usually performed by the male head of the household. He faces Mecca, recites the appropriate ritual words, and then cuts the animal's throat in a single stroke so that it bleeds to death quickly. Women who head households usually ask a male relative or the imam of the local mosque to perform the sacrifice for them, although it is permissible for them to perform the sacrifice themselves if no suitable male can be found.

There is no need for a special license to sacrifice animals in Muslim countries. In Western countries, however, a special license may be required. Sometimes a group of license holders will go to the slaughterhouse and sacrifice the animals on behalf of the Muslim community.

The meat from the sacrificed animal is normally divided into three portions, one of which is distributed to the poor. The second portion is given to friends and relatives, and the third portion is eaten at home by the family. In the West, where there may not be any poor Muslims who need the food, the meat is often given to nursing homes.

FURTHER READING

Ahsan, M.M. *Muslim Festivals*. Vero Beach, FL: Rourke Enterprises, 1987.

Bellenir, Karen. *Religious Holidays and Calendars*. 3rd ed. Detroit: Omnigraphics, 2004.

Gaer, Joseph. *Holidays Around the World*. Boston: Little, Brown, 1953.

Glassé, Cyril. *The Concise Encyclopedia of Islam*. 2nd ed. San Francisco: Harper & Row, 1999.

Gulevich, Tanya. *Understanding Islam and Muslim Traditions*. Detroit: Omnigraphics, 2004.

Henderson, Helene, ed. *Holidays, Festivals, and Celebrations of the World Dictionary*. 3rd ed. Detroit: Omnigraphics, 2005.

Smith, Huston. *The Illustrated World's Religions*. San Francisco: HarperSanFrancisco, 1994.

WEB SITE

Islam Keighley
i-keighley.com/news/View.php?ArticleID=27

Id al-Fitr
(Feast of Fast Breaking, The Lesser Feast)

Type of Holiday: Religious (Muslim)
Date of Observation: First day of the tenth Islamic lunar month of Shawwal
Where Celebrated: Africa, Egypt, India, Indonesia, Iran, Iraq, Jordan, Lebanon, Morocco, Pakistan, Saudi Arabia, Syria, Thailand, Turkey, and throughout the Muslim world
Symbols and Customs: Alms, Id Prayer, Moon
Related Holidays: Id al-Adha, Ramadan

ORIGINS

Id al-Fitr is one of the traditions of Islam, one of the world's largest religions. According to some estimates, there are more than one billion Muslims worldwide, with major populations found in the Middle East, North and sub-Saharan Africa, Turkey, Central Asia, and Southeast Asia. In Europe and the United States, Islam is the second largest religious group, with some seven million adherents in the United States. During the early years of Islam, the faith spread throughout the Arabian Peninsula into regions that are today occupied by Saudi Arabia, Syria, Iraq, and Jordan. Contrary to popular opinion, however, Muslims are not just Arabs. Muslims—followers of Islam—are found in many different ethnic groups all over the globe. In fact, Arabs make up less than twenty percent of Muslims.

The word Islam is an Arabic word that means "surrender to God." Its other meanings include peace, safety, and health. The central focus of Islam is a personal commitment and surrender to Allah, the Arabic word for God. In Islam, the concept of Allah is universal and eternal. Allah is the same in every religion and throughout the history of humankind. A person who follows Islam is called a Muslim, which means one who surrenders or submits to Allah's will. But Islam is not just a religion of belief; it is a religion of action. Five specific deeds are required of followers; these are called *The Five Pillars of Islam*. They are 1) *Shahadah*—confession of faith; 2) *Salat*—prayer/worship; 3) *Zakat*—charity; 4) *Sawm*—fasting; and 5) *Hajj*—pilgrimage.

The message of Islam was brought by Muhammad (570-632 C.E.), who is considered a prophet of Allah. The holy book of Islam is the *Qur'an* (also sometimes spelled *Koran* or *Alcoran*). According to Islamic belief, the Qur'an was revealed to Muhammad by Allah over a period of twenty-three years. Authorship of the Qur'an is attributed to Allah, and not to Muhammad; Muhammad merely received it. Muslims believe that because it originated with Allah, the Qur'an is infallible.

There are two main sects within Islam: Sunni and Shi'ite. Sunni Muslims are the majority (estimated at about eighty percent). They recognize the authority of the first four Caliphs, including Ali, and they believe that the Sunna (the example of the Prophet Muhammad) is interpreted through the consensus of the community. Shi'ite Muslims also look to special teachers, called imams. The imams are the direct descendants of Muhammad through Fatimah and Ali. These individuals are believed to be inspired and to possess secret knowledge. Shi'ites, however, do not recognize the same line of Islamic leaders acknowledged by the Sunnis. Shi'ites hold to a doctrine that accepts only leaders who are descended from Muhammad through his daughter Fatimah and her husband Ali. Many Shi'ite subsects believe that true imams are errorless and sinless. They receive instruction from these leaders rather than relying on the consensus of the community.

Also known as the Little Festival or the Lesser Feast, the Id al-Fitr is the second most important major holiday (after the **ID AL-ADHA**, or Great Feast) in the Islamic calendar. It follows the sighting of the new MOON that signifies the end of the month-long fast of **RAMADAN** and the beginning of a three-day period of feasting and celebration. Sometimes it is called the "sugar" festival, because of the sweets that are exchanged as gifts on this occasion.

Because it marks the end of an entire month of fasting and devotion, the Little Festival is observed with even more enthusiasm than the Great Festival. Although both feasts last three to four days and involve special prayer services, the Id al-Fitr is characterized by more spontaneous shows of joy and generosity. Muslims dress in their newest or best clothes and begin the day by gathering to recite the ID PRAYER. When the prayers are over, everyone embraces, greeting each other with the words *Id Mubarak* or "Happy Id." The day is often celebrated with camel races, puppet shows, and carnival rides.

Id refers to a festival of great joy and never-ending happiness, a time when Muslim families get together to give thanks and forget their differences. Much like Christians preparing for **CHRISTMAS**, Muslims decorate their houses, buy gifts for their friends and relatives, and send out Id cards. Shopping is such a big part of the festival that stores in many Muslim countries stay open all night during Ramadan. Muslims living in Western countries usually take a day off work (as opposed to the three-day holiday observed in Muslim countries) and let their children stay home from school. In some countries, the Id al-Fitr is a popular time to invite non-Muslim friends over for a visit, to foster greater understanding among different ethnic and religious groups.

Foods traditionally served at the Lesser Feast include *shir khorma*, made from milk, vermicelli, sugar, dates, and nuts. In Pakistan, this special treat is known as *saween*.

SYMBOLS AND CUSTOMS

Alms

A special offering, known as the zakat al-fitr and consisting of a measure of grain (or its equivalent) for each member of the household, is given to the poor during the Id al-Fitr. Every Muslim who can afford to do so is also asked to donate money to the poor in advance of the holiday, so that the poor have time to prepare for the celebration. In Western countries, money is often collected and sent to less wealthy Islamic countries, such as Bangladesh.

Id Prayer

On the first morning of Id al-Fitr, Muslims wake up early and flock to mosques or outdoor prayer grounds—such as parks, fields, and playgrounds—to offer special

Id prayers. Muslims living in London, for example, often hold their Id prayers in Regents' Park.

There are three different types of prayer in the Islamic religion. One is the spontaneous, individual prayer in which a worshipper expresses his personal feelings and petitions God. The second, known as *salah* ("worship"), is the ritual prayer that must be performed five times each day. Special forms of *salah* are prescribed for religious festivals, such as the Id al-Fitr, or to ask for guidance in particular circumstances. The third type of prayer is the inward prayer of "remembrance" of God, which often involves rhythmic chanting to induce a state of ecstasy.

Since Id al-Fitr is supposed to be a gathering for the entire Islamic community, women and children are also encouraged to come to the prayers. Many women, however, prefer to stay at home and prepare the foods that will be served during the three-day feast.

Moon

Because it marks the end of the fast of **RAMADAN**, the first appearance of the new moon of Shawwal generates great excitement—even greater than that at the beginning of Ramadan. As soon as the moon is sighted, everyone rushes to congratulate each other and begin celebrating. If the moon can't be seen because of clouds, which often happens in Western countries, people consult their local mosque or Islamic center, which receives information from Muslim countries by radio and telephone about where and when the Id moon is due to appear. Because of the distance between the various Muslim countries, however, the Id al-Fitr does not always begin at the same time.

FURTHER READING

Ahsan, M.M. *Muslim Festivals.* Vero Beach, FL: Rourke Enterprises, 1987.

Bellenir, Karen. *Religious Holidays and Calendars.* 3rd ed. Detroit: Omnigraphics, 2004.

Glassé, Cyril. *The Concise Encyclopedia of Islam.* 2nd ed. San Francisco: Harper & Row, 1999.

Gulevich, Tanya. *Understanding Islam and Muslim Traditions.* Detroit: Omnigraphics, 2004.

Henderson, Helene, ed. *Holidays, Festivals, and Celebrations of the World Dictionary.* 3rd ed. Detroit: Omnigraphics, 2005.

MacDonald, Margaret R., ed. *The Folklore of World Holidays.* Detroit: Gale Research, 1992.

Von Grunebaum, Gustave E. *Muhammadan Festivals.* New York: Schuman, 1951.

WEB SITE

Religion Facts
www.religionfacts.com/islam/holidays/fitr.htm

Iditarod

Type of Holiday: Sporting
Date of Observation: Begins first Saturday in March
Where Celebrated: Alaska
Symbols and Customs: Red Lantern, Sled Dog Teams, Widow's Lamp

ORIGINS

Each year on the first Saturday in March, dozens of the fastest SLED DOG TEAMS in the world assemble in Anchorage, Alaska. They come to participate in the Iditarod, a sporting event that has been called "the last great race on earth." The contest starts promptly at 10:00 a.m., when the racers and their teams of dogs begin their 1,150-mile dash across some of the most rugged terrain in the United States, all the while enduring the coldest weather this continent has to offer. The race ends in Nome, Alaska. These days most teams take anywhere between ten and seventeen days to complete the race.

The Iditarod race follows a close approximation of what was once the old Iditarod Trail. The trail takes its name from the small town of Iditarod, which lies along its route. In 1909, Iditarod was the site of the last gold rush in Alaska. In the nineteenth and early twentieth centuries, sled dog teams carried mail, people, and supplies to the towns, villages, and mining camps along this 1,000-mile course. The Alaskan settlers learned how to use dogs for this purpose from the Native American peoples. In those days the average sled dog driver, or "musher," ran a team of about twenty dogs and carried with him a half a ton or more of freight. So important was the Iditarod Trail to the settling of Alaska that the U.S. Congress has named it one of the National Historic Trails.

With the arrival of airplanes in Alaska in the 1920s, the need for sled dog teams began to fade. What's more, the population in some of the old mining towns had dwindled as the days of the Alaskan Gold Rush faded further into memory. Nevertheless, some hardy Alaskans still kept sled dog teams for short runs in remote areas. In the 1960s the arrival of the snowmobile in Alaska dealt a death blow to the custom of sled dog transport.

In 1967 a woman named Dorothy Page, a planner for the Alaska Centennial Celebration, planned the first Iditarod race. Concerned that Alaskans might soon forget this important part of their history and heritage, she arranged for a short sled dog race to be run along a part of the old Iditarod Trail. A similar race was run again in 1969. In the years that followed, with the help of the army, work began on clearing the full length of the Iditarod Trail. In 1973 the full-length race, from Anchorage to Nome, was run for the first time. The course was still so rugged that supplies could not be stored along the way, so each sled carried everything the racer and the dogs would need. The winner took three weeks to cross the finish line.

The decision to set the course of the race along the old Iditarod Trail not only paid tribute to its role in the settling of Alaska, but also to an important event in Alaskan history. In the winter of 1925 an outbreak of diphtheria threatened the town of Nome, Alaska. The local doctors found that they did not have the serum needed to cure this lethal disease. Fresh serum was located in Anchorage, but the winter weather made it too risky for pilots to fly. Moreover, the coastal city of Nome was located so far to the north that it was icebound during the winter and impossible to reach by boat. The authorities decided that the only way to get the serum to Nome was to send it by sled dog team.

The serum traveled the first leg of the journey, from Anchorage to Nenana, by train. After that, twenty mushers and more than 160 dogs transported the serum the rest of the way, passing it from one team to another like a baton in a relay race. In 127 hours, or about six days, the serum traveled 700 miles, directly to the door of Dr. Welch in Nome, Alaska. The brave men and dogs that ran this race did it in temperatures that rarely rose above forty degrees below zero, in winds that sometimes blew the dogs and the sled right off the trail, and in the murk and darkness of the long nights and short days of an Alaskan winter. The icy weather claimed the lives of four of the dogs and crippled several others, but all of the mushers survived. The event was reported across the United States and the lead dogs in the team that ran the last leg into Nome became temporarily famous. Today you can still see a statue that was erected to one of them—Balto—in New York City's Central Park. Today's Iditarod race pays tribute to this earlier, life-saving race, sometimes called the "great serum run."

The Iditarod is run along a slightly different course in even and odd numbered years. This gives different towns along the trail the chance to participate in what has become an important commemoration of Alaskan history, as well as a significant moneymaking event.

The first races attracted local Alaskans, many of whom were among the few people left in the state who still knew how to run sled dogs and survive in the tough conditions the trail had to offer. As the fame of the Iditarod spread, it attracted mushers from the lower forty-eight states as well as foreign countries. Nowadays more than sixty teams compete each year. The first place winner takes home a purse of around $75,000. Significant cash awards also go to those who finish in the other top twenty places. Everyone else who finishes receives $1,049, to help defray the costs of returning home.

SYMBOLS AND CUSTOMS

Red Lantern

Race organizers award a red lantern to the musher and team that cross the finish line last. The first red lantern award for a last place finish in a sled dog racing competition was awarded in the Fur Rendevous Race in 1953. Although it began as a joke, the red lantern prize has come to symbolize the sheer endurance that characterizes all long distance sled dog racers.

Sled Dog Teams

Each musher runs a team of twelve to sixteen dogs. Many mushers breed and train sled racing dogs throughout the year. Hardy northern breeds, like huskies and malamutes, are among the mushers' favorite animals, but many top racing dogs are mutts. In the early years of the race, harsh conditions led to the deaths of a number of dogs. In more recent years, regulations aimed at protecting the dogs and humans that run the race have made dog deaths a more rare occurrence. For example, mushers are required to provide booties for their dogs' feet and must submit all of their dogs to a number of veterinarian checks along the course of the race. To ensure that the dogs are properly fed, mushers send food for themselves and their dogs on ahead to various stopping points along the route.

Widow's Lamp

In the days when sled dog teams carried mail and freight to many of Alaska's remote towns and villages, a series of roadhouses along the sled dog routes provided safe havens for the mushers and their dogs. When word reached the roadhouse that a team had set out in their direction, a kerosene lamp was lit and hung outside to guide the musher and his dogs safely to their destination. The lamp also signaled the local people that there was a sled dog team out on the trail. The lamp was not extinguished until the musher and his team had arrived safely and taken shelter.

To honor this old Alaskan tradition, Iditarod organizers light a kerosene lamp in Nome at the time the race begins. This beacon, known as the Widow's Lamp, is hung on the burled arch that serves as the finishing line of the race. Race organizers keep it burning until the very last racer has crossed the finish line.

FURTHER READING

Beeman, Susan. "The Iditarod." *Alaska Geographic.* Vol. 28, No. 4, 2001.
Miller, Debbie S. *The Great Serum Race.* New York: Walker and Company, 2002.

WEB SITE

The Official Site of the Iditarod
www.iditarod.com

Imbolc
(Imbolg, Oimelg)

Type of Holiday: Ancient, Religious (Neopagan)
Date of Observation: February 1
Where Celebrated: British Isles
Symbols and Customs: Brigit, Lamb
Colors: Imbolc is identified with the worship of BRIGIT, with whom the color white is associated.
Related Holidays: Beltane, Candlemas (Groundhog Day), Lughnasa, Mabon, Samhain, St. Bridget's Day, Summer Solstice, Winter Solstice, Vernal Equinox

ORIGINS

Celtic peoples lived in Ireland, Scotland, England, and northern France from around 500 B.C.E. until around 100 C.E., when the Romans conquered most of Celtic Europe. Little is definitely known about ancient Celtic religion. The Celts themselves left sparse written accounts. Julius Caesar, who led the Romans into Celtic lands, wrote of his impressions of the people, as did other ancient Greco-Roman writers.

During the 1960s the modern Neopagan and Wiccan movements emerged in Great Britain, the United States, and other English-speaking countries. They follow a nature-oriented religion loosely linked to ancient Celtic and other beliefs and inspired by old European folk practices. They celebrate eight sabbats, known as the eight spokes of the wheel of the year, which include Imbolc as well as **SUMMER SOLSTICE, WINTER SOLSTICE, VERNAL EQUINOX, BELTANE, SAMHAIN, LUGHNASA,** and **MABON.**

Imbolc was an ancient Druidic festival dedicated to the mysteries of motherhood, which is why its ceremonies were usually carried out by Druid priestesses rather than by male members of the order. It was one of the "Greater Sabbats" of the Wiccan year ("Wicca" being the name used by believers in neopagan witchcraft to avoid the stigma attached to "witchcraft"), which were huge seasonal get-togethers for witches that involved all-night dancing, singing, and feasting. Like the other Sabbats (or Sabbaths) celebrated on April 30 (*see* **BELTANE**), July 31 (*see* **LUGHNASA**), and October 31 (*see* **SAMHAIN**), Imbolc revolved around the changing season and the breeding of animals (*see* LAMB).

Imbolc was dedicated to BRIGIT, the ancient Irish goddess whose name means "the shining one" (*breo* in Irish is a firebrand or torch, and *breoch* means glowing). Primarily a goddess of fertility, Brigit was frequently depicted as three goddesses in one: the virgin, the mother, and the crone. When Ireland became Roman Catholic, Brigit was transformed into a Christian saint, St. Bridget or Brigid, whose worship dates back to very early times. **ST. BRIDGET'S DAY** is a festival associated with this saint.

As one of the four occasions during the year when witches gathered, often on mountaintops or at crossroads, to perform their black rites and reaffirm their obedience to the devil, Imbolc was often characterized by wild sex orgies and other activities that can be traced to its origin as a pagan fertility celebration. It took place on the eve of February 2, later known to Christians as **CANDLEMAS**.

SYMBOLS AND CUSTOMS

Brigit

Brigit was the archetypal mother-goddess, protectress of women in labor and childbirth. Because she stood as a symbol of motherhood and fertility in general, cows and their milk were dedicated to Brigit, as were ewes and their LAMBS. Although it is not certain exactly why, Brigit was also associated with brewing beer. According to a Christianized version of an old medieval tale, she presided over a brewing at **EASTER** in which she produced enough beer for seventeen churches from a single measure of malt.

Brigit, with whom the color white is associated, is often shown carrying a white rod similar to the hazel rods carried by the Druid priests as symbols of their authority. The white rod symbolizes both the serpent and the swan, which is a bird with a serpent-like neck and a serpent's hiss.

Brigit has much in common with the Virgin Mary, and it is no coincidence that the Purification of the Virgin Mary and the Presentation of Jesus at the Temple in Jerusalem are commemorated on February 2 (*see* **CANDLEMAS**). In fact, it is traditional on Candlemas to offer prayers to both St. Brigit and the Blessed Virgin, and to honor motherhood in general.

Lamb

Imbolc took place at the beginning of the lambing season, so it was closely associated with the ewes and milking. This marked a vital turning point in the winter, since the first sheep's milk and cheese would have been very important at a time when stored meats and grains were beginning to run out and no other fresh foods were available.

Representing all things newborn and innocent, the lamb is an ancient symbol. A real newborn lamb may have been paraded through the streets or worshipped during Imbolc, and there is also reason to believe that some of the ancient ceremonies held on this day involved drinking the first sheep's milk of the year. When Christianity arrived, of course, the lamb became a symbol of Christ, who was referred to as the "Lamb of God."

FURTHER READING

Bellenir, Karen. *Religious Holidays and Calendars*. 3rd ed. Detroit: Omnigraphics, 2004.

Heinberg, Richard. *Celebrate the Solstice: Honoring the Earth's Seasonal Rhythms through Festival and Ceremony*. Wheaton, IL: Quest Books, 1993.

Henderson, Helene, ed. *Holidays, Festivals, and Celebrations of the World Dictionary*. 3rd ed. Detroit: Omnigraphics, 2005.

Hutton, Ronald. *The Pagan Religions of the Ancient British Isles: Their Nature and Legacy*. Oxford: Blackwell, 1991.

King, John. *The Celtic Druids' Year: Seasonal Cycles of the Ancient Celts*. London: Blandford, 1995.

Leach, Maria, ed. *Funk & Wagnalls Standard Dictionary of Folklore, Mythology & Legend*. San Francisco: Harper & Row, 1984.

WEB SITE

BBC (British Broadcasting Corporation)
www.bbc.co.uk/religion/religions/paganism/holydays/imbolc.shtml

Incwala

Type of Holiday: Calendar/Seasonal, National
Date of Observation: December-January
Where Celebrated: Swaziland
Symbols and Customs: Bull, Gourd

ORIGINS

The most sacred national ceremony that takes place in the independent kingdom of Swaziland in southeast Africa is the annual kingship ceremony known as the Incwala. It is held around the time of the **SUMMER SOLSTICE**, which falls in late December in Africa, and lasts for about three weeks. In addition to marking the beginning of a new year, the Incwala features rites aimed at strengthening the king's authority and increasing the strength and cohesiveness of the nation as a whole.

The phase of the moon and the positions of the sun and stars are constant topics of conversation as everyone waits for the precise moment when the sun appears to stand still, rising and setting in the same place for several days. The Swazi believe that the full or waxing moon brings strength and health, while the waning moon is associated with weakness. It is important, therefore, that the ceremony coincide not only with the **SUMMER SOLSTICE** but also with a favorable phase of the moon. If the wrong day is chosen, it is considered a national calamity because it means the king will not be strong enough to endure the trials of the coming year. Since the new moon that marks the beginning of the festival rarely coincides with the solstice, special rituals have been devised to compensate for the unfavorable timing.

The Little Incwala, which lasts for two days, begins when the moon is dark and the king is at his weakest. Because one purpose of the ceremony is to temporarily separate him from society and make a symbolic break with the old year, the king is sequestered in a special enclosure—just as the sun is said to be "resting in its hut" at the solstice.

The Big Incwala, which begins on the night of the full moon and lasts for six days, marks the symbolic rebirth and revitalization of the king. On the first day, a group of young, unmarried (and therefore "pure") men is sent to gather branches from a magic tree and bring them back to the king's councilors, who use them to build the sanctuary in which the king's powers will be symbolically reborn. On the third day, the king strikes a black BULL with a rod that is believed to possess the power of fertility. The pure young men must catch the animal and kill it with their bare hands, after which it is dragged into the sanctuary and sacrificed. All of this is considered preparation for the fourth day, when the king symbolically overcomes his rivals and gets rid of the evils and pollution of the old year. He comes out of his enclosure dressed in a frightening costume of green grass and wild animal skins, his body gleaming with black ointments. While the people sing and dance in the background, the young men or princes alternately drive the king back and beg him to return. The climax occurs when the king throws a bright green GOURD toward his warriors. Then he is led back to his hut.

On the final day of the Incwala, all of the ritual implements that have been used in the ceremony are burned in a huge fire, symbolically ridding the kingdom of evil. The king is bathed, and the drops of water that fall from his body are believed to attract the coming rains, which will reenergize the forces of nature.

It was common in ancient cultures to associate the health and vitality of the king with the health of the kingdom. In some cases, old kings were removed at the time of the solstice. Getting rid of an old king was a common means of ridding the kingdom of bad influences and cleansing the country as a whole.

SYMBOLS AND CUSTOMS

Bull

The main event of the third day of the Big Incwala is the killing of the bull, who symbolizes potency. Parts of the bull's body are used to prepare royal medicines, and the rest is given as an offering to the dead ancestors. The "Day of the Bull" is believed to fortify the king for the following day, when he appears in his terrifying costume and must "overcome" the young princes who symbolize his rivals.

Gourd

The bright green gourd used in the climax of the Incwala ceremony is known as the "Gourd of Embo"—"Embo" meaning North, or the direction from which the royal clan originally came. The king throws the gourd carefully on the upturned shield of one of his subjects, who must not let the fruit touch the ground. The gourd symbolizes the continuity of the past. In discarding it, the king proves his strength and opens the way to the future.

FURTHER READING

Heinberg, Richard. *Celebrate the Solstice: Honoring the Earth's Seasonal Rhythms through Festival and Ceremony.* Wheaton, IL: Quest Books, 1993.

Henderson, Helene, ed. *Holidays, Festivals, and Celebrations of the World Dictionary.* 3rd ed. Detroit: Omnigraphics, 2005.

MacDonald, Margaret R., ed. *The Folklore of World Holidays*. Detroit: Gale Research, 1992.

WEB SITES

Swaziland Government Ministry of Tourism
www.gov.sz/home.asp?pid=1254

Swaziland Tourism Authority
www.welcometoswaziland.com/index.php?option=com_content&task=view&
id=168&Itemid=77

Indianapolis 500

Type of Holiday: Sporting
Date of Observation: Sunday of Memorial Day Weekend in May
Where Celebrated: Indianapolis, Indiana
Symbols and Customs: Indianapolis Speedway, Victory Milk
Related Holidays: Daytona 500

ORIGINS

The first automobile race in America was held on November 2, 1895, at a time when there were fewer than 100 working cars in the nation. The course ran through the streets of Chicago, but only seven cars showed up, and only two of them were fully prepared to race. The winner was a Benz automobile whose average speed was only ten miles per hour—including the time spent on electrical problems, pit stops, and getting lost.

By the early 1900s, automobile racing was dominated by wealthy sportsmen, who came together at Ormond Beach and Daytona Beach in Florida (*see* **DAYTONA 500**) to race on the hard-packed sand. The nation's first track race took place at the 1896 Rhode Island State Fair in Narragansett Park, where spectators laughed at the sight of cars chugging around a track meant for horses. But eventually the popularity of track racing in America outstripped that of road racing.

The INDIANAPOLIS SPEEDWAY was the first track in the nation built especially for automobile racing. The Indianapolis businessmen who put up the money for it hoped that it would be used as a test track to improve American cars in general and Indiana-built cars in particular. The first 500-mile auto race was held there in 1911, and it became an overnight tradition. Although the race was an all-day affair—it took six hours and forty-two minutes for the winner to cover 500 miles— it drew 90,000 spectators. Happily, the winner was driving a Marmon, made by an Indianapolis manufacturer just across town.

Attendance at the "Indy 500," as it became known, slumped during the two world wars, but racing fans returned in 1946 and the sport continued to grow in popularity. Today, as many as 450,000 people come to the Speedway to watch the 500-mile race, and over thirty million watch it on television. Although stock car racing has become more popular—"stock cars" being Ford, Chrysler, or General Motors cars that have been adapted for racing—the Indy 500 remains the single most important auto racing event in America.

The cars that race at Indianapolis are usually powered by turbo-charged engines and run on a blend of fuels, such as methanol and nitromethane. They can finish the race in less than three hours. Officially, the Indy 500 is a testing-ground for devices that will eventually be used in passenger cars. The annual race has been credited with such improvements as the rear view mirror, balloon tires, and ethyl gasoline.

A name closely associated with the Indy 500 is A.J. Foyt, who was only twenty-six when he won his first race in 1961. He went on to become the first driver to win the Indy 500 four times. Even after a serious crash in Wisconsin in September of 1990 that shattered his legs, he was able to squeeze into an Indy car eight months later and start the race for the thirty-fourth year in a row.

On May 29, 2005, Danica Patrick changed the race forever when she became not only the fourth woman in history to start at the Indy 500, but the first woman ever to lead it. She maintained the front position for nineteen laps and finished in fourth place, breaking the 1978 record held by Janet Guthrie. Danica Patrick continues to place in top-five finishes in a field dominated by men, attracting increased spectator and TV viewer interest and extensive media coverage. In 2005, for example, on the day of her record-breaking race, Indy 500 TV ratings jumped by forty percent, the highest ratings for the Indy since 1997.

SYMBOLS AND CUSTOMS

Indianapolis Speedway

The 559-acre Indianapolis Speedway is a two-and-a-half mile rectangle with four rounded corners, gently banked at a little more than nine degrees at the bottom and sixteen degrees at the top. It was originally paved with bricks to reduce dust, but then "board tracks," with wooden surfaces, sprang up everywhere after World War I and became more popular. It fell into disrepair, and at one point developers were planning to subdivide it. But Eddie Rickenbacker, the World War I flying ace and former Indy driver who owned the track, turned down the developers' offer and sold the property to Anton Hulman, an Indiana businessman, for the same price he'd paid for it in 1927. Hulman rebuilt the track and restored its position as the symbolic home of championship auto racing.

Victory Milk

In 1936, three-time Indy winner Louis Meyer drank buttermilk after the race to refresh himself, as his mother had told him it would. The milk industry seized a golden opportunity after they saw a newspaper photograph of Meyer enjoying his milk in Victory Lane. An executive made sure milk was offered to the next year's winner, and a tradition began. There were several years in which milk was not offered to the victor, but the custom was revived in 1956 and has been in practice ever since.

FURTHER READING

Henderson, Helene, ed. *Holidays, Festivals, and Celebrations of the World Dictionary.* 3rd ed. Detroit: Omnigraphics, 2005.

Shemanski, Frances. *A Guide to World Fairs and Festivals.* Westport, CT: Greenwood Press, 1985.

WEB SITE

Indianapolis 500
www.indy500.com

Indra Jatra

Type of Holiday: National, Religious (Hindu, Buddhist)
Date of Observation: September-October; late Bhadrapada to early Asvina
Where Celebrated: Katmandu, Nepal
Symbols and Customs: Ceremonial Pole, Kumari, Mask of Bhairava, Upaku Route

ORIGINS

Both Hindus and Buddhists in Nepal observe the festival known as Indra Jatra, a weeklong celebration that combines paying homage to the Hindu god Indra with the commemoration of an historical event: the day when Prithwi Narayan Shah (1730-1775) achieved his goal of unifying Nepal's many separate kingdoms and became the country's first king. According to legend, Indra, the Hindu god of rain and chief of the gods, came to the Katmandu Valley to find some special flowers for his mother. He was caught trying to steal them and put in prison by the valley's inhabitants, who didn't realize who their prisoner was until his mother came looking for him. To show how sorry they were, they held a festival in his honor.

The celebration goes on for eight days, beginning with the erection of a CEREMONIAL POLE in Durbar Square, in front of the Royal Palace at Hanuman Dhoka. On the evening of the festival's opening day, families who have lost someone during the year follow the UPAKU ROUTE around the city of Katmandu. Traditional dances are performed in the square throughout the festival, and it is believed that the spirits of the gods are actually present in the bodies of the masked dancers.

The third day of the festival is the day on which young boys representing the Hindu gods Ganesh and Bhairava are pulled through the streets of Katmandu on chariots, while a twelve-foot-high MASK OF BHAIRAVA, the city's guardian deity, is put on public display with beer spouting from its mouth. But the highlight of Indra Jatra is the appearance of the living goddess KUMARI, a young girl in the third chariot who is dressed in red robes and sparkling jewels. These chariot processions take place three times during the festival week, and their route is often illuminated by butter lamps. The king of Nepal himself asks for Kumari's blessing, since it is she who has the power to reassert his authority over the people of Nepal.

Indra Jatra ends with the lowering of the CEREMONIAL POLE that was set up in front of the palace on the festival's opening day, accompanied by religious rituals and sacrifices.

SYMBOLS AND CUSTOMS

Ceremonial Pole

The ceremonial pole raised in front of the Hanuman Dhoka Palace is a phallic symbol representing the power of Indra, who brings monsoon rains to the Katmandu Valley and makes the harvest possible. It can be fifty feet tall, and its appearance on the first day of Indra Jatra is usually accompanied by music and the shooting of cannons.

Kumari

Kumari or the "Living Goddess" is actually a young girl who is believed to be the incarnation of the Hindu goddess Taleju Bhawani, later known as Durga. She is chosen by a group of senior priests when she is only four years old, and she must meet a number of strict physical standards to prove that her body is perfect. She is also subjected to tests of her courage, and her horoscope must be compatible with that of the current king.

Once she has been selected, the young Kumari is sequestered in Taleju Temple on the south side of Durbar Square, where she is schooled by a private tutor and allowed to leave only once a year for the Indra Jatra processions. She remains there until her first menstrual period, which is considered a sign that she is no longer "pure." Then she is replaced by a new Kumari and allowed to resume a somewhat normal life, except for the fact that she can never marry. The Nepalese believe that any man who marries a former Kumari is likely to meet an untimely death, and for this reason an aura of bad luck surrounds her for the rest of her life.

Mask of Bhairava

Images of the god Bhairava can be seen throughout Nepal, particularly during festivals, but the huge masklike image that is revealed to the public during Indra Jatra is one that was consecrated in 1795 and is seldom seen because it spends most of the year hidden behind a latticework screen.

The beer that appears to flow from Bhairava's mouth during Indra Jatra comes from a clay pot concealed within the mask. Gravity draws the beer out through a copper pipe and a small hole between the teeth, and those who come to see the mask try to catch a little in their mouths as a symbolic blessing from Bhairava.

Upaku Route

The route referred to as the Upaku Route, which is followed by families in mourning on the first day of Indra Jatra, marks the outer boundary of the old medieval city of Katmandu and is a popular "culture walk" for tourists visiting the city today.

FURTHER READING

Bellenir, Karen. *Religious Holidays and Calendars*. 3rd ed. Detroit: Omnigraphics, 2004.
MacDonald, Margaret R., ed. *The Folklore of World Holidays*. Detroit: Gale Research, 1992.

WEB SITES

Nepal Home Page
www.nepalhomepage.com/society/festivals/indrajatra.html

Visit Nepal Network
www.visitnepal.com/nepal_information/nepal_festivals.php

Inti Raymi Festival
(Inti Raymi Pageant, Sun Festival, Feast of the Sun)

Type of Holiday: Calendar/Seasonal
Date of Observation: June 24
Where Celebrated: Peru
Symbols and Customs: Golden Rod, Maize
Related Holidays: Winter Solstice

ORIGINS

The Inti Raymi Festival marks the changing of the seasons, which people in all parts of the world have honored since ancient times. Many cultures divided the year into two seasons, summer and winter, and marked these points of the year at or near the summer and winter solstices, during which light and warmth began to increase and decrease, respectively. In pre-industrial times, humans survived through hunting, gathering, and agricultural practices, which depend on the natural cycle of seasons, according to the climate in the region of the world in which they lived. Thus, they created rituals to help ensure enough rain and sun in the spring and summer so crops would grow to fruition at harvest time, which was, in turn, duly celebrated. Vestiges of many of these ancient practices are thought to have survived in festivals still celebrated around seasonal themes.

Inti Raymi is a **WINTER SOLSTICE** festival observed by the Incas in Peru. By the late fifteenth century their empire, which they believed lay at the center of the earth, extended along the Pacific coast of South America from northern Ecuador to central Chile. On the day of the solstice, the Incas would gather to honor Inti, their sun god, at the foot of the hill of La Marca, not far from where the equator is now known to be located. Just before dawn, the emperor and his entourage would go to a ceremonial plaza in central Cuzco, the empire's capital. They took off their shoes in deference to the sun, faced northeast, and waited for the sun to rise. When it appeared on the horizon, everyone crouched down and blew kisses in the sun's direction. Then the emperor lifted two golden cups of *chicha,* a sacred drink made of fermented MAIZE, and offered the cup in his left hand to the sun. It was poured into a basin that was designed to drain quickly. When the chicha disappeared, everyone thought the sun had consumed it. After sipping the chicha in the other cup, the emperor shared it with the others present and then proceeded to the Coricancha or Sun Temple. A fire was lit in the temple's innermost shrine, a room lined with magnificent gold "sun discs," by focusing the sun's rays with a convex mirror. Animal sacrifices and other ceremonies followed.

Today the main celebration still takes place in Cuzco, where there is a special procession and mock sacrifice to the sun, followed by a week-long celebration involving folk dances, tours of archaeological ruins, and displays of South American Indian arts and crafts. Bonfires are still lit in the Andes Mountains to celebrate the rebirth of the sun, and the Incas burn their old clothes as a symbolic way of destroying poverty and marking the end of the harvest cycle.

The Incas also observed a **SUMMER SOLSTICE** festival, known as Capac Raymi, in December.

SYMBOLS AND CUSTOMS

Golden Rod

According to the Incas' creation myth, the first Incas were sent down to earth by their father, the Sun, to find the place where a golden rod he had given them could be plunged into the soil with one blow, indicating that the ground was good for planting. This mythical rod probably represents the vertical rays of the sun at noon on the solstice, when it stands directly overhead. The place where it sank into the ground was marked at first with a humble shrine, later expanded into the Temple of the Sun or Coricancha ("Golden Enclosure"). The Coricancha soon became a religious center and place of pilgrimage as well as a model for other sun temples throughout the vast Inca empire.

In 1600 Garcilaso de la Vega, the nephew of the eleventh Inca ruler, documented the existence of a sacred group of gnomons or sunsticks near Quito, which is located very close to the Equator, where the sun passes through the zenith at noon on the equinox. According to Garcilaso, this was the seat that Inti, the sun god, liked best, because he sat straight up rather than leaning to the side. The Incas observed the equinoxes by watching their gnomons until the sun bathed all sides of the column equally, and there were no shadows cast. Then they decorated the gnomons with flowers and herbs and placed the Sun's throne on top.

Maize

Maize (corn) and chicha (fermented maize drink) were specially prepared by a group of chosen women, referred to as the "wives of the sun," for the Inti Raymi Festival. Because maize was symbolic of the Sun's gifts, it was important to eat it during the Sun Festival. The maize used for the festival was grown in the garden of the Coricancha, and during major festivals like the Inti Raymi, maize plants made of gold were displayed there. Given the fact that the Incas' empire was situated primarily in high altitudes where frost and hail were common, it is not surprising that sun worship was so intimately connected to the growing of maize.

FURTHER READING

Eliade, Mircea. *The Encyclopedia of Religion*. New York: Macmillan, 1987.

Heinberg, Richard. *Celebrate the Solstice: Honoring the Earth's Seasonal Rhythms through Festival and Ceremony*. Wheaton, IL: Quest Books, 1993.

Henderson, Helene, ed. *Holidays, Festivals, and Celebrations of the World Dictionary*. 3rd ed. Detroit: Omnigraphics, 2005.

Leach, Maria, ed. *Funk & Wagnalls Standard Dictionary of Folklore, Mythology & Legend*. San Francisco: Harper & Row, 1984.

MacDonald, Margaret R., ed. *The Folklore of World Holidays*. Detroit: Gale Research, 1992.

Shemanski, Frances. *A Guide to World Fairs and Festivals*. Westport, CT: Greenwood Press, 1985.

Ironman Triathlon World Championship

Type of Holiday: Sporting
Date of Observation: Saturday nearest the full moon in October
Where Celebrated: Kailua-Kona, Hawaii
Symbols and Customs: Awards Dinner, Carbo-Loading Party, Leg-Shaving, Lottery, Underwear Run

ORIGINS

The Ironman Triathlon began with a challenge from a naval commander named John Collins in 1978. He was sitting at the awards ceremony for a local running race in Honolulu, where he was stationed at the time, and got involved in a heated debate over which athletes were in the best shape, runners or swimmers. Collins, who was both a runner and a swimmer himself, had been reading about Tour de France legend Eddie Merckx and suggested that cyclists were the fittest of all. Then he issued a challenge he was certain would settle the matter: a race that would combine the Waikiki Rough Water Swim (a local swimming race), a bike ride around the entire island of Oahu, and the Honolulu Marathon. His enthusiasm for the idea inspired him to jump up on the stage during a break in the ceremony, grab the microphone, and announce the competition to everyone present, saying that the winner would be declared the "Ironman."

Only fifteen people rose to the challenge that first time in February 1978, and only twelve—Collins among them—actually crossed the finish line. The winner was Gordon Haller, an amateur athlete and taxi cab driver who completed the three events in eleven hours, forty-six minutes, and fifty-eight seconds. The Navy transferred Collins a couple of years later, and the owners of a local health club to whom he bequeathed the event ended up getting divorced. But Valerie Silk, the wife, took charge of the race and moved it from Oahu, the most populous and traffic-congested of the islands, to Kona, on the western side of the Big Island of Hawaii, in 1981. Instead of fighting traffic, the competitors now had to battle "mumuku" crosswinds and scorching temperatures as they ran 26.2 miles and biked 112 miles along the highway that cut through Kona's fields of rough black lava. When combined with a 2.4 mile ocean swim around a rectangular course, the event represented a little over 140 miles of grueling physical effort.

The Ironman Triathlon remained a relatively unrecognized event until ABC's "Wide World of Sports" began covering it in 1980. Then, in 1982, television viewers watched in horror as the women's leader, a college student named Julie Moss who had entered the race to gather information for her senior thesis on exercise physiology, collapsed from exhaustion and dehydration just a few yards from the finish line. Another competitor passed her but Moss wouldn't give up. She crawled the last twenty yards on her hands and knees, inspiring the admiration of athletes everywhere and triggering a boom in the event's popularity by showing that finishing the race was a huge accomplishment in itself. Now the race is watched on television by more than 100 million people worldwide.

Today the Ironman Triathlon World Championship, as it has been named to distinguish it from other triathlons that have sprung up around the world, attracts over 1,700 competitors from more than fifty countries and 5,500 volunteers. Another 50,000 spectators gather to watch, especially along Ali'i Drive in downtown Kona, where the running race ends. Women have participated in the event almost from the beginning, and there is now a physically challenged division in which wheelchair-bound athletes can compete. The date has been moved to the Saturday nearest the full moon in October to give athletes from colder climates more time to train and to make it easier for competitors who don't finish the race before dark.

Belgian Luc Van Lierde was the race's first international winner, running his record-breaking contest in 8:04:08 in 1996. He won the Triathlon again in 1999. The fastest women's time is held by eight-time champion Paula Newby-Fraser. The Zimbabwean ran the Triathlon in 8:55:28 in 1992 for her fifth victory.

SYMBOLS AND CUSTOMS

Awards Dinner

On the day after the triathlon, an awards dinner is held at the King Kamehameha Kona Beach Hotel, which has served as the triathlon's headquarters since 1988, for about 4,000 people. The winners of each division of the race are recognized and $560,000 in prize money is handed out, but the biggest applause is reserved for the first-place man and woman, who receive $110,000 each.

Carbo-Loading Party

The King Kamehameha Kona Beach Hotel also caters a carbo-loading party for competitors and Ironman enthusiasts—usually more than 2,000 people—on Thursday evening before the Saturday event. Although the hotel must hire dozens of extra people just to keep the buffet line from running out of plates or pasta, the hotel regards it as a great boost for business.

Leg-Shaving

It is customary for all Ironman competitors, even the men, to shave their legs before the race. In addition to keeping their legs cooler and making it easier for them to take off their wet suits after the swim, it's less painful to treat "road rash"—abrasions caused by falling during the running or biking race—on hairless legs.

Lottery

Before John Collins left Hawaii, he was assured by the new organizers of the triathlon that a few spots would always be kept open for "ordinary" athletes—in other words, not elite Ironman competitors—because these were the kind of people who entered the first race in 1978. Today, with a qualifying system to restrict the number of entrants and a seventeen-hour time limit, the Ironman still awards 200 spots by lottery to individuals who have not been in any of the qualifying races. There have been a number of notable competitors among this group, including the oldest (Robert McKeague, age eighty, who finished the race in 16:21:55) and the first to complete the race using a wheelchair and a hand-powered bike (Dr. Jon Franks, 1994).

Underwear Run

On the Thursday before the Saturday on which the triathlon takes place, there is a light-hearted race down Ali'i Drive by Ironman athletes—women as well as men—wearing only their underwear. The run is held early in the morning so as not to tire the runners by making them race in the heat of the day, and it gives them a chance to run off some of their nervous tension while at the same time raising money for the Ironman Foundation.

WEB SITE

Ironman Triathlon World Championship
ironman.com/worldchampionship

Iroquois Midwinter Ceremony

Type of Holiday: Calendar/Seasonal, Religious (Iroquois)
Date of Observation: January-February; begins five days after the first new moon in January
Where Celebrated: New York, Wisconsin, Canada
Symbols and Customs: Bear Dance, Big Heads, Dreamsharing, False Face Society, Great Feather Dance, Peach Stone Game, Stirring of the Ashes, Tobacco Invocation, White Dog Sacrifice

ORIGINS

The Iroquois Midwinter Ceremony is a Native American event related to religious traditions and seasonal change. The history of this and other Native American cultures dates back thousands of years into prehistoric times. According to many scholars, the people who became the Native Americans migrated from Asia across a land bridge that may have once connected the territories presently occupied by Alaska and Russia. The migrations, believed to have begun between 60,000 and 30,000 B.C.E., continued until approximately 4,000 B.C.E. This speculation, however, conflicts with traditional stories asserting that the indigenous Americans have always lived in North America or that tribes moved up from the south.

The historical development of religious belief systems among Native Americans is not well known. Most of the information available was gathered by Europeans who arrived on the continent beginning in the sixteenth century C.E. The data they recorded was fragmentary and oftentimes of questionable accuracy because the Europeans did not understand the native cultures they were trying to describe and the Native Americans were reluctant to divulge details about themselves.

The tribes belonging to what is known as the Iroquois Confederacy or Six Nations—the Mohawk, Oneida, Onondaga, Cayuga, Seneca, and Tuscarora—celebrate their Midwinter Ceremony in January or February, beginning on the fifth day after the first new moon in January and lasting for nine days. Also known as the New Year's Ceremony because it marks the beginning of a new ritual year, the celebration is announced by the masked messengers known as the BIG HEADS, who visit the longhouse—formerly a bark-covered structure in which the Iroquois lived, but now used primarily as a public activity space—and invite everyone to participate in the ceremonies that are about to begin.

Although the order in which the rituals take place varies according to the tribe and the location, the Midwinter Ceremony usually begins with the STIRRING OF THE ASHES to show people's gratitude for all the blessings that have been bestowed on them during the preceding year. There is a public naming ceremony at which all the children born during the year receive their Indian names, and the performance of ceremonial dances, including the GREAT FEATHER DANCE and the BEAR DANCE. Tobacco plays an important role in many Native American celebrations, and the TOBACCO INVOCATION ritual performed during the Midwinter Ceremony is a way of communicating a message of thanksgiving and a plea for a successful growing season directly to the Creator.

Communal DREAMSHARING is an important part of the Midwinter Ceremony. The Iroquois believe that dreams, rather than being merely fantasies or random images, represent a cure for diseases as well as mental disorders. By sharing their dreams in public and getting other tribe members' opinions about what these dreams represent, the Iroquois believe that they are better able to resolve whatever problems or conflicts gave rise to the dreams in the first place. The FALSE FACE SOCIETY also plays a role in dreamsharing by performing whatever curing rites are needed once the dreams have been interpreted.

One of the highlights of the Midwinter Ceremony, the WHITE DOG SACRIFICE, is no longer practiced. The Iroquois love their dogs, and to have one of their pets killed as a sacrifice was an indication of how seriously they took this thanksgiving ritual. The dog was strangled and decorated with beads, ribbons, and wampum. Its carcass was then burned, and people believed that the smoke would carry their gratitude and prayers to heaven. Nowadays a fancy white basket is considered an adequate substitute for a dog.

The Midwinter Ceremony concludes with a speaker who summarizes the events of the preceding nine days and makes a brief thanksgiving address. The new council members who have been chosen for the coming year are introduced at the longhouse and the rest of the tribe's members, now purified and released from the burden of their dreams, welcome a new year.

The traditional Iroquois ceremonial year is divided into two parts: winter, which is controlled by men, and summer, which is under women's domain. Thus, men take charge of winter ceremonies. After the Midwinter Ceremony, the women are formally given charge of the ceremonies for the next half of the year.

SYMBOLS AND CUSTOMS

Bear Dance

The Bear Dance, which is performed by many North American Indian tribes, is part of the curing rites associated with the Iroquois Midwinter Ceremony. The Iroquois bear dancers, which include women as well as men, imitate the lumbering, waddling movements of the bear as they dance in a counterclockwise circle. Although the Bear Dance may be performed privately for an individual who is ill, it is also performed at communal festivals like the Midwinter Ceremony to help "cure" the people of the problems and misfortunes that have beset them over the past year.

Big Heads

Often referred to by the Iroquois as "our uncles" because they represent the tribes' founders, the messengers known as Big Heads dress in buffalo skins and cornhusk masks with braids, thus symbolizing both the hunt and the harvest. They make visits throughout the village at the New Year to announce that the festivities are about to begin, carrying the wooden mallets used to mash corn and using them to stir up the ashes in household fires (*see* STIRRING OF THE ASHES).

Dreamsharing

Also known as "dream guessing," dreamsharing is a sacred activity through which the Iroquois try to rid themselves of troubling thoughts and make their wishes come true. They describe their dreams in front of the assembled tribe members, who then offer their interpretations and suggestions. The idea is to help the dreamer identify what need, wish, or desire the dream is trying to express; sometimes people reenact each other's dreams and then invite the spectators to guess what they mean. Those who come up with the most accurate interpretation are then required to help see that the dream is fulfilled, either by presenting the dreamer with symbolic gifts or by actually helping the dreamer satisfy his or her needs.

Dreamsharing is central to the Iroquois Midwinter Ceremony because it helps to cure people of the "illnesses" that are symptomatic of unresolved conflicts and unfulfilled desires. To correctly interpret someone's dream and then help resolve the situation it represents is considered not so much an obligation as an honor, one that cements tribal friendships and traditions.

False Face Society

The False Face Society is an Iroquois medicine society whose members are believed to possess the power to scare off the evil spirits that cause illness. This power resides primarily in the masks they wear, which are carved out of the wood of a living tree and have deep-set slits for eyes and large noses that often extend across the forehead with a spiny ridge or crease. The society holds its most important annual meeting in the longhouse during the Midwinter Ceremony, and its members participate in the ceremony's curing rituals, often reaching into the hot ashes of a fire without burning their hands and rubbing or blowing the ashes on those in need of a cure (*see* STIRRING OF THE ASHES). Although both men and women can belong to the False Face Society, only men are allowed to wear the society's frightening masks.

Great Feather Dance

The Great Feather Dance is held to give thanks to the Creator for all he has bestowed on the people during the year. The dancers wear full tribal regalia and dance to the accompaniment of only two singers, who sit face-to-face and use turtle-shell rattles to establish the rhythm. The Feather Dance is usually held on the next-to-last night of the nine-day Midwinter Ceremony. Along with the PEACH STONE GAME, it is one of the "Four Sacred Ceremonies" named by the eighteenth-century Seneca prophet Handsome Lake as being essential for salvation.

Peach Stone Game

Also known as the Bowl Game, this is a sacred Iroquois game that symbolizes the game played by the Creator and his evil brother as they competed with each other during the creation of the earth. Six peach stones, each with one side burned or blackened, are shaken in a bowl, and the score is based on whatever combination of "black" sides and "white" sides ends up showing, much as dice are used in other games of chance.

As played during the Midwinter Ceremony, the Peach Stone Game symbolizes the renewal of the earth, particularly the battle for survival that fruits and vegetables wage against the harsh elements of Nature, and the outcome is used to predict the success of the next year's harvest. It also symbolizes the good luck that the Creator has bestowed on the inhabitants of the earth. Men play against women, or one clan challenges another. The game can last two or three days, and bets are often placed on who is going to win.

Stirring of the Ashes

Stirring or blowing the ashes in both household and longhouse fires at the start of the Midwinter Ceremony is a symbolic means of showing gratitude to the Creator and of asking that the New Year bring renewal and fertility to the earth. Ashes symbolize the earth to which all living things return when they die and from which new life springs.

Tobacco Invocation

The STIRRING OF THE ASHES is often accompanied by the sprinkling of tobacco on the burning embers. The smoke from the tobacco is believed to rise up to heaven, taking with it the Iroquois' messages of thanks to their Creator. In fact, the Iroquois are often referred to as the "Tobacco People" or "Tobacco Nation" because their name comes from the word *ierokwa,* meaning "they who use tobacco."

In addition to its use as a ceremonial offering and a means of communicating with the spirit world, the Iroquois used tobacco to treat burns, sores, the pain of toothache, and diseases. Tobacco was indigenous to the New World, and it was the one crop that women were not responsible for cultivating. When Native American men got together to make peace or conduct business, they often shared a long-stemmed pipe of tobacco called the calumet, which was believed to induce "good thoughts."

White Dog Sacrifice

The central sacrificial rite of the Midwinter Ceremony traditionally involved the killing of a white dog because it symbolized purity, and the sacrifice was a symbolic way of purifying the entire community. The dog was strangled so there would be no blood or marks on it, and it was decorated with red paint, feathers, and ribbon. After it was laid on the fire, a basket of tobacco was thrown on the flames. Today, of course, the basket itself is white and is burned in place of the dog.

FURTHER READING

Bellenir, Karen. *Religious Holidays and Calendars*. 3rd ed. Detroit: Omnigraphics, 2004.

Cohen, Hennig, and Tristram Potter Coffin. *The Folklore of American Holidays*. 3rd ed. Detroit: Gale Research, 1999.

Gill, Sam D., and Irene Sullivan. *Dictionary of Native American Mythology*. Santa Barbara: ABC-CLIO, 1992.

Hirschfelder, Arlene B., and Paulette Fairbanks Molin. *Encyclopedia of Native American Religions*. Updated edition. New York: Facts on File, 2000.

Leach, Maria, ed. *Funk & Wagnalls Standard Dictionary of Folklore, Mythology & Legend*. San Francisco: Harper & Row, 1984.

Van Straalen, Alice. *The Book of Holidays Around the World*. New York: Dutton, 1986.

WEB SITES

First Nations Technical Institute on the Tyendinaga Mohawk Territory in Ontario, Canada
www.tyendinaga.net/amsp/youth99/tradcal/midwin1.htm

Janmashtami
(Krishna's Birthday)

Type of Holiday: Religious (Hindu)
Date of Observation: August-September; eighth day of the Hindu month of
   Bhadrapada
Where Celebrated: India
Symbols and Customs: Curd Pots

ORIGINS

Janmashtami is a celebration in Hinduism, which many scholars regard as the
world's oldest living religion. The word Hindu is derived from the Sanskrit term
Sindhu (or *Indus*), which meant river. It referred to people living in the Indus valley
in the Indian subcontinent.

Hinduism has no founder, one universal reality (or god) known as Brahman,
many gods and goddesses (sometimes referred to as devtas), and several scriptures. Hinduism also has no priesthood or hierarchical structure similar to that
seen in some other religions, such as Christianity. Hindus acknowledge the
authority of a wide variety of writings, but there is no single, uniform canon. The
oldest of the Hindu writings are the *Vedas*. The word "veda" comes from the Sanskrit word for knowledge. The *Vedas*, which were compiled from ancient oral traditions, contain hymns, instructions, explanations, chants for sacrifices, magical
formulas, and philosophy. Another set of sacred books includes the *Great Epics,*
which illustrate Hindu faith in practice. The *Epics* include the *Ramayana*, the
Mahabharata, and the *Bhagavad Gita*.

The Hindu pantheon includes approximately thirty-three million gods. Some of these are held in higher esteem than others. Over all the gods, Hindus believe in one absolute high god or universal concept. This is Brahman. Although he is above all the gods, he is not worshipped in popular ceremonies because he is detached from the day-to-day affairs of the people. Brahman is impersonal. Lesser gods and goddesses (devtas) serve him. Because these are more intimately involved in the affairs of people, they are venerated as gods. The most honored god in Hinduism varies among the different Hindu sects. Although Hindu adherents practice their faith differently and venerate different deities, they share a similar view of reality and look back on a common history.

The Hindu gods appeared in human or animal forms at certain times in history so they could perform great deeds. Each time a god went through another incarnation, it became the occasion for a new Hindu holiday. Vishnu appeared first as a fish, then as a tortoise and a boar. Later he appeared as a man-lion, a dwarf, the son of a great sage, and a prince. His most memorable incarnation, however, was when he appeared as Krishna, whose life and heroic deeds are described in the great Hindu epic, the *Mahabharata.*

The birthday of Lord Krishna, the eighth incarnation of Vishnu, is one of the most important Hindu festivals. Born at Mathura, in Uttar Pradesh, a state in northern India, Krishna's mission on earth was to get rid of the demon Kamsa, who had seized the throne, imprisoned the real king, and persecuted good people while making life easy for the wicked. His evil ways became so unbearable that Vishnu decided to incarnate himself as a man and bring about Kamsa's destruction.

Krishna grew up among the herdsmen of Gokul. As a child, he was adored for his mischievous pranks as well as his miracles. As a young cowherd, he became renowned as a lover, and the sound of his flute lured the wives and daughters of other cowherds to leave their homes to dance with him in the forest. When he finally returned to Mathura to slay the wicked Kamsa, he found the kingdom unsafe and led the people to the western coast of India, where he reestablished his court in what is today the state of Gujarat.

Janmashtami—the name comes from *Janma*, birth, and *ashtami*, the eighth—is celebrated on the eighth day of Bhadrapada by Hindus of all sects and castes throughout India, particularly in and around Mathura. The celebrations there include dancing, in imitation of the young Krishna's moonlight dances with the cow-girls, the singing of religious songs and hymns, and recitations from the great Hindu epics. Everyone, even children, fasts for twenty-four hours. The floor from the doorway to the inner meditation room of the house is often marked with a child's footprints, made by mixing flour and water, to create the impression that Krishna himself has walked through the house. Pilgrims from all over India visit the temple of Shri Rangji, where Krishna is known to have spent his childhood.

When the fast is broken at midnight, the ringing of temple bells, the jingling of cymbals, and the blowing of conch shells is ongoing. The image of Lord Krishna as a child is bathed in milk while his name is chanted, and, at the hour of his birth, the image is rocked in a cradle decorated with garlands of flowers.

SYMBOLS AND CUSTOMS

Curd Pots

Dairy foods are usually served on Janmashtami because Krishna was very fond of milk and butter as a child. In some parts of India, the celebration includes the shattering of curd pots (unglazed ceramic pots containing sour milk), which are hung up high over the streets by young men forming human pyramids, or suspended from a pole supported by two uprights. The pots are knocked down and broken in imitation of the young Krishna, who was so fond of milk that he used to steal, with the help of his friends, curds and butter that had been hung in earthen pots from the kitchen ceiling to keep it out of children's hands. After the curd pots are broken, the celebrants dance as Krishna danced during his stay among the herdsmen of Gokul.

FURTHER READING

Bellenir, Karen. *Religious Holidays and Calendars*. 3rd ed. Detroit: Omnigraphics, 2004.

Gaer, Joseph. *Holidays Around the World*. Boston: Little, Brown, 1953.

Gupte, B.A. *Hindu Holidays and Ceremonials*. 2nd ed. Calcutta: Thacker, Spink & Co., 1919.

Henderson, Helene, ed. *Holidays, Festivals, and Celebrations of the World Dictionary*. 3rd ed. Detroit: Omnigraphics, 2005.

Sharma, Brijendra Nath. *Festivals of India*. New Delhi: Abhinav Publications, 1978.

Sivananda, Swami. *Hindu Fasts and Festivals*. 8th ed. Shivanandanagar, India: Divine Life Society, 1997.

Thomas, Paul. *Festivals and Holidays in India*. Bombay: D.B. Taraporevala Sons, 1971.

WEB SITE

Society for the Confluence of Festivals in India
www.krishnajanmashtami.com

John Canoe Festival
(Jonkonnu Festival, Junkanoo Festival)

Type of Holiday: Folkloric
Date of Observation: December 26, January 1
Where Celebrated: Bahamas, Belize, Guatemala, Jamaica
Symbols and Customs: Goombay, John Canoe
Related Holidays: Carnival (Mardi Gras)

ORIGINS

Held on various Caribbean islands, the John Canoe Festival represents a combination of Mardi Gras (**CARNIVAL**), mummers' parades, and ancient African tribal rituals. Perhaps the best-known celebration is the one held in Nassau on December 26, Boxing Day (**ST. STEPHEN'S DAY**), and on January 1, **NEW YEAR'S DAY**. Masqueraded marchers wearing colorful headpieces and costumes that have taken months to prepare dance to the beat of an Afro-Bahamian rhythm called GOOMBAY. The Jonkonnu parade, which begins at four o'clock in the morning and continues until sunrise, is followed by the judging of costumes and awarding of prizes. There are Jonkonnu parades in Freeport and elsewhere in the Bahamas as well.

When slaveholders in the American South observed holidays, their slaves would usually celebrate by holding their own parties and barbecues. In North Carolina, these celebrations always included the appearance of JOHN CANOE, dressed in a colorful costume made from many scraps of material and wearing a white mask that was frightening to children and adults alike. He would dance down the street with a jerking, gyrating motion, often accompanied by musicians. He sang songs, told stories, and accepted contributions from spectators. The procession would last all day, and the party that followed went on all night. It was a way for African-American slaves to have their own fun on holidays observed primarily by whites. The custom known as "Kunering" (John Canoe was sometimes known as John Kuner), which only took place between Christmas and the New Year, was outlawed by the North Carolina police around 1900 because educated blacks regarded it as degrading to members of their race.

Today, celebrations featuring John Canoe can be found primarily in the West Indies. In Belize and Guatemala, the John Canoe masqueraders dance from house to house, wearing wire-screen masks painted white or pink with staring eyes, red lips, black eyebrows, and thin mustaches. In Jamaica, the Jonkonnu procession includes a King and Queen with their courtiers; a Sailor Boy, who uses a whip to keep the audience in line; Babu, an East Indian cowboy with a long cattle prod; and Pitchy Patchy, another traditional figure. The Jonkonnu processions held in remote villages are even rowdier, featuring a Whore Girl who raises her skirts and a Belly Woman who shakes her belly in time with the music.

SYMBOLS AND CUSTOMS

Goombay

Historically, "goombay" referred to the drumbeats and rhythms of Africa, which were brought to the Bahamas by slaves. The term was used during jump-in dances, when the drummer would shout "Gimbey!" at the beginning of each dance. The Igbo tribes in West Africa have a drum they called Gamby, from which the name "goombay" probably derived.

Today, Goombay refers to all Bahamian secular music, although it is particularly associated with the John Canoe Festival. It is played by a variety of unusual native instruments, including goat-skin drums, lignum vitae sticks, pebble-filled "shik-shaks," and steel drums.

John Canoe

There are a number of theories as to where the name "John Canoe" came from. Some believe he is a symbol for John Conny, the West African tribal chief who out-witted Dutch merchantmen and maintained control of the Prussian Fort Branden-burg (later known as "Conny's Castle"), which he commanded during the early eighteenth century at Prince's Town. John Conny, who lived from 1660 to 1732, promoted trade between the Ashanti and the Germans for more than a decade and was sometimes called the "Last Prussian Negro Prince."

In the United States, John Canoe was a precursor of the unofficial governor chosen by African-American slaves in New England on Election Day. For about 100 years, beginning in 1750, New England slaves would hold an election of their own, which would be followed by a parade featuring their newly elected governor. Thousands of slaves participated in such parades throughout Massachusetts, Connecticut, and Rhode Island. Although the unofficial governor had no legal power, he was usually a very able man who exercised considerable authority over New England blacks.

Still another theory about the name John Canoe is that it came from the French *gens inconnus*, or "unknown people," referring to the masked dancers who appear at the John Canoe Festival.

FURTHER READING

Anyike, James C. *African American Holidays*. Revised and expanded edition. Chicago: Popular Truth Pub., 1997.

Gay, Kathlyn. *African-American Holidays, Festivals, and Celebrations*. Detroit: Omnigraphics, 2007.

Cohen, Hennig, and Tristram Potter Coffin. *The Folklore of American Holidays*. 3rd ed. Detroit: Gale Research, 1999.

Henderson, Helene, ed. *Holidays, Festivals, and Celebrations of the World Dictionary*. 3rd ed. Detroit: Omnigraphics, 2005.

Shemanski, Frances. *A Guide to World Fairs and Festivals*. Westport, CT: Greenwood Press, 1985.

WEB SITE

Official Site of Junkanoo by Tajiz Ltd.
www.junkanoo.com

Juneteenth

Type of Holiday: Historic
Date of Observation: June 19 and other dates
Where Celebrated: United States
Symbols and Customs: Celebrations
Related Holidays: Lincoln's Birthday

ORIGINS

Juneteenth—an abbreviation for June 19—is the oldest African-American observance in the United States. Also known as Emancipation Day, Freedom Day, and Jun-Jun, it is a celebration of freedom from slavery that began spontaneously and spread across the country.

Juneteenth is a holiday that commemorates a significant historical event. Peoples throughout the world commemorate such significant events in their histories through holidays and festivals. Often, these are events that are important for an entire nation and become widely observed. The marking of such anniversaries serve not only to honor the values represented by the person or event commemorated, but also to strengthen and reinforce communal bonds of national, cultural, or ethnic identity. Victorious, joyful, and traumatic events are remembered through historic holidays. The commemorative expression reflects the original event through festive celebration or solemn ritual. Reenactments are common activities at historical holiday and festival gatherings, seeking to bring the past alive in the present.

Slavery was one of the major issues leading up to the Civil War in 1861. By 1862, laws abolishing slavery had been passed in the territories of Oklahoma, Nebraska, Colorado, and New Mexico. On September 22, 1862, President Abraham Lincoln issued a proclamation notifying the rebellious states that had seceded from the Union (Alabama, Florida, Georgia, Louisiana, Mississippi, South Carolina, and Texas, joined later by North Carolina, Arkansas, Virginia, and Tennessee) that if they didn't return to the Union by January 1, 1863, he would declare their slaves "forever free." This led to the Emancipation Proclamation, which declared that slaves in the eleven rebel states were free (*see* **LINCOLN'S BIRTHDAY**). Two years later, on January 31, 1865, Congress passed the thirteenth Amendment, abolishing slavery throughout the United States.

Even though slaves in the South were declared free in 1863, word didn't reach the slaves in Texas until June 19, 1865, the day General Gordon Granger and his federal troops arrived in Galveston with the intention of forcing slave owners to release their slaves. There are a number of theories as to why it took so long for the news of the Emancipation Proclamation to reach East Texas. Some people say that the news was delayed by mule travel, while others believe that the original messenger was murdered. The most popular explanation is that the news was deliberately withheld by wealthy landowners who wanted their slaves to bring in one last crop.

Juneteenth, the commemoration of General Granger's arrival, was originally celebrated not only in Texas but in Louisiana, perhaps because Granger left from New Orleans to begin his historic journey. Eventually the celebration spilled over into southwestern Arkansas. Then, as blacks began to migrate into the territory that was soon to become Oklahoma, they took their freedom festival with them.

In the late 1930s and early 1940s, there was a second migration of blacks from the southwestern states to California. These West Coast settlers continued to observe Juneteenth, but the celebration had dwindled to picnics sponsored by African Americans from the same state. For example, an "Oklahoma picnic" is still held in Los Angeles' Lincoln Heights Park every year on June 19. But what really emerged following these migrations was the idea of "homecoming": West Coast blacks who originally came from east Texas and the surrounding area began to migrate back home for a visit on the weekend nearest the nineteenth—a practice that is still common today.

Juneteenth is observed on a number of different dates, due to the fact that enforcement of the slaves' liberation came about only after the defeat of local Confederate forces. It is observed on January 1 in New York City, Boston, Alabama, Georgia, North and South Carolina, Virginia, Tennessee, and Maryland; on February 1 in Philadelphia; on May 8 in eastern Mississippi; on May 20 in Florida; on August 1 in Ontario (Canada); on August 4 in northeastern Arkansas, north central Tennessee, central Oklahoma, southeastern Missouri, and southwestern Illinois; on August 8 in southwestern Kentucky; and on September 22 in Indiana, the rest of Illinois, and Ohio. East Texas, Oklahoma, Louisiana, southwestern Arkansas, southern Oklahoma, and California continue to observe it on June 19 with festivities that include parades, picnics, singing and dancing, and baseball games.

SYMBOLS AND CUSTOMS

Celebrations

Juneteenth is typically spent in celebration. Games, picnics, barbecues, beauty pageants, talent contests, and sporting events are common on this day. Almost every celebration includes dancing and singing, including the song "Lift Ev'ry Voice and Sing." These expressions of joy are symbolic of the celebrations that took place on **NEW YEAR'S EVE** in 1862, as blacks awaited President Lincoln's official announcement that the slaves in the eleven southern states that had seceded from the Union were free.

FURTHER READING

Anyike, James C. *African American Holidays*. Revised and Expanded ed. Chicago: Popular Truth Pub., 1997.

Cohen, Hennig, and Tristram Potter Coffin. *The Folklore of American Holidays*. 3rd ed. Detroit: Gale Research, 1999.

Dunkling, Leslie. *A Dictionary of Days*. New York: Facts on File, 1988.

Gay, Kathlyn. *African-American Holidays, Festivals, and Celebrations*. Detroit: Omnigraphics, 2007.

Henderson, Helene, ed. *Holidays, Festivals, and Celebrations of the World Dictionary*. 3rd ed. Detroit: Omnigraphics, 2005.

Wiggins, William H. Jr. *O Freedom! Afro-American Emancipation Celebrations*. Knoxville: University of Tennessee Press, 2000.

WEB SITES

Juneteenth.com World Wide Celebration
www.juneteenth.com

"Juneteenth," Texas State Library & Archives Commission
www.tsl.state.tx.us/ref/abouttx/juneteenth.html

Kamakura Matsuri
(Snow Hut Festival)

Type of Holiday: Promotional
Date of Observation: Mid-February
Where Celebrated: Japan (several locations)
Symbols and Customs: Rice Cakes, Snow Huts, Snow Sculptures

ORIGINS

Some parts of Japan get as much snow and cold weather as the northernmost states in the United States. In fact, the snow often gets so deep that people must rely on skis and sleds to get around. One way to celebrate the winter weather is to hold what are known as "snow hut" festivals, which provide activity and entertainment for visitors and locals alike.

Since 1950, a week-long snow hut festival has been held every February in Sapporo, site of the 1972 Winter **OLYMPIC GAMES** and the capital of Hokkaido, the northern island of Japan. Although the festival started out as a secondary event to winter sports such as skiing and skating, it has developed over the years into a major tourist attraction that brings almost two million visitors to the city. Hundreds of huge SNOW SCULPTURES are erected in Odori Park and along the city's main street. The sculptures reflect the festival's theme, which is different each year. In past years, the sculptures have portrayed characters and themes from well-known fairy tales and television shows, as well as famous historical buildings. The week's activities also include a colorful parade and winter sports competitions.

More Ice and Snow Sculpture Festivals

laska: The World Ice Art Championships (formerly known as part of the Fairbanks Winter Carnival) is held in March each year. The Championships have been held in Fairbanks since 1934.

Canada: The Caribou Carnival features ice sculpture each year in March in Yellowknife, Northwest Territories. The Carnival has been held since 1955.

China: The Harbin Ice and Snow Festival, held in January and February, has featured sculptures since 1985.

Minnesota: The St. Paul Winter Carnival, which takes place in late January, includes displays of ice sculpture, most prominently the Ice Palace. The event has been held since 1886.

A snow hut festival is also held at Yokote in the Akita Prefecture of northern Japan from February 15 to 17, when the snow is usually at its deepest. The original purpose of the festival was to offer prayers to Suijin-sama, the water god, for a good rice crop. Children build SNOW HUTS and have parties inside, while their families gather to drink sweet sake and eat RICE CAKES and fruits.

Another well-established snow hut festival is held in mid-February at Tokamachi in Niigata Prefecture. The celebration includes a fashion and talent show presented on a stage made out of snow and a costume parade, photography contest, ski race, and exhibit of SNOW SCULPTURES.

SYMBOLS AND CUSTOMS

Rice Cakes

The rice cakes that are served during the Snow Hut Festival are made in the shape of cranes and turtles, which are traditional symbols of longevity, and of dogs called inukko, believed to offer protection against evil spirits.

Snow Huts

The snow hut or snow cave, known as kamakura, for which this midwinter festival is named, is much like the Alaskan igloo. The inside is furnished with a tatami (straw mat), an altar to the god of water, and a hibachi or charcoal stove that keeps the hut warm and can be used to heat soup, tea, or rice wine. Japanese children leave their boots outside the hut, just as they would normally do when entering a real house, and spend their time inside playing games and eating sweets. Sometimes they spend the night in the kamakura, which is illuminated by candles or electric lamps.

Snow Sculptures

Work on the snow sculptures for which the Kamakura Matsuri is famous begins three weeks in advance of the festival itself. The Japanese Self-Defense Force helps by transporting thousands of tons of snow to the site. A wooden frame is constructed and packed with snow; then the frame is removed and the carving begins. As the snow is shaped, it is sprayed with water to form ice. Some sculptures are intricately carved and several stories high.

FURTHER READING

Bauer, Helen, and Sherwin Carlquist. *Japanese Festivals*. Garden City, NY: Doubleday, 1965.

Buell, Hal. *Festivals of Japan*. New York: Dodd, Mead, 1965.

Henderson, Helene, ed. *Holidays, Festivals, and Celebrations of the World Dictionary*. 3rd ed. Detroit: Omnigraphics, 2005.

MacDonald, Margaret R., ed. *The Folklore of World Holidays*. Detroit: Gale Research, 1992.

Thurley, Elizabeth. *Through the Year in Japan*. London: Batsford Academic and Educational, 1985.

Trawicky, Bernard, and Ruth W. Gregory. *Anniversaries and Holidays*. 5th ed. Chicago: American Library Assocation, 2000.

Van Straalen, Alice. *The Book of Holidays Around the World*. New York: Dutton, 1986.

WEB SITES

Caribou Carnival
www.cariboucarnival.com

Harbin Ice and Snow Festival
www.china.org.cn/english/travel/198585.htm

Japan National Tourist Organization
www.jnto.go.jp/eng/indepth/history/traditionalevents/a10_fes_Yokote.html

The St. Paul Winter Carnival
www.winter-carnival.com

World Ice Art Championships
www.icealaska.com/index.html

Kartika Snan

Type of Holiday: Religious (Hindu)
Date of Observation: October-November; Hindu month of Kartika
Where Celebrated: India
Symbols and Customs: Lamps, Tulsi Plant
Related Holidays: Dewali

ORIGINS

Kartika Snan is a religious celebration in Hinduism, which many scholars regard as the world's oldest living religion. The word Hindu is derived from the Sanskrit term *Sindhu* (or *Indus*), which meant river. It referred to people living in the Indus valley in the Indian subcontinent.

Hinduism has no founder, one universal reality (or god) known as Brahman, many gods and goddesses (sometimes referred to as devtas), and several scriptures. Hinduism also has no priesthood or hierarchical structure similar to that seen in some other religions, such as Christianity. Hindus acknowledge the authority of a wide variety of writings, but there is no single, uniform canon. The oldest of the Hindu writings are the *Vedas*. The word "veda" comes from the Sanskrit word for knowledge. The *Vedas*, which were compiled from ancient oral traditions, contain hymns, instructions, explanations, chants for sacrifices, magical formulas, and philosophy. Another set of sacred books includes the *Great Epics*, which illustrate Hindu faith in practice. The *Epics* include the *Ramayana*, the *Mahabharata*, and the *Bhagavad Gita*.

The Hindu pantheon includes approximately thirty-three million gods. Some of these are held in higher esteem than others. Over all the gods, Hindus believe in one absolute high god or universal concept. This is Brahman. Although he is above all the gods, he is not worshipped in popular ceremonies because he is detached from the day-to-day affairs of the people. Brahman is impersonal. Lesser gods and goddesses (devtas) serve him. Because these are more intimately involved in the affairs of people, they are venerated as gods. The most honored god in Hinduism varies among the different Hindu sects. Although Hindu adherents practice their faith differently and venerate different deities, they share a similar view of reality and look back on a common history.

The Hindu months of Vaisakha (April-May), Kartika (October-November) and Magha (January-February) are regarded as especially holy and therefore suitable for acts of religious devotion. Throughout the month of Kartika, Hindus bathe in a sacred river, stream, pond, or well early in the morning. A month-long bathing festival is held on sacred rivers like the Ganges and the Yamuna. People set up tents on the riverbank, have regular morning baths, eat only a single meal each day, and spend their time in prayer and meditation.

Hindu women get up early in the morning and visit the sacred streams in groups, singing hymns along the way. After bathing, they visit a nearby temple. They also fast, keep sky LAMPS burning throughout the month, and worship the TULSI PLANT, which is considered sacred and is cultivated in homes and temples.

SYMBOLS AND CUSTOMS

Lamps

Lamps hung in small baskets from the tops of poles or from bamboo plants growing along the riverbanks during Kartika are sometimes referred to as "sky lamps." They are kept burning throughout the holy month of Kartika because they are believed to light the path of departed souls across the sky.

In Madras, the capital of Tamil Nadu in southeastern India, the full moon day of the month of Kartika is celebrated in much the same way as **DEWALI** is observed in northern India—that is, by lighting lamps in temples and private homes.

Tulsi Plant

Hindus believe that watering, cultivating, and worshipping the Tulsi plant ensures happiness. When Tulsi leaves are put into water, it becomes as holy as water from the Ganges. When placed in the mouth of those who are dying, along with some Ganges water, Tulsi leaves make their departure from this life easier. Tulsi leaves offered to Vishnu during Kartika are said to please him more than the gift of a thousand cows.

The Tulsi plant is a symbol for Vishnupriya (beloved of Vishnu), and their marriage is celebrated on the eleventh day of the waxing half of Kartika.

FURTHER READING

Bellenir, Karen. *Religious Holidays and Calendars*. 3rd ed. Detroit: Omnigraphics, 2004.

Henderson, Helene, ed. *Holidays, Festivals, and Celebrations of the World Dictionary*. 3rd ed. Detroit: Omnigraphics, 2005.

Welbon, Guy Richard, and Glenn E. Yocum. *Religious Festivals in South India and Sri Lanka*. New Delhi: Manohar Publications, 1982.

Kataklysmos Day
(Festival of the Flood)

Type of Holiday: Religious (Orthodox Christian)
Date of Observation: Between May 10 and June 13; coincides with Pentecost
Where Celebrated: Cyprus
Symbols and Customs: Chattismata, Water
Related Holidays: Pentecost

ORIGINS

Kataklysmos is a religious and popular festival celebrated on Cyprus, with its roots in both the Bible and Greek mythology. *Kataklysmos* is the Greek word meaning "flood," and it refers to the Bible's story about Noah in the book of Genesis as well as to a Greek creation myth.

In the Bible story, God decides that all humankind is corrupt. He causes a flood that will destroy all life—except Noah, his wife, their sons and sons' wives, and a male and female pair of every kind of animal and bird. Noah builds an ark to hold this menagerie, and they all live on it while it rains for forty days and forty nights. They eventually land on what is now thought to be Mt. Ararat, and Noah and his family and animals replenish the earth's population.

In the Greek story, Zeus decides to destroy the earth because of human wickedness. Floods cover the earth, leaving only a small area of dry land on top of Mt. Parnassus. After nine days and nine nights of rain, a great wooden chest drifts to the spot. Inside are Deucalion and his wife, Pyrrha. Deucalion had been warned by his father, Prometheus, that the flood was coming and was able to save himself and his wife by building the chest. As they walked down the mountain into the flood-devastated world, Deucalion and Pyrrha heard a voice telling them to "cast behind you the bones of your mother." They realized that the earth was their mother and stones were her bones. They began to throw stones, and the stones took human form. His stones became men, while hers became women. To celebrate the end of the flood, Deucalion held a festival, which may have been the forerunner of today's Kataklysmos.

The celebration, which begins on a Friday and lasts until Monday, is usually held in seaside towns. Activities include games, folk dancing, boat races, swimming competitions, feasting, and listening to CHATTISMATA. The most popular custom is throwing WATER at one another, in memory of the flood that once destroyed nearly all life on earth.

SYMBOLS AND CUSTOMS

Chattismata

Chattismata or "arguments in verse" are often held on Kataklysmos Day. The contestants exchange rhyming insults until one person can't think of a quick response, and his or her opponent wins. The responses must be immediate, appropriate, and clever. Skilled contestants can battle each other for hours.

Water

Sprinkling water on each other is so much a part of the Kataklysmos festival that Cypriots consider it bad luck *not* to be sprinkled. Since they believe that the sea is blessed by the Holy Spirit on this day, having water sprinkled over one's head is symbolic of sharing in this blessing. It also symbolizes the purification of both body and soul.

In one of the traditional dances performed on Kataklysmos Day, a man balances a stack of six full glasses of water on top of his head.

FURTHER READING

Henderson, Helene, ed. *Holidays, Festivals, and Celebrations of the World Dictionary*. 3rd ed. Detroit: Omnigraphics, 2005.
MacDonald, Margaret R., ed. *The Folklore of World Holidays*. Detroit: Gale Research, 1992.
Van Straalen, Alice. *The Book of Holidays Around the World*. New York: Dutton, 1986.

WEB SITE

Cyprus Insider
www.cyprusinsider.com/cidom/about/customs.asp

Kattestoet
(Festival of the Cats)

Type of Holiday: Folkloric
Date of Observation: Second Sunday in May, every three years (2006, 2009, 2012)
Where Celebrated: Ypres (Ieper), Belgium
Symbols and Customs: Cats, Parade, Witch

ORIGINS

Every three years, the people of Ypres (Ieper), Belgium, host a festival celebrating cats and their role in the town's history. The festival features a cat costume PARADE, an unusual ceremony whereby toy CATS are thrown off the roof of a tall building called the Cloth Hall, and the mock burning of a WITCH in the town square.

The Kattestoet, or Festival of the Cats, got its start in the late Middle Ages. The festival's history began with the rise of Ypres as a major center of the northern European cloth trade in the twelfth century. Located between France, England, and Germany, the town of Ypres prospered by selling its cloth to people in all three countries. As the fame and wealth of the cloth merchants grew, they decided to raise a large building in the center of town to serve as the headquarters of the cloth trade. Construction began in 1260 and was completed in 1304. This building, called the Cloth Hall, included a large covered market area for cloth trading and a tall bell tower. In order to keep their looms well-stocked, the Ypres cloth merchants stored an enormous amount of raw wool and linen fiber. The wool and linen attracted mice. Cloth merchants kept cats to control the mice, but soon the cats had so many kittens that stray cats swarmed all over the city. According to some, the Kattestoet began as a means of ridding the city of the stray cats. On the last day of the town's largest yearly fair, the town jester would gather up as many stray cats as possible and take them to the top of the Cloth Hall belfry. There he would fling them off the tower to their death below. This cruel custom was last practiced in 1817. The custom was revived with modification in 1938, when stuffed toy cats were substituted for living animals.

Some people offer another explanation for the cat killing custom. They claim that Count Baudoin III, ruler of Flanders (the region in which Ypres is located), tossed several cats from his castle tower in the year 962. Local folklore linked cats to witches and pagan religious practices. Count Baudoin had recently converted to

Christianity. It is said that the count killed the cats in order to show that he was not afraid of them, or of witches either.

Ypres' economy declined in the fourteenth century, due to widespread disease and military attacks. Although Ypres lost its prominence in the cloth trade, local tradition insists that the cat killing custom remained in place until the early ninteenth century.

The town of Ypres was almost completely destroyed in World War I. Undaunted, the town's citizens rebuilt the city, including the old Cloth Hall, which was reproduced according to its original design between the years 1934 and 1958. The Festival of the Cats was reinstituted as well, and new customs were added. The first cat parade was held in 1946. The parade expanded in 1955, when the towns of Metz (Lorraine), Hertogenbosch (the Netherlands), Luxembourg, and Sittingbourne (England), all of which have their own lore and legends concerning cats, were invited to attend. In 1958, festival organizers abandoned the traditional date of the event, the second Sunday in **LENT**, and instituted a new date: the second Sunday in May. The contemporary festival also features a mock witch burning.

SYMBOLS AND CUSTOMS

Cats

For hundreds of years, European folk legends and beliefs have linked cats with witches and occult practices. For this reason, many people feared cats, and folk customs permitted or encouraged people to harm and even kill them. The Ypres custom of tossing cats off of a tower is just one example of these past practices. Attitudes towards cats changed in the last 200 years, however. These days, Europeans view cats as charming household pets.

In spite of its origin, today's Kattestoet reflects the Belgian people's love for cats. The cat is the main symbol of the festival and its image can be found everywhere. The town's merchants display all manner of goods with cat images on them, toy dealers sell stuffed cats, and confectioners offer candy cats in all shapes, sizes, and flavors. What's more, festival participants dress as cats, complete with face paint and furry leotards.

Finally, the cat tossing event serves as the highlight of the entire festival. Spectators crowd around the Cloth Hall's highest tower, hoping to take home one of the toy cats. A man chosen to play the role of the town's jester (or clown) flings the plush toys over the edge in various directions. These prizes thrill those lucky enough to catch them as they fall.

Parade

About 2,500 people march in the Kattestoet parade. Some dress as pages or Flemish noblemen and women, while others are flag bearers or play in marching bands. The rest of the parade participants, however, dress as cats or work with the floats and giant cat figures. The parade features floats depicting cats throughout history. Popular float subjects include the history of cat worship, cats in ancient Egypt, cats in the Middle Ages, Celtic cats, cats in lore and legend, and cats around the world.

Since 1955, two male cartoon cats named Pietje Pek and Cieper have served as mascots for the Kattestoet. In 1971, Cieper found a mate in the female cat Minneke Poes, a new addition to the festival. In 1974, the couple showed off their first kitten, Pieperke. These characters are represented by giant cat puppets that bring up the rear of the parade.

Witch

In the Middle Ages, many Europeans believed in and were terrified of witches. They feared that witches' supernatural powers came from the devil. As a result, they often harassed or killed suspected witches. In many places, suspected witches were burned to death. The contemporary Kattestoet closes with a symbolic witch burning reminiscent of the Middle Ages, even though there is no evidence that witch burnings were included in the medieval festival. The burning takes place after the cat tossing event. Mock judges proclaim the witch guilty and the verdict is announced to the crowd. A mass of red and white balloons is released at the same time. Then the witch effigy, surrounded by a large heap of wood and brush, is set aflame.

FURTHER READING

Henderson, Helene, ed. *Holidays, Festivals, and Celebrations of the World Dictionary.* 3rd ed. Detroit: Omnigraphics, 2005.

Shapiro Devreux, Anne. "Medieval Sorcery, Modern Fest." *New York Times.* Travel Section. May 7, 1989.

WEB SITES

City of Ieper
www.ieper.be/ieper_en.aspx

Trabel.com
www.trabel.com/ieper/ieper.htm
www.trabel.com/ieper/ieper-history.htm
www.trabel.com/ieper/ieper-clothhall.htm

Kentucky Derby

Type of Holiday: Sporting
Date of Observation: First Saturday in May
Where Celebrated: Louisville, Kentucky
Symbols and Customs: Fancy Hats, Mint Julep, Red Roses

ORIGINS

One of the top sporting events in the United States, the horse race known as the Kentucky Derby has been held at Churchill Downs racetrack in Louisville, Kentucky, since 1875. It was originally modeled on England's Epsom Derby, and the stylish clothes and parties associated with the race represent a deliberate attempt to recreate the social atmosphere of the English derby. The Kentucky Derby is unquestionably the most important social event of the year in Louisville, as evidenced by the more than 10,000 parties held there during Derby week.

Kentucky has a long tradition of horse racing and horse breeding. With its relatively mild climate, rich vegetation, and bluegrass meadows, Kentucky offers the ideal environment for raising thoroughbred horses. The first horse races in the state were held in Lexington in 1787, and the first jockey club was organized ten years later. Colonel Meriwether Lewis Clark Jr. established Churchill Downs (named after the family that owned the land on which the track stands) as the home of the Louisville Jockey Club, and he served as the track's president from 1875 until 1894. He offered the Kentucky Derby as part of the Churchill Downs program, confining the race to three-year-old thoroughbreds carrying weight not in excess of 126 pounds.

On the day of the first Kentucky Derby, Colonel Clark gave a Derby breakfast for his friends—a custom that is still popular today. As soon as the race is over, the owner of the winning horse is invited to a private party given by the president of Churchill Downs, where he or she sips a MINT JULEP from a special sterling silver cup decorated with a wreath of roses (*see* RED ROSES) and a replica of a thoroughbred horse's shoe, authentic in every detail. The cup later becomes part of the collection of cups on display at the Downs.

The race is usually run in slightly over two minutes, although in 1964, Northern Dancer was the first to win the Derby in two minutes flat. The great Secretariat, fondly known as Big Red, is still the only horse to run the Derby in less than two minutes—although only fractions of a second less. Ridden by jockey Ron Turcotte, Secretariat then went on to win the Triple Crown, which means that he also won the Belmont Stakes (run in June at Belmont Park, near New York City) and the Preakness (run in late May at the Pimlico Race Course near Baltimore). Only a horse that has won all three races in a single year, as Secretariat did in 1973, qualifies as a Triple Crown winner.

Although the race takes only a couple of minutes, the festivities surrounding it go on for the better part of a week and include parades, a steamboat race on the Ohio River, and countless dinner parties and balls.

SYMBOLS AND CUSTOMS

Fancy Hats

In the late 1800s, it was customary for women to wear hats while attending social events. The Kentucky Derby's early runnings were thought to be social affairs as much as sporting events, and women dressed in their finest. While ladies' dress hats are less commonplace today, the most outlandish, festooned, and adorned hats are still flaunted at the Derby.

Mint Julep

How the drink known as the mint julep came to be so closely associated with the Kentucky Derby is not really known. The julep has been a Kentucky tradition since before the Civil War, and most Kentuckians pride themselves on their own special recipes. The basic ingredients are fresh-picked mint, sugar, and Kentucky bourbon, served over crushed ice in a frosted silver cup or souvenir Derby glass. The drink symbolizes southern hospitality and social grace, both of which are on display throughout Derby week.

Red Roses

Since 1932, it has been a Derby tradition for a group of Louisville women to sew hundreds of red rosebuds into a blanket to be worn by the winning horse. A wreath of red roses is also placed on the horse's neck in the winners' circle—an event that takes place in front of more than 150,000 spectators and over twenty million tuned in via television and radio worldwide. Both are symbolic of victory, much like the victory wreath that crowns the winner of the **BOSTON MARATHON**.

FURTHER READING

Christianson, Stephen G., and Jane M. Hatch. *The American Book of Days*. 4th ed. New York: H.W. Wilson, 2000.
Cohen, Hennig, and Tristram Potter Coffin. *The Folklore of American Holidays*. 3rd ed. Detroit: Gale Research, 1999.

Henderson, Helene, ed. *Holidays, Festivals, and Celebrations of the World Dictionary*. 3rd ed. Detroit: Omnigraphics, 2005.

Shemanski, Frances. *A Guide to World Fairs and Festivals*. Westport, CT: Greenwood Press, 1985.

WEB SITES

Churchill Downs
www.kentuckyderby.com

Kentucky Derby Festival
www.kdf.org

Keretkun

Type of Holiday: Religious (Chukchi)
Date of Observation: Late summer
Where Celebrated: Siberia, Russia
Symbols and Customs: Blanket Toss, Dancing, Keretkun's Net, Offerings

ORIGINS

The Chukchi are an ancient people native to the northeast Siberian region of Russia, near the Arctic Circle and across the Bering Strait from Alaska. Life in the harsh polar environment is challenging, and the extreme climate caused a cultural split early in Chukchi history. Two separate but interdependent ways of life evolved within Chukchi society. Some Chukchi became nomadic reindeer herders and hunters, constantly moving throughout the evergreen forests and frozen tundra of Siberia. Others formed coastal settlements beside the Bering or East Siberian seas and survived by fishing and hunting sea mammals. Through the development of these two different lifestyles, the ancient Chukchi created a balanced unity with their surroundings. The "reindeer" Chukchi and the "maritime" Chukchi worked together, trading food and supplies for mutual benefit.

Chukchi religious tradition is based in shamanic understanding, which fundamentally views the world as being occupied and governed by numerous spirits of various types. Basic Chukchi belief holds that humans are not superior to anything in the natural world, and the natural world is therefore not man's to possess or control. Everything in the natural world is thought to have a spirit, including plants, animals, fish, trees, rocks, wind, water, land, and sky. Spirits control inanimate objects as well as natural phenomena such as weather, fire, and the sea, and Chukchi strive to live in harmony with these spirits. Chukchi beliefs also include special respect for the spirits of the forest, the spirit masters of all animals (particularly the wild reindeer), and the sea spirit Keretkun.

The coastal Chukchi hold an annual celebration to honor Keretkun, who is regarded as the spirit who owns all of the sea animals on which the Chukchi depend for their livelihood. Because Keretkun is believed to provide almost everything that is necessary for the coastal Chukchi to survive, this festival is considered to be one of the most important of the year. The Keretkun festival usually takes place in late summer during the peak of the maritime hunting and fishing season. Traditional observance includes sacrificial OFFERINGS presented to Keretkun in a ceremonial fashion. These ceremonies are normally followed by DANCING, socializing, and athletic competitions such as sled races, foot races, wrestling, and the BLANKET TOSS.

SYMBOLS AND CUSTOMS

Blanket Toss

Chukchi festival celebrations typically include the traditional competitive pastime of blanket tossing, in which many people hold a blanket suspended between them to form a sort of handheld trampoline. One competitor sits or stands on the blanket while the blanket-holders move it up and down, tossing the person into the air—often as high as thirty feet. The person who jumps or bounces the highest is considered the winner. Blanket tossing began in ancient whaling communities where it was used to celebrate a successful hunt. It was also used to improve a hunter's ability to spot game by elevating him to a point from which he could see over greater distances.

Dancing

Coastal Chukchi observe the Keretkun festival with the performance of ancient ceremonial folk dances that honor Keretkun. These dances—performed in a sitting position, usually by women—involve elaborate head, neck, and arm movements in a stylized imitation of sea mammals such as seals, walrus, and whales.

Keretkun's Net

A focal point of the Keretkun festival is Keretkun's net, which was traditionally woven from reindeer tendons and painted with seal blood. The net is typically suspended inside a large tent over a fire and then decorated with symbolic offerings that represent what is needed for the coming year. In this way the net receives the Chukchi wishes and symbolic offerings, which are believed to be carried to Keretkun as the net is burned.

Offerings

During the Keretkun festival, hunters approach the shore to ceremonially offer their harpoons and other weapons to the sea and to request that Keretkun provide a plentiful hunt in the coming year. Offerings are also made to honor Keretkun by symbolically returning all the animals that had been killed during the hunting season to the sea, thus replenishing the resource that had been plundered. This is accomplished through the burning of Keretkun's net, which has been filled with painted oars and figures of birds and sea mammals. Food offerings are sometimes also made, including special dishes that are not part of the Chukchi's normal diet, such as reindeer sausage and blood soup.

FURTHER READING

Gall, Timothy L. "Chukchi." In *Worldmark Encyclopedia of Cultures and Daily Life*. Detroit: Gale Research, 1998.

Henderson, Helene, ed. *Holidays, Festivals, and Celebrations of the World Dictionary*, 3rd ed. Detroit: Omnigraphics, 2005.

Hutton, Ronald. *Shamans: Siberian Spirituality and the Western Imagination*. New York: Hambledon and London, 2001.

Levinson, David, and Timothy O'Leary, eds. *Encyclopedia of World Cultures*. New York: Macmillan Reference USA, 1996.

Vitebsky, Piers. *The Reindeer People: Living with Animals and Spirits in Siberia*. New York: Houghton Mifflin, 2005.

WEB SITES

Chukot Autonomous District (Okrug)
www.chukotka.org

Smithsonian Institution
alaska.si.edu/culture_ne_siberian.asp

King Kamehameha Day

Type of Holiday: Historic
Date of Observation: June 11
Where Celebrated: Hawaii
Symbols and Customs: Floral Parades, Hula Dancing, Statue Decoration

ORIGINS

King Kamehameha Day honors Kamehameha I, who unified the Hawaiian islands under the rule of a single monarch. Kamehameha I was born on the island of Hawaii sometime between 1748 and 1761. He died in 1819. The holiday created in his honor is the only holiday in the United States celebrating a monarch who reigned in a territory that is now included in the United States of America.

Prophecy and intrigue surrounded the future king from birth. His father was a high chief, and his mother was the daughter of Alapai, the former king. They gave him the name "Paiea," which means hard-shelled crab. Near the time of his birth, a very bright star appeared in the heavens. Historians suspect that this might have been Halley's Comet, which approached the earth in 1758. Hawaiian prophets declared the star to be a herald, announcing the birth of a great king who would conquer the warring tribal chiefs and reign supreme over all the Hawaiian islands. The former king Alapai grew anxious at this prediction and, when the child was identified as Paiea, the king ordered the infant to be put to death. Local people spirited the child away to safety, however. He was raised as a warrior and took for himself the name "Kamehameha," which means "the one set apart," or "the very lonely one."

When King Kalaniopuu died in 1782, the island of Hawaii was divided up between his two sons. War broke out among tribal chiefs in that same year. Kamehameha took this opportunity to begin a campaign to conquer and unify the Hawaiian Islands. By 1795 he had just about succeeded in this endeavor, with all but the small islands of Kauai and Niihau in his grasp. In 1810, peaceful negotiations resulted in the assimilation of these two islands into Kamehameha's Hawaiian kingdom.

King Kamehameha I was a shrewd politician who won the love of his people by protecting them from the violent retribution of powerful local chiefs. Moreover, realizing that he couldn't fend off European trade, he decided to profit from it. He taxed European ships that docked in Hawaii and established a government monopoly on the production and sale of sandalwood. He also encouraged agriculture and industry and oversaw the importation of new plants and animals. In addition, King Kamehameha outlawed human sacrifice and brought years of peace to the islands by putting an end to the frequent battles between rival chiefs and their followers.

In 1871, Kamehameha's grandson, King Kamehameha V, declared June 11 to be King Kamehameha I Day. Celebrations have taken place on this date since that time. The first King Kamehameha I Day, celebrated in 1872, featured various athletic contests, such as horse races, velocipede races, sack races, foot races, and wheelbarrow races. In 1883 a statue of the former king was erected on the island of Hawaii. In 1901, a small group of people celebrated the holiday by decorating the statue with garlands of flowers (called leis) for the holiday. Since that day, the decoration of King Kamehameha statues with leis has been an important part of the commemoration. The holiday continued to grow in importance until 1939, when the state of Hawaii established the King Kamehameha Celebration Commission. The commission took on the responsibility of planning and managing all the public events that take place during the holiday. The holiday is honored throughout the Hawaiian Islands, but the celebrations are especially fervent in Kohala, on the island of Hawaii, the district where King Kamehameha I was born and where he grew up.

SYMBOLS AND CUSTOMS

Flower Parades

King Kamehameha Day parades usually feature flower-covered floats and pa'u riders. A pa'u is a nineteenth century, full-length Hawaiian culotte-skirt. These flowing garments, made of twelve yards of brightly colored material, permitted women to retain their modesty while still riding horses astride. The women selected as pa'u riders for King Kamehameha Day prepare for the event by practicing their riding, sewing their pa'u costume, gathering flowers, and preparing the eleborate leis worn by the horses and their riders. Marching units, composed of student and community groups, often accompany these parades.

In North Kohala, a pa'u queen leads a retinue of princesses, representing the various islands that make up the state of Hawaii. Pages, outriders, and attendants accompany the pa'u queen and princesses. The parade passes by the statue of King Kamehameha, where the pa'u riders offer ho'okupu, ceremonial gifts symbolizing respect, to the illustrious monarch.

Hula Dancing

Civic celebrations of King Kamehameha Day usually feature displays of time-honored Hawaiian arts and crafts. Hula dancing to traditional Hawaiian music often serves as a focal point of the celebrations. In Honolulu, this custom has turned into an international competition. For the past 33 years, the city has hosted the annual King Kamehameha Hula competition on or around King Kamehameha Day. Hula groups from as far away as California, Nevada, and Japan take part in the event.

Statue Decoration

On King Kamehameha Day, statues of the monarch are draped in full-length leis of various colors and types of flowers. In the town of North Kohala, both individuals and organizations craft twenty-two-foot-long leis to drape over the arms and body of the nine-foot bronze statue. These leis are offered in admiration and respect for the once-powerful king. Some of the local groups that participate in the ceremony are the Royal Order of Kamehameha, Na papa Kanaka 'O Pu'ukohola, and the Kaahumanu Society. A ceremony accompanies the draping of the garlands. The ceremony includes the recounting of historical facts concerning the king, musical performances, hula dancing, and chanting.

North Kohala's Kamehameha statue is the oldest in Hawaii. In 1878, the Hawaiian legislature commissioned a French artist to make the statue, originally intended to stand outside the Judiciary Building in Honolulu. After French sculptors completed the piece, they shipped it from Paris to Hawaii. Sadly, the ship carrying the statue sunk near the Falkland Islands. Another statue was made for the city of Honolulu. The original statue was eventually recovered, however, and installed in North Kohala in 1912. The king's statue in Honolulu is also the site of an important statue decoration ceremony on King Kamehmeha Day.

WEB SITES

King Kamehameha Celebration Commission
www.hawaii.gov/dags/king_kamehameha_commission

Library of Congress Local Legacies
lcweb2.loc.gov/cocoon/legacies/HI?200002873.html

North Kohala Kamehameha Day
www.kamehamehadaycelebration.org

Kodomo-No-Hi
(Children's Day)

Type of Holiday: Folkloric
Date of Observation: May 5
Where Celebrated: Japan
Symbols and Customs: Carp, Horse, Iris

ORIGINS

What is known today as Kodomo-No-Hi or Children's Day originated as Tango-No-Sekku or Boys' Day. It can be traced back to China, where many years ago a young man named Ch'ü Yuan was so upset by the terrible conditions of his time that he drowned himself in a river, believing that from another world he would be better able to assist his countrymen. His self-sacrifice took place on May 5, which became known as Boys' Day during the ninth century because parents hoped that their sons would display the same spirit of devotion and selflessness. Each household would erect tall bamboo poles outside and attach streamers in the shape of CARP for each of their sons, while inside they would display figures of famous Samurai warriors from Japanese history or legend, dressed in shining suits of armor.

In 1948, Boys' Day was expanded to include girls, and it was renamed Children's Day. The purpose of this day is to impress upon both boys and girls the importance of being good citizens and of showing courage and strength in the face of adversity. But in fact, the customs and activities associated with this day still tend to focus on boys. Families fly carp wind-socks and display military heirlooms and small images of famous feudal warriors—complete with miniature swords, armor, and helmets—which are meant to inspire courage and bravery. Many local shrines and communities hold special festivities for children, including lion dances, sumo wrestling, *kendo* (fencing with bamboo staves), and climbing competitions.

SYMBOLS AND CUSTOMS

Carp

The custom of flying banners or wind-socks in the shape of carp dates back to the Tokugawa period in Japanese history, when farmers frightened away insects by hanging bright banners and grotesque figures in their fields and gardens. Later, these were transformed into representations of warriors and, instead of acting as scarecrows, were displayed indoors to remind young boys of the bravery and accomplishments of the Samurai.

The carp replaced the warrior figures around 1772 because people wanted a more visible, outdoor display. The carp is a symbol of strength and determination because it swims against the current, leaps up waterfalls, and is said not to quiver when touched with a knife. As the carp banners that are suspended from poles outside people's houses on Children's Day billow in the wind, they appear to swim against an invisible upstream current, embodying the virtues of perseverance and courage that families hope their children will display.

Horse

The original observance of Boys' Day was called Tango-No-Sekku. Tango means "First Day of the Horse," and the display of horses during this festival symbolized the attributes of manliness, bravery, and strength desired in boys.

Iris

During the Nara period, Tango-No-Sekku (*see* above) was also known as Shobu-No-Sekku or the Feast of the Iris, a plant believed to have magical restorative qualities. The swordlike leaves were placed at the entrances to houses, on the rooftops, and under the eaves to ward off evil. In the early seventeenth century, young boys would tie shobu leaves into bundles and strike them against the ground, making a loud noise. Today, boys carry wooden swords known as *shobu-katana* or "iris swords."

It is still a tradition on this day for young people to bathe in hot water in which iris leaves have been steeped. The leaves not only give the bathwater an unusual fragrance but are also believed to drive away illness and to instill in them the spirit of the warrior. Some people chop up the leaves and mix them with sake, the rice wine once enjoyed by the Samurai. Rice balls wrapped in iris leaves, known as *chimaki*, are also served on May 5.

FURTHER READING

Bauer, Helen, and Sherwin Carlquist. *Japanese Festivals*. Garden City, NY: Doubleday, 1965.
Buell, Hal. *Festivals of Japan*. New York: Dodd, Mead, 1965.
Cohen, Hennig, and Tristram Potter Coffin. *The Folklore of American Holidays*. 3rd ed. Detroit: Gale Research, 1999.

Henderson, Helene, ed. *Holidays, Festivals, and Celebrations of the World Dictionary.* 3rd ed. Detroit: Omnigraphics, 2005.

Humphrey, Grace. *Stories of the World's Holidays.* 1923. Reprint. Detroit: Omnigraphics, 1990.

Ickis, Marguerite. *The Book of Festivals and Holidays the World Over.* New York: Dodd, Mead, 1970.

Leach, Maria, ed. *Funk & Wagnalls Standard Dictionary of Folklore, Mythology & Legend.* San Francisco: Harper & Row, 1984.

MacDonald, Margaret R., ed. *The Folklore of World Holidays.* Detroit: Gale Research, 1992.

Spicer, Dorothy Gladys. *The Book of Festivals.* 1937. Reprint. Detroit: Omnigraphics, 1990.

Thurley, Elizabeth. *Through the Year in Japan.* London: Batsford Academic and Educational, 1985.

Van Straalen, Alice. *The Book of Holidays Around the World.* New York: Dutton, 1986.

Zabilka, Gladys. *Customs and Culture of Okinawa.* 2nd ed. Rutland, VT: C.E. Tuttle, 1973.

WEB SITE

Japanese Culture and Community Center of Northern California
www.jccnc.org/events/childrensday.htm

Korea National Foundation Day (Tangun Day, Tangun Accession Day)

Type of Holiday: National
Date of Observation: October 3
Where Celebrated: North Korea, South Korea
Symbols and Customs: Offerings, Speeches

ORIGINS

Also known as Tangun Day or Tangun Accession Day, Korea National Foundation Day commemorates the establishment of the Choson Kingdom in 2333 B.C., marking the beginning of the Korean society and way of life.

According to Korean legend, Tangun (alternately, Dangun or Tan-gun) was the son of a god and a bear-woman. As the first leader of the Korean people, Tangun created a system of government that instituted laws and moral codes of behavior. He also gave the Korean people skills in such areas as art, medicine, and agriculture. Tangun is thought to have ruled Korea for more than 1,000 years before becoming a mountain god.

Korea National Foundation Day, which celebrates Korean culture and the achievements of the Korean people, is a national holiday in South Korea. National holidays can be defined as those commemorations that a nation's government has deemed important enough to warrant inclusion in the list of official public holidays. They tend to honor a person or event that has been critical in the development of the nation and its identity. Such people and events usually reflect values and traditions shared by a large portion of the citizenry. It is a day of national pride for Koreans all over the world, although most public celebrations occur in South Korea. North Korea does not recognize the day as an official national holiday. In 2002, however, North Korean leaders participated with South Korea in a joint observance of the day for the first time since the Korean peninsula was divided in 1948.

SYMBOLS AND CUSTOMS

Offerings

Each year on National Foundation Day, a ceremony to honor Tangun is held at the Chamseongdan altar, located at the summit of Mt. Manisan on the southwestern point of Ganghwado Island in South Korea. This altar is said to have been built by Tangun and is itself a legendary place of worship and sacrifice favored by ancient kings throughout Korean history.

Speeches

National Foundation Day has become an occasion for politically themed speeches delivered by South Korean government leaders.

FURTHER READING

Cumings, Bruce. *Korea's Place in the Sun: A Modern History*. New York: W.W. Norton, 2005.

Henderson, Helene, ed. *Holidays, Festivals, and Celebrations of the World Dictionary*, 3rd ed. Detroit: Omnigraphics, 2005.

Rees, David. *Korea: An Illustrated History from Ancient Times to 1945*. New York: Hippocrene Books: 2001.

WEB SITE

Life in Korea
www.lifeinkorea.com/Information

Kristallnacht
(Crystal Night, Night of Broken Glass)

Type of Holiday: Historic
Date of Observation: November 9-10
Where Celebrated: Austria, Croatia, France, Germany, Netherlands, Poland, Romania, Spain, Sweden, United Kingdom, United States, and by Jewish communities all over the world
Symbols and Customs: Antiracism Demonstrations, Candlelight Vigils, Marches, Synagogue Ceremonies

ORIGINS

European Jews, particularly those living in Germany, suffered greatly during the 1930s. Adolf Hitler (1889-1945), the chancellor of Germany, started passing laws early in the decade that prevented Jews from observing the customs of their faith, and by 1935 they had lost their citizenship rights and could no longer vote in parliamentary elections. Laws passed in 1938 made it increasingly difficult for them to earn a living, and by 1939 all Jews living in Germany had to carry identification cards. But the situation reached crisis proportions later in 1938, when thousands of Polish Jews who had been living in Germany for many years were rounded up, loaded into boxcars, and sent to "relocation camps" on the Polish border because the Polish government refused to allow them back into their homeland.

When Herschel Grynszpan, a seventeen-year-old Polish Jew living with his uncle in Paris at the time, found out that his parents were among those who had been forced to leave their homes, he decided to seek revenge. He went to the German embassy and assassinated a German diplomat—an act that Germany's Nazi leaders used as an excuse to launch a "pogrom" or violent, organized attack against German Jews. On the night of November 9, 1938, Nazi storm troopers and members of the Nazi secret police and Hitler Youth groups went on a rampage through

453

Jewish neighborhoods in Germany, Austria, and other areas controlled by the Nazis. They broke into Jewish homes and businesses, smashing the windows, beating or murdering the inhabitants, and destroying whatever they found inside. They even entered synagogues and destroyed sacred Torah scrolls, setting the buildings themselves on fire. All told, nearly 100 Jews were killed that night, 7,500 Jewish businesses were ruined, and about 200 synagogues were destroyed—although Jewish groups claim that more than 1,000 were seriously damaged. About 25,000 Jewish men were torn from their homes and families and later sent to concentration camps, where many of them died.

The night of November 9-10 became known as "Kristallnacht," which is German for "Crystal Night," because of the broken glass strewn in the streets in the wake of the attacks. It was actually a Nazi who came up with the name, which some scholars believe was designed to mock the seriousness of the event in the same way that the concentration camp victims were said to receive *Sonderbehandlung* or "special treatment" when they were gassed to death. In any case, the name stuck, and this event is widely acknowledged as the beginning of the Holocaust, which would eventually claim the lives of six million Jews.

Kristallnacht commemorates a significant historical event. Peoples throughout the world commemorate such significant events in their histories through holidays and festivals. Often, these are events that are important for an entire nation and become widely observed. The marking of such anniversaries serves not only to honor the values represented by the person or event commemorated, but also to strengthen and reinforce communal bonds of national, cultural, or ethnic identity. Victorious, joyful, and traumatic events are remembered through historic holidays. The commemorative expression reflects the original event through festive celebration or solemn ritual.

Today, Kristallnacht is commemorated in cities throughout Germany as well as by Jewish communities all over the world. Many of the commemoration ceremonies are held at synagogues or Jewish cemeteries and involve the recitation of the Kaddish, an ancient Jewish prayer for the dead. In Germany, Kristallnacht observations coincide with those surrounding another, more recent, event: the 1989 breaching of the Berlin Wall, the ninety-six-mile-long concrete wall built in 1961 to prevent East Germans from escaping Communist rule after World War II (1939-45).

SYMBOLS AND CUSTOMS

Antiracism Demonstrations

Because the Holocaust stands as a symbol for racism and hate crimes, many antiracist organizations choose to hold demonstrations on Kristallnacht. Colleges and universities often invite Holocaust survivors to give lectures, and speakers at other public venues remind people of the connection between what happened in 1938 and the treatment that many minority groups are receiving today.

These demonstrations are particularly noticeable in Berlin, where the neo-Nazi movement and recent attacks on immigrants and Jewish synagogues have been a sad reminder of the 1938 anti-Jewish pogrom.

Candlelight Vigils

Candlelight vigils are a popular way to commemorate any historic event in which lives have been lost. Kristallnacht is often observed with the lighting of torches or candles, their flames symbolizing the souls of those who lost their lives not only on November 9, 1938, but afterward in the Holocaust.

Marches

Solemn marches, especially in large cities, are another way in which Jews and others commemorate Kristallnacht. In Berlin, the capital of Germany, more than 200,000 people marched through the city on November 9, 2000, both in memory of the event's Jewish victims and as a form of protest against more recent attacks on Jews and other minority groups.

Synagogue Ceremonies

Special ceremonies in honor of the victims of Kristallnacht are held in the historic synagogues at Wroclaw, Cracow, and Auschwitz, Poland, as well as in synagogues throughout the world. The Polish city of Wroclaw, which used to be the German city of Breslau was at one time the site of Germany's second largest Jewish congregation and two of its most historic synagogues, which have recently been restored.

FURTHER READING

Blackburn, Bonnie, and Leofranc Holford-Stevens. *The Oxford Companion to the Year*. New York: Oxford University Press, 2003.

Bowker, John, ed. *The Oxford Dictionary of World Religions*. New York: Oxford University Press, 1997.

Crim, Keith R. *The Perennial Dictionary of World Religions*. San Francisco: Harper & Row, 1989.

Trawicky, Bernard, and Ruth W. Gregory. *Anniversaries and Holidays*. 5th ed. Chicago: American Library Assocation, 2000.

WEB SITES

Center for Holocaust and Genocide Studies at the University of Minnesota
www.chgs.umn.edu/Educational_Resources/Curriculum/Broken_Threads/
    Kristallnacht/kristallnacht.html

The History Place
www.historyplace.com/worldwar2/timeline/knacht-bio.htm

*Kumbh Mela
(Pitcher Fair)*

Type of Holiday: Religious (Hindu)
Date of Observation: Every twelve years on a date calculated by astrologers; next
    fair scheduled for 2013
Where Celebrated: Allahabad, India
Symbols and Customs: Ganges River, Kumbh, Sadhus

ORIGINS

The Kumbh Mela, or Pitcher Fair, is part of the traditions of Hinduism, which
many scholars regard as the world's oldest living religion. The word Hindu is
derived from the Sanskrit term *Sindhu* (or *Indus*), which meant river. It referred to
people living in the Indus valley in the Indian subcontinent.

Hinduism has no founder, one universal reality (or god) known as Brahman, many
gods and goddesses (sometimes referred to as devtas), and several scriptures. Hinduism also has no priesthood or hierarchical structure similar to that seen in some
other religions, such as Christianity. Hindus acknowledge the authority of a wide
variety of writings, but there is no single, uniform canon. The oldest of the Hindu
writings are the *Vedas*. The word "veda" comes from the Sanskrit word for knowledge. The *Vedas*, which were compiled from ancient oral traditions, contain hymns,
instructions, explanations, chants for sacrifices, magical formulas, and philosophy.
Another set of sacred books includes the *Great Epics*, which illustrate Hindu faith in
practice. The *Epics* include the *Ramayana*, the *Mahabharata*, and the *Bhagavad Gita*.

The Hindu pantheon includes approximately thirty-three million gods. Some of
these are held in higher esteem than others. Over all the gods, Hindus believe in

one absolute high god or universal concept. This is Brahman. Although he is above all the gods, he is not worshipped in popular ceremonies because he is detached from the day-to-day affairs of the people. Brahman is impersonal. Lesser gods and goddesses (devtas) serve him. Because these are more intimately involved in the affairs of people, they are venerated as gods. The most honored god in Hinduism varies among the different Hindu sects. Although Hindu adherents practice their faith differently and venerate different deities, they share a similar view of reality and look back on a common history.

Believed to be the largest periodic gathering of human beings in the world, the Kumbh Mela or Pitcher Fair takes place every twelve years in the holy city of Prayag (now Allahabad) in north central India. It is the highpoint of a pilgrimage that also stops at Hardwar, Nasik, and Ujjain, but it is at Allahabad where the GANGES RIVER meets the Yamuna River, and where the mythical river of enlightenment, known as the Sarasvati, flows. About two million Hindu pilgrims from all over India travel here to take a dip at the confluence of the two rivers.

Why is it called the Pitcher Fair? According to legend, the Hindu gods and demons (*ashuras*) had been fighting for a long time, but neither could conquer the other. Both knew about a KUMBH (pitcher) filled with *amrit,* the nectar of immortality, that lay on the ocean floor. It was the gods, of course, who eventually found the pitcher, drank the nectar, and became immortal. But during the struggle, according to one version of the legend, drops of nectar fell at Prayag (Allahabad), Hardwar, Nasik, and Ujjain. Another version says that as the gods carried the pitcher off to heaven, they stopped at these four places. The journey took twelve days, which for the gods are much longer than earthly days—hence the twelve-year cycle on which the fair is held.

The fair that commemorates this journey has been held for centuries. A Chinese traveler in the seventh century mentioned seeing half a million Hindus gathered at Prayag, and today, of course, it is even easier for pilgrims to get there. A vast tent city is erected to house them, temporary water and power lines are installed, and ten pontoon bridges are laid across the Ganges. Movies of Hindu gods and heroes are shown from the backs of trucks, and plays recounting Hindu myths are performed. So many people attend the festival that the government often has difficulty controlling them, and tragedies cannot always be avoided. In 1954, for example, hundreds were killed or injured in a rush toward the water where the two rivers meet.

SYMBOLS AND CUSTOMS

Ganges River

The Ganges (Ganga in Sanskrit) is not only a sacred river but is believed by Hindus to be the source of all sacred waters. The place where it joins the Yamuna at

Allahabad is called the *sangam* and is considered by some to be the holiest place in India; a single dip in the waters of the confluence guarantees salvation. Hardwar, where the river leaves the hills and enters the plains of Hindustan, is also an important place of pilgrimage.

Bathing in the Ganges washes away sins, and throwing the bones and ashes of the dead into the holy waters sends the deceased immediately to heaven. Many orthodox Hindus will drink no water except that of the Ganges, which is transported by a supply service to those who live far away. Because it is believed to flow on and on forever, the Ganges is a symbol of eternity.

Kumbh

Translated literally, kumbh means "a pot of water," but it is also an astrological sign of the zodiac that corresponds to Aquarius, the Water Bearer. Every twelve years, when Jupiter enters into the sign of Kumbh and the Kumbh Mela is held, it becomes a symbol for salvation and immortality, due to its association with the fabled jar of nectar over which the gods and the demons fought so hard.

Sadhus

One of the biggest attractions at the Kumbh Mela is the procession of Sadhus or holy men. Emaciated from fasting and blinded by their constant gazing at the sun, the Sadhus emerge from seclusion in the forest or mountains to appear at this festival. Their faces and bodies are smeared with ashes, and they wear only loincloths as they carry images of the gods down to the water to be immersed. Some lie on beds of spikes or swing in the air with their heads down; others use microphones to attract large crowds to their lectures. People throng the roads to see them and often break through the barriers holding them back to receive the Sadhus' blessing.

FURTHER READING

Bellenir, Karen. *Religious Holidays and Calendars*. 3rd ed. Detroit: Omnigraphics, 2004.

Crim, Keith R. *The Perennial Dictionary of World Religions*. San Francisco: Harper & Row, 1989.

Henderson, Helene, ed. *Holidays, Festivals, and Celebrations of the World Dictionary*. 3rd ed. Detroit: Omnigraphics, 2005.

Holm, Jean, and John Bowker, eds. *Worship*. New York: St. Martin's Press, 1994.

Sanon, Arun. *Festive India*. New Delhi: Frank Bros., 1986.

Sharma, Brijendra Nath. *Festivals of India*. New Delhi: Abhinav Publications, 1978.

Thomas, Paul. *Hindu Religion, Customs, and Manners*. 6th ed. New York: APT Books, 1981.

Trawicky, Bernard, and Ruth W. Gregory. *Anniversaries and Holidays*. 5th ed. Chicago: American Library Assocation, 2000.

WEB SITE

Kumbh Mela Consultancy Bureau
www.kumbh.net

Kupalo Festival

Type of Holiday: Calendar/Seasonal
Date of Observation: June 24
Where Celebrated: Ukraine, United States
Symbols and Customs: Fern, Tree
Related Holidays: Midsummer Day

ORIGINS

This Ukrainian festival takes its name from Kupalo, the god of summer and fertility, who sleeps under a TREE during the winter and awakens in the spring. Since ancient times, people in all parts of the world have honored the changing of the seasons. Many cultures divided the year into two seasons, summer and winter, and marked these points of the year at or near the summer and winter solstices, during which light and warmth began to increase and decrease, respectively. In pre-industrial times, humans survived through hunting, gathering, and agricultural practices, which depend on the natural cycle of seasons, according to the climate in the region of the world in which they lived. Thus, they created rituals to help ensure enough rain and sun in the spring and summer so crops would grow to fruition at harvest time, which was, in turn, duly celebrated. Vestiges of many of these ancient practices are thought to have survived in festivals still celebrated around seasonal themes.

Many of the customs associated with the Kupalo Festival are directly linked to encouraging fertility in both the human and natural worlds. For example, young women often gather flowers to make a wreath that is tossed into a nearby river. Where the wreath touches the shore is believed to indicate what family the young woman will marry into. Another custom for girls is to make an effigy of Marena, the goddess of cold, death, and winter. After singing special holiday songs, they burn or drown the effigy to reduce the goddess's power over the coming winter. The Ukrainian winters are very harsh.

The Kupalo Festival dates back to pagan times, when people believed that the seasons were governed by supernatural forces. If certain yearly rituals were not carried out properly, the weather might not warm up in time to yield a good harvest. Today, the festival is still observed in parts of the Ukraine and in Ukrainian communities in the United States.

SYMBOLS AND CUSTOMS

Fern

Young men go into the forest on Kupalo to look for a type of fern that, according to legend, blooms only on the night of **MIDSUMMER DAY**. They take with them a special cloth, white powder, and a knife. If they find the fern and are strong enough to ward off the enticements of the wood nymphs, they draw a circle with the white powder and sit down in the middle to wait for the fern to bloom. When it does, they cut off the blossom with the knife and wrap the flower in the special cloth. They must never tell anyone that they have found the fern, or they will lose the luck and power it is believed to symbolize. This story explains why some people have more luck and talent than others.

Tree

A young sapling decorated with flowers, seeds, and fruit is probably the most recognizable symbol of the Kupalo Festival. It represents Kupalo himself, who awakens in the spring and shakes the tree he's been sleeping under, making the seeds fall and symbolically making the earth fertile again. During the festival young boys and girls dance around the tree and sing special songs to please this image of the fertility god.

FURTHER READING

Henderson, Helene, ed. *Holidays, Festivals, and Celebrations of the World Dictionary.* 3rd ed. Detroit: Omnigraphics, 2005.

Kwakiutl Midwinter Ceremonies

Type of Holiday: Calendar/Seasonal, Religious (Kwakiutl)
Date of Observation: February
Where Celebrated: Northwestern United States and Vancouver Island
Symbols and Customs: Hamatsa Dance, Raven, Salmon
Related Holidays: Iroquois Midwinter Ceremonies

ORIGINS

The Kwakiutl Midwinter Ceremonies are part of the Native American religious traditions. The history of this and other Native American cultures dates back thousands of years into prehistoric times. According to many scholars, the people who became the Native Americans migrated from Asia across a land bridge that may have once connected the territories presently occupied by Alaska and Russia. The migrations, believed to have begun between 60,000 and 30,000 B.C.E., continued until approximately 4,000 B.C.E. This speculation, however, conflicts with traditional stories asserting that the indigenous Americans have always lived in North America or that tribes moved up from the south.

The historical development of religious belief systems among Native Americans is not well known. Most of the information available was gathered by Europeans who arrived on the continent beginning in the sixteenth century C.E. The data they recorded was fragmentary and oftentimes of questionable accuracy because the Europeans did not understand the native cultures they were trying to describe and the Native Americans were reluctant to divulge details about themselves.

The Kwakiutl are one of the Indian tribes that inhabit the coastal region stretching from northern California to southeastern Alaska. They believe that long ago, before their people even existed, the world was ruled by animals—including bears, wolves, seals, ravens, bees, owls, and killer whale—with fantastic powers. These supernatural beings gave some of their power to humans, who were the ancestors of today's Kwakiutl.

During their winter ceremonial season, the Kwakiutl acknowledge and reaffirm their connection with the supernatural world by performing dramatic dances or *tseka* (*see* HAMATSA DANCE). The performers dress in strips of cedar bark and wear ornately carved masks that are designed to evoke the spirits of their supernatural forebears. The dances themselves illustrate characters and incidents from Kwakiutl mythology.

The midwinter ceremonies also include feasting. Favorite foods served during the ceremonies include SALMON, salal berries, cranberries, huckleberries, blackberries, crabapples, and soapberries that have been whipped up into a froth. Many of the elaborately carved dishes in which ceremonial foods were once served can now be seen in museum collections.

SYMBOLS AND CUSTOMS

Hamatsa Dance

The most important dance performed during the midwinter ceremonies of the Kwakiutl is the Hamatsa Dance. It is performed by members of the Cannibal Society, the most prestigious of the secret societies for which initiation rites are held during this period. The members must undergo special training and long periods of withdrawal from normal society, in return for which they are bestowed with the power of the Cannibal Spirit.

The Hamatsa Dance is characterized by magical effects, ghostly calls, and wild behavior. The dancers wear stylized masks, the most outstanding being that of the black-and-red Fool dancer. With his huge nose, he threatens audience members and occasionally throws stones at them to make sure they behave.

Raven

The Kwakiutl believe that it was the supernatural being known as the Raven who was responsible for placing the sun, moon, and stars in the sky, the SALMON in the rivers, and the fish in the sea. According to the legends of Alaska's coastal natives, the Raven also gave the Kwakiutl people fire and water and the foods they eat. Because he could turn himself into anything he wanted, the Raven loved to trick people by changing shape and form. Folklorists have collected a long series of stories, known as the "Raven cycle," about this supernatural being. During the midwinter ceremonies, tribal leaders and shamans (who serve as intermediaries between the natural and supernatural worlds) often wear raven masks.

The raven is also important to other Northwest coastal tribes. It can be found on the crest of the Tlingit and Haida of southeastern Alaska.

Salmon

The salmon was as important to the tribes of the Northwest coast as the buffalo was to the Plains Indians. It was in this region where salmon were caught in great numbers every year, and where they were a staple of the Native American diet. According to Kwakiutl legend, salmon were supernatural beings who lived in their own villages under the sea. They had their own rites and ceremonies, some of which were passed on to the Kwakiutl ancestors. Because they swim against the current when they make their annual "runs" up the inland waterways to spawn, salmon have often been regarded as a symbol of extraordinary power and perseverance.

The attitude of the Kwakiutl people to the salmon is best illustrated by the "first salmon" ceremony. When the first salmon is caught, it is ceremonially cleaned and placed on a mat or bed of fern leaves. It is welcomed with a prayer of thanks and promised good treatment. The bones and entrails are wrapped in a mat and thrown back into the river where it was caught, so that its soul can return to its village and tell the other supernaturals that the Kwakiutl remember them and have treated it well. Then the salmon is carried home by a select group—usually children, women only, or the family of the fisherman who caught it—and roasted for eating.

FURTHER READING

Bellenir, Karen. *Religious Holidays and Calendars*. 3rd ed. Detroit: Omnigraphics, 2004.

Henderson, Helene, ed. *Holidays, Festivals, and Celebrations of the World Dictionary*. 3rd ed. Detroit: Omnigraphics, 2005.

Kavasch, E. Barrie. *Enduring Harvests: Native American Foods and Festivals for Every Season*. Old Saybrook, CT: Globe Pequot Press, 1995.

Leach, Maria, ed. *Funk & Wagnalls Standard Dictionary of Folklore, Mythology & Legend*. San Francisco: Harper & Row, 1984.

WEB SITE

Smithsonian Institution, National Museum of Natural History
www.si.edu/harcourt/nmnh/native/native2.html

Kwanzaa

Date of Observation: December 26 - January 1
Where Celebrated: United States, Canada, Caribbean, and parts of Europe
Symbols and Customs: Candle Holder (Kinara), Corn (Muhindi), Crops (Mazao), Gifts (Zawadi), Mat (Mkeka), Seven Candles (Mishumaa Saba), Seven Principles (Nguzo Saba), Unity Cup (Kikombe Cha Umoja)
Colors: Kwanzaa is associated with red, black, and green—the colors of the national flag or *bendara* of the African-American people as designed by Marcus Garvey, father of the modern Black nationalist movement. Red symbolizes the continuing struggle of the African-American people, black is symbolic of their faces, and green stands for their hopes and aspirations for the future.
Related Holidays: Christmas, Hanukkah

ORIGINS

The name of this holiday comes from the Swahili phrase *matunda ya kwanza*, which means "first fruits." It was established in 1966 by Dr. Maulana "Ron" Karenga, a UCLA professor from Nigeria. After the August 1965 Watts riots in Los Angeles, Dr. Karenga, at that time a graduate student, felt that his people had lost touch with their African heritage. After completing his Ph.D., he began teaching African-American history and studied the culture of the Yorubas, Igbos, Ashantis, Zulus, and other African tribes. All of these tribes celebrated some type of harvest festival (*see* **NEW YAM FESTIVAL**), during which they remembered their ancestors, celebrated their good fortune, and made their plans for the coming year. Using this as his model, Dr. Karenga decided to create a cultural holiday that African Americans of all faiths could celebrate and that would shift their attention away from **CHRISTMAS** and other traditional "white" holidays. Dr. Karenga added a second "a" to the Swahili word meaning "first" so that the name of this newly created holiday would have seven letters—a number possessing great symbolic value in many African cultures. He also made it a seven-day celebration, not only because most of the other first fruits festivals lasted between seven and nine days, but because each day could then be dedicated to one of the SEVEN PRINCIPLES.

Among the activities associated with the celebration of Kwanzaa is the pouring of the *tambiko* or libation for the ancestors; the *Harambee*, which is a raised-arm gesture combined with a verbal call, the general meaning of which is "Let's all pull together"; and the lighting of the *mishumaa saba* or SEVEN CANDLES. Central to every Kwanzaa celebration is the *mkeka* or MAT, on which are arranged various symbolic items such as CORN, CROPS, a CANDLE HOLDER, and the UNITY CUP.

A communal feast or *Karamu* is held on the night of December 31, to which each participating family contributes a particular dish—usually made from okra, sesame seeds, black-eyed peas, peanuts, or other foods that African slaves brought to the United States. Before and during the feast, there is a program that combines information about African customs, traditions, and symbols with entertainment. The seventh and last day of Kwanzaa is also a time for opening GIFTS and thinking of ways to make the coming year better—not unlike the resolutions that other Americans make on **NEW YEAR'S DAY**.

Many African Americans wear African-style clothing during the Kwanzaa celebration. The women may wear a *buba* or loose-fitting gown, or a robe with a scarf at the waist called a *busuti*. Some women cover their hair with a *gele* or head wrap. Men may wear a shirt called a *dashiki*, or a long robe known as a *kanza*.

Kwanzaa shares many values and customs with the African harvest festivals from which it was derived. It is a time to strengthen the bonds among people, just as the harvest was an occasion to gather together and to give thanks to the Creator for a bountiful life. It is also a time for African Americans to honor their roots and heritage and to commemorate the struggles and survival of their people. Above all, it is a time to reassess their own lives and the lives of their communities and to recommit themselves to certain cultural ideals.

SYMBOLS AND CUSTOMS

Candle Holder (Kinara)

The kinara or seven-branched candle holder used in the celebration of Kwanzaa started out as a symbol of Nkulunkulu, the first ancestor and father of the African people. Nkulunkulu was referred to as the "corn stalk" that produced the "corn"—i.e., that went on to multiply as the African people. But now it has come to symbolize the African ancestors as a collective whole.

Corn (Muhindi)

As one of the fundamental foods grown in Africa, corn has always been central to African agriculture and society. The life cycle of corn is regarded as a symbol of the human life cycle. Along with the "stalk" or *kinara* (*see* CANDLE HOLDER), therefore, the corn used in Kwanzaa celebrations symbolizes the relationship between parents and children and between ancestors and their descendants.

Each family places as many ears of corn in the Kwanzaa display as there are children in the family. But even in households where there are no children, there is always at least one ear of corn. This is because in African society, parenthood is both biological and social. In other words, even individuals who are not personally responsible for children have a social responsibility for the children of the community. Kwanzaa is a time for reaffirming this responsibility.

Crops (Mazao)

The mazao is a bowl of fruits and vegetables that represents the harvest. Because it refers back to the roots of the celebration in African agricultural festivals, it is considered the most important of the symbols displayed on the Kwanzaa MAT or mkeka. It symbolizes the rewards of collective and productive labor.

Gifts (Zawadi)

When Kwanzaa was first established, there was some discussion over whether gift-giving should be a part of the celebration. There was a strong feeling that the kind of gift-giving associated with **CHRISTMAS**—which often involves spending money to impress or punish the receiver rather than to express love and bring pleasure—should be avoided. At the same time, it was recognized that gifts were symbolic of the fruits of labor, and that African gift-giving traditionally focused on items that were either made or grown.

In the end, it was decided that Kwanzaa gifts would be different. They would be instructive and inspirational and would be linked to the needs of the African people and their struggle. Rather than relying on a Santa Claus-like figure who promises things that parents cannot always deliver, Kwanzaa gift-giving would underscore the hard work and sacrifice involved in providing children with gifts. The presents would not be purchased until after Christmas was over, and they would be given only to children. To avoid the shopping frenzy and undisciplined spending associated with Christmas, the gifts would be equal in value to the children's achievements.

Kwanzaa gifts may be exchanged at any time, but they are usually opened on January 1, the last day of the celebration. Most are educational or inspirational items—for example, books by or about Africa or African Americans, tickets to African-American cultural events, or works by African-American artists. Favorite gifts include African games and toys, handmade clothes and accessories, and ethnic dolls. No gift should be purchased if it causes financial hardship for the giver, and the emphasis is on homemade rather than store-bought items.

Despite all the efforts that have been made to avoid the commercialization associated with **CHRISTMAS**, today Kwanzaa cards and wrapping paper are sold in the stores, along with specially manufactured Kwanzaa gifts such as teddy bears dressed in African costumes.

Mat (Mkeka)

The woven straw mat or mkeka on which all of the other Kwanzaa symbols are placed serves as a "foundation" for these items, just as tradition and history are the foundations necessary for self-knowledge and understanding of the African-American people. There is an old African proverb that says "No matter how high a house is built, it must stand on something." In a symbolic sense, the mkeka provides such a foundation.

Seven Candles (Mishumaa Saba)

Seven candles are placed in the *kinara* or candle holder: one black, three red, and three green—the colors of the national flag of the African-American people. The black candle is placed in the center of the kinara, while the red ones are placed on the left and the green ones on the right. Each day, a candle is lit to symbolize one of the SEVEN PRINCIPLES. The person who lights it then explains what it stands for, and this becomes the main topic of discussion for that day.

The black candle in the center represents the unity of the African-American people, which is the first of the Seven Principles. Beginning with the second day, candles are lit on the left and right alternately. Because red symbolizes struggle and green represents hope for the future, this method of lighting the candles underscores the message that there can be no future without a struggle. Each candle that has been lit before is relit along with the candle of the day, until all seven are burning on the last day of the festival.

The lighting of the seven candles is a daily ritual, similar to that of lighting the menorah during **HANUKKAH**, that symbolizes both the illumination of the SEVEN PRINCIPLES and the ancient African concept of "raising up light" to dispel the darkness in both a spiritual and intellectual sense.

Seven Principles (Nguzo Saba)

One of the reasons that Dr. Karenga created Kwanzaa was to introduce and reinforce what are known as the Seven Principles or *Nguzo Saba*, defined as the values needed to build and sustain the African-American family, community, and culture. These principles are: (1) Unity (*umoja*), (2) Self-determination (*kujichagulia*), (3) Collective work and responsibility (*ujima*), (4) Cooperative economics (*ujamma*), (5) Purpose (*nia*), (6) Creativity (*kuumba*), and (7) Faith (*imani*).

Each of the seven days of Kwanzaa is dedicated to one of the seven principles. Every evening during the festival, families gather together to discuss the principle to which that day has been dedicated and to light the candle (*see* SEVEN CANDLES) that symbolizes that principle. The Seven Principles are also described on a poster that is displayed during the celebration of Kwanzaa.

Unity Cup (Kikombe Cha Umoja)

The Unity Cup is part of the arrangement of symbolic objects displayed on the MAT or *mkeka* throughout the seven days of Kwanzaa. It serves two basic functions: (1) it is used to pour the *tambiko*, which is usually wine or grape juice accompanied by a "libation statement" or *tamshi la tambiko* in honor of the ancestors; and (2) it is passed around so that everyone can drink from it, a symbolic ritual designed to reinforce unity in the family and the African-American community. Pouring the *tambiko* and making a libation statement is a way of honoring the ancestors and reaffirming the link between them and their living African-American descendants.

After the cup has been passed around and is placed back on the table, the *kutoa majina* begins, which is the calling-out of the names of family ancestors. When the last name has been called, a drummer plays African-style rhythms, which is the signal for the start of the feast or *karamu*. The feast is followed by singing, dancing, and storytelling. The final evening of the celebration concludes with a Farewell Statement (*tamshi la tutaonana*) composed by Dr. Karenga. Then everyone shouts "Harambee!" seven times, and Kwanzaa is over.

FURTHER READING

Gay, Kathlyn. *African-American Holidays, Festivals, and Celebrations*. Detroit: Omni-graphics, 2007.

Gulevich, Tanya. *Encyclopedia of Christmas and New Year's Celebrations*. 2nd ed. Detroit: Omnigraphics, 2003.

Henderson, Helene, ed. *Holidays, Festivals, and Celebrations of the World Dictionary*. 3rd ed. Detroit: Omnigraphics, 2005.

Karenga, Maulana. *The African American Holiday of Kwanzaa*. Los Angeles: University of Sankore Press, 1988.

McClester, Cedric. *Kwanzaa: Everything You Always Wanted to Know but Didn't Know Where to Ask*. 30th anniversary edition. New York: Gumbs and Thomas, 1997.

Medearis, Angela S. *The Seven Days of Kwanzaa*. New York: Scholastic, 1994.

Santino, Jack. *All Around the Year: Holidays and Celebrations in American Life*. Urbana: University of Illinois Press, 1994.

Schmidt, Leigh Eric. *Consumer Rites: The Buying and Selling of American Holidays*. Princeton: Princeton University Press, 1995.

WEB SITE

Official Kwanzaa Web Site
www.officialkwanzaawebsite.org

Labor Day

Type of Holiday: National
Date of Observation: First Monday in September
Where Celebrated: United States and Canada
Symbols and Customs: Last Weekend in Summer, Parades and Rallies, Picnics,
  Political Speeches

ORIGINS

Labor Day is the only American holiday honoring the efforts of working people in building this country. It also commemorates the accomplishments of the labor movement in gaining decent wages and legal protections for workers. Both Americans and Canadians celebrate Labor Day on the first Monday in September.

Labor Day is a national holiday in the United States. National holidays can be defined as those commemorations that a nation's government has deemed important enough to warrant inclusion in the list of official public holidays. They tend to honor a person or event that has been critical in the development of the nation and its identity. Such people and events usually reflect values and traditions shared by a large portion of the citizenry.

The American Labor movement can be traced back to the founding of this country. The movement didn't become strong until the late nineteenth century, however, because until that time the U.S. was primarily an agricultural country. From 1860 to 1900, a remarkable change took place. The growth of American industry transformed this country from one where most people worked in agriculture to one where most people worked in mines and factories. As more people became factory

469

workers, the possibility of a strong, U.S. labor movement grew. Nevertheless, organizing proved difficult because workers had no protection from angry employers and desperately needed their meager wages. In those days, most factory employees worked ten to fourteen hours a day, six days a week. Wages were so low that not only did both parents work, but many families also had to send their children to work as well. There was no minimum wage, no laws against child labor, no sick leave, no vacations, no pension, no social security, and no protection against being fired without reason.

In the 1880s, an economic boom provided favorable conditions for labor leaders to demand shorter hours and higher wages. In 1882, leaders of New York's Central Labor Union decided to hold a parade and picnic on September 5. Some say the man who first proposed the idea was Peter J. McGuire, secretary of the Brotherhood of Carpenters and Joiners. More recent research suggests that it was Matthew McGuire, a machinist who served as secretary of the Central Labor Union in 1882. In any case, the event was a great success, even though the working people who participated lost a day's wages in order to attend the event. About 10,000 to 20,000 people marched in the parade, carrying the tools of their trade with them as symbols of their profession. The parade demonstrated to the public that workers could wield considerable power when they united to defend their interests. The picnic offered laborers an opportunity to relax, to form friendships with one another, and to listen to speeches by labor leaders. Musical entertainments and fireworks were also provided.

The parade and picnic in New York City served as a blueprint for similar events all over the country. Baltimore, Boston, Chicago, Detroit, Newark, and St. Paul all hosted Labor Day events in the 1880s. These events demonstrated the power of organized labor to both politicians and factory owners. They also publicized the plight of workers and inspired public sympathy for their cause. On February 21, 1887, Oregon became the first state to declare Labor Day a legal holiday. Colorado, Massachusetts, New Jersey, and New York followed suit later in that same year.

In some cities organizers scheduled Labor Day celebrations for May 1, in order to coincide with the **MAY DAY** rallies held by European labor leaders. Others stuck to the September date. By the end of the nineteenth century, however, American labor leaders had by and large decided to steer clear of any association with European communist, socialist, and anarchist labor leaders. May Day labor rallies disappeared and the September celebration established itself as Labor Day in the United States.

By 1894, twenty-three states had already made Labor Day into a legal holiday. In that same year, Congress declared Labor Day, the first Monday in September, to be a national holiday.

SYMBOLS AND CUSTOMS

Last Weekend in Summer

Although Labor Day has its roots in the labor movement, it has become a leisure-oriented holiday. For many Americans, Labor Day weekend symbolizes the last weekend in summer. Technically this isn't true, since fall begins on the **AUTUMN EQUINOX**. Nevertheless, in many parts of the U.S. the weather starts to cool down in early September, the days grow noticeably shorter, and children return to school after the summer break. For these reasons, many people treat Labor Day as the last weekend of summer and accordingly plan to picnic outside, go to the beach, or take a final summer vacation. Many stores hold Labor Day Weekend sales featuring discounted summer merchandise. Schools and colleges often wait until after Labor Day to begin their fall term. Some segments of the population suggest that Labor Day is the last day of the year on which fashion-conscious people wear white shoes and clothing (the first days being **MEMORIAL DAY** weekend). White shoes and clothing are associated with the heat of summer.

Parades and Rallies

In the early decades of the holiday's history, parades and rallies organized by labor unions often served as the main feature of civic Labor Day observances. In large cities tens of thousands of workers marched in these parades. They helped reinforce the values and aims of the union and kept members feeling united with one another. Indeed, in the first half of the twentieth century a strong American labor movement influenced politicians to pass laws that established a minimum wage, created a social security program to benefit people too old to work, eliminated child labor, and much more. By the 1960s organized labor had created working conditions that Americans living in the 1880s, when Labor Day first got its start, could scarcely dream of.

In the second half of the twentieth century, even as the labor movement achieved its goals, it began to lose strength and membership. Labor Day parades and rallies began to occur more sporadically and eventually died out in some places. Though parades are becoming rarer, some labor organizations still host picnics that include pro-labor speeches.

Picnics

Many Americans enjoy hosting or attending picnics with family and friends on Labor Day. Barbecued meats are often served, especially such typically American fare as hot dogs and hamburgers. The fruits and vegetables of summer, such as watermelon, tomatoes, green beans, summer squash, and corn, often play a starring role in the meal as well. Cold drinks and cold desserts, such as ice cream, usually round out the celebration.

Many political groups and labor organizations combine fun and politics by hosting large picnics at which speeches will be made. This tradition dates back to the founding of the holiday.

Political Speeches

Political candidates sometimes wait until Labor Day to make the first big speech of their campaign. Thus the day often serves as the start of the campaign trail, with two months of intense political activity ahead until the November elections. Some politicians try to make their speeches at large Labor Day picnics, where many of their supporters are likely to be gathered.

FURTHER READING

Henderson, Helene. *Patriotic Holidays of the United States: An Introduction to the History, Symbols, and Traditions Behind the Major Holidays and Days of Observance.* Detroit: Omnigraphics, 2006.

Henderson, Helene, ed. *Holidays, Festivals, and Celebrations of the World Dictionary.* 3rd ed. Detroit: Omnigraphics, 2005.

WEB SITES

History Now, American History Online
www.historynow.org/06_2005/historian4.html

Library of Congress Local Legacies
lcweb2.loc.gov/cocoon/legacies/MN/200003181.html

U.S. Department of Labor
www.dol/gov/opa/aboutdol/laborday.htm

Lag Ba-Omer

Type of Holiday: Religious (Jewish)
Date of Observation: Eighteenth day of the Jewish lunar month of Iyar (usually falls in May), or the thirty-third of the fifty days separating Passover and Shavuot
Where Celebrated: United States, Israel, and by Jews throughout the world
Symbols and Customs: Bonfires, Bow and Arrow
Related Holidays: Passover, Shavuot

ORIGINS

Lag Ba-Omer is one of the traditions of Judaism, one of the oldest continuously observed religions in the world. Its history extends back beyond the advent of the written word. Its people trace their roots to a common ancestor, Abraham, and then back even farther to the very moment of creation.

According to Jewish belief, the law given to the Jewish people by God contained everything they needed to live a holy life, including the ability to be reinterpreted in new historical situations. Judaism, therefore, is the expression of the Jewish people, attempting to live holy (set apart) lives in accordance with the instructions given by God.

Although obedience to the law is central to Judaism, there is no one central authority. Sources of divine authority are God, the Torah, interpretations of the Torah by respected teachers, and tradition. Religious observances and the study of Jewish law are conducted under the supervision of a teacher called a rabbi.

There are several sects within Judaism. Orthodox Judaism is characterized by an affirmation of the traditional Jewish faith, strict adherence to customs such as keeping the Sabbath, participation in ceremonies and rituals, and the observance of dietary regulations. Conservative Jewish congregations seek to retain many ancient traditions but without the accompanying demand for strict observance. Reform Judaism stresses modern biblical criticism and emphasizes ethical teachings more than ritualistic observance. Hasidism is a mystical sect of Judaism that teaches enthusiastic prayer as a means of communion with God. The Reconstructionist movement began early in the twentieth century in an effort to "reconstruct" Judaism with the community rather than the synagogue as its center.

The name of this Jewish holiday, Lag Ba-Omer, means "thirty-three omer," *omer* being the Hebrew word for a sheaf of barley or wheat. According to the book of

473

Leviticus, God told the Jews to make an offering of a sheaf of barley on each of the fifty days between **PASSOVER** and **SHAVUOT**. After the evening service, the number of the day was solemnly announced, and this ceremony was known as "the counting of the omer." When the fifty days were over, it was time to celebrate the harvest and to bring to the Temple two loaves of bread made from the new wheat.

Why the thirty-third day of this period was singled out may have something to do with an ancient pagan festival that was celebrated around the same time of year. The Romans believed that it was unlucky to marry in May before the harvest because this was the season when the souls of the dead came back to earth to haunt the living, and they could only be appeased by funerals, not weddings. This unlucky period lasted thirty-two days and ended with a festival on the thirty-third day, which was an occasion for celebration because the prohibition on joyful events had been lifted.

Why the seven weeks between **PASSOVER** and the harvest came to be regarded as a period of semi-mourning for the Jews is not entirely clear. No doubt the character of this period changed after the destruction of the second Temple, when people realized they could no longer bring the season's first barley and the two loaves of bread there as offerings. It was also natural for farmers to feel some anxiety at this time of year, when the success or failure of the crops depended on the weather and other factors beyond their control. The thirty-third day may have been intended as a much-needed break from the otherwise anxious and somber *omer* period.

There are other theories about the origins of this holiday as well. One is that it was the anniversary of the day when Bar Kochva and his Jewish warriors temporarily captured Jerusalem from the Romans in their fight to reestablish the Jewish nation. Another is that it marked the end of the epidemic that killed 24,000 students of the famous Rabbi Akiva during the first century. Still another links the holiday to the anniversary of the death of Rabbi Bar Yohai, a great Hebrew scholar who refused to obey the Romans when they forbade him to teach or to study the Torah.

Like the Christian **LENT**, the *omer* days are associated with certain restrictions. It is forbidden to get married, to shave or cut hair, to wear new clothes, to listen to music, or to attend any kind of public entertainment during the seven weeks. Whether this is because it was originally a period of mourning for certain historical events or because the weeks preceding the harvest were regarded as a time of "suspended animation," the fact remains that these prohibitions are lifted for a twenty-four-hour period on the thirty-third day. It is a popular day for Jewish weddings, for concerts and musical events, for wearing new clothes, and for lighting BONFIRES. In many American cities, Lag Ba-Omer is observed as Jewish Book

Day or Scholars' Day in memory of Rabbi Akiva, Bar Yohai, and other scholars who upheld the right of Jews to follow the dictates of their religion and culture. Jewish books are exhibited in public libraries, and lectures on Jewish literature are held. At Meron, the burial place of Bar Yohai, Hasidic Jews from all over Israel and neighboring countries gather in his honor.

For children, particularly in Israel, Lag Ba-Omer is a day for outings and picnics. Armed with BOWS AND ARROWS, they go with their teachers out in the woods, where a picnic lunch is followed by archery contests. Hebrew schools usually arrange their annual outings to coincide with this holiday. Pageants and plays depicting the historical events associated with the eighteenth day of Iyar are also popular.

Lag Ba-Omer is not regarded as a sacred holiday, nor is it distinguished by any special service or prayer in the synagogue.

SYMBOLS AND CUSTOMS

Bonfires

According to legend, the war hero Bar Kochva and his men lit fires in Jerusalem as a way of signaling villages far away that they had captured the city from the powerful Roman army. These villages, in turn, lit more fires—until the whole country knew about the victory. To commemorate this event, children throughout Israel start gathering scraps of wood, dry branches, rags, and other burnable items a few days before Lag Ba-Omer. They light huge bonfires on every empty lot they can find, sing songs, dance around the fire, and eat potatoes that have been baked in the hot embers.

Another Lag Ba-Omer custom associated with bonfires dates back to the sixteenth century. Orthodox Jewish parents bring their three-year-old boys to Meron, the village in Galilee where Rabbi Bar Yohai, the father of Jewish mysticism, and his son are buried. There a rabbi or other Jewish dignitary gives the young boys their first haircut, and the locks of hair are thrown into a bonfire. As a result of the Meron celebration, this custom has spread throughout Israel.

It has long been traditional in many parts of the world to light bonfires at the end of April or the beginning of May to scare off witches and demons. In ancient Rome, fires were lit at the **PARILIA** on April 21; in England, fires are still kindled at crossroads on **ST. GEORGE'S DAY**, April 23. The ancient Celtic festival of **BELTANE** (May 1) was also marked with bonfires, a custom that still survives in the Scottish Highlands and parts of Ireland. In fact, this Jewish holiday has much in common with the European **MAY DAY**, which would appear to support the theory that it originated as a rustic festival linked to the harvest.

Bow and Arrow

The Israeli custom of sending children out in the woods on Lag Ba-Omer to shoot with bows and arrows has its roots in both legend and folklore. In Germany, April 30 was **WALPURGIS NIGHT**, a time when demons and evil spirits were believed to roam the earth. It was common at one time to shoot arrows at these troublesome spirits, and in Germany, it is still common for rural people to go out in the woods and shoot arrows on the morning of May 1. In England, it is a popular day for archery contests—the bow and arrow being associated with Robin Hood, who is derived from the chief of the goblins and mischievous spirits, Robin o' the Wood. It is interesting to note that Israeli children take their bows and arrows to the cemetery as well as the forest. This might represent another link with ancient **MAY DAY** customs (*see* BONFIRES), which often included dances and gatherings in graveyards.

There are other explanations for the custom in Israel. After the destruction of the Temple in Jerusalem by Titus, the Roman general, Rabbi Akiva decided that the best way to get rid of the Roman conquerors was to teach his students how to fight. To avoid arousing suspicion, they dressed up as hunters with bows and arrows and went out in the woods to practice.

Another tradition links the bow and arrow to Rabbi Bar Yohai. Because he refused to obey the Roman decree against the study of the Torah and continued to teach his students, his life was perpetually in danger. He finally escaped to a cave in the mountains of Galilee, where he lived for 13 years by eating the fruit of the carob tree and drinking from a nearby spring. His students visited him each year on Lag Ba-Omer, disguising themselves as hunters by carrying bows and arrows.

FURTHER READING

Bellenir, Karen. *Religious Holidays and Calendars*. 3rd ed. Detroit: Omnigraphics, 2004.

Edidin, Ben. *Jewish Holidays and Festivals*. 1940. Reprint. Detroit: Omnigraphics, 1993.

Gaer, Joseph. *Holidays Around the World*. Boston: Little, Brown, 1953.

Gaster, Theodor H. *Festivals of the Jewish Year*. New York: William Sloane Associates, 1953.

Henderson, Helene, ed. *Holidays, Festivals, and Celebrations of the World Dictionary*. 3rd ed. Detroit: Omnigraphics, 2005.

Renberg, Dalia Hardof. *The Complete Family Guide to Jewish Holidays*. New York: Adama Books, 1985.

WEB SITES

Chabad-Lubavitch Media Center
www.chabad.org/library/article.asp?AID=42944

Judaica Guide
www.judaica-guide.com/lag_ba'omer

Lammas

Type of Holiday: Calendar/Seasonal
Date of Observation: August 1
Where Celebrated: British Isles
Symbols and Customs: Loaf of Bread
Related Holidays: Candlemas, Harvest Home Festival, Martinmas, Pentecost, Shavuot, Thanksgiving

ORIGINS

Originally called the Gule of August, Lammas was a celebration of the grain harvest and one of the four great pagan festivals of Britain. When Christianity was introduced, the day continued to be celebrated, and a LOAF OF BREAD made from the newly harvested grain was the usual offering at church. For this reason it was called *Hlaf-mass* (loaf mass), subsequently shortened to Lammas. Another theory about the name's origin is that it came from **LUGHNASA**, the ancient autumn festival in honor of Lugh, the Celtic sun god. Yet another explanation, although based on a custom apparently confined to the cathedral at York, is that it was called Lammas because it was traditional to bring a lamb to church as an offering on this day.

Lammas marked the changing of the seasons, which people in all parts of the world have honored since ancient times. Some cultures divided the year into two seasons, summer and winter, and marked these points of the year at or near the summer and winter solstices, during which light and warmth began to increase and decrease, respectively. In pre-industrial times, humans survived through hunting, gathering, and agricultural practices, which depend on the natural cycle of seasons, according to the climate in the region of the world in which they lived. Thus, they created rituals to help ensure enough rain and sun in the spring and summer so crops would grow to fruition at harvest time, which was, in turn, duly celebrated. Vestiges of many of these ancient practices are thought to have survived in festivals still celebrated around seasonal themes.

Although it is no longer observed, Lammas is important as an ancestor of other special days that are still celebrated. It was the forerunner of England's and Canada's modern Harvest Festival (*see* **HARVEST HOME FESTIVAL**) and of America's **THANKSGIVING.** Nowadays, harvest festivals tend to be observed later in the year, usually between September and November, when all of the autumn crops are in instead of just the early ones, like grain.

Up until the mid-eighteenth century, young herdsmen would band together in different companies and build towers out of stones or sod. On Lammas morning, the bands would assemble, waving flags and blowing horns, and set out to tear down one another's sod towers. Each carried a club or a cudgel, and victory was seldom gained without bloodshed. The day's activities usually ended with footraces.

In Scotland, Lammas was also one of the four cross-quarter days (along with **CANDLEMAS,** Whitsunday [*see* **PENTECOST**], and **MARTINMAS**) when tenants paid their rents—originally in the form of newly harvested grain—to their landlords. The phrase "at the Latter Lammas" meant "never" or "not in this lifetime." Tenants would often say, "I will pay him at the Latter Lammas," by which they meant, "I'll pay him when I get good and ready." In the Highlands, people sprinkled their cows and the floors of their houses with menstrual blood, which was believed to be especially potent against evil on May 1 and August 1.

SYMBOLS AND CUSTOMS

Loaf of Bread

As a symbol of the harvest and therefore of God's bounty, the loaf of bread has always played a part in the celebration of Lammas. It was made from grain that had just been harvested and brought to the church as an offering. Scholars believe that Lammas was closely related to the Jewish **SHAVUOT** or Feast of Weeks, which also came at the end of the grain harvest and entailed offering two loaves of bread at the Temple in Jerusalem.

FURTHER READING

Bellenir, Karen. *Religious Holidays and Calendars*. 3rd ed. Detroit: Omnigraphics, 2004.

Brewster, H. Pomeroy. *Saints and Festivals of the Christian Church*. 1904. Reprint. Detroit: Omnigraphics, 1990.

Chambers, Robert. *The Book of Days*. 2 vols. 1862-64. Reprint. Detroit: Omnigraphics, 1990.

Dunkling, Leslie. *A Dictionary of Days*. New York: Facts on File, 1988.

Harper, Howard V. *Days and Customs of All Faiths*. 1957. Reprint. Detroit: Omnigraphics, 1990.

Henderson, Helene, ed. *Holidays, Festivals, and Celebrations of the World Dictionary.* 3rd ed. Detroit: Omnigraphics, 2005.

Leach, Maria, ed. *Funk & Wagnalls Standard Dictionary of Folklore, Mythology & Legend.* San Francisco: Harper & Row, 1984.

MacDonald, Margaret R., ed. *The Folklore of World Holidays.* Detroit: Gale Research, 1992.

Urlin, Ethel L. *Festivals, Holy Days, and Saints' Days.* 1915. Reprint. Detroit: Omnigraphics, 1992.

WEB SITE

Eastborne Lamas Festival
www.lammasfest.org

Lantern Festival
(Teng Chieh, Feast of the First Full Moon)

Type of Holiday: Folkloric, Calendar/Seasonal
Date of Observation: Usually February; fifteenth through the eighteenth day of the first Chinese lunar month
Where Celebrated: China, Japan, Malaysia, Taiwan, Tibet
Symbols and Customs: Dragon Parade, Lantern Riddles, Lanterns, Lion Dance, Rice Flour Dumplings (Yuanxiao)
Related Holidays: Chinese New Year

ORIGINS

The Lantern Festival is believed to have originated with the emperors of China's Han Dynasty (206 B.C.E. to 221 C.E.), who paid tribute to the First Cause or origins of the universe on this night. Because the ceremony was held in the evening, LANTERNS were used to light the palace. Normally the Han rulers imposed a curfew on their subjects; but on this night, the curfew was lifted so that everyone could see the illuminated palace.

Today, whatever cosmic or religious significance the festival may originally have had is lost. The three-day Lantern Festival marks the end of the **CHINESE NEW YEAR** celebration and is primarily an occasion for hanging out lanterns, eating RICE FLOUR DUMPLINGS, and solving LANTERN RIDDLES. Merchants hang paper lanterns outside their shops for several days before the full-moon day, and homeowners hang them from their porches and in their gardens. On the night of the festival, people throng the streets to see the lantern displays. The most popular lanterns are cutouts of running horses that revolve with the heat of the candles that burn under them. In Taipei, Taiwan's capital city, high-tech lanterns with mechanical animation, dry-ice "smoke," and laser beams take the form of fire-spewing dragons and other fantastic creatures. In Hong Kong, it is traditional for any man who has had a son born during the year to bring a lantern to the Ancestral Hall, where the fathers gather for a meal. There are processions of clowns, stilt-walkers, and actors in costume, and the popular LION DANCE is performed in the streets.

The timing of the Lantern Festival derives from the Chinese lunisolar calendar, the oldest system of time measurement still in use. It is widely employed in Asian countries to set the dates of seasonal festivals. The **Chinese New Year** takes place on the new moon nearest to the point which is defined in the West as the fifteenth degree on the zodiacal sign of Aquarius. Each of twelve months in the Chinese year is twenty-nine or thirty days long and is divided into two parts, each of which is two weeks long. The Chinese calendar, like all lunisolar systems, requires periodic adjustment to keep the lunar and solar cycles integrated; therefore, an intercalary month is added when necessary.

The names of each of the twenty-four two-week periods sometimes correspond to seasonal festivals celebrated during the period. Beginning with the New Year, which takes place in late January or early February, these periods are known by the following names: Spring Begins (New Year and **LI CH'UN**), the Rain Water, the Excited Insects, the **VERNAL EQUINOX**, the Clear and Bright (**CHING MING**), the Grain Rains, the Summer Begins, the Grain Fills, the Grain in Ear, the **SUMMER SOLSTICE** (**DOUBLE FIFTH**), the Slight Heat, the Great Heat, the Autumn Begins, the Limit of Heat, the White Dew (**MID-AUTUMN FESTIVAL**), the **AUTUMN EQUINOX**, the Cold Dew, the Hoar Frost Descends, the Winter Begins, the Little Snow, the Heavy Snow, the **WINTER SOLSTICE,** the Little Cold, and the Great Cold.

SYMBOLS AND CUSTOMS

Dragon Parade

The dragon is a mythical creature symbolic of vigor, fertility, and spring rain. It has been described as having the head of a camel, the horns of a deer, the eyes of a rabbit, the ears of a cow, the neck of a serpent, the scales of a fish, and the talons of a hawk. On the last day of the Lantern Festival, a huge dragon made of bamboo rods and satin cloth in sections three to four feet long and traditionally illuminated by candles is carried through the streets by dozens of men and boys. Strings of firecrackers are set off wherever the dragon parade goes.

The Golden Dragon Parade in San Francisco, where there is a large Chinese population, has been an annual event since 1953. The dragon is 160 feet long and is accompanied by floats, marching bands, dance troupes, bell-and-drum corps, and various carnival-like characters. The San Francisco parade is considered the largest event of its kind in the world.

Lantern Riddles

The fifteenth day of the first month is also associated with a literary game that was popular at one time among elderly, educated people. Known as *Cai Deng Mi* or "Guessing the Lantern's Riddle," it consisted of writing riddles on slips of paper and pasting them lightly on LANTERNS hung either inside or outside the house. There might be hints in the form of objects hung from the lanterns with a written clue—a Chinese character, a line of verse, someone's name, etc.—pointing to the correct answer. Anyone who guessed the correct answer was rewarded on the spot.

Although lantern riddles are not as popular anymore, crossword puzzle lanterns with riddles pasted on their sides are still hung outside scholars' homes for the amusement of their literary friends.

Lanterns

The lanterns for which this festival is named probably date back to an ancient ceremony welcoming spring. The lantern, a source of light, was symbolic of the lengthening days of spring, and willow branches were used to symbolize spring rains. Another explanation is that evil spirits were believed to roam the earth on this night, and lanterns were used to scare them off. According to legend, a Ming Dynasty emperor ordered 10,000 lanterns to be set afloat on the lake at Nanking, and the sight was so beautiful that Buddha himself came down from Heaven to see it.

In rural areas of China, people hang lanterns at crossroads, near wells, and by marshes and rivers—places where the spirits of those who have died before their time and are therefore doomed to wander the earth are most likely to be found—in the hope that the light will lead these spirits to judgment and reincarnation. In the industrial city of Harbin in northeast China, fantastic lanterns have been carved from huge blocks of river ice for centuries. Now they are illuminated with colored electric lights and left standing until spring comes and the ice melts.

Chinese children make or buy lanterns in all shapes and put candles inside. The most popular shapes are those of whatever animal is the patron protector of that particular Chinese year—the rabbit, the tiger, the rat, the monkey, the horse, etc. Older children may take sticks of bamboo and stuff the hollow center with paper and oil-soaked rags to form a torch that will burn for several hours. Couples without children may purchase lanterns in the shape of little boys, and extra lanterns are often hung outside the house to indicate a desire for more children.

Lion Dance

Songs, dances, plays, and variety acts are performed throughout the Lantern Festival, but the Lion Dance is perhaps the most popular entertainment. Two men are concealed inside a huge papier-maché lion. One operates the moving jaws and lolling tongue of the head, which is decorated with bells. The other manipulates the lion's hindquarters. Accompanied by drums and gongs, the lion dances through the streets, crouching and leaping or bowing and hunching its back. Sometimes a "lion tamer" teases the lion. In some areas, the lion chases after a "pearl" or ball.

The Lion Dance reached its peak during the Tang dynasty (618-907 C.E.), when it featured five lions more than nine feet tall dressed in different colors. With wooden heads, silk tails, gilded eyes, and silver-plated teeth, the lions performed the Dance of the Five Directions while "lion boys" teased them with red whisks.

Because the lion is not indigenous to China, it took on a mythical aura. Sometimes lions were brought from Persia to the emperor as a form of tribute. They were highly valued and became symbolically associated with purity and protection.

Rice Flour Dumplings (Yuanxiao)

Sweet-tasting glutinous rice flour balls known as *yuanxiao* are traditionally served during the Lantern Festival. They are symbolic of the first full moon of the year and, because of their perfectly round shape, of the family as well. They may be filled with hawthorn, black bean, date, or sesame paste; in the southern part of China, pork, chicken, and vegetable fillings are popular. They are cooked just long enough to make the outer skin slippery.

How did the rice flour dumplings get their name? According to legend, the Lantern Festival originated because a young woman living in the emperor's household by the name of Yuan Xiao longed to see her parents. To help her out, a resourceful friend named Dongfang Shuo spread a rumor that the god of fire was going to burn down the city of Chang-an. The ensuing panic was widespread, and when he was summoned by the emperor, Dongfang Shuo advised him to have everyone leave the palace and hang LANTERNS on every streetcorner and building. This would make the fire god think that the city was already burning. The emperor followed his advice, and Yuan Xiao was able to go off and see her family.

In the north, it is customary to make the rice flour dumplings on the seventh day of the New Year and sell them on the eighth. They are served in restaurants throughout the three days of the Lantern Festival.

FURTHER READING

Bredon, Juliet, and Igor Mitrophanow. *The Moon Year: A Record of Chinese Customs and Festivals*. Shanghai: Kelly & Walsh, 1927.

Gaer, Joseph. *Holidays Around the World*. Boston: Little, Brown, 1953.

Henderson, Helene, ed. *Holidays, Festivals, and Celebrations of the World Dictionary*. 3rd ed. Detroit: Omnigraphics, 2005.

Ickis, Marguerite. *The Book of Festivals and Holidays the World Over*. New York: Dodd, Mead, 1970.

MacDonald, Margaret R., ed. *The Folklore of World Holidays*. Detroit: Gale Research, 1992.

Stepanchuk, Carol, and Charles Wong. *Mooncakes and Hungry Ghosts: Festivals of China*. San Francisco: China Books & Periodicals, 1991.

Van Straalen, Alice. *The Book of Holidays Around the World*. New York: Dutton, 1986.

WEB SITES

Chinese Culture Center of San Francisco
www.c-c-c.org/chineseculture/festival/lantern/lantern.html

Hong Kong Tourism Board
www.discoverhongkong.com/eng/heritage/festivals/he_fest_spri.jhtml

Laylat al-Bara'ah
(Shab-i-Barat, Fifteenth of Shaban, Night of Forgiveness, Night of Deliverance, Night of Record, Night of Destiny, Night of Fate, Birthday of the Twelfth Imam)

Type of Holiday: Religious (Muslim)

Date of Observation: Fifteenth Day of Shaban, the eighth month of the Muslim calendar

Where Celebrated: Bangladesh, India, Indonesia, Pakistan, and the Muslim countries of the Middle East and North Africa

Symbols and Customs: Charity, Fasting, Fireworks, Prayer Vigils, Qur'an Reading, Sweets, Tree of Life

Related Holidays: Ramadan

ORIGINS

Laylat al-Bara'ah is a holiday in the religious tradition of Islam, one of the world's largest religions. According to some estimates, there are more than one billion Muslims worldwide, with major populations found in the Middle East, North and sub-Saharan Africa, Turkey, Central Asia, and Southeast Asia. In Europe and the United States, Islam is the second largest religious group, with some seven million adherents in the United States. During the early years of Islam, the faith spread throughout the Arabian Peninsula into regions that are today occupied by Saudi Arabia, Syria, Iraq, and Jordan. Contrary to popular opinion, however, Muslims are not just Arabs. Muslims—followers of Islam—are found in many different ethnic groups all over the globe. In fact, Arabs make up less than twenty percent of Muslims.

The word Islam is an Arabic word that means "surrender to God." Its other meanings include peace, safety, and health. The central focus of Islam is a personal commitment and surrender to Allah, the Arabic word for God. In Islam, the concept of Allah is universal and eternal. Allah is the same in every religion and throughout the history of humankind. A person who follows Islam is called a Muslim, which means one who surrenders or submits to Allah's will. But Islam is not just a religion of belief; it is a religion of action. Five specific deeds are required of followers; these are called *The Five Pillars of Islam*. They are 1) *Shahadah*—confession of faith; 2) *Salat*—prayer/worship; 3) *Zakat*—charity; 4) *Sawm*—fasting; and 5) *Hajj*—pilgrimage.

The message of Islam was brought by Muhammad (570-632 C.E.), who is considered a prophet of Allah. The holy book of Islam is the *Qur'an* (also sometimes spelled *Koran* or *Alcoran*). According to Islamic belief, the Qur'an was revealed to Muhammad by Allah over a period of twenty-three years. Authorship of the Qur'an is attributed to Allah, and not to Muhammad; Muhammad merely received it. Muslims believe that because it originated with Allah, the Qur'an is infallible.

There are two main sects within Islam: Sunni and Shi'ite. Sunni Muslims are the majority (estimated at about eighty percent). They recognize the authority of the first four Caliphs, including Ali, and they believe that the Sunna (the example of the Prophet Muhammad) is interpreted through the consensus of the community. Shi'ite Muslims also look to special teachers, called imams. The imams are the direct descendants of Muhammad through Fatimah and Ali. These individuals are believed to be inspired and to possess secret knowledge. Shi'ites, however, do not recognize the same line of Islamic leaders acknowledged by the Sunnis. Shi'ites hold to a doctrine that accepts only leaders who are descended from Muhammad through his daughter Fatimah and her husband Ali. Many Shi'ite subsects believe that true imams are errorless and sinless. They receive instruction from these leaders rather than relying on the consensus of the community.

The origins of Laylat al-Bara'ah can be traced back to the founding of Islam. Contemporaries of the Prophet Muhammad report that he taught his followers that the fifteenth of Shaban was a holy day. Muhammad told them, "When the middle night of Shaban comes, spend the night in prayer and fast during the day, for in it God most high comes down at sunset to the lowest heaven and says, 'Is there no one who asks forgiveness so that I may forgive him? Is there no one afflicted so that I may relieve him." The belief that God is especially inclined to be merciful on this night led to the name "Laylat al-Bara'ah," which means "Night of Forgiveness" in Arabic.

Other beliefs surrounding Laylat al-Bara'ah include the notion that God determines one's fate for the year to come on this day. It is said that God completes the list of those who will be born, die, complete the Hajj pilgrimage, and experience other important milestones in the coming year on Laylat al-Bara'ah. In south Asia, the holiday is called "Shab-i-Barat," which means "Night of Destiny" or "Night of Fate." This name reflects the belief that God shapes one's destiny on this day.

Shia Muslims celebrate the Birthday of the Twelfth Imam on the fifteenth of Shaban. In Sunni Islam an imam is a prayer leader. Shia Muslims also use the word to refer to one of the early Muslim religious leaders, men who were also direct descendants of the Prophet. The Twelfth and last Imam, named Muhammad, was born in 869. He disappeared at the age of four, and no one knows what became of him. It is said among the Shias that he will reappear on earth at the end of time, when he will become known as the Mahdi, or the "Guided One."

SYMBOLS AND CUSTOMS

Charity

Islam strongly encourages Muslims to give to those less fortunate than themselves. The Qur'an assures Muslims many times over that this merciful act is sure to find favor with God. Some Muslims honor Laylat al-Bara'ah by giving to charity. They hope that God will reward them with blessings in the year to come for such an honorable deed.

Fasting

Muslims practice fasting in order to remind themselves of the plight of the poor and to develop spiritual strength. Muhammad himself recommended fasting during the month of Shaban. He believed that the practice honored God and felt that it boded well to fast during the month in which God took account of one's deeds on earth. As **RAMADAN**, the month of fasting, comes just two weeks after Laylat al-Bara'ah, Muhammad never fasted past the fifteenth of Shaban. Today very devout Muslims still fast during the daylight hours of Laylat al-Bara'ah.

Fireworks

Laylat al-Bara'ah is an especially important holiday for Muslims in India, Bangladesh, and Pakistan. Many towns in this region honor the holiday with fireworks displays. Children often create their own dazzling displays by setting off firecrackers.

Prayer Vigils

The most important customs associated with this holiday take place at night. Many Muslims attend religious gatherings in mosques on this evening. Some mosques also hold lectures and other educational events. It is customary to stay up late into the night, listening to recitations from the Qur'an and praying. The especially devout stay up all night, praying for the forgiveness of their sins and asking for blessings in the year ahead.

Qur'an Reading

The holy book of Islam is called the Qur'an. Islamic tradition links Chapter 36 of the Qur'an with Laylat al-Bara'ah. Titled "Ya Sin," this chapter addresses the themes of death and judgment. In it, God warns humans that they will be held accountable for their actions and attitudes. Many Muslims honor Laylat al-Bara'ah by reading this chapter. In verses eleven and twelve, God warns humanity that a record is kept of everyone's deeds, but that the heavens are merciful to those who follow the way of life taught by God (the Compassionate One) and passed down to humanity through the Prophet Muhammad:

> You can only warn those
> Who follow the Reminder
> And fear the Compassionate One is secret:
> Give them news of forgiveness
> And a generous, noble reward.
> For We give life to the dead,
> And We record what they sent before
> And what they left after them:
> And We have taken account of all things in a clear
> book of examples (Qur'an 36:11-12, Cleary trans.)

Both the record keeping and the mercy and blessings bestowed on the devout are especially associated with Laylat al-Bara'ah.

Sweets

Many Muslims enjoy special sweets on the evening of the fifteenth of Shaban, made all the tastier by the knowledge that the month of fasting lies just around the corner. In India and Pakistan, carrot halvah is a favorite dish associated with the holiday. This confection is made by simmering together shredded carrots, milk, and cream. After the liquid boils down, sugar, cardamom, ground almonds, and butter are added. The mixture is cooked a bit more, then cooled and served.

Tree of Life

According to Sunni Muslim folklore, God shakes the Tree of Life on the fifteenth of Shaban. This mythological tree is said to exist in heaven. It has numerous counterparts in other religions and mythologies, in which it is sometimes called the World Tree. According to Muslim folk belief, each leaf on this tree represents a living human being. When God shakes the tree, the leaves that fall from it indicate those who are destined to die in the coming year. Tradition holds that Israfil, the angel of death, collects the fallen leaves and escorts these souls to the afterlife in the year ahead.

FURTHER READING

Bellenir, Karen. *Religious Holidays and Calendars*. 3rd ed. Detroit: Omnigraphics, 2004.

Biedermann, Hans. *Dictionary of Symbolism: Cultural Icons and the Meanings Behind Them*. Translated by James Hulbert. New York: Meridian Books, 1994.

Cleary, Thomas, trans.. *The Essential Koran: The Heart of Islam*. San Francisco: Harper, 1994.

Gulevich, Tanya. *Understanding Islam and Muslim Traditions*. Detroit: Omnigraphics, 2004.

Renard, John. *Seven Doors to Islam: Spirituality and the Religious Life of Muslims*. Berkeley: University of California Press, 1996.

Sakr, Ahmad. *Feasts, Festivities, and Holidays*. Lombard, IL: Foundation for Islamic Knowledge, 1999.

Laylat al-Miraj
(The Ascent, The Night Journey)

Type of Holiday: Religious (Muslim)
Date of Observation: Twenty-seventh day of the seventh Islamic lunar month of Rajab
Where Celebrated: Africa, Egypt, India, Indonesia, Iran, Iraq, Jordan, Lebanon, Morocco, Pakistan, Saudi Arabia, Syria, Thailand, Turkey, and throughout the Muslim world
Symbols and Customs: Dome of the Rock, Seven Heavens
Related Holidays: Laylat al-Qadr, Mawlid al-Nabi

ORIGINS

Laylat al-Miraj is a holiday in the tradition of Islam, one of the world's largest religions. According to some estimates, there are more than one billion Muslims worldwide, with major populations found in the Middle East, North and sub-Saharan Africa, Turkey, Central Asia, and Southeast Asia. In Europe and the United States, Islam is the second largest religious group, with some seven million adherents in the United States. During the early years of Islam, the faith spread throughout the Arabian Peninsula into regions that are today occupied by Saudi Arabia, Syria, Iraq, and Jordan. Contrary to popular opinion, however, Muslims are not just Arabs. Muslims—followers of Islam—are found in many different ethnic groups all over the globe. In fact, Arabs make up less than twenty percent of Muslims.

The word Islam is an Arabic word that means "surrender to God." Its other meanings include peace, safety, and health. The central focus of Islam is a personal commitment and surrender to Allah, the Arabic word for God. In Islam, the concept of Allah is universal and eternal. Allah is the same in every religion and throughout the history of humankind. A person who follows Islam is called a Muslim, which means one who surrenders or submits to Allah's will. But Islam is not just a religion of belief; it is a religion of action. Five specific deeds are required of followers; these are called *The Five Pillars of Islam*. They are 1) *Shahadah*—confession of faith; 2) *Salat*—prayer/worship; 3) *Zakat*—charity; 4) *Sawm*—fasting; and 5) *Hajj*—pilgrimage.

The message of Islam was brought by Muhammad (570-632 C.E.), who is considered a prophet of Allah. The holy book of Islam is the *Qur'an* (also sometimes spelled *Koran* or *Alcoran*). According to Islamic belief, the Qur'an was revealed to Muhammad by Allah over a period of twenty-three years. Authorship of the Qur'an is attributed to Allah, and not to Muhammad; Muhammad merely received it. Muslims believe that because it originated with Allah, the Qur'an is infallible.

There are two main sects within Islam: Sunni and Shi'ite. Sunni Muslims are the majority (estimated at about eighty percent). They recognize the authority of the first four Caliphs, including Ali, and they believe that the Sunna (the example of the Prophet Muhammad) is interpreted through the consensus of the community. Shi'ite Muslims also look to special teachers, called imams. The imams are the direct descendants of Muhammad through Fatimah and Ali. These individuals are believed to be inspired and to possess secret knowledge. Shi'ites, however, do not recognize the same line of Islamic leaders acknowledged by the Sunnis. Shi'ites hold to a doctrine that accepts only leaders who are descended from Muhammad through his daughter Fatimah and her husband Ali. Many Shi'ite subsects believe that true imams are errorless and sinless. They receive instruction from these leaders rather than relying on the consensus of the community.

Laylat al-Miraj commemorates the ascent of the Prophet Muhammad into heaven, which is why it is often referred to as the Night Journey or the Ascent. The original account of this event is sketchy, and most of the details have been supplied by tradition. But according to the legend, the Prophet was sleeping in the sanctuary next to the Kaaba (see **HAJJ**) one night when the Angel Gabriel woke him and traveled with him to Jerusalem on the winged horse Buraq. There he prayed at the site of the Temple of Solomon (which lay in ruins after being destroyed by the Romans) with Abraham, Moses, Jesus, and other prophets. Muhammad was offered two vessels from which to drink, one of which contained wine and the other milk. He chose the milk, which Gabriel interpreted as his selecting "the primordial path" for himself and his followers. Then he was carried by Gabriel up to heaven from the rock of the Temple Mount, also known as Mt. Moriah, where it was believed that Abraham built the altar on which to sacrifice his son, Ishmael. The DOME OF THE ROCK sanctuary stands at this site today, and nearby is the al-Aqsa mosque, which takes its name from the word from the Qur'an for the Temple Mount.

The Prophet ascended through the SEVEN HEAVENS and as he did so, the Angel Gabriel and the prophets with whom he had prayed assumed their spiritual forms. At the summit of the ascent was the Lote Tree of the Uttermost Limit (see SEVEN HEAVENS), where Muhammad received the command from God that men should pray fifty times a day. When he descended, Moses advised him to go back and request that the number be reduced to something more realistic. He did, and the prayer requirement was finally reduced to five.

As he was returning from Jerusalem to Mecca, Muhammad saw caravans crossing the desert. When he told people that he had visited Jerusalem during the night and they didn't believe him, he described the caravans he'd seen on his return journey as proof that he was telling the truth. When the caravans arrived in Mecca, it confirmed his version of the night's events.

The journey from Mecca to Jerusalem is called the *Isra,* and the ascent from Jerusalem to heaven is called the *Mi'raj.* Together these two events are known as the Night Journey, which has often been portrayed in books of Persian miniatures. Although the exact date of the Mi'raj is not known, the event is usually celebrated on the twenty-seventh of Rajab.

SYMBOLS AND CUSTOMS

Dome of the Rock

The Dome of the Rock, a shrine in Jerusalem, was built between 685 and 691 C.E. and is the oldest existing Islamic monument. The Dome stands over the rock on the Temple Mount from which the Prophet is believed to have ascended to heaven. The rock is sacred not only to Muslims but also to Jews, because it was here that Abraham, the first patriarch of the Jewish people, is said to have prepared to sacrifice his son Isaac. It may also have been the site of the Holy of Holies, the innermost sanctuary of the Temple of Solomon, where the Ark of the Covenant was kept. After Mecca and Medina, the Temple Mount was the third holiest place in Islam. The early Muslims prayed in the direction of the Temple Mount, although later on they prayed facing Mecca. It was also the goal of the **HAJJ**, later supplanted by Mecca as well.

The rock itself is oblong, approximately fifty-six by forty-two feet. Below it is a small chamber, reached by a stairway, in which worshippers can pray, although a larger area has been set aside for this purpose on the ground level above. A crack in the rock, which is visible from the grotto below, is supposed to have appeared when the Prophet ascended to heaven. The rock, according to legend, wanted to follow and split in its effort to do so.

The sanctuary above the rock, with its golden dome dominating the skyline of old Jerusalem, was built by the Caliph 'Abd al-Malik ibn Arwan. The wooden dome, approximately sixty feet in diameter, is decorated with calligraphic designs typical of Islamic art, and there are 240 yards of inscriptions from the Qur'an. The Dome of the Rock's octagonal structure became the model for domed sanctuaries and saints' tombs from Morocco to China. The dome itself is a symbol: one step in the mathematical sequence leading from the square, representing the earth, to the circle, representing the perfection of heaven. The architecuture of the Dome of the Rock therefore symbolizes the Prophet's ascent to heaven.

Seven Heavens

The degrees of Being that separate creation from the Absolute in Islam are described symbolically in the Qur'an as the seven spheres, skies, or heavens. The seventh heaven is the furthest from the material world and the nearest to the state known as Beyond-Being. The final gulf between the two is marked by the Lote Tree of the Uttermost Limit, which is considered the limit of Being itself.

The concept of the seven heavens appears in early Jewish mysticism. It is probably of Babylonian or Persian origin, also with the seven heavens being the spheres of the seven planets visible to the human eye.

FURTHER READING

Ahsan, M.M. *Muslim Festivals*. Vero Beach, FL: Rourke Enterprises, 1987.

Bellenir, Karen. *Religious Holidays and Calendars*. 3rd ed. Detroit: Omnigraphics, 2004.

Crim, Keith R. *The Perennial Dictionary of World Religions*. San Francisco: Harper & Row, 1989.

Glassé, Cyril. *The Concise Encyclopedia of Islam*. 2nd ed. San Francisco: Harper & Row, 1999.

Gulevich, Tanya. *Understanding Islam and Muslim Traditions*. Detroit: Omnigraphics, 2004.

Henderson, Helene, ed. *Holidays, Festivals, and Celebrations of the World Dictionary*. 3rd ed. Detroit: Omnigraphics, 2005.

MacDonald, Margaret R., ed. *The Folklore of World Holidays*. Detroit: Gale Research, 1992.

WEB SITE

BBC (British Broadcasting Corporation)
www.bbc.co.uk/religion/religions/islam/holydays/lailatalmiraj.shtml

Laylat al-Qadr
(Night of Destiny, Night of Power)

Type of Holiday: Religious (Muslim)
Date of Observation: One of the last ten days of Ramadan, the ninth month of the Islamic lunar calendar; usually the 27th
Where Celebrated: Africa, Egypt, India, Indonesia, Iran, Iraq, Jordan, Lebanon, Morocco, Pakistan, Saudi Arabia, Syria, Thailand, Turkey, and throughout the Muslim world
Symbols and Customs: Lanterns, Qur'an
Related Holidays: Laylat al-Miraj, Mawlid al-Nabi

ORIGINS

Laylat al-Qadr is a holiday in the tradition of Islam, one of the world's largest religions. According to some estimates, there are more than one billion Muslims worldwide, with major populations found in the Middle East, North and sub-Saharan Africa, Turkey, Central Asia, and Southeast Asia. In Europe and the United States, Islam is the second largest religious group, with some seven million adherents in the United States. During the early years of Islam, the faith spread throughout the Arabian Peninsula into regions that are today occupied by Saudi Arabia, Syria, Iraq, and Jordan. Contrary to popular opinion, however, Muslims are not just Arabs. Muslims—followers of Islam—are found in many different ethnic groups all over the globe. In fact, Arabs make up less than twenty percent of Muslims.

The word Islam is an Arabic word that means "surrender to God." Its other meanings include peace, safety, and health. The central focus of Islam is a personal commitment and surrender to Allah, the Arabic word for God. In Islam, the concept of Allah is universal and eternal. Allah is the same in every religion and throughout the history of humankind. A person who follows Islam is called a Muslim, which means one who surrenders or submits to Allah's will. But Islam is not just a religion of belief; it is a religion of action. Five specific deeds are required of followers; these are called *The Five Pillars of Islam*. They are 1) *Shahadah*—confession of faith; 2) *Salat*—prayer/worship; 3) *Zakat*— charity; 4) *Sawm*—fasting; and 5) *Hajj*—pilgrimage.

The message of Islam was brought by Muhammad (570-632 C.E.), who is considered a prophet of Allah. The holy book of Islam is the *Qur'an* (also sometimes spelled *Koran* or *Alcoran*). According to Islamic belief, the Qur'an was revealed to Muhammad by Allah over a period of twenty-three years. Authorship of the Qur'an is attributed to Allah, and not to Muhammad; Muhammad merely received it. Muslims believe that because it originated with Allah, the Qur'an is infallible.

There are two main sects within Islam: Sunni and Shi'ite. Sunni Muslims are the majority (estimated at about eighty percent). They recognize the authority of the first four Caliphs, including Ali, and they believe that the Sunna (the example of the Prophet Muhammad) is interpreted through the consensus of the community. Shi'ite Muslims also look to special teachers, called imams. The imams are the direct descendants of Muhammad through Fatimah and Ali. These individuals are believed to be inspired and to possess secret knowledge. Shi'ites, however, do not recognize the same line of Islamic leaders acknowledged by the Sunnis. Shi'ites hold to a doctrine that accepts only leaders who are descended from Muhammad through his daughter Fatimah and her husband Ali. Many Shi'ite subsects believe that true imams are errorless and sinless. They receive instruction from these leaders rather than relying on the consensus of the community.

Also known as the "Night of Power" or "Night of Destiny," Laylat al-Qadr celebrates the night on which, in 610 C.E., the QUR'AN, or holy book of the Islamic religion, was first revealed to the Prophet Muhammad. While Muhammad was engaged in meditation in the cave of Hira, near the summit of the mountain Jabal Nur, the Angel Gabriel appeared to him with the first of the revelations that would continue on a sporadic basis for twenty-three years. The Prophet had no control over when Gabriel would speak, but when this occurred, Muhammad's state would visibly change. Once, for example, he was addressed by Gabriel while riding a camel. By the time the revelation was over, the camel was lying flat on the ground with its legs splayed out. Gabriel's words, according to Muhammad, physically assaulted him as if they were solid, heavy objects. In a trancelike state, Muhammad would repeat the words that Gabriel spoke, and his followers would record them on whatever was available—bones, bark, leaves, or scraps of parchment.

The first revelation is believed to have taken place during the last ten days of the holy month of **RAMADAN**. The widespread belief that the Qur'an was revealed on the twenty-seventh day of the month originated with Manicheism, a religion founded in the third century C.E. by Mani, who died on the twenty-seventh of Ramadan. Because no one is certain of the exact date, Muslims are asked to spend the last ten nights of Ramadan praying and reading the Qur'an. Some spend the entire night in the mosque during this period, or go out of their way to provide food and help for the poor.

SYMBOLS AND CUSTOMS

Lanterns

In Freetown, Sierra Leone, Laylat al-Qadr is known as the Day of Light or the Lanterns Festival. The custom of parading through the streets carrying lanterns on the twenty-sixth of Ramadan was introduced by a trader known as Daddy Maggay in the 1930s. Originally simple paper boxes, the lanterns were meant to symbolize the divine light of the Qur'an, sent down to earth by God (Allah). But as they grew into elaborate, floatlike structures, the competition among lantern-builders grew fierce, often erupting in violence. The Young Men's Muslim Association took control of the festival in the 1950s, in the hope that they could reduce the violence through better organization of the lantern-building competition.

Qur'an

The Qur'an—an Arabic word meaning "recitation"—contains the laws for Islamic society, warnings about the end of the world, descriptions of heaven and hell, and stories about both biblical figures and events that do not appear in the Bible. Muslims regard the Qur'an as a continuation of God's revelations to the Jews and the Christians, whose Bibles record only portions of the truth. Many of the stories found in the Bible were partially corrupted in transmission, according to Muslim scholars, which explains why the Qur'an's version of certain Bible stories often differs considerably from those found in the Hebrew scripture.

The Qur'an is divided into 114 chapters known as Surahs. The longer Surahs precede the shorter ones, and the whole is divided into thirty sections of approximately equal length known as *ajza'* (singular *juz'*) to make it easier to read the Qur'an on a regular basis. One *juz'* is supposed to be read every day of the month, and these divisions are usually indicated in the margins. Although parts of the Qur'an were written down during its revelation, large portions of it were also committed to memory, as was the custom in preliterate cultures. Until recently, the first step in a Muslim's education was to memorize the entire Qur'an. Even today, many Muslims know the book by heart.

Reciting passages from the Qur'an is the primary activity associated with Laylat al-Qadr. The written book is considered by Muslims to be the earthly or material manifestation of the Uncreated Qur'an in much the same way that Christians regard Jesus as the human incarnation of God.

FURTHER READING

Ahsan, M.M. *Muslim Festivals*. Vero Beach, FL: Rourke Enterprises, 1987.
Bellenir, Karen. *Religious Holidays and Calendars*. 3rd ed. Detroit: Omnigraphics, 2004.

Glassé, Cyril. *The Concise Encyclopedia of Islam*. 2nd ed. San Francisco: Harper & Row, 1999.

Gulevich, Tanya. *Understanding Islam and Muslim Traditions*. Detroit: Omnigraphics, 2004.

Henderson, Helene, ed. *Holidays, Festivals, and Celebrations of the World Dictionary*. 3rd ed. Detroit: Omnigraphics, 2005.

Ickis, Marguerite. *The Book of Festivals and Holidays the World Over*. New York: Dodd, Mead, 1970.

MacDonald, Margaret R., ed. *The Folklore of World Holidays*. Detroit: Gale Research, 1992.

Smith, Huston. *The Illustrated World's Religions*. San Francisco: HarperSanFrancisco, 1994.

Von Grunebaum, Gustave E. *Muhammadan Festivals*. New York: Schuman, 1951.

WEB SITE

BBC (British Broadcasting Corporation)
www.bbc.co.uk/religion/religions/islam/holydays/lailatalqadr.shtml

Lazarus Saturday

Type of Holiday: Religious (Christian)
Date of Observation: Between March 27 and April 30; Saturday before Palm Sunday
Where Celebrated: Eastern Europe, Greece, Russia
Symbols and Customs: Willow
Related Holidays: Easter, Palm Sunday

ORIGINS

Lazarus Saturday is a religious holiday in the Eastern Orthodox Christian church. The word Christian refers to a follower of Christ, a title derived from the Greek word meaning Messiah or Anointed One. The Christ of Christianity is Jesus of Nazareth, a man born between 7 and 4 B.C.E. in the region of Palestine. According to Christian teaching, Jesus was killed by Roman authorities using a form of execution called crucifixion (a term meaning he was nailed to a cross and hung from it until he died) in about the year 30 C.E. After his death, he rose back to life. His

495

death and resurrection provide a way by which people can be reconciled with God. In remembrance of Jesus' death and resurrection, the cross serves as a fundamental symbol in Christianity.

With nearly two billion believers in countries around the globe, Christianity is the largest of the world's religions. There is no one central authority for all of Christianity. The pope (the bishop of Rome) is the authority for the Roman Catholic Church, but other sects look to other authorities. Orthodox communities look to patriarchs and emphasize doctrinal agreement and traditional practice. Protestant communities focus on individual conscience. The Roman Catholic and Protestant churches are often referred to as the Western Church, while the Orthodox churches may also be called the Eastern Church. All three main branches of Christianity acknowledge the authority of Christian scriptures, a compilation of writings assembled into a document called the Bible. Methods of biblical interpretation vary among the different Christian sects.

In the Russian and other Orthodox churches, the Saturday before **PALM SUNDAY** is set aside to honor Lazarus, the brother of Martha and Mary. According to the Gospel of St. John, Jesus went to see Mary and Martha in Bethany when he heard that their brother was ill. But by the time he arrived, Lazarus had already been dead in his grave for four days. Jesus told Martha to take the stone away from the tomb where Lazarus had been buried. When she did, Jesus called out, "Lazarus, come forth." Lazarus walked out of the tomb, still wearing his graveclothes.

Lazarus Saturday was an important holiday in Bulgaria up until the early twentieth century. Young girls dressed up in bridal costumes went from house to house singing songs they had learned especially for this day and receiving eggs and sometimes small coins in return. On Palm Sunday, the older girls did the same thing, singing songs that dealt with various aspects of love, marriage, and family life. They made small wreaths out of WILLOW twigs and floated them on a river or in the village fountain. The girl whose wreath was the first to float after being submerged was given the title of *kumitsa*. The other girls were not allowed to speak to the kumitsa from Palm Sunday until **EASTER**. Then, on Easter Day, they would bring her presents of Easter eggs and a special kind of bread, in return for which the kumitsa would forgive them for their enforced silence.

In Greece, children still go from house to house singing songs about the resurrection of Lazarus on the day before Palm Sunday, usually carrying a picture of the story with them. Sometimes Lazarus is represented by a doll or a staff decorated with ribbons and cloth. In Cyprus, a boy covered with yellow flowers impersonates Lazarus. As he is led from house to house, he pretends to be dead and then rises when the girls say, "Lazarus! Come out!" This ritual so closely resembles the resurrection of Christ that it is often referred to as the "first Easter."

In Russia, the morning church service on this day is devoted to the memory of Lazarus. At the evening service, pussy willows are brought into the church to be blessed (*see* WILLOW). In Greece, Romania, and the former Yugoslavia, groups of children carry willow branches from house to house and act out the story of Christ raising Lazarus from the dead. In return, they receive gifts of fruit and candy. They believe that the resurrection of Lazarus is symbolic of the renewal of spring.

SYMBOLS AND CUSTOMS

Willow

Because the willow flourishes no matter how many of its branches are cut off, it stands as a symbol for the gospel of Christ, which remains intact no matter how widely it is spread over the world.

The willow is also known for its strength and flexibility. In Russia, the willow branches (or pussy willows) that are blessed in the church on Lazarus Saturday are never thrown out, but are later burned as sacred objects. According to an ancient folk belief, people who beat their children with willow branches are merely trying to impart the virtues of the willow tree—which is tall, healthy, and resilient—to the child.

FURTHER READING

Bellenir, Karen. *Religious Holidays and Calendars*. 3rd ed. Detroit: Omnigraphics, 2004.

Ferguson, George. *Signs and Symbols in Christian Art*. New York: Oxford University Press, 1954.

Harper, Howard V. *Days and Customs of All Faiths*. 1957. Reprint. Detroit: Omnigraphics, 1990.

Henderson, Helene, ed. *Holidays, Festivals, and Celebrations of the World Dictionary*. 3rd ed. Detroit: Omnigraphics, 2005.

MacDonald, Margaret R., ed. *The Folklore of World Holidays*. Detroit: Gale Research, 1992.

Spicer, Dorothy Gladys. *The Book of Festivals*. 1937. Reprint. Detroit: Omnigraphics, 1990.

WEB SITE

New Advent Catholic Encyclopedia
www.newadvent.org/cathen/09096a.htm

Leap Year Day
(Leap Day)

Type of Holiday: Calendar/Seasonal
Date of Observation: Every four years on February 29
Where Celebrated: British Isles, Europe, United States
Symbols and Customs: Proposals of Marriage

ORIGINS

Although a calendar year is thought of as being 365 days long, it actually takes the earth an additional five hours, forty-eight minutes, and forty-five seconds longer than that to complete its trip around the sun. When Julius Caesar initiated his calendar reform in 45 B.C.E., he tried to accommodate this discrepancy by fixing the solar year at 365 days, six hours—or 365 1/4 days. Every four years, the extra six hours per year added up to a whole day, which was added to February because it was the shortest month.

The calendar year still didn't correspond exactly to the astronomical year, however, and the discrepancy between the Julian calendar and the seasons of the year continued to increase—about three days every 400 years. In March of 1582, Pope Gregory XIII abolished the use of the Julian or Old Style calendar and instituted the Gregorian or New Style calendar. The Gregorian calendar subtracted ten days from the month of October so that October 6 was instead October 15. This shift brought the calendar more in line with the seasons. It also created Leap Year Day and established January 1 as the day of the new year throughout the Christian world. Catholic countries, such as Italy, France, Luxembourg, Spain, and Portugal, switched to the new calendar that year. Other European nations, predominantly Protestant or Orthodox, did not. Protestant Germany accepted the change in 1700, Orthodox Russia, in 1706. Great Britain accepted the Gregorian calendar and the New Year on January 1, in 1752. By the twentieth century most of the world had accepted the Gregorian calendar for civic and business purposes.

By instituting the new calendar, Pope Gregory not only canceled ten days but corrected the discrepancy in the length of the year. Pope Gregory decided that from this point on, Leap Year should be omitted in all centenary years, except those that are divisible by 400. Therefore, 1600 was a Leap Year, but 1700, 1800, and 1900 were not. The Gregorian calendar managed to bring the solar year much closer to the astronomical year, reducing the discrepancy to only twenty-six seconds a year—which won't add up to a full day until 3,323 years have passed.

Why is it called Leap Year? One explanation is that the additional day did not have any legal status in the English courts. February 29 was therefore "leaped over" in the records, and whatever happened on that day was dated February 28.

SYMBOLS AND CUSTOMS

Proposals of Marriage

Leap Year Day is sometimes referred to as Ladies' Day. There is an old tradition that women can propose marriage to men not only on Leap Day (February 29) but throughout Leap Year. It can be traced back to an ancient Irish legend concerning St. Patrick and St. Bridget in the fifth century. Bridget complained that her nuns were unhappy because they never had a chance to propose marriage—at the time, celibacy in religious orders was based on private vows and not required by the church. Patrick suggested that women be given this privilege every seven years, but that wasn't good enough for Bridget. She pleaded for granting it every four years, and Patrick obliged by offering them Leap Year—a so-called "compromise" that shows how passive women were expected to be in such matters. Bridget then proposed to Patrick, who declined—promising her instead a kiss and a silk gown.

In the British Isles during the Middle Ages, there was an unwritten law stating that any single man who declined a woman's proposal during Leap Year had to compensate her with a kiss and either a silk dress or a pair of gloves. Any woman who intended to propose to a man during Leap Year was expected to let a red petticoat show beneath the hem of her skirt. Similar laws were soon introduced in Europe, and the custom was legalized throughout France and in parts of Italy by the fifteenth century. It eventually spread to the United States, where it is no longer taken seriously. The tradition of having a man soften his refusal of a woman's proposal with a silk gown continued in Europe and the British Isles until its demise in the nineteenth century.

FURTHER READING

Bellenir, Karen. *Religious Holidays and Calendars*. 3rd ed. Detroit: Omnigraphics, 2004.

Christianson, Stephen G., and Jane M. Hatch. *The American Book of Days*. 4th ed. New York: H.W. Wilson, 2000.

Cohen, Hennig, and Tristram Potter Coffin. *The Folklore of American Holidays*. 3rd ed. Detroit: Gale Research, 1999.

Henderson, Helene, ed. *Holidays, Festivals, and Celebrations of the World Dictionary*. 3rd ed. Detroit: Omnigraphics, 2005.

Tuleja, Tad. *Curious Customs: The Stories Behind 296 Popular American Rituals*. New York: Harmony, 1987.

Van Straalen, Alice. *The Book of Holidays Around the World*. New York: Dutton, 1986.

WEB SITE

U.S. Naval Observatory, Astronomical Applications Department, in Washington DC

aa.usno.navy.mil/AA/faq/docs/leap_years.html

Leif Erikson Day

Type of Holiday: Historic
Date of Observation: October 9
Where Celebrated: Canada, Greenland, Iceland, Norway, United States
Symbols and Customs: Leif Erikson Festival, Parade

ORIGINS

Leif Erikson Day commemorates the arrival of the Vikings in North America, which is thought to have occurred nearly 500 years before the arrival of Christopher Columbus in 1492. Leif the Lucky, or Leif Erikson (so named because he was the son of Erik the Red), is thought to have landed on the northeastern shore of what is now Canada some time around the year 1000. The details of Erikson's exploration are uncertain, mainly because most of the historical information about his voyages is found in ancient Norse sagas. Sagas were often composed to honor and entertain rather than to record events with accuracy.

Several Norse sagas describe Erikson's arrival during the fall in a coastal land that was flat, lush, and fertile. Erikson named this place "Vinland" after the wild grapes that grew there. The exact location of Vinland is not known, although historians and archaeologists have identified several possible locations. In the early 1960s, archaeologists discovered the ruins of a Viking settlement in L'Anse aux Meadows in northern Newfoundland, Canada. The site contained important archaeological remains and included evidence of eight buildings. No direct link between Erikson and the site exists, but the location and layout of the buildings corresponds to ancient descriptions of the Vinland settlement. The area was declared a historic site by the Canadian government in 1976 and a World Heritage Site by the United Nations in 1978.

Norwegian-American cultural organizations began lobbying for an official U.S. holiday in honor of Leif Erikson as early as 1906. By that time, Leif Erikson Day was already being observed in Minnesota and Wisconsin by such groups as the Norwegian National League and the Sons of Norway. Although the exact date of Erikson's landing is not known, October 9 was chosen to commemorate Erikson's arrival during the fall and also to recognize the first organized group of Norwegian immigrants who landed in the port of New York on that date in 1825. On September 2, 1964, a joint resolution of the U.S. Congress was approved by President Lyndon B. Johnson, creating a national holiday in honor of Leif Erikson, to be observed annually on October 9.

As a historic holiday, Leif Erikson Day commemorates a significant historical event. People throughout the world remember significant events in their histories. Often, these are events that are important for an entire nation and become widely observed. The marking of such anniversaries serves not only to honor the values represented by the person or event commemorated, but also to strengthen and reinforce communal bonds of national, cultural, or ethnic identity. Victorious, joyful, and traumatic events are remembered through historic holidays. The commemorative expression reflects the original event through festive celebration or solemn ritual. Reenactments are common activities at historical holiday and festival gatherings, seeking to bring the past alive in the present.

Observances of Leif Erikson Day typically celebrate Viking history while acknowledging Erikson's courage, determination, and spirit of exploration. The cultures of Iceland and Norway are showcased as Erikson is honored as a "brave son of Iceland and grandson of Norway." Celebrations are held mainly in parts of the U.S. and Canada that have strong ties to Nordic and Scandinavian heritage. In Greenland, Iceland, and Norway, Erikson is generally regarded as an important historical figure, and the day may be observed as a celebration of the Nordic pioneering spirit.

SYMBOLS AND CUSTOMS

Leif Erikson Festival

These festivals are usually sponsored by Norwegian-American cultural organizations in celebration of Viking life and culture. Historically accurate depictions and/or reenactments of life in the Viking era may be staged. Other common festival features may include replica Viking ships, staged battles, craft demonstrations, folk music and dancing, speakers and presentations, and a Viking feast.

Parade

In areas with a large population of Norwegian Americans, including parts of Minnesota, New York, Washington, and Wisconsin, communities may hold a parade in honor of Leif Erikson Day. Parades often feature representations of Viking life and culture, floats, and marchers from various cultural heritage groups.

FURTHER READING

Henderson, Helene, ed. *Holidays, Festivals, and Celebrations of the World Dictionary,* 3rd ed. Detroit: Omnigraphics, 2005.

WEB SITES

Norwegian National League
nnleague.org

Scandinavica.com Monthly Magazine
www.scandinavica.com/culture/history/vinland.htm#ericson

Lemuralia
(Lemuria)

Type of Holiday: Ancient
Date of Observation: May 9, 11, 13
Where Celebrated: Rome, Italy
Symbols and Customs: Beans, Lemures
Related Holidays: All Souls' Day, Setsubun

ORIGINS

Lemuralia was a holiday in the ancient Roman religion, which scholars date back to the sixth century B.C.E. Roman religion dominated Rome and influenced territories in its empire until Emperor Constantine's conversion to Christianity in the third century C.E.

Ancient Roman religion was heavily influenced by the older Greek religion. Roman festivals therefore had much in common with those of the ancient Greeks.

Not only were their gods and goddesses mostly the same as those in the Greek pantheon (though the Romans renamed them), but their religious festivals were observed with similar activities: ritual sacrifice, theatrical performances, games, and feasts.

In ancient Rome, where even-numbered days were considered unlucky, the festival of the dead known as the Lemuralia was held on May 9, 11, and 13. It was established by Romulus, one of the legendary founders of Rome, to atone for killing his twin brother, Remus. Legend has it that when Romulus was raising the walls of Rome, Remus—who had been defeated in choosing the city's location—jumped over the wall in a gesture of scorn, for which his brother killed him.

The Lemures were the wandering spirits of the dead, who returned to visit and sometimes to threaten their kinfolk. To ward them off, the father or head of the household would get up at midnight, make a special gesture (holding his thumb between his closed fingers), wash his hands in pure water, and walk through the house spitting black BEANS from his mouth. He would repeat this ritual nine times without looking back, assuming that the ghosts of the dead would pick up the beans he left behind. Then he would wash his hands again and repeat the phrase "Ghosts of my fathers, be gone" nine times. After this, it was considered safe for him to look back, and all the ghosts would be gone.

The Lemuralia was a private and domestic rite rather than a public celebration. It was similar to the Parentalia observed in February (*see* LEMURES), but probably descended from a more ancient, superstitious period in Roman history. The February celebration in honor of the dead was more cheerful and civilized, while the Lemuralia was rooted in a time when fear of the dead was a powerful factor in most people's minds. The custom of ridding the house of spirits may have evolved from the periodic expulsion of demons performed on behalf of the community. May was considered an appropriate time to get rid of these demons because they were more likely to be rampant at the turn of the year in spring.

Temples were closed and marriages were prohibited during the three days of the Lemuralia. On the third day, a merchants' festival was held to ensure a prosperous year for business.

SYMBOLS AND CUSTOMS

Beans

Beans were associated with ghosts, witches, and supernatural spirits in ancient times. If a person dreamed about black beans, it was supposed to mean that grave danger awaited him or her. Sometimes beans were regarded as taboo, and priests would not touch them or even mention them—probably because of their association with the powers of the underworld. But their significance is uncertain; they may have been fertility symbols, or possibly surrogates for living family members, whom ghosts might try to snatch away.

Why would the ghosts of the dead pick up the beans scattered through the house at the Lemuralia? There is some reason to believe that by eating this traditional symbol of fertility, the ghosts hoped to obtain a new lease on life. It is also possible that people believed the souls of the dead resided in the beans. In any case, spitting beans was a widely used remedy against ghosts among the ancient Greeks and Romans. People often threw black beans on the graves of the deceased or burned them, as the dead were supposed to be unable to tolerate the smell.

The Japanese have a similar ceremony for driving out demons. On February 3, the head of the household puts on his best clothes and goes through all the rooms at midnight, scattering roasted beans and saying, "Out, demons! In, luck!" (*see* **SET-SUBUN**).

Lemures

Lemures is a general term for spirits after they have left the body, while those who haunt houses are called *larvae*. Both are considered hostile ghosts, unlike the *manes*, who were the benign spirits honored at the Parentalia in February. Both the lemures and the larvae terrified the good and haunted the wicked. The custom of celebrating festivals in their honor appears to have been instituted by Romulus, who wanted to appease the ghost of his twin brother, Remus. In fact, the Lemuralia (or Lemuria) was originally known as the Remuria.

The Lemures were believed to be particularly restless in May, which is probably why this month was considered an unlucky time to get married.

FURTHER READING

Bell, Robert E. *Dictionary of Classical Mythology*. Santa Barbara: ABC-CLIO, 1982.

Fowler, W. Warde. *The Roman Festivals of the Period of the Republic*. New York: Macmillan Co., 1925.

Henderson, Helene, ed. *Holidays, Festivals, and Celebrations of the World Dictionary*. 3rd ed. Detroit: Omnigraphics, 2005.

James, E.O. *Seasonal Feasts and Festivals*. 1961. Reprint. Detroit: Omnigraphics, 1993.

Leach, Maria, ed. *Funk & Wagnalls Standard Dictionary of Folklore, Mythology & Legend*. San Francisco: Harper & Row, 1984.

Lemprière, John. *Lemprière's Classical Dictionary*. Rev. ed. London: Bracken, 1994.

Scullard, H.H. *Festivals and Ceremonies of the Roman Republic*. Ithaca, NY: Cornell University Press, 1981.

Lent

Type of Holiday: Religious (Christian)
Date of Observation: Forty days, beginning on Ash Wednesday and ending on Easter eve
Where Celebrated: By Christians all over the world
Symbols and Customs: Birch Branches, Fasting, Lenten Fires
Colors: Lent is associated with the color purple, which symbolizes penance.
Related Holidays: Ash Wednesday, Carnival, Easter, Good Friday, Maslenitsa, Shrove Tuesday

ORIGINS

The observance of Lent is part of the religious tradition of Christianity, the largest of the world's religions, with nearly two billion believers in countries around the globe. The word Christian refers to a follower of Christ, a title derived from the Greek word meaning Messiah or Anointed One. The Christ of Christianity is Jesus of Nazareth, a man born between 7 and 4 B.C.E. in the region of Palestine. According to Christian teaching, Jesus was killed by Roman authorities using a form of execution called crucifixion (a term meaning he was nailed to a cross and hung from it until he died) in about the year 30 C.E. After his death, he rose back to life. His death and resurrection provide a way by which people can be reconciled with God. In remembrance of Jesus' death and resurrection, the cross serves as a fundamental symbol in Christianity.

There is no one central authority for all of Christianity. The pope (the bishop of Rome) is the authority for the Roman Catholic Church, but other sects look to other authorities. Orthodox communities look to patriarchs and emphasize doctrinal agreement and traditional practice. Protestant communities focus on individual conscience. The Roman Catholic and Protestant churches are often referred to as the Western Church, while the Orthodox churches may also be called the Eastern Church. All three main branches of Christianity acknowledge the authority of Christian scriptures, a compilation of writings assembled into a document called the Bible. Methods of biblical interpretation vary among the different Christian sects.

Self-denial during a period of intense religious devotion is a long-standing tradition in both the Eastern and Western churches. In the early days, Christians prepared for **EASTER** by fasting from **GOOD FRIDAY** until Easter morning. It wasn't until the ninth century that the Lenten season was fixed at forty days (with

Sundays omitted), perhaps reflecting the importance attached to the number: Moses went without food for forty days on Mount Sinai, the children of Israel wandered for forty years, Elijah fasted for forty days, and so did Jesus, who also spent forty hours in his tomb.

"Lent" comes from an Anglo-Saxon word meaning "spring" or "lengthening days." It is a period of self-examination and repentance in preparation for Easter and a time to strengthen one's faith in God through repentance and prayer. Lent has been observed for centuries with periods of strict FASTING, abstinence from meat (and in the East, from dairy products, wine, and olive oil as well), additional prayer services, and other penitential activities. It is customary for modern-day Christians to "give up something for Lent" —a favorite food or other worldly pleasure. It is also customary for the church organs to remain silent during this period, and for weddings and other celebrations to be prohibited.

Although the observation of Lent is usually associated with Roman Catholics, Protestant churches also observe Lent. Most offer Holy Communion on each of the Sundays during Lent, and some organize special Bible study classes for children and adults. Many churches set aside Sunday evenings during Lent for performances of cantatas, oratorios, and other Lenten music.

SYMBOLS AND CUSTOMS

Birch Branches

In Sweden, the Lenten season is called Fastlagen. It falls at a time of year when the ground is still frozen and the trees are bare. People cut birch branches and tie colored chicken or rooster feathers to the boughs. At one time, the decorated branches were used to beat one another, a cleansing ritual designed to get rid of anything evil or unholy. The custom of "birching" also served as a symbolic reminder of the beatings that Jesus received on his way to be crucified. Today, the branches are used to decorate windowsills.

Fasting

From the time of the Apostles, the church had singled out Friday as a weekly day of fast. In addition, many early Christians observed a strict two-day fast from Good Friday to Easter Sunday. Eventually a longer period of fasting was introduced in preparation for Easter, although its observance varied widely. Some churches fasted only during Holy Week, while others extended the fast for two or more weeks. Sunday was always an exception, and, in the Eastern church, so was Saturday. During the third and fourth centuries most churches adopted a forty-day fast in imitation of Christ, who had fasted for forty days in the wilderness after he was baptized.

Back in the days when there were no calendars to tell people how close they were to the end of the fasting period, they invented their own methods of keeping track of the time. One of these primitive calendars looked like a nun cut out of paper, with no mouth (symbolizing the abstention from food) and with her hands crossed in prayer. She had seven feet, all facing in the same direction. Every Saturday one of the feet was torn off, until the fast was over. Another approach, used in Greece, was to stick seven chicken feathers in a boiled potato or onion hanging from the ceiling by a string. A feather was removed as each week passed.

For nearly 1,000 years, the Catholic Church followed the fasting rules laid down by Pope Gregory the Great: no meat or animal products, such as milk, cheese, eggs, or butter. This is still the routine among members of the Eastern Catholic Church and the Greek Orthodox Church in the United States. But a new ruling of the Ecumenical Council in Rome says that Catholics are obligated to fast on only two days during Lent: **ASH WEDNESDAY** and **GOOD FRIDAY**.

Lenten Fires

The custom of lighting fires on the first Sunday in Lent was widespread in Europe at one time and is still common in parts of Belgium, northern France, and Germany. Children go around collecting fuel and cutting down bushes for days in advance. The fires are lit in the evening, often by the individual who has most recently married. Young people sing and dance around the bonfire, leaping over the embers to guarantee a good harvest or a happy marriage within the year, or to guard themselves against colic. In some areas, torches are lit from the fire and carried into the surrounding orchards, gardens, and fields. Ashes from the torches may be shaken on the ground or put in hens' nests so there will be plenty of eggs. In Switzerland, where the first Sunday in Lent is known as Spark Sunday, a "witch"—usually made from old clothes and fastened to a pole—is stuck in the middle of the fire. Sometimes old wheels are wrapped in straw and thorns, lit on fire, and sent rolling down a nearby hill.

There is an old peasant saying that neglecting to kindle the fire on the first Sunday in Lent means that God will light it himself—i.e., that he will burn the house down. It was common at one time to roast cats alive over the Lenten fires. The cats symbolized the devil, who could never be put through too much suffering.

FURTHER READING

Bellenir, Karen. *Religious Holidays and Calendars*. 3rd ed. Detroit: Omnigraphics, 2004.

Dobler, Lavinia G. *Customs and Holidays Around the World*. New York: Fleet Pub. Corp., 1962.

Frazer, Sir James G. *The Golden Bough: A Study in Magic and Religion*. New York: Macmillan, 1931.

Harper, Howard V. *Days and Customs of All Faiths*. 1957. Reprint. Detroit: Omnigraphics, 1990.

Henderson, Helene, ed. *Holidays, Festivals, and Celebrations of the World Dictionary*.
3rd ed. Detroit: Omnigraphics, 2005.

Ickis, Marguerite. *The Book of Festivals and Holidays the World Over*. New York:
Dodd, Mead, 1970.

Ickis, Marguerite. *The Book of Religious Holidays and Celebrations*. New York: Dodd,
Mead, 1966.

Santino, Jack. *All Around the Year: Holidays and Celebrations in American Life*.
Urbana: University of Illinois Press, 1994.

Spicer, Dorothy Gladys. *Festivals of Western Europe*. 1958. Reprint. Detroit: Omnigraphics, 1993.

Spicer, Dorothy Gladys. *The Book of Festivals*. 1937. Reprint. Detroit: Omnigraphics,
1990.

Urlin, Ethel L. *Festivals, Holy Days, and Saints' Days*. 1915. Reprint. Detroit: Omnigraphics, 1992.

Weiser, Franz Xaver. *Handbook of Christian Feasts and Customs*. New York: Harcourt,
Brace, 1958.

WEB SITES

Christian Resource Institute in Warr Acres, Oklahoma
www.cresourcei.org/cylent.html

New Advent Catholic Encyclopedia
www.newadvent.org/cathen/09152a.htm

Li Ch'un

Type of Holiday: Calendar/Seasonal
Date of Observation: Early February
Where Celebrated: China, and by Chinese communities throughout the world
Symbols and Customs: Meng Shan, Ox
Colors: Five colors are associated with Li Ch'un: black, white, red, green, and yel-
low. They represent the five elements (fire, water, metal, wood, earth), the five
planets that rule the elements (Mercury, Venus, Mars, Jupiter, and Saturn), the five
kinds of grain grown in China, and the five kinds of weather conditions (*see* OX).
Related Holidays: Chinese New Year, Ching Ming

ORIGINS

Li Ch'un is the Chinese festival welcoming the start of spring. The Chinese lunisolar calendar is based on the oldest system of time measurement still in use. It is widely employed in Asian countries to set the dates of seasonal festivals. The **CHINESE NEW YEAR** takes place on the new moon nearest to the point which is defined in the West as the fifteenth degree on the zodiacal sign of Aquarius. Each of twelve months in the Chinese year is twenty-nine or thirty days long and is divided into two parts, each of which is two weeks long. The Chinese calendar, like all lunisolar systems, requires periodic adjustment to keep the lunar and solar cycles integrated; therefore, an intercalary month is added when necessary.

The names of each of the twenty-four two-week periods sometimes correspond to seasonal festivals celebrated during the period. Beginning with the New Year, which takes place in late January or early February, these periods are known by the following names: Spring Begins (New Year and Li Ch'un), the Rain Water, the Excited Insects, the **VERNAL EQUINOX**, the Clear and Bright (**CHING MING**), the Grain Rains, the Summer Begins, the Grain Fills, the Grain in Ear, the **SUMMER SOLSTICE (DOUBLE FIFTH)**, the Slight Heat, the Great Heat, the Autumn Begins, the Limit of Heat, the White Dew (**MID-AUTUMN FESTIVAL**), the **AUTUMN EQUINOX**, the Cold Dew, the Hoar Frost Descends, the Winter Begins, the Little Snow, the Heavy Snow, the **WINTER SOLSTICE**, the Little Cold, and the Great Cold.

At one time Li Ch'un marked the traditional beginning of the farmer's agricultural year, which consisted of twenty-four "solar breaths" or "joints"—fifteen-day periods calculated according to the solar rather than the lunar calendar and named after the characteristics of each season. Li Ch'un means "Spring is here."

In rural areas, Li Ch'un is still observed with plowing ceremonies. A government representative dressed in his official robes arrives early in the morning at an appointed field, where a plow and oxen (or water buffaloes) are waiting near a small shrine. He makes an offering of fruit and sweets to the god of spring and the god of husbandry. After burning incense on the altar, he plows the first furrow in the field.

In towns and urban areas, long and colorful processions are held to welcome spring. There are usually more participants in these processions than spectators. Only soldiers and military officers are prohibited from joining the procession, because the gods who dwell in the heavens consider it a bad omen to see soldiers in the spring. The most prominent figure in the procession is the OX, made of paper and bamboo. When the procession reaches the temple, the image of the ox is burned so that its spirit will ascend to heaven and plead for a prosperous growing season.

The first day of spring is considered an auspicious time for weddings, and many people attend marriage ceremonies on the evening of Li Ch'un.

SYMBOLS AND CUSTOMS

Meng Shan

Meng Shan or the "spirit driver" plays a prominent part in the spring processions held on Li Ch'un. Made out of stiff paper, he is dressed in a way that is believed to foretell the weather for the coming year. If he is wearing a hat, it will be a dry year; no hat means rain. If he is wearing lots of clothing, it is considered an indication that weather will be hot; little clothing means cold weather. Since Meng Shan is a spirit, he dresses exactly opposite to the way a living man would dress for certain types of weather. If he wears a red belt, there will be a great deal of sickness and many deaths in the coming year; if he wears his white one, good health will be widespread. He drives before him the paper effigy of the OX.

Ox

The ox, or water buffalo, is the Chinese symbol for spring, because it is the animal that pulls the plow and draws new life out of the fields. In early observances of Li Ch'un, a live ox was slaughtered, but it was later replaced by a clay effigy. Nowadays the ceremonial ox is made of bamboo (symbolic of long life) covered with strips of paper in five colors: black, white, red, green, and yellow. After the bamboo frame for the ox is built, it is taken to a blind man (or a man who has been blindfolded). He is given an equal number of pieces of each of the five colors, all mixed together, and he pastes them on the framework at random. When the ox is taken out in the streets for the Li Ch'un procession, people study the colors carefully to see which one predominates. If there is more red than any other color, it means that the summer will be hot and dry; yellow means that it will be very windy; green means rain, and so forth.

The ox is prodded and beaten with bamboo poles decorated with strips of colored paper. Sometimes the effigy is filled with grain, which spills out when the ox is beaten. The grain-filled ox is probably a representation of the ancient corn-spirit, responsible for bringing fertility to the fields. The Chinese often put stalks of bamboo stuffed with chicken feathers in the ground in front of their houses on Li Ch'un. The first spring breeze is supposed to blow at the exact moment when the ox is being beaten, and it carries the feathers up into the sky. Sometimes the ox is whipped with willow twigs—willow being a traditional symbol of springtime. This "beating of the spring" is believed to hasten the season's arrival and promote fertilization of the soil.

After the procession is over, both the ox and the spirit driver are burned, and the pieces of charred paper that drift down are kept as good luck charms.

FURTHER READING

Bredon, Juliet, and Igor Mitrophanow. *The Moon Year: A Record of Chinese Customs and Festivals*. Shanghai: Kelly & Walsh, 1927.

Frazer, Sir James G. *The Golden Bough: A Study in Magic and Religion*. New York: Macmillan, 1931.

Gaer, Joseph. *Holidays Around the World*. Boston: Little, Brown, 1953.

Henderson, Helene, ed. *Holidays, Festivals, and Celebrations of the World Dictionary*. 3rd ed. Detroit: Omnigraphics, 2005.

Ickis, Marguerite. *The Book of Festivals and Holidays the World Over*. New York: Dodd, Mead, 1970.

Stepanchuk, Carol, and Charles Wong. *Mooncakes and Hungry Ghosts: Festivals of China*. San Francisco: China Books & Periodicals, 1991.

Lincoln's Birthday

Type of Holiday: Historic
Date of Observation: February 12
Where Celebrated: United States
Symbols and Customs: Gettysburg Address, Lincoln Memorial
Related Holidays: Juneteenth, Washington's Birthday

ORIGINS

Abraham Lincoln, the sixteenth president of the United States, was born on February 12, 1809. Lincoln began his political career in the Illinois state legislature, to which he was elected when he was only twenty-five years old. In 1837 he became a lawyer and moved from his home in New Salem to Springfield, where he met and married Mary Todd in 1842. He was a member of the U.S. House of Representatives from 1847 to 1849, but then he left politics and went back to his law career in Illinois.

Eventually he was lured into politics again. Although he lost his race against Stephen A. Douglas for the U.S. Senate in 1858, he so impressed the public with his speaking ability during a series of debates against Douglas that in 1860 he was nominated at the Republican Convention for the presidency and elected in November of that year.

As president, Lincoln's stand on the issue of slavery was clear: He was against it, and he believed that the government would not survive if half the states allowed slavery and the other half didn't. Less than six weeks after he was inaugurated, the Civil War (1861-65) began. Although his primary concern was to keep the nation whole, he soon realized that nothing would be resolved as long as the institution of slavery remained in force. He issued his famous Emancipation Proclamation, which freed five million slaves, on January 1, 1863.

Lincoln was elected for a second term in November 1864. But on April 15, 1865, just six days after General Robert E. Lee surrendered at Appomattox and the Civil War ended, Lincoln was shot by John Wilkes Booth as he sat with his wife watching a performance at Ford's Theatre in Washington. After his death, a funeral train carried Lincoln's body through the country for two weeks, and crowds gathered at every station to pay tribute to their slain president. This popular feeling for Lincoln remains strong to this day, as evidenced by the number of books, plays, and poems that are still being written about him.

Lincoln's Birthday is a holiday that commemorates a significant historical event. Peoples throughout the world commemorate significant events in their histories through holidays and festivals.. Often, these are events that are important for an entire nation and become widely observed. The marking of such anniversaries serve not only to honor the values represented by the person or event commemorated, but also to strengthen and reinforce communal bonds of national, cultural, or ethnic identity. Victorious, joyful, and traumatic events are remembered through historic holidays. The commemorative expression reflects the original event through festive celebration or solemn ritual. Reenactments are common activities at historical holiday and festival gatherings, seeking to bring the past alive in the present.

Lincoln's actual birthday, February 12, is a legal holiday in fifteen states, while others observe it on the second Monday in February. Some states combine it with **WASHINGTON'S BIRTHDAY** and observe it on the third Monday in February as either Presidents' Day or Washington-Lincoln Day. A special observance is held in Lincoln's long-time home town of Springfield, Illinois, where members of the American Legion, Veterans of Foreign Wars, and other patriotic groups make an annual pilgrimage to his tomb.

Race Relations Sunday is always celebrated on the Sunday nearest February 12. Commemorating the role Lincoln played in freeing the slaves during the Civil War, this occasion is observed by Roman Catholic and Jewish as well as Protestant and Eastern Orthodox churches.

SYMBOLS AND CUSTOMS

Gettysburg Address

Perhaps the most famous of all Lincoln's speeches, the Gettysburg Address was delivered the year after the Emancipation Proclamation, at the dedication of the national cemetery at the Gettysburg battlefield. It is a poignant and inspiring speech that has been praised all over the world as an example of beautifully written English prose, even though Lincoln had no time to prepare it and spoke from a few notes scribbled on a piece of paper. It begins with the words every American recognizes: "Four score and seven years ago our fathers brought forth upon this continent a new nation, conceived in liberty and dedicated to the proposition that all men are created equal."

The recitation of the Gettysburg Address is a popular way to observe Lincoln's Birthday, particularly in schools.

Lincoln Memorial

The Lincoln Memorial in Washington DC was designed by New York architect Henry Bacon in the classic Greek style, and the huge statue of Lincoln seated on a chair inside was the work of sculptor Daniel Chester French. The building, which is located at the end of a long reflecting pool, was dedicated on **MEMORIAL DAY** in 1922. Cut into the marble walls are the words of Lincoln's Second Inaugural Address, as well as the more famous GETTYSBURG ADDRESS.

One of the best known commemorations of Lincoln's birthday takes place at the Memorial, where government officials and foreign diplomats, led by the president of the United States or his representative, gather at noon to place wreaths before the massive statue of Lincoln. The president usually issues a Lincoln's Birthday Address focusing on the nation's accomplishments and shortcomings in the area of race relations and civil rights.

FURTHER READING

Christianson, Stephen G., and Jane M. Hatch. *The American Book of Days*. 4th ed. New York: H.W. Wilson, 2000.

Dunkling, Leslie. *A Dictionary of Days*. New York: Facts on File, 1988.

Henderson, Helene, ed. *Holidays, Festivals, and Celebrations of the World Dictionary*. 3rd ed. Detroit: Omnigraphics, 2005.

Humphrey, Grace. *Stories of the World's Holidays*. 1923. Reprint. Detroit: Omnigraphics, 1990.

McSpadden, J. Walker. *The Book of Holidays*. New York: Crowell, 1958.

Schaun, George and Virginia, and David Wisniewski. *American Holidays and Special Days*. 3rd ed. Lanham: Maryland Historical Press, 2002.

Spicer, Dorothy Gladys. *The Book of Festivals*. 1937. Reprint. Detroit: Omnigraphics, 1990.

Trawicky, Bernard, and Ruth W. Gregory. *Anniversaries and Holidays*. 5th ed. Chicago: American Library Assocation, 2000.

Van Straalen, Alice. *The Book of Holidays Around the World*. New York: Dutton, 1986.

WEB SITES

Abraham Lincoln Online
showcase.netins.net/web/creative/lincoln.html

Library of Congress
lcweb2.loc.gov/ammem/today/mar04.html

National Park Service
www.nps.gov/linc

Loi Krathong

Type of Holiday: Religious (Buddhist)
Date of Observation: November; fifteenth day of waxing moon in twelfth lunar
  month
Where Celebrated: Thailand
Symbols and Customs: Krathong, Lotus

ORIGINS

Loi Krathong is part of the religious tradition of Buddhism, one of the four largest religious families in the world. Buddhism is based on the teachings of Siddhartha Gautama (c. 563-483 B.C.E.), who came to be known as Buddha, or "The Enlightened One." The basic tenets of Buddhism can be summarized in the Four Noble Truths and the Eightfold Path. The Four Noble Truths are 1) the truth and reality of suffering; 2) suffering is caused by desire; 3) the way to end suffering is to end desire; and 4) the Eightfold Path shows the way to end suffering. The Eightfold Path consists of 1) right view or right understanding; 2) right thoughts and aspirations; 3) right speech; 4) right conduct and action; 5) right way of life; 6) right effort; 7) right mindfulness; and 8) right contemplation.

Loi Krathong, which is considered the most beautiful festival in Thailand, is said to have originated more than 800 years ago. King Ramakhamhaeng of Sukhotai, the first capital of Thailand, was making a pilgrimage on the river from temple to temple. One of his wives, Nang Nophames, wanted to please both her husband and Lord Buddha, so she made a KRATHONG or paper lantern resembling a LOTUS flower, put a candle in it, and set it afloat. The king was so delighted he decreed that his subjects should follow this custom every year.

Another theory about the origin of Loi Krathong claims that it goes back even further, to the ancient practice of paying tribute to Me Khongkha, the Mother of Water. The small coins and other items placed in the bottom of the krathong are meant as tokens to ask forgiveness for the ways in which humankind has abused its most precious natural resource. Yet another theory claims that the festival celebrates the lotus blossoms that sprang up when the Buddha took his first baby steps, or that it atones for the sin of passing in boats over the footprints of Buddha, which may be imbedded in the riverbottom.

Thais celebrate the "Festival of the Floating Leaf Cups" by going down to the nearest river or canal and floating small lamps or lanterns in the shape of animals, birds, dragons, airplanes, battleships, or other objects on the water. If there is no moving water nearby, the lanterns are set afloat on irrigation ditches. They are usually made out of banana leaves or paper. As they float out of sight, the individuals who launched them makes a wish. If the candle stays lit until the krathong disappears, it is believed that the wish will come true.

Houses and temples are decorated with colored streamers and lights throughout the three days of the festival, particularly in villages that are not located on rivers or canals. The monks, who are forbidden to take part in the floating of the krathong, conduct services three times a day in the *wat* or temple. The women and girls attend all three services, but the men and boys usually attend only the evening service, after which drums and gongs are beaten, firecrackers are exploded, and the festivities continue until dawn.

Although Loi Krathong is celebrated throughout the country, it is especially significant in Sukhotai, which is where Nang Nophames set the first krathong afloat. A beauty contest is usually part of the celebration, and the winner gets to represent Nophames throughout the three days of the festival.

SYMBOLS AND CUSTOMS

Krathong

Loi means "to float" and *krathong* is a "leaf cup" or "bowl." On the evening of the festival, Thais gather at the water after sunset to launch small lotus-shaped banana leaf or paper boats, each of which holds a lighted candle, a flower, and a small coin to honor the water spirits. Some say that the krathong is also a tribute to the snake named Phrajanag who lives at the bottom of the river or canal. According to legend, Phrajanag literally followed in the Buddha's footsteps and succeeded in reaching Nirvana.

Krathong or leaf cups, usually in the shape of a boat or a bird, go on sale several days before the festival. These commercially made krathong are really more like toys, and the stalls selling them are confined largely to cities and towns. In rural areas, people still make their own by hand.

The individual who has set the krathong afloat makes a wish as it drifts out of sight. If the candle is still burning when it disappears from view, it is believed that the wish will come true.

The paper or banana-leaf krathong are both an offering to appease the spirits of the river and a way of freeing oneself of the sins of the preceding year.

Lotus

Krathong are often made in the shape of a lotus blossom, which symbolizes the flowering of the human spirit under Buddhism. As a symbol, the lotus was adopted from the Hindus by the Buddhists in India, who introduced it into their sculpture, painting, and literature. It is identified with purity and perfection because it grows out of the mud and yet is not defiled by it. In much the same way, humankind should be able to live in an evil and impure world without being influenced by it.

FURTHER READING

Bellenir, Karen. *Religious Holidays and Calendars*. 3rd ed. Detroit: Omnigraphics, 2004.

Dobler, Lavinia G. *Customs and Holidays Around the World*. New York: Fleet Pub. Corp., 1962.

Henderson, Helene, ed. *Holidays, Festivals, and Celebrations of the World Dictionary*. 3rd ed. Detroit: Omnigraphics, 2005.

MacDonald, Margaret R., ed. *The Folklore of World Holidays*. Detroit: Gale Research, 1992.

Shemanski, Frances. *A Guide to World Fairs and Festivals*. Westport, CT: Greenwood Press, 1985.

Van Straalen, Alice. *The Book of Holidays Around the World*. New York: Dutton, 1986.

WEB SITE

Tourism Authority of Thailand
www.tatnews.org/events/events/nov/2375.asp

Losar
(Tibetan New Year)

Type of Holiday: Calendar/Seasonal, Religious (Tibetan Buddhism)
Date of Observation: February-March; first day of first Tibetan lunar month
Where Celebrated: India, Nepal, Tibet
Symbols and Customs: Dakar, Guthuk, Mystery Play of Tibet, Pebbles
Related Holidays: Dosmoche

ORIGINS

Losar, the Tibetan New Year, is part of Buddhism, one of the four largest religious families in the world. Buddhism is based on the teachings of Siddhartha Gautama (c. 563-483 B.C.E.), who came to be known as Buddha, or "The Enlightened One." The basic tenets of Buddhism can be summarized in the Four Noble Truths and the Eightfold Path. The Four Noble Truths are 1) the truth and reality of suffering; 2) suffering is caused by desire; 3) the way to end suffering is to end desire; and 4) the Eightfold Path shows the way to end suffering. The Eightfold Path consists of 1) right view or right understanding; 2) right thoughts and aspirations; 3) right speech; 4) right conduct and action; 5) right way of life; 6) right effort; 7) right mindfulness; and 8) right contemplation.

Tibetan Buddhism is defined not only by Buddhist teachings, but also by Tibetan indigenous religious traditions and folk practices. Tibetans observe a form of Buddhism known as Lamaism, Lama Buddhism, or Tibetan Buddhism. The Dalai Lama is the spiritual leader of Tibetan Buddhists. Their religion involves belief in evil spirits, magic, and the spirits of nature.

Many of the traditions surrounding the celebration of Losar, the Tibetan New Year, are associated with these beliefs. It was at one time observed only in Tibet, but since the People's Republic of China invaded Tibet in 1950 and the Dalai Lama was forced to flee to India, Losar is now celebrated by Tibetan refugees living in India and Nepal as well. The exact date is determined by Tibetan astrologers in Dharmsala, India, where the current Dalai Lama lives.

Before the new year actually arrives, bad memories from the old year must be chased away. Houses are cleaned and whitewashed and the lucky signs on them are repainted; a small amount of the dirt collected is thrown away at a crossroads where spirits might dwell. On the last day of the old year, Tibetan Buddhist monks conduct ceremonies aimed at driving out evil spirits and negative forces. In one such ritual, known as the MYSTERY PLAY OF TIBET, monks wearing grotesque masks and exotic robes perform a dance in which they portray the struggle between good and evil.

As the new year dawns, people try to get to a river, lake, stream, or pond for a ritual drink of water, which they believe will ensure a lucky year without problems or obstacles. Another way of ensuring good luck in the coming year is to eat rice cooked with butter and garnished with other flavorings. The rest of the new year's celebration, which lasts three days, is spent eating, drinking, and merrymaking, with dances, operas, and archery competitions.

Tibetan exiles living in India celebrate Losar by flocking to the temple in Dharmsala, where the Dalai Lama maintains a residence and works to preserve the cultural and religious heritage of Tibet. On the second day of the new year, he blesses people by touching their heads and giving them a piece of red-and-white string. They tie the string around their necks in the belief that it will protect them from illness. Losar is also observed in Ladakh, in the eastern part of Kashmir, as well as among refugee Tibetans living elsewhere in India.

SYMBOLS AND CUSTOMS

Dakar

The figure who goes from door to door on Losar, dressed like a beggar but performing like an acrobat, is known as the Dakar. He delivers good luck messages and, in return, is welcomed and given snacks or money.

Guthuk

Guthuk is a special dish prepared for the Losar celebration. In it are dumplings that contain omens: a pebble symbolizes a long, healthy life; cayenne pepper suggests that the individual has a temperamental personality; a piece of charcoal means that the recipient has a black heart.

Mystery Play of Tibet

Originally performed by a devil-dancing cult to drive out the old year along with its demons and human enemies, this annual dramatic performance is known to Tibetans as the Dance of the Red Tiger Devil and to Europeans as the Pageant of the Lamas or the Mystery Play of Tibet. It symbolizes the triumph of the Indian missionary monks over the pagan devils; more recently, it has been changed to represent the assassination of Langdarma, the king who tried to rid Tibet of Lamaism. Despite its many transformations over the years, however, the play continues to retain the devil-dancing features of its earliest form.

The play is performed on the last day of the year in the courtyards of Buddhist temples or monasteries and continues for two days. A group of priests in black miters (tall hats) is confronted by one group of demons after another, which they manage to exorcise. On the second day, an effigy representing the enemies of Tibet and Lamaism is dismembered and disemboweled. Pieces of the effigy, which is made out of dough, are thrown to the audience, who eat them or keep them to use as good-luck charms. All of this is accompanied by the blowing of long horns and the clash of huge cymbals.

The dance reenacts a ritual combat of good against evil. It ends with the burning of a pyramid-shaped object with a skull-like head at the apex. This sacrifice is interpreted as a sign that the temple has been rid of evil.

Pebbles

Tibetan Buddhists believe that an account of each person's good and evil deeds is kept in the form of white and black pebbles, and that on the Day of Judgment the two lots are weighed against each other to decide the individual's fate. On Losar, therefore, Tibetans repent for the sins that they have committed during the past year and promise to display only good conduct in the coming year, hoping that they can secure a favorable balance of black and white pebbles.

FURTHER READING

Bellenir, Karen. *Religious Holidays and Calendars*. 3rd ed. Detroit: Omnigraphics, 2004.

Crim, Keith R. *The Perennial Dictionary of World Religions*. San Francisco: Harper & Row, 1989.

Henderson, Helene, ed. *Holidays, Festivals, and Celebrations of the World Dictionary*. 3rd ed. Detroit: Omnigraphics, 2005.

Leach, Maria, ed. *Funk & Wagnalls Standard Dictionary of Folklore, Mythology & Legend*. San Francisco: Harper & Row, 1984.

MacDonald, Margaret R., ed. *The Folklore of World Holidays*. Detroit: Gale Research, 1992.

Sanon, Arun. *Festive India*. New Delhi: Frank Bros., 1986.

Van Straalen, Alice. *The Book of Holidays Around the World*. New York: Dutton, 1986.

WEB SITE

BBC (British Broadcasting Corporation)
www.bbc.co.uk/religion/religions/buddhism/holydays/losar.shtml

Lotus, Birthday of the

Type of Holiday: Religious (Buddhist)
Date of Observation: Twenty-fourth day of the sixth Chinese lunar month
Where Celebrated: Beijing, China
Symbols and Customs: Lotus

ORIGINS

The birthday of the Lotus is part of the tradition of Buddhism, one of the four largest religious families in the world. Buddhism is based on the teachings of Siddhartha Gautama (c. 563-483 B.C.E.), who came to be known as Buddha, or "The Enlightened One." The basic tenets of Buddhism can be summarized in the Four Noble Truths and the Eightfold Path. The Four Noble Truths are 1) the truth and reality of suffering; 2) suffering is caused by desire; 3) the way to end suffering is to end desire; and 4) the Eightfold Path shows the way to end suffering. The Eightfold Path consists of 1) right view or right understanding; 2) right thoughts and aspirations; 3) right speech; 4) right conduct and action; 5) right way of life; 6) right effort; 7) right mindfulness; and 8) right contemplation.

The Chinese celebrate the birthday of flowers in general (Moon 2, Day 12 or 15) and honor Wei Shen, the protectress of flowers (Moon 4, Day 19). But the LOTUS is singled out for special attention because of its importance to Buddhism. Gautama Buddha is described, in fact, as having "lotus eyes, lotus feet, and lotus thighs." His image is often shown seated or standing on a lotus.

The Birthday of the Lotus is observed at the time of year when lotuses bloom in the ponds and moats around Beijing, and people flock to the city to see them—much as they do in Japan and Washington DC during cherry blossom time (*see* **HANAMI**). The sixth moon of the Chinese calendar is called the "Lotus Moon" for this reason. Their blooms are a sign that prayers to the Dragon Prince have been answered and that the summer rains will start soon. Special lanes for rowboats are cut through the thick layer of lotus blossoms that cover the lakes of Beijing's Winter Palace.

SYMBOLS AND CUSTOMS

Lotus

As a symbol, the lotus has been sacred to many cultures and religions. It was adopted from the Hindus by the Buddhists in India, who introduced it into their sculpture, painting, and literature. From India, it went with the Buddhists to Nepal, Burma, China—where it is held sacred above all other flowers—and finally Japan.

The lotus symbolizes purity and perfection because it grows out of the mud and yet is not defiled by it. In much the same way, humankind should be able to live in an evil and impure world without being influenced by it. The open flower resting quietly on the water signifies meditation; in full bloom, it symbolizes spiritual enlightenment. Just as the lotus has its roots in the mud but its flower rises to achieve great beauty, devout Buddhists expected to rise above passion and selfish striving.

The many-petaled spread of the lotus blossom also has a more cosmic significance. It symbolizes the space in which all existence is supported and passes away. It is also a symbol of knowledge, which leads believers out of the cycle of reincarnation to Nirvana.

FURTHER READING

Biedermann, Hans. *Dictionary of Symbolism: Cultural Icons and the Meanings Behind Them.* New York: Meridian Books, 1994.

Bredon, Juliet, and Igor Mitrophanow. *The Moon Year: A Record of Chinese Customs and Festivals.* Shanghai: Kelly & Walsh, 1927.

Henderson, Helene, ed. *Holidays, Festivals, and Celebrations of the World Dictionary.* 3rd ed. Detroit: Omnigraphics, 2005.

Johnson, F. Ernest, ed. *Religious Symbolism.* New York: Institute for Religious and Social Studies, 1955.

Lughnasa

Type of Holiday: Ancient, Religious (Neopagan)
Date of Observation: August 1
Where Celebrated: England, Ireland, Scotland
Symbols and Customs: Funeral Processions, Hilltops, Oak Tree, Teltown Marriage
Related Holidays: Beltane, Imbolc, Lammas, Mabon, Reek Sunday, Samhain, Summer Solstice, Winter Solstice, Vernal Equinox

ORIGINS

Celtic peoples lived in Ireland, Scotland, England, and northern France from around 500 B.C.E. until around 100 C.E., when the Romans conquered most of Celtic Europe.

J. Albert Adams
Academy Media Center

Little is definitely known about ancient Celtic religion. The Celts themselves left sparse written accounts. Julius Caesar, who led the Romans into Celtic lands, wrote of his impressions of the people, as did other ancient Greco-Roman writers.

During the 1960s the modern Neopagan and Wiccan movements emerged in Great Britain, the United States, and other English-speaking countries. They follow a nature-oriented religion loosely linked to ancient Celtic and other beliefs and inspired by old European folk practices. They celebrate eight sabbats, known as the eight spokes of the wheel of the year, which include Lughnasa as well as **SUMMER SOLSTICE, WINTER SOLSTICE, VERNAL EQUINOX, BELTANE, SAMHAIN, IMBOLC**, and **MABON**.

Along with **BELTANE, SAMHAIN**, and **IMBOLC**, Lughnasa was one of the four major Celtic festivals observed in the British Isles during pre-Christian times. It takes its name from the ancient sun-god Lugh and the Celtic *nasadh*, meaning "commemoration." August 1 marked the midpoint of the warm or "summer" half of the year, which extended from May through October. Since the Celts measured their year from midsummer to midsummer, this festival was both a commemoration of the passing of the old year, as symbolized by FUNERAL PROCESSIONS for the sun-god Lugh, and a celebration of the arrival of the new year with games, feasting, and magic shows.

In Ireland, two important gatherings took place during Lughnasa: the assembly of Tailte, named after the goddess who was also the foster-mother of Lugh; and the assembly of Carman, which commemorated the grief of the mother-goddess Carman when her sons were expelled from Ireland. It was therefore an important gathering time for Celtic women, and there is evidence that ceremonies associated with marriage (*see* TELTOWN MARRIAGE), fertility, childbirth, and other female rites of passage took place during the festival.

In England, August 1 was called the festival of the Gule of August, a harvest celebration that was the forerunner of the American **THANKSGIVING**. When Christianity arrived, it was called **LAMMAS**, which may have come either from Lughmass or from "loaf-mass," since it was customary for loaves made from the first ripe grain to be blessed in the church on this day. Another theory is that the name derived from "lamb-mass," because it was the time of year when worshippers would bring a live lamb as an offering to the church.

While Beltane remained a pagan holiday and Samhain was largely replaced by the Christian festival of All Saints' Day, Lughnasa retained a mixture of pagan and Christian customs. In the Scottish Highlands, people used to sprinkle their cows and the floors of their houses with menstrual blood, which they believed would ward off evil on this day. Elsewhere in Scotland, Lammas was one of the so-called Quarter Days, when tenants paid their rents—an obvious Christianization of the harvest festival custom of having tenants bring the first new grain to their land-lords. In Ireland, where the celebration of Lughnasa waned during the late nine-teenth century and then was revived in the twentieth, it has survived primarily as a seasonal celebration.

SYMBOLS AND CUSTOMS

Funeral Processions

Because Lughnasa was originally a festival of mourning for the death of the sun-god Lugh, funerary rites and processions were a common practice. It is possible that at one time the victims were real, and that eventually they were replaced by effigies of the dead, carried in procession and buried in symbolic graves. Some scholars believe that in ancient times, when the Celtic kings reigned for only a year, the old king allowed himself to be put to death so that a new king could take his place. Since the Celts normally crowned their kings at midsummer, this would explain the necessity for funeral processions at Lughnasa.

In any case, the festival was an occasion for paying homage to the dead—particu-larly warriors and heroes in the style of Lugh—and eulogies or poems praising ancient gods and heroes were often recited. Even today, mock-funeral processions are occasionally held in Yorkshire and Lancashire, England, with groups of young men carrying an empty coffin for many miles along an ancient path.

Hilltops

Lughnasa was a popular time for gathering berries, particularly bilberries. In Ire-land, where Lughnasa began in mid-July and lasted until mid-August, the first Sunday of this four-week period was known as Bilberry Sunday. Young people would go off to the hilltops, where berries were plentiful, and not return until dusk. The boys would make bilberry bracelets for the girls by stringing the berries along short pieces of thread, competing with each other to see who could make the most beautiful bracelet for his girlfriend.

Many of the hilltop sights originally visited for berrypicking were later taken over by the Catholic Church and turned into pilgrimage sites. Croagh Patrick in County Mayo, Ireland, is a good example. Also known as The Reek, it is Ireland's holiest mountain, and pilgrims flock to it on the last Sunday in July, which is known as **REEK SUNDAY**. Although the Christians who climb Croagh Patrick do so because they want to pray on the spot where Ireland's patron saint is believed to have start-ed his ministry, this hilltop's fame may also be rooted in pagan celebrations.

As recently as the nineteenth century, people in Ireland were still visiting more than 100 hilltop sites on August 1 for berrypicking and pilgrimages.

Oak Tree

It is possible that the Druids, an ancient Celtic class of priests, venerated oak trees. If so, they were not the first to do so. There were oak cults in ancient Greece and Libya, and scholars believe that the oak cult came to Britain somewhere between 1600 and 1400 B.C.E., at least 500 years before the Celts.

According to some writers, the trees associated with the midsummer months are oak and holly, with the oak representing the god of the old year and the holly the god of the new year. The sun-god Lugh is associated with the oak in Celtic mythology because he symbolizes the old year (or the old king) who must yield to the new year (or new king) on August 1.

Teltown Marriage

Lughnasa was a time for the king to reconfirm his divine "marriage" to the well-being of his kingdom. Midsummer was also a popular time for real marriages, since the harvest was in, food was abundant, and agricultural chores were less demanding. In many ways, it was the most relaxed time of year, when people had the leisure to celebrate.

In medieval Ireland, there was a special kind of "trial" marriage that could only take place at Lughnasa. Called a Tailtean or Teltown marriage—after Tailte, a powerful goddess and the foster-mother of Lugh—it lasted only a year and a day. It could be dissolved without any social stigma, but only if both individuals returned on the next Lughnasa and went through a ritual in which they walked away from each other—one heading north and the other south.

Teltown, located in Ireland's County Meath, was also the scene of one of the most important gatherings that took place on August 1: the assembly of Tailte (*see* "Origins").

FURTHER READING

Bellenir, Karen. *Religious Holidays and Calendars*. 3rd ed. Detroit: Omnigraphics, 2004.

Chambers, Robert. *The Book of Days*. 2 vols. 1862-64. Reprint. Detroit: Omnigraphics, 1990.

Heinberg, Richard. *Celebrate the Solstice: Honoring the Earth's Seasonal Rhythms through Festival and Ceremony*. Wheaton, IL: Quest Books, 1993.

Henderson, Helene, ed. *Holidays, Festivals, and Celebrations of the World Dictionary*. 3rd ed. Detroit: Omnigraphics, 2005.

Hutton, Ronald. *The Pagan Religions of the Ancient British Isles: Their Nature and Legacy*. Oxford: Blackwell, 1991.

King, John. *The Celtic Druids' Year: Seasonal Cycles of the Ancient Celts*. London: Blandford, 1995.

Leach, Maria, ed. *Funk & Wagnalls Standard Dictionary of Folklore, Mythology & Legend*. San Francisco: Harper & Row, 1984.

MacDonald, Margaret R., ed. *The Folklore of World Holidays*. Detroit: Gale Research, 1992.

Urlin, Ethel L. *Festivals, Holy Days, and Saints' Days*. 1915. Reprint. Detroit: Omnigraphics, 1992.

Luilak
(Lazybones Day)

Type of Holiday: Folkloric
Date of Observation: Between May 9 and June 12; Saturday before Pentecost
Where Celebrated: Netherlands
Symbols and Customs: Branches, Wagons
Related Holidays: Pentecost

ORIGINS

Luilak or Lazybones Day is a youth festival celebrated in Zaandam, Haarlem, Amsterdam, and other towns in the western Netherlands. The holiday begins at four o'clock in the morning on the Saturday before **PENTECOST**, when groups of young people awaken their neighbors by whistling, banging on pots and pans, and ringing doorbells. Any boy or girl who refuses to get up and join in the noise-making is referred to as *Luilak* or "Lazybones" throughout the coming year. The Lazybones must also treat their companions to candy or cakes, and they are the butt of all sorts of jokes and teasing.

According to legend, the holiday originated in 1672 when a watchman named Piet Lak fell asleep while French invaders entered the country. He was known thereafter as *Luie-Lak*, or "Lazy Lak." In many parts of the country, *Luilakbollen* or "Lazybones Cakes," traditionally baked in the shape of fat double rolls and served hot with syrup, are specialties of the season.

SYMBOLS AND CUSTOMS

Branches

In some parts of the Netherlands, boys and girls get up early on the Saturday before Whitsunday (**PENTECOST**) and gather green branches from the woods.

Then they dip the branches in water and fasten them over the doors of late-sleepers in such a way that, when the door is opened, the branches fall on the unsuspecting "Lazybones" and give them a drenching. Then the children, who are usually lurking nearby, chase the Lazybones and beat them with the branches.

The custom of beating each other with branches as a way of welcoming spring dates back to very ancient times, when it was probably intended as a purification rite.

Wagons

Children often celebrate Luilak by making little wagons shaped like boots and decorated with branches and thistles, known as *luilakken*. Pulling the wagons over the cobblestone streets often generates enough friction to set the wheels smoking. The children then either watch their wagons go up in flames or douse them in the nearest canal.

Although the exact origin of the smoking wagons is not known, they are believed to be connected to an ancient spring fertility ceremony.

FURTHER READING

Henderson, Helene, ed. *Holidays, Festivals, and Celebrations of the World Dictionary.* 3rd ed. Detroit: Omnigraphics, 2005.

Ickis, Marguerite. *The Book of Festivals and Holidays the World Over.* New York: Dodd, Mead, 1970.

MacDonald, Margaret R., ed. *The Folklore of World Holidays.* Detroit: Gale Research, 1992.

Spicer, Dorothy Gladys. *Festivals of Western Europe.* 1958. Reprint. Detroit: Omnigraphics, 1993.

Spicer, Dorothy Gladys. *The Book of Festivals.* 1937. Reprint. Detroit: Omnigraphics, 1990.

WEB SITE

Catholic Culture
www.catholicculture.org/lit/recipes/view.cfm?id=1171

Lupercalia

Type of Holiday: Ancient
Date of Observation: February 15
Where Celebrated: Rome
Symbols and Customs: Blood, Februa, Goat, Milk, Wolf
Colors: Red and white, in the form of BLOOD and MILK, both played a part in the earliest observance of the Lupercalia. Nowadays these are the colors associated with Valentine's Day, to which this ancient festival has been linked.
Related Holidays: Valentine's Day

ORIGINS

The Lupercalia was a festival in the ancient Roman religion, which scholars trace back to the sixth century B.C.E. Roman religion dominated Rome and influenced territories in its empire until Emperor Constantine's conversion to Christianity in the third century C.E. Ancient Roman religion was heavily influenced by the older Greek religion. Roman festivals therefore had much in common with those of the ancient Greeks. Not only were their gods and goddesses mostly the same as those in the Greek pantheon (though the Romans renamed them), but their religious festivals were observed with similar activities: ritual sacrifice, theatrical performances, games, and feasts.

The Lupercalia festival was held in honor of the WOLF who mothered Romulus and Remus, the legendary twin founders of Rome. During the original Roman celebration, members from two colleges of priests gathered at a cave on the Palatine Hill called the Lupercal—supposedly the cave where Romulus and Remus had been suckled by a she-wolf—and sacrificed a GOAT and a dog. The animals' BLOOD was smeared on the foreheads of two young priests and then wiped away with wool dipped in MILK. The two young men stripped down to a goatskin loincloth and ran around the Palatine, striking everyone who approached them, especially the women, with thongs of goat skin called FEBRUA. It is believed that this was both a fertility ritual and a purification rite. It may also have been a very early example of "beating the bounds" (*see* **ASCENSION DAY**), or reestablishing the borders of the early Palatine settlement.

There is some confusion over which god the Luperci or priests served; some say it was Faunus, a rural deity, and some say it was Pan, the god of shepherds who protected sheep from the danger of wolves. All that is certain is that by Caesar's time, the annual ceremony had become a spectacular public sight, with young men running half-naked through the streets and provoking much good-natured hysteria among the women. February 15 was also the day when Mark Antony offered Julius Caesar the crown. Thanks to this historic event, and Shakespeare's account of it in his play *Julius Caesar*, the Lupercalia is one of the best known of all Roman festivals.

It is interesting that such a rustic festival continued to be celebrated in Rome for centuries after it had been Christianized. Its survival can be partially credited to Augustus, who rebuilt the Lupercal in the first century B.C.E., thus giving the celebration a boost. It continued to be observed until 494 C.E., when Pope Gelasius I changed the day to the Feast of the Purification of the Virgin Mary (*see* **CANDLEMAS**). There is some reason to believe that the Lupercalia was a forerunner of the modern **VALENTINE'S DAY**: Part of the ceremony involved putting girls' names in a box and letting boys draw them out, thus pairing them off until the next Lupercalia.

SYMBOLS AND CUSTOMS

Blood

Blood played an important role in the observation of the Lupercalia. The blood of the animals sacrificed at the festival was smeared across the foreheads of two young priests with a knife—perhaps to symbolize death without actually killing anyone. Some accounts of the early observation of this festival say that the youths had to laugh after the blood had been wiped off (*see* MILK), which may have been another symbolic act designed to prove that they had been reborn or revived.

Red, the color of blood, is still closely identified with the celebration of **VALENTINE'S DAY** on February 14. There is reason to believe that what started out as a pagan fertility ritual was eventually transformed into a Christian feast in honor of St. Valentine. Then the Christian festival gradually turned into a secular celebration of young lovers. If this is the case, then the red that dominates so many modern Valentine cards may have derived from the sacrificial blood of the Lupercalia.

Februa

The skins of the goats sacrificed at the Lupercalia were cut into long, thin strips, from which whips were made. The loinskin-clad youths ran through the streets, whipping everyone they met. Women in particular were eager to receive these lashes, as they believed that the whipping would cure infertility and ease the pains of childbirth.

The goatskin thongs used as whips were called *februa*. Both this name and the name of the month in which the festival was observed, February, were derived from the word *februum*, which was an ancient instrument of purification. Whipping certain parts of the body with an instrument believed to possess magical powers was considered an effective way of driving off the evil spirits that interfered with human fertilization. The goatskin thongs were believed to possess such powers.

Running around the settlement on the Palatine Hill in Rome wearing the skins and carrying the februa appears to have been an attempt to trace a magic circle around the city to shut out evil influences. This would make the Lupercalia a precursor of the ceremony that came to be known as "beating the bounds."

Goat

In pre-Christian times, the goat was a symbol of virility and unbridled lust. Christians saw the goat as an "impure, stinking" creature in search of gratification. In portrayals of the Last Judgment, the goat is the creature who is eternally condemned to the fires of Hell, and it's no coincidence that the devil has many goat-like characteristics. In the Middle Ages, witches were often shown riding through the air on goats, and the devil appears as a male goat whose rump the witches kiss.

If the Lupercalia was primarily a fertility ritual, it makes sense that the women were whipped with thongs made from the skins of an animal identified with lust and virility. But why was a dog sacrificed as well? It is important to remember here that the Lupercalia was both a fertility rite and a purification rite, held to protect the fields and herds from evil. Perhaps dogs were involved in the sacrifice because they are the traditional guardians of the sheepfold.

Goats today are considered a symbol of sexual drive, and February is the month during which they mate.

Milk

After the Luperci were smeared with the blood of the sacrifice, the blood was wiped from their foreheads with wool dipped in milk. Just as the blood symbolized death, the milky wool was symbolic of new life, because milk represents the source of life. Some scholars have theorized that the milk was a symbol of sperm and the red symbolized menstrual blood. According to an ancient theory of procreation, new life came from the union of white sperm with red menses.

Today, red and white are the colors associated with **VALENTINE'S DAY**.

Wolf

The Latin word for wolf is *lupus*, from which both the Lupercal (cave) and the Lupercalia derived their names. While the festival may originally have been held in honor of the she-wolf who cared for Romulus and Remus, wolves also represented a threat to the herds on which the early Romans depended for food. The wolf is therefore a symbol not only for the wild, unrestrained forces of nature but also for the benevolent guardian of helpless creatures like Romulus and Remus.

Why were the priests called Luperci? The word *Lupercus* might have come from a phrase meaning "to purify by means of a goat"; or it might have come from a combination of *lupus* and *arcere*, meaning "he who wards off wolves." Whether the Luperci were protectors from wolves or wolf-priests who took the form of wolves as a means of bringing them under control is a question that has never been satisfactorily answered. Some scholars suggest that the dead revealed themselves in the form of wolves, against whom the community had to be defended.

FURTHER READING

Biedermann, Hans. *Dictionary of Symbolism: Cultural Icons and the Meanings Behind Them.* New York: Meridian Books, 1994.

Fowler, W. Warde. *The Roman Festivals of the Period of the Republic.* New York: Macmillan Co., 1925.

Henderson, Helene, ed. *Holidays, Festivals, and Celebrations of the World Dictionary.* 3rd ed. Detroit: Omnigraphics, 2005.

James, E.O. *Seasonal Feasts and Festivals.* 1961. Reprint. Detroit: Omnigraphics, 1993.

Lemprière, John. *Lemprière's Classical Dictionary.* Revised ed. London: Bracken, 1994.

Santino, Jack. *All Around the Year: Holidays and Celebrations in American Life.* Urbana: University of Illinois Press, 1994.

Scullard, H.H. *Festivals and Ceremonies of the Roman Republic.* Ithaca, NY: Cornell University Press, 1981.

Mabon

Type of Holiday: Calendar/Seasonal, Ancient, Religious (Neopagan)
Date of Observation: Autumn Equinox, September 22 or 23
Where Celebrated: United States and Europe
Symbols and Customs: Circle Ceremonies, Harvest Feasts, Mabon
Related Holidays: Autumn Equinox, Beltane, Harvest Home, Imbolc, Lughnasa, Samhain, Summer Solstice, Winter Solstice, Vernal Equinox

ORIGINS

Mabon is derived from the Celtic peoples who lived in Ireland, Scotland, England, and northern France from around 500 B.C.E. until around 100 C.E., when the Romans conquered most of Celtic Europe. Little is definitely known about ancient Celtic religion. The Celts themselves left sparse written accounts. Julius Caesar, who led the Romans into Celtic lands, wrote of his impressions of the people, as did other ancient Greco-Roman writers.

Mabon honors the arrival of the fall season and the change in the balance of light and dark that occurs with the **AUTUMN EQUINOX**. The holiday is celebrated on the date of equinox, which falls on either September 22 or 23.

The ancient stone monuments of the British Isles provide some evidence that the prehistoric people that lived there honored the equinoxes and the solstices. Quite a number of stone monuments appear to have been built to identify the dates on which these celestial events occur. This prehistoric civilization was replaced, however, by the Celtic people in ancient times, and then later by the Anglo-Saxon peoples in early medieval times. No direct evidence exists to suggest that the Celts or

Anglo-Saxons continued these early observances. Nevertheless, the Anglo-Saxon word for September, "haleg-monath," translates as "holy month." This seems to suggest that some important holiday took place during this month. The Christian feast of **MICHAELMAS** falls on September 29, but it is unclear how widely celebrated it was in Anglo-Saxon times.

Neopagans and Wiccans, people who follow a nature-oriented religion loosely linked to ancient pagan beliefs and inspired by old European folk practices, began to celebrate the autumn equinox in the twentieth century. In doing so, they were guided by the belief that ancient pagan people often celebrated this event. Some call the holiday Mabon, while others refer to it simply as autumn harvest, autumn sabbat, or **AUTUMN EQUINOX.** It forms one of the eight sabbats of modern witchcraft (or Wicca), the other seven being **SUMMER SOLSTICE, WINTER SOLSTICE, VERNAL EQUINOX, BELTANE, SAMHAIN, IMBOLC,** and **LUGHNASA**. Together these holidays form the eight spokes of what is known as the wheel of the year. These holidays are distributed more or less evenly throughout the year, falling on the solstices, the equinoxes, and the four cross-quarter days; that is, the four days that fall between the solstices and the equinoxes.

SYMBOLS AND CUSTOMS

Circle Ceremonies

Many Wiccans and Neopagans celebrate Mabon by participating in circle ceremonies that highlight the themes of the holiday. The altar, or area where the ceremony takes place, is decorated with such harvest symbols as corn, apples, and wine, or perhaps equinox symbols, including black and white candles. Participants stand in a circle and a leader takes the group through a ceremony that may involve some combination of listening to stories, lighting candles, chanting, dancing, honoring various gods and goddesses, and responding in unison to invocations offered by the group leader.

Some groups may choose to focus their ceremony on the legend of Mabon, or Persephone, and the spiritual lessons contained therein. Other groups will focus on the change in season and thanksgiving for the harvest. The balance of light and darkness that occurs on the equinox is another popular theme of Mabon celebrations. This time of year is often associated with a turning inwards, and Mabon ceremonies may encourage group members to spend more time in introspection and meditation during the colder, darker months.

Harvest Feasts

Mabon occurs in an important time during the agricultural year, when the late summer harvest is drawing to a close. Neopagans and Wiccans honor this seasonal event in their Mabon celebrations. In fact, many Mabon celebrations revolve around communal meals in which harvest foods are shared and enjoyed. In North America such feasts might include corn, squash, tomatoes, grapes, apples, wine, bread, and other local foods.

Mabon

Some Wiccans have named the autumn equinox holiday that they celebrate "Mabon" after the Welsh legend about a magical youth of the same name. The legend of Mabon circulated within the ancient Celtic lands (Ireland, the British Isles, and northwestern France). In early Welsh tales Mabon is a heroic warrior, and in later accounts he becomes a semi-divine or magical figure. In the later stories associated with the King Arthur tales, Mabon is stolen from his mother, Modron, when he is only three days old and shut away in a magical cave. The child's full name, Mabon ap Modron, literally means "mother's son." Mabon grows up in captivity but is known to be the finest hunter in the land. He is finally rescued by the great Welsh hero Culhwch, who receives the aid of an owl, a stag, a blackbird, an otter, and a salmon in his long and arduous quest.

There are many variations on this tale. Its association with the **AUTUMN EQUINOX** comes from the role of darkness in the story. The kidnappers hide the baby in the darkness of the earth (the cave) just as the nights appear to overpower the days around the time of the equinox. The search for the divine child constitutes another important theme in the story. This search represents the universal search for the child in ourselves, or our desire to discover our true, inner nature. The use of animal guides in the search is very important. They alert us to the need to follow nature's wisdom if we are to be successful in our search.

Some neopagans compare the myth of Mabon to the more well-known Greek myth of Persephone, the spring goddess. Persephone, who is the daughter of the harvest goddess Demeter, is abducted and taken to the underworld by Hades, the Lord of the Dead. Although Persephone is rescued, she has to return to the underworld for six months of every year because she ate the food of the dead. During the time of Persephone's imprisonment, the days grow cold and the nights long. As the time of her emergence draws near, the earth again begins to show signs of life. Many neopagans associate the time of Persephone's disappearance with the **AUTUMN EQUINOX** and the time of her yearly emergence with the **VERNAL EQUINOX**. The story of Mabon's kidnapping has also been associated with the **AUTUMN EQUINOX**. Nevertheless, while Persephone languishes in her dark and dreary captivity, Mabon grows and flourishes in a bright and magical enclosure. Some interpreters of the tale have suggested that Mabon's presence underground blesses the earth, just as the fallow seasons of fall and winter restore the earth and permit new fertility to burst forth in the spring.

FURTHER READING

Buckland, Raymond. *Wicca for Life: The Way of the Craft, From Birth to the Summerland*. Citadel, NY: 2001.

Cabot, Laurie. *Celebrate the Earth: A Year of Holidays in the Pagan Tradition*. Delta, NY: 1994.

Dugan, Ellen. *Autumn Equinox: The Enchantment of Mabon*. St. Paul: Llewellyn, 2005

Hawkes, Elen. *The Sacred Round: A Witch's Guide to Magical Practice*. St. Paul: Llewellyn, 2002.

Hutton, Ronald. *The Pagan Religions of the Ancient British Isles: Their Nature and Legacy*. Oxford: Blackwell, 1991.

Grimassi, Rave. *Encyclopedia of Wicca and Witchcraft*. St. Paul: Lwellellyn, 2000.

Magha Puja
(Maka Buja, Full Moon Day)

Type of Holiday: Religious (Buddhist)
Date of Observation: February-March; full moon day of the third lunar month
Where Celebrated: India, Laos, Thailand, and by Buddhists around the world
Symbols and Customs: Circumambulation, Five Precepts, Meritorious Deeds, Ovadha Patimokha

ORIGINS

Magha Puja is part of the religious tradition of Buddhism, one of the four largest religious families in the world. Buddhism is based on the teachings of Siddhartha Gautama (c. 563-483 B.C.E.), who came to be known as Buddha, or "The Enlightened One." The basic tenets of Buddhism can be summarized in the Four Noble Truths and the Eightfold Path. The Four Noble Truths are 1) the truth and reality of suffering; 2) suffering is caused by desire; 3) the way to end suffering is to end desire; and 4) the Eightfold Path shows the way to end suffering. The Eightfold Path consists of 1) right view or right understanding; 2) right thoughts and aspirations; 3) right speech; 4) right conduct and action; 5) right way of life; 6) right effort; 7) right mindfulness; and 8) right contemplation.

Magha Puja is an important day for Buddhists everywhere and a national holiday in Thailand. It commemorates two events in Buddhist history. The first event was the day on which 1,250 Arahants or enlightened monks—all of whom had been ordained by the Buddha himself—spontaneously gathered at the Veluvan Monastery in Rajagriha, India, the capital of the ancient kingdom of Magadha. This was considered a miraculous occurrence because none of them had been specifically invited, nor did they know that so many others would be there. The Buddha delivered a sermon to them, known as the OVADHA PATIMOKHA, in which he laid down the basic precepts of Buddhism. The second event commemorated on this day occurred shortly before the Buddha's death, when he told his disciples that his earthly life would end and he would enter into Nirvana on the full moon day of the sixth lunar month, exactly three months after Magha Puja.

Magha Puja was not observed in Thailand until the reign of King Rama IV, who realized its significance and declared in 1851 that it would henceforth be celebrated annually. Today, Buddhists in Thailand and elsewhere observe Magha Puja by gathering at their local temples, where they observe the FIVE PRECEPTS, listen to sermons, carry out MERITORIOUS DEEDS, and join in the CIRCUMAMBULATION ritual.

SYMBOLS AND CUSTOMS

Circumambulation

One of the highlights of the Magha Puja celebration is the candlelight procession known as wien tien, which takes place in the temple at dusk when the full moon is rising. Led by praying monks, Buddhist worshippers carrying candles, incense sticks, and flowers make three complete circuits around the main chapel or shrine where the image of the Buddha is kept. They walk with their right sides turned toward Buddha, a sign of respect, and focus on the basic precepts of Buddhism (*see* FIVE PRECEPTS and OVADHA PATIMOKHA).

Five Precepts

The so-called "five precepts" of Buddhism are the basic rules governing moral conduct: to refrain from injuring others and to avoid stealing, lying, and unchaste or intemperate behavior, which includes the use of intoxicants. Magha Puja is a time for reflecting on these principles and on how they can be manifested in one's daily life.

Meritorious Deeds

The meritorious or "merit-making" deeds performed by Buddhists on Magha Puja include preparing and offering food to monks, giving alms to the poor, practicing meditation, attending sermons, chanting prayers, and participating in the wien tien or CIRCUMAMBULATION ritual. It is also common on this day to free birds and fish who have lived in captivity.

Ovadha Patimokha

It was during the sermon, referred to as Ovadha Patimokha (Fundamental Teaching), given by the Buddha to the 1,250 Buddhist monks assembled at the Veluvan Temple that he proclaimed the basic tenets of Buddhist belief: to refrain from evil acts, to perform good deeds, and to purify the mind.

FURTHER READING

Bechert, Heinz, and Richard Gombrich. *The World of Buddhism*. New York: Facts on File, 1984.

Bellenir, Karen. *Religious Holidays and Calendars*. 3rd ed. Detroit: Omnigraphics, 2004.

MacDonald, Margaret R., ed. *The Folklore of World Holidays*. Detroit: Gale Research, 1992.

Parrinder, Geoffrey. *A Dictionary of Non-Christian Religions*. Philadelphia: Westminster Press, 1971.

Van Straalen, Alice. *The Book of Holidays Around the World*. New York: Dutton, 1986.

WEB SITE

Thai Folk Library
www.thaifolk.com/Doc/maghapuja_e.htm

Mahavira Jayanti

Type of Holiday: Religious (Jain)
Date of Observation: March-April; thirteenth day of the waxing half of Caitra
Where Celebrated: India and throughout the Jain world
Symbols and Customs: Abhishek, Cradle Processions, Fasting

ORIGINS

Mahavira Jayanti is part of the tradition of Jainism, a religion based on the principles of nonviolence, truthfulness, chastity, and the avoidance of stealing and attachment to earthly things. Jainism originated in India around the same time that Buddhism developed. Jains believe in a sequence of reincarnations: animals must become human, and lay people must become monks in order to attain salvation from the world. Salvation, called mokhsa, is attained by liberating the soul from the contamination of matter (karma). This liberation results in omniscience and bliss for eternity.

One of the fundamental doctrines of Jainism is the separation of living matter (called jiva) and non-living matter (called ajiva). In order to achieve freedom from karma, Jains must completely avoid harming any living thing and practice perfect asceticism. Three concepts govern the affairs of the Jain people. These are known collectively as the Triratna (Three Jewels) and consist of right faith, right knowledge, and right conduct.

The name Jain comes from the Sanskrit word Jina, which means Conqueror. The conquerors honored by the Jains are people who have overcome and won enlightenment. The name Jinas also applies specifically to twenty-four spiritual guides from history and the legendary past who are collectively called the Tirthankaras (which means ford-markers). Each of the Tirthankaras achieved liberation, and by his model taught others how to do the same. There is no personal god in Jainism. Although several gods and goddesses are recognized (and a few of them are also included in the Hindu pantheon), they take a subordinate position to the twenty-four Tirthankaras.

Jainism teaches that the universe is eternal—it was not created, it has no beginning, and it will have no end. It passes through cycles during which civilizations rise and fall, men attain large size, and life-spans lengthen. In each cycle, twenty-four Tirthankaras appear. The last (twenty-fourth) Tirthankara was Vardhamana Mahavira, who lived about the same time as Buddha. Jain sects place the date of his death in 527 B.C.E., and some researchers place the event in 477 B.C.E. Mahavira taught a path of passionless detachment and, according to Jain teaching, had achieved omniscience (knowledge of all things) before he started preaching.

Lord Mahavira is the founder of Jainism. The Jains have two main sects: the Digambaras ("sky-clad"), whose monks do not wear clothes, and the Svetambaras ("white-clad"), whose monks wear white robes. The Digambaras believe that their monks should be totally nude, but Indian law requires that they wear a loincloth in public. Nakedness implies that they have left their sexual identity and all forms of desire behind them. Digambaras believe that only men can achieve liberation from the cycle of rebirths. Unlike Svetambaras, they believe that after his enlightenment, Mahavira no longer became involved in human relationships or participated in such human activities as eating, drinking, and talking.

Both sects agree that Mahavira was conceived by Devananda, a Brahmin wife, and that the embryo was miraculously transferred to the womb of Queen Trisala, who had sixteen prophetic dreams (or fourteen, according to the Svetambaras) shortly before his birth. These dreams were interpreted by astrologers, who said that the child would grow up to be either an emperor or a *tirthankar*—a human who,

537

through meditation and self-realization, has reached a state of enlightenment and serves as a kind of teacher or spiritual guide.

After renouncing the physical world at the age of thirty and meditating for twelve years, Vardhamana attained enlightenment and became known as Mahavira ("Great Hero"), the last of the twenty-four tirthankaras. He spent the next thirty years teaching the people of India how they could liberate themselves from the earthly cycle of birth and death and attain the blissful state known as Nirvana. Like his contemporary, the Buddha, Siddhartha Gautama (c.563 B.C.E. to c.483 B.C.E.), he challenged the ritualism and animal sacrifices associated with Hinduism. He believed in *ahimsa* or nonviolence to the point where he and his followers covered their mouths and noses to avoid inhaling germs and insects. Even today, the most devout Jains wear masks and carry brooms with which they sweep the ground in front of them as they walk, so as not to step on any living thing.

Jains celebrate their founder's birth in a solemn and sedate way, visiting the sacred sites associated with his life and worshipping the tirthankaras. Flags decorate Jain temples, where worshippers gather to offer their prayers, recite from the Jain scriptures, and focus on the teachings of Mahavira. They make a special effort to refrain from harming living things, and they often donate food, clothes, and money to the poor. Although there are few if any rituals associated with most Jain festivals, it may be the influence of Hinduism that has led members of the Jain community to carry out ABHISHEK or ritual bathing as well as PROCESSIONS through the streets so that everyone can honor the image of Mahavira. Offerings of milk, fruit, rice, and incense to such images on this day are also reminiscent of Hindu celebrations.

The observation of Mahavira Jayanti is more elaborate in places associated with Mahavira's life or where important Jain temples are located. Jains flock to the ancient shrines of Girnar and Palitana in Gujarat, to Pawapuri and Vaishali in Bihar, and to the Parasnath temple in Calcutta to celebrate Mahavira's birthday.

SYMBOLS AND CUSTOMS

Abhishek

Abhishek, a Sanskrit word meaning "to sprinkle water," refers to the ceremonial bathing of Mahavira's image on this day. The custom is symbolic of what happened when Vardhamana (Mahavira) was born: the gods and goddesses who came down from heaven to honor this exceptionally beautiful child, a future tirthankar, gave him a ceremonial bath.

Cradle Processions

After the ABHISHEK ritual is over, the image of Mahavira is placed in a cradle and carried through the streets so that everyone can admire it, Depending on where these processions take place, the image may be accompanied by drummers and other musicians, horses, elephants, and tableaux based on the events in Mahavira's life. Sometimes the image is carried in an elaborate chariot, and sometimes it is pulled through the streets in a simple wooden cart.

Fasting

Most Jains fast on Mahavira Jayanti, eating only one meal before sunset or refraining from eating altogether, breaking their fast the next morning.

FURTHER READING

Bellenir, Karen. *Religious Holidays and Calendars*. 3rd ed. Detroit: Omnigraphics, 2004.

Bowker, John, ed. *The Oxford Dictionary of World Religions*. New York: Oxford University Press, 1997.

Crim, Keith R. *The Perennial Dictionary of World Religions*. San Francisco: Harper & Row, 1989.

Henderson, Helene, ed. *Holidays, Festivals, and Celebrations of the World Dictionary*. 3rd ed. Detroit: Omnigraphics, 2005.

MacDonald, Margaret R., ed. *The Folklore of World Holidays*. Detroit: Gale Research, 1992.

Trawicky, Bernard, and Ruth W. Gregory. *Anniversaries and Holidays*. 5th ed. Chicago: American Library Assocation, 2000.

WEB SITE

Harvard University
www.fas.harvard.edu/~pluralsm/affiliates/jainism/jainedu/mahavir.htm

Martenitza

Type of Holiday: Calendar/Seasonal, Folkloric
Date of Observation: March 1
Where Celebrated: Albania, Bulgaria, Canada, Cyprus, Greece, Macedonia, Romania
Symbols and Customs: Martenitza
Colors: This festival is associated with the colors red and white. Red, symbolizing life, is believed to possess the power to drive away evil. White symbolizes the sun and purity.

ORIGINS

Martenitza, celebrated on the first day of March, marks the beginning of spring in Bulgaria and the beginning of summer in Greece. The holiday marks the changing of the seasons, which people in all parts of the world have honored since ancient times. Many cultures divided the year into two seasons, summer and winter, and marked these points of the year at or near the summer and winter solstices, during which light and warmth began to increase and decrease, respectively. In pre-industrial times, all humans survived through hunting, gathering, and agricultural practices, which depend on the natural cycle of seasons, according to the climate in the region of the world in which they lived. Thus, they created rituals to help ensure enough rain and sun in the spring and summer so crops would grow to fruition at harvest time, which was, in turn, duly celebrated. Vestiges of many of these ancient practices are thought to have survived in festivals still celebrated around seasonal themes.

The custom of exchanging MARTENITZAS, or tassels made of red and white threads, on the first day of March is most widespread in Bulgaria, although it is common in southern Romania, Albania, Greece, and Cyprus as well.

The rites associated with the holiday are varied. In some regions, the women dress completely in red on this day. In northeastern Bulgaria, the lady of the house tosses a red cloth over a fruit tree, or spreads a red woolen cloth on the fields to improve their fertility. In stock-breeding areas, a red-and-white thread is tied to the cattle. In Greece, the martenitza (which means "March") is tied to the wrist or big toe of children to protect them from the intense March sun. There is a widespread folk belief that children should wear their martenitza until they see the first swallow of the year. Then they should hide it under a stone. When the stone is lifted forty days later, ants indicate that wealth and happiness will come to the owner of the martenitza; but if there are worms, it means bad luck. Sometimes the martenitza is thrown on a rosebush in the garden, or tossed in the air when the first swallow is sighted. How these customs originated has been forgotten, but it is likely that the fate of the martenitza and of the person who wore it were somehow connected.

Bulgarians and Macedonians living in Canada exchange twists of red and white thread, known as *marteniki*, on the first day of March. When they see the first robins, they toss down the threads for the birds to use in their nest-building.

SYMBOLS AND CUSTOMS

Martenitza

The red-and-white thread tassel that gives this holiday its name can be traced back to the ancient Thracians, who attached silver or gold coins to their martenitzas.

March was the first month of the year in ancient Greece, and it is believed that the martenitza was originally a means of wishing each other good luck in the coming year. Since that time it has remained a symbol of good health and happiness, an appropriate token to exchange at a time of year when life is renewing itself.

FURTHER READING

Henderson, Helene, ed. *Holidays, Festivals, and Celebrations of the World Dictionary*. 3rd ed. Detroit: Omnigraphics, 2005.
MacDonald, Margaret R., ed. *The Folklore of World Holidays*. Detroit: Gale Research, 1992.

WEB SITE

Bulgarian Guide
www.bulgarian-guide.com/bulgarian-traditions/martenitsa

Martin Luther King Jr. Day

Type of Holiday: Historic, National
Date of Observation: Third Monday in January
Where Celebrated: Throughout the United States and U.S. territories, and by more than 100 nations around the world
Symbols and Customs: "I Have a Dream" Speech

ORIGINS

Born on January 15, 1929, Martin Luther King Jr. was the son of Martin Luther King Sr., the pastor of the Ebenezer Baptist Church in Atlanta, Georgia. He achieved national prominence in 1955, when he led the Montgomery, Alabama, bus boycott. The boycott was designed to end segregation in the city's transit system after Rosa Parks, a black seamstress, refused to obey a bus driver's order to give up her seat to a white male passenger and was fined $14. In 1960 King was chosen to head the Southern Christian Leadership Conference, giving him the organizational base he needed to extend his campaign for civil rights throughout the South. He organized many protests and marches, among them the August 1963 "March on Washington," at which he delivered his now famous "I HAVE A DREAM" SPEECH. Throughout his life he practiced nonviolent resistance and advocated peaceful protest against his country's segregationist practices. He received the Nobel Peace Prize in 1964.

Martin Luther King was assassinated in Memphis, Tennessee, by James Earl Ray on April 4, 1968. He had come to Memphis to help organize a strike of the city's sanitation workers, most of whom were black. He was shot while standing on the balcony outside his motel room. The assassination sparked riots in 120 American cities that year and led to a tremendous increase in the kind of violence that King had worked for more than a decade to prevent.

Eight days later, U.S. Representative John Conyers from Michigan called for a federal holiday honoring Dr. King. Atlanta was the first city to designate King's birthday as a paid holiday for city employees in 1971, and in 1973, Illinois became the first state to declare January 15 a statewide holiday. On January 15, 1981, which would have been King's fifty-second birthday, more than 100,000 people gathered at the Washington Monument to rally for a national holiday. Legislation was finally passed by Congress in 1983 setting aside the third Monday in January to honor King. This day is only the tenth national holiday approved by Congress, and it is the only one honoring an American other than past U.S. presidents.

National holidays can be defined as those commemorations that a nation's government has deemed important enough to warrant inclusion in the list of official public holidays. They tend to honor an event or a person, like King, who has been critical in the development of the nation and its identity. Such people and events usually reflect values and traditions shared by a large portion of the citizenry. In the United States, patiotism and identity were nurtured by the very act of celebrating new events as national holidays. The invention of traditions and the marking of important occasions in the life of the new nation were crucial in creating a shared bond of tradition and a sense of common belonging to a relatively new homeland through the shared experience of celebrating common holidays. As more and diverse peoples migrated to the United States, it became even more important to celebrate significant annual anniversaries, and Martin Luther King Jr. Day has become one of the nation's most important shared celebrations.

SYMBOLS AND CUSTOMS

"I Have a Dream" Speech

Oratory was Martin Luther King's greatest talent. The speech he delivered at the Lincoln Memorial in Washington DC, on August 28, 1963, almost immediately became a symbol of the civil rights movement. It was heard by an audience of 250,000 who had assembled there during the famous March on Washington to win the support of Congress and the president for pending civil rights legislation. When King was assassinated five years later, the speech became a symbol of his lifelong effort to end segregation through nonviolent means.

King repeated the phrase "I Have a Dream" at several points during the speech, building intensity with each repetition. Those who were close to King at the time say that he spent days agonizing over each paragraph, sentence, and punctuation mark—as if he knew it would be the speech by which he would be remembered. Excerpts from the "I Have a Dream" speech are still broadcast on television and radio around the time of the King holiday. It is often accompanied by the singing of "We Shall Overcome," widely regarded as the theme song of the civil rights movement.

FURTHER READING

Anyike, James C. *African American Holidays*. Revised and Expanded ed. Chicago: Popular Truth Pub., 1997.

Christianson, Stephen G., and Jane M. Hatch. *The American Book of Days*. 4th ed. New York: H.W. Wilson, 2000.

Gay, Kathlyn. *African-American Holidays, Festivals, and Celebrations*. Detroit: Omnigraphics, 2007.

Henderson, Helene, ed. *Holidays, Festivals, and Celebrations of the World Dictionary*. 3rd ed. Detroit: Omnigraphics, 2005.

Henderson, Helene. *Patriotic Holidays of the United States*. Detroit: Omnigraphics, 2006.

Santino, Jack. *All Around the Year: Holidays and Celebrations in American Life*. Urbana: University of Illinois Press, 1994.

Schaun, George and Virginia, and David Wisniewski. *American Holidays and Special Days*. 3rd ed. Lanham: Maryland Historical Press, 2002.

WEB SITES

Library of Congress
memory.loc.gov/ammem/today/jan15.html

The King Center
www.thekingcenter.com

Martinmas

Type of Holiday: Religious (Christian), Folkloric
Date of Observation: November 11
Where Celebrated: British Isles, Scandinavia, Western Europe
Symbols and Customs: Bonfires, Goose, Rod

ORIGINS

Martinmas is part of the religious tradition of Christianity. The word Christian refers to a follower of Christ, a title derived from the Greek word meaning Messiah or Anointed One. The Christ of Christianity is Jesus of Nazareth, a man born between 7 and 4 B.C.E. in the region of Palestine. According to Christian teaching, Jesus was killed by Roman authorities using a form of execution called crucifixion (a term meaning he was nailed to a cross and hung from it until he died) in about the year 30 C.E. After his death, he rose back to life. His death and resurrection provide a way by which people can be reconciled with God. In remembrance of Jesus' death and resurrection, the cross serves as a fundamental symbol in Christianity.

With nearly two billion believers in countries around the globe, Christianity is the largest of the world's religions. There is no one central authority for all of Christianity. The pope (the bishop of Rome) is the authority for the Roman Catholic Church, but other sects look to other authorities. Orthodox communities look to patriarchs and emphasize doctrinal agreement and traditional practice. Protestant communities focus on individual conscience. The Roman Catholic and Protestant churches are often referred to as the Western Church, while the Orthodox churches may also be called the Eastern Church. All three main branches of Christianity acknowledge the authority of Christian scriptures, a compilation of writings assembled into a document called the Bible. Methods of biblical interpretation vary among the different Christian sects.

Martinmas is the popular name for the feast day of St. Martin of Tours (316-397 C.E.), the patron saint of France. Pope Martin I (649-654 C.E.) made it a great church festival, probably in an attempt to Christianize the old Teutonic custom of slaughtering animals in mid-November because they couldn't be kept alive throughout the long winter.

During the Middle Ages, November 11 was regarded as both the beginning of the year and the beginning of winter, a time when rents for pastures were paid and farm servants changed jobs. It was called the Martinalia because it took the place of the Vinalia or vintage feast of ancient Rome and was observed by opening the first cask of the year's vintage.

In addition to giving thanks for the new wine, Martinmas was also a day of thanksgiving for the harvest. For rural people, Martinmas came at a happy time of year: The crops were in, the new wine was ready, the animals had been slaughtered, and it was time to relax. Not surprisingly, St. Martin became the patron saint of tavern keepers, wine-growers, and drunkards. The Feast of St. Martin is still observed as a harvest festival in Scandinavia and rural parts of Europe, with roast GOOSE being the traditional dish of the harvest feast.

Over the centuries, Martinmas has shifted from a religious feast to a folk festival. In Belgium and other western European countries, St. Martin's role is much like that of St. Nicholas. He appears dressed as a bishop in red robes, riding on a white horse. To children who have behaved well, he throws apples, nuts, and cakes; an ill-behaved child receives a ROD. Sometimes children fill their stockings with hay for St. Martin's horse and find them full of gifts the next morning.

Martinmas is also associated with the weather. In fact, the mild weather that often occurs in Europe in early November is referred to as "St. Martin's summer"— much like Indian summer in the United States. This goes back to an old legend that says St. Martin cut his cloak in two and gave half to a beggar who was nearly frozen with the cold. God sent warm weather so that the saint would be comfortable until he was able to find another cloak.

SYMBOLS AND CUSTOMS

Bonfires

The bonfires that can still be seen in Belgium, Holland, and parts of Germany on St. Martin's Day (or the night before) can be traced back to pagan times, when they were lit to ward off evil spirits and promote fertility. During the fifteenth century, so many fires were lit in Germany on this day that the festival was called Funkentag (Spark Day).

In northwestern Germany today, the fire is often contained in lanterns made of paper or carved-out turnips (*see* **HALLOWEEN**), carried through the streets by processions of children on St. Martin's Eve. Jumping over lighted candles set in the floor is another popular German fire custom. Elsewhere, young people dance around bonfires and leap through the flames. Later, the ashes are scattered over the fields to make them fertile.

Goose

As mentioned above, mid-November was the season for slaughtering farm animals among the Teutonic peoples. In fact, the original Anglo-Saxon name for November was *Blot-monath* or "blood month," associated not only with animal sacrifices but with feasting on meat. The tradition of slaughter has been preserved in the British custom of killing cattle on St. Martin's Day—referred to as "Martlemas beef"—and in the German custom of eating "St. Martin's Goose."

Why goose? According to an old legend, when St. Martin heard that he had been elected Bishop of Tours, the thought so intimidated him that he hid in a barn. But a goose found him there and made such a racket that his whereabouts were soon discovered.

In Denmark, a goose is eaten for the Martinmas meal and then its breastbone is examined for clues regarding the approaching winter. A very white bone is a sign of snow, while brown means extreme cold.

In parts of Ireland, it was common in the nineteenth century to kill an animal on Martinmas and sprinkle its blood over the threshold. Neglecting this custom—which may have been a holdover from the old Celtic festival of **SAMHAIN**—would bring bad luck.

Rod

In Bavaria and Austria, a *gerte* or rod is associated with St. Martin's Day. Used to promote fertility among cattle and prosperity in general, the rods are given to farmers, to be used in the springtime when they drive the cattle out to pasture for the first time. In Bavaria, the rods are made from birch boughs with all the leaves and twigs stripped off—except at the top, where oak leaves and juniper twigs are fastened. Flogging is common in folk rituals, and in this case its purpose is to drive away evil influences and transfer the life-giving virtues of the tree from which the rod is made.

There is some connection between the custom of flogging and St. Martin's role as a European Santa Claus. In Antwerp, Belgium, St. Martin throws down rods for naughty children as well as nuts and apples for good ones—just as Santa Claus leaves gifts for good children and a lump of coal for those who have misbehaved. In ancient times, beating someone didn't have the negative connotations it has today, but was instead a positive gesture meant to bestow virtue and vitality. In any case, it is interesting to note that so many pagan customs have gathered about the festival of a Christian saint.

FURTHER READING

Harper, Howard V. *Days and Customs of All Faiths.* 1957. Reprint. Detroit: Omnigraphics, 1990.

Henderson, Helene, ed. *Holidays, Festivals, and Celebrations of the World Dictionary.* 3rd ed. Detroit: Omnigraphics, 2005.

Miles, Clement A. *Christmas in Ritual and Tradition, Christian and Pagan.* 1912. Reprint. Detroit: Omnigraphics, 1990.

Pike, Royston. *Round the Year with the World's Religions.* 1950. Reprint. Detroit: Omnigraphics, 1992.

Purdy, Susan. *Festivals for You to Celebrate.* Philadelphia: Lippincott, 1969.

Urlin, Ethel L. *Festivals, Holy Days, and Saints' Days.* 1915. Reprint. Detroit: Omnigraphics, 1992.

Weiser, Franz Xaver. *Handbook of Christian Feasts and Customs.* New York: Harcourt, Brace, 1958.

WEB SITE

Irish Culture and Customs
www.irishcultureandcustoms.com/ACalend/Martinmas.html

Maskal
(Masqual, Meskel)

Type of Holiday: Religious (Christian)
Date of Observation: September 27
Where Celebrated: Ethiopia
Symbols and Customs: Cross, Demara, Maskal Flowers
Related Holidays: Exaltation of the Cross

ORIGINS

Christianity was established in Ethiopia in the fourth century, when a Christian from Syria named Frumentius traveled there and influenced the local ruler. At the time, Christianity in Syria was under the domain of the Orthodox Patriarch of Alexandria, Egypt. Thus, so was the new church in Ethiopia until 1959, when the Ethiopian Orthodox Church separated from the Coptic Church of Egypt.

Maskal is primarily a Christian festival observed in Ethiopia to commemorate the finding of the True Cross (i.e., the cross on which Christ was crucified). According to legend, the CROSS was found by Queen (later Saint) Helena—mother of the Roman emperor, Constantine—while she was on a religious pilgrimage to Jerusalem in the fourth century. She was very interested in the Mount of Calvary, where Jesus Christ had been crucified, and she organized an excavation there. Although all three crosses that had originally stood on Calvary were unearthed, St. Helena was able to determine which one was the True Cross by asking a man who was very ill to touch each of them. When he touched the True Cross, he was miraculously cured (*see* **EXALTATION OF THE CROSS**).

A relic or fragment of the True Cross was brought to Ethiopia during the Middle Ages as a reward to the Christian kings who had protected Coptic minorities from invaders. They received the relic a week before Maskal, which at that time was primarily a festival celebrating the arrival of spring. Since that time, the holiday has combined both Christian and pagan traditions.

Because Maskal comes at the end of the rainy season in Ethiopia, the fields are usually blooming with small yellow daisies known as MASKAL FLOWERS. The flowers are cut and fastened to special poles (*see* DEMARA) that each family brings to a central clearing. The poles are used to build a bonfire, around which young men dance, shouting war chants. On the following day, people draw a cross on their foreheads with the charcoal from the fire.

SYMBOLS AND CUSTOMS

Cross

The cross is one of the oldest and most universal of all symbols. It stands for Christ, who was sacrificed on a cross, as well as for the Christian religion and the idea of redemption or salvation through Christianity.

Maskal celebrates the finding of the True Cross by St. Helena, who is often depicted carrying a cross, along with a hammer and nails. Sometimes she is shown with the cross borne by angels who are appearing to her in a vision.

Demara

On the eve of Maskal, every town and village erects its own demara, which is a tall, conical arrangement of wooden poles decorated with maskal flowers and with a cross on top. The demara is blessed with incense, after which a procession of villagers or townspeople, led by the priests and local clergy, circle it three times in honor of the Trinity. When nightfall comes, the demara is set aflame to symbolize the burning incense that guided St. Helena to the exact location of the True Cross in Jerusalem.

Maskal Flowers

The yellow daisies known as maskal flowers are usually in full bloom at the time of year when this festival is observed. They are symbolic of the arrival of spring, since Maskal used to be a pagan festival celebrating the end of the rainy season—known as "winter" even though Ethiopia lies north of the equator.

FURTHER READING

Ferguson, George. *Signs and Symbols in Christian Art*. New York: Oxford University Press, 1954.

Henderson, Helene, ed. *Holidays, Festivals, and Celebrations of the World Dictionary*. 3rd ed. Detroit: Omnigraphics, 2005.

MacDonald, Margaret R., ed. *The Folklore of World Holidays*. Detroit: Gale Research, 1992.

Shemanski, Frances. *A Guide to World Fairs and Festivals*. Westport, CT: Greenwood Press, 1985.

Van Straalen, Alice. *The Book of Holidays Around the World*. New York: Dutton, 1986.

WEB SITE

Ethiopian Embassy of the United Kingdom
www.ethioembassy.org.uk/articles/articles/focus%20electronic-00/Ermias%20 Gulilat%20-%201.htm

Maslenitsa
(Butter Week, Cheese Week)

Type of Holiday: Religious (Christian), Folkloric
Date of Observation: Last week before the beginning of Orthodox Lent
Where Celebrated: Russia, Greece
Customs and Symbols: Blinis, Burning Festival Effigies, Maslenitsa Legend, Outdoor Activities, Snow Fortresses
Related Holidays: Carnival, Forgiveness Sunday, Lent

549

ORIGIN

Maslenitsa is a Christian holiday celebrated by Orthodox Christians. The word Christian refers to a follower of Christ. Christ is a title derived from the Greek word meaning Messiah or Anointed One. The Christ of Christianity is Jesus of Nazareth, a man born between 7 and 4 B.C.E. in the region of Palestine. According to Christian teaching, Jesus was killed by Roman authorities using a form of execution called crucifixion (a term meaning he was nailed to a cross and hung from it until he died) in about the year 30 C.E. After his death, he rose back to life. His death and resurrection provide a way by which people can be reconciled with God. In remembrance of Jesus's death and resurrection, the cross serves as a fundamental symbol in Christianity.

With nearly two billion believers in countries around the globe, Christianity is the largest of the world's religions. There is no one central authority for all of Christianity. The pope (the bishop of Rome) is the authority for the Roman Catholic Church, but other sects look to other authorities. Orthodox communities look to patriarchs and emphasize doctrinal agreement and traditional practice. Protestant communities focus on individual conscience. The Roman Catholic and Protestant churches are often referred to as the Western Church, while the Orthodox churches may also be called the Eastern Church. All three main branches of Christianity acknowledge the authority of Christian scriptures, a compilation of writings assembled into a document called the Bible. Methods of biblical interpretation vary among the different Christian sects.

Maslenitsa is the Russian name for the last week before the beginning of **LENT**. It may be translated as "Butter Week." This festival grew out of the Orthodox Christian custom of fasting during Lent. Devout Orthodox Christians refrain from eating meat and dairy products during Lent. One week before the start of Lent they stop eating meat, although they continue to eat dairy products. During this week, observant Russian Orthodox people sate themselves on butter-rich dishes, such as BLINIS, knowing that they will soon have to forego these treats. In Greece, this same festival is known as Cheese Week. Although Greeks also enjoy dairy-rich foods during this period of time, many of their festival customs differ from those associated with Maslenitsa.

Maslenitsa may be thought of as the Russian version of **CARNIVAL**, a European festival that takes place during the last four days before the start of Lent. The earliest historical document noting the occurrence of Carnival celebrations in Europe dates back to the year 965 C.E. In those days, Christians living in Western Europe also practiced the rigorous fasting regimen still maintained in Orthodoxy today. So they were inspired to indulge in as many rich foods as possible in the days before the start of Lent. Religious teachings also insisted that people maintain a somber demeanor and introspective state of mind during Lent. In fact, church officials insisted that people officially confess their sins on the day before Lent began. This day became known as **SHROVE TUESDAY**. These foreboding religious customs encouraged medieval Christians to celebrate Carnival with frivolous, outrageous, and often irreverent behavior. Wearing masks and costumes gave people the opportunity to frolic in the streets, and also to play pranks on one other while remaining anonymous. Under the cover of disguise and holiday humor, clowns or jesters offered social commentary that might otherwise have landed them in trouble. Many communities burned or buried an effigy of Carnival on the last day of the festival.

Some of these customs can be seen in the Maslenitsa celebrations of past centuries. In the nineteenth century, Russians donned masks or costumes to celebrate the festival. They also enjoyed the antics of traveling troupes of actors. The well-to-do took sleigh rides, often carrying a warm basket of BLINIS on their lap. One old custom encouraged people to visit the gravesites of their relatives on the first Sunday of Butter Week, bringing with them blinis that had been blessed in church and leaving some at the grave. Some Russians thought each day of Maslenitsa should have its own special activity. They believed that Monday was the day on which to construct the winter effigy, Tuesday the day for costumes and pranks, Wednesday the day for feasting, Thursday the day for rougher activities (such as boxing), Friday the day for newlyweds to visit their mothers-in-law, and Saturday the day to entertain one's sister-in-law. Most of these customs died out during the Communist era (1917-1991).

Old Maslenitsa customs that still remain include eating blinis and participating in OUTDOOR ACTIVITIES, such as sledding, snowball fights, and sleigh rides. BURNING FESTIVAL EFFIGIES and building SNOW FORTRESSES are also popular Maslenitsa activities. Forgiving friends, family, and neighbors for any way in which they may have offended takes place on the last day of the festival, known among Orthodox Christians as **FORGIVENESS SUNDAY.**

SYMBOLS AND CUSTOMS

Blinis

Blinis are thin buckwheat pancakes about the size of a saucer. Nowadays they may be made with other types of flour, but the batter usually contains both butter and eggs. The warm pancakes are rolled around a variety of fillings, including sour cream, butter, mushrooms, caviar, sturgeon, jam, and many other delicacies.

Some commentators feel that the association between blinis and Maslenitsa may date back to pre-Christian times. They see the round pancakes as symbols of the sun and believe that Russians of past times celebrated the return of the sun at this time of year. Indeed, the return of the sun and the hope for warmer weather is still one of the important themes of this holiday, though it may still be quite cold in Russia at this time of year.

Burning Festival Effigies

Some Russian communities build an effigy representing **CARNIVAL**, or winter, out of straw. During the festival, these scarecrow-like dolls may be given a royal title, such as "lady" or "prince." On the last day, however, they are set upon a pile of wood and burned, as a means of officially drawing Maslenitsa to an end. In some places this ceremony is also understood as a farewell to winter. The ashes from the fire may be gathered and sprinkled on newly sown crops. An old Russian folk belief asserts that the ashes will enhance the crops' fertility.

Maslenitsa Legend

An old Russian folk tale explains the origins of the holiday and its connection with blinis. Long ago, on a bitterly cold winter's day, a peasant man is walking through the woods. To his surprise he finds a merry, rosy-cheeked girl wandering there by herself. Striking up a conversation, he discovers that she is the daughter of Frost, a fear-inspiring magical being who personifies the grueling Russian winters. Her name is Maslenitsa. The man feels hopeful in the pretty young girl's presence, so he asks her to return with him to his home so that all the villagers might draw strength and courage from her presence. Maslenitsa does so, and the villagers love her. They experience hope, joy, and warmth in her presence. They begin to dance and keep on till the point of exhaustion. Maslenitsa stays as long as she can, but after a couple of days she tells the villagers that she must return to the forest. The villagers beg her to stay. The winter had been especially cold that year, and they dread the return of the gloom and chill they will feel when Maslenitsa leaves. Maslenitsa feels sorry for their suffering. Before she departs, she teaches them a magical charm to drive away the cold. She advises them to cook pancakes in the shape of the sun and have a great feast. Seeing this, the sun will be attracted to them and grow stronger in the sky each day. Maslenita's charm works. Thus, the tale concludes, the Russian people established a festival to honor this event, named after the young girl who taught them how to drive away winter. It takes place just as the harsh grip of winter begins to fade and the first signs of spring appear.

Outdoor Activities

Many Russians participate in outdoor sports or games during Maslenitsa. Some enjoy the old-fashioned fun of a sleigh ride. Others thrill to the excitement of a snowball fight or a fast, downhill ride on a sled. Outdoor singing and dancing also takes place during this holiday.

Snow Fortresses

In a related custom, some people enjoy building snow fortresses during the last few days of Maslenitsa. These fortresses represent the harsh Russian winter. On the last day of the festival, people storm and conquer the fortress. Their victory represents the defeat of winter by the forces of spring.

FURTHER READING

Gulevich, Tanya. *Encyclopedia of Easter, Carnival, and Lent.* Detroit: Omnigraphics, 2002.

WEB SITES

Center for Slavic, Eurasian, and East European Studies, University of North Carolina-Chapel Hill
www.unc.edu/depts/slavic/publications/brochure2.html

Passport Moscow Magazine
www.passportmagazine.ru/article/196

Masters Golf Tournament

Type of Holiday: Sporting
Date of Observation: First full week in April
Where Celebrated: Augusta, Georgia
Symbols and Customs: Green Jacket, Champions Dinner

ORIGINS

The golf tournament known simply as "The Masters" was created at a time when neither of the other major American golf tournaments—the U.S. Open or the PGA (Professional Golfers' Association) Championship—had ever been played in the Deep South. It was established in 1934 by Bobby Jones, a famous golfer who had come from the South and who had also designed the course at the exclusive Augusta National Golf Club, where the tournament is held. Together with his friend Clifford Roberts, the chairman of Augusta National who oversaw every detail of the tournament for forty-three years, Jones was so closely identified with The Masters that crowds flocked to see him for years after he ceased to be a serious competitor.

It was Bobby Jones who set the strict standards for spectators' behavior that are still printed in the spectators' guide, and who conducted the traditional interview with the new champion before presenting him with his GREEN JACKET.

The tournament started by Jones received a boost from General Dwight D. Eisenhower, a World War II hero and president of the United States (1953-61). Eisenhower vacationed in Augusta in 1948 and returned there frequently during his presidency to play golf, drawing nationwide attention to Augusta National and its yearly spring tournament. Up until this point, golf had been regarded as a sport for the elite, but Eisenhower made it a more acceptable pastime for common people.

It was professional golfer Arnold Palmer, however, who really put The Masters on the map. He was followed by Jack Nicklaus and Gary Player, and together they were known as the "Big Three." In the nine years beginning in 1958, when Palmer won his first Masters, the Big Three won eight times, ushering in what was later referred to as "the golden age of golf."

Qualifying rounds for the tournament are held on Thursday and Friday of the four-day tournament, and the top forty-four finishers participate in the final round. The top twenty-four finishers are automatically invited back the next year and do not have to requalify. In addition to a cash prize, the winner of the tournament receives a trophy and a green blazer.

It wasn't until September 1990 that the Augusta National Golf Club admitted its first black member, Ron Townsend, president of the Gannett Television Group. But the stage had been set by Lee Trevino, a Mexican-American golfer who declined the Club's invitations to play in the tournament in 1970 and 1971 because he said he felt uncomfortable in what remained a largely white, southern organization. The PGA now has rules forbidding discriminatory membership practices.

In 1997 Tiger Woods, at age twenty-one, won the Masters with a record 270 strokes for three days. At twenty-one, he became the youngest golfer to win the tournament and the first African American or Asian (his father is African American and his mother is Thai) to wear the green blazer. Woods also won the Masters in 2001, 2002, and 2005.

SYMBOLS AND CUSTOMS

Green Jacket

The 300 or so members of the Augusta National Golf Club, who come from all over America, wear blazers that are the green of well-tended grass. They are not allowed to remove their Club jackets from the premises. About one-third of the members, who are known collectively as the "Green Jackets," work actively on the tournament every year. They are not all superior golfers, but they have shown their dedication to the game.

The winner of The Masters is presented with a green jacket to symbolize his victory and acceptance into the golf elite. He may take it home with him and keep it for twelve months, until the next year's tournament.

Champions Dinner

An exclusive club gathers for dinner the Tuesday night of the week of every Masters. The menu is selected by the previous year's Masters champion. He hosts the group of previous champions and is given his inscribed gold locket in the form of the Masters Club emblem. Perhaps the most talked-about menu was that of Tiger Woods, who selected cheeseburgers, chicken sandwiches, French fries, milk shakes, and strawberry shortcake. This is the dinner he hosted at the age of twenty-two, after his first Masters victory. Other notable menus include Vijay Singh's Indian feast and Mike Weir's wild game spread.

FURTHER READING

Henderson, Helene, ed. *Holidays, Festivals, and Celebrations of the World Dictionary.* 3rd ed. Detroit: Omnigraphics, 2005.

Owen, David. *The Making of the Masters: Clifford Roberts, Augusta National, and Golf's Most Prestigious Tournament.* New York: Simon & Schuster, 1999.

Sampson, Curt. *The Masters: Golf, Money, and Power in Augusta.* New York: Villard, 1998.

Taylor, Dawson. *The Masters: Golf's Most Prestigious Tournament.* Chicago: Contemporary Books, 1986.

WEB SITES

Augusta Metropolitan Convention and Visitors Bureau
www.augustaga.org

Masters Golf Tournament Official Web Site
www.masters.org

Maundy Thursday
(Holy Thursday)

Type of Holiday: Religious (Christian)
Date of Observation: Between March 19 and April 22 in the West; between April 1 and May 5 in the East; Thursday before Easter
Where Celebrated: England, Europe, United States, South America, and throughout the Christian world
Symbols and Customs: Blessing the Oils, Foot Washing, Maundy Money, Silencing the Bells
Colors: The liturgical color for this day is white, the symbol of joy.
Related Holidays: Corpus Christi, Easter, Good Friday, Passover

ORIGINS

Maundy Thursday is part of the religious tradition of Christianity. The word Christian refers to a follower of Christ, a title derived from the Greek word meaning Messiah or Anointed One. The Christ of Christianity is Jesus of Nazareth, a man born between 7 and 4 B.C.E. in the region of Palestine. According to Christian teaching, Jesus was killed by Roman authorities using a form of execution called crucifixion (a term meaning he was nailed to a cross and hung from it until he died) in about the year 30 C.E. After his death, he rose back to life. His death and resurrection provide a way by which people can be reconciled with God. In remembrance of Jesus' death and resurrection, the cross serves as a fundamental symbol in Christianity.

With nearly two billion believers in countries around the globe, Christianity is the largest of the world's religions.There is no one central authority for all of Christianity. The pope (the bishop of Rome) is the authority for the Roman Catholic Church, but other sects look to other authorities. Orthodox communities look to patriarchs and emphasize doctrinal agreement and traditional practice. Protestant communities focus on individual conscience. The Roman Catholic and Protestant churches are often referred to as the Western Church, while the Orthodox churches may also be called the Eastern Church. All three main branches of Christianity acknowledge the authority of Christian scriptures, a compilation of writings assembled into a document called the Bible. Methods of biblical interpretation vary among the different Christian sects.

The day before **GOOD FRIDAY** has been observed since very early times with acts of humility in imitation of Jesus Christ, who washed the feet of his disciples on the eve of his crucifixion. The name "Maundy" probably came from the Latin *mandatum*, meaning "commandment." After the FOOT WASHING took place, Christ said, "A new commandment I give unto you, that you love one another as I have loved you." (John 13:34) Some say that "Maundy" came from an old word meaning "basket" in England, where the poor used baskets to carry the food and money distributed to them on this day (*see* MAUNDY MONEY).

The real significance of Maundy Thursday lies in the fact that it was the day of the Last Supper, when Jesus and his twelve apostles gathered to share the traditional Passover meal, as many others were doing all over Jerusalem. Jesus took the bread and the wine and described them in symbolic terms as his body and his blood, thus instituting the ceremony known as the Eucharist. He was trying to tell his disciples that just as the Jews had been saved from bondage in Egypt by the blood of a lamb smeared on their doors (*see* **PASSOVER**), all of mankind would be saved from the bondage of sin by the sacrifice he was about to make. He wanted his disciples to use this ceremony as a pattern for a memorial service they could hold later in his memory.

In some western European countries, the Thursday before **EASTER** is called Green Thursday. In Germany it's called *Gründonnerstag*, a name that is thought to have derived from *grunen* or *greinen*, meaning "to mourn," later corrupted into *grün* (green). In Austria and Hungary, it is customary to eat spinach and green salad on this day—perhaps because the Jews ate green vegetables or herbs at their Passover feast.

At one time, this day was known as Pure or Clean Thursday, from the ancient tradition of cleansing the soul as well as the body in preparation for Easter. The Old English name Shere (or Shier) Thursday referred to the practice of men shaving their beards on this day.

SYMBOLS AND CUSTOMS

Blessing the Oils

The ceremony performed on the morning of Maundy Thursday and known as the Blessing of the Oils takes place at St. Peter's in Rome and in cathedrals elsewhere. It dates back to an ancient rite, the renewal of the supply of oils used to anoint people who are baptized at **EASTER**. There are actually three types of oils that are blessed: (1) the oil of catechumens, used in baptizing people, consecrating churches, ordaining priests, and crowning sovereigns; (2) the oil used in administering extreme unction to those who are dying; and (3) the oil of chrism, used in confirmation, the consecration of bishops, and the blessing of bells. These oils are kept in a chrismatory or casket made of silver or brass.

Two of the oils blessed on Maundy Thursday are actually olive oil. But the chrism is an ointment based on olive oil to which balsam or a perfume has been added, symbolizing "the sweet savor of Christ." In the morning service, the bishop not only blesses the oils but invites his priests to renew their commitment to their calling.

Foot Washing

The act of washing someone's feet was a courtesy offered to a guest and usually performed by a female servant, or by the women of the family if there were no servants. When Jesus washed the feet of his twelve disciples at the Last Supper, it was more than a dramatic gesture on the eve of his crucifixion: he was teaching them that by humbling themselves, they could show their love for one another.

Foot washing has been a Maundy Thursday custom since the early days of the Church. Bishops, abbots, prelates, and other religious officials participated in the ceremony, as did the popes. In medieval times—and in some countries up to the present century—Christian emperors, kings, and lords washed the feet of poor men on Holy Thursday, after which they were given money and provided with a meal. The king of England used to have poor men brought to him—one man for each year of his age. Then he washed their feet and gave them food, money, and clothing. The last British monarch to perform the foot-washing ceremony was James II (1685-88). Today, British rulers attend a special Maundy Thursday service and distribute MAUNDY MONEY to the poor afterward.

At St. Peter's Cathedral in Rome, it used to be the custom for the Pope to wash the feet of subdeacons on Maundy Thursday. He no longer takes part in the ceremony, which is performed at the Church of the Ara Caeli. The biblical account of the event is chanted and then the bishop, who wears a linen cloth at his waist, kneels to wash the right foot of each of the thirteen men selected for the occasion. Twelve of them represent the apostles and the thirteenth represents the angel who, according to legend, appeared to Gregory the Great when he was performing an act of charity on this day in the late sixth century. Some say the thirteenth man represents St. Matthias, who replaced Judas Iscariot after he betrayed Jesus.

Some Roman Catholic churches still carry out the foot-washing ceremony on the Thursday preceding Easter. It symbolizes Jesus' commandment that his followers show humility.

Maundy Money

At one time in England, the king would have as many men brought before him as he was years old. Then he would wash their feet with his own hands and distribute *maunds,* which consisted of meat, clothing, and money. Queen Elizabeth in 1572 gave each person enough cloth for a gown, half a side of salmon, six red herring, bread, and wine. In 1838 Queen Victoria gave out woolen and linen clothing, shoes and stockings, and new coins minted specially for the occasion, which were referred to as "Maundy money."

Today, it is the Archbishop of Canterbury who distributes the Maundy money, which is carried into London's Westminster Abbey on a huge platter by the Yeoman of the Guard. The Archbishop and the Dean of Westminster wear only plain white instead of their usual elaborate robes, and they carry linen towels on their shoulders to commemorate the FOOT WASHING ceremony, which is no longer performed. The Maundy money, contained in red and white purses, consists of specially minted silver coins that total in value the monarch's age. Although they are considered legal tender, most recipients keep the coins as souvenirs.

England is one of very few countries where the ancient custom of distributing royal Maundy gifts is still continued.

Silencing the Bells

There is a universal legend among children that all the church bells "fly to Rome" after the Gloria of the Mass is sung on Holy Thursday. In Germany and central Europe, children are told that the bells make a pilgrimage to the tomb of the apostles, or that they go to the pope to be blessed and then sleep on the roof of St. Peter's Cathedral until Easter. In France, they are told that the bells fly to Rome to fetch the Easter eggs.

Whatever the reason for their departure, the silencing of the bells after the Gloria on Maundy Thursday has produced the popular expression that "the bells have gone to Rome" and will return after the Gloria is sung on Holy Saturday. Children run through the streets shaking various types of rattles and clappers to communicate the great sorrow associated with this period. In rural parts of Austria, boys with wooden clappers go through the villages announcing the time, because even the church clock is stopped.

After the Holy Thursday Mass is sung in Rome's Sistine Chapel, no bells are allowed to ring in the city until the following Saturday morning. This means that all the bells in Rome are silent from about 11:30 a.m. Thursday until the same time on Holy Saturday. Even the hand-held bells used to summon hotel guests to dinner are silent, although occasionally wooden clappers are used instead. Since the ringing of bells symbolizes a joyous event, their silence is an appropriate symbol for the sorrow associated with Jesus' suffering and death on the cross.

FURTHER READING

Bellenir, Karen. *Religious Holidays and Calendars.* 3rd ed. Detroit: Omnigraphics, 2004.

Chambers, Robert. *The Book of Days*. 2 vols. 1862-64. Reprint. Detroit: Omnigraphics, 1990.

Dobler, Lavinia G. *Customs and Holidays Around the World*. New York: Fleet Pub. Corp., 1962.

Ferguson, George. *Signs and Symbols in Christian Art*. New York: Oxford University Press, 1954.

Gulevich, Tanya. *Encyclopedia of Easter, Carnival, and Lent*. Detroit: Omnigraphics, 2002.

Harper, Howard V. *Days and Customs of All Faiths*. 1957. Reprint. Detroit: Omnigraphics, 1990.

Henderson, Helene, ed. *Holidays, Festivals, and Celebrations of the World Dictionary*. 3rd ed. Detroit: Omnigraphics, 2005.

Hole, Christina. *English Custom & Usage*. 1941. Reprint. Detroit: Omnigraphics, 1990.

Ickis, Marguerite. *The Book of Religious Holidays and Celebrations*. New York: Dodd, Mead, 1966.

James, E.O. *Seasonal Feasts and Festivals*. 1961. Reprint. Detroit: Omnigraphics, 1993.

Metford, J.C.J. *The Christian Year*. New York: Crossroad, 1991.

Monks, James L. *Great Catholic Festivals*. New York: Henry Schuman, 1951.

Pike, Royston. *Round the Year with the World's Religions*. 1950. Reprint. Detroit: Omnigraphics, 1992.

Urlin, Ethel L. *Festivals, Holy Days, and Saints' Days*. 1915. Reprint. Detroit: Omnigraphics, 1992.

Weiser, Franz Xaver. *Handbook of Christian Feasts and Customs*. New York: Harcourt, Brace, 1958.

WEB SITE

New Advent Catholic Encyclopedia
www.newadvent.org/cathen/10068a.htm

Mawlid al-Nabi
(Muhammad's Birthday, Birthday of the Prophet, Mulid al-Nabi, Maulid al-Nabi, Maulidi, Mawlid an-Nabi)

Type of Holiday: Religious (Muslim)
Date of Observation: Usually August or September; twelfth day of the Islamic lunar month of Rabi al-Awwal
Where Celebrated: Egypt, Indonesia, Iran, Kenya, Lebanon, Libya, West Africa, South Africa, Turkey, and throughout the Islamic world
Symbols and Customs: Attending Mosque, Burdah, Dhikr, Food, Gifts, Poems, Processions
Related Holidays: Laylat al-Miraj, Laylat al-Qadr

ORIGINS

Mawlid al-Nabi, the Birthday of the Prophet, is a holiday in the religious tradition of Islam, one of the world's largest religions. According to some estimates, there are more than one billion Muslims worldwide, with major populations found in the Middle East, North and sub-Saharan Africa, Turkey, Central Asia, and Southeast Asia. In Europe and the United States, Islam is the second largest religious group, with some seven million adherents in the United States. During the early years of Islam, the faith spread throughout the Arabian Peninsula into regions that are today occupied by Saudi Arabia, Syria, Iraq, and Jordan. Contrary to popular opinion, however, Muslims are not just Arabs. Muslims—followers of Islam—are found in many different ethnic groups all over the globe. In fact, Arabs make up less than twenty percent of Muslims.

The word Islam is an Arabic word that means "surrender to God." Its other meanings include peace, safety, and health. The central focus of Islam is a personal commitment and surrender to Allah, the Arabic word for God. In Islam, the concept of Allah is universal and eternal. Allah is the same in every religion and throughout the history of humankind. A person who follows Islam is called a Muslim, which means one who surrenders or submits to Allah's will. But Islam is not just a religion of belief; it is a religion of action. Five specific deeds are required of followers; these are called *The Five Pillars of Islam*. They are 1) *Shahadah*—confession of faith; 2) *Salat*—prayer/worship; 3) *Zakat*—charity; 4) *Sawm*—fasting; and 5) *Hajj*—pilgrimage.

The message of Islam was brought by Muhammad (570-632 C.E.), who is considered a prophet of Allah. The holy book of Islam is the *Qur'an* (also sometimes spelled *Koran* or *Alcoran*). According to Islamic belief, the Qur'an was revealed to Muhammad by Allah over a period of twenty-three years. Authorship of the Qur'an is attributed to Allah, and not to Muhammad; Muhammad merely received it. Muslims believe that because it originated with Allah, the Qur'an is infallible.

There are two main sects within Islam: Sunni and Shi'ite. Sunni Muslims are the majority (estimated at about eighty percent). They recognize the authority of the first four Caliphs, including Ali, and they believe that the Sunna (the example of the Prophet Muhammad) is interpreted through the consensus of the community. Shi'ite Muslims also look to special teachers, called imams. The imams are the direct descendants of Muhammad through Fatimah and Ali. These individuals are believed to be inspired and to possess secret knowledge. Shi'ites, however, do not recognize the same line of Islamic leaders acknowledged by the Sunnis. Shi'ites hold to a doctrine that accepts only leaders who are descended from Muhammad through his daughter Fatimah and her husband Ali. Many Shi'ite subsects believe that true imams are errorless and sinless. They receive instruction from these leaders rather than relying on the consensus of the community.

Mawlid al-Nabi celebrates the birth of the Prophet Muhammad, the founder of Islam. Born in Mecca on August 20, 570 C.E., he was a shepherd and a trader who began to receive revelations from God when he was forty years old. Over the next twenty-three years, he not only established the Islamic religion, but also brought an unprecedented degree of political unity to the Arab tribes. His birth is considered an event of major importance in the Muslim world because he was the last of the prophets and the one to whom the Qur'an (the holy book of the Islamic faith) was revealed.

Joyful but low-key observance of the Prophet's birthday dates back to early centuries of Muslim history. These observances grew larger and more complex over time. The biggest Mawlid al-Nabi celebrations in the Middle East usually take place in Egypt. Official Egyptian celebrations can be traced back to the time of the Fatimid Dynasty (909-1171), whose rulers traced their own ancestry back to Muhammad. In those days, the festivities began with prayers at the al-Azar mosque and concluded with readings from the Qur'an given in the royal palace. Poor people, mosque guardians, and religious officials who attended the palace event were given specially prepared sweets.

The first evidence of major celebrations of Mawlid al-Nabi comes from the city of Irbil (then Arabala), a town now located in the nation of Iraq. These celebrations took place in the year 1207. The town's Sufi community was very active in these festivities. Sufi missionaries are credited with spreading the festival to East Africa. Later that century, the Mamluk sultans (1254-1517) expanded the Mawlid al-Nabi celebrations. They ordered the streets to be decorated with lamps and large swaths of silk cloth. They also hosted a festival at Cairo's Citadel in which musicians, Sufi groups, and singers were invited to perform. In addition, poor people, soldiers, and government workers were given presents of clothes and money.

In the fifteenth century, the Sultan Qaitbey acquired an enormous outdoors tent that was erected every year to serve as headquarters for the festival. Sufi groups marching behind large banners converged on the tent, accompanied by drummers, singers, and other musicians. Army and government officials brought up the rear. Once assembled, the crowd settled in to eat, listen to speeches, and to pray. As in previous generations, the sultan gave away money and gifts.

In the sixteenth century, the sultans got rid of the tent and tried to dismantle the celebrations. The Sufi groups continued their processions and celebrations, however, and invited the king to join them. They issued these invitations right up until the reign of the last king of Egypt, King Farouk (r. 1936-52). Over time, the idea of celebrating the Prophet's birthday spread from Egypt to other areas, first in the Middle East and then wherever Muslims live.

Today, Mawlid al-Nabi is a public holiday in more than forty countries around the world. Muslims gather together in groups to remember Muhammad on his birthday. They honor the birth of Muhammad in a wide variety of ways that reflect their heritage, culture, and local customs. In Lebanon, for example, the celebration includes nine days of fairs and parades. Children are told stories about the night when Muhammad was born in Mecca—particularly about the 7,000 angels who brought Muhammad's mother a golden vessel filled with dew to bathe the holy infant. In Egypt, Muhammad's birthday is celebrated by illuminating the city of Cairo and with special ceremonies and performances, including a DHIKR.

Other common means of celebrating the Prophet's birth include singing songs, reading POEMS, and ATTENDING MOSQUE for special recitations or lectures concerning the life and teachings of the Prophet. Public PROCESSIONS take place in some Muslim countries. FOOD and GIFTS are important elements for many. Still, conservative and fundamentalist Muslims, especially those in the Wahhabi sect, do not celebrate Muhammad's birthday. They criticize Muslims who do celebrate for adopting a festival that is not authorized in the Qur'an or the hadith. Nevertheless, in much of the Muslim world, large numbers of believers mark the twelfth of Rabi al-Awwal with recitations and festivities.

Muslims gather together in groups to remember Muhammad on his birthday. They tell each other the story of his life, his character, and his sufferings. These so-called "Mawlid gatherings" take place throughout the month of Rabi al-Awwal. Another popular way of celebrating this day is to take part in large processions, often led by colorfully decorated elephants.

SYMBOLS AND CUSTOMS

Attending Mosque

Many Muslims attend mosque on Mawlid al-Nabi to pray and listen to special recitations. The celebration of the Prophet's birthday usually includes a recitation of the Qur'an and stories about the life of the Prophet, often in verse or in a combination of poetry and prose. These recitations, called mawlids, may have been inspired by the sermons given at the festivals of Christian saints. They might focus on a variety of topics, including the life of the Prophet, the example he set, his teachings, his character, his sufferings, and his mission. Some mosques might also include lectures on other important religious or social topics. Mawlid poems, of which many have been written in both Turkish and Arabic, have become so popular that they are sometimes recited on other festive occasions as well.

Burdah

Burdah refers to one of the Prophet's cloaks or mantles, which was made out of goat hair. It was the inspiration for two famous poems—one by a contemporary of Muhammad named Ka'b ibn Zuhayr and the other by the thirteenth-century poet Muhammad ibn Said al-Busiri. In the first poem, the Prophet gives away one of his many cloaks to Ka'b ibn Zuhayr, an outlaw who repents and asks for Muhammad's pardon. The mantle given to Ka'b became part of the national treasury after the poet's death, and today it is kept in the Topkapi Museum in Istanbul. In the second poem, al-Busiri describes the nature of the Prophet and praises him for his virtues. It is customary to recite this poem during the celebration of the Prophet's birthday.

Dhikr

The word *dhikr* means "remembrance" in Arabic. Among Sufi Muslims, dhikr refers to the chanting of certain words or phrases in praise of God. Its purpose is to induce an ecstatic experience or momentary union with God. Although the actual sequence of phrases can vary, the pattern is always the same. Such phrases as "There is no god but Allah," or "God is greatest" are repeated innumerable times to a certain rhythm, sometimes to the accompaniment of drums or pipes. Although dhikr meetings are held frequently by the Sufi, or dervish, fraternities, these litanies are particularly associated with the celebration of Mawlid al-Nabi.

Food

Feasting is an important part of Mawlid al-Nabi. Muslims in different regions prepare their own special foods in honor of the Prophet's birthday. In Egypt, for example, people celebrate with hummus, special sweets, and candy dolls. In Kenya, Muslims enjoy shrimp pilaf, curried eggplant, cassava with coconut sauce, mango chutney, and roasted red pepper. In Pakistan, Muslims feast on rice with meat and spices, as well as sweet rice. Candy and other sweet treats are on the menu in many areas. Other favorite foods served on this day include *tabboul,* made from grains of wheat that have been boiled and mixed with chopped mint, onions, parsley, and tomatoes, then mixed again with olive oil and lemon juice; *djaje mihshi,* or roast chicken filled with rice, spices, and ground lamb; and *baclava* a typical Mawlid dessert made from thin layers of pastry with crushed nuts and honey in between.

Gifts

Giving gifts is a tradition for some Muslims. Families often honor the day quietly at home by giving friends and neighbors gifts of peanut, pistachio, or hazelnut candy. Children receive candy dolls, made from hot, molten sugar poured into special molds. Girls often get female figures, while boys usually receive the figure of a man seated on a horse. Giving gifts to the poor is a frequent part of Mawlid al-Nabi.

Poems

One of the main features of the holiday in many countries is the recitation of long poems or litanies that express gratitude toward both God and Muhammad and praise the Prophet in the highest possible terms. In fact, this practice gave rise to a special genre of poetry. In Turkey and lands once under Turkish rule, a poem called the *al-Burdah* ("The Mantle") is a traditional favorite recited every year on Mawlid al-Nabi. It was written by Muhammad ibn Said al-Busiri (1213-1295), a Berber poet born in Cairo, Egypt. His inspiration came to him in a dream that occurred during a period in his life when he suffered from paralysis. In his dream, Muhammad approached him and wrapped his own mantle, or cloak, around him. Upon waking, al-Busiri discovered that he had been cured. In gratitude, al-Busiri composed "The Mantle." The poem recounts the life story of the Prophet and attempts to describe his exquisitely beautiful nature and his profound spiritual gifts. A famous line from the poet asserts that he is

> Like a flower in tenderness, and like the full moon in glory,
> And like the ocean in generosity, and like all Time brought into one point
> (Glassé: 80).

Over the years, both gifted poets and ordinary devotees have written poems praising the Prophet. These poems, too, may be read or recited around the time of the Prophet's birthday.

Processions

In some countries, Muslims celebrate the birth of the Prophet in a public fashion, by walking in large street processions and singing hymns. There might also be a public celebration in a town square, where Muslims may decorate the area and set up tents or booths for nighttime entertainment. These celebrations might also be held at a Sufi shrine. Sufi dancing, music, and devotional chants would fill the night air and create a mystical feeling.

FURTHER READING

Ahsan, M.M. *Muslim Festivals*. Vero Beach, FL: Rourke Enterprises, 1987.

Bellenir, Karen. *Religious Holidays and Calendars*. 3rd ed. Detroit: Omnigraphics, 2004.

Dobler, Lavinia G. *Customs and Holidays Around the World*. New York: Fleet Pub. Corp., 1962.

Glassé, Cyril. *The Concise Encyclopedia of Islam*. 2nd ed. San Francisco: Harper & Row, 1999.

Gulevich, Tanya. *Understanding Islam and Muslim Traditions*. Detroit: Omnigraphics, 2004.

Henderson, Helene, ed. *Holidays, Festivals, and Celebrations of the World Dictionary*. 3rd ed. Detroit: Omnigraphics, 2005.

MacDonald, Margaret R., ed. *The Folklore of World Holidays*. Detroit: Gale Research, 1992.

Renard, John. *Seven Doors to Islam: Spirituality and the Religious Life of Muslims*. Berkeley: University of California Press, 1996.

Von Grunebaum, Gustave E. *Muhammadan Festivals*. New York: Schuman, 1951.

WEB SITES

Mawlid an-Nabi: The Celebration of Prophet Muhammad's Birthday, Islamic Supreme Council of America
www.islamicsupremecouncil.org/bin/site/wrappers/spirituality-mohammads_bday.html

Ontario Consultants on Religious Tolerance
www.religioustolerance.org/main_day3.htm

Valuing our Differences: Celebrating Diversity, University of Kansas
www3.kumc.edu/diversity/ethnic_relig/mawlid.html

May Day

Type of Holiday: Calendar/Seasonal
Date of Observation: May 1
Where Celebrated: England, Europe, United States, former Soviet Union
Symbols and Customs: Flowers, Jack in the Green, May Baskets, May Dolls, Maypole, Queen of the May
Related Holidays: Beltane, Floralia, Vernal Equinox

ORIGINS

May Day is a festival of purely pagan origin. The Celts observed **BELTANE** on May 1 by lighting bonfires to honor the sun god and welcome the return of spring. The Romans observed their festival of flowers, the **FLORALIA**, for six days at the end of April and beginning of May, and many of the customs associated with May Day—such as gathering FLOWERS and weaving them into garlands or wreaths—can be traced back to ancient Greece and Rome.

May Day marks the changing of the seasons, which people in all parts of the world have honored since ancient times. Many cultures divided the year into two seasons, summer and winter, and marked these points of the year at or near the summer and winter solstices, during which light and warmth began to increase and decrease, respectively. In pre-industrial times, humans survived through hunting, gathering, and agricultural practices, which depend on the natural cycle of seasons, according to the climate in the region of the world in which they lived. Thus, they created rituals to help ensure enough rain and sun in the spring and summer so crops would grow to fruition at harvest time, which was, in turn, duly celebrated. Vestiges of many of these ancient practices are thought to have survived in festivals still celebrated around seasonal themes.

European communities celebrated the arrival of spring by decorating their homes with early-blooming flowers, selecting a QUEEN OF THE MAY, and dancing around the MAYPOLE. Women washed their faces in the early morning dew on May 1, believing that it would improve their complexions and bring them eternal youthfulness. Throughout the Middle Ages, the Renaissance, and even into the nineteenth century, May Day was widely observed throughout Europe and America—although the Puritans persecuted those who participated in the "heathen" customs associated with May Day and urged their children to spend the day reading the Bible.

Although May Day is primarily a festival to welcome spring, it also has political significance in some countries. At an international meeting of Socialists in 1889, it was decided that May Day should be renamed Labor Day and turned into a holiday honoring the working man. Countries with Socialist or Communist forms of government still celebrate May 1 with speeches and displays of military strength. The May Day Parade in Moscow's Red Square is one of the better known examples, although it has been toned down somewhat since the dissolution of the Soviet Union. The United States observes its Labor Day in early September. Ironically, May 1 marks the anniversary of the 1886 Chicago labor rally that resulted in the infamous Haymarket Riot and the subsequent decline of the labor anarchist movement.

May Day is not a national holiday in the United States, but people in Hawaii observe it as Lei Day by exchanging the traditional Hawaiian flower necklaces as symbols of friendship and good luck.

SYMBOLS AND CUSTOMS

Flowers

As the quintessential symbol of spring, flowers have played a central role in May Day celebrations since the time of the Roman **FLORALIA**. Garlands of flowers were such an important part of the May Day ceremonies in England that it was often called Garland Day. The custom of "bringing in the May"—going out to the field or woods early in the morning on May 1 and returning with baskets full of flowers—was widespread throughout Europe and America. Sometimes the flowers would be strung together in long chains. Another popular custom was tying a single blossom to the end of a long wand. Sometimes the flowers were used to make a crown for the May Queen (*see* QUEEN OF THE MAY) or to fill MAY BASKETS. In Greece, wild flowers are still gathered and woven into May Day wreaths. The wreaths are then hung up to dry until St. John's Eve (June 23), when they are burned in the midsummer bonfires (*see* **MIDSUMMER DAY**).

Up until the mid-nineteenth century in England, the "May Birchers" would go from house to house on May Day Eve and decorate the doors with boughs of trees or flowers that expressed their opinion of the person who lived there. In some areas, the plants were chosen because they rhymed with the word describing the person. For example, the "fair" of face might find a pear bough placed over her door, while someone who was "glum" might find a branch of plum. Not surprisingly, this custom caused so much ill feeling that it was eventually discontinued.

Jack in the Green

Until recently, a leaf-covered figure known as Jack in the Green was an important part of May Day celebrations in England. He was usually a young chimney sweep concealed inside a six-to-ten-foot-high wicker framework made of hoops and completely covered in holly and ivy. This leafy green figure danced at the head of a procession of chimney sweeps that meandered through the village, singing songs and collecting pennies.

Along with the QUEEN OF THE MAY, Jack in the Green is believed to be a relic of ancient European tree worship. The Gypsies of Romania and Transylvania still observe their Green George Festival on April 23—Green George being a tree-spirit represented by a boy dressed in branches, leaves, and flowers. These humans disguised as trees are another example of May Day's pagan origins.

May Baskets

The custom of hanging up small baskets filled with flowers became popular in the United States during the nineteenth century and is still enjoyed in some areas by children today. The baskets are often made from woven strips of colored paper decorated with lace-paper doilies and ribbons. They're filled with flowers, candy, perhaps a short poem, and the name of the person for whom they are intended. The usual practice is to hang the basket on the person's front door, ring the bell, and then run away before the door is opened—much like trick-or-treating at **HALLOWEEN**. In Iowa, school-age children leave May baskets at the doors of those they have crushes on, flowers being symbolic of love, fertility, and the arrival of spring.

May Dolls

The Romans welcomed the month of May by dedicating it to Flora, the goddess of flowers. They spent the first day of the month gathering flowers as offerings to the goddess. Sometimes Roman children made small images of Flora and decorated them with flowers. After Christianity was introduced and the Church tried to replace some of the pagan customs associated with May Day, these May dolls were turned into likenesses of the Virgin Mary. (*See also* QUEEN OF THE MAY)

Maypole

The Maypole is probably the best known of the symbols associated with May Day. The earliest Maypoles were trees (usually fir or birch) brought in solemn procession to the village square. But in the sixteenth and seventeenth centuries, many towns in England and Europe erected permanent poles that were left standing throughout the year and could be decorated for May Day. The shaft was sometimes painted with stripes, and a flower doll (*see* MAY DOLLS) was frequently fastened to the top. A tuft of greenery was always left on the end of the pole as a reminder that it was a symbol of the newly awakened spirit of fertility and vegetation.

Colorful ribbons or streamers were hung from the pole, and people would dance around it holding the ends of the streamers in such a way that they were woven into a pattern as the dancers progressed. Today, the Maypole dance is often performed by traditional English Morris dancers—men wearing hats decorated with ribbons and flowers, streamers on their wrists and elbows, bells strapped to their shins, and holding white handkerchiefs and clacking wooden sticks. The bells and sticks were originally used to frighten off evil spirits, and the dancers' high leaps were believed to encourage the crops to grow tall.

The Puritans hated the idea of dancing around the Maypole because they saw the pole as a phallic symbol and the dance as a pagan fertility ritual that had no place in a civilized Christian society. Although they tried to stamp out the custom, they were never altogether successful in repressing this and other May Day ceremonies that obviously had their roots in very primitive human instincts.

Queen of the May

The custom of crowning a Queen of the May commemorates Maia, the ancient Roman mother goddess associated with growth and the spring season, as well as Flora, the goddess of flowers. The Queen is usually chosen from the girls of the town or village, and at one time she was accompanied by a May King, their court, and villagers dressed up as shepherds, jesters, chimney sweeps, Morris dancers, and JACK IN THE GREEN, a mythical figure who symbolized the spirit of seasonal growth. Nowadays the May King has largely disappeared, but schoolchildren in London still choose their own May Queen.

In the United States, attempts to Christianize May Day focused on Mary, the mother of Jesus. In many places where May Day is celebrated with the crowning of a May Queen, there is often a procession to a local church, where the Queen places a crown of flowers on the statue of Mary.

FURTHER READING

Dobler, Lavinia G. *Customs and Holidays Around the World*. New York: Fleet Pub. Corp., 1962.

Frazer, Sir James G. *The Golden Bough: A Study in Magic and Religion*. New York: Macmillan, 1931.

Gaer, Joseph. *Holidays Around the World*. Boston: Little, Brown, 1953.

Henderson, Helene, ed. *Holidays, Festivals, and Celebrations of the World Dictionary*. 3rd ed. Detroit: Omnigraphics, 2005.

Hole, Christina. *English Custom & Usage*. 1941. Reprint. Detroit: Omnigraphics, 1990.

Ickis, Marguerite. *The Book of Festivals and Holidays the World Over*. New York: Dodd, Mead, 1970.

Leach, Maria, ed. *Funk & Wagnalls Standard Dictionary of Folklore, Mythology & Legend*. San Francisco: Harper & Row, 1984.

Long, George. *The Folklore Calendar*. 1930. Reprint. Detroit: Omnigraphics, 1990.

Purdy, Susan. *Festivals for You to Celebrate*. Philadelphia: Lippincott, 1969.

Santino, Jack. *All Around the Year: Holidays and Celebrations in American Life*. Urbana: University of Illinois Press, 1994.

Tuleja, Tad. *Curious Customs: The Stories Behind 296 Popular American Rituals*. New York: Harmony, 1987.

Memorial Day

Type of Holiday: National
Date of Observation: Last Monday in May
Where Celebrated: United States
Symbols and Customs: American Flag, Decoration of Graves, Poppy
Colors: Memorial Day is associated with the colors of the AMERICAN FLAG: red, symbolizing courage; white, symbolizing liberty or purity; and blue, symbolizing loyalty.
Related Holidays: Confederate Memorial Day, Flag Day, Fourth of July

ORIGINS

Memorial Day is a national holiday in the United States. National holidays can be defined as those commemorations that a nation's government has deemed important enough to include in the list of official public holidays. They tend to honor a person or event that has been critical in the development of the nation and its identity. Such people and events usually reflect values and traditions shared by a large portion of the citizenry. In the United States, patiotism and identity were nurtured from the beginning of the nation by the very act of celebrating new events in holidays like the Fourth of July, battle anniversaries, and other notable occasions. The invention of traditions and the marking of important occasions in the life of the new nation were crucial in creating a shared bond of tradition and a sense of common belonging to a relatively new homeland through the shared experience of celebrating common holidays, and Memorial Day has become one of the nation's most important shared celebrations.

Memorial Day was originally a day set aside to honor the northern Civil War dead by decorating their graves with flowers (*see* DECORATION OF GRAVES). Waterloo, New

York, is generally credited with having held the first Memorial Day observance on May 5, 1866. Henry C. Welles, a Waterloo pharmacist, suggested to veterans' organizations that the graves of the dead be decorated with flowers. Referred to at the time as "Decoration Day," this early celebration included flying AMERICAN FLAGS at half-staff, a veterans' parade, and a march to the village cemetery to hear patriotic speeches.

The first nationwide Decoration Day was held on May 30, 1868, by a group of Union Army veterans known as the Grand Army of the Republic. The May 30 date had no real significance, although it roughly coincided with the anniversary of the surrender of the last Confederate army on May 26, 1865. Many southern states felt that Decoration Day was really observed in honor of Union soldiers, so in 1891, Florida designated the birthday of Confederate president Jefferson Davis as **CONFEDERATE MEMORIAL DAY**. Nine other states followed suit, with dates ranging from April 26, the anniversary of the surrender of General George Johnson at Durham Station (North Carolina), to June 3, Jefferson Davis's birthday. After World War I, the American Legion took over the task of planning the observance, which became known as Memorial Day and honored American servicepeople from all wars.

Both religious services and patriotic parades mark the modern-day observation of Memorial Day. In the national official observance, a wreath is placed on the Tomb of the Unknown Soldier in Arlington National Cemetery in Virginia. One of the more moving observances is held in the Gettysburg National Cemetery in Pennsylvania, where schoolchildren scatter flowers over the graves of unknown Civil War soldiers. In 1986, Hands Across America—originally an effort to raise money for the homeless—was held on Sunday of Memorial Day weekend. The idea was to have an unbroken chain of people holding hands across the entire continent, but not enough people pledged to participate. They were urged to celebrate America anyway, and the event ended up merging with the observation of Memorial Day.

SYMBOLS AND CUSTOMS

American Flag

There are many theories about the origin of the American flag. Best known is the story of Betsy Ross, an expert seamstress and upholsterer who based her design on a sketch given to her by a committee appointed by Congress, one of whose members happened to be her deceased husband's uncle. It had thirteen stars, symbolic of the thirteen colonies, placed in a circle on a sky blue background to signify that the Union would be "without end." There were also thirteen red and white stripes, the red symbolizing the Mother Country (Great Britain), and the white symbolizing liberty or purity. They were carefully arranged so that red would appear at the top and bottom edge, making the flag easier to see from a great distance. The separation of red stripes by white stripes was also supposed to symbolize America's separation from England.

On Memorial Day the flag is displayed at half-mast, a symbol of mourning, from sunrise until noon, and at full staff from noon until sunset. This rule does not apply, however, to the millions of smaller flags that line American streets and sidewalks. There are also very specific rules governing how the flag should be displayed in churches.

Decoration of Graves

The practice of decorating graves with flowers and wreaths on Memorial Day officially dates back to the first observance in Waterloo, New York, in 1866, although the town of Boalsburg, Pennsylvania, has proclaimed itself the "Birthplace of Memorial Day" because it was decorating soldiers' graves two years earlier. Both of these towns may have gotten the idea from a paragraph in the Troy, New York, *Tribune* two years after the Civil War ended. It described how the women of Columbus, Mississippi, strewed flowers on the graves of both Confederate and Union soldiers, an act that quickly became a symbol of friendship and understanding between the North and the South.

Visiting cemeteries and decorating graves was hardly an American invention. Festivals in both Europe and Asia have featured this custom since very ancient times. In China and Japan, for example, people decorate graves at the **LANTERN FESTIVAL**, **OBON FESTIVAL**, and **CHING MING.** Observances for **ALL SOULS' DAY** and **DÍA DE LOS MUERTOS** usually involve visiting and decorating graves as well.

Poppy

Red paper poppies, symbolic of the war dead because real poppies bloomed everywhere in the battlefield graveyards of France, are traditionally sold by veterans on Memorial Day. The Veterans of Foreign Wars conducted the first nationwide "poppy sale" to raise money for disabled and destitute veterans in 1922. At one time, people referred to Memorial Day as Poppy Day.

FURTHER READING

Christianson, Stephen G., and Jane M. Hatch. *The American Book of Days*. 4th ed. New York: H.W. Wilson, 2000.

Cohen, Hennig, and Tristram Potter Coffin. *The Folklore of American Holidays*. 3rd ed. Detroit: Gale Research, 1999.

Henderson, Helene, ed. *Holidays, Festivals, and Celebrations of the World Dictionary*. 3rd ed. Detroit: Omnigraphics, 2005.

Ickis, Marguerite. *The Book of Patriotic Holidays*. New York: Dodd, Mead, 1962.

Santino, Jack. *All Around the Year: Holidays and Celebrations in American Life.* Urbana: University of Illinois Press, 1994.

Tuleja, Tad. *Curious Customs: The Stories Behind 296 Popular American Rituals.* New York: Harmony, 1987.

WEB SITES

Arlington National Cemetery
www.arlingtoncemetery.org

Gettysburg National Cemetery
www.nps.gov/getc/index.htm

Library of Congress
memory.loc.gov/ammem/today/may30.html
www.americaslibrary.gov/cgi-bin/page.cgi/jb/recon/memorial_1

Michaelmas
(St. Michael's Day,
Feast of St. Michael and All Angels)

Type of Holiday: Religious (Christian)
Date of Observation: September 29 in the West, November 8 in the East
Where Celebrated: Europe, Norway, Russia, United States, and by Christians all over the world
Symbols and Customs: Blackberries, Dragon, Goose, Scales
Related Holidays: Autumn Equinox

ORIGINS

Michaelmas is part of the Christian religious tradition. The word Christian refers to a follower of Christ, a title derived from the Greek word meaning Messiah or Anointed One. The Christ of Christianity is Jesus of Nazareth, a man born between 7 and 4 B.C.E. in the region of Palestine. According to Christian teaching, Jesus was killed by Roman authorities using a form of execution called crucifixion (a term meaning he was nailed to a cross and hung from it until he died) in about the year 30 C.E. After his death, he rose back to life. His death and resurrection provide a way by which people can be reconciled with God. In remembrance of Jesus' death and resurrection, the cross serves as a fundamental symbol in Christianity.

With nearly two billion believers in countries around the globe, Christianity is the largest of the world's religions. There is no one central authority for all of Christianity. The pope (the bishop of Rome) is the authority for the Roman Catholic Church, but other sects look to other authorities. Orthodox communities look to patriarchs and emphasize doctrinal agreement and traditional practice. Protestant communities focus on individual conscience. The Roman Catholic and Protestant churches are often referred to as the Western Church, while the Orthodox churches may also be called the Eastern Church. All three main branches of Christianity acknowledge the authority of Christian scriptures, a compilation of writings assembled into a document called the Bible. Methods of biblical interpretation vary among the different Christian sects.

Michael, the leader of the heavenly host of angels, is an important figure in the Christian, Jewish, and Muslim religious traditions; he even has a counterpart among the Babylonian and Persian angels. The Jews think of Michael as the special guardian of Israel. In Christianity, it is Michael who will sound the last trumpet on Judgment Day and escort the souls of the faithful departed into the presence of God. Sometimes he is represented as the only archangel, and sometimes as the head of a fraternity of archangels that includes Gabriel, Raphael, and others.

The veneration of St. Michael the Archangel dates back to very early times. He was the patron saint of the sick among the early Christians, and a church bearing his name existed in fourth-century Constantinople (for which reason the Eastern Church celebrates the Feast of St. Michael on November 8). In the fifth century, a basilica was dedicated to St. Michael on September 29 in the Via Salaria, about six miles from Rome. His feast day, originally celebrated only at this church, gradually spread to a number of holy places under his patronage. By the Middle Ages, the archangel Michael was widely revered throughout the Christian world, including Russia. He became even more popular after supposedly appearing in a vision on the top of Monte Gargano in Apulia, southern Italy, during the reign of Pope Gelasius I in the late fifth century. It is probably because of this that he came to be regarded as the angel of mountains. Many of the churches and chapels dedicated to him were erected on the tops of hills or mountains in western Europe. The French monastery known as Mont-Saint-Michel, located off the Normandy coast, is probably the most famous. Up until the seventeenth century, the red velvet buckler worn by Michael in his fight against Satan was displayed there (*see* DRAGON).

In England, where it is known as Michaelmas, St. Michael's Day was one of the four "quarter days" on which rents were due and contracts affecting houses and property were assumed or terminated. It is also associated with the opening of the fall term at public schools and universities.

In the mountains of Norway, *Mikkelsmesse* is the time of year when cows and goats are herded down from the mountain pastures to the valley farms. Dancing, singing, and feasting generally follow.

SYMBOLS AND CUSTOMS

Blackberries

Arriving as it did at the end of the harvest season, St. Michael's Day was a natural time to overindulge in eating and drinking. Perhaps to give people something to blame for the way they felt the next morning, a legend developed that blackberries were poisoned on the eve of this day because Satan stepped on them. Anyone who felt ill after a St. Michael's Day feast could always lay the blame on eating the poisoned berries.

In some places it is still considered very unlucky to eat blackberries on or after Michaelmas because the devil spits on them to get even with St. Michael, who was responsible for getting him thrown out of heaven (*see* DRAGON).

Dragon

Perhaps the best-known story concerning St. Michael the archangel comes from the Book of Revelation. There was a war in heaven during which Michael and the other angels fought against a dragon with seven heads, also known as Satan or the devil. Michael won, and the dragon was cast out, along with the angels who had fought beside him.

In Renaissance paintings, St. Michael is often shown dressed as a warrior, with wings on his shoulders and a dragon under his foot, symbolic of his victory over the powers of evil and darkness.

Goose

In rural England, where Michaelmas was the day on which tenant farmers paid their rents, it was customary to include in the payment "one goose fit for the lord's dinner." Although there is no question that geese were plentiful at this time of year, the goose has always played an important role in folklore and mythology. There were sacred geese in the Greek temples, and the geese from the Roman temple of Juno are credited with saving Rome from the invasion of the Gauls in the fourth century B.C.E. The Chinese, the Hindus, and the North American Indians also held the goose in high regard.

The custom of bringing a goose to the landlord at Michaelmas in hopes of making him more lenient gave rise to the superstition that eating goose on this day will prevent worries about money for an entire year. Goose is also eaten in Ireland on St. Michael's Day, supposedly as an act of gratitude for a miracle of St. Patrick's that was performed with the help of the archangel. Queen Elizabeth I is said to have been eating her Michaelmas goose when she received the good news about the defeat of the Spanish Armada.

Scales

The archangel Michael is frequently shown carrying a pair of scales, a symbol of his responsibility for "weighing" souls after they are released from death.

FURTHER READING

Bellenir, Karen. *Religious Holidays and Calendars*. 3rd ed. Detroit: Omnigraphics, 2004.

Brewster, H. Pomeroy. *Saints and Festivals of the Christian Church*. 1904. Reprint. Detroit: Omnigraphics, 1990.

Chambers, Robert. *The Book of Days*. 2 vols. 1862-64. Reprint. Detroit: Omnigraphics, 1990.

Christianson, Stephen G., and Jane M. Hatch. *The American Book of Days*. 4th ed. New York: H.W. Wilson, 2000.

Dunkling, Leslie. *A Dictionary of Days*. New York: Facts on File, 1988.

Harper, Howard V. *Days and Customs of All Faiths*. 1957. Reprint. Detroit: Omnigraphics, 1990.

Henderson, Helene, ed. *Holidays, Festivals, and Celebrations of the World Dictionary*. 3rd ed. Detroit: Omnigraphics, 2005.

Leach, Maria, ed. *Funk & Wagnalls Standard Dictionary of Folklore, Mythology & Legend*. San Francisco: Harper & Row, 1984.

MacDonald, Margaret R., ed. *The Folklore of World Holidays*. Detroit: Gale Research, 1992.

Urlin, Ethel L. *Festivals, Holy Days, and Saints' Days*. 1915. Reprint. Detroit: Omnigraphics, 1992.

WEB SITE

New Advent Catholic Encyclopedia
www.newadvent.org/cathen/10275b.htm

Mid-Autumn Festival
(Birthday of the Moon)

Type of Holiday: Calendar/Seasonal, Folkloric
Date of Observation: Full moon nearest September 15; fifteenth day of the eighth Chinese lunar month
Where Celebrated: China and throughout the Far East; in Asian communities all over the world
Symbols and Customs: Moon Cakes (Yueh Ping), Moon Hare, Moon Toad, Moon Viewing, Round Fruit
Related Holidays: Autumn Equinox

ORIGINS

The Chinese lunisolar calendar is based on the oldest system of time measurement still in use. It is widely employed in Asian countries to set the dates of seasonal festivals. The **CHINESE NEW YEAR** takes place on the new moon nearest to the point which is defined in the West as the fifteenth degree on the zodiacal sign of Aquarius. Each of twelve months in the Chinese year is twenty-nine or thirty days long and is divided into two parts, each of which is two weeks long. The Chinese calendar, like all lunisolar systems, requires periodic adjustment to keep the lunar and solar cycles integrated; therefore, an intercalary month is added when necessary.

The names of each of the twenty-four two-week periods sometimes correspond to seasonal festivals celebrated during the period. Beginning with the New Year, which takes place in late January or early February, these periods are known by the following names: Spring Begins (New Year and **LI CH'UN**), the Rain Water, the Excited Insects, the **VERNAL EQUINOX**, the Clear and Bright (**CHING MING**), the Grain Rains, the Summer Begins, the Grain Fills, the Grain in Ear, the **SUMMER SOLSTICE (DOUBLE FIFTH)**, the Slight Heat, the Great Heat, the Autumn Begins, the Limit of Heat, the White Dew (**MID-AUTUMN FESTIVAL**), the **AUTUMN EQUINOX**, the Cold Dew, the Hoar Frost Descends, the Winter Begins, the Little Snow, the Heavy Snow, the **WINTER SOLSTICE,** the Little Cold, and the Great Cold.

According to the Chinese lunar calendar, the autumn season extends throughout the seventh, eighth, and ninth months. This makes the fifteenth day of the eighth lunar month the season's midpoint. From this point onward, the power of the sun begins to wane; the days grow shorter and cooler, and the nights grow longer.

According to the Gregorian calendar, mid-September marks the time when the full moon—commonly called the Harvest Moon or Hunter's Moon—is at its lowest angle to the horizon, making it appear larger and brighter than usual. The Chinese celebrate the moon's birthday on this day, believing that it is the only night of the year when the moon is perfectly round. The Mid-Autumn Festival is therefore a double feast—a time for worshipping the moon goddess and for expressing gratitude for the harvest.

The Mid-Autumn Festival has been compared to the American **THANKSGIVING**, and there are some similarities. Family reunions are common, with family members often travelling long distances to be together. They feast, exchange gifts, and eat MOON CAKES. Many of these reunions take place out-of-doors in the evening, where the size and brightness of the moon can be admired.

Village theatricals are a popular way of entertaining the gods on this day. They are usually held in open-air theaters attached to temples, or in special sheds erected for the purpose. These temple-dramas are similar to the medieval miracle plays in Europe, which were performed on the porches of cathedrals. But they tend to avoid religious messages and focus instead on plots taken from legend or history, or from episodes in famous novels. Other popular entertainments include lion dancers and stilt walkers.

The Mid-Autumn Festival continues for three days. The evenings are devoted to MOON VIEWING parties, and the days are usually spent hiking and picnicking in the mountains. In addition to being a harvest festival and a celebration of the moon's birthday, it is also a festival of liberation, commemorating the day on which the ancient Chinese people overthrew the Mongol overlords and brought Mongolia under Chinese rule (*see* MOON CAKES).

SYMBOLS AND CUSTOMS

Moon Cakes (Yüeh Ping)

Made of grayish flour to resemble the color of the moon and often stacked in a pyramid thirteen-cakes high to represent the thirteen months of the Chinese lunar year, moon cakes are the most distinctive offering of the Mid-Autumn Festival. They are round like the moon and filled with melon seeds, cassia blossoms, orange peel, walnuts, date paste, or smashed bean. They are sent from neighbor to neighbor and exchanged among friends during the festival. In cities, confectioners make moon cakes and donate them to the poor. In rural villages, "moon cake societies" are formed to make sure that everyone has an adequate supply of cakes when the festival arrives. While most moon cakes are only a few inches in diameter, imperial chefs have made them as large as several feet across, decorated with images of the moon palace, the cassia tree, or the rabbit (*see* MOON HARE).

Legend says that during the Yuan dynasty (1279-1368), these cakes were used to convey secret instructions to Chinese patriots concerning the overthrow of their Mongol rulers. There was a Mongol spy living in every household, and the only way the Chinese people could communicate with each other was to conceal their messages in moon cakes. Information about the time and place of the revolution was spread by hiding it on small squares of paper inside the moon cakes that were sent to friends and relatives during the Mid-Autumn Festival in 1353. The midnight attack came as a complete surprise and hastened the dynasty's downfall.

Today there are twenty to thirty varieties of moon cakes. Their roundness makes them a perfect symbol not only for the moon, but also for family unity.

Moon Hare

In China, the association between the hare and the moon is very ancient. Shepherds or nomads who slept under the open sky would see figures outlined on the face of the moon and make up stories about how they came to be there. The hare and the frog (*see* MOON TOAD) are probably the best-known inhabitants of the moon, which Chinese mythology says is populated by both humans and animals. There is an old superstition that the hare, who never closes her eyes, gives birth with her eyes fixed on the moon. How brightly the moon shines on the night of this festival determines how many hares will be born during the coming year.

Images of the Moon Hare appear everywhere during the Mid-Autumn Festival, usually in the form of small clay statues. This legendary rabbit comes from an old Buddhist tale brought to China from India. The animals of the forest were scrambling to prepare offerings to the Buddha, who had taken the form of a Brahmin (or saint) and asked for food and water. The rabbit, embarrassed by the meager collection of herbs and grasses he'd managed to gather, caught sight of the cooking fire and leaped into it, offering himself to the Buddha but pausing first to remove any small creatures who had lodged in his fur. He was rewarded by having his image appear on the face of the moon where everyone could admire the example of his self-sacrifice.

The moon is a symbol of longevity in Chinese mythology because it is the dwelling place of the immortals. The Moon Hare is traditionally pictured under the Sacred Cassia Tree, pounding the Pill of Immortality with his mortar and pestle. The cassia tree blooms just in time for the moon's birthday, and Chinese physicians believe that its aromatic bark cures disease. Next to the hare is the woodcutter Wu Gang, who is doomed to continually chop down a cassia tree as punishment for a mistake he made while studying to become an immortal. Every time the axe makes a cut, the tree miraculously heals itself and the cut closes up.

Moon Toad

The Moon Toad (or frog) comes from the legend of Chang E, the goddess who inhabits the moon and who was changed into a three-legged toad because she found her husband's supply of the elixir of life and drank it all. When her misdeed was discovered, she fled to the moon, where she has lived ever since. Once a month, on the fifteenth day, her husband leaves his palace on the sun and comes to visit her. This explains why the moon is at its most beautiful on this day.

Just as the MOON HARE promises long life to those who are virtuous, the three-legged Moon Toad offers wealth to those who please the Moon Queen. He is often depicted with a string of gold coins.

Moon Viewing

In Japan, the custom of tsukimi or "moon viewing" is observed at the same time as the Chinese Mid-Autumn Festival. People set up a table facing the horizon where the moon will rise and place offerings on the table for the spirit of the moon. These offerings might include a vase holding the seven grasses of autumn, cooked vegetables, and tsukimi dango or "moon-viewing dumplings" made of rice flour. Moon-viewing festivals are particularly popular in Tokyo and in Kyoto, where people watch the moon from boats with dragons on their bows.

Round Fruit

The fruits associated with the Mid-Autumn Festival include apples, pomegranates, honey peaches, crab apples, sour betel nuts, and grapes—round fruits whose shape symbolizes the fullness of the moon and family harmony. Pears are excluded—not only because they are not perfectly round, but because the word for pear is *li*, which is pronounced the same as the word meaning "separation." On a day set aside for family reunions, pears would be considered an unlucky offering.

Chinese women set up an altar in the courtyard with five round plates filled with the fruits listed above. In the center are MOON CAKES baked especially for the holiday, and nearby are red candles and bundles of incense. Behind the family altar is a large paper scroll on which the MOON HARE appears, sitting under the Sacred Cassia Tree. Sometimes the scroll will show the MOON TOAD entangled in a string of coins. After a brief service in honor of the Moon Queen at midnight, the festival meal is eaten outdoors under the full moon.

FURTHER READING

Bredon, Juliet, and Igor Mitrophanow. *The Moon Year: A Record of Chinese Customs and Festivals*. Shanghai: Kelly & Walsh, 1927.

Eberhard, Wolfram. *A Dictionary of Chinese Symbols: Hidden Symbols in Chinese Life and Thought*. New York: Routledge & Kegan Paul, 1986.

Gaer, Joseph. *Holidays Around the World*. Boston: Little, Brown, 1953.

Henderson, Helene, ed. *Holidays, Festivals, and Celebrations of the World Dictionary*. 3rd ed. Detroit: Omnigraphics, 2005.

Stepanchuk, Carol, and Charles Wong. *Mooncakes and Hungry Ghosts: Festivals of China*. San Francisco: China Books & Periodicals, 1991.

WEB SITES

Hong Kong Tourism Board
www.discoverhongkong.com/eng/heritage/festivals/he_fest_mida.jhtml

National Heritage Board of Singapore
www.nhb.gov.sg/discover_heritage/heritagekids/feature_articles/feature_festival_chinese.shtml

Taiwan Government Information Office
www.gio.gov.tw/info/festival_c/moon_e/moon.htm

Mid-Lent Sunday
(Laetare Sunday, Mothering Sunday, Rose Sunday)

Type of Holiday: Religious (Christian: Roman Catholic, Anglican, Episcopalian)
Date of Observation: March-April; fourth Sunday in Lent
Where Celebrated: England, Scotland, United States
Symbols and Customs: Golden Rose, Simnel Cakes
Colors: Rose-colored vestments are worn in Roman Catholic churches on this day, in place of the purple vestments worn on the other Sundays in Lent.
Related Holidays: Ash Wednesday, Easter, Lent

ORIGINS

Mid-Lent Sunday is part of the Christian religious tradition. The word Christian refers to a follower of Christ, a title derived from the Greek word meaning Messiah or Anointed One. The Christ of Christianity is Jesus of Nazareth, a man born between 7 and 4 B.C.E. in the region of Palestine. According to Christian teaching, Jesus was killed by Roman authorities using a form of execution called crucifixion (a term meaning he was nailed to a cross and hung from it until he died) in about the year 30 C.E. After his death, he rose back to life. His death and resurrection provide a way by which people can be reconciled with God. In remembrance of Jesus' death and resurrection, the cross serves as a fundamental symbol in Christianity.

With nearly two billion believers in countries around the globe, Christianity is the largest of the world's religions. There is no one central authority for all of Christianity. The pope (the bishop of Rome) is the authority for the Roman Catholic Church, but other sects look to other authorities. Orthodox communities look to patriarchs and emphasize doctrinal agreement and traditional practice. Protestant communities focus on individual conscience. The Roman Catholic and Protestant churches are often referred to as the Western Church, while the Orthodox churches may also be called the Eastern Church. All three main branches of Christianity acknowledge the authority of Christian scriptures, a compilation of writings assembled into a document called the Bible. Methods of biblical interpretation vary among the different Christian sects.

The name "Mid-Lent Sunday" is not really accurate, since the halfway point in the forty days of **LENT** falls several days before the fourth Sunday. This may reflect an earlier method of computing the duration of Lent, but it is more likely that this holiday was moved up to a Sunday because Sundays were generally exempt from the Lenten fast, and breaking the fast on a weekday represented too great a departure from the restrictions of the season. In any case, there is no shortage of alternate names for this day. In the Roman Catholic Church it is called Laetare Sunday, from the Latin word meaning "rejoice," which begins the Introit of the Mass. Up until 1969, when Roman Catholic reforms reinstated all Sundays as festivals, it was also known as Refreshment Sunday because the usual Lenten restrictions were relaxed.

In the Church of England, as well as in the Episcopal Church in the United States, the fourth Sunday in Lent is known as Mothering Sunday. This designation goes back to the ancient Roman Hilaria, held on the Ides of March (March 15) in honor of Cybele, mother of the gods. The Christians took this pagan festival, symbolic of the high esteem in which motherhood was held, and turned it into a day on which offerings were brought to the "Mother Church" instead of to private chapels. As the Christian calendar took shape, this Sunday festival was shifted from mid-March to mid-Lent, and the idea of visiting the Mother Church spilled over into the family. Children living away from home returned to visit their parents, and servants were given a day off so they could do the same. They brought gifts for their mothers, typically flowers and a SIMNEL CAKE. The fourth Sunday in Lent became a popular time for family reunions throughout England, and a young person who made such a visit was said to go "a-mothering."

A popular dish served at these family get-togethers was furmety, a kind of sweet porridge made from wheat grains boiled in milk and spiced. In northern England and Scotland, the preferred dish was peas that had been fried in butter with salt and pepper and made into pancakes known as "carlings." For this reason, the day was sometimes referred to as Carling Sunday.

SYMBOLS AND CUSTOMS

Golden Rose

Mid-Lent Sunday is also known as Rose Sunday. Beginning in the eleventh century, it was the custom for the Pope to carry a golden rose in his hand while celebrating Mass on this day. Although it was originally a single rose of normal size, since the fifteenth century it has been a cluster or branch of roses made of pure gold and set with precious stones. This custom may originally have been connected with the arrival of spring, when flowering branches were carried by the Pope from the Lateran Palace, his official residence in Rome, to Santa Croce in Gerusalemme, where he celebrated the Mass. It may also have something to do with the medieval devotion to the Virgin Mary, known as the "Rose of Sharon." The rose itself is considered a symbol of spiritual joy.

After being blessed by the Pope, the rose is sometimes sent to a particular parish in recognition of its special devotion to the Church, or to a distinguished person who has shown an unusual degree of religious spirit and loyalty. Then a new rose is made for the following year.

According to an old superstition, the Golden Rose brings bad luck to its owner. This probably dates back to the story of Joanna of Sicily, the first queen to whom the rose was sent. She was dethroned soon afterward and strangled by her nephew.

Simnel Cakes

The earliest simnel cakes were unleavened cakes or buns made of wheat flour and boiled. Sometimes they were marked with a figure of Christ or the Virgin Mary, which would seem to indicate that they were originally linked to a pagan celebration and then Christianized—like the hot cross buns originally eaten in honor of the pagan goddess Eostre, then later marked with a cross to make them more acceptable to the Christian clergy (*see* **EASTER**).

Over the years, the simple flat cake with currants and spices evolved into an elaborate raised cake with a saffron-flavored crust and a ring of almond paste on the top. The center was filled with plums, candied lemon peel, and other fruits, and the entire cake was tied up in a cloth and boiled for several hours. Then it was brushed with egg and baked, giving the crust a consistency not unlike that of wood, with an ornamental border that made it look like a crown. As early as the fourteenth century, it was the custom for young people to carry simnels as gifts for their mothers on Mid-Lent (or Mothering) Sunday. Simnel cakes were made at **EASTER** and **CHRISTMAS** as well.

There are a number of theories about the origin of the name "simnel." It may have come from the Latin *simila,* a very fine flour. Another theory is that the cakes were named after Lambert Simnel, a baker during the reign of Henry VII. There is also a legend about an elderly couple named Simon and Nelly. They combined the unleavened dough left over at the end of Lent with the plum pudding left over from Christmas. Then they got into an argument over whether the cake should be boiled or baked. They finally compromised and decided to do both. The result was the "Simon-Nelly" cake.

These cakes are still made in England and sent all over the world during Lent. In the towns of Devizes and Bury, the baking begins right after Christmas to allow time for delivery of cakes to people living abroad. Many emigrants left standing orders many years ago for simnels to be sent to them, and these orders have been renewed by their children and grandchildren.

FURTHER READING

Brewster, H. Pomeroy. *Saints and Festivals of the Christian Church.* 1904. Reprint. Detroit: Omnigraphics, 1990.

Chambers, Robert. *The Book of Days.* 2 vols. 1862-64. Reprint. Detroit: Omnigraphics, 1990.

Harper, Howard V. *Days and Customs of All Faiths.* 1957. Reprint. Detroit: Omnigraphics, 1990.

Henderson, Helene, ed. *Holidays, Festivals, and Celebrations of the World Dictionary.* 3rd ed. Detroit: Omnigraphics, 2005.

Hole, Christina. *English Custom & Usage.* 1941. Reprint. Detroit: Omnigraphics, 1990.

Ickis, Marguerite. *The Book of Religious Holidays and Celebrations.* New York: Dodd, Mead, 1966.

Leach, Maria, ed. *Funk & Wagnalls Standard Dictionary of Folklore, Mythology & Legend.* San Francisco: Harper & Row, 1984.

Metford, J.C.J. *The Christian Year.* New York: Crossroad, 1991.

Urlin, Ethel L. *Festivals, Holy Days, and Saints' Days.* 1915. Reprint. Detroit: Omnigraphics, 1992.

WEB SITES

Ireland Now
www.irelandnow.com/mothersday.html

New Advent Catholic Encyclopedia
www.newadvent.org/cathen/06394b.htm

Midsummer Day
(St. John's Day)

Type of Holiday: Calendar/Seasonal, Folkloric, Religious (Christian)
Date of Observation: June 24, or nearest Friday
Where Celebrated: Brazil, Europe, Scandinavia
Symbols and Customs: Bonfires, Wheel
Related Holidays: Beltane, Inti Raymi Festival, Summer Solstice

ORIGINS

This ancient pagan festival celebrating the **SUMMER SOLSTICE** was originally observed on June 21, the longest day of the year. Like **BELTANE** in Ireland, Midsummer Day in Europe and the Scandinavian countries was a time to light BON-FIRES and drive out evil. At one time it was believed that all natural waters had medicinal powers on this day, and people bathed in rivers and streams to cure their illnesses.

When Christianity spread throughout the pagan world, the Midsummer festival on June 24 became St. John's Day, in honor of St. John the Baptist. Christian symbolism was attached to many of the pre-Christian rites associated with this day. The bonfires, for example, were renamed "St. John's Fires," and the herbs that were picked on this day for their healing powers were called "St. John's herbs." But the pagan customs and beliefs surrounding Midsummer Day never really disappeared, and the Feast of St. John is still associated with the solstice and solstitial rites.

Midsummer Day marks the changing of the seasons, which people in all parts of the world have honored since ancient times. Many cultures divided the year into two seasons, summer and winter, and marked these points of the year at or near the summer and winter solstices, during which light and warmth began to increase and decrease, respectively. In pre-industrial times, humans survived through hunting, gathering, and agricultural practices, which depend on the natural cycle of seasons, according to the climate in the region of the world in which they lived. Thus, they created rituals to help ensure enough rain and sun in the spring and summer so crops would grow to fruition at harvest time, which was, in turn, duly celebrated. Vestiges of many of these ancient practices are thought to have survived in festivals still celebrated around seasonal themes.

In Sweden, the *Midsommar* celebration begins on a Friday and lasts through Sunday. Every town and village sets up a maypole (*see* **MAY DAY**), which is decorated with flowers, leaves, and flags. One of the most popular places to spend the Midsommar weekend is in the province of Dalarna, where some of Sweden's oldest wooden cottages have been preserved. Because Sweden is located so far north, Midsommar is called "the day that never ends." The sun doesn't begin to set until 10:00 p.m., and it rises again at 2:00 a.m. In areas of Norway and Sweden that lie above the Arctic Circle, the sun shines twenty-four hours a day in the summer.

SYMBOLS AND CUSTOMS

Bonfires

Fire festivals were held all over Europe on June 23 (the **SUMMER SOLSTICE**) or on Midsummer Day (June 24) during pre-Christian times. The solstice is the turning point in the sun's journey across the sky: After climbing higher and higher, it stops and begins to retrace its steps. Ancient peoples believed they could stop the sun's decline by kindling their own "suns" in the form of bonfires.

Bonfires were originally called "bone fires" because young boys would often throw bones and other noxious-smelling things on the fire to drive away monsters and evil spirits. Over the centuries, these fires attracted many folk beliefs and rituals. For example, people believed that their crops would grow as high as the flames reached, or as high as they could jump over the burning embers. Farmers drove their cattle through the fires to guard them against disease and to promote their fertility. Sometimes ashes from the bonfires were scattered over the fields to protect the crops from blight and to ensure a good harvest.

Midsummer bonfires were associated with courtship and fertility rituals as well. Young girls would often make wreaths out of leaves and ribbons, then hang them in a tall fir tree that had been cut down and erected in the middle of the fire. As the flames licked at their heels, young boys would climb the tree, take down the wreaths, and stand on one side of the fire while their girlfriends stood on the other. Sometimes the girls would throw the wreaths across the fire to the boys they wanted to marry. Then, as the flames died down, the couples would join hands and leap over the fire three times for good luck.

In Bohemia, a region in the western Czech Republic, young boys would collect all the worn-out brooms they could find, dip them in pitch, and after setting them on fire, wave them around or throw them up in the air. Sometimes they would run headlong down a hillside, brandishing their torches and shouting. The burned stumps of the brooms would then be stuck in their families' gardens to protect them from caterpillars and gnats. Some people put them in their fields or on the roofs of their houses as a charm against lightning, fire, and bad weather.

In Sweden, Denmark, and Norway, midsummer bonfires were known as "Balder's balefires." Lighting them was a way of reenacting the myth of Balder, the Scandinavian god of poetry who was killed when Loki, a divine mischief-maker, struck him with a bough of mistletoe. His body was burned on a pyre at the time of the summer solstice. Later on, effigies of Balder were thrown into the midsummer bonfires.

When Midsummer Day became St. John's Day, the Church gave new meaning to the bonfires. Since Jesus had once called John the Baptist "a burning and a shining light" (John 5:35), church officials decided that the fires should stand for St. John instead of the sun. The fact that it was St. John who baptized Jesus in the River Jordan dovetailed nicely with the pagan belief in the medicinal powers of water on Midsummer Day.

Although at one time midsummer bonfires were popular from Ireland in the west to Russia in the east, and from Norway and Sweden all the way south to Greece and Spain, today the bonfire tradition is still alive in only a few countries—primarily Sweden, Finland, and Lithuania. Roman Catholics in Brazil build large bonfires in front of their houses on St. John's Day to commemorate Elizabeth, St. John's mother and a cousin of the Virgin Mary. According to legend, Elizabeth promised to notify Mary of the birth of her child by building a bonfire in front of her house and setting off fireworks. In the United States, midsummer bonfires have been moved to the **FOURTH OF JULY**.

Wheel

Sometimes the straw that had been collected for the Midsummer BONFIRE was attached to a wheel and set on fire. As the wheel burned, two young men would grab the handles that projected from the axle and run downhill with it, often extinguishing the flames in a river or stream at the bottom of the hill. The wheel, of course, represented the sun, and letting it roll downhill was a demonstration of the fact that having reached its highest point in the sky, the sun was now beginning its descent. In Germany, the sun's "falling" is still celebrated on St. John's Day with burning wheels rolled down hills. It is considered good luck if a wheel burns all the way to the bottom of the hill.

In some European countries, burning discs were hurled into the night sky after being kindled in bonfires. Their flight made them resemble fiery dragons, symbolic of the monsters believed to roam the earth on this night.

FURTHER READING

Dobler, Lavinia G. *Customs and Holidays Around the World*. New York: Fleet Pub. Corp., 1962.

Frazer, Sir James G. *The Golden Bough: A Study in Magic and Religion*. New York: Macmillan, 1931.

Heinberg, Richard. *Celebrate the Solstice: Honoring the Earth's Seasonal Rhythms through Festival and Ceremony*. Wheaton, IL: Quest Books, 1993.

Henderson, Helene, ed. *Holidays, Festivals, and Celebrations of the World Dictionary*. 3rd ed. Detroit: Omnigraphics, 2005.

Ickis, Marguerite. *The Book of Festivals and Holidays the World Over*. New York: Dodd, Mead, 1970.

Purdy, Susan. *Festivals for You to Celebrate*. Philadelphia: Lippincott, 1969.

Santino, Jack. *All Around the Year: Holidays and Celebrations in American Life*. Urbana: University of Illinois Press, 1994.

WEB SITE

Estonian Ministry of Foreign Affairs
www.vm.ee/estonia/kat_174/pea_174/1190.html

Miss America Pageant

Type of Holiday: Promotional
Date of Observation: September or October for one week
Where Celebrated: Atlantic City, New Jersey
Symbols and Customs: Bert Parks, Evening Wear Competition, Interview, Judging Format, Rose Walk, Scholarships, Swimsuit Competition, Talent Competition, "There She Is, Miss America"

ORIGINS

Although the Miss America Pageant has for decades been identified with former master of ceremonies BERT PARKS, it was a group of New Jersey businessmen who first came up with the idea of staging a "bathing beauty" pageant to give the economy of their beachfront community, Atlantic City, a boost. Then two local reporters suggested at a newspaper convention that the editors assembled there might increase their circulation by holding entry-level contests where readers could send in photographs of beautiful girls in bathing suits. The winners of these photographic contests would then compete against each other live in Atlantic City, and the overall winner, to be crowned "Miss America," would be chosen by a panel of well-known artists.

The competitors in that first pageant, held in 1921, wore wool "bathing dresses" with baggy tunic tops over leggings or bloomers. They posed on wicker chairs and paraded along the beach with local officials. The winner, sixteen-year-old Margaret Gorman, was chosen for her athletic good looks and potential "to shoulder the responsibilities of homemaking and motherhood," in the words of one judge. But no sooner had the annual contest gotten off the ground than it was discontinued in 1928 due to charges of indecency by women's clubs—not only because the bathing suits were too revealing but because it was discovered that one of the contestants was married and another had a young infant. The pageant didn't start up again until the 1930s, this time under the direction of Leonora Slaughter, who focused on getting more refined young women—ages eighteen to twenty-eight who had never been married—to compete. Slaughter established the Miss America Pageant as it is known today and remained in charge for more than thirty years.

Since then the weeklong competition has undergone numerous transformations and survived many controversies. Landmark events include the first Jewish Miss America (Bess Myerson in 1945), the first African-American Miss America (Vanessa Williams in 1984, who was also the first to have her crown taken away when it was discovered that she had once posed for sexually explicit photographs), the first contestant with a visible disability (Theresa Uchytil in 2000, who was born without a left hand but proceeded to perform an impressive baton-twirling routine), and the first disabled woman to win the Miss America crown (Heather Whitestone in 1995, who was deaf). Feminist protesters disrupted the 1968 pageant by throwing bras, girdles, and makeup into a trash can outside Convention Hall and setting them on fire, giving rise to the term "bra-burners," and in 1999 pageant directors briefly considered dropping the requirement that contestants sign a sworn statement that they had never been married or pregnant. In other words, the evolution of the pageant has paralleled changing attitudes toward women in American society.

Today the pageant is a weeklong series of events, beginning when the winners of the fifty state pageants arrive in Atlantic City on Monday and ending with Saturday night's judging of the ten semifinalists and five finalists, a live television extravaganza that involves choreographed song-and-dance numbers. Many contestants in the Miss America Pageant are veterans of smaller local and regional pageants before they make it to Atlantic City. Each contestant is the winner of her state's pageant. Before that, contestants may have participated in any number of state and other local pageants as well as pageants for younger ages.

To minimize the emphasis on physical beauty, current Miss America Pageant contestants are judged in four different categories: the TALENT COMPETITION, the SWIMSUIT COMPETITION, the EVENING WEAR COMPETITION, and the INTERVIEW. In addition to being recognized for their poise and articulateness, the winners, finalists, and semifinalists receive hefty SCHOLARSHIPS they can use to pursue a college or graduate school education. Bert Parks no longer hosts the pageant, which has been televised since 1954, but the coronation song he made famous, "THERE SHE IS, MISS AMERICA," is still what most Americans associate with the pageant. Other major pageants include Miss USA, Miss World, and Miss Universe.

SYMBOLS AND CUSTOMS

Bert Parks

Bert Parks joined the Miss America Pageant as master of ceremonies in 1955, the year after it was first televised, and he quickly became an indispensable part of the show. In addition to his easygoing onstage personality, it was his rendition of the pageant's theme song, "THERE SHE IS, MISS AMERICA," which he sang every year as the newly crowned queen made her first walk down the carpeted runway in Atlantic City's Convention Hall, that particularly endeared him to both the contestants and television audiences across America. The event's most memorable moments include the time Parks' microphone went dead in the middle of the song and the year he was given the list of the top ten finalists to read, only to discover that it contained the previous year's winners.

Parks was replaced in 1979 after twenty-five years as the pageant's emcee. Following in his footsteps were actor Ron Ely (for two years), then television personality Gary Collins, who happened to be married to Mary Ann Mobley, Miss America 1959. Collins served as emcee until 1990, and his successors since then have included the team of Regis Philbin and Kathie Lee Gifford as well as brother-and-sister act Donny and Marie Osmond.

Evening Wear Competition

The earliest Miss Americas were crowned wearing their bathing suits, but in 1948 Beatrice (BeBe) Shopp inaugurated a new tradition by being crowned in her evening gown. The evening gown competition was a relatively low-key fashion parade in the 1920s, but it has since become an important part of the pageant, giving contestants an opportunity to show how successful they are in choosing a gown that fits their personality and self-image. Over the years gown styles have changed from loose-fitting "flapper-style" dresses to elaborate full-skirted ball gowns with layers of netting and heavily beaded, form-fitting dresses that make the wearers look, in the words of one judge, like "walking chandeliers."

In a bow to feminist concerns about the pageant, and in an attempt to de-emphasize the way the women look in their gowns in favor of the poise they display while wearing them, the evening gown competition was renamed "On-Stage Personality in Evening Wear."

Interview

Since 1990, Miss America contestants have been expected to participate in an interview so they can display their ability to handle the unexpected and to answer questions under the pressure of public scrutiny. At first it was an extemporaneous, onstage interview based on a single question, but the nature of the questions and the often amusing responses they provoked made pageant planners look for a better way to showcase contestants' intelligence. From 1972 until 1987, the candidates memorized short speeches which they delivered during the EVENING GOWN COMPETITION, and this approach eventually gave way to questioning each contestant about a public issue of her choice.

Beginning in the 1990s, contestants were asked to write an essay on whatever issue they had committed themselves to support or pursue if they won the title. Contestants in past years have chosen such subjects as sexual abstinence, under-age drinking, and organ donation. The interview accounts for 30 percent of a candidate's score in the preliminary competition and twenty percent of the final score.

Judging Format

Contestants in the original Miss America Pageant were judged on the basis of body measurements, but by the 1940s, the contestants' ranking in evening gown, talent, swimsuit, and "personality" categories each accounted for twenty-five percent of their total score. Talent counted for thirty percent by 1960, and the current judging system, where talent is worth forty percent, was implemented in 1986.

Contestants in the Miss America Pageant are given scores in five basic categories—the TALENT COMPETITION, the INTERVIEW, the EVENING GOWN COMPETITION, the SWIMSUIT COMPETITION, and on-stage question—by a preliminary panel of seven judges, who choose the top ten semifinalists. This group of ten is then narrowed down by the final panel of judges, usually well-known people or celebrities, to five finalists, and the winner is the one with the highest score of the five.

In the preliminary scoring, the talent competition accounts for thirty-five percent of the score, the interview twenty-five percent, "On-Stage Personality in Evening Wear" twenty percent, "Lifestyle and Fitness in Swimsuit" fifteen percent, and On-Stage Question five percent. During the final scoring, the judges compile the contestant's "Composite Score"—a category based on the individual's performance in the preliminary phases of competition in conjunction with the degree to which she exhibits the qualities and attributes listed in the Miss America job description. The composite score accounts for thirty percent of the score. The swimsuit and evening wear scores are worth twenty percent each, and talent is worth thirty percent.

In 1996, television viewers were included in the judging for the first time. Viewers were invited to call in their choice for the five finalists, in effect serving as an eighth judge.

Rose Walk

Unveiled on September 7, 1997, the Rose Walk was designed as a tribute to all Miss America winners. Designed by artist Lauren Ewing, it consists of a series of bronze plaques set into the sidewalk on Michigan Avenue and extending from the Atlantic City Convention Center, where the pageant is held, all the way to Atlantic Avenue. Beginning with the first Miss America in 1921, each plaque bears the name of the winner, the year she held the crown, and a quotation describing her response to her new role. The $250,000 monument is illuminated by rose-colored lights, and it has proved to be a popular Atlantic City tourist attraction.

Scholarships

The Miss America Organization, based in Atlantic City, is one of the nation's largest scholarship providers for young women. It was Leonora Slaughter who came up with the idea of offering scholarships to pageant finalists, emphasizing that she wanted the winners "to become something" rather than heading off to Hollywood at the end of their reign. Bess Myerson was the first Miss America (1945) to receive a scholarship, which she used to pursue graduate studies at Columbia University.

The winner of the pageant currently receives a $50,000 scholarship; the four runners-up receive $25,000, $20,000, $15,000, and $10,000, respectively; the next three finalists receive scholarships worth $7,000 each; and the last two finalists are awarded $6,000 each. Scholarships of up to $6,000 are also given out at the preliminary level of competition for "Talent" "Lifestyle & Fitness," "Presence and Poise," "Miss Congeniality," and "Quality of Life Winner." The winner of the Bernie Wayne Performing Arts Award (*see* "THERE SHE IS, MISS AMERICA") receives a scholarship as well.

Swimsuit Competition

The swimsuit competition dates back to the very first year the pageant was held, but the Miss America Organization has retitled it "Physical Fitness in Swimsuit" to de-emphasize the pageant's reputation as a "bathing beauty" contest. Swimsuit styles, just like evening gown styles, have changed over the years, and contestants no longer have to wear identical suits. Two-piece suits have been allowed since 1997, although thongs and bikinis are still forbidden. Competitors must register their swimsuits in advance so that pageant officials can make sure they aren't too risqué.

Yolande Betbeze, Miss America 1951, refused to participate in any activities during her reign that involved wearing a bathing suit. Catalina, the well-known bathing suit manufacturer that had provided suits for pageant contestants since the early 1940s, withdrew its sponsorship soon after. Nowadays competitors choose their own suits, and the emphasis is on physical fitness rather than body measurements. Jill Renee Cummings, Miss Vermont in the 1997 competition, raised eyebrows when she appeared in a two-piece bathing suit with a belly-button ring. But with the swimsuit competition accounting for only fifteen percent of the score in the preliminary judging and only ten percent in the finals, candidates tend to spend more time developing their talent and public speaking skills.

Talent Competition

The Talent Competition became a mandatory part of the pageant in 1938. Perhaps because so many Miss America contestants hope to pursue a career in show business, singers and dancers predominate in these widely watched displays on the stage at the Atlantic City Convention Center, although the pageant has seen its share of hula dancers, baton twirlers, and gymnasts doing handsprings across the stage. Performances that involve bringing animals on stage were banned after 1949, when the horse on which a contestant was riding just missed plunging into the orchestra, and a fire-baton that ended up in the judges' booth led to a ban on anything that might injure spectators. But many contestants have given professional-quality performances of opera, classical music, and ballet, and there's no question that a talented competitor has an edge when it comes to winning the pageant.

Judges for this part of the competition look at the amount of discipline involved in developing the talent, how difficult it is, and how accomplished the performer appears to be. They also consider such intangible factors as stage presence, facial expressions, and showmanship. The idea here is not to select someone who will then take her act "on the road" as the reigning Miss America, but someone who is comfortable being in the spotlight and has the poise and confidence to handle the many public appearances Miss America is required to make. Because only the five finalists get to perform their talent on the Saturday night live television broadcast, a separate award is given to the winner of the preliminary talent competition.

"There She Is, Miss America"

The song that BERT PARKS made famous was written by Bernie Wayne (1919-1993), who also wrote the hit song "Blue Velvet." Wayne was inspired to write a song about Miss America when he read in the newspaper in 1954 that the pageant was going to be televised for the first time, and it only took him an hour to do it. But once Bert Parks started performing the song in 1955, it became so closely identified with the pageant that almost every American who watched the show was able to sing along, at least with the opening lines:

There she is, Miss America
There she is, your ideal
The dream of a million girls
Who are more than pretty
May come true in Atlantic City

Wayne died in 1993, but every year a special award is given in his memory to a national Miss America contestant who wants to pursue a career in the performing arts.

FURTHER READING

Bivans, Ann-Marie. *Miss America: In Pursuit of the Crown*. New York: MasterMedia, 1991.

Christianson, Stephen G., and Jane M. Hatch. *The American Book of Days*. 4th ed. New York: H.W. Wilson, 2000.

WEB SITES

Miss America
www.missamerica.org

Miss Universe
www.missuniverse.com

Miss USA
www.missusa.com

Miss World
www.missworld.tv

Miwok Big Time
(Miwok Acorn Festival)

Type of Holiday: Calendar/Seasonal
Date of Observation: Fourth weekend in September
Where Celebrated: California
Symbols and Customs: Cha'ka, Grinding Rock, Roundhouse

ORIGINS

The Miwok (MEE-wahk) Indians lived at one time in what is now northern and central California. There were three groups: the Lake Miwok, who lived south of Clear Lake; the Coast Miwok, who lived just north of what is now San Francisco; and the Eastern Miwok, who lived south of what is now Sacramento. Like other California Indian tribes, the Miwok relied heavily on acorns for food, which they harvested from valley oaks in the autumn and stored in CHA'KA or granaries. But before the acorns could be eaten, they had to go through a special process designed to get rid of the tannin, which prevented the human body from absorbing their nutrients and gave them a bitter taste. The acorns were cracked open and the "meat" was ground into meal by using stone pestles in the mortar holes formed in huge slabs of marbleized limestone known as *chaw'se* or GRINDING ROCKS. These can still be seen, particularly in California's Grinding Rock State Historic Park in the foothills of the Sierra Nevada Mountains. Here a huge, flat expanse of limestone containing more than a thousand mortar holes stands as evidence of the Miwok's efforts.

The acorn meal was rinsed repeatedly with stream water to wash the tannin away. Then it was used to make soup, acorn mush, or acorn bread. Acorns are extremely high in nutritional value, and the average adult Miwok consumed about 2,000 pounds of them a year, which is why the harvest was such an important event.

The Miwok would celebrate the acorn harvest every year at a tribal gathering known as Big Time. Families from widely scattered Miwok villages would come together to share the fruits of the harvest, exchange news and supplies, and perform ceremonial dances. Although the Gold Rush in 1848 disrupted the Miwok's way of life and forced them to leave the land they had occupied for centuries, Big Time is still celebrated at Miwok Park in Novato, California, at Point Reyes National Seashore, and elsewhere. But the best-known celebration takes place at

Grinding Rock State Park in Pine Grove, where an entire Miwok village—including acorn granaries, a ceremonial ROUNDHOUSE, and typical Miwok bark dwellings—has been reconstructed. Descendants of the original Miwok (who number about 3,400, according to the last census) and other California Indian tribes come to this event on the fourth weekend in September to perform traditional dances, play hand games, and engage in storytelling.

SYMBOLS AND CUSTOMS

Cha'ka

The Miwok Indians stored the acorns they would eat during the winter months in granaries known as cha'ka. These were structures several feet high, consisting of poles through which branches had been woven to form sides, with a thatched roof of fir or cedar to keep out the rain and a lining of pine needles and wormwood to ward off deer, rodents, and insects. Each family had its own cha'ka, and these structures, which resembled tall baskets, have been reconstructed at various Miwok Indian sites, where they stand as a symbol of Miwok culture and tradition.

Grinding Rock

The huge limestone grinding rock or chaw'se that can be seen in an open meadow at Grinding Rock State Park has become a monument to the Miwok's survival. It has more grinding cups or mortar holes (1,185) than any other grinding rock in North America, and when the cups fill with rainwater, they look like round, glistening footprints across the stone.

The chaw'se at Grinding Rock State Park is also distinguished by the presence of 363 petroglyphs or rock carvings that depict circles, wavy lines, and human and animal tracks. It is believed that these carvings, estimated to be between two and three thousand years old, tell the history of the Miwok in this area. With the exception of one other, much smaller, site, this is the only Native American grinding rock known to have been decorated in this way.

Because the limestone of the grinding rock is relatively soft and fragile, visitors are not allowed to walk on it, but are encouraged to admire it from a wooden observation platform and to respect it as a symbol of the Miwok way of life.

Roundhouse

The reconstructed roundhouse or hun'ge at Grinding Rock State Park is one of the largest in existence. It is 60 feet in diameter, and its inside walls consist of cedar poles through which wild grapevine has been woven. The roof, which slopes gradually upward from ground level, is made of cedar bark slabs. There is a clay floor on which ceremonial dances are performed, with a huge oak post at each corner. Ceremonies are held here on several occasions each year, Big Time being one of them.

Many Native Americans were very upset when the roundhouse was remodeled in the early 1990s and a fire exit was added to comply with state safety laws. Because the circular structure of the building is considered to be symbolic of Mother Earth, and because the addition of the fire exit tampered with that structure, some people now see the roundhouse as "ruined" and refuse to go inside.

FURTHER READING

Eagle Walking Turtle. *Indian America: A Traveler's Companion.* Santa Fe: J. Muir Publications, 1989.

WEB SITES

Indian Grinding Rock State Historic Park
www.parks.ca.gov/?page_id=553

Federated Indians of the Graton Rancheria
www.gratonrancheria.com

Moors and Christians Fiesta

Type of Holiday: Historic
Date of Observation: April 22-24
Where Celebrated: Spain
Symbols and Customs: Costumes, Entradas, Filaes, Mock Battle, St. George
Related Holidays: St. George's Day

ORIGINS

The Moors, who were Muslims from Northern Africa, conquered Spain in the eighth century, but by the late 1200s they had lost most of the territory they'd gained to the Christians, with whom they were constantly doing battle. By the end of the fifteenth century Spain was a Christian country under the Catholic rule of King Ferdinand and Queen Isabella. Dozens of Moors and Christians fiestas are held throughout Spain at varying times of the year to commemorate the Christians' victory, and traces of them can even be seen in the celebrations of other countries where the Spanish influence remains strong. But none is more elaborate or colorful than the Moors and Christians Fiesta held in Alcoy, in the southeastern province of Alicante, Spain, on April 22-24.

The date of the festival has less to do with the day on which, in 1276, the Christians defeated the Moorish leader, Al-Azraq, than with the fact that April 23 is **ST. GEORGE'S DAY.** According to legend, the Moors seized the castle of Alcoy in the morning and were on the verge of winning the battle. But then the Christians made a fervent appeal to ST. GEORGE and were able to reverse their fortunes in the afternoon.

The Moors and Christians Fiesta is a festival that commemorates a significant historical event. Peoples throughout the world commemorate such significant events in their histories through holidays and festivals. Often, these are events that are important for an entire nation and become widely observed. The marking of such anniversaries serve not only to honor the values represented by the person or event commemorated, but also to strengthen and reinforce communal bonds of national, cultural, or ethnic identity. Victorious, joyful, and traumatic events are remembered through historic holidays. The commemorative expression reflects the original event through festive celebration or solemn ritual. Reenactments are common activities at historical holiday and festival gatherings, seeking to bring the past alive in the present.

Today the celebration of this event begins when a papier-mâché castle is built in Alcoy's main plaza. The first day of the fiesta opens with a special Mass for all those who will participate in the MOCK BATTLE, followed by the colorful ENTRADAS or entry parades as the companies of Moorish and Christian soldiers, known as FILAES, march into the city accompanied by bands. On the second day, St. George's relics are moved from his temple to the Church of Santa Maria, where another Mass is held. A second procession is held later in the day to return the relics to the temple, after which there is a huge display of fireworks. The battle itself takes place on the third day. After a messenger on horseback announces the confrontation that is about to take place, the two armies roam the streets firing muskets at one another that leave a dense fog of gunpowder and make enough noise to be heard far beyond the city limits. The Moors seize the castle by mid-morning and hoist their flag on the ramparts; but in the afternoon, after St. George appears on his white horse, the Moors retreat and the Christians become the victors.

In the fifteenth through the seventeenth centuries, the battle between the Moors and Christians was performed as a dance-drama, complete with music, costumes, and spoken dialogue. It was known as the "Dance of the Conquest," and it can still be seen in some locations. But commemoration in the form of a mock battle has proved to be far more popular.

SYMBOLS AND CUSTOMS

Costumes

The elaborate costumes worn by the soldiers participating in the MOCK BATTLE between the Moors and the Christians are not strictly historical; if anything, they tend to be fanciful and flamboyant—particularly those worn by the Moors. Many of the costumes are made from expensive silks and brocades, with jewel-encrusted swords and fancy helmets. The costumes cost so much, in fact, that many members of the FILAES or armies have to save their money all year to pay for them. After the fiesta in Alcoy is over, the captains of these armies often donate their costumes to the local Moors and Christians museum.

These modern-day soldiers are allowed to wear wristwatches and eyeglasses but must otherwise avoid anything that looks contemporary. The huge cigars that they hold in their mouths are another interesting costume tradition, although its source is unknown.

Entradas

The entradas—which means "entries" or entry processions—that take place on the morning and afternoon on the first day of the fiesta are basically an opportunity for members of the FILAES to show off their COSTUMES. The Christians enter the city first, while the Moors come later in the day. Tourists and townspeople gather along the streets to watch these magnificent parades, which can be even more spectacular than the fighting that follows.

Filaes

There are fourteen filaes or armies—fourteen Christian and fourteen Moorish—that participate in the fiesta. Membership in these groups is more than a once-a-year commitment, as meetings are held throughout the year to plan and raise money for the event. Many of the members pay for their costumes out of their own pockets, but the competition among the various filaes to be the "best dressed" is so intense that most feel it is worth it. Some people sign their children up for membership in the filaes at birth, so the loyalties to various groups run deep and are often passed on to the next generation.

Although no one is exactly sure how the filaes originated, they are believed to date back to the seventeenth century, when many Spanish towns established their own militias to fight the Barbary pirates. One of the biggest problems facing today's filaes is where to find enough horses, since most of the farmers in the countryside around Alcoy use tractors.

Mock Battle

The mock battle that is the highlight of the Moors and Christians Fiesta represents a tradition that goes back to the Middle Ages, when men liked to dress up as soldiers and engage in make-believe combat, with plenty of gunpowder to create the right "special effects." Whatever historical information has survived about the 1276 conflict on which the mock battle in Alcoy is based has been largely forgotten by the organizers of the modern-day festival, who see it as symbolic of the battle between Good and Evil, with Evil (i.e., the Moors) winning the upper hand for a while but eventually succumbing to the power of Good (the Christians).

St. George

St. George is the patron saint of Alcoy, the city he is believed to have saved from the Moors in 1276. He is usually seen riding his white horse—traditionally regarded as a symbolic messenger from the world of the dead—and he appears near the end of the MOCK BATTLE as a kind of ghost or apparition on the ramparts of the castle, signifying the power of Christianity to overcome all odds.

FURTHER READING

Epton, Nina. *Spanish Fiestas*. New York: A.S. Barnes, 1969.

MacDonald, Margaret R., ed. *The Folklore of World Holidays*. Detroit: Gale Research, 1992.

Merin, Jennifer, and Elizabeth B. Burdick. *International Directory of Theatre, Dance, and Folklore Festivals*. Westport, CT: Greenwood Press, 1979.

WEB SITE

Turespaña (Fiestas de Moros y Christians)
www.spain.info/TourSpain/Eventos/Fiestas/?language=EN

Mother's Day

Type of Holiday: Promotional
Date of Observation: Second Sunday in May
Where Celebrated: Australia, England, United States
Symbols and Customs: Carnation
Colors: Mother's Day is associated with the colors red and white. Some people wear white CARNATIONS on this day to honor mothers who have died and red or pink carnations for those who are living.
Related Holidays: Father's Day, Mid-Lent Sunday

ORIGINS

The observation of a national holiday in honor of mothers is due largely to the efforts of Anna Jarvis, who was born in Grafton, West Virginia, in 1864 and spent most of her adult life in Philadelphia. Her constant longing for the West Virginia countryside and for the family and friends she'd grown up with provided her with the theme for her Mother's Day movement, and it struck a familiar chord with other sons and daughters who had moved away from their home towns.

Jarvis's own mother was a model of domestic nurturing and responsibility. Although she had lived through many tragedies, including the deaths of seven of her eleven children, she never lost her faith in God. She cared for her children when they were ill, looked after a husband who was considerably older than she, and gave up her own dream of a college education. After she died, Jarvis helped arrange a special service at the church in Grafton to commemorate the work her mother had done there.

Eventually Jarvis decided that she wanted to honor her mother on a much larger scale—by honoring all mothers with their own special day on the second Sunday in May. She wrote letters to politicians, newspaper editors, and church leaders, and organized a committee, known as the Mother's Day International Association, to promote the new holiday. As a church organist and Sunday school teacher herself, Jarvis was familiar with Children's Day (the second Sunday in June), which had been observed since the 1870s. She wanted Mother's Day to stand closer to **MEMORIAL DAY**, so that people would remember the sacrifices their mothers had made for their families, just as they remembered the sacrifices their sons had made for their country. Jarvis's home church, Andrews Methodist Episcopal, dedicated the International Mother's Day Shrine in 1962. The shrine hosts events each May to honor mothers, including a tea and a concert.

The first official Mother's Day services were held in May of 1908. President Woodrow Wilson gave the day national recognition in 1914, and by the late 1920s, Mother's Day was one of the more prominent American holidays. But what Jarvis had originally envisioned as a church-based celebration of maternal love and sacrifice gradually came to embody the mounting tension in American culture between Christianity and commercialism. Greeting card manufacturers were quick to jump on the Mother's Day bandwagon, and the new holiday soon became the fourth largest for card buying in the United States—after **CHRIST-MAS**, **VALENTINE'S DAY**, and **EASTER**.

Mother's Day has also served as a focal point for various cultural debates involving women, justice, and inequality. Coretta Scott King, the wife of slain civil rights leader Martin Luther King Jr., led a Mother's Day march in 1968 to rally support for poor mothers and their children. In the 1970s the National Organization for Women used Mother's Day to stage rallies for the Equal Rights Amendment, to promote access to child care, and to stage banquets supporting equality for women. In the 1980s, the Women's Party for Survival, founded by Helen Caldicott, used the holiday to stage antinuclear demonstrations.

Other events commemorating Mother's Day are held to raise awareness for women's health concerns. The Y-ME National Breast Cancer Organization, founded in 1978 to provide support for breast cancer patients, holds Walk to Empower events on Mother's Day. Based in Chicago, the Walk to Empower spread to twelve cities by 2007, with more than 40,000 participants. Australia's annual Mother's Day Classic Run/Walk raises funds for the National Breast Cancer Foundation. Held since 1998, the Classic has spread to numerous cities throughout the country. More than 50,000 participated in 2007.

Sometimes Mother's Day is confused with Mothering Sunday (*see* **MID-LENT SUNDAY**), an English holiday that falls on the fourth Sunday in **LENT.** But Mother's Day is now observed in England as well, and the traditions associated with Mothering Sunday have been largely forgotten. A growing number of Protestant churches celebrate the second Sunday in May as the Festival of the Christian Home, an attempt to emphasize the role of the family as a whole, rather than just mothers.

SYMBOLS AND CUSTOMS

Carnation

During Victorian times, specific flowers had served as symbols for such complex emotions as sorrow, remembrance, hope, faith, longing, and love. Because they were associated with women and the home, flowers were a natural symbol of femininity and domestic happiness. Commercial florists in the United States reinforced these symbolic associations with great effectiveness. By 1918, the advertising slogan of the Society of American Florists was "Say It with Flowers."

Because her own mother had loved white carnations, Anna Jarvis urged people to wear them in honor of their mothers on the first national observance of Mother's Day. The unprecedented demand for white carnations boosted prices and caused shortages in some areas. To avoid similar problems in subsequent years, the floral industry tried to shift the focus from white carnations to flowers in general, encouraging people to decorate their homes, churches, and cemeteries with flowers and offering special Mother's Day bouquets. Year after year, the industry came up with elaborate campaigns urging people to buy roses, potted plants, corsages, spring flowers in baskets, and other floral arrangements for their mothers.

Jarvis lobbied hard against the floral industry's "profiteering." She even proposed substituting celluloid buttons for white carnations as the official badge of the holiday, and urged people to stop buying flowers or any other gifts for the occasion. Although she was not able to rid the holiday of its commercial aspects, it was the carnation—her mother's favorite—that survived as the main symbol for maternal purity, faithfulness, and love. Chronic shortages in the supply of white carnations led florists to promote the idea of wearing red (or pink) carnations to honor living mothers and white flowers to honor the deceased.

FURTHER READING

Henderson, Helene, ed. *Holidays, Festivals, and Celebrations of the World Dictionary.* 3rd ed. Detroit: Omnigraphics, 2005.

Ickis, Marguerite. *The Book of Religious Holidays and Celebrations.* New York: Dodd, Mead, 1966.

Schmidt, Leigh Eric. *Consumer Rites: The Buying and Selling of American Holidays.* Princeton: Princeton University Press, 1995.

WEB SITES

International Mother's Day Shrine
www.mothersdayshrine.com

Library of Congress
www.americaslibrary.gov/cgi-bin/page.cgi/jb/jazz/mother_1

Mother's Day Central
www.mothersdaycentral.com

Mother's Day Classic Run/Walk
www.mothersdayclassic.org

Y-ME National Breast Cancer Organization
main.y-me.org

Naadam
(Nadam, Nadaam)

Type of Holiday: Sporting
Date of Observation: July 11-13
Where Celebrated: Ulaanbaatar, Mongolia
Symbols and Customs: Airag, Archery, Eagle Dance, Horse Racing, Uukhai Song, Wrestling

ORIGINS

The sporting and cultural festival known as Naadam dates back more than 2,000 years, to a time when the nomadic tribes that inhabited Mongolia celebrated the skills—strength, speed, and marksmanship—on which their survival depended. They held competitions in what they called "the three manly games"—ARCHERY, HORSE RACING, and WRESTLING—before going into battle and after winning a war, and often when a new king was crowned. When the legendary Genghis Khan united the nomadic tribes and became ruler of the Mongolian Empire in the early thirteenth century, the games' popularity was widespread, and the top competitors were often war heroes. Starting sometime in the seventeenth century, the games were held in conjunction with Buddhist religious holidays, and then, beginning in 1922, they were held to celebrate the anniversary of the revolution that drove out the Chinese and led to the establishment of the Mongolian People's Republic. Nowadays, Naadam, which means "game" or "competition" in Mongolian, is primarily regarded as a traditional sporting event that celebrates the Mongolians' proud history and culture.

Although smaller competitions are held throughout the country, the main Naadam celebration takes place in the capital city of Ulaanbaatar for three days in July. Spectators and competitors arrive from all over, setting up their *ghers* or yurts—the collapsible canvas and felt tents stretched over a wooden framework used by the early nomadic tribes—on the open grasslands surrounding the capital. The festival opens with a huge parade of monks, military brass bands, and athletes dressed in traditional Mongolian costumes. Three days of fierce competition and equally enthusiastic merrymaking follow. Although the festival still focuses on the "three manly games," women are now allowed to compete in everything but the wrestling.

SYMBOLS AND CUSTOMS

Airag

Airag is made from fermented mare's milk. It is a popular drink in Mongolia and a traditional cure for everything from digestive ailments to anemia, tuberculosis, and impotence. The winning five jockeys (usually children) of the HORSE RACING event are each given a cup or bowl of this beverage to drink, and they sprinkle the remainder over their horses so the animals can share in the victory celebration.

Archery

The archery contests held during Naadam date back to the time of Genghis Khan, but archery itself has played an important role in Mongolian history since 300-200 B.C.E. The Mongols use bows made from layers of wood, horn, birch bark, fish glue, and other traditional substances, which make them very strong and difficult to bend. The arrows are made from the wood of willow or pine trees, with heads made of bone and vulture feather "fins" that help them travel farther. The target is unusual as well: a wall of leather cylinders that is placed about seventy-five meters away from the male archers and sixty meters from the women; for younger competitors, it is placed at a distance of three (for girls) or four meters (for boys) per year of age.

Archers compete as individuals as well as in teams. The men shoot forty arrows and the women twenty, wearing a special glove to protect the hand that pulls back on the string and protective clothing around the arm that pushes against the bow. Referees standing near the target raise their arms and sing the UUKHAI SONG when the target is hit. The winner of the archery competition is honored with the title of *mergen*, which means "sharpshooter" or "marksman."

Eagle Dance

The devekh or eagle dance is performed both before and after the WRESTLING competition. With arm movements that imitate an eagle in flight, the dance serves as a warm-up exercise beforehand—not to mention a way of displaying the competitor's well-developed physique. At the end of a round, the loser must walk under the winner's arm, and the winner then performs the eagle dance again, this time to symbolize his invincibility.

Horse Racing

The horse was for many centuries as central to the nomadic Mongolian way of life as the car is to the lifestyle of modern-day Americans. Although most Mongolian families no longer raise their own horses, herdsmen continue to do so for the races that are such an important part of Naadam.

What makes the Naadam horse races so different from races held elsewhere is that instead of running around a track or set course, the race is run in the open, over distances of roughly ten to twenty miles (depending upon the age of the horse) of grasslands with many natural obstacles. Although originally the competitors were adult men riding horses who had not yet been broken, today's jockeys are young children aged five to twelve who have been riding horses since they were born. Their lighter weight poses less of a burden for the horses, who have been specially trained for this event by charging up steep hills in midsummer heat, wrapped in sheepskins, and who are of a pony-like breed that can run for hours without getting tired. Although the young jockeys, many of whom prefer to ride bareback, are very skillful when it comes to maneuvering their horses, knowing just when to restrain them and when to let them run at full speed, falls and injuries are fairly common. The winner of the race is the horse that successfully completes a round trip—with or without its rider—from the starting line out to a designated point and then back again. The start of the race is particularly exciting, with all the young jockeys circling the starting line yelling "Giingo!"—an ancient Mongolian war-cry.

The fact that the winning horse receives more attention than its rider—songs of praise are traditionally sung in honor of the five horses that come in first—is an indication of the symbolic role horses have played in the survival of the Mongolian people. Even more significant is the fact that after the medals are awarded to the winners, the losing horse and its rider are invited up to the judges' stand, where the national storyteller (similar to the poet laureate of the United States) recites an ode designed to cheer up the jockey and give him the confidence to try again the following year.

Uukhai Song

Sung during the ARCHERY competition, the folk song known as uukhai is an ancient one, dating back to the days when the distance from the archer to the target was about three times as long as it is now. Because the judges were standing near the target and the archer was too far away to hear them, they would start singing the uukhai song as the archer drew back his bow and then, through hand signals and changes in the song's melody, indicate how accurate the shot was.

Wrestling

Wrestling has always been the most popular sport in Mongolia, dating back thousands of years. It differs from American wrestling in two important ways: there are no separate weight classes and no time limits. It is possible, therefore, to see a relatively small man wrestling with someone twice his size, or to see two wrestlers locked together for long periods of time, each waiting for the other to make a false move. All of the wrestlers wear small, tight briefs or loincloths, velvet caps, boots with turned-up toes known as gutuls, and a small jacket known as a zodog that covers only the arms and the back of the shoulders, leaving the chest bare so that the competitors can prove their manliness. Many of them look more like Japanese sumo wrestlers than their somewhat trimmer American counterparts.

The wrestling competition goes on for two days, with hundreds of wrestlers from all over Mongolia competing simultaneously. The trick is to get one's opponent to lose his balance and touch the ground with a knee or an elbow, after which the winner performs the celebratory ritual known as the EAGLE DANCE. The winning wrestlers are awarded titles—"Falcon" if they win five rounds, "Elephant" if they win seven, and "Lion" if they win all of their matches. If a Lion goes on to win the following year, he earns the title of "Titan," and subsequent wins add epithets like "Nation-wide" or "Invincible" to his title.

FURTHER READING

Freeman, Dave, et al. *100 Things to Do Before You Die: Travel Events You Just Can't Miss*. Dallas: Taylor Pub. Co., 1999.

MacDonald, Margaret R., ed. *The Folklore of World Holidays*. Detroit: Gale Research, 1992.

Trawicky, Bernard, and Ruth W. Gregory. *Anniversaries and Holidays*. 5th ed. Chicago: American Library Assocation, 2000.

WEB SITES

Center for the Study of Eurasian Nomads
www.csen.org/Mongol.Nadaam/Mongol.text.html

EurasiaNet
www.eurasianet.org/departments/culture/articles/eav082401.shtml

Mongolia Today Magazine
www.mongoliatoday.com/issue/1/naadam.html

Nachi No Hi Matsuri
(Kumano Fire Festival, Nachi Fire Festival)

Type of Holiday: Religious (Shinto)
Date of Observation: July 14
Where Celebrated: Kumano, Japan
Symbols and Customs: Fire, Mikoshi, Religious Dances, Torches

ORIGINS

The Nachi No Hi Matsuri, or Nachi Fire Festival, is part of the Shinto tradition. Shinto is an ancient religion that originated in Japan. Most Shinto adherents live in Japan, but small communities also exist in Europe, Latin America, North America, and in the Pacific island nations.

The name Shinto was first employed during the sixth century C.E. to differentiate indigenous religions in Japan from faith systems that originated in mainland Asia (primarily Buddhism and Confucianism). The word is derived from two Chinese characters, *shen* (gods) and *tao* (way). Loosely translated, Shinto means "way of the gods." Its roots lie in an ancient nature-based religion. Some important concepts in Shinto include the value of tradition, the reverence of nature, cleanliness (ritual purity), and the veneration of spirits called kami. Strictly speaking, kami are not deities. The literal translation of the word kami is "that which is hidden."

Kami (which is both the singular and plural term) are honored but do not assert their powers upon humans in the traditional manner of deities or gods in other religions. People may be descended from the kami, and kami may influence the course of nature and events. The kami can bestow blessings, but they are not all benign. Kami are present in natural things such as trees, mountains, rocks, and rivers. They are embodied in religious relics, especially mirrors and jewels. They also include spirits of ancestors, local deities, holy people, and even political or literary figures. The human role is to venerate the kami and make offerings. The ultimate goal of Shinto is to uphold the harmony among humans and between people and nature. In this regard, the principle of all kami is to protect and sustain life.

The central authorities in Shinto are the priests. Traditionally, the duties of the priest were passed through heredity lines, but in modern times priests are trained on the basis of recommendation. The priests' duties include communicating with the kami and ensuring that ceremonies are properly carried out. Shinto does not have a single collection of sacred texts analogous to the Christian Bible or Islamic Qur'an. Instead, several important books provide information and guidance: *Koji-ki* (*Records of Ancient Events*), *Nihongi* (*Chronicles of Japan*), and *Engishiki* (*Chronicles of the Engi*).

Nachi No Hi Matsuri takes place in Kumano, Japan, located near the city of Kyoto. This Shinto festival honors the spirits associated with the nearby Nachi waterfall. The local people have venerated this beautiful waterfall—133 meters in height—for centuries. The nearby Kumano Nachi Grand Shrine provides a sanctuary for the local deities that sprang from the waterfall.

Shinto believers also worship spirits. These spirits include the souls of the departed, as well as kami that represent features of the natural landscape. Shinto spirituality emphasizes the sacredness of the natural world and promotes the worship of nature spirits as a means of forging deeper connections with the gods and with the processes of creation itself. These beliefs explain the existence of so many sacred sites in Japan. The Nachi waterfall is one of these sacred sites.

Participating in festivals is an important activity for Shinto believers. Festivals provide people with a means of honoring the gods and spirits, thereby drawing blessing to themselves. In addition to the nationally celebrated festivals, many towns and villages have their own festivals to honor local deities. Popular local festivals, such as the Nachi Fire Festival, may attract many people from other areas, as well as local residents.

Throughout the year the Kumano Nachi Grand Shrine houses the small portable shrines that provide dwelling places for the twelve kami associated with the Nachi falls. It is also said that the twelve mini-shrines, called MIKOSHI, represent the twelve months of the year. The Nachi fire festival provides the deities with their yearly excursion to the waterfall. After being carried to the waterfall in a grand torchlit procession, the mikoshi are positioned so that the mist of the waterfall sprays over them. This refreshes the kami, who in turn bless the land and the people.

SYMBOLS AND CUSTOMS

Fire

In the Shinto religion, fire is considered a purifying force. The huge torches that festival participants carry are purposefully brought close to the mikoshi, in order that the flames exert their purifying force on the shrine and the spirit within. Festival participants, too, are purified by their proximity to the fires. The Nachi No Hi Matsuri is one of the three most famous Shinto fire festivals in Japan.

Mikoshi

A mikoshi is a portable shrine that provides a home or resting place for a Shinto god. Many Shinto festivals feature processions in which mikoshi are paraded through the streets of town as a means of providing festival goers with the opportunity to greet and honor the god, and also as a means of allowing the deity to bless the people. Mikoshi are designed to look like tiny temples set atop litters. Two sturdy wooden poles run along each side of the carrying platform. The poles make it possible for the bearers to carry the mikoshi on their shoulders as if they were carrying an important dignitary on a litter. Designers usually beautify the mikoshi by fitting it with elaborate brass ornaments and silken cords.

The Kumano Nachi Grand Shrine houses twelve mikoshi, one for each of the twelve local deities associated with the Nachi waterfall. These vermillion-colored mikoshi are six meters tall, decorated with gold gilt, and shaped like waterfalls. They are further adorned with fans and mirrors. The beautiful fans that decorate these mikoshi have led to a nickname for the festival, Ogi Matsuri, or "Fan Festival." On the very top of each mikoshi sits a representation of the mythical phoenix bird, an emblem of divinity.

The religious highpoint of the festival is the procession of the mikoshi down to the waterfall and the sacred ceremonies that are performed there. Then the bearers carry the mikoshi back to the Nachi Grand shrine, where they will stay until the next year's festival.

Religious Dances

Before the mikoshi leave the Shinto temple, sacred dances are performed within the temple precinct. Some of these dances represent the planting of the fields. Sacred dances are also performed in front of the mikoshi when they are stationed next to the waterfall. The harvesting of the fields is an important theme represented in these dances.

Torches

Specially designated festival participants, dressed all in white, meet the mikoshi on their journey from the shrine to the waterfall, carrying twelve huge torches. Each of these torches weighs fifty kilograms and requires three or four strong people to carry it. The torch bearers keep the torches close to the mikoshi so that the fire can exercise its purifying effect. Once the mikoshi are positioned near the falls, the bearers continue to keep the huge torches moving alongside them.

Many of the spectators who follow the procession also carry torches. These much smaller torches can easily be held in one hand. Even children may be allowed tiny torches for the occasion.

FURTHER READING

Bauer, Helen and Sherwin Carlquist. *Japanese Festivals.* Garden City, NY: Doubleday, 1965.

Henderson, Helene, ed. *Holidays, Festivals and Celebrations of the World Dictionary.* 3rd ed. Detroit: Omnigraphics, 2005.

WEB SITES

Encyclopedia of Shinto, Kokugakuin University, Tokyo, Japan
eos.kokugakuin.ac.jp/modules/xwords/entry.php?entryID=715

Japan National Tourist Organization
www.jnto.go.jp/eng/indepth/history/traditionalevents/a33_fes_nachi.html

Kumano Field Museum
kumano-world.org/english/fire_festival.html#1

Religious Movements, University of Virginia
religiousmovements.lib.virginia.edu/nrms/shinto.html

Naga Panchami (Naag Panchami)

Type of Holiday: Religious (Hindu)
Date of Observation: July-August; fifth day of Sravana
Where Celebrated: India and Nepal
Symbols and Customs: Snake

ORIGINS

Naga Panchami is a festival that includes both Hinduism and early Indian religious beliefs. *Panchami* means "fifth," the day on which this Hindu festival is celebrated, and *Naga* refers to a group of serpent deities in early Indian religion. The mythical Nagas were semi-divine beings said to have sprung from Kadru, the wife of Rishi Kashyapa. Although they live and rule below the earth, the Nagas were believed to roam the earth wearing jewels and ornaments. SNAKE worship was fairly widespread in India at one time and is still an important part of popular religious practice in some regions.

When Naga culture was incorporated into Hinduism, many of the snake deities were accepted by the Hindus into their belief systems. The thousand-headed serpent Ananta, for example, is the most powerful of the Nagas. It is on the coils of Ananta that the Hindu god Vishnu is often seen resting. Shrines to the nagas can be found throughout India, and Hindu women often worship at "snake-stones" when they want to bear sons or avoid illness.

As a festival in honor of the snake deities, Naga Panchami goes back to very ancient times. It is an occasion for fasting and worshipping cobras, since the Nagas were often depicted as cobras with extended hoods. If cobras are not available, huge cloth effigies of serpents are made and displayed in public, as are snakes made from metal, stone, and clay. Images of snake deities are often painted on walls as well. Worshippers offer milk and flowers to the cobras and coins to the snake charmers who gather in town for the festival. Because serpents live underground, digging in the earth is prohibited on this day.

The Hindu god Shiva is also worshipped at this festival, since he is traditionally shown wearing snakes as ornaments. In temples dedicated to Shiva, particularly those in Ujjain and Varanasi, hundreds of cobras are brought in by trappers and released before the god's image. Worshippers then empty their pots of milk over the snakes' heads to protect themselves against snakebite throughout their lives. At the end of the day, there are serpent dances in open fields, and the snakes are freed.

Many scholars regard Hinduism as the oldest living religion. The word Hindu is derived from the Sanskrit term *Sindhu* (or *Indus*), which meant river. It referred to people living in the Indus valley in the Indian subcontinent.

Hinduism has no founder, one universal reality (or god) known as Brahman, many gods and goddesses (sometimes referred to as devtas), and several scriptures. Hinduism also has no priesthood or hierarchical structure similar to that seen in some other religions, such as Christianity. Hindus acknowledge the authority of a wide variety of writings, but there is no single, uniform canon. The oldest of the Hindu writings are the *Vedas*. The word "veda" comes from the Sanskrit word for knowledge. The *Vedas*, which were compiled from ancient oral traditions, contain hymns, instructions, explanations, chants for sacrifices, magical formulas, and philosophy. Another set of sacred books includes the *Great Epics*, which illustrate Hindu faith in practice. The *Epics* include the *Ramayana*, the *Mahabharata*, and the *Bhagavad Gita*.

The Hindu pantheon includes approximately thirty-three million gods. Some of these are held in higher esteem than others. Over all the gods, Hindus believe in one absolute high god or universal concept. This is Brahman. Although he is above all the gods, he is not worshipped in popular ceremonies because he is detached from the day-to-day affairs of the people. Brahman is impersonal. Lesser gods and goddesses (devtas) serve him. Because these are more intimately involved in the affairs of people, they are venerated as gods. The most honored god in Hinduism varies among the different Hindu sects. Although Hindu adherents practice their faith differently and venerate different deities, they share a similar view of reality and look back on a common history.

SYMBOLS AND CUSTOMS

Snake

Because the snake sheds its skin, it is regarded by Hindus as a symbol of immortality. In Hindu art, eternity is often represented by a serpent eating its own tail. The cobras worshipped on Naga Panchami are raised at special snake shrines. In places that are frequented by wild snakes, worshippers often leave out dishes of milk to feed them.

FURTHER READING

Bellenir, Karen. *Religious Holidays and Calendars*. 3rd ed. Detroit: Omnigraphics, 2004.

Crim, Keith R. *The Perennial Dictionary of World Religions*. San Francisco: Harper & Row, 1989.

Henderson, Helene, ed. *Holidays, Festivals, and Celebrations of the World Dictionary*. 3rd ed. Detroit: Omnigraphics, 2005.

Sharma, Brijendra Nath. *Festivals of India*. New Delhi: Abhinav Publications, 1978.

Thomas, Paul. *Festivals and Holidays in India*. Bombay: D.B. Taraporevala Sons, 1971.

WEB SITE

Festivals of India
www.festivalsofindia.in/nagpanchami

Navajo Mountain Chant

Type of Holiday: Calendar/Seasonal, Religious (Navajo)
Date of Observation: Nine days at the end of winter
Where Celebrated: Arizona
Symbols and Customs: Circle of Evergreens, Fire, Plumed Arrow, Sand Paintings
Colors: Blue and black play an important symbolic role in the Mountain Chant (*see* CIRCLE OF EVERGREENS below).
Related Holidays: Navajo Night Chant

ORIGINS

The Navajo Mountain Chant is part of Native American religious tradition. The history of this and other Native American cultures dates back thousands of years into prehistoric times. According to many scholars, the people who became the Native Americans migrated from Asia across a land bridge that may have once connected the territories presently occupied by Alaska and Russia. The migrations, believed to have begun between 60,000 and 30,000 B.C.E., continued until approximately 4,000 B.C.E. This speculation, however, conflicts with traditional stories asserting that the indigenous Americans have always lived in North America or that tribes moved up from the south.

The historical development of religious belief systems among Native Americans is not well known. Most of the information available was gathered by Europeans who arrived on the continent beginning in the sixteenth century C.E. The data they recorded was fragmentary and oftentimes of questionable accuracy because the Europeans did not understand the native cultures they were trying to describe and the Native Americans were reluctant to divulge details about themselves.

The Navajo call themselves *Diné* (or *Dineh*), meaning "people." Their deities are known as the Holy People and include Changing Woman (*see also* **APACHE GIRLS' SUNRISE CEREMONY**), Talking God, the Sun, Earth, Moon, and Sky. Navajo religious practices emphasize healing rituals, in terms of curing diseases as well as healing relationships among all living things.

The nine-day Mountain Chant marks a transition in the seasons. It takes place in late winter, at the end of the thunderstorms but before the spring winds arrive. Members of the Navajo Nation believe that if this ceremony were to be held at any other time of year, the result would be death from lightning or snake-bite. The chant is also considered a curing ceremony, performed not only for individuals who are sick, but also to restore order and balance in human relationships.

The legend on which the Mountain Chant is based chronicles the adventures of Dsilyi Neyani, the eldest son of a wandering Navajo family. He is captured by the Utes while hunting one day, but he manages to escape with the help of the gods (known as the Yei). During his long journey to rejoin his family, he encounters many hazards and learns a great deal about magic and ceremonial acts. For example, he learns how to make the SAND PAINTINGS that are used in the Mountain Chant, how to make the feathers dance, how to swallow swords (*see* PLUMED ARROW), how to make a weasel appear and do magic, how to handle FIRE without getting burned, and how to make the mystical "hu-hu-hu-hu" cry used in the Mountain Chant dance.

When Dsilyi Neyani returns to his family, he discovers that they have grown into an entire tribe during his long absence. It takes him four days and four nights to tell the story of his wanderings, but the rituals he brings back are so compelling that messengers are immediately sent out to invite guests to witness what he has learned. Even today, the Mountain Chant remains an event to which visitors from outside the Navajo Nation are especially welcome.

The Mountain Chant consists of four ceremonies, all based on the same legend but differing considerably in terms of their presentation and the wording of the songs that are sung. Perhaps the most moving ceremony takes place on the final day. The medicine man emerges from the lodge or hogan at sunset and begins to chant, while a CIRCLE OF EVERGREENS eight to ten feet tall—each concealing the man who handles it—rises as if by magic and forms a circular enclosure about 100 feet in diameter with only one opening, facing east. The ground within this circle is considered sacred, and there is a cone-shaped bonfire in the center.

The final ceremony begins when the central bonfire is lit. Dancers with their bodies whitened by clay rush into the circle, leaping wildly and waving their arms and legs. They circle the fire from south to west to north and then south again, the white clay on their bodies protecting them from the heat of the flames (*see* FIRE). Sometimes they throw sumac wands tipped with rings of fluffy eagle down into the fire. The down flares briefly and burns away, but the dancer conceals a second ring of fluff, which he then shakes to the end of the wand, creating the impression that the fluffy ball has been magically restored. A similar illusion is involved in the "yucca trick," in which a yucca plant appears to grow miraculously from a bare root, then blossoms, and finally reveals its fruit.

The Fire Dance takes place just before dawn, when the central bonfire has burned down to embers. Young men drag in huge trees to feed the central fire, and the dancers make a sound with their tongues that imitates the sound of a hot fire.

They carry large bundles of shredded cedar bark, which are ignited with coals from the base of the fire. Once they are burning, the bundles are thrown over the fence to the east first and then in the other three directions. The men dance in a circle around the fire, beating their own and each others' bodies with the flaming brands. Spectators later gather up bits of the burned cedar, which is believed to offer protection against fire for the coming year.

In 1926 the Mountain Chant was made into a film directed by Roman Hubbell. The star of the film was named "Crawler" because his lower limbs were paralyzed—supposedly while attempting to learn the **NAVAJO NIGHT CHANT**. But his disability did not prevent him from learning and practicing the Mountain Chant.

SYMBOLS AND CUSTOMS

Circle of Evergreens

The first time the Mountain Chant was performed, the circle of trees within which it took place was six miles in diameter and crowded with people. Today it is no longer this large a celebration, but the dark circle formed by the branches continues to play an important part in the ceremony. The trees represent the black and the blue spruce, both of which are mentioned in the legend of Dsilyi Neyani. In the songs sung during the Mountain Chant, black symbolizes the male principle and blue is the female.

The pairing of blue and black is common in Navajo legend. Black is usually associated with the north, the direction where evil and danger dwell. Blue is associated with the south. The home of the mountain sheep, as described in the Mountain Chant, consists of two black rooms and two blue rooms.

Fire

Fire is a symbol of annihilation among the Navajo, as it is among most Native American tribes who believe in magic. Fire is said to burn evil, and the exposure to intense heat that takes place during the Fire Dance on the final night of the Mountain Chant symbolizes the ability to control fire, which in turn controls evil.

Plumed Arrow

One of the dances performed during the Navajo Mountain Chant is the Dance of the Great Plumed Arrows. Plumed arrows are considered the most sacred of healing devices, although there is a trick involved in this particular dance. Each dancer holds his arrow up over the "patient" who is being cured by the ceremony and then thrusts it down his own throat, causing the spectators to gag in sympathy. In reality, however, this "sword-swallowing" is made possible by holding the arrowhead between the teeth and running the shaft of the arrow into a hollow casing. The patient is then touched with the arrows, which are believed to chase evil from the body.

Sand Paintings

The preparation of sand paintings takes place before the Mountain Chant begins. A large space is covered with fine sand, smoothed out as flat as a canvas. As many as twelve men may work on the sand painting at one time, letting colored sand—normally red, blue, yellow, and white—dribble through their fingers to form the desired pattern. The medicine man oversees the process and is quick to catch any errors, since a single mistake can undermine the effectiveness of the entire ceremony.

The sand painting plays an important role in the healing process. When the patient is admitted to the hogan or lodge—a typical Navajo building with earth walls reinforced by timbers—the medicine man begins to chant. When the chanting is over, he sprinkles the patient and the sand painting with a feather dipped in water. He then takes sand from various parts of the painting and applies it to parts of the patient's body. Spectators in the hogan may take sand and touch their own bodies with it, so they can share in the "cure." Afterward, the sand painting is destroyed, and the sand is taken away.

The sand paintings typically illustrate events in the legend of Dsilyi Neyani. In one sand painting, for example, there are four figures known as the Long Bodies, who helped Dsilyi during his long journey home. The black Long Body is said to belong to the north, the one under it (white) to the east, the next (blue) to the south, and the bottom one (yellow) to the west. (*See* discussion of sand paintings under **NAVAJO NIGHT CHANT.**)

FURTHER READING

Fergusson, Erna. *Dancing Gods: Indian Ceremonials of New Mexico and Arizona.* New York: A.A. Knopf, 1931.

Reichard, Gladys. *Navajo Religion: A Study of Symbolism.* 2nd ed. Princeton: Princeton University Press, 1974.

Navajo Night Chant
(Nightway)

Type of Holiday: Religious (Navajo)
Date of Observation: Late fall or winter for nine days
Where Celebrated: Arizona
Symbols and Customs: Masks, Sacred Bundle, Sand Paintings
Related Holidays: Navajo Mountain Chant

ORIGINS

The Navajo Night Chant is part of Native American religious tradition. The history of this and other Native American cultures dates back thousands of years into prehistoric times. According to many scholars, the people who became the Native Americans migrated from Asia across a land bridge that may have once connected the territories presently occupied by Alaska and Russia. The migrations, believed to have begun between 60,000 and 30,000 B.C.E., continued until approximately 4,000 B.C.E. This speculation, however, conflicts with traditional stories asserting that the indigenous Americans have always lived in North America or that tribes moved up from the south.

The historical development of religious belief systems among Native Americans is not well known. Most of the information available was gathered by Europeans who arrived on the continent beginning in the sixteenth century C.E. The data they recorded was fragmentary and oftentimes of questionable accuracy because the Europeans did not understand the native cultures they were trying to describe and the Native Americans were reluctant to divulge details about themselves.

The nine-night ceremony known as the Night Chant or Nightway is believed to date from around 1000 B.C.E., when it was first performed by the Indians who lived in Canyon de Chelly (now eastern Arizona). It is considered to be the most sacred of all Navajo ceremonies and one of the most difficult and demanding to learn, involving the memorization of hundreds of songs, dozens of prayers, and several very complicated SAND PAINTINGS. And yet the demand for Night Chants is so great that as many as fifty such ceremonies might be held during a single season, which lasts eighteen to twenty weeks.

The Navajo call themselves *Diné* (or *Dineh*), meaning "people." Their deities are known as the Holy People, and include Changing Woman (*see also* **APACHE**

GIRLS' SUNRISE CEREMONY), Talking God, the Sun, Earth, Moon, and Sky. Navajo religious practices emphasize healing rituals, in terms of curing diseases as well as healing relationships among all living things.

Like the **NAVAJO MOUNTAIN CHANT**, the Night Chant is basically a healing ritual, designed both to cure people who are sick and to restore the order and balance of human relationships within the Navajo universe. Led by a trained medicine man—a combination doctor-priest—who has served a long apprenticeship and learned the intricate and detailed practices that are essential to the chant, the ceremony itself is capable of scaring off sickness and ugliness through the use of techniques that shock or arouse. Once disorder has been removed, order and balance are restored through song, prayer, sand painting, and other aspects of the ceremony.

Before the chant itself takes place, young children undergo a tribal initiation. After being stripped of their clothing and then struck with a yucca whip, young boys are allowed to see the "gods" (i.e., the dancers who impersonate the gods) without their masks for the first time. Girls are not whipped but rather touched with ears of corn covered with sprays of spruce.

On the day of the chant, crowds gather expectantly outside the lodge where rehearsals have been taking place. The outdoor area in which the ceremony will be held is cleared of spectators, and many fires are lit to take the chill out of the night air. The dancers, who represent the gods, are led in by the medicine man and Hastse-yalti, the maternal grandfather of the gods, along a path of meal that has been laid down for them to follow. The patient emerges from the lodge, sprinkles the gods with meal from his or her basket, and gives each one a sacrificial cigarette. The medicine man intones a long prayer for the patient, repeating each phrase four times. Then the four gods dance, with Hastse-yalti moving rhythmically back and forth and hooting at the end of every verse to show his approval.

The original Night Chant involved four teams who danced twelve times each with half-hour intervals in between—a total of ten hours. Today, however, there are often so many teams dancing that there is no time for intermissions. The dance movements resemble a Virginia Reel, with two lines facing each other. Each of the six male dancers takes his female partner, dances with her to the end of the line, drops her there, and moves back to his own side. The chant itself is performed without variation and has a hypnotic effect on the listeners. The only relief is provided by the rainmaker-clown named Tonenili, who sprinkles water around and engages in other playful antics.

The medicine men who supervise the Night Chant insist that everything—each dot and line in every sand painting, each verse in every song, each feather on each mask—be arranged in exactly the same way each time the curing ceremony is performed or it will not bring about the desired result. There are probably as many active Night Chant medicine men today as at any time in Navajo history, due to the general increase in the Navajo population, the popularity of the ceremony, and the central role it plays in Navajo life and health. But it is getting more difficult to find apprentices willing to learn the elaborate rituals. Although a medicine man typically earns between $500 and $1,000 for a nine-day Night Chant, compensation often comes in the form of livestock, baskets, cloth, jewelry, blankets, buckskin, and food for the duration of the ceremony.

SYMBOLS AND CUSTOMS

Masks

There are typically twenty-four Nightway masks, although the ceremony can be performed with fewer. These masks are worn by the God Impersonators who perform the ritual dances. Some of these impersonators—Calling God, Gray God, Whistling God, Whipping God, and Humpedback God among them—wear the masks of ordinary male gods with special ornaments attached at the time of the ceremony. Other masks include the yellow and blue Fringed Mouth of the Water mask, the Black and Red God masks, the Monster Slayer mask, the Talking God mask, and the Born for Water mask.

In addition to being worn by the God Impersonators who dance on the dramatic final night of the nine-day ceremony, the masks are vital to the application of many "medicines" (including the SAND PAINTINGS) to the patient. They also play a vital role in the initiation of the young. The masks of the female goddesses are actually worn by men, since women are not allowed to minister to the person for whom the chant is being sung.

The masks used in the Nightway ceremony are made of sacred buckskin, which must be obtained without shedding the animal's blood. The usual method consists of chasing the deer into a blind, throwing it to the ground, and smothering it by stuffing sacred meal into its nostrils. Buckskin is a symbol of life to the Navajo people.

Sacred Bundle

The medicine man's sacred bundle or *jish* is made up of ceremonial items such as bags of pollen, feathers, stones, skins, pieces of mountain sheep horn, and a flint blade believed to belong to the god known as the Monster Slayer. The sacred bundle also includes gourd rattles and the sacred buckskin MASKS worn by the God Impersonators.

Although the medicine man might carry other necessary items in his jish—such as incense, spruce collars, and the ground pigments used in SAND PAINTING—they are not considered part of the sacred bundle. Most of the items in the jish are permanent; they are not used up during the ceremony itself.

Sand Paintings

As in the **NAVAJO MOUNTAIN CHANT**, sand paintings play an important role in the healing rituals of the Night Chant. Twelve different sand paintings are considered appropriate for the Nightway, of which a maximum of six are usually chosen: four large and two small. The patient and his or her family normally have a say in which sand paintings are used. Each one is associated with a particular story and is accompanied by specific songs, prayers, and ceremonial procedures.

It is rarely the medicine man himself who makes the sand paintings, although he is responsible for overseeing their preparation. Usually his assistants do the actual painting, dribbling small amounts of colored sand through their fingers onto a smooth sand surface. The resulting works of art must be perfect; in other words, there can be no deviations from the design set down by the gods.

Every detail in each sand painting has a special meaning. If the plumes on the heads of the figures are on the same side as the rattle, for example, it means that rain is desired. If they are on the opposite side from the hand holding the rattle, it means that the growth of corn is the desired outcome. Standard Nightway sand painting designs include First Dancers, Whirling Logs, Water Sprinklers, Fringed Mouth Gods, Black Gods, and Corn People.

The purpose of the sand paintings is to allow the patient to absorb the powers depicted in the painting, often by sitting or sleeping on it. The medicine man applies items from the *jish* or SACRED BUNDLE to the gods depicted in the sand painting and then to the corresponding part of the patient's body. It is considered wrong—if not downright dangerous—to reproduce these sand paintings in any way, since they might attract the attention of the gods to a situation where no real healing is intended. Sketching and photographing them is therefore prohibited, although sometimes this prohibition can be sidestepped by removing the prayer-plumes set around the painting or omitting some other detail, so that the painting itself is not really "finished."

FURTHER READING

Faris, James C. *The Nightway: A History and a History of Documentation of a Navajo Ceremonial.* Albuquerque: University of New Mexico Press, 1990.

Fergusson, Erna. *Dancing Gods: Indian Ceremonials of New Mexico and Arizona.* New York: A.A. Knopf, 1931.

Reichard, Gladys. *Navajo Religion: A Study of Symbolism.* 2nd ed. Princeton: Princeton University Press, 1974.

American Indian Heritage Foundation
www.indians.org/welker/nightcha.htm

Nawruz
(Naw Roz, Navroz, No Ruz, New Year)

Type of Holiday: Calendar/Seasonal
Date of Observation: Beginning March 21 for thirteen days
Where Celebrated: Afghanistan, India, Iran
Symbols and Customs: Egg and Mirror, Gardens of Adonis, Seven S's (Haft-sin), Water Sprinkling, Wheat Cakes

ORIGINS

Nawruz, which means "new day" in Persian, celebrates the beginning of spring and the start of the new year. It is observed by all religious groups in Iran and Afghanistan; in India, it is celebrated by the Parsis as Jamshed Navroz. This holiday dates back further than Islam and is believed to have come from Zoroastrian Persia, where it coincided with the **VERNAL EQUINOX** and was observed in honor of the solar new year.

Nawruz marks the changing of the seasons, which people in all parts of the world have honored since ancient times. Many cultures divided the year into two seasons, summer and winter, and marked these points of the year at or near the summer and winter solstices, during which light and warmth began to increase and decrease, respectively. In pre-industrial times, humans survived through hunting, gathering, and agricultural practices, which depend on the natural cycle of seasons, according to the climate in the region of the world in which they lived. Thus, they created rituals to help ensure enough rain and sun in the spring and summer so crops would grow to fruition at harvest time, which was, in turn, duly celebrated. Vestiges of many of these ancient practices are thought to have survived in festivals still celebrated around seasonal themes.

In fifteenth-century Egypt, Persian Nawruz customs were combined with those of a typical **SATURNALIA** or **CARNIVAL** celebration. People crowned a "Prince of the New Year," who smeared flour all over his face, rode through the streets on a donkey, and collected money. Anyone who failed to make a suitable contribution was doused with water or dirt. Sometimes teachers were attacked by their students and thrown into a fountain, from which they had to "buy" their way out. Eventually the government succeeded in suppressing the more outrageous festival customs.

In modern Iran, houses are cleaned and children are given new clothes in preparation for the thirteen-day New Year's celebration. The evening before Nawruz begins, a traditional omelette made with greens is served, along with pilaf, a rice dish symbolizing the wish for an abundant year. Friends and relatives visit each other and exchange gifts that include colored eggs (*see* EGG AND MIRROR), fruit, and bunches of narcissus. Banquets featuring seven foods beginning with the letter S (*see* SEVEN S'S) are held, and the New Year's dinner is typically eaten sitting around a tablecloth spread out on the floor. In Muslim homes, it is customary to pop a piece of candy into someone's mouth on Nawruz while reciting a brief passage from the Qur'an. Sometimes each member of the family will eat a piece of candy while a passage is read from the Qur'an. Then they embrace each other and say, "May you live a hundred years."

The thirteenth day of Nawruz is called Sizdan-Bedar or "Thirteenth Day Out." It is considered unlucky to remain at home on this day, so the entire family usually goes to the country or a city park to spend the day picnicking and to welcome the arrival of spring. Folk singers, dancers, clowns, and costumed actors wander about entertaining people on this day. Children bring their GARDENS OF ADONIS with them and throw them into a stream of running water.

In Afghanistan, Nawruz is a favorite time to play *buzkashi* or "goat-grabbing." The object of the game is for a team of horse riders to grab the carcass of a goat that has been placed in a pit, carry it around a goal post, and put it back in the pit. The game is believed to have developed on the plains of Mongolia and Central Asia using a prisoner of war instead of a goat. Since there are several hundred horsemen on each team galloping at breakneck speed and lashing at each other with buzkashi whips, the game often results in fatalities.

SYMBOLS AND CUSTOMS

Egg and Mirror

Muslim families observe Nawruz with a dinner consisting of foods that begin with the letter S (*see* SEVEN S'S). These dishes are laid out on a tablecloth on the floor, along with a colored egg, a mirror, and a candle for each family member. At the precise moment when the new year begins, the egg is placed on the mirror. To everyone's delight, the egg usually trembles a bit—probably because of all the cannons that are fired at midnight.

Eggs are a traditional symbol of fertility and new life, and their use at the new year festival may date back to the time when it was a pastoral festival marking the change from winter to summer. The light reflected in the mirror symbolizes the brightness of the future.

Gardens of Adonis

A couple of weeks before Nawruz arrives, Iranian families plant quick-growing seeds such as wheat, celery, and lentils in shallow bowls containing a little dirt and water. They soon turn into masses of green, symbolizing life and good fortune. Then, on the thirteenth day of the festival, children take the sprouted seeds and throw them over the garden wall or into a stream of running water. This act is symbolic of doing away with family quarrels so that the new year can begin in friendliness and peace (*see* WHEAT CAKES).

The name for these miniature gardens dates back to ancient mythology. Adonis— originally the Babylonian god Tammuz—was a young Greek god beloved by Aphrodite. He was killed by a wild boar while hunting in the mountains, and Aphrodite was so grief-stricken that the gods arranged to let him spend half the year on earth with her and the other half in the underworld. The story of the dying god who was resurrected each year became a symbol for the seasonal shift from winter to spring. A funeral cult was founded in his honor, and each spring the women of Greece and western Asia would plant seeds in vases and sprinkle them with warm water. These Gardens of Adonis, as they were called, would be cast into the sea along with images of the young god. The blooming of the red anemone seven days later was considered to be symbolic of his return.

Seven S's (Haft-sin)

The most outstanding feature of the Nawruz celebration is the festival table, a cloth spread out on the floor containing the *Haft-sin* or "Seven S's," all food items that represent happiness in the new year: *sabyeh* or green sprouts grown from seed; *sonbul* or hyacinth; *samanoo* or sweet wheat pudding; *serkeh* or vinegar; *sumac* from the sumac plant; *seeb* or apple; and *senjed* or Bohemian olives. The Haft-sin represent the seven archangels of God who embody the principles of ethical behavior in the Zoroastrian religion.

Other foods served at the festival include roast chicken, fruit, bread, sweets, and rose water. After the feast is over, candy is passed around while passages from the Qur'an are read aloud.

Water Sprinkling

In ancient Persia, Syria, and Egypt, Nawruz was originally a celebration of the arrival of spring. People woke up early, drew running water in a vase, and then poured it over themselves in a symbolic act designed to stave off bad luck and harm.

There are a number of theories as to where this custom originated. Legend has it that once, after a very long drought, rain fell on New Year's Day. From that time onward, rain was considered a good omen, and pouring water over each other became a new year's tradition. Another theory is that it is simply an act of purification designed to cleanse the body of the smoke and dirt associated with tending the winter fires.

Yet another explanation is that when the prophet Solomon lost his kingdom and his powers—symbolized by the loss of his signet ring—because one of his wives had returned to the worship of her old idols, he was forced to wander unrecognized through Jerusalem and beg for his food. According to the Qur'an, Solomon was not really at fault for this lapse, and as soon as he realized why he was being punished, he sought God's forgiveness. His signet ring was restored to him and with it, his sovereignty. The swallows were so overjoyed that they celebrated by splashing each other with water.

Wheat Cakes

The wheat cakes associated with Nawruz are not ordinary cakes for eating. They are uncooked, and they contain whole grains of wheat. The cake is kept moist until the wheat sprouts and turns into a miniature garden. In many homes, there is a layer of the cake for each member of the family, and the children wait anxiously for the wheat to sprout on their layer. On the thirteenth day of the new year festival, the family takes the cake out into the fields and throws it away. Like GARDENS OF ADONIS, the wheat cakes take with them all the bad feelings and quarrels that have accumulated within the family, clearing the way for a peaceful new year.

FURTHER READING

Dobler, Lavinia G. *Customs and Holidays Around the World*. New York: Fleet Pub. Corp., 1962.

Gaer, Joseph. *Holidays Around the World*. Boston: Little, Brown, 1953.

Glassé, Cyril. *The Concise Encyclopedia of Islam*. 2nd ed. San Francisco: Harper & Row, 1999.

Henderson, Helene, ed. *Holidays, Festivals, and Celebrations of the World Dictionary*. 3rd ed. Detroit: Omnigraphics, 2005.

Ickis, Marguerite. *The Book of Festivals and Holidays the World Over*. New York: Dodd, Mead, 1970.

Ickis, Marguerite. *The Book of Religious Holidays and Celebrations*. New York: Dodd, Mead, 1966.

Leach, Maria, ed. *Funk & Wagnalls Standard Dictionary of Folklore, Mythology & Legend*. San Francisco: Harper & Row, 1984.

MacDonald, Margaret R., ed. *The Folklore of World Holidays*. Detroit: Gale Research, 1992.

Purdy, Susan. *Festivals for You to Celebrate*. Philadelphia: Lippincott, 1969.

Von Grunebaum, Gustave E. *Muhammadan Festivals*. New York: Schuman, 1951.

WEB SITE

BBC (British Broadcasting Corporation)
www.bbc.co.uk/religion/religions/bahai/holydays/nawruz.shtml

New Yam Festival

Type of Holiday: Calendar/Seasonal, Religious (Igbo, Yoruba)
Date of Observation: Late June
Where Celebrated: Nigeria
Symbols and Customs: Divination Rites, Yam

ORIGINS

The New Yam Festival marks the changing of the seasons, which people in all parts of the world have honored since ancient times. Many cultures divided the year into two seasons, summer and winter, and marked these points of the year at or near the summer and winter solstices, during which light and warmth began to increase and decrease, respectively. In pre-industrial times, humans survived through hunting, gathering, and agricultural practices, which depend on the natural cycle of seasons, according to the climate in the region of the world in which they lived. Thus, they created rituals to help ensure enough rain and sun in the spring and summer so crops would grow to fruition at harvest time, which was, in turn, duly celebrated. Vestiges of many of these ancient practices are thought to have survived in festivals still celebrated around seasonal themes.

The New Yam Festival is a holiday celebrated annually by almost all of the ethnic groups in Nigeria. It usually takes place around the end of June, and it is considered taboo to eat the newly harvested YAM before this date. The high priest sacrifices a goat and pours its blood over a symbol representing the god of the harvest. Then the carcass is cooked and a soup is made from it, while the yams are boiled and pounded to make *foofoo*. After the priest has prayed for a better harvest in the coming year, he declares the feast open by eating the pounded yam and the soup. Then everyone joins in, and there is dancing, drinking, and merrymaking. After the festival is over, it is permissible for anyone in the community to eat the new yam.

Why is the yam so important? An old Igbo myth says that during a severe famine Igbo (from whom the tribe takes its name) was told that he must sacrifice his son, Ahiajoku, and his daughter, Ada, in order to save his other children. After they were killed, their flesh was cut into pieces and buried in several different mounds. A few days later, yams sprouted from the flesh of Ahiajoku, while cocoyams sprouted from the flesh of Ada. Igbo and his other children survived the famine by eating them. The spirit of Ahiajoku became the God of Yam.

The myth of Ahiajoku is reenacted during the New Yam Festival each year. Each householder places four or eight new yams on the ground near a shrine. After saying some prayers, he cuts small portions off each end of the yams to symbolize the sacrifice of Ahiajoku. The yams are then cooked with palm oil, water, and chicken to make a dish that symbolizes the body and blood of Ahiajoku. The Igbo people consider the yam to be so sacred that at one time, anyone caught stealing it would be put to death. Today, such thieves are banished.

The Yoruba people celebrate the New Yam Festival, known to them as Eje, for two days around the time of the harvest. They fast, give thanks for the harvest, and carry out special DIVINATION RITES to determine the fate of the community, and particularly its crops, in the coming year. Most of the festival activities take place in a sacred grove and at a sacred shrine, both of which are purified for the occasion. There are very specific rules governing how the new yams must be presented to the appropriate religious authorities.

The Igbo people celebrate what they call the Onwasato Festival in August, which marks the beginning of the harvest. There is a thanksgiving ritual in which the senior member of every family kills at least one fowl and sprinkles its blood on the *Okpensi* (symbol of the family), giving thanks to the family's ancestors. The feathers are removed and spread on the threshold to demonstrate the family's determination to forsake evil. One of the fowls is roasted and put aside, while the others are consumed during the day's feasting. On the second day, the roasted fowls are shared by members of the extended family.

SYMBOLS AND CUSTOMS

Divination Rites

A highlight of the New Yam Festival, particularly among the Yoruba people, is the divination rite that determines the destiny of the community and the likelihood of an abundant harvest. One of the recently harvested yams is taken and divided in two. The two parts are thrown up in the air, and if one part lands face up and the other face down, it is considered a very promising sign. If both fall either face up or face down, it is taken as a bad omen.

Yam

Yams are a staple of life in Nigeria, and a great deal depends on the success of the crop. Since it can be affected by many different religious powers, from the ancestors to the gods, it is essential that these powers be treated with respect and offered special prayers and sacrifices at the time of the yam harvest.

Among the Igbo, the yam is symbolic of a human being who was sacrificed so that other humans might survive. Ahiajoku (*see* "Origins") is the only example of a human hero who is deified in Igbo mythology, since his spirit became the God of Yam.

FURTHER READING

Bellenir, Karen. *Religious Holidays and Calendars*. 3rd ed. Detroit: Omnigraphics, 2004.

Henderson, Helene, ed. *Holidays, Festivals, and Celebrations of the World Dictionary*. 3rd ed. Detroit: Omnigraphics, 2005.

MacDonald, Margaret R., ed. *The Folklore of World Holidays*. Detroit: Gale Research, 1992.

WEB SITE

Family Culture
www.familyculture.com/holidays/yamfestival.htm

New Year's Day

Type of Holiday: Calendar/Seasonal
Date of Observation: January 1
Where Celebrated: Australia, British Isles, North and South America, Europe, Scandinavia, and in all countries using the Gregorian calendar
Symbols and Customs: Baby, First-footing, Football Games, Gifts, Pig, Resolutions
Related Holidays: Chinese New Year, Dewali, Hogmanay, Nawruz, New Year's Eve, Oshogatsu, Rosh Hashanah, Saturnalia, Sol, Songkran, Tet

ORIGINS

Celebrating the first day of the year on January 1 is a relatively modern practice. Up until the time of Julius Caesar, the Romans generally celebrated New Year's Day in March, the first month of the Roman year. January 1 marked the beginning of the civil year for the ancient Romans, a time when new consuls were inducted into office. Although there were games and feasting at this time, March 1 was still observed as New Year's Day with a festival to Mars, the Roman god of war.

Caesar changed the Roman New Year's Day to January 1 in honor of Janus, the god of all beginnings and the keeper of the gates of heaven and earth. Janus was always represented with two faces, one looking back to the old year and the other looking forward to the new year. It was customary to celebrate the festival in his honor by exchanging GIFTS and making RESOLUTIONS to be friendly and good to one another.

When the Romans under Constantine accepted Christianity as their new faith, they retained the Festival of Janus as their New Year's Day but turned it into a day of fasting and prayer. It was a time for all good Christians to turn over a new leaf, but not all Christians observed it. Even after the Gregorian calendar was adopted by Roman Catholic countries in 1582, Great Britain and the English colonies in America continued to begin the year in March. It wasn't until 1752 that Britain and its possessions adopted the so-called New Style calendar (Gregorian) and accepted January 1 as the beginning of the year. But among the Puritans in New England, the old associations with the pagan god Janus were offensive enough to persuade many of them to ignore the day altogether and refer to January simply as "First Month."

The Gregorian calendar is named after Pope Gregory XIII, who in 1582 instituted a calendar that corrected time-keeping errors in Julius Caesar's Julian calendar, which had been in use since 45 B.C.E. In 1852 the Gregorian calendar subtracted ten days from the month of October so that October 6 was instead October 15. This shift brought the calendar more in line with the seasons. It also created Leap Year Day and established January 1 as the day of the new year throughout the Christian world. Catholic countries such as Italy, France, Luxembourg, Spain, and Portugal switched to the new calendar that year. Other European nations, predominantly Protestant or Orthodox, did not. Protestant Germany accepted the change in 1700, Orthodox Russia in 1706. Great Britain accepted the Gregorian calendar, and the New Year on January 1, in 1752. By the twentieth century most of the world had accepted the Gregorian calendar for civic and business purposes.

Today, New Year's Day is geared toward feasting and family. Almost everywhere it is a day for receiving visitors (*see* FIRST-FOOTING) and recovering from **NEW YEAR'S EVE** festivities. Watching FOOTBALL GAMES is often part of the day.

January 1st is also known as Emancipation Day. During the Civil War, President Abraham Lincoln issued a preliminary proclamation to free slaves in states and parts of states "in rebellion aganst the United States." The Emancipation Proclamation became effective on January 1, 1863. After the signing of the proclamation, Emancipation Day was observed on January 1 in many areas of the United States. Emancipation celebrations began to diminish by the 1950s and 1960s, when the emphasis was on gaining civil rights and equality. When Emancipation Day is observed today, parades and speeches highlight the importance of freedom.

SYMBOLS AND CUSTOMS

Baby

Just as the old man is a traditional symbol of the year that is ending, the image of the newborn baby is both a religious symbol of the Christ Child as well as a secular symbol of rebirth and renewal at the beginning of a new year. The "New Year Baby" that appears on holiday greeting cards and in New Year's decorations is usually a playful rather than a solemn child and is often shown wearing a party hat.

First-footing

Many modern New Year's Day customs originated in Scotland and England. First-footing is a good example. It is still observed in Scotland, where a family's fortunes in the coming year are believed to be influenced by the first guest who sets foot in the door after the New Year strikes. If it's a woman, a light-haired man, an undertaker, or anyone who walks with his toes pointing inward, it is considered a bad omen. A dark-haired man, on the other hand, brings good luck. In some villages, dark-haired men hire themselves out as professional first-footers whose job it is to go from house to house immediately after the New Year arrives. Female first-footers are considered to be such bad luck that male restaurant owners will sometimes make a point of opening the restaurant themselves before the waitresses arrive on New Year's Day.

Just as it is bad luck for a fair-haired or red-haired person to "let in" the New Year, there are folk beliefs surrounding what the first-footer brings with him or her. When entering the house, he or she must bring a *handsel*—a piece of bread, an orange, or an ear of corn carried in his or her hand for good luck. Sometimes the first footer brings cheese or cakes to share with the family being visited. The Scottish name for New Year's Eve is **HOGMANAY**, and one of the traditional foods shared with the first footer is Hogmanay shortbread, baked in the shape of a sun—perhaps a survival of pagan sun worship at the **WINTER SOLSTICE**.

The Dutch who came to settle in New York introduced the custom of making calls on New Year's Day, and by the 1840s, visiting on New Year's Day was a widespread practice among the middle classes in America. Gentlemen arrived with engraved calling cards, and women set out beautifully decorated tables full of food and served coffee or whiskey punch. This custom continues in the popular "open house" parties held on New Year's today.

Football Games

Perhaps no pastime is as closely identified with New Year's Day in the United States as watching football games on television—especially the **ROSE BOWL** game in Pasadena, California; the Cotton Bowl in Dallas, Texas; the Sugar Bowl in New Orleans, Louisiana; and the Orange Bowl in Miami, Florida. In many homes, having friends over to watch football has replaced the more social visits paid on this day in past centuries.

Gifts

The ancient Romans exchanged gifts on New Year's Day—usually coins bearing the portrait of the two-faced god, Janus. These gifts were called *strenae*, a name that survives in the French word *étrennes*, meaning New Year's presents. They were the precursor to our modern **CHRISTMAS** presents, and they were based on the belief that acting wealthy (i.e., by spending money on gifts) would attract good financial luck in the coming year. Feasting and drinking were popular for the same reason, serving as a kind of charm to guarantee abundance. In fact, many of the customs now associated with New Year's Day were based on the principle that whatever happened on the first day of the year would affect one's fortunes throughout the year.

Although gift-giving at New Year's is rare in the United States, it remains popular in France, Italy, and some other European countries.

Pig

Roast pork or suckling pig is a favorite dish to serve at New Year's dinner. The pig is a symbol of good luck in many countries. But in this case the custom arose because the pig roots in a forward direction, making it an apt symbol of a prosperous future. Eating turkey, goose, or any other fowl is equivalent to inviting bad luck, since all fowl scratch backward in their search for food.

Resolutions

Ancient peoples indulged themselves in alcoholic and sexual excess at New Year's as a way of acting out the chaos that they hoped the new year would banish. The New Year's festival was an attempt to start over, and it was customary to purge oneself of excess energy and to confess one's sins in the hope that the New Year would somehow be different.

The Puritans, who were never in favor of New Year's revelry, thought that this was a good time for religious renewal and spiritual resolve. They urged young people not to waste the holiday on vain and foolish amusements but to make New Year's an occasion for changing the way they lived their lives. Like Christians elsewhere, they often made New Year's vows or pledges designed to conquer their own weaknesses, to capitalize on their God-given talents, or to make themselves more useful to others.

The custom of making more secular New Year's resolutions came into vogue at the turn of the twentieth century. People started promising to be more moderate in their eating and drinking habits and to patch up their quarrels with friends, family, and business associates. But it was always understood that most of these vows would not be kept—at least not for long—since humans were backsliders by nature.

The New Year's resolutions that are so widely encouraged and talked about today are a secularized version of the vows that more religious individuals once made in their never-ending journey toward spiritual perfection. Although often made with the best of intentions, such pledges are rarely carried out and must be renewed on an annual basis.

FURTHER READING

Gaer, Joseph. *Holidays Around the World.* Boston: Little, Brown, 1953.

Gay, Kathlyn. *African-American Holidays, Festivals, and Celebrations.* Detroit: Omnigraphics, 2007.

Gulevich, Tanya. *Encyclopedia of Christmas and New Year's Celebrations.* 2nd ed. Detroit: Omnigraphics, 2003.

Henderson, Helene, ed. *Holidays, Festivals, and Celebrations of the World Dictionary.* 3rd ed. Detroit: Omnigraphics, 2005.

Ickis, Marguerite. *The Book of Festivals and Holidays the World Over.* New York: Dodd, Mead, 1970.

Kachun, Mitch. *Festivals of Freedom: Memory and Meaning in African-American Emancipation Celebrations.* Amherst: University of Massachusetts Press, 2003.

Miles, Clement A. *Christmas in Ritual and Tradition, Christian and Pagan.* 1912. Reprint. Detroit: Omnigraphics, 1990.

Purdy, Susan. *Festivals for You to Celebrate.* Philadelphia: Lippincott, 1969.

Santino, Jack. *All Around the Year: Holidays and Celebrations in American Life.* Urbana: University of Illinois Press, 1994.

Schmidt, Leigh Eric. *Consumer Rites: The Buying and Selling of American Holidays.* Princeton: Princeton University Press, 1995.

Scullard, H. H. *Festivals and Ceremonies of the Roman Republic.* Ithaca, NY: Cornell University Press, 1981.

Spicer, Dorothy Gladys. *The Book of Festivals*. 1937. Reprint. Detroit: Omnigraphics, 1990.

Tuleja, Tad. *Curious Customs: The Stories Behind 296 Popular American Rituals*. New York: Harmony, 1987.

Wiggins, William H. Jr. *O Freedom! Afro-American Emancipation Celebrations*. Knoxville: University of Tennessee Press, 2000.

WEB SITES

New Advent Catholic Encyclopedia
www.newadvent.org/cathen/11019a.htm

"The African-American Mosaic: A Library of Congress Resource Guide for the Study of Black History and Culture"
www.loc.gov/exhibits/african/intro.html

"The Slave Experience: Freedom and Emancipation," part of PBS online exhibit "Slavery and the Making of America"
www.pbs.org/wnet/slavery/experience/freedom/index.html

New Year's Eve

Type of Holiday: Calendar/Seasonal
Date of Observation: December 31
Where Celebrated: Australia, British Isles, North and South America, Europe, Scandinavia, former Soviet Union, and in all countries using the Gregorian calendar
Symbols and Customs: "Auld Lang Syne," Noisemaking, Old Man, Wassail Bowl
Related Holidays: Chinese New Year, Dewali, Hogmanay, Nawruz, New Year's Day, Oshogatsu, Rosh Hashanah, Saturnalia, Sol, Tet, Watch Night

ORIGINS

Midnight on December 31 marks the transition between the Old Year and the New Year, an occasion that is celebrated with everything from prayer to parties. Some people wear silly hats, drink champagne, and use noisemakers; they're apt to kiss their bosses, throw their arms around strangers on the street, and generally engage in behavior that would be considered scandalous at other times of the year. Others attend midnight church services, while still others congregate in public places like New York City's Times Square or London's Trafalgar Square to count down the closing seconds of the old year.

It is likely that our New Year's Eve customs are related, if only indirectly, to the ancient Roman **SATURNALIA**, which was observed around the time of the **WINTER SOLSTICE** in December. This pagan holiday was characterized by the suspension of discipline and rules governing behavior, and like New Year's Eve celebrations today, it occasionally got out of hand. In eighteenth-century America, the New Year's Eve revelry in such cities as Philadelphia, New York, and Baltimore often ended in street demonstrations and violence. Groups of men and boys would blow tin horns, set off firecrackers, knock down gates and fences, shatter windows, and even break into the homes of the wealthy, demanding money or hospitality.

Unlike **CHRISTMAS**, which is traditionally celebrated indoors, New Year's Eve festivities frequently take place in the out-of-doors, particularly in urban areas. A popular trend that has emerged in recent years is attending "First Night" celebrations. These originated in Boston in 1976 and are now held in more than 65 American cities. They represent a deliberate attempt to replace the partying and drinking that have traditionally marked New Year's Eve with a wide variety of cultural events and performances in both indoor and outdoor settings. Those who prefer a quiet New Year's Eve at home often get their outdoor experience vicariously by watching the illuminated ball that descends on Times Square during the closing minutes of the old year.

SYMBOLS AND CUSTOMS

"Auld Lang Syne"

The custom of singing "Auld Lang Syne" on New Year's Eve is all that remains of a much broader custom that originated in the British Isles in the late eighteenth century, when all parties ended with the guests standing in a circle singing this traditional song. The custom first took hold in Scotland, probably because the lyrics were written in 1788 by Robert Burns, the country's favorite folk poet. There were other versions of the song, however, one of which was used in the 1783 opera *Rosina* by composer William Shield. Most musicologists agree that the tune came from a traditional Scottish folk melody, and that Burns and others merely tinkered with the words.

In the Scots dialect, *auld lang syne* means "old long since"—in other words, the good old days. Even the rowdiest New Year's Eve parties often end with a relatively quiet, if drunken, rendition of this simple tribute to times past.

Noisemaking

The custom of using noise to welcome in the New Year dates back to ancient times, when noise was believed to scare off evil spirits. Although few people today link New Year's Eve with any kind of evil influence, noisemaking still plays a prominent role in their celebrations. In Denmark, young people "smash in the New Year" by banging on their friends' doors and throwing pieces of broken pottery against the sides of houses. In Japan, dancers go from house to house at **OSHOGATSU** making strange noises by rattling bamboo sticks and pounding drums. In Vietnam, Hawaii, and South America, New Year's Eve is celebrated by setting off firecrackers. And in the United States, New Year's Eve parties almost always feature the inexpensive plastic, paper, or tin noisemakers normally associated with children's birthday parties.

Old Man

If the baby is often used to symbolize the New Year, the old man is the classic symbol of the year that is drawing to an end. Holiday greeting cards used to feature these symbols regularly, although they are less common today. In some ways, Santa Claus (see **CHRISTMAS**) is the old man we now associate with the passing year. In any case, the baby and the old man serve as a useful metaphor for the birth and death of a calendar year.

Wassail Bowl

In England at one time, New Year's Eve was an occasion for feasting and celebrating. Family and friends would gather around a bowl of hot ale spiced with cloves, nutmeg, and ginger, from which the head of the house would drink to their health. Then each family member or friend would drink from the bowl and pass it on, saying "Waes Hael!" as they drank—an Anglo-Saxon expression meaning, "May you be in good health." The bowl came to be known as the "wassail" bowl, and "wassailing" became a general term for merrymaking during the holiday season.

FURTHER READING

Henderson, Helene, ed. *Holidays, Festivals, and Celebrations of the World Dictionary*. 3rd ed. Detroit: Omnigraphics, 2005.

Gulevich, Tanya. *Encyclopedia of Christmas and New Year's Celebrations*. 2nd ed. Detroit: Omnigraphics, 2003.

Ickis, Marguerite. *The Book of Festivals and Holidays the World Over*. New York: Dodd, Mead, 1970.

Pike, Royston. *Round the Year with the World's Religions*. 1950. Reprint. Detroit: Omnigraphics, 1992.

Santino, Jack. *All Around the Year: Holidays and Celebrations in American Life.* Urbana: University of Illinois Press, 1994.

Schmidt, Leigh Eric. *Consumer Rites: The Buying and Selling of American Holidays.* Princeton: Princeton University Press, 1995.

Tuleja, Tad. *Curious Customs: The Stories Behind 296 Popular American Rituals.* New York: Harmony, 1987.

WEB SITE

Times Square Alliance
www.timessquarenyc.org/nye/nye.html

Niman Kachina Festival
(Niman Festival, Going-Away of the Gods, Going Home Ceremony)

Type of Holiday: Religious (Hopi)
Date of Observation: July
Where Celebrated: Arizona
Symbols and Customs: Kachinas, Masks
Related Holidays: Powamû Festival, Wuwuchim

ORIGINS

The Niman Kachina Festival is part of the Hopi religious tradition. The history of this and other Native American cultures dates back thousands of years into prehistoric times. According to many scholars, the people who became the Native Americans migrated from Asia across a land bridge that may have once connected the territories presently occupied by Alaska and Russia. The migrations, believed to have begun between 60,000 and 30,000 B.C.E., continued until approximately 4,000 B.C.E. This speculation, however, conflicts with traditional stories asserting that the indigenous Americans have always lived in North America or that tribes moved up from the south.

The historical development of religious belief systems among Native Americans is not well known. Most of the information available was gathered by Europeans who arrived on the continent beginning in the sixteenth century C.E. The data they recorded was fragmentary and oftentimes of questionable accuracy because the Europeans did not understand the native cultures they were trying to describe and the Native Americans were reluctant to divulge details about themselves.

The KACHINAS are the ancestral spirits of the Hopi Indians. For six months of the year, they leave their home in the mountains and visit the tribe, bringing health to the people and rain to their crops. Their arrival in January or February is celebrated as the **POWAMÛ FESTIVAL**, and their departure in July is observed as the Niman Kachina Festival, with ceremonial dances at all four Hopi pueblos. These dances are actually the last in a series that take place throughout the six months when the kachinas are present in the pueblo.

The Hopi observe a ceremonial calendar in which the year is divided into two parts. According to tradition, during one half of the year the kachinas (nature, ancestral, and guardian spirits) live in the village and reveal themselves to the people through ceremonial dances. During the other half of the year, the kachinas separate themselves from the village and return to live in their homes in the mountains. The Kachina season begins around the time of **WINTER SOLSTICE**, as people begin to prepare the ground for planting, and it closes in late July with the bringing in of the first harvest.

In the Niman Kachina Festival, the masked dancers who represent the kachinas perform their dances in the plaza, pounding their feet rhythmically, chanting, and sprinkling sacred meal on the ground. Their arms are filled with green cornstalks—symbolic of the crops for which the tribe is so thankful—and some carry musical instruments made from hollow gourds painted yellow and green. Notched sticks are laid across the gourds, and the scapulae (shoulder blades) of deer serve as bows for these primitive fiddles. The dance is repeated at intervals throughout the day.

During the dance, a procession of men and women emerges from the kiva—a large underground room used for ceremonial purposes. These are the Hopi priests and priestesses. One carries an ancient water bowl from which he flings drops of water, symbolic of rain, with an eagle feather; one has a ceremonial pipe, from which he blows smoke, symbolic of clouds. The women place meal in each dancer's hand—another indication that the Niman Kachina is a ceremony of gratitude for the harvest as well as a going-away party for the ancestral spirits.

The dancers hand out gifts to the children: gourd rattles and bows and arrows for the boys, and kachina dolls for the girls. They also distribute baskets, bowls, or wash-pans filled with foods symbolic of the harvest—small ears of corn, peaches, melon, and other first fruits.

Young Hopi women who have married during the year are barred from observing any ceremonial dances until the Niman Kachina, at which their attendance is required. They all wear the pure white wedding blanket made by the groom from native cotton and wool. This blanket is worn at all ceremonial occasions after the wedding, and when the woman dies, it serves as her burial shroud.

The kachinas don't actually depart until the second morning of the festival. There is a brief ceremony at sunrise that involves throwing meal, pouring water, and other symbolic acts. The priest stands at the top of the ladder that leads down into the kiva and offers a prayer. The masked kachinas leave the village by way of a trail leading west, disappearing just as the sun appears over the horizon.

SYMBOLS AND CUSTOMS

Kachinas

The word *kachina* means "spirit." It applies both to the ancestral spirits whose arrival and departure are celebrated each year and to the men wearing MASKS who impersonate these supernatural beings. Men, animals, plants, stones, mountains, storms, the sky, and the underground all have spirits personified as kachinas, who come into the modern world carrying the legends of the Hopi past. Although the kachinas themselves are not gods, they act as intermediaries between mortals and the Hopi deities. Prayers for sun and rain, or for more children, are made to the kachinas in the belief that they will bring these appeals to the gods' attention.

Kachina also applies to the dolls carved out of cottonwood and painted, dressed, and feathered to look exactly like the Niman Kachina dancers. Children play with kachina dolls, which can also be seen standing on special altars erected around the time of the festival.

There are a number of legends concerning the kachinas' origin, most of which agree that the chief kachina was a badger who came from the underworld. Many of the ceremonies featuring kachinas are conducted in a language so ancient that even the participants do not understand it.

Masks

The kachina's most distinguishing feature is his mask or ceremonial helmet. The face may represent a bird, beast, monster, or man—or a combination thereof, with many variations in color. These masks usually bear symbols representing clouds, rain, or rainbows, since the Niman Kachina Festival takes place at a time of year when rain is apt to be scarce. The male kachinas often carry an object associated with the spirits they represent—for example, a bow and arrow, yucca whip, pine branch, or feathers. The women kachinas, known as *kachinamana*, are represented by men as well. They wear wigs, with their hair styled in flat swirls over the ears known as squash-blossoms, a symbol of virginity.

Before the final kachina dance takes place, the masks are repainted and refinished with a ruff of feathers, fur, or spruce at the neck—spruce, according to the Hopis, having a magnetic attraction for rain. The remainder of the costume consists of a white ceremonial kirtle (kilt) and sash, with a turtle-shell rattle under the knee, moccasins, and jewelry. A fox skin hangs from the rear of the belt or sash—all that remains of the animal skins in which the Hopi kachinas once clothed their entire bodies.

FURTHER READING

Bellenir, Karen. *Religious Holidays and Calendars*. 3rd ed. Detroit: Omnigraphics, 2004.

Fergusson, Erna. *Dancing Gods: Indian Ceremonials of New Mexico and Arizona*. New York: A.A. Knopf, 1931.

Fewkes, Jesse Walter. *Tusayan Katcinas and Hopi Altars*. Albuquerque: Avanyu Pub., 1990.

Heinberg, Richard. *Celebrate the Solstice: Honoring the Earth's Seasonal Rhythms through Festival and Ceremony*. Wheaton, IL: Quest Books, 1993.

Henderson, Helene, ed. *Holidays, Festivals, and Celebrations of the World Dictionary*. 3rd ed. Detroit: Omnigraphics, 2005.

Nyepi
(Balinese Lunar New Year, Saka New Year)

Type of Holiday: Calendar/Seasonal
Date of Observation: Late March; first day of the tenth lunar month
Where Celebrated: Bali, Indonesia
Symbols and Customs: Cockfighting, Kissing, Noisemaking, Ogoh-ogoh
Related Holidays: Galungan

ORIGINS

Nyepi marks the beginning of a new year according to the *saka (caka)*, or twelve-month lunar calendar, which originated in India and was introduced to Indonesia in the first century C.E. Each month in the saka year ends on the day of the new moon, and the year as a whole begins on the day after the new moon of the **VERNAL EQUINOX**, which is also the first day of the tenth lunar month. Balinese people also follow the *wuku*, or 210-day ritual calendar, and **GALUNGAN** is the celebration of the new year in Bali according to that calendar.

Preparations for Nyepi begin three days beforehand, when all the religious statues are carried in procession from the Balinese Hindu temples to the sea for the ritual known as *melasti*. Everyone wears traditional Balinese sarongs, and the sound of bells and gongs accompanies the bathing of the images in seawater that has been blessed by the priests. The priests then sprinkle holy water on the people themselves, so that they will begin the new year in a purified state.

The dominant religion of the island of Bali in Indonesia is known as Bali Hindu, or Agama Tirtha, the Religion of Holy Water. Claiming more than two million adherents in Bali, the faith is a blend of ancient indigenous Balinese beliefs and strong Hindu and Buddhist influences. The emergence of Bali Hindu as a distinct religion is thought to have occurred sometime between the fourteenth and nineteenth centuries.

On the day before Nyepi, the last day of the old year, the exorcism ritual known as *Tawur Agung Kesanga* is held. It is marked by intense NOISEMAKING and the parading of effigies or OGOH-OGOH through the streets, which are thought to drive the evil spirits away from the villages. People bang pots and pans together, children set off firecrackers, and the sound of the gamelan (a traditional Indonesian instrumental ensemble) can be heard during these parades. Nyepi falls at the end of the rainy season, which leaves the earth in a soiled and spiritually unbalanced state. Getting rid of evil this way, it is believed, will restore the earth's harmony, balance, and purity.

The day of Nyepi itself is spent in complete silence. Everyone adheres to four basic rules: no light (including cooking fires); no physical work; no travel or movement (including driving, opening doors and windows, or even leaving the house), and no entertainment or amusement (including music, art, or sexual intercourse). Starting at dawn and lasting for twenty-four hours, the Balinese people stay in their homes and spend their time fasting, praying, and meditating. It is a day for purifying themselves spiritually and readying themselves mentally for the start of a new year. Even tourists are warned not to go anywhere or make any noise on this day. The streets are empty and the beaches are closed, so most visitors spend the day in their hotels.

The day after Nyepi is usually devoted to visiting relatives. Just outside the capital city of Denpasar, this is the day when the unusual custom of public KISSING takes place.

SYMBOLS AND CUSTOMS

Cockfighting

Although gambling has been officially outlawed in Bali since the early 1980s, cock-fighting is permitted on the day before Nyepi. Cockfights take place in every village, and after the cocks die, they are plucked and cooked right away, since no cooking is allowed during the observation of the holiday. The blood from the dead cocks is sprinkled over the nearest crossroad, a ritual that is believed to purify the earth.

Kissing

One of the most unusual customs associated with Nyepi takes place in the village of Banjar Kaja, in the southern part of the capital city of Denpasar. Known as med-medan, it involves two groups of teenagers, one male and one female, who, after walking in a procession to the local temple for prayers, face each other and move closer and closer until they are kissing. Although no one is certain how or where this public display of affection originated, it is widely believed that the kissing ritual offers protection from the unexpected in the coming year.

Perhaps influenced by what they have seen in Western movies and on television, the young Balinese who participate in the ritual often get carried away, exchanging passionate kisses rather than the recommended chaste, ceremonial ones. Only those who live in Banjar Kaja are allowed to join in the kissing, although tourists and nonresidents usually gather to watch. Should they get caught up in the spirit of the event and be unable to restrain themselves, there are always adult "referees" standing by to hose them down with cold water.

Noisemaking

Nyepi is known as much for the noise it creates the day beforehand as it is for the silence of the holiday itself. The noisemaking begins at dusk, accompanied by torches, which are used to drive the demons out of every possible hiding place. People bang on drums, tin cans, cymbals and gongs, pots and pans, and whatever else they can find that will make a loud noise. They light firecrackers and beat the earth and the trees with sticks. The noise subsides around midnight, and it is believed that after several hours of this racket, no evil spirits will be left in the villages.

Ogoh-ogoh

Ogoh-ogoh are the huge and usually frightening effigies that each village makes to represent the demons or evil spirits that are plaguing the lives of its inhabitants. Made from bamboo or wood and covered with styrofoam or papier-mâché, they usually resemble mythical giants or creatures from Balinese folklore, although they occasionally take the form of more modern demons, such as motorcycle gang members. Held aloft by young men, they are paraded through the streets as part of the noisy processions that take place on the eve of Nyepi. At the end of the evening's festivities, the ogoh-ogoh are often burned as a symbolic way of getting rid of evil.

FURTHER READING

Freeman, Dave, et al. *100 Things to Do Before You Die: Travel Events You Just Can't Miss*. Dallas: Taylor Pub. Co., 1999.
MacDonald, Margaret R., ed. *The Folklore of World Holidays*. Detroit: Gale Research, 1992.

WEB SITE

International Herald Tribune
www.iht.com/articles/2006/03/24/opinion/edhogue.php

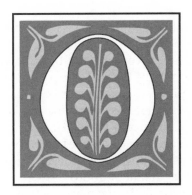

Obon Festival
(Bon Festival, Festival of Lanterns,
Festival of the Dead)

Type of Holiday: Religious (Buddhist)
Date of Observation: July 13-15 or August 13-15
Where Celebrated: Japan, and by Japanese Buddhists throughout the world
Symbols and Customs: Bonfires, Bon-Odori, Lanterns
Related Holidays: All Souls' Day, Ching Ming, Hungry Ghosts Festival

ORIGINS

The Obon Festival has been observed by Buddhist families in Japan ever since Buddhism was introduced there around 552 B.C.E. Although it was originally celebrated only by the court and noblemen, the celebration eventually spread to the general population. It was a festival in honor of the dead, similar to the Christian **ALL SOULS' DAY**.

Buddhism is one of the four largest religious families in the world. It is based on the teachings of Siddhartha Gautama (c. 563-483 B.C.E.), who came to be known as Buddha, or "The Enlightened One." The basic tenets of Buddhism can be summarized in the Four Noble Truths and the Eightfold Path. The Four Noble Truths are 1) the truth and reality of suffering; 2) suffering is caused by desire; 3) the way to end suffering is to end desire; and 4) the Eightfold Path shows the way to end suffering. The Eightfold Path consists of 1) right view or right understanding; 2) right thoughts and aspirations; 3) right speech; 4) right conduct and action; 5) right way of life; 6) right effort; 7) right mindfulness; and 8) right contemplation.

Although the Obon Festival is still a fairly solemn occasion, people take joy in the knowledge that their dead relatives can return to earth for a visit. Preparations include cleaning houses and graveyards and lighting small BONFIRES to welcome the spirits home. The graves of the deceased are often decorated with the branches of the Japanese umbrella pine (*koya-maki*), rice balls (*mochi*), fruit, and incense. In the main room of the house, where the altar is located, a small mat is spread on the floor. The *ihai* or record of ancestry is placed on the mat, along with appropriate decorations. A miniature fence made of leaves surrounds this arrangement, and a table is set with foods that the dead particularly enjoy, which include potatoes cooked with sesame seeds, eggplant or gourds, sweets, fruits, and cakes. Throughout the three days of the festival, the dead are spoken to as if they were alive and present. On the final day, they are offered special "farewell rice balls" to sustain them on their return journey.

The purpose of the Obon Festival is to keep the memory of the deceased alive and to encourage obedience from sons and daughters. Obon celebrations are held not only in Japan, but in other countries where there is a large Japanese Buddhist population. In the United States, for example, there is a big Obon celebration in Chicago, as well as in several California cities. Obon celebrations take place in either July or August, depending upon the location.

SYMBOLS AND CUSTOMS

Bonfires

Bonfires are lit outside Japanese homes twice during Obon. At the start of the festival, they are lit to welcome the spirits of the dead as they return to earth to visit the living. On the third and final day of the festival, they are lit to guide the spirits back to their celestial home. Just as certain foods are prepared to satisfy the spirits' appetites, the light of the bonfires is regarded as necessary to help them find their way around.

In Kyoto, Japan, giant bonfires are lit on the mountainsides. They are made in the shape of the character that means "large."

Bon-Odori

The climax of the Obon Festival is the Bon-Odori, or "Dance of Rejoicing," a folk dance that is held in every town, by the light of paper LANTERNS, to comfort the souls of the dead. It was originally a dance of lamentation in which close relatives of the deceased would dance and sing to the music of a flute and a drum. The early

Bon dances were performed at a variety of local festivals, many of which coincided with Obon. These other festivals eventually merged, and what began as a religious celebration for the spirits of the dead evolved into a gala festival of dancing.

In Buddhist temples during Obon, dancers perform to the beat of a huge *taiko* (drum) mounted on a platform. Both men and women wear a light summer kimono known as a *yukata*, and most carry large sandalwood fans. Sometimes their steps are slow and graceful as they assume postures that resemble living statues. At other times, their bodies sway in unison and spin faster and faster as the tempo of the drumbeat increases. Although some people practice the traditional steps with instructors for weeks in advance, almost anyone can join in simply by following the person in front of him or her. Bon dances, which can continue throughout the night, express the joyous side of the Obon Festival, just as the lantern ceremonies (*see* LANTERNS) reflect its more serious side.

Lanterns

Lanterns play an important role throughout the three days of Obon. At night, families go to the cemetery carrying lanterns designed to light the path for the ancestral spirits. Sometimes lanterns are left burning on the graves, casting an eery glow over the otherwise dark cemetery. Lanterns are often left burning in front of each house as well, serving as signposts for both guests and the souls of the departed. Then, on the final day of the festival, little boats with paper lanterns on the bow are set adrift on lakes and rivers. The boats contain the names of the ancestors who are being honored.

The Todaji Temple in Honolulu, which is the only member of Buddhism's oldest sect in the United States, holds a procession of floating spirits in Ala Moana Park during Obon. After a short service in the temple, its members launch several hundred wooden boats, each about three feet long, decorated with colored lanterns and filled with offerings of food and incense and memorial tablets with the names of ancestors written on them. Each family launches one boat—even if it's only a waxed paper carton. The fleet is led by the mother boat or *oyabune*, which is usually five feet long.

FURTHER READING

Araki, Nancy K., and Jane M. Horii. *Matsuri Festival: Japanese-American Celebrations and Activities*. San Francisco: Heian International Pub. Co., 1978.

Bauer, Helen, and Sherwin Carlquist. *Japanese Festivals*. Garden City, NY: Doubleday, 1965.

Bellenir, Karen. *Religious Holidays and Calendars*. 3rd ed. Detroit: Omnigraphics, 2004.

Dobler, Lavinia G. *Customs and Holidays Around the World*. New York: Fleet Pub. Corp., 1962.

Eberhard, Wolfram. *A Dictionary of Chinese Symbols: Hidden Symbols in Chinese Life and Thought*. New York: Routledge & Kegan Paul, 1986.

Henderson, Helene, ed. *Holidays, Festivals, and Celebrations of the World Dictionary*. 3rd ed. Detroit: Omnigraphics, 2005.

WEB SITE

Shingon Buddhist International Institute
www.shingon.org/library/archive/Obon.html

Obzinky

Type of Holiday: Calendar/Seasonal
Date of Observation: Late August to mid-September
Where Celebrated: Czech Republic
Symbols and Customs: Baba, Wreath
Related Holidays: Thanksgiving

ORIGINS

Obzinky marks the changing of the seasons, which people in all parts of the world have honored since ancient times. Many cultures divided the year into two seasons, summer and winter, and marked these points of the year at or near the summer and winter solstices, during which light and warmth began to increase and decrease, respectively. In pre-industrial times, humans survived through hunting, gathering, and agricultural practices, which depend on the natural cycle of seasons, according to the climate in the region of the world in which they lived. Thus, they created rituals to help ensure enough rain and sun in the spring and summer so crops would grow to fruition at harvest time, which was, in turn, duly celebrated. Vestiges of many of these ancient practices are thought to have survived in festivals still celebrated around seasonal themes.

There are actually two harvest celebrations in the Czech and Slovak Republics. One of them, known as Posviceni, is the church consecration of the harvest. The other, Obzinky, is a secular festival where the field workers celebrate the end of the harvest by making a WREATH out of corn, wheat, or rye and wildflowers. Sometimes the wreath is placed on the head of a pretty young girl, and sometimes it is placed in a wagon along with decorated rakes and scythes and pulled in procession to the home of the landowner. Ribbons are braided into the horses' manes and tails, and the reapers wear their most colorful clothes. The laborers present the wreath and congratulate their employers on a good harvest, after which they are invited to participate in dancing, singing, and feasting at the farmowner's expense. Foods served at this feast traditionally include roast pig, roast goose, and *Kolace*—square cakes filled with plum jam or a stuffing made from sweetened cheese or poppy seed. Beer and slivovice, a prune liquor, accompany the food.

SYMBOLS AND CUSTOMS

Baba

The woman who binds the last sheaf of corn or wheat in the harvest is known as the *Baba* or "old woman." In some areas, the Baba is a doll made from the last sheaf of grain and decorated with ribbons and flowers. Like the WREATH, the Baba is carried in procession to the landowner's home, where it occupies a place of honor until the next harvest.

The custom of making a "corn dolly" or puppet representing the corn goddess or spirit of the harvest is a very ancient one (*see* CORN DOLLY under **THANKSGIVING**). Sometimes the reaper herself was wrapped up in cornstalks and brought to the farmhouse, where she was often the object of ridicule and teasing. The general belief behind all of these customs was that the spirit of the corn was driven out with the cutting of the last sheaf. After spending the winter in the barn, the corn spirit would go out again to the fields to resume her activity as the force that made the corn grow.

Wreath

The wreath made of corn, wheat, or rye and brought to the landowner's house at the completion of the harvest serves much the same purpose as the BABA. It symbolizes the fruits of the fields, and presenting it to the landowner is a way of presenting him with the bounty of the harvest.

FURTHER READING

Frazer, Sir James G. *The Golden Bough: A Study in Magic and Religion*. New York: Macmillan, 1931.

Henderson, Helene, ed. *Holidays, Festivals, and Celebrations of the World Dictionary*. 3rd ed. Detroit: Omnigraphics, 2005.

MacDonald, Margaret R., ed. *The Folklore of World Holidays*. Detroit: Gale Research, 1992.

Spicer, Dorothy Gladys. *The Book of Festivals*. 1937. Reprint. Detroit: Omnigraphics, 1990.

WEB SITE

Australian Media
www.harvestfestivals.net/czechrepublicfestivals.htm

October Horse Sacrifice

Type of Holiday: Ancient
Date of Observation: October 15
Where Celebrated: Rome, Italy
Symbols and Customs: Blood, Horse's Head
Related Holidays: Parilia

ORIGINS

In ancient Rome, a two-horse chariot race was held in the Campus Martius (Field of Mars) on October 15. After the race was over, the right-hand horse of the winning chariot was killed with a spear as a sacrifice to Mars, the god of war. The HORSE'S HEAD was cut off first, and decorated with a necklace of loaves or cakes. Then there was a battle between the inhabitants of two different quarters of the city to see who could seize the head and hang it up in a place where everyone could see it. Meanwhile, the horse's tail, still dripping with BLOOD, was rushed to the king's house, where the blood was allowed to drip on the sacred hearth. The rest of the blood was preserved until April 21, when the **PARILIA** (a festival in honor of Pales, the protector of shepherds and their flocks) was held. It would then be burned as part of a purifying ceremony, and both men and animals would leap over the fire.

Scholars find the beginnings of ancient Roman religion in the sixth century B.C.E. Roman religion dominated Rome and influenced territories in its empire until Emperor Constantine's conversion to Christianity in the third century C.E. Ancient Roman religion was heavily influenced by the older Greek religion. Roman festivals therefore had much in common with those of the ancient Greeks. Not only were their gods and goddesses mostly the same as those in the Greek pantheon (though the Romans renamed them), but their religious festivals were observed with similar activities: ritual sacrifice, theatrical performances, games, and feasts.

Many of the rituals associated with the October Horse Sacrifice have their roots in ancient agricultural customs. Horse racing was a common activity on farms at certain seasons of the year, and a wreath—similar to the necklace of loaves—was often hung around the neck of the winning horse. The men and women who worked on the farm also raced against each other in pursuit of a calf, a kid, a sheep, or some other animal believed to represent the corn-spirit or goddess of vegetation.

While there is strong evidence that the October Horse Sacrifice was originally an agricultural fertility rite, some scholars believe that it was more of a military rite, designed to purify the army when it returned from its summer campaign. The fact that a horse was sacrificed (as opposed to an ox or some other farm animal) would seem to support this theory, since horses were closely linked to war in ancient times. It is also possible that what started out as a fertility rite later developed into a martial one, with army horses taking the place of farm horses. In any case, the blood, the hearth, and the necklace of loaves hung around the horse's head all have strong associations with the fertility of the fields.

SYMBOLS AND CUSTOMS

Blood

The blood of the sacrificed horse was a symbol of life. When dripped on the sacred hearth or burned in the fires of the **PARILIA**, it was believed to purify and ward off evil. Anyone who breathed in the smoke of the fire in which the blood had been scattered would therefore gain new life and strength and avoid the evil forces that might otherwise hinder survival.

Horse's Head

The horse's head represents the corn-spirit. In ancient times, it was common after the harvest was over to hang up some object in a prominent place on the farm or in the village—usually a bunch of corn or flowers—and call it by the name of an animal. Eventually a real animal's head was used for the same purpose. Hanging a necklace of loaves around the horse's head showed that it was an object that possessed the power to make the fields more fertile.

FURTHER READING

Fowler, W. Warde. *The Roman Festivals of the Period of the Republic*. New York: Macmillan Co., 1925.

Henderson, Helene, ed. *Holidays, Festivals, and Celebrations of the World Dictionary*. 3rd ed. Detroit: Omnigraphics, 2005.

Leach, Maria, ed. *Funk & Wagnalls Standard Dictionary of Folklore, Mythology & Legend*. San Francisco: Harper & Row, 1984.

Scullard, H.H. *Festivals and Ceremonies of the Roman Republic*. Ithaca, NY: Cornell University Press, 1981.

Odunde Festival

Type of Holiday: Religious (Ifa, Santeria, Yoruba)
Date of Observation: Second Sunday in June
Where Celebrated: Philadelphia, Pennsylvania
Symbols and Customs: Offerings, Procession, Street Fair

ORIGINS

The Odunde Festival (formerly known as the Oshun Festival) was created in 1975 by Lois Fernandez, who organized friends, family members, and the residents of her south Philadelphia community to stage the one-day event. Odunde (oh-doon-day), which means "Happy New Year" in the Yoruba language of western Africa, celebrates the coming of another year for people who observe traditional African cultural and religious systems, particularly the Ifa, Santeria, and Yoruba faiths. In accordance with these belief systems, hundreds of spirits known as orishas are directly involved with the earthly activities of humans. Devotees venerate the orishas with rituals either individually or in ceremonies conducted by priests or priestesses.

Fernandez was inspired to create the festival by her earlier visits to Africa, where she first attended festivals honoring orishas. She was particularly impressed by ceremonies honoring Oshun (alternately, Ochun), a feminine orisha associated with rivers. Having observed festivals for Oshun at riverbanks first in Nigeria and later in various U.S. cities, Fernandez was moved to organize such a festival near the Schuylkill River in Philadelphia. There were many bureaucratic and organizational challenges posed by critics of the idea. But Fernandez and her supporters convinced the community that they could stage a cultural event that would bring African Americans together for a rewarding and long-lasting celebration.

The first festival was a huge success, drawing hundreds of people to participate in a ceremonial PROCESSION to honor Oshun with chanting, dancing, drumming, and

OFFERINGS made at the Schuylkill River. Within two years the event had grown to include a STREET FAIR featuring a variety of African and African-American vendors and entertainers. The festival now typically draws more than 500,000 attendees each year, with nearly one fourth of the participants traveling to Philadelphia from other areas of the U.S. as well as several African countries. Many festival participants and attendees dress in traditional African clothing, particularly the observers of the Yoruba, Santeria, Ifa, and Voudun faiths, who typically dress in traditional white robes.

The Odunde Festival itself is held on the second Sunday in June, although related activities are held over the whole weekend. Typically included in the weekend are events such as workshops, seminars, cultural presentations, and a reception for the ambassadors of African nations participating in the festival. These events are sponsored by Odunde, Inc., an organization that produces year-round educational and cultural programs in addition to the Odunde Festival.

SYMBOLS AND CUSTOMS

Offerings

The Odunde Festival procession leads devotees to the Schuylkill River, where offerings of fruit, flowers, honey, and coins are made to Oshun. Offerings are made to ask Oshun for blessings or to thank her for blessings bestowed in the previous year.

Procession

Overseen by a Yoruba priest or priestess, the Odunde Festival ceremonies begin with a procession led by traditional dancers wearing masks that represent ancestral spirits. Sacred drummers chant and drum to the orishas, and devotees dance and sing as they proceed toward the Schuylkill River, where offerings are made to Oshun. The procession then returns to its starting point for the opening of the street fair.

Street Fair

The Odunde Festival includes a street fair that takes places along ten city blocks in south Philadelphia. More than 300 vendors from throughout the U.S. as well as many South American, Caribbean, and African nations sell food, crafts, and other merchandise. Attendees are entertained by performers on several stages and at various street corners.

FURTHER READING

Gay, Kathlyn. *African-American Holidays, Festivals, and Celebrations*. Detroit: Omnigraphics, 2007.

Wiggins, William H. Jr., and Douglas DeNatale, eds. *Jubilation!: African American Celebrations in the Southeast*. Columbia: University of South Carolina Press, 1994.

WEB SITES

Odunde Festival
www.odundeinc.org

Philadelphia Folklore Project
www.folkloreproject.org/programs/exhibits/odunde

Odwira

Type of Holiday: Calendar/Seasonal
Date of Observation: September-October; December-January
Where Celebrated: Ghana
Symbols and Customs: Animal Sacrifice, Drumming, Golden Stool, Ivory Trumpet, Twins

ORIGINS

The Akan people of southern Ghana, a West African country located along the Atlantic between Togo and the Ivory Coast, celebrate the festival known as Odwira either in September-October, at the time of the yam harvest, or in December-January, during the planting season. The timing of this important festival, which dates back more than 300 years, varies among the different Akan groups, although the best known observation is probably that of the Ashanti (or Asante), which is held in the autumn.

Odwira serves a number of purposes: It gives people an opportunity to show their gratitude for the yam harvest, to honor their ancestors and renew their family bonds, and to reconfirm their support for their king. The weeklong series of events varies from one location to the next, but it usually begins with a parade in which the king is carried on an elaborately decorated palanquin through the streets, accompanied by DRUMMING and the blowing of IVORY TRUMPETS. Then he sits in state in the town square to receive visits from the chiefs of other villages and the homage paid by local residents. Other events include dancing and drumming, the offering of the new yam to the gods, feasting, and the cleansing of the sacred stools (*see* ANIMAL SACRIFICE, GOLDEN STOOL). The Friday before the festival ends is set aside for honoring TWINS.

The idea for the first Odwira celebration is believed to have come from Osei Tutu, the first Ashanti king and founder of the Ashanti nation in the late seventeenth century. It was Osei Tutu who built Kumasi, the capital city of the Ashanti region, and who established the legend of the Golden Stool to ensure the continuation of the king's power and authority. A special Odwira celebration, more elaborate than the annual observation, takes place three years after a new king has been installed so that everyone can pay homage to the Golden Stool and show their respect for the new king's authority.

SYMBOLS AND CUSTOMS

Animal Sacrifice

During the cleansing and purification rituals for the sacred stools, which are believed to embody the spirits of the dead male ancestors of the Akan people, it is traditional to sprinkle the stools with the blood of a sheep that has been sacrificed for the purpose. The stools may also be purified with consecrated water from a nearby stream.

Drumming

Drumming is a highly evolved art form among the Akan. Drummers gather in the town square during Odwira to demonstrate their talents—particularly on the fontonfrom drum, which can be six feet tall, making it necessary for the drummer to stand on something that will put him up high enough to reach the top. Drummers also accompany the parades that take place during the festival and play for the king as he sits in state in the town square.

Golden Stool

Ancestor worship is central to the Akan religious beliefs and rituals. When a man reaches the age of maturity, he buys a carved wooden stool, which stands as a symbol of his existence and of his ancestry. When he dies, his stool is placed in a room with the stools of his ancestors. Once a year, during the Odwira festival, these stools are brought out and purified, traditionally with sanctified water and the blood from an ANIMAL SACRIFICE.

The Golden Stool is the most important of all. It represents the spirit or soul of the people as a whole, rather than a particular individual, and is therefore an object of great veneration. When a new king comes into power, tradition dictates that he sit on the stool so that he can make symbolic contact with his people. But his contact with the stool must be only symbolic, for it is believed that if he actually makes physical contact with the stool, it will cause sterility. To avoid this, he is often suspended over the stool.

Ivory Trumpet

The ivory trumpets that are blown during the celebration of Odwira are made from the tusks of elephants, which Africans regard as the king of all the animals. When such a horn is blown, it makes a sound very similar to that made by an elephant, which is considered the highest form of praise by the Akan people.

Twins

The Friday of Odwira week is called the Abam Day—Abam meaning "twins." It is named after the twin rulers Atta Panin and Atta Obuom, who succeeded their mother, Queen Dokua, in the nineteenth century. All twins and their parents dress in white and attend a special ceremony that culminates in the purification of the Abam shrine with holy water.

FURTHER READING

MacDonald, Margaret R., ed. *The Folklore of World Holidays*. Detroit: Gale Research, 1992.
Opoku, A.A. *Festivals of Ghana*. Accra, Ghana: Ghana Pub. Corp., 1970.
Van Straalen, Alice. *The Book of Holidays Around the World*. New York: Dutton, 1986.

WEB SITE

Okyeman Cultural Association
www.okyeman.com/odwira.htm

Ogun Festival
(Olojo Festival)

Type of Holiday: Religious (Yoruba)
Date of Observation: July
Where Celebrated: Ife, Oyo State (Nigeria)
Symbols and Customs: Crown, Iron

ORIGINS

The Ogun Festival is observed by the Yoruba people of Nigeria, whose religion is based on ancient oral traditions. Beliefs and practices are preserved by passing history, customs, and traditions from one generation to the next. Authority for interpreting events and establishing proper conduct of ethics and morals rests with a bureaucratic structure of rulers who function in both religious and political realms.

According to traditional Yoruba belief, all power in the universe emanates from a supreme being, Olodumare. Olodumare, known as the owner of everlasting abundance, among many other praise names, holds all power and is the giver of all life. Olodumare is the mystical remote source of all things and is not identified by gender. All that exists, including supernatural divine realities and natural earth realities, are part of Olodumare.

As the supreme almighty source, Olodumare is directly involved in the affairs of the earth through a complex core of sub-divinities called orisa. The orisa are authoritative divine emissaries and serve as intermediaries between the people of earth and Olodumare. They are the major objects of veneration and ritual obligation. The names and number of orisa vary according to national and local custom, but they number in the hundreds. Some are more nationally known while others may be only venerated according to localized custom.

The Ogun Festival commemorates the god Ogun, a mythical warrior, and the birth of his son, Oranmiyan, who later became king of Yorubaland. Ogun is the god of IRON and of war, as well as the patron of blacksmiths and hunters. He was the first god to descend to earth while it was still a marshy wasteland. Since he was the only one who possessed a tool—an iron cutlass—that could penetrate the dense vegetation, he cleared the way for the other deities to descend. When Obatala had finished molding the physical form of the first ancestors, it was Ogun who added the finishing touches—a role he played throughout all of creation. He continues to preside over the "finishing touches" of culture, such as circumcisions and the cutting of tribal marks.

The Ogun Festival lasts for three days. It begins with the vigil known as the *Ilagun* or *Asoro,* which takes place at midnight. On behalf of its blacksmiths, the city of Ife donates two new hoes and several iron bell-gongs needed for the ritual. The Ogun shrine in Ife is decorated with palm fronds, and two dogs are prepared for sacrifice. A libation is poured, prayers to the god are offered, and a ritual dance is held around the shrine.

The city is in a festive mood for the remainder of the festival, when the war chiefs in full regalia dance to the tune of the *ibembe* drums and bell-gongs made of iron while traditional Ogun songs are sung. The highlight is the procession from the palace to Oke Mogun, where Ogun finally settled after abdicating the throne. The chief, who wears the royal CROWN of Ife, is accompanied by priests and priestesses of the various other gods and goddesses worshipped by the Yoruba. Guns are fired when they arrive at the shrine. Special rituals are carried out there, and a ram is sacrificed to the dead ancestors or *Oonis*.

The dances performed at the Ogun Festival reenact mythical themes and are choreographed according to traditional models. Sometimes they consist of simple gestures—such as swinging a machete—that recall the god's powers. Although Ogun is traditionally regarded as the patron of blacksmiths, who unlock the secrets of the earth and forge them into tools, nowadays he is worshipped by drivers and surgeons as the god of automobiles, trucks, and the operating room. Since metal makes the creation and expansion of civilization possible, Ogun is seen as the god who "opens the way"; that is, he makes it possible for the powers of other gods to be effective.

SYMBOLS AND CUSTOMS

Crown

In the procession that is the highlight of the Ogun Festival, the chief wears the beaded crown known as Are, which is supposed to be as heavy as the load that an average man can carry. The crown symbolizes a living deity and therefore attracts many invisible spirits when it is brought out for the annual event. The people of Ife believe that it is the power of the crown that usually causes rain to fall on this day.

Iron

Ogun is the god or *orisha* of iron, which can be transformed into the peaceful tools of agriculture as well as the terrible weapons of war. His iron cutlass stands as a symbol of his power, which can be channeled toward both creative and destructive ends. People who are asked to swear to tell the truth in a court of law and who will not swear on the Bible or the Qur'an are sometimes asked to put their tongue and lips on a cutlass made of iron. In one of the palaces of Ife, there is a large lump of iron that people touch to guarantee that they're telling the truth.

As the one who shapes iron, the blacksmith plays an important role in African mythology. The ability to turn fire and earthy substances into the products of civilization is seen as a parallel to the creation of the world. The smith is regarded as the chief agent of God on earth, the one who shapes the world.

FURTHER READING

Bellenir, Karen. *Religious Holidays and Calendars*. 3rd ed. Detroit: Omnigraphics, 2004.

Eliade, Mircea. *The Encyclopedia of Religion*. New York: Macmillan, 1987.

King, Noel Q. *Religions of Africa: A Pilgrimage into Traditional Religions*. New York: Harper & Row, 1970.

MacDonald, Margaret R., ed. *The Folklore of World Holidays*. Detroit: Gale Research, 1992.

Murphy, Joseph M. *Santería: African Spirits in America*. Boston: Beacon Press, 1988.

Oktoberfest

Type of Holiday: Calendar/Seasonal, Historic
Date of Observation: Second to last Saturday in September until the First Sunday in October
Where Celebrated: Munich, Germany, and various towns and cities in the United States, Canada, and throughout the world
Symbols and Customs: Beer, Beer Halls, Parades, Tapping the First Keg

ORIGINS

Oktoberfest began as an open-to-the-public wedding celebration. On October 12, 1810, Crown Prince Ludwig of Bavaria married Princess Therese of Saxony-Hildburghausen. Five days later, an outdoor party took place in a meadow just outside Munich, the capital city of the German state of Bavaria. This location permitted the family to celebrate the marriage with horse races, a popular pastime of that era. The large, open-air setting also allowed the residents of Munich to attend the celebration.

The event proved so popular that the following year, local people recreated it. The horse races were repeated, and, in addition, local farmers organized an agricultural show. In 1818 Oktoberfest included beer stands, a carousel, and various musical performances. The festival continued to grow throughout the nineteenth century, attracting new activities and a greater variety of entertainment. The *trachenfest*, or costume parade, began in 1835, and the grand entry parade began in 1887. Beer stands were replaced by beer tents in the late nineteenth century, expanding seating capacity and offering customers greater comfort.

The festival took its current shape in the twentieth century. Festival organizers dropped the horse races, which had been the original attraction. The agricultural show has continued till this day, though nowadays it takes place only every third year. The beer tents, or halls, grew in popularity, size, and number during the twentieth century. These days the most popular festival activities, drinking beer and listening to music, take place in the beer halls. Carnival rides, parades, and children's activities are also important elements of Oktoberfest.

Although Oktoberfest began as an October wedding celebration, not many vestiges of the original inspiration for the festival remain. The celebrations still take place in the same field, however. This land, which is now within the Munich city limits, is called "Theresienwiese," or "Therese's meadow," in honor of the princess and her wedding festivities. Sometimes locals refer to the festival itself simply as the *wiesn*, in reference to its location. Oktoberfest, which means "October festival," originally took place during the month of October. It now begins in September and ends during the first weekend of October. Festival organizers made this change because the October weather in Munich is unreliable, and cold rain, blustery winds, and even sleet have driven away festival participants in past years.

Munich's Oktoberfest attracts about six million party-goers yearly. It is certainly the largest folk festival in Germany. Over the past 150 years, German immigrants have established Oktoberfest celebrations around the globe. It is estimated that over 3,000 towns worldwide celebrate Oktoberfest each September and October. About a thousand of these festivals take place in North America. Cincinnati's celebration attracts about half a million people yearly. In Canada, the Kitchener-Waterloo Oktoberfest hosts about three quarters of a million festival-goers. Other American cities with notable Oktoberfest celebrations include Milwaukee (Wisconsin), Torrance (California), Mt. Angel (Oregon), Columbus (Ohio), Fredericksburg (Texas), Tulsa (Oklahoma), and Frankenmuth (Michigan).

SYMBOLS AND CUSTOMS

Beer

Drinking beer has become the primary pastime of Oktoberfest. In Munich about 1.3 million gallons of beer are consumed each year during the festival. Only locally brewed beer is served during the city's Oktoberfest. The six Munich breweries represented at the festival are Hacker-Pschorr, Spaten, Lowenbrau, Augustiner, Paulaner, and Hofbrauhaus.

In Munich, breweries make a special beer for Oktoberfest called *wiesenbier*, or "meadow beer." *Marzen bier*, meaning "March beer," is also popular during Oktoberfest. In past times, March was the last month in which beer was brewed before summer. Beer wasn't brewed at all during the summer because it tended to go bad during the hotter months. In the early fall, people were ready to brew again, so the March beer had to be drunk up to make room for the new brews. March beer was purposefully brewed to be somewhat stronger and sweeter than ordinary beer, and somewhat reddish in color. The high alcohol content helped to preserve it. Even though modern technology has eliminated the need for these traditional brewing styles, March beer is still popular during Oktoberfest. In the U.S. specialty brewers have produced a lighter-tasting, lighter-colored beer, called Oktoberfest beer.

Beer Halls

Nowadays Munich's Oktoberfest boasts fourteen beer halls: Armbrustschützen-zelt, Augustiner-Festhalle, Bräurosi, Fischer-Vroni, Hacker-Festzelt, Hippodrom, Hofbräu-Festzelt, Käfers Wiesn Schänke, Löwenbräu-Festhalle, Ochsenbraterei, Schottenhamel, Schützen-Festhalle, Weinzelt, and Winzerer-Fähndl. Each hall features different beers, foods, décor, and entertainment. Schottenhamel is both the oldest and the largest of the beer halls, with a seating capacity of 10,000. Traditionally, the festive atmosphere inside the halls was enhanced by German brass bands performing traditional German drinking songs and oom-pah-pah waltzes. These days taped music, rock and roll, and even non-German music may be heard. Inside the beer halls, hungry festival-goers can order German sausages, roast chicken, and other hearty German foods to accompany their steins of beer.

Parades

Munich's Oktoberfest begins with the Grand Entry parade led by the mayor. It features beautifully decorated horse-drawn carts representing Munich's breweries, on top of which ride the brewers and Oktoberfest beer hall owners. Beer waitresses in traditional German dress march behind the brewery floats, as well as the members of German brass bands who will entertain the Oktoberfest crowds. Men, women, and children in traditional German dress follow. The four-mile-long parade moves through the city streets and leads to the *Theresienwiese*, where the mayor of Munich officially opens the festival. About 7,000 people take part in this parade.

Another parade takes place on the second day of Oktoberfest. Called the *Trachen-fest*, which means, "celebration of traditional clothing," this parade features groups of marchers from various locations throughout Germany and the rest of Europe, all in traditional dress. The men representing Bavaria wear white shirts, knee-high stockings, and leather shorts held up by suspenders. These shorts are called *lederhosen*. The German women wear flowery dresses referred as *dirndl*. Folk music and dancing accompany this parade.

Tapping the First Keg

In Munich, Oktoberfest begins with a ceremonial tapping of the first keg. This ceremony dates back to 1950. At noon on the opening day, the mayor of Munich enters into the Schottenhamel beer tent to tap the first keg of the festival. Schottenhamel receives this privilege because it is the oldest of the beer tents, having been established in 1867. Festival organizers arrange for a cannon to shoot twelve times. Then the mayor taps the first keg of beer. He fills his stein and declares "Ozapft is!" meaning "the keg is tapped!" Oktoberfest beer drinking officially begins after this moment.

FURTHER READING

Festivals and Holidays. New York: Macmillan Library Reference, 1999.
"German Life's North American Oktoberfest Picks." *German Life*, October/ November 1998. www.germanlife.com/Archives/1998/9810_01.html

WEB SITES

Munich Oktoberfest
www.oktoberfest.de/en/index.php

Munich Tourist Office
www.muenchen.de/Rathaus/tourist_office/oktoberfest/126032/oktoberfest_ geschichte.html

Olympic Games

Type of Holiday: Sporting
Date of Observation: Every four years
Where Celebrated: Various countries around the world
Symbols and Customs: Olympic Flame, Olympic Rings

ORIGINS

There were four major religious festivals in ancient Greece that entailed athletic competitions: the Olympic Games, the Pythian Games, the Nemean Games, and the Isthmian Games. The Olympic Games, held in honor of Zeus, were especially popular. First held in 776 B.C.E. at Olympia, Greece, they continued to be held once every four years for 1,168 years. Then Greece came under Roman rule, and the games declined. They were finally abolished in 393 C.E. by the Christian Roman emperor, Theodosius I, who probably objected to some of the pagan rites associated with the games.

At first the Olympic Games were confined to a single day and a single event: a footrace the length of the stadium. Additional races were added later, along with the discus throw, javelin throw, broad (or long) jump, boxing, wrestling, pentathlon (consisting of five different track and field events), chariot racing, and other contests. There were competitions for poets, orators, and dramatists as well. The length of the games was later extended to five days, and the winners were celebrated as national heroes.

It wasn't until the late nineteenth century that the games were revived, largely through the efforts of Baron Pierre de Coubertin of France, an educator and scholar who wanted to discourage professionalism in sports by holding amateur world championships. The first Olympiad of modern times was held under the royal patronage of the King of Greece in 1896 in a new stadium built for the purpose in Athens. Since that time, the games have been held in cities all over the world at four-year intervals, except for lapses during the First and Second World Wars. A separate cycle of winter games was initiated in 1924.

The modern Olympic Games consist of the Summer Games, held in a large city, and the Winter Games, held at a winter resort. Since 1994, the games have been held on a four-year cycle, but two years apart (i.e., Winter Games in 1994 and 1998, Summer Games in 1996 and 2000). There are twenty-eight approved sports for the Summer Games, which include archery, basketball, boxing, canoeing, cycling, equestrian events, fencing, football (soccer), gymnastics, modern pentathlon, rowing, swimming, diving, volleyball, water polo, weight lifting, wrestling, and yachting. The Winter Games offer competition in such events as biathlon (skiing and shooting), bobsled, ice hockey, luge, ice skating, and skiing. Newer Olympic sports include snowboarding and beach volleyball.

In recent years, about 200 nations have sent over 10,000 male and female athletes to the Summer Olympics, and almost four billion have watched the competition on television. The Winter Olympics are somewhat smaller, with about eighty nations participating.

SYMBOLS AND CUSTOMS

Olympic Flame

The highlight of the opening ceremonies at both the Winter and Summer Olympics is the lighting of the Olympic flame, said to represent the "Olympic spirit" of competition. A cross-country relay runner carries a torch first lit at Olympia, Greece, and ignites the flame that burns throughout the fifteen or sixteen days of the games. Thousands of runners, representing each country between Greece and the host country, take part in the four-week torch relay. The lighting of the torch is followed by a spectacular production of fireworks, strobe lights, fly-overs, music, dance, and other entertainments.

Olympic Rings

The Olympic rings were proposed by Olympic Games founder Baron Pierre de Coubertin in 1914. They first appeared on Olympic medals in 1924. The five rings are blue, black, red, yellow, and green. These colors were selected because one of them can be found in the flag of each nation competing in the Olympics. Each ring represents a continent, and their interlacing shows the universality of the Olympics. Also reflected in the joining of the rings is the meeting of the athletes of the world.

FURTHER READING

Henderson, Helene, ed. *Holidays, Festivals, and Celebrations of the World Dictionary.* 3rd ed. Detroit: Omnigraphics, 2005.
Van Straalen, Alice. *The Book of Holidays Around the World.* New York: Dutton, 1986.

WEB SITES

International Olympic Committee
www.olympic.org

Olympic Museum
www.museum.olympic.org

Onam

Type of Holiday: Religious (Hindu)
Date of Observation: August-September
Where Celebrated: Kerala, India
Symbols and Customs: Boxing, Flower Carpets, Kathakali, Snake-Boat Races

ORIGINS

Onam is a four-day Hindu festival held in the state of Kerala, India. Many scholars regard Hinduism as the oldest living religion. The word Hindu is derived from the Sanskrit term *Sindhu* (or *Indus*), which meant river. It referred to people living in the Indus valley in the Indian subcontinent.

Hinduism has no founder, one universal reality (or god) known as Brahman, many gods and goddesses (sometimes referred to as devtas), and several scriptures. Hinduism also has no priesthood or hierarchical structure similar to that seen in some other religions, such as Christianity. Hindus acknowledge the authority of a wide variety of writings, but there is no single, uniform canon. The oldest of the Hindu writings are the *Vedas*. The word "veda" comes from the Sanskrit word for knowledge. The *Vedas*, which were compiled from ancient oral traditions, contain hymns, instructions, explanations, chants for sacrifices, magical formulas, and philosophy. Another set of sacred books includes the *Great Epics,* which illustrate Hindu faith in practice. The *Epics* include the *Ramayana*, the *Mahabharata*, and the *Bhagavad Gita.*

The Hindu pantheon includes approximately thirty-three million gods. Some of these are held in higher esteem than others. Over all the gods, Hindus believe in one absolute high god or universal concept. This is Brahman. Although he is above all the gods, he is not worshipped in popular ceremonies because he is detached from the day-to-day affairs of the people. Brahman is impersonal. Lesser gods and goddesses (devtas) serve him. Because these are more intimately involved in the affairs of people, they are venerated as gods. The most honored god in Hinduism varies among the different Hindu sects. Although Hindu adherents practice their faith differently and venerate different deities, they share a similar view of reality and look back on a common history.

The Onam festival is explained in a legend known to the people of Kerala. According to legend, the ancient King Mahabalia, also known as Bali, was so powerful and his subjects so prosperous that those who worshipped the Hindu god Vishnu were afraid of losing their status. So Vishnu, disguised as a dwarf named Vamana, decided to trick Bali into giving up his kingdom. Bali was conducting a great sacrifice and told Vamana he could have anything he wanted as a sacrificial gift. Vamana asked only for a piece of land he could cover with three strides. Bali readily agreed, but as soon as he poured the sacrificial water into Vamana's hands to confirm the gift, Vamana suddenly transformed himself into a giant. His first step occupied the entire earth, his second step took him all the way to heaven, and there was nowhere left for him to take his third step. Seeing no other alternative, Bali offered his own head. As Vamana placed his third step on Bali's head, he pushed him down to the underworld as king of the Ashuras (demons). Bali asked if he could be allowed to return once a year to make sure that his people were well and happy, and Vamana agreed.

To welcome him, the people of Kerala clean their houses and yards, which they then decorate with flowers and leaves. The first day of the festival is devoted to feasting, exchanging gifts, singing songs, and dancing. The second day of the festival, known as Thiruvonam, is the day of Bali's return to his former kingdom. Celebrations include BOXING demonstrations, the traditional clapping dance (*kyekot-tikali*) around a brass lamp, and reenactments of stories from the lives of epic heroes (*see* KATHAKALI). There is also a spectacular procession of caparisoned elephants, SNAKE-BOAT RACES, folk dancing, and fireworks displays.

SYMBOLS AND CUSTOMS

Boxing

Thallu or open-palm boxing is a martial art indigenous to Kerala. The boxers use the flat of their palms instead of closed fists, although this does not necessarily make the competition any less brutal. Even those who end up bleeding profusely are often reluctant to give in.

During the Onam festival, every village organizes boxing tournaments, and local dignitaries distribute prizes to the winners. The dexterity of the boxers and the skill with which they fight are exceptional.

Flower Carpets

One of the festival's more unusual features is the displays of elaborately designed carpets made entirely out of flowers. These offer a symbolic welcome to the returning King Bali.

Kathakali

The Kathakali is a pantomime dance that begins shortly after sunset and continues throughout the night. The theme of the dance is an episode from the *Ramayana* or the *Mahabharata,* both Hindu religious epics, and it usually tells a story with a moral. The headgear worn by the dancers indicates which role they play—a king, a god, a demon, etc.—but all other expressions of character are limited to gestures and miming. The control that a skilled Kathakali dancer must have over the muscles of his or her face is considerable; the *Nava-rasas* or Nine Emotions must be accurately portrayed through facial expressions and supported by the appropriate gestures.

Background music is provided by a small orchestra consisting of the Chenda (a drum peculiar to Malabar and noted for its shrill sound), Chengalam (gongs), and Elathalam (a pair of big cymbals), in addition to wind instruments and voices.

Snake-Boat Races

The so-called "snake boats" or *Kalivallaigal* are rowing boats with a high, narrow stern that resembles the neck of a serpent. The largest is 100 to 130 feet long and requires sixty pairs of rowers. Its ornate stern is decorated with brass and rises fifteen to twenty feet above the water. Smaller versions are manned by crews of about thirty. As many as 100 boats enter the competition in different categories. Success in the races depends on a perfect sense of timing and the strength of the crew. If one oarsman is out of synch, the entire boat may capsize, throwing everyone into the water. An elevated platform in the middle of the boat holds a small group of musicians who provide a rhythm for the rowers with cymbals and drums.

Wealthy patrons commission the building of the boats, and the colorful silk umbrellas hung with gold coins and tassels that provide shade on the boats are considered an indication of the owner's economic status. The more umbrellas a boat holds, the wealthier its patron.

The most spectacular snake-boat races are held at Aranmula, Champakulam, and Kottayam.

FURTHER READING

Bellenir, Karen. *Religious Holidays and Calendars*. 3rd ed. Detroit: Omnigraphics, 2004.

Henderson, Helene, ed. *Holidays, Festivals, and Celebrations of the World Dictionary*. 3rd ed. Detroit: Omnigraphics, 2005.

Sanon, Arun. *Festive India*. New Delhi: Frank Bros., 1986.

Sharma, Brijendra Nath. *Festivals of India*. New Delhi: Abhinav Publications, 1978.

Shemanski, Frances. *A Guide to World Fairs and Festivals*. Westport, CT: Greenwood Press, 1985.

Thomas, Paul. *Hindu Religion, Customs, and Manners*. 6th ed. New York: APT Books, 1981.

Trawicky, Bernard, and Ruth W. Gregory. *Anniversaries and Holidays*. 5th ed. Chicago: American Library Assocation, 2000.

Van Straalen, Alice. *The Book of Holidays Around the World*. New York: Dutton, 1986.

WEB SITE

Society for the Confluence of Festivals in India
www.onamfestival.org

Oshogatsu
(New Year's Day in Japan)

Type of Holiday: Calendar/Seasonal
Date of Observation: January 1
Where Celebrated: Japan
Symbols and Customs: Bells, Camellia, Crane and Tortoise, Daruma, Dreams, Gifts, Kadomatsu, Manzai, Mochi, Narcissus, Plum Bough, Rake, Shimenawa or Shimekazari, Utagaruta
Related Holidays: Chinese New Year, Sol

ORIGINS

Several countries in Asia celebrate the new year at about the same time—including China, Japan, Korea, and Vietnam—and with many of the same customs, such as offerings to household god(s), housecleaning and new clothes, banquets, ancestor worship, and fireworks. The date of the new year in the countries mentioned above is based on a lunisolar calendar, similar to or the same as the one used in China. The exception for this timing is Japan, which has employed the Gregorian calendar since 1873 and thus observes New Year's Day on January 1, though many older traditions remain.

The Chinese lunisolar calendar is based on the oldest system of time measurement still in use. It is widely employed in Asian countries to set the dates of seasonal festivals. The **CHINESE NEW YEAR** takes place on the new moon nearest to the point which is defined in the West as the fifteenth degree on the zodiacal sign of Aquarius. Each of twelve months in the Chinese year is twenty-nine or thirty days long and is divided into two parts, each of which is two weeks long. The Chinese calendar, like all lunisolar systems, requires periodic adjustment to keep the lunar and solar cycles integrated; therefore, an intercalary month is added when necessary.

Oshogatsu or **NEW YEAR'S DAY** is the most important festival in the Japanese calendar. Schools, banks, and offices traditionally close from January 1 until January 3, a period during which people visit their friends, relatives, and superiors. Visits made during the first three days of the New Year are usually very brief, and they focus on relatives and superiors, as dictated by the rules of Japanese etiquette. Individuals of less importance may be visited anytime within the first two weeks.

Shogatsu means "standard month," a reference to the fact that the standards people set for their own behavior during the first few days of the year can influence their fortunes for the next twelve months. Businesses, clubs, and groups of friends get together and hold year-end parties, a good opportunity to promote good will and patch up any lingering quarrels or misunderstandings. All unfinished business is taken care of, debts are paid, and the house gets a thorough cleaning. The idea is to start the New Year with a clean slate.

The preparations for Oshogatsu are quite elaborate. They begin on the twenty-third day of the twelth month with the burning of the Kitchen God's effigy. The Kitchen God is a minor deity who lives with the family all year and sets out on the twenth-third day of the last month to file his annual report on the family's behavior, returning just before midnight on **NEW YEAR'S EVE** (*see* **CHINESE NEW YEAR**). The burning of his effigy releases the Kitchen God for his "ascent" to heaven. While he is gone, the house is cleaned. At one time, a symbolic house-cleaning was carried out with a green bamboo duster whose feathery twigs and leaves represented prosperity and good fortune. Nowadays, cleaning house includes recovering or replacing all tatami mats, repapering sliding doors and screens, and burning the old paper charms pasted up in the kitchen or bedroom and replacing them with new ones. There is an old Japanese saying that the New Year must be greeted with a swept garden, a mended roof, a new dress, a clean body, a clear conscience, and an honest purse (i.e., no debts).

The actual arrival of the New Year is announced by the ringing of BELLS in all the Buddhist temples. In the morning, *wakamizu* or "young water" is drawn from the well with a wooden bucket to ensure good health for the coming year. Family members rise early, wash in *wakamizu*, put on new clothing, and sit together at the table for the first meal of the year. *O-toso* or sweet, spiced wine is served before breakfast as a token of celebration, first to the youngest member of the family and last to the oldest. According to tradition, the family that drinks *o-toso* will have no sickness, for the drink has the power to destroy evil spirits and invigorate the human body. Pink and white rice cakes (*see* MOCHI) and many kinds of fruit are placed before the ancestral tablets in the family shrine. After the family feast is over, people toast each other and pay visits to their friends and relatives. Young girls and women play shuttlecock in long-sleeved kimonos, while men and boys fly kites and play with spinning tops.

Oshogatsu is believed to have evolved out of ancient Japanese rituals associated with seasonal changes, which were very important to farmers. The New Year celebration originally coincided with the **WINTER SOLSTICE**. It was believed that the dead visited the living at this time of year, and masked figures and troupes of dancers would go from house to house rattling bamboo sticks to scare off evil spirits. When the Western calendar was adopted in 1873, the New Year celebration was moved to January 1.

A number of special foods are served on Oshogatsu. The national dish of the New Year's festival is *o-zoni* (literally "boiled mixture"), a clear or bean-mash soup that might contain vegetables or bits of fish or chicken. Other foods served during the festival have symbolic value—for example, *kazu-no-ko* or herring roe ("many children"); *mame* or black beans ("good health"); *kachiguri* or hulled, baked chestnuts ("victory"); and *kombu* or kelp ("happiness").

SYMBOLS AND CUSTOMS

Bells

The arrival of the New Year is announced by ringing the bells in Buddhist temples 108 times. The ringing of the joya no kane or "end-of-year bell" is said to represent the leaving behind of 108 worldly concerns of the old year. Some say that ringing the bell purges the 108 weaknesses described by Buddha's teaching.

Camellia

The flower associated with the entire first month of the Japanese New Year is the tsubaki or camellia, which blossoms from December right through to March. A hardy perennial, it symbolizes a long and healthy life. But because the blossom can just as easily drop from its stem before the petals are withered, it also serves as a reminder of inconstancy. Among the warriors of feudal Japan, the camellia stood as a symbol of the Samurai's readiness to have his own head fall at the stroke of an enemy's sword.

Crane and Tortoise

Both the crane (*tsuru*) and the tortoise (*kame*) are symbols of longevity. Cranes made by folding paper in a square are hung in homes at Oshogatsu or placed on trays of food as symbols of good fortune and long life. Crane-inspired designs can also be found on dishes, containers, and other household articles used during the New Year's festival.

A common song sung at New Year's in the Tokyo area is based on an early poem written by a Zen priest: "Cranes have a life of a thousand years;/Tortoises have the joy of ten thousand years./May your life prosper and continue/Longer than the cranes, tortoises, and bamboo."

Daruma

The Daruma is a good-luck charm in the form of a doll. It takes its name from an Indian Buddhist priest named Bodhidharma, who sat facing a cliff in silent meditation for nine years. Because of this, he lost the use of his arms and legs. But he continued to travel throughout China, teaching people about Buddha. The Daruma doll therefore symbolizes inner strength and determination.

The Japanese purchase Daruma dolls during the New Year season in the hope that they will bring good fortune. Made of wood, clay, stone, or papier-mâché, the dolls have rounded bottoms, so that they'll return to an upright position if knocked over. They are usually painted red all over with the exception of the face. The eyes are very prominent and may be entirely black or white. The purchaser of the doll can then paint in the iris while making a wish. When the wish comes true, the other iris is painted in.

Dreams

According to Japanese belief, the first dream of the New Year (hatsuyume) foretells one's fate in the coming year. Someone who dreams about ships loaded with treasures will have a happy and prosperous year. Dreams about the rising sun are also symbolic of good fortune, as are dreams about sea voyages. Although dreams involving snakes and swords would not ordinarily be associated with good luck, on this particular night they indicate that wealth lies in store for the dreamer. Dreams about rain mean that worries can be expected, while dreams about moonlight mean that things will get better. Earthquake dreams foretell a change in residence, snow portends happiness, and ice signifies that an arranged marriage will take place.

Gifts

Oshogatsu is a popular time for gift-giving, particularly among adults. Servants are given new kimonos and pocket money, while all employees receive at least an extra month's salary. Typical gifts include eggs (symbolizing the wish for a well-rounded, complete life), fruit (especially round fruit, which represents good luck), and dried cuttlefish (symbolizing numerous offspring). Among casual acquaintances, typical gifts exchanged might include printed cotton towels, folding fans, or even a packet of matches. Unless the gift is a single object, it must be given in sets of three, five, or nine, which are the most auspicious numbers. Seven is considered an unlucky number, as are all even numbers with the exception of ten and, in some cases, two.

Oshogatsu gifts are usually wrapped in paper and string that is half red, half white—colors that represent the *yin* and *yang* principles of Chinese philosophy and together represent "completeness." The ceremonial string or *mizuhiki* might have originated as a rain-charm. Under it there is a square of red and white paper folded into the shape of a lozenge with a tiny piece of seaweed in the middle, meant to convey the idea that "This gift is but a seaweed in the ocean of your prosperity."

The gifts are opened after the caller has left. If a particular gift is found to be useless, or is too similar to something that the person already owns, a fresh piece of paper is wrapped around it, a new string is tied, and the package is passed on to somebody else.

Kadomatsu

First used in the seventeenth century, the *kadomatsu* is a decoration made from pine and bamboo that is placed at the front gate or on either side of the door to the house. It is put up at the start of the New Year season to ward off evil, promote growth and fertility, and bring blessings to the household. The pine (*matsu*) symbolizes constancy, morality, and the power to resist old age and adversity. Pine needles, which occur in pairs joined at the end, also symbolize married love and unity. Their sharp points are good for scaring off ghosts and evil spirits. The bamboo (*take*) symbolizes great strength under adversity, since it bends under a load of snow but springs back upright after shedding it. The bamboo is always cut on a slant so that any evil spirits will be snagged on its sharp points. Sometimes the fern (*shida*) is added to the arrangement to symbolize vigor and progeny.

Like Christmas wreaths, kadomatsu can be either very simple or quite elaborate. Although some houses have only a cluster of pine boughs, larger houses have far more elegant arrangements consisting of pine, bamboo, and plum blossoms—all cold-weather plants as well as symbols of congratulations and good luck. The kadomatsu is placed in front of the house to express the hope that the New Year will bring vigor, long life, and strength to everyone in the family. It is left in place until the seventh day, when only a sprig of pine remains as a reminder of the holiday that has passed and as an omen of the future. All decorations come down around January 14, when they are burned in a huge community bonfire. In rural areas, the kadomatsu is often thrown into a stream or river so that it will carry off any lingering sins or illnesses.

Nowadays the kadomatsu is not complete without an orange. A mandarin orange is often used, but it should really be a *daidai*, which grows into a real tree. The fruit matures in winter and, if left on the branch, becomes green again the following spring, making it an apt symbol of rebirth. The daidai's many pips represent offspring, and its color and shape resemble that of the sun. The daidai must never be eaten, since this would be symbolic of destroying prosperity. Sometimes the orange is accompanied by a boiled crayfish or *ebi* (prawn), a reference to the ancient Japanese saying, "May you grow so old that your back becomes bent like an ebi's!" And because the prawn turns red when it is boiled, it also symbolizes rebirth into a more prosperous future.

Manzai

Manzai are like Christmas carolers. Dressed in ancient costumes and wearing tall hats known as *eboshi,* the singers go from house to house during the New Year's season singing songs and beating their *tsuzumi* or hand drums. This custom originated more than 1,000 years ago, when artists from China danced and sang in the imperial court as a way of conveying the season's greetings. Most manzai today are professional groups who sing and dance in return for a nominal payment, although amateur manzai can often be found in rural areas.

The original manzai dancer was a semi-religious figure, called in by high-ranking noblemen to purify their houses by chanting good-luck songs. Then he evolved into an amusing beggar who sang and danced to the accompaniment of an hourglass-shaped drum shouting, *Manzai! Manzai!* meaning "ten thousand years!"—a good luck wish. The traditional manzai dancer wears a black-and-white striped hat with a red sun-disk on one side and a silver full moon on the other. His face is covered by a smiling mask, and he holds a folding fan that he uses to "blow in" good luck.

Mochi

Mochi or pounded rice cakes are a traditional part of the Japanese New Year celebration. They are made from steamed rice that has been pounded into a sticky paste and shaped into small round buns. In earlier times, families would get together to make their own mochi, and traveling *mochi tsuki* men would come around with their special pounding equipment. Although mechanized pounding machines have taken over the task in most areas, some rural families continue to make mochi from scratch.

A *sambo* or raised wooden tray holds the mochi, which are made somewhat larger than usual for New Year's. Because of their circular shape, with a flat bottom and slightly convex top, they are often compared to a mirror. *Kagami mochi* or "mirrored mochi" consist of a large rice cake surmounted by a smaller one and placed on clean white paper in the center of a *sambo* stand. They are a symbol of the hope for a brighter and happier new year. Rather than being eaten, the kagami mochi stand in the alcove or household shrine as an offering to the gods. On January 11, they are removed from the alcove and, if they're not too hard, are cut up and served to family members.

Sometimes *kagami mochi* are embellished with other New Year's symbols: the fern for progeny; seaweed for joy; the lobster or prawn for longevity; the persimmon for fecundity and a happy family; and the daidai (*see* KADOMATSU), a type of orange symbolizing many generations.

The custom of eating mochi at New Year's goes back to the early ninth century, when it was widely believed that for each mochi a person ate, one year would be added to his or her age.

Narcissus

The *suisen* or narcissus is a symbol of purity and fertility (sui means "water") and of the life that lies beneath the frozen snow. It was the holy flower of the temple for the Hindus, and some of the Indian lore attached to it may have reached Japan via Buddhism. Because the narcissus blooms right around New Year's Day, it has always been associated with luck in the coming year. A spray of narcissus wrapped in folded paper and tied with a red and white string (*see* GIFTS) is a special emblem of the Oshogatsu festival.

Plum Bough

The blossoming plum tree (*ume*) is considered a symbol of feminine beauty, charm, and chastity—the counterpart of the masculine pine. Because the plum blossoms while the ground is still covered with snow, it is also a symbol of courage.

The arrangement of pine, bamboo, and plum known as *shochikubai* appears frequently in Japanese art. It represents the beginning of a new year and the wish for happiness and fulfilled hopes. If the season is advanced enough, a plum bough may be added to the vase of pine branches in the entrance hall and main room during the Oshogatsu festival.

Rake

One of the most popular objects purchased during Oshogatsu is a rake covered in trinkets. It stands as a symbol of "raking in" good fortune and prosperity during the New Year season.

Shimenawa or Shimekazari

The *shimenawa* or rice-straw rope is one of the most important household decorations during the New Year's festival. It is hung over the front and back doors, barn door, around the well, and up over the roof or under the eaves to bring good luck and keep out evil. The use of the shimenawa can be traced back to an old myth about Amaterasu-omikami, the Sun Goddess. After being abused by her brother, the goddess withdrew into a rocky cave and refused to come out and shine. The world was plunged into darkness. To draw her out, the other gods and goddesses staged a dance and played music. When she came out of the cave to see where the music was coming from, they stretched a rice-straw rope across the entrance so she couldn't go back in. For hundreds of years, the shimenawa has been used to designate the boundaries of a sacred area, whether it be a shrine, a temple, a tree, or a home. It stands as a reminder that the place is sanctified and free of evil spirits.

The wisps of straw that are twisted into the rope are designed to prick intruders or demons, who are very susceptible to being hurt by sharp things. Other symbolic objects may be woven into the shimenawa or attached to it, such as fern-fronds (symbolic of expanding good fortune), a small orange (the word for which in Japanese sounds the same as the word meaning "generation to generation"), or a section of lobster (symbolizing old age because of its bent back). Some scholars theorize that the shimenawa is related to the sheaves of corn hung up in European homes and barns as a charm protecting the crops from disease.

Sometimes the shimenawa is twisted into a knot like a pretzel—knots and loops having magical powers in Japanese mythology. The name for this ornament is *shimekazari*. Shimekazari charms are hung up near every entrance and on the walls of stables and warehouses to bring prosperity and good luck.

Unlike a normal rope, the shimenawa is twisted from right to left. In Japan, anything done in reverse is considered good magic. While the shimenawa is used locally at all Shinto festivals, either draped around a shrine or to festoon the streets, only at Oshogatsu is it used in the home.

Utagaruta

A traditional pastime among young people in Japan around this time of year is utagaruta, an unusual game based on the work of Fujiwara Sadaie, a poet who died in 1242. He collected what he considered to be the best poems of his time and published them as "Single Songs of a Hundred Poets." In the game of utagaruta, these poems are divided into two sets, each set having one half of each poem. The object of the game is to find the matching halves and put them together as quickly as possible. Expert players are able to find a match almost as soon as the first syllable of the poem has been read. Sometimes utagaruta games are broadcast on the radio.

FURTHER READING

Araki, Nancy K., and Jane M. Horii. *Matsuri Festival: Japanese-American Celebrations and Activities*. San Francisco: Heian International Pub. Co., 1978.

Bauer, Helen, and Sherwin Carlquist. *Japanese Festivals*. Garden City, NY: Doubleday, 1965.

Casal, U. A. *The Five Sacred Festivals of Ancient Japan*. Rutland, VA: Sophia University in cooperation with Tuttle, 1967.

Dobler, Lavinia G. *Customs and Holidays Around the World*. New York: Fleet Pub. Corp., 1962.

Heinberg, Richard. *Celebrate the Solstice: Honoring the Earth's Seasonal Rhythms through Festival and Ceremony*. Wheaton, IL: Quest Books, 1993.

Henderson, Helene, ed. *Holidays, Festivals, and Celebrations of the World Dictionary*. 3rd ed. Detroit: Omnigraphics, 2005.

Ickis, Marguerite. *The Book of Festivals and Holidays the World Over*. New York: Dodd, Mead, 1970.

Purdy, Susan. *Festivals for You to Celebrate*. Philadelphia: Lippincott, 1969.

WEB SITES

BBC (British Broadcasting Corporation)
www.bbc.co.uk/religion/religions/shinto/holydays/oshogatsu.shtml

Family Culture
www.familyculture.com/holidays/japanese_new_year.htm

Our Lady of Guadalupe, Fiesta of

Type of Holiday: Religious (Roman Catholic)
Date of Observation: December 12
Where Celebrated: Mexico City, Mexico
Symbols and Customs: Dark Madonna, "Las Mañanitas," Matachin Dance, Roses, Tilma

ORIGINS

The celebration in honor of Our Lady of Guadalupe, also known as the DARK MADONNA, is a Christian festival that is held in Mexico City each year on December 12. The word Christian refers to a follower of Christ, a title derived from the Greek word meaning Messiah or Anointed One. The Christ of Christianity is Jesus of Nazareth, a man born between 7 and 4 B.C.E. in the region of Palestine. According to Christian teaching, Jesus was killed by Roman authorities using a form of execution called crucifixion (a term meaning he was nailed to a cross and hung from it until he died) in about the year 30 C.E. After his death, he rose back to life. His death and resurrection provide a way by which people can be reconciled with God. In remembrance of Jesus' death and resurrection, the cross serves as a fundamental symbol in Christianity.

With nearly two billion believers in countries around the globe, Christianity is the largest of the world's religions. There is no one central authority for all of Christianity. The pope (the bishop of Rome) is the authority for the Roman Catholic Church, but other sects look to other authorities. Orthodox communities look to patriarchs and emphasize doctrinal agreement and traditional practice. Protestant communities focus on individual conscience. The Roman Catholic and Protestant

churches are often referred to as the Western Church, while the Orthodox churches may also be called the Eastern Church. All three main branches of Christianity acknowledge the authority of Christian scriptures, a compilation of writings assembled into a document called the Bible. Methods of biblical interpretation vary among the different Christian sects.

The Fiesta of Our Lady of Guadalupe dates back to 1531, just ten years after Hernando Cortez, the Spanish conquistador, overthrew Tenochtitlan, the capital city of the Aztec Indian empire. That was also only a few years after the first Christian missionaries arrived there. An Aztec Indian who had just recently been converted to Christianity was walking through the dry, rugged hills just north of the newly renamed capital, Mexico City, on his way to church when he passed a hill called Tepeyac, where a temple dedicated to the Aztec earth goddess had once stood. Suddenly he heard music, and the Virgin Mary appeared and called him by his Christian name, Juan Diego. She instructed him to go to the bishop of Mexico and tell him to build a church on the same site where the Aztecs had worshipped their goddess. The bishop thought Juan Diego had fabricated his story and refused to take him seriously. The Virgin appeared to Juan Diego again the next day, and he dutifully made another appeal to the bishop, who told him to go away and not to return until he could present proof of this divine request.

When Juan Diego encountered the Virgin a third time on December 12, 1531, she told him to pick some of the ROSES that were growing nearby—roses that were in full bloom despite the fact that it was winter—and bring them to the bishop. Diego gathered them in his TILMA or cloak and opened it in front of the bishop, who immediately recognized the red Castillian roses that grew only in his homeland, Spain. What's more, he saw imprinted on the tilma the image of a beautiful dark-skinned woman, dressed in clothing that made her pregnancy unmistakable, framed by the rays of the sun. The bishop immediately knew that this was a sign from God and that Diego was telling the truth. A shrine was built on the site, and it was named "Guadalupe" for two reasons. First, the Virgin had identified herself as the "ever-virgin Holy Mary coatlaxopeuh"—a Nahuatl word for "who crushes the serpent"—and the Spanish religious officials had misunderstood the word, which is pronounced kwat-la-supe. Second, Guadalupe was the name of a village in Spain where a similar miracle had occurred. The Basilica of Guadalupe was built near this same site in the early eighteenth century.

Today, thousands of pilgrims flock to the Basilica—many of them walking on their knees—to participate in a special Mass and to see the image of Our Lady that has been miraculously preserved since it first appeared on Juan Diego's cloak more than 450 years ago. There are processions through the streets, with people in traditional Mexican dress carrying red roses or poinsettias, and it is a popular time for the performance of the MATACHIN dance and the singing of the traditional Mexican folk song known as "LAS MAÑANITAS." Although the largest celebration is held in Mexico City, there are fiestas in honor of the Virgin of Guadalupe all over Mexico on December 12 as well as in areas of the southwestern United States where the Spanish influence remains strong. It is said that only the French shrine at Lourdes attracts as many pilgrims as the Basilica of Guadalupe.

SYMBOLS AND CUSTOMS

Dark Madonna

The image of the dark-skinned Virgin who appeared to Juan Diego in 1531 and who can still be seen on his TILMA wears a blue-green outer cloak covered with stars, supposedly in the same configuration as they appeared in the sky that night. She is surrounded by the rays of the sun, symbolic of the fact that Christianity superseded the worship of the Aztec sun god, and she is standing on a crescent moon. She also has a black sash around her waist, which is something that pregnant women wore in sixteenth-century Mexico. In the shapes formed by the reflections in her eyes, scientists have found the profiles of as many as eighteen different people, one of whom is believed to be Juan Diego.

The Dark Madonna remains not only a symbol of Mexican Christianity but of Mexican nationalism. With her coppery skin and Indian features, she symbolizes the pride of the indigenous Mexican people, who were forced to give up their gods and rituals when the light-skinned Europeans arrived.

"Las Mañanitas"

It is popular, particularly for children, to sing the folk song known as "Las Mañanitas" at the Fiesta of Our Lady of Guadalupe. It is both a morning song and a birthday song, used to greet people and to honor the Virgin Mary on her special day.

Matachin Dance

The Matachin dance-drama, which is still performed on this day in Mexican villages and in the Indian pueblos of the southwestern United States, originally reenacted the conflict between the Moors and the Christians (see **MOORS AND CHRISTIANS FIESTA**). The Spanish brought it to Mexico and used it to dramatize the arrival of Catholicism there. Although Matachin dances vary from one location to another, there are certain standard characters who always appear. They include La Malinche, who stands for innocence and is usually played by a young girl; El Toro, the bull, who is killed; El Abuelo, a clown-like figure; and El Monarca, the leader of the dance. A central feature of the performance is La Transa (the Braids), in which the dancers weave ribbons around a maypole.

The Matachin dancers wear colorful outfits and tall headdresses, with handkerchiefs or fringes partially concealing their faces. The music is provided by a violin and a guitar, and the dancers keep time by shaking gourd rattles. The dance represents an unusual merging of European music with Native American movements.

Roses

The red roses that Juan Diego gathered to prove to the bishop that he had really seen the Virgin Mary were miraculous on two counts: No roses at all—let alone the red Castillian variety (from Castile in central Spain)—were native to Mexico, and surely none would be blooming on such inhospitable ground in early December. Although several varieties of roses were eventually introduced by the Spanish colonists, they were a rarity in Mexico in the early sixteenth century.

Today, roses and poinsettias, which traditionally bloom in December, are carried in the processions that take place at the Fiesta of Our Lady of Guadalupe as a symbol of the Virgin's miraculous appearance to Juan Diego in 1531.

Tilma

The tilma on which the Dark Madonna's image appears is a simple handmade cape or cloak with a seam running down the center whose fabric is made from the tropical plant known as agave, which is a succulent similar to cactus. Such a fabric would normally be expected to last no more than twenty years, but Juan Diego's tilma has remained intact despite being repeatedly touched for many years, on display for centuries thereafter, and, at one point, having nitric acid spilled all over it. As far as the authenticity of the image is concerned, scientists who have examined the tilma have never been able to find any evidence of ink or paint, which would suggest that the image had been deliberately drawn or painted by someone.

FURTHER READING

Christianson, Stephen G., and Jane M. Hatch. *The American Book of Days*. 4th ed. New York: H.W. Wilson, 2000.

Cohen, Hennig, and Tristram Potter Coffin. *The Folklore of American Holidays*. 3rd ed. Detroit: Gale Research, 1999.

Harper, Howard V. *Days and Customs of All Faiths*. 1957. Reprint. Detroit: Omnigraphics, 1990.

Haven, Kendall. *New Year's to Kwanzaa: Original Stories of Celebration*. Golden, CO: Fulcrum Resources, 1999.

MacDonald, Margaret R., ed. *The Folklore of World Holidays*. Detroit: Gale Research, 1992.

Merin, Jennifer, and Elizabeth B. Burdick. *International Directory of Theatre, Dance, and Folklore Festivals*. Westport, CT: Greenwood Press, 1979.

Spicer, Dorothy Gladys. *The Book of Festivals*. 1937. Reprint. Detroit: Omnigraphics, 1990.

WEB SITES

Inside Mexico
www.inside-mexico.com/guadalupe.htm

Mexico Connect
www.mexconnect.com/mex_/guadalupe.html
www.mexconnect.com/ mex_/travel/ldumois/ldguadalupe.html

Palio, Festival of the

Type of Holiday: Sporting
Date of Observation: July 2, August 16
Where Celebrated: Siena, Italy
Symbols and Customs: Masgalano, Pacifier, Palio, Partiti, Rincorsa, Tratta

ORIGINS

The horse race known as the Palio has been run in one form or another since the thirteenth century, and it has been run twice annually for more than 340 years. It is a combination of theater, religious ritual, and athletic competition that takes place in Siena, Italy, every July and August, when ten horses representing the city's *contrade* or districts run three laps around the perimeter of the fan-shaped Piazza del Campo. The winning contrada takes home the PALIO, which is also the name of the silk banner symbolizing victory in the centuries-old race.

There are actually seventeen contrade in Siena, but only ten get to race because there simply isn't room for more horses on the track, which is only twenty yards wide and involves two hazardous ninety-degree turns. Three days before the race, the horses that will compete are selected by the *Capitanos*, who are the individuals in charge of organizing each district's challenge for the Palio (*see* TRATTA). The jockeys are usually mercenaries hired from outside the city—individuals who can be bribed by rival contrade and by each other to obstruct their opponents, hold them back by grabbing their jackets, or push them off course. Rivalry among the contrade runs deep, and there are no rules that prevent the race captains—chosen by their contrada to devise a winning strategy—from doing whatever it takes to better their chances of winning (*see* PARTITI).

The race itself is preceded by four days of elimination heats. Then, about two hours before the start, there is a magnificent procession around the race course. Each contrada has its own drummers and flag-throwers (who can hurl their flags three or four stories into the air) dressed in medieval costumes whose colors symbolize the district they represent. They are followed by the horses with their jockeys, who have already been blessed at the altar of their neighborhood churches.

It is the tenth horse or RINCORSA who actually signals the beginning of the race. It takes less than two minutes to run three laps (slightly more than a kilometer) around the Piazza del Campo, but what goes on during those two minutes is a wild spectacle unlike any other horse race in the world. The jockeys ride bareback and carry whips that they use on their own and each other's horses. They wear high-top sneakers and splash water on the insides of their pant legs for a better grip, but falling off is a common occurrence. Negotiating the two right-angle turns is so dangerous that mattresses are strapped along the outside. Horses crash into them so frequently that "going to the mattresses" has become a common Sienese expression when something falls apart or goes off course. Even a riderless horse can win the race, provided that its head ornament bearing the colors of the contrada is still in place.

In recent years, animal rights groups have objected to the Palio's brutality. Horses are often drugged to improve their performance and, in the course of their run, they are sometimes crippled. But given the fact that more than 60,000 spectators routinely crowd the stands that are erected around the track, hang out the windows and balconies of the surrounding buildings, and jam the center of the piazza just to catch a glimpse of the action, it seems unlikely that Siena's greatest festival would be discontinued.

SYMBOLS AND CUSTOMS

Masgalano

Fastened at the top of the banner known as the PALIO is the Masgalano (from the Spanish for "best-looking"), an embossed silver plate. It is awarded to the best dressed and best coordinated comparsa, which is the costumed group that represents each contrada in the parade that precedes the race.

Pacifier

An unusual and fairly recent symbol of Siena's devotion to the Virgin Mary, whose image appears on the PALIO itself, is a child's pacifier. During the period of the race, many Sienese can be seen sucking on pacifiers or wearing them tied in the scarves

Siena's Contrade

Names and Translations of the Seventeen Contrade:

Aquila – Eagle

Bruco – Caterpillar

Chiocciola – Snail

Civetta – Owl

Drago – Dragon

Giraffa – Giraffe

Istrice – Porcupine

Leocorno – Unicorn

Lupa – She-Wolf

Montone – Ram

Nicchio – Shell

Oca – Goose

Onda – Wave

Pantera – Panther

Selva – Forest

Tartuca – Tortoise

Torre – Tower

they wear to represent the colors of their contrada. Some even tie baby bottles filled with wine around their necks so they can celebrate whenever they feel like it. These childish objects are symbolic not only of their relationship to the Holy Mother but to the contrada whose loyal sons and daughters they are.

Palio

A painted silk or heavy canvas banner mounted vertically on a long black staff, the Palio is a symbol of victory in the competition that bears its name. Because the banner is often subjected to rough treatment—particularly before the race, when it is brought to the church of Provenzano to be blessed and is occasionally damaged by the pages who try to touch it with their sharp-pointed flags for good luck—a new Palio is painted for each race by a prominent Italian artist.

The Palio depicts the Virgin Mary and is drawn around the track by four white oxen during the procession before the race. After the race is over, the banner and members of the winning contrada head up the hill to the town's thirteenth-century cathedral, where it is hung above the altar while the winning jockey kneels and offers a prayer of thanks.

Partiti

A *partito* is a secret agreement between the captains of two different contrade concerning the course of the race. Although each contrada has a traditional enemy within the group, which never changes, alliances and counter-alliances with other contrade may be negotiated by the race captains.

Every night for a week before the Palio, the Capitanos and their lieutenants are busy cutting deals (*partiti*). A contrada that has not drawn a good horse, for example, might swap its jockey with another contrada so that a third contrada can be beaten—in return for which the captain of the winning contrada will give the other a sum of money. Only two rules govern this behind-the-scenes wheeling and dealing: One cannot make a partito with one's historical enemy, and only the winner pays. It has been estimated that mounting a successful campaign to win the Palio can cost a contrada more than $500,000.

Rincorsa

The rules for starting the race are the same as those used during the elimination heats. The first nine jockeys position their horses between two starting-ropes, trying to keep an appropriate distance from their competitors. Then the tenth horse, known as the *rincorsa*, comes from behind at a full gallop, and the moment he reaches the first rope, it is dropped and the race begins. The tenth jockey is alerted by the starter when the other nine have arranged themselves in a suitable line-up and can choose the moment at which his horse enters.

The start of the Palio is usually a lot more chaotic than it sounds. The jockeys try to guess the exact moment at which the rope will be lowered, and they kick their horses in the flanks to get them ready to set off. False starts are common and can be dangerous, especially if the starter isn't quick to lower the rope and prevent the horses from colliding with it.

Tratta

The ritual known as *tratta* (drawing lots for horses) takes place in the Piazza del Campo on the morning of the third day before the race. Anyone who owns a horse can present it as a potential competitor; the horses are examined by a veterinarian and, if selected, turned over to the contrade for the trial races.

Once the heats are over and the animals have been examined one more time by the vet, they are presented individually to the Capitanos, who vote on which horses will actually participate in the final race. A horse is as likely to be rejected for its obvious superiority as for its lack of speed; because the Capitanos must choose ten horses without knowing to whom they will be assigned, they tend to select those with more or less equal qualifications. The voting is open unless one or more of the captains requests that it be carried out in secret. A secret vote is held according to an old Sienese custom where black (signifying "No") and white (signifying "Yes") balls are held in a closed fist and placed inside a silver urn.

FURTHER READING

Falassi, Alessandro, and Giuliano Catoni. *Palio*. Milan: Electa, 1983.

Henderson, Helene, ed. *Holidays, Festivals, and Celebrations of the World Dictionary*. 3rd ed. Detroit: Omnigraphics, 2005.

Shemanski, Frances. *A Guide to World Fairs and Festivals*. Westport, CT: Greenwood Press, 1985.

Spicer, Dorothy Gladys. *Festivals of Western Europe*. 1958. Reprint. Detroit: Omnigraphics, 1993.

Spicer, Dorothy Gladys. *The Book of Festivals*. 1937. Reprint. Detroit: Omnigraphics, 1990.

Trawicky, Bernard, and Ruth W. Gregory. *Anniversaries and Holidays*. 5th ed. Chicago: American Library Assocation, 2000.

Van Straalen, Alice. *The Book of Holidays Around the World*. New York: Dutton, 1986.

WEB SITE

Comune of Siena Official Web Site
www.comune.siena.it/contenuti/palio/inglese/index_ingl.htm

Palm Sunday (Passion Sunday)

Type of Holiday: Religious (Christian)

Date of Observation: Between March 15 and April 18 in the West; between March 28 and May 1 in the East; the Sunday preceding Easter

Where Celebrated: British Isles, Europe, United States, Mexico, Latin America, Scandinavia, and by Christians all over the world

Symbols and Customs: Palm Branches

Colors: Purple or violet is used throughout Holy Week to symbolize the passion or suffering of Christ.

Related Holidays: Ash Wednesday, Easter, Good Friday, Lent, Maundy Thursday

ORIGINS

Palm Sunday is a Chistian holiday that celebrates Jesus' return to Jerusalem. The word Christian refers to a follower of Christ, a title derived from the Greek word meaning Messiah or Anointed One. The Christ of Christianity is Jesus of Nazareth, a man born between 7 and 4 B.C.E. in the region of Palestine. According to Christian teaching, Jesus was killed by Roman authorities using a form of execution called crucifixion (a term meaning he was nailed to a cross and hung from it until he died) in about the year 30 C.E. After his death, he rose back to life. His death and resurrection provide a way by which people can be reconciled with God. In remembrance of Jesus' death and resurrection, the cross serves as a fundamental symbol in Christianity.

With nearly two billion believers in countries around the globe, Christianity is the largest of the world's religions. There is no one central authority for all of Christianity. The pope (the bishop of Rome) is the authority for the Roman Catholic Church, but other sects look to other authorities. Orthodox communities look to patriarchs and emphasize doctrinal agreement and traditional practice. Protestant communities focus on individual conscience. The Roman Catholic and Protestant churches are often referred to as the Western Church, while the Orthodox churches may also be called the Eastern Church. All three main branches of Christianity acknowledge the authority of Christian scriptures, a compilation of writings assembled into a document called the Bible. Methods of biblical interpretation vary among the different Christian sects.

Palm Sunday commemorates the triumphant return of Jesus Christ to Jerusalem, where he received a hero's welcome from the people who had heard about the miracles he'd performed and regarded him as the leader who would deliver them from the domination of the Roman Empire. He rode into the city on an ass, and the people greeted him by waving PALM BRANCHES and strewing them in his path, shouting, "Hosanna: Blessed is the King of Israel that cometh in the name of the Lord" (John 12: 12, 13).

Although Jesus entered Jerusalem in triumph, later events proved that his popularity was largely superficial. The city was already filled with holiday pilgrims because it was the Jewish feast of **PASSOVER**, and it is likely that Jesus deliberately chose this time so that his final showdown with the Jewish authorities would take place in front of as many people as possible. The happy crowd of pilgrims, many of whom probably knew Jesus as a popular rabbi, made a special event of his arrival, cheering and throwing down palm branches for him to ride over.

As a Christian observance, Palm Sunday dates back to the tenth century. But the persistence of ancient folk beliefs about the power of palm branches would seem to indicate a link with much earlier celebrations. At one time it was customary to use a wooden ass mounted on wheels with a human figure riding on it to represent Jesus. As soon as the ass passed over the willow or palm branches that had been strewn on the ground, people would rush to gather them up because they were regarded as protection against storms and lightning. Crosses made of woven palm were a popular charm against disease.

Probably the greatest present-day observance of Palm Sunday takes place in Rome, where the Pope, carried in St. Peter's Chair on the shoulders of eight men, comes out of St. Peter's Basilica to bless the palms. After the service, golden palm branches are distributed among the clergy and olive branches, a symbol of spiritual anointing, are given to the congregation. Then the thousands of worshippers who have gathered in St. Peter's Square march through the basilica and around the portico, emerging from one door and reentering through another to symbolize the entry of Jesus into Jerusalem. Some of the palm branches are saved and later burned to make ashes for the following year's **ASH WEDNESDAY**.

SYMBOLS AND CUSTOMS

Palm Branches

The palm branch is a symbol of victory and a sign of reverence. In Europe, where palm branches are hard to find, branches of box, yew, or willow are often carried in procession on Palm Sunday to commemorate Jesus' triumphant entry into Jerusalem.

After the Reformation in the sixteenth century, Henry VII declared that carrying palms on Palm Sunday was a custom that should be maintained. By the nineteenth century in many parts of England, it was customary for young people to go "a-palming" on the Saturday before Palm Sunday—in other words, to go into the woods and gather willow twigs (in the absence of palms) and return with armloads of cuttings as well as sprigs of willow in their hats or buttonholes. Like the palm branches, the willow cuttings were collected and burned, and the ashes were set aside for the following **ASH WEDNESDAY**.

The belief that palm branches offered protection from disease and natural disasters can still be seen in the customs of some European countries. In Austria and the Bavarian region of Germany, for example, farmers make *Palmbuschen* by attaching holly leaves, willow boughs, and cedar twigs to the top of long poles. After these have been blessed in the local church on Palm Sunday, farmers set them up in their fields or barns to ward off illness and to protect their crops from hail and drought.

In the Netherlands, the *Palmpaas* is a stick to which a hoop has been attached. The hoop is covered with boxwood and decorated with paper flags, eggshells, sugar rings, oranges, figs, raisins, and chocolate eggs. Sometimes there is a figure of a swan or a cock on the top, made from baked dough. It is generally believed that the Palmpaas was originally a fertility symbol representing the arrival of spring and the resurgence of life after the long winter.

On Palm Sunday in Italy, the piazzas in front of most small churches are filled with people dressed up in new spring clothes and with vendors selling olive and palm branches. The olive branches may be gilded or painted silver, and the palms are often braided into crosses and decorated with roses, lilies, or other flowers. After the palms have been blessed in the church, they are often exchanged as peace offerings or as a sign of reconciliation between those who have quarreled.

In Czechoslovakia, the priests bless pussy willows. Farmers wave the willow branches over their fields of grain to protect them from hail or violent rainstorms. Sometimes pussy willow branches are placed on the roof to protect the house from fire.

FURTHER READING

Bellenir, Karen. *Religious Holidays and Calendars*. 3rd ed. Detroit: Omnigraphics, 2004.

Chambers, Robert. *The Book of Days*. 2 vols. 1862-64. Reprint. Detroit: Omnigraphics, 1990.

Dobler, Lavinia G. *Customs and Holidays Around the World*. New York: Fleet Pub. Corp., 1962.

Gulevich, Tanya. *Encyclopedia of Easter, Carnival, and Lent*. Detroit: Omnigraphics, 2002.

Harper, Howard V. *Days and Customs of All Faiths*. 1957. Reprint. Detroit: Omnigraphics, 1990.

Henderson, Helene, ed. *Holidays, Festivals, and Celebrations of the World Dictionary*. 3rd ed. Detroit: Omnigraphics, 2005.

Ickis, Marguerite. *The Book of Festivals and Holidays the World Over*. New York: Dodd, Mead, 1970.

Metford, J.C.J. *The Christian Year*. New York: Crossroad, 1991.

Monks, James L. *Great Catholic Festivals*. New York: Henry Schuman, 1951.

Pike, Royston. *Round the Year with the World's Religions*. 1950. Reprint. Detroit: Omnigraphics, 1992.

Santino, Jack. *All Around the Year: Holidays and Celebrations in American Life*. Urbana: University of Illinois Press, 1994.

WEB SITES

Greek Orthodox Archdiocese of America
lent.goarch.org/palm_sunday/learn

New Advent Catholic Encyclopedia
www.newadvent.org/cathen/11432b.htm

Parilia

Type of Holiday: Ancient
Date of Observation: April 21
Where Celebrated: Rome, Italy
Symbols and Customs: Bonfires, Foliage, Laurel, Olive
Related Holidays: Beltane, May Day, Midsummer Day, October Horse Sacrifice, St. George's Day

ORIGINS

The Parilia was a festival in the ancient Roman religion, which scholards date to the sixth century B.C.E. Roman religion dominated Rome and influenced territories in its empire until Emperor Constantine's conversion to Christianity in the third century C.E. Ancient Roman religion was heavily influenced by the older Greek religion. Roman festivals therefore had much in common with those of the ancient Greeks. Not only were their gods and goddesses mostly the same as those in the Greek pantheon (though the Romans renamed them), but their religious festivals were observed with similar activities: ritual sacrifice, theatrical performances, games, and feasts.

The Parilia was a Roman agricultural festival designed to purify and protect the flocks. Pales was the protector of shepherds and their sheep, an ancient god usually regarded as male, but sometimes as female. Shepherds would pray to Pales for forgiveness if they or their sheep had unwittingly trespassed on sacred ground and frightened the woodland deities, or if they disturbed the sacred fountains or cut the branches of sacred trees. They would also pray to Pales that their sheep be kept free of disease and not fall prey to wolves or dogs, that the rainfall and vegetation would be plentiful, that many lambs would be born, and that their wool would be thick and soft. They prepared for the Parilia by cleaning and sweeping out their folds with brooms made of LAUREL twigs, by decorating their stalls with FOLIAGE and green boughs, and by hanging wreaths over the entrances. Sometimes they would burn sulphur along with OLIVE wood, laurel, and rosemary, with the smoke passing through their sheepfolds and cattle sheds to purify their flocks and herds. Or they would drive their beasts through BONFIRES, then jump over the flames themselves three times to ensure the welfare of their flocks—a practice that was common throughout Europe on **EASTER**, **MAY DAY**, and **MIDSUMMER DAY**. The blood that had been preserved from the **OCTOBER HORSE SACRIFICE** six months earlier was burned, as were bean shells and the ashes of the cattle sacrificed at the Fordicidia, the April 15 fertility festival in which unborn calves were torn from their mothers' wombs and burned. The festival would end with an open-air feast.

The Parilia was one of the oldest Roman festivals. One of the reasons why the festival remained so popular is that it fell on the day widely regarded as the birthday of the city of Rome, which was founded in 753 B.C.E. A public holiday known as the *Natalis urbis Romae* (birthday of the city of Rome) was observed with music, street dancing, and general revelry. **ST. GEORGE'S DAY,** which is believed to have been the medieval counterpart of the ancient Parilia, was also observed with revelry and dancing in the streets in honor of England's patron saint. But both of these observances had their roots in ancient fertility and purification rites involving turning the herds and flocks out to new pastures.

SYMBOLS AND CUSTOMS

Bonfires

As a symbol of the sun, fire—in the form of bonfires, torches, burning embers, and even ashes—was believed to be capable of stimulating the growth of crops as well as the health and vigor of humans and animals. Ancient festivals observed, like the Parilia, with fire were designed to ensure the continued supply of light and heat from the sun as well as purification and the destruction of evil. As a symbol, fire combines both positive elements (heat, light) as well as negative (destruction, conflagration). To pass through the fire, as celebrants at the Parilia would do, symbolized transcending the human condition. Driving flocks through a bonfire was a well-known purification rite in ancient times, familiar from the celebration of **BELTANE** in Scotland and Ireland on May 1.

According to legend, Romulus, the founder of Rome, played a significant role in conducting the purification rituals of the Parilia. This is probably why April 21 was set aside not only to honor the pastoral god Pales, but also the founding of Rome.

Foliage

The custom of decorating the enclosures where sheep and cattle were kept with green boughs and wreaths at the Parilia probably descended from the primitive rites used by ancient peoples to influence the gods of vegetation. It is still common to decorate houses by bringing leaves and branches indoors at certain special seasons— among them **MAY DAY, MIDSUMMER DAY**, the harvest, and **CHRISTMAS**.

Laurel

Laurel leaves were prized not only for their medicinal properties but also for their ability to cleanse the soul of guilt. In ancient Rome, laurel was believed to possess the power to purge those who had shed the blood of others, and according to legend, laurel was the one tree that was never struck by lightning. By using brooms made of laurel twigs to sweep out their sheep folds, the shepherds were carrying out a symbolic purification that would guarantee the health and safety of their sheep.

Olive

For the Romans, the olive tree was associated with Pax, the goddess of peace. A messenger asking for peace or asylum often carried olive branches wrapped in wool, and wreaths made of olive or LAUREL were often used to crown the victors in military battles. As one of the ingredients in the purifying fires used on the Parilia to cleanse sheep folds and cattle stalls, olive wood was intended to protect the animals from danger and disease.

FURTHER READING

Biedermann, Hans. *Dictionary of Symbolism: Cultural Icons and the Meanings Behind Them*. New York: Meridian Books, 1994.

Christianson, Stephen G., and Jane M. Hatch. *The American Book of Days*. 4th ed. New York: H.W. Wilson, 2000.

Cirlot, J.E. *A Dictionary of Symbols*. New York: Philosophical Library, 1962.

Fowler, W. Warde. *The Roman Festivals of the Period of the Republic*. New York: Macmillan Co., 1925.

Frazer, Sir James G. *The Golden Bough: A Study in Magic and Religion*. New York: Macmillan, 1931.

Henderson, Helene, ed. *Holidays, Festivals, and Celebrations of the World Dictionary*. 3rd ed. Detroit: Omnigraphics, 2005.

James, E.O. *Seasonal Feasts and Festivals*. 1961. Reprint. Detroit: Omnigraphics, 1993.

Olderr, Steven. *Symbolism: A Comprehensive Dictionary*. Jefferson, NC: McFarland, 1986.

Scullard, H.H. *Festivals and Ceremonies of the Roman Republic*. Ithaca, NY: Cornell University Press, 1981.

Paro Tsechu

Type of Holiday: Religious (Buddhist)
Date of Observation: Early spring; tenth through fifteenth day of second month of Buddhist lunar calendar
Where Celebrated: Paro, Bhutan
Symbols and Customs: Cham, Thongdrel

ORIGINS

Paro Tsechu is one of the festivals of Buddhism, one of the four largest religious families in the world. It is based on the teachings of Siddhartha Gautama (c. 563-483 B.C.E.), who came to be known as Buddha, or "The Enlightened One." The basic tenets of Buddhism can be summarized in the Four Noble Truths and the Eightfold Path. The Four Noble Truths are 1) the truth and reality of suffering; 2) suffering is caused by desire; 3) the way to end suffering is to end desire; and 4) the Eightfold Path shows the way to end suffering. The Eightfold Path consists of 1) right view or right understanding; 2) right thoughts and aspirations; 3) right speech; 4) right conduct and action; 5) right way of life; 6) right effort; 7) right mindfulness; and 8) right contemplation.

One of the most popular festivals of Bhutan, a principality northeast of India in the Himalaya Mountains, is held in the town of Paro. *Tsechu* means "tenth day" and refers to the birth of the Buddha. It is also used in much the same way as "festival" is used in English.

The Paro festival commemorates the life and deeds of Padmasambhava. Known in Bhutan as Guru Rimpoche, he was a mystic who brought Buddhism to Bhutan from Tibet. The purpose of the festival is to exorcise evil influences and to ensure good fortune in the coming year. The highlight of the five-day festival occurs before dawn on the final day, when a huge appliqued scroll known as the THONG-DREL is displayed at the local administrative and religious center known as the Dzong.

Dressed in their best clothes, people bring dried yak meat and *churra*, a puffed rice dish, to the Dzong, where they watch masked dancers perform (*see* CHAM). Other festival activities include folk dancing and singing, and performances by clowns called *atsaras*. Many of the dances and performances associated with Paro Tsechu are typical of Buddhist traditions observed in Tibet and the Ladakh area of India.

SYMBOLS AND CUSTOMS

Cham

A series of dances called cham are performed for the festival. One of these, the Black Hat Dance, tells of the victory over a Tibetan king who tried to stamp out Buddhism. The Dance of the Four Stags commemorates the defeat of the god of the wind by Guru Rimpoche. Yet another dance, known as the Deer Dance, tells the story of how Guru Rimpoche taught Buddhism while traveling through the country on the back of a deer. The dances are performed by monks who play the roles of deities, heroes, and animals, dressed in brilliantly colored silks and brocades. They wear carved wooden or papier-mâché masks symbolizing the figures they portray. The dances are accompanied by the music of drums, bells, gongs, conch-shell trumpets, and horns—some of which are so long they touch the ground.

Thongdrel

The huge scroll known as the Thongdrel is unfurled from the top of the wall of the Dzong just before the first rays of the sun touch it. It is a type of thangka (a term that refers to a religious scroll of any size) and is so big that it covers the monastery's three-story-high wall. The Thongdrel is said to have the power to confer blessings and to provide an escape from the cycle of existence. It depicts various events in the life of Guru Rimpoche.

FURTHER READING

Henderson, Helene, ed. *Holidays, Festivals, and Celebrations of the World Dictionary.* 3rd ed. Detroit: Omnigraphics, 2005.
Van Straalen, Alice. *The Book of Holidays Around the World.* New York: Dutton, 1986.

Paryushana

Type of Holiday: Religious (Jain)
Date of Observation: August-September; Hindu month of Bhadrapada
Where Celebrated: India
Symbols and Customs: Ten Cardinal Virtues

ORIGINS

Paryushana is a religious holiday in Jainism, which originated in India around the same time that Buddhist thought developed. Jains believe in a sequence of reincarnations: animals must become human and lay people must become monks in order to attain salvation from the world. Salvation, called mokhsa, is attained by liberating the soul from the contamination of matter (karma). This liberation results in omniscience and bliss for eternity.

One of the fundamental doctrines of Jainism is the separation of living matter (called jiva) and non-living matter (called ajiva). In order to achieve freedom from karma, Jains must completely avoid harming any living thing and practice perfect asceticism. Three concepts govern the affairs of the Jain people. These are known collectively as the Triratna (Three Jewels) and consist of right faith, right knowledge, and right conduct.

The name Jain comes from the Sanskrit word Jina, which means Conqueror. The conquerors honored by the Jains are people who have overcome and won enlightenment. The name Jinas also applies specifically to twenty-four spiritual guides from history and the legendary past who are collectively called the Tirthankaras (which means ford-markers). Each of the Tirthankaras achieved liberation, and by his model taught others how to do the same. There is no personal god in Jainism. Although several gods and goddesses are recognized (and a few of them are also included in the Hindu pantheon), they take a subordinate position to the twenty-four Tirthankaras.

Jainism teaches that the universe is eternal—it was not created, it has no beginning and will have no end. It passes through cycles during which civilizations rise and fall, men attain large size and life-spans lengthen. In each cycle, twenty-four Tirthankaras appear. The last (twenty-fourth) Tirthankara was Vardhamana Mahavira who lived about the same time as Buddha. Jain sects place the date of his death in 527 B.C.E., and some researchers place the event in 477 B.C.E. Mahavira taught a path of passionless detachment and, according to Jain teaching, had achieved omniscience (knowledge of all things) before he started preaching.

The followers of Jainism, also known as the Faith of the Conquerors, devote their lives to conquering themselves and their own human weaknesses. They adhere strictly to certain rules, the first of which (known as *ahimsa*) is that they cannot kill or hurt any living thing. This means that they can't eat meat or swat a mosquito. They can't go to war or retaliate against anyone who attacks them. They can't even be farmers, because plowing the fields would kill worms and insects. To avoid injuring living creatures, they often carry a small broom or brush with which they can sweep them out of harm's way.

The growth of Jainism and the scattering of its followers eventually led to a division over whether or not their monks should be allowed to wear clothing. One group believed that they should avoid any concession to human comfort, and that the body should not be protected from heat, cold, or rough surfaces. This group became known as the Digambaras, which means "clad in the four directions"—in other words, naked. The other group, known as the Svetambaras ("clad in white"), believed that a single white garment was permissible.

During the month of Bhadrapada in the Hindu calendar, the Jains observe an eight-day fast known as Paryushana. They confess their sins and ask forgiveness for any harm they might have caused, consciously or unconsciously, to any living thing. The fast, which allows them to eat only once a day, is observed by both the Svetambar and Digambar sects at different times. Svetambar Jains begin their fast on the thirteenth day of the waning half of the month, ending on the fifth day of the waxing half. Digambar Jains begin their observation on the fifth day of the waxing half and end on the thirteenth lunar day. They spend this period analyzing themselves and criticizing their own behavior. They beg forgiveness from one another for offenses they may have committed, whether deliberately or unknowingly, in the hope that they can restore lost friendships. They also worship the Tirthankaras or "crossing-makers"—the twenty-four great teachers of the Jain religion.

SYMBOLS AND CUSTOMS

Ten Cardinal Virtues

A major focus of the self-examination that goes on during Paryushana is what are known as the Ten Cardinal Virtues: forgiveness, charity, simplicity, contentment, truthfulness, self-restraint, fasting, detachment, humility, and continence. Jain leaders lecture on the importance of pursuing these virtues and stress their cultivation. The process of cultivating the Ten Cardinal Virtues symbolizes man's emergence from an evil and depraved world to one of spiritual and moral refinement.

FURTHER READING

Bellenir, Karen. *Religious Holidays and Calendars.* 3rd ed. Detroit: Omnigraphics, 2004.

Crim, Keith R. *The Perennial Dictionary of World Religions.* San Francisco: Harper & Row, 1989.

Gaer, Joseph. *Holidays Around the World.* Boston: Little, Brown, 1953.

Henderson, Helene, ed. *Holidays, Festivals, and Celebrations of the World Dictionary.* 3rd ed. Detroit: Omnigraphics, 2005.

MacDonald, Margaret R., ed. *The Folklore of World Holidays.* Detroit: Gale Research, 1992.

The Pluralism Project at Harvard University
www.pluralism.org/resources/tradition/essays/jain4.php

Passover (Pesach)

Type of Holiday: Religious (Jewish)
Date of Observation: Begins between March 27 and April 24; between 15 and 21 (or 22) Nisan
Where Celebrated: Europe, Israel, United States, and by Jews all over the world
Symbols and Customs: Afikomen, Bitter Herbs, Egg, Elijah's Cup, Four Cups of Wine, Four Questions, Haggadah, Haroset, Karpas, Lamb Bone, Salt Water, Unleavened Bread (Matzoh)

ORIGINS

Passover is a Jewish holiday that celebrates Moses leading the Jews out of slavery. Their religion, Judaism, is one of the oldest continuously observed religions in the world. Its history extends back beyond the advent of the written word. Its people trace their roots to a common ancestor, Abraham, and then back even farther to the very moment of creation.

According to Jewish belief, the law given to the Jewish people by God contained everything they needed to live a holy life, including the ability to be reinterpreted in new historical situations. Judaism, therefore, is the expression of the Jewish people, attempting to live holy (set apart) lives in accordance with the instructions given by God. Although obedience to the law is central to Judaism, there is no one central authority. Sources of divine authority are God, the Torah, interpretations of the Torah by respected teachers, and tradition. Religious observances and the study of Jewish law are conducted under the supervision of a teacher called a rabbi.

There are several sects within Judaism. Orthodox Judaism is characterized by an affirmation of the traditional Jewish faith, strict adherence to customs such as keeping the Sabbath, participation in ceremonies and rituals, and the observance of dietary regulations. Conservative Jewish congregations seek to retain many ancient traditions but without the accompanying demand for strict observance.

Reform Judaism stresses modern biblical criticism and emphasizes ethical teachings more than ritualistic observance. Hasidism is a mystical sect of Judaism that teaches enthusiastic prayer as a means of communion with God. The Reconstructionist movement began early in the twentieth century in an effort to "reconstruct" Judaism with the community rather than the synagogue as its center.

The story of Passover is told as follows. According to the Old Testament of the Bible, the Jews settled in Egypt, in the area around the Nile, at the invitation of Joseph. When the Pharoahs launched an ambitious building program, the Hebrews were forced into service and gradually became slaves. The Book of Exodus tells the story of their suffering and how their leader, Moses, brought them out of bondage and led them to the land that had been promised to their forefathers—an event considered to be the birth of the Jewish nation.

When the Pharoah referred to in Exodus (believed by scholars to be Ramses II) refused to let Moses lead the Jews out of Egypt, God sent nine plagues—including frogs, lice, locusts, fire, and hailstones—to change Pharoah's mind. But Pharoah remained unmoved, so God devised a tenth plague, sending the Angel of Death to kill the first-born son of every Egyptian household. The Jews, however, were warned ahead of time to sacrifice a lamb and sprinkle the blood on their doorposts so that the Angel of Death would "pass over" and spare their sons. Pharoah finally relented, and the Jews were allowed to leave.

Passover is an eight-day celebration of the Jews' deliverance from slavery in Egypt, but it appears that its roots go back even further. The early inhabitants of the region known as Canaan (now Palestine) were farmers, and they held seasonal rites to honor their local gods. Their spring festival was known as Pesach, which in Hebrew meant "skipping" or "gamboling," and it apparently involved the sacrifice of lambs. When Moses led the Hebrew tribes out of slavery in Egypt and the people chose Jehovah to be their God—an event that occurred during the Hebrew month of Nisan (March-April)—the ancient spring festival of Pesach was reinterpreted to mean the "skipping over" or "passing over" of Jewish homes by the Angel of Death. Today, Pesach and Passover refer to the same holiday.

Passover is traditionally observed for seven days, from the fifteenth to the twenty-first of Nisan. Today, however, only the Jews of Israel and Reform Jews of other countries do this. Orthodox and Conservative Jews observe it for eight days, the first two of which are the most important. The primary activity is a special feast called the *seder*, which means "order" and consists of several symbolic foods that are eaten in a particular sequence, including a hard-boiled EGG, a roasted LAMB BONE, parsley dipped in SALT WATER, BITTER HERBS, HAROSET, and matzoh or UNLEAVENED BREAD. The HAGGADAH, or story of the exodus from Egypt, is read aloud to explain the historical and religious meaning of the holiday. As the seder comes to an end, people eat the last piece of matzoh, known as the AFIKOMEN, and thank God for the gift of their freedom.

Several features of the seder and the accompanying narrative seem to indicate that these rituals have not been handed down intact from a particular age but have evolved from a number of different ages, providing a capsule history of the Jews. The custom of reclining on cushions while eating the meal, the preliminary dipping of parsley in salted water, and the eating of eggs as an hors d'oeuvre, for example, are all characteristic of a typical Roman banquet. Reciting the Haggadah may also have been modeled after the Roman practice of reading literary works aloud at mealtime.

The exact dates of the events related in the story of Passover are not known with any certainty. According to the Book of Exodus, some 600,000 Hebrews left Egypt after living there for 430 years. On the basis of this biblical account, scholars have calculated that they became slaves there in the fourteenth century B.C.E. and that they fled Egypt around 1270 B.C.E.

SYMBOLS AND CUSTOMS

Afikomen

The *afikomen* is a piece broken off the middle of three matzoth traditionally placed under a special Pesach napkin on the seder table. It serves both as a treat for the children and as a concluding bite for the adults. In order to keep the children awake and interested during the lengthy ritual of the seder, the afikomen is hidden from them. At the end of the meal, they are asked to search for it, and the one who finds it is rewarded with a gift. Another variation on this custom allows the children to "steal" the afikomen and exchange it at the end of the meal for a gift. When the afikomen gets back to the seder table, it is broken in pieces and served to each participant as a dessert.

Little is known about the origins of the custom. The Talmud, a collection of writings about Jewish law and tradition, says that "men must not leave the paschal [Passover] meal *epikomin*." This last word was the Greek *epi komon,* a popular expression for "going out on the town" to celebrate. This advice was later misinterpreted as "Men must not leave out the *afikomen* after the paschal meal," and this curious expression was taken to mean that some sort of special dessert had to be served at the conclusion of the seder. This is probably where the custom of distributing small pieces of UNLEAVENED BREAD at the conclusion of the meal originated.

Another theory about the origin of the afikomen is that this piece of matzoh was a symbolic substitute for the sacrifice of a lamb at Passover, which was discontinued after the destruction of the second Temple in Jerusalem. The fact that the afikomen is usually wrapped in a napkin reminds seder participants that the Hebrews left Egypt with their kneading troughs wrapped up in their clothes and carried on their shoulders.

Bitter Herbs

The maror or bitter herbs, usually horseradish, eaten at the seder symbolize the hardships endured by the Jews when they were slaves in Egypt. These are served in a "sandwich" between pieces of matzoh, thereby obeying the Old Testament commandment (Exodus 12:8) that UNLEAVENED BREAD and bitter herbs be eaten together.

Egg

The hard-boiled egg served at the Passover seder represents the spiritual strength of the Jews. The fact that the egg is "roasted" serves as a reminder that in the days of the Temple in Jerusalem, animals were roasted (i.e., sacrificed) for God on this and other holidays.

Like the Easter egg in Christianity, the seder egg also symbolizes the beginning of new life in the spring and recalls the holiday's agricultural origins (*see* **EASTER**).

Elijah's Cup

In addition to the FOUR CUPS OF WINE traditionally drunk during the Passover meal, a fifth cup is filled but not drunk. Instead, the door is left open for the prophet Elijah. According to tradition, Elijah will be the forerunner for the Messiah who will redeem Israel and the rest of the world. He will arrive on the night of the seder, dressed as a beggar to see how people accept him, and will judge by their behavior whether or not they are ready for the Messiah. After the fifth cup is filled with wine, therefore, the children watch it eagerly to see if the level miraculously goes down, indicating that Elijah has visited their home.

The practice of leaving the door open for Elijah goes back to the Middle Ages. Its original purpose may have been to disprove the belief that Jews used the blood of Christian children to prepare matzoh. The door was left open so that everyone could see exactly how it was made. Even today, leaving the door open expresses the spirit of freedom and safety that Jews feel on this occasion, in spite of the false accusations they have had to endure.

Four Cups of Wine

Four cups of red wine are supposed to be drunk during the seder. But because the Jews do not encourage or enjoy drunkenness, they usually space out the designated drinking times and make sure that the wine is accompanied by food or diluted with water.

Why four cups? The most popular explanation links them with the four phrases in Exodus describing how God will redeem Israel: (1) "and I will take you out"; (2) "and I will deliver you"; (3) "and I will redeem you"; and (4) "and I will take you."

The custom is first mentioned in accounts dating from the middle of the second century. Scholars trace it back to the destruction of the second Temple in Jerusalem, after which the Jews, under Roman rule, were exposed to the customs of Roman banquets. The Romans would first drink wine while eating vegetables dipped in vinegar (*see* KARPAS) or in fruit sauce (*see* HAROSET). After these appetizers, they would move into the dining room for the main course and a second glass of wine. They would have a third glass following the meal. The fourth cup is the one drunk during the *Kiddush,* or blessing over the wine, that is traditionally offered at Passover and other Jewish holidays.

Four Questions

The seder begins with the chanting of the Kiddush prayer, the filling of the wine glasses (*see* FOUR CUPS OF WINE), the breaking of the middle matzoh (*see* AFIKOMEN), and the chanting of passages in either Hebrew or English from the HAGGADAH. Then the youngest child present at the table asks the well-known Four Questions:

(1) Why is this night different from all other nights? On all other nights we may eat either leavened bread or unleavened. Why, on this night, do we eat only unleavened?

(2) On all other nights, we may eat all kinds of herbs. Why, on this night, do we eat only bitter herbs?

(3) On all other nights, we don't dip some foods into other foods. Why do we dip parsley into salt water and bitter herbs into haroset tonight?

(4) On all other nights, we may sit at table erect or leaning. Why on this night do we sit reclining?

The answers to these questions are also contained in the HAGGADAH, which is read aloud by the head of the family.

Haggadah

The Haggadah is a compilation of stories, passages from the Bible, interpretations, benedictions, hymns, and instructions for conducting the seder. Although portions of it are more than 2,000 years old, the basic text was put together by Rabbi Shimeon ben Gamaliel in the second century B.C.E. The story of Passover, which is read during the seder, is introduced by a series of FOUR QUESTIONS asked by the youngest member of the family, beginning with "Why is this night different from all other nights?" Everything that follows constitutes the answer to this question. The Haggadah explains what each of the special Passover foods stands for and tells the story of how Moses led the Jewish slaves out of Egypt. The narrative is interspersed with expressions of gratitude to God for helping the Israelites escape and for guiding them on their journey to the Promised Land.

Haroset

Haroset (or charoset) is a mixture of wine, chopped apples, nuts, sugar, and cinnamon. It symbolizes the clay used by the Jewish slaves to make bricks to build Pharoah's cities.

Karpas

Karpas refers to a green vegetable, usually parsley, dipped in SALT WATER before being eaten. Because it is green, it symbolizes hope and new growth in the spring.

Lamb Bone

The lamb bone is set on a special seder plate, along with a roasted EGG and three matzoh (see UNLEAVENED BREAD). It symbolizes the lambs sacrificed by the Jews in Egypt, so that the blood could be painted on their doorposts and the Angel of Death would pass over their houses.

Salt Water

The salt water in which parsley (see KARPAS) and other vegetables are dipped symbolizes the tears shed by the Hebrew slaves in Egypt.

Unleavened Bread (Matzoh)

Unleavened bread is flat, because it is made without yeast. The unleavened bread that is served at Passover and other Jewish holidays is known as matzoh. It serves as a reminder of the Jews' hurried departure from Egypt, when there was no time to wait for the bread to rise. In addition to symbolizing the freedom gained by the Jews, matzoh also recalls the bread baked from the first grain harvested by the Jewish farmers in Palestine, thus recalling the festival's ancient agricultural roots.

Three pieces of matzoh are placed on the table at the start of the seder. Together, they stand for unity. The top one represents the *Kohen* or priest, the middle one is called the Levite, and the bottom one is known as the Israelite—three of the earliest divisions among Jews. All Jews, the leader of the seder explains, are brothers. Then he takes the middle of the three pieces and breaks it in half. One of these halves is the AFIKOMEN, which is spirited away from the table and hidden somewhere in the house, to be searched for later by the children. The afikomen is also the last thing eaten at the seder, so that the taste of matzoh stays in everyone's mouth.

The best type of matzoh is made of only flour and water, without even salt to flavor it. This is the type of matzoh normally used at the seder, and it is called the "bread of poverty" or "bread of affliction." The matzoth intended for use at Passover are usually labeled "Kosher for Pesach" on the box. While the original matzoh was round and soft, the invention of matzoh-making machines in the nineteenth century popularized the more brittle, rectangular matzoh that is eaten today.

FURTHER READING

Bellenir, Karen. *Religious Holidays and Calendars*. 3rd ed. Detroit: Omnigraphics, 2004.

Cashman, Greer Fay. *Jewish Days and Holidays*. New York: SBS Pub., 1979.

Cuyler, Margery. *Jewish Holidays*. New York: Holt, Rinehart and Winston, 1978.

Edidin, Ben. *Jewish Holidays and Festivals*. 1940. Reprint. Detroit: Omnigraphics, 1993.

Gaer, Joseph. *Holidays Around the World*. Boston: Little, Brown, 1953.

Gaster, Theodor H. *Festivals of the Jewish Year*. New York: William Sloane Associates, 1953.

Henderson, Helene, ed. *Holidays, Festivals, and Celebrations of the World Dictionary*. 3rd ed. Detroit: Omnigraphics, 2005.

Ickis, Marguerite. *The Book of Festivals and Holidays the World Over*. New York: Dodd, Mead, 1970.

Purdy, Susan. *Festivals for You to Celebrate*. Philadelphia: Lippincott, 1969.

Santino, Jack. *All Around the Year: Holidays and Celebrations in American Life*. Urbana: University of Illinois Press, 1994.

WEB SITE

Union of Orthodox Jewish Congregations in America
www.ou.org/chagim/pesach

Pentecost (Whitsunday)

Type of Holiday: Religious (Christian)
Date of Observation: Seventh Sunday (fifty days) after Easter
Where Celebrated: British Isles, Europe, United States, and throughout the Christian world
Symbols and Customs: Dew, Dove, Rose, Smoke Money
Colors: Pentecost is associated with the colors red and white—red for the tongues of fire that descended on the Apostles' heads, and white for the robes worn by the newly baptized.
Related Holidays: Easter, Pinkster, Shavuot

ORIGINS

Pentecost is a Christian holiday that takes place fifty days after **EASTER**. The word Christian refers to a follower of Christ, a title derived from the Greek word meaning Messiah or Anointed One. The Christ of Christianity is Jesus of Nazareth, a man born between 7 and 4 B.C.E. in the region of Palestine. According to Christian teaching, Jesus was killed by Roman authorities using a form of execution called crucifixion (a term meaning he was nailed to a cross and hung from it until he died) in about the year 30 C.E. After his death, he rose back to life. His death and resurrection provide a way by which people can be reconciled with God. In remembrance of Jesus' death and resurrection, the cross serves as a fundamental symbol in Christianity.

With nearly two billion believers in countries around the globe, Christianity is the largest of the world's religions. There is no one central authority for all of Christianity. The pope (the bishop of Rome) is the authority for the Roman Catholic Church, but other sects look to other authorities. Orthodox communities look to patriarchs and emphasize doctrinal agreement and traditional practice. Protestant communities focus on individual conscience. The Roman Catholic and Protestant churches are often referred to as the Western Church, while the Orthodox churches may also be called the Eastern Church. All three main branches of Christianity acknowledge the authority of Christian scriptures, a compilation of writings assembled into a document called the Bible. Methods of biblical interpretation vary among the different Christian sects.

As recorded in the New Testament of the Bible, it was fifty days after **EASTER** that the Apostles gathered in Jerusalem to celebrate the Jewish festival of **SHAVUOT**. As they prayed together, the Holy Spirit descended on them in the form of "tongues of fire," enabling them to speak in other languages. Transformed from rather timid men into courageous missionaries, they immediately began to preach about Jesus Christ to the Jews from many nations who had flocked to Jerusalem for Shavuot. More than 3,000 were baptized, an event now considered to mark the birth of the Christian Church. According to tradition, this is also the day on which, centuries earlier, Moses received the Ten Commandments on Mount Sinai, giving the Jewish religious community its start.

"Pentecost" comes from the Greek word meaning "fiftieth." Just as the Jewish feast of Shavuot comes fifty days after **PASSOVER**, Pentecost is observed fifty days after Easter. In the beginning, Pentecost included the entire fifty-day period from Easter to the Descent of the Holy Spirit, although a special festival was observed on the last day. It was a period of continual rejoicing during which fasting was not permitted and prayers had to be offered while standing rather than kneeling, in honor of Jesus' resurrection. The first mention of Pentecost as a separate feast occurred in the third century, when it became the second official date of the year (after Easter) when infants and catechumens (those who had been instructed in the basics of Christianity) could be baptized. The English called it Whitsunday (White Sunday), probably because of the white robes worn by the newly baptized. Eventually the number of children left unchristened because their parents were waiting for Whitsuntide became too unwieldy, and the rules regarding when people could be baptized were relaxed.

The period known as Whitsuntide (the week beginning on the Saturday before Whitsunday and ending the following Saturday) has traditionally been associated with the return of good weather and the emergence of green grass and spring flowers. A common way of observing Whitsuntide in many countries is to go out in the fields or woods and bring back green boughs to decorate a member of the village. Known variously as Green George, Jack-in-the-Green, the Leaf Man, and the Whitsuntide Lout, these woodland characters are believed to be a survival of pagan spring rites. In a game called "hunting the green man," children search for a young man dressed in leaves and moss.

In the early Christian Church, Pentecost was second in importance only to Easter. Nowadays no special ceremonies take place on this day in Roman Catholic churches, aside from the Saturday vigil and the Mass celebrated on Sunday with symbolic red vestments. In the Episcopal and Protestant churches, Pentecost is still a day for the confirmation and baptism of new members. All Christian churches celebrate Holy Communion on this day.

SYMBOLS AND CUSTOMS

Dew

In rural areas of northern Europe, people still believe in the special healing power of the dew that falls during the night on the eve of Pentecost. They walk barefoot through the grass early on Sunday morning in the belief that the dew that touches their feet will cure their ills and protect them from harm. They also collect dew on pieces of bread and feed them to their pets and farm animals as protection against accidents and disease.

Dove

In both ancient and Christian art, the dove is a symbol of purity and peace. But since the earliest years of the Christian era, it has symbolized the Holy Ghost, based on the Bible's description of the descent of the Holy Spirit in John 1:32: "And John bore record, saying, I saw the spirit descending from heaven like a dove, and it abode upon him." Nowadays the dove can be seen on priestly vestments, on altars, sacred utensils, and in many religious paintings. It is customary to have a painted dove suspended over the altar during Mass on Pentecost, and some families hang a carved and painted dove over their dining room table during Whitsuntide.

Christians have come up with a number of ingenious ways of incorporating the dove into their celebration of Pentecost. At one time, real doves were often let loose during Pentecost services, or pieces of white wool were thrown down from the "Holy Ghost hole" in the church ceiling. Sometimes a slowly revolving disk bearing the figure of a white dove on a blue background would descend horizontally to announce the arrival of the Holy Spirit. In some central European countries, pieces of burning straw or wick were dropped from the hole to represent the tongues of fire (*see* ROSE). In France, trumpets were blown during Mass on Pentecost to signify the rushing wind that accompanied the Spirit's descent.

In Germany and Austria, it is customary to suspend a painted wooden dove over the altar on Pentecost. At Orvieto, Italy, a wooden dove with extended wings runs along a wire in the great square in front of the cathedral, giving the illusion that the Holy Spirit is descending on the Apostles, who are gathered together on a platform set up in front of the cathedral doors.

Rose

Just as the DOVE is a symbol of the Holy Spirit, the red rose has become a symbol for the tongues of fire that descended on the Apostles during the Holy Spirit's visit on Pentecost. Centuries ago, people used to shoot real flames from the church roof or use lit torches to represent the tongues of fire, but safety concerns eventually put a stop to the practice. Red roses became a less dangerous substitute for real flames, and huge quantities of them were often let down from the church ceiling during the Pentecost service.

In Germany, Pentecost is called Pfingsten, and the prevailing symbol of the feast is the pink and red peonies known as Pfingstrosen or "Whitsun roses."

Smoke Money

In Scotland, Whitsunday was one of the so-called Quarter Days, the days on which rents and other payments fell due. In England, it was the day on which people paid their money to support the church. Because they were assessed on the basis of how many fireplaces they had in their houses, or according to the number of chimneys, the Whitsunday collection came to be known as "hearth" or "smoke" money.

FURTHER READING

Appleton, LeRoy H., and Stephen Bridges. *Symbolism in Liturgical Art*. New York: Scribner, 1959.

Barz, Brigitte. *Festivals with Children*. Edinburgh: Floris Books, 1987.

Bellenir, Karen. *Religious Holidays and Calendars*. 3rd ed. Detroit: Omnigraphics, 2004.

Chambers, Robert. *The Book of Days*. 2 vols. 1862-64. Reprint. Detroit: Omnigraphics, 1990.

Dobler, Lavinia G. *Customs and Holidays Around the World*. New York: Fleet Pub. Corp., 1962.

Ferguson, George. *Signs and Symbols in Christian Art*. New York: Oxford University Press, 1954.

Gulevich, Tanya. *Encyclopedia of Easter, Carnival, and Lent*. Detroit: Omnigraphics, 2002.

Henderson, Helene, ed. *Holidays, Festivals, and Celebrations of the World Dictionary*. 3rd ed. Detroit: Omnigraphics, 2005.

Ickis, Marguerite. *The Book of Festivals and Holidays the World Over*. New York: Dodd, Mead, 1970.

Ickis, Marguerite. *The Book of Religious Holidays and Celebrations*. New York: Dodd, Mead, 1966.

Monks, James L. *Great Catholic Festivals*. New York: Henry Schuman, 1951.

Spicer, Dorothy Gladys. *Festivals of Western Europe*. 1958. Reprint. Detroit: Omnigraphics, 1993.

Spicer, Dorothy Gladys. *The Book of Festivals*. 1937. Reprint. Detroit: Omnigraphics, 1990.

Urlin, Ethel L. *Festivals, Holy Days, and Saints' Days*. 1915. Reprint. Detroit: Omnigraphics, 1992.

Weiser, Franz Xaver. *Handbook of Christian Feasts and Customs*. New York: Harcourt, Brace, 1958.

WEB SITE

Christian Resource Institute
www.cresourcei.org/cypentecost.html

Pinkster

Type of Holiday: Historic
Date of Observation: May
Where Celebrated: Sleepy Hollow, New York
Symbols and Customs: Dancing, Drumming, Games, Pinkster King
Related Holidays: Pentecost

ORIGINS

Pinkster was originally celebrated by seventeenth century Dutch immigrants who settled in New Jersey and in the Hudson Valley and western Long Island in New York. Historically celebrated in May or early June, Pinkster roughly corresponded with observances of **PENTECOST**, the Christian commemoration of the coming of the Holy Spirit to Jesus's followers after his death and resurrection. The festival name is derived from *Pinksteren*, which is the Dutch name for Pentecost. Early observances of Pinkster combined the religious significance of Pentecost with secular celebrations of spring and renewal of life.

Unlike most other holidays during the period before the abolition of slavery in the United States, Pinkster was celebrated jointly by enslaved Africans and Dutch slave owners. During Pinkster festivities, Africans and Europeans often gathered together for games, dancing, drinking, and feasting. Many people associate slavery with the South, but in fact there were more than 32,700 slaves in New York and New Jersey by the late 1700s. Slaves were normally given time off during Pinkster, and many were allowed to travel to visit family and friends during the holiday. For this reason, Pinkster became the most important holiday of the year for many slaves.

Pinkster celebrations were most popular between 1790 and 1810, particularly around Albany, New York. By this time, the holiday had grown to a four-day celebration combining Dutch traditions and African slave customs. Preparations began weeks before the festival as tents and shelters were erected on Pinkster Hill—now the site of the New York State Capitol—where most of the Pinkster festivities took place.

Gradually, however, Dutch participation tapered off and Pinkster became an increasingly African-American holiday. As observances became more exclusively African, slaves used the occasion to subtly ridicule European culture by creating caricatures of European fashion, behavior, and customs. This was done through speeches, storytelling, and the crowning of the Pinkster King. Over time the Dutch objected to the slaves' observance of Pinkster, and the celebrations were made illegal in 1811.

Each year in May, an authentic recreation of a Pinkster celebration takes place in Sleepy Hollow, New York. The event is held at Philipsburg Manor, a historic Colonial-era milling and trading complex that was originally owned by Dutch immigrants and worked by twenty-three African slaves. Traditional DANCING, DRUMMING, GAMES, and food are featured along with the election of the Pinkster King, storytelling, and living history demonstrations drawn from more than 100 years of Pinkster celebrations held in the Hudson Valley area. A smaller event takes place for one day in June in Brooklyn, New York. There, a carnival is held at the Wyckoff Farmhouse Manor, and it includes African-inspired music and dance, plus sports competitions.

SYMBOLS AND CUSTOMS

Dancing

Dance was an important part of the original Pinkster celebrations. Dutch settlers preferred the organized European-style dances of the Colonial period, while slaves created improvised dances with steps that combined certain European elements with traditional African movements. Early African-American dances such as the jig, the double shuffle, and the breakdown are thought to have originated with Pinkster. Modern tap and break dancing are thought to have evolved from these early African-American forms of dance.

Drumming

As with other early African-American celebrations, drumming played a critical role in celebrations of Pinkster. Intense dancing, drumming, and chanting sessions were common and often went on for many hours. Drummers who were able to perform for hours on end were highly respected for their stamina.

Games

Dutch and African games were popular features of the original Pinkster celebrations. Children played a bowling game called ninepins and participated in stilt-walking competitions. People of all ages joined in European-style country dancing and egg-dyeing.

Pinkster King

One of the most important aspects of Pinkster was the crowning of the Pinkster King. During the height of Pinkster celebrations, this position was held every year by a well-known and highly respected slave named King Charles. Upon his arrival in Albany, King Charles conducted a procession through the town and up Pinkster Hill, where he presided over a royal ceremony. King Charles was also responsible for conducting the Pinkster celebrations, including regulation of the dancing and drumming sessions.

FURTHER READING

Abraham, Roger D. *Singing the Master.* New York: Penguin Books, 1992.

Gay, Kathlyn. *African-American Holidays, Festivals, and Celebrations.* Detroit: Omnigraphics, 2007.

Henderson, Helene, ed. *Holidays, Festivals, and Celebrations of the World Dictionary*, 3rd ed. Detroit: Omnigraphics, 2005.

Palmer, Colin, ed. *Encyclopedia of African-American Culture and History*, 2nd ed. Detroit: Macmillan Reference USA, 2006.

Williams-Myers, Albert James. *Long Hammering: Essays on the Forging of an African-American Presence in the Hudson River Valley in the Early Twentieth Century.* Trenton, NJ: Africa World Press, 1994.

WEB SITE

Historic Hudson Valley
hudsonvalley.org/pinkster

Pitra Paksa Festival
(Pitra Visarjana Amavasya)

Type of Holiday: Religious (Hindu)
Date of Observation: September-October; Asvina
Where Celebrated: India
Symbols and Customs: Kalasa, Rice, Vegetables
Related Holidays: All Souls' Day, Día de los Muertos, Obon Festival

ORIGINS

The Pitra Paksa Festival is part of Hinduism, which many scholars regard as the oldest living religion. The word Hindu is derived from the Sanskrit term *Sindhu* (or *Indus*), which meant river. It referred to people living in the Indus valley in the Indian subcontinent. Hinduism has no founder, one universal reality (or god) known as Brahman, many gods and goddesses (sometimes referred to as devtas), and several scriptures. Hinduism also has no priesthood or hierarchical structure similar to that seen in some other religions, such as Christianity. Hindus acknowledge the authority of a wide variety of writings, but there is no single, uniform canon. The oldest of the Hindu writings are the *Vedas*. The word "veda" comes from the Sanskrit word for knowledge. The *Vedas*, which were compiled from ancient oral traditions, contain hymns, instructions, explanations, chants for sacrifices, magical formulas, and philosophy. Another set of sacred books includes the *Great Epics*, which illustrate Hindu faith in practice. The *Epics* include the *Ramayana*, the *Mahabharata*, and the *Bhagavad Gita*.

The Hindu pantheon includes approximately thirty-three million gods. Some of these are held in higher esteem than others. Over all the gods, Hindus believe in one absolute high god or universal concept. This is Brahman. Although he is above all the gods, he is not worshipped in popular ceremonies because he is detached from the day-to-day affairs of the people. Brahman is impersonal. Lesser gods and goddesses (devtas) serve him. Because these are more intimately involved in the affairs of people, they are venerated as gods. The most honored god in Hinduism varies among the different Hindu sects. Although Hindu adherents practice their faith differently and venerate different deities, they share a similar view of reality and look back on a common history.

Hindus believe that the dead still need to be fed and clothed. They will become angry if they are not fed, and they need the clothing that is offered to them each year so they can gain admission to the resting place of dead souls, known as Swaraga, and avoid going to hell, or Naraka. If they aren't provided with what they need, accident, illness, or misfortune might befall their descendants. The two-week Pitra Paksa ("ancestors' fortnight") Festival observed in southern India is therefore one of the most important family rituals of the Hindu year, a time when people devote themselves to tending the needs of their deceased relatives.

Preparations for the festival include whitewashing houses, buying new clothes, and bathing. On the first day of the festival, one or two senior members of each family fast by avoiding all nonliquid foods, while the others eat only snacks. The floor of the area where the ancestor worship will take place—usually near the kitchen or front door—is cleaned carefully with cow dung, and *rangolli* designs are drawn on the floor with flour. A low wooden platform is placed on top of the design. A plantain leaf is laid on top of the platform (or directly on top of the rangolli design), some RICE is poured on the leaf, and the KALASA vessel is filled with water and set on top of the rice. Two butter-burning lamps are placed on either side.

The high point of the festival is the offering of a special meal to the deceased ancestors. It includes two meat dishes, no less than three VEGETABLE dishes, several kinds of snacks, and three or more (always an odd number) banana leaves filled with food. Three of these meals are prepared; one is placed on the roof, to be eaten by crows and sparrows, while the other two are consumed by humans. Sometimes Brahmins (members of the highest Hindu caste) are invited to partake of these special foods in the belief that they will ensure that the offerings reach the souls of departed family members. Occasionally one meal is fed to a cow in the belief that animals (as well as birds) are somehow connected to the ancestral spirits. During the entire two-week period, no male member of the family shaves, and no one is allowed to wear new clothes or cut his or her hair or nails. The eldest son usually performs the required religious ceremonies each day, which include offering water to the departed ancestors. On the last day of the two-week festival, known as *Amavasya*, or new moon, offerings are made to all ancestors whose day of death is unknown.

Brahmins and non-Brahmins honor the dead in quite different ways. Brahmins observe the lunar anniversaries of both parents' deaths, rather than attributing any particular importance to the Pitra Paksa fortnight. For non-Brahmins, however, the Pitra Paksa Festival is very similar to **ALL SOULS' DAY** for Christians, **DÍA DE LOS MUERTOS** for Mexicans, and the **OBON FESTIVAL** for Japanese Buddhists. It honors the ancestral spirits as a group, rather than individual family members who have died more recently.

SYMBOLS AND CUSTOMS

Kalasa

The vessel known as the *kalasa* is either a new clay pot, which guarantees its purity, or one that has been cleaned thoroughly before being filled. There is no fixed rule determining who fills the kalasa with water; it may be the family member who is fasting, the head of the household, or the unmarried daughter. The water is drawn from a nearby river, irrigation channel, or well. A very specific procedure must be followed while filling the vessel, which includes chanting the name of the eldest female ancestor and placing some betel leaves and a coconut in the open top of the filled vessel.

Once the kalasa has been set in the place of worship, it is decorated with vermilion, a garland of yellow chrysanthemums (a symbol of life and prosperity), or necklaces. Sometimes it is wrapped in a sari as well. Most household shrines separate the male and female offerings that are set before the vessel. Male offerings, which might include a *pance* (waist-cloth), liquor, tobacco, and a towel, are placed on the right. Female offerings, including palm-leaf earrings and other items of jewelry, combs, and saris, are placed on the left.

The kalasa symbolizes the deceased ancestors to whom food, water, and clothing are being offered. Once the kalasa has been installed, decorated, clothed, and "fed," the family continues its worship throughout the two-week festival by burning incense and camphor.

Rice

Rice plays an important part in this and other Hindu festivals. Raw rice is considered "hot," while cooked rice is "cool." Cooked rice is associated with funeral and mourning rituals, as well as with the spirits of the departed. Hindus of all castes put a small amount of raw rice in the corpse's mouth before it is cremated or buried. By the end of the ten-day period that is believed to mark the transition to a peaceful death, the deceased Hindu's soul is considered to be as "cool," or as peaceful, as rice that has been cooked.

During the Pitra Paksa Festival, cooked rice is served in several different forms. *Khir,* or rice boiled in milk, is sometimes offered to Brahmins in the belief that whatever is given to them will also reach the souls of the departed. Some Hindus serve yogurt rice shaped into balls called "kalasa balls." Rice flour is also an important ingredient in several of the snacks and desserts eaten during the festival. Plain boiled rice is the main festival offering, symbolic of the ancestors' state of peaceful repose after having passed through all the stages of life. Cooked white rice is also a metaphor for their having given life to their descendants, and for the integrity of the family as a whole.

Vegetables

Certain vegetables are a required element in the meal that is offered to the deceased ancestors, while others are taboo. This is because, as all Hindus know, the ancestors have their own preferences which must be catered to. Gourds and squashes feature prominently on the list of required vegetables because they are filled with seeds and grow on tendril-bearing vines, both of which symbolize the fertility and continuity of the family. Eggplant and potato are usually required as well, probably because they embody the principle of whiteness and purity. White is also the color of milk and of rice, and is therefore associated with nourishment and family ties. But other gourds, particularly those whose seeds are white when immature and then turn black when they're ready for planting, are strictly taboo.

Not every Hindu family has the same list of required vegetables for the ancestral feast. Some families might choose okra, for example, because it is filled with white seeds. But its skin is quite rough, and it lacks the pulpy white flesh that some other vegetables have. So while one family might be attracted to okra because of the white seeds, another family might reject it because of its rough skin and lack of white flesh. The list of vegetables offered to the ancestors at the festival is based on the characteristics of the vegetables themselves as well as on the habits and customs of each individual family.

Brahmins prepare a mixture called *saubhagya sunti* or "fortune-bestowing ginger," which they claim possesses the qualities of a thousand vegetables and can be used in the ancestors' meal to replace all other vegetables.

FURTHER READING

Bellenir, Karen. *Religious Holidays and Calendars*. 3rd ed. Detroit: Omnigraphics, 2004.

Hanchett, Suzanne. *Coloured Rice: Symbolic Structure in Hindu Family Festivals*. Delhi: Hindustan Pub. Corp., 1988.

Henderson, Helene, ed. *Holidays, Festivals, and Celebrations of the World Dictionary*. 3rd ed. Detroit: Omnigraphics, 2005.

MacDonald, Margaret R., ed. *The Folklore of World Holidays*. Detroit: Gale Research, 1992.

Plough Monday

Type of Holiday: Religious (Christian)
Date of Observation: January; first Monday after Epiphany
Where Celebrated: England
Symbols and Customs: Blessing the Plough, Plough Light, Sword Dance, The Bessy
Related Holidays: Compitalia

ORIGINS

Plough Monday is an ancient rustic holiday that later became part of the Christian tradition. The word Christian refers to a follower of Christ, a title derived from the Greek word meaning Messiah or Anointed One. The Christ of Christianity is Jesus of Nazareth, a man born between 7 and 4 B.C.E. in the region of Palestine. According to Christian teaching, Jesus was killed by Roman authorities using a form of execution called crucifixion (a term meaning he was nailed to a cross and hung from it until he died) in about the year 30 C.E. After his death, he rose back to life. His death and resurrection provide a way by which people can be reconciled with God. In remembrance of Jesus' death and resurrection, the cross serves as a fundamental symbol in Christianity.

With nearly two billion believers in countries around the globe, Christianity is the largest of the world's religions. There is no one central authority for all of Christianity. The pope (the bishop of Rome) is the authority for the Roman Catholic Church, but other sects look to other authorities. Orthodox communities look to patriarchs and emphasize doctrinal agreement and traditional practice. Protestant communities focus on individual conscience. The Roman Catholic and Protestant churches are often referred to as the Western Church, while the Orthodox churches may also be called the Eastern Church. All three main branches of Christianity acknowledge the authority of Christian scriptures, a compilation of writings assembled into a document called the Bible. Methods of biblical interpretation vary among the different Christian sects.

Also known as Fool Plough, Fond Plough, or Fond Pleeaf, the ancient rustic holiday Plough Monday was observed in England up through the late 1800s. It was believed to have started in the days of the medieval Roman Catholic Church, when farmers (or ploughmen, as they were called in England) kept candles called PLOUGH LIGHTS burning in churches before the images of their own special saints. Once a year, on the Monday after **EPIPHANY**, just before they resumed plowing after the

CHRISTMAS holidays—or sometimes at the end of **LENT**, to celebrate the end of plowing—they gathered in villages to collect money to pay for the plough lights. They would draw a plow through the village streets, accompanied by dancers and musicians, and demand money from passersby. This custom can be traced back to an even older tradition whereby a decorated plow was dragged from house to house by plowmen who shouted "God speed the plough!" and asked for money or gifts. If they didn't receive anything, they plowed up the yard in front of the house.

The sixteenth-century Reformation put an end to the adulation of saints, but the festivities associated with Plough Monday continued. The money that was originally collected for plough lights was used instead for eating and drinking. By the nineteenth century, the festival had become a day filled with music, dancing, processions, and trick-or-treating (*see* **HALLOWEEN**) by local farmers. A man known as THE BESSY would often dress up as a buffoon in women's clothing, and another, known as "The Fool," would wear animal skins or a fur hat and tail. They would parade from door to door, demanding money to buy not plough lights, but ale in the local tavern.

Dances were often performed around the plow, as if the dancers were acting out the revival of the earth in spring. The grain was supposed to grow as high that year as the dancers could jump—which gave rise to some wild dancing. In some places a plow, or even a log, was dragged over the fields in a symbolic plowing motion to ensure that the earth would be fertile when the time for real plowing arrived.

SYMBOLS AND CUSTOMS

Blessing the Plough

The custom of blessing the plow on the previous day, sometimes called Plough Sunday, is one that has survived in some English towns to this day. Plows that are to be used in preparing the fields for spring sowing are decorated and brought to the local church to be blessed.

Plough Light

The plough light or candle that was kept burning in the church before the image of the plowman's favorite saint was a symbol of the connection between the fertility of the fields and the blessings of God. Farmers believed that if they kept these lights burning, they would be assured of a successful harvest.

Sword Dance

It was very common at one time, especially in the rural areas of northeastern Yorkshire, for traditional Sword Dances to be performed on Plough Monday. Like the Morris Dance, the Sword Dance consisted of many intricate movements executed with precision and restraint. The dancers held swords in their right hands and at some point interlaced them to form a hexagon, known as "the lock," that was so firmly constructed it could be held aloft in a single dancer's hand. The geometrical figure would then be undone as each dancer took back his own sword.

The climax of the dance was the beheading scene. A character in the dance, often the one called The Fool, appeared to be decapitated by the swords. As he lay still on the ground, the other dancers would start shouting for a doctor, who would arrive and bring The Fool back to life with something from a bottle.

The Sword Dance was traditional in midwinter—as opposed to the Morris Dance, which was not confined to a particular season but usually accompanied **EASTER**, **MAY DAY**, or **MIDSUMMER DAY** festivities. The central feature of the Sword Dance was always a make-believe death followed by a magical resurrection, symbolic of the miraculous rebirth of nature in springtime. Such dances have enjoyed a rebirth themselves in recent years, and they are often performed at fairs and festivals in both England and the United States.

The Bessy

The female impersonator known as The Bessy is probably a remnant of an ancient mother goddess. Plough Monday itself is believed to have descended from the Roman **COMPITALIA,** celebrated by servants when their plowing was over. The Bessy remains a stock character in pantomime, mummers' parades, and SWORD DANCES, but is especially associated with Plough Monday.

FURTHER READING

Bellenir, Karen. *Religious Holidays and Calendars*. 3rd ed. Detroit: Omnigraphics, 2004.

Brewster, H. Pomeroy. *Saints and Festivals of the Christian Church*. 1904. Reprint. Detroit: Omnigraphics, 1990.

Chambers, Robert. *The Book of Days*. 2 vols. 1862-64. Reprint. Detroit: Omnigraphics, 1990.

Dunkling, Leslie. *A Dictionary of Days*. New York: Facts on File, 1988.

Harper, Howard V. *Days and Customs of All Faiths*. 1957. Reprint. Detroit: Omnigraphics, 1990.

Helfman, Elizabeth. *Celebrating Nature: Rites and Ceremonies Around the World*. New York: Seabury Press, 1969.

Henderson, Helene, ed. *Holidays, Festivals, and Celebrations of the World Dictionary*. 3rd ed. Detroit: Omnigraphics, 2005.

Hole, Christina. *English Custom & Usage*. 1941. Reprint. Detroit: Omnigraphics, 1990.

Leach, Maria, ed. *Funk & Wagnalls Standard Dictionary of Folklore, Mythology & Legend*. San Francisco: Harper & Row, 1984.

MacDonald, Margaret R., ed. *The Folklore of World Holidays*. Detroit: Gale Research, 1992.

Spicer, Dorothy Gladys. *Yearbook of English Festivals*. 1954. Reprint. Detroit: Omnigraphics, 1993.

Urlin, Ethel L. *Festivals, Holy Days, and Saints' Days*. 1915. Reprint. Detroit: Omnigraphics, 1992.

WEB SITE

Pulse of the Planet
www.pulseplanet.com/archive/Jan02/2576.html

Pongal
(Makara Sankranti)

Type of Holiday: Religious (Hindu)
Date of Observation: Three days in mid-January
Where Celebrated: India
Symbols and Customs: Cow, Rice

ORIGINS

The three-day Pongal festival is part of Hinduism, which many scholars regard as the oldest living religion. The word Hindu is derived from the Sanskrit term *Sindhu* (or *Indus*), which meant river. It referred to people living in the Indus valley in the Indian subcontinent. Hinduism has no founder, one universal reality (or god) known as Brahman, many gods and goddesses (sometimes referred to as devtas), and several scriptures. Hinduism also has no priesthood or hierarchical structure similar to that seen in some other religions, such as Christianity. Hindus acknowledge the authority of a wide variety of writings, but there is no single, uniform canon. The oldest of the Hindu writings are the *Vedas*. The word "veda" comes from the Sanskrit word for knowledge. The *Vedas*, which were compiled from ancient oral traditions, contain hymns, instructions, explanations, chants for sacrifices, magical formulas, and philosophy. Another set of sacred books includes the

717

Great Epics, which illustrate Hindu faith in practice. The *Epics* include the *Ramayana,* the *Mahabharata,* and the *Bhagavad Gita.*

The Hindu pantheon includes approximately thirty-three million gods. Some of these are held in higher esteem than others. Over all the gods, Hindus believe in one absolute high god or universal concept. This is Brahman. Although he is above all the gods, he is not worshipped in popular ceremonies because he is detached from the day-to-day affairs of the people. Brahman is impersonal. Lesser gods and goddesses (devtas) serve him. Because these are more intimately involved in the affairs of people, they are venerated as gods. The most honored god in Hinduism varies among the different Hindu sects. Although Hindu adherents practice their faith differently and venerate different deities, they share a similar view of reality and look back on a common history.

Pongal, one of the most colorful festivals observed in southern India, honors the sun, the earth, and the COW. Believed to be the survival of an ancient harvest festival because it falls around the time of the **WINTER SOLSTICE**, the three-day festival coincides with the harvest season and with the end of the monsoons. It is called Pongal in the state of Tamil Nadu; in Andhra Pradesh, Karnataka; and in Gujarat it is known as Makara Sankranti because it takes place when the sun starts to move south in the zodiac from Cancer to the House of Makara (the Alligator), otherwise known as Capricorn (the Goat).

The first day, known as Bhogi Pongal, is observed as a family festival and is usually spent cleaning everything in the house. Shops, offices, and factories are cleaned as well—a symbolic washing-away of material sins. The second day is Surya Pongal, and it is set aside for worship of the Sun God, Surya. The third day, Mattu Pongal, is reserved for worshipping cattle (*see* COW). The fourth day, which is not always observed, is spent paying visits, reestablishing old relationships and forgotten connections.

Orthodox Hindus make a pilgrimage to Allahabad, the holy city where the Ganges and the Jumna Rivers meet, on Makara Sankranti. Sometimes as many as a million people arrive in this northern city to have their sins washed away by bathing in the Ganges. Because the festival is a time for banishing quarrels, it is common to serve visitors sugared sesamum seed, advising them to "Eat sweetly, speak sweetly." Chewing on raw sugar cane is another favorite pastime during the festival.

In some parts of India, women who want to have children take coconuts and secretly leave them in a Brahmin home—or they bring gifts of betel nuts and spices to Brahmin wives. Sometimes they take coconuts to their neighbors and exchange them for fruit, saying, "Take a boy and give a child."

In Ahmedabad in the state of Gujarat, Makara Sankranti is a time for competitive kite-flying. Kitemakers from other cities gather here to make their kites and see whose flies the highest. As darkness falls, the battle of the kites ends. But new kites, each carrying its own paper lamp, fill the sky with flickering lights.

SYMBOLS AND CUSTOMS

Cow

The third day of Pongal is known as the Festival of the Cow. Cows and oxen are bathed, their horns are cleaned and polished, and garlands of flowers are hung around their necks. The main event in many Indian villages is bull-chasing: Bags of money are tied to the horns of ferocious bulls, who are allowed to stampede through the streets of the town. Young men try to catch a bull by the horns and claim the bag of money. Sometimes the horns have been sharpened and painted, which makes the chase even more dangerous and exciting.

Although bull-chasing is popular, Pongal is really a day to recognize the importance of cattle to the agricultural community. They are fed some of the newly harvested rice and showered with affection and attention. No cow is expected to work on Pongal; instead, they roam the countryside in all their flowers and finery (*see* RUNNING OF THE BULLS under **SAN FERMIN FESTIVAL**).

Rice

The most characteristic feature of Pongal in southern India, where rice is the staple food, is the cooking and eating of rice from the newly gathered harvest. On the second day of the festival, rice boiled in milk is offered to the Sun God, Surya—a symbolic expression of thanksgiving for the bounty of the harvest. Friends greet one another by asking, "Is it boiled?" The answer is always, "Yes, it is cooked." One of the literal meanings of pongal, in fact, refers to the foaming of milk without its boiling over, which is considered a very auspicious sign.

FURTHER READING

Bellenir, Karen. *Religious Holidays and Calendars*. 3rd ed. Detroit: Omnigraphics, 2004.

Gaer, Joseph. *Holidays Around the World*. Boston: Little, Brown, 1953.

Henderson, Helene, ed. *Holidays, Festivals, and Celebrations of the World Dictionary*. 3rd ed. Detroit: Omnigraphics, 2005.

MacDonald, Margaret R., ed. *The Folklore of World Holidays*. Detroit: Gale Research, 1992.

Oki, Morihiro. *India: Fairs and Festivals*. Tokyo: Gakken Co., 1989.

Sharma, Brijendra Nath. *Festivals of India*. New Delhi: Abhinav Publications, 1978.

Thomas, Paul. *Festivals and Holidays in India*. Bombay: D.B. Taraporevala Sons, 1971.

WEB SITE

Society for the Confluence of Festivals in India
www.pongalfestival.org

Pooram

Type of Holiday: Religious (Hindu)
Date of Observation: April-May; ten days during the Hindu month of Vaisakha
Where Celebrated: Trichur and elsewhere in Kerala, India
Symbols and Customs: Elephants, Pandimelam, Parasols
Related Holidays: Great Elephant March

ORIGINS

Pooram is one of the celebrations of Hinduism, which many scholars regard as the oldest living religion. The word Hindu is derived from the Sanskrit term *Sindhu* (or *Indus*), which meant river. It referred to people living in the Indus valley in the Indian subcontinent. Hinduism has no founder, one universal reality (or god) known as Brahman, many gods and goddesses (sometimes referred to as devtas), and several scriptures. Hinduism also has no priesthood or hierarchical structure similar to that seen in some other religions, such as Christianity. Hindus acknowledge the authority of a wide variety of writings, but there is no single, uniform canon. The oldest of the Hindu writings are the *Vedas*. The word "veda" comes from the Sanskrit word for knowledge. The *Vedas*, which were compiled from ancient oral traditions, contain hymns, instructions, explanations, chants for sacrifices, magical formulas, and philosophy. Another set of sacred books includes the *Great Epics,* which illustrate Hindu faith in practice. The *Epics* include the *Ramayana,* the *Mahabharata*, and the *Bhagavad Gita.*

The Hindu pantheon includes approximately thirty-three million gods. Some of these are held in higher esteem than others. Over all the gods, Hindus believe in one absolute high god or universal concept. This is Brahman. Although he is above all the gods, he is not worshipped in popular ceremonies because he is detached from the day-to-day affairs of the people. Brahman is impersonal. Lesser gods and goddesses (devtas) serve him. Because these are more intimately involved in the affairs of people, they are venerated as gods. The most honored god in Hinduism varies among the different Hindu sects. Although Hindu adherents practice their faith differently and venerate different deities, they share a similar view of reality and look back on a common history.

Pooram was first held in Trichur during the reign of Sakthan Thampuran (1775-90), who was the Raja of Kochi (Cochin). Thampuran renovated the Vadakku-nathan Temple complex, which includes not only the main temple dedicated to Shiva but two smaller temples dedicated to the sister goddesses Paramekkavu and Thiruvambadi. He also cut down the trees surrounding the temples to create the Thekkinkadu Maidan, the huge open space named after the teak forest that once stood there and the main venue for the spectacle of Pooram.

The word *pooram* means "meeting," and the original purpose of the event was for the gods and goddesses of neighboring provinces to meet ceremonially on an annual basis. Today, the highlight of the festival occurs when two groups of fifteen ELEPHANTS, one representing the Paramekkavu Temple and the other the Thiru-vambadi Temple, meet face to face on the maidan in front of the Vadakkunathan Temple. One of the elephants in each group carries the image of the temple's deity, and all are caparisoned, which means they wear rich ornamental coverings that resemble chain mail. Three Brahmin priests sit atop each elephant, and in their hands are the symbols of royalty—yak-hair whisks with silver handles, circular fans made of peacock feathers, and brightly colored silk PARASOLS—which they wave to the rhythm of the music provided by the traditional instrumental group known as the PANDIMELAM. Other temples send elephants carrying deities to partic-ipate in the procession as well, and when all have made their way slowly through the streets and gathered at the Vadakkunathan Temple, there is a spectacular dis-play of color and movement in which parasols are twirled and exchanged while the tempo of the music gradually increases from slow and majestic to a frenzy (*see* PANDIMELAM). The festival ends with fireworks that extend into the next morning and a farewell between the two goddess-carrying elephants, which link trunks before parting. The entire show takes about thirty hours.

Although Pooram is observed in many locations throughout Kerala, a state at the southwestern tip of India, the largest and most widely attended celebration is in Trichur (Thrissur), where thousands gather to see the "Pooram of all Poorams." The events there center around the Vadakkunathan Temple, but the festival is not exclusively a Hindu one. Muslims and Christians play an active role in planning for Pooram, and virtually everyone turns out to see the **GREAT ELEPHANT MARCH**, for which the festival is world famous.

SYMBOLS AND CUSTOMS

Elephants

Each temple participating in Pooram sends a contingent of elephants to accompa-ny the image of its god or goddess. Smaller temples may send only three or four elephants, while the Paramekkavu and Thiruvambadi temples send the largest contingents of fifteen elephants each. If a temple doesn't own any elephants, they can usually be borrowed or hired, and it is considered a great honor for the elephant's owner when his animal is asked to participate.

Each elephant wears a *nettipattam,* which is a piece of cloth to which hundreds of gold pieces have been stitched, giving the overall effect of large sequins. What is even more impressive than the huge beasts' willingness to wear this heavy decoration in the hot sun is the patience with which they stand in the temple grounds while surrounded by exploding fireworks and the sound of the *chenda* drums.

Pandimelam

The Pandimelam is a group of four instrumentalists who perform at Kerala's temple festivals and play traditional music. Their instruments are the chenda, a cylindrical drum; the ilathalam, which is similar to cymbals; the kuzhal, a wind instrument that resembles a hollow pipe; and the kombu, a C-shaped trumpet made of brass or copper. The Chenda Melam, an orchestra of drums, also performs at Pooram, particularly during the parasol exchange (*see* PARASOLS).

Parasols

The parasols carried by the Brahmins during the elephant procession are a symbol of royalty. They are usually made out of patterned silk with silver pendants along the edge, and the colors range from red, purple, and orange to turquoise, black, and gold. In the ceremony known as Kudamattam, the Brahmins from one temple face those from the other temple and engage in a competition that involves each side exchanging parasols in time with the music provided by the PANDIMELAM. The spectacle of all these ceremonial umbrellas swaying and twirling is probably Pooram's most unforgettable sight.

FURTHER READING

Bellenir, Karen. *Religious Holidays and Calendars*. 3rd ed. Detroit: Omnigraphics, 2004.

WEB SITE

Emerging Planet India
www.trichur.net/pooram.html

Posadas, Las

Type of Holiday: Religious (Christian)
Date of Observation: December 16-24
Where Celebrated: Mexico, United States
Symbols and Customs: Piñata
Related Holidays: Christmas, Christmas Eve

ORIGINS

Las Posadas is a Christian religious tradition related to the birth of Jesus Christ. The word Christian refers to a follower of Christ, a title derived from the Greek word meaning Messiah or Anointed One. The Christ of Christianity is Jesus of Nazareth, a man born between 7 and 4 B.C.E. in the region of Palestine. According to Christian teaching, Jesus was killed by Roman authorities using a form of execution called crucifixion (a term meaning he was nailed to a cross and hung from it until he died) in about the year 30 C.E. After his death, he rose back to life. His death and resurrection provide a way by which people can be reconciled with God. In remembrance of Jesus' death and resurrection, the cross serves as a fundamental symbol in Christianity.

With nearly two billion believers in countries around the globe, Christianity is the largest of the world's religions. There is no one central authority for all of Christianity. The pope (the bishop of Rome) is the authority for the Roman Catholic Church, but other sects look to other authorities. Orthodox communities look to patriarchs and emphasize doctrinal agreement and traditional practice. Protestant communities focus on individual conscience. The Roman Catholic and Protestant churches are often referred to as the Western Church, while the Orthodox churches may also be called the Eastern Church. All three main branches of Christianity acknowledge the authority of Christian scriptures, a compilation of writings assembled into a document called the Bible. Methods of biblical interpretation vary among the different Christian sects.

Las Posadas is a Mexican tradition whose popularity is growing in the United States, especially in southern California and the southwestern states. For nine nights, beginning on December 16, groups of friends and neighbors visit each other's houses and reenact Mary's and Joseph's search for shelter (Spanish *posada*) as they traveled from Nazareth to Bethlehem during the days preceding the birth of the infant Jesus. Each night the group knocks on someone's door, requests lodging, and is refused. Finally, on **CHRISTMAS EVE**, their request is granted. Once everyone is inside the house, there is feasting and merrymaking.

Las Posadas can take many different forms. Sometimes the processions are held in the streets and churches, with villagers carrying lighted candles and children pulling a wagon on which a nativity scene has been erected. There are also larger, more public presentations of *las posadas* that are open to townspeople and tourists. In some areas, *posadas* is synonymous with "parties," which are given on each of the nine nights leading up to **CHRISTMAS**. Everyone gathers at a particular house on the ninth evening, and the search by Mary and Joseph for lodgings is reenacted at the door of each room. On the stroke of midnight, the hostess leads them to a room where a table has been prepared. Images of Mary and Joseph are placed on the table and the feasting begins. An essential element of the *posadas* party is a PIÑATA for the children.

Among the poor, it is customary for friends and neighbors to get together and share the expenses involved in celebrating Las Posadas. This is especially true in Mexico, where Christmas is more of a community than a family event. In the United States, one of the most famous Posadas celebrations takes place on Olvera Street in Los Angeles.

SYMBOLS AND CUSTOMS

Piñata

The piñata was originally a clay or pottery container covered with papier-mâché and colored tissue paper to resemble an animal, bird, clown, ball, or some other playful object. It originated in Italy during the Renaissance, where it was used as an entertainment at adult masquerade balls. But today it is primarily a party game for children. Blindfolded, they take turns trying to break the piñata, which is hung from a tree or a hook in the ceiling, with a stick. Once it shatters, everyone scrambles to collect the small toys and candy that have been concealed inside.

The last piñata of the Christmas season in Mexico is broken on Christmas Eve. After the final posada is held earlier in the evening and everyone has returned from midnight Mass, there is a big feast. The children get so excited trying to break open the piñata that they often start swinging the stick at each other.

FURTHER READING

Bellenir, Karen. *Religious Holidays and Calendars.* 3rd ed. Detroit: Omnigraphics, 2004.
Crippen, T.G. *Christmas and Christmas Lore.* 1923. Reprint. Detroit: Omnigraphics, 1990.

Gulevich, Tanya. *Encyclopedia of Christmas and New Year's Celebrations*. 2nd ed. Detroit: Omnigraphics, 2003.

Henderson, Helene, ed. *Holidays, Festivals, and Celebrations of the World Dictionary*. 3rd ed. Detroit: Omnigraphics, 2005.

MacDonald, Margaret R., ed. *The Folklore of World Holidays*. Detroit: Gale Research, 1992.

Purdy, Susan. *Festivals for You to Celebrate*. Philadelphia: Lippincott, 1969.

Santino, Jack. *All Around the Year: Holidays and Celebrations in American Life*. Urbana: University of Illinois Press, 1994.

Spicer, Dorothy Gladys. *The Book of Festivals*. 1937. Reprint. Detroit: Omnigraphics, 1990.

WEB SITE

Herbert Hoover Presidential Library & Museum
hoover.archives.gov/exhibits/christmasworld/mexico.html

Poson

Type of Holiday: Religious (Buddhist)
Date of Observation: May-June; full moon day of the Hindu month of Jyestha
Where Celebrated: Sri Lanka
Symbols and Customs: Bodhi Tree, Mango-Tree Stupa, Thuparama Stupa

ORIGINS

The full moon day of every month is a holiday in Sri Lanka (formerly Ceylon), an independent island state off the southern tip of India. But the full moon day of the Hindu month of Jyestha, known as Poson, is the second most important holiday (after **VESAK**) of the year for Sri Lankan Buddhists. It commemorates the day on which, in 306 B.C.E., Buddhism was introduced there, triggering a widespread and profound revolution in Sri Lanka's cultural and religious life.

Buddhism, one of the four largest religious families in the world, is based on the teachings of Siddhartha Gautama (c. 563-483 B.C.E.), who came to be known as Buddha, or "The Enlightened One." The basic tenets of Buddhism can be summarized in the Four Noble Truths and the Eightfold Path. The Four Noble Truths are 1) the truth and reality of suffering; 2) suffering is caused by desire; 3) the way to

725

end suffering is to end desire; and 4) the Eightfold Path shows the way to end suffering. The Eightfold Path consists of 1) right view or right understanding; 2) right thoughts and aspirations; 3) right speech; 4) right conduct and action; 5) right way of life; 6) right effort; 7) right mindfulness; and 8) right contemplation.

The Sri Lankans have a legend about how Buddhism was introduced to their island. King Tissa was out hunting when he saw a deer grazing near the mountain known as Mihintale, about seven miles from the capital city of Anuradhapura. Because he was a true sportsman, he alerted the deer to his presence so he wouldn't have to shoot it while it was feeding. The deer took off up the mountain with King Tissa in pursuit. Suddenly the deer disappeared and in its place stood a yellow-robed monk. This was Mahinda, the son of the great Buddhist Emperor Asoka of India. After a brief conversation designed to test King Tissa's readiness to receive instruction (*see* MANGO-TREE STUPA), Mahinda introduced him to the basic tenets of Buddhism. The king was so impressed that he built sixty-eight caves at Mihintale for Mahinda and his companions to live in while they did their missionary work, and it wasn't long before the entire island had been converted to Buddhism.

Mahinda had been sent to Sri Lanka by his father, Asoka, who was a friend of King Tissa and wanted to share with him and his people the rewards of the Buddhist religion. Mahinda stayed in Sri Lanka until his death at age eighty, by which time Buddhism was well established there. A monument, known as the MANGO-TREE STUPA, was built near the place where he and King Tissa first met, and now more than 1,800 stone steps lead pilgrims up the mountain to the shrine that houses Mahinda's relics.

Poson is celebrated throughout Sri Lanka, but especially at Anuradhapura and Mihintale, where the buildings and streets are lit up and reenactments of the meeting between Mahinda and King Tissa are a popular entertainment. In addition to visiting Mahinda's shrine, Buddhists make a point of paying homage to the BODHI TREE growing at Anuradhapura, which is believed to have descended from a branch of the original Bodhi Tree in India that is associated with the Buddha's Enlightenment.

SYMBOLS AND CUSTOMS

Bodhi Tree

According to Buddhist belief, the Buddha (Siddhartha Guatama) was meditating under a ficus or fig tree at Bodh Gaya, a village in central Bihar (India), when he reached the spiritual state known as Enlightenment. Thereafter this fig tree was known as the Bodhi (or Bo) Tree.

While Mahinda was preaching Buddhism to the people of Sri Lanka, his sister Sangamitta brought a branch of the original Bodhi Tree to Anuradhapura. It was planted in the royal garden there and can still be seen, with monks standing guard around it as they have done since it was planted. Many believe that it is the world's oldest living tree.

Forty saplings grew from the seeds of this tree and were planted at every Buddhist temple on the island. Although there is no way of ascertaining that fig trees weren't already growing in Sri Lanka when Sangamitta arrived, it is widely believed that all those now in existence are descendants of the branch she brought from India. In any case, the Bodhi Tree remains a symbol of Buddhism.

Mango-Tree Stupa

The Ambasthala or Mango-Tree Stupa, where Mahinda's relics are enshrined, got its name from a series of questions that Mahinda posed to King Tissa as a way of judging his readiness to receive Buddhist teachings. Pointing to a mango tree that was growing nearby, Mahinda asked the king to identify it and then used it as the basis for a riddle. King Tissa solved the riddle brilliantly, thus proving that he was the right person to help Mahinda bring Buddhism to the people of Sri Lanka.

The Mango-Tree Stupa was built just below the peak of Mihintale, where this conversation took place, by one of King Tissa's successors. Many mango trees are now growing in the area, where they stand as a symbol of the historic meeting that resulted in the spread of Buddhism to Sri Lanka.

Thuparama Stupa

In addition to bringing a branch of the original Bodhi Tree to Sri Lanka, Mihintale's sister Sangamitta also brought some relics of the Buddha. A commemorative monument or stupa was built for his collarbone in Anuradhapura, where it served as an ongoing source of inspiration for Buddhist worshippers. The original stupa was fairly primitive, but it was later rebuilt and eventually turned into a vadatage or relic house, with many columns supporting a circular roof. The remains of these columns can still be seen surrounding the more solid, domelike stupa, now known as Thuparama.

FURTHER READING

Bechert, Heinz, and Richard Gombrich. *The World of Buddhism*. New York: Facts on File, 1984.

Bellenir, Karen. *Religious Holidays and Calendars*. 3rd ed. Detroit: Omnigraphics, 2004.

Bowker, John, ed. *The Oxford Dictionary of World Religions*. New York: Oxford University Press, 1997.

Powamû Festival (Bean-Planting Festival)

Type of Holiday: Religious (Hopi)
Date of Observation: Late January-early February for eight days
Where Celebrated: Arizona
Symbols and Customs: Bean Sprouts, Flogging, Masks, Soyokmana
Related Holidays: Niman Kachina Festival, Wuwuchim

ORIGINS

The Powamû Festival is a midwinter religious celebration of the Hopi Indians. The historical development of religious belief systems among many Native American groups is not well known. Most of the information available was gathered by Europeans who arrived on the continent beginning in the sixteenth century C.E. The data they recorded was fragmentary and oftentimes of questionable accuracy because the Europeans did not understand the native cultures they were trying to describe and the Native Americans were reluctant to divulge details about themselves.

The history of Native American cultures dates back thousands of years into prehistoric times. According to many scholars, the people who became the Native Americans migrated from Asia across a land bridge that may have once connected the territories presently occupied by Alaska and Russia. The migrations, believed to have begun between 60,000 and 30,000 B.C.E., continued until approximately 4,000 B.C.E. This speculation, however, conflicts with traditional stories asserting that the indigenous Americans have always lived in North America or that tribes moved up from the south.

The Hopi observe a ceremonial calendar in which the year is divided into two parts. According to tradition, during one half of the year the kachinas (nature, ancestral, and guardian spirits) live in the village and reveal themselves to the people through ceremonial dances. During the other half of the year, the kachinas separate themselves from the village and return to live in their homes in the mountains. The Kachina season begins around the time of **WINTER SOLSTICE**, as people begin to prepare the ground for planting, and it closes in late July with the bringing in of the first harvest.

The Hopi Indians believe that for six months of the year, ancestral spirits called the Kachinas leave their mountain homes and visit the tribe, bringing health to the people and rain for their crops. The midwinter ceremony known as the Powamû celebrates their return, just as the **NIMAN KACHINA FESTIVAL** in July celebrates their departure.

Preparations for the ceremony include repainting the MASKS that will be worn by the individuals impersonating the Kachinas. On the third day, young men bring in baskets of wet sand, which they leave near the entrance to the kiva, or ceremonial meeting room. A hot fire burns throughout the eight days of the Powamû in the kiva of every Hopi village, and blankets are stretched across the opening so that the atmosphere inside is like that of a hothouse. Each man who enters the kiva during this period carries a basket or bowl of sand into it and plants a handful of beans, which sprout quickly in all the heat and humidity.

The Powamû culminates in a dance that takes place in the nine kivas that dot the mesa in northeastern Arizona. The dancers' bodies are painted red and white, and they wear squash blossoms—actually yucca fiber twisted into the shape of a squash blossom—in their hair. They put on white kilts and sashes and leggings with a fringe of shells tied down the side. The dance takes place in two lines facing each other, inside the sweltering kiva. When it is over, the dancers leave for the next village's kiva, and another group arrives. During the course of the night, each group dances at all nine kivas.

Wearing masks and with painted bodies, the next morning the Kachinas arrive bringing dolls and rattles for the girls, bows and arrows for the boys, and for both the green BEAN SPROUTS that have been growing in the overheated kivas. Clowns run around making jokes, tripping each other, and performing pantomimes for everyone's enjoyment. The festival concludes with a huge feast in which bean sprouts are the main ingredient. From this time until their departure in July, the Kachinas appear regularly in masked ceremonies performed in the Hopi villages.

SYMBOLS AND CUSTOMS

Bean Sprouts

Sprouted beans are a symbol of fertility. Since the Hopis depend on the kachinas to bring rain and other conditions essential to the growth of their crops, bean sprouts also symbolize the approaching spring.

Flogging

Until the age of nine or ten, Hopi children believe that the Kachinas who appear at the Powamû and other ceremonial dances are superhuman. When they have matured, they are told that the real Kachinas no longer visit the earth but are impersonated by men wearing MASKS. The price for acquiring this knowledge, however, is participation in a ritual flogging or whipping ceremony. The children are never struck hard enough to cause real pain, and the ritual is not intended to be cruel. Sometimes a child who is particularly frightened is not actually flogged at all, but instead has a yucca whip whirled over his or her head. Occasionally an adult will be flogged as well, which is believed to promote healing.

On four successive mornings, the child who has been flogged is taken to a place on the mesa where he or she makes an offering at a shrine and casts meal toward the sun. During this period the child is not allowed to eat salt or meat, but on the fourth day these restrictions are lifted. From this time onward, the child is allowed to look at the Kachinas without their masks and at other sacred objects in the kiva without incurring any punishment.

The flogging ceremony symbolizes the revelation of the secret of Hopi life: the knowledge that the Kachinas are not really spirits but men dressed to represent them.

Masks

The masks worn by the men who impersonate the Kachinas during the Powamû Festival may vary from year to year, but some of the masks remain constant. Before the dance takes place, the masks are repainted and refurbished. They are designed to fit closely over the head, hiding it completely, with a ruff of feathers, fur, or spruce at the neck. The face usually resembles a bird, beast, monster, or man—or some combination thereof. Those who wear the Kachina masks usually carry an object associated with the being they represent—for example, a bow and arrow, a yucca whip, or feathers.

The female Kachinas, who are impersonated by men, wear wigs of long hair styled in the flat swirls over the ears known as squash blossoms, a symbol of virginity.

Soyokmana

The group of Kachinas that visit each Hopi village during the Powamû Festival usually includes Soyokmana, a witch-like creature carrying a crook and a bloody knife. The group goes from house to house demanding food, receiving gifts, and presenting BEAN SPROUTS. When the food they are offered does not meet their standards, the Kachinas make hooting and whistling noises and refuse to leave until they have been properly fed. Sometimes Soyokmana uses her crook to hook a child around the neck and hold him or her there, screaming in terror. Parents tell their children that this is a punishment for being naughty.

FURTHER READING

Bellenir, Karen. *Religious Holidays and Calendars*. 3rd ed. Detroit: Omnigraphics, 2004.

Cohen, Hennig, and Tristram Potter Coffin. *The Folklore of American Holidays*. 3rd ed. Detroit: Gale Research, 1999.

Fergusson, Erna. *Dancing Gods: Indian Ceremonials of New Mexico and Arizona*. New York: A.A. Knopf, 1931.

Fewkes, Jesse Walter. *Tusayan Katcinas and Hopi Altars*. Albuquerque: Avanyu Pub., 1990.

Henderson, Helene, ed. *Holidays, Festivals, and Celebrations of the World Dictionary*. 3rd ed. Detroit: Omnigraphics, 2005.

Leach, Maria, ed. *Funk & Wagnalls Standard Dictionary of Folklore, Mythology & Legend*. San Francisco: Harper & Row, 1984.

Procession of the Swallow

Type of Holiday: Folkloric, Calendar/Seasonal
Date of Observation: March 1
Where Celebrated: Greece
Symbols and Customs: Ivy, Swallow

ORIGINS

The Procession of the Swallow marks the changing of the seasons, which people in all parts of the world have honored since ancient times. Many cultures divided the year into two seasons, summer and winter, and marked these points of the year at or near the summer and winter solstices, during which light and warmth began to increase and decrease, respectively. In pre-industrial times, humans survived through hunting, gathering, and agricultural practices, which depend on the natural cycle of seasons, according to the climate in the region of the world in which they lived. Thus, they created rituals to help ensure enough rain and sun in the spring and summer so crops would grow to fruition at harvest time, which was, in turn, duly celebrated. Vestiges of many of these ancient practices are thought to have survived in festivals still celebrated around seasonal themes.

The Procession of the Swallow is a Greek custom observed on March 1 in celebration of the arrival of spring. Children go from house to house in pairs, carrying a rod from which a basket full of IVY is hung. At the end of the rod is an effigy of a bird made of wood with tiny bells around its neck. This is the SWALLOW from which the festival takes its name.

As they proceed through the village, the children sing "swallow songs" that go back more than 2,000 years. The woman of the house takes a few ivy leaves from the basket and places them in her hen's nest in the hope that they will encourage the hen to lay more eggs. The children receive a few eggs in return, and they move on to the next house.

SYMBOLS AND CUSTOMS

Ivy

Because it stays green all year long, the ivy that is carried from house to house during the Procession of the Swallow is a symbol of health and growth. It is believed to possess the power to keep hens and other domestic animals from succumbing to disease and to increase their fertility.

Swallow

At one time it was widely believed that the swallow hibernated in the mud during the winter, reemerging with the advent of spring. For this reason it became a symbol for spring itself.

In Christian art, the swallow often appears in scenes of the Annunciation and of the Nativity, where it is usually shown nesting under the eaves or in holes in the wall. Just as it symbolized a rebirth from the death-like state of winter, it also became a symbol of the Resurrection of Christ.

FURTHER READING

Ferguson, George. *Signs and Symbols in Christian Art*. New York: Oxford University Press, 1954.

Henderson, Helene, ed. *Holidays, Festivals, and Celebrations of the World Dictionary*. 3rd ed. Detroit: Omnigraphics, 2005.

Ickis, Marguerite. *The Book of Festivals and Holidays the World Over*. New York: Dodd, Mead, 1970.

Leach, Maria, ed. *Funk & Wagnalls Standard Dictionary of Folklore, Mythology & Legend*. San Francisco: Harper & Row, 1984.

Purim
(Feast of Lots)

Type of Holiday: Religious (Jewish)
Date of Observation: February-March; fourteenth day of Adar
Where Celebrated: Europe, Israel, United States, and by Jews all over the world
Symbols and Customs: Hamantaschen, Kreplach, Megillah, Noisemakers, Purim Plays, Queen Esther, Shalachmanot
Related Holidays: Carnival, Halloween

ORIGINS

Purim is a Jewish holiday dating back over 2,600 years. Judaism is one of the oldest continuously observed religions in the world. Its history extends back beyond the advent of the written word. Its people trace their roots to a common ancestor, Abraham, and then back even farther to the very moment of creation.

According to Jewish belief, the law given to the Jewish people by God contained everything they needed to live a holy life, including the ability to be reinterpreted in new historical situations. Judaism, therefore, is the expression of the Jewish people, attempting to live holy (set apart) lives in accordance with the instructions given by God. Although obedience to the law is central to Judaism, there is no one central authority. Sources of divine authority are God, the Torah, interpretations of the Torah by respected teachers, and tradition. Religious observances and the study of Jewish law are conducted under the supervision of a teacher called a rabbi.

There are several sects within Judaism. Orthodox Judaism is characterized by an affirmation of the traditional Jewish faith, strict adherence to customs such as keeping the Sabbath, participation in ceremonies and rituals, and the observance of dietary regulations. Conservative Jewish congregations seek to retain many ancient traditions but without the accompanying demand for strict observance. Reform Judaism stresses modern biblical criticism and emphasizes ethical teachings more than ritualistic observance. Hasidism is a mystical sect of Judaism that teaches enthusiastic prayer as a means of communion with God. The Reconstructionist movement began early in the twentieth century in an effort to "reconstruct" Judaism with the community rather than the synagogue as its center.

The story of Purim takes place six hundred years before the Christian era, when most of the Jews were slaves in Persia. Ahasuerus, the Persian king, had married the most beautiful girl he could find, Esther, without knowing that she was Jewish. Mordecai, her cousin and guardian, advised her not to reveal her identity as a Jew. After the marriage took place, Mordecai overheard two of the king's soldiers plotting to kill him. Their plans were foiled, and Mordecai was praised for having saved the king's life.

Mordecai's fortunes were reversed, however, when the king decided to appoint Haman as prime minister. Haman took a dislike to Mordecai, who refused to bow down before the new prime minister. Haman decided that Mordecai should be killed and persuaded the king to let him destroy the empire's entire Jewish population along with him. He cast lots (*pur* is the ancient Akkadian word for "lot") to find out which day would be the most auspicious for carrying out his evil plan. This means that he threw small sticks or stones on the ground, using them in much the same way that dice are used today to make a decision based on chance. The lots told him that things would go especially well on the fourteenth of Adar.

When Mordecai heard about Haman's plan, he rushed to tell Queen Esther, knowing that if she told the king she was Jewish, the slaughter would not take place. Esther was worried that her husband might be angry with her for concealing her background, and she told Mordecai she needed to summon her strength before she could confront the king. So Mordecai, Esther, and all the Persian Jews fasted and prayed for three days, at the end of which she felt brave enough to tell Ahasuerus the truth. Recalling that Mordecai had once saved his life, the king was grateful to Esther and Mordecai for revealing Haman's evil nature. Haman and his ten sons were hung from the gallows, and Mordecai became the new prime minister. In his first official act as the king's top adviser, Mordecai sent letters rolled into scrolls (*see* MEGILLAH) to everyone in the kingdom, telling them what had happened and declaring the next day a holiday.

Purim was not observed widely until the second century, when it was referred to as the Day of Mordecai or Day of Protection. But even the earliest celebrations included reciting the story of Esther and exchanging gifts (*see* SHALACHMANOT). It is customary to serve a large meal, known as the *Seudah,* in the afternoon rather than the evening. Turkey is a popular main dish at this meal, and there are usually KREPLACH in the soup. HAMANTASCHEN are the favorite Purim dessert.

Scholars have pointed out that the story of Esther cannot possibly be factual, since none of the Persian kings had a wife named Esther, and none had a prime minister named Haman. It is also highly unlikely that a Persian king could marry a Jewish bride without knowing it, since Persian kings were only allowed to marry into one of the seven leading families of the realm. How do they account, then, for the origin of Purim? Since the name of the holiday is similar to the Persian word meaning "first," some scholars think that Purim goes back to the old Persian New Year festival, which was celebrated around the time of the **VERNAL EQUINOX**.

Whatever its origins, Purim remains a happy occasion. Children dress up in costumes and put on PURIM PLAYS that tell the story of the holiday. It is also a time for sharing food with friends and for charity to the poor.

SYMBOLS AND CUSTOMS

Hamantaschen

Hamantaschen are small pastries filled with a mixture of honey and poppy seeds. In Israel they are called *Oznei Haman,* which means "Haman's ears" and refers to the old European custom of cutting off a criminal's ears before hanging him. Elsewhere they are called "Haman's pockets," a reference to the fact that the legendary Haman's pockets were filled with money from all the bribes he had taken. Some claim that hamantaschen look like the three-cornered hat that Haman wore, but there is no evidence that such hats were in use at that time.

The custom of eating pastries filled with poppy seeds at Purim already existed in the Middle Ages. Sometimes the pastries are filled with prune jam, in commemoration of a plum merchant from Bohemia who, along with the rest of the Bohemian Jews, was saved from persecution in the early eighteenth century.

Kreplach

On the eve of Purim, it is traditional among European Jews to eat kreplach, small pockets of dough filled with ground meat or cheese, boiled, and usually served in soup. For reasons that are not entirely clear, eating kreplach is also associated with beating and banging. They are eaten on the eve of **YOM KIPPUR** because people beat their breasts while reciting their sins. They are also eaten on the last day of **SUKKOT**, when the willow branches are beaten, and on Purim because of the banging that accompanies the mention of Haman's name (*see* PURIM PLAYS).

Megillah

The Megillah is a scroll containing the Book of Esther, symbolic of the rolled letters that Mordecai sent throughout the Persian Empire, explaining how the Jews had been saved and declaring an official holiday. On Purim, the Megillah is read in the synagogue using a special melodic rhythm. Sometimes it is read in a comical way; for example, when the reader comes to the names of Haman's ten sons, it is common to read them very quickly so that they all blend together. Whenever Haman's name is mentioned, people boo and stamp their feet. The same spirit of celebration and merriment that is seen in the PURIM PLAYS and in the election of a QUEEN ESTHER carries over into the synagogue. Sometimes Haman's name is written in chalk on the soles of slippers so that the stomping and shuffling will make it wear off.

The Megillah (Book of Esther) is the only book of the Bible in which illustrations are permitted. The Jewish religion forbids drawing an image of God, but God's name is not mentioned in the Megillah, which has been illustrated by a number of artists over the centuries. The container in which the Megillah was traditionally kept was often decorated as well.

Noisemakers

The *grager* (also spelled *gregger*) is the most popular noisemaker on Purim. It is used to drown out the sound of Haman's name during the reading of the MEGILLAH. Because the Bible instructs Jews to wipe out the memory of Amalek, the leader of the tribe from which Haman was descended, the use of noisemakers symbolically eliminates the evil prime minister who was nearly responsible for wiping out the Persian Jews. In Israel, children often use pop guns or cap guns as their noisemakers.

Haman was so universally detested that, in some Jewish communities, making noise was not enough. The people also made effigies of Haman and burned them.

Purim Plays

During the Middle Ages, the celebration of Purim included masquerades, jesters, musicians, and actors. It was, in fact, the Jewish counterpart of the Christian **CAR-NIVAL** celebration. But Purim plays didn't really become popular until the sixteenth century. Young men and women dressed in costumes would go from house to house in the Jewish community, parodying the characters described in the MEGILLAH. Ahasuerus, for example, might resemble the local sheriff, and Haman was often modeled after the town drunkard. They also poked fun at other biblical figures and at contemporary Jewish life. A surefire way to get laughs was to mock the rabbi's recital of the prayer known as the Kiddush by reeling off a meaningless string of Hebrew words or by chanting obscure verses from the Bible that had nothing to do with one another. In return for the entertainment they provided, the players received money or treats.

This kind of door-to-door theater eventually gave way to actual stage performances and folklore plays. Up until World War II, such plays were common in Germany and eastern Europe during the month of Adar. Although they were more formal, these Purim plays still retained their burlesque character, often degenerating into vulgarity and even obscenity. They were tolerated rather than encouraged by the Jewish authorities—and, in some cases, prohibited.

In western Europe, North America, and Israel, the plays gave way to masquerade parties for adults and children, and to beauty contests held to select a QUEEN ESTHER. Masquerading remains especially popular in Israel, where Purim is an official school holiday and children roam the streets in all kinds of costumes, much as they do on **HALLOWEEN** in the United States.

Queen Esther

Just as the celebration of **TWELFTH NIGHT** involved the crowning of a mock "king," a young boy was crowned Purim King, a custom that dates back to the fourteenth century. In modern times, especially in the United States and at the Purim Carnival in Tel Aviv, the winner of a beauty contest is crowned as Queen Esther.

Scholars believe that these mock kings and queens who are chosen to reign for just the brief period of the festival are actually a survival of a very ancient custom, which was to install a temporary monarch during the brief period between the end of one year and the beginning of the next.

Shalachmanot

Shalachmanot is the word used to describe the Purim gifts that parents give to children and that friends and relatives exchange with each other. Gifts are also made to rabbis and teachers. Donating to the poor and the needy is part of the Purim tradition as well. In the United States, it usually takes the form of presenting Purim baskets to poor families and making contributions to various Jewish funds.

Cakes, candies, and fruit have always been popular Shalachmanot items, along with books, clothing, and other useful items. Sephardic children (the descendants of Jews from Spain and Portugal) prefer cakes baked in the shape of the MEGILLAH, QUEEN ESTHER, or Mordecai riding on a horse. Jewish bakers in Jerusalem and other communities compete with one another to see who can make the most interesting Purim cakes.

FURTHER READING

Bellenir, Karen. *Religious Holidays and Calendars*. 3rd ed. Detroit: Omnigraphics, 2004.

Cashman, Greer Fay. *Jewish Days and Holidays*. New York: SBS Pub., 1979.

Crim, Keith R. *The Perennial Dictionary of World Religions*. San Francisco: Harper & Row, 1989.

Cuyler, Margery. *Jewish Holidays*. New York: Holt, Rinehart and Winston, 1978.

Edidin, Ben. *Jewish Holidays and Festivals*. 1940. Reprint. Detroit: Omnigraphics, 1993.

Gaer, Joseph. *Holidays Around the World*. Boston: Little, Brown, 1953.

Gaster, Theodor H. *Festivals of the Jewish Year*. New York: William Sloane Associates, 1953.

Henderson, Helene, ed. *Holidays, Festivals, and Celebrations of the World Dictionary*. 3rd ed. Detroit: Omnigraphics, 2005.

MacDonald, Margaret R., ed. *The Folklore of World Holidays*. Detroit: Gale Research, 1992.

WEB SITES

Union for Reform Judaism
urj.org/holidays/purim

Union of Orthodox Jewish Congregations of America
www.ou.org/chagim/purim

*Pushkar Mela
(Pushkar Camel Fair)*

Type of Holiday: Religious (Hindu); Promotional
Date of Observation: October-November; four days around the full moon day of the Hindu month of Kartika
Where Celebrated: Pushkar, India
Symbols and Customs: Brahma Temple, Camel Trading, Pushkar Lake

ORIGINS

The annual camel fair Pushkar Mela began as a religious event that was part of Hinduism, which many scholars regard as the world's oldest living religion. The word Hindu is derived from the Sanskrit term *Sindhu* (or *Indus*), which meant river. It referred to people living in the Indus valley in the Indian subcontinent.

Hinduism has no founder, one universal reality (or god) known as Brahman, many gods and goddesses (sometimes referred to as devtas), and several scriptures. Hinduism also has no priesthood or hierarchical structure similar to that seen in some other religions, such as Christianity. Hindus acknowledge the authority of a wide variety of writings, but there is no single, uniform canon. The oldest of the Hindu writings are the *Vedas*. The word "veda" comes from the Sanskrit word for knowledge. The *Vedas*, which were compiled from ancient oral traditions, contain hymns, instructions, explanations, chants for sacrifices, magical formulas, and philosophy. Another set of sacred books includes the *Great Epics*, which illustrate Hindu faith in practice. The *Epics* include the *Ramayana*, the *Mahabharata*, and the *Bhagavad Gita*.

The Hindu pantheon includes approximately thirty-three million gods. Some of these are held in higher esteem than others. Over all the gods, Hindus believe in one absolute high god or universal concept. This is Brahman. Although he is above all the gods, he is not worshipped in popular ceremonies because he is detached from the day-to-day affairs of the people. Brahman is impersonal. Lesser gods and goddesses (devtas) serve him. Because these are more intimately involved in the affairs of people, they are venerated as gods. The most honored god in Hinduism varies among the different Hindu sects. Although Hindu adherents practice their faith differently and venerate different deities, they share a similar view of reality and look back on a common history.

The annual Camel Fair held in Pushkar, a small town several miles from Ajmer in the state of Rajasthan, is not only the largest camel fair in the world but one of India's most colorful events. It takes place during the month of Kartika, beginning two days prior to the full moon day and ending the day after, but the 50,000 camels, horses, and cattle to be traded at the fair usually start arriving with their owners several days in advance. Pushkar's population of 11,000 swells to more than twenty times that during the week of the fair as pilgrims, tourists, singers, dancers, and craftsmen gather for the festivities.

Although no one is certain how the fair came to be held in Pushkar, there is reason to believe that it began as a religious event. A well-known lake was created there, according to Hindu belief, when Lord Brahma, the god of creation, took revenge on the demon Vajra Nabha, who had killed Brahma's children, by striking him with his special weapon, the lotus flower. The demon was killed instantly, and lakes formed in the three places where the lotus petals fell to Earth, one of which was in Pushkar. But when Brahma wanted to sanctify the place by performing a sacrifice there on the full moon day of Kartika, his wife Sarasvati was nowhere to be found. He sent someone to fetch her, but Sarasvati took her time. Knowing that he couldn't perform the sacrifice without a wife at his side and that the full moon was slipping away, Brahma hurriedly married a local milkmaid named Gayatri. When Sarasvati arrived, she was furious. She punished her husband by declaring that Pushkar was the only place on Earth where he would be worshipped, and that the full moon day of Kartika was the only day of the year when this could occur.

PUSHKAR LAKE became one of the five most highly revered pilgrimage sites in India. At one point there were 500 temples and fifty-two palaces built around the lake,

400 of which remain today (*see* BRAHMA TEMPLE). How a religious pilgrimage led to the establishment of a livestock and commercial fair is a mystery, but there is no question that the lake and its temples put Pushkar on the map. Today the fair manages to encompass both ritual bathing and CAMEL TRADING, along with a broad range of commercial ventures and amusements that include snake charmers, fire-eaters, and acrobats. There are performances of folk dancing and singing, hand-crafts for sale, and an atmosphere of celebration as well as religious devotion throughout the week in which the fair is held.

SYMBOLS AND CUSTOMS

Brahma Temple

For more than 700 years, Pushkar has been a focal point for the worship of Brahma. In fact, there are only two temples dedicated to Brahma in all of India: the one at Pushkar and another at Khedbrahma in Kerala. The former is the most important of the hundreds of temples located on PUSHKAR LAKE, and the thousands of pilgrims who flock here for the Pushkar Mela consider a visit to the temple, with its red spire and hamsa (wild goose or swan, the vehicle on which Brahma rides) over the entryway, to be essential. There is also a temple dedicated to Sarasvati, but it is located some distance away—which is perhaps appropriate, given Sarasvati's anger and disdain when she discovered that her husband had replaced her with a milkmaid.

Camel Trading

The primary purpose of the Pushkar Mela is to give the buyers and sellers of camels, along with horses and cattle, an opportunity to bargain with each other. Livestock traders from all over the country bring their animals to Pushkar in the hope of doing some business, and it is not uncommon for more than 25,000 camels to change hands in the course of a few days. These ungainly but trustworthy beasts are washed and groomed for the event; many wear jewelry around their ankles and have their coats shaved to form decorative patterns. The haggling over prices can get quite heated, and tourists will often gather just to watch the traders and buyers argue with each other.

There is a "camel beauty contest," in which the owners parade their camels before huge crowds in the hope that they will impress potential buyers, and camel races where the jockeys frequently end up on the ground. One of the more amusing events is the "camel rush," where people jump onto camels one after the other to see how many a single camel can hold. Some people hire camels just to get around the fair, because the size of the crowds makes driving almost impossible.

Pushkar Lake

Hindus regard Pushkar Lake to be the tirtharaja—the king of the shrines or pilgrimage places—because it was blessed by Brahma himself. They believe that those who take a dip in the lake during the full moon of Kartika, therefore, will have all their sins washed away and will be guaranteed salvation. The lake has fifty-two ghats, which are flights of stairs leading down into the water, so that Hindus who come there to worship Brahma can take a ritual bath.

FURTHER READING

Freeman, Dave, et al. *100 Things to Do Before You Die: Travel Events You Just Can't Miss*. Dallas: Taylor Pub. Co., 1999.

Shemanski, Frances. *A Guide to World Fairs and Festivals*. Westport, CT: Greenwood Press, 1985.

Van Straalen, Alice. *The Book of Holidays Around the World*. New York: Dutton, 1986.

Queen's Birthday
(Sovereign's Official Birthday, Trooping the Colour)

Type of Holiday: National
Date of Observation: Second Saturday in June
Where Celebrated: United Kingdom, Australia, Bermuda, Canada, and other countries with close ties to the UK
Symbols and Customs: Colours, Horse Guards Parade, Inspection, Royal Salute, Trooping the Colour
Colors: Red, which is the color of Queen Elizabeth's flag

ORIGINS

The birthday of Queen Elizabeth II is a national holiday in the United Kingdom. National holidays can be defined as those commemorations that a nation's government has deemed important enough to warrant inclusion in the list of official public holidays. They tend to honor a person or event that has been critical in the development of the nation and its identity. Such people and events usually reflect values and traditions shared by a large portion of the citizenry.

Although the British have celebrated their sovereign's birthday for centuries, it was Queen Victoria, who ruled the British Empire from 1837 until 1901, who came up with the idea of an "official" birthday celebration. Her real birthday was May 24, but it was decided that a public celebration would be held in June. Edward VII (reigned 1901-10), whose birthday was in early November, decided to let the June celebration stand, and George V (reigned 1910-36), who was born on June 3, decided to use his real birthday for the national holiday. George VI (reigned 1936-52) was born in mid-December and Elizabeth (reigned 1952-present) was born on April 21—both times of year when the weather in England is notoriously unreliable. So it made sense to continue to observe the Sovereign's Official Birthday in June, at a time when the weather is more likely to cooperate. Because Queen Elizabeth II has reigned over England for such a long time—her coronation was on June 2, 1952—this day is commonly referred to as the Queen's Birthday. It is usually observed on the second Saturday in June, although the queen's other obligations occasionally necessitate moving it up or back a week.

The official birthday celebration is closely identified with the ceremony known as TROOPING THE COLOUR, an event that takes place on HORSE GUARDS PARADE in Whitehall, an area of London where many government offices are now located and where Whitehall Palace, the official residence of England's royal family in the sixteenth and seventeenth centuries, once stood. The queen is escorted from her home in Buckingham Palace by her Household Cavalry to the parade grounds, where she sits on horseback and carries out an INSPECTION of the Household Troops assembled there. The flag or COLOUR of a particular regiment (a different one is chosen each year) is then "trooped" or carried through the ranks where each and every soldier can see it. The troops then march or ride on horseback past the queen, after which she returns to Buckingham Palace. A ROYAL SALUTE of forty-one guns in London's Green Park brings the event to a close.

SYMBOLS AND CUSTOMS

Colours

"Colours" is a British term for the regimental flags that were traditionally carried into battle and used to rally the soldiers and help them recognize the other members of the group they were fighting with. Although this is no longer done, the colour still symbolizes a regiment's spirit and is carried in parades as a memorial to its fallen soldiers.

The Queen's Colour is solid crimson. If she is present during the ceremony, her colour is carried through the ranks of her Household Troops, as is the colour of the particular regiment (Coldstream, Grenadier, Scots, Irish, or Welsh Guards) in residence in London at the time.

Horse Guards Parade

The Horse Guards Parade, where the Trooping of the Colour takes place in June, is London's largest open space. Built in 1745 to house the guards for the royal palace of Whitehall, it has also served a jousting ground and a tennis court. The Parade is entered through a low arch, where two sentries stand guard, and a number of government offices and the prime minister's Downing Street residence are located along the perimeter.

Inspection

The queen's "inspection" of her assembled troops at Horse Guards Parade is more of a formality than an actual, soldier-by-soldier inspection. Since every soldier has already been inspected a number of times beforehand to make sure that his uniform is spotless and his equipment is clean and in perfect condition, the inspection is a symbolic way of letting the soldiers know that the queen acknowledges their presence.

Royal Salute

The Royal Salute—the firing of forty-one guns in London's Green Park—after the queen has returned to Buckingham Palace is a symbol of the people's respect for their sovereign. Gun salutes originated in the sixteenth century as a naval tradition: A warship entering a foreign port would demonstrate its peaceful intentions by emptying all of its guns first. By 1688 rules had been established regarding how many guns should be fired to show respect for an admiral (nineteen) and a member of the royal family (twenty-one)—the latter number being chosen because most naval ships at the time had ten guns on each side, and an extra shot would be fired as a signal to begin. The forty-one-gun Royal Salute represents two complete rounds from the gun deck of a ship plus the shot that serves as a starting signal.

Trooping the Colour

The ceremony known as Trooping the Colour has been part of the celebration of the king or queen's birthday since the mid-eighteenth century. Symbolizing the soldiers' loyalty to their sovereign, it consists of an intricate series of fast and slow marches and other parade maneuvers that take months of rehearsal to execute without error. The ceremony was originally known as "Lodging the Colour" because the flag that is carried past the troops was lodged or returned to the regiment's quarters afterward for safekeeping. The ceremony is accompanied by military music, typically drums and pipes, and it takes about an hour. The public is invited to watch dress rehearsals for the event, which take place on the two preceding Saturdays.

Trooping the regimental flag was at one time necessary so that new recruits would learn to recognize their flag and rally around it in the confusion of battle. Nowadays it serves a largely ceremonial purpose.

FURTHER READING

Dobler, Lavinia. National Holidays Around the World. New York: Fleet Press Corp., 1968.

Dunkling, Leslie. *A Dictionary of Days*. New York: Facts on File, 1988.

Trawicky, Bernard, and Ruth W. Gregory. *Anniversaries and Holidays*. 5th ed. Chicago: American Library Assocation, 2000.

Van Straalen, Alice. *The Book of Holidays Around the World*. New York: Dutton, 1986.

WEB SITE

British Monarchy's Official Web Site
www.royal.gov.uk

Raksha Bandhan
(Janai Purnima, Brother and Sister Day)

Type of Holiday: Religious (Hindu, Buddhist)
Date of Observation: July-August; Hindu month of Sravana
Where Celebrated: India, Nepal
Symbols and Customs: Rakhi

ORIGINS

Raksha Bandhan is a day for brothers and sisters to reaffirm their bonds of affection. It is observed by the Hindus in northern India and by both Hindus and Buddhists in Nepal, where members of both religions often celebrate in each other's temples. Sisters tie colorful threads or amulets (*see* RAKHI) on their brothers' wrists and put dots of vermilion paste on their brothers' foreheads while praying for them to live a long life. Brothers, in turn, give their sisters gifts—usually a piece of jewelry or clothing, or perhaps some money—while promising to protect them throughout their lives. In families where there are only boys or only girls, a friend or relative is asked to act as a brother or sister during the festival.

In Nepal, the Brahmins (members of the highest caste) put golden threads around everyone's wrists while reciting a mantra or sacred word to give the thread the power to protect its wearer. The *Janai* or "sacred threads" that all Brahmins wear around their necks are also changed at this time.

The word Hindu is derived from the Sanskrit term *Sindhu* (or *Indus*), which meant river. It referred to people living in the Indus valley in the Indian subcontinent. Many scholars regard Hinduism as the oldest living religion.

Hinduism has no founder, one universal reality (or god) known as Brahman, many gods and goddesses (sometimes referred to as devtas), and several scriptures. Hinduism also has no priesthood or hierarchical structure similar to that seen in some other religions, such as Christianity. Hindus acknowledge the authority of a wide variety of writings, but there is no single, uniform canon. The oldest of the Hindu writings are the *Vedas*. The word "veda" comes from the Sanskrit word for knowledge. The *Vedas*, which were compiled from ancient oral traditions, contain hymns, instructions, explanations, chants for sacrifices, magical formulas, and philosophy. Another set of sacred books includes the *Great Epics*, which illustrate Hindu faith in practice. The *Epics* include the *Ramayana*, the *Mahabharata*, and the *Bhagavad Gita*.

The Hindu pantheon includes approximately thirty-three million gods. Some of these are held in higher esteem than others. Over all the gods, Hindus believe in one absolute high god or universal concept. This is Brahman. Although he is above all the gods, he is not worshipped in popular ceremonies because he is detached from the day-to-day affairs of the people. Brahman is impersonal. Lesser gods and goddesses (devtas) serve him. Because these are more intimately involved in the affairs of people, they are venerated as gods. The most honored god in Hinduism varies among the different Hindu sects. Although Hindu adherents practice their faith differently and venerate different deities, they share a similar view of reality and look back on a common history.

SYMBOLS AND CUSTOMS

Rakhi

Usually made from a few colorful cotton or silk threads, or sometimes from silver and gold threads, the *rakhi* symbolizes protection against evil during the coming year. According to legend, when Sultan Babar, the Mohammedan Emperor at Delhi, received a portion of a silken bracelet from the Rajputanan princess who was in grave danger, he immediately rushed to help her. Such a relationship was considered to be like that of brother and sister, and it became customary in India for men who had received *rakhis* to risk their lives, if necessary, to help their "sisters" and rescue them from danger.

Another legend says that Sachi, the consort of the Hindu god Indra, tied such a thread bracelet around the right wrist of her husband when he was disgraced in battle by the demon forces. Indra fought the demons again and was victorious this time.

Old, worn-out *rakhis* must be discarded in the water of a pool, sacred tank, or river.

FURTHER READING

Bellenir, Karen. *Religious Holidays and Calendars*. 3rd ed. Detroit: Omnigraphics, 2004.

Henderson, Helene, ed. *Holidays, Festivals, and Celebrations of the World Dictionary*. 3rd ed. Detroit: Omnigraphics, 2005.

MacDonald, Margaret R., ed. *The Folklore of World Holidays*. Detroit: Gale Research, 1992.

Spicer, Dorothy Gladys. *The Book of Festivals*. 1937. Reprint. Detroit: Omnigraphics, 1990.

WEB SITE

Society for the Confluence of Festivals in India
www.raksha-bandhan.com

Ram Navami

Type of Holiday: Religious (Hindu)
Date of Observation: March-April; ninth day of the waxing half of the Hindu month of Caitra
Where Celebrated: India
Symbols and Customs: Coconut, Rama Lila Pageant, *Ramayana*

ORIGINS

The festival Ram Navami, which honors the birth of Rama, is part of the the Hindu faith, which many scholars regard as the oldest living religion. The word Hindu is derived from the Sanskrit term *Sindhu* (or *Indus*), which meant river. It referred to people living in the Indus valley in the Indian subcontinent.

Hinduism has no founder, one universal reality (or god) known as Brahman, many gods and goddesses (sometimes referred to as devtas), and several scriptures. Hinduism also has no priesthood or hierarchical structure similar to that seen in some other religions, such as Christianity. Hindus acknowledge the authority of a wide variety of writings, but there is no single, uniform canon. The oldest of the Hindu writings are the *Vedas*. The word "veda" comes from the Sanskrit word for knowledge. The *Vedas*, which were compiled from ancient oral traditions, contain hymns, instructions, explanations, chants for sacrifices, magical formulas, and philosophy. Another set of sacred books includes the *Great Epics*, which illustrate Hindu faith in practice. The *Epics* include the *Ramayana*, the *Mahabharata*, and the *Bhagavad Gita*.

The Hindu pantheon includes approximately thirty-three million gods. Some of these are held in higher esteem than others. Over all the gods, Hindus believe in one absolute high god or universal concept. This is Brahman. Although he is above all the gods, he is not worshipped in popular ceremonies because he is detached from the day-to-day affairs of the people. Brahman is impersonal. Lesser gods and goddesses (devtas) serve him. Because these are more intimately involved in the affairs of people, they are venerated as gods. The most honored god in Hinduism varies among the different Hindu sects. Although Hindu adherents practice their faith differently and venerate different deities, they share a similar view of reality and look back on a common history.

Also known as Ramnavami, this Hindu festival celebrates the birth of Rama, the first son of King Dasaratha of Ayodhya, an ancient town in eastern Uttar Pradesh. According to Hindu belief, the god Vishnu was incarnated in ten different human forms, of which Rama was the seventh. He and his wife, Sita, are venerated as the ideal man and wife.

Rama was a popular epic hero before he came to be considered an incarnation of Vishnu. In the early books of the RAMAYANA, the great Hindu religious epic poem, there is no mention of Rama as a divinity. He is a human hero-prince, and it was not until Book VII (the last of the seven books, written much later) and the second century that the theory of his divinity was put forward. Since that time, however, Rama worship has been widespread. The places associated with his life are places of pilgrimage, and his birthday is a day of rejoicing at the temples dedicated to him.

Among the Vaishnavas, the Hindu sect whose devotees honor Vishnu as the supreme god, the celebration of Rama's birthday begins on the first day of Caitra and continues until the ninth, the day on which he was born at noon. In all the important Vaishnava temples, as soon as the sun reaches its highest point in the noonday sky, the priest displays a COCONUT, which he puts in a cradle as he announces the birth of the god. Worshippers are regaled with stories of the great Hindu hero who conquered the island of Ceylon and destroyed the demon king

Ravana. Religious dances and plays depicting episodes from Rama's life are also performed (*see* RAMA LILA PAGEANT).

Ayodhya, the birthplace of Rama, is the main location for the observation of Ram Navami. The Kanaka Bhawan temple here attracts a large number of people, who come to pay homage. The *RAMAYANA* is read and recited, and a fair is held. Elsewhere, statues of Rama are adorned and worshipped; people chant his name and attend lectures on his life and teachings. Hindus believe that Ram-Nam is a magic formula or *mantra* that should be repeated, recited, and meditated upon frequently.

SYMBOLS AND CUSTOMS

Coconut

The coconut palm is particularly sacred to the Hindus because it is a "milk-yielding tree," and the epic poem known as the *Mahabharata* describes in detail the milk-yielding trees of paradise. It is considered auspicious to break coconuts before beginning any sort of important undertaking, and the kernel of the nut is traditionally one of the objects offered to the gods at the time of worship.

When the priest places a coconut in a cradle on Ram Navami, it becomes a symbolic offering in honor of the deity's birth.

Rama Lila Pageant

Plays about Rama are very popular in the former Indian state of the United Provinces (now mainly Uttar Pradesh), where the ancient kingdom of Ayodhya was once located. This is where Rama was born and where, upon his return from exile, he ruled. The Rama Lila Pageant, which is also performed during the **DURGA PUJA** festival, portrays events described in the epic poem RAMAYANA, which tells the story of Rama's life. Most Hindus are so familiar with the events portrayed in the pageant that they can anticipate what is about to happen and call out certain standard responses.

Ramayana

A Hindu epic written in Sanskrit by the poet-sage Valmiki, the *Ramayana* recounts the life of Prince Rama, the seventh incarnation of Vishnu, and his love for Sita, his wife. Rama and Sita are forced into exile by the manipulations of his stepmother. While in exile, Sita is abducted by the demon Ravana. Rama is able to rescue her with the help of the monkey-god Hanuman. Rama eventually returns to reclaim his kingdom.

The recitation of passages from the *Ramayana* or "story of Rama" is an important part of the Ram Navami celebration.

FURTHER READING

Bellenir, Karen. *Religious Holidays and Calendars*. 3rd ed. Detroit: Omnigraphics, 2004.

Henderson, Helene, ed. *Holidays, Festivals, and Celebrations of the World Dictionary*. 3rd ed. Detroit: Omnigraphics, 2005.

Kennedy, Richard S. *The International Dictionary of Religion*. New York: Crossroad, 1984.

Leach, Maria, ed. *Funk & Wagnalls Standard Dictionary of Folklore, Mythology & Legend*. San Francisco: Harper & Row, 1984.

Parrinder, Geoffrey. *A Dictionary of Non-Christian Religions*. Philadelphia: Westminster Press, 1971.

Sharma, Brijendra Nath. *Festivals of India*. New Delhi: Abhinav Publications, 1978.

Thomas, Paul. *Hindu Religion, Customs, and Manners*. 6th ed. New York: APT Books, 1981.

Underhill, Muriel M. *The Hindu Religious Year*. London: Oxford University Press, 1921.

WEB SITE

Festivals in India
www.festivalsinindia.net/ramnavami

Ramadan

Type of Holiday: Religious (Muslim)
Date of Observation: Ninth month of the Islamic lunar calendar
Where Celebrated: Africa, Egypt, India, Indonesia, Iran, Iraq, Jordan, Lebanon, Morocco, Pakistan, Saudi Arabia, Syria, Thailand, Turkey, and throughout the Muslim world
Symbols and Customs: Fasting, Five Pillars, Iftar, New Moon, Sahur
Related Holidays: Hajj, Id al-Fitr, Laylat al Bara'ah, Laylat al-Qadr

ORIGINS

Ramadan, a significant period of fasting, reflection, and prayer for all Muslims, is a holiday in the religious tradition of Islam, one of the world's largest religions. According to some estimates, there are more than one billion Muslims worldwide, with major populations found in the Middle East, North and sub-Saharan Africa, Turkey, Central Asia, and Southeast Asia. In Europe and the United States, Islam is the second largest religious group, with some seven million adherents in the United States. During the early years of Islam, the faith spread throughout the Arabian Peninsula into regions that are today occupied by Saudi Arabia, Syria, Iraq, and Jordan. Contrary to popular opinion, however, Muslims are not just Arabs. Muslims—followers of Islam—are found in many different ethnic groups all over the globe. In fact, Arabs make up less than twenty percent of Muslims.

The word Islam is an Arabic word that means "surrender to God." Its other meanings include peace, safety, and health. The central focus of Islam is a personal commitment and surrender to Allah, the Arabic word for God. In Islam, the concept of Allah is universal and eternal. Allah is the same in every religion and throughout the history of humankind. A person who follows Islam is called a Muslim, which means one who surrenders or submits to Allah's will. But Islam is not just a religion of belief; it is a religion of action. Five specific deeds are required of followers; these are called *The Five Pillars of Islam*. They are 1) *Shahadah*—confession of faith; 2) *Salat*—prayer/worship; 3) *Zakat*—charity; 4) *Sawm*—fasting; and 5) *Hajj*—pilgrimage.

The message of Islam was brought by Muhammad (570-632 C.E.), who is considered a prophet of Allah. The holy book of Islam is the *Qur'an* (also sometimes spelled *Koran* or *Alcoran*). According to Islamic belief, the Qur'an was revealed to Muhammad by Allah over a period of twenty-three years. Authorship of the Qur'an is attributed to Allah, and not to Muhammad; Muhammad merely received it. Muslims believe that because it originated with Allah, the Qur'an is infallible.

There are two main sects within Islam: Sunni and Shi'ite. Sunni Muslims are the majority (estimated at about eighty percent). They recognize the authority of the first four Caliphs, including Ali, and they believe that the Sunna (the example of the Prophet Muhammad) is interpreted through the consensus of the community. Shi'ite Muslims also look to special teachers, called imams. The imams are the direct descendants of Muhammad through Fatimah and Ali. These individuals are believed to be inspired and to possess secret knowledge. Shi'ites, however, do not recognize the same line of Islamic leaders acknowledged by the Sunnis. Shi'ites hold to a doctrine that accepts only leaders who are descended from Muhammad through his daughter Fatimah and her husband Ali. Many Shi'ite subsects believe that true imams are errorless and sinless. They receive instruction from these leaders rather than relying on the consensus of the community.

Ramadan is the ninth month of the Islamic year, and it marks the anniversary of more than one significant event. It was during Ramadan that the Qur'an was first revealed to the Prophet Muhammad (*see* **LAYLAT AL-QADR**). According to legend, as Muhammad sat alone in the wilderness, the angel Gabriel came to him with a golden tablet in his hands and told the Prophet to read what was written on it. This was the essence of the Qur'an, just as the Tablets of the Law received by Moses on Mount Sinai were the essence of the Old Testament. The Battle of Badr—the first battle between the idol worshippers of Mecca and the Muslims of Medina—also occurred during Ramadan, resulting in a glorious victory for the Muslims.

FASTING during the holy month of Ramadan is one of the FIVE PILLARS or requirements of the Islamic faith. It begins with the sighting of the NEW MOON, usually on the 28th day of the previous month. In many Islamic countries, the start of Ramadan is announced with the firing of a gun or cannon on the eve of the first day, since the Islamic "day" begins at sunset. Cannon fire is also used to signal the beginning and end of each day's fast. The morning hours are typically spent reciting the Qur'an, while the remainder of the day is spent sleeping, reading, and praying. As sunset approaches, Muslims gather in the mosque to chant the Qur'an and pray. When the gun announcing the end of the fast is fired, they return home to eat. It is compulsory for every Muslim over the age of twelve to observe the fast. Children learn to fast by doing so gradually, until they are old enough to do so without injuring their health.

Because the Islamic calendar is lunar, the observation of Ramadan moves through the year, eventually occurring in each of the seasons. When it falls at the height of summer, the fast is even more difficult to observe. The days can be nearly sixteen hours long, and although Muslims are permitted to hold water in their mouths for a moment, they cannot drink any until the sun goes down.

Like the Christian **LENT** or the period between **ROSH HASHANAH** and **YOM KIPPUR** for Jews, Ramadan is a time for self-examination and increased religious devotion. The fast ends when the new moon is again sighted and the month of Shawwal begins. It is followed by the **ID AL-FITR**, the Festival of Breaking Fast, which lasts for three days and is marked by feasting and the exchange of gifts.

SYMBOLS AND CUSTOMS

Fasting

The rules regarding the Ramadan fast are very stringent. No food or drink is permitted between sunrise and sunset; kissing, smoking, bathing, sexual intercourse, and receiving injections are forbidden as well. Some Muslims even try to avoid swallowing their saliva or opening their mouths more than is absolutely necessary to draw in fresh air. Only travelers, mothers with young babies, young children, the aged, and those who are very ill are excused from the requirements of the fast. Menstruating women are also exempt, but they must make up for the lost fast days at some point during the year. The same rule applies to days lost for health or travel reasons.

While the days are spent fasting, each night the fast is broken with a feast. It is customary to begin with a white soup made of wheat broiled in meat broth. This is followed later by a regular dinner of meat, rice, and vegetables. The rule is that when it becomes light enough outside to distinguish a white thread from a black one, the fast must be resumed. Muslims believe that whoever observes the fast faithfully and with pure intentions will have his or her sins forgiven. Fasting during Ramadan is said to be thirty times more effective than doing so at any other time of year.

The purpose of fasting is to teach the self-discipline that is needed to prepare for the suffering that Muslims may have to face in the course of obeying their God. It is also a powerful means of defeating Satan, because the passions that are Satan's weapons are strengthened by eating and drinking. Finally, fasting is a communal experience that makes everyone more aware of what it is like to feel hunger.

According to the Prophet, there are five things that will undo the good that has been acquired through fasting: telling a lie, denouncing someone behind his or her back, slander, a false oath, and greed or covetousness.

Five Pillars

The Five Pillars of Islam are the fundamental tenets or requirements that are accepted by all branches of the Muslim faith. They are as follows:

(1) *Shahadah:* The duty to recite the creed of Islam: "There is no god but Allah, and Muhammad is His Prophet."

(2) *Salat:* The duty to worship God with prayer five times each day.

(3) *Zakat:* The duty to be charitable, to distribute alms, and to help the needy.

(4) *Sawm:* The observance of the Fast of Ramadan.

(5) *Hajj:* The duty to make a pilgrimage to Mecca at least once in a lifetime.

Fasting during Ramadan is the Fourth Pillar, although the first two Pillars are considered the most essential (i.e., no one who disregards them can be considered a Muslim).

Iftar

When the fast ends at sunset each day during Ramadan, the meal that is taken to break the fast is called *iftar.* It is a happy occasion in most Muslim families. Foods that have been prepared at home or purchased at the market are spread out on a table while everyone sits around and waits for the sun to go down.

The timing of iftar is usually announced on radio and television, but the old tradition is to listen for the call from the minarets of the mosque. Muslims usually break their fast by first eating a date or taking a drink of water—in imitation of the Prophet, who broke his fast in a similar manner.

New Moon

The Islamic calendar is lunar, which means that each month begins with the appearance of the new moon. In Muslim countries, everyone comes out of the house to see the new moon of Ramadan. Many climb up on their roofs or go to the tops of nearby hills to get a better view. Once the new moon has been sighted, everyone congratulates each other and hurries back inside to prepare for the early morning meal (*see* SAHUR).

If the weather is cloudy and the moon is difficult to see, Islamic countries broadcast the news of its sighting. Once the appearance of the new moon is confirmed by at least two people, the news is announced on radio and television. Before these means of communication were invented, it was traditionally announced by firing a cannon.

Sahur

The *sahur* is a meal taken just before dawn and the start of the day's fast during the month of Ramadan. In cities and towns, many people walk through the streets in the early morning hours, beating drums and playing flutes or calling out to let people know that it is time to partake of the pre-dawn meal.

If Ramadan falls during the winter, when the nights are long and people have plenty of time to rest, sahur is a full meal. But on short summer nights, because of the limited amount of time between IFTAR and sahur, the early morning meal is very light and simple. After it is over, everyone prepares for morning prayer, worshipping either at the mosque or at home.

FURTHER READING

Ahsan, M.M. *Muslim Festivals*. Vero Beach, FL: Rourke Enterprises, 1987.

Bellenir, Karen. *Religious Holidays and Calendars*. 3rd ed. Detroit: Omnigraphics, 2004.

Crim, Keith R. *The Perennial Dictionary of World Religions*. San Francisco: Harper & Row, 1989.

Gaer, Joseph. *Holidays Around the World*. Boston: Little, Brown, 1953.

Glassé, Cyril. *The Concise Encyclopedia of Islam*. 2nd ed. San Francisco: Harper & Row, 1999.

Gulevich, Tanya. *Understanding Islam and Muslim Traditions*. Detroit: Omnigraphics, 2004.

Henderson, Helene, ed. *Holidays, Festivals, and Celebrations of the World Dictionary.* 3rd ed. Detroit: Omnigraphics, 2005.

Pike, Royston. *Round the Year with the World's Religions.* 1950. Reprint. Detroit: Omnigraphics, 1992.

Von Grunebaum, Gustave E. *Muhammadan Festivals.* New York: Schuman, 1951.

WEB SITES

BBC (British Broadcasting Corporation)
www.bbc.co.uk/religion/religions/islam/practices/ramadan_1.shtml

IslamiCity
www.islamicity.com/ramadan

Rath Yatra
(Jagannatha Festival, Car Festival)

Type of Holiday: Religious (Hindu)
Date of Observation: June-July; Hindu month of Asadha
Where Celebrated: India
Symbols and Customs: Chariot

ORIGINS

The Rath Yatra festival celebrates the god Krishna and is part of the Hindu faith, which many scholars regard as the world's oldest living religion. The word Hindu is derived from the Sanskrit term *Sindhu* (or *Indus*), which meant river. It referred to people living in the Indus valley in the Indian subcontinent. Hinduism has no founder, one universal reality (or god) known as Brahman, many gods and goddesses (sometimes referred to as devtas), and several scriptures. Hinduism also has no priesthood or hierarchical structure similar to that seen in some other religions, such as Christianity. Hindus acknowledge the authority of a wide variety of writings, but there is no single, uniform canon. The oldest of the Hindu writings are the *Vedas*. The word "veda" comes from the Sanskrit word for knowledge. The *Vedas*, which were compiled from ancient oral traditions, contain hymns, instructions, explanations, chants for sacrifices, magical formulas, and philosophy. Another set of sacred books includes the *Great Epics*, which illustrate Hindu faith in practice. The *Epics* include the *Ramayana*, the *Mahabharata*, and the *Bhagavad Gita*.

The Hindu pantheon includes approximately thirty-three million gods. Some of these are held in higher esteem than others. Over all the gods, Hindus believe in one absolute high god or universal concept. This is Brahman. Although he is above all the gods, he is not worshipped in popular ceremonies because he is detached from the day-to-day affairs of the people. Brahman is impersonal. Lesser gods and goddesses (devtas) serve him. Because these are more intimately involved in the affairs of people, they are venerated as gods. The most honored god in Hinduism varies among the different Hindu sects. Although Hindu adherents practice their faith differently and venerate different deities, they share a similar view of reality and look back on a common history.

The Rath Yatra festival celebrates Jagannatha, a form of the Hindu god Krishna worshipped primarily in the state of Orissa, India. Jagannatha means "Lord of the World." The Jagannatha Temple in Puri, one of the largest Hindu temples in India, is a pilgrimage site for his worshippers and the focus of Rath Yatra, a major festival observed at the end of June. Wooden images of Jagannatha, his brother Balabhadra, and his sister Subhadra are carried in procession in three huge CHARIOTS or carts that resemble temples and are called *raths*. Jagannatha's is the largest—as high as a three-story building—and all three chariots are drawn along the processional route by thousands of devotees.

Early on the morning of the festival, 108 pitchers of water are drawn from a well reserved for the occasion, and the images of Jagannatha and his siblings are washed with reverence and placed in their respective chariots. These huge, ornate vehicles are then dragged from the temple to Gundicha Mandir, the god's summer house, a distance of about a mile and a half. Seven days later, the chariots return to the temple, where they are disassembled and their materials used to make religious relics.

At one time, worshippers would throw themselves under the wheels of the chariot as it moved forward in the belief that they would be guaranteed a holy death. Nowadays this practice has been forbidden, but people still flock to Puri to take part in the procession and the feast that follows. Similar festivals are held in other Indian cities where there are temples dedicated to Jagannatha, but participation in the procession at Puri is considered to be the greatest honor.

The Jagannatha Festival is very popular because distinctions among the castes are suspended on this day. All Hindus are considered equal, and everyone has to eat the food prepared at the shrine by low caste men.

SYMBOLS AND CUSTOMS

Chariot

The main chariot containing the image of Jagannatha has a yellow-and-orange striped canopy forty-five feet high, with sixteen wheels seven feet in diameter. As it is pulled through the city along the established processional path, devotees have an opportunity for *darsana* or "sight" of the god. They may toss flowers, break coconuts, or sprinkle the image with water as the cart passes before them. Because the moving chariot represents an inexorable force that can crush anything in its path, Jagannatha's name has entered the English language as the word "juggernaut."

The journey of the huge chariot commemorates Krishna's journey from the village of Gokul, where he had been raised by cowherds, back to Mathura, the city of his birth, where his divine mission was to kill the wicked king, Kamsa.

FURTHER READING

Bellenir, Karen. *Religious Holidays and Calendars*. 3rd ed. Detroit: Omnigraphics, 2004.

Crim, Keith R. *The Perennial Dictionary of World Religions*. San Francisco: Harper & Row, 1989.

Eliade, Mircea. *The Encyclopedia of Religion*. New York: Macmillan, 1987.

Gaer, Joseph. *Holidays Around the World*. Boston: Little, Brown, 1953.

Henderson, Helene, ed. *Holidays, Festivals, and Celebrations of the World Dictionary*. 3rd ed. Detroit: Omnigraphics, 2005.

Leach, Maria, ed. *Funk & Wagnalls Standard Dictionary of Folklore, Mythology & Legend*. San Francisco: Harper & Row, 1984.

WEB SITE

ISCKON
www.rathayatra.co.uk

Reek Sunday

Type of Holiday: Religious (Roman Catholic)
Date of Observation: Last Sunday in July
Where Celebrated: County Mayo, Ireland
Symbols and Customs: The Reek
Related Holidays: Lughnasa

ORIGINS

Reek Sunday is an Irish Christian event celebrating St. Patrick. The word Christian refers to a follower of Christ, a title derived from the Greek word meaning Messiah or Anointed One. The Christ of Christianity is Jesus of Nazareth, a man born between 7 and 4 B.C.E. in the region of Palestine. According to Christian teaching, Jesus was killed by Roman authorities using a form of execution called crucifixion (a term meaning he was nailed to a cross and hung from it until he died) in about the year 30 C.E. After his death, he rose back to life. His death and resurrection provide a way by which people can be reconciled with God. In remembrance of Jesus' death and resurrection, the cross serves as a fundamental symbol in Christianity.

With nearly two billion believers in countries around the globe, Christianity is the largest of the world's religions. There is no one central authority for all of Christianity. The pope (the bishop of Rome) is the authority for the Roman Catholic Church, but other sects look to other authorities. Orthodox communities look to patriarchs and emphasize doctrinal agreement and traditional practice. Protestant communities focus on individual conscience. The Roman Catholic and Protestant churches are often referred to as the Western Church, while the Orthodox churches may also be called the Eastern Church. All three main branches of Christianity acknowledge the authority of Christian scriptures, a compilation of writings assembled into a document called the Bible. Methods of biblical interpretation vary among the different Christian sects.

Reek Sunday is the day on which thousands of pilgrims climb the mountain known as Croagh Patrick in County Mayo to pray on the spot where Ireland's patron saint, St. Patrick, is believed to have started his ministry. The tradition has been in existence for more than 1,500 years: It was here that Patrick, according to legend, fasted for forty days and forty nights in 441, and where he banished the snakes from Ireland. But the date for the pilgrimage was not set until 1432, when the pope sent a letter granting a relaxation of penances to those who climbed to the top of Croagh Patrick on the Sunday before the Feast of St. Peter's Chains (August 1) and gave alms for the support of the chapel there.

Because it is so much easier for modern-day pilgrims to get to Croagh Patrick and because their numbers have increased so dramatically, the pilgrimage season has been expanded to run from June into September. Local people make their own pilgrimage on the Friday before Reek Sunday, while other groups make their pilgrimages either in early July or on August 15, the **FEAST OF THE ASSUMPTION OF THE BLESSED VIRGIN MARY**. But it is on the last Sunday in July that the largest number of pilgrims—at least 25,000—make their ascent.

To climb the mountain, they follow a winding trail about three miles long that rises from the village of Murrisk at the southern shore of Clew Bay. Many climb in bare feet with rosary beads wrapped around their fingers as they pray. There are three "stations" where the pilgrims pause. The first is the statue of St. Patrick a few hundred yards up the trail, which they circle seven times while reciting prayers. This is followed by a steep climb, where many pilgrims fall victim to the stones, gravel, and mud covering the precipitous slope. Volunteers from the Order of Malta are standing by to take the injured down on stretchers, although occasionally an Air Force helicopter must be called in from Donegal. Most falls actually occur on the way down, where people are more likely to be overcome by weakness or vertigo. A number of people have died while climbing THE REEK, as the mountain is known locally.

At the summit, pilgrims observe the second station at Leaba Phadraig (Patrick's Bed) or, more traditionally, by walking fifteen times around the whitewashed stone oratory built in 1905, again reciting prayers. Masses are said on the summit every half hour from 8:00 a.m. until 4:00 p.m. by twenty priests, who also hear confessions. The third station, an ancient mound known as Reilig Mhuire (Our Lady's Cemetery), is just a short distance down from the summit on the west. Once all three stations are completed, the pilgrim obtains a plenary indulgence (a remission of all temporal punishment due to sin).

At one time it was customary to engage in dancing, singing, and feasting after the pilgrimage was completed, but the festivities often got out of hand and the Church put a stop to them. Enterprising vendors are always waiting at the foot of the hill, however, to sell the weary pilgrims sandwiches, lemonade, and souvenir "certificates" to prove they've made the climb.

SYMBOLS AND CUSTOMS

The Reek

Local people have referred to Croagh Patrick as "The Reek" for as far back as anyone can remember. The cone-shaped mountain is 2,510 feet tall, with a volcanic quartzite peak. Leading up to the summit are two rough tracks—one from the east and one from the west. Most pilgrims climb the track from the east, setting out in the dark so they will reach the top shortly after dawn.

Some scholars believe that The Reek is part of a pre-Christian pilgrimage route that stretched for 32 miles. There are actually a number of reasons to believe that it played a part in pre-Christian tradition. Reek Sunday is still known as Domhnach Chrom Dubh in the west of Ireland—Chrom Dubh being the pagan god of the harvest, and August 1 being the original date for celebrating the start of the harvest season. It was during the pre-Christian festival of **LUGHNASA**, also observed on August 1, that people traditionally visited hilltop sites to pick berries.

FURTHER READING

Bellenir, Karen. *Religious Holidays and Calendars*. 3rd ed. Detroit: Omnigraphics, 2004.

Henderson, Helene, ed. *Holidays, Festivals, and Celebrations of the World Dictionary*. 3rd ed. Detroit: Omnigraphics, 2005.

Long, George. *The Folklore Calendar*. 1930. Reprint. Detroit: Omnigraphics, 1990.

MacDonald, Margaret R., ed. *The Folklore of World Holidays*. Detroit: Gale Research, 1992.

Trawicky, Bernard, and Ruth W. Gregory. *Anniversaries and Holidays*. 5th ed. Chicago: American Library Assocation, 2000.

Weiser, Franz Xaver. *The Holyday Book*. New York: Harcourt, Brace, 1956.

WEB SITES

Croagh Patrick Visitor Centre
www.croagh-patrick.com/mountain.html

Westport Tourist Office
westport.mayo-ireland.ie/CroaghPatrick3.htm

*Ridvan
(Rizwhan)*

Type of Holiday: Religious (Baha'i)
Date of Observation: April 21-May 2
Where Celebrated: Worldwide
Symbols and Customs: Abstaining from Work, Elections, Reenactments

ORIGINS

The Baha'i faith was established in 1863 by Baha'u'llah, a Persian (Iranian) prophet who is regarded by the faithful as the Messenger of God. Ridvan (alternately Rizwhan) commemorates the events that occurred over the course of twelve days that Baha'u'llah spent in a rose garden in Baghdad, Iraq. There he revealed himself to be the fulfillment of the prophecies of all previous religions. In doing so, Baha'u'llah founded the Baha'i religion, which is based on his teachings. He established this as the "Most Great Festival" and specified that the first, ninth, and twelfth days of Ridvan should be observed as holidays and that work should be suspended.

Ridvan is regarded as the King of Festivals and is one of the most important holidays of the Baha'i year. During the twelve-day observance, the faithful meet for communal prayer and socializing, with specific customs varying according to local cultural practices. Meeting rooms may be decorated with roses or draped with white cloth to represent the outdoor canopy used by Baha'u'llah in the garden. Accounts of Baha'u'llah's revelations may be read aloud. In some Baha'i communities, reenactments depict significant events of Ridvan, while music and choral performances may also be staged.

On a less spiritual note, administrative business for the worldwide Baha'i organization is also conducted during Ridvan, including elections of religious leaders.

SYMBOLS AND CUSTOMS

Abstaining from Work

The first (April 21), ninth (April 29), and twelfth (May 2) days of Ridvan are observed as holy days. These three days commemorate the anniversaries of Baha'u'llah's arrival in the garden, the subsequent arrival of his relatives, and his departure for Constantinople (now known as Istanbul, Turkey). On these days Baha'is abstain from work to spend time in individual or communal prayer and reflection.

Elections

The worldwide Baha'i religious community is administered by the members of Spiritual Assemblies, which operate at the local, national, and international level. Spiritual Assembly members are elected annually during Ridvan. All members of the Baha'i faith are equally eligible to vote in these elections.

Reenactments

Some Baha'i communities stage pageants or theatrical reenactments to depict the significant events of Ridvan. These presentations typically focus on the arrival of Baha'u'llah at the garden, his declaration of himself as the Messenger of God, pertinent teachings he delivered during the twelve days of Ridvan, and his departure for Turkey from Iraq.

FURTHER READING

Bellenir, Karin. *Religious Holidays and Calendars*, 3rd ed. Detroit: Omnigraphics, 2004.

Bowers, Kenneth E. *God Speaks Again: An Introduction to the Baha'i Faith*. Wilmette, IL: Baha'i Publications, 2004.

Henderson, Helene, ed. *Holidays, Festivals, and Celebrations of the World Dictionary*, 3rd ed. Detroit: Omnigraphics, 2005.

Smith, Peter. *A Concise Encyclopedia of the Baha'i Faith*. Boston: Oneworld, 2000.

WEB SITE

National Spiritual Assembly of the Baha'is of the U. S.
www.bahai.us/festival-of-ridvan

Rocket Festival
(Boun Bang Fay, Bun Bang Fai)

Type of Holiday: Calendar/Seasonal, Folkloric, Religious (Buddhist)
Date of Observation: April-May; full moon day of Vaisakha
Where Celebrated: Laos, Thailand, United States
Symbols and Customs: Rocket
Related Holidays: Vesak

ORIGINS

The Rocket Festival in Laos marks the coming of the rainy season. It provides people with an excuse to get together and celebrate during a time when the weather makes almost any work impossible. Known as Bun Bang Fai (*bun* means "festival" in Laos), the festival was originally intended to guarantee good crops. But with the arrival of Buddhism, it also became a commemoration of the birth, enlightenment, and death of Buddha.

Buddhism, one of the four largest religious families in the world, is based on the teachings of Siddhartha Gautama (c. 563-483 B.C.E.), who came to be known as Buddha, or "The Enlightened One." The basic tenets of Buddhism can be summarized in the Four Noble Truths and the Eightfold Path. The Four Noble Truths are 1) the truth and reality of suffering; 2) suffering is caused by desire; 3) the way to end suffering is to end desire; and 4) the Eightfold Path shows the way to end suffering. The Eightfold Path consists of 1) right view or right understanding; 2) right thoughts and aspirations; 3) right speech; 4) right conduct and action; 5) right way of life; 6) right effort; 7) right mindfulness; and 8) right contemplation.

The Rocket Festival takes its name from the main event: a contest among *wat* (temple) communities to see which can build and launch the most successful ROCKET. After the religious ceremonies associated with the festival are over, people dress in traditional costumes and gather outdoors. The rockets are traditionally bamboo poles up to 20 feet in length, decorated with dragons and colored streamers and filled with a special gunpowder mix. They are judged not only on the basis of how far they fly when launched, but on how beautifully they are decorated. Buddhist monks are generally the best rocket makers.

The Rocket Festival was brought to the United States by Laotians who immigrated in the 1970s and 1980s. Since there is no rainy season in the United States, Bun Bang Fai is observed there primarily for nostalgic reasons, and to introduce Americans to Laotian culture.

SYMBOLS AND CUSTOMS

Rocket

Bun Bang Fai dates back to a time when Laotians believed in many gods and would fire rockets in hopes of persuading them to send the rain needed for the rice harvest. The rocket was seen as a much more immediate way of communicating with the gods than the traditional methods of prayer and sacrifice.

The rocket contests that are held today have less to do with religion and agriculture than with competition among neighborhoods and between civic and military groups. Officials judging the contest usually watch from a grandstand and give prizes for the most brilliant, the fastest, and the highest rocket.

FURTHER READING

Henderson, Helene, ed. *Holidays, Festivals, and Celebrations of the World Dictionary.* 3rd ed. Detroit: Omnigraphics, 2005.

MacDonald, Margaret R., ed. *The Folklore of World Holidays.* Detroit: Gale Research, 1992.

Van Straalen, Alice. *The Book of Holidays Around the World.* New York: Dutton, 1986.

WEB SITE

Smithsonian National Air and Space Museum
www.nasm.si.edu/research/dsh/artifacts/RM-BounBangFai.htm

Rogation Days (Rogationtide, Soil and Water Stewardship Week)

Type of Holiday: Religious (Christian)
Date of Observation: April 25 and the three days preceding Ascension Day
Where Celebrated: England, France, Germany, United States, and by Christians all over the West
Symbols and Customs: Beating the Bounds, Litanies, Reconciliation
Related Holidays: Ember Days

ORIGINS

Rogation Days is a three-day period in the Christian faith that involves prayers, processions, and asking for God's help. The word Christian refers to a follower of Christ, a title derived from the Greek word meaning Messiah or Anointed One. The Christ of Christianity is Jesus of Nazareth, a man born between 7 and 4 B.C.E. in the region of Palestine. According to Christian teaching, was killed by Roman authorities using a form of execution called crucifixion (a term meaning he was nailed to a cross and hung from it until he died) in about the year 30 C.E. After his death, he rose back to life. His death and resurrection provide a way by which people can be reconciled with God. In remembrance of Jesus' death and resurrection, the cross serves as a fundamental symbol in Christianity.

With nearly two billion believers in countries around the globe, Christianity is the largest of the world's religions. There is no one central authority for all of Christianity. The pope (the bishop of Rome) is the authority for the Roman Catholic Church, but other sects look to other authorities. Orthodox communities look to patriarchs and emphasize doctrinal agreement and traditional practice. Protestant communities focus on individual conscience. The Roman Catholic and Protestant churches are often referred to as the Western Church, while the Orthodox churches may also be called the Eastern Church. All three main branches of Christianity acknowledge the authority of Christian scriptures, a compilation of writings assembled into a document called the Bible. Methods of biblical interpretation vary among the different Christian sects.

The word "rogation" comes from the Latin *rogare,* meaning "to ask or beseech." It was Bishop Mamertus of Viennes, France, who came up with the idea of setting aside the Monday, Tuesday, and Wednesday before **ASCENSION DAY** for processions and LITANIES to ask not only for God's blessings but for his protection. During the years when Mamertus was bishop (461-475 C.E.), France was struck by more than the usual number of natural disasters, including floods, fires, earthquakes, and plagues, as well as by rioting, looting, and invasions. Mamertus called for three days of prayer, fasting, and penitence in the hope that God would forgive the people for their sins and protect them from further catastrophe. He led processions on these three days in which the entire community participated, reciting prayers and asking God to bring them peace, good weather, and a bountiful harvest.

The idea caught on, and by 511 C.E. the custom of holding processions with litanies on these three days, known as the Minor Rogations, had spread throughout the country. Soon the entire Western Church was observing the Rogation Days, which in England were called "Gang" or "Gange" Days, from the Anglo-Saxon word *gangen,* meaning "to go" or "to walk." The Church of England used these days as an opportunity to reconfirm parish boundaries (*see* BEATING THE BOUNDS) and to settle differences among church members (*see* RECONCILIATION). Over the centuries, Rogationtide became primarily a time to bless the fields and the crops, although prayers for protection from natural disasters never disappeared from the observation entirely. In Cold Springs, Minnesota, for example, the Rogation Days are devoted to commemorating the end of the grasshopper plague that devastated the crops in 1877. There is a procession to the "Grasshopper Chapel" that was built afterward to show appreciation to God for answering the farmers' prayers. Elsewhere in the United States, the fifth Sunday after **EASTER** is known as Rural Life Sunday or Soil Stewardship Sunday, and the week that follows is known as Soil and Water Stewardship Week. Since 1955 the National Association of Conservation Districts (NACD) has sponsored this observance, setting it aside as a time to focus on the importance of soil and water conservation.

April 25 is known as the Major Rogation because it dates back even further than the time of Mamertus. Scholars believe that it was instituted by the Roman Catholics to replace the Robigalia, an ancient Roman feast held on this date in honor of the bisexual corn god Robigus (also known as the goddess Robigo), in hopes that he/she would protect the corn crop from blight. Observation of the Robigalia involved a procession to the grove that served as a shrine to Robigus about four miles outside the city of Rome, where animal sacrifices were made and a celebration with games and amusements followed. Like the Minor Rogations, the Major Rogation was essentially a time to bless the fields and crops and ask for protection from natural disasters.

SYMBOLS AND CUSTOMS

Beating the Bounds

The ancient Romans held processions on April 25 to win the favor of Robigus/Robigo, the corn god/goddess. When Christianity came to Rome, it retained the processions but held them in honor of the Christian God and included LITANIES. Bishop Mamertus instituted processions on the three days preceding **ASCENSION DAY,** and in England the Ascension Day processions were used to reconfirm the existence of parish boundaries—a practice known as "beating the bounds." The congregation would follow the parish priest while reciting a Litany of the Saints, pausing from time to time while the priest sprinkled holy water on the trees, stones, and other natural objects that served as boundary markers. In the days before modern maps and techniques of surveying had been invented, this was the only method available to impress on people's memories just where the limits of the parish lay. Sometimes young people were tossed into streams, bumped against stones, and dragged over walls and hedges so that it was unlikely that in their lifetimes they would ever forget where these markers lay. Some villages in England still "beat the bounds" during Rogationtide or on Ascension Day, stopping at boundary stones or trees while a clergyman reads from the Bible or recites a prayer.

Litanies

The public prayers known as litanies, which involve invocations by one or more persons followed by set responses—for example, "His mercy endureth forever"— from a group, are derived from ancient Jewish tradition. Litanies were often used while marching in processions because they gave people a rhythm to march to and a chance to rest and catch their breath, and the two terms eventually became synonymous. When Mamertus established the processions associated with the Minor Rogations in 470 C.E., he called them "litanies" because of their penitential nature. The word "litany," in fact, comes from the Greek litaneia, meaning "supplication," which makes it equivalent to the Latin rogare, "to beseech," from which the Rogation Days take their name.

Reconciliation

During the Middle Ages, the Rogation Days were dedicated not only to blessing the harvest and asking for God's protection but to settling arguments among parishioners. By participating in communitywide processions, individuals who were angry with one another would often settle their disputes and put their personality conflicts to rest.

FURTHER READING

Bellenir, Karen. *Religious Holidays and Calendars*. 3rd ed. Detroit: Omnigraphics, 2004.

Dunkling, Leslie. *A Dictionary of Days*. New York: Facts on File, 1988.

Harper, Howard V. *Days and Customs of All Faiths*. 1957. Reprint. Detroit: Omnigraphics, 1990.

Lemprière, John. *Lemprière's Classical Dictionary*. Revised ed. London: Bracken, 1994.

MacDonald, Margaret R., ed. *The Folklore of World Holidays*. Detroit: Gale Research, 1992.

Trawicky, Bernard, and Ruth W. Gregory. *Anniversaries and Holidays*. 5th ed. Chicago: American Library Assocation, 2000.

Urlin, Ethel L. *Festivals, Holy Days, and Saints' Days*. 1915. Reprint. Detroit: Omnigraphics, 1992.

Weiser, Franz Xaver. *Handbook of Christian Feasts and Customs*. New York: Harcourt, Brace, 1958.

WEB SITE

New Advent Catholic Encylopedia
www.newadvent.org/cathen/13110b.htm

Rose Bowl
(Tournament of Roses)

Type of Holiday: Sporting
Date of Observation: January 1
Where Celebrated: Pasadena, California
Symbols and Customs: Football Game, Parade, Rose Queen

ORIGINS

The first Tournament of Roses took place in 1890. Members of Pasadena's hunt club cooked up the idea as a way of promoting their town's mild climate and fertile land. Club members modeled the Tournament of Roses on the Battle of the Flowers, which takes place in Nice, France. The tournament consisted of a PARADE of flower-decked carriages, foot races, polo matches, and tug-of-war contests. The event pleased the townsfolk and so became an annual event. The first participants in the Tournament of Roses would hardly recognize the celebration that takes place today. Although the parade remains, an annual college FOOTBALL GAME has come to dominate the day's events, which are broadcast on television to over sixty million viewers in the U.S. and abroad.

In 1895 the Hunt Club turned over the organization and management of the Tournament of Roses to a new, non-profit group called the Tournament of Roses Association. The Association added new features to the yearly event, including ostrich races and bronco busting. In 1902 they added a football match to the festival. Tournament organizers envisioned an east-versus-west contest, and so pitted Stanford University's team against the team from the University of Michigan. Michigan squashed Stanford 49 to 0 in this first ever post-season college football game. In fact, Stanford was so far behind in the third quarter that they simply admitted defeat and called off the rest of the game, much to the disappointment of the fans. This unimpressive ending led tournament organizers to replace football with

Roman chariot races until 1916, when football games returned and claimed a permanent place at the center of the day's festivities.

As time went on, the football game became the central and most important event in the Tournament of Roses. In fact, today the Tournament of Roses is often referred to as the Rose Bowl, a title that refers specifically to the football game. The game takes its name from Rose Bowl stadium, built in the early 1920s specifically for the game. Rose Bowl Stadium was named after the Yale Bowl, a bowl-shaped structure many deem to be the first modern football stadium. In 1952, when NBC broadcast the game, the Rose Bowl became the first college football game to be nationally televised.

The flower-covered carriages that graced the first years of the Tournament of Roses have long since been replaced with motorized parade floats. The parade, which precedes the football game, is also covered on television. Each year a different celebrity Grand Marshall presides over the parade, along with the ROSE QUEEN, a young beauty queen from the Pasadena area.

The Tournament of Roses Association continues to organize both the parade and the football game. Although the Association hires a few paid employees, it relies heavily on the efforts of more than 900 volunteers who give about 80,000 hours of labor each year to help pull off this massive undertaking. The Rose Bowl is usually played on January 1, but festival organizers try not to schedule the game on a Sunday, and so it is put off in some years until January 2.

SYMBOLS AND CUSTOMS

Football Game

The Rose Bowl Game has been nicknamed "the granddaddy of them all" because it was the first national, post-season collegiate football game. Each year it pits the winner of the Big Ten conference against the winner of the Pacific Ten conference. The proceeds from the game benefit each school in the Pacific Ten and Big Ten, whether their team is playing in the Rose Bowl that year or not. In 2005, the Rose Bowl payout totaled about $30 million. Each university in the two conferences received over one million dollars in revenue. These football games have sold out each year since 1947. In addition, it is estimated that about 68.5 million Americans watch the game on TV.

Parade

The Rose Parade is about five-and-a-half miles long and lasts about two-and-a-half hours. About one million people line the parade route every year. The Tournament of Roses Parade features beautiful floats that, according to parade rules, must be entirely covered in some combination of flowers, petals, leaves, seeds, bark, and twigs. Associations, corporations, or cities sponsor most of the floats entered in the Rose Parade. Most are professionally designed and built, and some even include computerized animation as well as computerized hydraulic systems. Each year tournament organizers select a theme for the parade, and floats must represent an aspect of that theme.

In addition, the parade also features beautifully costumed equestrians. About 300 horses and their riders take part. Many different breeds of horses are represented. Marching bands have been a feature of the parade since 1891, when the Monrovia Town Band became the first to march in a Tournament of Roses parade. These days sixteen musical groups are selected to participate in the parade every year. Over fifty bands compete for these positions.

Each year the president of the Tournament of Roses Association chooses a celebrity Grand Marshall to preside over the parade. Politicians, actors, actresses, athletes, generals, musicians, writers, astronauts, lawyers, and doctors have been selected in past years.

Rose Queen

In 1930 tournament organizers added a beauty contest to the day's festivities. The winner of the contest, dubbed the Rose Queen, presides over the day's celebrations. Current contest rules state that only single, childless women who are full-time students, who are between the ages of seventeen and twenty-one, and who live in the Pasadena area are eligible to serve as the Rose Queen. Approximately 1,000 young women compete for this honor every year. Contestants are judged on personality, poise, public speaking ability, and academic achievement. Six princesses are also chosen. Together they represent the queen and her court. All seven young women will ride on a special float in the parade. The Rose Queen and the Rose Princesses are expected to attend about 150 media and public events throughout the year, where, as goodwill ambassadors, they will promote the Rose Bowl and the city of Pasadena.

FURTHER READING

Gulevich, Tanya. *Encyclopedia of Christmas and New Year's Celebrations.* 2nd ed. Detroit: Omnigraphics, 2003.

Michelson, Herb, and David Newhouse. *Rose Bowl Football since 1902.* New York: Stein and Day, 1977.

WEB SITE

Tournament of Roses Association
www.tournamentofroses.com

Rosh Hashanah
(Jewish New Year, Day of Remembrance)

Type of Holiday: Religious (Jewish), Calendar/Seasonal
Date of Observation: 1 and 2 Tishri; between September 6 and October 4
Where Celebrated: By Jews all over the world
Symbols and Customs: Book of Life, Challah, Honey, Kittel, Shanah Tovah Cards, Shofar, Tashlikh Ceremony
Colors: Many Jews wear white clothing on Rosh Hashanah to remind themselves of the holiness and purity of the festival.
Related Holidays: New Year's Day, Yom Kippur

ORIGINS

In Judaism, Rosh Hashanah is part of the new year and the beginning of the High Holy Days. Judaism is one of the oldest continuously observed religions in the world. Its history extends back beyond the advent of the written word. Its people trace their roots to a common ancestor, Abraham, and then back even farther to the very moment of creation.

According to Jewish belief, the law given to the Jewish people by God contained everything they needed to live a holy life, including the ability to be reinterpreted in new historical situations. Judaism, therefore, is the expression of the Jewish people, attempting to live holy (set apart) lives in accordance with the instructions given by God. Although obedience to the law is central to Judaism, there is no one central authority. Sources of divine authority are God, the Torah, interpretations of the Torah by respected teachers, and tradition. Religious observances and the study of Jewish law are conducted under the supervision of a teacher called a rabbi.

There are several sects within Judaism. Orthodox Judaism is characterized by an affirmation of the traditional Jewish faith, strict adherence to customs such as keeping the Sabbath, participation in ceremonies and rituals, and the observance of dietary regulations. Conservative Jewish congregations seek to retain many ancient traditions but without the accompanying demand for strict observance. Reform Judaism stresses modern biblical criticism and emphasizes ethical teachings more than ritualistic observance. Hasidism is a mystical sect of Judaism that teaches enthusiastic prayer as a means of communion with God. The Reconstruc-

tionist movement began early in the twentieth century in an effort to "reconstruct" Judaism with the community rather than the synagogue as its center.

The Jewish year begins around the time of the **AUTUMN EQUINOX** (September 21-23), at the beginning of the month of Tishri. The first ten days of the month are known as the High Holy Days. The new year celebration, Rosh Hashanah, is observed on the first and second of these days, when God opens the sacred BOOK OF LIFE and judges people on the basis of their actions over the past year. The next several days are known as the Days of Penitence, a period during which Jews can influence their fate by making amends for the wrongs they have committed during the year. The tenth and last of the High Holy Days is **YOM KIPPUR**, the Day of Atonement, or the day on which their fates for the coming year are inscribed and sealed.

Unlike the secular observance of **NEW YEAR'S DAY**, Rosh Hashanah marks the start of a very solemn season. The story of Abraham is read in the synagogue, and the blowing of the SHOFAR serves as a call to penitence and a reminder of Abraham's willingness to obey God. Jews ponder their behavior and think about what they can do to make themselves better people. All debts from the past year are supposed to be settled before Rosh Hashanah, and many Jews ask forgiveness from their friends and families for any slights or transgressions they may have committed.

Rosh Hashanah is observed for two days in countries outside of Israel. Back in the days when travel was dangerous and difficult, and messages often failed to arrive on time, Jews living in foreign countries weren't sure exactly when certain holidays should be celebrated. In such instances they would observe two days, because one of them was bound to be correct. This gave rise to the custom of observing Rosh Hashanah, **PASSOVER, SHAVUOT,** and **SUKKOT** over a two-day period. This custom was retained for Jews living outside Israel, while Reform Jews and those living in Israel observe only one day.

The turning of the year was closely related to the turning of the seasons. At one time, the three great Jewish festivals (Rosh Hashanah, Yom Kippur, and Sukkot) may have been one great harvest festival. But today they are distinct.

SYMBOLS AND CUSTOMS

Book of Life

The Book of Life is divided into three sections: one for the wicked, one for the righteous, and one for those who fall in between. The names of the righteous are immediately inscribed in the Book of Life for good fortune in the coming year, while the wicked are condemned to death. Judgments about those who fall in between is made on **YOM KIPPUR**, which gives them time to repent and change their ways. It is for this reason that Jews often wish each other not only "Happy New Year" but "Have a good signature."

Challah

Challah is a special bread served on Rosh Hashanah that is braided and baked in a circular shape, symbolizing the roundness of the year and the cycle of the seasons. Sometimes it is shaped like a ladder, a bird, or a crown. The ladder serves as a reminder that people are judged on this day, and that some are destined to climb and prosper while others will descend and suffer. The bird is a symbol of God's mercy, which extends to even the smallest of animals. The crown is a symbol of the kingship of God, which Rosh Hashanah emphasizes.

Honey

It is customary at Rosh Hashanah to eat pieces of CHALLAH dipped in honey, which is symbolic of sweet life in the new year. It is also customary to eat a new fruit of the year, such as apples, dipped in honey, and to have honey cake for dessert.

Kittel

During the morning service at Rosh Hashanah, it is customary for rabbis, cantors, and some adult male worshippers to wear a long white robe known as a kittel. It stands as a symbol of purity and a reminder of the white linen robe that the high priest used to wear in the Temple of Jerusalem. Very pious Jews are married and buried in a kittel, which is also worn on **YOM KIPPUR** and at the seder on **PASSOVER**.

Shanah Tovah Cards

Many Jews send out Shanah Tovah greeting cards that say "Leshanah Tovah Tikatevu," or "May you be written down for a good year." Although the custom of extending good wishes at Rosh Hashanah started among German Jews during medieval times, these wishes weren't expressed in writing until the fifteenth century, when Jews both in and outside Germany started ending their letters and notes with such messages during the month preceding the holiday. The custom of sending New Year's cards evolved from this practice.

Shanah Tovah cards are sent to rabbis, relatives, friends, and teachers, as well as to business associates and community leaders. Some Jews print their own personal cards, while others buy them at a stationery store. Schoolchildren often make their own. In Israel, they can be purchased from stalls set up in the streets. The cards often feature figures from comic strips, portraits of political and military figures, and sometimes planes, tanks, and guns, symbolic of the violence that has plagued the Middle East in recent decades.

Shofar

Rosh Hashanah is also known as the Day of Blowing the Shofar or Ram's Horn. It recalls the story of Abraham, who was willing to sacrifice his son, Isaac, to prove the strength of his faith in God. At the last minute, he heard God's voice telling him not to harm his son but to sacrifice an animal instead. Miraculously, he saw a ram caught by its horns in a nearby thicket.

The shofar is also associated with other important events in Jewish history. It sounded when Moses called the Israelites together to give them the Ten Commandments on Mount Sinai and when the Temple in Jerusalem was destroyed. The shofar is still used in Israel to announce the arrival of the Sabbath on Friday afternoons and during the swearing-in of a new president.

The shofar makes three distinct sounds: *Shevarim,* which consists of three broken notes said to resemble sobbing; *Teruah,* or nine short notes resembling wailing; and *Tekiah,* a long, unbroken sound. These three tones, which honor Abraham, Isaac, and Jacob, are repeated several times in different sequences. Blowing this ancient instrument properly on Rosh Hashanah requires a trained expert; the notes are prescribed by tradition, and their order cannot be changed in any way. Its call summons worshippers to search their consciences and to repent before it is too late.

Although the shofar is usually made from a ram's horn, it can be the horn of any kosher (clean) animal, with the exception of cows, which might remind people of the disgraceful incident involving the Golden Calf (Exodus 32). A curved horn is preferred because it symbolizes the natural posture of the humble, or man bowing in submission to God.

Primitive peoples regarded the New Year as a time when demons were likely to be roaming about. To scare them away, it was customary to make noise by beating drums, sounding gongs, blowing trumpets, and cracking whips. The blowing of the shofar is probably related to this ancient custom, but it is regarded today as a symbol of the history and faith of the Jewish people.

Tashlikh Ceremony

Orthodox Jews, whose ancestors came from northern Europe, observe the ceremony of *Tashlikh* ("you will cast"), a symbolic throwing away of one's sins into a body of water. On the afternoon of the first day of the New Year (or the second day, if the first day is the Sabbath), they go to the nearest body of flowing water and recite in Hebrew the closing words of the Book of Micah: "He will turn again, he will have compassion upon us; he will subdue our iniquities; and thou wilt cast all their sins into the depths of the sea." As these words are being recited, people empty their pockets of lint and bread crumbs, throwing them into the water so their sins will be carried away. If flowing water is not available, the ceremony can take place by a well, or facing in the direction of a distant body of water.

Some scholars think that the origin of this custom can be found in the ancient Roman practice of throwing offerings to the river spirits at certain critical times of the year.

FURTHER READING

Bellenir, Karen. *Religious Holidays and Calendars*. 3rd ed. Detroit: Omnigraphics, 2004.

Cashman, Greer Fay. *Jewish Days and Holidays*. New York: SBS Pub., 1979.

Cuyler, Margery. *Jewish Holidays*. New York: Holt, Rinehart and Winston, 1978.

Edidin, Ben. *Jewish Holidays and Festivals*. 1940. Reprint. Detroit: Omnigraphics, 1993.

Gaer, Joseph. *Holidays Around the World*. Boston: Little, Brown, 1953.

Gaster, Theodor H. *Festivals of the Jewish Year*. New York: William Sloane Associates, 1953.

Henderson, Helene, ed. *Holidays, Festivals, and Celebrations of the World Dictionary*. 3rd ed. Detroit: Omnigraphics, 2005.

Ickis, Marguerite. *The Book of Festivals and Holidays the World Over*. New York: Dodd, Mead, 1970.

Purdy, Susan. *Festivals for You to Celebrate*. Philadelphia: Lippincott, 1969.

Renberg, Dalia Hardof. *The Complete Family Guide to Jewish Holidays*. New York: Adama Books, 1985.

Santino, Jack. *All Around the Year: Holidays and Celebrations in American Life*. Urbana: University of Illinois Press, 1994.

WEB SITES

Union for Reform Judaism
urj.org/holidays/roshhashanah

Union of Orthodox Jewish Congregations of America
www.ou.org/chagim/roshhashannah

Royal Ascot

Type of Holiday: Sporting
Date of Observation: Four days in mid-June
Where Celebrated: Ascot, England
Symbols and Customs: Ascot Racecourse, Gold Cup, Grand Stand, Hats, Royal Enclosure, Royal Procession, Tailgate Picnics

ORIGINS

It was Queen Anne, the second daughter of the English King James II and an enthusiastic horsewoman herself, who first spotted a broad, flat field near the village of East Cote (later called Ascot), just a few miles south of Windsor Castle in Berkshire, and thought it would be a good location for a racecourse. The first races were held there on August 11, 1711, with Queen Anne presiding over the festivities.

When George II came to the throne in 1760, the Royal Meeting at Ascot (or Royal Ascot) rose from its humble beginnings to become the second most celebrated race in all of England—after the race at Epsom, which had been held since the early seventeenth century. A grandstand was built in 1822 and, after that, a permanent stand for the king and the royal family that included reception rooms and a suite from which they could view the races. The buildings surrounding the racecourse were added to and enlarged several times during the nineteenth century, and soon there were private boxes, hundreds of open and closed stalls, a paddock for saddling the horses, accommodation for carriages, and a large dining hall with a verandah.

The social festivities and balls surrounding the races at Ascot have always played an important role, and today Royal Ascot is widely regarded as the high point of the English social season. Members of the royal family traditionally attend the races, and the English upper classes can be seen flaunting their finest fashions before the cameras of the international press (*see* HATS). The broad neck scarf worn by well-dressed English gentlemen took its name from the event, and Ascot is also the setting for Cecil Beaton's famous "black and white" scene in *My Fair Lady*. Many of the social events for which Royal Ascot is famous take place in the private luncheon rooms of the GRAND STAND or in the large dining halls on the lawn behind it. Various private clubs also set up tents for refreshments.

Despite its identification with the wealthy, the Royal Meeting at Ascot has also attracted more than its share of thieves, gamblers, and con artists. The erection of gambling booths was eventually prohibited, but this didn't put a stop to the gam-

Food & Beverages Consumed During Royal Ascot 2006

185,000 bottles of champagne

176,000 pints of beer

15,000 bottles of wine

11,000 lobsters

4.5 British tonnes (almost 10,000 pounds) of beef

100,000 scones

bling, which frequently led to arguments, brawls, and riots. New rules and regulations adopted in the mid-nineteenth century curtailed such behavior, but it has never been stopped altogether.

The races last for four days, but the principal event is the Ascot GOLD CUP, established in 1807 and run over an almost two-mile course by horses more than three years old.

SYMBOLS AND CUSTOMS

Ascot Racecourse

The course at Ascot is built on a geological formation known as the Bagshot Sands. The sandy soil is unusually dry for England and makes growing grass difficult. Many attempts to bring about a permanent change in the nature of the ground at Ascot have been made over the years: large quantities of manure have been spread, the hardiest possible grass seed has been sown, and the course has been irrigated. At one point it was decided that allowing sheep to graze over the course would be a good idea, but in fact, they nearly ruined it.

The course is more or less circular and measures sixty-six yards short of two miles. The first half is on a gradual descent and the second half, known as the Old Mile Course, is for the most part uphill. The New Course (also known as the New Mile) measures a little over one mile, and it is both straight and uphill.

Gold Cup

The first time that a cup was raced for at Ascot was in 1772, when the Duke of Cumberland instituted a race for five-year-old horses over a four-mile course. This was the beginning of the competition for what, in 1807, was first called The Gold Cup, which by that time had become the most highly prized trophy in horse racing. Although it is not the only race run at Ascot, it is certainly the most important. Other popular races include the Gold Vase and the Royal Hunt Cup.

The Cup itself was originally made by Garrard's of London, the same company that made the original **AMERICA'S CUP**. It is shaped like a wide urn, with two ornately decorated handles on either side.

Grand Stand

The rough wooden buildings that once served as a grandstand at Ascot, with tents for the royal family's reception rooms, were eventually replaced by a range of buildings whose facade extends for almost a quarter of a mile along the course. It is called, appropriately, the Grand Stand, and its most prominent feature is the clock tower, from which the spectator gets a panoramic view of the course and the surrounding neighborhood.

The ground floor is mostly waiting rooms and refreshment lounges, which include the Japanese Tea Room. The balcony of the first floor has private boxes, each of which has room for about six people. There is usually a waiting list for boxes, and many years may elapse before one becomes free. Immediately behind the uncovered stalls of the first floor is a large room known as the Drawing Room, which contains free seats for the public—as does the roof, which is fitted with benches arranged in tiers extending up to the clock tower.

Hats

Ladies' Day, which falls on the Thursday of Ascot week, is a long-standing tradition. It features a parade of women displaying their hats, which are often so elaborate that it can be difficult to recognize who is underneath them. Hats have always been in style in England, but tradition demands that women wear them at the Royal Meeting. In fact, women cannot enter the exclusive ROYAL ENCLOSURE without wearing "a hat covering the crown of the head." All during the week of the races, photographs of the more outrageous hats fill the pages of the British tabloid newspapers.

Many of the hats that can be seen at Ascot were made by Herbert Johnson Ltd. of London, which has been creating hats for more than 200 years and has made them for kings, czars, and Princess Diana. A custom-made hat costs from $500 to several thousand dollars.

Royal Enclosure

In 1822, King George IV commissioned architect John Nash to build a two-story Royal Box. Only guests with an invitation from the king could enter the lawn surrounding the box, which is now referred to as the Royal Enclosure. Those who are admitted to the enclosure wear a small badge on their lapel that bears their name and title; many are lords, dukes, marquesses, viscounts, earls, ambassadors, or Members of Parliament. Cameras are strictly forbidden except by the press in prescribed areas—lest an aristocrat be caught in a less-than-flattering pose.

Royal Procession

George IV instituted what is now known as the Royal Procession in 1825, and it has changed very little in the years since. At 2:00 p.m. each day during Ascot week, Queen Elizabeth and Prince Philip lead the procession in their elegant horse-drawn carriage, followed by other family members, friends, and race officials, who also ride in open carriages while tens of thousands of patrons stand and cheer.

Tailgate Picnics

Several hours before the races begin, cars fill up the vast fields that serve as Ascot's parking lots. People spread blankets, set up tables and chairs, and open bottles of champagne. Picnics are also held in the private tree-filled parking area adjacent to the ROYAL ENCLOSURE, but here the cars are mostly Rolls Royces and Bentleys, with butlers pouring vintage champagne and serving poached salmon or lobster. These tailgate picnics are an elaborate version of what takes place before football games in the United States.

FURTHER READING

Cawthorne, George J., and Richard S. Herod. *Royal Ascot: Its History and Its Associations*. London: Longmans, Green, 1900.

Henderson, Helene, ed. *Holidays, Festivals, and Celebrations of the World Dictionary*. 3rd ed. Detroit: Omnigraphics, 2005.

WEB SITE

Ascot Racecourse
www.ascot.co.uk

Royal National Eisteddfod

Type of Holiday: Folkloric
Date of Observation: First week in August
Where Celebrated: Location alternates between North Wales and South Wales
Symbols and Customs: Chairing Ceremony, Choral Singing, Crowning Ceremony, Floral Dance, Gorsedd, Homecoming, Welsh Language

ORIGINS

The Royal National Eisteddfod is a weeklong celebration of poetry, CHORAL SINGING, drama, art, and the WELSH LANGUAGE that takes place in either North Wales or South Wales every year in early August. It is derived from the tournaments in which Welsh bards (epic poets who recited their work) and musicians competed against one another for the patronage of the wealthy back in the tenth century. The first truly national eisteddfod (which means "sitting down together" or "gathering") was held in 1176, when the Welsh prince known as Lord Rhys ap Gruffudd held a festival at his castle in Cardigan featuring two competitions, one for bards and the other for musicians who played the traditional Welsh instruments—the harp, the crwth (similar to a lyre), and the pibcorn (hornpipe). He awarded a chair—literally a seat at his table, which also meant steady employment—to the best musician and the best poet. The ceremony known as "Chairing the Bard" remains a highlight of the Royal National Eisteddfod today (*see* CHAIRING CEREMONY).

After that it became customary for wealthy noblemen all over Wales to hold *eisteddfodau* at which poets and musicians (both singers and instrumentalists) competed according to very strict rules regarding composition and performance. A hierarchy was established whereby apprentice poets and musicians could work their way up to professional status by mastering various techniques and areas of knowledge in their field. But then, when Wales became politically unified with England in 1536, London became the center of cultural life, and these annual gatherings lost momentum. It was Edward Williams (1747–1826), better known as the bard Iolo Morganwg (John of Glamorgan), who stirred up feelings of Welsh patriotism and drew attention to the idea of a national eisteddfod as a good way to revive ancient Welsh traditions. By 1881 the National Eisteddfod Association had been formed for the express purpose of organizing an annual cultural festival, the location alternating between North and South Wales, and the event has been held regularly since that time, with only brief interruptions during the First and Second World Wars.

The Royal National Eisteddfod's most outstanding feature is the fact that all of the competitions—which today encompass poetry, prose, music, drama, and art—take place entirely in the WELSH LANGUAGE. About 6,000 competitors in these fields prepare all year, often by achieving prominence at smaller eisteddfodau around the country, for the main events, which include the "Crowning of the Bard" (*see* CROWNING CEREMONY) on Monday of the festival week, the Prose Medal Ceremony on Wednesday, and the "Chairing of the Bard" on Friday. There are also competitions for visual artists and craftspeople, theater groups, and even Welsh pop and rock bands. The "Welsh Learner's Pavilion" is dedicated to promoting Welsh culture, with cooking demonstrations, dance and drama workshops, and instruction in the Welsh language.

SYMBOLS AND CUSTOMS

Chairing Ceremony

Although the scope of the Royal National Eisteddfod has expanded over the years to include a wide variety of art forms, it is still poetry that takes center stage during the weeklong festival. There are two main competitions, one for "the Chair" and one for "the Crown" (*see* CROWNING CEREMONY). The former is known in Welsh as Y Cadeirio (The Chairing), and it involves awarding a chair or seat of honor to the poet who has composed the best long poem in strict metres. All entries are submitted anonymously to avoid favoritism, and the Chair is awarded in front of the assembled GORSEDD of the Bards.

Choral Singing

In ancient Wales the art of singing, particularly choral singing, was very well established and passed down from teacher to student. Some people even believe that the Welsh invented part-singing or harmony, although this is unlikely. Welsh "mastersingers" never used music that had been written down because they wanted to keep their art form exclusive, and because the frequency of war meant that they had to be prepared to pack up and leave on a moment's notice, carrying their skills and traditions in their heads.

The period from 1840 until the First World War (1914-18) represented a "golden age" for Welsh male choirs. Community hymn-singing festivals were common, and the singing that took place in chapel every Sunday was of an unusually high standard, often involving four-part harmony. Many Welsh chapels had their own orchestras, which would join the choirs in performing oratorios. Today the popularity and strength of the choirs remains, although many of them now admit women.

Crowning Ceremony

The "Crowning of the Bard" ceremony is held to honor the best free-verse poet. Like the CHAIRING CEREMONY, it takes place in front of the GORSEDD, and the winner's identity is not revealed until he or she mounts the stage to accept the crown. The ceremony usually takes place on Monday of festival week in the main pavilion, where thousands of people gather to hear the winning bard recite.

Floral Dance

A flower dance is performed after the CHAIRING CEREMONY as well as after the Prose Medal competition and the CROWNING CEREMONY. The dancers are young Welsh girls, and the steps they follow are based on a pattern designed to suggest the gathering of wildflowers from a field.

Gorsedd

Gorsedd means "high seat" in Welsh. It is a group of poets, writers, musicians, artists, and other individuals—who have included athletes and opera stars—recognized for their contributions to sustaining the Welsh culture, language, and traditions. It was Edward Williams (alias John of Glamorgan) who founded the Gorsedd in 1792 in London and brought it to the Eisteddfod held in Carmarthen in 1819. It was also Williams who put the Gorsedd members in Druids' robes to make them look like members of an ancient bardic court. The group's full name is Gorsedd Beirdd Ynys Prydain or "Court of the Bards of the Island of Britain," and it is their job to organize the ceremonies at which the Chair, the Crown, and the Prose Medal are awarded.

Although the Gorsedd members are dressed to resemble Druids, their connection with Druidism as a religion and with the Druids who guarded the secrets of the ancient Celts is purely imaginary. When he established the group in the late eighteenth century, Edward Williams did everything he could think of to convince people that its members were descended from these ancient Celtic priests.

Homecoming

Welsh people from all over the world return home to attend the Royal National Eisteddfod. A special ceremony, known as Cymru a'r Byd, is held to welcome them back to their homeland. Although this was not part of the original eisteddfod as it developed in the nineteenth century, it has been a tradition since 1948, when the ceremony was first held to welcome returning Welshmen who had served in the Middle East during World War II (1939-45).

Welsh Language

As mentioned above, the Welsh language is used at all Royal National Eisteddfod events. It was spoken throughout the country up until the late eighteenth century, and less educated people, especially in rural areas, continued to speak it for another 100 years. But as workers began to leave Wales to find jobs in the factories of England, Scotland, and Ireland, English became more common. Nowadays it is estimated that less than a fifth of the people actually know Welsh, which some scholars believe is the oldest language still spoken in all of Europe. Most native Welsh speakers live in the more rural areas of the north and west.

Since the passage of the Welsh Language Act of 1993, there has been a widespread effort to promote the use of Welsh in public contexts, to teach it to students between the ages of five and sixteen, and to make road signs bilingual. But there is probably no other factor as instrumental in promoting the use of Welsh as the growing popularity of the Royal National Eisteddfod. Although simultaneous translation is available for tourists at many events, encouraging people to speak and understand Welsh is clearly a primary purpose of the festival.

FURTHER READING

Leach, Maria, ed. *Funk & Wagnalls Standard Dictionary of Folklore, Mythology & Legend*. San Francisco: Harper & Row, 1984.

Merin, Jennifer, and Elizabeth B. Burdick. *International Directory of Theatre, Dance, and Folklore Festivals*. Westport, CT: Greenwood Press, 1979.

Rabin, Carol Price. *Music Festivals in Europe and Britain*. Rev. ed. Stockbridge, MA: Berkshire Traveller Press, 1984.

Shemanski, Frances. *A Guide to World Fairs and Festivals*. Westport, CT: Greenwood Press, 1985.

Spicer, Dorothy Gladys. *The Book of Festivals*. 1937. Reprint. Detroit: Omnigraphics, 1990.

Trawicky, Bernard, and Ruth W. Gregory. *Anniversaries and Holidays*. 5th ed. Chicago: American Library Assocation, 2000.

Van Straalen, Alice. *The Book of Holidays Around the World*. New York: Dutton, 1986.

WEB SITES

BBC (British Broadcasting Corporation)
www.bbc.co.uk/wales/catchphrase/eisteddfod/whatisit.shtml

Royal National Eisteddfod
www.eisteddfod.org.uk/english

Samhain

Type of Holiday: Ancient, Religious (Neopagan)
Date of Observation: November 1
Where Celebrated: British Isles
Symbols and Customs: Bonfires, Harp, Swan
Related Holidays: All Souls' Day, Beltane, Halloween, Lughnasa, Mabon, Samhain, Summer Solstice, Winter Solstice, Vernal Equinox

ORIGINS

Celtic peoples lived in Ireland, Scotland, England, and northern France from around 500 B.C.E. until around 100 C.E., when the Romans conquered most of Celtic Europe. Little is definitely known about ancient Celtic religion. The Celts themselves left sparse written accounts. Julius Caesar, who led the Romans into Celtic lands, wrote of his impressions of the people, as did other ancient Greco-Roman writers.

During the 1960s the modern Neopagan and Wiccan movements emerged in Great Britain, the United States, and other English-speaking countries. They follow a nature-oriented religion loosely linked to ancient Celtic and other beliefs and inspired by old European folk practices. They celebrate eight sabbats, known as the eight spokes of the wheel of the year, which include Samhain as well as **SUMMER SOLSTICE, WINTER SOLSTICE, VERNAL EQUINOX, BELTANE, IMBOLC, LUGHNASA,** and **MABON.**

Samhain (pronounced *sah-win*) is an Irish word meaning "summer's end." Along with **IMBOLC** (February 1), **BELTANE** (May 1), and **LUGHNASA** (August 1), it was one of the four major Celtic festivals observed in ancient times. Samhain was the Celtic **NEW YEAR'S DAY**, a time of transition between the old and new year when the souls of those who had died during the previous year gathered to travel to the land of the dead. The festival actually began at sundown on October 31, and many of the symbols now associated with **HALLOWEEN**—including witches, ghosts, and goblins—derived from the pagan belief that the gates to the underworld were opened on this day and that the spirits of the dead were free to roam the earth. Since Samhain was also a harvest festival, people made offerings of fruits and vegetables to honor the dead.

Some of the customs associated with Samhain—and later with **HALLOWEEN**—can be traced back to the ancient Roman festival dedicated to Pomona, the goddess of fruit, held at around the same date. When the Romans conquered Britain, they brought these customs with them. The tradition of bobbing for apples, for example, probably comes from the Roman games played during Pomona's festival.

The early Christian missionaries particularly disliked Samhain's emphasis on the supernatural, and they tried to convince people that the spirits of the dead were actually delusions sent by the devil. Due largely to their efforts, the Celtic underworld eventually became associated with the Christian hell, and the concept of honoring the benevolent spirits of the dead gradually gave way to fears about evil spirits and witchcraft.

Although Samhain is widely regarded as the Celtic New Year's Day, some scholars believe that the Celts actually began their year in midsummer, somewhere between **BELTANE** and **LUGHNASA**.

SYMBOLS AND CUSTOMS

Bonfires

In pagan times, it is possible that human sacrifices occurred around Samhain. All fires had to be extinguished, and they could only be rekindled from the main bonfire. It is still common in parts of Ireland and Scotland to extinguish the peat fires on **HALLOWEEN** and relight them from the bonfires that burn on the hilltops.

Bonfires were also a way of illuminating the path for the souls of the dead as they wandered from the world of the living back to the Celtic underworld. Some people hoped that their fires would scare off any spirits that meant them harm.

In addition to lighting bonfires, special lanterns were carved out of gourds or turnips. These were meant to symbolize the life-giving energy of the sun and to encourage its regeneration at a time of year when the days were growing shorter. Although carving and displaying pumpkins at **HALLOWEEN** is often assumed to be an American tradition, it is likely that the custom goes back much further.

Harp

An old Irish legend associated with Samhain tells the story of the annual destruction of Tara, the magical hill which was also the ancestral seat of the gods. Every year at Samhain a goblin called Aillen played the harp so skillfully that everyone was charmed into sleep, allowing him to set fire to the palace. A hero named Finn finally overcame Aillen's magic by holding the sharp point of a spear against his own forehead. The pain kept him awake while everyone else fell asleep.

As a symbol, the harp is regarded as a bridge between heaven and earth. This is why heroes often requested that a harp be buried with them, to facilitate their access to heaven. Along with the SWAN, the harp is considered one of the essential symbols of the journey from the world of the living to the world of the dead.

Swan

According to Irish folklore, a god named Oenghus fell in love with a young girl named Caer (also known as Rhiannon), who was capable of taking on the form of a swan at the festival of Samhain. Because her father would not let Oenghus woo Caer, the only way he could be with her was to wait for the festival and then transform himself into a swan. United at last, the pair flew three times around a lake, putting everyone else into a dream-sleep that lasted three days and three nights, giving the lovers an opportunity to fly off to the god's palace.

Along with the HARP, the swan is symbolically associated with the journey to the land of the dead, and it is often shown harnessed to funerary wagons. The festival of Samhain may have celebrated, through the legend of people and gods shape-shifting into swans, the transformation of life from one state to another. There is also some evidence that swan-dances were held at Samhain.

FURTHER READING

Cirlot, J.E. *A Dictionary of Symbols.* New York: Philosophical Library, 1962.

Heinberg, Richard. *Celebrate the Solstice: Honoring the Earth's Seasonal Rhythms through Festival and Ceremony.* Wheaton, IL: Quest Books, 1993.

Henderson, Helene, ed. *Holidays, Festivals, and Celebrations of the World Dictionary.* 3rd ed. Detroit: Omnigraphics, 2005.

Hutton, Ronald. *The Pagan Religions of the Ancient British Isles: Their Nature and Legacy.* Oxford: Blackwell, 1991.

King, John. *The Celtic Druids' Year: Seasonal Cycles of the Ancient Celts.* London: Blandford, 1995.

Leach, Maria, ed. *Funk & Wagnalls Standard Dictionary of Folklore, Mythology & Legend.* San Francisco: Harper & Row, 1984.

Santino, Jack. *All Around the Year: Holidays and Celebrations in American Life.* Urbana: University of Illinois Press, 1994.

San Fermin Festival

Type of Holiday: Sporting
Date of Observation: Week that includes July 7
Where Celebrated: Pamplona, Spain
Symbols and Customs: Bull, Running of the Bulls, Safety Barriers

ORIGINS

The Feast of San Fermin was originally observed in Pamplona, Spain, on October 10 with prayers and a procession in honor of the city's patron saint. But in 1591 the Pamplona city council proposed to the Church that the celebration be transferred to July 7, to coincide with a fair that was traditionally held in the city and that featured the running of bulls through the streets. Some scholars believe that this was a deliberate attempt to link the saint's name to an event that was an entirely secular celebration, while others believe that the date was changed simply to take advantage of the summer weather. In any case, as time went on, the fair declined in importance while the RUNNING OF THE BULLS became the most prominent feature of the day's events.

Today, the start of the San Fermin Festival is announced with a gun fired from the balcony of the town hall. Bands of *txistularis* (a Basque word pronounced chees-too-LAH-rees)—with dancers, drummers, and *txistu* (a musical instrument similar to a flute) players—march through the town and its suburbs playing songs announcing the RUNNING OF THE BULLS, an event that has now been part of the festival for more than 400 years. At 8:00 a.m., the bulls are allowed to run from the corrals in which they are kept through the streets to the bullring. Before them run the young men of the city, often accompanied by tourists who have come to Pamplona to risk their lives and display their bravery. When the bulls reach the arena, the running ends and they are locked up in their pens until the bullfight takes place later in the day. Although the race lasts barely five minutes, participants are frequently injured and occasionally killed by the stampeding animals.

The killing of the BULL didn't become an official part of the San Fermin Festival until the end of the seventeenth century. Up to that time, the bull was simply run until he was exhausted and of no further use. Then he was taken back to the corral and eventually returned to the country to recover from any injuries he might have suffered. Nowadays, the bull usually falls victim to a professional bullfighter in the bullring.

The San Fermin Festival received a huge boost in popularity after the publication of Ernest Hemingway's novel *The Sun Also Rises*, in which the RUNNING OF THE BULLS at Pamplona is described in vivid detail. Thousands of people now come to Pamplona in July to watch from behind the wooden barriers that line the streets to the arena as the bulls are prodded and taunted until they are ready to charge anyone or anything that stands in their way.

SYMBOLS AND CUSTOMS

Bull

The bull has long been regarded as a sacred animal in Spain. Because of its great size and strength, the bull is also a symbol of sexual vigor and fecundity. Any man who comes in direct contact with a bull, either by fighting it or by eating its flesh, is believed to partake of the bull's power.

Running of the Bulls

For many centuries in Spain, people used bulls on a rope or with burning pitch on their horns to celebrate important saints' days or special occasions, such as weddings, betrothals, and religious festivals. Before a wedding, for example, the bridegroom and his male friends would run a bull, tied with a heavy rope, through the streets of town to the bride's house, where it was killed. What the groom was trying to do was to bring his clothing in contact with the animal, thus acquiring its sexual powers. The present-day bullfight represents, in a symbolic way, the transmission of the bull's power, at the precise moment of its death, to the *matador* or bullfighter. But rather than being a sacred rite, it has become a public entertainment.

The "runners of bulls" were originally lower-class people skilled at running in front of the bull or handling the rope tied to its horns. They were often athletes, acrobats, or dancers who could move quickly and get out of the animal's way. Eventually, the more highly skilled performers began to charge for their participation. As time passed, they were replaced by professional bullfighters or matadors.

Today's runners are usually young men—and occasionally young women dressed as men—who want to prove their courage and agility.

Safety Barriers

First used in 1776 to mark the route of the running bulls, the safety barriers are made of fir wood. Along the course, these barriers are made up of 1,800 boards, forty gates, 590 posts, 200 palisades (fences), 2,400 wedges, and 2,000 bolts. Every year, twenty boards must be replaced because of damage.

FURTHER READING

Henderson, Helene, ed. *Holidays, Festivals, and Celebrations of the World Dictionary.* 3rd ed. Detroit: Omnigraphics, 2005.

Serran-Pagan, Gines. *Pamplona-Grazalema: From the Public Square to the Bullring.* New York: Enquire Print & Pub., 1980.

Shemanski, Frances. *A Guide to World Fairs and Festivals.* Westport, CT: Greenwood Press, 1985.

Spicer, Dorothy Gladys. *Festivals of Western Europe.* 1958. Reprint. Detroit: Omnigraphics, 1993.

Trawicky, Bernard, and Ruth W. Gregory. *Anniversaries and Holidays.* 5th ed. Chicago: American Library Assocation, 2000.

Van Straalen, Alice. *The Book of Holidays Around the World.* New York: Dutton, 1986.

WEB SITES

Council of Pamplona, Spain
www.pamplona.net

San Fermin Guide
www.sanfermin.com/guia/in_sanfermin.shtml

San Gennaro Festival

Type of Holiday: Religious (Christian)
Date of Observation: Last two weeks of September
Where Celebrated: Little Italy, New York City
Symbols and Customs: Church Services, Fundraising, Procession, Street Fair
Colors: The San Genarro Festival area is usually festooned with decorations in green, white, and red, which are the colors of the Italian flag.

ORIGINS

San Gennaro is a Christian festival that honors the patron saint of Naples, Italy. The word Christian refers to a follower of Christ. Christ is a title derived from the Greek word meaning Messiah or Anointed One. The Christ of Christianity is Jesus of Nazareth, a man born between 7 and 4 B.C.E. in the region of Palestine. According to Christian teaching, Jesus was killed by Roman authorities using a form of execution called crucifixion (a term meaning he was nailed to a cross and hung from it until he died) in about the year 30 C.E. After his death, he rose back to life. His death and resurrection provide a way by which people can be reconciled with God. In remembrance of Jesus' death and resurrection, the cross serves as a fundamental symbol in Christianity.

With nearly two billion believers in countries around the globe, Christianity is the largest of the world's religions. There is no one central authority for all of Christianity. The pope (the bishop of Rome) is the authority for the Roman Catholic Church, but other sects look to other authorities. Orthodox communities look to patriarchs and emphasize doctrinal agreement and traditional practice. Protestant communities focus on individual conscience. The Roman Catholic and Protestant churches are often referred to as the Western Church, while the Orthodox churches may also be called the Eastern Church. All three main branches of Christianity acknowledge the authority of Christian scriptures, a compilation of writings assembled into a document called the Bible. Methods of biblical interpretation vary among the different Christian sects.

San Gennaro, or St. Januarius, a fourth-century bishop of Benevento, is the patron saint of Naples, Italy. According to legend, he survived being thrown into a fiery furnace and then a den of wild beasts, but was eventually beheaded during the reign of Diocletian. His body was brought to Naples, along with two vials containing some of his blood. The congealed blood, preserved since that time in the Cathedral of San Gennaro in Naples, is believed to liquefy on the anniversary of his death each year—an event that has drawn crowds to Naples since 1389. The mystery of San Gennaro's blood is regarded by the faithful as a miracle.

Each year in Naples, San Gennaro Day is observed on September 19 with an elaborate ceremony. Statues of various saints and other religious artifacts are carried in a procession that winds through the streets to the cathedral. The highlights of this procession are two silver reliquaries. One, in the shape of a bust of San Gennaro, is believed to contain the head of the saint. The second is a smaller square container with glass sides enclosing the two ancient vials of blood. Once inside the cathedral, the two reliquaries are placed on the altar. Traditional prayers are recited amidst an atmosphere of increasing urgency and fervent pleas for the miracle to occur. At the point when the officiant declares that the blood has liquefied, the faithful erupt in wild, enthusiastic cheering and the cathedral's bells ring to signal the miraculous event. The miracle is said to occur consistently almost every year, with documented accounts dating back to the twelfth century.

U.S. observances of San Gennaro Day began in New York City in 1926 as an informal community celebration organized by recent Italian immigrants who had settled in the Little Italy district of Manhattan. Originally held as a one-day neighborhood block party, the event has grown over the years into an eleven-day street fair that is attended by some two million people annually. The San Gennaro Festival is now billed as the largest and longest-running religious street festival in New York City.

The festival is held in Little Italy during the last two weeks of September, with most of the religious ceremonies occurring on September 19. Special church services are held on that day, including a procession in which a statue of San Gennaro is carried through the streets.

The custom of celebrating Italian-American culture by holding a San Gennaro Festival has recently begun to spread to other U.S. cities. San Genarro Festivals are now also held at various times of the year in Las Vegas, Nevada; Los Angeles, California; and Reston, Virginia.

SYMBOLS AND CUSTOMS

Church Services

A special celebratory mass is offered in honor of San Gennaro on September 19. The mass is usually held in the afternoon of that day at the Most Precious Blood Church in Little Italy in New York City.

Fundraising

One of the primary purposes of the San Gennaro Festival street fair is to raise money for charitable causes. In New York City, the festival has donated millions of dollars to benefit the community over the years.

Procession

A procession is held in Little Italy on the evening of September 19 immediately after church services. The statue of San Gennaro is taken from Most Precious Blood Church, which houses the national shrine of San Gennaro, and carried through the festival in emulation of the ceremonies held in Naples. A second procession to close the festival usually takes place on the last Saturday or Sunday of September in the afternoon.

Street Fair

During the San Gennaro Festival, a carnival atmosphere prevails throughout Little Italy. Diversions include free entertainment, games, contests, and vendors selling various Italian foods and desserts. The streets are decorated with red, white, and green banners and Italian flags.

FURTHER READING

Henderson, Helene, ed. *Holidays, Festivals, and Celebrations of the World Dictionary*, 3rd ed. Detroit: Omnigraphics, 2005.
Thurston, Herbert. "St. Januarius." In *Catholic Encyclopedia*. New York: Robert Appleton Company, 1910.

WEB SITES

San Gennaro Festival, Little Italy District of New York City
www.littleitalynyc.com/sg_page1.asp

San Gennaro Festival, Las Vegas, Nevada
www.sangennarofeast.net

San Gennaro Festival, Los Angeles, California
www.sangennarofoundation.org

San Gennaro Festival, Reston, Virginia
www.sgfva.org

San Jacinto Day

Type of Holiday: Historic
Date of Observation: April 21
Where Celebrated: Texas
Symbols and Customs: Memorial Services, Reenactment

ORIGINS

San Jacinto Day is observed as a Texas state holiday in commemoration of the battle to free Texas from Mexico. On April 21, 1836, General Sam Houston led 900 Texan fighters in an attack on the 1,200 Mexican soldiers of General Antonio Lopez de Santa Anna. The surprise attack resulted in a battle that lasted only eighteen minutes, with victory for Texas. More than 600 Mexican soldiers were killed, while only nine Texans died in the battle.

The Battle of San Jacinto is regarded by some historians as one of the most significant events in history, with lasting worldwide impact. This battle started a chain of events that would ultimately make the United States a continental force with growing international power. The liberation of Texas from Mexico at San Jacinto eventually resulted in the Mexican-American War. In winning that war, the U.S. permanently annexed almost a million square miles of territory, growing to reach the Pacific coast. This land is now occupied by the states of Arizona, California, Colorado, Kansas, Nevada, New Mexico, Oklahoma, Texas, Utah, and Wyoming. The growth of the U.S. during this era positioned the country to become a leading power in North America.

San Jacinto Day is a historic holiday, one through which people remember significant events in their histories. Often, historic holidays are events that are important for an entire nation and become widely observed. The marking of such anniversaries serves not only to honor the values represented by the person or event commemorated, but also to strengthen and reinforce communal bonds of national, cultural, or ethnic identity. Victorious, joyful, and traumatic events are remembered through historic holidays. The commemorative expression reflects the original event through festive celebrations or the solemn ritual of MEMORIAL SERVICES. A REENACTMENT is a common activity at historical holiday and festival gatherings, seeking to bring the past alive in the present.

In 1936, a monument was dedicated in La Porte, Texas, at the site of the battle, with construction completed in 1939. The octagonal concrete obelisk stands 570 feet high and is topped with a giant Texas star. It is the tallest monument column in the world, and the second tallest monument in the U.S. A museum is housed within the building at the monument's base.

SYMBOLS AND CUSTOMS

Memorial Services

Memorial services are held on San Jacinto Day in honor of all those who died in the battle. The largest such ceremony is conducted each year at the San Jacinto Battlegrounds. General Houston's battle report is read aloud and a wreath is placed at the base of the San Jacinto Monument.

Reenactment

A reenactment of the Battle of San Jacinto is staged each year at the San Jacinto Monument. Related activities focus on living history demonstrations, including replicas of the Texan and Mexican military camps and historical presentations on various aspects of daily life in Texas in 1836.

FURTHER READING

Haley, James L. *Passionate Nation: The Epic History of Texas*. New York: Free Press, 2006.

Henderson, Helene, ed. *Holidays, Festivals, and Celebrations of the World Dictionary*, 3rd ed. Detroit: Omnigraphics, 2005.

Tolbert, Frank X. *The Day of San Jacinto*. New York: McGraw-Hill Book Company, 1959.

WEB SITE

Friends of the San Jacinto Battleground
www.friendsofsanjacinto.com

Saturnalia

Type of Holiday: Ancient
Date of Observation: December 17-23
Where Celebrated: Rome, Italy
Symbols and Customs: Candles, Clay Dolls (Sigillaria), Holly and Ivy, Mock King
Related Holidays: Christmas, Feast of Fools, Twelfth Night, Winter Solstice

ORIGINS

Saturnalia was an ancient festival that was part of ancient Roman religion, which scholars trace back to the sixth century B.C.E. Roman religion dominated Rome and influenced territories in its empire until Emperor Constantine's conversion to Christianity in the third century C.E. Ancient Roman religion was heavily influenced by the older Greek religion. Roman festivals therefore had much in common with those of the ancient Greeks. Not only were their gods and goddesses mostly the same as those in the Greek pantheon (though the Romans renamed them), but their religious festivals were observed with similar activities: ritual sacrifice, theatrical performances, games, and feasts.

The ancient Roman **WINTER SOLSTICE** festival known as the Saturnalia was held in honor of Saturn, the god of agriculture and mythical king of Italy during its fabled "Golden Age." For seven days, all social distinctions and public business were suspended: The law courts and schools closed down, wars were interrupted or postponed, and slaves exchanged places with their masters. They sat down at the table, wearing their masters' clothes and the *pilleus* or badge of freedom. They could drink as much as they wanted and exhibit behavior that would normally have been punished by death or imprisonment. This temporary reversal of the social order was typical of ancient New Year's rites, which celebrated the "turning" of the year. It was often accompanied by masquerading or change of dress between the sexes, drinking, gambling, and other forms of frivolity and self-indulgence. The idea was to recapture "the good old days," when Saturn ruled and everyone was happy.

Although the festivities lasted for only seven days, the entire month leading up to the kalends (first day) of January was dedicated to Saturn. There were thanksgiving ceremonies at shrines and temples, public feasting, and private family feasts. People exchanged gifts, often in the form of artificial fruit (a symbol of fertility), CLAY DOLLS, or CANDLES. The most popular foods to serve at this time of year were figs, dates, plums, pears, and apples; fresh pomegranates and melons; sweet breads, cakes, and pastries in the shape of stars; nuts; and cider or mulled wine—all of which is now associated with **CHRISTMAS**. In fact, the date of Jesus' birth was deliberately set to coincide with this pagan festival, which had degenerated over the centuries into a week-long spree of debauchery and crime. It is for this reason that the term "saturnalia" is now used to describe a period of unrestrained license and revelry.

SYMBOLS AND CUSTOMS

Candles

The Saturnalia was a fire festival, when homes were decorated with candles and colored lanterns. One of the gifts frequently exchanged at the Saturnalia was wax tapers (cerei), believed to be a survival of the fires that traditionally burned at the **WINTER SOLSTICE,** the darkest time of the year. Much like the Yule log in northern Europe, burning candles was a means of bringing fire—symbol of the blessings of the sun god—into the house. Burning candles at the time of the solstice was also meant to symbolize—and perhaps to ensure—the return of the sun's power.

Clay Dolls (Sigillaria)

Part of the celebration of the Saturnalia was a fair known as the *sigillariorum celebritas*, at which people could buy the small clay images they later gave away as gifts. At one time there was actually a separate festival called the Sigillaria or Feast of Dolls, held on December 22. But it was eventually absorbed into the seven days of the Saturnalia.

Although there is no hard evidence that these earthenware dolls had symbolic value or that they served as more than playthings, some scholars believe that the little clay figures of the Holy Family—Mary, Joseph, and Jesus—traditionally sold in Rome's Piazza Navona at Christmastime are the modern-day counterparts of the *sigillaria* exchanged as gifts during the pagan Saturnalia.

Holly and Ivy

The two plants associated with the Christmas season, holly and ivy, are also associated with the Saturnalia. Saturn's club was made from holly wood, and his sacred bird, the gold-crested wren, made its nest in ivy. The advent of Christianity, however, linked holly (spelled "holi" in Middle English) with Jesus. The berry and leaf of the holly became symbols for the blood of Christ and the crown of thorns that Jesus wore when he was crucified.

Mock King

In the early days of the Saturnalia, a mock king was chosen by drawing lots. His role was to preside over the revels, which often included making ridiculous demands of his subjects—such as asking them to dance naked. It is possible that his behavior represented the last relic of a very ancient custom, which was to have a young man take on the role of Saturn for the duration of the festival and then, when his brief reign ended, be killed or sacrifice himself on the altar by cutting his own throat. Although this bloodshed was supposed to symbolize the renewal of life at the **WINTER SOLSTICE**, it is also possible that the mock king acted as a scapegoat—that is, by taking his own life, he took with him the offenses of the community as a whole. But as Roman society became more civilized, this human sacrifice was no longer considered acceptable. The mock king or Lord of Misrule survived, however, and can still be found in modern-day celebrations of **CARNIVAL** and **TWELFTH NIGHT**, as well as in the medieval **FEAST OF FOOLS**.

FURTHER READING

Crippen, T.G. *Christmas and Christmas Lore.* 1923. Reprint. Detroit: Omnigraphics, 1990.

Frazer, Sir James G. *The Golden Bough: A Study in Magic and Religion.* New York: Macmillan, 1931.

Heinberg, Richard. *Celebrate the Solstice: Honoring the Earth's Seasonal Rhythms through Festival and Ceremony.* Wheaton, IL: Quest Books, 1993.

Henderson, Helene, ed. *Holidays, Festivals, and Celebrations of the World Dictionary.* 3rd ed. Detroit: Omnigraphics, 2005.

James, E.O. *Seasonal Feasts and Festivals.* 1961. Reprint. Detroit: Omnigraphics, 1993.

King, John. *The Celtic Druids' Year: Seasonal Cycles of the Ancient Celts.* London: Blandford, 1995.

Leach, Maria, ed. *Funk & Wagnalls Standard Dictionary of Folklore, Mythology & Legend.* San Francisco: Harper & Row, 1984.

Miles, Clement A. *Christmas in Ritual and Tradition, Christian and Pagan.* 1912. Reprint. Detroit: Omnigraphics, 1990.

Santino, Jack. *All Around the Year: Holidays and Celebrations in American Life.* Urbana: University of Illinois Press, 1994.

WEB SITE

New Advent Catholic Encyclopedia
www.newadvent.org/cathen/03724b.htm

Saut d'Eau Pilgrimage (Fête de Saut d'Eau)

Type of Holiday: Religious (Roman Catholic and Voodoo)
Date of Observation: July 16
Where Celebrated: Haiti
Symbols and Customs: Bathing, Cloth Strips, Offerings, Possession

ORIGINS

In the days approaching July 16, tens of thousands of people from all over the island nation of Haiti make their way to a remote village named Ville Bonheur. In the nineteenth century, a vision of a voodoo goddess appeared by Saut d'Eau, a waterfall near the village. Ever since that time, people have commemorated the appearance with an annual pilgrimage to the site. There they honor Ezili Danto, a voodoo goddess that Haitians consider an African version of the Blessed Virgin Mary. Haitians living as far away as the United States sometimes come home in July to attend the three-day festival at Saut d'Eau.

Most Haitians trace their ancestry back to West African slaves imported by the French colonizers in the sixteenth and seventeenth centuries. These slaves, who hailed from various ethnic groups, brought their deities and religious rituals with them. Once in Haiti, all these spiritual beliefs and practices blended together, along with new ideas that the African slaves learned from French Roman Catholic priests. The resulting religious mixture has come to be called "Voodoo." Today, the two official religions of Haiti are Voodoo and Roman Catholicism. Many Haitians practice both at the same time.

Voodoo encourages its followers to serve the many unseen spirit beings that watch over human affairs. In return, the spirits will grant favors, protection, and good health. One such spirit is Ezili Danto, sometimes spelled Erzulie Dantor. Ezili Danto is a beautiful mother goddess who has many children and several different male partners. Many Voodoo believers see this female spirit as equivalent to the Virgin Mary. Indeed, the pilgrimage to Saut d'Eau, which is dedicated to Ezili Danto, takes place on July 16, the feast day of Our Lady of Mt. Carmel.

The festival traces its history back to the year 1849. Haitians say that in that year Ezili Danto appeared alongside a palm tree near Saut d'Eau. The young man who saw the beautiful and mysterious woman noticed that when she disappeared her image remained behind, imprinted on one of the palm leaves. By the time the leaf fell off the tree, the image transferred itself to a new leaf. Visitors began to come to see the miraculous tree. Some took the opportunity to bathe in the nearby waterfall. When news spread that one of the bathers experienced a miraculous healing, more and more people began to visit the tree, pray, and make offerings to the goddess.

The local Catholic priests were not pleased with these developments. One of them cut down the palm tree in order to abolish the superstitious practices that took place there. According to legend, he died of mysterious causes that same day. The visitors then transferred their devotions to a nearby palm tree. Another zealous priest cut the tree down. The second priest had a stroke and died a few months later. Eventually Catholic officials built a church in the village dedicated to Our Lady of Mt. Carmel. By so doing they suggested that she was behind the miraculous occurrences at Saut d'Eau. Since most Haitians see Ezili Danto and the Blessed Virgin as one and the same, they easily incorporated Roman Catholic masses and devotions into the religious observances of the Saut d'Eau pilgrimage.

Saut d'Eau pilgrims begin arriving weeks in advance of the feast day. Many have serious diseases or disabilities and seek healing. Others have made vows that include a pilgrimage to Saut d'Eau, either in thanksgiving for favors granted or in hopes of future favors. Although transport to the village is difficult and often expensive, people arrive in a happy mood. Since there are no hotels in the village, pilgrims must rent a room from a villager or camp out. A festival atmosphere begins to blossom as musicians play and listeners dance in the streets. Early arrivers can attend the novena—a Roman Catholic prayer service that takes place on nine consecutive days. What's more, local people erect a crucifixion scene near the entrance to the village. Pilgrims visit it in order to pray to Jesus, touch the crucifix, and light candles there. On July 16 the village church holds many Roman Catholic masses. Pilgrims strain to get close enough to the statue of the Virgin Mary to touch or kiss it. In addition, a religious procession tours the village. Pilgrims also trek from the village to the Saut d'Eau waterfall. Here they hope Ezili Danto will hear their prayers, grant their requests, and perhaps even take POSSESSION of their bodies. They remove most of their outer clothing, BATHING under the falling water and in the pool it creates.

SYMBOLS AND CUSTOMS

Bathing

When the pilgrims arrive at the Saut d'Eau waterfall, they remove most of their outer clothes and bathe themselves under the falls. They scrub themselves clean with soap or with herbs and ask Ezili Danto for favors. Tradition encourages bathers to leave their old clothes behind in the water.

Cloth Strips

Ezili Danto's favorite colors are blue and pink. She is thought to have a huge wardrobe of pink and blue dresses to wear on different occasions. To honor the goddess, Saut d'Eau pilgrims tie strips of pink and blue cloth around their waists. When they reach the waterfall, they remove the cloths and tie them around the nearby trees. By doing so, they hope to rid themselves or their communities of disease and misfortune.

Offerings

The pilgrimage at Saut d'Eau gives worshippers an opportunity to make an offering to Ezili Danto. Some people collect alms and make a donation to the church on the Blessed Virgin's feast day. Others leave flowers and candles near Mary's image in the church. Still others leave candles near the waterfalls, hoping to make an offering directly to Ezili Danto. Voodoo priests and priestesses sometimes arrange animal sacrifices to take place near the waterfalls, a practice that is also believed to please the goddess.

Possession

In Voodoo, it is considered a blessing to have the spirit of a god or goddess enter the body and express him or herself through a living person. Pilgrims bathing in the sacred waterfalls at Saut d'Eau are hoping for just such an experience. Those who undergo spirit possession at Saut d'Eau often cry out in a loud voice, sing, and roll their eyes. They stagger about the pools in such a way that they seem unaware of sharp rocks and rapidly flowing currents. Other pilgrims hurry towards them, hoping to make their petition directly into the ear of the Ezili Danto, as she takes possession of a devotee.

FURTHER READING

Bellenir, Karen. *Religious Holidays and Calendars*. 3rd ed. Detroit: Omnigraphics, 2004.

Desmangles, Leslie G. *The Faces of the Gods: Vodou and Roman Catholicism in Haiti*. Chapel Hill: University of North Carolina Press, 1992.

Laguerre, Michel. "Haitian Pilgrimage to O.L. of Saut d'Eau: A Sociological Analysis." *Social Compass*, Vol. 36, no. 1 (1986): 5-21.

Regan, Jane. "Haitians Seek Saint and Spirit, Pilgrimage Blends Vodou, Catholic Rites." *Miami Herald*, July 17, 2003.

WEB SITES

Haiti Embassy
www.haiti.org

Hartford Web Publishing's World History Archives
www.hartford-hwp.com/archives/43a/355.html

Sennin Gyoretsu

Type of Holiday: Historic
Date of Observation: May 17-18
Where Celebrated: Nikko, Japan
Symbols and Customs: Fox Masks, Hawks, Lions, Mirrors, Samurai

ORIGINS

Also known as Toshogu Haru-No-Taisai (Great Spring Festival of the Toshogu Shrine) or the Procession of 1,000 People, Sennin Gyoretsu commemorates the reburial of Shogun Tokugawa Ieyasu (1543-1616), the first of the Tokugawa shoguns (rulers) and the founder of the powerful Tokugawa shogunate. When Ieyasu died, he requested that his remains be transferred to a simply built mausoleum in Nikko. His grandson, Iemitsu, erected an elaborate shrine to house the mausoleum, using more than a million sheets of gold and thousands of the finest builders, craftsmen, and artists to produce the vermilion-lacquered buildings known today as the Toshogu Shrine.

The original procession to the shrine took place in May 1617. It crossed the vermilion-lacquered bridge that spans the nearby Daiya River, slowly mounted the stairs that led to a long lane of cryptomeria (Japanese cedar) trees, and finally brought the body of Shogun Ieyasu to its final resting place. Today, dignitaries and descendants of the Tokugawa family gather on May 17, the day before the procession, and cross the vermilion bridge that leads to the shrine to make offerings to the three shoguns buried there (*see* MIRRORS). The spirits of the shoguns are carried on portable shrines through the famous Gate of Sunlight to the nearby Futaarasan Shrine, where they remain until the next day's procession.

Sennin Gyoretsu is a holiday that commemorates a significant historical event. Peoples throughout the world commemorate such significant events in their histories through holidays and festivals. Often, these are events that are important for an entire nation and become widely observed. The marking of such anniversaries serves not only to honor the values represented by the person or event commemorated, but also to strengthen and reinforce communal bonds of national, cultural, or ethnic identity. Victorious, joyful, and traumatic events are remembered through historic holidays. The commemorative expression reflects the original event through festive celebration or solemn ritual. Reenactments are common activities at historical holiday and festival gatherings, seeking to bring the past alive in the present.

On May 18, huge crowds gather around the Futaarasan Shrine to await the start of the historic procession. It begins with a hundred soldiers marching in two lines, accompanied by costumed SAMURAI guardsmen. Then there are several groups of men carrying weapons—spears, bows and arrows, and old matchlock guns—followed by warriors wearing helmets with antlers and ornamental armor with bright orange shields. Among the many other groups marching are page boys dressed in hats that resemble animal heads, men wearing FOX MASKS, and Shinto priests carrying flags and streamers of all sizes, colors, and designs. The procession reaches a climax when the Shinto musicians arrive, marching in time to the beating of huge drums and the chiming of bells. Before the celebration ends and the portable shrines are returned to the Toshogu Shrine, spectators gather around the shrine's sacred stage to see the *asuma-asobi* dance performed and to watch an arrow-shooting ceremony (*yabusame*) based on a game that was played during the Kamakura period.

The Procession of 1,000 People is watched by hundreds of thousands of Japanese and foreign tourists, who flock to Nikko for what is said to be the most spectacular display of ancient samurai costumes and weaponry in Japan.

SYMBOLS AND CUSTOMS

Fox Masks

The men wearing fox masks who march in the procession symbolize the fox-like phantoms that are believed to live in the mountains around Nikko. It is their job to watch over the Toshogu Shrine, protecting it from damage or intruders.

Hawks

During the Tokugawa shogunate, certain huntsmen were given the job of training hawks to catch small birds. The men carrying stuffed hawks in the procession represent these hawk-trainers.

Lions

Because lions are believed to ward off evil, a large group of men wearing shaggy manes march in the procession.

Mirrors

Metallic mirrors symbolizing the spirits of the three shoguns—Tokugawa Ieyasu, Minamoto Yoritomo (1147-1199), and Toyotomi Hideyoshi (1537-1598)—enshrined at Nikko are transferred to palanquins or portable shrines and carried on the shoulders of young men through the tree-lined streets. The main palanquin is believed to carry the spirit of Tokugawa Ieyasu, the shogun whose remains were moved from their resting place and taken to the newly erected shrine on this day in 1617.

Samurai

The samurai, whose name means to serve or guard, were members of Japan's hereditary warrior class that rose to power in the twelfth century and dominated the Japanese government until the mid-nineteenth century. They reached their position of greatest power under the rule of Tokugawa Ieyasu, and they remained powerful for more than 200 years after his death in 1616. The men who dress like ancient samurai for the Procession of 1,000 People wear the elaborate helmets and square, wing-like body armor of the Tokugawa era (1603-1867). They stand as a symbol of the bravery, honor, and loyalty that characterized this elite group at its peak.

FURTHER READING

Bauer, Helen, and Sherwin Carlquist. *Japanese Festivals*. Garden City, NY: Doubleday, 1965.

Buell, Hal. *Festivals of Japan*. New York: Dodd, Mead, 1965.

Henderson, Helene, ed. *Holidays, Festivals, and Celebrations of the World Dictionary*.
3rd ed. Detroit: Omnigraphics, 2005.

Shemanski, Frances. *A Guide to World Fairs and Festivals*. Westport, CT: Greenwood
Press, 1985.

WEB SITE

Japan National Tourist Organization
www.jnto.go.jp/eng/indepth/history/traditionalevents/a25_fes_nikko.html

Setsubun
(Bean-Throwing Festival)

Type of Holiday: Folkloric, Calendar/Seasonal
Date of Observation: February 3
Where Celebrated: Japan
Symbols and Customs: Bean Throwing
Related Holidays: Lemuralia

ORIGINS

At one time the Japanese believed that the new year started when the season
changed from winter to spring. The first day of spring, according to the ancient
Japanese lunar calendar, fell on February 4, and Setsubun, also known as the Bean-
Throwing Festival, has been celebrated since that time on February 3, or the eve of
the first day of the new year.

Setsubun is a holiday that commemorates seasonal change. Since ancient times
people in all parts of the world have honored the changing of the seasons. Many
cultures divided the year into two seasons, summer and winter, and marked these
points of the year at or near the summer and winter solstices, during which light
and warmth began to increase and decrease, respectively. In pre-industrial times,
humans survived through hunting, gathering, and agricultural practices, which

depend on the natural cycle of seasons, according to the climate in the region of the world in which they lived. Thus, they created rituals to help ensure enough rain and sun in the spring and summer so crops would grow to fruition at harvest time, which was, in turn, duly celebrated. Vestiges of many of these ancient practices are thought to have survived in festivals still celebrated around seasonal themes.

The rituals associated with Setsubun focus on bidding farewell to winter and welcoming the approach of spring. People gather at shrines or temples where local dignitaries—or, in some cases, well-known celebrities such as athletes, actors, politicians, or sumo wrestlers—throw dried beans at the crowd and shout their good wishes. Before any beans are thrown, the individuals who will participate are blessed inside the shrine by monks; after this blessing, the chief monk of the shrine goes out and throws the first beans to the people. Those who catch the beans thrown by celebrities often keep them for the entire year as good luck charms, and some hold out their hats to catch as many as possible.

The Japanese throw fistfuls of beans in their homes as well, calling out *Oni wa soto, fuku wa uchi* or "Devils go out! Come in, good luck!" The bean-thrower or *toshiotoko* is traditionally someone who was born in a particular "animal" year according to the Chinese calendar—for example, the Year of the Rat or the Year of the Monkey. But nowadays, it is usually the head of the household. The bean-thrower aims particularly at the dark corners of rooms, where the evil spirits of winter may still be lurking.

To keep the festivities under control, each person is supposed to throw one bean for each year that has passed since his or her birth, plus an extra bean for the coming year. It is also an old custom to eat as many beans as the years one has lived in order to ward off bad luck. Some people decorate their doorways with sardine heads, believing that devils don't like their smell, and with branches, to poke out the devils' eyes.

SYMBOLS AND CUSTOMS

Bean Throwing

The throwing of beans at Setsubun is symbolic of sowing or scattering seeds in the spring, an activity that was traditionally believed to cast out the devils that had caused bad luck in the preceding year.

FURTHER READING

Buell, Hal. *Festivals of Japan*. New York: Dodd, Mead, 1965.
Helfman, Elizabeth. *Celebrating Nature: Rites and Ceremonies Around the World*. New York: Seabury Press, 1969.

Henderson, Helene, ed. *Holidays, Festivals, and Celebrations of the World Dictionary*. 3rd ed. Detroit: Omnigraphics, 2005.

Leach, Maria, ed. *Funk & Wagnalls Standard Dictionary of Folklore, Mythology & Legend*. San Francisco: Harper & Row, 1984.

MacDonald, Margaret R., ed. *The Folklore of World Holidays*. Detroit: Gale Research, 1992.

Spicer, Dorothy Gladys. *The Book of Festivals*. 1937. Reprint. Detroit: Omnigraphics, 1990.

Thurley, Elizabeth. *Through the Year in Japan*. London: Batsford Academic and Educational, 1985.

Trawicky, Bernard, and Ruth W. Gregory. *Anniversaries and Holidays*. 5th ed. Chicago: American Library Assocation, 2000.

Van Straalen, Alice. *The Book of Holidays Around the World*. New York: Dutton, 1986.

WEB SITE

British Airways
events.britishairways.com/sisp/?fx=event&event_id=24310

Seville Fair
(Feria de Sevilla, April Fair, Feria de Abril)

Type of Holiday: Folkloric, Historic
Date of Observation: Late April
Where Celebrated: Seville, Spain
Symbols and Customs: Bullfighting, Casetas, Flamenco Dress, Flamenco Music and Dancing, Food and Wine, Horse Parades

ORIGINS

The Seville Fair is a week-long, city-wide celebration. It features local FOOD AND WINE, music, and dancing, as well as displays of horsemanship and bravery in BULLFIGHTING.

The Seville Fair began as a springtime agricultural and livestock market in the mid-nineteenth century. In 1847 the town of Seville granted permission to two well-to-do residents, José María Ybarra and Narciso Bonaplata, to organize a livestock fair in April of that year. The affair was a success and was enjoyed by local people as much for the livestock trading as it was for the singing, dancing, and bull fighting that also took place on that occasion.

In the early years of the fair, simple CASETAS—covered canvas stalls or tents— were set up for the livestock dealers. The local elite quickly adopted the idea of setting up their own casetas so that they could enjoy the fair without having to mingle with the middle and lower classes all day long. By 1850, the city council sanctioned the installation of coffee stalls, candy and pastry sellers, and bars. As time went by, the livestock dealing became less important, and the festivities became more important. Livestock dealing disappeared in the mid-twentieth century, but the number of private casetas continued to grow, in spite of the expense involved in renting and furnishing these stalls for a private party. Carnival attractions, too, such as rides and games, have been added to the fair.

The Seville Fair has completely shed its origins as a livestock market, yet it retains some of its old reputation as a playground for Seville's wealthier classes. The enduring customs of the Seville Fair lend themselves to displays of wealth and status. Indeed, the yearly fair gives Seville's elite a chance to show off their horses, their beautiful clothing, and their luxurious casetas. In the 1960s such famous foreign visitors as Prince Rainier and Princess Grace of Monaco, the American actor Orson Welles, and American First Lady Jacqueline Kennedy brought the fair international attention and prestige, which it still enjoys today.

The Seville Fair always falls in late April and lasts one week. It opens on a Tuesday at 12:00 a.m. with the illumination of the ceremonial gate constructed at the entrance of the fairgrounds. People stream through the arch, and the festivities begin. The Fair ends the following Sunday night with a display of fireworks. Monday is a city-wide day off from work, which gives people time to recover and return to their normal lives. The city government sets and announces the dates for the April Fair in December of the previous year.

SYMBOLS AND CUSTOMS

Bullfighting

Bullfighting is an ancient sport that has become a spectacular cultural symbol for Spain. Bullfighters known as *matadors* train from childhood to perform the intricate, stylized rituals of the fight. Years of practice are required to prepare to become a matador, and many of the top matadors in Spain are members of traditional bullfighting families. Spanish bullfights typically take place during festivals, fairs, and holiday celebrations.

During the Seville Fair, bullfights are scheduled every day. People with tickets for the fight drift away from the fairgrounds in the late afternoon, leisurely making their way to Seville's bullfighting ring. The event usually begins around 5:00 p.m. These contests pit some of Spain's best matadors against some of Spain's fiercest bulls and are considered to be the best bullfights of the season. Each day's contests involve individual matches between six bulls and three matadors, with one matador and one bull in the ring at the same time. Each match plays out according to traditional maneuvers and rules of engagement and usually lasts about fifteen minutes.

Casetas

The Seville Fair takes place at a fairgrounds some distance away from the city center. People with means set up little houses, or *casetas*, for the duration of the fair. These casetas, which resemble the covered stalls set up by vendors at an American fair, provide shelter from the sun, a place to sit down, and the backdrop for a party. Over 1,000 casetas have been erected in recent years, from small, private parties to large, public pavilions. Since it costs a fair amount of money to rent the space, most casetas belong to well-to-do families, businesses, trade unions, government agencies, membership organizations, politicians, bars, restaurants, and social clubs. Casetas are typically decorated with banners, streamers, flags, and flowers to reflect a unique theme. Each caseta hosts a private party—in fact, most of the fair's nighttime activity takes place in the casetas. Guards at the door make sure that only those whose names appear on the guest list enter. Inside, guests enjoy food, drink, music, dancing, laughter, and conversation until late at night. Music and dancing are the primary entertainment.

The rows of casetas create streets and lanes that are given names in order to help people navigate the fair. Most are named after famous bullfighters, underlining the importance of bull fighting to the Seville Fair.

Flamenco Dress

Many Sevillians enjoy dressing up in folk costume for the fair. For the men, this means a *traje de corto*, or "short suit." The traje de corto consists of a short, bolero-style jacket, white shirt, tight-fitting trousers, and boots. A broad brimmed black hat completes the outfit. For the women, this means a flamenco dress, called dressing *de faralaes* (dressing "in ruffles"). The name comes from the rows and rows of ruffles that cover the skirt from the knees down to the floor. These dresses hug the figure from the bust to the thigh and flare out below. They are often made from bright, polka-dotted fabric.

Flamenco dresses are not only the traditional costume of the Seville Fair, but also the traditional garb of Flamenco dancers. This style of dress was first worn by late nineteenth-century gypsy women in Andalusia, Spain's southern region. For this reason, wearing this kind of dress is referred to as dressing *de gitana*, "gypsy style," or *de flamenca*, "flamenco style." The flamenco dress was later adopted by the middle and upper classes as a style of folk dress. Outside of Spain the flamenco dress is viewed as typically Spanish, although inside Spain it is understood to be typically Andalusian.

While the men's short suit is well-suited to equestrian activities, the women's flamenco dress is not. Women who are planning to ride a horse to the fair sometimes opt for the female equivalent of the men's suit, which consists of a short, tight-fitting jacket of dark material, a white blouse, and a long skirt, also of dark-colored material. This type of dress is referred to as *de amazona*, or "Amazon style."

Flamenco Music and Dancing

Flamenco songs, or *Sevillanas*, combine traditional Andalusian folk songs and a regional form of flamenco dancing. As symbols of the region's culture and history, many area residents learn the songs and dances in school as young children. The dances are performed in pairs of either a man and a woman or two women and include a set of steps executed in different sequences. Musical accompaniment typically includes guitar, hand claps, flute, drums, tambourines, and *castanets*, a traditional Spanish handheld percussion instrument that produces a clacking sound.

The Seville Fair is a celebration of all things Sevillian, and Flamenco music and dancing thus play an important role in the festivities. Although the roots of Flamenco music lie throughout southern Spain, Flamenco enjoys a particularly strong association with the city of Seville. At the Seville Fair, people play Sevillanas on their boom boxes inside their casetas and dance when the mood strikes them. At night, after the bullfighting is finished, fair goers return to the fair grounds where more Flamenco music and dancing takes place.

Food and Wine

Fairgoers indulge in feasts of food and wine during the entire week, enjoying small amounts continually throughout the day and night rather than sitting down for full meals. The traditional Spanish appetizers known as *tapas* are the food of choice. Tapas range from simple, cold trays of cheese and meat to more elaborately prepared hot seafood and egg dishes and small pastries with rich fillings known as *empanadas*.

Andalusia specializes in the production of sherry, a fortified wine ranging from pale yellow to mahogany brown in color, and from very dry to very sweet in taste. Sherry is the most popular alcoholic drink served at the Seville Fair. People who prefer a less alcoholic drink sometimes mix sherry with fizzy lemonade.

Horse Parades

The livestock market that was once central to the Seville Fair is long gone, yet a small echo remains in the horse parades that wealthy Sevillians still put on. These daily parades allow members of Seville's upper class to show off their wealth and finery. The parade begins at midday. Those who can't afford to ride come to watch the well-to-do Sevillians, wearing Flamenco dress, parade on horseback or in their horse-drawn carriages. Costumed riders travel in groups, sometimes stopping at different entertainment tents where tapas and wine are brought out to them. Others ride in colorful carriages. Sometimes both a man and a woman will ride a horse, with the man sitting in front and the women behind him, riding in a side-saddle position with her arms around his waist. In this way she can take part in the parade and still wear her fabulous Flamenco dress. The parade also includes musicians and singers who perform traditional ballads while walking alongside those on horseback. The parade ends in the mid-to-late afternoon, as the horses and carriages make their way to the bullring.

FURTHER READING

Henderson, Helene, ed. *Holidays, Festivals, and Celebrations of the World Dictionary.* 3rd ed. Detroit: Omnigraphics, 2005.

Nash, Elizabeth. Seville. *Córdoba, and Granada: A Cultural History.* New York: Oxford University Press, 2005.

WEB SITES

Andalucía magazine
www.andalucia.com/magazine/english/ed2/seville-feria.htm

Exploreseville.com
www.exploreseville.com/events/feriadeabril.htm

Flamenco magazine
www.esflamenco.com/scripts/news/ennews.asp?frmIdPagina=36

Tourist Office of Spain
www.okspain.org

Shalako Ceremony

Type of Holiday: Calendar/Seasonal, Religious (Zuni)
Date of Observation: Late November-early December
Where Celebrated: New Mexico
Symbols and Customs: Shalako
Related Holidays: Winter Solstice

ORIGINS

The Shalako Ceremony is part of the religious tradition of the Zuni Indians. The history of this and other Native American cultures dates back thousands of years into prehistoric times. According to many scholars, the people who became the Native Americans migrated from Asia across a land bridge that may have once connected the territories presently occupied by Alaska and Russia. The migrations, believed to have begun between 60,000 and 30,000 B.C.E., continued until approximately 4,000 B.C.E. This speculation, however, conflicts with traditional stories asserting that the indigenous Americans have always lived in North America or that tribes moved up from the south.

The historical development of religious belief systems among Native Americans is not well known. Most of the information available was gathered by Europeans who arrived on the continent beginning in the sixteenth century C.E. The data they recorded was fragmentary and oftentimes of questionable accuracy because the Europeans did not understand the native cultures they were trying to describe and the Native Americans were reluctant to divulge details about themselves.

The Shalako Ceremony is the most important event of the year for the Zuni Indians of New Mexico. It takes place in the early winter, after the crops are in, and the timing is crucial. Like several other Native peoples, the Zuni divide their ceremonial year into two parts: winter and summer. Winter begins at the **WINTER SOLSTICE**; ceremonies during this half of the year tend to emphasize healing, conflict, and fertility. Summer ceremonies, which begin at the **SUMMER SOLSTICE**, are concerned with agriculture and the necessity for rain.

In former days, it was the duty of the Sun Priest to ensure that the Shalako Ceremony coincided as closely as possible with both the **WINTER SOLSTICE** and the full moon. During the eight days preceding the solstice, the Sun Priest would pray and fast, making pilgrimages to the sacred Thunder Mountain to commune with the Sun Father. On the ninth morning, he announced the approach of the solstice with a low, mournful call.

Nowadays everyone knows when the Shalako Ceremony will be held, and it attracts more outside visitors than any other Zuni festival. Preparations begin a full year in advance. Each of the SHALAKO must be housed and entertained during the festival—an expense that can take a family years to recover from. Although other members of the village help each host bring in his crop and fix up his house, the brunt of the expense falls to the individual. Sometimes a new house must be built to accommodate the Shalako dancers. At the very least, the existing house must be replastered.

About eight days before the ceremony, the Mudheads—clown-like figures wearing mud-daubed masks that resemble deformed human faces—announce the arrival of the SHALAKO. Early on the morning of the ceremony, the "impersonators of the gods" and their attendants leave the village quietly, carrying their masks and other paraphernalia hidden under their blankets. The Fire God—usually a young boy with his body painted black and spotted with red, yellow, blue, and white—and his ceremonial father visit each house where the Shalako will be staying and leave two prayer-plumes, symbolizing the original man and woman, in a box. The Council of the Gods arrives next, making the same rounds that the Fire God has made and pausing in front of each house to dance and shake bunches of deer bones. The Council includes Sayatasha, the Rain God of the North, and Hu-tu-tu, the Rain God of the South. They enter the house designated for Sayatasha through a hatchway in the roof and are greeted by the host and his family, who sprinkle them with sacred meal. Food is put out for the Council members, and everyone eats.

By the time the Council of the Gods disappears, it is sunset and time for the Shalako to appear and perform their dance. Spectators gather behind a barbed-wire fence set up in an open field. The SHALAKO appear just at dusk—six huge figures who tower above their attendants, wearing headdresses with eagle feathers that fan out like the rays of the sun. They carry their masks on long poles hidden under blankets, and the same man who carries the pole manipulates the mask's bulging eyes and clacks its wooden beak. Each Shalako has two attendants: a manager and a man who will relieve him when he tires of dancing while maneuvering the heavy superstructure. The switch in dancers takes place behind blankets so that no one will see what is going on and the children won't know that these images aren't really gods. The dancers take great pride in balancing their masks and never missing a step as they bend their knees, dip their heads, and then right themselves. At the end of the ceremony, each Shalako enters the house that has been prepared for him, and a welcoming ceremony is performed there.

More dancing begins at midnight in the SHALAKO houses, where the men take turns handling the heavy, swaying masks. The departure of the gods takes place around noon, with the Fire God followed by the Council of the Gods and finally the Shalako themselves. Long lines of spectators watch them leave, with their peculiar swooping motion and clacking wooden beaks. Since the Shalako act as messengers to the gods, their departure is the final prayer for rain to fill the rivers, wells, and springs before summer arrives.

SYMBOLS AND CUSTOMS

Shalako

According to Zuni legend, their ancestors emerged from the underworld to the earth's surface and searched for their "center," where they would find water and security. The Water Spider led them to an anthill, which he proclaimed was the center of the earth, instructing them to build their village there.

The Shalako, who are believed to have first appeared at Zuni around 1840, retrace the wanderings of the Zunis from the center of the earth to the modern pueblo. Since they are the couriers of the gods, they run back and forth all year carrying messages, bringing moisture and rain when it is needed. When they leave, they carry the Zunis' prayers for rain with them.

FURTHER READING

Bellenir, Karen. *Religious Holidays and Calendars*. 3rd ed. Detroit: Omnigraphics, 2004.

Fergusson, Erna. *Dancing Gods: Indian Ceremonials of New Mexico and Arizona*. New York: A.A. Knopf, 1931.

Heinberg, Richard. *Celebrate the Solstice: Honoring the Earth's Seasonal Rhythms through Festival and Ceremony*. Wheaton, IL: Quest Books, 1993.

Henderson, Helene, ed. *Holidays, Festivals, and Celebrations of the World Dictionary*. 3rd ed. Detroit: Omnigraphics, 2005.

Leach, Maria, ed. *Funk & Wagnalls Standard Dictionary of Folklore, Mythology & Legend*. San Francisco: Harper & Row, 1984.

WEB SITE

Pueblo Cultural Center
www.indianpueblo.org/ipcc/zunipage.htm

Shavuot
(Feast of Weeks)

Type of Holiday: Religious (Jewish)
Date of Observation: Between May 16 and June 13; sixth day of Sivan
Where Celebrated: Europe, Israel, United States, and by Jews all over the world
Symbols and Customs: Bikkurim, Milk and Honey, Roses
Related Holidays: Lag Ba-Omer, Passover, Sukkot

ORIGINS

Shavuot is one of the holidays of the Jewish faith, one of the oldest continuously observed religions in the world. Its history extends back beyond the advent of the written word. Its people trace their roots to a common ancestor, Abraham, and then back even farther to the very moment of creation.

According to Jewish belief, the law given to the Jewish people by God contained everything they needed to live a holy life, including the ability to be reinterpreted in new historical situations. Judaism, therefore, is the expression of the Jewish people, attempting to live holy (set apart) lives in accordance with the instructions given by God. Obedience to the law is central to Judaism, but there is no one central authority. Sources of divine authority are God, the Torah, interpretations of the Torah by respected teachers, and tradition. Religious observances and the study of Jewish law are conducted under the supervision of a teacher called a rabbi.

There are several sects within Judaism. Orthodox Judaism is characterized by an affirmation of the traditional Jewish faith, strict adherence to customs such as keeping the Sabbath, participation in ceremonies and rituals, and the observance of dietary regulations. Reform Judaism stresses modern biblical criticism and emphasizes ethical teachings more than ritualistic observance. Conservative Jewish congregations seek to retain many ancient traditions but without the accompanying demand for strict observance. Hasidism is a mystical sect of Judaism that teaches enthusiastic prayer as a means of communion with God. The Reconstructionist movement began early in the twentieth century in an effort to "reconstruct" Judaism with the community rather than the synagogue as its center.

Shavuot—which means "weeks" in Hebrew—originated as an agricultural festival that took its name from the seven weeks between Pesach (or **PASSOVER**), when the first sheaf of barley was brought to the Temple in Jerusalem, and the beginning of the wheat harvest. Because the Jews had no written calendar, the exact date of Shavuot would be determined by counting seven weeks from the second day of **PASSOVER**, with the holiday taking place on the fiftieth day. When a fixed calendar was later adopted, the sixth of Sivan was designated as the date of the harvest festival.

Every housewife would grind some fresh flour from the new grain and bake cakes and loaves of bread for the family feast. At the Temple in Jerusalem, there was a ceremonial sacrifice of two loaves baked from the new wheat crop. Pilgrims would come from all parts of the country to participate in the harvest ceremonies at the Temple, often bringing an offering of wheat as well as grapes, figs, and pomegranates (*see* BIKKURIM). Sometimes families would gather in each farming village and walk to Jerusalem together, forming a long column as they approached the temple. At the front of these processions there would be an ox whose horns were painted gold and decorated with olive branches. Behind the ox there would be musicians playing tambourines, flutes, and other instruments. They would bring their offerings to the Temple, where the priests would bless them.

After the Second Temple was destroyed, the Jews no longer had a place to perform this annual ritual. The rabbis looked for a way to preserve the holiday and give it new meaning. In the middle of the second century, they designated Shavuot as the anniversary of the day on which the Ten Commandments were given to the children of Israel at Mount Sinai. The agricultural and spiritual aspects of the festival formed a meaningful parallel: Just as Shavuot marked the end of seven weeks' collaboration between God and man in gathering the harvest, it also celebrated the end of a spiritual harvest, which began with the deliverance of the Jews from Egypt and reached its climax with the Covenant (or contract) between God and the people of Israel that was made on Mount Sinai.

Many Shavuot customs are related to the Torah, or Jewish Bible, the contents of which were also revealed to Moses on Mount Sinai. On the eve of the holiday, many pious Jews wash in the *mikvah* or ritual bath and put on new clothes so that they will be clean when they receive the Torah. They dedicate the evening to studying portions of the Torah and the Talmud, a collection of writings that constitute Jewish civil and religious law. The Book of Ruth is a popular selection to read on Shavuot because it manages to combine both the holiday's agricultural and religious roots. It tells the story of a pagan woman who was converted to Judaism, but the events take place against the background of the barley harvest.

Shavuot's agricultural roots have not been entirely forgotten. Houses and synagogues are decorated with flowers (*see* ROSES) and greenery; in Israel, children fill baskets with vegetables and fruits from their garden and carry them to school, where they are donated to charity.

SYMBOLS AND CUSTOMS

Bikkurim

The Mishnah or first part of the Talmud describes how the *bikkurim* or first fruits used in the celebration of Shavuot are selected: "When a man comes down to his field and sees a ripe fig, or a ripe cluster of grapes, or a ripe pomegranate, he ties each with a red thread, saying, 'These are bikkurim.'"

In modern Israel, many kibbutzim (community settlements) and other agricultural communities have revived the bikkurim ceremony. Fresh produce is brought to a designated place by tractors, carts, and wheelbarrows that have been decorated with flowers and greenery. There is singing, folk dancing to the music of ancient instruments, and poetry reading. Sometimes there are pageants that re-create the traditional pilgrimage and ceremony at the Temple of Jerusalem.

One of the most colorful bikkurim ceremonies is held in Haifa, where Jews from the Sharon, Emek, and Jordan valleys gather to offer their first fruits to the Jewish National Fund (Keren Kayemet). There is a procession of young people carrying decorated baskets filled with ripe fruits and vegetables, sheaves of fresh-cut barley and wheat, jugs of honey *(see* MILK AND HONEY), and young fowl or lambs. After handing over the first fruits to the Keren Kayemet, everyone takes a seat in the open-air theater to enjoy the pageant known as *Hatene* or "The Basket," which is a reenactment of ancient bikkurim ceremonies. In the United States, an impressive bikkurim festival is held annually in one of the city parks of Chicago.

Milk and Honey

Cheese and dairy dishes are often served at Shavuot because, according to legend, the Israelites were too exhausted after witnessing the revelation on Mount Sinai to slaughter an animal and cook its meat. It is also said that when they returned to their tents after spending all day at Mount Sinai and discovered that their milk had gone sour, they turned it into cheese. Modern Jews eat cheese blintzes (pancakes filled with cottage cheese), ice cream, and cheese-filled kreplach (dumplings). Any food made from milk is considered symbolic, for milk plays the same role in physical growth that the Torah plays in moral and spiritual growth.

Honey, usually in the form of honey cakes, is also eaten on Shavuot. According to Jewish scholars, this is because the Torah is as sweet as honey and as nourishing as milk to those who study and live by its teachings.

Roses

Flowers and greenery are used to decorate homes and synagogues at Shavuot for two reasons. Like **SUKKOT**, it originated as a celebration of the harvest. The flowers and green branches are symbols of the farming life that the Jewish people led in ancient times. It is also said that Mount Sinai was unusually green on the day that Moses received the Ten Commandments. According to one version of the events of that day, the mountain was actually covered in roses. The custom of decorating with roses, either fresh or cut out of paper, was so prevalent at one time that the Persian Jews referred to Shavuot as the Feast of the Flowers, while Italian Jews called it the Feast of the Roses.

FURTHER READING

Bellenir, Karen. *Religious Holidays and Calendars*. 3rd ed. Detroit: Omnigraphics, 2004.

Christianson, Stephen G., and Jane M. Hatch. *The American Book of Days*. 4th ed. New York: H.W. Wilson, 2000.

Cohen, Hennig, and Tristram Potter Coffin. *The Folklore of American Holidays*. 3rd ed. Detroit: Gale Research, 1999.

Crim, Keith R. *The Perennial Dictionary of World Religions*. San Francisco: Harper & Row, 1989.

Edidin, Ben. *Jewish Holidays and Festivals*. 1940. Reprint. Detroit: Omnigraphics, 1993.

Gaer, Joseph. *Holidays Around the World*. Boston: Little, Brown, 1953.

Gaster, Theodor H. *Festivals of the Jewish Year*. New York: William Sloane Associates, 1953.

Harper, Howard V. *Days and Customs of All Faiths*. 1957. Reprint. Detroit: Omnigraphics, 1990.

Henderson, Helene, ed. *Holidays, Festivals, and Celebrations of the World Dictionary*. 3rd ed. Detroit: Omnigraphics, 2005.

Ickis, Marguerite. *The Book of Festivals and Holidays the World Over*. New York: Dodd, Mead, 1970.

MacDonald, Margaret R., ed. *The Folklore of World Holidays*. Detroit: Gale Research, 1992.

Renberg, Dalia Hardof. *The Complete Family Guide to Jewish Holidays*. New York: Adama Books, 1985.

Urlin, Ethel L. *Festivals, Holy Days, and Saints' Days*. 1915. Reprint. Detroit: Omnigraphics, 1992.

WEB SITE

Union of Orthodox Jewish Congregations of America
www.ou.org/chagim/shavuot

Shawnee Death Feast

Type of Holiday: Religious (Shawnee)
Date of Observation: Varies
Where Celebrated: Oklahoma
Customs and Symbols: Darkened Room, Food, Speaking to the Spirits

ORIGINS

The Shawnee Death Feast is part of the Native American religious tradition. The history of Native American cultures dates back thousands of years into prehistoric times. According to many scholars, the people who became the Native Americans migrated from Asia across a land bridge that may have once connected the territories presently occupied by Alaska and Russia. The migrations, believed to have begun between 60,000 and 30,000 B.C.E., continued until approximately 4,000 B.C.E. This speculation, however, conflicts with traditional stories asserting that the indigenous Americans have always lived in North America or that tribes moved up from the south.

The historical development of religious belief systems among the Shawnee and other Native Americans is not well known. Most of the information available was gathered by Europeans who arrived on the continent beginning in the sixteenth century C.E. The data they recorded was fragmentary and oftentimes of questionable accuracy because the Europeans did not understand the native cultures they were trying to describe and the Native Americans were reluctant to divulge details about themselves.

The Shawnee Death Feast is an annual ceremony held in memory of loved ones who have died. One of the traditional beliefs of the Shawnee is that the spirits of the dead have the ability to influence the circumstances of the living, for better or worse. The Death Feast is offered to assure the dead that they are remembered fondly and to respectfully request that the living remain undisturbed by their spirits. Although many older Native American religious practices have been overtaken by Christianity, some Shawnee continue to observe the Death Feast as a way of honoring ancestors and other deceased loved ones.

The Death Feast is normally conducted in private, at the home of the family or friends of the deceased. Special FOOD is prepared and served on a table just as it would be for any guest. This is usually also an opportunity for SPEAKING TO THE SPIRITS. The food is then left in a DARKENED ROOM for a period of time. The family and/or friends of the deceased return to the room later to clear away the food, which can then be eaten by the living. It is believed that the spirits of the departed consume the essence (aroma) of the food, although sometimes portions of the food are missing when the family returns.

CUSTOMS AND SYMBOLS

Darkened Room

The feast is left undisturbed in a darkened room for a few hours or overnight. It is believed that during this time the spirits of the dead will consume the feast.

Food

The food that is left out for the spirits usually includes traditional Native American dishes but can include anything that was preferred by the deceased in life.

Speaking to the Spirits

After the feast is set on the table, someone present usually addresses the spirits of the deceased, speaking aloud of fond memories and asking for help, insight, and guidance from the spirits.

FURTHER READING

Hirschfelder, Arlene B., and Paulette Molin. "Death Feast." In *Encyclopedia of Native American Religions*. New York: Facts on File, 2000.

Hultkrantz, Ake. "North American Indian Religions: An Overview." In *Encyclopedia of Religion*. Edited by Lindsay Jones. 2nd ed. New York: Macmillan Reference USA, 2005.

WEB SITE

Native American Sites, Information on Individual Native Nations
www.nativeculturelinks.com/nations.html

Shichi-Go-San
(Seven-Five-Three Festival)

Type of Holiday: Religious (Shinto)
Date of Observation: November 15
Where Celebrated: Japan
Symbols and Customs: Guardian Bag, Thousand-Year Candy, Toy Dog
Colors: Red is the most popular color for girls to wear on this day. Boys usually
   dress in gray and black.

ORIGINS

The Shichi-Go-San festival is part of the Shinto tradition, an ancient religion that originated in Japan. Most Shinto adherents live in Japan, but small communities also exist in Europe, Latin America, North America, and in the Pacific island nations.

The name Shinto was first employed during the sixth century C.E. to differentiate indigenous religions in Japan from faith systems that originated in mainland Asia (primarily Buddhism and Confucianism). The word is derived from two Chinese characters, *shen* (gods) and *tao* (way). Loosely translated, Shinto means "way of the gods." Its roots lie in an ancient nature-based religion. Some important concepts in Shinto include the value of tradition, the reverence of nature, cleanliness (ritual purity), and the veneration of spirits called *kami*. Strictly speaking, kami are not deities. The literal translation of the word kami is "that which is hidden."

Kami (which is both the singular and plural term) are honored, but they do not assert their powers upon humans in the traditional manner of deities or gods in other religions. People may be descended from the kami, and kami may influence the course of nature and events. The kami can bestow blessings, but they are not all benign. Kami are present in natural things such as trees, mountains, rocks, and rivers. They are embodied in religious relics, especially mirrors and jewels. They also include spirits of ancestors, local deities, holy people, and even political or literary figures. The human role is to venerate the kami and make offerings. The ultimate goal of Shinto is to uphold the harmony among humans and between people and nature. In this regard, the principle of all kami is to protect and sustain life.

The central authorities in Shinto are the priests. Traditionally, the duties of the priest were passed through heredity lines, but in modern times priests are trained on the basis of recommendation. The priests' duties include communicating with the kami and ensuring that ceremonies are properly carried out. Shinto does not have a single collection of sacred texts analogous to the Christian Bible or Islamic Qur'an. Instead, several important books provide information and guidance: *Kojiki* (*Records of Ancient Events*), *Nihongi* (*Chronicles of Japan*), and *Engishiki* (*Chronicles of the Engi*).

The Shichi-Go-San festival is believed to have originated back in the days when children often died young and parents wanted to express their gratitude for those who had survived. It has long been traditional in Japan to take girls aged seven, boys of five, and all three-year-olds, dressed in their finest, to the neighborhood Shinto shrine on November 15 to invoke the blessings of the family's guardian gods. Three-year-old girls wear their hair fully dressed for the first time in the style worn by their mothers. Five-year-old boys put on traditional skirt-like trousers, and seven-year-old girls wear their first *obi*, or wide kimono sash.

After the young children have assembled at the shrine where they were registered at birth, the priest performs an old Shinto ritual in which he waves a branch in circles high over the children's heads. At the close of the brief ceremony, the priest's attendants come out, carrying white box-like trays with pyramids of small white paper packages, two for each child. One contains cakes in the form of the Shinto emblems—the mirror, the sword, and the jewel—while the other contains a small quantity of uncooked rice, which is considered sacred because it has been in front of the altar. The mothers take the rice home and mix it with the rice they serve at the evening meal, where family members offer their congratulations to the child before lifting their chopsticks to eat.

Seven, five, and three are considered lucky numbers in Japan, and the most fortunate mother of all is the one who has three children of the appropriate ages and sexes. Fathers often videotape their children as they receive the priest's blessings and a bag of THOUSAND-YEAR CANDY.

SYMBOLS AND CUSTOMS

Guardian Bag

Many children carry a bag made of brocade or some other brightly colored cloth. It often contains a piece of writing that the priest gave to the child on his or her first visit to the shrine as an infant. Both boys and girls carry these so-called guardian bags, which are considered a symbolic protection against evil.

Thousand-Year Candy

When they get to the shrine, the children who have come to celebrate the Seven-Five-Three festival are given sacks full of pink candy known as "Thousand-Year Candy." It is supposed to bring them good luck and a long life.

Toy Dog

Almost every child carries a toy dog to the shrine. These dogs are usually black-and-white, with a cape-like red collar or a red band with a tiny bell. Friends and relatives give the toy dogs to the children as gifts on the festival, and some children are burdened with so many dogs that they must have help carrying them. The dogs, which can range in size from very small to eighteen or more inches high, are considered to be good luck guardians for small children.

FURTHER READING

Bauer, Helen, and Sherwin Carlquist. *Japanese Festivals*. Garden City, NY: Doubleday, 1965.

Bellenir, Karen. *Religious Holidays and Calendars*. 3rd ed. Detroit: Omnigraphics, 2004.

Dobler, Lavinia G. *Customs and Holidays Around the World*. New York: Fleet Pub. Corp., 1962.

Henderson, Helene, ed. *Holidays, Festivals, and Celebrations of the World Dictionary*. 3rd ed. Detroit: Omnigraphics, 2005.

MacDonald, Margaret R., ed. *The Folklore of World Holidays*. Detroit: Gale Research, 1992.

Van Straalen, Alice. *The Book of Holidays Around the World*. New York: Dutton, 1986.

WEB SITE

Web Japan
web-japan.org/kidsweb/explore/calendar/november/shichigosan.html

Shick-Shack Day
(Royal Oak Day, Restoration Day)

Type of Holiday: Historic
Date of Observation: May 29
Where Celebrated: England
Symbols and Customs: Oak Sprig
Related Holidays: May Day

ORIGINS

Also known as Restoration Day, Shick-Shack Day commemorates the restoration of King Charles II to the throne in 1660, ending the Puritan Commonwealth that had been introduced in 1649. After his defeat by the English Parliamentarians (also known as Roundheads, because they wore their hair cut short), Charles II hid in an oak tree near Boscobel to escape the soldiers who were pursuing him. He was forced to remain there all day, unable to speak or shift his position for fear of being discovered.

This event occurred in September of 1651. He was restored to the throne in 1660, much to the relief of most of the English people. He is particularly remembered at the Royal Hospital in Chelsea, founded in 1682 as a refuge for old soldiers no longer able to earn a living. They celebrate their Founders' Day on May 29 by parading in his honor, by covering the statue of Charles II that stands in the center of the main courtyard with oak boughs, and by wearing a sprig of oak in their lapels.

Although it occurs at the end of May, Shick-Shack Day has much in common with **MAY DAY**. Maypoles are displayed along the streets of many English villages, and people dance around them much as they do elsewhere on May 1. Young women often bathe their faces in the early morning dew, and children bring branches and blossoms in from the woods—both popular May Day customs.

The *Oxford English Dictionary* suggests that this day takes its name from a corruption of *shitsack*, a derogatory name for the Nonconformists, Protestants who did not follow the doctrines and practices of the established Church of England. The term was later applied to anyone who didn't wear an oak leaf or oak-apple in memory of Charles II on May 29, and nowadays refers to the OAK SPRIG itself.

Shick-Shack Day is a holiday that commemorates a significant historical event. Peoples throughout the world commemorate such significant events in their histories through holidays and festivals. Often, these are events that are important for an entire nation and become widely observed. The marking of such anniversaries serves not only to honor the values represented by the person or event commemorated, but also to strengthen and reinforce communal bonds of national, cultural, or ethnic identity. Victorious, joyful, and traumatic events are remembered through historic holidays. The commemorative expression reflects the original event through festive celebration or solemn ritual. Reenactments are common activities at historical holiday and festival gatherings, seeking to bring the past alive in the present.

There are a number of local names for Shick-Shack Day. In some areas it is known as Oak Apple Day because people wear oak-apples as well as sprigs of oak leaves, and children gather twigs with oak-apples still attached and try to sell them in the streets. In the town of Ulverston, it is known as Bobby Ack Day—"bobby" referring to the knob-like oak-apple, and "ack" representing an older pronunciation of "oak." In other towns it is called Nettle Day, because children punish those who forget to wear an oak sprig by pushing them into a bed of nettles.

"The Royal Oak" is one of the most popular names for pubs in England today. The signs usually show Charles II peering through the leaves of an oak tree, looking more like a boy who's been caught stealing apples than a king escaping his enemies.

SYMBOLS AND CUSTOMS

Oak Sprig

The sprig of oak worn by people on Shick-Shack Day is a symbol of the oak tree that concealed King Charles II when he was under attack by the Roundheads. The oak sprig also recalls the king himself, who was one of the most popular English monarchs and is still remembered for his many good deeds.

FURTHER READING

Chambers, Robert. *The Book of Days*. 2 vols. 1862-64. Reprint. Detroit: Omnigraphics, 1990.

Dunkling, Leslie. *A Dictionary of Days*. New York: Facts on File, 1988.

Henderson, Helene, ed. *Holidays, Festivals, and Celebrations of the World Dictionary*. 3rd ed. Detroit: Omnigraphics, 2005.

Hole, Christina. *English Custom & Usage*. 1941. Reprint. Detroit: Omnigraphics, 1990.

MacDonald, Margaret R., ed. *The Folklore of World Holidays*. Detroit: Gale Research, 1992.

WEB SITE

BBC (British Broadcasting Corporation)
www.bbc.co.uk/wiltshire/moonraking/folklore_oak_apple.shtml

Shivaratri
(Sivaratri)

Type of Holiday: Religious (Hindu)
Date of Observation: February-March; thirteenth and fourteenth day of the waning half of the Hindu month of Phalguna
Where Celebrated: India, Mauritius, Nepal
Symbols and Customs: Bel Tree, Lingam

ORIGINS

Shivaratri is a festival in the tradition of Hinduisim, which many scholars regard as the oldest living religion. The word Hindu is derived from the Sanskrit term *Sindhu* (or *Indus*), which meant river. It referred to people living in the Indus valley in the Indian subcontinent. Hinduism has no founder, one universal reality (or god) known as Brahman, many gods and goddesses (sometimes referred to as devtas), and several scriptures. Hinduism also has no priesthood or hierarchical structure similar to that seen in some other religions, such as Christianity. Hindus acknowledge the authority of a wide variety of writings, but there is no single, uniform canon. The oldest of the Hindu writings are the *Vedas*. The word "veda" comes from the Sanskrit word for knowledge. The *Vedas*, which were compiled from ancient oral traditions, contain hymns, instructions, explanations, chants for sacrifices, magical formulas, and philosophy. Another set of sacred books includes the *Great Epics*, which illustrate Hindu faith in practice. The *Epics* include the *Ramayana*, the *Mahabharata*, and the *Bhagavad Gita*.

The Hindu pantheon includes approximately thirty-three million gods. Some of these are held in higher esteem than others. Over all the gods, Hindus believe in one absolute high god or universal concept. This is Brahman. Although he is above all the gods, he is not worshipped in popular ceremonies because he is detached from the day to day affairs of the people. Brahman is impersonal. Lesser gods and goddesses (devtas) serve him. Because these are more intimately involved in the affairs of people, they are venerated as gods. The most honored god in Hinduism varies among the different Hindu sects. Although Hindu adherents practice their faith differently and venerate different deities, they share a similar view of reality and look back on a common history.

Shivaratri is the main festival held in honor of Shiva (or Siva), the Hindu god of destruction and regeneration. According to Hindu teaching, this is the night on which Shiva danced the *Tandav,* his celestial dance of Creation, Preservation, and Destruction. Throughout India and in other countries where he is venerated, Hindus eat only once on the thirteenth day of Phalguna; after this, they fast in preparation for the Great Night of Shiva, as the festival is also known. It is the sacred duty of every worshipper to keep a vigil throughout the night and to worship him at midnight by offering leaves from the wood-apple or BEL TREE. There is an old Hindu saying that even an intelligent dog will not touch its food on this day.

Huge gatherings take place in temples all over India on Shivaratri—even in rural areas, where the bells ring all night and people stay awake by chanting Shiva's name, singing songs about his glory, and recounting his legends. Special celebrations are held at the Shiva shrines in Tamil Nadu, Andhra Pradesh, and Uttar Pradesh, and hundreds of thousands of Hindus make the pilgrimage to Pashupatinath Temple in Katmandu, Nepal, for worship, feasting, and ritual bathing in the holy Bagmati River. In Port Louis, Mauritius, wooden arches covered with flowers are carried to the holy lake known as Grand Bassin, to get water with which the images of Shiva can be washed. A large number of fairs are also held on Shivaratri, and bathing in holy tanks or sacred rivers is a common activity.

Members of all castes or divisions of Hindu society are allowed to participate in the worship of Shiva. While the wealthy perform elaborate rites that include expensive offerings to Shiva and substantial gifts to the poor, members of the lower castes must content themselves with pouring water on the Shiva-LINGAM. The ceremonies surrounding Shivaratri are particularly popular with Hindu women, especially those wishing to become pregnant.

SYMBOLS AND CUSTOMS

Bel Tree

The bel tree—also known as the *bilwa* or *bilva* tree—is sacred to Lord Shiva. According to legend, a disreputable hunter was going out to hunt one day (which happened to be the day of the festival) when he passed one of Shiva's temples and saw a number of people worshipping the LINGAM and calling out Shiva's name. Mockingly, he imitated their cries; without realizing it, uttering the god's name on that holy day removed some of his sins. His hunting was unsuccessful, which meant that he had to fast. Then, as night approached, he climbed up into a bel tree to escape the wild animals and wait for morning. Unable to sleep, he kept an involuntary vigil; and shivering from the cold, he accidentally shook down some of the bel leaves, which fell onto a stone LINGAM beneath the tree. Although none of these acts was deliberate, the hunter ended up performing exactly those rites that the worshippers of Shiva perform on Shivaratri, and he was instantly released from his past sins and made a saint.

The message here is that anyone who consciously observes the rituals associated with Shivaratri will be granted prosperity in life and salvation thereafter.

Lingam

According to Hindu legend, Shiva manifested himself in the form of a huge, flaming *linga* or phallic symbol in order to get the better of both Brahma and Vishnu, who were busy arguing over which among the three was the most powerful god. To settle the matter, Brahma and Vishnu agreed that whoever was the first to find the end of the blazing column of fire that appeared before them would be considered the greatest of the Hindu gods. Vishnu, in the form of a boar, started looking for the bottom of the lingam, while Brahma, in the form of a swan, started looking for the top. After years of searching, neither was successful, and they were both forced to acknowledge Shiva's superiority.

The use of the lingam (also known as the *linga* or *Shiva-linga*) as a symbol for Shiva was introduced after the Aryan immigration into India, having been taken from aboriginal worship. Gradually it was adopted by the lower Hindu castes, who were in closer touch with the aboriginal tribes, and finally it was accepted by all castes as the emblem of Shiva.

The lingam—whose name is Sanskrit for "sign" or "distinguishing symbol"—represents Shiva's generative powers. It is usually a short, cylindrical pillar with a rounded top, made out of stone or wood and decorated with carvings of the god along its sides. The lingam is worshipped with offerings of fresh flowers, pure water, young sprouts of grass, fruit, leaves from the BEL TREE, and sun-dried rice.

FURTHER READING

Bellenir, Karen. *Religious Holidays and Calendars*. 3rd ed. Detroit: Omnigraphics, 2004.

Crim, Keith R. *The Perennial Dictionary of World Religions*. San Francisco: Harper & Row, 1989.

Henderson, Helene, ed. *Holidays, Festivals, and Celebrations of the World Dictionary*. 3rd ed. Detroit: Omnigraphics, 2005.

MacDonald, Margaret R., ed. *The Folklore of World Holidays*. Detroit: Gale Research, 1992.

Sanon, Arun. *Festive India*. New Delhi: Frank Bros., 1986.

Sharma, Brijendra Nath. *Festivals of India*. New Delhi: Abhinav Publications, 1978.

Thomas, Paul. *Hindu Religion, Customs, and Manners*. 6th ed. New York: APT Books, 1981.

Trawicky, Bernard, and Ruth W. Gregory. *Anniversaries and Holidays*. 5th ed. Chicago: American Library Assocation, 2000.

Underhill, Muriel M. *The Hindu Religious Year*. London: Oxford University Press, 1921.

Van Straalen, Alice. *The Book of Holidays Around the World*. New York: Dutton, 1986.

Welbon, Guy Richard, and Glenn E. Yocum. *Religious Festivals in South India and Sri Lanka*. New Delhi: Manohar Publications, 1982.

WEB SITE

Kashmir News Network
www.ikashmir.net/festivals/festivals.html#17

Shrove Tuesday

Type of Holiday: Religious (Christian)
Date of Observation: Between February 3 and March 9; day before Ash Wednesday
Where Celebrated: England, Europe, Scandinavia, United States, and by Christians all over the world
Symbols and Customs: Games, Pancakes, Shrovetide Bear
Related Holidays: Ash Wednesday, Carnival, Lent

ORIGINS

Shrove Tuesday is a Christian holiday related to **ASH WEDNESDAY** and **LENT**. The word Christian refers to a follower of Christ, a title derived from the Greek word meaning Messiah or Anointed One. The Christ of Christianity is Jesus of Nazareth, a man born between 7 and 4 B.C.E. in the region of Palestine. According to Christian teaching, Jesus was killed by Roman authorities using a form of execution called crucifixion (a term meaning he was nailed to a cross and hung from it until he died) in about the year 30 C.E. After his death, he rose back to life. His death and resurrection provide a way by which people can be reconciled with God. In remembrance of Jesus' death and resurrection, the cross serves as a fundamental symbol in Christianity.

With nearly two billion believers in countries around the globe, Christianity is the largest of the world's religions. There is no one central authority for all of Christianity. The pope (the bishop of Rome) is the authority for the Roman Catholic Church, but other sects look to other authorities. Orthodox communities look to patriarchs and emphasize doctrinal agreement and traditional practice. Protestant communities focus on individual conscience. The Roman Catholic and Protestant churches are often referred to as the Western Church, while the Orthodox churches may also be called the Eastern Church. All three main branches of Christianity acknowledge the authority of Christian scriptures, a compilation of writings assembled into a document called the Bible. Methods of biblical interpretation vary among the different Christian sects.

The term Shrove Tuesday comes from the verb "to shrive" originally meant "to write." In medieval England, a priest would hear someone's confession and write down or prescribe an appropriate penance. After absolution, the person was said to have been "shriven." The last three days before **ASH WEDNESDAY** were referred to as "Shrovetide," traditionally a period of penitence. The final day, Shrove Tuesday, was the last opportunity for Christians to confess their sins before the start of **LENT**.

Also known as Fat Tuesday (*Mardi Gras* in French) or Pancake Tuesday, Shrove Tuesday was also a time for merrymaking. Back in the days when **LENT** required wearing dark clothing, eating meals without meat, and banning all forms of pleasure and entertainment for forty days, it was customary for people to have a good time on the day before these restrictions went into effect. Because they had to use up all the fat, eggs, and butter in the house, housewives used these ingredients to make doughnuts, PANCAKES, and other rich foods. In England, Shrove Monday was sometimes referred to as Collop Monday for the same reason—a *collop* being a slice of meat. In addition to eating more than usual, people would play GAMES and hold costume parades. The Mardi Gras celebration in New Orleans is typical of the masquerades and dancing in the streets that still take place in many countries on this day.

SYMBOLS AND CUSTOMS

Games

It was customary to hold seasonal games and contests on Shrove Tuesday in England and elsewhere in Europe. Such activities may originally have been designed to promote fertility and conquer the forces of evil at the beginning of spring. In England, it was customary for parishes to divide themselves into two opposing groups and engage in "rough and tumbles" or a game of football. The earliest recorded game of Shrove Tuesday football took place at Chester in 1533. By the eigtheenth century, Shrovetide games had become considerably more brutal, and often involved cockfighting or hen-thrashing. Even the football games had a tendency to get out of hand, resulting in broken legs and other injuries. As many as a thousand or more people would congregate at these events, and many would end up dunking each other in the nearest river. Shop windows were often shattered by tugs-of-war going on in the streets.

Although Shrovetide games were a widespread form of pre-Lenten celebration, they eventually died out in most areas because they were too dangerous and caused too much damage. They survived in a few small towns, however, up until the present century.

Pancakes

Shrove Tuesday is believed to be a survival of the ancient Roman Fornacalia, or Feast of Ovens, which took place around February 17. A movable feast that lasted a week, it involved making an offering of *far*, a flour made from the oldest kind of Italian wheat, which was then roasted in the oven and crushed in a primitive mill and served in the form of cakes.

Centuries later, Shrove Tuesday became associated with frying pancakes, which gave housewives an opportunity to use up their leftover lard before the Lenten fast. Before the Reformation, eating anything made with fats or butter was strictly forbidden during Lent, and making pancakes (called *bannocks* in Scotland), doughnuts, or sweet buns was a form of thrift as well as self-indulgence. The typical menu served on this day in many European countries is still pancakes with sausages, bacon, or meat scraps.

Because so many pancakes were made on this day, they also featured prominently in the GAMES that were played. The most famous is the Pancake Race held since 1445 in Olney, England. The participants must wear a skirt, an apron, and a headscarf and flip their pancakes in the air three times as they run the 415-yard course.

Shrovetide Bear

In Western Europe, especially in rural areas, it was traditional at one time to dramatize the "death" of **CARNIVAL** on Shrove Tuesday by condemning to death a scarecrow or strawman dressed in an old pair of trousers and known as the Shrovetide Bear or *Fastnachtsbär*. The effigy would often be beheaded, laid in a coffin, and buried in the churchyard on **ASH WEDNESDAY**. Sometimes it would be hanged, burned, drowned, or thrown in the village dump. In some areas, it was believed that if the last woman to marry jumped over the fire in which the Shrovetide Bear was burned, it would make her fertile.

In Bohemia in the eastern Czech Republic, a person in a mask or disguise, known as the "Oats Goat," is led from house to house on Shrove Tuesday. He dances with the women and, in return, receives food, money, and drink. Like the Shrovetide

Bear, the Oats Goat is dressed in straw and wears horns on his head. He is also associated with fertility, because at one time it was believed that dancing with him ensured the growth of crops. Women would pluck bits of straw from him and put them in their hens' nests to guarantee a good supply of eggs.

FURTHER READING

Dobler, Lavinia G. *Customs and Holidays Around the World*. New York: Fleet Pub. Corp., 1962.

Frazer, Sir James G. *The Golden Bough: A Study in Magic and Religion*. New York: Macmillan, 1931.

Harper, Howard V. *Days and Customs of All Faiths*. 1957. Reprint. Detroit: Omnigraphics, 1990.

Henderson, Helene, ed. *Holidays, Festivals, and Celebrations of the World Dictionary*. 3rd ed. Detroit: Omnigraphics, 2005.

Hole, Christina. *English Custom & Usage*. 1941. Reprint. Detroit: Omnigraphics, 1990.

Ickis, Marguerite. *The Book of Festivals and Holidays the World Over*. New York: Dodd, Mead, 1970.

James, E.O. *Seasonal Feasts and Festivals*. 1961. Reprint. Detroit: Omnigraphics, 1993.

Jobes, Gertrude. *Dictionary of Mythology, Folklore, and Symbols*. New York: Scarecrow Press, 1962.

Long, George. *The Folklore Calendar*. 1930. Reprint. Detroit: Omnigraphics, 1990.

Metford, J.C.J. *The Christian Year*. New York: Crossroad, 1991.

Urlin, Ethel L. *Festivals, Holy Days, and Saints' Days*. 1915. Reprint. Detroit: Omnigraphics, 1992.

Weiser, Franz Xaver. *Handbook of Christian Feasts and Customs*. New York: Harcourt, Brace, 1958.

WEB SITES

BBC (British Broadcasting Corporation)
www.bbc.co.uk/religion/religions/christianity/holydays/lent_2.shtml

New Advent Catholic Encyclopedia
www.newadvent.org/cathen/09152a.htm

Simhat Torah
(Festival of Rejoicing in the Law)

Type of Holiday: Religious (Jewish)
Date of Observation: Between September 28 and October 26; twenty-third day of Tishri
Where Celebrated: Europe, Israel, United States, and by Jews all over the world
Symbols and Customs: Candles or Flags, Hakafot, Torah
Related Holidays: Shemini Aztaret, Sukkot

ORIGINS

The holiday Simhat Torah is part of Judaism, one of the oldest continuously observed religions in the world. Its history extends back beyond the advent of the written word. Its people trace their roots to a common ancestor, Abraham, and then back even farther to the very moment of creation.

According to Jewish belief, the law given to the Jewish people by God contained everything they needed to live a holy life, including the ability to be reinterpreted in new historical situations. Judaism, therefore, is the expression of the Jewish people attempting to live holy (set apart) lives in accordance with the instructions given by God. Obedience to the law is central to Judaism, but there is no one central authority. Sources of divine authority are God, the Torah, interpretations of the Torah by respected teachers, and tradition. Religious observances and the study of Jewish law are conducted under the supervision of a teacher called a rabbi.

There are several sects within Judaism. Orthodox Judaism is characterized by an affirmation of the traditional Jewish faith, strict adherence to customs such as keeping the Sabbath, participation in ceremonies and rituals, and the observance of dietary regulations. Conservative Jewish congregations seek to retain many ancient traditions but without the accompanying demand for strict observance. Reform Judaism stresses modern biblical criticism and emphasizes ethical teachings more than ritualistic observance. Hasidism is a mystical sect of Judaism that teaches enthusiastic prayer as a means of communion with God. The Reconstructionist movement began early in the twentieth century in an effort to "reconstruct" Judaism with the community rather than the synagogue as its center.

Simhat Torah, which follows **SUKKOT**, celebrates the annual completion of the public reading of the Jewish holy book known as the TORAH, which consists of the first five books of the Old Testament. In Hebrew, *Simhat Torah* means "rejoicing in the law," since the Torah is often referred to as "the Law" of the Jewish faith.

Unlike other major Jewish holidays, Simhat Torah is of relatively recent origin. The observance was established in Western Europe around the eleventh century. In ancient times, the public reading of the Torah took place on a three-year cycle, and it wasn't until the fourteenth century that the custom of reading the beginning of the Torah immediately after its completion was made official. To be chosen as the "Bridegroom of the Law," who reads the final verses of the last book (Deuteronomy), or the "Bridegroom of the Beginning," who reads the opening verses of the first book (Genesis), is considered a great honor. After the final portion has been read and special prayers have been recited, members of the congregation take the scrolls in their arms and dance in circles around the synagogue (*see* HAKAFOT).

In Israel and among Reform Jews, this festival is observed on the twenty-second day of Tishri, concurrently with Shemini Aztaret (*see* **SUKKOT**). All other Jews celebrate Simhat Torah separately on the twenty-third day. Israelis also hold a second HAKAFOT or procession around the synagogue on the night after Simhat Torah, frequently accompanied by bands and choirs.

Simhat Torah customs have varied from country to country. In Afghanistan, all the scrolls are taken out of their Arks and heaped in a pyramid that reaches almost to the synagogue's roof. In Cochin, China, a carpet was traditionally laid on the courtyard flagstones, coconut oil lamps were stacked up in a pyramid in front of the synagogue entrance, and the Scrolls of the Law were carried around the outside of the synagogue. One synagogue in Calcutta, India, has fifty scrolls, and the women go from scroll to scroll, kissing them. Young Yemeni children are taken to the synagogue for the first time on this holiday.

In southern France, two mourners stand on either side of the reader, crying bitterly as the death of Moses is related. The Bridegroom of the Law in Holland is escorted home in a torchlight parade accompanied by music. A crown was placed on the head of every reader in medieval Spain, and in some places in Eastern Europe the reader wore a large paper hat decorated with bells and feathers.

SYMBOLS AND CUSTOMS

Candles or Flags

The procession in which the scrolls of the TORAH are carried around the synagogue is usually led by children waving flags and carrying poles topped by scooped-out apples in which candles have been inserted. These candles are considered symbolic of the Law or Torah itself, which is said to "enlighten the eyes."

In former times, the children leading the procession around the synagogue carried dried willow branches left over from **SUKKOT** and used them as torches. Concern for their safety prompted rabbis to prohibit this practice and ask children to substitute small candles. But some rabbis considered any form of fire unsafe and replaced the candles with flags topped with apples or beets in which candles have been inserted before being lighted, or flags topped with candles that remain unlit. During the eighteenth century, special Simhat Torah flags were introduced for the purpose of making the holiday more fun for children and encouraging their participation. These flags often display the Hebrew words meaning "Flag of the camp of Judah."

Hakafot

The highlight of the evening service held on Simhat Torah is the series of seven ceremonial processions around the synagogue in which people take turns carrying the Torah scrolls. Known as *hakafot* or "encirclements," the custom is designed to be an expression of joy. A similar custom characterizes the traditional Jewish wedding, which includes walking seven times around the bridal couple in order to "close the circle" and protect the bride and groom from the demons believed to be hovering around them. The service held in the synagogue on Simhat Torah is really an imitation of the Jewish wedding service, symbolizing the "marriage" of Israel to the Law.

As a part of the Simhat Torah celebration, the hakafot custom began in the late sixteenth century, probably as an adaptation of the procession that already took place on **SUKKOT** with palm and willow branches. In Israel, where the celebration of Simhat Torah often continues well into the night, there is often a public hakafot with bands, singing, and dancing in public squares.

Torah

The Jewish holy book is divided into three parts: (1) the Torah (The Law); (2) the Nevi'im (The Prophets); and (3) the Ketuvim (The Writings). While all three are considered sacred, it is the Torah that receives the most reverence. It consists of the first five books of the Old Testament in the Christian Bible, written by Moses and often referred to as the Pentateuch: Genesis, Exodus, Leviticus, Numbers, and Deuteronomy.

The essential element and symbol of Simhat Torah, the Torah scroll is made of parchment (from the hides of kosher animals) attached at each end to a wooden roller. The scribe who copies the Torah onto the parchment, using a quill from a kosher bird and special black ink, cannot make a mistake when writing any words that refer to God or he must throw away the entire sheet. Mistakes in any other words can be erased with a pumice stone. After he has finished writing on the parchment, the sheets are sewn together with special threads made from the foot-tendons of a kosher animal.

The rollers are usually topped with silver ornaments called *rimonim*, which is Hebrew for "pomegranates"—perhaps a reference to their original form. When the Torah is rolled up, it is put inside an embroidered silk or velvet cover for protection, usually topped by an ornamental silver crown. A silver breastplate or *hoshen* is hung by chains on the cover of the Torah and decorated with pictures of various Jewish motifs. A silver pointer (*yad*), usually in the shape of a hand with one finger extended, is used while reading the Torah because the parchment may not be touched.

FURTHER READING

Bellenir, Karen. *Religious Holidays and Calendars*. 3rd ed. Detroit: Omnigraphics, 2004.

Cashman, Greer Fay. *Jewish Days and Holidays*. New York: SBS Pub., 1979.

Christianson, Stephen G., and Jane M. Hatch. *The American Book of Days*. 4th ed. New York: H.W. Wilson, 2000.

Cohen, Hennig, and Tristram Potter Coffin. *The Folklore of American Holidays*. 3rd ed. Detroit: Gale Research, 1999.

Crim, Keith R. *The Perennial Dictionary of World Religions*. San Francisco: Harper & Row, 1989.

Gaer, Joseph. *Holidays Around the World*. Boston: Little, Brown, 1953.

Gaster, Theodor H. *Festivals of the Jewish Year*. New York: William Sloane Associates, 1953.

Henderson, Helene, ed. *Holidays, Festivals, and Celebrations of the World Dictionary*. 3rd ed. Detroit: Omnigraphics, 2005.

MacDonald, Margaret R., ed. *The Folklore of World Holidays*. Detroit: Gale Research, 1992.

Renberg, Dalia Hardof. *The Complete Family Guide to Jewish Holidays*. New York: Adama Books, 1985.

WEB SITE

Union of Orthodox Jewish Congregations of America
www.ou.org/chagim/shmini-simchat

Sol
(Lunar New Year in Korea)

Type of Holiday: Calendar/Seasonal
Date of Observation: January-February; first day of first lunar month
Where Celebrated: Korea
Symbols and Customs: Kite-Flying, Luck Ladle, Seesaw, Sieve, Tug of War, Yut
Related Holidays: Chinese New Year, Oshogatsu, Tet

ORIGINS

Sol, named after the ancient Korean sun god, is the Lunar New Year celebration in Korea. Government offices, shops, and other places of business close from the first until the third day of January, but the New Year's celebration actually goes on for fifteen days. It begins on the first day of the first lunar month, when offerings of food and wine are arranged in front of the ancestral shrine in each Korean home. Then family members dress up in new clothes and pay visits to their relatives and neighbors. Each New Year visitor is entertained and offered food and wine; small children are given money, cakes, or fruit. Rice-cake soup, also known as New Year's soup or *duggook,* is a favorite.

Because each year has a corresponding animal symbol in Korea, the first day of the year bears that animal's name: the rat, the ox, the tiger, the rabbit, the dragon, the serpent, the horse, the sheep, the monkey, the cock, the dog, or the pig. For example, in the Year of the Rat, the first day would be known as the Prime Rat Day, just as the first day of the Year of the Tiger is called the Prime Tiger Day. Each of these animal symbols has certain superstitions attached to it. For example, farmers believe that milling grain on the Prime Rat Day will cause rats to disappear during the year. In farming villages, therefore, young boys build "rat fires" in the fields out of dried weeds and straw in the belief that the more brilliant the rat fire, the richer the crop. Similarly, there is a folk belief that if any member of a family combs his or her hair on Prime Serpent Day, a snake is likely to invade the house during the coming year.

A number of rituals are performed on the fifteenth day of the New Year, also known as the "Great Fifteenth," which marks the end of the holiday season. The number nine is considered lucky on this day, and people routinely repeat their actions nine times—particularly children, who compete with each other to see how many "lucky nines" they can achieve before the day is over.

Other East Asian New Years

he new year is celebrated at about the same time by several countries in Asia—including China, Japan, Korea, and Vietnam—and with many of the same customs, such as offerings to household god(s), housecleaning and new clothes, banquets, ancestor worship, and fireworks. The date of the new year in these countries is based on a lunisolar calendar, similar to or the same as the one used in China. The exception for this timing is Japan, which has employed the Gregorian calendar since 1873 and thus observes New Year's Day on January 1, though many older traditions remain.

The Chinese lunisolar calendar is based on the oldest system of time measurement still in use. It is widely employed in Asian countries to set the dates of seasonal festivals. The **CHINESE NEW YEAR** takes place on the new moon nearest to the point that is defined in the West as the fifteenth degree on the zodiacal sign of Aquarius. Each of twelve months in the Chinese year is twenty-nine or thirty days long and is divided into two parts, each of which is two weeks long. The Chinese calendar, like all lunisolar systems, requires periodic adjustment to keep the lunar and solar cycles integrated; therefore, an intercalary month is added when necessary.

Many of the customs associated with the Lunar New Year are derived from ancient folk beliefs regarding one's fortunes during the coming year. For example, farmers used to measure the shadow of a stick by moonlight on the fifteenth day of the first month, when the moon was high in the sky. They would place a pole in their gardens or fields and measure the shadow, whose length would tell them how much wind and rain they could expect in the coming year, how successful their crops would be, whether there would be pestilence and flooding, and whether the harvest would be plentiful. Similarly, women traditionally save all their loose hair by collecting it when they comb it and then burn it outside their front gates on the first day of the new year. They believe this will ensure a year's protection from disease.

SYMBOLS AND CUSTOMS

Kite-Flying

It is common to celebrate the Great Fifteenth with kite-flying and kite-fighting, which is done by covering the kite strings with dried glue to which glass dust has been added. When the strings from two kites cross and rub together, the string held by the more skillfully maneuvered kite eventually cuts through the string of the other kite, sending it crashing to the ground.

In some areas, the kite flying goes on throughout the fifteen days of the New Year's season. On the last day, the kite-fliers write the letters that mean "warding off bad luck" on the kite and fly it as high as they can, then cut the string and let it escape. This is a symbolic act that represents sending their bad luck for the year as far away as they can.

Luck Ladle

It is customary for Koreans to buy ladles made out of bamboo on New Year's Day. Ladle sellers begin making their rounds soon after midnight on the eve of Sol, so that everyone will have a new ladle to use in the kitchen. The ladle is thought to symbolize good luck because it was originally used to scoop and sort grains. By using the so-called Luck Ladle, people can only "scoop up" good luck.

In South Korea, rakes are hung on the wall or door in addition to bamboo Luck Ladles or baskets. The rake is used to gather kindling wood—an act which, like the scooping up of grain, is regarded as symbolic of good luck.

Seesaw

Bouncing on seesaws is a women's folk sport played in Korea during the New Year's holiday. Two women bounce each other up in the air by jumping on either end of a long board with a straw pillow or some other device in the middle to make it act like a seesaw.

There are a number of explanations for this unusual custom. One is that in ancient times, when the military arts were much admired and women were more active, they often rode horses with the men and even played polo. Board bouncing and other games were part of their training, designed to prepare them for any kind of national emergency that might occur. Another explanation is that seesaw bouncing can be traced back to the early Yi Dynasty, when women were forbidden to have any outdoor exercise. Desperate to see their sweethearts, they would seesaw in the hopes of catching a glimpse of them over the garden wall.

Sieve

There is a legend in Korea about a night spirit that sneaks into houses during the night of the first day of the New Year and tries on the family's shoes. When it finds a pair that fits, it steals the shoes, giving their owner a year's worth of bad luck.

840

To ward off this spirit, family members bring all of their shoes into the living room and go to bed early. They hang a sieve on the front gate so that when the back luck spirit arrives, it will start counting the holes in the sieve and be distracted. The hope is that it will have to start counting over several times—long enough for the night to end and dawn to break, at which point the spirit must leave. In some areas, people set off firecrackers to scare the night spirit away.

Sometimes people stretch a straw rope across their front gates to keep out the evil spirit and hide all their shoes indoors.

Tug of War

Tug of war has been a popular sport in Korea since the very earliest times. During the celebration of Sol, all of the inhabitants of a village will contribute straw, from which a huge rope is braided to about the thickness of a man's fist. The village is divided into two teams, and occasionally more people are recruited from neighboring towns. On some occasions, more than 10,000 people have gathered to take part in a tug of war, complete with trumpet-blowers, battle flags, and "cheerleaders" with gongs and cymbals. Since the contest often continues for hours, there is usually an intermission with singing and dancing, after which the tug resumes. A typical tug of war lasts three to four days, beginning at 11 a.m. and stopping at 11 p.m. every night. It is believed that the winning side will have a good harvest and will be protected from disease in the coming year.

Yut

Yut (also *Yud*) is a very ancient game that is played only in Korea during the New Year holiday. It is played with a set of four carved blocks of uniform size, with a flat side as the face and a rounded or convex side as the back. Although the rules of the game are too complicated to explain in detail, the blocks are cast three or four feet into the air, and the player is given a score based on the combination of flat and round sides facing up. This number determines how many spaces the player may advance his or her token on a game board or mat. The player or team that reaches "home" first is the winner.

Although Yut is played today mostly for amusement, at one time it was a popular method of divination used by farmers to see what the year's crops would be like or what their personal fortunes would be.

FURTHER READING

Henderson, Helene, ed. *Holidays, Festivals, and Celebrations of the World Dictionary.* 3rd ed. Detroit: Omnigraphics, 2005.

MacDonald, Margaret R., ed. *The Folklore of World Holidays*. Detroit: Gale Research, 1992.

Sang-su, Choe. *Annual Customs of Korea*. Seoul: Seomun-dang, 1983.

WEB SITE

Korean Cultural Center of Los Angeles
www.kccla.org/html/specialevent_detail.asp?ID=38

Songkran
(Water Festival, New Year's Day in Thailand)

Type of Holiday: Calendar/Seasonal, Religious (Buddhism)
Date of Observation: April 13-15
Where Celebrated: Thailand
Symbols and Customs: Water
Related Holidays: Holi

ORIGINS

Songkran is part of the tradition of Buddhism, one of the four largest religious families in the world. Buddhism is based on the teachings of Siddhartha Gautama (c. 563-483 B.C.E.), who came to be known as Buddha, or "The Enlightened One." The basic tenets of Buddhism can be summarized in the Four Noble Truths and the Eightfold Path. The Four Noble Truths are 1) the truth and reality of suffering; 2) suffering is caused by desire; 3) the way to end suffering is to end desire; and 4) the Eightfold Path shows the way to end suffering. The Eightfold Path consists of 1) right view or right understanding; 2) right thoughts and aspirations; 3) right speech; 4) right conduct and action; 5) right way of life; 6) right effort; 7) right mindfulness; and 8) right contemplation.

Songkran is the traditional New Year's Day celebration in Thailand, observed near the time of the **VERNAL EQUINOX**. The festivities, which are secular as well as religious, take place over a three-day period and include colorful processions and traditional games. The most widespread custom on this day, however, is throwing or sprinkling WATER on images of the Buddha, a traditional purification rite which usually leads to people throwing water at each other. Water-filled plastic bags are sold everywhere, so that everyone—even tourists—can join in the celebration. Not surprisingly, the most popular gift on this holiday is a towel.

The tendency among young people to douse each other with water can often get out of hand. But most people are careful to show respect to their elders by sprinkling water on their hands or feet. Monks, too, are shown respect by bringing them offerings of rice, meat, and fruit and by blessing them with a small amount of water.

SYMBOLS AND CUSTOMS

Water

It is considered a blessing to be soaked with water on Songkran because it symbolizes the washing away of all the old year's evils and the giving of new life. For the same reason, it is common for people to release pet birds from their cages and to pour fish from their fishbowls into the river.

The custom of throwing water at one another is believed to have derived from the Hindu celebration of **HOLI**. It should also be remembered that, while New Year's Day in the United States falls at the coldest time of year, in Thailand it can be extremely hot in April, which makes the water-splashing custom more welcome than it might be elsewhere.

FURTHER READING

Bellenir, Karen. *Religious Holidays and Calendars*. 3rd ed. Detroit: Omnigraphics, 2004.

Henderson, Helene, ed. *Holidays, Festivals, and Celebrations of the World Dictionary*. 3rd ed. Detroit: Omnigraphics, 2005.

Ickis, Marguerite. *The Book of Festivals and Holidays the World Over*. New York: Dodd, Mead, 1970.

MacDonald, Margaret R., ed. *The Folklore of World Holidays*. Detroit: Gale Research, 1992.

Shemanski, Frances. *A Guide to World Fairs and Festivals*. Westport, CT: Greenwood Press, 1985.

Van Straalen, Alice. *The Book of Holidays Around the World*. New York: Dutton, 1986.

Soyaluna
(Soyal, Soyala, Sol-ya-lang-eu)

Type of Holiday: Calendar/Seasonal, Religious (Hopi)
Date of Observation: December 22
Where Celebrated: Arizona
Symbols and Customs: Plumed Snake, Sun Shield
Related Holidays: Hopi Snake Dance, Winter Solstice, Wuwuchim

ORIGINS

Soyaluna is part of the tradition of the Hopi Indians, one of the Native American tribes of North America. The history of this and other Native American cultures dates back thousands of years into prehistoric times. According to many scholars, the people who became the Native Americans migrated from Asia across a land bridge that may have once connected the territories presently occupied by Alaska and Russia. The migrations, believed to have begun between 60,000 and 30,000 B.C.E., continued until approximately 4,000 B.C.E. This speculation, however, conflicts with traditional stories asserting that the indigenous Americans have always lived in North America or that tribes moved up from the south.

The historical development of religious belief systems among Native Americans is not well known. Most of the information available was gathered by Europeans who arrived on the continent beginning in the sixteenth century C.E. The data they recorded was fragmentary and oftentimes of questionable accuracy because the Europeans did not understand the native cultures they were trying to describe and the Native Americans were reluctant to divulge details about themselves.

Soyaluna is related to sun worship, which was common among early peoples. In North America, the Hopi Indians observed the sun rising and setting at different points on the horizon. They also noticed that it reached its most vertical position in the sky in summer and that, when it rose lower in the sky, the weather was cold and the earth was barren. In midsummer, when they imagined the sun close to the earth, the Hopis performed their Snake Dance (*see* **HOPI SNAKE DANCE**), asking the snake to bring their request for rain to the gods of the underworld. But when the sun started to withdraw, their attention shifted to preventing it from forsaking them altogether. At the time of the **WINTER SOLSTICE** in December, they believed that the Sun God had traveled as far from the earth as he ever did. It required the most powerful humans—in this case, the warriors—to persuade the

Sun God to turn around and come back to the pueblo. The purpose of the Soyaluna ceremony, which is still held among the Hopi today, is to prevent the disappearance of the sun at the time of year when the days are at their shortest.

Preparations for the ceremony begin with cutting pieces of cotton string and tying feathers and pinyon needles to the end. These are exchanged among friends and relatives during the day, and are sometimes tied in the recipient's hair. When the person who made the feathered string presents it to a friend, he says, "May all the Kachinas grant you your wishes tomorrow"—the Kachinas being the spirits of the Hopi ancestors. Then the giver holds his or her gift vertically and moves it back and forth horizontally. At night, everyone takes a willow branch and attaches all the strings that he or she has received to it. The sticks are carried to the *kiva* or ceremonial meeting room and placed in the rafters, making the room look like a bower of feathers and pinyon needles.

The main celebration takes place in the kiva. The chief of the resident Hopi society wears a headdress decorated with symbols of rain clouds and carries a shield on which the sun appears. Representatives of other societies carry shields on which a star, an antelope, or other symbolic objects have been drawn. Someone carries an effigy of Palulukonuh, the PLUMED SNAKE, carved from the woody stalk of the agave plant.

The shield bearers enter the kiva and take turns stamping on the *sipapu,* a shallow hole covered by a board, which is the symbolic entrance to the underworld. Then they arrange themselves into two separate groups—one on the north and one on the south side of the room—and start singing, while the bearer of the SUN SHIELD rushes to one side and then to the other. He is driven back by the shield bearers on both sides, whose movements symbolize the attack of hostile powers on the sun. It is not uncommon for one or more of the participants in this mock struggle to faint from the heat and exhaustion.

On the west wall of the kiva, there is an altar consisting of a stack of corn, two or more ears of which have been contributed by each family in the pueblo, surrounded by stalks and husks. There is also a large gourd with an opening in it, from which the head of the Plumed Snake effigy protrudes. Manipulated by someone behind the altar, the snake's head rises slowly to the center of the opening and makes a roaring noise. The shield bearers throw meal to the effigy and in response to each offering, the snake roars again. During the ceremony the Hopi priest sprinkles sand on the floor of the kiva. When the Sun God's footprints appear in the sand, everyone knows that he has been persuaded to return.

One of the most sacred ceremonies held by the Hopi, Soyaluna means "Prayer-Offering Ceremony." It is a time for saying prayers for the New Year and for wishing each other prosperity and health.

SYMBOLS AND CUSTOMS

Plumed Snake

The effigy of the Plumed (or Plumed-Head) Snake that appears in the kiva during the Soyaluna ceremony is painted black, with a tongue-like appendage protruding from its mouth. The snake symbolizes the evil influences that are driving the sun away. The assembled chiefs make their offerings of prayer and meal to the Plumed Snake to persuade him not to "swallow" the sun, as he does when there is an eclipse.

Sun Shield

The Hopis have their own explanation for why the days grow shorter in winter and longer in summer. They envision the sun as being driven away by hostile forces and then, after a considerable struggle, persuaded to return. Without the Soyaluna ceremony, the sun might never return, bringing the warmer weather that is needed for growing corn and other food. The bearer of the Sun Shield, therefore, represents the Hopi Sun God, whose favors are crucial to the tribe's survival.

FURTHER READING

Fewkes, Jesse Walter. *Tusayan Katcinas and Hopi Altars*. Albuquerque: Avanyu Pub., 1990.

Heinberg, Richard. *Celebrate the Solstice: Honoring the Earth's Seasonal Rhythms through Festival and Ceremony*. Wheaton, IL: Quest Books, 1993.

Henderson, Helene, ed. *Holidays, Festivals, and Celebrations of the World Dictionary*. 3rd ed. Detroit: Omnigraphics, 2005.

Leach, Maria, ed. *Funk & Wagnalls Standard Dictionary of Folklore, Mythology & Legend*. San Francisco: Harper & Row, 1984.

St. Anthony of Padua, Feast of

Type of Holiday: Religious (Christian)
Date of Observation: June 13
Where Celebrated: France, Italy, Portugal, Puerto Rico, Spain, United States
Symbols and Customs: Blessing the Animals, Brides of St. Anthony, St. Anthony's Bread

ORIGINS

Although he is named for the Italian city of Padua, where he spent much of his life, St. Anthony was born in 1195 in Lisbon, Portugal. He was studying at a monastery in Coimbra when he met some Franciscan missionaries who were on their way to preach Christianity in Morocco. They were martyred there soon afterward, and when their remains were sent back to Coimbra, St. Anthony was so inspired by their example that he decided to follow in their footsteps. Although he became a Franciscan and managed to get sent to Africa to preach, he fell ill almost immediately upon his arrival and had to return to Portugal by boat. He was caught up in a huge storm en route and sought refuge on the island of Sicily, where he was cared for by Franciscans. Eventually he made his way to Assisi to meet St. Francis himself.

As the Franciscans soon discovered, St. Anthony had a gift for preaching. He often had to deliver his sermons in the open air, because the crowds he attracted were so large that no church could hold them. According to legend, when a group of heretics refused to hear what he had to say, he addressed himself to the fish instead, who poked their heads up out of the water to listen. Although the exact origin of the association is uncertain, St. Anthony is primarily remembered for his ability to restore lost things. An ancient Portuguese story claims it was St. Anthony who, when a book of chants was stolen from a monastery, inspired the thief to return it. Today, people pray to St. Anthony when they have lost or misplaced something.

St. Anthony died at the age of thirty-six on June 13, 1231, and was buried in Padua, where a basilica was erected in his honor and still houses his relics. He was canonized as a saint in 1232. His feast day is celebrated not only in Italy but also in Portugal, where he is the patron saint of Lisbon. Groups of singers and musicians, known as *marchas*, parade along the Avenida da Liberdade on the eve of St. Anthony's Day, while children make altars decorated with candles and pictures of the saint and beg for money that is used to pay for a children's feast (*see* ST. ANTHONY'S BREAD).

The basis of saint day remembrances is found in ancient Roman tradition. On the anniversary of a death, families would share a ritual meal at the grave site of an ancestor. This practice was adopted by Christians who began observing a ritual meal on the death anniversary of ancestors in the faith, especially martyrs. As a result, most Christian saint days are associated with the death of the saint. There are three important exceptions. John the Baptist, the Virgin Mary, and Jesus are honored on their nativities (birthdays). Many who suffered martyrdom are remembered on saint days in the calendars of several Orthodox, Catholic, and Protestant sects.

In the United States, the Feast of St. Anthony is observed primarily by Native Americans in the Southwest, who celebrate with traditional Indian dances, and by the inhabitants of New York City's Greenwich Village, where the Shrine Church of St. Anthony, the city's oldest Italian church, sponsors a ten-day outdoor festival.

SYMBOLS AND CUSTOMS

Blessing the Animals

As the patron saint of animals, St. Anthony has much in common with his friend and spiritual mentor, St. Francis of Assisi. In Rome, back in the days before cars became the standard mode of transportation, people used to bring their horses and mules to St. Anthony's Church on June 13 to be blessed.

Brides of St. Anthony

St. Anthony is also known as the "wedding saint," and in Padua it was customary at one time for all the single women in town to dress in white robes on the evening of June 12 and walk through the city streets while praying to St. Anthony for a husband. Nowadays only very young girls participate in the procession.

In Lisbon, "St. Anthony's Day weddings" are held in the town hall on June 13. Although this is a tradition that was discontinued for a number of years, it has been revived recently as a way of encouraging young couples to move to the city after they marry, rather than raising their families in the suburbs. Young women who hope to marry soon visit St. Anthony shrines, where they offer flowers, candles, and photographs of their boyfriends. Another Portuguese tradition is to write letters to St. Anthony requesting that he send a suitable mate. Much like letters to Santa Claus at **CHRISTMAS**, they are dropped in a special box on St. Anthony's feast day.

St. Anthony's Bread

Begging and donating money have long been associated with the Feast of St. Anthony. When the church known as San António da Sé in Lisbon was destroyed by an earthquake in 1755, the city's children began collecting money to rebuild it. They set up altars on the street, decorated with pictures of the saint, flowers, candles, and cut paper decorations, and begged "a little penny for Santo António" from passersby. The existing church, which was completed in 1812, was largely paid for by these contributions.

In the nineteenth century, according to legend, a young woman in France asked St. Anthony for a favor, promising that if he granted it she would donate loaves of bread to the poor. This gave rise to the practice of giving money or alms, referred to as "St. Anthony's Bread," to the poor on June 13. Donation boxes for the poor with this label can still be found in French churches.

FURTHER READING

Christianson, Stephen G., and Jane M. Hatch. *The American Book of Days*. 4th ed. New York: H.W. Wilson, 2000.

Cohen, Hennig, and Tristram Potter Coffin. *The Folklore of American Holidays*. 3rd ed. Detroit: Gale Research, 1999.

Harper, Howard V. *Days and Customs of All Faiths*. 1957. Reprint. Detroit: Omnigraphics, 1990.

MacDonald, Margaret R., ed. *The Folklore of World Holidays*. Detroit: Gale Research, 1992.

Spicer, Dorothy Gladys. *Festivals of Western Europe*. 1958. Reprint. Detroit: Omnigraphics, 1993.

Spicer, Dorothy Gladys. *The Book of Festivals*. 1937. Reprint. Detroit: Omnigraphics, 1990.

Weiser, Franz Xaver. *Handbook of Christian Feasts and Customs*. New York: Harcourt, Brace, 1958.

WEB SITE

New Advent Catholic Encyclopedia
www.newadvent.org/cathen/01556a.htm

St. Barbara's Day

Type of Holiday: Religious (Christian)
Date of Observation: December 4
Where Celebrated: Czech Republic, France, Germany, Poland, Syria, and by Christians throughout the world
Symbols and Customs: Barbara Branch, St. Barbara's Grain
Related Holidays: Christmas

ORIGINS

According to legend, St. Barbara's father, a wealthy pagan, was so afraid that his daughter would fall in love and leave him that he locked her up in a richly furnished tower. She heard about Christianity, however, and arranged to receive a visit from a Christian disciple disguised as a physician. She was eventually converted to Christianity and baptized. One day, while her father was away, she had some workmen install a third window in her tower, which only had two. When she confessed her new faith to her father, she explained that the Christian soul received its light through three windows: the Father, the Son, and the Holy Ghost. At the time, Christianity was considered a criminal offense. Her father was so angry that he took her before a judge, who sentenced her to death by beheading. One version of the story says that Barbara's father carried out the sentence himself, but was killed by lightning on his way home. Another says that he was struck by lightning just as he was about to behead her. In any case, St. Barbara today is usually represented by a tower with three windows, for which reason she is somewhat inaccurately known as the patron saint of forts and of artillerymen. She is also called upon to protect people from lightning, storms, and sudden death.

In parts of France, Germany, and Syria, St. Barbara's Day is considered the beginning of the **CHRISTMAS** season. In Poland, St. Barbara's Day is associated with prophecies concerning the weather. If it rains on December 4, it will be cold and icy on Christmas Day; if it's cold and icy on St. Barbara's Day, Christmas will be warmer and rainy.

The basis of saint day remembrances is found in ancient Roman tradition. On the anniversary of a death, families would share a ritual meal at the grave site of an ancestor. This practice was adopted by Christians who began observing a ritual meal on the death anniversary of ancestors in the faith, especially martyrs. As a result, most Christian saint days are associated with the death of the saint. There are three important exceptions. John the Baptist, the Virgin Mary, and Jesus are honored on their nativities (birthdays). Many who suffered martyrdom are remembered on saint days in the calendars of several Orthodox, Catholic, and Protestant sects.

Because sufficient evidence for Barbara's life has not been determined, the Roman Catholic Church removed her day from the calendar of saints in 1969.

SYMBOLS AND CUSTOMS

Barbara Branch

It was customary among Czechs and Slovaks, as well as other central Europeans, to break a branch off a cherry tree on St. Barbara's Day. It was placed in a pot of water in the kitchen and kept warm. If the girl who tended the twig was successful in making it bloom on **CHRISTMAS EVE**, it was considered an omen that she would find a good husband within a year.

The custom of cutting a dormant branch of the flowering cherry and bringing it indoors on St. Barbara's Day in the hope that it will bloom in time for Christmas is once again regaining its popularity among western Christians. The cherry blossom is a symbol of spring as well as of spiritual or feminine beauty. The sweet fruit of the cherry symbolizes the sweetness of character that is derived from good works. In some countries, Barbara branches are cut from apple, plum, almond, forsythia, jasmine, or horse chestnut trees.

St. Barbara's Grain

In southern France, particularly Provence, it is customary to set out dishes with grains of wheat soaked in water on sunny window sills. There is a folk belief that if the "St. Barbara's grain" grows quickly, it means a good year for crops. But if it withers and dies, the crops will be ruined.

On **CHRISTMAS EVE**, the grain is placed near the crèche as a symbol of the coming harvest.

FURTHER READING

Barz, Brigitte. *Festivals with Children*. Edinburgh: Floris Books, 1987.

Eliade, Mircea. *The Encyclopedia of Religion*. New York: Macmillan, 1987.

Ferguson, George. *Signs and Symbols in Christian Art*. New York: Oxford University Press, 1954.

Harper, Howard V. *Days and Customs of All Faiths*. 1957. Reprint. Detroit: Omnigraphics, 1990.

Henderson, Helene, ed. *Holidays, Festivals, and Celebrations of the World Dictionary*. 3rd ed. Detroit: Omnigraphics, 2005.

Olderr, Steven. *Symbolism: A Comprehensive Dictionary*. Jefferson, NC: McFarland, 1986.

Weiser, Franz Xaver. *Handbook of Christian Feasts and Customs*. New York: Harcourt, Brace, 1958.

WEB SITE

U.S. Army's Fort Sill, Oklahoma
sill-www.army.mil/pao/pabarbar.htm

St. Basil's Day

Type of Holiday: Religious (Orthodox Christian)
Date of Observation: January 1
Where Celebrated: Greece
Symbols and Customs: Gift Giving, Good Luck Charms, St. Basil's Water, Ship, Vasilopita

ORIGINS

In Greece, January 1 is observed as St. Basil's Day. St. Basil was born in the year 329 C.E. in a region of central Turkey called Cappadocia. He died on January 1, 379. Among Orthodox Christians, he is revered as one of the most important leaders of the early Church. Through his writing and preaching, he made lasting contributions to Christian theology.

Basil came from a distinguished Cappadocian family that lived in the town of Caesarea. One of his uncles was a bishop, and his sister, Macrina, became a nun and later an abbess. Basil received a liberal education and considered following in his father's footsteps by becoming a lawyer. His sister Macrina encouraged him to enter the religious life, however, and he decided to take her advice. Basil's two brothers also pursued careers within the church, later both becoming bishops. Basil was attracted to monastic life, so he set up a little monastery on his family's estate in Pontus. Later he became involved in the theological debates of his day, arguing strongly against a point of view called Arianism. His prominence in these debates inspired him to become a priest and later the bishop of Cappadocia. As bishop, Basil established charitable institutions to help the poor, the sick, and travelers. He maintained his involvements in theological debates and even defied the emperor when he felt that the emperor sided with the wrong point of view.

Today Basil is best known for his writings on the nature of God and on monastic life. Among Orthodox Christians these works have earned him the title of St. Basil the Great. A church hymn honors him as "the revealer of heavenly things." In addition, St. Basil is remembered for the Liturgy of St. Basil, though some scholars question whether or not he is the sole author. In any case, Orthodox churches perform the Liturgy of St. Basil on his feast day, as well as nine other times throughout the church year.

The basis of saint day remembrances—for St. Basil as well as other saints—is found in ancient Roman tradition. On the anniversary of a death, families would share a ritual meal at the grave site of an ancestor. This practice was adopted by Christians who began observing a ritual meal on the death anniversary of ancestors in the faith, especially martyrs. As a result, most Christian saint days are associated with the death of the saint. There are three important exceptions. John the Baptist, the Virgin Mary, and Jesus are honored on their nativities (birthdays). Many who suffered martyrdom are remembered on saint days in the calendars of several Orthodox, Catholic, and Protestant sects.

An old legend about St. Basil explains the origin of VASILOPITA (Basil's bread). According to the story, jewelry and gold coins from many of Caesarea's well-to-do families came into Bishop Basil's possession. Some say that he foiled a thief, others that he was charged with returning taxes that had been assessed too heavily. In any case, the people of Caesarea fell to arguing about who owned what. Basil, trusting God to solve this dilemma asked some women to bake the valuables into several loaves of bread. Each claimant received a slice of the bread. They rejoiced as they discovered their own money and jewelry within the slice of bread that they received.

SYMBOLS AND CUSTOMS

Gift Giving

According to Greek folk tradition, holiday gifts should be opened on St. Basil's Day, rather than on Christmas Day. In fact, St. Basil, rather than Santa Claus or St. Nicholas, is the **CHRISTMAS** gift bringer in Greece. Some families bring out their gifts on **CHRISTMAS EVE**, displaying them until St. Basil's Day, when they are opened.

Good Luck Charms

Events that take place on St. Basil's Day are thought to set the tone for the entire year. According to Greek folklore, a household's luck in the coming year depends on who enters first. This person symbolizes the household's fortunes in the year to come. Many families hope that a strong, healthy person will be the first to cross their threshold after the stroke of midnight. In this case, the family would be blessed with good health. Others prefer to have an icon (a religious image) enter first, held in someone's outstretched arms. This is thought to confer spiritual blessings. Tradition encourages householders to welcome the first person to enter the house in the new year with coins and sweets. Some people insist that the person must cross the threshold with his or her right foot in order to bring good luck.

Because the events on St. Basil's Day are so important, a number of superstitions advise people to think happy thoughts, to avoid crying and quarreling, and to eat abundantly. Wearing new clothes will help to insure a good wardrobe in the year to come.

St. Basil's Water

Some Greek families perform a ceremony called the "renewal of the waters" on St. Basil's Day. Family members empty all the containers of water in their home and then refill them with St. Basil's water (water collected on St. Basil's Day). Some people also ask a priest to come to the home and bless it with holy water.

Ship

The ship is a symbol of St. Basil's Day because folk tradition insists that St. Basil used this mode of transport to journey from Turkey, his ancestral homeland, to Greece. On December 24, Greek youth go caroling from house to house. They often carry with them small boats made of wood, cardboard, or tin. These ships represent St. Basil's journey across the Aegean Sea to bring gifts to Greek children. The children use the ships to collect the coins and sweets given to them by their neighbors.

Vasilopita

St. Basil's eve is also **NEW YEAR'S EVE**. Many Greek families stay up late, entertaining guests and playing cards. At the hour of midnight, everyone shouts "kali chronia" (good year) and "chronia polla" (many years). Then the host cuts the vasilopita, (Basil's bread). This sweetened bread is made especially for the holiday. A coin is placed inside the dough before baking. Many Greek families follow a custom whereby the head of the household cuts the bread, reserving the first piece of bread for Christ, the second for St. Basil, the third for the Virgin Mary, and the fourth for the poor. After that, each family member and guest receives a slice of bread. Whoever receives the coin in their slice will have good luck in the year to come. New Year's carols, whose lyrics offer respect to St. Basil and express hope for good fortune in the new year, are also sung on **NEW YEAR'S EVE** and **NEW YEAR'S DAY.**

FURTHER READING

Gulevich, Tanya. *Encyclopedia of Christmas and New Year's Celebrations.* 2nd ed. Detroit: Omnigraphics, 2003.

Rouvelas, Marilyn. *A Guide to Greek Traditions and Customs In America.* Bethesda, MD: Nea Attiki, 1993.

WEB SITES

Greek Orthodox Archdiocese of America
www.goarch.org/en/special/listen_learn_share/basil/learn/index.asp?printit=yes

Museum of Science and Industry, Chicago, IL
www.msichicago.org/temp_exhibit/catw2006/traditions/countries/greece.html

St. Basil's Academy, Garrison, NY
www.stbasil.goarch.org/about/vasilopita.asp

St. Blaise's Day

Type of Holiday: Religious (Christian)
Date of Observation: February 3
Where Celebrated: England, France, Germany, Spain, United States, and by Christians all over the world
Symbols and Customs: Blessing the Draft Horses, Blessing the Throat, Bonfires, Candles, Comb, St. Blaise's Loaves

ORIGINS

St. Blaise (or Blasius) was the child of rich and noble parents, who raised him as a Christian. He was a physician by profession and was made Bishop of Sebaste in Armenia sometime early in the fourth century. All of the legends about his life portray him as a kind and generous man who loved animals and birds.

One legend in particular tells how Blaise escaped the persecution of Christians in Armenia by fleeing to the mountains and living in a remote cave. The wild beasts around him immediately saw that he was a friend and neither feared nor attacked him. Instead, they came to his cave every day, waiting patiently outside until he was finished with his devotions, and asked for his blessing. He also healed their injuries and cured their diseases, in return for which the wild birds brought him food in their beaks. Eventually his hiding place was discovered, and he was dragged off for punishment by Agricolaus, the governor of Cappadocia and Lower Armenia.

On his way back to the city, he met a woman whose only pig had been carried off by a wolf. He rescued the pig by demanding that the wolf give up its prey. Later, when he was in prison, this same woman secretly brought him food and CANDLES to lighten the darkness of his cell. But even her kindness could not prevent his being tortured and beheaded in 316.

Today, St. Blaise's Day is observed by those who are afflicted with throat troubles (*see* BLESSING THE THROAT) and, to a lesser extent, by people who care for wild beasts and working animals (*see* BLESSING THE DRAFT HORSES). At one time, he was the patron saint of wool-combers (*see* COMB).

The basis of the remembrance of St. Blaise, as well as other saints, is found in ancient Roman tradition. On the anniversary of a death, families would share a ritual meal at the grave site of an ancestor. This practice was adopted by Christians, who began observing a ritual meal on the death anniversary of ancestors in the faith, especially martyrs. As a result, most Christian saint days are associated with the death of the saint. There are three important exceptions. John the Baptist, the Virgin Mary, and Jesus are honored on their nativities (birthdays). Many who suffered martyrdom are remembered on saint days in the calendars of several Orthodox, Catholic, and Protestant sects.

SYMBOLS AND CUSTOMS

Blessing the Draft Horses

According to legend, on the journey back from his mountain hideaway with his captors St. Blaise stopped to bless the draft horses he passed on his way. For this reason, February 3 is often associated with the blessing of work horses. In Bavaria, farmers used to bring their work horses to church on St. Blaise's Day to be blessed by the parish priest. In some areas, the horses would be led to church wearing a small brass COMB behind one ear.

Blessing the Throat

Another event said to have occurred either on the way to his trial or just before St. Blaise was executed explains why he is the patron saint of sufferers from throat afflictions. A child who had swallowed a fishbone was on the verge of choking to death when St. Blaise touched his throat, dislodging the bone and saving the child's life. Perhaps his training as a physician helped him to do what was needed, but the incident was hailed as a miracle.

In some Roman Catholic churches, the ceremony known as Blessing the Throat is observed on February 3, St. Blaise's Day. In the church of St. Etheldreda in London, for example, two long CANDLES are blessed, lighted, and tied together with ribbons to form a cross. Those who suffer from throat ailments kneel while the ribboned cross is laid under their chins. Their throats are touched gently with the ends of the lighted candles while the priest says, "May the Lord deliver you from the evil of the throat, and from every other evil."

Bonfires

The custom of lighting a hilltop bonfire on St. Blaise's night has often been explained by the connection between the saint's name and the word "blaze." A more likely explanation is the saint's association with fire and light (*see* CANDLES) and the fact that his feast day is the day after **CANDLEMAS**, also a festival of fire and light.

Candles

The candles that are lit in churches on St. Blaise's Day or tied in a cross and used to bless throats commemorate the candles brought to him in prison by the woman whose pig he had rescued. St. Blaise told her that every year on the anniversary of his death she should offer a candle in church in his memory. He also promised that good things would happen to her and to others who followed this practice faithfully.

Comb

Before he was executed, St. Blaise was tortured by having his flesh torn with sharp iron combs, similar to those used in the preparation of wool for weaving. Because of this, he became the patron saint of wool combers, and his cult flourished during the Middle Ages in Germany, France, Italy, England, Scotland, and other countries where the wool trade was important.

Until fairly recently in England, St. Blaise's Day was observed as a holiday in all of the major wool-producing towns, which held processions and pageants. Everyone involved in the production of wool—from young apprentices to wealthy merchants, from shepherds and sheep shearers to weavers, spinners, and dyers—participated in these processions, which were usually accompanied by lively music. St. Blaise was represented by a man dressed as a bishop riding on horseback, carrying a book in one hand and a comb in the other. Sometimes a shepherdess would ride in a carriage, carrying a live lamb in her lap. Speeches and poems were recited in honor of the wool trade and its patron saint.

St. Blaise's Loaves

In Spain, small loaves called *tortas de San Blas* or *panecillos del sants* (little breads of the saint) are baked in preparation for St. Blaise's Day. They are then blessed during Mass and eaten by the children to prevent them from choking during the coming year.

FURTHER READING

Chambers, Robert. *The Book of Days*. 2 vols. 1862-64. Reprint. Detroit: Omnigraphics, 1990.

Cohen, Hennig, and Tristram Potter Coffin. *The Folklore of American Holidays*. 3rd ed. Detroit: Gale Research, 1999.

Dunkling, Leslie. *A Dictionary of Days*. New York: Facts on File, 1988.

Harper, Howard V. *Days and Customs of All Faiths*. 1957. Reprint. Detroit: Omnigraphics, 1990.

Henderson, Helene, ed. *Holidays, Festivals, and Celebrations of the World Dictionary*. 3rd ed. Detroit: Omnigraphics, 2005.

Hole, Christina. *Saints in Folklore*. New York: M. Barrows, 1965.

Jobes, Gertrude. *Dictionary of Mythology, Folklore, and Symbols*. New York: Scarecrow Press, 1962.

MacDonald, Margaret R., ed. *The Folklore of World Holidays*. Detroit: Gale Research, 1992.

Urlin, Ethel L. *Festivals, Holy Days, and Saints' Days*. 1915. Reprint. Detroit: Omnigraphics, 1992.

FURTHER READING

New Advent Catholic Encyclopedia
www.newadvent.org/cathen/02592a.htm

St. Bridget's Day

Type of Holiday: Religious (Christian)
Date of Observation: February 1
Where Celebrated: England, Ireland, Scotland
Symbols and Customs: Bridie Doll, Fire, Rush Cross
Related Holidays: Imbolc, St. Patrick's Day

ORIGINS

St. Bridget (or Bride) is the female patron saint of Ireland. She was an Irish princess who converted to Christianity and became the first Irish nun. In 585 she built a cell for herself under a large oak that may have been the site of pagan ceremonies in earlier times. Her hermitage there was known as Kill-Dara, or "the cell of the oak." She established a convent there, around which the Irish city of Kildare eventually grew.

The customs associated with St. Bridget's Day resemble in many ways those of the ancient Celtic festival of **IMBOLC**, observed at the same time of year and considered to mark the first day of spring and the beginning of the planting season. Bridget was therefore associated with a number of legends and superstitions regarding the weather and agricultural prosperity. For example, every other day between St. Bridget's Day and **ST. PATRICK'S DAY** (March 17) is supposed to be fair, according to Irish folklore. After that, every day is supposed to be fair. And like the groundhog on **CANDLEMAS**, the hedgehog's behavior on St. Bridget's Day is believed to predict the upcoming weather.

The custom of having women propose marriage to men during Leap Year (*see* **LEAP YEAR DAY**) can be traced back to St. Bridget, who complained to St. Patrick about the fact that men always took the initiative. She persuaded him to grant women the right to propose to men one year out of every four. Then Bridget proposed to Patrick, who turned her down but softened his refusal by giving her a kiss and a silk gown.

The basis of the remembrance of St. Bridget, as well as other saints, is found in ancient Roman tradition. On the anniversary of a death, families would share a ritual meal at the grave site of an ancestor. This practice was adopted by Christians who began observing a ritual meal on the death anniversary of ancestors in the faith, especially martyrs. As a result, most Christian saint days are associated with the death of the saint. There are three important exceptions. John the Baptist, the Virgin Mary, and Jesus are honored on their nativities (birthdays). Many who suffered martyrdom are remembered on saint days in the calendars of several Orthodox, Catholic, and Protestant sects.

SYMBOLS AND CUSTOMS

Bridie Doll

"Bride" or "Bridie" is another form of "Bridget." Bridie dolls were small figures made of straw and decorated with flowers. Women would bring them to the door on St. Bridget's Day and call out, "Let Bride come in!" The doll was then placed in a cradle inside the house with a wand of birch, broom, or willow beside it to represent Bride's husband.

The custom of displaying Bridie dolls originated in Scotland but has recently been revived in the area around Glastonbury, England. Irish children still go from door to door carrying a large doll, which they call "St. Bridget's baby," and ask for money to buy candles for the saint.

Fire

The pagan sun god in Ireland had a daughter named Brighit, usually shown with a child in her arms. Her chief temple, in what later became known as Kildare, was served by virgins of noble birth called "the daughters of fire." It was their duty to keep Brighit's sacred fire burning without interruption. When the temple later became the site of St. Bridget's Christian convent, the nuns continued to tend the fire that had originally been dedicated to the pagan goddess, whose name was close enough to the Christian saint's name to be easily confused.

Brighit was associated with fire because *breo* is Irish for a firebrand or torch, and *breoch* means "glowing." St. Bridget's fire continued to burn for several hundred years, but it was suppressed by an order from the Archbishop of Dublin in the year 1220, perhaps because of its pagan origins. But the custom of lighting a fire on St. Bridget's Day survived for many years in Scotland, where schoolchildren would build a "Candlemas blaze" on the first of February.

Rush Cross

In some parts of Ireland, children are still sent out on St. Bridget's Eve to pull up rushes, which cannot be cut with a knife. When the rushes are brought into the house, everyone gathers around the fire and makes crosses from them, which are then sprinkled with holy water. The wife or eldest daughter prepares tea and pancakes, and a plate of pancakes is laid on top of the rush crosses. After the food has been eaten, the crosses are hung up over doors and beds to bring good luck.

The rush crosses are probably a survival of a pre-Christian custom associated with a pagan demigoddess who was considered to be a patroness of the Irish bards. They were adapted by the Christian missionaries, for whom the cross was a symbol of Jesus Christ.

FURTHER READING

Brewster, H. Pomeroy. *Saints and Festivals of the Christian Church*. 1904. Reprint. Detroit: Omnigraphics, 1990.

Crippen, T.G. *Christmas and Christmas Lore*. 1923. Reprint. Detroit: Omnigraphics, 1990.

Henderson, Helene, ed. *Holidays, Festivals, and Celebrations of the World Dictionary*. 3rd ed. Detroit: Omnigraphics, 2005.

King, John. *The Celtic Druids' Year: Seasonal Cycles of the Ancient Celts*. London: Blandford, 1995.

Santino, Jack. *All Around the Year: Holidays and Celebrations in American Life*. Urbana: University of Illinois Press, 1994.

Urlin, Ethel L. *Festivals, Holy Days, and Saints' Days*. 1915. Reprint. Detroit: Omnigraphics, 1992.

WEB SITE

New Advent Catholic Encyclopedia
www.newadvent.org/cathen/02784b.htm

St. Casimir's Day

Type of Holiday: Religious (Christian)
Date of Observation: March 4
Where Celebrated: Lithuania
Symbols and Customs: Casimir Fair, Heart-Shaped Cookies, Palms

ORIGIN

St. Casimir is the patron saint of Lithuania and Poland. He is especially popular in Lithuania because he is the only Roman Catholic saint that the people of that country consider to be Lithuanian. He is buried in Vilnius, the capital of Lithuania. His feast day, March 4, is widely celebrated in Lithuania. The activities that take place on that day reflect the pride Lithuanians take in their culture and their love for their patron saint.

Casimir was born in Cracow, Poland, on October 3, 1458. His grandfather, King Wladislaus II Jagiello, is credited with converting Lithuania from Orthodox Christianity to Roman Catholicism. His father, King Casimir IV, served as King of Lithuania and later become the King of Poland. His mother was Princess Elizabeth of Austria. The couple had six sons and six daughters, of which Casimir was the second oldest son. Though raised in Poland, the children had strong ties to Lithuania.

Young Casimir was given a fine education with strong religious overtones. His tutors included Father Dlugosz, the Polish historian, a Roman Catholic canon, and even an archbishop. This exposure to Roman Catholic piety deeply affected the young boy. His parents placed him in the care of Father Dlugosz when he was nine years old. Even at this young age, Casimir demonstrated considerable religious devotion. At the age of thirteen, Casimir journeyed to Hungary, where he had been offered the crown if he would lead the Hungarians in their fight against the invading Turkish Muslims. The military campaign was a failure, however, and Casimir returned to Poland.

Casimir's reputation for piety grew as he became a young man. He was known to have a special devotion to the Virgin Mary. It is said that he would kneel in prayer outside the doors of locked churches, praying there for hours during the night, even in bad weather. He also gained a reputation for his chastity and for his devotion to fasting.

In 1479, when Casimir was twenty-one years old, his father left Poland and returned to Lithuania to help put the country's political affairs in order. Casimir served as the ruler of Poland in his father's absence. The people acclaimed him a just and prudent leader. During these years, Casimir's father tried to arrange a marriage for him, but the young prince refused all offers, preferring to remain single. In 1484 he journeyed to Lithuania, where he became extremely ill. He died at the court in Grodno on March 4, 1484.

Not long after Prince Casimir's death, people began to pray at his tomb. Some of these people claimed that miracles happened to them after asking for Casimir's help. His most famous miracle occurred in 1518, when the Russian army attacked the Lithuanian town of Polotsk. It is said that St. Casimir appeared before the Lithuanian troops on a white horse, and led them on the charge across the Dauguva River. Inspired by this miraculous apparition, the Lithuanians fought off the Russian invasion.

In 1521, the Roman Catholic Church began the proceedings to officially declare Prince Casimir a saint of the church. These proceedings finally came to a close on November 7, 1602, when Pope Clement VIII proclaimed Casimir an official Roman Catholic saint.

The basis of saint day remembrances—for St. Casimir as well as other saints—is found in ancient Roman tradition. On the anniversary of a death, families would share a ritual meal at the grave site of an ancestor. This practice was adopted by Christians who began observing a ritual meal on the death anniversary of ancestors in the faith, especially martyrs. As a result, most Christian saint days are associated with the death of the saint. There are three important exceptions. John the Baptist, the Virgin Mary, and Jesus are honored on their nativities (birthdays). Many who suffered martyrdom are remembered on saint days in the calendars of several Orthodox, Catholic, and Protestant sects.

In addition to serving as the patron saint of Lithuania, Casimir has also become the patron saint of youth. Pope Pius XII assigned St. Casimir this position on June 11, 1948. St. Casimir is often depicted holding a lily, a traditional Christian symbol for chastity or purity.

SYMBOLS AND CUSTOMS

Casimir Fair

Hundreds of years ago, many Lithuanians journeyed to Vilnius to celebrate St. Casimir's Day near the saint's tomb. Once there, they stayed a day or two to shop in the big city. Open-air markets sprang up to cater to these tourists. These markets provided the pilgrims with souvenirs of St. Casimir's Day, such as PALMS and HEART-SHAPED COOKIES, as well as Lithuanian handicrafts, food, and other useful items. These fairs became known as *Kaziuko muges* in Lithuanian, or "Little

Casimir Fairs." Nowadays Casimir Fairs can be found in many towns in Lithuania. They feature Lithuanian handicrafts, folk music, and folk dancing. They are usually scheduled for March 4, or the weekend closest to that date.

Casimir Fairs also take place in towns outside Lithuania that host people of Lithuanian descent. In the United States, churches or scouting organizations often take on the responsibility of hosting a Casimir Fair. These events usually feature Lithuanian foods, books, music, and handicrafts. Many Lithuanian Americans attend these fairs in order to reconnect with their cultural heritage and with other members of their ethnic community.

Heart-Shaped Cookies

Lithuanians make heart-shaped cookies called *muginukus* on St. Casimir's Day. The recipe for these cookies calls for honey instead of sugar as the main sweetener. Other ingredients include flour, eggs, butter, cream, cinnamon, and cloves. The dough is chilled, rolled out flat, and cut with heart-shaped cookie cutters. After the cookies are baked, they are decorated with colored sugar. Typical designs include flowers, birds, dots, and zigzags.

An old custom encouraged bakers who set up shop at Casimir Fairs to add a commonly used Lithuanian name to each cookie. People who attended a Casimir Fair often bought cookies with the names of friends and relatives who couldn't come. Upon returning to their residence, they distributed these souvenirs to those who had remained at home. These days Lithuanian families often bake their own *muginukus*. They make sure to embellish at least one cookie with the name of each family member.

Palms

One of the most commonly seen items at Casimir Fairs are *verbos*, or palms. Artisans make the palms by twisting together grasses and flowers to form the outlines of typical Lithuanian designs. Then they attach these geometrical designs to short sticks. Alternately, herbs, grasses, and flowers can be twined around or glued to very thin sticks.

Lithuanians save their St. Casimir's day palms and carry them to church on **PALM SUNDAY**. Afterwards they bring them home and use them as household decorations.

FURTHER READING

Bindokiene, Danute Brazyte. *Lithuanian Customs and Traditions*. Chicago: Lithuanian World Community, 1998.

WEB SITES

Catholic Encyclopedia
www.newadvent.org/cathen/03402a.htm

Lithuania Embassy
www.ltembassyus.org

Lithuanian Customs and Traditions
lietuviu-bendruomene.org/educat/tradicijos

St. Catherine's Day

Type of Holiday: Religious (Christian)
Date of Observation: November 25
Where Celebrated: England, France
Symbols and Customs: Catherine Bonnet, Catherine Wheel, Cattern Cake, Lighthouse

ORIGINS

St. Catherine is now believed to be a writer's invention rather than a historical person, and for this reason her feast day is no longer observed in the Roman Catholic Church calendar. Because sufficient evidence for Catherine's life has not been determined, her day was removed from the calendar of saints in 1969. But Catherine was one of the most admired and popular saints in western Europe during the latter Middle Ages, and some of the customs associated with her feast survive to this day.

According to legend, St. Catherine was born a pagan in Alexandria, but she loved books and learning so much that she eventually became interested in Christianity. Her family's high rank, if not her youth, might have protected her from being persecuted along with the other Alexandrian Christians, but she insisted on confronting Emperor Maxentius, scolding him for his cruelties and trying to persuade him that paganism was wrong. The emperor tried to seduce her but was rebuffed, and in anger he threw her into prison, where she managed to convert 200 soldiers of the guard. She was condemned to death by torture on a spiked wheel that would tear her flesh to pieces as it revolved. But the wheel broke and the spikes, flying off in all directions, ended up killing some of the spectators who had gathered to watch her die (*see* CATHERINE WHEEL). She was finally beheaded with a sword in 310 C.E. Upon her death, her body is said to have been carried by angels to the top of Mount Sinai and buried on the site where a great monastery containing her shrine was later built.

The returning Crusaders spread St. Catherine's legend to western Europe at the end of the eleventh and the beginning of the twelfth centuries. Her cult quickly took root, and she was even more admired and popular in the West than she was in her original Eastern home. Her feast day, November 25, was observed with great solemnity until well into the nineteenth century, especially by spinners, lacemakers, carters, and ropemakers. She was also the patron saint of carpenters, wheelwrights, millers, and others whose work was in some way connected with wheels. In eighteenth-century England, young women in the textile industry engaged in merrymaking or "catherning" on this day, which they sometimes referred to as "Cathern Day."

The basis of saint day remembrances is found in ancient Roman tradition. On the anniversary of a death, families would share a ritual meal at the grave site of an ancestor. This practice was adopted by Christians who began observing a ritual meal on the death anniversary of ancestors in the faith, especially martyrs. As a result, most Christian saint days are associated with the death of the saint. There are three important exceptions. John the Baptist, the Virgin Mary, and Jesus are honored on their nativities (birthdays). Many who suffered martyrdom are remembered on saint days in the calendars of several Orthodox, Catholic, and Protestant sects.

SYMBOLS AND CUSTOMS

Catherine Bonnet

Because she died a virgin and refused to save her own life by sacrificing her virginity, St. Catherine is the patron saint of old maids and young, unmarried girls. She is still celebrated in France by unmarried women under the age of twenty-five, particularly those who work in the millinery and dressmaking industries. They wear "Catherine Bonnets"—homemade creations of paper and ribbon—on November 25 in her honor. If a young French woman reaches the age of 25 without being married or engaged, she is said to coiffer Sainte Catherine—to "do St. Catherine's hair" or "don St. Catherine's bonnet," which is a warning that she is likely to become a spinster.

Catherine Wheel

In England, the Catherine Wheel is a type of firework that revolves like a pinwheel as it burns and throws off sparks. Lighting Catherine Wheels is a popular activity there on **GUY FAWKES DAY.** In the United States, cheerleaders and aspiring gymnasts perform "cartwheels," repeating the motion of St. Catherine on her wheel of torture as they turn head-over-heels.

The wheel is both the symbol of St. Catherine's martyrdom and an ancient fire symbol, an image of the life-giving sun.

Cattern Cake

In England, St. Catherine's Day or Cattern Day was a holiday for lacemakers right up through the nineteenth century. Young girls who worked in the lacemaking trade would go from house to house, often dressed up in boys' clothing, to receive cattern cakes, known as "wiggs" because of their wig-like shape, and a special drink made from warm beer, beaten eggs, and rum. They sang traditional working songs as they made their rounds, and at night they feasted, played games, and lit fireworks, particularly CATHERINE WHEELS.

Cattern Day was also a holiday for spinners. They would exchange their normally drab attire for white dresses decorated with scarlet and other colored ribbons. One of them would be chosen as Queen, and she would lead a procession around the village, stopping at all of the wealthier homes to ask for gifts of food or money. "Catterning" soon became a synonym for going house to house, begging for food, drink, or money and singing traditional songs.

Lighthouse

Many of the churches built in honor of St. Catherine were, like her grave, located on hilltops near the sea. From these high points of land, beacons frequently burned to guide travelers, especially sailors. Her chapel on a hill at Abbotsbury in Dorset, England, once had such a beacon, as did her chapel on St. Catherine's Point on the Isle of Wight. It has been suggested that her association with lighthouses derived from her birth at Alexandria, where the most famous lighthouse of the ancient world was located. Today, St. Catherine's association with light and fire is seen primarily in the burning CATHERINE WHEEL.

FURTHER READING

Dunkling, Leslie. *A Dictionary of Days*. New York: Facts on File, 1988.

Harper, Howard V. *Days and Customs of All Faiths*. 1957. Reprint. Detroit: Omnigraphics, 1990.

Henderson, Helene, ed. *Holidays, Festivals, and Celebrations of the World Dictionary*. 3rd ed. Detroit: Omnigraphics, 2005.

Hole, Christina. *Saints in Folklore*. New York: M. Barrows, 1965.

Leach, Maria, ed. *Funk & Wagnalls Standard Dictionary of Folklore, Mythology & Legend*. San Francisco: Harper & Row, 1984.

MacDonald, Margaret R., ed. *The Folklore of World Holidays*. Detroit: Gale Research, 1992.

Spicer, Dorothy Gladys. *Festivals of Western Europe*. 1958. Reprint. Detroit: Omnigraphics, 1993.

Spicer, Dorothy Gladys. *The Book of Festivals*. 1937. Reprint. Detroit: Omnigraphics, 1990.

Urlin, Ethel L. *Festivals, Holy Days, and Saints' Days*. 1915. Reprint. Detroit: Omnigraphics, 1992.

WEB SITE

New Advent Catholic Encyclopedia
www.newadvent.org/cathen/03445a.htm

St. Christopher's Day

Type of Holiday: Religious (Christian)
Date of Observation: July 25 in the West; May 9 or 22 in the East
Where Celebrated: Nesquehoning, Pennsylvania, and by Christians all over the world
Symbols and Customs: Blessing of the Cars, Staff, St. Christopher Medal

ORIGINS

Very little is known for sure about the man whose Christian name was Christopher, aside from the fact that he was martyred in Asia Minor around 250 C.E. during a series of persecutions ordered by Emperor Decius. By the sixth century, however, his following was well established in the East, and it had spread to the West by the ninth century.

The most popular legend concerning St. Christopher is that he started out as a pagan named Offerus, who lived in Canaan and was so proud of his strength that he vowed to serve only the most powerful man he could find. He started out serving the emperor, who turned out to be afraid of the devil. Then he served the devil, who turned out to be afraid of a cross. Finally he was converted to Christianity by a hermit, who baptized him with the name "Christopher" and suggested that the best way for him to serve God was to perform the earthly work for which he was best suited. So he became a ferryman, carrying pilgrims on his strong shoulders across a swift-moving river while using a STAFF to maintain his balance.

One day a young child approached and asked to be ferried across the stream. Halfway across, the weight of the child became so great that he feared they wouldn't make it. When they finally arrived safely on the other side, the child explained that he had been carrying the weight of the sins of the world. Christopher knew then that he had been carrying Christ, and that he'd met the all-powerful god for whom he'd been searching. The name "Christopher" means "Christ-bearer," and he is usually shown supporting the Christ child on his shoulders.

The basis of saint day remembrances—for St. Christopher as well as other saints—is found in ancient Roman tradition. On the anniversary of a death, families would share a ritual meal at the grave site of an ancestor. This practice was adopted by Christians who began observing a ritual meal on the death anniversary of ancestors in the faith, especially martyrs. As a result, most Christian saint days are associated with the death of the saint. There are three important exceptions. John the Baptist, the Virgin Mary, and Jesus are honored on their nativities (birthdays). Many who suffered martyrdom are remembered on saint days in the calendars of several Orthodox, Catholic, and Protestant sects.

By the thirteenth century, the Roman Catholic Church had instituted canonization, the process of making a person a saint. Before that, Christians venerated people they considered saints. In some cases, the pope would formally condone that veneration. In 1120 Pope Callistus II approved the cult that surrounded Christopher.

Although the Roman Catholic church removed his name from its universal calendar in 1969—largely because of the lack of reliable information about his life—St. Christopher's reputation has not diminished. As the patron saint of motorists, travelers, pilgrims, sailors, and ferrymen, his popularity extends beyond the walls of any one church and even beyond Christianity. Statues of St. Christopher can often be seen on car dashboards (*see* BLESSING OF THE CARS), and ST. CHRISTOPHER MEDALS often appear on car sun-visors and key chains.

SYMBOLS AND CUSTOMS

Blessing of the Cars

In Nesquehoning, Pennsylvania, St. Christopher's Day is the occasion for the Blessing of the Cars. The custom began in 1933, when the pastor of Our Lady of Mount Carmel Church started blessing automobiles after he himself had been involved in three serious car accidents.

Sometimes it takes an entire week to bless all the cars that arrive in Nesquehoning from throughout Pennsylvania and other nearby states. In recent years, other Catholic churches have taken up the custom and perform their own blessing ceremonies.

Staff

According to legend, after St. Christopher carried the Christ child safely to the far side of the river, he was told to plant his staff in the ground, whereupon it immediately turned into a tree and put forth leaves and fruit. It was this miracle that convinced him of his passenger's true identity and confirmed his vow to spend the rest of his life in the service of God.

The staff has more than one symbolic meaning in relation to St. Christopher. On the one hand, it is a symbol for travelers and pilgrims. But it is also a symbol of Jesus' strength and power, since its miraculous transformation into a tree proved beyond any doubt that God was more powerful than the emperor or the devil.

St. Christopher Medal

In the Middle Ages, there was a widespread belief that whoever looked upon a picture or statue of St. Christopher would be free from harm for the rest of the day. This led to the practice of hanging his picture or image across from the church doors, where everyone who entered would gaze upon it. The popularity of St. Christopher medals today, particularly among soldiers and travelers, is an extension of this custom.

FURTHER READING

Chambers, Robert. *The Book of Days*. 2 vols. 1862-64. Reprint. Detroit: Omnigraphics, 1990.

Christianson, Stephen G., and Jane M. Hatch. *The American Book of Days*. 4th ed. New York: H.W. Wilson, 2000.

Cohen, Hennig, and Tristram Potter Coffin. *The Folklore of American Holidays*. 3rd ed. Detroit: Gale Research, 1999.

Harper, Howard V. *Days and Customs of All Faiths*. 1957. Reprint. Detroit: Omnigraphics, 1990.

Henderson, Helene, ed. *Holidays, Festivals, and Celebrations of the World Dictionary*. 3rd ed. Detroit: Omnigraphics, 2005.

Jobes, Gertrude. *Dictionary of Mythology, Folklore, and Symbols*. New York: Scarecrow Press, 1962.

Urlin, Ethel L. *Festivals, Holy Days, and Saints' Days*. 1915. Reprint. Detroit: Omnigraphics, 1992.

WEB SITE

New Advent Catholic Encyclopedia
www.newadvent.org/cathen/03728a.htm

St. David's Day

Type of Holiday: Religious (Christian)
Date of Observation: March 1
Where Celebrated: Wales
Symbols and Customs: Leek

ORIGINS

The patron saint of Wales, St. David was a monk, an ascetic, and a bishop who founded or restored many monasteries and greatly influenced religious life in Wales. Although his dates are not known for certain, he may have died around the late sixth century. He died on March 1 in the Pembrokeshire town where he'd founded his first monastery, known today as St. David's, but his remains were later moved to the Abbey of Glastonbury.

St. David's Day is observed not only in Wales but by Welsh groups all over the world. It has been observed in the United States since very early times, due to the extensive migration of Welsh people to Pennsylvania at the end of the seventeenth century. Their presence eventually led to the establishment of the St. David's Society (sometimes called the Welsh Society), whose members are known for wearing LEEKS in their hats on St. David's Day and who have worked hard to preserve Welsh history and traditions. Such groups exist in Ohio, Wisconsin, and Florida as well as in New York City, where the St. David's Society has held an annual banquet on March 1 since 1835. This is a popular day on which to hold *Eisteddfodau*, which are traditional Welsh festivals involving competition in singing and literature. Another popular way to observe St. David's Day is with choral singing, for which the Welsh are noted.

The basis of saint day remembrances—for St. David as well as other saints—is found in ancient Roman tradition. On the anniversary of a death, families would share a ritual meal at the grave site of an ancestor. This practice was adopted by Christians who began observing a ritual meal on the death anniversary of ancestors in the faith, especially martyrs. As a result, most Christian saint days are associated with the death of the saint. There are three important exceptions. John the Baptist, the Virgin Mary, and Jesus are honored on their nativities (birthdays). Many who suffered martyrdom are remembered on saint days in the calendars of several Orthodox, Catholic, and Protestant sects.

SYMBOLS AND CUSTOMS

Leek

The leek is an herb similar to an onion and is also the floral emblem of Wales. The association of St. David with the leek is said to date back to a battle fought in the seventh century between the Welsh and the Saxons. St. David suggested that the Welsh wear a leek in their caps so they could recognize one another and avoid killing their own men. He is also said to have lived for many years on the site of what would later become one of his monasteries, eating only bread, water, and wild leeks.

To this day, new Welsh army recruits must eat ritual leeks on March 1.

FURTHER READING

Chambers, Robert. *The Book of Days*. 2 vols. 1862-64. Reprint. Detroit: Omnigraphics, 1990.

Christianson, Stephen G., and Jane M. Hatch. *The American Book of Days*. 4th ed. New York: H.W. Wilson, 2000.

Cohen, Hennig, and Tristram Potter Coffin. *The Folklore of American Holidays*. 3rd ed. Detroit: Gale Research, 1999.

Dunkling, Leslie. *A Dictionary of Days*. New York: Facts on File, 1988.

Harper, Howard V. *Days and Customs of All Faiths*. 1957. Reprint. Detroit: Omnigraphics, 1990.

Henderson, Helene, ed. *Holidays, Festivals, and Celebrations of the World Dictionary*. 3rd ed. Detroit: Omnigraphics, 2005.

Leach, Maria, ed. *Funk & Wagnalls Standard Dictionary of Folklore, Mythology & Legend*. San Francisco: Harper & Row, 1984.

MacDonald, Margaret R., ed. *The Folklore of World Holidays*. Detroit: Gale Research, 1992.

Urlin, Ethel L. *Festivals, Holy Days, and Saints' Days*. 1915. Reprint. Detroit: Omnigraphics, 1992.

WEB SITE

New Advent Catholic Encyclopedia
www.newadvent.org/cathen/04640b.htm

St. Elmo's Day

Type of Holiday: Religious (Christian)
Date of Observation: June 2
Where Celebrated: Italy and by Christians, particularly sailors, around the world
Symbols and Customs: St. Elmo's Fire

ORIGINS

St. Elmo has been confused with St. Erasmus, an earlier patron saint of sailors. Erasmus was a third-century Italian bishop who was martyred around 304 during the persecution of Christians by the Roman emperor Diocletian. He was at the height of his popularity in the thirteenth century when Elmo, who had spent much of his life working among the seafaring people of the Spanish coast, came along. Over the centuries, the two saints became identified with one another in the minds of the sailors who asked for their protection, and eventually no distinction was made between them.

Some scholars think that Elmo is merely a variation of the name Erasmus, and that the two saints are actually the same person. According to legend, Erasmus was martyred by being disemboweled, and for this reason his name is often invoked by people who suffer from intestinal problems.

The basis of saint day remembrances—for St. Elmo as well as other saints—is found in ancient Roman tradition. On the anniversary of a death, families would share a ritual meal at the grave site of an ancestor. This practice was adopted by Christians who began observing a ritual meal on the death anniversary of ancestors in the faith, especially martyrs. As a result, most Christian saint days are associated with the death of the saint. There are three important exceptions. John the Baptist, the Virgin Mary, and Jesus are honored on their nativities (birthdays). Many who suffered martyrdom are remembered on saint days in the calendars of several Orthodox, Catholic, and Protestant sects.

SYMBOLS AND CUSTOMS

St. Elmo's Fire

Because St. Elmo is the patron saint of sailors, it seemes appropriate that a natural phenomenon which can only be observed at sea should be named after him. "St. Elmo's Fire" is a pale, brush-like spray of electricity occasionally seen at the top of a ship's mast on a stormy night. This association apparently arose because the legend of St. Erasmus (also called Elmo) describes him preaching during a thunderstorm, undeterred by a bolt of lightning that strikes nearby. Sailors, who had good reason to be afraid of sudden storms, thought that seeing St. Elmo's Fire was a sign of the saint's protection.

The Greeks were familiar with this phenomenon long before the time of any Christian saint. If it appeared as a single brush of light, they called it "Helena," after the exceptionally beautiful daughter of Leda and Jupiter who married Menelaus and was seduced by Paris and carried off to Troy, thus triggering the Trojan War. If it appeared as a double stroke of light, they called it "Castor and Pollux," after Helena's twin brothers.

The scientific name for this electrical phenomenon is "corona discharge." But since the Middle Ages, it has been referred to as St. Elmo's Fire. Sailors at sea used to think these lights in the sky were the souls of the departed, rising to glory through the intercession of St. Elmo.

FURTHER READING

Farmer, David Hugh. *The Oxford Dictionary of Saints*. 5th ed. New York: Oxford University Press, 2003.

Harper, Howard V. *Days and Customs of All Faiths*. 1957. Reprint. Detroit: Omnigraphics, 1990.

Henderson, Helene, ed. *Holidays, Festivals, and Celebrations of the World Dictionary*. 3rd ed. Detroit: Omnigraphics, 2005.

Jobes, Gertrude. *Dictionary of Mythology, Folklore, and Symbols*. New York: Scarecrow Press, 1962.

Trawicky, Bernard, and Ruth W. Gregory. *Anniversaries and Holidays*. 5th ed. Chicago: American Library Assocation, 2000.

St. Francis of Assisi, Feast of

Type of Holiday: Religious (Christian)
Date of Observation: October 4
Where Celebrated: Italy, United States
Symbols and Customs: Blessing of the Animals
Related Holidays: Christmas

ORIGINS

St. Francis was the son of a wealthy family who lived in the Italian town of Assisi. When he was about twenty, he was held prisoner for a year as the result of a war between two neighboring towns. This experience, combined with a serious illness he suffered at about the same time, prompted him to reexamine his life. He ended up forsaking any claim to his family's fortune and going off to live in a hut, where he spent his time ministering to the poor and the sick. A group of his boyhood friends left their homes and joined him. These were the first Franciscans, as the members of the religious order started by St. Francis eventually came to be known. In the beginning, however, they were called the Penitents of Assisi.

The Penitents were known for their high spirits and appreciation of the simple things in life. Like St. Francis, their leader, they were troubadours who went around singing about God's goodness. Their numbers increased rapidly, and they made their headquarters at the Portiuncula, a small chapel of the church of Santa Maria degli Angeli. Even though the Franciscans were ragged and underfed, they all shared the joy and enthusiasm that had originally drawn them to St. Francis. They spent much of their time renovating churches that had fallen into disrepair and taking care of lepers and other outcasts.

The basis of saint day remembrances—of St. Francis and other saints—is found in ancient Roman tradition. On the anniversary of a death, families would share a ritual meal at the grave site of an ancestor. This practice was adopted by Christians who began observing a ritual meal on the death anniversary of ancestors in the faith, especially martyrs. As a result, most Christian saint days are associated with the death of the saint. There are three important exceptions. John the Baptist, the Virgin Mary, and Jesus are honored on their nativities (birthdays). Many who suffered martyrdom are remembered on saint days in the calendars of several Orthodox, Catholic, and Protestant sects.

By the thirteenth century, the Roman Catholic Church had instituted canonization, the process of making a person a saint. Before that, Christians venerated people they considered saints. In 1228 Pope Gregory IX formally canonized Francis of Assisi.

Although St. Francis died when he was only in his forties, he is believed to have been responsible for instituting two widespread **CHRISTMAS** traditions. He gave instructions for building the first crèche, in the town of Greccio, so that he could see with his own eyes the scene that must have surrounded the infant Jesus as he lay in the manger. St. Francis is also credited with the custom of caroling, since it was the Franciscans who composed and sang the first Italian Christmas carols.

The Feast of St. Francis is one of the most important festivals of the year in Assisi, Italy. For two days, the entire town is illuminated by oil lamps burning consecrated oil brought from a different Italian town each year. A parchment in St. Francis's handwriting, believed to be the saint's deathbed blessing to his follower, Brother Leo, is taken to the top of the Santa Maria degli Angeli basilica, and the people are blessed by a representative of the Pope.

SYMBOLS AND CUSTOMS

Blessing of the Animals

St. Francis loved animals because they were God's creatures. He instituted the custom of showing special kindness to animals at Christmastime, urging farmers to provide their oxen and asses with extra corn and hay in commemoration of the night when the infant Jesus lay between an ox and an ass in the manger. He also encouraged people to scatter grain and corn on the streets so that the birds would have enough to eat. He had a great fondness for songbirds, especially larks.

In the United States, it is not uncommon for children to bring their pets to the church to be blessed on St. Francis's feast day. The annual blessing of the animals held at the Cathedral of St. John the Divine in New York City on this day has turned into quite a spectacle. Among the animals that have come there to be blessed are a camel, an 8,000-pound elephant, a macaw with a thirty-word vocabulary, and a turtle that was rescued from a Chinese restaurant, where it was about to be made into soup.

FURTHER READING

Brewster, H. Pomeroy. *Saints and Festivals of the Christian Church*. 1904. Reprint. Detroit: Omnigraphics, 1990.

Christianson, Stephen G., and Jane M. Hatch. *The American Book of Days*. 4th ed. New York: H.W. Wilson, 2000.

Cohen, Hennig, and Tristram Potter Coffin. *The Folklore of American Holidays*. 3rd ed. Detroit: Gale Research, 1999.

Dobler, Lavinia G. *Customs and Holidays Around the World*. New York: Fleet Pub. Corp., 1962.

Harper, Howard V. *Days and Customs of All Faiths*. 1957. Reprint. Detroit: Omnigraphics, 1990.

Henderson, Helene, ed. *Holidays, Festivals, and Celebrations of the World Dictionary*. 3rd ed. Detroit: Omnigraphics, 2005.

WEB SITE

New Advent Catholic Encyclopedia
www.newadvent.org/cathen/06221a.htm

St. George's Day
(Georgemas)

Type of Holiday: Religious (Christian), National
Date of Observation: April 23 in England and the United States, February 25 in the Republic of Georgia
Where Celebrated: England, United States, Republic of Georgia
Symbols and Customs: Armor, Blessing of the Horses, Cross, Dragon, Green George, Lance
Colors: St. George's Day is associated with the colors scarlet and blue. Scarlet can be seen in the banner of the Church of England, which has a red cross on a white background in honor of the country's patron saint. It was also the custom in England on St. George's Day for men of fashion to wear a blue coat, perhaps in imitation of the blue mantle worn by the Knights of the Garter, the highest order of British knighthood. In the April 23 service held in St. Paul's Cathedral in London, members of the Order of St. Michael and St. George still dress in blue capes lined with scarlet.
Related Holidays: May Day, Parilia

ORIGINS

The patron saint of England, St. George is best known for slaying the vicious DRAGON who had terrorized a village in Cappadocia, a country in Asia Minor that became a Roman province in 17 C.E. After demanding to be fed two sheep a day, the dragon started asking for human victims. Lots were drawn to determine who would be sacrificed, and eventually the lot fell to the king's daughter. Dressed as a bride, the princess was led to the dragon's lair. St. George, an officer in the Roman army, happened to be riding by at the time and, in the name of Christ, stopped to help the princess. Making the sign of the CROSS, he engaged in combat and finally succeeded in pinning the dragon to the ground with his LANCE and then slaying it with his sword. In another version of the legend, he made a leash out of the princess's sash and led the dragon back to the city like a pet dog. The king and all his people were so impressed by St. George's victory that they were converted to the Christian faith.

Most Romans were still pagan at this time, and Christians were routinely persecuted. After killing the dragon, St. George continued on his journey to Palestine. There he defied the Roman emperor Diocletian's decree outlawing Christianity, refusing to give up his faith. He was seized and tortured, and eventually beheaded on April 23 in the year 300 C.E. By the Middle Ages he had become the model for

Christian soldiers and warriors everywhere. He was made the patron saint of England around 1344.

The basis of saint day remembrances—for St. George as well as other saints—is found in ancient Roman tradition. On the anniversary of a death, families would share a ritual meal at the grave site of an ancestor. This practice was adopted by Christians who began observing a ritual meal on the death anniversary of ancestors in the faith, especially martyrs. As a result, most Christian saint days are associated with the death of the saint. There are three important exceptions. John the Baptist, the Virgin Mary, and Jesus are honored on their nativities (birthdays). Many who suffered martyrdom are remembered on saint days in the calendars of several Orthodox, Catholic, and Protestant sects.

St. George's Day, sometimes referred to as Georgemas, has been observed as a religious feast as well as a holiday since the thirteenth century. In the United States, St. George's Societies in Philadelphia; New York City; Charleston, South Carolina; and Baltimore, Maryland dedicated to charitable causes hold their annual dinners on April 23. In the former Soviet Union, St. George's Day is celebrated on February 25 as the national day of the Georgian Republic. In the Alps, shepherds pay special homage to St. George, probably because his feast day coincides with the time of year when they move their flocks up to mountain pastures (*see* **PARILIA**).

SYMBOLS AND CUSTOMS

Armor

St. George was a favorite subject among Renaissance artists. He is usually represented as a young knight in shining armor emblazoned with a red CROSS, riding on his horse. Armor is a symbol not only of chivalry but of the Christian faith as a safeguard against evil. In Ephesians 6:11-17, St. Paul says, "Put on the whole armor of God, that ye may be able to stand against the wiles of the devil ... having on the breastplate of righteousness ... the shield of faith ... the helmet of salvation, and the sword of the Spirit, which is the word of God."

Blessing of the Horses

In Germany, St. George is the protector of horses and their riders. On April 23, in the villages of upper Bavaria, people bring their horses to church and the parish priest blesses the animals and their masters, sprinkling both with holy water. In the Swiss Canton of Valais, farmers lead their donkeys, mules, and horses to church on April 23 to be blessed, believing that the ceremony will protect their animals from disease and accident throughout the year.

In parts of Greece, St. George's Day is observed with games and horse races. The prize for the winner is often a saddle or harness. (*See also* **ST. STEPHEN'S DAY**.)

Cross

The cross known as St. George's Cross is the one that appears on the banner of the Church of England. The cross is red on a white background, in imitation of the red cross popularly shown on St. George's ARMOR.

In the former Soviet Union, this festival honors the patron of the Military Order of St. George's Cross. It is observed with special church services and reunions among military officers. Celebratory dinners are held for military men of all ranks.

Dragon

The dragon is an imaginary animal that combines characteristics from various other aggressive and dangerous animals, such as crocodiles, lions, and snakes. Found in the majority of the world's cultures, the dragon usually stands as a symbol of the primordial enemy who must be confronted in combat as a supreme test of one's power or faith. In Christianity, the dragon often symbolizes the devil or Satan. He is usually depicted as a devouring monster who destroys his victims in an attempt to get even with God for casting him out of heaven.

In stark contrast to Western ideas about the dragon, the Chinese dragon is a benign, good-natured creature symbolizing fertility and male vigor (*see* DRAGON BOATS under **DOUBLE FIFTH**).

Green George

The gypsies of Transylvania and Romania celebrate the festival of Green George on April 23. On the eve of St. George's Day, a young willow tree is cut down, set in the ground, and decorated with leaves and garlands. Pregnant women place a piece of their clothing under the tree and leave it there overnight. If they find a leaf lying on the garment the following morning, they know they will have an easy delivery. Sick and elderly people visit the tree as well, spitting on it and asking for a long life.

On the morning of St. George's Day, a young man dressed from head to toe in green leaves and blossoms appears. He is known as Green George, the human double of the willow tree. While the power of granting an easy delivery to pregnant women and vital energy to the sick and elderly belongs to the willow, Green George throws a few handfuls of grass to the farm animals so they won't lack fodder during the year. It is also Green George's responsibility to gain the favor of the water spirits. He does this by taking three iron nails and, after knocking them into the willow, pulling them out and throwing them into a running stream. Sometimes a puppet version of

Green George is thrown into the stream as well. This is supposed to ensure the rain that will be needed to make the fields and meadows green in summer.

Like other tree spirits, the appearance of Green George in April is seen as necessary to the regeneration that is taking place in the natural world. His counterpart in England is known as Jack-in-the-Green (*see* **MAY DAY**).

Lance

According to the legend of St. George and the dragon, the saint pierced the dragon with his lance, which then broke, forcing him to kill the dragon with his sword. A symbol of war—in this case, the struggle between the Christian spirit and evil—the lance is considered an earthly weapon, in contrast to the spiritual implications of the sword. The broken lance is considered a symbol of St. George and also of the Passion, since it was a lance that was used to pierce the side of Jesus as he hung on the cross.

FURTHER READING

Brewster, H. Pomeroy. *Saints and Festivals of the Christian Church*. 1904. Reprint. Detroit: Omnigraphics, 1990.

Cirlot, J.E. *A Dictionary of Symbols*. New York: Philosophical Library, 1962.

Dobler, Lavinia G. *Customs and Holidays Around the World*. New York: Fleet Pub. Corp., 1962.

Ferguson, George. *Signs and Symbols in Christian Art*. New York: Oxford University Press, 1954.

Frazer, Sir James G. *The Golden Bough: A Study in Magic and Religion*. New York: Macmillan, 1931.

Henderson, Helene, ed. *Holidays, Festivals, and Celebrations of the World Dictionary*. 3rd ed. Detroit: Omnigraphics, 2005.

Ickis, Marguerite. *The Book of Festivals and Holidays the World Over*. New York: Dodd, Mead, 1970.

Leach, Maria, ed. *Funk & Wagnalls Standard Dictionary of Folklore, Mythology & Legend*. San Francisco: Harper & Row, 1984.

Olderr, Steven. *Symbolism: A Comprehensive Dictionary*. Jefferson, NC: McFarland, 1986.

Urlin, Ethel L. *Festivals, Holy Days, and Saints' Days*. 1915. Reprint. Detroit: Omnigraphics, 1992.

WEB SITE

VisitBritain
www.enjoyengland.com/attractions/events/calendar/april/st-george.aspx

St. James the Apostle, Feast of

Type of Holiday: Religious (Roman Catholic)
Date of Observation: July 25
Where Celebrated: Mexico, Philippines, Puerto Rico, Spain, United States, and by
   Spanish-speaking countries and communities around the world
Symbols and Customs: Bomba, Caballeros, Pilgrimage, Vejigantes

ORIGINS

St. James the Apostle, or Santiago as he is known in Spain, was St. John the Evangelist's brother and the first of the twelve apostles to be martyred for his faith. He went to Spain as a missionary before returning to Palestine, where King Herod Agrippa beheaded him around 44 C.E. His remains were brought back to Spain by boat and buried in a field not far from the coast of Galicia in northwestern Spain. The exact location of his grave was eventually forgotten, and it lay neglected for almost 800 years, until the site was miraculously illuminated by starlight in the early ninth century. The discovery of the tomb provided a much-needed boost to the morale of the Spanish troops, who were fighting the Moors at the time, and a vision of the saint on a white horse galloping across the sky is believed to have given them the strength and spirit they needed to drive the Moors out of Spain. A church known as Santiago de Compostela (St. James of the Field of the Star) was built on the site, and it soon became a popular destination for pilgrims (*see* PIL-GRIMAGE) from all over Europe.

The basis of saint day remembrances—for St. James as well as other saints—is found in ancient Roman tradition. On the anniversary of a death, families would share a ritual meal at the grave site of an ancestor. This practice was adopted by Christians who began observing a ritual meal on the death anniversary of ancestors in the faith, especially martyrs. As a result, most Christian saint days are associated with the death of the saint. There are three important exceptions. John the Baptist, the Virgin Mary, and Jesus are honored on their nativities (birthdays). Many who suffered martyrdom are remembered on saint days in the calendars of several Orthodox, Catholic, and Protestant sects.

Because he is the patron saint of Spain, St. James's feast day is celebrated throughout the country but particularly in Santiago de Compostela, where there are processions, bull fights, and fireworks. Mexicans observe July 25 with the Dance of the Tastoanes, which reenacts the struggle between the Mexican natives and the Spanish invaders.

The Fiesta of St. James is the year's most important celebration, however, in Loíza, Puerto Rico, a town largely populated by the descendants of the African slaves who once worked on the plantations there. In fact, St. James has taken on many of the characteristics of Shangó, the African (Yoruba) god of war and thunder.

The festival in Loíza centers around three images of the saint—one for the women, one for the men, and one for the children—which are kept throughout the year in the homes of *mantenedoras* or maintainers and taken out in procession during the yearly festival. The townspeople dress up as CABALLEROS or traditional Spanish gentlemen, as VEJIGANTES or Moors, and as *viejos* or old men who wear ragged clothing and whose job it is to provide music for the festival and solicit gifts for St. James. The dances and pantomimes performed by these masked figures are of primarily African origin, although they incorporate certain elements of Spanish history and Christian legend.

The celebration of St. James the Apostle's Day in the United States is most notable among the Pueblo Indians of New Mexico, where the influence of the early Spanish missionaries can still be seen. The inhabitants of the Taos, Santa Ana, Laguna, and Cochiti pueblos hold traditional Native American dances on this day, and at Acoma July 25 is celebrated with a rooster pull.

SYMBOLS AND CUSTOMS

Bomba

The music known as bomba, which is played at the St. James Festival in Loíza, Puerto Rico, is characterized by chanting and drumming. It represents a combination of Spanish and African elements. Foremost among the instruments are the bombas themselves—tall wooden drums with goatskin parchment heads—along with bongo drums, tambourines, maracas, guitars, and palillos, which are wooden sticks.

Caballeros

Of the several different types of costumed characters who participate in the celebration of St. James Day in Loíza, the caballeros represent all that is good and Christian. They are dressed in the traditional costume of the old-fashioned Spanish gentleman, with brightly colored silk or satin jackets and trousers and masks on which the features of such a gentleman, including a mustache, have been painted. Their hats are usually decorated with ribbons, bells, and tiny mirrors, and they typically appear at the festival on horseback.

Pilgrimage

Christian pilgrims from all over the world have traveled to Santiago de Compostela since the eleventh century to kneel before the saint's tomb in the crypt of the Romanesque cathedral that was built between 1078 and 1211 C.E., replacing the original ninth century church. So many pilgrims began arriving there after the cathedral was completed that King Ferdinand and Queen Isabella of Spain built a hotel across from it, called the Hostal de los Reyes Católicos, in the early sixteenth century. As a pilgrimage site, Santiago de Compostela rivals Jerusalem and Rome.

Most pilgrims follow the Camino de Santiago or St. James Way, which begins in the foothills of the Pyrenees Mountains of southern France and ends at Santiago de Compostela, a distance of 800 kilometers (500 miles). Most pilgrims follow the route on foot, which takes about a month, staying in rustic inns and monasteries along the way.

Vejigantes

In contrast to the CABALLEROS, who represent good, the vejigantes who participante in the St. James Fiesta in Loíza, Puerto Rico, symbolize evil and are identified with the Moors, against whom St. James and the cabelleros do battle. They wear batlike costumes and grotesque three-horned masks made of dried coconut husks, painted with the traditional Yoruba (African) colors of red and black. They roam the streets of the city, making howling noises and striking passersby with a paper bag—formerly an inflated bladder known as a vejiga—tied to the end of a stick. It is said that back in the days when pirates would frequently come ashore, plantation owners would have their slaves dress up as vejigantes to scare the invaders away.

FURTHER READING

Bellenir, Karen. *Religious Holidays and Calendars*. 3rd ed. Detroit: Omnigraphics, 2004.

Christianson, Stephen G., and Jane M. Hatch. *The American Book of Days*. 4th ed. New York: H.W. Wilson, 2000.

Cohen, Hennig, and Tristram Potter Coffin. *The Folklore of American Holidays*. 3rd ed. Detroit: Gale Research, 1999.

Eagle Walking Turtle. *Indian America: A Traveler's Companion*. Santa Fe: J. Muir Publications, 1989.

Harper, Howard V. *Days and Customs of All Faiths*. 1957. Reprint. Detroit: Omnigraphics, 1990.

Leach, Maria, ed. *Funk & Wagnalls Standard Dictionary of Folklore, Mythology & Legend*. San Francisco: Harper & Row, 1984.

MacDonald, Margaret R., ed. *The Folklore of World Holidays*. Detroit: Gale Research, 1992.

Spicer, Dorothy Gladys. *Festivals of Western Europe*. 1958. Reprint. Detroit: Omnigraphics, 1993.

Urlin, Ethel L. *Festivals, Holy Days, and Saints' Days*. 1915. Reprint. Detroit: Omnigraphics, 1992.

St. Joseph's Day
(Dia de San Giuseppe, Fallas)

Type of Holiday: Religious (Christian)
Date of Observation: March 19 in the West; July 29 in the East
Where Celebrated: Italy, Sicily, Spain, United States, and by Christians all over the
  world
Symbols and Customs: Breads, Fruits, and Grains; Fish; Flowering Rod

ORIGINS

Joseph, husband of the Virgin Mary and foster-father of Jesus, has been honored as
a saint since the earliest days of the Christian Church. But very little is known
about his life, or even the exact date of his death, which is believed to have
occurred when Jesus Christ was eighteen.

The basis of saint day remembrances—for St. Joseph as well as other saints—is
found in ancient Roman tradition. On the anniversary of a death, families would
share a ritual meal at the grave site of an ancestor. This practice was adopted by
Christians who began observing a ritual meal on the death anniversary of ancestors in the faith, especially martyrs. As a result, most Christian saint days are associated with the death of the saint. There are three important exceptions. John the
Baptist, the Virgin Mary, and Jesus are honored on their nativities (birthdays).
Many who suffered martyrdom are remembered on saint days in the calendars of
several Orthodox, Catholic, and Protestant sects.

By the thirteenth century, the Roman Catholic Church had instituted canonization,
the process of making a person a saint. Before that, Christians venerated people
they considered saints. In 1870 Pope Pius IX formally proclaimed Joseph the
patron of the universal church.

St. Joseph's Day is widely celebrated in Italy as a day of feasting and sharing with
the poor, of whom he is the patron saint. Each village prepares a "table of St.
Joseph" by contributing money, candles, flowers, and food (*see* FISH). Then they
invite three guests of honor—representing Mary, Joseph, and Jesus—to join in
their feast, as well as others representing the twelve apostles. They also invite the
orphans, widows, beggars, and poor people of the village to eat with them. The
food is blessed by the village priest and by the child chosen to represent Jesus;

then it is passed from one person to the next. Dia de San Giuseppe, as the day is known, is celebrated by Italians in the United States and in other countries as well.

In Valencia, Spain, it is a week-long festival (March 12-19) called Fallas de San Jose (Bonfires of St. Joseph). Its roots can be found in medieval times, when the carpenters' guild (of whom Joseph was the patron saint) made a huge bonfire on St. Joseph's Eve out of the wood shavings that had accumulated over the winter. This was considered the end of the winter and the last night on which candles and lamps would have to be lighted. In fact, the carpenters often burned the *parot,* or wooden candelabrum, in front of their shops.

In Valencia nowadays the *parots* have become *fallas,* or huge floats of intricate scenes made of wood and papier-mâché, satirizing everything from the high cost of living to political personalities. On St. Joseph's Eve, March 18, the *fallas* parade through the streets. At midnight on March 19, the celebration ends with a spectacular ceremony known as the *crema,* when all the *fallas* are set on fire.

Among Sicilian Catholics living in the United States, St. Joseph's Day is a major event—the equivalent of **ST. PATRICK'S DAY** among Irish-Americans. This is particularly true in New Orleans, Milwaukee, and other cities where there are large Sicilian populations. In Southern California, a custom similar to the Hispanic **POSADAS** takes place on St. Joseph's Day: Mary's and Joseph's search for shelter is reenacted by children, who go from house to house requesting lodging for the night. When they reach the third house, they are greeted by a large St. Joseph's Altar and an elaborate meal.

SYMBOLS AND CUSTOMS

Breads, Fruits, and Grains

Cards exchanged by Roman Catholics on St. Joseph's Day often show specially baked breads, fruits, and grains along with images of the saint. They are a symbol of fertility and abundance, although now the day is more of an ethnic festival than a celebration of spring.

Fish

The tables or altars set up in Sicilian homes on St. Joseph's Day are often used to display the special foods associated with the holiday. Fish is a favorite choice, probably because this holy day falls during **LENT**, when meat is forbidden. But it may also have something to do with fish as a fertility symbol (*see* BREADS, FRUITS, AND GRAINS) and a symbol of Christianity. The fish often stands for Christ in Christian art and literature because the five Greek letters forming the word "fish" are the initial letters of the five words, "Jesus Christ God's Son Savior." The fish is also a symbol of baptism: Just as the fish cannot live out of the water, the true Christian cannot live except through the waters of baptism.

Flowering Rod

Mary didn't choose Joseph to be her husband. According to legend, the priest Zacharius was told by an angel to gather together all the widowers, instructing them to bring their rods (or staffs) with them. Joseph appeared with the rest, and their rods were placed in the temple overnight in the hope that God would provide a sign to indicate which of them he favored. The next morning, it was discovered that Joseph's rod had burst into flower, and a white dove flew out of it. This was taken to be a clear sign of God's intentions for him. In paintings of the subject, the rejected suitors are often shown breaking their rods with expressions of envy and disgust. Joseph's rod is usually shown in the form of a stalk of lilies—the lily being a symbol of purity and the flower most often associated with the Virgin Mary (*see* LILY under **ANNUNCIATION OF THE BLESSED VIRGIN MARY**).

FURTHER READING

Appleton, LeRoy H., and Stephen Bridges. *Symbolism in Liturgical Art.* New York: Scribner, 1959.

Bellenir, Karen. *Religious Holidays and Calendars.* 3rd ed. Detroit: Omnigraphics, 2004.

Biedermann, Hans. *Dictionary of Symbolism: Cultural Icons and the Meanings Behind Them.* New York: Meridian Books, 1994.

Brewster, H. Pomeroy. *Saints and Festivals of the Christian Church.* 1904. Reprint. Detroit: Omnigraphics, 1990.

Ferguson, George. *Signs and Symbols in Christian Art.* New York: Oxford University Press, 1954.

Henderson, Helene, ed. *Holidays, Festivals, and Celebrations of the World Dictionary.* 3rd ed. Detroit: Omnigraphics, 2005.

Santino, Jack. *All Around the Year: Holidays and Celebrations in American Life.* Urbana: University of Illinois Press, 1994.

WEB SITE

Fallas of Valencia
www.fallas.com

St. Lucy's Day
(Luciadagen)

Type of Holiday: Religious (Christian)
Date of Observation: December 13
Where Celebrated: Denmark, Finland, Norway, Sweden, United States
Symbols and Customs: Candles, Eyes, Lucia Cats
Colors: St. Lucy's Day is associated with the colors white and red. In Scandinavia, it is traditional to observe this day by dressing the oldest daughter in the family in a white robe tied with a crimson sash.
Related Holidays: Winter Solstice

ORIGINS

According to tradition, St. Lucy or Santa Lucia was born in Syracuse, Sicily, in the third century. She was so beautiful that she attracted the unwanted attentions of a pagan nobleman, to whom she was betrothed against her will. In an attempt to end the affair, she cut out her EYES, which her suitor claimed "haunted him day and night." But God restored them as a reward for her sacrifice. She then gave away her entire dowry to the poor people of Syracuse. This made her lover so angry that he tried to force her to perform a sacrifice to his pagan gods. She refused and was taken off to prison. There she was again ordered to perform the sacrifice or be condemned to death. But when the soldiers tried to move her to the place of execution, they could not budge her. They lit a fire on the floor around her, used ropes and pulleys, and finally stabbed her in the neck with a dagger. For this reason she is the patron saint for protection from throat infections.

According to the Julian or Old Style calendar, St. Lucy blinded herself on the **WINTER SOLSTICE**—the shortest, darkest day of the year. When the Vikings were converted to Christianity, they adopted the Italian saint as the day's patroness because her name, Lucia, meant "light." To the sun-starved inhabitants of Sweden, Norway, Finland, and Denmark, this was the joyful day after which winter began yielding to spring, and they brought to it many of their pagan light and fire customs (*see* CANDLES). Their belief in the saint's power to break winter's spell gave rise to the popular folk custom of writing her name on doors and fences, along with the drawing of a girl, in the hope that Lucia would drive winter away.

The basis of saint day remembrances—for. St. Lucy as well as other saints—is found in ancient Roman tradition. On the anniversary of a death, families would share a ritual meal at the grave site of an ancestor. This practice was adopted by Christians who began observing a ritual meal on the death anniversary of ancestors in the faith, especially martyrs. As a result, most Christian saint days are associated with the death of the saint. There are three important exceptions. John the Baptist, the Virgin Mary, and Jesus are honored on their nativities (birthdays). Many who suffered martyrdom are remembered on saint days in the calendars of several Orthodox, Catholic, and Protestant sects.

In Sweden, where St. Lucy's Day is known as Luciadagen, it marks the official start of the **CHRISTMAS** season. Before sunrise on December 13, the oldest (or, in some cases, the prettiest) girl in the house goes among the sleeping family members dressed in a white robe with a red sash and wearing a metal crown covered with whortleberry (sometimes lingonberry) leaves and encircled by nine lighted CANDLES. The younger girls also dress in white and wear haloes of glittering tinsel. The boys—known as *Starngossar* or Star Boys—wear white robes and tall cone-shaped hats made of silver paper, and they carry star-topped scepters. The "Lucia Bride," as she is called, leads the Star Boys and younger girls through the house, awakening the rest of the family by singing a special song and bringing them coffee and buns (*see* LUCIA CATS).

The Lucy celebrations were brought to the United States by Swedish immigrants, whose customs survive in Swedish-American communities throughout the country. Chicago holds a major citywide festival on the afternoon of December 13 each year at the downtown Chicago Civic Center. A similar celebration takes place in Philadelphia, with Swedish Christmas songs, folk dances, and a procession of Lucia brides.

SYMBOLS AND CUSTOMS

Candles

The bonfires traditionally kindled on the **WINTER SOLSTICE** were designed to encourage the return of the sun at the darkest time of year. Even after the arrival of Christianity and the New Style calendar, light and fire were considered an essential part of St. Lucy's Day observations. The candles that the Lucia bride wears in her crown are one of the forms of light associated with this holiday. It was also common at one time for people to keep candles burning in their homes all day on December 13. Although St. Lucy's Day now falls several days before the solstice, it is still associated with light and the lengthening days.

Eyes

St. Lucy is often shown carrying her eyes on a platter, although there is no support for this in early accounts of her life. The eyes are a familiar symbol associated with the saint, however, and they serve as a good example of how a symbolic idea can be converted into a fact. Her name in Latin, Lucia, comes from lux, meaning "light." St. Lucy was often invoked by the blind for this reason, and eventually this gave rise to the story that she blinded herself by gouging out her eyes. Both the eyes and the lamp that Lucy is often shown carrying symbolize her divine light and wisdom.

Lucia Cats

Special buns are served on the morning of December 13. Although they come in a variety of shapes, the most popular are the *Lussekatter* or "Lucia cats," with raisins for eyes and baked dough that curls up at either end.

Cats have been a symbol of good luck since ancient times. They were also used as a sign to keep the devil out of the house, because he was believed to appear in the form of a cat.

FURTHER READING

Appleton, LeRoy H., and Stephen Bridges. *Symbolism in Liturgical Art*. New York: Scribner, 1959.

Brewster, H. Pomeroy. *Saints and Festivals of the Christian Church*. 1904. Reprint. Detroit: Omnigraphics, 1990.

Dobler, Lavinia G. *Customs and Holidays Around the World*. New York: Fleet Pub. Corp., 1962.

Ferguson, George. *Signs and Symbols in Christian Art*. New York: Oxford University Press, 1954.

Henderson, Helene, ed. *Holidays, Festivals, and Celebrations of the World Dictionary*. 3rd ed. Detroit: Omnigraphics, 2005.

Miles, Clement A. *Christmas in Ritual and Tradition, Christian and Pagan*. 1912. Reprint. Detroit: Omnigraphics, 1990.

Purdy, Susan. *Festivals for You to Celebrate*. Philadelphia: Lippincott, 1969.

Santino, Jack. *All Around the Year: Holidays and Celebrations in American Life*. Urbana: University of Illinois Press, 1994.

Weiser, Franz Xaver. *Handbook of Christian Feasts and Customs*. New York: Harcourt, Brace, 1958.

WEB SITE

Skansen Museum in Stockholm, Sweden
www.skansen.se

St. Mennas's Day

Type of Holiday: Religious (Orthodox Christian)
Date of Observation: November 11
Where Celebrated: Greece
Symbols and Customs: Scissors

ORIGINS

The name Mennas means "messenger, revealer." It is believed that St. Mennas has the power to reveal where lost or stolen items lie hidden. He is therefore very important to shepherds who have lost their sheep or who wish to protect them against wolves. In Greece, his day is observed by the many shepherds who must guide their sheep through the rough, mountainous terrain.

There are actually two different saints by the name of Mennas. One was a camel driver in Egypt who enlisted in the Roman army. When his legion reached Phrygia, he discovered that the Roman emperor, Diocletian, had started persecuting Christians. He left the army and hid in a mountain cave there to avoid persecution. But then, during the annual games held in the arena at Cotyaeum, he boldly entered the arena and announced that he was a Christian—an act of courage for which he was beheaded in 295 C.E. The other St. Mennas was a Greek from Asia Minor who became a hermit in the Abruzzi region of Italy and died in the sixth century.

There is an old proverb that says winter announces its arrival on St. Mennas's Day, November 11, and arrives on St. Philip's Day, November 15.

The basis of saint day remembrances—for St. Mennas as well as other saints—is found in ancient Roman tradition. On the anniversary of a death, families would share a ritual meal at the grave site of an ancestor. This practice was adopted by Christians who began observing a ritual meal on the death anniversary of ancestors in the faith, especially martyrs. As a result, most Christian saint days are associated with the death of the saint. There are three important exceptions. John the Baptist, the Virgin Mary, and Jesus are honored on their nativities (birthdays). Many who suffered martyrdom are remembered on saint days in the calendars of several Orthodox, Catholic, and Protestant sects.

SYMBOLS AND CUSTOMS

Scissors

In Greece, shepherds' wives refrain from using scissors on St. Mennas's Day. Instead, they wind a thread around the points of their scissors—a symbolic action designed to keep the jaws of wolves closed and the mouths of the village gossips shut.

FURTHER READING

Henderson, Helene, ed. *Holidays, Festivals, and Celebrations of the World Dictionary.* 3rd ed. Detroit: Omnigraphics, 2005.

Ickis, Marguerite. *The Book of Festivals and Holidays the World Over.* New York: Dodd, Mead, 1970.

MacDonald, Margaret R., ed. *The Folklore of World Holidays.* Detroit: Gale Research, 1992.

St. Patrick's Day

Type of Holiday: Religious (Christian)
Date of Observation: March 17
Where Celebrated: Ireland, United States
Symbols and Customs: Bonfires, Drinking, Harp, Leprechaun, Parades, Shamrock, Shillelagh
Colors: St. Patrick's Day is associated with the colors green, white, and orange. In addition to being a symbol of spring and fertility, green has been Ireland's national color since the nineteenth century. Whether they're Irish or not, many Americans wear something green on this day. In Ireland, young girls wear green hair ribbons, and boys often wear a green badge with a golden HARP on it. Everyone wears sprigs of green SHAMROCK on St. Patrick's Day. The three broad stripes on the flag of the Republic of Ireland are green, white, and orange: green for the Gaelic and Catholic majority, orange for Ireland's Protestants (after William of Orange, the Protestant son-in-law of the British King James II), and white for peace between the two groups.
Related Holidays: Beltane, Reek Sunday, St. Bridget's Day, Vernal Equinox

ORIGINS

St. Patrick, the patron saint of Ireland, was not actually Irish. He was born on March 17 around 385 somewhere in Roman Britain, possibly near Dumbarton in Scotland. At the age of sixteen he was captured by Irish raiders looking for slaves and carried off to Ireland, where he spent much of his time tending his master's sheep. He was lonely and homesick there, but he believed that he deserved to be punished for ignoring God's commandments.

After six years of slavery, he heard a voice telling him, "Thy ship is ready for thee." He ran away, heading for the coast, and was taken aboard a ship as a crew member. He ended up deserting his shipmates and wandering through southern Gaul (France) and Italy. After spending several years in Europe making up for the education he'd never received, he had a vision from God telling him to return to Ireland and convert the pagans to Christianity.

St. Patrick landed in County Wicklow, south of what is now Dublin, around 432. He made his way through the country as a missionary, visiting the Irish chieftains and telling them about the new religion he represented. Although his life was in constant danger, he somehow managed to survive to old age, and when he died in 464, the entire country went into mourning. He is probably best remembered for ordering all the snakes to leave Ireland—an event that, according to legend, occurred on the mountain later known as Croagh Patrick. On the last Sunday in July every year, hundreds of pilgrims gather there to commemorate their patron saint (*see* **REEK SUNDAY**).

The basis of saint day remembrances—for St. Patrick as well as other saints—is found in ancient Roman tradition. On the anniversary of a death, families would share a ritual meal at the grave site of an ancestor. This practice was adopted by Christians who began observing a ritual meal on the death anniversary of ancestors in the faith, especially martyrs. As a result, most Christian saint days are associated with the death of the saint. There are three important exceptions. John the Baptist, the Virgin Mary, and Jesus are honored on their nativities (birthdays). Many who suffered martyrdom are remembered on saint days in the calendars of several Orthodox, Catholic, and Protestant sects.

The first St. Patrick's Day celebration in the United States was held in Boston in 1737. The potato famine of 1845-49 brought many Irish immigrants to the United States, where St. Patrick's Day became an opportunity to express pride in their national heritage. In cities like Boston, New York, Philadelphia, and Los Angeles, it was observed with PARADES, banquets, speeches, and Irish plays, pageants, and dancing. People wore green and displayed the SHAMROCK and the green Irish flag with the gold HARP.

Today, there are more people of Irish descent in the United States than there are in Ireland, and the holiday has become a time for the Irish everywhere to show their unity and express their feelings about freedom—particularly freedom from British rule. In Ireland, it is a far less rowdy and commercial event than it is in the United States. People in Ireland attend sporting events or stay home and watch the New York St. Patrick's Day Parade on television, but they don't drink green beer, wear green derbies (an English invention), or put green carnations in their lapels.

Popular foods served in the U.S. on St. Patrick's Day include corned beef and cabbage, mulligatawny soup, Irish stew, and Irish soda bread. In Ireland, the preferred dish is colcannon, made from mashed potatoes combined with shredded kale or cabbage, minced onion, and melted butter.

SYMBOLS AND CUSTOMS

Bonfires

According to legend, St. Patrick was driven out of County Wicklow not long after he arrived. He sailed north and ended up in Tara, the legendary seat of Ireland's high kings. He arrived just as **BELTANE** was being celebrated, and all the fires had to be extinguished until the king had kindled his fire on the hill of Tara. St. Patrick lit his own campfire, and the flames were spotted by the king, Laoghaire. Outraged at this show of disrespect, he took a group of Druids to St. Patrick's camp to confront the missionary. But the Druids were afraid of Patrick's power and advised the king not to enter the camp. Instead, Patrick came out and settled the dispute, delivering a sermon during which he picked a SHAMROCK and used it to demonstrate the concept of the Holy Trinity.

St. Patrick was wise enough not to try to eliminate pagan rites and customs altogether. Instead, he tried to find a way to combine them with Christian customs. Since the Irish had traditionally honored their gods with bonfires on the hilltops in the spring, St. Patrick instituted the custom of lighting **EASTER** fires as a symbol for the Christian faith, which could never be extinguished.

Drinking

Drinking is a popular activity on St. Patrick's Day. St. Patrick is said to have brought the art of distilling spirits to Ireland, and the traditional cottage dweller's drink known as *poteen*, made from Irish white potatoes, has long been regarded as a way of warding off the ills associated with the country's damp climate. In the traditional custom known as "drowning the Shamrock," families with servants would put SHAMROCKS in a bowl and cover them with Irish whiskey, giving the remainder of the bottle to the servants. Nowadays, pub-crawling has become a popular way to spend the holiday.

Although the Irish are only moderately heavy drinkers by European standards (Belgians and Germans both consume more beer), the stereotype of the drunken Irishman remains common in America. In Ireland, both the churches and the government have tried to discourage the custom in recent years by putting more emphasis on the religious aspects of the holiday.

Harp

The harp is a symbol of St. Patrick's Day and of Ireland itself. It appears on Irish coins and on some Irish flags. It is also part of the national coat of arms, the presidential flag, and the royal arms of the United Kingdom. Harp music is often played in Irish castles that are open to the public, as well as in hotels and other public places. One of the world's oldest musical instruments, the harp has a long history in Irish mythology and legend.

The old Irish harp, known as the *clarsach,* was relatively small, with a sound box carved from a solid block of wood. The harpist held it on his or her knee and plucked the heavy brass strings with the fingernails of the other hand. Irish stone carvings and early Christian metal work often show people playing harps, so it is likely that the harp was a popular instrument by the time St. Patrick arrived in Ireland. Kings, church officials, princes, and poets often gathered to recite tales about Ireland to the accompaniment of harp music. The well-known Irish song, "The Harp That Once Through Tara's Halls," written by the Irish poet Thomas Moore, describes such a gathering in the hall of the Irish kings at Tara, a hill in County Meath.

Leprechaun

The legendary creatures known in Ireland as leprechauns were part of a group of fairies known as *Luchorpan,* which means "the wee ones." Over the years, the name luchorpan became confused with an Irish word meaning "one-shoemaker." Since shoemakers had a reputation for living alone and having a grumpy nature, the leprechaun was depicted as a solitary creature, usually working on a single shoe rather than a pair. He was a wizened, bearded dwarf who wore a green suit and cap and worked day and night mending the shoes of the other fairies.

The Irish were generally afraid of fairies, who could kidnap brides and snatch babies from their cradles. They believed that listening to fairy music could make a person lose all sense of human sympathy, after which the person might become a seer, a great poet, or a musician. Some scholars believe that fairies were the gods of ancient Ireland and that when the Christian gods took their place, they dwindled in both status and size to the miniature beings they are today.

Parades

The St. Patrick's Day Parade is largely an American invention. It was well established in Boston, Philadelphia, Atlanta, Cleveland, and many other American cities by the 1850s; by the 1870s, there were enough Irish living in Los Angeles to make the parade there an annual event. Today there are parades on March 17 in at least thirty states.

The largest takes place in New York City. It began in 1763, when small groups of Irish settlers banded together and followed the cobblestone streets to celebrate at their local taverns. Such informal marches became more organized after the Revolutionary War, when a veterans' group called the Friendly Sons of St. Patrick began advertising their ancestry on March 17. The growing number of Irish immigrants who poured into New York following the 1840s potato famine gave rise to religious and political tensions, particularly with British Protestants, and the St. Patrick's Day parade often erupted in fights and violence. It was the Ancient Order of Hibernians who finally converted the parade from a rough, informal social outing to a large, well-organized civil rights demonstration. As the Irish became more influential in New York City politics, the parade gradually quieted down. But even today the parade often provokes controversy, as it did when gay and lesbian Irish-Americans wanted to march as a group up Fifth Avenue.

No matter where the parades take place, they usually feature marching bands, fife and drum corps, and musicians wearing kilts and playing such favorite Irish songs as "Danny Boy," "The Minstrel Boy," and "Garryowen." Local dignitaries in morning coats and top hats wear green, white, and orange sashes and carry SHILLE-LAGHS. There are green hats, green banners, and green carnations everywhere.

Shamrock

Shamrock is an English name for the plant known in Gaelic as *seamrog*. It is a small, three-leaved plant similar to clover. The ancient Druids associated it with the coming of spring and the rebirth of the natural world at the **VERNAL EQUINOX**. Even today, it is customary in Ireland to plant something new in the garden each day during "Patrick's Week," the week following March 17.

St. Patrick is said to have used the shamrock when he explained the theological doctrine of the Holy Trinity (three persons in one God) to the unconverted Irish pagans, pointing out that the shamrock has three separate leaves but is a single plant with a single stem. This legend may have arisen after the fact to justify the high esteem in which the shamrock was traditionally held by the Irish people.

The shamrock still grows freely all over Ireland, where the mild climate keeps it green all year. Although it started out as a symbol of St. Patrick and his teachings, over the centuries it became symbolic of the way the Irish felt about their country. In the nineteenth and twentieth centuries, it became an emblem of Irish rebellion and, more than ever, a symbol of national pride.

Shillelagh

Shillelagh is an old Irish word for a short, stout club or cudgel made of oak. It is also the name of a famous oak forest that once stood in County Wicklow. A club or cudgel cut from one of these oaks was referred to as a "sprig of shillelagh." Eventually the name was used to describe any cudgel made of oak, and it served as an apt symbol of the staunch spirit of the Irish.

The shillelagh was often used as a weapon. Ancient feuds between families were often fought with shillelaghs at county fairs. Sometimes two of the clubs were used, so that the fighter could strike with one hand and fend off his opponent with the other. The typical Irishman is often depicted swinging a shillelagh, even though a real shillelagh was never swung but was grasped in the middle.

When the English cut down most of Ireland's oak trees, Irishmen started cutting their clubs or walking sticks from blackthorn hedges. Tourists today bring back mock shillelaghs made of blackthorn bound with green ribbons as souvenirs. In St. Patrick's Day PARADES, officials often carry blackthorn walking sticks, while children in the crowd wave toy shillelaghs made of green plastic.

FURTHER READING

Appleton, LeRoy H., and Stephen Bridges. *Symbolism in Liturgical Art*. New York: Scribner, 1959.

Barth, Edna. *Shamrocks, Harps, and Shillelaghs: The Story of the St. Patrick's Day Symbols*. New York: Seabury Press, 1977.

Bellenir, Karen. *Religious Holidays and Calendars*. 3rd ed. Detroit: Omnigraphics, 2004.

Christianson, Stephen G., and Jane M. Hatch. *The American Book of Days*. 4th ed. New York: H.W. Wilson, 2000.

Cohen, Hennig, and Tristram Potter Coffin. *The Folklore of American Holidays*. 3rd ed. Detroit: Gale Research, 1999.

Crim, Keith R. *The Perennial Dictionary of World Religions*. San Francisco: Harper & Row, 1989.

Danaher, Kevin. *The Year in Ireland*. 4th ed. St. Paul, MN: Irish Books and Media, 1984.

Harper, Howard V. *Days and Customs of All Faiths*. 1957. Reprint. Detroit: Omnigraphics, 1990.

Henderson, Helene, ed. *Holidays, Festivals, and Celebrations of the World Dictionary*. 3rd ed. Detroit: Omnigraphics, 2005.

Ickis, Marguerite. *The Book of Festivals and Holidays the World Over*. New York: Dodd, Mead, 1970.

MacDonald, Margaret R., ed. *The Folklore of World Holidays*. Detroit: Gale Research, 1992.

Santino, Jack. *All Around the Year: Holidays and Celebrations in American Life*. Urbana: University of Illinois Press, 1994.

Tuleja, Tad. *Curious Customs: The Stories Behind 296 Popular American Rituals*. New York: Harmony, 1987.

Urlin, Ethel L. *Festivals, Holy Days, and Saints' Days*. 1915. Reprint. Detroit: Omnigraphics, 1992.

Weiser, Franz Xaver. *Handbook of Christian Feasts and Customs*. New York: Harcourt, Brace, 1958.

WEB SITES

Library of Congress
www.americaslibrary.gov/cgi-bin/page.cgi/jb/modern/stpatric_1

St. Patrick's Festival of Dublin, Ireland
www.stpatricksday.ie

St. Stephen's Day
(Boxing Day)

Type of Holiday: Religious (Christian)
Date of Observation: December 26
Where Celebrated: Australia, Austria, Canada, England, Germany, Ireland, Poland, Sweden, and other Christian nations
Symbols and Customs: Christmas Box, Horse, Wren
Related Holidays: Christmas

ORIGINS

St. Stephen became the first Christian martyr on this day, December 26, somewhere between 31 and 35 C.E. According to the New Testament book of Acts, Stephen was chosen by the Apostles as one of the first seven deacons of the church in Jerusalem. He was later denounced as a blasphemer by the Sanhedrin, the Jewish council in ancient Palestine, and stoned to death outside the gate of Jerusalem that now bears his name. Stephen's death is considered an example of the highest class of martyrdom, because he intentionally gave his life for Christ.

The basis of saint day remembrances—for St. Stepehen as well as other saints—is found in ancient Roman tradition. On the anniversary of a death, families would share a ritual meal at the grave site of an ancestor. This practice was adopted by Christians who began observing a ritual meal on the death anniversary of ancestors in the faith, especially martyrs. As a result, most Christian saint days are associated with the death of the saint. There are three important exceptions. John the Baptist, the Virgin Mary, and Jesus are honored on their nativities (birthdays). Many who suffered martyrdom are remembered on saint days in the calendars of several Orthodox, Catholic, and Protestant sects.

In England, Australia, Canada, and many other countries, the day after **CHRIST-MAS** is Boxing Day. There are a number of theories about where this holiday got its name. Some point to the church alms-box, the contents of which were not dispensed until the day after Christmas. The most popular explanation is that it was named after the earthenware CHRISTMAS BOXES that servants and tradespeople used to carry around to collect tips and end-of-the-year bonuses. Some people believe that it comes from the Arabic *backsheesh*, meaning "gratuity." Crusaders brought this word back with them, and it became common for anyone who had rendered service to another person during the year to expect *backsheesh* at Christmas.

SYMBOLS AND CUSTOMS

Christmas Box

At one time, every ship that went off on a long voyage kept a box on board for donations to the priest who, in return, was expected to offer masses for the safety of the ship and its sailors. The box was not to be opened until the vessel returned. If the voyage had been rough, it was usually quite full. Because mass at that time was called Christ-mass, the boxes kept to pay for it were called "Christmass Boxes."

A relic of these ancient boxes can be seen in the earthenware or wooden boxes with slits in the top used by servants and children in nineteenth-century England to gather money during the Christmas season, giving rise to the name Boxing Day. Servants, apprentices, and tradespeople, especially in London, broke their boxes open as soon as Christmas was over. Christmas boxes were also associated with the custom of "doling," in which bands of young, poor, and often rowdy people went around demanding gifts of money and food from the wealthy and privileged. In the 1820s and 1830s, the English custom of Christmas boxes was transformed into the Victorian custom of exchanging Christmas gifts.

The earthen savings box can still be found in the Netherlands, where it is commonly made in the shape of a pig, much like the American piggy bank. It is considered bad luck to break open this box, known as "The Feast Pig," before Christmas.

Horse

St. Stephen is the patron saint of horses. According to a Swedish legend, he had five of them. As he made his rounds preaching the word of God and one of his horses got tired, he simply mounted the next. After his death, his body was tied to the back of an unbroken colt, which brought him back to his hometown, Norrala, to be buried. The church that was later built on the site of his grave became a place of pilgrimage to which owners brought their sick animals, particularly horses, for healing. Some scholars think that this legendary Swedish St. Stephen is a mythical figure rather than the New Testament martyr, and that the legend surrounding him and his horses was an attempt to account for the folk customs that were already well established on this day.

In England, at one time horses were bled on St. Stephen's Day in the belief that it would benefit them—a custom that is still carried out in some parts of Austria. During St. Stephen's Day services in Munich, Germany, it was customary for more than 200 men on horseback to ride three times around the interior of a church, a practice that wasn't abolished until 1876. Horse races are common on this day, and horses are often fed consecrated salt or bread as a good-luck charm.

The customs associated with horses on this day appear to be non-Christian in origin. It is possible that horses were sacrificed or slaughtered on this day in pagan times, and that the horse races that often took place were a prelude to some kind of purification ceremony for houses and fields. (*See also* **ST. GEORGE'S DAY.**)

Wren

In England and Ireland it was the custom on the day after Christmas to "hunt the wren." Young men and boys would dress up in leaves and branches to go out hunting, and after they had killed a bird, they fastened it to the top of a long pole and went from house to house collecting money. In some areas, a feather from the wren was exchanged for a small donation and then kept as protection against shipwreck during the coming year. After all the houses in the village had been visited, the wren was laid out on a funeral bier and carried to the churchyard, where it was buried with great solemnity. Sometimes the bird was boiled and eaten.

Known as "the king of birds," the wren was probably once regarded as sacred. Hunting it at Christmastime may have been all that remained of the primitive custom of slaying the divine animal. Carrying its body from door to door was apparently intended to convey to each house a portion of the bird's virtues. Eating the bird may have originally been some sort of communion feast.

FURTHER READING

Bellenir, Karen. *Religious Holidays and Calendars.* 3rd ed. Detroit: Omnigraphics, 2004.
Brewster, H. Pomeroy. *Saints and Festivals of the Christian Church.* 1904. Reprint. Detroit: Omnigraphics, 1990.

Crippen, T.G. *Christmas and Christmas Lore*. 1923. Reprint. Detroit: Omnigraphics, 1990.

Henderson, Helene, ed. *Holidays, Festivals, and Celebrations of the World Dictionary*. 3rd ed. Detroit: Omnigraphics, 2005.

Hervey, Thomas K. *The Book of Christmas*. Boston: Roberts Brothers, 1888.

Miles, Clement A. *Christmas in Ritual and Tradition, Christian and Pagan*. 1912. Reprint. Detroit: Omnigraphics, 1990.

Santino, Jack. *All Around the Year: Holidays and Celebrations in American Life*. Urbana: University of Illinois Press, 1994.

Schmidt, Leigh Eric. *Consumer Rites: The Buying and Selling of American Holidays*. Princeton: Princeton University Press, 1995.

Urlin, Ethel L. *Festivals, Holy Days, and Saints' Days*. 1915. Reprint. Detroit: Omnigraphics, 1992.

WEB SITES

Australian Media
www.irishfestivals.net/saintstephensday.htm

New Advent Catholic Encyclopedia
www.newadvent.org/cathen/14286b.htm

St. Swithin's Day

Type of Holiday: Religious (Christian)
Date of Observation: July 15
Where Celebrated: British Isles, United States
Symbols and Customs: Rain

ORIGINS

The humble monk known as Swithin (or Swithun) was chosen by King Egbert of the Anglo-Saxon kingdom of Wessex to tutor his son, Ethelwulf. When Ethelwulf succeeded his father in 839, he chose Swithin as bishop of Winchester, the capital of Wessex. When Swithin died in 862, he left instructions that he was to be buried outside in the churchyard—not inside the cathedral, as most bishops were—because he hated any kind of ostentation or show and wanted the money that his monks were going to spend on a mausoleum to be spent helping the poor instead. He chose as his gravesite a place where rain from the church eaves poured down and saturated the earth. It was taken as a sign of St. Swithin's humility that he chose this wet and undesirable area.

A hundred years passed, and a number of healing miracles were reported by those who visited St. Swithin's grave. Eventually the church authorities decided it wasn't right to have such a great man buried anywhere except under the altar, so they made arrangements to move St. Swithin's bones. As the solemn procession started out, however, there was such an intense storm that the event had to be postponed. The RAIN continued for forty days, causing widespread flooding, and the church authorities began to get the idea that St. Swithin didn't want to be moved. So they called the whole thing off, and the rain immediately stopped.

The only problem with this story is that it isn't true. St. Swithin's bones were moved to Winchester Cathedral without incident on July 15, 971—a sunny day. But his legend, which spread from medieval England into Ireland, has made predictions concerning the weather the most enduring part of his feast day.

The basis of saint day remembrances—for St. Swithin and other saints—is found in ancient Roman tradition. On the anniversary of a death, families would share a ritual meal at the grave site of an ancestor. This practice was adopted by Christians who began observing a ritual meal on the death anniversary of ancestors in the faith, especially martyrs. As a result, most Christian saint days are associated with the death of the saint. There are three important exceptions. John the Baptist, the Virgin Mary, and Jesus are honored on their nativities (birthdays). Many who suffered martyrdom are remembered on saint days in the calendars of several Orthodox, Catholic, and Protestant sects.

SYMBOLS AND CUSTOMS

Rain

There is an old saying in England that "On Swithin's Day, if it should rain, for forty days it will remain"—a reference to the six-week downpour that supposedly occurred when the saint's remains were moved from the churchyard into the cathedral. A few gentle showers on July 15 are not usually considered a bad thing; in fact, such weather is described as St. Swithin "christening the apples." But no one wants a heavy rain, for fear that it will last as long as that legendary storm.

Just like St. Médard of France and St. Isidor of Spain, St. Swithin is frequently called up when rain is needed—particularly by farmers, even though they greet rain on St. Swithin's Day with considerable anxiety. He is widely known as "the rain saint of England."

FURTHER READING

Brewster, H. Pomeroy. *Saints and Festivals of the Christian Church*. 1904. Reprint. Detroit: Omnigraphics, 1990.

Chambers, Robert. *The Book of Days*. 2 vols. 1862-64. Reprint. Detroit: Omnigraphics, 1990.

Christianson, Stephen G., and Jane M. Hatch. *The American Book of Days*. 4th ed. New York: H.W. Wilson, 2000.

Cohen, Hennig, and Tristram Potter Coffin. *The Folklore of American Holidays*. 3rd ed. Detroit: Gale Research, 1999.

Coulson, John, ed. *The Saints: A Concise Biographical Dictionary*. New York: Hawthorn Books, 1958.

Danaher, Kevin. *The Year in Ireland*. 4th ed. St. Paul, MN: Irish Books and Media, 1984.

Dunkling, Leslie. *A Dictionary of Days*. New York: Facts on File, 1988.

Farmer, David Hugh. *The Oxford Dictionary of Saints*. 5th ed. New York: Oxford University Press, 2003.

Harper, Howard V. *Days and Customs of All Faiths*. 1957. Reprint. Detroit: Omnigraphics, 1990.

Henderson, Helene, ed. *Holidays, Festivals, and Celebrations of the World Dictionary*. 3rd ed. Detroit: Omnigraphics, 2005.

MacDonald, Margaret R., ed. *The Folklore of World Holidays*. Detroit: Gale Research, 1992.

Spicer, Dorothy Gladys. *The Book of Festivals*. 1937. Reprint. Detroit: Omnigraphics, 1990.

Urlin, Ethel L. *Festivals, Holy Days, and Saints' Days*. 1915. Reprint. Detroit: Omnigraphics, 1992.

WEB SITE

New Advent Catholic Encyclopedia
www.newadvent.org/cathen/14357c.htm

St. Sylvester's Day

Type of Holiday: Religious (Christian)
Date of Observation: December 31
Where Celebrated: Austria, Belgium, France, Germany, Hungary, Switzerland
Symbols and Customs: Bells, Pig
Related Holidays: New Year's Eve

ORIGINS

St. Sylvester was Pope in the year 325 C.E., when the Emperor Constantine declared that the pagan religion of Rome would be replaced by Christianity as the official religion of the Empire. Although it is unclear exactly what role, if any, St. Sylvester played in this important event, he is usually given at least some of the credit for stamping out paganism. A number of European countries—including Belgium, Germany, and Switzerland—observe a holiday on the anniversary of Pope Sylvester's death in 335.

The basis of saint day remembrances—for St. Sylvester and other saints—is found in ancient Roman tradition. On the anniversary of a death, families would share a ritual meal at the grave site of an ancestor. This practice was adopted by Christians who began observing a ritual meal on the death anniversary of ancestors in the faith, especially martyrs. As a result, most Christian saint days are associated with the death of the saint. There are three important exceptions. John the Baptist, the Virgin Mary, and Jesus are honored on their nativities (birthdays). Many who suffered martyrdom are remembered on saint days in the calendars of several Orthodox, Catholic, and Protestant sects.

These remembrances take place in many countries. In Belgium, the last girl or boy to get out of bed on December 31 is nicknamed "Sylvester" and must pay a fine to his or her sisters and brothers—which means that most young people get up very early in the morning on this day. There is a superstition that the young girl who does not finish her work by sunset will not have any marriage prospects in the coming year.

In Switzerland, there is an old folk tradition that the spirits of darkness are out and about on the last night of the year. These demons must be frightened away by ringing BELLS and lashing whips. For centuries men and boys have dressed up as "Sylvesterklause" in costumes made from twigs, mosses, and other natural things. They walk through the countryside, stopping at every farmhouse to yodel a greeting and to receive coins and mulled wine. They perform dances designed to scare off demons and ring the huge bells they carry before moving on to the next house. Because St. Sylvester's Day is also **NEW YEAR'S EVE**, the Swiss celebrate by lighting bonfires in the mountains and ringing church bells to signal the passing of the old year and the beginning of the new. In some Swiss villages, grain is threshed on specially constructed platforms to ensure a plentiful harvest in the coming year.

In Germany, it is considered lucky to eat the traditional St. Sylvester's Day carp and to keep a few of the fish scales as a New Year's charm.

SYMBOLS AND CUSTOMS

Bells

The custom of making noise—in this case, by ringing bells—to scare off evil demons can be traced back to very ancient times, long before the arrival of Christianity. The Sylvesterklause who go from house to house on this day in Switzerland wear costumes that include enormous bells, and church bells are rung in every village. In Geneva, Switzerland, a huge crowd gathers in front of the Gothic Cathedral of St. Pierre to listen to the midnight chiming of the bells, especially "La Clémence," believed to be the oldest and most beautiful bell in all of Europe.

Pig

In Austria and Hungary, it is not uncommon in restaurants and cafés for the owner to set a pig loose at midnight on St. Sylvester's Day. Everyone tries to touch it because it is considered a symbol of good luck. In private homes, a pig made of marzipan might be hung from the ceiling or chandelier, with a gold piece placed in its mouth to symbolize the wish for wealth. At midnight, everyone touches the pig for good luck. In Vienna, people sometimes lead young pigs by pink satin leashes along fashionable city streets on St. Sylvester's Day.

FURTHER READING

Brewster, H. Pomeroy. *Saints and Festivals of the Christian Church*. 1904. Reprint. Detroit: Omnigraphics, 1990.

Christianson, Stephen G., and Jane M. Hatch. *The American Book of Days*. 4th ed. New York: H.W. Wilson, 2000.

Dobler, Lavinia G. *Customs and Holidays Around the World*. New York: Fleet Pub. Corp., 1962.

Henderson, Helene, ed. *Holidays, Festivals, and Celebrations of the World Dictionary*. 3rd ed. Detroit: Omnigraphics, 2005.

Spicer, Dorothy Gladys. *Festivals of Western Europe*. 1958. Reprint. Detroit: Omni-
    graphics, 1993.

Spicer, Dorothy Gladys. *The Book of Festivals*. 1937. Reprint. Detroit: Omnigraphics,
    1990.

Van Straalen, Alice. *The Book of Holidays Around the World*. New York: Dutton, 1986.

WEB SITE

St. Anthony Messenger Press
www.americancatholic.org/Features/SaintOfDay/default.asp?id=1246

St. Thomas the Apostle's Day

Type of Holiday: Religious (Christian)
Date of Observation: December 21 by Anglicans and Malabar Christians; July 3
    by Roman Catholics; October 6 in the East
Where Celebrated: England, Guatemala, India, Pakistan, United States, and by
    Christians all over the world
Symbols and Customs: Barring the Door, Divination Rites, Doleing, Flying Pole
    Dance
Related Holidays: Winter Solstice

ORIGINS

St. Thomas the Apostle is often referred to as "Doubting Thomas" because he
refused to believe the other Apostles when they told him that Jesus had appeared
to them on the evening of the first **EASTER** and showed them the wounds he had
received when he was crucified. Thomas, who wasn't with them at the time, insisted that he had to touch Jesus' wounds with his own hands before he could believe.
Eight days later he had an opportunity to do just that, but he is still remembered
for his skeptical nature.

When the Apostles left Jerusalem and went out into the world to spread the
Gospel, Thomas went to India. He worked as a carpenter there, preaching the
word of God until he was captured and killed by King Mazdai, whose wife and
son he had already converted. Along India's Malabar coast, there is still a community of Christians who call themselves the "Christians of St. Thomas" and claim
that their ancestors were converted by St. Thomas the Apostle. Thomas is the

patron saint of India and Pakistan, and his feast day is a major celebration among the Malabar Christians.

The basis of saint day remembrances—for St. Thomas and for other saints—is found in ancient Roman tradition. On the anniversary of a death, families would share a ritual meal at the grave site of an ancestor. This practice was adopted by Christians who began observing a ritual meal on the death anniversary of ancestors in the faith, especially martyrs. As a result, most Christian saint days are associated with the death of the saint. There are three important exceptions. John the Baptist, the Virgin Mary, and Jesus are honored on their nativities (birthdays). Many who suffered martyrdom are remembered on saint days in the calendars of several Orthodox, Catholic, and Protestant sects.

St. Thomas's Day falls on December 21, the **WINTER SOLSTICE**, which explains why he appears in folklore as a saint of light and darkness. Because of his connection with the mysterious turning of the year, St. Thomas is often invoked for protection against evil and clues about what the future will hold (*see* DIVINATION RITES). Roman Catholics used to celebrate his feast in December but later shifted it to July 3, the day on which his relics were transferred. Episcopalian, Lutheran, and some other Protestant churches continue to observe December 21 as St. Thomas's Day, while Orthodox Christians observe it on October 6.

SYMBOLS AND CUSTOMS

Barring the Door

In western Europe, it was customary for schoolchildren to bar their teacher from entering the school on St. Thomas's Day. They would rush to school as early as possible in the morning so they would be there before their teacher arrived. Then they would barricade the door, refusing to let him enter until he promised them a day off. In Belgium, students demanded a feast of cakes and ale, and children would often bar the door against their parents as well. In Denmark, St. Thomas's Day was a school festival, when children brought gifts of money or candles to their teacher and he, in return, gave them a feast.

The custom of barring schoolmasters probably had less to do with St. Thomas than with the fact that December 21 usually coincided with the end of the school term.

Divination Rites

St. Thomas was often consulted for predictions about the future because of his connection with the ominous time of year when the world turned from darkness to light. One common practice on St. Thomas's Eve was to throw a pair of shoes backwards over the shoulder and then leave the room without looking to see how they fell. If, in the morning, they were found pointing towards the door, it was a sign that the person to whom they belonged would leave home during the coming year, perhaps to be married. If they pointed inward, the person knew that he or she would not be changing homes for the next 12 months.

Young English girls used to peel an onion, wrap it up in a handkerchief, and sleep with it under their pillows on the eve of St. Thomas's Day, a practice that would make them dream of their future husbands. The actual feast day was sometimes thought to be unlucky for weddings; because it was the shortest day of the year, it was regarded as an omen of a short married life. But in some areas it was deliberately chosen for weddings because the brief hours of daylight on the solstice left the young couple with less time to have second thoughts about getting married.

Doleing

In England at one time, it was customary on St. Thomas's Day for the poorer inhabitants of the parish to call on their wealthier neighbors and receive a gift or "dole" of food or money. In return, they would give their benefactor a sprig of holly or mistletoe. This custom gave rise to the name "Doleing Day," although in some parts of England it was known as Gooding Day or Mumping Day, since those who had to beg were said to be "on the mump."

During the nineteenth century in England, workmen often received groceries and other goods in lieu of wages. They would be given vouchers that could only be exchanged for food at their employer's "tommy" shop. The loaves of bread that were traditionally distributed as charity on St. Thomas's Day became known as "tommy," and the word was later used to describe any kind of food or provisions distributed to workers or soldiers.

Flying Pole Dance

On St. Thomas's Day in Guatemala, the Mayan Indians honor the sun god they worshipped long before they became Christians with a dangerous ritual known as the palo voladore or 'flying pole dance.' Three men climb to the top of a 50-foot pole. As one beats a drum and plays a flute, the other two wind a long rope attached to the pole around one foot and jump. If they land on their feet, it is believed that the sun god will be pleased and that the days will start getting longer—a safe bet in view of the fact that St. Thomas's day coincides with the **WINTER SOLSTICE** (*see also* **CORPUS CHRISTI, FEAST OF**).

FURTHER READING

Bellenir, Karen. *Religious Holidays and Calendars*. 3rd ed. Detroit: Omnigraphics, 2004.

Chambers, Robert. *The Book of Days*. 2 vols. 1862-64. Reprint. Detroit: Omnigraph-ics, 1990.

Christianson, Stephen G., and Jane M. Hatch. *The American Book of Days*. 4th ed. New York: H.W. Wilson, 2000.

Dunkling, Leslie. *A Dictionary of Days*. New York: Facts on File, 1988.

Harper, Howard V. *Days and Customs of All Faiths*. 1957. Reprint. Detroit: Omni-graphics, 1990.

Henderson, Helene, ed. *Holidays, Festivals, and Celebrations of the World Dictionary*. 3rd ed. Detroit: Omnigraphics, 2005.

Hole, Christina. *Saints in Folklore*. New York: M. Barrows, 1965.

MacDonald, Margaret R., ed. *The Folklore of World Holidays*. Detroit: Gale Research, 1992.

Spicer, Dorothy Gladys. *The Book of Festivals*. 1937. Reprint. Detroit: Omnigraphics, 1990.

Urlin, Ethel L. *Festivals, Holy Days, and Saints' Days*. 1915. Reprint. Detroit: Omni-graphics, 1992.

Van Straalen, Alice. *The Book of Holidays Around the World*. New York: Dutton, 1986.

WEB SITES

New Advent Catholic Encyclopedia
www.newadvent.org/cathen/14658b.htm

St. Anthony Messenger Press
www.americancatholic.org/Features/SaintOfDay/default.asp?id=1433

St. Urho's Day

Type of Holiday: Folkloric
Date of Observation: March 16
Where Celebrated: Minnesota, Michigan, and by Finnish-American communities across the United States and Canada
Symbols and Customs: Chant, Fish Soup, Ode to St. Urho, St. Urho Statue
Colors: Purple, the color of grapes, and Nile green, the color of grapevines and grasshoppers
Related Holidays: St. Patrick's Day

ORIGINS

St. Urho's Day is a celebration of fairly recent origin. It was invented in the spring of 1956 by Richard L. Mattson, a manager at Ketola's Department Store in Virginia, Minnesota, a town about ninety minutes north of Duluth whose population included many immigrant iron mine workers. One of Mattson's coworkers, a woman of Irish descent named Gene McCavic, was teasing him about the fact that the Finns did not have a famous patron saint like St. Patrick. In a burst of inspiration and national pride he made one up, naming him St. Urho and giving him credit for chasing the poisonous frogs out of Finland in much the same way that St. Patrick drove the snakes out of Ireland. Urho is a fairly common name in Finland, and it just so happened that the president of Finland at the time was Urho Kekkonen. With Mattson's help, McCavic wrote an ODE TO ST. URHO that told the story of a *poika* (Finnish for "boy") named Urho who uses his powerful voice—part of the great strength he has developed from eating FISH SOUP and sour milk—to chase away the frogs that have been plaguing his homeland.

The idea caught on, and a few years later a professor from Bemidji State University named Sulo Havumaki elaborated on the St. Urho legend by changing the plague from frogs to grasshoppers (locusts), which destroyed the grapes that were at one time so plentiful in Finland. Although St. Urho's Day was originally supposed to be May 24, it was shifted to March 16, the day before **ST. PATRICK'S DAY**, so that Finnish-Americans could get their celebration underway before the Irish-Americans started. The holiday spread from a few towns in Minnesota—Virginia, Menahga, New York Mills, Wolf Lake, and Finland—to the Upper Peninsula of Michigan and parts of Montana and Ontario. Today it is recognized in both Canada and all fifty American states, although it is only celebrated in areas with a large Finnish-American population. There is even evidence that the holiday has been carried back to Finland by native Finns who have visited the United States.

The typical St. Urho's Day observance begins at dawn on March 16. The women and children gather along the shore of the nearest lake and repeat the legendary CHANT that St. Urho used to get rid of the frogs in Finland so many years ago. The men, who are all dressed in green, form a procession to the lake, waving pitchforks and making hopping or kicking movements like the imaginary grasshoppers who litter their path. Along the way, they change from green to purple clothing, symbolizing the disappearance of the grasshoppers and the reemergence of the grapes. Afterward, there is a celebration at which people sing, dance to polka music, and drink wine or grape juice.

Richard Mattson died on June 5, 2001, shortly before his 88th birthday. He was the manager at Ketola's Department Store for forty-two years but is probably best remembered for his creation of the St. Urho legend.

SYMBOLS AND CUSTOMS

Chant

The chant that is repeated wherever Finnish-Americans gather to celebrate St. Urho's Day is "Heinäsirkka, heinäsirkka, meine täätä hiiteen," which means, roughly, "Grasshopper, grasshopper, go away."

Fish Soup

Mojakkaa (moy-yah-kah) or fish soup is a favorite Finnish dish. Along with sour whole milk, it is mentioned in Gene McCavic's original ODE TO ST. URHO as one of the foods that made the young Urho so strong.

Ode to St. Urho

The original "Ode to St. Urho," written on a piece of wrapping paper in Ketola's Department Store, has been preserved at the Iron World Museum in Chisholm, Minnesota. It is written in Finnish dialect and goes like this:

> Ooksie kooksie coolama vee
> Santia Urho is ta poy for me!
> He sase out ta hoppers as pig as birds
> Neffer peefor haff I hurd dose words!
> He reely told dose pugs of kreen
> Braaffest finn I effer seen!
> Some celebrate for St. Pat unt hiss nakes
> Putt Urho poyka kot what it takes.
> He got tall and trong from feelia sour
> Unt ate culla moyakka effery hour.
> Tat's why day guy could sase does peetles
> What crew as thick as chack bine needles.
> So let's give a cheer in hower pest vay
> On this sixteenth of March, St. Urho's Tay!

St. Urho Statue

Statues of St. Urho can be seen in both Menahga and Finland, Minnesota. The St. Urho in Menagha was originally carved in 1982 by a chainsaw sculptor from a 2,000-pound oak block, but it has since been replaced with a fiberglass replica to make it more resistant to the harsh Minnesota weather. It shows a twelve-foot-high figure of a bearded man with a grasshopper at the end of his pitchfork. The one in Finland is eighteen feet tall and resembles a totem pole rather than an actual human figure.

FURTHER READING

Trawicky, Bernard, and Ruth W. Gregory. *Anniversaries and Holidays*. 5th ed. Chicago: American Library Assocation, 2000.

WEB SITE

Roadside America
www.roadsideamerica.com/sights/sightstory.php?tip_AttrId=%3D11468

Sukkot
(Sukkoth, Succoth)

Type of Holiday: Religious (Jewish)
Date of Observation: 15-21 Tishri (begins between September 20 and October 18)
Where Celebrated: Europe, Israel, United States, and by Jews all over the world
Symbols and Customs: Beating the Willow, Four Species, Sukkah, Water Libation Ceremony
Related Holidays: Simhat Torah, Yom Kippur

ORIGINS

The holiday of Sukkot is part of the traditions of Judaism, one of the oldest continuously observed religions in the world. Its history extends back beyond the advent of the written word. Its people trace their roots to a common ancestor, Abraham, and then back even farther to the very moment of creation.

According to Jewish belief, the law given to the Jewish people by God contained everything they needed to live a holy life, including the ability to be reinterpreted in new historical situations. Judaism, therefore, is the expression of the Jewish people, attempting to live holy (set apart) lives in accordance with the instructions given by God. Obedience to the law is central to Judaism, but there is no one central authority. Sources of divine authority are God, the Torah, interpretations of the Torah by respected teachers, and tradition. Religious observances and the study of Jewish law are conducted under the supervision of a teacher called a rabbi.

There are several sects within Judaism. Orthodox Judaism is characterized by an affirmation of the traditional Jewish faith, strict adherence to customs such as keeping the Sabbath, participation in ceremonies and rituals, and the observance of dietary regulations. Conservative Jewish congregations seek to retain many ancient traditions but without the accompanying demand for strict observance. Reform Judaism stresses modern biblical criticism and emphasizes ethical teachings more than ritualistic observance. Hasidism is a mystical sect of Judaism that teaches enthusiastic prayer as a means of communion with God. The Reconstructionist movement began early in the twentieth century in an effort to "reconstruct" Judaism with the community rather than the synagogue as its center.

The Jewish holiday of Sukkot can be traced back to an ancient Canaanite holiday held after the grape harvest, around the time of the **AUTUMN EQUINOX**. Jewish farmers made little booths or SUKKAHS from the branches of fruit trees and evergreens and lived in them throughout the seven days of the celebration. It was primarily a festival of thanksgiving, a time to celebrate the fruit harvest—as opposed to **SHAVUOT**, which marked the end of the grain harvest. Many farmers collected some of their produce, gathered up their families, and made a pilgrimage to Jerusalem for the festival. Often referred to as the Feast of the Ingathering because of its associations with the gathering of the harvest and the close of the agricultural year, Sukkot also involved the performance of special ceremonies designed to induce rainfall.

After the Jews were released from slavery in Egypt, they wandered for forty years before entering the Promised Land. During this period they lived in tents or booths (called *succot* or *sukkot*), which they pitched wherever they happened to stop for the night. When they finally reached the Promised Land, most of them became farmers. Because the fields were so far from their homes, they would often live in the fields for the entire period of the harvest, once again building *succot* to protect themselves from the sun during the day and the cold wind at night. The holiday that originally celebrated the ingathering of the harvest, therefore, took on added significance as the Feast of Tabernacles or the Feast of Booths, commemorating the period in Jewish history when the *sukkah* was the only home that the Jews knew.

Sukkot begins at sundown on the fourteenth day of Tishri. On the first two days, people build small huts out of branches to recall the sukkot in which their ancestors lived. The inside is hung with apples, grapes, corn, pomegranates, and other fruits and vegetables to commemorate the harvest. In the synagogue, Jews give thanks to God for the plants He has created by waving the FOUR SPECIES in all directions. The seventh day is more of a holiday than the third through sixth days, which are considered half-holidays. According to tradition, this is the last possible day on which one can seek and obtain forgiveness for the sins of the previous year—an extension of the Day of Atonement or **YOM KIPPUR**. Pious Jews stay up half the night chanting psalms and reading sacred books. Most try to stay awake until midnight, when they believe that the heavens open up. Children in particular believe that if they make a wish at the moment the skies open, it is certain to come true.

The eighth day of Sukkot, known as Shemini Aztaret, is the Day of Solemn Assembly. A more serious mood prevails on this day, and it is customary to eat meals in the SUKKAH. Special services for people who have died are held in the synagogue, and prayers are offered for rain in Israel. No matter where they live, Jews pray for rain in their homeland during this season because it is needed there to ensure a good spring harvest. The afternoon of Shemini Aztaret is spent visiting and receiving friends and relatives. The following day, known as **SIMHAT TORAH**, celebrates the completion of the reading of the Torah, which immediately begins again. Simhat Torah is now celebrated as a separate holiday by Orthodox and Conservative Jews.

Sukkot has remained a major festival throughout the centuries. Ceremonies that were originally held in the Temple have been moved to the synagogue and the home, but the holiday has retained both its agricultural and historical significance. But of all the Jewish festivals, Sukkot has suffered the most from the changes brought about by modern life. It is difficult to build a sukkah in many modern cities, and because the festival is based on events that occurred more than 3,000 years ago, modern Jews have found it difficult to identify with the customs and hardships they are commemorating.

SYMBOLS AND CUSTOMS

Beating the Willow

On the last day of Sukkot, willow twigs (*see* FOUR SPECIES) are beaten against the altar until all the leaves fall off. The usual explanation for this custom is that it symbolizes the fragility of human life, which fades and falls like autumn leaves. Some say that the falling leaves are also symbolic of sins that have been cast away.

The tradition is probably rooted in the primitive belief that the willow is a symbol of fertility and that beating people with willow branches ensures potency and fertility. The beating of the willow branches on the seventh day of Sukkot is not unlike the "Easter smacks" used in some European countries to promote fertility.

Four Species

In the religious services held each morning during Sukkot, Jews engage in a thanksgiving ritual involving four symbolic plants: the *lulav* or date palm, the myrtle, the willow, and the *etrog*, a fragrant citrus fruit that resembles a large lemon. Three myrtle twigs and two willow branches are tied around a long branch of lulav, while the etrog is taken out of its special, well-padded box. As prayers are said, the lulav and the etrog are waved in all directions, and the worshippers thank God for the good things that come from the earth. Because Sukkot has its roots in farming, harvesting, and the world of nature, these prayers usually include a plea for rain to help the crops grow.

These four fruits or "species" were chosen because they were abundant in ancient Israel and would last throughout the seven-day festival without wilting. But over the years, they have accumulated symbolic meaning as well. Some say they stand for the four most important bodily organs: the heart (etrog), the spine (lulav), the eye (myrtle), and the lips or mouth (willow). Another interpretation is that they stand for four different types of people: The etrog represents the person who possesses both beauty and character; the lulav is the person who is beautiful but has no character; the myrtle is the person with character who lacks beauty; and the willow is the person who lacks both. Yet another theory is that they symbolize the four periods of Jewish history: The stately lulav recalls the period of kings and prophets; the fragrant myrtle is a reminder of the Talmudic era of learning and wisdom; the drooping willow symbolizes the Jews' period of exile and wandering; and the etrog, which is both beautiful and fragrant, symbolizes their hope for the future.

A simpler explanation is that the Four Species represent all forms of vegetation. The etrog tree, whose fruit resembles an oversize lemon, is fragrant but needs human attention to help it grow. The lulav or date palm, which has no scent, represents those fruit-bearing trees that can survive on rainwater alone. The myrtle is a pleasant-smelling, ornamental shrub that does not yield edible fruit. And the willow, which needs a great deal of water to grow, has neither fruit nor fragrance but is useful for building things and for making fires.

In the synagogue, there is a procession in which the lulav and the etrog are waved in unison each day during Sukkot. On the seventh day, the procession is repeated seven times. After the service, the lulav is given to the children, who weave rings, bracelets, and baskets from strips of palm leaf.

Sukkah

Building a sukkah in the backyard—or on a terrace or rooftop—is the primary tradition associated with Sukkot. It must have at least two standing walls, and the roof must be made of leaves and twigs so that the stars can shine through and people will be reminded of God in heaven. Some Jews avoid using nails when they build the sukkah because metal is associated with the tools of war.

The sukkah represents the huts in which Jewish farmers traditionally lived during the harvest season in Palestine and the tents in which the exiled Jews were sheltered during their desert wanderings. It also stands as a symbol of the brevity and insecurity of human life. For modern Jews, it serves as a reminder of the lack of safety and security experienced by millions of Jews in Germany, Italy, Poland, Romania, Hungary, and other countries. According to the Talmud, the sukkah's frail roof should remind people not to put too much trust in the power of man.

Traditionally, all meals are eaten in the sukkah throughout the festival. But since it is often impossible to do this in modern cities, the rules have been modified to require that at least one meal be taken in the booth each day and each night of the festival. Since building a sukkah may be impossible for those who live in apartment buildings, the usual solution is a communal sukkah set up in the courtyard of the synagogue. The greens, fruits, and flowers with which it is decorated are more likely to come from the local florist or grocery store, and a perfunctory visit to the sukkah after the synagogue service often substitutes for spending the night in it.

The task of building the sukkah, as well as eating and sleeping in it, usually falls to the male members of the family. The mother and girls are responsible for decorating it, typically with the seven Israeli farm products mentioned in the Bible (grapes, figs, pomegranates, wheat, barley, olives, and honey). In Europe, the decorations often include cutout paper chains and lanterns, pictures of holy men and places, and birds made out of egg shells and feathers.

Water Libation Ceremony

At one time, the second day of Sukkot marked the ancient water-drawing (or water-pouring) ceremony described in the Talmud. A golden pitcher was filled with water from a spring outside Jerusalem. The person who carried the pitcher was greeted by three blasts of the shofar (or ram's horn) and by shouts of joy from several thousand pilgrims who had gathered at the city's Water Gate. They joined the procession to the altar, where the priest took the golden vase and poured water over the altar while the pilgrims sang. That night, the Temple court was illuminated with candles and torches, and people danced and sang around the pillars. At a given signal, they formed a huge procession and marched to the eastern gate of the city accompanied by harps, lutes, cymbals, and trumpets.

The water libation ceremony is based on "sympathetic magic," the ancient notion that the things men do may induce similar actions on nature's part. Pouring water, for example, was probably designed to induce rain, and lighting candles and torches might originally have been a magical rite that would rekindle the sun at the time of the **AUTUMN EQUINOX**.

Nowadays, the once elaborate water-pouring ceremony has dwindled to a special celebration in the synagogue on the night of the second day. Psalms are chanted and the evening is spent eating, drinking, and being entertained. Jewish organizations often organize special parties on this evening, which they call Simhat Bet Hashoevah gatherings.

FURTHER READING

Bellenir, Karen. *Religious Holidays and Calendars*. 3rd ed. Detroit: Omnigraphics, 2004.

Cashman, Greer Fay. *Jewish Days and Holidays*. New York: SBS Pub., 1979.

Cuyler, Margery. *Jewish Holidays*. New York: Holt, Rinehart and Winston, 1978.

Edidin, Ben. *Jewish Holidays and Festivals*. 1940. Reprint. Detroit: Omnigraphics, 1993.

Gaer, Joseph. *Holidays Around the World*. Boston: Little, Brown, 1953.

Gaster, Theodor H. *Festivals of the Jewish Year*. New York: William Sloane Associates, 1953.

Henderson, Helene, ed. *Holidays, Festivals, and Celebrations of the World Dictionary*. 3rd ed. Detroit: Omnigraphics, 2005.

Ickis, Marguerite. *The Book of Festivals and Holidays the World Over*. New York: Dodd, Mead, 1970.

Penner, Lucille Recht. *The Thanksgiving Book*. New York: Hastings House, 1986.

Purdy, Susan. *Festivals for You to Celebrate*. Philadelphia: Lippincott, 1969.

Renberg, Dalia Hardof. *The Complete Family Guide to Jewish Holidays*. New York: Adama Books, 1985.

Santino, Jack. *All Around the Year: Holidays and Celebrations in American Life*. Urbana: University of Illinois Press, 1994.

WEB SITES

Union for Reform Judaism
urj.org/holidays/sukkot

Union of Orthodox Jewish Congregations of America
www.ou.org/chagim/sukkot

Summer Solstice

Type of Holiday: Calendar/Seasonal, Ancient, Religious (Neopagan)
Date of Observation: June 21 or 22 in the Northern Hemisphere; December 21 or 22 in the Southern Hemisphere
Where Celebrated: Modern observances of the Summer Solstice are rare, but in ancient times it was observed throughout Europe, the British Isles, China, Egypt, North Africa, and Scandinavia.
Symbols and Customs: Bonfires, Herbs, Midsummer Bride, Mock Funerals
Related Holidays: Beltane, Imbolc, Incwala, Inti Raymi Festival, Lughnasa, Mabon, Midsummer Day, Samhain, Sun Dance, Winter Solstice, Vernal Equinox

ORIGINS

Few celebrations can be traced back as far as the Summer Solstice, the day when the sun is at its furthest point from the equator. It reaches its northernmost point around June 21, which is the longest day of the year for those living north of the equator, and its southernmost point around December 22, which is the longest day for those living in the Southern Hemisphere. The word "solstice" comes from the Latin *solstitium* meaning "sun-stopping," because the point in the sky where the sun appears to rise and set stops and reverses direction after this day.

The Summer Solstice marks the changing of the seasons, which people in all parts of the world have honored since ancient times.. Many cultures divided the year into two seasons, summer and winter, and marked these points of the year at or near the summer and winter solstices, during which light and warmth began to increase and decrease, respectively. In pre-industrial times, humans survived through hunting, gathering, and agricultural practices, which depend on the natural cycle of seasons, according to the climate in the region of the world in which they lived. Thus, they created rituals to help ensure enough rain and sun in the spring and summer so crops would grow to fruition at harvest time, which was, in turn, duly celebrated. Vestiges of many of these ancient practices are thought to have survived in festivals still celebrated around seasonal themes.

One of the oldest celebrations of the Summer Solstice took place in ancient Egypt at the Temple of Amen-Ra at Karnak, whose foundations date back to about 3700 B.C.E. On the day of the solstice, a beam of light would illuminate a sanctuary in the temple's interior for about two to three minutes, during which the brightness would reach a peak and then begin to subside. This dramatic spotlighting effect enabled the Egyptian priests to calculate the length of the solar year with a high degree of accuracy.

A similar phenomenon was observed at Stonehenge in the Wiltshire plain of southwest England. Built by pre-Celtic peoples over a period of many centuries, beginning around 2800 B.C.E., this ancient monument composed of enormous stone arches was a gathering place for ancient tribes throughout southern England at the time of the Summer Solstice. If one stands at the center of the monument and faces northeast along its axis, the thirty-five-ton Heel Stone appears 256 feet away, marking the approximate place on the horizon where the sun rises on the Summer Solstice. In recent years, astronomers have discovered at least two dozen other solar and lunar alignments that the ancient builders of Stonehenge incorporated into its structure.

The earliest Chinese emperors observed the Summer Solstice in ways designed to stimulate the earthy, feminine *yin* forces. The solstice rites took place on the Altar of the Earth just north of the Forbidden City. Unlike the Round Mound used to observe the **WINTER SOLSTICE**, the altar was square and had a stairway leading in each of the four cardinal directions (north, south, east, and west). While the human sacrifice that took place at the **WINTER SOLSTICE** was burned, in summer the sacrificial victim was buried, thus maintaining a healthy balance in the earth's natural rhythms.

If the **WINTER SOLSTICE** is an occasion for hope, when the days begin to grow longer, the Summer Solstice is often tinged with sadness. Although it is a time of warmth, abundance, and fertility, when the days are long and nature is at her peak, it is also the point after which the days begin to get shorter and the darkness increases. While **WINTER SOLSTICE** traditions can still be found in modern **CHRISTMAS** and **NEW YEAR'S DAY** celebrations, the ancient Summer Solstice rites have largely disappeared.

One exception is related to the modern Neopagan and Wiccan movements, which emerged during the 1960s in Great Britain, the United States, and other English-speaking countries. They follow a nature-oriented religion loosely linked to ancient Celtic and other beliefs and inspired by old European folk practices. They celebrate eight sabbats, known as the eight spokes of the wheel of the year, which include **SUMMER SOLSTICE, WINTER SOLSTICE, VERNAL EQUINOX, BELTANE, SAMHAIN, IMBOLC, LUGHNASA,** and **MABON**. At the time of the Summer Solstice, Neopagans and Wiccans gather to celebrate at Stonehenge.

SYMBOLS AND CUSTOMS

Bonfires

Lighting bonfires was one of the most universal of ancient midsummer rites—one that still survives in some northern European countries. In Denmark and Norway, the fires were believed to prevent cattle from being struck by disease. The Germans looked into the fire through branches of larkspur in the belief that this would keep their eyes healthy. In Scotland, cowherds walked around their cattle three times carrying burning torches in order to purify and protect the animals.

Solstice bonfires were also associated with fertility and courtship. In Bohemia, girls and boys would stand on opposite sides of the fire and look at one another through wreaths they'd made to see whether they would be true to one another and who would marry whom. Then the girls would throw their wreaths across the flames toward their sweethearts. The singed wreaths were taken home afterward and kept in the house, in the belief that they offered protection from illness and thunderstorms throughout the year. When the fire had burned down a little, the couples would join hands and leap across the embers three times.

At San Pedro Manrique in Spain, people still build a bonfire and light it at six o'clock on Midsummer Eve. At midnight, they spread its coals into a carpet and walk barefoot across the glowing path, each carrying another person on his or her back. Midsummer bonfires are also common in North Africa, even though the Islamic calendar is lunar and therefore independent of the seasons. This would seem to suggest that the custom of lighting fires is even older than the arrival of Islam.

Herbs

The solstice was considered one of the best times of year to gather the herbs that would cure diseases and offer protection against evil. When the Christian Church tried to draw attention away from the pagan rites of the solstice by making June 24 St. John the Baptist's Day, these herbs were referred to as "St. John's herbs."

Mugwort was gathered at the solstice and made into garlands. Herbalists still use mugwort to cure rheumatism, fevers, and ague. When sewn into a pillow, its dried leaves are said to induce vivid dreams. In France, mugwort is known as the "herb of St. John"—a clear attempt to Christianize an old pagan remedy.

Verbena, also referred to as *vervain*, was gathered after sunset on Midsummer Eve and soaked overnight in water, or dried and worn around the neck. It was highly valued for its ability to strengthen the nervous system and relieve stress. The ancients used it as an aphrodisiac.

St. John's wort blooms around the time of the Summer Solstice, putting out masses of bright yellow flowers that resemble the sun. Its oil is still used to relieve sunburn, and the ancients believed that one whiff of this strong-scented plant would send evil spirits running.

Among Christians, *Hawkweed* or *Mouse-ear* root was believed to contain the blood of St. John. But the ancients valued the milky, reddish juice of the plant as a remedy for whooping cough and respiratory diseases.

Ancient peoples believed that *ferns* bloomed at midnight on Midsummer Eve. Whoever saw the blooming take place would be endowed with miraculous knowledge and power. But if the magical flower was touched by a human hand, it would vanish instantly.

Other herbs associated with the Summer Solstice and midsummer in general include chamomile, geranium, thyme, rue, chervil seed, giant fennel, and pennyroyal, all of which were prized for the aromas they gave off when they were thrown on BONFIRES.

Midsummer Bride

Because it marked the peak of the summer season, the solstice was associated with fertility and sexuality. Even today, June remains the most popular month for weddings, although most people know nothing about the ancient ceremonies involving symbolic marriage that once took place at midsummer.

In Sweden, each village chose a Midsummer Bride, who in turn selected a mock-bridegroom. Young men of the village also took advantage of the season to choose temporary brides. In Sardinia, these summer solstice couples were known as "Sweethearts of St. John," and the celebration featured pots of sprouting wheat and barley that suggested a symbolic link between human sexuality and the fertility of nature.

These marriage rituals were more than play-acting; they were designed to make the crops grow and the flowers bloom. The ancients believed that human sexual intercourse exercised a harmonizing influence on nature and society—an influence that was particularly needed at the solstices, when Heaven and Earth were at their extremes.

Mock Funerals

The Summer Solstice was the point after which the days grew shorter and the light declined. Many of the ancient rites that took place at the solstice were designed to postpone the sun's decline by celebrating life and fertility, or to mourn its passing. Midsummer was therefore a popular time for both weddings (*see* MIDSUMMER BRIDE) and funerals. In Tsarist Russia, midsummer was celebrated by dressing a straw man in women's clothes and decorating it with a crown of flowers. Young people would take this effigy in their arms and leap over a bonfire; on the following day, it would be stripped and thrown into a stream. In some areas, the straw figure was attacked and torn to bits, after which its "death" would be loudly mourned. Sometimes it was carried in a coffin through the streets.

The point of these mock-funeral rites was to mourn the "death" of the sun and the beginning of the cycle of decay in the natural world. Both weddings and funerals were seen as moments of transformation, when energy was released and Heaven and Earth were momentarily reunited.

FURTHER READING

Frazer, Sir James G. *The Golden Bough: A Study in Magic and Religion*. New York: Macmillan, 1931.

Heinberg, Richard. *Celebrate the Solstice: Honoring the Earth's Seasonal Rhythms through Festival and Ceremony*. Wheaton, IL: Quest Books, 1993.

Henderson, Helene, ed. *Holidays, Festivals, and Celebrations of the World Dictionary*. 3rd ed. Detroit: Omnigraphics, 2005.

King, John. *The Celtic Druids' Year: Seasonal Cycles of the Ancient Celts*. London: Blandford, 1995.

WEB SITE

BBC (British Broadcasting Corporation)
www.bbc.co.uk/religion/religions/paganism/holydays/summersolstice.shtml

Sun Dance

Type of Holiday: Religious (various Native American)
Date of Observation: Late June-early July (full moon closest to the summer solstice)
Where Celebrated: North America
Symbols and Customs: Buffalo, Sage, Sun Pole, Willow
Colors: The Sun Dance is associated with the colors red (symbol of the sunset), yellow (forked lightning), white (light), and black (night).
Related Holidays: Summer Solstice

ORIGINS

The Sun Dance is associated with many Native American tribes, whose cultures date back thousands of years into prehistoric times. According to many scholars, the people who became the Native Americans migrated from Asia across a land bridge that may have once connected the territories presently occupied by Alaska and Russia. The migrations, believed to have begun between 60,000 and 30,000 B.C.E., continued until approximately 4,000 B.C.E. This speculation, however, conflicts with traditional stories asserting that the indigenous Americans have always lived in North America or that tribes moved up from the south.

The historical development of religious belief systems among Native Americans is not well known. Most of the information available was gathered by Europeans who arrived on the continent beginning in the sixteenth century C.E. The data they recorded was fragmentary and oftentimes of questionable accuracy because the Europeans did not understand the native cultures they were trying to describe and the Native Americans were reluctant to divulge details about themselves.

Seasonal and celestial cycles were very important to the nomadic Native Americans who at one time inhabited the Great Plains of North America. Most of the tribes, particularly the Sioux, participated in a common ceremonial event known as the Sun Dance, traditionally held at the time of the full moon closest to the **SUMMER SOLSTICE**. The entire ceremony lasted sixteen days: Eight days were spent in preparation, the performance itself took four days, and there were four days of abstinence. It was a time of renewal and healing, and it was crucial that it take place at midsummer, when the SAGE plant was succulent and when the sun was at its highest point in the sky.

The participants did not eat or drink during the dance itself. They took a sweat bath in the morning on the first day and painted their bodies in the symbolic colors of red, blue, yellow, white, and black (*see* "Colors"). They dressed in a deerskin apron, wristlets and anklets made of rabbit fur, and a feather in their hair. Members of tribes from many miles around would set up their tipis to form a circular dance enclosure around the SUN POLE, which had been cut and painted in advance. To the accompaniment of a large drum and special ceremonial songs, the dancers circled in procession and paid homage to the sun.

Pain and self-sacrifice were an essential part of life to many Native American tribes, and the Sun Dance provided them with an opportunity to renew themselves and give thanks to the sun by sacrificing their own flesh. Certain participants in the dance, known as "pledgers," would have wooden skewers (or sometimes eagle claws) inserted under the skin of their chests. The skewers were then attached to a strong rope and tied to the Sun Pole. The dancers formed a circle around the pole, and after going toward it four times to place their hands on it and pray, they would pull back as hard as they could until the skewers were torn free. An alternative method was to have two skewers inserted under the skin of the shoulder blades. Heavy buffalo skulls (*see* BUFFALO) would be hung from the skewers by thongs and dragged around until their weight eventually tore the skewers loose. Yet another variation was for the dancers to suspend themselves from the pole with ropes attached to the skewers or tie the ropes to a horse. The dancers would continue this way until they fell unconscious from the pain or tore themselves loose, after which they believed they would receive a divine vision. Although such self-inflicted tortures sound barbaric today, at the time the participants had the moral support of the entire tribe. The ceremony was popular at one time among the Kiowa, Bungi, Mandan, Hidatsa, Arapaho, Cheyenne, Blackfoot, and Crow. The Shoshone, Ute, Comanche, and other tribes performed the dance without the self-torture.

Many Indian tribes believe that the sun "died" after the solar eclipse of August 7, 1869. The Sioux performed their last Sun Dance in 1881. The torture elements of the dance were widely misunderstood, which resulted in its being condemned in many areas. It survives, however, among some of the northern and western tribes, particularly the Southern Utes and the Arapaho, who hold their Sun Dance without any sacrifice of flesh.

SYMBOLS AND CUSTOMS

Buffalo

The buffalo head is a symbol of plenty, because at one time Native Americans killed and ate the animals and used their skins for clothing. The buffalo also symbolizes strength and comfort. It was often featured in the Sun Dance because the buffalo feeds on SAGE and WILLOW, which means that it ultimately depends on the sun.

The buffalo figures prominently in the Sun Dance held by the Arapaho Indians on the Wind River Reservation near Fort Washakie, Wyoming. A huge center pole (*see* SUN POLE) with a buffalo head on top and twelve outer poles surrounding it form a circular enclosure within which the dance is performed. The buffalo head faces west, toward the Rocky Mountains, and freshly picked SAGE is placed on its nose. The dancers approach the pole and then step back, always keeping their eyes on the buffalo head.

Sage

Sage was often placed on the nose of the buffalo head that surmounted the central SUN POLE in the dance enclosure. Since sage is known for its strong scent and was a common symbol for healing as well as breathing, placing it on the buffalo's nose made it seem as though the buffalo were still alive and able to breathe.

Sun Pole

The tall pole, usually cottonwood, that occupies the center of the circular enclosure in which the Sun Dance is performed is both a phallic symbol and a symbol of the sun. Among the Sioux, it represented Wakan-Tanka, the all-pervading power of the universe. The ceremonial cutting of the Sun Pole was conducted by four young virgins, two male and two female. Among some tribes, a sword or stick was substituted.

Willow

Both the Ute and the Cheyenne fastened a willow branch in the fork at the top of the cottonwood SUN POLE. In fact, the Northern Cheyenne refer to the ceremony as the Willow Dance, ignoring the sun worship aspect of the dance altogether. The willow is a symbol of water and of growing things.

FURTHER READING

Bellenir, Karen. *Religious Holidays and Calendars*. 3rd ed. Detroit: Omnigraphics, 2004.

Dobler, Lavinia G. *Customs and Holidays Around the World*. New York: Fleet Pub. Corp., 1962.

Heinberg, Richard. *Celebrate the Solstice: Honoring the Earth's Seasonal Rhythms through Festival and Ceremony*. Wheaton, IL: Quest Books, 1993.

Henderson, Helene, ed. *Holidays, Festivals, and Celebrations of the World Dictionary*. 3rd ed. Detroit: Omnigraphics, 2005.

Leach, Maria, ed. *Funk & Wagnalls Standard Dictionary of Folklore, Mythology & Legend*. San Francisco: Harper & Row, 1984.

Super Bowl Sunday

Type of Holiday: Sporting
Date of Observation: Usually the last Sunday in January
Where Celebrated: United States
Symbols and Customs: Gambling, Pre-Game Show, Super Bowl Parties, Vince Lombardi and the Green Bay Packers

ORIGINS

Like the slaying of the old king and the crowning of the new king that took place at the start of the new year in ancient times, the Super Bowl is the result of a long series of elimination games that culminate in a single showdown (*see* **WINTER SOLSTICE**). The champions of the National Football League's American Football Conference (AFC) and National Football Conference (NFC) play each other at a pre-selected site, usually a warm-weather city or one that has a covered stadium. This annual football ritual takes place at the end of January, and rather than being just another championship event, it has become the equivalent of a national holiday. Even criminals take the day off: When the San Francisco 49ers played at the 1985 Super Bowl in Palo Alto, California, San Francisco's crime rate dropped nearly seventy-five percent.

The first Super Bowl game was played on January 15, 1967, in the Los Angeles Coliseum, where the Green Bay Packers beat the Kansas City Chiefs by a score of 35-10 (*see* VINCE LOMBARDI AND THE GREEN BAY PACKERS). It had been suggested that the event be called "The Final Game" or even "The Big One," but then Lamar Hunt, a Texas financier and owner of the Kansas City Chiefs, came up with the idea of calling it the "Super Bowl" after watching his daughter play with a Super Ball—a small, high-bouncing ball that was a popular toy at the time. The games have traditionally been identified by Roman numerals, but it wasn't until Super Bowl IV in 1970 that the name "Super Bowl" actually appeared on the tickets.

At the time of the first Super Bowl, there were two football leagues, the National Football League (NFL) and the American Football League (AFL). The NFL's Green Bay Packers dominated the first couple of Super Bowls, but then the AFL's New York Jets and their star quarterback Joe Namath—dubbed "Broadway Joe" for his celebrity status—won Super Bowl III, proving that the two leagues could compete equally and adding to the event's popularity. In 1970 the two leagues merged into one and created two conferences, which now compete for the Super Bowl title. Other milestones include Super Bowl X in 1976, when the first PRE-GAME SHOW was broadcast on television, and Super Bowl XII in 1978, the first time the event was held indoors, drawing the largest audience at the time to have ever watched a sporting event on television. At Super Bowl XV in 1981, a huge yellow bow was erected over the main entrance of the Louisiana Superdome in New Orleans to commemorate the fifty-two American hostages who had just been released by Iran after 444 days in captivity.

At the beginning, the price of television advertising during the game sold for $85,000 a minute. After Joe Namath and the Jets won Super Bowl III, the price suddenly jumped to $200,000. By Super Bowl XIX, it was costing advertisers $1 million a minute. By Super Bowl XLI in 2007, the cost of ads had risen to over $2 million for just thirty seconds. It has been estimated that about forty percent of all U.S. households owning television sets tune in to the Super Bowl, which has made the advertisements almost as important as the game itself. Advertisers have started running commercials days before the game that promote the commercials they will show during the game—just as Apple Computer did so successfully during Super Bowl XVIII, with a memorable commercial introducing its Macintosh computer. Corporate logos have appeared on everything from the seat cushions in the stadium to the blimps that jockey for position in the sky overhead. Even the U.S. government has used the Super Bowl as a marketing tool, making it the kickoff event of the 1976 bicentennial celebration.

Although the Super Bowl is always held on a Sunday, religious leaders have never seemed to mind. Norman Vincent Peale once said that "If Jesus were alive today, he would be at the Super Bowl." Even U.S. presidents routinely get involved in the game, recommending plays beforehand and delivering their congratulations to the winning team by telephone at the end.

SYMBOLS AND CUSTOMS

Gambling

It has become a tradition in schools, offices, and at SUPER BOWL PARTIES for everyone to put a certain amount of money into a "pool" and bet not only on which team will win but on the "point spread" between the two scores. Sometimes partygoers will draw slips of paper from a hat on which various outcomes have been written—an approach that reduces the emphasis on knowledge of the two teams and their relative strength and gives everyone an equal chance of winning.

Pre-Game Show

It was NFL Commissioner Pete Rozelle who made sure that the Super Bowl provided entertainment on a grand scale. The first pre-game show for spectators and television viewers climaxed with the release of 4,000 pigeons, and subsequent pre-game shows have featured Hollywood celebrities and jets trailing plumes of red, white, and blue smoke. The popularity of "The Star-Spangled Banner," which is traditionally played before all types of American sporting events, skyrocketed after it became part of the pre-game ceremonies at the Super Bowl. It is usually sung by a well-known American pop singer.

The half-time show has also become a major entertainment spectacle. In the past, half-time shows have included hot-air balloons and reenactments of historic American battles.

Super Bowl Parties

A few weeks after **NEW YEAR'S DAY,** many Americans—even those who aren't particularly interested in football—attend Super Bowl parties. These are typically day-long events held at a friend's house with chips, beer, and a potluck supper. The highlight, of course, is the game—and finding out who wins the Super Bowl pool (see GAMBLING).

Vince Lombardi and the Green Bay Packers

Wisconsin's Green Bay Packers and their coach, the legendary Vince Lombardi, were the original symbols of the Super Bowl, representing the tradition of hard work and competitiveness for which the event stands. When Lombardi became the Packers' coach in 1959, he took over a team that had lost nearly every game during the preceding season. But within two years he had turned them into NFL champions They won the first two Super Bowl games in 1967 and 1968, and although their two-game winning streak cannot be compared to that of the San Francisco 49ers, the Pittsburgh Steelers, or the Dallas Cowboys, they remain the team that best represents the spirit of the Super Bowl.

The trophy given to the winning team is named for Lombardi, whose game plan, in the words of one of his former players, was "Attack! Attack! Attack!" The trophy is symbolic of the values Lombardi exemplified and the excellence he demanded from his players.

The sterling silver Vince Lombardi Trophy of a football in the kicking position is handcrafted by Tiffany & Co. Standing twenty-two inches tall, the prize weighs seven pounds and is worth $12,500. The trophy is awarded to the owner of the winning team by the NFL Commissioner.

FURTHER READING

Dienhart, Tom, Joe Hoppel, and Dave Sloan, eds. *The Complete Super Bowl Book*. St. Louis: The Sporting News, 1994.

Henderson, Helene, ed. *Holidays, Festivals, and Celebrations of the World Dictionary*. 3rd ed. Detroit: Omnigraphics, 2005.

Santino, Jack. *All Around the Year: Holidays and Celebrations in American Life*. Urbana: University of Illinois Press, 1994.

WEB SITES

National Football League
www.nfl.com
www.superbowl.com

Vince Lombardi
www.vincelombardi.com

Sweetest Day

Type of Holiday: Promotional
Date of Observation: Third Saturday in October
Where Celebrated: United States, particularly Illinois, Indiana, Michigan, New York, Ohio, and Wisconsin
Symbols and Customs: Candy, Cards, Flowers
Related Holidays: Valentine's Day

ORIGINS

Many people assume that Sweetest Day originated fairly recently with retailers who were interested in promoting the sale of cards and gifts. But the day was actually created in 1922 by Herbert Birch Kingston, a philanthropist in Cleveland, Ohio. Kingston worked for a local candy maker, and he wanted to brighten the lives of those who were isolated, lonely, or without family. He chose a Saturday in October to distribute candy and other small gifts to hospitals, nursing homes, and orphanages in the Cleveland area.

Kingston's idea soon caught on, and the practice of setting aside a day for remembering special people with a thoughtful gesture grew in popularity. Within a few years the third Saturday of October was designated as Sweetest Day in the city of Cleveland. The day's name was chosen as a reference to the gifts of candy and other sweets that were commonly distributed on that day.

Although Sweetest Day is slowly spreading throughout the U.S., the day is most often observed in the upper Midwest and northeastern regions of the U.S., particularly in the cities of Buffalo, New York; Chicago, Illinois; Cleveland, Ohio; and Detroit, Michigan. The typical Sweetest Day gifts are CANDY, FLOWERS, and CARDS. Sweetest Day is sometimes regarded as a second **VALENTINE'S DAY;** however, where Valentine's Day usually focuses on appreciation of a romantic partner, any special person can be acknowledged on Sweetest Day.

SYMBOLS AND CUSTOMS

Candy

Gifts of candy have been a part of Sweetest Day since the first observances of the holiday. In early Sweetest Day celebrations, celebrities and public figures often arranged for the delivery of thousands of boxes of chocolates to individuals in the

Cleveland area. One film actress paid for the distribution of candy to hospital patients and also to everyone who came to see her movies, while another sent treats to all the newsboys in the city in thanks for their service to the community.

Cards

Sweetest Day cards have been given alone or with gifts for many years. The tradition became commercialized in the 1960s when greeting card companies began offering Sweetest Day cards for sale. Over the years, demand for Sweetest Day cards has increased significantly—approximately fifty different card designs were offered by one company in 2000, increasing to more than 150 in 2006.

Flowers

Flowers have become another popular Sweetest Day gift, particularly for loved ones, although special platonic or family relationships may also be acknowledged with flowers on Sweetest Day.

FURTHER READING

Henderson, Helene, ed. *Holidays, Festivals, and Celebrations of the World Dictionary*, 3rd ed. Detroit: Omnigraphics, 2005.

WEB SITE

Sweetest Day
sweetestday.com

Tanabata
(Star Festival)

Type of Holiday: Folkloric
Date of Observation: July 7
Where Celebrated: Japan
Symbols and Customs: Bamboo, Kusudama, Magpies, Mulberry Leaves
Colors: The colored strips of paper that are used to decorate the BAMBOO branches that are displayed during the Tanabata festival come in five colors: green, yellow, red, white, and dark blue (or purple) as a substitute for black. They were originally colored threads representing the cloth that the Weaving Girl in the legend used to make for the gods.

ORIGINS

Tanabata, which means "Weaving Loom Festival," is a Japanese festival based on an old Chinese legend about two lovers who were parted. The daughter of the celestial emperor, Tentei, lived on the eastern bank of the River of Heaven (also known as the Milky Way), where she spent her days weaving the cloth needed by the gods who lived in her father's mansion. Known as Shokujo or the Weaving Girl, she was betrothed to Kengyu, a simple cowherd. Their honeymoon lasted so long that they neglected their other duties: Kengyu's cows grew thin, and the gods complained that they didn't have enough clothing. In a fit of anger, Tentei punished the couple by forcing them to live on opposite sides of the River of Heaven, allowing them to see each other only once a year, on the seventh night of the seventh moon. Since there was no bridge across the river, a flock of MAGPIES extended their wings to form a bridge that the Weaving Girl could walk across.

The lovers wept so hard when they were forced to leave each other that it provided the fields with abundant summer rain.

There are many versions of this legend throughout China and Korea. It may have been linked to an ancient fertility rite, and several generations ago it was still common in rural parts of Japan for young men and women to climb a nearby mountain on the night of Tanabata and sleep there together. The fact that the hero of the legend is a cowherd would appear to support this theory, since cows and bulls were a well-established symbol of fertility. In rural areas, the Tanabata festival was observed by planting young trees in fields and gardens where they could protect the crops from harmful insects.

The Japanese took over what had been essentially a Chinese festival in 755 C.E., and eventually it was declared one of the five most important festivals of Japan, along with **OSHOGATSU** or New Year's Day, **HINA MATSURI** (Doll Festival), Tango No Sekku (Boys' Festival; *see* **KODOMO-NO-HI**), and the **CHRYSAN-THEMUM FESTIVAL**. Today it is primarily a women's and children's festival, since the Weaving Girl is the patroness of women and of needlework. At one time the festival was observed with embroidery contests and needle-threading competitions: Only a superior needlewoman could thread a needle while holding it under a table or while sitting in a room lit only by a glowing ember or by moonlight. But today the primary activity is laying out offerings to the Star Goddess or Weaving Girl, consisting usually of watermelons, cakes, and various feminine toilet articles such as combs, mirrors, and rouge-pots. Unmarried girls typically lay out their offerings in sets of seven, one for the Weaver Princess and the others for her six sisters. In more educated households, there may be a *koto* (harp) and a flute laid out with the rest of the offerings to symbolize the "harmony" of music and of a happy marriage. In cities and towns, people often go to the theater to see a special play, "Crossing the Milky Way," which is performed only on this holiday.

Tanabata was observed on the seventh day of the seventh lunar month until use of the Gregorian calendar transposed it to July 7. Those who observe the festival believe that if the night is cloudy or rainy, the magpies will not form their bridge, and the celestial lovers must wait another year.

SYMBOLS AND CUSTOMS

Bamboo

The Japanese consider bamboo a sacred plant, admired for its ability to bend and withstand adversity. But it is also a womanly plant, full of grace and capable of being influenced by wind or soil.

It is customary to stick branches of freshly cut bamboo in the ground in front of the house or to attach them to the doors or the eaves on the day of the Tanabata festival. These bamboo branches were originally decorated with multicolored threads in honor of the Weaver Princess. Today these threads have been replaced by strips of paper in many different colors, which are believed to scare off evil spirits by fluttering in the wind. Love poems may be written on some of the strips, or poems in praise of the Weaver Princess. Children sit around the table on the eve of the festival and, with their parents' help, try to compose these poems, although sometimes they are copied out of anthologies. Other symbolic items may be hung in the bamboo branches as well, such as a crane (for long life), a brush (for improvement of calligraphy), a net (for good crops and a bountiful catch), a kimono (for protection of the body), a lottery basket (for luck), and a money pouch (for the spirit of saving).

Like other forms of greenery associated with spring and rebirth, the branches serve as a reminder of the life-giving qualities of bamboo, which spreads very rapidly. On the day after the festival, the branches are taken down and thrown in the nearest river, where they are allowed to float away with the current.

Kusudama

Kusudama are balls or pompoms made from paper, cloth, or celluloid with long tassels of many colors. The original kusudama were medicinal balls made of herbs and used to get rid of evil spirits and ward off illnesses. The emperor would give them to his guests and noblemen, but eventually they became common household ornaments and were often used as playthings for children.

In the Japanese city of Sendai, where Tanabata is a very elaborate celebration observed a month later than usual (August 6-8), colorful kusudama are hung all along the streets and in train stations, a testament to the Japanese love of papercraft.

Magpies

Crows, magpies, and ravens were interchangeable in China and Japan. These birds were all regarded as messengers of the gods, and they possessed supernatural powers enabling them to predict the future. Although all three are considered birds of ill omen, under certain circumstances they can prophesy happiness as well. The magpie in particular is associated with good news or the arrival of a guest. The joy it symbolizes is often associated with marital bliss, due to its role in the legend of the cowherd and the weaver.

According to legend, magpies cannot be seen in the trees after the hour of noon on the day of the Tanabata festival. If any are spotted, children throw stones at them to punish them for not doing their duty. They are supposed to be up in heaven, helping to build a bridge across the Milky Way for the thwarted lovers.

Mulberry Leaves

On the night of Tanabata, people used to dip leaves from a mulberry tree in a large bowl of water while standing outdoors and studying the reflection of the stars on the water's surface. The way the leaves behaved and the appearance of the water were then interpreted as omens regarding marriage, offspring, and prospects for the rice crop. Since the mulberry tree was connected with the making of silk in China (silkworms feed on mulberry leaves), it was a natural symbol to use on a day devoted to a weaver of cloth.

The custom of "reading" mulberry leaves on Tanabata is rarely practiced nowadays. It survives only in very rural areas of Japan.

FURTHER READING

Araki, Nancy K., and Jane M. Horii. *Matsuri Festival: Japanese-American Celebrations and Activities*. San Francisco: Heian International Pub. Co., 1978.

Bauer, Helen, and Sherwin Carlquist. *Japanese Festivals*. Garden City, NY: Doubleday, 1965.

Bredon, Juliet, and Igor Mitrophanow. *The Moon Year: A Record of Chinese Customs and Festivals*. Shanghai: Kelly & Walsh, 1927.

Casal, U.A. *The Five Sacred Festivals of Ancient Japan*. Rutland, VA: Sophia University in cooperation with Tuttle, 1967.

Eberhard, Wolfram. *A Dictionary of Chinese Symbols: Hidden Symbols in Chinese Life and Thought*. New York: Routledge & Kegan Paul, 1986.

Gaer, Joseph. *Holidays Around the World*. Boston: Little, Brown, 1953.

Henderson, Helene, ed. *Holidays, Festivals, and Celebrations of the World Dictionary*. 3rd ed. Detroit: Omnigraphics, 2005.

Stepanchuk, Carol, and Charles Wong. *Mooncakes and Hungry Ghosts: Festivals of China*. San Francisco: China Books & Periodicals, 1991.

WEB SITE

Japan National Tourist Organization
www.jnto.go.jp/eng/indepth/history/traditionalevents/a69a_fes_tanabata.html

Tano Festival
(Dano)

Type of Holiday: Calendar/Seasonal
Date of Observation: May-June; fifth day of the fifth lunar month
Where Celebrated: Korea
Symbols and Customs: Amulets, Date Tree Wedding, Fan, Iris, Mask Dance, Mugwort, Swinging, Wrestling
Related Holidays: Double Fifth

ORIGINS

The Tano Festival celebrates the changing seasons and the coming of spring. Since ancient times people in all parts of the world have honored the changing of the seasons. Many cultures divided the year into two seasons, summer and winter, and marked these points of the year at or near the **SUMMER SOLSTICE** and **WINTER SOLSTICE**, during which light and warmth began to increase and decrease, respectively. In pre-industrial times, humans survived through hunting, gathering, and agricultural practices, which depend on the natural cycle of seasons, according to the climate in the region of the world in which they lived. Thus, they created rituals to help ensure enough rain and sun in the spring and summer so crops would grow to fruition at harvest time, which was, in turn, duly celebrated. Vestiges of many of these ancient practices are thought to have survived in festivals still celebrated around seasonal themes.

Also known as Dano Day or Swing Day, the Tano Festival is an ancient spring agricultural festival in Korea that started as a planting ritual and a time to pray for a good harvest. It falls in the farming season between the planting of rice seedlings and their transplanting to the paddy fields. Along with **SOL** or New Year's Day and the **MID-AUTUMN FESTIVAL**, it is one of the country's three great national holidays.

In ancient times, people got up early on Tano, washed, and put on new clothes. They performed the ceremony of worshipping their ancestors with special foods arranged before the home altar. After the ceremony, everyone enjoyed eating the sacrificial foods and spent the day celebrating with friends. In modern Korea, people still make offerings of new summer foods at the family shrine, and women and children gather together in their new clothes to play games and engage in SWING-ING contests. Rice cakes in the shape of the Chinese characters meaning "long life" and "blessings" are a festival favorite, as are rainbow rice cakes made with rice flour that has been dyed in bright colors.

According to oriental philosophy, the number five is regarded as having a positive character because it is an odd number. There is a tendency to emphasize all double-odd days, but the double fifth day is regarded as particularly auspicious.

SYMBOLS AND CUSTOMS

Amulets

It is customary for each household to make Dano Day amulets or good-luck charms by writing in red ink sentences that guarantee the annihilation of disease and invite heavenly blessings and good fortune for every member of the family. The amulets are then posted over the name plate at the front gate of the house. Up until the end of the Yi Dynasty in Korea, cabinet ministers and other officials used to make Dano amulets and post them on the pillars of the royal palace. This practice probably derived from the ancient belief in using a red seal on a piece of paper as a means of warding off evil spirits.

Date Tree Wedding

In rural areas, there is a custom known as the "date tree wedding," which involves inserting a round stone between two branches of a date tree. If this is done at noon on the Tano Festival, it is believed that the tree will bear more fruit. A similar result can be achieved by chopping many branches off the tree at noon on this day.

Fan

There are two types of fans in Korea: the folding type and the flat, round fan. Folding fans have white bamboo struts and are often painted with lacquer, with pictures of peach blossoms, butterflies, locusts, white herons, and other symbolic objects. The flat, round fan is called a *danseon* and can be made to resemble various leaf shapes. Men traditionally use the round fan at home but take a folding fan when they go out in public. Women and young people usually use the round fan. Some round fans are large enough to shade the sunlight, and some have long handles so they can be used to chase away flies and mosquitoes.

Up until the end of the Yi Dynasty, it was traditional to make fans and present them to the king, who in turn gave them to cabinet ministers and other government officials on Dano Day. Local governors and military officers also used to present fans to the palace and distribute them as gifts. The fan is still considered an important symbol of the festival.

Iris

One of the first things that Korean boys and girls do on the day of the Tano Festival, before changing into their new clothes, is to wash their hair and faces in hot water that has been boiled with iris or calamus plants. The root of the plant is then carved to make a hairpin with letters meaning "long life" and "luck" painted in vermilion—a custom that is believed to chase bad spirits away.

Mask Dance

The Mask Dance was at one time a popular part of the Tano celebration, particularly in the Bongsan and Haeju areas. The dancers were usually local officials who had some singing and dancing talent; they put together a company in which membership was hereditary. About a month before the festival, they went off to a Buddhist monastery to prepare for their performance.

Nowadays, it is usually local merchants who bear the expense of the mask dance and then invite their customers and business associates to be their guests. The dance is performed at night, with a wood fire to illuminate the scene, and it lasts until dawn. Because people believe that the masks and costumes attract evil spirits during the performance, it is customary to burn them in the fire when it is over. The performers gather around the fire and pray with their hands pressed together, which marks the end of the ritual dance.

Mugwort

There was an ancient custom in Korea of making a tiger out of artemisia or mugwort plants on Dano Day. It resembled a scarecrow and was called the *ssug-beom* or 'artemisia tiger.' Occasionally the tiger was made from colored cloth, and artemisia leaves were used only on the outside.

In rural areas, people still get up early on Dano Day to cut artemisia in the fields and make a bundle of it to hang on their front gates. Because of its strong smell, it is believed to ward off bad luck and disaster. Mugwort is a common ingredient in herbal medicines, and at one time it was believed that only plants dug at noon on this day and dried in the shade would have the desired medicinal effect.

Swinging

For women in both urban and rural areas, swinging is a popular activity on Dano Day. A long, heavy rope is tied at both ends to the branch of a large tree—or, more often nowadays, to the cross-piece of a tall frame—and women swing by riding on the U-shaped bottom of the rope. The swinger wears a colorful dress and hair ribbons. Sometimes young women swing in pairs, and there are contests to see who can swing the highest and kick a suspended bell. They wear colorful Korean dresses with billowing skirts, and, in Pyongyang, where swinging is particularly popular, blue skirts with white jackets or red skirts with yellow jackets.

Although boys and men may participate in the swinging contests as well, this is a sport that is traditionally reserved for women and girls.

Wrestling

Boys and men often spend the day of the festival participating in *ssirum,* a form of native Korean wrestling that dates back to 400 C.E. Each village selects its biggest, strongest man to represent them in these contests, and the rivalry can be intense. Only the hands and feet are used, which keeps it from getting too violent.

The two wrestlers begin by facing each other kneeling down; they get ready by holding each other, their right hand grasping the opponent's waistband and their left hand holding the opponent's leg. When the starting signal is given, they stand up together and start wrestling. The one whose body or hand touches the ground first loses. Ssirum matches are very popular in Korea and are often televised nationally.

FURTHER READING

Henderson, Helene, ed. *Holidays, Festivals, and Celebrations of the World Dictionary.* 3rd ed. Detroit: Omnigraphics, 2005.

MacDonald, Margaret R., ed. *The Folklore of World Holidays.* Detroit: Gale Research, 1992.

Sang-su, Choe. *Annual Customs of Korea.* Seoul: Seomun-dang, 1983.

Van Straalen, Alice. *The Book of Holidays Around the World.* New York: Dutton, 1986.

WEB SITE

Korean Air
www.skynews.co.kr/skynews_main/ENGLISH/culture/culture_006.htm

Teej
(Tij, Green Teej)

Type of Holiday: Religious (Hindu)
Date of Observation: July-August; third day of the waxing half of the Hindu month of Sravana
Where Celebrated: India, Nepal
Symbols and Customs: Henna, Parvati, Swing
Related Holidays: Gauri Festival

ORIGINS

Teej is a festival in the religious tradition of Hinduism, which many scholars regard as the oldest living religion. The word Hindu is derived from the Sanskrit term *Sindhu* (or *Indus*), which meant river. It referred to people living in the Indus valley in the Indian subcontinent. Hinduism has no founder, one universal reality (or god) known as Brahman, many gods and goddesses (sometimes referred to as devtas), and several scriptures. Hinduism also has no priesthood or hierarchical structure similar to that seen in some other religions, such as Christianity. Hindus acknowledge the authority of a wide variety of writings, but there is no single, uniform canon. The oldest of the Hindu writings are the *Vedas*. The word "veda" comes from the Sanskrit word for knowledge. The *Vedas*, which were compiled from ancient oral traditions, contain hymns, instructions, explanations, chants for sacrifices, magical formulas, and philosophy. Another set of sacred books includes the *Great Epics,* which illustrate Hindu faith in practice. The *Epics* include the *Ramayana*, the *Mahabharata*, and the *Bhagavad Gita*.

The Hindu pantheon includes approximately thirty-three million gods. Some of these are held in higher esteem than others. Over all the gods, Hindus believe in one absolute high god or universal concept. This is Brahman. Although he is above all the gods, he is not worshipped in popular ceremonies because he is detached from the day-to-day affairs of the people. Brahman is impersonal. Lesser gods and goddesses (devtas) serve him. Because these are more intimately involved in the affairs of people, they are venerated as gods. The most honored god in Hinduism varies among the different Hindu sects. Although Hindu adherents practice their faith differently and venerate different deities, they share a similar view of reality and look back on a common history.

The Hindu festival of Teej is celebrated throughout India, but particularly in the dry, desert-like state of Rajasthan in the northwestern part of the country. It welcomes the monsoon season, when the wind off the Indian Ocean brings the heavy rains that provide a respite from the hot summer weather and that are so necessary for a good harvest. Because the monsoon is associated with crops and fertility, Teej is also a celebration for women and is dedicated to the Hindu goddess PARVATI, consort of Lord Shiva and the patron goddess of women.

In preparation for the festivities, Hindu women traditionally paint delicate designs on their hands and feet with HENNA. They wear green, red, or yellow dresses and new glass or lacquer bangles on their arms. Married women go to their parents' homes to receive gifts of clothing and jewelry, while unmarried girls are given sweets, jewelry, and clothing by their mothers. Decorated SWINGS are hung from trees, in houses, and in gardens, and women and young girls spend the day swinging on them and singing songs that honor Parvati. In households where there are boys, it is customary for brothers to put up swings for their sisters. There are also fairs and processions that involve carrying images of Parvati through the streets.

It is not difficult to see the connection between the arrival of the monsoon and the fertility that is associated with marriage. Married Hindu women worship Parvati on this day in the hope that they will have long, happy married lives and that their children will find peace and prosperity. The new clothes and jewelry they put on are symbols of such a life, and Teej is said to be a particularly important day for newly married women.

In Katmandu, Nepal, Hindu women visit Pashupatinath Temple on this day to worship Shiva and Parvati. Ritual bathing in the sacred Bagmati River is believed to wash away the sins of the preceding year.

SYMBOLS AND CUSTOMS

Henna

Decorating her hands and feet with henna expresses a Hindu woman's optimism about the future, since henna itself symbolizes happiness and is believed to bring good luck. The most popular designs include flowers and leaves, vertical lines on the palms (symbolic of the monsoon rains), and ghevar, which is the form of a round, sweet dish made especially for the festival. In addition to its symbolic meaning, henna also serves the purpose of cooling the skin in the hot summer weather.

Parvati

The Hindu goddess Parvati is a symbol for complete womanhood. Although she has many different names and manifestations, representing every imaginable aspect of Mother Nature, she is best known as Gauri, the goddess of abundance (*see* **GAURI FESTIVAL**), Uma, the ascetic, and Parvati, the devoted housewife.

Teej celebrates the day on which Parvati left her father's home to go to that of her new husband, Lord Shiva. For this reason, a bridal car or carriage is often taken out in a procession of decorated elephants, camels, horses, dancers, and musicians, with an image of the goddess carried in a palanquin.

Swing

In folklore and mythology, swinging is an activity that is usually indulged in by gods and goddesses when they want to have fun. The swinging that Hindu women do on this day is basically a form of play and an opportunity for them to relax and enjoy themselves. Because the act of swinging creates wind, it is also possible that the swing is a symbol for the wind off the ocean that brings the monsoon.

The swings that are used on Teej are supposed to be hung from mango trees, since the mango is a symbol of fertility.

FURTHER READING

Bellenir, Karen. *Religious Holidays and Calendars*. 3rd ed. Detroit: Omnigraphics, 2004.

Henderson, Helene, ed. *Holidays, Festivals, and Celebrations of the World Dictionary*. 3rd ed. Detroit: Omnigraphics, 2005.

MacDonald, Margaret R., ed. *The Folklore of World Holidays*. Detroit: Gale Research, 1992.

Sanon, Arun. *Festive India*. New Delhi: Frank Bros., 1986.

Sharma, Brijendra Nath. *Festivals of India*. New Delhi: Abhinav Publications, 1978.

Trawicky, Bernard, and Ruth W. Gregory. *Anniversaries and Holidays*. 5th ed. Chicago: American Library Assocation, 2000.

Van Straalen, Alice. *The Book of Holidays Around the World*. New York: Dutton, 1986.

Tenjin Matsuri
(Tenjin Festival)

Type of Holiday: Religious (Shinto)
Date of Observation: July 24 and July 25
Where Celebrated: Osaka, Japan
Symbols and Customs: Boat Parade, Hand Clapping, Parade, Tenjin Ritual

ORIGIN

Tenjin Matsuri is part of the Shinto tradition, an ancient religion that originated in Japan. Most Shinto adherents live in Japan, but small communities also exist in Europe, Latin America, North America, and in the Pacific island nations.

The name Shinto was first employed during the sixth century C.E. to differentiate indigenous religions in Japan from faith systems that originated in mainland Asia (primarily Buddhism and Confucianism). The word is derived from two Chinese characters, shen (gods) and tao (way). Loosely translated, Shinto means "way of the gods." Its roots lie in an ancient nature-based religion. Some important concepts in Shinto include the value of tradition, the reverence of nature, cleanliness (ritual purity), and the veneration of spirits called kami. Strictly speaking, kami are not deities. The literal translation of the word kami is "that which is hidden."

Kami (which is both the singular and plural term) are honored, but do not assert their powers upon humans in the traditional manner of deities or gods in other religions. People may be descended from the kami, and kami may influence the course of nature and events. The kami can bestow blessings, but they are not all benign. Kami are present in natural things such as trees, mountains, rocks, and rivers. They are embodied in religious relics, especially mirrors and jewels. They also include spirits of ancestors, local deities, holy people, and even political or literary figures. The human role is to venerate the kami and make offerings. The ultimate goal of Shinto is to uphold the harmony among humans and between people and nature. In this regard, the principle of all kami is to protect and sustain life.

The central authorities in Shinto are the priests. Traditionally, the duties of the priest were passed through heredity lines, but in modern times priests are trained on the basis of recommendation. The priests' duties include communicating with the kami and ensuring that ceremonies are properly carried out. Shinto does not have a single collection of sacred texts analogous to the Christian Bible or Islamic

Qur'an. Instead, several important books provide information and guidance: *Koji-ki* (*Records of Ancient Events*), *Nihongi* (*Chronicles of Japan*), and *Engishiki* (*Chronicles of the Engi*).

Many Japanese people consider Osaka's Tenjin Matsuri to be one of the three greatest festivals in Japan. This celebration honors the ninth-century scholar Sugawara-no-Michizane (845-903). The people of Japan respected this man so greatly that, after his death, they began to regard him as a god of learning and literature. This promotion earned him a new name, Tenman Tenjin, or Tenjin for short. The citizens of Osaka built the Temmangu Shrine in the new god's honor in the early tenth century. The festival in his name dates back to the year 951 C.E. Many towns and cities besides Osaka also have shrines and festivals dedicated to this popular Shinto god.

Osaka's festival began as an offering to Tenjin for his protection against the plague. According to local records, hot weather wilted the people of Osaka in the year 951. Moreover, they worried about the diseases that tended to spread under these conditions. As a means of protecting themselves from illness, each resident of the city brought a piece of paper cut into the shape of a human being to the Temmangu Shrine. The Shinto priests that kept the shrine took all the pieces of paper and prayed over them while performing a ritual that involved rubbing the papers on their bodies. To complete the ritual and perfect that protection from disease that it offered, the people removed the papers from the city. They deposited the paper dolls onto boats and set sail for the mouth of the river, where they dumped the paper dolls overboard.

Some say that Osaka's Tenjin Festival reached its height during the Edo period (1603-1868). In those days, the parade from the temple to the river featured seventy float, called *danjiri* in Japanese. Nowadays, only one traditionally designed float remains. In past centuries, people from each of the city's neighborhoods fashioned eight-foot-tall dolls. During the PARADE, they would stand the dolls in front of their homes to greet the gods as they were carried by in their *mikoshi*, or portable shrine. About fifteen of these antique dolls still exist. Many of them are displayed in the Temmangu Shrine during the festival.

SYMBOLS AND CUSTOMS

Boat Parade

The boat parade takes place on the last night of the festival. The people of Osaka call this event *funatogyo*. Hundreds of lantern-lit boats and barges float down the Okawa River, which runs through the town of Osaka. Fires may be built on a ship to further illuminate their entertainments on board, which include traditional Japanese music, dance, and drama. In addition, a huge fireworks display bedazzles the night sky. Those who are not lucky enough to be on board a boat enjoy the spectacle from the water's edge. The mikoshi, too, are placed on boats and travel on the river. Afterwards they are returned to the temple in the same procession of dancers, musicians, and costumed citizens that escorted the mikoshi down to the riverside.

Hand Clapping

Groups of festival participants clap their hands in a syncopated fashion throughout the land and boat parades. Many of the local people enjoy this ritual and view it a typically Osakan gesture.

Parade

The parade begins with a Shinto religious ceremony in which the spirit of the god Tenjin is ushered from his shrine to his mikoshi, or portable shrine. A mikoshi provides a temporary dwelling place for gods and spirits. The mikoshi resemble beautifully decorated miniature temples set atop a litter. It takes a team of strong men to carry them through the streets on their shoulders. The mikoshi procession gives the god a chance to visit the people and see their level of well-being. The mikoshi of a number of other gods also participate in the Tenjin festival parade.

The land parade is one of the highlights of the festival. About 3,000 people march in this parade, dressed in the fashions of eighth-to-twelfth-century Japan. Costumed children, dancers, drummers, musicians, young ladies dressed as geishas, and political dignitaries add to the spectacle. Specially selected bearers dressed in white carry Tenjin's mikoshi through the streets and down to the river.

Tenjin Ritual

Sugawara-no-Michizane, later Tenjin, achieved great success as a poet, scholar, and statesman. He rose to great prominence as a politician in the royal court in Kyoto but lost his post due to the successful schemes of his rival. Thereafter, he was sent to Dazaifu, then a remote region, in a kind of exile. Michizane devoted the rest of his life to study and became the greatest expert on literature of his day. When he died, the people began to consider him a minor deity. This transformation is in keeping with Shinto religious beliefs that acknowledge that especially noble or successful people join the ranks of the *kami* (spirits, gods) after death.

During the Tenjin festival, the people of Osaka honor the scholar god Tenjin in a Shinto ritual. A child is chosen to play the role of Tenjin in this ceremony. The child playing Tenjin carries a halberd—a ceremonial, long-handled axe—which is called a *hoko* in Japanese. In this ritual the hoko represents the diseases that plague the city. The hoko ceremony begins at the Temmangu shrine with a ritual that includes dance and prayers. At the end of the ceremony, the shrine officials give the hoko to the child playing the role of Tenjin. The child and a shrine guardian journey together to the river and board a small white boat with a slender tree placed in the front and in the back. A rower maneuvers the boat into the center of the river. After more prayers and rituals, the child dumps the halberd overboard, symbolizing removal of the city's diseases.

FURTHER READING

Bauer, Helen, and Sherwin Carlquist. *Japanese Festivals.* Garden City, NY: Doubleday, 1965.

Henderson, Helene, ed. *Holidays, Festivals and Celebrations of the World Dictionary.* 3rd ed. Detroit: Omnigraphics, 2005.

WEB SITES

City of Osaka
www.Osaka-info.jp/tenjin_matsuri/main_en.html

Japan Atlas
web-japan.org/atlas/festivals/fes16.html

Japan National Tourist Organization
www.jnto.go.jp/eng/indepth/history/traditionalevents/a37_fes_tenjin.html

Terminalia

Type of Holiday: Ancient
Date of Observation: February 23
Where Celebrated: Rome, Italy
Symbols and Customs: Boundary Stones

ORIGINS

Terminalia was part of ancient Roman religion, which scholars date back to the sixth century B.C.E. Roman religion dominated Rome and influenced territories in its empire until Emperor Constantine's conversion to Christianity in the third century C.E. Ancient Roman religion was heavily influenced by the older Greek religion. Roman festivals therefore had much in common with those of the ancient Greeks. Not only were their gods and goddesses mostly the same as those in the Greek pantheon (though the Romans renamed them), but their religious festivals were observed with similar activities: ritual sacrifice, theatrical performances, games, and feasts.

Terminalia was a festival to worship Terminus, the god of boundaries. The festival was established by Numa, the second king of Rome. Numa founded a public festival to correspond with farmers' private worship of the spirits that inhabited the BOUNDARY STONES marking their property's borders. Terminalia, as the celebration was called, was probably the basis for a number of later ceremonies that involved marking boundaries, such as Common Ridings Day in Scotland, Beating the Bounds in England (*see* **ASCENSION DAY**), and the Boundary Walk Festivals (Grenzumgang) held in many German towns.

The terminus or boundary stones marking the outer limits of ancient Rome stood between the fifth and sixth milestones on the road to Laurentum. During the observance of the Terminalia, property owners would gather there or at the boundary stones marking their private lands. Each landowner decorated his side of the stone and helped to build the altar on which a fire would be kindled and sacrifices made. Someone would throw corn from a basket into the fire three times while the others, dressed in white, looked on in silence. The stone was then sprinkled with blood. Afterward, there would be singing and socializing among family members and servants.

On the Capitoline Hill in Rome, an ancient boundary stone was located in the temple of Jupiter. The stone was placed under an opening in the roof so that it could be worshipped under an open sky as farmers had traditionally done. How Terminus came to be associated with Jupiter is uncertain. But according to legend, when Jupiter was to be introduced into the Capitoline Temple, all of the gods made way for him except Terminus, who insisted on sharing Jupiter's space. Another theory is that the temple was erected on the site of an ancient boundary stone that was so sacred it couldn't be moved.

SYMBOLS AND CUSTOMS

Boundary Stones

The stones that marked the boundaries of privately owned property in ancient Rome were regarded as the dwelling place of *numina*, spirits that can be traced back to very primitive times. These spirits helped to promote good relationships among neighbors and to keep strong territorial feelings under control. Their purpose can perhaps best be summarized by a line from the American poet Robert Frost: "Good fences make good neighbors."

Certain rites were carried out every time a boundary stone was put in place. Fruits of the earth, honey, and wine, along with the bones, ashes, and blood of a lamb or a suckling pig, were placed in a hole located where property owned by two or three farmers converged. A stone or a stump of wood was then rammed down on top of these offerings and fixed in place. The fact that sacrificial blood was considered essential to the ritual indicates just how important it was.

FURTHER READING

Fowler, W. Warde. *The Roman Festivals of the Period of the Republic*. New York: Macmillan Co., 1925.

Henderson, Helene, ed. *Holidays, Festivals, and Celebrations of the World Dictionary*. 3rd ed. Detroit: Omnigraphics, 2005.

Hole, Christina. *English Custom & Usage*. 1941. Reprint. Detroit: Omnigraphics, 1990.

James, E.O. *Seasonal Feasts and Festivals*. 1961. Reprint. Detroit: Omnigraphics, 1993.

Lemprière, John. *Lemprière's Classical Dictionary*. Rev. ed. London: Bracken, 1994.

Scullard, H.H. *Festivals and Ceremonies of the Roman Republic*. Ithaca, NY: Cornell University Press, 1981.

Tet

Type of Holiday: Calendar/Seasonal
Date of Observation: Usually late January or early February; first to seventh day of first lunar month
Where Celebrated: Vietnam
Symbols and Customs: Cay Neu, Peach Tree
Colors: It is customary at Tet to give children red envelopes with money in them. The color red is symbolic of happiness.
Related Holidays: Chinese New Year, Sol

ORIGINS

The Tet festival is a Vietnamese celebration of the new year. The new year is celebrated at about the same time by several countries in Asia—Vietnam as well as China, Japan, and Korea—and with many of the same customs, such as offerings to household god(s), housecleaning and new clothes, banquets, ancestor worship, and fireworks. The date of the new year in these countries is based on a lunisolar calendar, similar to or the same as the one used in China. The exception for this timing is Japan, which has employed the Gregorian calendar since 1873 and thus observes New Year's Day on January 1, though many older traditions remain.

The Chinese lunisolar calendar is based on the oldest system of time measurement still in use. It is widely employed in Asian countries to set the dates of seasonal festivals. The **CHINESE NEW YEAR** takes place on the new moon nearest to the point which is defined in the West as the fifteenth degree on the zodiacal sign of Aquarius. Each of twelve months in the Chinese year is twenty-nine or thirty days long and is divided into two parts, each of which is two weeks long. The Chinese calendar, like all lunisolar systems, requires periodic adjustment to keep the lunar and solar cycles integrated; therefore, an intercalary month is added when necessary.

"Tet" is an abbreviation for *Tet Nguyen Dan*, which means "first day" in Vietnamese. It is the most important festival of the year in Vietnam, signifying both the beginning of the year and the arrival of spring. People wear new clothes, settle their old debts and quarrels, clean and repaint their houses, and visit their friends and relatives. Tet is also a time for making sacrifices and setting out special foods for the family's deceased ancestors, who are invited to come back for a few days and share in the festivities with the living members of the family.

The seven days of Tet officially begin with a ceremony bidding farewell to the kitchen god or spirit of the household, who leaves at midnight on the last day of the old year to travel to the celestial court of the Jade Emperor and report on the family's affairs. After he has left, firecrackers are set off to usher in the new year. Because the first visitor to arrive at the house after midnight is believed to influence the family's happiness and well-being for the entire year, many families invite certain guests to drop by early and encourage others, who might be unlucky, to come later. If a rich man should be the first caller, for example, it means that the family's fortunes will increase during the coming year. Whatever happens on the first day of Tet is believed to set the "tone" for the rest of the year, so everyone tries to be as polite, cheerful, and optimistic as possible.

On the first day of the new year, the adults of the household get up early and set up an altar to honor the departed ancestors. Twice a day, special foods are prepared and placed on the family altar for the ancestors who come back to visit. The second day is spent visiting friends and relatives, and the third day is spent visiting one's teachers. The ancestors are believed to depart on the fourth day of Tet, after which most people return to work, and life resumes a more normal pace. This is also a popular day to visit graveyards, where family members escort their departing relatives back to the land of the dead.

Tet became known all over the world in 1968 for the "Tet Offensive" of the Vietnam War. The lunar New Year truce was shattered on January 31 by attacks from

North Vietnam and the National Liberation Front against more than 100 South Vietnamese cities. The attacks were repulsed, and the United States and South Vietnam claimed victory. But television viewers who had seen the ferocity of the attack knew otherwise, and the Tet Offensive led to increased pressure from Americans to end the war.

SYMBOLS AND CUSTOMS

Cay Neu

The Cay Neu is a high bamboo pole set up in front of the house on the last day of the old lunar year. Various items are placed on top, including red paper with special inscriptions and a small basket containing various gifts for the good spirits of the household—including betel and areca nuts, wind chimes, a small square of woven bamboo (a symbolic barrier to stop evil spirits), and cock feathers for decoration. The Vietnamese believe that since the good spirits of the household must report to heaven during Tet, special precautionary measures must be taken to scare off the evil spirits, who might otherwise take advantage of the situation. But even the Cay Neu cannot stop a bad spirit, so many families take the added precaution of scattering lime powder around the house and using it to draw a bow and arrow in front of the threshold—a symbolic weapon to drive away evil.

Peach Tree

It is very common to place a flowering branch of the peach tree in a vase for the duration of the Tet holiday. A symbol of longevity and immortality, the peach boughs placed in and around the house at the new year are believed to drive away evil spirits.

Certain Vietnamese villages specialize in cultivating peach trees particularly for this purpose. But factories in Hanoi also make artificial peach tree branches that resemble the real thing and last much longer.

FURTHER READING

Cohen, Hennig, and Tristram Potter Coffin. *The Folklore of American Holidays*. 3rd ed. Detroit: Gale Research, 1999.

Eberhard, Wolfram. *A Dictionary of Chinese Symbols: Hidden Symbols in Chinese Life and Thought*. New York: Routledge & Kegan Paul, 1986.

Henderson, Helene, ed. *Holidays, Festivals, and Celebrations of the World Dictionary*. 3rd ed. Detroit: Omnigraphics, 2005.

Ickis, Marguerite. *The Book of Festivals and Holidays the World Over*. New York: Dodd, Mead, 1970.

MacDonald, Margaret R., ed. *The Folklore of World Holidays*. Detroit: Gale Research, 1992.

Santino, Jack. *All Around the Year: Holidays and Celebrations in American Life*. Urbana: University of Illinois Press, 1994.

WEB SITE

University of Kansas Medical Center
www3.kumc.edu/diversity/ethnic_relig/tet.html

Thaipusam (Thai Poosam)

Type of Holiday: Religious (Hindu)
Date of Observation: January-February for three days
Where Celebrated: India, Malaysia, Sri Lanka, Singapore, South Africa, Mauritius
Symbols and Customs: Kavadi (Kavadee)

ORIGINS

The Thaipusam festival is part of the traditions of Hinduism, which many scholars regard as the oldest living religion. The word Hindu is derived from the Sanskrit term *Sindhu* (or *Indus*), which meant river. It referred to people living in the Indus valley in the Indian subcontinent. Hinduism has no founder, one universal reality (or god) known as Brahman, many gods and goddesses (sometimes referred to as devtas), and several scriptures. Hinduism also has no priesthood or hierarchical structure similar to that seen in some other religions, such as Christianity. Hindus acknowledge the authority of a wide variety of writings, but there is no single, uniform canon. The oldest of the Hindu writings are the *Vedas*. The word "veda" comes from the Sanskrit word for knowledge. The *Vedas*, which were compiled from ancient oral traditions, contain hymns, instructions, explanations, chants for sacrifices, magical formulas, and philosophy. Another set of sacred books includes the *Great Epics*, which illustrate Hindu faith in practice. The *Epics* include the *Ramayana*, the *Mahabharata*, and the *Bhagavad Gita*.

The Hindu pantheon includes approximately thirty-three million gods. Some of these are held in higher esteem than others. Over all the gods, Hindus believe in one absolute high god or universal concept. This is Brahman. Although he is above all the gods, he is not worshipped in popular ceremonies because he is detached from the day-to-day affairs of the people. Brahman is impersonal. Lesser gods and goddesses (devtas) serve him. Because these are more intimately involved in the affairs of people, they are venerated as gods. The most honored god in Hinduism varies among the different Hindu sects. Although Hindu adherents practice their faith differently and venerate different deities, they share a similar view of reality and look back on a common history.

Thaipusam is one of the most dramatic Hindu festivals and marks the birthday of Lord Subramaniam (Subramanya), second son of the goddess Parvati. Hindus show their devotion to Subramaniam in a number of ways on this day, many of which involve testing their ability to withstand physical pain (*see* KAVADI).

In Malaysia, the highlight of the festival is the procession from Kuala Lumpur to the Batu Caves about eight miles away. The statue of Subramanya is decorated with jewels and finery and placed on an elaborately carved chariot drawn by bullocks. The devotees who join in the procession through the main streets of the city to the caves chant the slogan, *vel-vel, vetri-vel*—a reference to the lance (*vel*) that Parvati gave to her son. The statue is later carried up the 272 steps to the cave and placed beside the permanent statue kept there. The next day, about one million devotees begin to pay homage, while movies, carousels, and other entertainments are provided for their amusement. Temporary sheds are erected to house the worshippers who have traveled a great distance and must stay there during the three-day festival.

Self-inflicted torture is part of the celebration of Thaipusam in some countries, particularly among the Tamil people in Mauritius and in Durban, South Africa.

SYMBOLS AND CUSTOMS

Kavadi (Kavadee)

The most extreme way of showing devotion to Subramanya during Thaipusam is known as "kavadi-carrying." A *kavadi* is a wooden arch on a wooden base, decorated with flowers, peacock feathers, and paper. It is carried on the devotee's shoulders, with various food offerings tied to the arch or balanced on the base. The kavadi bearers prepare for their ordeal by abstaining from all meat and sex during the ten days preceding the festival. Before they begin their journey, they undergo a special ceremony to put them in a trance-like state. Then they subject themselves to various degrees of physical torture, which may include having their upper bodies symmetrically pierced with vels (lances) and skewers thrust through their cheeks and tongues.

The procession begins, with the devotees carrying the kavadis on their shoulders. Some draw a small chariot behind them by means of chains fixed to hooks dug into their sides; others wear sandals studded with nails. In some areas, as many as 600-800 kavadis appear in the procession, and the people carrying them are usually in a state of utter frenzy or exhaustion by the time they deposit their burdens at the feet of the statue of Subramanya.

Some Hindus believe that carrying the kavadi washes away sins through self-inflicted suffering. Others see it as a symbol of the triumph of good over evil. Most Hindus who choose to carry the kavadi during this festival do so to achieve a desired objective or to pay back the gods for helping them avoid a calamity. Someone who has recently recovered from a life-threatening illness, or who has finally given birth to a child, for example, may take a vow to bear kavadi on Thaipusam day.

FURTHER READING

Bellenir, Karen. *Religious Holidays and Calendars*. 3rd ed. Detroit: Omnigraphics, 2004.

Henderson, Helene, ed. *Holidays, Festivals, and Celebrations of the World Dictionary*. 3rd ed. Detroit: Omnigraphics, 2005.

MacDonald, Margaret R., ed. *The Folklore of World Holidays*. Detroit: Gale Research, 1992.

Shemanski, Frances. *A Guide to World Fairs and Festivals*. Westport, CT: Greenwood Press, 1985.

WEB SITE

Malaysian Tourism Promotion Board
www.visitmalaysia.com/holthaipusam.html

Thanksgiving

Type of Holiday: Historic, National
Date of Observation: Fourth Thursday in November (United States); second Monday in October (Canada)
Where Celebrated: Canada, United States
Symbols and Customs: Corn Dolly, Cornucopia, Indian Corn, Parades, Pilgrims, Plymouth Rock, Turkey
Colors: The colors of the autumn harvest—orange, brown, and gold—can be seen in Thanksgiving decorations and table settings. Because it is not strictly a religious festival, there are no liturgical colors associated with the day.
Related Holidays: Harvest Home Festival, Lammas, Sukkot, Wampanoag Pow-wow

ORIGINS

Thanksgiving is a national holiday in the United States. National holidays can be defined as those commemorations that a nation's government has deemed important enough to warrant inclusion in the list of official public holidays. They tend to honor a person or event that has been critical in the development of the nation and its identity. Such people and events usually reflect values and traditions shared by a large portion of the citizenry.

In the United States, patiotism and identity were nurtured from the beginning of the nation by the very act of celebrating new events in holidays like the Fourth of July, battle anniversaries, and other notable occasions. This was even more important in the country's early years because the nation was composed of people from a variety of backgrounds and traditions. The invention of traditions and the marking of important occasions in the life of the new nation were crucial in creating a shared bond of tradition and a sense of common belonging to a relatively new homeland through the shared experience of celebrating common holidays. As more and diverse peoples migrated to the United States, it became even more important to celebrate significant annual anniversaries, and Thanksgiving soon became one of the nation's most important shared celebrations.

The autumn harvest has always been a cause for celebration. The ancient Greeks honored Demeter, their corn goddess, at the annual festival known as the **THES-MOPHORIA** in October, when the seeds for the next year's crop were about to be planted. The Romans had their Cerealia, held each year on October 4 in honor of the grain goddess, Ceres. They offered her the first fruits of the harvest and paraded through the field, participating in games and sports and sharing a huge thanksgiving feast. The Jews observed **SUKKOT**, or the Feast of Tabernacles, in the autumn as well. They hung the walls of the small huts built for this festival with apples, grapes, corn, pomegranates, and other fruits and vegetables. Both the North American and South American Indians celebrated the harvest as well. All of these early thanksgiving ceremonies were social as well as religious occasions, providing those whose work in the fields was completed with an opportunity to sing, dance, feast, and play games.

In America, there were at least two thanksgiving celebrations before the one that took place at Plymouth in 1621. In 1607, a group of English settlers led by Captain George Popham met with a group of Abnaki Indians near the mouth of the Kennebec River to share a harvest feast and prayer meeting. On December 14, 1619, there was a celebration in Virginia led by Captain John Woodleaf and thirty-nine colonists who had traveled up the James River from Jamestown to a place called Berkeley Hundred, where they went ashore and gave thanks.

Most Americans, however, think of the first "official" Thanksgiving as being the one that took place at Plymouth Colony in October 1621, a year after the PILGRIMS first landed on the New England coast (*see* PLYMOUTH ROCK). They were joined in their three-day feast by Massasoit, the chief of the Wampanoag tribe, and about ninety of his fellow tribesmen. Only fifty of the original 100 Pilgrims had survived the first winter, and those who did owed their survival to the Indians. The feast they shared with them in 1621 was primarily a harvest celebration rather than a religious one (*see* **WAMPANOAG POWWOW**).

During the next several years, no one specific day was set aside in the American colonies for giving thanks. A day would be named when there was a special reason to be thankful, such as a bumper crop or escape from an epidemic. It was largely due to the efforts of a women's magazine editor named Sarah Hale that Thanksgiving came to be a national holiday. She petitioned presidents and government officials for more than twenty years to establish a national day of thanksgiving. On October 3, 1863, President Abraham Lincoln finally proclaimed the fourth Thursday in November as Thanksgiving Day. President Franklin D. Roosevelt moved it up a week to stimulate the economy by allowing more time for **CHRISTMAS** shopping. But the tradition was already so well established that the change created an uproar. Finally, Congress ruled in 1941 that the fourth Thursday in November would be the legal federal holiday. Canadians celebrate their Thanksgiving Day on the second Monday in October.

The Pilgrims' Thanksgiving can be traced back to the English **HARVEST HOME FESTIVAL** and Dutch thanksgiving traditions, which some Pilgrims learned about during the ten years they spent in the city of Leyden before coming to America. Today, Thanksgiving is a time for family reunions, most of which center around the preparation of an elaborate meal featuring TURKEY and a dozen or so accompanying dishes. Although some people go to special church services on Thanksgiving Day, far more line the streets to watch PARADES or sit in front of the television watching football games. In many American cities and towns, the day after Thanksgiving marks the official start of the **CHRISTMAS** shopping season.

SYMBOLS AND CUSTOMS

Corn Dolly

Many rituals were associated with the cutting of the last sheaf of corn at the harvest. At one time, people believed that the corn spirit or corn goddess ran from plant to plant, just ahead of the advancing sickles. Sometimes farmers "caught" the corn spirit by making the last sheaf into a doll, who was believed to possess magical powers. The corn doll was then decorated with ribbons or crowned with a wreath of flowers and hung up on the farmhouse wall until it was time to plow for the next year's crops. Then the farmer's wife would cut the doll into pieces and bring it to the fields as food for the horses; or she would burn it, and the farmer would plow the ashes back into the earth as a way of ensuring a plentiful harvest. In some places, the corn doll would be thrown into a river in the hope that it would guarantee sufficient rainfall.

At the traditional English festival known as Harvest Home, the last of the corn was piled on a cart decorated with flowers, ribbons, and green branches. A "lord" and "lady" of the harvest were chosen to ride in the cart, and as it passed, people hiding in the bushes would throw buckets of water at it—another rain charm.

In America today, small dolls made from corn husks are a popular household decoration at Thanksgiving.

Cornucopia

Also known as the "horn of plenty," the cornucopia is not only a harvest symbol but a symbol of early America, with its seemingly endless supply of game and produce. In ancient Rome, a goat's horn overflowing with fruit and other foods was an attribute of both Flora, the goddess of flowers, and Fortuna, the goddess of fortune. In Greece, it was associated with Amalthea, a nymph in the form of a goat who nursed the infant Zeus in a cave on the island of Crete. According to legend, Amalthea broke off one of her horns and, filling it with fruits and flowers, gave it to Zeus. To show his gratitude, Zeus set the goat's image in the sky as the constellation Capricorn. In another version of the myth, the grateful young Zeus breaks off a goat's horn and gives it to Amalthea, his foster mother, telling her it will supply her with whatever she needs.

Cornucopia—from the Latin *cornu copiae,* meaning "horn of plenty"—is a longstanding symbol of fruitfulness and abundance. Americans often place cornucopia baskets on their Thanksgiving tables to symbolize their gratitude for the feast they are about to share.

Indian Corn

The Pilgrims didn't know about corn when they first arrived in America, but the Indians showed them how to plant the kernels and fertilize the mounds with fish. Because they didn't want the Indians to know how many of the original settlers had died that first winter, the Pilgrims planted corn over the graves to disguise them. The ears of maize or Indian corn, as it was known, were small and knobby, with red, yellow, blue, green, and blackish kernels. Sometimes they were roasted and eaten, but more often they were dried and pounded into cornmeal for cornbread and cornmeal mush.

While it is not part of the traditional Thanksgiving menu, Indian corn is a favorite household decoration at this time of year. Although corn is an ancient symbol of fertility, prosperity, and growth, the irregularly shaped and colored Indian corn is a more recent American symbol of the harvest.

Parades

In ancient Greece and Rome, harvest celebrations often included farm wagons decorated with sheaves of grain. Today, many Americans celebrate Thanksgiving with parades featuring floats reminiscent of these early harvest wagons. In fact, some scholars see the harvest queens who ride in modern-day Thanksgiving parades as the descendants of the pagan corn goddesses.

The oldest Thanksgiving Day parade, which dates back to 1920, is the one held by Gimbel's department store in Philadelphia. Macy's department store in New York held its first parade in 1924. Today the Macy's parade features characters from story books, movies, television, and toyland. In recent years, it has attracted more than three million spectators, while another sixty million Americans have watched it on television. In Hollywood, television and movie stars parade through the streets on floats.

Pilgrims

Originally the Pilgrims were called Puritans because they wanted to "purify" the Church of England, which they felt was too concerned with ritual and with telling people what to believe. They met secretly in homes to study the Bible and listen to sermons. Those who were prepared to leave the Church of England and set up their own church—without bishops, altars, candles, incense, or organ music—were known as Separatists. Because the English church and government were one and the same in the 1600s, separating from the church was considered an act of treason. One group of Separatists, under the leadership of William Brewster, decided to move to Holland. They lived in Leyden for ten years, but worried about their children forgetting English language and customs. Fifty or sixty of these, along with other passengers who had their own reasons for wanting to leave—102 in all—decided to make the journey to the New World on board the *Mayflower*. Among the best-known Pilgrims are Miles Standish and John Alden, who were not Separatists at all but who became famous as characters in Henry Wadsworth Longfellow's 1858 poem, "The Courtship of Miles Standish."

The Pilgrims as seen today—on Thanksgiving posters, greeting cards, paper table-cloths and napkins, and in the form of candles or figurines—wear gray, black, or dun-colored clothing with white collars and cuffs. They have tall black hats with broad brims and a silver buckle in front; their shoes have silver buckles as well. The women and girls usually wear long dresses in drab colors with white aprons and caps. In reality, however, Pilgrim women often wore red, purple, bright blue, or green dresses colored with vegetable dyes. The ornamental buckles seen on the Pilgrims' hats and shoes weren't introduced until later in the seventeenth century.

The figures of Pilgrims seen at Thanksgiving today are a symbol of the bravery and determination of America's earliest settlers. They are often portrayed as male-female couples because they represent the "parents" of the American people.

Plymouth Rock

Perhaps the most famous landmark in America today is the granite boulder on which the Pilgrims first stepped when they came ashore at Plymouth, Massachusetts. But until just before the American Revolution, it was simply another rock. During the next century it was moved first to Plymouth's town square, then to a local museum known as Pilgrim Hall. Finally it was brought back to the water-front and placed under a stone canopy with a box believed to contain Pilgrim bones. Eventually, to prevent souvenir-hunters from chipping off pieces, the rock was placed in a pit surrounded by an iron railing, with a portico overhead to shelter visitors from the weather.

Whether or not the Pilgrims actually stepped ashore on this rock is not known with any certainty. Apparently there was a huge boulder about forty feet from shore along the sandy coast of Massachusetts in 1620. But since there is no documentation about exactly where the Pilgrims landed, there is no way of knowing whether this rock provided them with a stepping-stone. Some historians have theorized that the Pilgrims used the rock as a landmark to help guide them into the harbor.

Plymouth Rock has long symbolized America's freedom. During the Revolutionary War, the residents of Plymouth took it as a good omen rather than a coincidence when the rock split in two while being pried from its bed for use as a pedestal for a liberty pole: Shortly after, the colonies officially split from England. The two halves were eventually reunited under a protective canopy at the foot of Coles Hill, where it now sits. Although originally estimated to have measured twelve feet in diameter and to have weighed seven or eight tons, over the years the rock has been whittled down considerably by souvenir-hunters and the difficulties of moving it.

Turkey

There is no record of what was eaten at the Pilgrims' first Thanksgiving feast. The Indians who had been sent out to hunt probably returned with wild geese and ducks, but there is no way of knowing whether they brought back a turkey—a large, stately bird with greenish-bronze feathers that was native to North America. Because of their size (twenty to thirty pounds) and because they were relatively easy to catch, however, wild turkeys quickly became an important source of food for the early American settlers.

Some say the turkey was named by the late sixteenth-century European explorers, who confused it with the European turkey cock, a completely different bird. Others claim that the word comes from the Hebrew *tukki*, meaning "big bird," which is what the doctor on Columbus's ship shouted when he saw one for the first time. In any case, the turkey did not become an American Thanksgiving tradition until the 1860s. After World War II, an aggressive marketing campaign by the poultry industry and the development of larger, hybrid turkeys combined to make the stuffed bird a symbol of American abundance and the traditional main course at Thanksgiving dinner.

The custom of snapping the turkey's wishbone, bringing luck to the person who gets the larger half, can be traced back to the Romans. It was certainly a well-established tradition in England by the time the Pilgrims brought it to America. Some word historians believe that the bone-snapping custom gave rise to the popular expression, "to get a lucky break."

Today, Americans eat more than 690 million pounds of turkey every Thanksgiving, accompanied by such traditional American dishes as cranberries, squash, mashed potatoes, sweet potatoes, pumpkin pie, and stuffing (which the Pilgrims referred to as "pudding in the belly"). After the United States won its independence, Congress debated the choice of a national bird. Benjamin Franklin thought the bald eagle was a bird of "bad moral character" and advocated the turkey as a "true, original Native of North America."

FURTHER READING

Barth, Edna. *Turkeys, Pilgrims, and Indian Corn: The Story of the Thanksgiving Symbols*. New York: Seabury Press, 1975.

Biedermann, Hans. *Dictionary of Symbolism: Cultural Icons and the Meanings Behind Them*. New York: Meridian Books, 1994.

Cirlot, J.E. *A Dictionary of Symbols*. New York: Philosophical Library, 1962.

Graham-Barber, Lynda. *Gobble!: The Complete Book of Thanksgiving Words*. New York: Bradbury Press, 1991.

Henderson, Helene, ed. *Holidays, Festivals, and Celebrations of the World Dictionary*. 3rd ed. Detroit: Omnigraphics, 2005.

Henderson, Helene. *Patriotic Holidays of the United States*. Detroit: Omnigraphics, 2006.

Penner, Lucille Recht. *The Thanksgiving Book*. New York: Hastings House, 1986.

Purdy, Susan. *Festivals for You to Celebrate*. Philadelphia: Lippincott, 1969.

Santino, Jack. *All Around the Year: Holidays and Celebrations in American Life*. Urbana: University of Illinois Press, 1994.

Tuleja, Tad. *Curious Customs: The Stories Behind 296 Popular American Rituals*. New York: Harmony, 1987.

WEB SITE

The History Channel
www.history.com/minisites/thanksgiving

Thesmophoria

Type of Holiday: Ancient
Date of Observation: October
Where Celebrated: Greece
Symbols and Customs: Pigs

ORIGINS

The Greek religion flourished in the ancient Greek city-states and surrounding areas between the eighth and fourth centuries B.C.E. The city-state of Athens was the center of ancient Greek civilization, and major ceremonies took place there. Within Athens, the Acropolis was the religious center, consisting of temples dedicated to the gods and goddesses. However, smaller sanctuaries to the gods and goddesses also existed throughout the region.

Ancient Greek religion pervaded every aspect of life, and there was no concept of a separation between sacred and secular observances. Thus, ancient Greek festivals were religious occasions. Ritual and sacrifice, athletic games, dramatic performances, and feasting were all elements of festivals.

The ancient Greek festival known as the Thesmophoria was observed only by women for three days in October (some say between the eleventh and the thirteenth; others say between the fourteenth and the sixteenth), at a time of year when the ground was being prepared for the autumn sowing of crops. It was held in honor of the corn goddess and earth mother Demeter, who was sometimes referred to as Thesmophorus. According to Greek mythology, Demeter's daughter Kore, the corn maiden, was gathering flowers near Eleusis one day when she was abducted by Pluto, god of the underworld, and taken away to his subterranean kingdom. By lowering PIGS into chasms in the earth, the women chosen to participate in the rituals of the Thesmophoria commemorated the abduction of Kore.

In Athens and other Greek cities, women dressed in white robes and observed a period of strict chastity for several days before and during the ceremony. They would strew their beds with herbs that were supposed to ward off venereal diseases and sit on the ground to promote the fertility of the corn that had just been sown. Although the festival itself was taken very seriously, it was not uncommon for the women to joke among themselves, as if in doing so they could cheer up the goddess Demeter, who suffered greatly over the loss of her daughter.

Scholars believe that the Thesmophoria can be traced back to an even more ancient festival that celebrated the bringing up of the corn from the underground silos in which it was stored after being threshed in June. During the four months when the grain was concealed in the earth, the fields were barren and parched by the sun. It wasn't until the winter rains began in October that they could be plowed and sown again, so this was an appropriate time to hold a festival celebrating the earth's fertility. The Romans had a similar festival in honor of Ceres, called the Cerealia.

SYMBOLS AND CUSTOMS

Pigs

Pigs were considered sacred to Demeter because, according to legend, when the earth opened up and Pluto emerged in his chariot to abduct Kore, the herdsman Eubouleus and his pigs were swallowed up as well.

To commemorate this event, pigs were let down into caves or clefts in the earth, together with cakes and the branches of pine trees. Each year at the Thesmophoria, women who had undergone special purification rituals for the purpose went down into these underground chasms and brought up the putrefied remains of the pigs that had been thrown in there the previous year. The rotted flesh was placed on altars and mixed with seed-corn, which was then sown in the fields as a kind of magical fertilizer to ensure a good crop.

The pigs are not only symbolic of Kore, the corn maiden, but of the corn itself, which was at one time stored in underground silos. Bringing the pig-flesh up out of the earth symbolizes the return of the earth's fertility at the beginning of the winter rainy season.

FURTHER READING

Henderson, Helene, ed. *Holidays, Festivals, and Celebrations of the World Dictionary.* 3rd ed. Detroit: Omnigraphics, 2005.

James, E.O. *Seasonal Feasts and Festivals.* 1961. Reprint. Detroit: Omnigraphics, 1993.

Lemprière, John. *Lemprière's Classical Dictionary of Proper Names Mentioned in Ancient Authors.* 3rd ed. London: Routledge, 1984.

Scullard, H.H. *Festivals and Ceremonies of the Roman Republic.* Ithaca, NY: Cornell University Press, 1981.

Tihar

Type of Holiday: Religious (Hindu)
Date of Observation: Five days in October-November; starting on the thirteenth day of the waning half of the Hindu month of Kartika
Where Celebrated: Nepal
Symbols and Customs: Brothers and Sisters, Cow, Crow, Dog, Gambling, Oil Lamps, Ox, Tika
Related Holidays: Dewali

ORIGINS

The festival Tihar is part of the religious tradition of Hinduism, which many scholars regard as the oldest living religion. The word Hindu is derived from the Sanskrit term *Sindhu* (or *Indus*), which meant river. It referred to people living in the Indus valley in the Indian subcontinent. Hinduism has no founder, one universal reality (or god) known as Brahman, many gods and goddesses (sometimes referred to as devtas), and several scriptures. Hinduism also has no priesthood or hierarchical structure similar to that seen in some other religions, such as Christianity. Hindus acknowledge the authority of a wide variety of writings, but there is no single, uniform canon. The oldest of the Hindu writings are the *Vedas*. The word "veda" comes from the Sanskrit word for knowledge. The *Vedas*, which were compiled from ancient oral traditions, contain hymns, instructions, explanations, chants for sacrifices, magical formulas, and philosophy. Another set of sacred books includes the *Great Epics*, which illustrate Hindu faith in practice. The *Epics* include the *Ramayana*, the *Mahabharata*, and the *Bhagavad Gita*.

The Hindu pantheon includes approximately thirty-three million gods. Some of these are held in higher esteem than others. Over all the gods, Hindus believe in one absolute high god or universal concept. This is Brahman. Although he is above all the gods, he is not worshipped in popular ceremonies because he is detached from the day-to-day affairs of the people. Brahman is impersonal. Lesser gods and goddesses (devtas) serve him. Because these are more intimately involved in the affairs of people, they are venerated as gods. The most honored god in Hinduism varies among the different Hindu sects. Although Hindu adherents practice their faith differently and venerate different deities, they share a similar view of reality and look back on a common history.

Tihar is a five-day festival observed in Nepal that roughly corresponds to what is known as the Festival of Lights or **DEWALI** in India and elsewhere. But the celebration in Nepal is unique. It focuses not just on Laxmi (known as Lakshmi in India), the Hindu goddess of wealth and wife of Lord Vishnu, but on the CROW, the DOG, the COW, and the OX—all domestic animals that have deep symbolic value to the Nepalese. It also emphasizes family bonds, particularly those between BROTHERS AND SISTERS.

According to Hindu belief, King Bali showed his devotion to Lord Vishnu by offering him everything he owned. In return, Vishnu said that, for a five-day period each year, Bali could rule over all three worlds—heaven, earth, and the underworld. During these five days, therefore, Yama, who is the king of the underworld and god of death, has to leave his kingdom and stay with his sister, Yamuna.

The first day of the five-day festival is dedicated to honoring CROWS—birds normally regarded as sacred in Nepal. Hindus put out food for them in the morning on small trays or plates made of leaves, or they offer the first serving of their own breakfast to the crows. Then they bathe in a nearby river and light an OIL LAMP. The second day is devoted to DOGS, who have garlands of flowers looped around their necks and a TIKA placed on their foreheads. Special meals are prepared, not only for family pets but for stray dogs, who can often be seen running around town wearing flower necklaces.

The festival's third day is the most important and the one that most closely resembles the celebration of **DEWALI** because it is dedicated to honoring Laxmi, the Hindu goddess of wealth. She is usually depicted as standing on or holding a lotus flower, and her image is often placed on doors and lintels so that she will bring good luck to all who enter. It is believed that at midnight on the third day of Tihar, Laxmi rides around the world on the owl that serves as her mode of transportation, stopping only at those houses where she is being worshipped properly. In anticipation of her midnight visit, Nepalese families scrub the entranceways to their houses and mark the area outside the door with red mud so that Laxmi cannot possibly miss seeing it. Sometimes they will also mark a path from the front door to the family's money box, where emergency funds are kept, in the hope that the goddess of wealth will increase the family's resources. The third day of Tihar is also dedicated to COWS, the national animal of Nepal and a sacred animal to all Hindus. It is common to see cows wearing marigold garlands around their necks and TIKAS on their foreheads. But the most beautiful spectacle on this third day is the thousands of tiny OIL LAMPS that burn in every door and window.

While the fourth day of Tihar is dedicated to worshipping the OX in much the same way that the other animals were worshipped—with garlands, TIKAS, and special meals—what makes this day different is the custom known as *Maha Puja*, which means "self worship." Since this is also New Year's Day according to the calendar used by Nepal's Newar community, worshipping oneself amounts to wishing oneself good health and happiness for the coming year. It is believed that performing this *puja* or worship of the self honors the spirit that dwells in each person's body.

The fifth and final day of the festival, known as Bhai Tika, is the day on which sisters honor their brothers—or, if they have no brothers, they are permitted to substitute a cousin or other close relative. Sisters pray to Yama, god of the underworld, so that he will grant their brothers a long life, and they perform certain rituals to protect their brothers from being claimed by Yama and carried off to his underground kingdom. In return, brothers often give their sisters gifts of cash and promise to protect their honor. The festival ends with a huge feast in celebration of family bonds.

SYMBOLS AND CUSTOMS

Brothers and Sisters

Sisters pay homage to their brothers during Tihar because Yama, the god of the underworld, leaves his kingdom to visit his sister Yamuna during the five-day period of the festival. Just as Yamuna worships Yama with special rituals throughout his stay, Nepalese women and girls honor their brothers by breaking a walnut, by drawing a ring of mustard oil around them, and by putting garlands of flowers around their necks and a multicolored TIKA on their foreheads.

Cow

The cow or gai is the Hindus' most sacred animal. Cows also symbolize wealth, which is why the cow is honored on the same day that Laxmi, the goddess of wealth, is worshipped.

Crow

In Hindu mythology the crow is the messenger of death. By honoring crows on the second day of Tihar, Nepalese Hindus hope to earn the crows' favor and thus salvation for themselves and their offspring.

Dog

As in American society, the dog plays the role of both household pet and companion as well as guardian of the house in Nepal. Bhairava, the Hindu god of destruction, is often depicted with a dog at his side or riding a dog like a horse. There is also a legendary dog who guards the gate to Yama's underworld kingdom. Dogs are therefore animals to be respected if not feared, and honoring them during Tihar is one way of avoiding the torments of hell.

Gambling

Gambling and games of chance have a long tradition as part of the celebration of **DEWALI** (*see* GAMES OF CHANCE). Although gambling is illegal in Nepal, such rules are suspended during the observation of Tihar, when games involving cards and dice are common. Unfortunately, in recent years Nepalese young people have become so fond of drinking and gambling during the holiday that they largely ignore its religious roots and significance as a time for families to get together. Gambling in many cases leads to disputes over money which, when fueled by alcohol, can result in violence. The older generation in Nepal has lamented this shift in the festival's focus, which is so contrary to its original purpose.

Oil Lamps

The oil lamps that sparkle everywhere during Tihar usually have cotton wicks and burn mustard oil. They are a symbolic means of welcoming Laxmi, the goddess of wealth, into the house, where it is hoped that she will improve the family's fortunes. The lamps also recall the return of Rama, hero of the Hindu epic Ramayana, to his home town of Ayodhya after his many years of exile. The entire city was lit with oil lamps to welcome him back.

Ox

The ox is the animal that helps the Nepalese plow their fields and perform other difficult tasks, for which it is highly esteemed. Like the cows and dogs who are honored earlier in the festival, oxen are draped with flower garlands and served special meals on the fourth day of Tihar. Some people also perform what is known as Gobardhan puja—the worship of Gobardhan Hill, which resembles the hump on an ox's back—by making a small hill of cow dung and covering it with grass before performing puja on it. It is believed that Lord Krishna created the Gobardhan Hill to save people and their cows from a terrible flood.

Tika

Also known as the bindhi or kumkum, the tika is a small red or maroon dot worn on the forehead between the eyebrows, in an area where energy is believed to accumulate in the human body. The red color is said to symbolize the blood sacrifices that were at one time offered to the Hindu gods and also to represent love. It is a symbol of good fortune; women whose husbands have died do not wear the tika, nor do those who have experienced a death in the family. Men used to wear the tika as a sign of spiritual achievement, but today they wear it primarily during religious ceremonies.

Traditionally, the tika is made from powdered spices and flowers that have been turned into a paste. But nowadays most tikas are of the "stick-on" variety. They come in many different shapes, colors, and sizes, and they are more of a fashion statement than an indicator of the wearer's status or spirituality.

FURTHER READING

Leach, Maria, ed. *Funk & Wagnalls Standard Dictionary of Folklore, Mythology & Legend*. San Francisco: Harper & Row, 1984.

MacDonald, Margaret R., ed. *The Folklore of World Holidays*. Detroit: Gale Research, 1992.

Stutley, Margaret, and James Stutley. *A Dictionary of Hinduism*. San Francisco: Harper & Row, 1977.

WEB SITE

Nepal Home Page
www.nepalhomepage.com/society/festivals/tihar.html

Timkat (Timqat)

Type of Holiday: Religious (Orthodox Christian)
Date of Observation: January 19
Where Celebrated: Ethiopia
Symbols and Customs: Guks, Mass Baptism, Tabot
Related Holidays: Epiphany, Ganna

ORIGINS

Timkat is celebrated in Ethiopia by Orthodox Christians. The word Christian refers to a follower of Christ, which is a title derived from the Greek word meaning Messiah or Anointed One. The Christ of Christianity is Jesus of Nazareth, a man born between 7 and 4 B.C.E. in the region of Palestine. According to Christian teaching, Jesus was killed by Roman authorities using a form of execution called crucifixion (a term meaning he was nailed to a cross and hung from it until he died) in about the year 30 C.E. After his death, he rose back to life. His death and resurrection provide a way by which people can be reconciled with God. In remembrance of Jesus's death and resurrection, the cross serves as a fundamental symbol in Christianity.

With nearly two billion believers in countries around the globe, Christianity is the largest of the world's religions. There is no one central authority for all of Christianity. The pope (the bishop of Rome) is the authority for the Roman Catholic Church, but other sects look to other authorities. Orthodox communities look to patriarchs and emphasize doctrinal agreement and traditional practice. Protestant communities focus on individual conscience. The Roman Catholic and Protestant churches are often referred to as the Western Church, while the Orthodox churches may also be called the Eastern Church. All three main branches of Christianity acknowledge the authority of Christian scriptures, a compilation of writings assembled into a document called the Bible. Methods of biblical interpretation vary among the different Christian sects.

Just as **EPIPHANY** is observed twelve days after **CHRISTMAS** (December 25), Timkat, the Ethiopian celebration of Epiphany, occurs twelve days after **GANNA**, the Ethiopian Christmas (January 7). Christianity was established in Ethiopia in the fourth century, when a Christian from Syria named Frumentius traveled there and influenced the local ruler. At the time, Christianity in Syria was under the domain of the Orthodox Patriarch of Alexandria, Egypt. Thus, so was the new church in Ethiopia until 1959, when the Ethiopian Orthodox Church separated from the Coptic Church of Egypt.

Timkat commemorates the baptism of Christ in the River Jordan and is celebrated in a unique manner. Timkat focuses on the Ark of the Covenant, the wooden chest containing the tablets on which the Ten Commandments or laws of the ancient Israelites are inscribed. Although no one is really certain what became of the original Ark, the Ethiopian Orthodox Church has largely based its identity on the fact that it resides in the holy city of Aksum (Axum), where it is housed in a special chapel next to the Church of Saint Mary of Zion and watched over day and night by a single guard who is both a monk and a virgin. Every Orthodox church in Ethiopia, however, has a TABOT or sacred replica of the Ark, which is taken out on the eve of Timkat by the priests and villagers and carried to a tent that has been erected near a stream or pool. The procession that accompanies the TABOT is a particularly colorful one, with all the villagers dressed in white and the priests wearing brightly colored satin robes and carrying velvet umbrellas studded with sequins. The TABOT remains in the tent throughout the night, while Orthodox Christians gather around it to sing, dance, and pray. A mass is held at 2:00 a.m., and people hold picnics by the dim light of oil lamps, drinking the Ethiopian beer that they have brewed especially for this holiday.

At dawn, the priest takes a ceremonial golden cross, dips it in the water, and uses it to extinguish a candle that sits on the makeshift altar or on a pole in the river. After this, he sprinkles water over the faithful who have gathered to commemorate the baptism of Christ. At this point it is not uncommon for people to start jumping into the water fully clothed, even though the water is often very cold (*see* MASS BAPTISM). After this, the TABOT is carried in procession back to the church, accompanied by the sound of bells, drums, trumpets, and singing. January 20 is the feast of the Archangel Michael, a popular saint in Ethiopia, which gives everyone an excuse to extend the celebration for another day.

One of the best places to witness the observance of Timkat is in the isolated northern mountain town of Lalibela, which is named after the king who ruled the country from 1167 to 1207. The town has eleven churches carved out of a single rock formation that date back to the period when Christianity first flourished in Ethiopia. According to legend, King Lalibela's stonemasons built the churches—some of which are four stories high—with the help of angels over a twenty-four-year period. Like churches elsewhere in the country, each contains a TABOT that is carried out in procession during Timkat.

SYMBOLS AND CUSTOMS

Guks

One of the most popular pastimes during Timkat is playing the national sport known as guks, which consists of "warriors" pursuing each other on horseback and hurling bamboo lances. The game takes place in an open field, and the players, who are organized in teams, wear white uniforms with capes and headdresses that resemble a lion's mane. They protect themselves against the blows of their opponents with shields made from animal hides —usually hippopotamus.

The game has its roots in actual warfare techniques, back in the days when Ethiopians pursued their enemies on horseback and relied on speed and accuracy with a javelin rather than armor and sophisticated weapons to avoid injury.

Mass Baptism

The custom of jumping into the water on Timkat is symbolic of Jesus' baptism in the River Jordan. Ethiopian Christians believe that when they immerse themselves in the water they are "born again" into the Christian faith, and some believe that the waters cure infertility and other ills.

Tabot

The term "tabot" seems to refer not just to the Ark—the acacia wood box that the Lord told Moses to build (Exodus 25:10) to house the stone tablets on which the Ten Commandments were written—but also to the sacred tablets themselves. In Ethiopian Orthodox churches, these tablets are usually made out of wood or stone, and laypeople are never allowed to actually look at them. On Timkat they are covered by several layers of richly decorated fabric before being carried in procession to the tent that has been set up for them.

What happened to the original Ark? It was given a special room, called the "Holy of Holies," in the Temple that Solomon built in Jerusalem, but when the city was destroyed by the Romans in 70 C.E., the Ark disappeared in the chaos. The Ethiopians aren't the only ones who claim to have the true Ark in their possession, but it is this belief that gives the replicas found in all their churches so much power and authority.

FURTHER READING

Harper, Howard V. *Days and Customs of All Faiths*. 1957. Reprint. Detroit: Omnigraphics, 1990.

Ickis, Marguerite. *The Book of Festivals and Holidays the World Over*. New York: Dodd, Mead, 1970.

MacDonald, Margaret R., ed. *The Folklore of World Holidays*. Detroit: Gale Research, 1992.

WEB SITE

PBS (Public Broadcasting Service)
www.pbs.org/wonders/Episodes/Epi4/4_cultr2.htm

Tisha be-Av
(Fast of Av)

Type of Holiday: Religious (Jewish)
Date of Observation: Between July 17 and August 14; ninth day of Av
Where Celebrated: Europe, Israel, United States, and by Jews throughout the
world
Symbols and Customs: Eggs and Ashes, Wailing Wall
Colors: Because it is observed as a day of mourning, Tisha be-Av is associated
with the color black. In many synagogues, the ark housing the Torah or Jewish
holy book is covered with a black cloth on this day.
Related Holidays: Lag Ba-Omer

ORIGINS

Tisha be-Av is a mourning period observed in Judaism, one of the oldest continuously observed religions in the world. Its history extends back beyond the advent
of the written word. Its people trace their roots to a common ancestor, Abraham,
and then back even farther to the very moment of creation.

According to Jewish belief, the law given to the Jewish people by God contained
everything they needed to live a holy life, including the ability to be reinterpreted
in new historical situations. Judaism, therefore, is the expression of the Jewish people, attempting to live holy (set apart) lives in accordance with the instructions
given by God. Obedience to the law is central to Judaism, but there is no one central authority. Sources of divine authority are God, the Torah, interpretations of the
Torah by respected teachers, and tradition. Religious observances and the study of
Jewish law are conducted under the supervision of a teacher called a rabbi.

There are several sects within Judaism. Orthodox Judaism is characterized by an
affirmation of the traditional Jewish faith, strict adherence to customs such as
keeping the Sabbath, participation in ceremonies and rituals, and the observance
of dietary regulations. Conservative Jewish congregations seek to retain many
ancient traditions but without the accompanying demand for strict observance.
Reform Judaism stresses modern biblical criticism and emphasizes ethical teachings more than ritualistic observance. Hasidism is a mystical sect of Judaism that
teaches enthusiastic prayer as a means of communion with God. The Reconstructionist movement began early in the twentieth century in an effort to "reconstruct"
Judaism, with the community rather than the synagogue as its center.

Tisha be-Av is a twenty-four-hour period of fasting, lamentation, and prayer in memory of the destruction of both the First and Second Temples in Jerusalem, two events that took place on the same day several centuries apart. The First Temple, built by King Solomon, was destroyed in 586 B.C.E. by the Babylonians under King Nebuchadrezzar, who sold many of the Jews into slavery and exiled thousands of others. When they were finally permitted to return to their land about seventy years later, the first thing they did was to build a new temple on the site of the first one. The Second Temple was in use for almost 600 years, although at one point the Greeks nearly ruined it by erecting statues of Zeus and other Greek gods in the temple and making it unholy. The Romans under Titus finally burned it down in 70 C.E., an even greater tragedy than the destruction of the First Temple in terms of lost life and property. The only piece of the temple that still remains standing is part of the western wall that surrounded it, also known as the WAILING WALL.

Other sad events have taken place on this day as well. In 132 C.E., the Romans plowed over the holy places of Jerusalem and started building their own city, ending any hopes the Jews might have had of rebuilding their temple. It was also on the ninth of Av in 135 C.E. that the town of Bethar, the last stronghold of Bar Kochva and his rebels, fell to the Romans (*see* **LAG BA-OMER**). In 1492, all Spanish Jews were ordered to leave the country on Tisha be-Av; in 1670, the Jews of Vienna were expelled from the city on this day.

Tisha be-Av marks the end of a three-week period of national mourning that begins on the seventeenth of Tammuz, the day on which, about 2,000 years ago, the Roman threat to Jerusalem became so menacing that sacrifices could no longer be offered in the Holy Temple. Any kind of festivity or entertainment is forbidden during this three-week period. No new clothes may be worn, no hair cut, no music played, and no weddings held. Celebration is only permitted on the Sabbath and on days of special events—a Bar Mitzvah, for example. Many Jews visit the cemetery during these weeks to pay their respects to friends and relatives who have died.

The feeling of mourning intensifies as the three weeks pass, culminating on Tisha be-Av. No flags are flown, no parades are held, and no bands are allowed to play on this day. Most Jews spend the day quietly in prayer and fasting. The principal feature of the service held in the synagogue is the recital of the Book of Lamentations. Believed to have been written by the prophet Jeremiah, Lamentations is really a collection of five dirges (mournful tales) on the subject of the Temple's destruction in 586 B.C.E. and the subsequent scattering of the Jewish people. The synagogue is lit only by candles, and worshippers take off their shoes and sit on the floor or on low benches. Like mourners, they do not greet one another. If Tisha be-Av falls on the Sabbath, the fast is postponed until the following day.

SYMBOLS AND CUSTOMS

Eggs and Ashes

The last meal eaten before the Fast of Av includes eggs and a pinch of ashes. Eggs are served, according to one Jewish poet, because "eggs have no mouth and our grief is too strong for words." Ashes are used as a symbol of mourning. Eggs and ashes are traditionally served to Jewish mourners when they return from a funeral.

Wailing Wall

Huge crowds of Jews assemble at the Wailing Wall in Jerusalem—believed to be the last remaining portion of the wall that once surrounded the Second Temple—on the 9th of Av. For many years following the Temple's destruction in 70 C.E., Jews could not visit the Wailing Wall (sometimes called the Western Wall) because the land on which it stood was ruled by Arabs, who would not permit the Jews to go there. But this part of Jerusalem was retaken by the Israeli army in 1967. Since that time, anyone who wants to can cry or pray at the wall. Some people have left notes with special prayers to God in the cracks between the stones.

FURTHER READING

Bellenir, Karen. *Religious Holidays and Calendars*. 3rd ed. Detroit: Omnigraphics, 2004.

Edidin, Ben. *Jewish Holidays and Festivals*. 1940. Reprint. Detroit: Omnigraphics, 1993.

Gaster, Theodor H. *Festivals of the Jewish Year*. New York: William Sloane Associates, 1953.

Henderson, Helene, ed. *Holidays, Festivals, and Celebrations of the World Dictionary*. 3rd ed. Detroit: Omnigraphics, 2005.

Renberg, Dalia Hardof. *The Complete Family Guide to Jewish Holidays*. New York: Adama Books, 1985.

WEB SITE

Union of Orthodox Jewish Congregations of America
www.ou.org/yerushalayim/tishabav

Tod Kathin
(Robe-Offering Month)

Type of Holiday: Religious (Buddhist)
Date of Observation: October-November
Where Celebrated: Cambodia, Laos, Myanmar (Burma), Thailand
Symbols and Customs: Kathin, Meritorious Deeds, Padetha Tree
Related Holidays: Waso

ORIGINS

Tod Kathin is part of the tradition of Buddhism, one of the four largest religious families in the world. Buddhism is based on the teachings of Siddhartha Gautama (c. 563-483 B.C.E.), who came to be known as Buddha, or "The Enlightened One." The basic tenets of Buddhism can be summarized in the Four Noble Truths and the Eightfold Path. The Four Noble Truths are 1) the truth and reality of suffering; 2) suffering is caused by desire; 3) the way to end suffering is to end desire; and 4) the Eightfold Path shows the way to end suffering. The Eightfold Path consists of 1) right view or right understanding; 2) right thoughts and aspirations; 3) right speech; 4) right conduct and action; 5) right way of life; 6) right effort; 7) right mindfulness; and 8) right contemplation.

Tod Kathin falls at the end of the Buddhist Lent—a three-month period also known as **WASO**, Vassa, or Vossa in Southeast Asia. This usually falls at the end of the rainy season in October, on the full moon day of the month of Thadingyut. It is marked by a three-day Festival of Lights commemorating the day when Buddha returned to earth after his three-month stay at the heavenly place known as Tava-timsa. His path was illuminated by thousands of lights, and today Buddhists in the Southeast Asian countries of Myanmar, Cambodia, Laos, and Thailand set off fireworks, launch fire balloons into the sky, and float tiny rafts with candles on the waters to celebrate.

The Festival of Lights is the beginning of what is known as Tod Kathin or Robe-Offering Month. It is a time for Buddhists to show their appreciation to the monks of their local monastery by bringing them food, useful household items and cleaning supplies, and above all, robes (*see* KATHIN). Because Lord Buddha believed that material possessions were the source of much human misery and longing, he instructed his monks not to burden themselves with anything beyond a simple robe and a few necessary personal items, such as razors and needles. The Buddhist community must supply them with everything else they need, and Tod Kathin provides a formal opportunity for them to do so while at the same time showing their gratitude to the monks for the services they have performed and the teachings they have kept alive.

Tod Kathin ceremonies are held wherever there are Buddhist monasteries, although they tend to be more elaborate where large or well-known monasteries are located. The offerings themselves are carried to the monastery in a procession, often involving brightly colored costumes and music, with the gifts piled up on floats or carried on lacquer trays. If the offering consists of money, it is usually presented in the form of a PADETHA TREE. When the procession arrives at the monastery, there is a formal ceremony during which the robes are presented to the monks, which is then followed by a blessing and other festivities.

The Buddhists who make these contributions do so willingly and joyfully because they know how important MERITORIOUS DEEDS are to following the Eightfold Path that leads to Nirvana, the state of bliss that is every Buddhist's ultimate goal.

SYMBOLS AND CUSTOMS

Kathin

A kathin was originally a wooden frame the Buddhist monks would use to stretch remnants of cloth. The scraps were then sewn together and dyed an orangey-yellow to make their robes. Although Buddha eventually decided that the resulting garments were too shabby-looking and permitted the monks to accept robes as gifts from lay people, the robes continued to be identified with the frames originally used to make them. Tod Kathin means "laying down of the holy cloth," but the word kathin has also come to be associated with the pilgrimages Buddhists make to deliver these gifts to the monastery.

Because Tod Kathin also marks the end of the monks' three-month Lenten seclusion, freeing them to go out into the world to preach and to visit their parents and teachers, it is an appropriate time for them to receive fresh robes.

Meritorious Deeds

According to Buddhist belief, there are various acts that bring merit to the individual, and supporting the monks, or members of the sangha, is one of these. Giving the monks food and clothing, contributing to the building and maintenance of the wat (monastery), and participating in ceremonies such as the Robe-Offering are among the most highly valued merit-making activities.

Padetha Tree

A common way of collecting gifts and money from local people for Robe-Offering Month is to set up a wooden structure that resembles a tree wrapped in silver or gold paper. People attach cash and other useful gifts to these so-called padetha trees, which are then presented to the monks. Such trees can often be seen standing by the side of the road or in the marketplace. Groups of people who work together or belong to the same profession will often organize their own padetha trees.

FURTHER READING

MacDonald, Margaret R., ed. *The Folklore of World Holidays*. Detroit: Gale Research, 1992.

Trawicky, Bernard, and Ruth W. Gregory. *Anniversaries and Holidays*. 5th ed. Chicago: American Library Assocation, 2000.

Van Straalen, Alice. *The Book of Holidays Around the World*. New York: Dutton, 1986.

WEB SITE

The Buddhist Association in Washington DC
www.watthaidc.org/index.php?section=90

Tori-no-ichi
(Bird Fair, Festival of the Rooster)

Type of Holiday: Religious (Shinto)
Date of Observation: November for two or three days
Where Celebrated: Japan
Symbols and Customs: Great Bird, Rake

ORIGINS

Tori-no-ichi is an observance in Shinto, an ancient religion that originated in Japan. Most Shinto adherents live in Japan, but small communities also exist in Europe, Latin America, North America, and in the Pacific island nations.

The name Shinto was first employed during the sixth century C.E. to differentiate indigenous religions in Japan from faith systems that originated in mainland Asia (primarily Buddhism and Confucianism). The word is derived from two Chinese characters, *shen* (gods) and *tao* (way). Loosely translated, Shinto means "way of the gods." Its roots lie in an ancient nature-based religion. Some important concepts in Shinto include the value of tradition, the reverence of nature, cleanliness (ritual purity), and the veneration of spirits called *kami*. Strictly speaking, kami are not deities. The literal translation of the word kami is "that which is hidden."

Kami (which is both the singular and plural term) are honored but do not assert their powers upon humans in the traditional manner of deities or gods in other religions. People may be descended from the kami, and kami may influence the course of nature and events. The kami can bestow blessings, but they are not all benign. Kami are present in natural things such as trees, mountains, rocks, and rivers. They are embodied in religious relics, especially mirrors and jewels. They also include spirits of ancestors, local deities, holy people, and even political or literary figures. The human role is to venerate the kami and make offerings. The ultimate goal of Shinto is to uphold the harmony among humans and between people and nature. In this regard, the principle of all kami is to protect and sustain life.

The central authorities in Shinto are the priests. Traditionally, the duties of the priest were passed through heredity lines, but in modern times priests are trained on the basis of recommendation. The priests' duties include communicating with the kami and ensuring that ceremonies are properly carried out. Shinto does not have a single collection of sacred texts analogous to the Christian Bible or Islamic Qur'an. Instead, several important books provide information and guidance: *Kojiki (Records of Ancient Events), Nihongi (Chronicles of Japan),* and *Engishiki (Chronicles of the Engi).*

Tori-no-ichi, also known as the Bird Fair or Rooster Festival, is held in November at Shinto shrines in Japan, particularly the Otori Shrine in Asakusa. The rooster is one of the twelve animals after which the years, days, and hours are named in the old Japanese calendar. Tori-no-ichi is held on days of the rooster in November. The day of the rooster occurs every twelve days, so Tori-no-ichi is held either two or three times in November, depending on the year. Legend suggests that when there are three days, the likelihood of fires is unusually high.

According to Shinto mythology, a sacred bird (sometimes referred to as a crow, an eagle, or a rooster) perched on the stringed instrument (known as a gen) used to lure the sun god out of her cave when the world was plunged in darkness. In Japanese, the name Tori-no-ichi not only refers to this mythological bird but also constitutes a play on the words signifying financial gain. This may be because most of the members of the Shinto sect who observe the festival are wealthy merchants who want to ensure a successful business year. Tori-no-ichi has been observed since the Edo Period (1603-1868).

The celebration's most visible feature is the bamboo RAKES sold at stalls that are set up around the shrine. Other good-luck emblems that are often used for advertising or decorative purposes during the festival include gold and silver coins, the account book, the magic key that is believed to have the power to unlock the door of fate, and the hammer, which can be used to hammer out whatever it is that a person wants from the bag carried by the god of wealth.

SYMBOLS AND CUSTOMS

Great Bird

"The Great Bird" in Shinto mythology has been variously regarded as a crow, an eagle, or a rooster. It is widely regarded as a symbol of prosperity and good fortune because of its role in the mythological incident described above and because it is believed to possess the strength to fly higher (i.e. closer to heaven) than any other bird.

Rake

The bamboo rakes that are sold and displayed everywhere during Tori-no-ichi are symbolic of the ability to attract good fortune because they resemble the outstretched claws of the kumade or "bear's paw." One who possesses the kumade has the power to attract or "rake in" any treasure or good fortune that he or she may desire.

The rakes that are sold in outdoor stalls surrounding the shrines where the festival is observed are similar to garden rakes but are usually decorated with many good-luck emblems and, in the center, the smiling mask of Okame, the so-called "laughing goddess" or goddess of good nature. They may be small enough to be worn as a hair ornament or tucked in the neckline of a woman's dress, or they may be so large and heavily decorated that it takes several men to carry them through the streets. It is not uncommon for merchants to boost their chances for prosperity by purchasing a successively larger and more elaborate kumade each year.

FURTHER READING

Henderson, Helene, ed. *Holidays, Festivals, and Celebrations of the World Dictionary.* 3rd ed. Detroit: Omnigraphics, 2005.
MacDonald, Margaret R., ed. *The Folklore of World Holidays.* Detroit: Gale Research, 1992.

WEB SITE

Japan National Tourist Organization
www.jnto.go.jp/eng/indepth/history/traditionalevents/a62_fes_tori.html

Tour de France

Type of Holiday: Sporting
Date of Observation: July
Where Celebrated: France
Symbols and Customs: Arc de Triomphe, Jerseys

ORIGINS

The cycling race known today as the Tour de France can be traced back to 1903, when two Parisian sports publications, *Le Vélo* and *L'Auto,* were competing for readers. *Le Vélo* had already organized the 400-mile Bordeaux-to-Paris race and the 700-mile Paris-Brest-Paris cycling marathon. So Henri Desgrange, a former cycling champ and editor of *L'Auto,* decided to create an even more grueling event that would last an entire month and take competitors on a 1,500-mile route through France that began and ended in Paris. "Le Tour de France Cycliste" was an instant success, drawing huge crowds and doubling the circulation of Desgrange's paper.

Although the course varies, today's Tour de France race averages 4,000 kilometers (2,500 miles) and always includes challenging stretches through the Alps, the Massif Central, and the Pyrenees mountains, with a finale in Paris (*see* ARC DE TRIOMPHE). What distinguishes the Tour from other long-distance cycling races are the physical demands it places on the riders. It is divided into twenty-three timed stages, or legs, which are covered over a three-week period, with one day of rest. Two hundred riders compete in teams of ten, and it is the job of certain team riders to help "clear the way" for the team's best cyclist. A well-balanced team will have riders who specialize in sprinting and climbing, some good all-around riders, and a few *domestiques* (servants), whose sole function it is to support and clear a path for the team leader, even if it means giving him their own bicycle when he has a flat tire. It is not uncommon for a rider to win four or five of the daily stages and still finish far behind the winner, who is the individual with the lowest cumulative time for all stages combined. Similarly, it is possible to win only one stage, or none at all, and still finish first by staying close to the leaders day after day and waiting for them to falter. The real keys to winning the Tour de France are consistency and endurance, and the victors usually become international celebrities.

The names most commonly associated with the Tour de France are the five-time winners: Jacques Anquetil (1957, 1961-64); Belgian Eddie Merckx (1969-72, 1974), considered by many the world's greatest all-time cycling champion; Bernard Hinault (1978-79, 1981-82, 1985); and Spaniard Miguel Indurain (1991-95). Greg LeMond was the first American to win the Tour (1986, 1989-90). But perhaps no one embodies the spirit of the Tour de France more than Lance Armstrong from Texas, who rode to victory in 1999—only three years after being diagnosed with cancer and given a fifty percent chance of survival. The fact that he became fit enough to ride in the race—let alone win it—was a testimonial to his vast personal strength. That victory was Armstrong's first of seven in a row, and his winning streak ended with his retirement after the 2005 race.

The Tour de France has always been marked by stories of extraordinary courage and commitment. Eugéne Christophe was in second place in the 1913 Tour when he broke the fork of his bike on a steep climb through the Pyrenees Mountains. Knowing that attacks by bears were a constant danger, he ran ten miles, carrying his bike, to the nearest village, where he used the local blacksmith's forge to make the necessary repairs.

Tom Simpson of England, a former world champion, collapsed and died while climbing Mont Ventoux in the 1967 Tour. His last words were, "Put me back on the bike." Unfortunately, the use of performance-enhancing drugs was found to have played a role in Simpson's death, and "doping" scandals have continued to plague the Tour to this day. Riders are now routinely tested for drug use throughout the race.

Like the modern sports world at large, the Tour de France has had its share of performance-enhancing drug scandals. In 2006, Tour winner Floyd Landis was stripped of his title after testing positive for anabolic steroids. Many people felt, however, that it was the 2007 Tour de France that hit rock bottom when two teams withdrew from the race due to team member doping. But the most shocking event in the season's string of doping scandals was the dismissal of race leader and expected winner Michael Rasmussen by his team, Rabobank, before Stage 17 of the Tour for lying to race officials about his whereabouts during mandatory drug tests.

The 2007 race ended in humiliation and disgrace, but many are optimistic that the new zero-tolerance drug policy instituted by the Union Cycliste Internationale (UCI), the governing body of cycling, will allow the Tour de France to regain the prestige it has enjoyed in previous years.

Despite these problems, the Tour de France continues to attract viewers. Over one billion people watch it on television and another fifteen million stand by the roadside to catch a glimpse of the racers. In 1984 the Tour Feminin, a special women's race, was added to the event as a stage race of about 1,000 kilometers (625 miles) that was run concurrently with the final two weeks of the men's tour. In 1998, the name Tour Feminin was changed to La Grande Boucle Feminine Internationale at the insistence of the organizers of the Tour de France, who felt that the name Tour should denote only the men's race. Although the course has been shortened, the dates changed, and the race has been plagued by financial and sponsorship woes, La Grande Boucle continues to survive as one of the most prestigious women's cycling races today.

SYMBOLS AND CUSTOMS

Arc de Triomphe

Although it has been estimated that more than a third of France's population turns out to watch part of the Tour de France, by far the largest crowd forms along the Champs-Elysées, the most famous boulevard in Paris. As the riders complete the final stretch of the last stage, they pass many of the city's well-known sights, including the Louvre, the Tuileries Gardens, the arcades of the Rue de Rivoli, the Place de la Concorde with its Egyptian obelisk, and, finally, the Arc de Triomphe (Arch of Triumph). Photographs of the winner passing in front of the Arc have appeared in newspapers all over the world, and the Arc itself has become a symbolic backdrop for victory in the world's greatest cycling race.

Commissioned by Napoleon in 1806, the Arc de Triomphe marks the tomb of the Unknown Soldier, who is buried under the center.

Jerseys

The leader at any given stage in the Tour de France is the rider who currently holds the lowest accumulated time. He can easily be recognized by the yellow jersey he wears, a tradition that started in 1919. In contrast, the last-place rider is referred to as "the Red Lantern."

In the 1930s, the "King of the Mountains" classification was created to reward the rider who excelled at climbing, and a white jersey with red polka dots became the sign of this distinction.

The rider with the most sprint points in the previous stage wears the green jersey. Sprint points are earned in finishes, along the route, and in individual time trials. The solid white jersey is given to the leading rider under the age of twenty-five.

FURTHER READING

Brunel, Philippe. *An Intimate Portrait of the Tour de France*. 2nd ed. Denver: Buonpane Pub., 1996.

Henderson, Helene, ed. *Holidays, Festivals, and Celebrations of the World Dictionary*. 3rd ed. Detroit: Omnigraphics, 2005.

Van Straalen, Alice. *The Book of Holidays Around the World*. New York: Dutton, 1986.

WEB SITE

Le Société du Tour de France
www.letour.fr/indexus.html

Tu Bishvat
(Bi-Shevat, Tu B'Shevat, New Year of the Trees)

Type of Holiday: Religious (Jewish), Calendar/Seasonal
Date of Observation: Between January 16 and February 13; fifteenth day of Shevat
Where Celebrated: Israel, United States, and by Jews throughout the world
Symbols and Customs: Trees
Related Holidays: Arbor Day

ORIGINS

Tu Bishvat is a holiday in Judaism, one of the oldest continuously observed religions in the world. Its history extends back beyond the advent of the written word. Its people trace their roots to a common ancestor, Abraham, and then back even farther to the very moment of creation.

According to Jewish belief, the law given to the Jewish people by God contained everything they needed to live a holy life, including the ability to be reinterpreted in new historical situations. Judaism, therefore, is the expression of the Jewish people, attempting to live holy (set apart) lives in accordance with the instructions given by God. Obedience to the law is central to Judaism, but there is no one central authority. Sources of divine authority are God, the Torah, interpretations of the Torah by respected teachers, and tradition. Religious observances and the study of Jewish law are conducted under the supervision of a teacher called a rabbi.

There are several sects within Judaism. Orthodox Judaism is characterized by an affirmation of the traditional Jewish faith, strict adherence to customs such as keeping the Sabbath, participation in ceremonies and rituals, and the observance of dietary regulations. Conservative Jewish congregations seek to retain many ancient traditions but without the accompanying demand for strict observance. Reform Judaism stresses modern biblical criticism and emphasizes ethical teachings more than ritualistic observance. Hasidism is a mystical sect of Judaism that teaches enthusiastic prayer as a means of communion with God. The Reconstruc-

tionist movement began early in the twentieth century in an effort to "reconstruct" Judaism with the community rather than the synagogue as its center.

Tu Bishvat is a minor Jewish holiday honoring TREES, similar to the American observation of **ARBOR DAY**. It originated in Israel, where the fifteenth of Shevat comes at the beginning of spring when the buds on the trees are beginning to open. The ancient Jews loved trees and treasured them for the fruit, shade, and lumber they provided. They assigned many trees special symbolic meanings (*see* TREES) and compared the Torah, their holy book, to "a tree of life." In fact, most of the forests seen in Israel today were originally planted by Jewish colonists.

It is said that the sap begins to rise in the fruit trees of the Holy Land on the fifteenth day of Shevat. It is customary, therefore, to sit up late the previous evening and recite passages from the Jewish scriptures dealing with trees, fruits, and the fertility of the earth. Israeli schoolchildren go outside with shovels and hoes and plant trees on Tu Bishvat, singing songs about trees and flowers as they work and dancing around the trees they have planted. Because there are relatively few trees in Israel, the task of planting them on this day is considered crucial to preserving the soil.

Tu Bishvat is primarily a children's holiday in Europe. In Jewish schools, they bring figs, dates, raisins, almonds, and other fruits native to Israel into their classrooms, where the teacher divides the supply equally so there will be no distinctions between rich and poor. In Jewish schools in the United States and other countries, Tu Bishvat is often celebrated with special assemblies, classroom parties, and entertainment for parents. Refreshments usually include fruits that grow in Israel, such as dates, figs, carobs, and Jaffa oranges. In some countries, Jewish children buy Jewish National Fund tree certificates, which can be purchased for the modest cost of a sapling and its planting, in honor of their parents, while parents often buy the certificates as educational gifts for their children. Many Jews in the United States have donated money for trees in honor of famous Americans such as George Washington, Harry S Truman, Eleanor Roosevelt, and Chief Justice Louis Brandeis.

Because Tu Bishvat is primarily a nature festival without any specific religious ceremonies, it is surprising that it was remembered after the Jews left Palestine. That it survived and is still observed in Western countries where there is often frost and snow during the month of Shevat shows how deeply Jews have longed for their homeland.

SYMBOLS AND CUSTOMS

Trees

There was a long-standing Jewish tradition, revived recently in Israel, of planting a cedar tree, symbolic of courage and strength, when a baby boy was born, and a cypress, which is smaller and more fragrant, to honor the birth of a girl.

When the child grew up, the wood of this tree was used to make the *huppa* or wedding canopy.

Because trees were associated with two of the most important events in a person's life, birth and marriage, Jewish children were raised with a great reverence for trees. Different types of trees were used to symbolize human characteristics: for example, the olive (wisdom), the grapevine (joy and childbearing), and the palm (beauty and stateliness). Planting trees to celebrate births and setting aside a day specifically for tree-planting has kept the Jewish homeland wooded from one generation to the next.

Tu Bishvat is also known as Rosh Hashanah Leilanot, or New Year of the Trees. It is widely believed to be the day on which trees are "judged"; in other words, it is the day on which each tree's fate is decided. This determines which trees will flourish and grow tall; which will wither and die; which will suffer from lightning, strong winds, or insects; and which will be strong enough to withstand all danger.

FURTHER READING

Bellenir, Karen. *Religious Holidays and Calendars*. 3rd ed. Detroit: Omnigraphics, 2004.

Cirlot, J.E. *A Dictionary of Symbols*. New York: Philosophical Library, 1962.

Dobler, Lavinia G. *Customs and Holidays Around the World*. New York: Fleet Pub. Corp., 1962.

Edidin, Ben. *Jewish Holidays and Festivals*. 1940. Reprint. Detroit: Omnigraphics, 1993.

Ferguson, George. *Signs and Symbols in Christian Art*. New York: Oxford University Press, 1954.

Gaer, Joseph. *Holidays Around the World*. Boston: Little, Brown, 1953.

Gaster, Theodor H. *Festivals of the Jewish Year*. New York: William Sloane Associates, 1953.

Henderson, Helene, ed. *Holidays, Festivals, and Celebrations of the World Dictionary*. 3rd ed. Detroit: Omnigraphics, 2005.

Renberg, Dalia Hardof. *The Complete Family Guide to Jewish Holidays*. New York: Adama Books, 1985.

WEB SITE

Union of Orthodox Jewish Congregations of America
www.ou.org/chagim/roshchodesh/shevat/tubshevat.htm

Twelfth Night
(Epiphany Eve)

Type of Holiday: Religious (Christian)
Date of Observation: January 5 or 6
Where Celebrated: Great Britain, Europe, United States
Symbols and Customs: Fire, Lord of Misrule, Twelfth Night Pageants
Related Holidays: Christmas, Epiphany

ORIGINS

The celebration of Twelfth Night is part of the Christian tradition. The word Christian refers to a follower of Christ, a title derived from the Greek word meaning Messiah or Anointed One. The Christ of Christianity is Jesus of Nazareth, a man born between 7 and 4 B.C.E. in the region of Palestine. According to Christian teaching, Jesus was killed by Roman authorities using a form of execution called crucifixion (a term meaning he was nailed to a cross and hung from it until he died) in about the year 30 C.E. After his death, he rose back to life. His death and resurrection provide a way by which people can be reconciled with God. In remembrance of Jesus' death and resurrection, the cross serves as a fundamental symbol in Christianity.

With nearly two billion believers in countries around the globe, Christianity is the largest of the world's religions. There is no one central authority for all of Christianity. The pope (the bishop of Rome) is the authority for the Roman Catholic Church, but other sects look to other authorities. Orthodox communities look to patriarchs and emphasize doctrinal agreement and traditional practice. Protestant communities focus on individual conscience. The Roman Catholic and Protestant churches are often referred to as the Western Church, while the Orthodox churches may also be called the Eastern Church. All three main branches of Christianity acknowledge the authority of Christian scriptures, a compilation of writings assembled into a document called the Bible. Methods of biblical interpretation vary among the different Christian sects.

As the last of the traditional Twelve Days of Christmas, Twelfth Night marks the end of the Christmas season. Why twelve days? The custom of extending **CHRISTMAS** may have derived from the pagan custom of marking the **WINTER SOLSTICE** for a number of days—a widespread tradition in Europe, particularly England, from the eleventh century onwards. But the exact day on which this season ends remains ambiguous. To some people, Twelfth Night means the evening before the Twelfth Day, or January 5. To others, it means the evening *of* the Twelfth Day, or January 6. In any case, it is often observed on the night of **EPIPHANY** rather than the night before.

Twelfth Night has been observed since the Middle Ages with games, masquerades, and other revelries. Elaborate pageants, processions, and pantomimes, combined with singing, dancing, and feasting, took place under the direction of a LORD OF MISRULE, a mock official assisted by a "fool" or jester. In rural parts of England, Twelfth Night celebrations included bonfires (*see* FIRE), masques, and the curious custom of "wassailing" the fruit trees, which meant carrying jugs of cider to the orchards and offering toasts to the apple trees to ensure a good yield. In France, Germany, and the Low Countries, young boys would dress up in exotic costumes and paper crowns. Representing the Three Kings, or Magi, they would go begging from house to house, carrying paper star lanterns on long poles.

By the eighteenth century, the lavish celebrations that had been associated with Twelfth Night began to lose their appeal; by the nineteenth century, they had practically died out, although remnants of the ancient festivities survived in some areas. The King of the Bean (*see* LORD OF MISRULE) is still a popular Twelfth Night tradition in Belgium, Portugal, England, France, Germany, and the Netherlands. In the United States, TWELFTH NIGHT PAGEANTS are still popular, including masked figures, costumed musicians, and the performance of traditional English dances like the Abbots Bromley Antler Dance or Horn Dance. In New Orleans, Twelfth Night marks the beginning of the **CARNIVAL** season, which ends on Mardi Gras, the day before **ASH WEDNESDAY**.

January 5 is also referred to as Old Christmas Eve, because according to the Old Style or Julian Calendar, **CHRISTMAS** fell on January 6. The inhabitants of some remote areas of Great Britain continue to observe ancient customs associated with Old Christmas Eve.

SYMBOLS AND CUSTOMS

Fire

At one time in England, it was customary to light twelve small fires and one large one in a field sown with wheat as a means of protecting it from disease. In Ireland, a sieve full of oats was set up as high as possible, and twelve lighted candles were set in the grain, with a larger one in the middle. Although the meaning of these customs has been largely forgotten, some say that the fires were intended to symbolize Jesus Christ and his twelve apostles. Others see them as a survival of heathen sun worship.

A similar Twelfth Night custom survived in Westmorland. A holly bush or young ash tree would have torches fastened to the branches. The torches were lit and the tree was carried around the village to the accompaniment of music. When the torches had burned out, two rival groups would scramble for the remains of the tree, and the rest of the night would be spent in merrymaking.

In the United States, it is traditional to take down the Christmas tree and other greenery used to decorate the house, pile it up outdoors, and burn it on Twelfth Night. In fact, the custom of lighting bonfires on Twelfth Night seems to be gaining in popularity.

Lord of Misrule

The custom of electing a king to rule over the festivities on Twelfth Night can be traced back to the reign of Edward II in England. The usual custom was to prepare a special cake, known as the Kings' Cake (Gâteau des Rois in France), and to conceal a bean (sometimes a pea or a coin) inside. The cake would be cut into as many pieces as there were guests at the Twelfth Night feast. The youngest member of the family would distribute the pieces, and whoever got the piece with the bean inside was crowned "King of the Bean" or "Lord of Misrule." If a woman got the bean, she would choose a king. A mock court would be assembled by drawing slips of paper from a hat, and these assumed characters would have to be maintained throughout the evening. The custom lasted far into the nineteenth century, but it was eventually discontinued because so many coarse and offensive characters had been introduced. Elaborately decorated Twelfth Cakes remained popular until late Victorian times and are still served in some parts of Europe today.

Twelfth Night Pageants

For hundreds of years, miracle plays about the Three Kings had been staged at this time of year, originally in church sanctuaries and then later, when the performances had become too secular, outside the church. Religious dramas were eventually joined by the staging of popular tragedies, comedies, and historical dramas. William Shakespeare's comedy *Twelfth Night* is believed to have been first presented for Queen Elizabeth I at Whitehall Palace in 1601.

The Twelfth Night pageants performed in the United States today are usually far more modest than the elaborate productions of Elizabethan England. But many of the dances and characters incorporated into these modern performances can be traced back to medieval times.

FURTHER READING

Bellenir, Karen. *Religious Holidays and Calendars*. 3rd ed. Detroit: Omnigraphics, 2004.

Chambers, Robert. *The Book of Days*. 2 vols. 1862-64. Reprint. Detroit: Omnigraphics, 1990.

Christianson, Stephen G., and Jane M. Hatch. *The American Book of Days*. 4th ed. New York: H.W. Wilson, 2000.

Cohen, Hennig, and Tristram Potter Coffin. *The Folklore of American Holidays*. 3rd ed. Detroit: Gale Research, 1999.

Crippen, T.G. *Christmas and Christmas Lore*. 1923. Reprint. Detroit: Omnigraphics, 1990.

Gulevich, Tanya. *Encyclopedia of Christmas and New Year's Celebrations*. 2nd ed. Detroit: Omnigraphics, 2003.

Henderson, Helene, ed. *Holidays, Festivals, and Celebrations of the World Dictionary*. 3rd ed. Detroit: Omnigraphics, 2005.

MacDonald, Margaret R., ed. *The Folklore of World Holidays*. Detroit: Gale Research, 1992.

Miles, Clement A. *Christmas in Ritual and Tradition, Christian and Pagan*. 1912. Reprint. Detroit: Omnigraphics, 1990.

Spicer, Dorothy Gladys. *The Book of Festivals*. 1937. Reprint. Detroit: Omnigraphics, 1990.

Urlin, Ethel L. *Festivals, Holy Days, and Saints' Days*. 1915. Reprint. Detroit: Omnigraphics, 1992.

WEB SITE

BBC (British Broadcasting Corporation)
www.bbc.co.uk/religion/religions/christianity/christmas/carols_3.shtml

Up Helly Aa

Type of Holiday: Folkloric
Date of Observation: January 24
Where Celebrated: Lerwick, Shetland Islands, Scotland
Symbols and Customs: Guizer Jarl, Guizers, Torchlit Procession, Up Helly Aa Bill, Viking Ship

ORIGIN

In the nineteenth century, the people of Lerwick, a town in Scotland's Shetland Islands, devised a holiday that closed the **CHRISTMAS** season with a bang. They dressed in costumes and marched through the streets with torches, singing songs and blowing horns. Up Helly Aa has continued to develop throughout the years and now features the burning of a replica of a Viking ship. This festival provides the people of the Shetland Islands with an opportunity for humorous, costumed revelry and all-night partying. This unusual celebration has gained fame in Scotland and throughout the United Kingdom.

Some researchers believe that the name "Up Helly Aa" comes from "Uphaliday," an old Scottish term for **EPIPHANY**. Epiphany marked the end of the midwinter revelries centered on **CHRISTMAS** and **NEW YEAR'S EVE**. Thus it was called Uphaliday, which historians suggest means something like "up holidays all." In its early years, Up Helly Aa was celebrated on various dates in January. By the late nineteenth century, the people of Lerwick settled on January 24 as the date for this festival.

The first Up Helly Aa celebrations took place around the mid-nineteenth century. In those days, the young men of Lerwick placed tar barrels atop sledges, set them on fire, and dragged them through the streets. They blew horns in order to add noise to the smoke and flames. After the flames died down, mummers, or GUIZERS, roamed the streets and paid visits to friends and family. They wore costumes and masks or make-up to disguise their identities, which allowed them to play pranks on people they knew or act out humorous little skits.

In the late nineteenth century, concerns about fire safety and messy molten tar prompted the replacement of the tar barrels with a TORCHLIT PROCESSION of local men dressed as Vikings. Recent research has suggested several intellectually oriented young men who began to participate in the festival around 1870 first introduced the Viking theme. They were also responsible for moving the festival to its current date, introducing the ship burning custom, and encouraging more elaborate guizing practices.

In the 1880s the first ship—which some say was actually an old rowboat—was burned at the climax of the procession. This symbol of a VIKING SHIP was meant to represent the 100-year period in history, which occurred about 1,000 years ago, when the Shetland Islands were under Norse rule. This ship-burning custom caught on and has served as the highlight of the festival ever since. In 1899, the head guizer, called GUIZER JARL, created the first UP HELLY AA BILL. This document, which is read aloud and then posted, makes fun of local events and people. This custom also became a hit and is a much-anticipated feature of the festival for the people of Lerwick. These days the festival is organized by a committee that works throughout the year to organize the event. Nearly 1,000 guizers take part each year, and around 5,000 people line the streets of Lerwick in order to view the spectacle.

After the procession and the burning of the boat, festival-goers attend large parties in social halls or restaurants. There are eleven of these large-scale events in Lerwick, and each squad of guizers is expected to make an appearance at each of the eleven parties. These parties last until daybreak. Many are private, but there are a few that can be attended by anyone who purchases a ticket.

SYMBOLS AND CUSTOMS

Guizer Jarl

The Guizer Jarl is the head of the Viking squad. As this is the most important role in the festival, it comes with special privileges. The Guizer Jarl chooses a character from Viking history to impersonate during his twenty-four-hour reign over the festival. Care is taken to devise an impressive and appropriate costume with which to impersonate this character. With his disguise in place, the Guizer Jarl kicks off the day's festivities with the reading and posting of the UP HELLY AA BILL. He also rides in the VIKING SHIP during the TORCHLIT PROCESSION, which is pulled through the streets by his Viking squad. Finally, he presides over the parties he attends after the ship is burnt.

Guizers

Guizing, or mumming, is an old midwinter custom in the British Isles. It involves dressing up in homemade costumes and parading through the streets. Guizers often pull pranks on neighbors and friends or go door-to-door performing short skits. In return, householders would usually give them something to eat or drink.

Up Helly Aa guizing began in just this way. In the twentieth century, as the festival grew more organized, rules sprang up to govern the guizing practices. About 1,000 guizers are divided into forty-nine squads, each of which takes on a theme. For example, the guizers that lead the torchlit march to the VIKING SHIP are all men dressed as Vikings. They wear helmets, carry shields, and are required to grow beards for the occasion. Other squads adopt different themes, taking their inspiration from politicians, celebrities, and many other sources. In recent years, junior squads, composed solely of young people, have also marched in the procession. After the burning of the ship there is one more duty to attend to. Each squad of guizers is required to perform a skit or an act at every party that the squad attends.

Torchlit Procession

The torchlit procession begins in the early evening. The guizers assemble in squads and parade through the streets of town, carrying torches and singing songs. The procession ends at the harbor, where the torches are thrown onto the VIKING SHIP, setting it ablaze.

Up Helly Aa Bill

The Up Helly Aa bill is a one or two-page proclamation that satirizes local personalities and events. The GUIZER JARL signs and posts the bill at the kickoff of the festival. The people of Lerwick enjoy this custom and take the jibes contained in the bill in a spirit of good humor.

Viking Ship

In recent decades, the members of the Viking squad have dedicated themselves to creating beautiful replicas of a small Viking ship. The men will begin this work about four months before the festival. The ship is designed so that it may be dragged through the city streets like a parade float. In the dark of the early evening GUIZER JARL steps into the replica of the Viking longboat that his squad has labored so many months to build. The men drag it through the city streets at the heart of the TORCHLIT PROCESSION. When the procession reaches the harbor, Guizer Jarl at last leaves the Viking ship. A volley of torches soon sets it ablaze to the delight of thousands of onlookers.

FURTHER READING

Gulevich, Tanya. *Encyclopedia of Christmas and New Year's Celebrations.* 2nd ed. Detroit: Omnigraphics, 2003.
MacDonald, Margaret Read. *The Folklore of World Holidays.* Detroit: Gale Research, 1992.

WEB SITES

Folk Radio UK
www.folkradio.co.uk/content/view/175/56

Shetland Tourism
www.shetlandtourism.com/pages/up_helly_aa.htm

Up-helly-aa.org, the Shetland Times, Ltd.
www.up-helly-aa.org.uk

Visit Shetland
www.visitshetland.com/events/up-helly-aa-event

Urs of Data Ganj Bakhsh

Type of Holiday: Religious (Muslim)
Date of Observation: Twentieth day of the Muslim Month of Safar
Where Celebrated: Pakistan
Symbols and Customs: Chaddar Procession, Charitable Distribution of Milk and Food, Naat Poetry Recitations, Qawwali Music, Religious Lectures and Discussions

ORIGINS

The Urs of Data Ganj Bakhsh is a holiday in the religious tradition of Islam, one of the world's largest religions. According to some estimates, there are more than one billion Muslims worldwide, with major populations found in the Middle East, North and sub-Saharan Africa, Turkey, Central Asia, and Southeast Asia. In Europe and the United States, Islam is the second largest religious group, with some seven million adherents in the United States. During the early years of Islam, the faith spread throughout the Arabian Peninsula into regions that are today occupied by Saudi Arabia, Syria, Iraq, and Jordan. Contrary to popular opinion, however, Muslims are not just Arabs. Muslims—followers of Islam—are found in many different ethnic groups all over the globe. In fact, Arabs make up less than twenty percent of Muslims.

The word Islam is an Arabic word that means "surrender to God." Its other meanings include peace, safety, and health. The central focus of Islam is a personal commitment and surrender to Allah, the Arabic word for God. In Islam, the concept of Allah is universal and eternal. Allah is the same in every religion and throughout the history of humankind. A person who follows Islam is called a Muslim, which means one who surrenders or submits to Allah's will. But Islam is not just a religion of belief; it is a religion of action. Five specific deeds are required of followers; these are called *The Five Pillars of Islam*. They are 1) *Shahadah*—confession of faith; 2) *Salat*—prayer/worship; 3) *Zakat*—charity; 4) *Sawm*—fasting; and 5) *Hajj*—pilgrimage.

The message of Islam was brought by Muhammad (570-632 C.E.), who is considered a prophet of Allah. The holy book of Islam is the *Qur'an* (also sometimes spelled *Koran* or *Alcoran*). According to Islamic belief, the Qur'an was revealed to Muhammad by Allah over a period of twenty-three years. Authorship of the Qur'an is attributed to Allah, and not to Muhammad; Muhammad merely received it. Muslims believe that because it originated with Allah, the Qur'an is infallible.

There are two main sects within Islam: Sunni and Shi'ite. Sunni Muslims are the majority (estimated at about eighty percent). They recognize the authority of the first four Caliphs, including Ali, and they believe that the Sunna (the example of the Prophet Muhammad) is interpreted through the consensus of the community. Shi'ite Muslims also look to special teachers, called imams. The imams are the direct descendants of Muhammad through Fatimah and Ali. These individuals are believed to be inspired and to possess secret knowledge. Shi'ites, however, do not recognize the same line of Islamic leaders acknowledged by the Sunnis. Shi'ites hold to a doctrine that accepts only leaders who are descended from Muhammad through his daughter Fatimah and her husband Ali. Many Shi'ite subsects believe that true imams are errorless and sinless. They receive instruction from these leaders rather than relying on the consensus of the community.

The Urs of Data Ganj Bakhsh celebrates the life and work of the Muslim mystic and saint Ali ibn Uthman al-Jullabi al-Hujwiri (died circa 1070). He is perhaps better known by his nickname, Data Ganj Bakhsh, which means "the master bestower of treasure." The word urs can be translated as "wedding celebration." Throughout Asia, the Middle East, and North Africa, Muslims celebrate the death anniversaries of many saints. These death anniversaries are called urs, or wedding celebrations, in affirmation of the belief that death brings the saints into union with God.

Relatively little is known about the life of Data Ganj Bakhsh. It is believed that he was born in the late tenth or early eleventh century in Gazna, Afghanistan. He traveled widely in the Middle East and Central Asia. For example, he is thought to have visited Azerbaijan, Tabriz, Baghdad, Damascus, Samarkand, Nishapur, Khurusan, Egypt and a number of other places. In 1039, the saint settled in Lahore, Pakistan. Data Ganj Bakhsh was a Muslim, but also a Sufi. This means that he followed Islam's mystical path, pursuing a genuine experience of connection with God through various spiritual pursuits and practices. In fact, the saint achieved fame for writing the first book on Sufism issued in the Persian language. This book, called *Kashf al-Mahjub li-Arbab al-Qulub,* or "The Unveiling of the Hidden for the Lords of the Heart," argues that Sufism is a distinctive path within Islam and explains the Sufi insights into God.

Data Ganj Bakhsh was also widely respected as a Sufi master—that is, an expert practitioner of Sufism and mentor to those wishing to become Sufis. It is said that he was first called "Data Ganj Bakhsh" by a devoted follower about 100 years after his death. This devotee, named Mu'in ad-Din Muhammad Chisti, felt that he had received so many spiritual insights and blessings after meditating at the tomb of Data Ganj Bakhsh that he needed to thank him. So Chisti faced the tomb of the saint and praised him, naming him "the master bestower of treasure" and the perfect guide for the illuminated saints as well as the struggling and imperfect people of this world. During his lifetime Chisti himself gained great renown as a spiritual master and was later known as a saint.

Data Ganj Bakhsh died and was buried in the city of Lahore, which falls within the state of Punjab, in eastern Pakistan. Soon after his death, a shrine and mosque were built to honor him. The mosque and shrine soon became a site of pilgrimage and remained a popular destination for Muslim pilgrims from all walks of life throughout the Middle Ages. Today the mosque is one of the most famous and visited shrines in south Asia. It is large enough to hold 50,000 people. Many devotees of the saint gather there on Thursday evenings to pray and read the Qur'an. (Thursday evenings are considered part of Friday, the Muslim holy day.)

The Urs of Data Ganj Bakhsh is one of Pakistan's most popular festivals. Each year it attracts around a million participants. Devotees of the saint come from all over Pakistan, India, Saudi Arabia, Europe, and the United States in order to participate in this three-day affair. Festival-goers enjoy visiting the saint's tomb, praying and reading the Qur'an in the saint's mosque, and shopping at the many stands that spring up around the mosque at the time of the festival.

SYMBOLS AND CUSTOMS

Chaddar Procession

Groups of devotees honor the saint by marching through Lahore holding the edges of sheet-like expanses of fabric called chaddars. These beautifully decorated cloths are thrown over the tomb as a respectful and prayerful gesture. Green colored cloths are favored during this festival, green being the color most closely associated with the Prophet Muhammad and with the Muslim religion itself. As the marchers pass through the neighborhood streets, well-wishers toss bills and coins onto the chaddar as an offering to the saint.

The festival officially begins with the laying of the first chaddar on the saint's grave. This task is usually undertaken by an important official from the Punjabi government, accompanied by high-level religious and political dignitaries.

Charitable Distribution of Milk and Food

Islam places great importance on feeding the poor and helping the needy. In fact, Muslims are expected to make a yearly charitable contribution of at least two percent of their wealth and income for this purpose. This principle can be seen in action at the Urs of Data Ganj Bakhsh, where milk and meals are distributed for free to the very poor. These meals consist mainly of a combination of grains and beans. Many pilgrims contribute to the food giveaway. The city's milkmen collect and donate milk during the three days of the festival

Naat Poetry Recitations

A naat is a poem honoring the Prophet Muhammad or one of his family members. These poems may be read or chanted like songs by a solo singer or by a singer accompanied by a drummer. Accomplished naat singers are often found performing before eager crowds at Islamic religious events. The Urs of Data Ganj Bakhsh is just such an occasion.

Qawwali Music

Qawwali music is a kind of Muslim devotional music that is especially popular in India, Afghanistan, and Pakistan. It features talented singers that express the devotion that they feel for God, the Prophet Muhammad, or the example set by a particular saint through their music. Good qawwali singers combine passionate lyrics and expressive singing styles. Popular qawwali singers travel to Pakistan specifically to perform during the Urs of Data Ganj Bakhsh. A special enclosure is constructed for these performances. In recent years festival organizers have arranged for round-the-clock performances of qawwali music and naat poetry recitations.

Religious Lectures and Discussions

Festival organizers draw together various scholars and Muslim religious officials to give public lectures on the writings and teachings of Data Ganj Bakhsh. These lectures, which take place over the course of the three-day festival, are free and open to the public.

FURTHER READING

Aslalm, Nareen. "960th Urs of Hazrat Data Ganj Bakhsh [RA] in Lahore form April-9." *Pakistan Times.* www.pakistantimes.net/2004/03/23/metro1.htm

Aslam, Nasreen. "962nd Urs of Hazrat Data Ganj Bakhsh [RA] Begins." *Pakistan Times.* www.pakistantimes.net/national030210601.htm

Bellenir, Karen. *Religious Holidays and Calendars.* 3rd ed. Detroit: Omnigraphics, 2004.

Gulevich, Tanya. *Understanding Islam and Muslim Traditions.* Detroit: Omnigraphics, 2004.

WEB SITES

Lahore Bazaar
www.lahorebazaar.com/lahore/saints/data_gunj_bakhsh.asp

Pakistan Embassy
www.pakistanembassy.com

Ute Bear Dance

Type of Holiday: Religious (Ute)
Date of Observation: Late May-early June
Where Celebrated: Towaoc and Ignacio, Colorado
Symbols and Customs: Bear, Morache, Plumes

ORIGINS

The Ute Bear Dance is part of the Ute Native American religious tradition. The history of this and other Native American cultures dates back thousands of years into prehistoric times. According to many scholars, the people who became the Native Americans migrated from Asia across a land bridge that may have once connected the territories presently occupied by Alaska and Russia. The migrations, believed to have begun between 60,000 and 30,000 B.C.E., continued until approximately 4,000 B.C.E. This speculation, however, conflicts with traditional stories asserting that the indigenous Americans have always lived in North America or that tribes moved up from the south.

The historical development of religious belief systems among Native Americans is not well known. Most of the information available was gathered by Europeans who arrived on the continent beginning in the sixteenth century C.E. The data they recorded was fragmentary and oftentimes of questionable accuracy because the Europeans did not understand the native cultures they were trying to describe and the Native Americans were reluctant to divulge details about themselves.

The Bear Dance performed every spring by the Ute Indians of Colorado is the oldest dance that the tribe performs, dating back even further than the fifteenth century, when it was first witnessed by Spanish explorers. It is also the only dance that the Utes themselves originated, first as a mating dance or courtship ritual and later as a celebration of the arrival of spring and an opportunity to get together and socialize.

The dance is rooted in a legend about two brothers who went out hunting and came upon a bear who was standing up on his hind legs, shuffling back and forth while clawing a tree or, in some versions, scratching his back against it. The first brother continued to hunt, while the second stayed behind to observe the bear's strange movements. In return for sparing his life, the bear taught the second brother how to perform the dance and the mysterious song that accompanied it. The bear told the hunter that he should teach the dance to his people so that they could show their respect for and, at the same time, draw strength from the spirit of the bear.

Today, the Bear Dance usually takes place in an open field or corral surrounded by a fence made of brush or woven branches. Traditional women's dress for the dance includes tall white buckskin moccasins and brightly colored shawls, although today it is not uncommon to see the dancers wearing shorts and sneakers or cowboy boots and jeans. While spectators line up against the fence, two lines of dancers, one male and one female, face each other and start shuffling toward each other and then back again to the accompaniment of a small group of singers and the sound of the MORACHE or rasp. Then the women select partners by flicking the fringe of their shawl at them, and the dance continues with the two lines divided into couples. One of the singers plays the role of "the Cat," using a willow switch to urge slow or shy dancers to move more quickly. The dancing continues for four or five days, ending when one of the couples falls down from exhaustion or the singers grow tired. There is a huge feast afterward, which is organized by the Bear Dance Chiefs.

Some scholars believe that the Bear Dance was primarily a fertility dance and that it was performed in the spring because this is when the bears emerged from hibernation and started looking for mates. This theory is supported by the fact that the dance remains a "ladies' choice," and that the women select their partners for the dance in much the same way that female bears awake first and chase the males.

Although the Bear Dance was originally held at the end of February or in early March and lasted a week or more, nowadays it is more of a late spring ritual. The Southern Utes hold their Bear Dance over Memorial Day weekend in Ignacio, Colorado, while the Ute Mountain Ute tribe holds its Bear Dance during the first week in June in Towaoc. Currently, there are a few more than 3,000 Utes, most of whom live on reservations. Visitors to the reservation are allowed to watch the Bear Dance, which was at one time closed to all but Native Americans.

SYMBOLS AND CUSTOMS

Bear

According to legend, the bear was created to teach strength, wisdom, and survival skills to the Ute people. To this day, the bear remains the symbolic source of the tribe's strength and a reminder of its former superiority in war. The bear is also believed to possess the power to heal and to communicate directly with the Spirit World.

Morache

The instrument known as a morache was originally made from the jawbone of a bear. Nowadays it is often made of two notched sticks or a notched stick and a piece of bone, which are then rubbed against each other over a wooden or tin box that serves as a resonator. The sound made by these "growl sticks" imitates both the noise made by the bear and the spring's first thunder, which is believed to awaken the bears from their winter hibernation.

Plumes

One of the purposes of the Bear Dance is to give the dancers an opportunity to rid themselves of the worries and tensions that have built up over the course of a long winter. When the dancers enter the corral, they wear plumes that symbolize these worries. Then, at the end of the dance, they hang these plumes on the branch of a cedar tree located at the corral's eastern entrance, symbolically shedding their psychological burdens.

FURTHER READING

Bellenir, Karen. *Religious Holidays and Calendars*. 3rd ed. Detroit: Omnigraphics, 2004.

Eagle Walking Turtle. *Indian America: A Traveler's Companion*. Santa Fe: J. Muir Publications, 1989.

Gill, Sam D., and Irene Sullivan. *Dictionary of Native American Mythology*. Santa Barbara: ABC-CLIO, 1992.

Hirschfelder, Arlene B., and Paulette Fairbanks Molin. *Encyclopedia of Native American Religions*. Updated edition. New York: Facts on File, 2000.

WEB SITES

Southern Ute Indian Tribe
www.southern-ute.nsn.us/culture/bear.html

Ute Mountain Ute Tribe
www.utemountainute.com/legends.htm#Spring%20Time

Vaisakh
(Baisakh, Baisakhi)

Type of Holiday: Religious (Sikh, Hindu), Calendar/Seasonal
Date of Observation: April 13; first day of Vaisakha
Where Celebrated: India, Malaysia
Symbols and Customs: Akhand Path, Bhangra, Charity, Five K's, Pahul Ceremony
Related Holidays: Guru Nanak's Birthday

ORIGINS

Vaisakh is a new year's celebration in both the Sikh and the Hindu faiths. Among the Sikhs who live in Malaysia and the region of northwestern India known as the Punjab, where the Sikh religion was founded, the first day of the month of Vaisakha is New Year's Day. Because the date is based on the solar calendar used in this part of the country, it normally coincides with April 13, although once every thirty-six years it falls on April 14.

Aside from being the first day of the year, Vaisakh is also the anniversary of several important historical events. It is the day on which Guru Gobind Singh, the tenth and last of the gurus whose teachings are central to Sikhism, founded the militant Khalsa brotherhood in 1699. And it was on this day in 1747 that the Sikhs decided to build a permanent fortress at Amritsar, which is why this city has become a focal point for their worship. On Vaisakh in 1919, the British lieutenant governor of the Punjab tried to prevent the Sikhs from gathering there. They assembled anyway and were fired on by the army, an act that resulted in the deaths of 337 men, forty-one boys, and a baby.

Because of the day's historical and religious significance, all Sikhs are required to visit the largest and most important *gurdwara* (public place of worship) they can get to. If possible, they should visit the Golden Temple in Amritsar, where a continuous reading of the Granth Sahib (*see* AKHAND PATH) and certain other rituals are held. After the religious ceremonies are over, there is feasting and folk dancing. Thousands of Sikhs visit the Golden Temple in Amritsar every year and bathe in the Pool of Immortality.

Among Hindus, Vaisakh marks the beginning of the new year. Early in the morning, people bathe in sacred rivers, pools, or wells. They then dress in festive clothes and visit houses of worship for prayers. A pilgrimage to the only shrine of Badrinath, in the Himalayas, begins on this day. Vaisakh is also a harvest festival in northern India, particularly in the Punjab, where most of the country's grain is grown.

SYMBOLS AND CUSTOMS

Akhand Path

For Sikhs, the main religious event that takes place on Vaisakh is the reading of the Granth Sahib, the Sikh holy book, from beginning to end. This takes approximately forty-eight hours and begins two days before the holiday so that the reading will end at dawn on the first of Vaisakha. It begins with the preparation of *karah parshad*, the "gift of God to his devotees," prepared in an iron bowl (*karah*) and made of equal portions of flour, sugar, and ghee (clarified butter). Then the Ardas, a three-part prayer, is recited by the entire congregation, standing with their palms pressed together facing the throne of the Guru Granth Sahib. Then the holy book is opened at random, a verse is read for spiritual guidance, and the akhand path begins with the *Japji,* written by Guru Nanak, the first guru.

Members of the community visit the gurdwara whenever they can during the two days during which the scripture is being read. A number of readers participate in the round-the-clock reading of the scripture, each reading for about two hours before the next one takes over. At the end, everyone gathers at the gurdwara and shares some karah parshad. Then the Granth Sahib is carried in a procession to the accompaniment of religious music. Five leaders of the congregation walk in front of the Granth with drawn swords in memory of the *panj pyares* (*see* PAHUL CEREMONY) of Guru Gobind Singh.

Bhangra

In the Punjab region, Vaisakh is a harvest festival for Hindus. People dance the strenuous folk dance known as the BHANGRA, which involves movements that reenact the entire agricultural process: plowing, sowing, weeding, reaping, and winnowing. The final sequence of the dance shows the farmer celebrating the harvest. In addition, these festivals might include singing folk songs accompanied by drums, feasting, and other merry-making.

Charity

Many Hindus believe that charity given during Vaisakh is especially worthy. Therefore, people are generous in giving money, grain, and other items to the poor.

Five K's

Members of the Khalsa or militant brotherhood of the Sikh religion distinguish themselves by the wearing of five symbols: the kesh (uncut hair), khanga (comb), kirpan (sword), kara (steel wrist band), and kacch (a pair of breeches that must not reach below the knee). The kesh and the khanga symbolize an orderly form of spirituality, since unlike other religious groups that wear uncut hair, the Sikhs are instructed to wash their hair regularly and comb it twice a day. The kacch symbolizes modesty and moral restraint. The kara, worn on the right wrist, is also a symbol of restraint, although some believe that it was originally a means of protecting the wrist from the bowstring. But the circular shape of the wristband serves as a reminder of the Sikh's unity with God and with the other members of the Khalsa. The sword or kirpan symbolizes dignity and self-respect. Khalsa members are supposed to be ready to fight, but only in self-defense or to protect the weak and the oppressed.

Pahul Ceremony

For Sikhs, Pahul means "baptism," and the initiation ceremony for new members of the Khalsa that frequently takes place on Vaisakh recalls the "baptism of the sword" used by Guru Gobind Singh to select the first members of this militant brotherhood in 1699. Since it was customary for Sikhs to gather on Vaisakh, Guru Gobind Singh took advantage of the annual gathering to remind his followers of the dangerous times in which they lived and the importance of being a strong, unified people. Then, drawing his sword, he asked any man who was willing to sacrifice his head as a show of faith to step forward. There was a prolonged silence during which no one responded. Then one man came forward and was taken into the guru's tent. When the guru reappeared with a bloody sword in his hand, four more men followed. After the last of the *panj pyares* ("beloved five") had disappeared into the tent, the guru emerged with his small band of dedicated followers. To celebrate their courage, he gave them nectar (*amrit*) made from water and sugar crystals prepared in an iron bowl and stirred with a double-edged sword.

Although new members may be initiated into the Khalsa at any time of year, Vaisakh is the most popular season for doing so. Initiates must be at least fourteen years of age and must possess the five symbols of their faith (*see* FIVE K'S above) and be devout members of the Sikh community. The initiation ceremony begins with an explanation of the principles of the Sikh faith, readings from the scriptures, and the preparation of amrit. Five men representing the original *panj pyares* kneel around an iron bowl and take turns stirring its contents with a double-edged sword (*khanda*). When the nectar is ready, the *panj pyares* lift up the bowl and offer a prayer. One by one the initiates come forward and are given a handful of amrit to drink. Then the remaining nectar is sprinkled five times on their hair and eyes. The initiation ceremony ends with the reading of a passage of scripture chosen at random and the sharing of *karah parshad*—flour, sugar, and ghee mixed in equal proportions in an iron bowl, symbolic of the equality and brotherhood of the Sikh faith.

FURTHER READING

Bellenir, Karen. *Religious Holidays and Calendars*. 3rd ed. Detroit: Omnigraphics, 2004.

Cole, William Owen, and Piara Singh Sambhi. *The Sikhs: Their Religious Beliefs and Practices*. 2nd ed. Portland: Sussex Academic Press, 1998.

Crim, Keith R. *The Perennial Dictionary of World Religions*. San Francisco: Harper & Row, 1989.

Henderson, Helene, ed. *Holidays, Festivals, and Celebrations of the World Dictionary*. 3rd ed. Detroit: Omnigraphics, 2005.

Kapoor, Sukhbir Singh. *Sikh Festivals*. Vero Beach, FL: Rourke Enterprises, 1989.

MacDonald, Margaret R., ed. *The Folklore of World Holidays*. Detroit: Gale Research, 1992.

WEB SITE

Society for the Confluence of Festivals in India
www.baisakhifestival.com

Valentine's Day

Type of Holiday: Folkloric
Date of Observation: February 14
Where Celebrated: Primarily Britain and the United States, although Valentine's Day was at one time celebrated widely in Italy, France, Austria, Hungary, Germany, and Spain
Symbols and Customs: Cupid, Heart and Arrow, Lovebirds, Valentine Cards
Colors: Valentine's Day is associated with red and white—the colors of blood and milk, both of which were central to the ancient Roman Lupercalia. Because it is the color of the human heart, red is a symbol of warmth and feeling. White stands for purity; some think that the bridal veil was the inspiration for the white lace traditionally used on VALENTINE CARDS. White is also a symbol of faith—in this case, the faith between two lovers.
Related Holidays: Candlemas, Lupercalia, Sweetest Day

ORIGINS

What is known as Valentine's Day descended from the ancient Roman celebration known as the **LUPERCALIA**, held on February 15. Although it started out as a fertility ritual, the Lupercalia quickly took on the character of a lovers' holiday. Roman boys chose their partners for the celebration by drawing girls' names from a box or urn; then the couple would exchange gifts on the day of the festival. When the Roman armies invaded what is now France and Britain, they brought their Lupercalia customs with them—including the drawing of names for partners or sweethearts. But the advent of Christianity in the fourth century necessitated putting a Christian face on what was essentially a pagan celebration. So in 469 C.E., Pope Gelasius set aside February 14 to honor St. Valentine, a young Roman who was martyred by Emperor Claudius II on this day in 270 C.E. for refusing to give up Christianity. Because of the proximity of the two dates, many customs associated with the Lupercalia were carried over to the Feast of St. Valentine.

One legend describes St. Valentine as a third-century priest who defied the Roman emperor's ban on marriages and engagements by marrying young people in secret and who was eventually arrested and put to death. Another story tells of a man named Valentine who was imprisoned for helping Christians who were being persecuted. While serving time in jail, he converted the jailer and his family to Christianity and restored the sight of the jailer's blind daughter, with whom he fell in love. On the morning of his execution, he sent her a farewell message signed, "From your Valentine."

There was a spring festival observed in Italy during the Middle Ages at which young people gathered in groves and gardens to listen to love poetry and romantic music. Afterward, they would pair off and stroll among the trees and flowers. Similar pairing-off customs were popular in France as well, but they often led to hard feelings and trouble, and were finally banned in 1776. Valentine's Day customs survived, however, in the British Isles, where young men were drawing names for "valentines" or sweethearts for centuries after the departure of the Roman armies. In England, young people played a popular game in which they would write down the names of all the young women on pieces of paper, roll them up tightly, and place them in a bowl. The young men, blindfolded, would then take turns drawing a name from the bowl. The girl whose name was drawn would be that boy's "Valentine" for the coming year.

Because it occurs seven weeks after the **WINTER SOLSTICE** and marks the progression from winter to spring, mid-February has traditionally been regarded as a time of fertility. In the Middle Ages, it was said that birds chose their mates on February 14 (*see* LOVEBIRDS). This was also the day on which Groundhog Day was originally observed (*see* **CANDLEMAS**), heralding the approach of spring.

SYMBOLS AND CUSTOMS

Cupid

Cupid, the Roman god of love, is a favorite symbol for VALENTINE CARDS, party decorations, and candy boxes. He was originally depicted as a young man carrying a bow and a quiver full of arrows. Over the years, Cupid's form was gradually altered, and the handsome youth of ancient mythology became a pudgy baby. This transformation of a god who was said to have sharpened his arrows on a grindstone whetted with blood to a helpless infant got a boost during the Victorian era, when merchants were eager to promote Valentine's Day as a holiday more suitable for women and children.

Cupid was the son of Venus, the Roman goddess of love and beauty. To the Romans, he was a symbol of passionate, playful, or tender love. His arrows were invisible, and his victims, who included gods as well as humans, would not be aware that they had been shot until they suddenly fell in love.

Heart and Arrow

A red or pink heart pierced by an arrow is the best known and most enduring symbol of Valentine's Day. It can be seen in VALENTINE CARDS and decorations as well as in candies, cookies, and cakes served on this day. The heart itself symbolizes vulnerability as well as love: By sending someone a Valentine, one is taking a risk that he or she will be rejected. The arrow that pierces the heart is a symbol of death and the vulnerability of the unprotected heart. Together, the heart and the arrow also represent the merging of the male and female principles.

As early as the twelfth century, the heart was considered the seat of love and affection. But the conventional heart shape, which is symmetrical and tapers to a point at the bottom, doesn't look anything like a real heart. Some scholars speculate that it was designed by a casual doodler to represent the human buttocks, a female torso with prominent breasts, or even the imprint that a woman wearing lipstick makes when she presses her lips against a piece of paper.

In the early 1800s, young British and American men sometimes wore slips of paper with their girlfriends' names written on them pinned to their sleeves for several days, thus giving rise to the expression "to wear one's heart on one's sleeve."

In the United States, the American Heart Association holds its "Save a Sweet Heart" program during Valentine's week. It is an anti-smoking campaign that uses the symbol of the heart to educate high school students about the health risks involved in smoking.

Lovebirds

The popular medieval folk belief that birds chose their mates on February 14 made doves a favorite symbol for VALENTINE CARDS. The dove was sacred to Venus and other love deities and had a reputation for choosing a lifelong mate. Known for their "billing and cooing," doves have long been a symbol of romantic love.

When printed Valentines first began to appear, many of them featured lovebirds. Toward the end of the nineteenth century, some even had a stuffed hummingbird or bird of paradise mounted on a satin cushion. The lovebirds that appear on today's Valentines are usually tiny parrots with brilliant feathers. In the wild, they are known for living in pairs and keeping to themselves, much like couples in love.

Valentine Cards

The custom of exchanging love notes on Valentine's Day can be traced back to the ancient Roman **LUPERCALIA**, when boys drew the names of girls from a box and escorted the girl whose name they had drawn to the festival. The Christian church tried to downplay the holiday's sexual aspects by initiating the custom of drawing saints' names from a box. The participants would then be expected to emulate the saint whose name they had drawn for the rest of the year. Needless to say, the idea never really caught on, and Valentine's Day remains an occasion for exchanging love messages.

One of the first Valentine cards was created by Charles, Duke of Orleans. Imprisoned in the Tower of London for several years following the Battle of Agincourt in 1415, he sent Valentine poems to his wife in France from his jail cell. Commercially made Valentines didn't appear in England until almost 1800, although handmade cards had been popular for some time. In the nineteenth century, "penny dreadfuls" took the place of romantic Valentines. These were insulting and sometimes cruel cards, meant to be funny and usually sent anonymously.

In America, handmade Valentines began to appear around 1740. They were sealed with red wax and left secretly on a lover's doorstep or sent by mail. They were often quite elaborate, with cutout or pinprick designs resembling lace. Another popular handmade Valentine was the "puzzle purse," which had verses hidden within its folds that had to be read in a certain order. Commercially made cards began to take over in the 1880s.

"Valentine" meant the person whose name was picked from the box, or who was chosen to be one's sweetheart, by 1450. By 1533, it meant the folded piece of paper with the name on it; by 1610 it referred to a gift given to the special person; and by 1824 it referred to the verse, letter, or message sent to that person. Some say that the word "Valentine" doesn't come from St. Valentine at all, but rather from the Old French *galantine,* meaning "a lover or gallant."

FURTHER READING

Barth, Edna. *Hearts, Cupids, and Red Roses: The Story of the Valentine Symbols.* New York: Seabury Press, 1974.

Buday, George. *The History of the Christmas Card.* 1971. Reprint. Detroit: Omnigraphics, 1991.

Gaer, Joseph. *Holidays Around the World.* Boston: Little, Brown, 1953.

Henderson, Helene, ed. *Holidays, Festivals, and Celebrations of the World Dictionary.* 3rd ed. Detroit: Omnigraphics, 2005.

Ickis, Marguerite. *The Book of Festivals and Holidays the World Over.* New York: Dodd, Mead, 1970.

Purdy, Susan. *Festivals for You to Celebrate.* Philadelphia: Lippincott, 1969.

Santino, Jack. *All Around the Year: Holidays and Celebrations in American Life.* Urbana: University of Illinois Press, 1994.

Schmidt, Leigh Eric. *Consumer Rites: The Buying and Selling of American Holidays.* Princeton: Princeton University Press, 1995.

Tuleja, Tad. *Curious Customs: The Stories Behind 296 Popular American Rituals.* New York: Harmony, 1987.

WEB SITE

Library of Congress
www.americaslibrary.gov/cgi-bin/page.cgi/jb/modern/valentin_1

Vasaloppet

Type of Holiday: Sporting
Date of Observation: First Sunday in March
Where Celebrated: Between Mora and Sälen, Sweden
Symbols and Customs: Blueberry Soup, Children's Races, Ladies' Race, Vasaloppet's Museum

ORIGINS

The idea for what is now the world's largest cross-country ski race came from a Swedish newspaper editor named Anders Pers. He wanted an event that would commemorate the heroic effort of Gustav Eriksson Vasa, a young Swede who tried to persuade his countrymen to revolt against their Danish rulers in the sixteenth century and was imprisoned in Denmark for his efforts. When he escaped from prison in 1520, he headed north to Mora, where he hoped to find some men who would join his revolt. Unfortunately, the men of Mora were not interested, and, in order to avoid being recaptured by the Danes, Vasa headed off on his skis for Norway. Soon after he left, the men of Mora reconsidered and decided Vasa was right. They sent their two fastest skiers to catch up with him, which they managed to do in Sälen. The three men then skied back to Mora—a distance of more than ninety kilometers (about fifty-five miles)—and organized an army that waged a two-and-a-half-year battle against the ruling Danes. When it was all over in 1523, Gustav Erkisson Vasa became a national hero and king of Sweden.

Pers wanted a cross-country ski race that would test the competitors' endurance, just as that of Vasa and his companions had been tested in the sixteenth century. The first Vasaloppet, as the race was called, took place on March 19, 1922, with the starting line in Sälen and the finish line in Mora. It took the winner more than seven-and-a-half hours to complete the race, and he received his trophy while standing in front of Vasa's monument. The Vasaloppet went on to become one of the world's most demanding cross-country races, ranking in prestige with the Winter Olympics.

A wide variety of skiers compete during Vasaloppet week, including young children, recreational skiers, and elite ski racers. More than 15,000 skiers from more than thirty countries compete in the main race, which is held on the first Sunday in March, and 3,000 volunteers are needed to run the food stations, which are located along the course at approximately ten-kilometer intervals (*see* BLUEBERRY SOUP). In addition to the ninety-kilometer race, there is a thirty-kilometer coed recreational race known as the Kort Vasan, a CHILDREN'S RACE, and a LADIES' RACE. The Öppet Spär is a two-day race over the regular 90-kilometer course that allows skiers to cover the same distance without the pressure of competition. There is also a Halv Vasan, introduced in 1997, that covers only half the Vasaloppet course, and a Skejt Vasan for cross-country skiers who use the now-popular "skating" technique. The time it takes the winner to complete the race has been cut in half since the 1920s, with the current record (set in 1998) standing at three hours, thirty-eight minutes, fifty-seven seconds.

Perhaps no name is more closely associated with the race than that of Nils Karlsson, who has won the Vasaloppet nine times. It was 1954 before a foreigner, Pekka Kuvaja of Finland, won the Vasaloppet, and then another seventeen years elapsed before a Norwegian won the race. Since that time there have been a number of foreign victors, but there is no question that the Swedes have dominated the race over its eighty-year history. Perhaps this is why the motto over the finish gate says, "In the footsteps of our fathers towards the victories of the future."

SYMBOLS AND CUSTOMS

Blueberry Soup

Blueberry soup is a traditional Swedish dish that has become closely identified with the Vasaloppet. It is a standard offering at the race's food stations, although not all foreign competitors enjoy the taste. Blueberries are high in vitamin C, iron, magnesium, and other minerals, and they are a good source of antioxidants, which help the body fight cancer, heart disease, arthritis, and the effects of aging. The skiers who compete in the Vasaloppet consume an impressive quantity of blueberry soup, as well as other food and drink, during the race: 128,320 litres (almost 33,900 gallons) of blueberry soup, 55,000 litres of porridge, 1,000 litres of gruel, 103,500 Vasaloppet buns, 54,600 litres of sport drinks, 12,500 litres of bouillon, and 5,220 litres of coffee.

Children's Races

The Vasaloppet has spawned a number of related events over the years. Since the mid-1980s many Swedish towns have organized their own "miniature Vasaloppet" ski races for children in nursery and elementary school. The course is usually

900 meters long and food stations are set up to serve the children BLUEBERRY SOUP and all of the other Vasaloppet favorites.

Ladies' Race

Although a woman successfully completed the Vasaloppet as early as 1923, it was 1981 before women were allowed to compete in the race officially. A separate women's competition, known as the Tjej Vasan, was introduced in 1988 over a thirty-kilometer course that runs from Oxberg to Mora—the same course, in fact, used in the recreational Kort Vasan. Eight thousand women are allowed to enter the Tjej Vasan, making it the largest all-female skiing competition in the world. But the Vasaloppet itself remains a test of male endurance: Just as American men may celebrate a "big" birthday by running a marathon, Swedish men frequently celebrate their fiftieth birthday by entering the Vasaloppet.

Vasaloppet's Museum

A museum honoring the history of the Vasaloppet opened in 1994 in Mora. Its displays include skis, sticks (poles), photographs, texts, and articles about the race. Its cinema shows films that discuss past challenges, modern-day skiing, and future development plans for the Vasaloppet. There are computers with race statistics and special exhibits honoring both female and male champions. The museum attracts around 15,000 visitors every year.

FURTHER READING

Van Straalen, Alice. *The Book of Holidays Around the World*. New York: Dutton, 1986.

WEB SITE

Vasaloppet Official Web Site
www.vasaloppet.se

Vasant Panchami
(Basant Panchami)

Type of Holiday: Calendar/Seasonal, Religious (Hindu)
Date of Observation: January-February; fifth day of the waxing half of the Hindu month of Magha
Where Celebrated: India
Symbols and Customs: Books, Sarasvati
Colors: Yellow—the color of the mustard flower that announces the arrival of spring.

ORIGINS

Vasant Panchami is a springtime festival in Hinduism, which many scholars regard as the oldest living religion. The word Hindu is derived from the Sanskrit term *Sindhu* (or *Indus*), which meant river. It referred to people living in the Indus valley in the Indian subcontinent.

Hinduism has no founder, one universal reality (or god) known as Brahman, many gods and goddesses (sometimes referred to as devtas), and several scriptures. Hinduism also has no priesthood or hierarchical structure similar to that seen in some other religions, such as Christianity. Hindus acknowledge the authority of a wide variety of writings, but there is no single, uniform canon. The oldest of the Hindu writings are the *Vedas*. The word "veda" comes from the Sanskrit word for knowledge. The *Vedas*, which were compiled from ancient oral traditions, contain hymns, instructions, explanations, chants for sacrifices, magical formulas, and philosophy. Another set of sacred books includes the *Great Epics*, which illustrate Hindu faith in practice. The *Epics* include the *Ramayana*, the *Mahabharata*, and the *Bhagavad Gita*.

The Hindu pantheon includes approximately thirty-three million gods. Some of these are held in higher esteem than others. Over all the gods, Hindus believe in one absolute high god or universal concept. This is Brahman. Although he is above all the gods, he is not worshipped in popular ceremonies because he is detached from the day-to-day affairs of the people. Brahman is impersonal. Lesser gods and goddesses (devtas) serve him. Because these are more intimately involved in the affairs of people, they are venerated as gods. The most honored god in Hinduism varies among the different Hindu sects. Although Hindu adher-

1008

ents practice their faith differently and venerate different deities, they share a similar view of reality and look back on a common history.

Vasant Panchami marks the changing of the seasons, which people in all parts of the world have honored since ancient times. Many cultures divided the year into two seasons, summer and winter, and marked these points of the year at or near the **SUMMER SOLSTICE** and **WINTER SOLSTICE**, during which light and warmth began to increase and decrease, respectively. In pre-industrial times, humans survived through hunting, gathering, and agricultural practices, which depend on the natural cycle of seasons, according to the climate in the region of the world in which they lived. Thus, they created rituals to help ensure enough rain and sun in the spring and summer so crops would grow to fruition at harvest time, which was, in turn, duly celebrated. Vestiges of many of these ancient practices are thought to have survived in festivals still celebrated around seasonal themes.

One such seasonal event is Vasant Panchami, a festival of spring celebrated by Hindus throughout India in late January or early February (*panchami* means "fifth"). People wear bright yellow clothes because yellow is a color associated with the blooming of the mustard flower and the arrival of spring. Men often wear yellow turbans, while women wear yellow saris or tunics over trousers with a yellow scarf. The main meal of the day is made with yellow rice cooked especially for the occasion.

Vasant Panchami is a time for families to get together and spend the day flying kites, listening to music, and dancing. Because it is also a festival that honors SARASVATI, the Hindu goddess of learning, her image is frequently displayed and worshipped. In West Bengal, where the veneration of Sarasvati is particularly widespread, there are processions in which images of her graceful figure are carried to the river for a ceremonial bath.

Many of the celebrations held on this day take place in schools and universities, where SARASVATI is held in high esteem for her association with literature and the fine arts. Some young people in India have started to celebrate Vasant Panchami in much the same way that Americans celebrate **VALENTINE'S DAY**, as a day for young couples who are in love.

SYMBOLS AND CUSTOMS

Books

As an appropriate symbol for learning and eloquence, books play an important role in the celebration of Vasant Panchami. In the hope that SARASVATI will help them with their exams, students place special offerings of pens, brushes, and books before the goddess's image. Young Hindu children start their education on this day by writing the 50 letters of the Sanskrit alphabet while seated before an image of Sarasvati, who is credited with the invention of the Sanskrit language. In some regions, it is a day for the dedication of books.

Sarasvati

Sarasvati is usually shown holding a *vina* or lute, reclining on a lotus blossom or riding a white swan. In later Hindu mythology, she is the wife of Brahma and the goddess of wisdom and eloquence. It is widely believed that without Sarasvati's blessing, no one can be skilled in poetry, music, or any other art.

Sarasvati was originally a river goddess, worshipped for her fertilizing and purifying powers. She was personified in the Sarasvati River, which was as sacred to early Indians as the Ganges is to them today. But the identification of the goddess with the river is controversial, and the name Sarasvati is now applied to two rivers: one flows through the Punjab region and the other arises in the Aravalli Range, a series of hills that run through northern India.

FURTHER READING

Bellenir, Karen. *Religious Holidays and Calendars*. 3rd ed. Detroit: Omnigraphics, 2004.

Henderson, Helene, ed. *Holidays, Festivals, and Celebrations of the World Dictionary*. 3rd ed. Detroit: Omnigraphics, 2005.

Kapoor, Sukhbir Singh. *Sikh Festivals*. Vero Beach, FL: Rourke Enterprises, 1989.

Leach, Maria, ed. *Funk & Wagnalls Standard Dictionary of Folklore, Mythology & Legend*. San Francisco: Harper & Row, 1984.

Sharma, Brijendra Nath. *Festivals of India*. New Delhi: Abhinav Publications, 1978.

Thomas, Paul. *Hindu Religion, Customs, and Manners*. 6th ed. New York: APT Books, 1981.

Trawicky, Bernard, and Ruth W. Gregory. *Anniversaries and Holidays*. 5th ed. Chicago: American Library Assocation, 2000.

Underhill, Muriel M. *The Hindu Religious Year*. London: Oxford University Press, 1921.

Van Straalen, Alice. *The Book of Holidays Around the World*. New York: Dutton, 1986.

WEB SITE

Hindu Council UK
www.hinducounciluk.org/newsite/vasant.asp

Vata Savitri

Type of Holiday: Religious (Hindu)
Date of Observation: May-June; last three days (or last day) of the bright half of Jyestha
Where Celebrated: India
Symbols and Customs: Banyan Tree

ORIGINS

Vata Savitri is a tradition in Hinduism, which many scholars regard as the oldest living religion. The word Hindu is derived from the Sanskrit term *Sindhu* (or *Indus*), which meant river. It referred to people living in the Indus valley in the Indian subcontinent.

Hinduism has no founder, one universal reality (or god) known as Brahman, many gods and goddesses (sometimes referred to as devtas), and several scriptures. Hinduism also has no priesthood or hierarchical structure similar to that seen in some other religions, such as Christianity. Hindus acknowledge the authority of a wide variety of writings, but there is no single, uniform canon. The oldest of the Hindu writings are the *Vedas*. The word "veda" comes from the Sanskrit word for knowledge. The *Vedas*, which were compiled from ancient oral traditions, contain hymns, instructions, explanations, chants for sacrifices, magical formulas, and philosophy. Another set of sacred books includes the *Great Epics*, which illustrate Hindu faith in practice. The *Epics* include the *Ramayana*, the *Mahabharata*, and the *Bhagavad Gita*.

The Hindu pantheon includes approximately thirty-three million gods. Some of these are held in higher esteem than others. Over all the gods, Hindus believe in one absolute high god or universal concept. This is Brahman. Although he is above all the gods, he is not worshipped in popular ceremonies because he is detached from the day-to-day affairs of the people. Brahman is impersonal. Lesser gods and goddesses (devtas) serve him. Because these are more intimately involved in the affairs of people, they are venerated as gods. The most honored god in Hinduism varies among the different Hindu sects. Although Hindu adherents practice their faith differently and venerate different deities, they share a similar view of reality and look back on a common history.

Vata Savitri is a fast observed by Hindu women who want to avoid widowhood. During the Middle Ages, being left a widow was the most dreaded misfortune that could befall a Hindu woman. Even now, orthodox Hindu women all hope to die before their husbands. On Vata Savitri, therefore, they perform special ceremonies designed to promote the health and longevity of their husbands.

Savitri was the daughter of King Ashvapati. When she was old enough to marry, her father told her she could choose the man she wanted as her husband. She chose Satyavan, a hermit who lived in the jungle. The seer Narad warned Savitri that Satyavan was destined to die within a year. But she refused to let this knowledge change her mind and married him anyway. She got rid of all her jewels and fancy dresses and wore the coarse garments of a hermit. During the last three days of his life, she vowed to fast. Then, on his final day, she followed him as he went out to cut wood. He was so tired he lay down with his head in her lap and fell asleep.

There are several versions of what happened next. One says that the branch of a tree fell on his head, while another claims he was bit by a snake. In any case, when Yama, the god of death, appeared to snatch his soul out of his body, Savitri chose to follow. Yama was so impressed by her devotion that he restored her husband to life and blessed them with a hundred sons.

Savitri is regarded as a symbol of marital fidelity. The festival held in her honor takes its name from the *vata* or BANYAN TREE, which she worshipped on the day of her husband's death. Hindu women get up early on this day and, after bathing, go out in groups to worship the banyan tree. They water the tree, sprinkle vermilion (red powder) on it, wrap raw cotton threads around its trunk, and then circle it seven times. They also observe a fast and make an offering of sugar and ghee (clarified butter). Women who are unable to get to a banyan tree worship a twig of it at home and distribute sweets to their family members and neighbors. They also pray for their husbands' prosperity and good health.

SYMBOLS AND CUSTOMS

Banyan Tree

The banyan tree, also known as the Indian fig tree, is a symbol of immortality because it never dies. Its aerial roots support new branches, and it can go on growing for hundreds of years. Savitri is usually shown holding a branch of the banyan in one hand and the tree's aerial root in the other. An offshoot of the banyan tree can be seen growing over her head.

Hindu women believe that worshipping the banyan tree on Vata Savitri will guarantee a long life for their husbands.

FURTHER READING

Bellenir, Karen. *Religious Holidays and Calendars*. 3rd ed. Detroit: Omnigraphics, 2004.

Gupte, B.A. *Hindu Holidays and Ceremonials*. 2nd ed. Calcutta: Thacker, Spink & Co., 1919.

Henderson, Helene, ed. *Holidays, Festivals, and Celebrations of the World Dictionary*. 3rd ed. Detroit: Omnigraphics, 2005.

MacDonald, Margaret R., ed. *The Folklore of World Holidays*. Detroit: Gale Research, 1992.

Spicer, Dorothy Gladys. *The Book of Festivals*. 1937. Reprint. Detroit: Omnigraphics, 1990.

WEB SITE

Hinduism Today
www.hinduismtoday.com/archives/2005/1-3/56-57_women.shtml

Vegetarian Festival
(Festival of the Nine Emperor Gods)

Type of Holiday: Religious (Buddhist)

Date of Observation: September-October; first nine days of the ninth Chinese lunar month

Where Celebrated: Malaysia, Singapore, Thailand, and by Chinese communities elsewhere

Symbols and Customs: Blade Ladder-Climbing, Fasting/Vegetarianism, Fire-Walking, Lantern-Raising Ceremony, Self-Mutilation, Wayang Performances, White Clothing

ORIGINS

The Vegetarian Festival, also known as the Festival of the Nine Emperor Gods, is part of the traditions of Buddhism, one of the four largest religious families in the world. Buddhism is based on the teachings of Siddhartha Gautama (c. 563-483 B.C.E.), who came to be known as Buddha, or "The Enlightened One." The basic tenets of Buddhism can be summarized in the Four Noble Truths and the Eightfold Path. The Four Noble Truths are 1) the truth and reality of suffering; 2) suffering is caused by desire; 3) the way to end suffering is to end desire; and 4) the Eightfold Path shows the way to end suffering. The Eightfold Path consists of 1) right view or right understanding; 2) right thoughts and aspirations; 3) right speech; 4) right conduct and action; 5) right way of life; 6) right effort; 7) right mindfulness; and 8) right contemplation.

What is known in Thailand as the Vegetarian Festival and in Singapore as the Festival of the Nine Emperor Gods has its roots in China, where star-worship was well established by the time of the Han Dynasty (202 B.C.E.-220 C.E.). The seven stars of the Big Dipper and two other nearby stars, invisible to the human eye, were deities referred to as the Nine Great Emperors or Nine Emperor Gods, and it was believed that they controlled the destiny of mortals.

In 1825, when a traveling Chinese opera company visited Phuket, the largest of the islands in Thailand, to entertain the Chinese who were working in the tin mines there, a terrible epidemic of malaria broke out, and many people lost their lives. The Chinese decided they had brought this fate upon themselves because they had forgotten that it was the ninth lunar month, a period during which they normally paid tribute to the Nine Emperor Gods by abstaining from eating meat or killing animals. When the members of the opera company purified their bodies by fasting and adhering to a strict vegetarian diet (*see* FASTING/VEGETARIANISM), the epidemic miraculously came to an end. Thereafter, everyone in the Chinese community made sure they honored these gods during the first nine days of the ninth lunar month, which usually falls in late September and early October.

This festival is still widely observed in Phuket, where it is called the Vegetarian Festival. Members of the Chinese Buddhist community celebrate by avoiding not only meat but also sex and alcoholic drinks. They abstain from killing any living thing, arguing, lying, and any other activities that are not in keeping with their efforts to purify themselves in both body and mind. They put on WHITE CLOTHING, attend WAYANG or Chinese opera performances, and participate in various acts of SELF-MUTILATION, which are both horrifying and fascinating to watch. Most of the ceremonies associated with the festival take place in Phuket's Chinese temples, and the dense smoke from the fires, candles, and burning incense in these temples helps the self-mutilators achieve the trancelike state that will protect them from harm.

A farewell procession is held on the ninth and last day of the festival, when images of the Nine Emperor Gods are carried through the streets, accompanied by those who have mutilated themselves to prove their devotion. An urn filled with burning benzoin (a gum resin), which was ignited on the first day of the festival and has been kept in a private place in the temple ever since, is also carried in the procession, usually to the waterfront where it is emptied into the sea in a symbolic farewell to the Nine Emperor Gods as they return to heaven.

SYMBOLS AND CUSTOMS

Blade Ladder-Climbing

One of the more impressive acts of SELF-MUTILATION that can be seen during the Phuket Vegetarian Festival is performed on the seventh night. Hundreds of young men climb forty-foot-high ladders with extremely sharp rungs that are erected outside the Chinese temples. While most are in a trance that protects them from serious injury, there are always a few whose feet are badly cut.

Fasting/Vegetarianism

The custom of fasting dates back to about 3000 B.C.E. in China, when it was believed to be the key to longevity. It was not widely practiced, however, until Buddhism came to China during the reign of the Eastern Han Dynasty Emperor Ming (58-76 C.E.).

Fasting during the Vegetarian Festival is not the same thing as starvation; it entails a strict avoidance of meat, eggs, chicken, and seafood, and sometimes vegetables with strong odors, such as onions and garlic, and certain spices. Some people are so fastidious about their vegetarianism during the festival that they use a different set of dishes for serving meals. The fasting can begin as much as several weeks before the festival itself and is regarded as an essential form of preparation for the trials of SELF-MUTILATION that follow.

Fire-Walking

One of the forms of SELF-MUTILATION performed during the Vegetarian Festival occurs in the evening outside the temple, where beds of hot charcoal fifteen or more feet in diameter are waiting. Those who have prepared themselves mentally and spiritually are able to walk over the hot coals barefoot without getting burned.

Lantern-Raising Ceremony

In Phuket, the lantern-raising ceremony is performed in the evening before the nine-day festival begins. A lantern with nine wicks, symbolic of the Nine Emperor Gods and hanging from a bamboo pole to which leaves and branches are still attached, is raised to the top of a post made from the trunk of a tree. Once the lantern has been lit and raised, it symbolizes the arrival of the Emperor Gods, which means that the festival itself can begin.

Self-Mutilation

It is the self-mutilation rituals that have made the Vegetarian Festival in Phuket a major tourist attraction in recent years. Those who have been preparing for this for weeks allow their faces to be pierced, usually through the cheek, by sharp objects such as knives, skewers, or shards of glass. Larger objects such as swords, umbrellas, chains, and poles have also been used. Sometimes several self-mutilators will be pierced by the same length of steel wire, forming a kind of human necklace, and sometimes rods that are several feet long with heavy objects attached to the ends are forced through the cheeks of the willing volunteers. The piercing itself is done with the utmost care, using antiseptic gloves and piercing tools that have been cleaned and sterilized. These people believe that the Nine Emperor Gods inhabit their bodies during the festival, which enables them to endure these hideous acts of self-mutilation. When they are able to do so successfully, they say it's proof of the Emperor Gods' power.

FIRE-WALKING and BLADE LADDER-CLIMBING are other forms of self-mutilation associated with the festival. "Human pincushions" can also be seen, with thousands of small pins piercing their necks, shoulders, and backs.

Wayang Performances

Chinese opera, known as wayang, is quite different from the elaborate theater productions associated with opera in Europe and the United States. It is usually performed in a much more casual setting, either on the street or in a temporary theater that has been set up outdoors. The stories are usually based on ancient legends with which everyone is familiar, and the actors wear colorful, ornate costumes and heavy makeup. Performances can last two days or even longer.

The wayang performances that take place during the Vegetarian Festival in Phuket are a reminder of how the festival originated—when a visiting Chinese opera troupe brought illness and death upon the local population because they failed to pay tribute to their own Emperor Gods while traveling away from home.

White Clothing

The white clothing people wear during the Vegetarian Festival is a symbol of the purity they are striving to achieve by observing a strict vegetarian diet and by engaging in acts of SELF-MUTILATION.

FURTHER READING

Freeman, Dave, et al. *100 Things to Do Before You Die: Travel Events You Just Can't Miss*. Dallas: Taylor Pub. Co., 1999.

MacDonald, Margaret R., ed. *The Folklore of World Holidays*. Detroit: Gale Research, 1992.

Phuket Vegetarian Festival
www.phuketvegetarian.com

Vernal Equinox

Type of Holiday: Calendar/Seasonal, Ancient, Religious (Neopagan)
Date of Observation: On or about March 21
Where Celebrated: All over the world
Symbols and Customs: Flowers
Related Holidays: Beltane, Easter, Imbolc, Lughnasa, Mabon, May Day, Nyepi, Passover, Samhain, Summer Solstice, Winter Solstice

ORIGINS

The vernal equinox—from the Latin *vernalis*, meaning "of spring," and *equinoxium*, meaning "time of equal days and nights"—is one of two times during the year (the other being the **AUTUMN EQUINOX**) when day and night are of equal length all over the world. This occurs because the ecliptic, or the sun's path through the sky, and the earth's equator intersect, with the sun above the equator. At this precise moment, known as the equinox, exactly one-half of the earth is illuminated by the sun's rays while the other half is in darkness, producing a day and a night that are both twelve hours long.

In ancient times, the vernal equinox marked the beginning of the year and the point from which the twelve constellations of the zodiac were calculated. For this reason, the vernal equinox was sometimes referred to as the "first point of Aries," because at one time spring began when the sun entered the zodiac sign of Aries. But because of a phenomenon known as the "precession of the equinoxes," which refers to a cyclical wobbling in the earth's axis of rotation, the vernal equinox has shifted westward over the centuries, and spring now begins when the sun is in Pisces, the next constellation to the west.

In terms of earthly weather, the astronomical seasons mean nothing. In many parts of the United States, for example, where spring is widely identified with the months of March, April, and May, winter weather can persist well into April and even into May. In Great Britain, on the other hand, spring is popularly thought to include February, March, and April. In the Southern Hemisphere, of course, the seasons are reversed: There, spring begins around September 23 and ends about December 21.

The vernal equinox marks the changing of the seasons, which people in all parts of the world have honored since ancient times. Many cultures divided the year into two seasons, summer and winter, and marked these points of the year at or near the **SUMMER SOLSTICE** and **WINTER SOLSTICE**, during which light and warmth began to increase and decrease, respectively. In pre-industrial times, humans survived through hunting, gathering, and agricultural practices, which depend on the natural cycle of seasons, according to the climate in the region of the world in which they lived. Thus, they created rituals to help ensure enough rain and sun in the spring and summer so crops would grow to fruition at harvest time, which was, in turn, duly celebrated. Vestiges of many of these ancient practices are thought to have survived in festivals still celebrated around seasonal themes.

As the season of planting and germination, when life and light replaced the darkness and death of the winter season, spring had a profound influence on ancient peoples and played an important role in their folklore, mythology, and art. Most ancient New Year rites taking place around the time of the vernal equinox involved one or more of the following elements: (1) fasting; (2) purgation, usually involving fire, the ringing of bells, and the cleansing of houses and temples; (3) invigoration, often in the form of a mock combat between the forces of life and death or the release of sexual energy; and (4) jubilation in the form of feasting and merriment.

The people of Bali, for example, celebrate the vernal equinox and the New Year by driving the devils out of their villages and then observing a day of stillness, known as **NYEPI**. After luring the evil spirits out of their hiding places with an elaborate offering of food, drink, and money, with samples of every kind of seed, fruit, and animal found on the island arranged in the shape of an eight-pointed star, the demons are driven out of the village by people running through the streets lighting firecrackers and banging on drums and tin cans. The following day, Nyepi, is observed as a day of absolute stillness: no cooking or fires, sexual intercourse, or work of any kind is permitted.

The early Christians, who regarded the seasons as symbolic of the course of human life, identified spring with rebirth and resurrection. The Christian festival of **EASTER**, which takes its name from Eostre, the Teutonic goddess of spring and fertility, is a joyful celebration of the resurrection of Christ observed on the Sunday after the first full moon following the vernal equinox. Even the Jewish feast of **PASSOVER** is rooted in ancient agricultural customs associated with spring and planting.

During the 1960s, the modern Neopagan and Wiccan movements emerged in Great Britain, the United States, and other English-speaking countries. They follow a nature-oriented religion loosely linked to ancient Celtic and other beliefs and inspired by old European folk practices. They celebrate eight sabbats, known as the eight spokes of the wheel of the year, which include **SUMMER SOLSTICE, WINTER SOLSTICE, VERNAL EQUINOX, BELTANE, SAMHAIN, IMBOLC, LUGHNASA,** and **MABON**.

SYMBOLS AND CUSTOMS

Flowers

Ancient sculptors and artists often depicted spring as a female figure carrying flowers. Flowers are a traditional symbol not only of spring but of the transitory beauty associated with this season. Flowers in a field are a popular Christian symbol of the Virgin Mary and the Church, and white flowers in particular are associated with the Virgin.

In the United States and other countries, spring remains a popular time for flower festivals and garden tours. Just as seeds are planted in the spring, it is also a time for other kinds of beginnings, including graduations and weddings.

FURTHER READING

Chambers, Robert. *The Book of Days*. 2 vols. 1862-64. Reprint. Detroit: Omnigraphics, 1990.

Christianson, Stephen G., and Jane M. Hatch. *The American Book of Days*. 4th ed. New York: H.W. Wilson, 2000.

Heinberg, Richard. *Celebrate the Solstice: Honoring the Earth's Seasonal Rhythms through Festival and Ceremony*. Wheaton, IL: Quest Books, 1993.

Henderson, Helene, ed. *Holidays, Festivals, and Celebrations of the World Dictionary*. 3rd ed. Detroit: Omnigraphics, 2005.

Leach, Maria, ed. *Funk & Wagnalls Standard Dictionary of Folklore, Mythology & Legend*. San Francisco: Harper & Row, 1984.

MacDonald, Margaret R., ed. *The Folklore of World Holidays*. Detroit: Gale Research, 1992.

Olderr, Steven. *Symbolism: A Comprehensive Dictionary*. Jefferson, NC: McFarland, 1986.

WEB SITE

National Maritime Museum
www.nmm.ac.uk/server/show/conWebDoc.3843

Vesak
(Wesak, Buddha's Birthday)

Type of Holiday: Religious (Buddhist)
Date of Observation: April-May; full moon of Vaisakha
Where Celebrated: China, India, Indonesia, Japan, Korea, Nepal, Singapore, Sri
 Lanka, Thailand, Tibet, and by Buddhists all over the world
Symbols and Customs: Bathing the Buddha, Bodhi Tree
Related Holidays: Rocket Festival

ORIGINS

Vesak is the holiest day of the year in Buddhism, one of the four largest religious families in the world. Buddhism is based on the teachings of Siddhartha Gautama (c. 563-483 B.C.E.), who came to be known as Buddha, or "The Enlightened One." The basic tenets of Buddhism can be summarized in the Four Noble Truths and the Eightfold Path. The Four Noble Truths are 1) the truth and reality of suffering; 2) suffering is caused by desire; 3) the way to end suffering is to end desire; and 4) the Eightfold Path shows the way to end suffering. The Eightfold Path consists of 1) right view or right understanding; 2) right thoughts and aspirations; 3) right speech; 4) right conduct and action; 5) right way of life; 6) right effort; 7) right mindfulness; and 8) right contemplation.

Vesak celebrates the Buddha's birth, enlightenment, and death, or attainment of Nirvana. While these anniversaries are observed in all Buddhist countries, they are not always celebrated on the same day. Theravada Buddhists, who practice the oldest form of their religion and can be found primarily in Southeast Asia, observe all three anniversaries on the full moon of the sixth month. In Japan and other Mahayana Buddhist countries, these three events are celebrated on separate days: the Buddha's birth on April 8, his enlightenment on December 8, and his death on February 15.

Although the celebrations differ from country to country, activities generally center on Buddhist temples, where people gather to listen to sermons on the life of Buddha. In the evening, there are candlelight processions around the temples, while homes are decorated with paper lanterns and oil lamps. Because it's considered important to practice the virtues of kindness to all living things, it's traditional in some countries to free caged birds on this day, or to set up booths to dispense food to the poor.

Siddhartha Gautama, who came to be called the Buddha ("the Enlightened"), was born into an aristocratic family. At the age of twenty-nine, distressed by the misery of mankind, he renounced his life of luxury and left his wife and infant son to become a wandering ascetic. For six years he practiced the most severe austerities, eating little and meditating regularly. But then he realized that self-deprivation wasn't leading him to what he sought. One morning in 528 B.C.E., while sitting in deep meditation under the BODHI TREE, he experienced a wider vision of his own existence and derived from that vision his blueprint for religious life. In the years that followed, he laid down rules of ethics and condemned the caste system. He taught that the aim of religion is to free oneself of worldly concerns in order to attain enlightenment, or Nirvana. The Buddha trained large numbers of disciples to continue his work. He died in about 483 B.C.E.

In Japan, Buddha's birthday is known as Hana Matsuri or Flower Festival because it marks the beginning of the cherry blossom season. The image of Buddha is covered by a miniature unwalled shrine called the *hana-mido* or "flowery temple." Sometimes the flower-decked temple is drawn through the streets by a horse or ox. In China, *sutras* (sermons of Buddha) are chanted to the accompaniment of drums and bells, brass cymbals, and tiny gongs. The fish, a symbol of watchfulness, appears in the form of wooden fish heads, which are struck with small sticks. In Sri Lanka, where the great festival of Wesak is held on the first full moon in May, people sit out in the moonlight in little shanties made of flowers and greenery and listen to the long sermons of the Bikkhus (priests), which tell stories from the life of Buddha.

SYMBOLS AND CUSTOMS

Bathing the Buddha

The tradition of bathing images of the Buddha on Vesak seems to have derived from an episode in the story of his life in which the two serpents, Nanda and Upananda, bathe him after his birth. Today, the bathing ritual takes many different forms. In China, his image is carried out of the temple and into the courtyard, where it is sprinkled with water that is exceptionally pure. Sometimes the image of Buddha is placed in a big jar of water, and believers take a spoonful of water and sprinkle it over his head as they pass through the courtyard.

In Japan, Buddha's image is bathed with *ama-cha*, a sweet tea prepared from hydrangea leaves that have been steamed and dried. The statue of the Buddha usually shows him with one hand raised high toward heaven and the other directed toward the earth. This posture is derived from the story of his birth, soon after which he raised his right hand and lowered his left, declaring, "I am my own Lord throughout heaven and earth." Worshippers take some of the tea home with them so their faith and good health will be perpetuated.

Bodhi Tree

The tree under which the Buddha was enlightened in 528 B.C.E. was a type of ficus or Asian fig tree that can grow as high as 100 feet. Like the banyan tree, it branches indefinitely and has thick "prop" roots that support the extended branches.

There are actually two points in Gautama's life where a tree plays a significant role. The first was when he was a boy and he slipped naturally into a trance while sitting under a rose-apple tree. When Gautama abandoned the ascetic life at the age of thirty-five, he recalled that early experience and again sought refuge under a tree to compose his thoughts and await enlightenment. The tree that sheltered him throughout the night came to be known as the Bodhi Tree—*bodhi* meaning "enlightenment" or "awakening."

When King Asoka of India sent his daughter to Sri Lanka as a Buddhist missionary, she took a branch of the famous Bodhi Tree with her. According to legend, the branch took root, a symbol of the new religion.

FURTHER READING

Bauer, Helen, and Sherwin Carlquist. *Japanese Festivals*. Garden City, NY: Doubleday, 1965.

Bellenir, Karen. *Religious Holidays and Calendars*. 3rd ed. Detroit: Omnigraphics, 2004.

Bredon, Juliet, and Igor Mitrophanow. *The Moon Year: A Record of Chinese Customs and Festivals*. Shanghai: Kelly & Walsh, 1927.

Crim, Keith R. *The Perennial Dictionary of World Religions*. San Francisco: Harper & Row, 1989.

Eberhard, Wolfram. *A Dictionary of Chinese Symbols: Hidden Symbols in Chinese Life and Thought*. New York: Routledge & Kegan Paul, 1986.

Eliade, Mircea. *The Encyclopedia of Religion*. New York: Macmillan, 1987.

Henderson, Helene, ed. *Holidays, Festivals, and Celebrations of the World Dictionary*. 3rd ed. Detroit: Omnigraphics, 2005.

Ickis, Marguerite. *The Book of Festivals and Holidays the World Over*. New York: Dodd, Mead, 1970.

Pike, Royston. *Round the Year with the World's Religions*. 1950. Reprint. Detroit: Omnigraphics, 1992.

WEB SITE

Buddha Dharma Education Association Inc.
www.buddhanet.net/vesak.htm

Veterans' Day
(Remembrance Day, Armistice Day)

Type of Holiday: Historic, National
Date of Observation: November 11
Where Celebrated: Canada, England, France, United States
Symbols and Customs: Poppy, Tomb of the Unknown Soldier

ORIGINS

The armistice that ended the fighting in World War I was signed in Marshal Ferdinand Foch's railroad car in the Forest of Compiègne, France, on November 11, 1918. There were huge public celebrations in Paris, London, and New York City, where more than a million Americans jammed Broadway, danced in the streets, and hurled ticker tape out their windows.

During the 1920s, the annual observance of the armistice became a tradition on both sides of the Atlantic. It was known as Remembrance Day in England and Canada and Armistice Day in the United States, or sometimes Victory Day. The United States started honoring its war dead in 1921 (*see* TOMB OF THE UNKNOWN SOLDIER), but November 11 didn't become a legal national holiday until 1938.

National holidays can be defined as those commemorations that a nation's government has deemed important enough to warrant inclusion in the list of official public holidays. They tend to honor a person or event that has been critical in the development of the nation and its identity. Such people and events usually reflect values and traditions shared by a large portion of the citizenry.

In the United States, patiotism and identity were nurtured from the beginning of the nation by the very act of celebrating new events in holidays like the Fourth of July, battle anniversaries, and other notable occasions. The invention of traditions and the marking of important occasions in the life of the new nation were crucial in creating a shared bond of tradition and a sense of common belonging to a relatively new homeland through the shared experience of celebrating common holidays. As more and diverse peoples migrated to the United States, it became even more important to celebrate significant annual anniversaries, and Veterans' Day became one of the nation's most important shared celebrations.

One of the reasons the armistice was such a cause for celebration is that people believed that the death and destruction of World War I would never be repeated. But the advent of World War II changed all that, and for many years afterward, celebrations of the 1918 ceasefire received little attention. Veterans' groups urged that November 11 be set aside to pay tribute to all those who had served in the armed forces—in other words, those who had fought in World War II and the Korean War as well. In 1954 President Dwight Eisenhower signed a bill specifying that Armistice Day would thereafter be commemorated as Veterans' Day.

Veterans' Day observances take place all over the United States, particularly in places associated with the American war effort—for example, the USS *North Carolina* Battleship Memorial, a restored World War II ship docked in Wilmington, North Carolina. The celebrations usually include parades, speeches, military balls, and religious services. In many places, the eleventh day of the eleventh month is celebrated by observing a two-minute silence at 11:00 in the morning, the hour at which the hostilities ceased.

SYMBOLS AND CUSTOMS

Poppy

The poppy is a small red flower that grows wild in the fields of Europe where many of those who died in the First World War are buried. It was popularized by the famous war poem written by John McCrae, whose best-known lines are, "In Flanders fields the poppies blow/ Between the crosses, row on row." Flanders was the site of heavy fighting during the war, and for many the poppy came to symbolize both the beauty of the landscape and the blood that was shed there.

Artificial paper poppies are sold by veterans' organizations in most countries on November 11. Poppies are also used to decorate the graves of those who died fighting in World War I.

Tomb of the Unknown Soldier

The United States didn't really start honoring its war dead on November 11 until 1921, when the remains of an unidentified American soldier who had died fighting in France were disinterred and transported back to the United States. The remains of the "unknown soldier," as he came to be called, lay in state in the rotunda of the Capitol in Washington DC for three days before being moved to their final resting place at Arlington National Cemetery in Virginia.

The principal observation of Veterans' Day in the United States still takes place at the Tomb of the Unknown Soldier, which symbolizes the nation's desire to honor its war dead. Throughout the year, sentries maintain a constant vigil at the grave site.

Since 1960, a flaming torch that was lighted in Antwerp, Belgium, and then brought to the United States has burned there to honor all those who have died while serving their country. Taps are sounded at the tomb on November 11 at exactly 11:00 a.m., and the President or his representative places a wreath on the shrine. Afterward, representatives of the armed forces and several thousand spectators listen to an address by a prominent public figure in the amphitheater behind the tomb.

FURTHER READING

Christianson, Stephen G., and Jane M. Hatch. *The American Book of Days*. 4th ed. New York: H.W. Wilson, 2000.

Dunkling, Leslie. *A Dictionary of Days*. New York: Facts on File, 1988.

Henderson, Helene, ed. *Holidays, Festivals, and Celebrations of the World Dictionary*. 3rd ed. Detroit: Omnigraphics, 2005.

Spicer, Dorothy Gladys. *The Book of Festivals*. 1937. Reprint. Detroit: Omnigraphics, 1990.

Van Straalen, Alice. *The Book of Holidays Around the World*. New York: Dutton, 1986.

WEB SITES

U.S. Department of Veterans Affairs
www.va.gov/opa/vetsday

Veterans Affairs Canada
www.vac-acc.gc.ca/general/sub.cfm?source=history/other/remember

Walpurgis Night (Walpurgisnacht)

Type of Holiday: Folkloric
Date of Observation: April 30
Where Celebrated: Austria, Germany, Scandinavia
Symbols and Customs: Bonfires, Witches
Related Holidays: Beltane, May Day

ORIGINS

April 30, the eve of **MAY DAY**, is named for St. Walpurga, an English missionary who became an abbess in Germany, where she died in 780 C.E. On the eve of May 1, her remains were moved from Heidenheim to Eichstätt, where her shrine became a popular place of pilgrimage. Legend has it that the rocks at Eichstätt give off a miraculous oil possessing curative powers. Walpurga is known as the saint who protects against magic.

The traditions associated with St. Walpurga's Day can be traced back to pre-Christian celebrations on the eve of **BELTANE**, one of the four major festivals of the ancient Celts who once inhabited much of the European continent. The people who lived in the Harz Mountains of Germany believed for many centuries that WITCHES rode across the sky on the eve of St. Walpurga's Day to hold a coven or gathering on Brocken Mountain. To frighten them off, they rang church bells, banged pots and pans, and lit torches topped with hemlock, rosemary, and juniper. The legend of Walpurgis Night is still celebrated in Germany, Austria, and

Scandinavia with BONFIRES and other festivities designed to welcome spring by warding off demons, disaster, and darkness.

Although Walpurgis Night is not widely observed in the United States, many Scandinavian clubs and associations, particularly in cities with large Swedish or Norwegian populations, hold celebrations on April 30 consisting primarily of BON-FIRES, speeches, folk dancing, and music.

SYMBOLS AND CUSTOMS

Bonfires

Bonfires have been lit to scare off witches and other evil creatures since ancient times. The fires that were lit on the eve of **BELTANE** were designed to promote fertility and to ward off bad luck and disease. They represented the life-giving power of the sun, and leaping through the flames or over the glowing embers was a way of sharing the sun's power.

It is still customary in parts of Sweden to build huge bonfires on Walpurgis Night and light them by striking two flints together. Every large village has its own fire, often built on a hilltop, and young people dance around it in a ring. If the flames blow toward the north, it means that the spring will be cold and slow to arrive; if they incline to the south, it will be mild. People leap over the glowing embers in a ceremony called "Burning the Witches." There is a widespread folk belief that the fields will be blessed for as far as the light of the bonfire reaches.

Witches

Witches symbolize the evil that is everywhere in the world and that must be guarded against. Because witches were believed to be out riding their broomsticks to a gathering on the tallest peak of Germany's Harz Mountains on Walpurgis Night, people tried to make light of their own fears by wearing costumes and holding parties. Straw effigies of witches were often paraded through the streets and burned in BONFIRES.

FURTHER READING

Christianson, Stephen G., and Jane M. Hatch. *The American Book of Days*. 4th ed. New York: H.W. Wilson, 2000.

Frazer, Sir James G. *The Golden Bough: A Study in Magic and Religion*. New York: Macmillan, 1931.

Gulevich, Tanya. *Encyclopedia of Easter, Carnival, and Lent*. Detroit: Omnigraphics, 2002.

Heinberg, Richard. *Celebrate the Solstice: Honoring the Earth's Seasonal Rhythms through Festival and Ceremony*. Wheaton, IL: Quest Books, 1993.

Henderson, Helene, ed. *Holidays, Festivals, and Celebrations of the World Dictionary*. 3rd ed. Detroit: Omnigraphics, 2005.

James, E.O. *Seasonal Feasts and Festivals*. 1961. Reprint. Detroit: Omnigraphics, 1993.

King, John. *The Celtic Druids' Year: Seasonal Cycles of the Ancient Celts*. London: Blandford, 1995.

Santino, Jack. *All Around the Year: Holidays and Celebrations in American Life*. Urbana: University of Illinois Press, 1994.

WEB SITE

Swedish Institute
www.sweden.se/templates/cs/Event_17130.aspx

Wampanoag Powwow

Type of Holiday: Historic
Date of Observation: Fourth of July weekend
Where Celebrated: Mashpee, Massachusetts
Symbols and Customs: Fireball
Related Holidays: Thanksgiving

ORIGINS

The Wampanoag Indians have lived for more than 12,000 years in southern New England, occupying parts of what are now Rhode Island and Massachusetts, including Martha's Vineyard and Nantucket. When the Pilgrims settled at Plymouth in 1620, Massasoit, the Wampanoag chief, made a peace treaty with the English that was observed until his death. However, in response to the white people who later encroached on Indian lands, his son, Metacomet (also known as King Philip), organized a confederacy of tribes to drive them out. He and many of the other chiefs were killed in what became known as King Philip's War, and the Wampanoag were almost entirely wiped out. The survivors fled to Martha's Vineyard and Nantucket or joined the Cape Cod Indians, who had remained neutral in the struggle.

Today, the town of Mashpee on the southeast coast of Cape Cod is home to more than 1,000 Wampanoag descendants of Massasoit and his son. For centuries the Indians held annual summer powwows—an opportunity for tribal members to gather around their chiefs and religious leaders for feasting and participation in healing and trading rites. Today, the Mashpee Wampanoag Powwow takes place over the **FOURTH OF JULY** weekend, and tribal peoples come together from all over the Northeast. Feasting continues to play a central role in the powwow, for it was the Wampanoag Indians who originally shared their **THANKSGIVING** harvest with the Pilgrims in the 1620s, thereby ensuring the new colony's survival.

Foods served at the gathering include shellfish, codfish, quohog fritters, and woodland teas made from black birch, sassafras, sweet fern, sumac, and other wild plants. Many who come to the powwow take the opportunity to visit the Old Indian Burial Ground nearby and the Indian Meeting House, built in 1684, where the Mashpee Tribe continues to worship and to hold civic and social gatherings.

SYMBOLS AND CUSTOMS

Fireball

One of the most celebrated events of the Wampanoag Powwow is the traditional game known as Fireball, which has been played for hundreds of years, but only on this particular night. It is similar to soccer, but freer and more dangerous, since it is played with a flaming ball made of leather strips soaked for days in whale oil and wound tightly around each other. This ancient "medicine game" was traditionally played by men who had chosen to participate on behalf of a sick relative or friend in need of healing. The bruises, burns, and wounds they suffered during the game were believed to relieve a loved one's illness. Many Wampanoag still believe in the healing powers of this display of manhood and bravado, which takes place at Mashpee's Memorial Park.

FURTHER READING

Kavasch, E. Barrie. *Enduring Harvests: Native American Foods and Festivals for Every Season.* Old Saybrook, CT: Globe Pequot Press, 1995.

WEB SITE

Mashpee Wampanoag Tribal Council
www.mashpeewampanoagtribe.com

Washington's Birthday
(Presidents' Day, Washington-Lincoln Day)

Type of Holiday: Historic, National
Date of Observation: February 22 or third Monday in February
Where Celebrated: United States
Symbols and Customs: Cherry Tree
Colors: Washington's Birthday is often associated with the colors red, white, and blue, symbolic of the American flag and of patriotism in general. These colors can be seen not only in the flags and bunting that decorate public streets and buildings on this day, but also in advertisements promoting Presidents' Day sales.
Related Holidays: Lincoln's Birthday

ORIGINS

As commander-in-chief of the Continental Army during the American Revolution and as the first president of the United States, George Washington has always played an important role in American literature and legend. People started celebrating his birthday while he was still alive, particularly during his two terms as president (1789-96). But they usually held their observances on February 11. The date wasn't shifted to February 22 until 1796, some years after the New Style or Gregorian calendar was adopted.

Richmond, Virginia, was the first town to sponsor a public celebration of George Washington's birthday, in 1782. Celebrations became more popular during his first term as president, then began to wane with the development of two political parties, the Federalists (with whom Washington sympathized) and the Jeffersonian Democratic-Republicans, who found such celebrations offensive. Partisan feelings weren't set aside until after Washington's death in 1799, when Congress passed a resolution calling on the nation to observe February 22, 1800, with appropriate activities.

George Washington's Birthday is a national holiday in the United States. National holidays can be defined as those commemorations that a nation's government has deemed important enough to warrant inclusion in the list of official public holidays. They tend to honor a person or event that has been critical in the development of the nation and its identity. Such people and events usually reflect values and traditions shared by a large portion of the citizenry. In the United States, patriotism and identity were nurtured from the beginning of the nation by the very act of celebrating new events in holidays like the **FOURTH OF JULY**, battle anniversaries, and other notable occasions. This was even more important in the country's early years because the nation was composed of people from a variety of backgrounds and traditions. The invention of traditions and the marking of important occasions in the life of the new nation were crucial in creating a shared bond of tradition and a sense of common belonging to a relatively new homeland through the shared experience of celebrating common holidays. As more and diverse peoples migrated to the United States, it became even more important to celebrate significant annual anniversaries, and Washington's Birthday became one of the nation's most important shared celebrations.

The observance of Washington's Birthday didn't really take hold until 1832, the centennial of his birth. One of the most memorable celebrations was held in Los Angeles in 1850. The town's leading citizens decided to mark the occasion with a fancy ball, but some of the community's less refined members were excluded. They retaliated by firing a cannon into the ballroom, killing several men and wounding others.

While the third Monday in February is observed as Washington's Birthday by the federal government and most states, some combine it with the February birthday of another famous American president, Abraham Lincoln, calling it Washington-Lincoln Day or Presidents' Day (*see* **LINCOLN'S BIRTHDAY**). Today it is primarily a commercial event, as store owners take advantage of the holiday weekend to empty their shelves of midwinter stock.

SYMBOLS AND CUSTOMS

Cherry Tree

Stories about George Washington's precocious adolescence were largely the invention of his biographers. Probably the most popular is the legend of how he chopped down one of his father's cherry trees and then owned up to his mistake by saying to his father, "I cannot tell a lie." There appears to be no historic basis for this tale, which first appeared in the 1806 edition of *The Life and Memorable Actions of George Washington,* by Parson Mason Weems. The cherry tree, along with the hatchet that chopped it down, has nevertheless come to represent the honesty and forthrightness for which Washington was revered.

Ironically, this and the other popular legend concerning George Washington—how he threw a silver dollar across the Potomac River—are remembered today primarily by merchandisers. Their advertisements often employ phrases like, "We're chopping our prices for you!" or "Silver Dollar Days" to lure shoppers into America's malls during the holiday weekend.

FURTHER READING

Chambers, Robert. *The Book of Days*. 2 vols. 1862-64. Reprint. Detroit: Omnigraphics, 1990.

Christianson, Stephen G., and Jane M. Hatch. *The American Book of Days*. 4th ed. New York: H.W. Wilson, 2000.

Dunkling, Leslie. *A Dictionary of Days*. New York: Facts on File, 1988.

Henderson, Helene, ed. *Holidays, Festivals, and Celebrations of the World Dictionary*. 3rd ed. Detroit: Omnigraphics, 2005.

Schaun, George and Virginia, and David Wisniewski. *American Holidays and Special Days*. 3rd ed. Lanham: Maryland Historical Press, 2002.

Tuleja, Tad. *Curious Customs: The Stories Behind 296 Popular American Rituals*. New York: Harmony, 1987.

WEB SITES

George Washington's Mount Vernon Estate and Gardens
www.mountvernon.org

Library of Congress
memory.loc.gov/ammem/today/feb22.html

Waso
(Buddhist Rains Retreat, Buddhist Lent, Vatsa, Vossa)

Type of Holiday: Religious (Buddhist)
Date of Observation: Mid-July through mid-October
Where Celebrated: Cambodia, China, Japan, Korea, Laos, Myanmar (Burma), Thailand
Symbols and Customs: Candles, Dhamma-cakkappavattana-sutta, Travel Restrictions
Related Holidays: Tod Kathin

ORIGINS

Waso is part of the religious tradition of Buddhism, one of the four largest religious families in the world. Buddhism is based on the teachings of Siddhartha

Gautama (c. 563-483 B.C.E.), who came to be known as Buddha, or "The Enlightened One." The basic tenets of Buddhism can be summarized in the Four Noble Truths and the Eightfold Path. The Four Noble Truths are 1) the truth and reality of suffering; 2) suffering is caused by desire; 3) the way to end suffering is to end desire; and 4) the Eightfold Path shows the way to end suffering. The Eightfold Path consists of 1) right view or right understanding; 2) right thoughts and aspirations; 3) right speech; 4) right conduct and action; 5) right way of life; 6) right effort; 7) right mindfulness; and 8) right contemplation.

Waso, the three-month period known as the Buddhist Lent or Buddhist Rains Retreat, is observed in Myanmar (formerly Burma), Thailand, and other Southeast Asian countries from the full moon day of the lunar month of Waso through the full moon day of Thadingyut, which roughly corresponds to the monsoon season from mid-July through mid-October every year. In Cambodia it is known as Vossa, and in Laos it is called Vatsa. The Buddhist Lent is also observed in countries that do not have a rainy season, including China, Japan, and Korea.

The first and last days of this Lenten period are the most important. The full moon day of Waso is the day on which the Buddha is believed to have been conceived in his mother's womb. Born as Prince Siddhartha Gautama, he was twenty-nine years old when he saw the suffering around him and decided to renounce the privileged world into which he had been born to become a wandering ascetic. Leaving his wife and son behind, he made what is referred to as his "Great Renunciation" on the full moon day of Waso. Then, after attaining the state of bliss known as Enlightenment in 528 B.C.E., he preached his first sermon (*see* DHAMMA-CAKKAPPAVATTANA-SUTTA) to five companions on the full moon day of Waso. This day, therefore, not only inaugurates the Buddhist Lent but commemorates the Buddha's conception, Great Renunciation, and first sermon as an enlightened being. It is observed by bringing gifts, food, and other offerings to Buddhist monks in the monasteries to which they will be confined for the next three months. The gifts that people may bring are usually restricted to the "Eight Requisites" that Buddha permitted a monk to own: robes, a belt, a bowl for begging, a razor, a sewing needle, a water strainer, a toothpick, and a staff.

Although the Lenten period primarily affects Buddhist monks living in monasteries, Buddhist laypeople are expected to be more restrained and spiritual during these three months, avoiding such acts as getting married or moving to a new house. Because it is a popular time for young men to enter the priesthood, ordinations are common. Monks, who are subjected to TRAVEL RESTRICTIONS during the rainy season, usually spend their time in the monastery praying and meditating, conserving their "spiritual energy" for when they are again allowed to resume their travels. The Lenten period concludes with a joyful celebration of the rainy season's end in the form of a Festival of Lights—a period of up to three days during which Buddhists illuminate their homes and temples with candles and colored lamps or lanterns.

SYMBOLS AND CUSTOMS

Candles

Candles play an important role in the observation of Waso. A large candle is often lit on the first day of the Buddhist Lent amidst much ceremony and then kept alight for the entire three-month period. In rural areas of Cambodia, for example, one of the villagers usually makes the Lenten candle and then it is carried in procession, often via boat, to the local monastery, where it is presented to the assembled monks along with other gifts and offerings. In Thailand, there is a candle festival at which beeswax candles many feet high, carved in the shape of birds and other figures, are carried through the streets in procession before being brought to the temple or monastery.

Dhamma-cakkappavattana-sutta

The Buddha's first sermon after achieving Enlightenment is known as the Dhamma-cakkappavattana-sutta, which means "the setting in motion of the Wheel of the Dhamma"—the Dhamma (or Dharma) being the Buddha's teachings or doctrine. The symbol of the many-spoked wheel, which is often associated with Buddhism, originally stood for the Buddha's proclamation of this doctrine during his first sermon, which took place, according to Buddhist belief, on the full moon day of Waso near the sacred city of Benares (now Varanasi) in India. In this sermon he explained the Four Noble Truths and the Eightfold Path, his basic message being that the root of all suffering is desire or attachment to earthly things—a state that can best be alleviated by following what is known as The Middle Way, which guides the believer along a path somewhere between complete self-indulgence and complete self-denial. The full moon day of Waso is often referred to as Dhamma-cakka Day, and Buddhists often recite passages from Buddha's sermon during the period between sunset and moonrise, which is believed to be the time of day when Buddha delivered the Dhamma-cakkappavattana-sutta.

Travel Restrictions

Buddhist monks are confined to the monasteries during the three-month Buddhist Lent for a very specific reason. When Buddha originally told his monks to go forth and spread his teachings throughout the world, they did so regardless of the weather. This meant that during the rainy season, they often ended up tramping through fields and forests, unwittingly hurting farmers' crops and killing insects and small animals they could not see in muddy or flooded areas. When the Buddha heard complaints about this, he decided to restrict the monks' travel during the three-month monsoon season. Today, the monks are allowed to travel short distances if they absolutely have to, but they are expected to return to the monastery at night to sleep.

FURTHER READING

Bechert, Heinz, and Richard Gombrich. *The World of Buddhism.* New York: Facts on File, 1984.

Bellenir, Karen. *Religious Holidays and Calendars.* 3rd ed. Detroit: Omnigraphics, 2004.

Bowker, John, ed. *The Oxford Dictionary of World Religions.* New York: Oxford University Press, 1997.

MacDonald, Margaret R., ed. *The Folklore of World Holidays.* Detroit: Gale Research, 1992.

Van Straalen, Alice. *The Book of Holidays Around the World.* New York: Dutton, 1986.

WEB SITE

Burmese Buddhist Temple in Singapore
www.bbt.org.sg/wasomessage.htm

Watch Night

Type of Holiday: Religious (Protestant Christian), Historic
Date of Observation: December 31
Where Celebrated: United States
Symbols and Customs: Dinner, Emancipation Proclamation, Interruptions, Prayers, Singing, Shouters
Related Holidays: New Year's Eve

ORIGINS

Watch Night takes place on **NEW YEAR'S EVE.** Watch Night celebrations began in Methodist and Moravian churches as a means of providing their congregations with a spiritual alternative to rowdy and drunken New Year's Eve celebrations. Today, Watch Night services are usually found in Methodist, Moravian, and evangelical Protestant churches, especially those with a largely African-American congregation.

Watch Night services are modeled after the ancient Christian custom of holding a prayer service on the evening before an important feast day. These prayer services were called "vigils," a name that comes from the Latin word *vigilia*, meaning "to watch." The late-night services comply with biblical teachings urging the faithful to watch and wait for the coming of God (Matthew 25:1-13).

The founder of the Methodist Church, John Wesley, did much to popularize Watch Night. He first observed Watch Night services in a Moravian Church when serving as an Anglican priest in Georgia from 1735 to 1737. Upon returning to Great Britain, he left the Church of England in order to found the Methodist Church. Methodists established the custom of holding Watch Night services monthly on the night of the full moon. The light of the moon made it easier for parishioners to find their way home after the service. English Methodists brought Watch Night services with them to the American colonies. The first Methodist Watch Night services in this country were scheduled in the year 1770. They took place at Wesley Chapel in New York City and also at St. George's Methodist Church in Philadelphia.

In the nineteenth century, monthly Watch Night services fell into decline. Methodist congregations began to schedule these services for **NEW YEAR'S EVE** instead. Pastors hoped that by doing so they could provide members of their congregation with a way to take stock of their spiritual and material lives on New Year's Eve, instead of abandoning themselves to drunken carousing. The custom of making New Year's resolutions, which are customarily aimed at self-improvement, comes from this religious movement to add a spiritual component to New Year's Eve. Methodist ministers also urged their congregations to meditate on the passing of time and their own mortality as they faced a new year, hopefully finding in this experience the inspiration to amend their lives. During the twentieth century, many Methodist congregations discontinued Watch Night services. In recent years, a new movement to reform New Year's Eve has produced another alternative celebration called "First Night."

Many African-American congregations have retained the custom of holding Watch Night services on New Year's Eve. This custom recalls the events that took place on Watch Night on December 31, 1862. That night, African Americans kept vigil, praying that a promise made to them 100 days earlier would be fulfilled. In September 1862, President Abraham Lincoln had announced that he intended to sign the EMANCIPATION PROCLAMATION on January 1, 1863. The proclamation would officially abolish slavery in the United States.

Lincoln kept his promise and signed the Emancipation Proclamation. Both black and white Americans who had opposed slavery celebrated the fulfillment of their hopes on January 1, 1863. One celebration took place in Boston, Massachusetts, where abolitionists planned a gala celebration at the city's music hall for that day. The event included a concert of Beethoven's Fifth Symphony and a poetry recitation by Ralph Waldo Emerson. Many well-known political and literary figures attended. Another celebration took place at the Tremont Temple Baptist Church in Boston. The famous African-American orator Frederick Douglass attended that event. News that Lincoln had just signed the Proclamation came over the telegraph wires during the ceremony, prompting wild cheering from the audience. In Washington DC, the Proclamation was read aloud to the rejoicing congregation at the Israel Bethel church. Spontaneous parties broke out all over Washington as news spread that Lincoln had actually signed the proclamation into law.

As a result of these events, January 1st became known as Emancipation Day in African-American communities. Ever since that time, African Americans have associated Watch Night with the special history, culture, and concerns of their community. In many black churches, Watch Night begins with a soul food DINNER, followed by services with SINGING and PRAYERS. In some churches, the EMANCIPATION PROCLAMATION is read at midnight.

SYMBOLS AND CUSTOMS

Dinner

Before Watch Night services begin, many African-American churches host a feast. The dinner typically features soul food, including black-eyed peas, turnip greens, chicken, and other traditional dishes. African drummers and dancers might perform.

Emancipation Proclamation

In many African-American churches, services on December 31 run from 9:00 or 10:00 p.m. to midnight or after. They feature prayer, singing, testimonies, and a sermon. In some churches, a pastor or a member of the congregation may recall the original Freedom's Eve and review the significance of events for congregants unfamiliar with its historical importance. Just before midnight, the lights may be dimmed or turned off for prayer. As the new year comes in, the Emancipation Proclamation is read.

Interruptions

In Moravian churches, carefully scheduled interruptions bring the service to a halt at midnight. As the hour approaches, the pastor usually begins a sermon. In some churches, the band starts to play when the clock strikes twelve. This blast from the band interrupts the pastor in the middle of his sermon. The bandleader usually selects the Moravian hymn, "Now Thank We All Our God" for this occasion. The abrupt interruption symbolizes the teaching that Christ may return at any moment and emphasizes the need for spiritual readiness. Another Moravian custom encourages the congregation to get up and leave at the stroke of midnight, even if the pastor is still speaking. This custom, too, represents spiritual readiness and the decision to respond immediately to the call of Christ.

Prayers

Watch Night services encourage attendees to pray for themselves, their communities, and the world. Traditional prayer and meditation themes include improving one's life, increasing devotion to God, reflecting on one's mortality, and petitioning God for peace and justice at home and abroad.

Singing

Most Watch Night services include some form of hymn singing. Often the hymns emphasize such themes as steadfast faith, the grace and power of God, or the coming of Christ.

Shouters

One uniquely American form of Watch Night singing was revived in the late twentieth century when the McIntosh County Shouters, an African-American singing group from Georgia, caught the public eye. These folk musicians had preserved a form of hymn singing called the "ring shout" that was practiced by African-American slaves. Before this group came to light, scholars believed that this art form had died out.

The ring shout is a form of hymn singing with circle dancing and shouts of praise to God thrown in. The singers begin by forming a circle and shuffling in a counterclockwise direction. They neither lift their feet from the ground nor cross their legs. A single singer begins a hymn, singing slowly at first and then speeding up. The other singers add rhythm by hand clapping, foot tapping, and stick beating, as they continue to move in a circular direction. The group singers answer the lead singer in a "call and response" pattern typical of African music. Some of the songs favored by ring shouters include veiled references to slavery and escape. The McIntosh County Shouters have been praised for preserving this African-American art form. They have released CDs, have performed at the Smithsonian Institution in Washington DC, and have appeared on documentaries. In spite of their growing fame, they continue to perform at Watch Night services held at the Mt. Calvary Baptist Church in Bolden, Georgia.

FURTHER READING

Gay, Kathlyn. *African-American Holidays, Festivals, and Celebrations*. Detroit: Omnigraphics, 2007.

Gulevich, Tanya. *Encyclopedia of Christmas and New Year's Celebrations.* 2nd ed. Detroit: Omnigraphics, 2003.

Henderson, Helene. *Patriotic Holidays of the United States.* Detroit: Omnigraphics, 2006.

Kachun, Mitch. *Festivals of Freedom: Memory and Meaning in African American Emancipation Celebrations.* Amherst: University of Massachusetts Press, 2003.

WEB SITES

African-American Odyssey: The Quest for Full Citizenship, Library of Congress
rs6.loc.gov/ammem/aaohtml/exhibit/aopart4.html

McIntosh County Shouters, Home Page
hometown.aol.com/ShoutforFreedom

McIntosh County Shouters, New Georgia Encyclopedia, a project of the Georgia Humanities Council
www.georgiaencyclopedia.org/nge/Article.jsp?id=h-520&hl=y

Westminster Dog Show

Type of Holiday: Sporting
Date of Observation: Second Monday and Tuesday in February
Where Celebrated: New York City
Symbols and Customs: Benching, Best in Show, Dog Fanciers' Luncheon, Dog Writers Association Awards Dinner, Scoring, Terminology

ORIGINS

Often referred to as the "World Series" or "Super Bowl" of dog shows, the Westminster Kennel Club Dog Show, as it is officially known, is the second oldest continuously held sporting event in the United States, surpassed only by the **KENTUCKY DERBY**, which is less than two years older. The idea for an annual dog show to be held in New York City came from a group of men who raised sporting dogs and met periodically at New York's Westminster Hotel. They decided to form the Westminster Kennel Club, which held its "First Annual New York Bench Show of Dogs" on May 8-10, 1877. It featured more than 1,200 dogs and was such a success that they added a fourth day to the competition.

By 1883 the show had found a permanent home at Madison Square Garden, where it has been held (with a few exceptions) ever since. Although it was eventually cut back to a three-day show and then to its present two-day format, the Westminster Dog Show quickly became an institution for dog-fanciers across the United States.

Although the judging itself lasts only two days, preparation for the show begins a year or more in advance with the selection of about forty judges who are divided into seven groups according to the type of dog: Sporting, Hound, Working, Terrier, Toy, Non-Sporting, and Herding. Since 1992, the show's 2,500 entries have been limited to American Kennel Club champions, which are dogs that have accumulated a certain number of points by winning at smaller dog shows. And although entry forms used to arrive by mail and were opened at random, which meant that the first 2,500 to be opened were the only dogs allowed to compete, this rule was changed in 2000. Now approximately 780 dogs—the top five in each breed at American Kennel Club shows during the preceding year—receive special invitations to enter, thus ensuring that the very best dogs in America get a chance to compete for Westminster's top honor, BEST IN SHOW.

What kind of dogs can be seen at Westminster? In 2007, 165 different breeds were represented, with dachshund, Irish setter, Chinese shar-pei, Australian shepherd, and rotweiler being some of the top breeds entered. The Westminster Kennel Club's logo, however, features a pointer—based on a photograph of Sensation, a legendary pointer once owned by the club who was said to have the most nearly perfect head of any dog in his breed at the time.

The show itself is covered by more than 600 journalists from more than twenty countries, including many members of the Dog Writers Association of America (*see* DOG WRITERS ASSOCIATION AWARDS DINNER). But it was the decision to televise the event in the early 1980s that led to expanded public interest in the show, which currently attracts about 35,000 spectators and almost five million television viewers in more than 140 countries. The show also received a tremendous boost with the 2000 release of the popular movie *Best in Show,* starring Christopher Guest, Eugene Levy, Catherine O'Hara, and Parker Posey.

SYMBOLS AND CUSTOMS

Benching

Since 1883 the Westminster Dog Show has been what is called a "benched" show. This means that all of the dogs who are competing on a particular day must stay on their assigned benches throughout the judging process, which goes on for several hours—unless, of course, they are being groomed or exercised. The benches are divided into separate areas for each dog by partitions, but the benching area is still very crowded. While benching makes it easier for spectators, breeders, and judges to view and discuss the various breeds being judged, it also puts tremendous pressure on the dogs to sit still and behave. There are currently fewer than ten benched shows held in the United States each year.

Best in Show

The award for "Best in Show" has been given since 1907. It goes to the dog who has received top honors from three separate judges: the one who judges the breed, the one who judges the group (Sporting, Hound, Working, Herding, etc.), and the Best in Show judge. The latter is someone with years of experience as a breed and a group judge who has raised champion dogs in the past. The owner of the dog judged Best in Show receives a silver trophy from the Westminster Kennel Club.

The judge normally looks at the dog's general appearance, condition, and carriage. Particular attention is paid to the head, including the dog's eyes, ears, skull, and muzzle. The color and texture of its coat are important, as are its hindquarters, forequarters, feet, and tail. Even temperament comes into play. Wire fox terriers have won Best in Show the most number of times, and the terrier group has produced more winners than any other group. Over the years, however, the winners have ranged from a 155-pound Newfoundland to a four-pound Pomeranian. The only dog to win Best in Show three times was a smooth fox terrier named Warren Remedy in 1907-1909. In 2008, the beagle Uno won Best in Show, the first time a beagle had ever won the top award at the Westminster Dog Show.

Dog Fanciers' Luncheon

A week of social gatherings accompanies the Westminster Dog Show, and the highlight is the Dog Fanciers' Luncheon on the day after the judging has concluded. Held at Sardi's, the well-known Manhattan restaurant, the luncheon gives the judges an opportunity to compare notes and to speak informally about their decisions. The annual "Fido" Awards are also presented at the luncheon for "Man of the Year," "Woman of the Year," "Handler of the Year," and "Writer of the Year." A place of honor is reserved at the luncheon for the dog who has been named Best in Show.

Dog Writers Association Awards Dinner

The Dog Writers Association of America (DWAA) was established in 1935 to make sure that the journalists who cover dog shows are provided with the facilities and equipment they need to do their jobs. The DWAA also holds an annual writing competition that is open to both amateurs and professionals who write about the sport of raising, breeding, and showing dogs as well as other aspects of dog ownership. The biggest event of the year for these dog writers is the annual dinner held on the Sunday night before the Westminster Dog Show. It is here that the writing competition awards are presented and that dog writers from all over the country get a chance to meet and discuss the next day's competition.

Scoring

The judging process is taken very seriously at Westminster, and the weight given to various aspects of a dog's appearance and behavior has been carefully worked out over the years. A maximum of thirty points is awarded for appearance, temperament, carriage, and condition. The dog's head, expression, ears, eyes, and teeth are worth a maximum of twenty points, and up to twenty points are given for the body, neck, legs, feet, and tail. Gait can earn up to twenty points, and the color and texture of the dog's coat make up the final ten points for a perfect score of 100.

Terminology

Standard – The written description of the traits and movement of the ideal specimen of a breed, generally based on form and function.

Conformation – The structure and physical characteristics of a dog.

Stack – The pose itself or the posing of the dog in its natural stance by a handler.

Gait – The action of movement of the dog.

WEB SITES

American Kennel Club
www.akc.org/index.cfm

Westminster Kennel Club
www.westminsterkennelclub.org

Wianki Festival of Wreaths

Type of Holiday: Folkloric
Date of Observation: June 23
Where Celebrated: Washington DC
Symbols and Customs: Wreath
Related Holidays: Midsummer Day

ORIGINS

The Wianki Festival of Wreaths (*wianki* means "wreath" in Polish) is observed by Polish-American young people in Washington DC on St. John's Eve, June 23. Girls make wreaths out of fresh greens, put a lit candle in the center, and set them afloat in the reflecting pool in front of the Lincoln Memorial. Young men gather around the pool in the hope that the wind will blow their girlfriends' wreaths toward them.

The origins of this festival can be traced back to pagan times. For centuries in Poland it has been customary for girls to wear a garland of wildflowers on St. John's Eve, decorate it with ribbons, and fasten a lighted candle to the center. Then they throw their wreaths far out into a moving river or stream. If the wreath drifts to shore, it is taken as a sign that the girl will never marry; it if sinks, she will die within the year; if it floats downstream, she will definitely be married. According to superstition, the boy who catches a wreath will marry the girl to whom it belongs. So the boys hide in boats along the river banks and try to capture their sweethearts' garlands. At the end of the festival, the boys take the girls upstream in their boats.

A very similar festival took place in pre-Revolutionary Russia. Known as Semik— meaning "seventh," because it was held on the seventh Thursday after **EASTER**— it involved young girls throwing wreaths into the water or hanging them on trees as an offering to the god of the woods. The fate of the wreath was regarded as evidence of the young girl's fate.

SYMBOLS AND CUSTOMS

Wreath

The myrtle wreath is traditionally considered to be the symbol of a bride, and the wreath in general has been used to symbolize immortality, victory, and mourning. The wreaths that young Polish and Polish-American girls set afloat on the water can therefore be seen as symbolic of the several different paths their lives may take: They may die within the year, they may marry, etc.

FURTHER READING

Henderson, Helene, ed. *Holidays, Festivals, and Celebrations of the World Dictionary.* 3rd ed. Detroit: Omnigraphics, 2005.

MacDonald, Margaret R., ed. *The Folklore of World Holidays.* Detroit: Gale Research, 1992.

Olderr, Steven. *Symbolism: A Comprehensive Dictionary.* Jefferson, NC: McFarland, 1986.

Spicer, Dorothy Gladys. *The Book of Festivals.* 1937. Reprint. Detroit: Omnigraphics, 1990.

Wild Horse Festival (Soma Nomaoi)

Type of Holiday: Historic
Date of Observation: July 23 to July 25
Where Celebrated: In and around Haramachi City, Japan
Symbols and Customs: Flags, Horse Race, Mock Battles, Opening Ceremony and Procession, Samurai Costumes, Wild Horse Capture

ORIGINS

The Wild Horse Festival commemorates the prowess of Japan's samurai warriors by recreating events and scenes that took place hundreds of years ago. In those days, samurai warriors belonging to the Soma clan used the plains around the city of Haramachi to carry out their military exercises. The Japanese people feared and admired these warriors and marveled at their skills. Each year during the military exercises, the head of the Soma Clan released wild horses and challenged the warriors to capture them. It is believed that this training technique can be traced back about 1,000 years, when Tairo Kojito Masakado, an ancestor of the Soma clan, challenged the warriors under his command with this feat as a means of improving their horsemanship. Today's festival features a ritualized WILD HORSE CAPTURE, as well as other military displays.

The Wild Horse Festival is a historic holiday, one that commemorates a significant historical event. People throughout the world remember significant events in their histories. Often, these are events that are important for an entire nation and become widely observed. The marking of such anniversaries serves not only to honor the values represented by the person or event commemorated, but also to strengthen and reinforce communal bonds of national, cultural, or ethnic identity. Victorious, joyful, and traumatic events are remembered through historic holidays. The commemorative expression reflects the original event through festive celebration or solemn ritual. Reenactments are common activities at historical holiday and festival gatherings, seeking to bring the past alive in the present.

Around 1,000 years ago, Japan's warriors began to develop their own culture. The values and ideals of samurai culture differed somewhat from those of the Japanese upper class. The samurai valued bravery, military skill, personal loyalty, the ability to suffer hardship without complaint, and a strong sense of personal honor. The power of the samurai class deepened between 1300 and 1600. In that era, under the influence of Zen Buddhism, samurai culture contributed important elements to the Japanese arts, such as the tea ceremony and flower arranging. According to some historians, the samurai became the most powerful group in Japanese society and contributed much to the unique culture of Japan. During the Tokugawa period (1603-1867) the samurai became a closed social caste, meaning that one had to be born into a samurai family in order to become a samurai. As the Tokugawa era waned, so did the power and influence of the samurai. Many became bureaucrats and lost the military prowess that had made them famous. When feudalism was abolished in the 1870s, the samurai class lost its special position within Japanese society.

Among all the samurai clans of days gone by, the Soma clan was especially renowned for its warriors' skill with horses. The Soma established themselves in the area around present-day Haramachi in the fourteenth century. Threatened by the constant conflict that characterized medieval Japan, the Soma clan developed yearly military exercises to keep its warriors in top shape for battle. During the relatively peaceful Tokugawa period, the value placed on military hardiness rather than the need to be constantly prepared to fight kept these military drills alive. When the samurai class was abolished in the late nineteenth century, the members of the Soma clan, proud of their samurai identity, continued their yearly military exercises. Gradually, these events lost their true military rigor and became a historic festival commemorating the values and skills of samurai culture. The head of the Soma clan still presides over the festival. He is called the *taicho*, or commander, of the event.

Some experts believe the Wild Horse Festival to be the most authentic samurai festival in Japan. Indeed, the government of Japan officially recognizes the Soma Nomaoi festival as one of the nation's important "folk cultural assets." In recent years the three-day festival has attracted about a quarter of a million spectators.

SYMBOLS AND CUSTOMS

Flags

All festival participants must have a banner, or flag, that displays their clan symbol. In past centuries, all the samurai clans devised flags that bore symbols representing the clan. Festival participants must research their clan symbol and submit their flag design to the festival committee, which will judge it historical accuracy. Once approved, the flags must be specially made to order.

Horse Race

The horse race is one of the highlights of the festival. Twelve riders in full samurai garb, including flags and katana swords, race a distance of 1,000 meters at top speeds. To demonstrate the tough samurai spirit, even those riders that are thrown from their horses are encouraged to remount and finish the race.

Mock Battles

In order to recreate something of the battles of olden days, clan banners are shot into the air along with fireworks. The festival participants then compete to take possession of the banners.

Opening Ceremony and Procession

On the first full day of the festival, the current head of the Soma clan offers prayers for success in battle at a local Shinto shrine. Then he sounds a blast on a conch shell. This signals the festival participants to assemble for the procession to the mock battleground. The sight of hundreds of horses and riders in magnificent samurai costumes marching through the city streets is a favorite with festival goers.

Samurai Costumes

About 600 men participate yearly in the events the make up the Wild Horse Festival. Those who wish to participate must fill out an application and be approved by the festival committee. Participating can be a very expensive proposition, as all participants are expected to wear genuine antique or good quality replica samurai costumes. These costumes include not only clothing, but also helmets and armor. What's more, one is expected to provide one's own horse for the three-day event. The horse, too, must wear historically accurate gear.

Many riders have authentic samurai regalia handed down to them by their ancestors. Spectators are thus treated to a display that rivals and sometimes outshines that available in any museum.

Wild Horse Capture

The wild horse capture, or Nomagake ritual, takes place on the last day of the festival. Samurai warriors drive a group of unsaddled and unbridled horses in to the precincts of a Shinto shrine. Other festival participants, dressed all in white, capture the horses with their bare hands. The horses are then presented as offerings at the shrine.

FURTHER READING

Buell, Hal. *Festivals of Japan*. New York: Dodd, Mead and Company, 1965.

Caesar, Ed. "Freeze Frame: Samurai Horse Race, Haramachi City, Japan, 24/07/06." *The Independent*. July 25, 2006. www.findarticles.com/p/articles/mi_qn4158/is_20060725/ai_n16640117

Henderson, Helene, ed. *Holidays, Festivals and Celebrations of the World Dictionary*. 3rd ed. Detroit: Omnigraphics, 2005.

WEB SITES

City of Haramachi, Japan
www.city.haramachi.fukushima.jp/english/nomaoi/nomaoi.html

Japan Atlas
web-japan.org/atlas/festivals/fes06.html

Japan National Tourist Organization
www.jnto.go.jp/end/indepth/history/traditionalevents/a36_fes_soma.html

Toraba.com
www.toraba.com/feature-soma-page-1.htm

Wimbledon

Type of Holiday: Sporting
Date of Observation: Late June-early July; six weeks before first Monday in August
Where Celebrated: Wimbledon, England
Symbols and Customs: Ball Boys and Ball Girls, Centre Court

ORIGINS

The Lawn Tennis Championships held at Wimbledon, England, for thirteen days every summer is the oldest and most prestigious tennis tournament in the world. It was in 1875 that the All-England Croquet Club was persuaded to set aside a portion of its grounds on Worple Road, Wimbledon, for the purpose of playing lawn tennis, which was more physically demanding than the relatively slow-moving game of croquet. The first lawn tennis tournament was held there in July of 1877, with heavy rackets shaped like showshoes and a net that was five feet high at each end but only a little over three feet in the middle—differences that were inherited from the ancient game known as court tennis or "Real Tennis," and from which lawn tennis had only recently been derived. Spencer Gore won the first All England Lawn Tennis Championship, and a sport that had been little more than a leisurely pastime for the wealthy was on its way to becoming the multimillion-dollar industry it is today.

The first American to win a Wimbledon championship was Bill Tilden in 1920, and in many ways he was a prototype for today's tennis champions. He was a natural when it came to drawing a crowd, yet he could be very temperamental in the eyes of the referees and linesmen. But Tilden never tested Wimbledon's reputation as the most polite tennis championship in the world the way John McEnroe did in the early 1980s. Although McEnroe was a formidable tennis player, the three-time Wimbledon singles champ whined, sulked, screamed, threatened, and called the umpire "the pits of the earth."

A ladies' championship was instituted in 1884, and the first female tennis superstar was Suzanne Lenglen of France, who dominated women's tennis from 1919 to 1926. The huge crowds who came to see Lenglen play were an important factor in the decision to move the championships to a new facility on Church Road in 1922. The courts were planted with Cumberland grass and mowed to the smoothness of a billiard table, and the new CENTRE COURT, where the championships would be held, was declared to be "the fastest lawn tennis court in the world." Lenglen was followed by a number of other outstanding women players, including Althea Gibson, the first black player to win a Wimbledon title in 1957, and Billie Jean King, who won six Wimbledon titles. King was known not only for her cockiness on the court, but also for dedicating herself to achieving equality with male players in terms of earning power.

Wimbledon suffered a decline in prestige during the 1950s and 60s, when many of the top tennis players left to join the professional ranks. The solution to this problem was to open the tournament up to both amateurs and professionals in 1968. It has remained an open tournament since that time, and today the world's best tennis players compete at Wimbledon for both singles and doubles titles. The event is watched on television by tennis fans all over the world, many of whom get up at dawn or conduct all-night vigils around their television sets so as not to miss a single match. Members of the English royal family, who have attended the tournament since 1907, usually watch the finals from the Royal Box.

SYMBOLS AND CUSTOMS

Ball Boys and Ball Girls

Ball boys and ball girls at Wimbledon know the rules of tennis and are physically fit. They must pass a written test and undergo vigorous physical trials involving sprinting, standing very still, and rolling, throwing, and catching tennis balls. The average age is fifteen, and the approximate ratio of boys to girls is fifty/fifty. Only boys were eligible for this position until 1977, when ball girls were introduced.

Centre Court

The "new" Centre Court at Wimbledon, which opened in 1922, was no longer in the center, but off to one side. It is where the championships are held every summer, and it is off-limits to members of the All England Lawn Tennis Club and to everyone else except the grounds staff. On the Saturday before the competition begins, four women club members play two or three sets of doubles to "bruise" the grass and make sure the courts are in good shape. On the Monday after the tournament is over, the Chairman's Four play doubles, which officially closes the use of the court for the season.

After sustaining considerable damage from bombing in World War II (1939-45), Centre Court underwent months of renovation. Today, the grass is repeatedly hand-weeded and mowed until it is only an eighth of an inch long. Then it is rolled in two directions by a two-ton roller, leaving a playing surface so even and firm that it produces a true bounce. During the championships, the head grounds-man and his staff are busy every evening watering, patching, trimming, rolling, and re-marking the turf. Centre Court also has a tent-like cover that can be quickly raised by a team of groundsmen in the event of a heavy rainfall. After the championships are over, Centre Court is usually resown with new seed before the next major tournament.

Centre Court is again undergoing major re-development, with renovations begun in 2006 scheduled for completion by the 2009 Championships. In addition to an increased seating capacity (from 13,800 to 15,000), the improvements will include: a translucent retractable roof that will complement the original 1920s Centre Court building, new and enhanced restaurants, and a completely re-designed tea lawn.

Tickets to Centre Court are almost impossible to obtain. Debenture seats, which provide tickets year after year, are traded on the London Stock Exchange for huge sums of money. Debentures, sold every five years, guarantee holders one seat per debenture per day for each of the Championships during the five year period. Each debenture in the current issue (covering 2006-2010 series) is priced at £23,150 ($45,000, U.S.) and supports maintenance and improvement projects at Wimbledon. In 1989, a new process was introduced, the so-called "White Market," in which the Club buys back tickets from debenture holders in order to resell them at higher cost to existing Debenture and Marquee holders. Membership in the All England Lawn Tennis Club helps, as members are entitled to purchase two tickets for each day of the championship. Tickets are also bought by corporations, which use them to reward favored employees and to woo clients.

FURTHER READING

Henderson, Helene, ed. *Holidays, Festivals, and Celebrations of the World Dictionary.* 3rd ed. Detroit: Omnigraphics, 2005.

Revie, Alastair. *Wonderful Wimbledon.* London: Pelham, 1972.

Robertson, Max. *Wimbledon: Centre Court of the Game.* 3rd ed. London: BBC Books, 1987.

WEB SITE

The All England Lawn Tennis and Croquet Club
www.wimbledon.org

Wind Festival

Type of Holiday: Folkloric
Date of Observation: February-March; first day of the second lunar month
Where Celebrated: Korea
Symbols and Customs: Bamboo Altars, Good Luck Papers

ORIGINS

Korean folk religion predates the arrival of Buddhism, Confucianism, and Taoism to the peninsula, but scholars are uncertain of its origins. Hundreds of deities are worshipped throughout Korea, many of whom are tied to specific locations and natural objects. Most of the deities are women, as are most of the religious specialists, called *mudang*. They perform services ranging from funeral rites to personal fortune-telling to community ceremonies.

The custom of praying to the Wind God exists in the southeast and some other coastal areas of Korea and is known as *Yeongdong halmanne*, which means "southeast grandmother," or *I-weol halmanne*, which means "grandmother of the second moon." According to legend, *Yeongdong halmanne* was a goddess-grandmother who came down from heaven during the second lunar month to see the world, accompanied by either her daughter or her daughter-in-law, and stayed from the first to the twentieth day. When the grandmother was accompanied by her daughter, nothing bad happened; but when her daughter-in-law came with her, things had a tendency to go wrong. The daughter-in-law, who was an epileptic, would raise storms that sank boats and damaged crops. People started offering special prayers on these days, asking the grandmother and her daughter-in-law not to cause trouble but to offer their families safety and good luck.

In coastal areas of Korea, farmers, fishermen, and sailors still offer special prayers and sacrifices to "Yeongdong Mama" and her daughter-in-law during the second lunar month. Tempting foods and boiled rice are set out in the kitchen or garden, where temporary altars have been fashioned out of bamboo (*see* BAMBOO ALTARS), and little pieces of white paper (*see* GOOD LUCK PAPERS) are burned. A "tabu rope" is placed in front of the house to keep out beggars and sick people, who are regarded as unlucky, and fresh earth is spread around the house.

SYMBOLS AND CUSTOMS

Bamboo Altars

In areas where storms are a constant threat, Koreans set up branches and leaves of bamboo in their kitchens or gardens and tie pieces of colored cloth and paper to them. They lay out sacrifices and offer prayers under these makeshift altars, which remain standing for twenty days. Each morning during this period, fresh well water is drawn and served in a new gourd placed under the altar.

Good Luck Papers

The custom of burning small pieces of white paper on which the birth dates of family members have been written is believed to bring good luck. The higher the ashes fly, the better the luck they will bring.

FURTHER READING

Henderson, Helene, ed. *Holidays, Festivals, and Celebrations of the World Dictionary*. 3rd ed. Detroit: Omnigraphics, 2005.

MacDonald, Margaret R., ed. *The Folklore of World Holidays*. Detroit: Gale Research, 1992.

Sang-su, Choe. *Annual Customs of Korea*. Seoul: Seomun-dang, 1983.

Winter Solstice

Type of Holiday: Calendar/Seasonal, Ancient, Religious (Neopagan)
Date of Observation: December 21 or 22 in the Northern Hemisphere; June 21 or 22 in the Southern Hemisphere
Where Celebrated: Modern observances of the Winter Solstice are rare, but in ancient times it was observed throughout Europe, the British Isles, China, India, and Scandinavia
Symbols and Customs: Fire, Tree
Related Holidays: Beltane, Christmas, Imbolc, Lughnasa, Mabon, Samhain, Saturnalia, Soyaluna, Summer Solstice, Vernal Equinox

ORIGINS

The word "solstice" comes from the Latin *sol stetit*, which means, "The sun stood still." In the Northern Hemisphere, the sun rises and sets further south on the horizon as the Winter Solstice approaches; it rises and sets further north as the **SUMMER SOLSTICE** approaches. For a period of about six days in late December and again in late June, the sun appears to rise and set in almost exactly the same place, giving the solstices their name.

The Winter Solstice marks the changing of the seasons, which people in all parts of the world have honored since ancient times. Many cultures divided the year into two seasons, summer and winter, and marked these points of the year at or near the summer and winter solstices, during which light and warmth began to increase and decrease, respectively. In pre-industrial times, humans survived through hunting, gathering, and agricultural practices, which depend on the natural cycle of seasons, according to the climate in the region of the world in which they lived. Thus, they created rituals to help ensure enough rain and sun in the spring and summer so crops would grow to fruition at harvest time, which was, in turn, duly celebrated. Vestiges of many of these ancient practices are thought to have survived in festivals still celebrated around seasonal themes.

The ancient Romans celebrated the Winter Solstice with a festival dedicated to Saturn, the god of agriculture (*see* **SATURNALIA**). When Emperor Constantine declared in the early fourth century that Christianity would be the new faith of the Roman Empire, the holiday was given an entirely new name and meaning: It became the birthday of Jesus of Nazareth, also known as Christ Mass or **CHRISTMAS.** Many familiar Yuletide customs—including the Christmas TREE and the

Yule log (*see* FIRE)—actually have more to do with the Winter Solstice than with Christian doctrine. Even Santa Claus may originally have been a "solstice shaman" who officiated at the rites that took place on the Winter Solstice.

The ancient Chinese people believed that, at sunrise on the Winter Solstice, the *yang* or masculine principle was born into the world and began a six-month period of ascendancy. The Hindus, even though their calendar was based on lunar cycles, held festivals on the solstices and equinoxes as well. In northern India, for example, people greeted the Winter Solstice with a ceremonial clanging of bells and gongs to frighten off evil spirits. In the British Isles, the Druids celebrated the overthrow of the old god, Bran, by the new god, Bel, at the time of the December solstice.

The Winter Solstice was marked by the victory of light over darkness, the end of the cycle of death and decay and the beginning of a new cycle of light and growth. It has traditionally been a time for people to celebrate the gradual lengthening of the days and the regeneration of the earth.

During the 1960s the modern Neopagan and Wiccan movements emerged in Great Britain, the United States, and other English-speaking countries. They follow a nature-oriented religion loosely linked to ancient Celtic and other beliefs and inspired by old European folk practices. They celebrate eight sabbats, known as the eight spokes of the wheel of the year, which include **SUMMER SOLSTICE**, **WINTER SOLSTICE**, **VERNAL EQUINOX**, **BELTANE**, **SAMHAIN**, **IMBOLC**, **LUGHNASA**, and **MABON**.

SYMBOLS AND CUSTOMS

Fire

The Winter Solstice was traditionally celebrated by lighting fires, symbolic of the sun, whose powers would increase as the days grew longer. The midwinter tradition of lighting a Yule log, for example, was an ancient Celtic fire ritual performed at the time of the December solstice. To bring the log indoors and burn it was symbolically to bring the blessing of the Sun God into the house. The log had to burn steadily without being extinguished or else bad luck would follow. Sometimes wine, cider, ale, or corn was sprinkled over the log before it was lit. In southern England, particularly Cornwall, the figure of a man was drawn in chalk on the log—perhaps a survival of what was originally a human sacrifice by fire. Part of the log was kept and used to ignite the new log a year later (*see* YULE LOG under **CHRISTMAS EVE**).

The Yule candle lit in many churches at the beginning of the **CHRISTMAS** season is another example of how pagan solstice rites were gradually absorbed by

Christianity. At one time only the head of the household was allowed to light or extinguish the flame, and an unused remnant was preserved as protection against thunder and lightning. In some countries, tallow from the Yule candle was rubbed on the farmer's plow to promote fertility in the fields. The electric candles that are displayed in so many American homes at Christmastime today reflect this ancient Celtic reverence for the candle as a symbol of light during the darkest time of the year.

Tree

Tree worship was central to the religious beliefs of the Teutons and the Druids, who built their temples in the woods. Trees were regarded as possessing spirits, and they were only cut down out of necessity. The ancient Norsemen and the people of Central Asia saw the tree as a symbol for the universe. Native Americans and the early people of India and China held similar ideas.

The Christmas tree probably derived from customs associated with pre-Christian tree worship. The Romans decorated evergreen trees and wreaths at the **SATURNALIA**, and an evergreen shrub called the "herb of the sun" was especially favored at the time of the Winter Solstice. Nowadays, the popularity of cut Christmas trees has been challenged by those whose concern for the environment favors the idea of planting a living tree around Christmas or the Winter Solstice (*see* CHRISTMAS TREE under **CHRISTMAS**).

FURTHER READING

Bellenir, Karen. *Religious Holidays and Calendars*. 3rd ed. Detroit: Omnigraphics, 2004.

Christianson, Stephen G., and Jane M. Hatch. *The American Book of Days*. 4th ed. New York: H.W. Wilson, 2000.

Gaer, Joseph. *Holidays Around the World*. Boston: Little, Brown, 1953.

Gulevich, Tanya. *Encyclopedia of Christmas and New Year's Celebrations*. 2nd ed. Detroit: Omnigraphics, 2003.

Heinberg, Richard. *Celebrate the Solstice: Honoring the Earth's Seasonal Rhythms through Festival and Ceremony*. Wheaton, IL: Quest Books, 1993.

Henderson, Helene, ed. *Holidays, Festivals, and Celebrations of the World Dictionary*. 3rd ed. Detroit: Omnigraphics, 2005.

King, John. *The Celtic Druids' Year: Seasonal Cycles of the Ancient Celts*. London: Blandford, 1995.

MacDonald, Margaret R., ed. *The Folklore of World Holidays*. Detroit: Gale Research, 1992.

Urlin, Ethel L. *Festivals, Holy Days, and Saints' Days*. 1915. Reprint. Detroit: Omnigraphics, 1992.

WEB SITE

National Maritime Museum
www.nmm.ac.uk/server/show/conWebDoc.3843

World AIDS Day

Type of Holiday: Promotional
Date of Observation: December 1
Where Celebrated: Worldwide
Symbols and Customs: Activism, Education, Fundraising, Memorial Ceremonies
Colors: The color red is associated with AIDS awareness campaigns. It is particularly featured in the looped red ribbons that have become a global symbol of AIDS awareness, remembrance, and activism.

ORIGINS

World AIDS Day was created by the World Health Organization and the United Nations General Assembly. The day is observed on December 1 to increase international awareness of HIV (human immunodeficiency virus) and AIDS (acquired immune deficiency syndrome), and to promote greater social tolerance and understanding of the issues faced by people living with the disease. More than sixty-five million people have been infected with HIV, and over twenty-five million people have died of AIDS worldwide since the first cases were diagnosed in 1981. The World Health Organization forecasts more than 117 million additional deaths from AIDS by 2030. World AIDS Day draws attention to the seriousness of HIV/AIDS and its impact on a global scale. Since the first observance of World AIDS Day in 1988, it has become one of the most widely recognized international health awareness campaigns.

In planning activities and programs for World AIDS Day each year, governmental agencies and independent nonprofit organizations join together to strengthen international efforts that address the worldwide AIDS pandemic. World AIDS Day programming typically focuses on ACTIVISM, EDUCATION, and FUNDRAISING in order to raise public awareness of, and engagement with, the problem of AIDS worldwide. In addition, those who have died of AIDS are remembered in MEMORIAL CEREMONIES held on World AIDS Day.

SYMBOLS AND CUSTOMS

Activism

World AIDS Day encourages members of the general public to participate in such activist events as marches, rallies, and demonstrations. These events typically include speeches calling for improved health care and treatment for those with AIDS. Other forms of individual action commonly include volunteerism and street outreach, which supports the one-to-one education of the general public, especially youth and members of medically underserved and vulnerable populations. Outreach programs directed at politicians and members of the media may include activities such as letter writing campaigns and phone banks.

Education

Educational programs are a key component of World AIDS Day observances. These programs take a variety of forms, often including workshops, seminars, public presentations, panel discussions, health fairs, and public service announcements or advertisements. Mobile HIV testing facilities are a common feature of World AIDS Day observances.

Fundraising

Special events are commonly held on World AIDS Day to raise money for charitable organizations that assist people living with HIV/AIDS. Any manner of event may be held in conjunction with World AIDS Day, with a wide range of possibilities including art exhibits, fashion shows, musical performances, theater performances, dances, sporting events, film screenings, private parties, and so on.

Memorial Ceremonies

Candlelight memorial ceremonies are often held on World AIDS Day to remember those who have died of AIDS. Some memorial ceremonies include the display of sections of the NAMES Project AIDS Memorial Quilt (www.aidsquilt.org), which is regarded as the largest ongoing community arts project in the world. Currently containing more than 40,000 individual squares—each representing someone who has died of AIDS—the quilt is composed entirely of personal memorials created and contributed by volunteers.

FURTHER READING

Henderson, Helene, ed. *Holidays, Festivals, and Celebrations of the World Dictionary*, 3rd ed. Detroit: Omnigraphics, 2005.

WEB SITES

U.S. Department of Health and Human Services
www.hhs.gov/aidsawarenessdays

World Health Organization, Regional Office for Southeast Asia
www.searo.who.int/en/Section10/Section18/Section351.htm

World Cup Soccer

Type of Holiday: Sporting
Date of Observation: Every four years
Where Celebrated: Location varies
Symbols and Customs: FIFA World Cup Trophy

ORIGINS

The World Cup is an international championship tournament of men's soccer, a team sport known in many countries as football. The tournament is organized and governed by the Fédération Internationale de Football Association (FIFA) and is officially known as the FIFA World Cup. The World Cup existed solely as a men's event for years, until a women's tournament was added in 1991.

FIFA was founded in 1904 by representatives of the national soccer organizations of seven European countries. Although FIFA members voted almost immediately to establish a worldwide championship tournament, it was many years before the first World Cup tournament was held. Factors that contributed to this delay included the establishment of soccer as a new sport throughout the world, differences in playing abilities of teams outside Europe at that time, and varying rules of game play. Most importantly, World War I disrupted normal life throughout most of Europe from 1914 to 1918.

Jules Rimet, a French attorney who had previously served as the president of the French Football Federation, was elected president of FIFA in 1921. Rimet is widely credited as the creator of the World Cup. Through his efforts to increase the international popularity of soccer, standardize the rules of play, and expand FIFA membership, Rimet developed soccer as a viable sport for both amateur and professional players. The success of soccer during the 1924 and 1928 Olympics demonstrated the increasing worldwide support for the game and hastened the development of the World Cup tournament.

The first World Cup was held in 1930 in Montevideo, Uruguay. Uruguay was chosen to host the event because its team won the gold medals for soccer in the two previous Olympic competitions. At that time the Olympics allowed only amateur players, but Rimet decided to allow professionals to enter the World Cup. Enormous controversy surrounded these two decisions, with disputes erupting over the chosen location as well as the status of qualifying players. In a dramatic protest, England resigned from FIFA, beginning a boycott that would ultimately continue through the first four World Cup tournaments. Many other European teams also objected to the distant location, which required several weeks of costly steamship travel to reach. The worldwide economic depression at that time resulted in many teams declining to participate, despite Uruguay's offer to pay the travel expenses of any team that wanted to come. In the end, thirteen countries chose to participate in the inaugural World Cup, including four teams from Europe.

After a turbulent beginning, interest in the World Cup grew steadily. Although some European countries continued to boycott the World Cup for political reasons, subsequent tournaments were attended by a growing number of countries. World War II interrupted the World Cup, with a twelve-year gap between the 1938 tournament in France and the 1950 tournament in Brazil. The 1954 World Cup match between Yugoslavia and France was the first to be televised, with a limited broadcast reaching fans in Lausanne, Switzerland. In 1966, England beamed the first global television broadcast by satellite. This was also the first World Cup to have an official mascot character—a lion cub named Willie—marking the beginning of the popular tournament mascot tradition.

World Cup Soccer has evolved to include teams from more than 200 countries around the world. An extensive regional qualifying system requires teams to win a place in the final tournament, which is limited to thirty-two teams. Games in the final championship tournament are generally held in several different cities within the host country and are attended by millions of fans. Television broadcasts reach billions of viewers throughout the world.

The phenomenal popularity and success of the men's World Cup prompted FIFA to create a Women's World Cup in 1991. The women's tournament, also held every four years, continues to grow in popularity and further extends the global appeal of the game.

SYMBOLS AND CUSTOMS

FIFA World Cup Trophy

The original World Cup prize was the Jules Rimet Trophy, a commissioned piece created by French sculptor Abel Lafleur in 1930. The trophy was a statue made of gold, standing almost twelve inches high (thirty centimeters) and weighing almost nine pounds (four kilograms), depicting a winged goddess of victory whose raised arms held an octagonal cup. The statue's base was made of lapis lazuli, a semi-precious blue stone. Four gold plates, one on each side of the base, were engraved with the names of the nine winning teams between 1930 and 1970.

Like the early years of the tournament it represented, the Jules Rimet Trophy itself had a colorful history. Near the end of World War II, the trophy was hidden in a shoe box under the bed of Ottorino Barassi, the FIFA vice president at the time and a resident of Italy. Barassi was responsible for hiding the prize from German soldiers. At that point in the war, German soldiers were retreating from Italy and were raiding homes along the way, looking for valuables. Then on March 20, 1966, the trophy was stolen from its public display in London, England. A frantic public search ensued. The trophy was discovered in a London garden a week later by a dog named Pickles, who became an instant national hero. In 1970 Brazil became the first to win three World Cup tournaments, and the Jules Rimet Trophy was retired in their honor. On December 20, 1983, the trophy was stolen again. This time it was never recovered, and it was eventually replaced with a replica donated by the Kodak Brazil Corporation.

After the retirement of the original trophy, FIFA held a competition to select a design for a new World Cup prize to be awarded at the 1974 tournament. Italian sculptor Silvio Gazzaniga's design was chosen, featuring two figures representing athletes in motion amidst curving lines rising to a sphere representing the earth. The trophy is made of solid gold, stands fourteen inches high (thirty-six centimeters), and weighs eleven pounds (almost five kilograms). The base is made of malachite, a semi-precious green stone, and includes enough space for the names of seventeen winning teams. FIFA plans to commission a new, third World Cup trophy for the tournament in 2038.

FURTHER READING

Cantor, Andres. *Goooal! A Celebration of Soccer*. New York: Simon & Schuster, 1996.

Fiore, Fernando. *The World Cup: The Ultimate Guide to the Greatest Sports Spectacle in the World*. New York: HarperCollins, 2006.

Henderson, Helene, ed. *Holidays, Festivals, and Celebrations of the World Dictionary*, 3rd ed. Detroit: Omnigraphics, 2005.

Lewis, Michael. *World Cup Soccer*. Wakefield, RI: Moyer Bell, 1994.

WEB SITE

World Cup Soccer
www.fifa.com/worldcup

World Eskimo-Indian Olympics

Type of Holiday: Sporting
Date of Observation: Mid-July or early August
Where Celebrated: Fairbanks, Alaska
Symbols and Customs: Blanket Toss, Eskimo Ice Cream, High Kick, Knuckle Hop, Miss WEIO Pageant, Muktuk-Eating Contest, Race of the Torch, Six-Ring Logo
Related Holidays: Arctic Winter Games, Olympic Games

ORIGINS

The native peoples of Alaska have a longstanding tradition of gathering together periodically for the purpose of playing games—not just the usual team sports, but games that test the specific qualities that are essential to surviving in a harsh climate where food must be hunted under extreme and often hazardous conditions. People from small villages would gather, usually during the **CHRISTMAS** season, to engage in informal competitions as well as dancing, storytelling, and feasting.

More than forty years ago a pilot for Wien Airlines named Frank Whaley, who had witnessed these traditional gatherings in his travels across the state and was concerned that they would soon disappear, convinced his employer and the Fairbanks Chamber of Commerce to include the games as part of the city's annual Golden Days Celebration. The first "World Eskimo Olympics" was held in 1961, just two years after Alaska became a state. The *Tundra Times*, Alaska's only native newspaper, took over sponsorship of the event nine years later, at which point the name was changed to the World Eskimo-Indian Olympics, reflecting the broad range of native peoples who were now participating in the games.

What hasn't changed over the years is the nature of the games themselves. They include events that test strength, like the KNUCKLE HOP and the Arm Pull, challenges to endurance and the ability to withstand pain, like the Ear Pull, and contests that hinge on balance and agility, like the Alaskan HIGH KICK and the Toe Kick. Some of the games are clearly derived from practices associated with hunting and whaling, like the BLANKET TOSS, and many are designed to build up the brute strength that is needed to haul seals and other animals through holes in the ice. Women started competing in the early 1970s and 1980s, and in 1998 they placed first, second, and third in the Ear Weight, a contest in which competitors lift weights that are attached to their ears by loops of twine. They must lift the weights

Special Awards

Several special awards are given annually to competitors in the World Eskimo-Indian Olympics:

A.E. "Bud" Hagberg Memorial Sportsmanship Athletic Award – the athlete who best exemplifies good sportsmanship; chosen by the athletes

Howard Rock Memorial Outstanding Athlete Award – the best athlete; chosen by the athletes

Frank Whaley Award Presentation for Outstanding Contributions – the individual or company who has consistently given their time, money, and effort in support of the Olympics

by standing up as straight as they can and then move forward over the greatest distance possible.

The World Eskimo-Indian Olympics have continued to draw larger crowds of spectators and to produce more record-breaking achievements over the past four decades, and there is now an independent, nonprofit organization dedicated to planning, organizing, and running the event. In addition to the athletic competitions, there are fish-cutting and seal-skinning contests, a Native Baby Contest in which both mother and child appear in tribal costumes, an Eskimo dance competition, and the ever-popular MISS WEIO PAGEANT.

SYMBOLS AND CUSTOMS

Blanket Toss

The Blanket Toss or Nalakatuk is just what it sounds like: The competitor is thrown as high as thirty feet into the air by sitting or standing in the middle of a walrus-skin "trampoline" that is held up by other team members. This practice was quite common in whaling communities, where it was used to celebrate a successful hunt. It was also used to improve a hunter's ability to spot game by elevating him to a point from which he could see over greater distances.

Eskimo Ice Cream

A favorite treat served during the World Eskimo-Indian Olympics is what is known as Eskimo ice cream or akutaq. Unlike the American ice cream treat known as an Eskimo Pie, this is made from whipped berries—usually northern-grown salmonberries, which are also known as cloudberries—mixed with snow and either seal or caribou oil.

High Kick

There are actually several events involving jumping off the floor and kicking a suspended target. In the One-Foot High Kick, the competitor must use both feet to propel himself or herself upward, then kick the target with one foot and land on that same foot without losing his or her balance. Such a move was at one time used by messengers to let other villagers or hunters know that a whale had been caught or that other game was approaching. The Two-Foot High Kick is similar, except that the competitor must kick the target with both feet and land on both feet. The Alaskan High Kick is even more complicated, requiring the competitor to hold one foot with the opposite hand and, using the other hand for elevation and balance, attempt to kick the target with the foot that is free, landing in the same position without losing his or her balance—the object being to achieve as much height as possible.

Knuckle Hop

Also known as the Seal Hop because the movement it requires is similar to that used by seals, the Knuckle Hop is a challenge to both strength and endurance. The competitor gets into the position normally used for a push-up, but with all his or her weight resting on the knuckles (rather than hands) and toes. Then, keeping the back straight and the elbows partially bent, he or she attempts to "hop" forward. The goal is to cover as great a distance as possible, but of course not much distance is usually achieved. This was a game designed to be played in a hut or other confined space during the winter, or on the ground outside during the summer.

Miss WEIO Pageant

The very first World Eskimo Olympics held in 1961 featured a "Miss Eskimo Olympics Queen" contest. This contest has since been renamed "Miss World Eskimo-Indian Olympics," and, like the **MISS AMERICA PAGEANT** after which it was originally modeled, the competition emphasizes not only physical attractiveness but also poise, talent, and other accomplishments. In addition to the winner, there are awards for Miss Congeniality, Most Traditional, Most Photogenic, and Most Talented.

Muktuk-Eating Contest

Muktuk is the skin of a whale and the thin layer of blubber beneath it, usually harvested from beluga whales. Like a pie-eating contest at a country fair, the Muktuk-

Eating Contest at the World Eskimo-Indian Olympics requires competitors to eat as much of this Eskimo delicacy as quickly as possible.

Race of the Torch

The Race of the Torch is a five-kilometer road race that takes place at the start of the World Eskimo-Indian Olympics. The male and female winners of the race are given the privilege of carrying the torches used to ignite the World Eskimo-Indian Olympic torch, which is modeled after the Olympic Flame (*see* **OLYMPIC GAMES**).

Six-Ring Logo

The World Eskimo-Indian Olympics logo consists of six interconnected rings symbolizing Alaska's six major tribes: Eskimo, Athabascan, Haida, Tlingit, Tsimshian, and Aleut. It is modeled after the logo used by the **OLYMPIC GAMES,** which consists of five interconnected rings signifying the five continents: Africa, America, Asia, Australia, and Europe.

FURTHER READING

Shemanski, Frances. *A Guide to World Fairs and Festivals*. Westport, CT: Greenwood Press, 1985.

WEB SITE

World Eskimo-Indian Olympics, Inc.
www.weio.org

World Series

Type of Holiday: Sporting
Date of Observation: Annually in October
Where Celebrated: Location varies
Symbols and Customs: Commissioner's Trophy, Parades, World Series Rings

ORIGINS

The World Series is a men's professional baseball championship played between the two leagues in Major League Baseball, the National League and American

League. The winning teams from each of these two leagues meet for a series of seven games, with the World Series championship going to the team that is the first to win four games. Despite its name, the World Series is not an international sporting event. Participation is limited to the teams that are part of Major League Baseball, which includes twenty-nine U.S. teams and one team in Toronto, Ontario, Canada. The World Series was named in the early 1900s when the American game of baseball was not yet being played outside the U.S., and the world of baseball was small.

The early years of professional baseball in the U.S. were fraught with scandal and controversy. The game had been played across the country in various forms throughout the 1800s, with the first professional teams being formed around 1867. Baseball games during this time were played in a somewhat disorganized fashion, as teams operated without a league structure and often did not even agree on the standard rules of play. These disagreements sometimes resulted in teams refusing to play each other at all. The National Association of Professional Baseball Players represented the first attempt to organize teams. The group was formed in 1871 but disbanded soon after due to gambling and bribery scandals.

The National League was formed in 1876, and a precursor to the American League existed by 1884. The first intra-league professional baseball championship was played in 1884, consisting of a three-game series featuring the Providence Grays of the National League against the New York Metropolitans of the American League. In what is regarded by many as baseball's first big upset, the Grays defeated the highly regarded Metropolitans.

By 1890, a third independent professional organization called the Players League had formed. With three leagues in competition for players and fans, the Players League and the American League both eventually folded. The American League was attempting to reorganize by 1899, but ongoing conflicts with the National League prevented intra-league games from being played. The two leagues ultimately reached an agreement in the early 1900s, and the return of a two-league professional baseball system stabilized the sport and revived public interest in the game.

The first World Series, called the World's Championship Series, was held in 1903 and is generally regarded as the precursor to the modern World Series. This nine-game series featured the National League Pittsburgh Pirates against the American League Boston Pilgrims. The Pirates were popularly favored to win but were unexpectedly defeated by the Pilgrims. The next year, the World Series was cancelled when the National League champion New York Giants refused to play against Boston. The World Series resumed in 1905 with the Giants against Philadelphia in a seven-game series. The seven-game format used today was adopted in 1905 as the World Series standard of play, with the exception of the series played from 1919 to 1921, which included nine games.

Public interest and excitement around the World Series spread as the number of baseball fans grew throughout the U.S. Before the advent of radio broadcasts, huge public message boards enabled fans to follow the developing game action. These boards were often attached to the exterior walls of buildings, usually those that housed newspaper offices. Play-by-play reports and updated scores were received by telegraph and manually posted on the boards, which usually included a drawing of the baseball field with players' figures that were moved from base to base by telegraph operators. The first radio studio broadcast of a World Series was in 1921, and the first live radio broadcast from a baseball stadium occurred in 1923.

One event that generated a lot of public interest in baseball was the 1919 World Series and its aftermath. In that series, the Cincinnati Reds beat the Chicago White Sox in eight games. The next year, after an investigation into baseball gambling, authorities charged that the series had been "fixed" by gamblers—meaning that they had made arrangements in advance to ensure a certain outcome. Authorities accused seven players from the White Sox of accepting bribes from gamblers to lose the series intentionally. An eighth player didn't accept a bribe but was said to have known about the fix and failed to stop it. Those eight players were banned from baseball for life. The event became known as the Chicago Black Sox Scandal, and it tarnished the image of baseball as America's pastime.

During this time, African Americans were not allowed to play for teams in the National League or American League. African Americans created a separate professional baseball organization in the 1920s, consisting of the Negro National League and the Eastern Colored League. The first Negro League World Series was played in 1924 and then held annually until 1927, when the Eastern Colored League disbanded. The Negro League World Series was restarted in 1942 and held each year until 1948. Major League Baseball became integrated in 1947 when Jackie Robinson—the first African-American player in the modern major leagues—was signed by the Brooklyn Dodgers. Once the practice of barring African Americans from Major League Baseball teams ended, so did the Negro League World Series.

Another World Series of baseball also began in the early 1940s. During World War II, the All-American Girls Professional Baseball League was formed because many players in the professional men's leagues had been drafted into military service. The women's professional league played from 1943 to 1954 and held the Women's World Series every year during that time.

The first World Series television broadcast occurred in 1948 to a limited audience of fans in Cleveland and Toledo, Ohio; Chicago, Illinois; Buffalo, New York;

Detroit, Michigan; Milwaukee, Wisconsin; and St. Louis, Missouri. The first national television broadcast of the World Series occurred in 1951.

Two series that were particularly gratifying to baseball fans occurred in recent years. In 2004, the Boston Red Sox beat the St. Louis Cardinals to win the World Series—after not winning for eighty-six years. The Red Sox had faced a particularly difficult American League Championship Series against their rival, the New York Yankees, falling behind 3-0 before winning four straight games. Then the following year, 2005, the Chicago White Sox won after an even longer wait—they hadn't won a World Series in eighty-eight years, since 1919.

Since its inception more than 100 years ago, professional baseball has become one of the fastest-growing sports in the world. Baseball is now played in more than 100 countries and enjoyed by millions of fans. The World Series continues to be one of the most highly anticipated sporting events in the U.S. In recognition of the globalization of the game, the World Baseball Classic—a true international championship—was held for the first time in 2006. Created by the Major League Baseball organization and the Major League Baseball Players Association, the World Baseball Classic is intended to be held every four years beginning in 2009.

SYMBOLS AND CUSTOMS

Commissioner's Trophy

Commonly known as the World Series Trophy, the Commissioner's Trophy was first awarded to the St. Louis Cardinals in 1967. Unlike other championship trophies in sports such as ice hockey and soccer, the Commissioner's Trophy is not passed from one winning team to the next each year. Instead, a new trophy is created for each winning team to own permanently.

The current design of the Commissioner's Trophy was created by renowned jewelers Tiffany & Co. in 2000. The handcrafted trophy, standing twenty-four inches high and weighing thirty pounds, features thirty gold flags—one for each of the Major League Baseball teams—arranged in a circle and rising above latitude and longitude lines representing the earth. The base is engraved with the words "Presented by the Commissioner of Baseball" and also includes the engraved signature of the Baseball Commissioner.

Parades

Playing in the World Series—and better yet, winning it—is a source of tremendous excitement, elation, and pride for hometown fans. After the series, the winning city often hosts a parade to honor the team's achievement. Players, coaches, owners, and other staffers ride in open vehicles through city streets. The route would be thronged with fans cheering for their team and their favorite players. A rally is usually held at the end of the route, giving team members and city officials a chance to speak and to display the World Series Trophy. For all—players, officials, and fans—it's a chance to celebrate.

World Series Rings

In a special ceremony that takes place at the beginning of each baseball season, elaborate rings are awarded to the winners of the previous season's World Series. Rings are usually given to players, coaches, staff, and others associated with the team. The design of the rings differs each year; a typical World Series ring can include more than twenty diamonds and thirty-five grams of solid gold.

FURTHER READING

Enders, Eric. *1903-2004: 100 Years of the World Series*. New York: Sterling Publishing, 2003.

Henderson, Helene, ed. *Holidays, Festivals, and Celebrations of the World Dictionary*, 3rd ed. Detroit: Omnigraphics, 2005.

Leventhal, Josh. *The World Series: An Illustrated Encyclopedia of the Fall Classic*. New York: Black Dog & Leventhal, 2001.

Schoor, Gene. *The History of the World Series: The Complete Chronology of America's Greatest Sports Tradition*. New York: William Morrow and Company, 1990.

WEB SITES

Major League Baseball
www.mlb.com

World Series
www.worldseries.com

Wuwuchim

Type of Holiday: Calendar/Seasonal, Religious (Hopi)
Date of Observation: Sixteen days in November
Where Celebrated: Arizona
Symbols and Customs: Closing of the Roads, Kachinas, Kiva, Masau'u, New Fire Ceremony, Wuwuchim Song
Related Holidays: Niman Kachina Festival, Powamû Festival, Soyaluna

ORIGINS

The Wuwuchim ceremony is part of the traditions of the Hopi Indians of North America. The history of this and other Native American cultures dates back thousands of years into prehistoric times. According to many scholars, the people who became the Native Americans migrated from Asia across a land bridge that may have once connected the territories presently occupied by Alaska and Russia. The migrations, believed to have begun between 60,000 and 30,000 B.C.E., continued until approximately 4,000 B.C.E. This speculation, however, conflicts with traditional stories asserting that the indigenous Americans have always lived in North America or that tribes moved up from the south.

The historical development of religious belief systems among Native Americans is not well known. Most of the information available was gathered by Europeans who arrived on the continent beginning in the sixteenth century C.E. The data they recorded was fragmentary and oftentimes of questionable accuracy because the Europeans did not understand the native cultures they were trying to describe and the Native Americans were reluctant to divulge details about themselves.

The Hopi Indian ceremony known as Wuwuchim takes place in November and marks the beginning of a new ceremonial year in the Hopi calendar. The name is believed to have derived from the Hopi word *wuwutani*, which means "to grow up," and the initiation of young men into the sacred societies that oversee this and other Hopi ceremonies is an important part of the celebration. The tribal elders close off all roads leading to the pueblo (*see* CLOSING OF THE ROADS), all fires are extinguished, and the women and children stay indoors. The initiation rituals take place in the underground chamber known as the KIVA, where the adolescent boys are gathered and where they participate in secret ceremonies that introduce them to Hopi religious customs and beliefs. Although visitors and even other tribe members are not allowed to witness these rites, they are overseen by a tribal chief who impersonates MASAU'U, the Hopi god of death and the ruler of the underworld. After they have undergone their initiation, the young men are treated as adults and allowed to dance as KACHINAS in other Hopi ceremonies throughout the year. Wuwuchim is therefore essential to the continuing cycle of Hopi ceremonial life.

The kindling of the new fire (*see* NEW FIRE CEREMONY) is the first ritual to take place during Wuwuchim. Other tribes observe this ritual around the time of the **WINTER SOLSTICE**, but the fact that it is part of Wuwuchim underscores the latter's importance as the start of the Hopi New Year. As the ceremony draws to a close, there are prayers, songs (*see* WUWUCHIM SONG), and dances designed to ensure the safety and success of the Hopi people in the coming year.

SYMBOLS AND CUSTOMS

Closing of the Roads

It is during Wuwuchim that the Hopi invite their dead ancestors (*see* KACHINAS) to return to the pueblo. A path must be kept open for them, but this necessitates closing all roads leading to the pueblo so that other people cannot enter during this sacred time of year. Tribal elders do this by laying down four parallel lines of cornmeal across each road that leads into the village. These lines serve as a symbolic barrier to the outside world.

Kachinas

Kachinas (also katsinas or katchinas) are the spirits or supernatural beings who possess the power of gods and represent the Hopi ancestors. They first begin to emerge from the underworld at Wuwuchim and remain on earth for about half the year, departing in July after the **SUMMER SOLSTICE**. Young Hopi children are taught from the very start to respect the power of the kachinas by being given dolls that represent these spirits. As they grow older, they are often disciplined by male tribe members wearing kachina masks, and, when they reach adolescence, they are initiated into the grown-up world when the men who impersonate the kachinas take off their masks and reveal their true identities. This is what happens during Wuwuchim.

One of the most powerful kachinas is MASAU'U, who is also known as the Blue Star Kachina. The Hopi believe that when the Blue Star Kachina finally removes his mask and reveals himself, this will herald the end of an era or cycle of Hopi life.

Kiva

The underground ceremonial chamber known as the kiva is a symbolic representation of the underworld from which the Hopi people emerged at the time of creation. It is the place where many of the Hopi's secret ceremonies are held and where ceremonial fires are lit and tended. The small hole in the floor of the kiva is known as a sipapu, and only spirits or KACHINAS can pass through it. The sipapu is also a symbolic umbilical cord that connects the "womb" of the earth to its inhabitants.

The kiva is a focal point for most Hopi ceremonies, Wuwuchim among them. The dancers use it to dress, rehearse, and rest after their public performances. It is also where the secret initiation rites are held for adolescent boys.

Masau'u

Masau'u (also Masaw, Masao, Masauwu) is the Hopi god of death, fire, darkness, and war. He rules the underworld and is said to wear raw animal hides for clothing and a frightening mask. As the god of fire, Masau'u is responsible for teaching the young Hopi men undergoing their initiation during Wuwuchim about fire. It is usually a chief who impersonates Masau'u during the ceremony.

New Fire Ceremony

The New Fire Ceremony takes place at dawn on the first day of Wuwuchim. Two Hopi priests use flint or the friction produced by rubbing two sticks together to kindle a fire, which they then feed with coal. Torches are ignited from this fire and carried throughout the pueblo, where they are used to light other fires. The fire itself is symbolic of the power of the sun, which is channeled through MASAU'U to warm the earth and its inhabitants.

Wuwuchim Song

A number of songs are sung during Wuwuchim, but in the past there has been one particular song that, according to legend, heralds the coming of war or disaster. It tells the story of the Blue Star Kachina and how a new cycle of Hopi life will begin when the Blue Star Kachina takes off his mask. It is said that this song was sung both in 1914, just before World War I erupted, and in 1940, just after World War II began.

FURTHER READING

Bellenir, Karen. *Religious Holidays and Calendars*. 3rd ed. Detroit: Omnigraphics, 2004.

Eagle Walking Turtle. *Indian America: A Traveler's Companion*. Santa Fe: J. Muir Publications, 1989.

Gill, Sam D., and Irene Sullivan. *Dictionary of Native American Mythology*. Santa Barbara: ABC-CLIO, 1992.

Hirschfelder, Arlene B., and Paulette Fairbanks Molin. *Encyclopedia of Native American Religions.* Updated edition. New York: Facts on File, 2000.

Jobes, Gertrude. *Dictionary of Mythology, Folklore, and Symbols.* New York: Scarecrow Press, 1962.

Leach, Maria, ed. *Funk & Wagnalls Standard Dictionary of Folklore, Mythology & Legend.* San Francisco: Harper & Row, 1984.

WEB SITE

Hopi Cultural Center
www.hopi.nsn.us

Yaqui Easter Ceremony

Type of Holiday: Religious (Christian, Yaqui)
Date of Observation: Seven weeks, ending on Easter Sunday
Where Celebrated: Arizona, Mexico
Symbols and Customs: Burning of the Masks, Caballeros, Chapayekas, Deer Dance, Fariseos, Flowers, Matachin Dance, Pascolas
Colors: Red, which symbolizes the blood of Jesus Christ
Related Holidays: Easter

ORIGINS

The Yaqui Easter Ceremony combines Christian beliefs with the traditions of the Yaqui Indians. The historical development of religious belief systems among this and other Native American groups is not well known. Most of the information available was gathered by Europeans who arrived on the continent beginning in the sixteenth century C.E. The data they recorded was fragmentary and oftentimes of questionable accuracy because the Europeans did not understand the native cultures they were trying to describe and the Native Americans were reluctant to divulge details about themselves.

The history of Native American cultures dates back thousands of years into prehistoric times. According to many scholars, the people who became the Native Americans migrated from Asia across a land bridge that may have once connected the territories presently occupied by Alaska and Russia. The migrations, believed to have begun between 60,000 and 30,000 B.C.E., continued until approximately 4,000 B.C.E. This speculation, however, conflicts with traditional stories asserting that the indigenous Americans have always lived in North America or that tribes moved up from the south.

The Yaqui Indians currently living in Tucson and Phoenix, Arizona, are descended from the original tribe that lived in northwestern Mexico near the Yaqui River. Jesuit missionaries arrived there in the early seventeenth century and began to teach the Yaqui about Christianity. But while they accepted certain Roman Catholic practices, they continued to hold onto many of their ancient beliefs. This mix of Christian and tribal rituals is particularly apparent in their annual Easter Ceremony, which is observed by both the Yaqui who remained in Mexico and those who fled to the southwestern United States during the wars with Spanish troops and the Mexican government in the eighteenth and nineteenth centuries.

Preparations for **EASTER** begin before **ASH WEDNESDAY** with the decoration of churches, the creation of ceremonial masks, and the setting up of crosses for the reenactment of the Passion of Christ. Public ceremonies and tribal dances, including the DEER DANCE, take place throughout the forty days of **LENT,** but it is during Easter week that the celebration reaches a climax. On Holy Thursday the CHAPAYEKAS, the soldiers who have been searching for Jesus throughout Lent, capture an effigy of Christ and seize control of the church. As part of the FARISEOS (Pharisees) or enemies of Christ, they carry out a symbolic crucifixion on Good Friday, but the Resurrection takes place that night and they don't realize at first that they have lost possession of the body. On Holy Saturday there is a final confrontation between the Fariseos and Chapayekas on one side and, on the other, several groups who are defending the church and have armed themselves with FLOWERS. The Fariseos and Chapayekas advance toward the church three times, but they are turned back by the Matachin Dancers (*see* MATACHIN DANCE), the Deer Dancers (*see* DEER DANCE), the PASCOLAS, and an avalanche of real and crepe paper flowers. Eventually the Fariseos are defeated, which they admit by throwing their ceremonial masks and the straw effigy of Judas into a huge fire (*see* BURNING OF THE MASKS). The Pascolas, along with the Deer Dancers and Matachin Dancers, perform at the celebration that follows, and when the news of Jesus' resurrection reaches them early on Sunday morning, they join the rest of the Yaqui in a final procession of joy that ends with a sermon in which the various parts of the Easter Ceremony are explained.

SYMBOLS AND CUSTOMS

Burning of the Masks

The act of throwing their ceremonial masks and the straw effigy of their leader, Judas, into a fire on Easter Sunday is not only an admission of defeat on the part of the chapayekas but a symbolic way of ridding themselves of Judas and, by implication, the sins of the entire Yaqui community. Like other aspects of the Easter Ceremony, this represents a blending of tribal rituals designed to drive out evil with the biblical story of how Judas betrayed Jesus shortly before his crucifixion.

Caballeros

The Caballeros are the cavalry or horsemen whose role during the reenactment of the Passion is to guard Jesus from those who are trying to capture him. They wear hats and swords and carry a blue flag, which symbolizes all that is good in the Yaqui community.

Chapayekas

Chapayeka means "long nose" in the Yaqui language, and the masks worn by these soldiers during the annual Easter Ceremony traditionally have long, slender noses. It is possible that the word chapayeka was originally used to describe the Spanish invaders of Mexico.

The chapayekas are members of the FARISEOS, or Pharisees—in other words, the enemies of Jesus—and they play an important role in his capture and crucifixion. In addition to helmet-like masks, they wear plaid blankets over their shoulders and cocoon rattles around their legs and waists. They are primarily known for their clowning and irreverent behavior, and their job is to distract everyone from what's going on by teasing and taunting the crowd with their red-tipped swords, symbolic of Jesus' blood. As a group, they are an extension of their leader, Judas, and as such they represent the evil or sinful elements in the Yaqui community.

Deer Dance

The Yaqui Deer Dancers wear deer heads with antlers and glass eyes on their own heads, which are covered by a piece of white cloth. They are usually bare-chested and carry rattles made from dried gourds in either hand, with cocoon rattles tied to their ankles. During the Easter Ceremony, the Deer Dancers perform with the PASCOLAS, who attempt to capture them. Their movements imitate those of the animal they impersonate—silent, skittish, and aloof—and they dance to the music of three singers who accompany themselves on rasping sticks, imitative of the deer's breathing, and a water drum made from a hollow gourd floating in water, which is meant to sound like the beating of the deer's heart.

The deer was at one time a crucial source of food and hides for the Yaqui, and the Deer Dance, which is performed not only at Easter but at other Yaqui fiestas, pays homage to their longstanding relationship with this animal, which they both fear and admire.

Fariseos

Along with the CABALLEROS or horsemen, the Fariseos or Pharisees are one of the two societies responsible for organizing the Yaqui Easter Ceremony. They are the infantry or foot soldiers, and they symbolize the evil forces that persecuted and eventually crucified Christ. Their leader is Pontius Pilate, the Roman official who presided over Jesus' trial and ordered his crucifixion, and they are often referred to as the Soldiers of Rome.

The Fariseos dress completely in black, with black scarves covering most of their faces. During the final confrontation that takes place on Holy Saturday, it is the Fariseos who are defeated by those defending the church, who pelt them with FLOWERS. After this symbolic death, they are welcomed back into the church and greeted as men who have been rebaptized into the Christian faith.

Flowers

Flowers—particularly those that grow in the Mexican desert—have always possessed symbolic value for the Yaqui. They appear in many Yaqui songs and stories, and they are also a symbol for the Virgin Mary, whose heaven is believed to be filled with flowers. At the final confrontation on Holy Saturday between the forces of evil (see FARISEOS) and the defenders of the Christian Church, the latter use flowers (or sometimes confetti to represent real flowers) as their weapon. These flowers symbolize the blood of Jesus, which has the power to overcome evil.

Matachin Dance

The Matachin Dancers who perform at the Easter Ceremony and other Yaqui fiestas represent the forces of good. They wear headdresses decorated with red flowers and brightly colored skirts, and they carry rattles made from hollow gourds and palma, which are wands shaped like a trident covered in feathers.

The Matachin Dance is considered to be the most sacred of all the Yaqui dances, because it honors the Virgin Mary, their patroness, and is performed to ensure that she continues to look favorably upon the Yaqui people. During the Easter Ceremony, the Matachin Dancers are not seen until Holy Saturday, when they participate in the final confrontation with the FARISEOS and perform their dance afterward.

Pascolas

The term pascola comes from the Yaqui word pahko, which means "fiesta," combined with ola, meaning "old man." They perform at all the Yaqui fiestas and other special occasions, accompanied by a harp, a violin, and a combination of drum and flute. Like the Deer Dancers, they wear cocoon rattles around their ankles and bells or rattles around their waists; their masks, which are normally black or brown with red or white decorations, resemble either human or animal faces, with long tufts of hair and a cross carved into the chin or forehead.

At the Easter Ceremony and other Yaqui fiestas, the Pascolas, who usually perform individually, play the role of clowns who try to get audience members more involved and who provide comic relief during otherwise serious religious ceremonies. They also serve as a unifying element throughout the ceremonial year, opening every Yaqui fiesta with their dancing, storytelling, and humorous antics.

FURTHER READING

Christianson, Stephen G., and Jane M. Hatch. *The American Book of Days*. 4th ed. New York: H.W. Wilson, 2000.

Eagle Walking Turtle. *Indian America: A Traveler's Companion*. Santa Fe: J. Muir Publications, 1989.

Gill, Sam D., and Irene Sullivan. *Dictionary of Native American Mythology*. Santa Barbara: ABC-CLIO, 1992.

Hirschfelder, Arlene B., and Paulette Fairbanks Molin. *Encyclopedia of Native American Religions*. Updated edition. New York: Facts on File, 2000.

Leach, Maria, ed. *Funk & Wagnalls Standard Dictionary of Folklore, Mythology & Legend*. San Francisco: Harper & Row, 1984.

WEB SITE

Pascua Yaqui Tribe
www.pascuayaquitribe.org

Yemanja Festival
(Iemanja)

Type of Holiday: Religious (Candomblé, Macumba)
Date of Observation: January 1 or February 2
Where Celebrated: Brazil
Symbols and Customs: Miniature Boats, Offerings, Yemanja Statue

ORIGINS

Yemanja is a powerful sea goddess from the Brazilian religion known as Macumba or Candomblé. Many practitioners of this religion see Yemanja as similar to the Blessed Virgin Mary in Roman Catholicism. In some regions of the country and in Rio de Janeiro, Brazil's capital city, people celebrate Yemanja on January 1. In the city of Salvador her festival takes place on February 2. The Yemanja festival is so popular that some of the most spectacular scenes from the celebrations are broadcast on Brazilian television.

Candomblé and Macumba are African-based religious traditions in Brazil and can be traced to the arrival of the first African slaves in the sixteenth century. However, these religious traditions became very popular during the nineteenth century. During the years of slavery, ceremonies were typically conducted in secret. Following the emancipation of Brazilian slaves in 1888, some gatherings were held in the open and others remained concealed. The gatherings, organized into communities, centered around a local leader, most often a priestess. Although individual Candomblé and Macumba centers share a common heritage, they may differ in religious practice. Some focus on maintaining the purity of African traditions; others freely incorporated Roman Catholic elements and even added some gods from indigenous Brazilians to their pantheon.

The origins of this festival can be traced back to the sixteenth century, when the Portuguese began to import slaves from Africa to Brazil. The slaves brought their West African religion with them, complete with various gods and goddesses, which they called "orishas." The Portuguese then tried to impose Roman Catholicism on the African slaves. This process gave birth to a new Brazilian religion, which mixes elements of the Yoruba religion of West Africa with certain Roman Catholic beliefs and practices. The black Brazilians found many parallels between the gods and goddesses of West Africa and the saints of Roman Catholicism. The sea goddess Yemanja, for example, became interchangeable with the Virgin Mary. There are several different variants of this Black Brazilian religion. The practices that are most closely aligned with the old Yoruba religion are called Candomblé. Macumba is a name applied to all of them, including those that involve the practice of black or white magic.

No one knows exactly when the first Yemanja festival took place. Until 1888, when slavery was abolished in Brazil, Macumba practitioners had to keep their religious practices secret. The first center for Candomblé was established in the city of Salvador, which is still regarded as the center of the nation's African-Brazilian religions. The ceremonies were presided over by women priestesses, and many women still serve in this role today.

Brazilians treat Yemanja as the patron saint of navigators and believe that she associates with mermaids. Moreover, they claim that she presides over the oceans and ensures a good fishing season. She also helps the faithful to have a happy family life and grants them favors.

The people of Rio de Janeiro host fabulous celebrations in honor of Yemanja on January 1. Several days beforehand, workers build stands and loud speakers along the long beachfront. On the afternoon of December 31, people begin to anticipate the night's festivities as office workers dump waste papers out of the windows of their high rise buildings, creating a snow storm effect. After dinner, people stroll towards the beaches. The locals wear white clothing to celebrate Yemanja's feast day.

As midnight approaches, crowds roam across the sands. People who practice Candomblé or some form of Macumba gather together to make little altars in the sand. Some people celebrate the excitement by setting off firecrackers and fireworks. The loudspeakers blare music out towards the sea. When the loudspeakers announce the arrival of midnight, fireworks splash bursts of color across in the night sky. People on the top floors of the beachfront high-rise hotels toss cascades of fireworks from the roofs of these buildings. The assembled crowds begin to move towards the sea to set free MINIATURE BOATS in the waves. People also toss flowers into the sea. Then they stroll along the beach enjoying the party-like atmosphere created by the large crowds, the food stalls, and the samba bands. For many, eating, drinking, and samba dancing complete the night's festivities. Those who make an early night of it leave the beach around three a.m. Others stay until dawn.

SYMBOLS AND CUSTOMS

Miniature Boats

In order to ensure that Yemanja receives the offerings presented to her, some of her followers place them in miniature boats. People also place statuettes of one or more of the Candomblé gods and goddesses on these boats. On the day of her festival they wade into the sea and release the boats, hoping that they will carry the offerings directly to the goddess. Some say Yemanja lives in the "seventh wave," and so a boat is needed to carry the devotees' gifts from the shore to her watery home.

Offerings

People make offerings to Yemanja in order to thank her for past favors and to ask for future favors. They give the goddess things that she is believed to enjoy, such as perfume, mirrors, combs, soap, flowers, and champagne. The goddess is also thought to prefer certain kinds of incense, which her devotees buy and burn for her on the day of her festival. Faithful followers of the goddess also provide Yemanja with miniature representations of things they would like the goddess to help them acquire, such as cars and homes. They hope that the goddess will appreciate the miniature and be inspired to grant them the real thing.

People leave the offerings on the beach or place them in miniature boats that they cast off into the sea. Lit candles sunk into the sand mark the beach offerings. Some people create a little altar in the sand, outlining it with candles. They place lit candles in a star-shaped pattern and arrange food, drink, and flowers inside. Then they stand around the altar, offering prayers or singing songs. Many people toss flowers into the sea as a tribute to the sea goddess. Folk tradition teaches that if the waves carry the flower out to sea, Yemanja will bless the giver with good fortune. If the sea returns the flower to shore, however, Yemanja frowns on the giver.

Some Macumba practitioners kill animals and present them as part of their offerings to Yemanja. Although city officials have outlawed animal sacrifice on the city's main beaches, those who wander further down the shore could run into scenes of animal sacrifice.

Yemanja Statue

In Brazil, followers of Yemanja often keep a small statue of the goddess in their homes. They dress the statue in blue and white clothing, because these colors symbolize the goddess. On the day of her festival, devotees carry large statues of Yemanja out into the streets. They end up at the ocean where the statue bearers carry the image a little ways out into the water.

FURTHER READING

Bellenir, Karen. *Religious Holidays and Calendars*. 3rd ed. Detroit: Omnigraphics, 2004.

Ferro, Jennifer. *Brazilian Foods and Culture*. Vero Beach, FL: Rourke Press, 1999.

Hess, David J. *Samba in the Night: Spiritism in Brazil*. New York: Columbia University Press, 1994.

Hillman, Elizabeth. "Rio Welcomes its New Year Goddess." *Contemporary Review*, January 1994.

Morwyn. *Magic From Brazil: Recipes, Spells and Rituals*. St. Paul, MN: Llewellyn, 2001.

WEB SITE

Brazil Embassy
www.brasilemb.org

Yom Kippur
(Day of Atonement, Day of Judgment)

Type of Holiday: Religious (Jewish)
Date of Observation: Between September 15 and October 13; tenth day of Tishri
Where Celebrated: Europe, Israel, United States, and by Jews all over the world
Symbols and Customs: Kapparot Ceremony, Kol Nidre, Scapegoat, Shofar
Colors: Yom Kippur is associated with the color white. The rabbi, cantor, and married men of the congregation wear the *kittel* or long white robe of purity. It is also customary to drape the scrolls of the Torah in white, to cover the ark or closet in which the scrolls are kept with a white curtain, and to spread white cloths over the cantor's reading desk and the pulpit. For this reason, Yom Kippur is sometimes known as "the White Fast."
Related Holidays: Rosh Hashanah, Sukkot

ORIGINS

Yom Kippur is a significant and solemn time in Judaism, one of the oldest continuously observed religions in the world. Its history extends back beyond the advent of the written word. Its people trace their roots to a common ancestor, Abraham, and then back even farther to the very moment of creation.

According to Jewish belief, the law given to the Jewish people by God contained everything they needed to live a holy life, including the ability to be reinterpreted in new historical situations. Judaism, therefore, is the expression of the Jewish people, attempting to live holy (set apart) lives in accordance with the instructions given by God. Obedience to the law is central to Judaism, but there is no one central authority. Sources of divine authority are God, the Torah, interpretations of the Torah by respected teachers, and tradition. Religious observances and the study of Jewish law are conducted under the supervision of a teacher called a rabbi.

There are several sects within Judaism. Orthodox Judaism is characterized by an affirmation of the traditional Jewish faith, strict adherence to customs such as keeping the Sabbath, participation in ceremonies and rituals, and the observance of dietary regulations. Conservative Jewish congregations seek to retain many ancient traditions but without the accompanying demand for strict observance. Reform Judaism stresses modern biblical criticism and emphasizes ethical teachings more than ritualistic observance. Hasidism is a mystical sect of Judaism that teaches enthusiastic prayer as a means of communion with God. The Reconstruc-

tionist movement began early in the twentieth century in an effort to "reconstruct" Judaism with the community rather than the synagogue as its center.

The ten-day period of penitence in the Jewish calendar between **ROSH HASHANAH**, the Jewish New Year, and Yom Kippur, or the Day of Atonement, is typical of similar periods in other cultures marking the transition between the old year and the new. It was a period during which all normal activities were suspended. It was regarded as being "outside time," because extra days were often inserted between the end of one year and the beginning of the next to bring the lunar and solar calendars into harmony. In Judaism, this ten-day period was dedicated to examining the soul.

The last of the ten High Holy Days, Yom Kippur is the most solemn day in the Jewish calendar. It is the day on which God examines people's lives and writes down His final decision concerning their future in the Book of Life, which is then sealed until the following year. Because it is their last chance to acknowledge their sins and ask God to forgive them, Jews often spend the entire twenty-four hours at the synagogue, where five services are held. They also abstain from food and water during this period, which keeps their minds clear for prayer and repentance.

God is said to open three books on Rosh Hashanah. The first contains the names of the virtuous, whose lives will be blessed during the next twelve months. The second contains the names of the wicked, who are doomed to death and disaster. In the third, however, are the names of those who still have a chance to redeem themselves and determine their own fates, because this book isn't sealed until twilight on Yom Kippur. If a person is genuinely sorry for what he or she has done and asks God to forgive and correct his or her wrongdoing, God will put a "good signature" next to the person's name and the coming year will be a happy one. When Jews meet each other in the synagogue on this day, they often say, "May you end this day with a good signature."

The celebration of Yom Kippur begins in the evening at the synagogue, where the prayer known as the KOL NIDRE is recited. Worshippers then read prayers from the Yom Kippur prayer book and spend the entire period of the holiday praying that they will be forgiven for their sins and thinking about how they might become better people. Many of these prayers are said out loud, with everyone in the synagogue joining in. On the afternoon of Yom Kippur, the story of the prophet Jonah and the whale is read from the Jewish scriptures as a reminder that God is eager for people to repent. The end of the service is marked by a long blast from the SHOFAR or ram's horn, after which people go home to eat their first meal following the day-long fast.

The *challah* or bread baked on Yom Kippur is often made in special shapes —usually a ladder, symbolic of the hope that Yom Kippur prayers will reach heaven, or wings, because the scriptures read on Yom Kippur compare men to angels.

SYMBOLS AND CUSTOMS

Kapparot Ceremony

In a very ancient ceremony held on the day before Yom Kippur and known as the *Kapparah* or *Kapparot*, it was customary to take a chicken (a rooster for a man, a hen for a woman) and swing it around one's head three times while reciting verses from the Psalms and the Book of Job. The chicken served as a kind of SCAPEGOAT: It took on the individual's sins and absorbed any punishment that he or she deserved. The custom of Kapparot is normally practiced only by very pious Jews. Today, many people observe it by swinging money tied in a handkerchief over their heads and then giving it to charity.

The act of making circles appears in many other Jewish customs, as well as in those of other ancient cultures. Making a "magic ring" was originally believed to ward off evil spirits. Some Jewish authorities have condemned the Kapparot ceremony as a display of heathen superstition, but it remains popular among Orthodox Jews.

Kol Nidre

On the eve of Yom Kippur, there is a service at the synagogue known as the Kol Nidre ("All Vows"). It dates back to the sixth century when, during the Spanish Inquisition, Jews were forced to become Christians. They tried to follow their religious beliefs in secret, asking God to forgive them for breaking vows they could not keep because of events beyond their control. The Kol Nidre prayer has also been used during other times in history when Jews have been forced, in one way or another, to abandon the practice of their religion.

To many Jews the Kol Nidre prayer is synonymous with Yom Kippur. Modern Reform Jews no longer recite the Kol Nidre because it has been criticized for providing a "loophole" by which they might avoid fulfilling their obligations. But the haunting melody to which the words of the Kol Nidre are sung, composed between the mid-fifteenth and mid-sixteenth centuries, can be very moving, and many people have tears in their eyes when they listen to it.

Scapegoat

A scapegoat is someone or something that bears the blame for the wrongs committed by others. The idea of using a scapegoat to atone for human sins goes back to the most primitive societies. The ancient Babylonians included in their ten-day New Year celebration a *Kapparu* day—a day for the cleansing of sins. They would kill a ram and rub its body against the walls of the temple so that any impurities would be absorbed. The next day, they would designate a criminal to act as a human scapegoat for the sins of the community. This unfortunate person would be paraded in the streets and beaten over the head. When the Jews took over this ceremony, it became more than an act of purgation; people had to be purified not just for their own sakes, but for the sake of their God. Sin was regarded as an obstacle not only to their material welfare but to the fulfillment of their duty to God. In fact, Yom Kippur gets its name from *kippurim,* which refers to the various procedures used to remove the taint of sin.

Why a scape*goat?* The male goat for pre-Christians was a symbol of virility and unbridled lust. But as sexuality became more and more repressed, the goat's status was reduced to that of an "impure, stinking" creature who only cared about gratifying its own appetites. In portrayals of the Last Judgment, the goat is used to symbolize those who are damned. This is based upon a passage in the Bible describing how Christ on Judgment Day will separate the believers from the non-believers as the shepherd separates the sheep from the goats.

In ancient times, two scapegoats were chosen. After special ceremonies were held transferring the sins of the community to the goats, one of them was sacrificed and the other was driven into the wilderness. When the Second Temple in Jerusalem was destroyed in 70 C.E., animal sacrifices were discontinued, and Yom Kippur underwent a profound change. The sins that used to be removed by the ritual of the scapegoat now had to be purged by each individual through confession and absolution. At the same time, atoning for one's sins by attending synagogue services on Yom Kippur remains a community experience.

Shofar

In Jerusalem, it was customary to signal the end of Yom Kippur by blowing the shofar or ram's horn at the Western Wall, also known as the Wailing Wall (*see* **TISHA BE-AV**). After the Arabs rioted against the Jewish population of Palestine in 1919, the British administrators ordered the Jews to stop the custom. Defying threats from both Arabs and the British police, certain dedicated Jews continued the practice; many were imprisoned for doing so.

In June 1967, after the old city of Jerusalem was freed from Jordanian control, one of the first things that the Chief Rabbi of the Israeli Defense Force did was to blow the shofar at the Western Wall. Since that time, the custom has been restored. Every year on Yom Kippur, thousands of Israelis gather at the wall to listen.

FURTHER READING

Bellenir, Karen. *Religious Holidays and Calendars.* 3rd ed. Detroit: Omnigraphics, 2004.

Biedermann, Hans. *Dictionary of Symbolism: Cultural Icons and the Meanings Behind Them.* New York: Meridian Books, 1994.

Cashman, Greer Fay. *Jewish Days and Holidays*. New York: SBS Pub., 1979.

Edidin, Ben. *Jewish Holidays and Festivals*. 1940. Reprint. Detroit: Omnigraphics, 1993.

Ferguson, George. *Signs and Symbols in Christian Art*. New York: Oxford University Press, 1954.

Frazer, Sir James G. *The Golden Bough: A Study in Magic and Religion*. New York: Macmillan, 1931.

Gaer, Joseph. *Holidays Around the World*. Boston: Little, Brown, 1953.

Gaster, Theodor H. *Festivals of the Jewish Year*. New York: William Sloane Associates, 1953.

Henderson, Helene, ed. *Holidays, Festivals, and Celebrations of the World Dictionary*. 3rd ed. Detroit: Omnigraphics, 2005.

Purdy, Susan. *Festivals for You to Celebrate*. Philadelphia: Lippincott, 1969.

Renberg, Dalia Hardof. *The Complete Family Guide to Jewish Holidays*. New York: Adama Books, 1985.

WEB SITE

Union of Orthodox Jewish Congregations of America
www.ou.org/chagim/yomkippur

Bibliography

Bibliography

The following bibliography lists the sources consulted in the preparation of this volume.

Abraham, Roger D. *Singing the Master.* New York: Penguin Books, 1992.

Adkins, Lesley, and Roy A. Adkins. *Dictionary of Roman Religion.* New York: Oxford University Press, 1996.

Ahsan, M.M. *Muslim Festivals.* Vero Beach, FL: Rourke Enterprises, 1987.

Anyike, James C. *African American Holidays.* Revised and expanded edition. Chicago: Popular Truth Pub., 1997.

Appleton, LeRoy H., and Stephen Bridges. *Symbolism in Liturgical Art.* New York: Scribner, 1959.

Araki, Nancy K., and Jane M. Horii. *Matsuri Festival: Japanese-American Celebrations and Activities.* San Francisco: Heian International Pub. Co., 1978.

Aveni, Anthony. *Empires of Time: Calendars, Clocks, and Cultures.* New York: Kodansha International, 1995.

Barth, Edna. *Hearts, Cupids, and Red Roses: The Story of the Valentine Symbols.* New York: Seabury Press, 1974.

Barth, Edna. *Shamrocks, Harps, and Shillelaghs: The Story of the St. Patrick's Day Symbols.* New York: Seabury Press, 1977.

Barth, Edna. *Turkeys, Pilgrims, and Indian Corn: The Story of the Thanksgiving Symbols.* New York: Seabury Press, 1975.

Barth, Edna. *Witches, Pumpkins, and Grinning Ghosts: The Story of the Halloween Symbols.* New York: Seabury Press, 1972.

Barz, Brigitte. *Festivals with Children.* Edinburgh: Floris Books, 1987.

Bauer, Helen, and Sherwin Carlquist. *Japanese Festivals.* Garden City, NY: Doubleday, 1965.

Bechert, Heinz, and Richard Gombrich. *The World of Buddhism.* New York: Facts on File, 1984.

Bell, Robert E. *Dictionary of Classical Mythology.* Santa Barbara: ABC-CLIO, 1982.

Bellenir, Karen. *Religious Holidays and Calendars.* 3rd ed. Detroit: Omnigraphics, 2004.

Biedermann, Hans. *Dictionary of Symbolism: Cultural Icons and the Meanings Behind Them.* New York: Meridan Book, 1994.

Bivans, Ann-Marie. *Miss America: In Pursuit of the Crown.* New York: MasterMedia, 1991.

Blackburn, Bonnie, and Leofranc Holford-Stevens. *The Oxford Companion to the Year.* New York: Oxford University Press, 2003.

Bowker, John, ed. *The Oxford Dictionary of World Religions.* New York: Oxford University Press, 1997.

Bredon, Juliet, and Igor Mitrophanow. *The Moon Year: A Record of Chinese Customs and Festivals.* Shanghai: Kelly & Walsh, 1927.

Brewster, H. Pomeroy. *Saints and Festivals of the Christian Church.* 1904. Reprint. Detroit: Omnigraphics, 1990.

Brunel, Philippe. *An Intimate Portrait of the Tour de France.* 2nd ed. Denver: Buonpane Pub., 1996.

Buday, George. *The History of the Christmas Card.* 1971. Reprint. Detroit: Omnigraphics, 1991.

Buell, Hal. *Festivals of Japan.* New York: Dodd, Mead, 1965.

Carmichael, Elizabeth, and Chloe Sayer. *The Skeleton at the Feast: The Day of the Dead in Mexico.* Austin: University of Texas Press, 1992.

Carrick, Robert W. *The Pictorial History of the America's Cup Races.* New York: Viking Press, 1964.

Casal, U.A. *The Five Sacred Festivals of Ancient Japan.* Rutland, VA: Sophia University in cooperation with Tuttle, 1967.

Cashman, Greer Fay. *Jewish Days and Holidays.* New York: SBS Pub., 1979.

Cawthorne, George J., and Richard S. Herod. *Royal Ascot: Its History and Its Associations.* London: Longmans, Green, 1900.

Chambers, Robert. *The Book of Days.* 2 vols. 1862-64. Reprint. Detroit: Omnigraphics, 1990.

Christianson, Stephen G., and Jane M. Hatch. *The American Book of Days.* 4th ed. New York: H.W. Wilson, 2000.

Cirlot, J.E. *A Dictionary of Symbols.* New York: Philosophical Library, 1962.

Cohen, Hennig, and Tristram Potter Coffin. *The Folklore of American Holidays.* 3rd ed. Detroit: Gale Research, 1999.

Cole, William Owen, and Piara Singh Sambhi. *The Sikhs: Their Religious Beliefs and Practices*. 2nd ed. Portland: Sussex Academic Press, 1998.

Coulson, John, ed. *The Saints: A Concise Biographical Dictionary*. New York: Hawthorn Books, 1958.

Crim, Keith R. *The Perennial Dictionary of World Religions*. San Francisco: Harper & Row, 1989.

Crippen, T.G. *Christmas and Christmas Lore*. 1923. Reprint. Detroit: Omnigraphics, 1990.

Cuyler, Margery. *Jewish Holidays*. New York: Holt, Rinehart and Winston, 1978.

Danaher, Kevin. *The Year in Ireland*. 4th ed. St. Paul, MN: Irish Books and Media, 1984.

Dawson, W.F. *Christmas: Its Origin and Associations*. 1902. Reprint. Detroit: Omnigraphics, 1990.

Dienhart, Tom, Joe Hoppel, and Dave Sloan, eds. *The Complete Super Bowl Book*. St. Louis: The Sporting News, 1994.

Dobler, Lavinia G. *Customs and Holidays Around the World*. New York: Fleet Pub. Corp., 1962.

Dobler, Lavinia. *National Holidays Around the World*. New York: Fleet Press Corp., 1968.

Drucker, Malka. *Hanukkah: Eight Nights, Eight Lights*. New York: Holiday House, 1980.

Dunkling, Leslie. *A Dictionary of Days*. New York: Facts on File, 1988.

Eagle Walking Turtle. *Indian America: A Traveler's Companion*. Santa Fe: J. Muir Publications, 1989.

Eberhard, Wolfram. *A Dictionary of Chinese Symbols: Hidden Symbols in Chinese Life and Thought*. New York: Routledge & Kegan Paul, 1986.

Eberhard, Wolfram. *Chinese Festivals*. New York: Henry Schuman, 1952.

Edidin, Ben. *Jewish Holidays and Festivals*. 1940. Reprint. Detroit: Omnigraphics, 1993.

Eliade, Mircea. *The Encyclopedia of Religion*. 16 vols. New York: Macmillan, 1987.

Epton, Nina. *Spanish Fiestas*. New York: A.S. Barnes, 1969.

Falassi, Alessandro, and Giuliano Catoni. *Palio*. Milan: Electa, 1983.

Faris, James C. *The Nightway: A History and a History of Documentation of a Navajo Ceremonial*. Albuquerque: University of New Mexico Press, 1990.

Farmer, David Hugh. *The Oxford Dictionary of Saints*. 5th ed. New York: Oxford University Press, 2003.

Ferguson, George. *Signs and Symbols in Christian Art*. New York: Oxford University Press, 1954.

Fergusson, Erna. *Dancing Gods: Indian Ceremonials of New Mexico and Arizona*. New York: A.A. Knopf, 1931.

Fewkes, Jesse Walter. *Hopi Snake Ceremonies*. Revised ed. Albuquerque: Avanyu Pub., 2000.

Fewkes, Jesse Walter. *Tusayan Katcinas and Hopi Altars*. Albuquerque: Avanyu Pub., 1990.

Fowler, W. Warde. *The Roman Festivals of the Period of the Republic*. New York: Macmillan Co., 1925.

Frazer, James G. *The Golden Bough: A Study in Magic and Religion*. New York: Macmillan, 1931.

Freeman, Dave, et al. *100 Things to Do Before You Die: Travel Events You Just Can't Miss*. Dallas: Taylor Pub. Co., 1999.

Gaer, Joseph. *Holidays Around the World*. Boston: Little, Brown, 1953.

Ganteaume, Cécile R. "White Mountain Apache Dance: Expressions of Spirituality." In *Native American Dance: Ceremonies and Social Traditions*, edited by Charlotte Heth. Washington DC: National Museum of the American Indian, Smithsonian Institution, 1992.

Gaster, Theodor H. *Festivals of the Jewish Year*. New York: William Sloane Associates, 1953.

Gay, Kathlyn. *African-American Holidays, Festivals, and Celebrations*. Detroit: Omnigraphics, 2007.

Giblin, James Cross. *Fireworks, Picnics, and Flags: The Story of the Fourth of July Symbols*. New York: Clarion Books, 1983.

Gill, Sam D., and Irene Sullivan. *Dictionary of Native American Mythology*. Santa Barbara: ABC-CLIO, 1992.

Glassé, Cyril. *The Concise Encyclopedia of Islam*. 2nd ed. San Francisco: Harper & Row, 1999.

Gordon, Matthew S. *Islam*. New York: Facts on File, 1991.

Graham-Barber, Lynda. *Gobble!: The Complete Book of Thanksgiving Words*. New York: Bradbury Press, 1991.

Griffin, Robert H., and Ann H. Shurgin. *Junior Worldmark Encyclopedia of World Holidays*. Vol. 2. Detroit: U*X*L, 2000.

Gulevich, Tanya. *Encyclopedia of Christmas and New Year's Celebrations*. 2nd ed. Detroit: Omnigraphics, 2003.

Gulevich, Tanya. *Encyclopedia of Easter, Carnival, and Lent*. Detroit: Omnigraphics, 2002.

Gulevich, Tanya. *Understanding Islam and Muslim Traditions*. Detroit: Omnigraphics, 2004.

Gupte, B.A. *Hindu Holidays and Ceremonials*. 2nd ed. Calcutta: Thacker, Spink & Co., 1919.

Gwynne, Walker. *The Christian Year: Its Purpose and Its History*. 1917. Reprint. Detroit: Omnigraphics, 1990.

Hanchett, Suzanne. *Coloured Rice: Symbolic Structure in Hindu Family Festivals*. Delhi: Hindustan Pub. Corp., 1988.

Harper, Howard V. *Days and Customs of All Faiths*. 1957. Reprint. Detroit: Omnigraphics, 1990.

Haven, Kendall. *New Year's to Kwanzaa: Original Stories of Celebration*. Golden, CO: Fulcrum Resources, 1999.

Hazeltine, Alice Isabel, and Elva Sophronia Smith. *The Easter Book of Legends and Stories*. 1947. Reprint. Detroit: Omnigraphics, 1992.

Heinberg, Richard. *Celebrate the Solstice: Honoring the Earth's Seasonal Rhythms through Festival and Ceremony*. Wheaton, IL: Quest Books, 1993.

Helfman, Elizabeth. *Celebrating Nature: Rites and Ceremonies Around the World*. New York: Seabury Press, 1969.

Henderson, Helene, ed. *Holidays, Festivals, and Celebrations of the World Dictionary*. 3rd ed. Detroit: Omnigraphics, 2005.

Henderson, Helene. *Patriotic Holidays of the United States*. Detroit: Omnigraphics, 2006.

Hervey, Thomas K. *The Book of Christmas*. Boston: Roberts Brothers, 1888.

Hill, Jeff, and Peggy Daniels. *Life Events and Rites of Passage*. Detroit: Omnigraphics, 2008.

Hirschfelder, Arlene B., and Paulette Fairbanks Molin. *Encyclopedia of Native American Religions*. Updated ed. New York: Facts on File, 2000.

Hoang, Vivi. "Spirits Live on Day of the Dead: Mexican Tradition of Dia de los Muertos Pays Respect to Deceased through Offerings, Communion." *Tennessean*, October 27, 2006.

Hoig, Stan. *It's the Fourth of July!* New York: Cobblehill Books, 1995.

Hole, Christina. *English Custom and Usage*. 1941. Reprint. Detroit: Omnigraphics, 1990.

Hole, Christina. *Saints in Folklore*. New York: M. Barrows, 1965.

Holm, Jean, and John Bowker, eds. *Worship*. New York: St. Martin's Press, 1994.

Humphrey, Grace. *Stories of the World's Holidays*. 1923. Reprint. Detroit: Omni-graphics, 1990.

Hutton, Ronald. *The Pagan Religions of the Ancient British Isles: Their Nature and Legacy*. Oxford: Blackwell, 1991.

Ickis, Marguerite. *The Book of Festivals and Holidays the World Over*. New York: Dodd, Mead, 1970.

Ickis, Marguerite. *The Book of Patriotic Holidays*. New York: Dodd, Mead, 1962.

Ickis, Marguerite. *The Book of Religious Holidays and Celebrations*. New York: Dodd, Mead, 1966.

Jacobs, Andrew. "As Joyous as It Is Macabre; A Mexican Holiday Ensures the Dead Have Their Day." *New York Times*, November 3, 1999.

James, E.O. *Seasonal Feasts and Festivals*. 1961. Reprint. Detroit: Omnigraphics, 1993.

Jarvie, Grant. *Highland Games: The Making of the Myth*. Edinburgh: Edinburgh University Press, 1991.

Jobes, Gertrude. *Dictionary of Mythology, Folklore, and Symbols*. New York: Scarecrow Press, 1962.

Johnson, F. Ernest, ed. *Religious Symbolism*. New York: Institute for Religious and Social Studies, 1955.

Jones, Lindsay, ed. *Encyclopedia of Religion*. 2nd ed. 15 vols. Detroit: Macmillan Reference USA, 2005.

Kachun, Mitch. *Festivals of Freedom: Memory and Meaning in African American Emancipation Celebrations*. Amherst: University of Massachusetts Press, 2003.

Kapoor, Sukhbir Singh. *Sikh Festivals*. Vero Beach, FL: Rourke Enterprises, 1989.

Karenga, Maulana. *The African American Holiday of Kwanzaa*. Los Angeles: University of Sankore Press, 1988.

Kavasch, E. Barrie. *Enduring Harvests: Native American Foods and Festivals for Every Season*. Old Saybrook, CT: Globe Pequot Press, 1995.

Kennedy, Richard S. *The International Dictionary of Religion*. New York: Crossroad, 1984.

King, John. *The Celtic Druids' Year: Seasonal Cycles of the Ancient Celts*. London: Blandford, 1995.

King, Noel Q. *Religions of Africa: A Pilgrimage into Traditional Religions*. New York: Harper & Row, 1970.

Leach, Maria, ed. *Funk & Wagnalls Standard Dictionary of Folklore, Mythology and Legend*. San Francisco: Harper & Row, 1984.

Lemprière, John. *Lemprière's Classical Dictionary*. Revised ed. London: Bracken, 1994.

Lemprière, John. *Lemprière's Classical Dictionary of Proper Names Mentioned in Ancient Authors*. 3rd ed. London: Routledge, 1984.

Long, George. *The Folklore Calendar*. 1930. Reprint. Detroit: Omnigraphics, 1990.

Lord, Priscilla Sawyer, and Daniel J. Foley. *Easter Garland*. 1963. Reprint. Detroit: Omnigraphics, 1999.

Lord, Priscilla Sawyer, and Daniel J. Foley. *Easter the World Over*. Philadelphia: Chilton Book Co., 1971.

MacDonald, Margaret R., ed. *The Folklore of World Holidays*. Detroit: Gale Research, 1992.

McClester, Cedric. *Kwanzaa: Everything You Always Wanted to Know but Didn't Know Where to Ask*. 30th anniversary edition. New York: Gumbs and Thomas, 1997.

McSpadden, J. Walker. *The Book of Holidays*. New York: Crowell, 1958.

Medearis, Angela S. *The Seven Days of Kwanzaa*. New York: Scholastic, 1994.

Menard, Valerie. *The Latino Holiday Book: From Cinco de Mayo to Día de los Muertos— The Celebrations and Traditions of Hispanic-Americans*. New York: Marlowe and Co., 2004.

Merin, Jennifer, and Elizabeth B. Burdick. *International Directory of Theatre, Dance, and Folklore Festivals*. Westport, CT: Greenwood Press, 1979.

Metford, J.C.J. *The Christian Year*. New York: Crossroad, 1991.

Miles, Clement A. *Christmas in Ritual and Tradition, Christian and Pagan*. 1912. Reprint. Detroit: Omnigraphics, 1990.

Miller, Mary, and Karl Taube. *An Illustrated Dictionary of the Gods and Symbols of Ancient Mexico and the Maya*. New York: Thames and Hudson, 1997.

Monks, James L. *Great Catholic Festivals*. New York: Henry Schuman, 1951.

Mowrey, Marc, and Tim Redmond. *Not in Our Backyard: The People and Events That Shaped America's Modern Environmental Movement*. New York: W. Morrow, 1993.

Murphy, Joseph M. *Santería: African Spirits in America*. Boston: Beacon Press, 1988.

Neely, William. *Daytona, U.S.A.* Tucson: AXTEX Corp., 1979.

Oki, Morihiro. *India: Fairs and Festivals*. Tokyo: Gakken Co., 1989.

Olderr, Steven. *Symbolism: A Comprehensive Dictionary*. Jefferson, NC: McFarland, 1986.

Opoku, A.A. *Festivals of Ghana*. Accra, Ghana: Ghana Pub. Corp., 1970.

Owen, David. *The Making of the Masters: Clifford Roberts, Augusta National, and Golf's Most Prestigious Tournament*. New York: Simon & Schuster, 1999.

Parise, Frank, ed. *The Book of Calendars*. New York: Facts on File, 1982.

Parrinder, Geoffrey. *A Dictionary of Non-Christian Religions*. Philadelphia: Westminster Press, 1971.

Penner, Lucille Recht. *The Thanksgiving Book*. New York: Hastings House, 1986.

Pike, Royston. *Round the Year with the World's Religions*. 1950. Reprint. Detroit: Omnigraphics, 1992.

Purdy, Susan. *Festivals for You to Celebrate*. Philadelphia: Lippincott, 1969.

Rabin, Carol Price. *Music Festivals in Europe and Britain*. Revised ed. Stockbridge, MA: Berkshire Traveller Press, 1984.

Reichard, Gladys. *Navajo Religion: A Study of Symbolism*. 2nd ed. Princeton: Princeton University Press, 1974.

Renard, John. *Seven Doors to Islam: Spirituality and the Religious Life of Muslims*. Berkeley: University of California Press, 1996.

Renberg, Dalia Hardof. *The Complete Family Guide to Jewish Holidays*. New York: Adama Books, 1985.

Rest, Friedrich. *Our Christian Symbols*. New York: Pilgrim Press, 1954.

Revie, Alastair. *Wonderful Wimbledon*. London: Pelham, 1972.

Richard, E.G. *Mapping Time: The Calendar and Its History*. Oxford: Oxford University Press, 1998.

Robertson, Max. *Wimbledon: Centre Court of the Game*. 3rd ed. London: BBC Books, 1987.

Sampson, Curt. *The Masters: Golf, Money, and Power in Augusta*. New York: Villard, 1998.

Sang-su, Choe. *Annual Customs of Korea*. Seoul: Seomun-dang, 1983.

Sanon, Arun. *Festive India*. New Delhi: Frank Bros., 1986.

Santino, Jack. *All Around the Year: Holidays and Celebrations in American Life*. Urbana: University of Illinois Press, 1994.

Santino, Jack. *Halloween and Other Festivals of Death and Life*. Knoxville: University of Tennessee Press, 1994.

Schaun, George, Virginia Schaun, and David Wisniewski. *American Holidays and Special Days*. 3rd ed. Lanham: Maryland Historical Press, 2002.

Schmidt, Leigh Eric. *Consumer Rites: The Buying and Selling of American Holidays*. Princeton: Princeton University Press, 1995.

Scullard, H.H. *Festivals and Ceremonies of the Roman Republic*. Ithaca, NY: Cornell University Press, 1981.

Serran-Pagan, Gines. *Pamplona-Grazalema: From the Public Square to the Bullring*. New York: Enquire Print & Pub., 1980.

Sharma, Brijendra Nath. *Festivals of India*. New Delhi: Abhinav Publications, 1978.

Shemanski, Frances. *A Guide to Fairs and Festivals in the United States*. Westport, CT: Greenwood Press, 1984.

Shemanski, Frances. *A Guide to World Fairs and Festivals*. Westport, CT: Greenwood Press, 1985.

Sivananda, Swami. *Hindu Fasts and Festivals*. 8th ed. Shivanandanagar, India: Divine Life Society, 1997.

Smith, Huston. *The Illustrated World's Religions*. San Francisco: HarperSanFrancisco, 1994.

Spicer, Dorothy Gladys. *Festivals of Western Europe*. 1958. Reprint. Detroit: Omnigraphics, 1993.

Spicer, Dorothy Gladys. *The Book of Festivals*. 1937. Reprint. Detroit: Omnigraphics, 1990.

Spicer, Dorothy Gladys. *Yearbook of English Festivals*. 1954. Reprint. Detroit: Omnigraphics, 1993.

Stepanchuk, Carol, and Charles Wong. *Mooncakes and Hungry Ghosts: Festivals of China*. San Francisco: China Books & Periodicals, 1991.

Stutley, Margaret, and James Stutley. *A Dictionary of Hinduism*. San Francisco: Harper & Row, 1977.

Taylor, Dawson. *The Masters: Golf's Most Prestigious Tournament*. Chicago: Contemporary Books, 1986.

Thomas, Paul. *Festivals and Holidays in India*. Bombay: D.B. Taraporevala Sons, 1971.

Thomas, Paul. *Hindu Religion, Customs, and Manners*. 6th ed. New York: APT Books, 1981.

Thompson, Sue Ellen. *Halloween Program Sourcebook*. Detroit: Omnigraphics, 2000.

Thurley, Elizabeth. *Through the Year in Japan*. London: Batsford Academic and Educational, 1985.

Trawicky, Bernard, and Ruth W. Gregory. *Anniversaries and Holidays*. 5th ed. Chicago: American Library Assocation, 2000.

Trepp, Leo. *The Complete Book of Jewish Observance*. New York: Summit Books, 1980.

Tuleja, Tad. *Curious Customs: The Stories Behind 296 Popular American Rituals*. New York: Harmony, 1987.

Underhill, Muriel M. *The Hindu Religious Year*. London: Oxford University Press, 1921.

Urlin, Ethel L. *Festivals, Holy Days, and Saints' Days*. 1915. Reprint. Detroit: Omnigraphics, 1992.

Van Straalen, Alice. *The Book of Holidays Around the World*. New York: Dutton, 1986.

Von Grunebaum, Gustave E. *Muhammadan Festivals*. New York: Schuman, 1951.

Weiser, Franz Xaver. *Handbook of Christian Feasts and Customs*. New York: Harcourt, Brace, 1958.

Weiser, Franz Xaver. *The Holyday Book*. New York: Harcourt, Brace, 1956.

Welbon, Guy Richard, and Glenn E. Yocum. *Religious Festivals in South India and Sri Lanka*. New Delhi: Manohar Publications, 1982.

Whibley, Leonard. *A Companion of Greek Studies*. 3rd ed. Cambridge: University Press, 1916.

Wiggins, William H. Jr. *O Freedom! Afro-American Emancipation Celebrations*. Knoxville: University of Tennessee Press, 2000.

Williams-Myers, Albert James. *Long Hammering: Essays on the Forging of an African-American Presence in the Hudson River Valley in the Early Twentieth Century*. Trenton, NJ: Africa World Press, 1994.

Zabilka, Gladys. *Customs and Culture of Okinawa*. 2nd ed. Rutland, VT: C.E. Tuttle, 1973.

Appendices

Appendix A
Calendars throughout History:
An Overview of
Calendar Systems around the World

This section provides information on calendars in various parts of the world and within major religious traditions. Following a general historical overview, these calendars are discussed in the order in which they were developed or established:

CALENDARS THROUGHOUT HISTORY: AN OVERVIEW

The calendar is so ordinary, and yet so important, that one can hardly imagine a time when it did not exist. It is a fundamental commodity of life. Its significance is so great that in some cultures the institution and maintenance of dating systems have sacred status, and they fall under the jurisdiction of religious authorities.

Around the globe, through centuries of human history, a wide range of different calendars have been used to order time in a systematic manner—a need that all human civilizations share. Today, the Western Gregorian calendar serves as an international standard for business and diplomatic purposes. On the world's stage, this is a recent development, and people of various religions, nations, and societies still employ many other calendars to mark the passing of time. The characteristics of these calendars are as diverse as the societies that developed them. All calendars, however, serve the common purpose of enabling people to work together to accomplish specific goals.

In the broadest sense, a calendar consists of the set of rules that a society uses to determine which days are ordinary and which are holy, or holidays.

Thousands of years ago, before the written historical record began, people lived in small tribal societies based on hunting and gathering. Activities were likely coordinated by word of mouth, and time-keeping methods were fairly uncomplicated. People probably used days as indications of time, and perhaps they even recognized periods similar to months through observing changes in the moon's appearance. They would have observed seasonal and annual patterns, but without a formal system of reckoning them. Almost certainly, their needs did not demand anything as complex as a decade or century.

Over the course of time, people began living in agricultural communities with larger populations and diversified work forces. This shift required that people become more interdependent. For example, if farmers and city dwellers were going to conduct business efficiently, they must come to the marketplace at the same time. As a result, the need for a tool to arrange societal events became apparent.

Ancient Egyptians and Babylonians Systematize Their Calendars

The first two cultures that influenced the development of the Western Gregorian calendar were the Babylonians and Egyptians. Both shared similar characteristics—an agricultural base, a large population spread over a significant expanse of land, and a need to gather together at regular intervals to observe religious festivals. The responsibility for forming a central time-reckoning system so that people would know when to arrive at these festivals was placed in the hands of the respective religious communities.

To develop their calendars, both groups followed similar approaches. They divided time into three major divisions—what we now recognize as days, months, and years—and then went about calculating the exact duration of each category. The questions faced by the ancient Babylonians and Egyptians were the same questions all subsequent calendar makers have had to address:

- How long is a day?
- How long is a month?
- How long is a year?

These values may seem obvious to a modern observer, but it took centuries of ongoing observations, measurements, and calculations to set them.

The Day

The basic building block of all calendars is the day. The length of the day is set by the amount of time in which the earth completes one rotation on its axis. During the fifth century B.C.E. (Before Common Era, which is equivalent to the term B.C.), the Babylonians divided this duration of time into twenty-four segments that we now know as hours. However, because accurate measurement of seconds and even minutes was not possible until the sixteenth century C.E. (Common Era, equivalent to A.D.), the length of those hours has not always been fixed.

The day was given scientific regularity only with the development of accurate clocks. The demand for this accuracy was a byproduct of the interest in maritime navigation that came with the Renaissance.

The Month

A lunar month, the period of a complete cycle of the phases of the moon, lasts approximately twenty-nine-and-a-half days. It is easy for all to recognize, short enough to be counted without using large numbers, matches closely with the female menstrual cycle and, given its relation to the tidal cycle, with the duration of cyclic behavior in some marine animals. Its simplicity and minimal ease of observation (if one discounts cloudy skies) led to its great significance, and it was widely used as the basis for calendars in many cultures. The length of each month varied according to the culture. For example, the Babylonians alternated between twenty-nine- and thirty-day months, while the Egyptians fixed them at thirty days.

The Seasons and the Year

But the problem inherent in the use of a lunar calendar is that the cycles of the sun, not the moon, determine the seasons, the predictability of which is essential to the success of agriculture. The seasons could be determined by solar observation, either by measuring the cycle of the midday shadow cast by a stick placed vertically in the ground or by sophisticated astronomical calculations. Either system resulted in a solar year of approximately 365 days, incompatible with the twelve twenty-nine-and-a-half-day lunar months that resulted in a 354-day year.

Civilizations attempted to reconcile lunar months with the solar year in varied ways. The most influential ancient effort was that of the Egyptian astronomers. Working from precise mathematical observations and borrowing from Babylonian astronomy, they drew up the Roman calendar that Julius Caesar introduced.

Perhaps the most difficult issue faced by calendar makers was establishing the length of the year. Although measuring a complete cycle of seasons may not seem complicated, it created significant problems for many calendar systems.

Each season in a cycle was marked by weather changes. Some seasons were warm, others cold; some had high levels of precipitation, others low. This cycling of the seasons originally defined the year—a period of time important to agrarian cultures that depended heavily on the ability to predict optimal planting and harvesting times.

Each season contained several new moons or months. The cycling of the moon and the cycling of weather patterns were not synchronized. This led to different systems for measuring a year's length.

Babylonians and Egyptians Disagree

In the fifth century B.C.E., the Babylonians and Egyptians both arrived at a specific number of days in the year, but their conclusions were different. The Babylonians claimed that the year was 360 days long while the Egyptians more accurately estimated the year at 365 days. The discrepancy between the two lengths of the year is puzzling.

One possibility for the difference is that the Babylonians simply miscalculated. This is unlikely, however, in light of their sophisticated astronomical and mathematical systems. Another explanation is that they rounded their figure from 365 to 360 to facilitate the interaction of the year with their base-twelve numerical system.

The problem with the Babylonians' five-day omission was that the months would not stay in line with the seasons of the year. Each year the beginning of each month would occur at least five days earlier in relation to the position of the sun. Eventually, the months would be completely dissociated from the seasons in which they originally occurred. To correct this problem, the Babylonians periodically added months to the calendar, a process termed intercalation, which can also be used to add "leap" days or weeks.

The Babylonians were not the only people to face the problem of keeping the months coordinated with the seasons. Even though the Egyptians calculated the length of the year more accurately, they too realized that their determination was not exactly perfect.

The Solar System Affects the Length of the Year

Precise division of a year into months or days is impossible because the seasons, the phases of the moon, and the ever-cycling periods of daylight and nighttime are determined by the earth's relationship to the sun and the moon. The movements of these heavenly bodies do not neatly coincide with the mathematical systems of any human civilization.

The quest to discover the secrets of how the universe fits together has motivated astronomers throughout history. In the second century C.E., Ptolemy, a Greek astronomer, formulated the theory that the earth was the center of the universe and that the sun, stars, moon, and other planets revolved around it. In the fifteenth century C.E., the Polish astronomer Copernicus advocated the notion that the earth rotated on an axis and, along with the other heavenly bodies in the solar system, revolved around the sun. Shortly after the Copernican assertion, Galileo presented supporting evidence based on observations he had made using his invention, the telescope.

The Gap between the Lunar and Solar Cycles

We now understand that an 11.25-day difference exists between the 354-day lunar cycle that determines the months and the 365.25-day solar cycle that determines the seasons. Calendar systems have applied three main strategies in their search for a solution to this discrepancy.

The first, called a lunar calendar, ignores the seasons and allows the lunar (moon) cycle to be the basis of the year, as the Islamic calendar does. A second is called a lunisolar calendar. It involves an elaborate system of calculations to add days or months to the lunar year until it coincides with the solar year. The Jewish calendar is one example. The third system, which originated with the Egyptians, is the pure solar calendar. It allows the sun to determine not only the seasons but the length of the months as well.

CHINESE CALENDAR

The Chinese calendar, widely used in Asian countries, is based on the oldest system of time measurement still in use, with its epoch believed to be 2953 B.C.E. Part of the reason that the Chinese calendar has survived intact for so long is that, until the middle of the twentieth century, the document was considered sacred. Any changes to the calendar were tightly controlled by imperial authorities, and the penalty for illegally tampering with the time-keeping system was death. Until the rise of Communism in China during the twentieth century, the official calendar was presented to the emperor, governors, and other dignitaries in an annual ceremony. Since 1912 the Gregorian calendar has been in use for civic purposes.

The Chinese New Year takes place on the new moon nearest to the point which is defined in the West as the fifteenth degree of the zodiacal sign of Aquarius. Each of the twelve months in the Chinese year is twenty-nine or thirty days long and is divided into two parts, each of which is two weeks long. The Chinese calendar, like all lunisolar systems, requires periodic adjustment to keep the lunar and solar cycles integrated; therefore, an intercalary month is added when necessary.

The names of each of the twenty-four two-week periods sometimes correspond to festivals that occur during the period. Beginning with the New Year, which takes place in late January or early February, these periods are known by the following names: Spring Begins (New Year), the Rain Water, the Excited Insects, the Vernal Equinox, the Clear and Bright, the Grain Rains, the Summer Begins, the Grain Fills, the Grain in Ear, the Summer Solstice, the Slight Heat, the Great Heat, the Autumn Begins, the Limit of Heat, the White Dew, the Autumnal Equinox, the Cold Dew, the Hoar Frost Descends, the Winter Begins, the Little Snow, the Heavy Snow, the Winter Solstice, the Little Cold, and the Great Cold.

INDIAN CALENDARS

Throughout its history, India has used a plethora of calendars and dating systems, of which there have been two basic types: a civil calendar that was changed with each new regime and a religious calendar that was maintained by the Hindus. In addition, each geographical region had its own Hindu calendar, although most of the calendars shared some elements that they gleaned from a common heritage.

India's Original Calendar

India's first time-reckoning system emerged before 1000 B.C.E. It was based on astronomical observations and consisted of a solar year of 360 days comprising twelve lunar months. The discrepancy between the length of the solar and lunar years was corrected by intercalating a month every sixty months.

In 1200 C.E., the Muslims brought the use of their calendar to India for administrative purposes, and the British introduced the Gregorian calendar in 1757. Even so, each separate state maintained a calendar that its citizens used in their daily interactions. Throughout India's colonial days, the entrenchment of these local calendars created havoc for the central government because any given date would yield up to six different interpretations throughout the country. The difficulties continued after independence, when an Indian government took control in 1947.

The Saka Era Calendar

When India became a unified and independent nation, the differences among regional calendars included more than thirty methods for determining the beginning of the era, the year, and the month. These variations in the Hindu calendar were the culmination of nearly 5,000 years of history.

In 1952 the Calendar Reform Committee was established and charged with devising a unified system that would adhere to modern astronomical calculations and accommodate the calculation of dates for religious festivals. As a result of the committee's work, the National Calendar of India was adopted in 1957.

The National Calendar of India is a twelve-month lunisolar calendar with traditional Hindu month names. Some months are thirty days in length; others are thirty-one days. The year is 365 days long, with an extra day added to the end of the first month every four years (coinciding with leap years in the Gregorian calendar).

The National Calendar of India counts years from the inception of the Saka Era (s.e.)—the spring equinox in 79 c.e. In the year in which it was adopted, the first day of the first month (Caitra) was Caitra 1, 1879 s.e., which corresponded to March 22, 1957 c.e. Using the Gregorian calendar for comparison, the year 1926 in the Saka Era began on March 22, 2004 c.e.

Dates for religious festivals, which depend on lunar and solar movements, are calculated annually by the India Meteorological Department, although regional variations still exist. For administrative purposes, the Indian government currently follows the Gregorian calendar.

Hindu Calendar

Although each geographical region of India has had its own calendar, all are based on an ancient calendar, the earliest time measurement system in India, found in texts thought to date from as early as 1000 b.c.e. Of the multitudinous regional Hindu calendars, used only for religious holidays, the majority divide an approximate solar year of 360 days into twelve months. Each day is 1/30th of a month, with the intercalation of a leap month every sixty months. Time measurements based on observations of the constellations are used along with the calendar. Each month is divided into two fortnights: *krsna* (waning or dark half) and *sukla* (waxing or bright half). In southern India, the month begins with the new moon. In other parts of the country, the full moon is considered to be the beginning of the month. Many references to the Hindu calendar (depending on the source) are given as follows: month, fortnight (either S=waxing or K=waning), and number of the day in that fortnight (e.g., Rama Navami: Caitra S. 9).

The names of the Hindu months (with variant spellings) are given below, with the Burmese name for the month in brackets:

> **Caitra or Chaitra [Tagu]:** March-April
> **Vaisakha [Kasone]:** April-May
> **Jyeshta or Jyaistha [Nayhone]:** May-June
> **Ashadha or Asadha [Waso]:** June-July
> **Sravana [Wagaung]:** July-August
> **Bhadrapada [Tawthalin]:** August-September
> **Asvina [Thadingyut]:** September-October
> **Kartika or Karttika [Tazaungmone]:** October-November
> **Margasirsa or Margashirsha [Nadaw]:** November-December
> **Pausa or Pausha [Pyatho]:** December-January

Magha [Tabodwei]: January-February
Phalguna [Tabaung]: February-March

Jain Calendar

The Indian calendars generally have lunar months, but the duration of an average year is a sidereal year. The dates of most all the Jain festivals are calculated using such a lunisolar calendar. In northern India, the beginning of the month occurs at the full moon. This means that the first fortnight is waning. People in southern India typically mark the beginning of the month at the new moon and the first fortnight is waxing. Jains begin the new year in the autumn with the Dewali festival commemorating the liberation (achievement of Nirvana) of their founder, Nataputta Mahavira. The Hindu new year generally occurs in the spring; however, in Gujarat, the Hindu new year also starts with Dewali.

Mahavira's achievement of Nirvana (at his death) in 527 B.C.E. also serves as the epoch for the Jain calendar. Dewali 2004 C.E., for example, begins the year 2531 V.N.S. (Vira Nirvana Samvat).

Cyclical Eras

The Jain concept of how time cycles through progressive and regressive eras also differs from that of the Hindus. Jains believe that a complete cycle of time consists of twelve separate units. Of these, six represent deteriorating conditions and six represent improving conditions. The third and fourth units of both half-cycles represent times when neither extreme predominates. Only during these units can the Tirthankaras be born.

Currently, the earth is experiencing the fifth unit in the declining part of the time cycle. Risabha, the first Tirthankara of the current age, is said to have been born during the third unit; Mahavira was born at the close of the fourth. Each of the last two units in the declining half-cycle has a duration of 21,000 years.

The months of the Jain calendar are given below. The names of the Jain months are nearly the same as those of the Hindu months, but the Jain new year begins in Kartika, rather than in Caitra.

Kartika: October-November
Margasira: November-December
Pausa: December-January
Magha: January-February
Phalguna: February-March
Caitra: March-April
Vaisakha: April-May
Jyestha: May-June

Asadha: June-July
Sravana: July-August
Bhadrapada: August-September
Asvina: September-October

Buddhist Calendar

The Buddhist calendar, which originated in India, varies among different geographic locations, as does the Hindu calendar, with which it shares many common elements. Buddhism spread outside India after the Buddha's death in 483 B.C.E. The method for determining the date of the new year is not uniform among Buddhist sects. Theravada Buddhists (those primarily in Sri Lanka, Laos, Burma/Myanmar, Thailand, and Cambodia), using a Hindu calendar as their basis, calculate the months by the moon and the new year by the sun's position in relation to the twelve segments of the heavens, each named for a sign of the zodiac. The solar new year begins when the sun enters Aries, usually between April 13th and 18th. The lunar months alternate between twenty-nine and thirty days in length. The first lunar month is usually sometime in December, except for the Burmese Buddhist calendar, which begins in April (see Hindu Calendar above for Burmese names). Periodically, the seventh month has an intercalary day, and an intercalary month is added every few years. Cambodia, Laos, and Thailand refer to the months by number. Tibetan Buddhists, whose calendar has been heavily influenced by the Chinese calendar, begin their new year at the full moon nearest to the midpoint of Aquarius. Mahayana Buddhists (those primarily in Tibet, Mongolia, China, Korea, and Japan) base their holidays on Buddhist, Chinese, or Gregorian calendars.

Sikh Calendar

The Sikh calendar dates from the religion's inception in the fifteenth century C.E. It is a lunar calendar that is based on the moon's movement from one zodiac sign into the next rather than on the phase of the moon. The dates of some festivals, however, derive from the phase of the moon. The beginning of a new month is called the Sangrand. It is announced in the Sikh house of worship (gurdwara) but it is not a festival day.

Sikh festivals are marked on a special calendar called the Sikh Gurpurab Calendar. A gurpurab is a date commemorating births, deaths (and martyrdoms), or other important events associated with the lives of the ten Sikh human gurus or with the Sikh scriptures, the *Guru Granth Sahib*. The Gurpurab Calendar also notes the anniversary dates of historic incidents important to the Sikh faith.

The Sikh Gurpurab Calendar begins with the month of Chait (March/April), showing its inspiration from the Hindu calendar. The Sikh New Year celebration, however, falls on the first day of the second month, Basakh.

The Sikh have used several calendars since their religious tradition began in the fifteenth century. Over time, the lunar calendar called the Bikrami calendar was used predominantly. The Bikrami calendar consisted of twelve months averaging twenty-nine-and-a-half days. This yields a year that is approximately eleven days shorter than the solar year. To keep the lunar calendar in line with the solar seasons, the Sikh calendar intercalated an extra lunar month whenever two new moons occur within the same solar month. The thirteenth lunar month then took the name of the solar month in which it fell. The names of the regular twelve lunar months are listed in the *Guru Granth Sahib*.

The solar component of the Bikrami calendar, however, did not correspond exactly to the natural solar year—every seventy years a discrepancy equal to one day accrued. To resolve this problem, two calendars were developed to accurately match the natural solar year: the Nanakshai Calendar, which is based on Guru Nanak's birth, and the Khalsa Calendar, which is based on the founding of the Khalsa. In 1999 C.E., the Sikhs adopted the Nanakshai Calendar. Although the choice generated some controversy, it is now used to observe all Sikh religious holidays and has grown increasingly popular, especially among Sikh communities outside India.

The Nanakshai calendar is devised in a manner that maintains consistency with the western Gregorian calendar so that holidays always fall on the same day of the year. It begins with the month of Chait (Chait 1 falls on March 14) and contains five months of thirty-one days and seven months of thirty days. The last month usually contains thirty days, but in leap years an extra day is added.

The Nanakshai calendar counts years from Guru Nanak's birth in 1469 C.E. The year 536 Nanakshai began in the year 2004 C.E.

The months of the Nanakshai calendar, along with variant spellings, are given below.

> **Chait** or **Chet**: March-April
> **Basakh** or **Vaisakhi**: April-May
> **Jaith** or **Jeth**: May-June
> **Har** or **Harh**: June-July
> **Sawan**: July-August
> **Bhadro** or **Bhadon**: August-September
> **Asun** or **Asu**: September-October
> **Katik**: October-November
> **Magar** or **Maghar**: November-December
> **Poh**: December-January
> **Magh**: January-February
> **Phagan** or **Phagun**: February-March

MAYAN AND AZTEC CALENDARS

The Mayan and Aztec civilizations both used what is commonly referred to as the Mesoamerican calendar. This ancient calendar may have derived from the Olmec civilization, which thrived between 1300 and 400 B.C.E. in what is now southeastern Mexico, along the Gulf. The Mesoamerican calendrical system, which probably originated between 1000 and 900 B.C.E., employed not just one calendar, but a system of two interconnecting calendars: a 260-day calendar and a 365-day calendar. These two calendars ran alongside each other. Every fifty-two years, a named day from the 260-day calendar would be the same as a named day from the 365-day calendar (there are 18,980 days in fifty-two years, and 18,980 is the least common multiple of both 365 and 260). This fifty-two-year cycle was observed by both the Mayans and the Aztecs.

Mayan civilization, in what is now southeastern Mexico, Belize, and portions of Guatemala and Honduras, flourished between about 300-900 C.E., a period known as the Classical Mayan era. The Mayans used the 260-day calendar—known as the *tzolkin*—for sacred purposes, and the 365-day solar-based calendar—called the *haab*—for agricultural purposes. The Mayan calendar system employed glyphs, small pictorial inscriptions, to represent such time periods as a day, a month, and a year, as well as to represent specific months of the year and specific days in the months. Each day was named for a god who was thought to be manifest as that day. The days' numbers were written using a combination of dots and bars. The 260-day Mayan calendar was divided into thirteen months of twenty named days. The 365-day calendar was divided into eighteen months of twenty named days plus a brief month of five days, called *Uayeb*, or "ominous days." The fifty-two-year Mayan cycle is known as the Calendar Round. The 260-day system is thought to be the only one of its kind in the world. Scholars are not certain what the significance of 260 is, though some have noted that the average duration of human pregnancy is approximately 260 days long. In addition, the Mayans had a highly developed knowledge of astronomy, and 260 was a number significant in calculating the appearance of Venus, the planet identified with the Mayan god Kukulcán. (Kukulcán was known as Quetzalcoatl to the Toltec people, who flourished in Mesoamerica—and dominated the Mayans—from the tenth century to the middle of the twelfth century.)

Mayans also developed the Long Count, an extensive system of time-reckoning that attempted to encompass the time of the world from its creation to its end. The Mayans are thought to have developed the Long Count between 400 B.C.E. and 100 C.E. From this system, they dated the creation of the world to have occurred in 3114 B.C.E. (or 3113 B.C.E., by some contemporary calculations). This Long Count, according to some scholars, will end in December 2011 (or 2012).

The Aztecs—they called themselves Mexica—dominated Mesoamerica after the Toltec empire collapsed, from the early 1300s up until the Spanish began colonization in the early 1600s. Like the Mayans, the Aztecs used the 260-day calendar divided into thirteen months of twenty days; they called it *tonalpohualli,* or "count of day." Their 365-day calendar also consisted of eighteen months of twenty days plus a period of five days that the Aztecs believed to be unlucky. The Aztecs also named their days after deities, but, unlike the Mayan system, Aztec numerical notation consisted only of dots. Aztecs probably did not use a Long Count. At the end of their fifty-two-year cycle—which they called *xiuhmolpilli,* or "year bundle"—the Aztecs celebrated the new beginning with a great renewal ceremony (*see* New Fire Ceremony).

Today, the 365-day civil calendar predominates throughout the region, though some contemporary Mayans also continue to use the 260-day calendar to observe sacred festivals.

BABYLONIAN CALENDAR

Babylonian, Sumerian, and Assyrian astronomers living in Mesopotamia hundreds of years B.C.E. developed calendars that would influence the later Roman Julian and Gregorian calendars. These earlier calendars were based on the phases of the moon and were closely related to the religious life of the cultures that developed them. The influence of the Mesopotamian civilizations on the global art of calendar making was far reaching because many of the techniques they developed were adopted by future societies.

Of the various cultures that thrived in Mesopotamia, the Babylonians seem to have most significantly influenced calendar making. Many details of the evolution of the Babylonian calendar have been lost over the centuries, but it is known that the calendar was lunar in nature, had a system of intercalation, had months divided into seven-day units, and had days with twenty-four hours.

Because these early calendar makers were pioneers in the field, they were among the first to be confronted with the discrepancy between the lunar and solar cycles—a problem that had the potential to render any calendar system ineffective. To reconcile the two natural courses, the Babylonians worked out a schedule whereby an extra month was periodically intercalated. The process of intercalation, termed *iti dirig,* seems to have been rather arbitrary at first, but by 380 B.C.E. a formal system was adopted, adding an extra month in the third, sixth, eighth, eleventh, seventeenth, and nineteenth years. Many other cultures, including the Greeks, developed similar intercalation schemes that may have drawn their inspiration from the Babylonian model.

Although the origin of the week has been a subject of much research and debate among scholars since the time of Plutarch (46-119 C.E.), most agree that the Babylonians are the primary source for the week in the Western civil calendar. Many researchers also conclude that the Babylonians devised the week as a part of their religious practices. They have observed that years, months, and days all reflect natural cycles, but the week does not. This observation has led to some questions: Why does the week have seven days? Why are the days named after celestial bodies? Why are the days not arranged according to the order of the planets in the solar system? Many proposed solutions to these questions have surfaced over the course of time.

Details of the Babylonian calendar are few, but some are known. It appears that the major festival was the New Year celebration that took place in the spring of the year during the Babylonian month of Nisanu. On the first day of the festival, a ritual marriage was performed between the king and the high priestess, who symbolized the sovereignty of the land. On this day, the Babylonian creation myth (called *Enuma elish* from its opening words, "When on high") was read aloud. On the fifth day, Rites of Atonement were observed. During the Rites the king, as a representative of the people, endured a ritual of abasement to atone for the sins of the people against the gods. On the seventh day, the Festival of the Sun, or spring equinox, took place.

Zoroastrian Calendars

Zoroastrianism originated in Persia (now Iran) and was founded by Zoroaster, who is thought to have lived around 628-551 B.C.E., although some scholars have posited that he lived several hundred years earlier. Zoroastrianism spread after he converted a tribal prince, Vishtaspa, to this new religion. By the time of the Sasanian dynasty (226-651 C.E.), Zoroastrianism was the Persian state religion. After the Muslim conquest of Persia in the middle of the seventh century, many Zoroastrians migrated to India, particularly the western state of Gujarat, where they became known as the "Parsi" (meaning "Persian") community.

The Zoroastrian calendar derived from the ancient Babylonian calendar, except that the former's days and months were dedicated to spiritual beings. In the mid-eighteenth century, some Parsis adopted the Persian calendar and called it the *qadimi* calendar, giving rise to the Zoroastrian sect known as Kadmi. Others remained with the traditional religion and calendar, though it was a month behind the Kadmi calendar, and were referred to as Shenshais, often rendered Shahanshahis. In 1906 the Fasli sect was founded. It advocated the use of a calendar closer to the Gregorian one, in which the new year would always begin at the vernal equinox and which would add an extra day every four years.

All three Zoroastrian calendars have the same twelve thirty-day months with five intercalary days called *Gatha* coming at the end of the twelfth month. The differences are in how each reconciles the lunar year with the natural solar year. As a result, a single date on each Zoroastrian calendar corresponds to three different

Gregorian dates. For example, in 2002, the first day of the first month (Frawardin 1) fell on March 21 according to the Fasli calendar, on July 22 according to the Kadmi calendar, and on August 21 according to the Shahanshai calendar.

The Zoroastrian month names and approximate English meanings are:

> **Frawardin or Fravardin** (Humanity): March-April*
> **Ardwahist or Ardibehest** (Truth and Righteousness): April-May
> **Hordad or Khordad** (Perfection): May-June
> **Tir** (Sirius, the Dog Star): June-July
> **Amurdad or Amardad** (Immortality): July-August
> **Shahrewar or Sherever** (Benevolent Dominion): August-September
> **Mihr or Meher** (Fair Dealing): September-October
> **Aban or Avan** (Water or Purity): October-November
> **Adar or Adur** (Fire): November-December
> **Dae or Deh** (Creator): December-January
> **Vohuman or Bahman** (Good Mind): January-February
> **Spendarmad or Aspandarmad** (Holy Devotion): February-March
> * Gregorian month ranges corresponding to the Fasli calendar

ROMAN JULIAN CALENDAR

Julius Caesar ordered the change of the reformed Roman lunar calendar to a solar-based one in 46 B.C.E. The intercalation of ninety days corrected a growing discrepancy between the seasons and the months in which they had traditionally fallen. Prior to this intercalation, the Roman civic year had come to be about three months "ahead" of the seasons, so spring began in June. The year 46 B.C.E. was assigned 445 days to make the adjustment; it was called *ultimus annus confusionis*, "the last year of the muddled reckoning." The new calendar, based on the Egyptian solar calendar, provided for a year of 365 days, with an additional day in February every fourth year. The addition of this leap year and day gives the Julian year an average length of 365.25 days—very close to the actual solar cycle. The Julian calendar (O.S., or Old Style) remained in civic use in the West for more than 1,600 years. It is still the basis of the "Old Calendarist" Orthodox Christian liturgical calendar and is used by all Orthodox Christian churches to determine the date of Easter.

JEWISH CALENDAR

In 358 C.E., Hillel II introduced a permanent calendar based on mathematical and astronomical calculations, eliminating the need for eyewitness sightings of the new moon with which the new month begins. Due to doubts as to when the new moon appeared, biblical law stated that those living outside Israel would observe two days rather than one for each festival, except for Yom Kippur, the Day of Atonement. The Talmud required that this custom continue even after the calendar was formulated. The Jewish era begins with the date of Creation, traditionally set in 3761 B.C.E.

Only slight modifications were made to Hillel's calendar, and it has remained unchanged since the tenth century. A day is reckoned from sundown to sundown, a week contains seven days, a month is either twenty-nine or thirty days long, and a year has twelve lunar months plus about eleven days, or 353, 354, or 355 days. To reconcile the calendar with the annual solar cycle, a thirteenth month of thirty days is intercalated in the third, sixth, eighth, eleventh, fourteenth, seventeenth, and nineteenth years of a nineteen-year cycle; a leap year may contain from 383 to 385 days. The civil calendar begins with the month of Tishri, the first day of which is Rosh Hashanah, the New Year. The cycle of the religious calendar begins on Nisan 15, Passover (Pesach).

The names of the months of the Jewish calendar were borrowed from the Babylonians. The pre-exilic books of the Bible usually refer to the months according to their numerical order, beginning with Tishri, but there are four months mentioned with different names: Nisan/Abib, Iyyar/Ziv, Tishri/Ethanim, and Heshvan/Bul:

Nisan: mid-March to mid-April
Iyyar: mid-April to mid-May
Sivan: mid-May to mid-June
Tammuz: mid-June to mid-July
Av: mid-July to mid-August
Elul: mid-August to mid-September
Tishri: mid-September to mid-October
Heshvan: mid-October to mid-November
Kislev: mid-November to mid-December
Tevet: mid-December to mid-January
Shevat: mid-January to mid-February
Adar: mid-February to mid-March
*The intercalary month of Adar II is inserted before Adar as needed.

ISLAMIC CALENDAR

The Islamic calendar, called *hijri* or Hegirian, is still strictly lunar-based. Moreover, the *actual* beginning of a month depends on the sighting of the new moon. Traditionally, if the sky is overcast and the new moon is not visible, the previous month runs another thirty days before the new month begins. However, the *practical* beginning of a month is according to astronomical calculations of lunar cycles. The

Islamic era begins July 16, 622 C.E., the date of the hegira or flight into exile of the Prophet Muhammad from Mecca to Medina.

There are twelve Islamic lunar months, some of twenty-nine, others of thirty days; these yield 354 days in the Islamic year. The fixed holidays set in the Islamic calendar thus move "backward" about ten days each year in relation to the Gregorian calendar. In roughly thirty-six years, Ramadan, the Islamic holy month of fasting, moves back through the entire solar year. The Islamic day runs from sundown to sundown.

Other calendars were developed in Islamic countries for the sake of agriculture, which depends on a solar calendar. The Coptic calendar, a variation of the Julian, was used until recently, but it is now limited primarily to Egypt and the Sudan, countries with large Coptic populations. The Turkish fiscal calendar, also Julian-based, was used in the Ottoman Empire. Nowadays, the Gregorian calendar is followed nearly everywhere for civic purposes, and the Islamic calendar determines only the days of religious observance. Saudi Arabia is one exception, and, at least officially, employs the Islamic calendar as the calendar of reference.

The names of the Islamic months are an ancient reflection of the seasons of the solar year:

> **Muharram:** the sacred month
> **Safar:** the month which is void
> **Rabi al-Awwal:** the first spring
> **Rabi ath-Thani:** the second spring
> **Jumada-l-Ula:** the first month of dryness
> **Jumada-th-Thaniyyah:** the second month of dryness
> **Rajab:** the revered month
> **Shaban:** the month of division
> **Ramadan:** the month of great heat
> **Shawwal:** the month of hunting
> **Dhu al-Qadah:** the month of rest
> **Dhu al-Hijjah:** the month of pilgrimage

GREGORIAN CALENDAR

By the late sixteenth century, the difference between the Julian calendar and the seasons had grown to ten days because the Julian year, averaging 365.25 days, was slightly longer than the actual length of a solar year, which, by modern calculation, is known to be 365.242199 days long. Fixed holy days began to occur in the "wrong" season, both for the church and for farmers, who used certain holy days to determine planting and harvesting. Pope Gregory XIII ordered the reform that deleted ten days from the year 1582; in that year, October 15 was the day after October 5. This change, coupled with the elimination of leap days in "century" years unless evenly divisible by 400 (e.g., 1600, 2000), corrected the calendar so that today only occasional "leap seconds" are needed to keep months and seasons synchronized. At first adopted only in Roman Catholic countries, the Gregorian calendar (N.S., or New Style) gradually came to be accepted throughout the West. Today, it has become the calendar used by most of the world, at least for business and government.

CHRISTIAN LITURGICAL CALENDARS

Both the Jewish and the Greek time-keeping systems are clearly visible within the Christian liturgical calendars. Most immediately recognizable, however, are the influences of the Jewish calendar. The movable feasts within Christianity, such as Easter and Pentecost, have connections to Jewish celebrations.

Many branches of Christianity follow similar calendars to mark the holy days of the year. The calendar focuses attention on special incidents in Jesus's life and also provides for the remembrance of many saints and historical events. It includes two types of dates: movable feasts, which are typically established based on their relationship to the Feast of the Resurrection (Easter), and fixed holidays.

Old and New Calendars

Throughout the centuries the Julian Calendar has been in use in both the Christian East and West. The introduction of the Gregorian Calendar fueled the ever accelerating animosity between the two Churches. Even though many in the East recognized the inadequacies of the Julian Calendar, leading some to go so far as to devise new calendars for themselves, it nevertheless remained in use throughout the Byzantine period and beyond.

With the introduction of the Gregorian Calendar, Pope Gregory tried to convince the Orthodox to adopt it, but the latter refused because it would alter the dating of Easter. Canon 7 of the Council of Nicea (325) set clear regulations for the dating of Easter. To adopt the Gregorian Calendar would mean having Easter coincide with the Jewish Passover, something clearly against the canonical stipulations.

Orthodox Churches continued to use the Julian Calendar until May 1923, when the Ecumenical Patriarch Meletios IV convened an "Inter-Orthodox Congress" in Constantinople. Not all Orthodox Churches were represented. Though invited, the Churches of Alexandria, Antioch, and Jerusalem did not attend. The Church of Bulgaria was never asked. Only the Orthodox Churches of Cyprus, Greece, Romania, and Serbia participated. Even then, no unanimous decision was reached regarding the calendar of choice. It has been only in recent years that the Churches of Alexandria, Antioch, Constantinople, Cyprus, Greece, Poland, Romania, and, in 1968, Bulgaria, voted to adopt the new Gregorian Calendar. The Churches of Jerusalem, Russia, and Serbia continue to adhere to the old Julian Calendar.

Western Calendar

The western Christian liturgical year begins in late November with a season called Advent. Four weeks long, Advent provides a time during which Christians prepare for Jesus's birth. Advent is followed by Christmas and the Christmas season, when his birth is celebrated. In early January, Epiphany commemorates Jesus's appearance to the Gentiles (non-Jews). Lent is a season of introspection and penance in preparation for Easter. It concludes with Holy Week, when events in the last week of Jesus's life are highlighted. The Easter season begins on Resurrection Sunday and lasts until Ascension Day, commemorating his ascension into heaven. The season of Pentecost begins with the celebration of the coming of the Holy Spirit. The longest season of the year, Trinity, completes the cycle.

The revised Roman Catholic calendar of 1969 changed some of the days on which certain saints were honored. Days that once had been universally honored became only locally honored. According to Catholic law, followers are obligated to participate in Mass weekly on either a Saturday evening or Sunday morning and on six other days identified as holy days of obligation: Christmas, Solemnity of Mary, Ascension, Assumption of the Blessed Virgin, All Saints Day, and Immaculate Conception.

Orthodox Calendars

In the Orthodox Church two different calendars determine holidays and feast days. The first—the Julian Calendar—is attributed to the Roman Emperor Julius Caesar and bears his name. The latter—the Gregorian Calendar—emerged in the sixteenth century as an effort to correct the discrepancy between calendar time and calculated astronomical time. It added thirteen days back into the year and was named for Pope Gregory XIII, who commissioned the work.

The Orthodox liturgical calendar has five main elements: the daily cycle, the weekly cycle, the Paschal cycle, the cycle of fixed feasts, and the cycle of eight tones.

Whereas many other Christian Churches start the liturgical year with the first Sunday in Advent, the Orthodox Christian Church starts the liturgical year on September 1. In the Ecumenical Patriarchate this is observed as the Day of the Environment, with the role in the salvation of the world of the Theotokos, the mother of God, being emphasized. The Nativity of the Virgin Mary on September 8 and her Dormition on August 15 come at opposite ends of the liturgical year. Other than those included among the twelve great feasts, the other Marian feast day is December 9, the Conception of the Virgin by St. Anne.

March 25, the Annunciation, is another major feast of the Theotokos, but it is also a feast of the Conception of Christ and begins a series of feasts of the Lord. The Nativity of the Lord, as well as the Visit of the Magi, is observed in the Orthodox Church on December 25. The Circumcision of Jesus falls on January 1, the feast of Saint Basil the Great. For the Orthodox Christian, Epiphany, or Theophany as it is sometimes known, is January 6 and commemorates Christ's baptism. The feast of the Transfiguration is held on August 6.

The Paschal cycle begins four weeks before Lent, on the Sunday of the Pharisee and the Publican. Lent itself begins on Pure Monday and ends on Lazarus Saturday, the day before Palm Sunday. The Passion, the Mystical Supper, the Agony, Betrayal, Trial, Sufferings, Death, Burial and Glorious Resurrection, the Assumption into heaven of the Lord, and the Sending of His Holy Spirit upon the Apostles are all celebrated in the feasts of the Paschal cycle. The cycle ends with Pentecost Sunday, the feast of the Holy Trinity, and the Sunday of All Saints.

In addition to the special feast days of the Lord or of Mary, every day on the Orthodox Calendar commemorates some saint. These may be saints venerated by all of Christendom, Latin Church saints from early centuries, saints particular to a specific locale, or the Righteous, or Dikaios, of the Old Law.

In the medieval period of the Church, all music was organized on the basis of a system of eight tones. These tones continue to have not only musical significance but a calendrical significance as well. Beginning the first Sunday after Easter, St. Thomas Sunday, each successive week uses the texts and music of the next of the eight tones for its offices. Each day of the week has its distinctive hymns and verses for each of these eight tones. The book which contains the texts for each day's services for all eight tones is called the Parakletike.

BAHA'I CALENDAR

The Baha'i calendar, called the Badí (meaning "wondrous"), consists of nineteen months, each with nineteen days. Four intercalary days—called Ayyam-i-Ha, the Days of Ha—occur after the eighteenth month in regular years, while five are inserted in leap years. Nineteen multiplied by nineteen equals 361, plus four intercalary days equals 365. But the number nineteen was chosen for more than its mathematical convenience. The Baha'i religion's first prophet, Mirza Ali Mohammad (also known as the Bab), devised a calendar for the new religion. He had eighteen followers; thus, these nineteen original Babis are remembered in the calendar's structure.

The Nineteen-Day Feast takes place on the first day of each month and constitutes the regular Baha'i worship gathering. Each Feast follows the same three-part format: prayer, congregational business, and fellowship with a shared meal.

The Baha'i year begins on the vernal equinox, March 21. Baha'i years are numbered. Year 1 was 1844, the year of the Bab's Declaration. Each Baha'i month is named for an attribute of God:

Bahá (Splendor): March 21
Jalál (Glory): April 9
Jamál (Beauty): April 28
Azamat (Grandeur): May 17
Núr (Light): June 5
Rahmat (Mercy): June 24
Kalimát (Words): July 13
Kamál (Perfection): August 1
Asmá (Names): August 20
'Izzat (Might): September 8
Mashiyyat (Will): September 27
'Ilm (Knowledge): October 16
Qudrat (Power): November 4
Qawl (Speech): November 23
Masá'il (Questions): December 12
Sharaf (Honor): December 31
Sultán (Sovereignty): January 19
Mulk (Dominion): February 7*
'Alá' (Loftiness): March 2* (month of fasting)
*Ayyam-i-Ha (Days of Ha; intercalary days): February 26-March 1
(February 26-March 2 in leap years)

Appendix B
Tourism Information Sources
for North America

The following list includes tourism information sources for the United States, Canada, and Mexico. Within the United States, the list is organized first by state, plus the District of Columbia. These listings start with the state-wide tourism and chamber of commerce offices. Those are followed by local offices for convention and visitors' bureaus and then chambers of commerce. Listings for both Canada and Mexico also include both tourism boards and chambers of commerce.

UNITED STATES

ALABAMA

Alabama Tourism & Travel Bureau
401 Adams Ave
Suite 126
Montgomery, AL 36104
Phone: 334-242-4169; Fax: 334-242-4554
Toll-free: 800-252-2262
www.touralabama.org

Business Council of Alabama
PO Box 76
Montgomery, AL 36101
Phone: 334-834-6000; Fax: 334-241-5984
Toll-free: 800-665-9647
www.bcatoday.org

Greater Birmingham Convention & Visitors
  Bureau
2200 9th Ave N
Birmingham, AL 35203
Phone: 205-458-8000; Fax: 205-458-8086
Toll-free: 800-458-8085
www.sweetbirmingham.com

Huntsville/Madison County Convention &
  Visitor's Bureau
500 Church St
Huntsville, AL 35801
Phone: 256-551-2230; Fax: 256-551-2324
Toll-free: 800-772-2348
www.huntsville.org

Mobile Bay Convention & Visitors Bureau
1 S Water St
Mobile, AL 36602
Phone: 251-208-2000; Fax: 251-208-2060
Toll-free: 800-566-2453
www.mobile.org

Montgomery Area Chamber of Commerce
  Convention & Visitor Bureau
300 Water St
Union Stn
Montgomery, AL 36104
Phone: 334-261-1100; Fax: 334-261-1111
Toll-free: 800-240-9452
www.visitingmontgomery.com

Tuscaloosa Convention & Visitors Bureau
1305 Greensboro Ave
Tuscaloosa, AL 35401

Phone: 205-391-9200; Fax: 205-759-9002
Toll-free: 800-538-8696
www.tcvb.org

Birmingham Regional Chamber of
   Commerce
505 N 20th St
Suite 200
Birmingham, AL 35203
Phone: 205-324-2100; Fax: 205-324-2560
www.birminghamchamber.com

Chamber of Commerce of
   Huntsville/Madison County
PO Box 408
Huntsville, AL 35804
Phone: 256-535-2000; Fax: 256-535-2015
www.huntsvillealabamausa.com

Chamber of Commerce of West Alabama
PO Box 020410
Tuscaloosa, AL 35402
Phone: 205-758-7588; Fax: 205-391-0565
www.tuscaloosachamber.com

Mobile Area Chamber of Commerce
451 Government St
Mobile, AL 36602
Phone: 251-433-6951; Fax: 251-432-1143
Toll-free: 800-422-6951
www.mobilechamber.com

Montgomery Area Chamber of Commerce
41 Commerce St
Box 79
Montgomery, AL 36101
Phone: 334-834-5200; Fax: 334-265-4745
www.montgomerychamber.com

ALASKA

Alaska Tourism Development Office
PO Box 11801
Juneau, AK 99811
Phone: 907-465-2012; Fax: 907-465-3767
www.commerce.state.ak.us/oed/toubus/
   home.cfm

Alaska State Chamber of Commerce
217 2nd St

Suite 201
Juneau, AK 99801
Phone: 907-586-2323; Fax: 907-463-5515
www.alaskachamber.com

Anchorage Convention & Visitors Bureau
524 W 4th Ave
Anchorage, AK 99501
Phone: 907-276-4118; Fax: 907-278-5559
Toll-free: 800-478-1255
www.anchorage.net

Fairbanks Convention & Visitors Bureau
550 1st Ave
Fairbanks, AK 99701
Phone: 907-456-5774; Fax: 907-452-2867
Toll-free: 800-327-5774
www.explorefairbanks.com

Juneau Convention & Visitors Bureau
One Sealaska Plaza
Suite 305
Juneau, AK 99801
Phone: 907-586-1737; Fax: 907-586-1449
Toll-free: 800-587-2201
www.traveljuneau.com

Anchorage Chamber of Commerce
1016 W 6th Ave
Suite 303
Anchorage, AK 99501
Phone: 907-272-2401; Fax: 907-272-4117
www.anchoragechamber.org

Fairbanks Chamber of Commerce
800 Cushman St
Suite 114
Fairbanks, AK 99701
Phone: 907-452-1105; Fax: 907-456-6968
www.fairbankschamber.org

Juneau Chamber of Commerce
3100 Channel Dr
Suite 300
Juneau, AK 99801
Phone: 907-463-3488; Fax: 907-463-3489
www.juneauchamber.com

ARIZONA

Arizona Tourism Office
1110 W Washington St
Suite 155
Phoenix, AZ 85007
Phone: 602-364-3700; Fax: 602-364-3701
Toll-free: 888-520-3434
www.arizonaguide.com

Arizona Chamber of Commerce & Industry
1850 N Central Ave
Suite 1010
Phoenix, AZ 85014
Phone: 602-248-9172; Fax: 602-265-1262
Toll-free: 800-498-6973
www.azchamber.com

Flagstaff Convention & Visitors Bureau
323 W Aspen Ave
Flagstaff, AZ 86001
Phone: 928-779-7611; Fax: 928-556-1305
Toll-free: 800-217-2367
www.flagstaffarizona.org

Greater Phoenix Convention & Visitors
  Bureau
400 E Van Buren St
1 Arizona Center Suite 600
Phoenix, AZ 85004
Phone: 602-254-6500; Fax: 602-253-4415
Toll-free: 877-225-5749
www.visitphoenix.com

Mesa Convention & Visitors Bureau
120 N Center St
Mesa, AZ 85201
Phone: 480-827-4700; Fax: 480-827-4704
Toll-free: 800-283-6372
www.mesacvb.com

Metropolitan Tucson Convention & Visitors
  Bureau
100 S Church Ave
Tucson, AZ 85701
Phone: 520-624-1817; Fax: 520-884-7804
Toll-free: 800-638-8350
www.visittucson.org

Scottsdale Convention & Visitors Bureau
4343 N Scottsdale Rd
Suite 170
Scottsdale, AZ 85251
Phone: 480-421-1004; Fax: 480-421-9733
Toll-free: 800-782-1117
www.scottsdalecvb.com

Tempe Convention & Visitors Bureau
51 W 3rd St
Suite 105
Tempe, AZ 85281
Phone: 480-894-8158; Fax: 480-968-8004
Toll-free: 800-283-6734
www.tempecvb.com

Flagstaff Chamber of Commerce
101 W Rt 66
Flagstaff, AZ 86001
Phone: 928-774-4505; Fax: 928-779-1209
www.flagstaffchamber.com

Glendale Chamber of Commerce
PO Box 249
Glendale, AZ 85311
Phone: 623-937-4754; Fax: 623-937-3333
Toll-free: 800-437-8669
www.glendaleazchamber.org

Greater Phoenix Chamber of Commerce
201 N Central Ave
Suite 2700
Phoenix, AZ 85073
Phone: 602-254-5521; Fax: 602-495-8913
www.phoenixchamber.com

Mesa Chamber of Commerce
120 N Center St
Mesa, AZ 85201
Phone: 480-969-1307; Fax: 480-827-0727
www.mesachamber.org

Scottsdale Area Chamber of Commerce
7343 Scottsdale Mall
Scottsdale, AZ 85251
Phone: 480-945-8481; Fax: 480-947-4523
www.scottsdalechamber.com

Tempe Chamber of Commerce
PO Box 28500
Tempe, AZ 85285

Phone: 480-967-7891; Fax: 480-966-5365
www.tempechamber.org

Tucson Metropolitan Chamber of Commerce
465 W St Mary's Rd
Tucson, AZ 85701
Phone: 520-792-2250; Fax: 520-882-5704
www.tucsonchamber.org

ARKANSAS

Arkansas Parks & Tourism Dept
1 Capitol Mall
Little Rock, AR 72201
Phone: 501-682-7777; Fax: 501-682-1364
Toll-free: 800-628-8725
www.arkansas.com

Arkansas State Chamber of Commerce
410 S Cross St
PO Box 3645
Little Rock, AR 72203
Phone: 501-372-2222; Fax: 501-372-2722
www.statechamber-aia.dina.org

Fort Smith Convention & Visitors Bureau
2 N 'B' St
Fort Smith, AR 72901
Phone: 479-783-8888; Fax: 479-784-2421
Toll-free: 800-637-1477
www.fortsmith.org

Hot Springs Convention & Visitors Bureau
134 Convention Blvd
Hot Springs, AR 71901
Phone: 501-321-2277; Fax: 501-321-2136
Toll-free: 800-543-2284
www.hotsprings.org

Little Rock Convention & Visitors Bureau
426 W Markham St
PO Box 3232
Little Rock, AR 72203
Phone: 501-376-4781; Fax: 501-374-2255
Toll-free: 800-844-4781
www.littlerock.com

Fort Smith Chamber of Commerce
612 Garrison Ave
Fort Smith, AR 72901

Phone: 479-783-6118; Fax: 479-783-6110
www.fschamber.com

Greater Hot Springs Chamber of Commerce
659 Ouachita Ave
Hot Springs, AR 71901
Phone: 501-321-1700; Fax: 501-321-3551
Toll-free: 800-467-4636
www.hotspringschamber.com

Greater Little Rock Chamber of Commerce
1 Chamber Plaza
Little Rock, AR 72201
Phone: 501-374-2001; Fax: 501-374-6018
www.littlerockchamber.com

CALIFORNIA

California Travel & Tourism Commission
PO Box 1499
Sacramento, CA 95812
Phone: 916-444-4429; Fax: 916-322-3402
www.visitcalifornia.com

California Chamber of Commerce
PO Box 1736
Sacramento, CA 95812
Phone: 916-444-6670; Fax: 916-325-1272
www.calchamber.com

Anaheim/Orange County Visitor &
   Convention Bureau
800 W Katella Ave
Anaheim, CA 92802
Phone: 714-765-8888; Fax: 714-991-8963
Toll-free: 888-598-3200
www.anaheimoc.org

Chula Vista Convention & Visitors Bureau
233 4th Ave
Chamber of Commerce Bldg
Chula Vista, CA 91910
Phone: 619-426-2882; Fax: 619-420-1269
www.chulavistaconvis.org

Fresno City & County Convention & Visitors
   Bureau
848 M St
3rd Fl
Fresno, CA 93721

Phone: 559-445-8300; Fax: 559-445-0122
Toll-free: 800-788-0836
www.fresnocvb.org

Garden Grove Visitors Bureau
12866 Main St
Suite 102
Garden Grove, CA 92840
Phone: 714-638-7950; Fax: 714-636-6672
www.gardengrovechamber.org

Greater Bakersfield Convention & Visitors
  Bureau
515 Truxtun Ave
Bakersfield, CA 93301
Phone: 661-325-5051; Fax: 661-325-7074
Toll-free: 866-425-7353
www.bakersfieldcvb.org

Huntington Beach Conference & Visitors
  Bureau
301 Main St
Suite 208
Huntington Beach, CA 92648
Phone: 714-969-3492; Fax: 714-969-5592
surfcityusa.com

Long Beach Convention & Visitors Bureau
1 World Trade Center
Suite 300
Long Beach, CA 90831
Phone: 562-436-3645; Fax: 562-435-5653
Toll-free: 800-452-7829
www.visitlongbeach.com

Los Angeles Convention & Visitors Bureau
333 S Hope St
18th Fl
Los Angeles, CA 90071
Phone: 213-624-7300; Fax: 213-624-9746
Toll-free: 800-228-2452
www.lacvb.com

Modesto Convention & Visitors Bureau
1150 9th St
Suite C
Modesto, CA 95354
Phone: 209-526-5588; Fax: 209-526-5586
Toll-free: 888-640-8467
www.visitmodesto.com

Monterey County Convention & Visitors
  Bureau
150 Oliver St
PO Box 1770
Monterey, CA 93942
Phone: 831-649-1770; Fax: 831-648-5373
Toll-free: 888-221-1010
www.montereyinfo.org

Oakland Convention & Visitors Bureau
463 11th St
Oakland, CA 94607
Phone: 510-839-9000; Fax: 510-839-5924
www.oaklandcvb.com

Oxnard Convention & Visitors Bureau
200 W 7th St
Oxnard, CA 93030
Phone: 805-385-7545; Fax: 805-385-7571
Toll-free: 800-269-6273
www.oxnardtourism.com

Palm Springs Desert Resorts Convention &
  Visitors Authority
70-100 Hwy 111
Rancho Mirage, CA 92270
Phone: 760-770-9000; Fax: 760-770-9001
Toll-free: 800-967-3767
www.palmspringsusa.com

Riverside Convention & Visitors Bureau
3750 University Ave
Suite 175
Riverside, CA 92501
Phone: 951-222-4700; Fax: 951-222-4712
Toll-free: 888-913-4636
www.riversidecvb.com

Sacramento Convention & Visitors Bureau
1608 'I' St
Sacramento, CA 95814
Phone: 916-808-7777; Fax: 916-808-7788
Toll-free: 800-292-2334
www.sacramentocvb.org

San Bernardino Convention & Visitors
  Bureau
201 N 'E' St
Suite 103
San Bernardino, CA 92401

Phone: 909-889-3980; Fax: 909-888-5998
Toll-free: 800-867-8366
san-bernardino.org

San Diego Convention & Visitors Bureau
2215 India St
San Diego, CA 92101
Phone: 619-232-3101; Fax: 619-696-9371
www.sandiego.org

San Francisco Convention & Visitors Bureau
201 3rd St
Suite 900
San Francisco, CA 94103
Phone: 415-974-6900; Fax: 415-227-2602
www.sfvisitor.org

San Jose Convention & Visitors Bureau
408 Almaden Blvd
San Jose, CA 95110
Phone: 408-295-9600; Fax: 408-277-3535
Toll-free: 800-726-5673
www.sanjose.org

Santa Barbara Visitors Bureau & Film
    Commission
1601 Anacapa St
Santa Barbara, CA 93101
Phone: 805-966-9222; Fax: 805-966-1728
Toll-free: 800-927-4688
www.santabarbaraca.com

Stockton/San Joaquin Convention & Visitors
    Bureau
445 W Webber Ave
Suite 220
Stockton, CA 95203
Phone: 209-547-2770; Fax: 209-466-5271
www.visitstockton.org

Anaheim Chamber of Commerce
201 E Center St
Anaheim, CA 92805
Phone: 714-758-0222; Fax: 714-758-0468
anaheimchamber.org

Chula Vista Chamber of Commerce
233 4th Ave
Chula Vista, CA 91910
Phone: 619-420-6602; Fax: 619-420-1269
www.chulavistachamber.org

Fremont Chamber of Commerce
39488 Stevenson Pl
Suite 100
Fremont, CA 94539
Phone: 510-795-2244; Fax: 510-795-2240
www.fremontbusiness.com

Fresno Chamber of Commerce
2331 Fresno St
Fresno, CA 93721
Phone: 559-495-4800; Fax: 559-495-4811
www.fresnochamber.com

Garden Grove Chamber of Commerce
12866 Main St
Suite 102
Garden Grove, CA 92840
Phone: 714-638-7950; Fax: 714-636-6672
Toll-free: 800-959-5560
www.gardengrovechamber.org

Glendale Chamber of Commerce
200 S Louise St
Glendale, CA 91205
Phone: 818-240-7870; Fax: 818-240-2872
www.glendalechamber.com

Greater Bakersfield Chamber of Commerce
1725 Eye St
Bakersfield, CA 93301
Phone: 661-327-4421; Fax: 661-327-8751
www.bakersfieldchamber.org

Greater Riverside Chambers of Commerce
3985 University Ave
Riverside, CA 92501
Phone: 951-683-7100; Fax: 951-683-2670
www.riverside-chamber.com

Greater Stockton Chamber of Commerce
445 W Weber Ave
Suite 220
Stockton, CA 95203
Phone: 209-547-2770; Fax: 209-466-5271
www.stocktonchamber.org

Huntington Beach Chamber of Commerce
19891 Beach Blvd
Suite 140
Huntington Beach, CA 92648

Phone: 714-536-8888; Fax: 714-960-7654
www.hbchamber.org

Long Beach Area Chamber of Commerce
1 World Trade Center
Suite 206
Long Beach, CA 90831
Phone: 562-436-1251; Fax: 562-436-7099
www.lbchamber.com

Los Angeles Area Chamber of Commerce
350 S Bixel St
Los Angeles, CA 90017
Phone: 213-580-7500; Fax: 213-580-7511
www.lachamber.org

Modesto Chamber of Commerce
PO Box 844
Modesto, CA 95353
Phone: 209-577-5757; Fax: 209-577-2673
www.modchamber.org

Monterey Peninsula Chamber of Commerce
380 Alvarado St
Monterey, CA 93940
Phone: 831-648-5360; Fax: 831-649-3502
www.mpcc.com

Oakland Metropolitan Chamber of
    Commerce
475 14th St
Suite 100
Oakland, CA 94612
Phone: 510-874-4800; Fax: 510-839-8817
www.oaklandchamber.com

Oxnard Chamber of Commerce
400 E Esplanade Dr
Suite 302
Oxnard, CA 93036
Phone: 805-983-6118; Fax: 805-604-7331
www.oxnardchamber.org

Palm Springs Chamber of Commerce
190 W Amado Rd
Palm Springs, CA 92262
Phone: 760-325-1577; Fax: 760-325-8549
www.pschamber.org

Sacramento Metro Chamber of Commerce
1 Capital Mall

Suite 300
Sacramento, CA 95814
Phone: 916-552-6800; Fax: 916-443-2672
www.metrochamber.org

San Bernardino Area Chamber of Commerce
PO Box 658
San Bernardino, CA 92402
Phone: 909-885-7515; Fax: 909-384-9979
www.sbachamber.org

San Diego Regional Chamber of Commerce
402 W Broadway
Suite 1000
San Diego, CA 92101
Phone: 619-544-1300
sdchamber.org

San Francisco Chamber of Commerce
235 Montgomery St
12th Fl
San Francisco, CA 94104
Phone: 415-392-4520; Fax: 415-392-0485
www.sfchamber.com

San Jose Silicon Valley Chamber of
    Commerce
310 S 1st St
San Jose, CA 95113
Phone: 408-291-5250; Fax: 408-286-5019
www.sjchamber.com

Santa Ana Chamber of Commerce
PO Box 205
Santa Ana, CA 92702
Phone: 714-541-5353; Fax: 714-541-2238
www.santaanachamber.com

Santa Barbara Region Chamber of
    Commerce
924 Anacapa St
Suite 1
Santa Barbara, CA 93101
Phone: 805-965-3023; Fax: 805-966-5954
www.sbchamber.org

COLORADO

Colorado Tourism Office
1625 Broadway

Suite 1700
Denver, CO 80202
Phone: 303-892-3885; Fax: 303-892-3848
Toll-free: 800-265-6723
www.colorado.com

Colorado Assn of Commerce & Industry
1600 Broadway
Suite 1000
Denver, CO 80202
Phone: 303-831-7411; Fax: 303-860-1439
www.cochamber.com

Aspen Chamber Resort Assn
425 Rio Grande Pl
Aspen, CO 81611
Phone: 970-925-1940; Fax: 970-920-1173
Toll-free: 800-670-0792
www.aspenchamber.org

Boulder Convention & Visitors Bureau
2440 Pearl St
Boulder, CO 80302
Phone: 303-442-2911; Fax: 303-938-2098
Toll-free: 800-444-0447
www.bouldercoloradousa.com

Colorado Springs Convention & Visitors
    Bureau
515 S Cascade Ave
Colorado Springs, CO 80903
Phone: 719-635-7506; Fax: 719-635-4968
Toll-free: 800-368-4748
www.experiencecoloradosprings.com

Denver Metro Convention & Visitors Bureau
1555 California St
Suite 300
Denver, CO 80202
Phone: 303-892-1112; Fax: 303-892-1636
Toll-free: 800-234-6257
www.denver.org

Durango Area Tourism Office
111 S Camino del Rio
Durango, CO 81301
Phone: 970-247-3500; Fax: 970-385-7884
Toll-free: 800-525-8855
www.durango.org

Fort Collins Convention & Visitors Bureau
19 Old Town Sq
Suite 137
Fort Collins, CO 80524
Phone: 970-232-3840; Fax: 970-232-3841
Toll-free: 800-274-3678
www.ftcollins.com

Greater Pueblo Chamber of Commerce &
    Visitors Council
302 N Santa Fe Ave
Pueblo, CO 81003
Phone: 719-542-1704; Fax: 719-542-1624
Toll-free: 800-233-3446
www.pueblo.org

Aspen Chamber Resort Assn
425 Rio Grande Pl
Aspen, CO 81611
Phone: 970-925-1940; Fax: 970-920-1173
Toll-free: 800-670-0792
www.aspenchamber.org

Aurora Chamber of Commerce
562 Sable Blvd
Suite 200
Aurora, CO 80011
Phone: 303-344-1500; Fax: 303-344-1564
www.aurorachamber.org

Boulder Chamber of Commerce
2440 Pearl St
Boulder, CO 80302
Phone: 303-442-1044; Fax: 303-938-8837
www.boulderchamber.com

Colorado Springs Chamber of Commerce
2 N Cascade Ave
Suite 110
Colorado Springs, CO 80903
Phone: 719-635-1551; Fax: 719-635-1571
www.coloradospringschamber.org

Denver Metro Chamber of Commerce
1445 Market St
Denver, CO 80202
Phone: 303-534-8500; Fax: 303-534-3200
www.denverchamber.org

Durango Area Chamber of Commerce
111 S Camino del Rio

PO Box 2587
Durango, CO 81303
Phone: 970-247-0312; Fax: 970-385-7884
Toll-free: 888-414-0835
www.durangobusiness.org

Fort Collins Area Chamber of Commerce
225 S Meldrum St
Fort Collins, CO 80521
Phone: 970-482-3746; Fax: 970-482-3774
www.fcchamber.org

Greater Pueblo Chamber of Commerce
302 N Santa Fe Ave
Pueblo, CO 81003
Phone: 719-542-1704; Fax: 719-542-1624
Toll-free: 800-233-3446
www.pueblochamber.org

CONNECTICUT

Connecticut Commission on Culture &
  Tourism
755 Main St
1 Financial Plaza
Hartford, CT 06103
Phone: 860-256-2800; Fax: 860-256-2811
www.cultureandtourism.org

Connecticut Tourism Div
505 Hudson St
Hartford, CT 06106
Phone: 860-270-8080; Fax: 860-270-8077
Toll-free: 888-288-4748
www.ctbound.org

Connecticut Business & Industry Assn
350 Church St
Hartford, CT 06103
Phone: 860-244-1900; Fax: 860-278-8562
www.cbia.com

Greater Hartford Convention & Visitors
  Bureau
31 Pratt St
4th Fl
Hartford, CT 06103
Phone: 860-728-6789; Fax: 860-293-2365
www.enjoyhartford.com

Greater New Haven Convention & Visitors
  Bureau
169 Orange St
New Haven, CT 06510
Phone: 203-777-8550; Fax: 203-782-7755
Toll-free: 800-332-7829
www.newhavencvb.org

Bridgeport Regional Business Council
10 Middle St
14th Fl
Bridgeport, CT 06604
Phone: 203-335-3800; Fax: 203-366-0105
www.brbc.org

Greater New Haven Chamber of Commerce
900 Chapel St
10th Fl
New Haven, CT 06510
Phone: 203-787-6735; Fax: 203-782-4329
www.gnhcc.com

MetroHartford Alliance
31 Pratt St
Suite 5
Hartford, CT 06103
Phone: 860-525-4451; Fax: 860-293-2592
www.metrohartford.com

Stamford Chamber of Commerce
733 Summer St
Suite 101
Stamford, CT 06901
Phone: 203-359-4761; Fax: 203-363-5069
www.stamfordchamber.com

DELAWARE

Delaware Tourism Office
99 Kings Hwy
Dover, DE 19901
Phone: 302-739-4271; Fax: 302-739-5749
Toll-free: 866-284-7483
www.visitdelaware.net

Delaware State Chamber of Commerce
PO Box 671
Wilmington, DE 19899
Phone: 302-655-7221; Fax: 302-654-0691

Toll-free: 800-292-9507
www.dscc.com

Greater Wilmington Convention & Visitors
   Bureau
100 W 10th St
Suite 20
Wilmington, DE 19801
Phone: 302-652-4088; Fax: 302-652-4726
Toll-free: 800-422-1181
www.wilmcvb.org

Kent County Tourism Corp
435 N DuPont Hwy
Dover, DE 19901
Phone: 302-734-1736; Fax: 302-734-0167
Toll-free: 800-233-5368
www.visitdover.com

Rehoboth Beach Convention Center
229 Rehoboth Ave
Rehoboth Beach, DE 19971
Phone: 302-227-4641; Fax: 302-227-4643
cityofrehoboth.com

Central Delaware Economic Development
   Council
435 N DuPont Hwy
Dover, DE 19901
Phone: 302-678-3028; Fax: 302-678-0189
Toll-free: 800-624-2522
www.cdedc.org

Rehoboth Beach-Dewey Beach Chamber of
   Commerce
501 Rehoboth Ave
Rehoboth Beach, DE 19971
Phone: 302-227-2233; Fax: 302-227-8351
Toll-free: 800-441-1329
www.beach-fun.com

DISTRICT OF COLUMBIA

District of Columbia Convention & Tourism
   Corp
901 7th Street NW
4th Fl
Washington, DC 20001
Phone: 202-789-7000; Fax: 202-789-7037

Toll-free: 800-422-8644
www.washington.org

District of Columbia Chamber of
   Commerce
1213 K St NW
Washington, DC 20005
Phone: 202-347-7201; Fax: 202-638-6762
www.dcchamber.org

US Chamber of Commerce
1615 H St NW
Washington, DC 20062
Phone: 202-659-6000; Fax: 202-463-5836
Toll-free: 800-638-6582
www.uschamber.com

Washington DC Convention & Tourism
   Corp
901 7th St NW
4th Fl
Washington, DC 20001
Phone: 202-789-7000; Fax: 202-789-7037
Toll-free: 800-422-8644
www.washington.org

FLORIDA

Florida Tourism Commission
661 E Jefferson St
Suite 300
Tallahassee, FL 32301
Phone: 850-488-5607; Fax: 850-224-2938
Toll-free: 888-735-2872
www.visitflorida.com

Florida Chamber of Commerce
136 S Bronough St
Tallahassee, FL 32301
Phone: 850-521-1200; Fax: 850-521-1219
Toll-free: 877-521-1200
www.flchamber.com

Alachua County Visitors & Convention
   Bureau
30 E University Ave
Gainesville, FL 32601
Phone: 352-374-5231; Fax: 352-338-3213
Toll-free: 866-778-5002
www.visitgainesville.net

Daytona Beach Area Convention & Visitors
  Bureau
126 E Orange Ave
Daytona Beach, FL 32114
Phone: 386-255-0415; Fax: 386-255-5478
Toll-free: 800-544-0415
www.daytonabeach.com

Greater Fort Lauderdale Convention &
  Visitors Bureau
100 E Broward Blvd
Suite 200
Fort Lauderdale, FL 33301
Phone: 954-765-4466; Fax: 954-765-4467
Toll-free: 800-356-1662
sunny.org

Greater Miami Convention & Visitors
  Bureau
701 Brickell Ave
Suite 2700
Miami, FL 33131
Phone: 305-539-3000; Fax: 305-530-5859
Toll-free: 800-933-8448
www.gmcvb.com

Greater Naples Marco Island Everglades
  Convention & Visitors Bureau
3050 N Horseshoe Dr
Suite 218
Naples, FL 34104
Phone: 239-403-2384; Fax: 239-403-2404
Toll-free: 800-688-3600
www.paradisecoast.com

Jacksonville & the Beaches Convention &
  Visitors Bureau
550 Water St
Suite 1000
Jacksonville, FL 32202
Phone: 904-798-9111; Fax: 904-798-9103
Toll-free: 800-733-2668
www.visitjacksonville.com

Monroe County Tourist Development
  Council
1201 White St
Suite 102
Key West, FL 33040

Phone: 305-296-1552; Fax: 305-296-0788
Toll-free: 800-648-5510
www.fla-keys.com

Orlando/Orange County Convention &
  Visitors Bureau
6700 Forum Dr
Suite 100
Orlando, FL 32821
Phone: 407-363-5800; Fax: 407-370-5000
Toll-free: 800-551-0181
www.orlandoinfo.com

Palm Beach County Convention & Visitors
  Bureau
1555 Palm Beach Lakes Blvd
Suite 800
West Palm Beach, FL 33401
Phone: 561-233-3000; Fax: 561-471-3990
Toll-free: 800-833-5733
www.palmbeachfl.com

Pensacola Convention & Visitors Bureau
1401 E Gregory St
Pensacola, FL 32502
Phone: 850-434-1234; Fax: 850-432-8211
Toll-free: 800-874-1234
www.visitpensacola.com

Saint Johns County Convention & Visitors
  Bureau
88 Riberia St
Suite 400
Saint Augustine, FL 32084
Phone: 904-829-1711; Fax: 904-829-6149
Toll-free: 800-653-2489
www.oldcity.com

Saint Petersburg/Clearwater Area
  Convention & Visitors Bureau
13805 58th St N
Suite 2-200
Clearwater, FL 33760
Phone: 727-464-7200; Fax: 727-464-7222
Toll-free: 800-345-6710
www.floridasbeach.com

Sarasota Convention & Visitors Bureau
6701 N Tamiami Trail

Sarasota, FL 34236
Phone: 941-957-1877; Fax: 941-951-2956
Toll-free: 800-522-9799
www.sarasotafl.org

Tallahassee Area Convention & Visitors
　Bureau
106 E Jefferson St
Tallahassee, FL 32301
Phone: 850-606-2305; Fax: 850-606-2301
Toll-free: 800-628-2866
www.seetallahassee.com

Tampa Bay Convention & Visitors Bureau
400 N Tampa St
Suite 2800
Tampa, FL 33602
Phone: 813-223-1111; Fax: 813-229-6616
Toll-free: 800-826-8358
www.visittampabay.com

Chamber of Commerce of the Palm Beaches
401 N Flagler Dr
West Palm Beach, FL 33401
Phone: 561-833-3711; Fax: 561-833-5582
www.palmbeaches.org

Daytona Beach-Halifax Area Chamber of
　Commerce
126 E Orange Ave
Daytona Beach, FL 32114
Phone: 386-255-0981; Fax: 386-258-5104
www.daytonachamber.com

Gainesville Area Chamber of Commerce
300 E University Ave
Suite 100
Gainesville, FL 32601
Phone: 352-334-7100; Fax: 352-334-7141
www.gainesvillechamber.com

Greater Fort Lauderdale Chamber of
　Commerce
512 NE 3rd Ave
Fort Lauderdale, FL 33301
Phone: 954-462-6000; Fax: 954-527-8766
www.ftlchamber.com

Greater Miami Chamber of Commerce
1601 Biscayne Blvd

Miami, FL 33132
Phone: 305-350-7700; Fax: 305-374-6902
Toll-free: 888-660-5955
www.greatermiami.com

Greater Sarasota Chamber of Commerce
1945 Fruitville Rd
Sarasota, FL 34236
Phone: 941-955-8187; Fax: 941-366-5621
www.sarasotachamber.org

Greater Tampa Chamber of Commerce
PO Box 420
Tampa, FL 33601
Phone: 813-228-7777; Fax: 813-223-7899
Toll-free: 800-298-2672
www.tampachamber.com

Hialeah Chamber of Commerce & Industries
240 E 1st Ave
Hialeah, FL 33010
Phone: 305-888-7780; Fax: 305-888-7804
www.hialeahchamber.org

Jacksonville Chamber of Commerce
3 Independent Dr
Jacksonville, FL 32202
Phone: 904-366-6600; Fax: 904-632-0617
www.myjaxchamber.com

Key West Chamber of Commerce
402 Wall St
Key West, FL 33040
Phone: 305-294-2587; Fax: 305-294-7806
Toll-free: 800-527-8539
www.keywestchamber.org

Miami Beach Chamber of Commerce
1920 Meridian Ave
3rd Fl
Miami Beach, FL 33139
Phone: 305-672-1270; Fax: 305-538-4336
www.miamibeachchamber.com

Naples Area Chamber of Commerce
2390 Tamiami Trail N
Naples, FL 34103
Phone: 239-262-6141; Fax: 239-435-9910
www.napleschamber.org

Orlando Regional Chamber of Commerce
PO Box 1234
Orlando, FL 32802
Phone: 407-425-1234; Fax: 407-835-2500
www.orlando.org

Pensacola Area Chamber of Commerce
117 W Garden St
Pensacola, FL 32502
Phone: 850-438-4081; Fax: 850-438-6369
www.pensacolachamber.com

Saint Augustine & Saint Johns County
    Chamber of Commerce
1 Riberia St
Saint Augustine, FL 32084
Phone: 904-829-5681; Fax: 904-829-6477
www.staugustinechamber.com

Saint Petersburg Area Chamber of
    Commerce
100 2nd Ave N
Suite 150
Saint Petersburg, FL 33701
Phone: 727-821-4069; Fax: 727-895-6326
www.stpete.com

Tallahassee Chamber of Commerce
PO Box 1639
Tallahassee, FL 32302
Phone: 850-224-8116; Fax: 850-561-3860
www.talchamber.com

GEORGIA

Georgia Tourism Div
285 Peachtree Center Ave NE
Suite 1000
Atlanta, GA 30303
Phone: 404-656-2000; Fax: 404-651-9063
Toll-free: 800-847-4842
www.georgiaonmymind.org

Georgia Chamber of Commerce
235 Peachtree St NE
Suite 2000
Atlanta, GA 30303
Phone: 404-223-2264; Fax: 404-223-2290

Toll-free: 800-241-2286
www.gachamber.com

Atlanta Convention & Visitors Bureau
233 Peachtree St NE
Suite 100
Atlanta, GA 30303
Phone: 404-521-6600; Fax: 404-584-6331
Toll-free: 800-285-2682
www.atlanta.net

Augusta Metropolitan Convention &
    Visitors Bureau
1450 Greene St
Suite 110
Augusta, GA 30901
Phone: 706-823-6600; Fax: 706-823-6609
Toll-free: 800-726-0243
www.augustaga.org

Columbus Convention & Visitors Bureau
900 Front Ave
Columbus, GA 31901
Phone: 706-322-1613; Fax: 706-322-0701
Toll-free: 800-999-1613
www.visitcolumbusga.com

Macon-Bibb County Convention/Visitors
    Bureau
450 ML King Blvd
Macon, GA 31201
Phone: 478-743-3401; Fax: 478-745-2022
Toll-free: 800-768-3401
www.maconga.org

Savannah Area Convention & Visitors
    Bureau
101 E Bay St
Savannah, GA 31401
Phone: 912-644-6401; Fax: 912-644-6499
Toll-free: 877-728-2662
www.savcvb.com

Augusta Metro Chamber of Commerce
PO Box 1837
Augusta, GA 30903
Phone: 706-821-1300; Fax: 706-821-1330
www.augustagausa.com

Greater Columbus Chamber of Commerce
1200 6th Ave
PO Box 1200
Columbus, GA 31902
Phone: 706-327-1566; Fax: 706-327-7512
Toll-free: 800-360-8552
www.columbusgachamber.com

Greater Macon Chamber of Commerce
305 Coliseum Dr
Macon, GA 31217
Phone: 478-621-2000; Fax: 478-621-2021
www.maconchamber.com

Metro Atlanta Chamber of Commerce
235 Andrew Young International Blvd NW
Atlanta, GA 30303
Phone: 404-880-9000; Fax: 404-586-8464
www.metroatlantachamber.com

Savannah Area Chamber of Commerce
101 E Bay St
Savannah, GA 31401
Phone: 912-644-6400; Fax: 912-644-6499
Toll-free: 877-728-2662
www.savannahchamber.com

HAWAII

Hawaii Business Economic Development &
   Tourism Dept
PO Box 2359
Honolulu, HI 96804
Phone: 808-586-2355; Fax: 808-586-2377
www.hawaii.gov/dbedt

Hawaii Tourism Authority
1801 Kalakaua Ave
Honolulu, HI 96815
Phone: 808-973-2255; Fax: 808-973-2253
www.hawaii.gov/tourism

Hawaii Chamber of Commerce
1132 Bishop St
Suite 402
Honolulu, HI 96813
Phone: 808-545-4300; Fax: 808-545-4369
Toll-free: 800-464-2924
www.cochawaii.com

Hawaii Visitors & Convention Bureau
2270 Kalakaua Ave
Suite 801
Honolulu, HI 96815
Phone: 808-923-1811; Fax: 808-924-0290
Toll-free: 800-464-2924
www.gohawaii.com

IDAHO

Idaho Tourism Development Div
700 W State St
PO Box 83720
Boise, ID 83720
Phone: 208-334-2470; Fax: 208-334-2631
Toll-free: 800-842-5858
www.visitid.org

Idaho Assn of Commerce & Industry
PO Box 389
Boise, ID 83701
Phone: 208-343-1849; Fax: 208-338-5623
www.iaci.org

Boise Convention & Visitors Bureau
312 S 9th St
Suite 100
Boise, ID 83702
Phone: 208-344-7777; Fax: 208-344-6236
Toll-free: 800-635-5240
www.boise.org

Pocatello Convention & Visitors Bureau
324 S Main St
Suite B
Pocatello, ID 83204
Phone: 208-235-7659; Fax: 208-233-1527
Toll-free: 877-922-7659
www.pocatellocvb.com

Boise Metro Chamber of Commerce
PO Box 2368
Boise, ID 83701
Phone: 208-472-5205; Fax: 208-472-5201
www.boisechamber.org

Greater Pocatello Chamber of Commerce
324 S Main St
Pocatello, ID 83204

Phone: 208-233-1525; Fax: 208-233-1527
www.pocatelloidaho.com

ILLINOIS

Illinois Tourism Bureau
100 W Randolph St
Suite 3-400
Chicago, IL 60601
Phone: 312-814-4732; Fax: 312-814-6175
Toll-free: 800-226-6632
www.enjoyillinois.com

Illinois State Chamber of Commerce
311 S Wacker Dr
Suite 1500
Chicago, IL 60606
Phone: 312-983-7100; Fax: 312-983-7101
www.ilchamber.org

Central Illinois Tourism Development Office
700 E Adams St
Springfield, IL 62701
Phone: 217-525-7980; Fax: 217-525-8004
www.visitcentralillinois.com

Champaign County Convention & Visitors
   Bureau
1817 S Neil St
Suite 201
Champaign, IL 61820
Phone: 217-351-4133; Fax: 217-359-1809
Toll-free: 800-369-6151
www.visitchampaigncounty.org

Chicago Convention & Tourism Bureau
2301 S Lake Shore Dr
McCormick Complex Lakeside Center
Chicago, IL 60616
Phone: 312-567-8500; Fax: 312-567-8533
www.choosechicago.com

Chicago Office of Tourism
78 E Washington St
4th Fl
Chicago, IL 60602
Phone: 312-744-2400; Fax: 312-744-2359
Toll-free: 877-244-2246
www.877chicago.com/

Peoria Area Convention & Visitors Bureau
456 Fulton St
Suite 300
Peoria, IL 61602
Phone: 309-676-0303; Fax: 309-676-8470
Toll-free: 800-747-0302
www.peoria.org

Rockford Area Convention & Visitors
   Bureau
102 N Main St
Rockford, IL 61101
Phone: 815-963-8111; Fax: 815-963-4298
Toll-free: 800-521-0849
www.gorockford.com

Springfield Convention & Visitors Bureau
109 N 7th St
Springfield, IL 62701
Phone: 217-789-2360; Fax: 217-544-8711
Toll-free: 800-545-7300
www.visitspringfieldillinois.com

Champaign County Chamber of Commerce
1817 S Neil St
Suite 201
Champaign, IL 61820
Phone: 217-359-1791; Fax: 217-359-1809
www.ccchamber.org

Chicagoland Chamber of Commerce
200 E Randolph St
Suite 2200
Chicago, IL 60601
Phone: 312-494-6700; Fax: 312-494-0660
www.chicagolandchamber.org

Greater Springfield Chamber of Commerce
3 S Old State Capitol Plaza
Springfield, IL 62701
Phone: 217-525-1173; Fax: 217-525-8768
www.gscc.org

Peoria Area Chamber of Commerce
124 SW Adams St
Suite 300
Peoria, IL 61602
Phone: 309-676-0755; Fax: 309-676-7534
www.peoriachamber.org

Rockford Regional Chamber of Commerce
308 W State St
Suite 190
Rockford, IL 61101
Phone: 815-987-8100; Fax: 815-987-8122
www.rockfordchamber.com

INDIANA

Indiana Tourism Development Office
1 N Capitol Ave
Suite 100
Indianapolis, IN 46204
Phone: 317-232-8860; Fax: 317-233-6887
Toll-free: 888-365-6946
www.in.gov/visitindiana

Indiana State Chamber of Commerce
115 W Washington St Suite 850-S
Indianapolis, IN 46204
Phone: 317-264-3110; Fax: 317-264-6855
www.indianachamber.com

Bloomington/Monroe County Convention &
Visitors Bureau
2855 N Walnut St
Bloomington, IN 47404
Phone: 812-334-8900; Fax: 812-334-2344
Toll-free: 800-800-0037
www.visitbloomington.com

Evansville Convention & Visitors Bureau
401 SE Riverside Dr
Evansville, IN 47713
Phone: 812-425-5402; Fax: 812-421-2207
Toll-free: 800-433-3025
www.evansvillecvb.org

Fort Wayne/Allen County Convention &
Visitors Bureau
1021 S Calhoun St
Fort Wayne, IN 46802
Phone: 260-424-3700; Fax: 260-424-3914
Toll-free: 800-767-7752
www.visitfortwayne.com

Indianapolis Convention & Visitors Assn
200 S Capitol Ave
1 RCA Dome Suite 100
Indianapolis, IN 46225

Phone: 317-639-4282; Fax: 317-639-5273
Toll-free: 800-323-4639
www.indy.org

South Bend/Mishawaka Convention &
Visitors Bureau
401 E Colfax Ave
Suite 310
South Bend, IN 46617
Phone: 574-234-0051; Fax: 574-289-0358
Toll-free: 800-828-7881
www.livethelegends.org

Chamber of Commerce of Saint Joseph
County
401 E Colfax Ave
Suite 310
South Bend, IN 46617
Phone: 574-234-0051; Fax: 574-289-0358
www.sjchamber.org

Greater Bloomington Chamber of Commerce
400 W 7th St
Suite 102
Bloomington, IN 47404
Phone: 812-336-6381; Fax: 812-336-0651
www.chamber.bloomington.in.us

Greater Fort Wayne Chamber of Commerce
826 Ewing St
Fort Wayne, IN 46802
Phone: 260-424-1435; Fax: 260-426-7232
www.fwchamber.org

Indianapolis Chamber of Commerce
111 Monument Cir
Suite 1950
Indianapolis, IN 46204
Phone: 317-464-2200; Fax: 317-464-2217
www.indychamber.com

Metropolitan Evansville Chamber of
Commerce
100 NW 2nd St
Suite 100
Evansville, IN 47708
Phone: 812-425-8147; Fax: 812-421-5883
www.evansvillechamber.com

IOWA

Iowa Tourism Office
200 E Grand Ave
Des Moines, IA 50309
Phone: 515-242-4705; Fax: 515-242-4718
Toll-free: 888-472-6035
www.traveliowa.com

Iowa Assn of Business & Industry
904 Walnut St
Suite 100
Des Moines, IA 50309
Phone: 515-280-8000; Fax: 515-244-8907
Toll-free: 800-383-4224
www.iowaabi.org

Cedar Rapids Area Convention & Visitors
  Bureau
119 1st Ave SE
PO Box 5339
Cedar Rapids, IA 52406
Phone: 319-398-5009; Fax: 319-398-5089
Toll-free: 800-735-5557
www.cedar-rapids.com

Dubuque Convention & Visitors Bureau
300 Main St
Suite 200
Dubuque, IA 52001
Phone: 563-557-9200; Fax: 563-557-1591
Toll-free: 800-798-4748

Greater Des Moines Convention & Visitors
  Bureau
400 Locust St
Suite 265
Des Moines, IA 50309
Phone: 515-286-4960; Fax: 515-244-9757
Toll-free: 800-451-2625
www.seedesmoines.com

Cedar Rapids Area Chamber of Commerce
424 1st Ave NE
Cedar Rapids, IA 52401
Phone: 319-398-5317; Fax: 319-398-5228
www.cedarrapids.org

Dubuque Area Chamber of Commerce
300 Main St

Suite 200
Dubuque, IA 52001
Phone: 563-557-9200; Fax: 563-557-1591
Toll-free: 800-798-4748
www.dubuquechamber.com

Greater Des Moines Partnership
700 Locust St
Suite 100
Des Moines, IA 50309
Phone: 515-286-4950; Fax: 515-286-4974
Toll-free: 800-376-9059
www.desmoinesmetro.com

KANSAS

Kansas Travel & Tourism Development Div
1000 SW Jackson St
Suite 100
Topeka, KS 66612
Phone: 785-296-5403; Fax: 785-296-6988
Toll-free: 800-252-6727
www.travelks.org

Kansas Chamber of Commerce & Industry
835 SW Topeka Blvd
Topeka, KS 66612
Phone: 785-357-6321; Fax: 785-357-4732
www.kansaschamber.org

Kansas City Kansas/Wyandotte County
  Convention & Visitors Bureau
727 Minnesota Ave
PO Box 171517
Kansas City, KS 66117
Phone: 913-321-5800; Fax: 913-371-3732
Toll-free: 800-264-1563
www.visitthedot.com

Visit Topeka Inc
1275 SW Topeka Blvd
Topeka, KS 66612
Phone: 785-234-1030; Fax: 785-234-8282
Toll-free: 800-235-1030
www.visittopeka.travel

Wichita Convention & Visitors Bureau
100 S Main St
Suite 100
Wichita, KS 67202

Phone: 316-265-2800; Fax: 316-265-0162
Toll-free: 800-288-9424
www.visitwichita.com

Greater Topeka Chamber of Commerce
120 SE 6th St
Suite 110
Topeka, KS 66603
Phone: 785-234-2644; Fax: 785-234-8656
www.topekachamber.org

Kansas City Kansas Area Chamber of
   Commerce
PO Box 171337
Kansas City, KS 66117
Phone: 913-371-3070; Fax: 913-371-3732
www.kckchamber.com

Wichita Area Chamber of Commerce
350 W Douglas Ave
Wichita, KS 67202
Phone: 316-265-7771; Fax: 316-265-7502
www.wichitachamber.org

KENTUCKY

Kentucky Travel Dept
500 Mero St
Suite 2200
Frankfort, KY 40601
Phone: 502-564-4930; Fax: 502-564-5695
Toll-free: 800-225-8747
www.kentuckytourism.com

Kentucky Chamber of Commerce
464 Chenault Rd
Frankfort, KY 40601
Phone: 502-695-4700; Fax: 502-695-6824
www.kychamber.com

Frankfort/Franklin County Tourist &
   Convention Commission
100 Capitol Ave
Frankfort, KY 40601
Phone: 502-875-8687; Fax: 502-227-2604
Toll-free: 800-960-7200
www.frankfortky.org

Lexington Convention & Visitors Bureau
301 E Vine St

Lexington, KY 40507
Phone: 859-233-7299; Fax: 859-254-4555
Toll-free: 800-845-3959
www.visitlex.com

Louisville & Jefferson County Convention &
   Visitors Bureau
401 W Main St
Suite 2300
Louisville, KY 40202
Phone: 502-584-2121; Fax: 502-584-6697
Toll-free: 800-792-5595
www.gotolouisville.com

Frankfort Area Chamber of Commerce
100 Capitol Ave
Frankfort, KY 40601
Phone: 502-223-8261; Fax: 502-223-5942
www.frankfortky.org

Greater Lexington Chamber of Commerce
330 E Main St
Suite 100
Lexington, KY 40507
Phone: 859-254-4447; Fax: 859-233-3304
www.lexchamber.com

Greater Louisville Inc
614 W Main St
Louisville, KY 40202
Phone: 502-625-0000; Fax: 502-625-0010
Toll-free: 800-500-1066
www.greaterlouisville.com

LOUISIANA

Louisiana Culture Recreation & Tourism
   Dept
PO Box 94361
Baton Rouge, LA 70804
Phone: 225-342-8115; Fax: 225-342-3207
www.crt.state.la.us

Louisiana Tourism Office
PO Box 94291
Baton Rouge, LA 70804
Phone: 225-342-8100; Fax: 225-342-8390
www.louisianatravel.com

Louisiana Assn of Business & Industry
3113 Valley Creek Dr
PO Box 80258
Baton Rouge, LA 70898
Phone: 225-928-5388; Fax: 225-929-6054
Toll-free: 888-816-5224
www.labi.org

Baton Rouge Convention & Visitors Bureau
730 North Blvd
Baton Rouge, LA 70802
Phone: 225-383-1825; Fax: 225-346-1253
Toll-free: 800-527-6843
www.visitbatonrouge.com

Jefferson Convention & Visitors Bureau
1221 Elmwood Park Blvd
Suite 300
Jefferson, LA 70123
Phone: 504-731-7083; Fax: 504-731-7089
Toll-free: 877-572-7474
www.gatewaytoneworleans.com

Lafayette Convention & Visitors
    Commission
1400 NW Evangeline Thwy
Lafayette, LA 70501
Phone: 337-232-3737; Fax: 337-232-0161
Toll-free: 800-346-1958
www.lafayettetravel.com

New Orleans Metropolitan Convention &
    Visitors Bureau
2020 St Charles Ave
New Orleans, LA 70130
Phone: 504-566-5011; Fax: 504-566-5046
Toll-free: 800-672-6124
www.neworleanscvb.com

Shreveport-Bossier Convention & Tourist
    Bureau
629 Spring St
Shreveport, LA 71101
Phone: 318-222-9391; Fax: 318-222-0056
Toll-free: 800-551-8682
www.shreveport-bossier.org

Bossier Chamber of Commerce
710 Benton Rd
Bossier City, LA 71111

Phone: 318-746-0252; Fax: 318-746-0357
www.bossierchamber.com

Greater Baton Rouge Chamber of Commerce
564 Laurel St
Baton Rouge, LA 70801
Phone: 225-381-7125; Fax: 225-336-4306
www.brchamber.org

Greater Lafayette Chamber of Commerce
804 E St Mary Blvd
Lafayette, LA 70503
Phone: 337-233-2705; Fax: 337-234-8671
www.lafchamber.org

Greater Shreveport Chamber of Commerce
400 Edwards St
Shreveport, LA 71101
Phone: 318-677-2500; Fax: 318-677-2541
Toll-free: 800-448-5432
www.shreveportchamber.org

Jefferson Chamber of Commerce
3421 N Causeway Blvd
Suite 203
Metairie, LA 70002
Phone: 504-835-3880; Fax: 504-835-3828
www.jeffersonchamber.org

New Orleans Chamber of Commerce
1515 Poydras St
Suite 1010
New Orleans, LA 70112
Phone: 504-522-7226; Fax: 504-522-1355
www.neworleanschamber.org

MAINE

Maine Tourism Office
59 State House Stn
Augusta, ME 04333
Phone: 207-287-5711; Fax: 207-287-8070
Toll-free: 888-624-6345
www.visitmaine.com

Maine State Chamber of Commerce
7 University Dr
Augusta, ME 04330
Phone: 207-623-4568; Fax: 207-622-7723
www.mainechamber.org

Convention & Visitors Bureau of Greater
  Portland
245 Commercial St
Portland, ME 04101
Phone: 207-772-5800; Fax: 207-874-9043
www.visitportland.com

Greater Bangor Convention & Visitors
  Bureau
40 Harlow Pl
Bangor, ME 04401
Phone: 207-947-5205; Fax: 207-942-2146
Toll-free: 800-916-6673
www.bangorcvb.org

Bangor Region Chamber of Commerce
519 Main St
Bangor, ME 04401
Phone: 207-947-0307; Fax: 207-990-1427
www.bangorregion.com

Bar Harbor Chamber of Commerce
93 Cottage St
PO Box 158
Bar Harbor, ME 04609
Phone: 207-288-5103; Fax: 207-288-2565
Toll-free: 888-540-9990
www.barharborinfo.com

Kennebec Valley Chamber of Commerce
21 University Dr
Augusta, ME 04330
Phone: 207-623-4559; Fax: 207-626-9342
www.augustamaine.com

Portland Regional Chamber
60 Pearl St
Portland, ME 04101
Phone: 207-772-2811; Fax: 207-772-1179
www.portlandregion.com

MARYLAND

Maryland Tourism Development Office
217 E Redwood St
9th Fl
Baltimore, MD 21202
Phone: 410-767-3400; Fax: 410-333-6643
Toll-free: 800-543-1036
www.mdisfun.org

Maryland Chamber of Commerce
60 West St
Suite 100
Annapolis, MD 21401
Phone: 410-269-0642; Fax: 410-269-5247
www.mdchamber.org

Annapolis & Anne Arundel County
  Conference & Visitors Bureau
26 West St
Annapolis, MD 21401
Phone: 410-268-8687; Fax: 410-263-9591
Toll-free: 888-302-2852
www.visit-annapolis.org

Baltimore Area Convention & Visitors Assn
100 Light St
12th Fl
Baltimore, MD 21202
Phone: 410-659-7300; Fax: 410-727-2308
Toll-free: 800-343-3468
www.baltimore.org

Ocean City Convention & Visitors Bureau
4001 Coastal Hwy
Ocean City, MD 21842
Phone: 410-289-8181; Fax: 410-723-8655
Toll-free: 800-626-2326
www.ococean.com

Annapolis & Anne Arundel County
  Chamber of Commerce
49 Old Solomons Island Rd
Suite 204
Annapolis, MD 21401
Phone: 410-266-3960; Fax: 410-266-8270
www.annapolischamber.com

Baltimore City Chamber of Commerce
312 N ML King Blvd
Baltimore, MD 21201
Phone: 410-837-7101; Fax: 410-837-7104
www.baltimorecitychamber.com

Ocean City Chamber of Commerce
12320 Ocean Gateway
Ocean City, MD 21842
Phone: 410-213-0144; Fax: 410-213-7521
Toll-free: 888-626-3386
www.oceancity.org

MASSACHUSETTS

Massachusetts Travel & Tourism Office
10 Park Plaza
Suite 4510
Boston, MA 02116
Phone: 617-973-8500; Fax: 617-973-8525
Toll-free: 800-227-6277
www.mass-vacation.com

New England Council Inc
98 N Washington St
Suite 201
Boston, MA 02114
Phone: 617-723-4009; Fax: 617-723-3943
www.newenglandcouncil.com

Greater Boston Convention & Visitors
    Bureau
2 Copley Pl
Suite 105
Boston, MA 02116
Phone: 617-536-4100; Fax: 617-424-7664
Toll-free: 888-733-2678
www.bostonusa.com

Greater Springfield Convention & Visitors
    Bureau
1441 Main St
Suite 136
Springfield, MA 01103
Phone: 413-787-1548; Fax: 413-781-4607
Toll-free: 800-723-1548
www.valleyvisitor.com

Worcester County Convention & Visitors
    Bureau
30 Worcester Center Blvd
Worcester, MA 01608
Phone: 508-755-7400; Fax: 508-754-2703
Toll-free: 800-231-7557
www.worcester.org

Cape Cod Chamber of Commerce
5 Shoot Flying Hill Road
Centerville, MA 02632
Phone: 508-362-3225; Fax: 508-362-3698
Toll-free: 888-332-2732
www.capecodchamber.org

Greater Boston Chamber of Commerce
75 State St
2nd Fl
Boston, MA 02109
Phone: 617-227-4500; Fax: 617-227-7505
www.bostonchamber.com

Greater Springfield Chamber of
    Commerce
1441 Main St
Suite 136
Springfield, MA 01103
Phone: 413-787-1555; Fax: 413-731-8530

Worcester Regional Chamber of
    Commerce
339 Main St
Worcester, MA 01608
Phone: 508-753-2924; Fax: 508-754-8560
www.worcesterchamber.org

MICHIGAN

Michigan Travel Michigan
300 N Washington Sq
Lansing, MI 48913
Phone: 517-373-0670; Fax: 517-373-0059
Toll-free: 888-784-7328
www.michigan.org

Michigan Chamber of Commerce
600 S Walnut St
Lansing, MI 48933
Phone: 517-371-2100; Fax: 517-371-7224
Toll-free: 800-748-0266
www.michamber.com

Ann Arbor Area Convention & Visitors
    Bureau
120 W Huron St
Ann Arbor, MI 48104
Phone: 734-995-7281; Fax: 734-995-7283
Toll-free: 800-888-9487
www.annarbor.org

Detroit Metropolitan Convention & Visitors
    Bureau
211 W Fort St
Suite 1000
Detroit, MI 48226

Phone: 313-202-1800; Fax: 313-202-1808
Toll-free: 800-225-5389
www.visitdetroit.com

Flint Area Convention & Visitors Bureau
316 Water St
Flint, MI 48502
Phone: 810-232-8900; Fax: 810-232-1515
Toll-free: 800-253-5468
flintcommercecenter.com

Grand Rapids/Kent County Convention &
Visitors Bureau
171 Monroe Ave NW
Suite 700
Grand Rapids, MI 49503
Phone: 616-459-8287; Fax: 616-459-7291
Toll-free: 800-678-9859
www.visitgrandrapids.org

Greater Lansing Convention & Visitors
Bureau
1223 Turner St
Suite 200
Lansing, MI 48906
Phone: 517-487-0077; Fax: 517-487-5151
Toll-free: 800-648-6630
www.lansing.org

Ann Arbor Area Chamber of Commerce
115 W Heron
3rd Fl
Ann Arbor, MI 48104
Phone: 734-665-4433; Fax: 734-665-4191
www.annarborchamber.org

Detroit Regional Chamber
1 Woodward Ave Suite 1900
PO Box 33840
Detroit, MI 48232
Phone: 313-964-4000; Fax: 313-964-0183
www.detroitchamber.com

Genesee Regional Chamber of Commerce
519 S Saginaw St
Suite 200
Flint, MI 48502
Phone: 810-232-7101; Fax: 810-233-7437
www.thegrcc.org

Grand Rapids Area Chamber of Commerce
111 Pearl St NW
Grand Rapids, MI 49503
Phone: 616-771-0300; Fax: 616-771-0318
www.grandrapids.org

Lansing Regional Chamber of Commerce
300 E Michigan Ave
Suite 300
Lansing, MI 48933
Phone: 517-487-6340; Fax: 517-484-6910
www.lansingchamber.org

MINNESOTA

Minnesota Tourism Office
121 7th Pl E
Suite 100
Saint Paul, MN 55101
Phone: 651-296-5029
Toll-free: 888-868-7476
www.exploreminnesota.com

Minnesota Chamber of Commerce
400 Robert St N
Suite 1500
Saint Paul, MN 55101
Phone: 651-292-4650; Fax: 651-292-4656
Toll-free: 800-821-2230
www.mnchamber.com

Duluth Convention & Visitors Bureau
21 W Superior St
Suite 100
Duluth, MN 55802
Phone: 218-722-4011; Fax: 218-722-1322
Toll-free: 800-438-5884
www.visitduluth.com

Greater Minneapolis Convention & Visitors
Assn
250 Marquette Ave
Suite 1300
Minneapolis, MN 55401
Phone: 612-767-8000; Fax: 612-335-5839
Toll-free: 800-445-7412
www.minneapolis.org

Rochester Convention & Visitors Bureau
111 S Broadway

Suite 301
Rochester, MN 55904
Phone: 507-288-4331; Fax: 507-288-9144
Toll-free: 800-634-8277
www.rochestercvb.org

Saint Paul River Centre Convention &
    Visitors Authority
175 W Kellogg Blvd
Suite 502
Saint Paul, MN 55102
Phone: 651-265-4900; Fax: 651-265-4999
Toll-free: 800-627-6101
www.stpaulcvb.org

Chamber of Commerce of Fargo Moorhead
202 1st Ave N
Moorhead, MN 56560
Phone: 218-233-1100; Fax: 218-233-1200
www.fmchamber.com

Duluth Area Chamber of Commerce
5 W 1st St
Suite 101
Duluth, MN 55802
Phone: 218-722-5501; Fax: 218-722-3223
www.duluthchamber.com

Minneapolis Regional Chamber of
    Commerce
81 S 9th St
Suite 200
Minneapolis, MN 55402
Phone: 612-370-9100; Fax: 612-370-9195
www.minneapolischamber.org

Rochester Area Chamber of Commerce
220 S Broadway
Suite 100
Rochester, MN 55904
Phone: 507-288-1122; Fax: 507-282-8960
www.rochestermnchamber.com

Saint Paul Area Chamber of Commerce
401 N Robert St
Suite 150
Saint Paul, MN 55101
Phone: 651-223-5000; Fax: 651-223-5119
www.saintpaulchamber.com

MISSISSIPPI

Mississippi Tourism Development Div
PO Box 849
Jackson, MS 39205
Phone: 601-359-3297; Fax: 601-359-5757
Toll-free: 866-733-6477
www.visitmississippi.org

Mississippi Economic Council
PO Box 23276
Jackson, MS 39225
Phone: 601-969-0022; Fax: 601-353-0247
Toll-free: 800-748-7626
www.msmec.com

Metro Jackson Convention & Visitors
    Bureau
921 N President St
Jackson, MS 39202
Phone: 601-960-1891; Fax: 601-960-1827
Toll-free: 800-354-7695
www.visitjackson.com

Mississippi Gulf Coast Convention &
    Visitors Bureau
PO Box 6128
Gulfport, MS 39506
Phone: 228-896-6699; Fax: 228-896-6788
Toll-free: 888-467-4853
www.gulfcoast.org

Tupelo Convention & Visitors Bureau
399 E Main St
Tupelo, MS 38804
Phone: 662-841-6521; Fax: 662-841-6558
Toll-free: 800-533-0611
tupelo.net

Area Development Partnership
1 Convention Center Plaza
Hattiesburg, MS 39401
Phone: 601-296-7500; Fax: 601-296-7505
Toll-free: 800-238-4288
www.theadp.com

MetroJackson Chamber of Commerce
PO Box 22548
Jackson, MS 39225

Phone: 601-948-7575; Fax: 601-352-5539
www.metrochamber.com

Mississippi Gulf Coast Chamber of Commerce
11975-E Seaway Rd
Gulfport, MS 39503
Phone: 228-604-0014; Fax: 228-604-0105
www.mscoastchamber.com

MISSOURI

Missouri Tourism Div
PO Box 1055
Jefferson City, MO 65102
Phone: 573-526-5900; Fax: 573-751-5160
Toll-free: 800-877-1234
www.missouritourism.org

Missouri Chamber of Commerce
PO Box 149
Jefferson City, MO 65102
Phone: 573-634-3511; Fax: 573-634-8855
www.mochamber.org

Branson/Lakes Area Chamber of Commerce/
    Convention & Visitors Bureau
PO Box 1897
Branson, MO 65615
Phone: 417-334-4136; Fax: 417-334-4139
Toll-free: 800-214-3661
www.bransonchamber.com

Columbia Convention & Visitors Bureau
300 S Providence Rd
Columbia, MO 65203
Phone: 573-875-1231; Fax: 573-443-3986
Toll-free: 800-652-0987
www.visitcolumbiamo.com

Convention & Visitors Bureau of Greater
    Kansas City
1100 Main St
Suite 2200
Kansas City, MO 64105
Phone: 816-221-5242; Fax: 816-691-3805
Toll-free: 800-767-7700
www.visitkc.com

Jefferson City Convention & Visitors Bureau
213 Adams St
Jefferson City, MO 65101

Phone: 573-632-2820; Fax: 573-638-4892
Toll-free: 800-769-4183
www.visitjeffersoncity.com

Saint Louis Convention & Visitors
    Commission
1 Metropolitan Sq
Suite 1100
Saint Louis, MO 63102
Phone: 314-421-1023; Fax: 314-421-0039
Toll-free: 800-325-7962
www.explorestlouis.com

Springfield Missouri Convention & Visitors
    Bureau
815 E Saint Louis St
Springfield, MO 65806
Phone: 417-881-5300; Fax: 417-881-2231
Toll-free: 800-678-8767
www.springfieldmo.org

Columbia Chamber of Commerce
300 S Providence Rd
Columbia, MO 65203
Phone: 573-874-1132; Fax: 573-443-3986
chamber.columbia.mo.us

Greater Kansas City Chamber of Commerce
911 Main St
Suite 2600
Kansas City, MO 64105
Phone: 816-221-2424; Fax: 816-221-7440
www.kcchamber.com

Independence Chamber of Commerce
210 W Truman Rd
Independence, MO 64050
Phone: 816-252-4745; Fax: 816-252-4917
www.independencechamber.com

Jefferson City Area Chamber of Commerce
213 Adams St
Jefferson City, MO 65101
Phone: 573-634-3616; Fax: 573-634-3805
www.jcchamber.org

Saint Louis Regional Commerce & Growth
    Assn
1 Metropolitan Sq
Suite 1300
Saint Louis, MO 63102

Phone: 314-231-5555; Fax: 314-444-1122
Toll-free: 877-785-7242
www.stlrcga.org

Springfield Area Chamber of Commerce
202 S John Q Hammons Pkwy
Springfield, MO 65806
Phone: 417-862-5567; Fax: 417-862-1611
Toll-free: 800-879-7504
www.springfieldchamber.com

MONTANA

Montana Promotion Div (Travel Montana)
PO Box 200533
Helena, MT 59620
Phone: 406-444-2654
Toll-free: 800-847-4868
www.visitmt.com

Montana Chamber of Commerce
PO Box 1730
Helena, MT 59624
Phone: 406-442-2405; Fax: 406-442-2409
www.montanachamber.com

Billings Chamber of Commerce &
    Convention & Visitors Bureau
815 S 27th St
PO Box 31177
Billings, MT 59107
Phone: 406-245-4111; Fax: 406-245-7333
Toll-free: 800-735-2635
billingscvb.visitmt.com

Helena Convention & Visitors Bureau
225 Cruse Ave
Helena, MT 59601
Phone: 406-447-1530; Fax: 406-447-1532
Toll-free: 800-743-5362
helenacvb.visitmt.com

Great Falls Area Chamber of Commerce
710 1st Ave N
Great Falls, MT 59401
Phone: 406-761-4434; Fax: 406-761-6129
Toll-free: 800-735-8535
www.greatfallschamber.org

Helena Area Chamber of Commerce
225 Cruse Ave

Helena, MT 59601
Phone: 406-442-4120; Fax: 406-447-1532
Toll-free: 800-743-5362
www.helenachamber.com

NEBRASKA

Nebraska Travel & Tourism Div
PO Box 98907
Lincoln, NE 68509
Phone: 402-471-3796; Fax: 402-471-3026
Toll-free: 877-632-7275
www.visitnebraska.org

Nebraska Chamber of Commerce &
    Industry
PO Box 95128
Lincoln, NE 68509
Phone: 402-474-4422; Fax: 402-474-5681
www.nechamber.com

Greater Omaha Convention & Visitors
    Bureau
1001 Farnam St
Suite 200
Omaha, NE 68102
Phone: 402-444-4660; Fax: 402-444-4511
Toll-free: 800-332-1819
www.visitomaha.com

Lincoln Convention & Visitors Bureau
1135 M St
3rd Fl
Lincoln, NE 68508
Phone: 402-434-5335; Fax: 402-436-2360
Toll-free: 800-423-8212
www.lincoln.org

Greater Omaha Chamber of Commerce
1301 Harney St
Omaha, NE 68102
Phone: 402-346-5000; Fax: 402-346-7050
www.omahachamber.net

Lincoln Chamber of Commerce
PO Box 83006
Lincoln, NE 68501
Phone: 402-436-2350; Fax: 402-436-2360
www.lcoc.com

NEVADA

Nevada Tourism Commission
401 N Carson St
Carson City, NV 89701
Phone: 775-687-4322; Fax: 775-687-6779
Toll-free: 800-237-0774
www.travelnevada.com

Carson City Convention & Visitors Bureau
1900 S Carson St
Suite 100
Carson City, NV 89701
Phone: 775-687-7410; Fax: 775-687-7416
Toll-free: 800-638-2321
www.carson-city.org

Las Vegas Convention & Visitors Authority
3150 S Paradise Rd
Las Vegas, NV 89109
Phone: 702-892-0711; Fax: 702-892-2824
Toll-free: 800-332-5333
www.lvcva.com

Reno-Sparks Convention & Visitors Authority
PO Box 837
Reno, NV 89504
Phone: 775-827-7600; Fax: 775-827-7686
Toll-free: 800-443-1482
www.visitrenotahoe.com

Carson City Area Chamber of Commerce
1900 S Carson St
Suite 200
Carson City, NV 89701
Phone: 775-882-1565; Fax: 775-882-4179
www.carsoncitychamber.com

Las Vegas Chamber of Commerce
3720 Howard Hughes Pkwy
Las Vegas, NV 89169
Phone: 702-735-1616; Fax: 702-735-2011
www.lvchamber.com

NEW HAMPSHIRE

New Hampshire Travel & Tourism
  Development Office
PO Box 1856
Concord, NH 03302

Phone: 603-271-2665; Fax: 603-271-6870
Toll-free: 800-386-4664
www.visitnh.gov

New Hampshire Business & Industry Assn
122 N Main St
3rd Fl
Concord, NH 03301
Phone: 603-224-5388; Fax: 603-224-2872
www.nhbia.org

Manchester Area Convention & Visitors
  Bureau
889 Elm St
3rd Fl
Manchester, NH 03101
Phone: 603-666-6600; Fax: 603-626-0910
www.manchestercvb.com

Greater Concord Chamber of Commerce
40 Commercial St
Concord, NH 03301
Phone: 603-224-2508; Fax: 603-224-8128
www.concordnhchamber.com

Greater Manchester Chamber of Commerce
889 Elm St
Manchester, NH 03101
Phone: 603-666-6600; Fax: 603-626-0910
www.manchester-chamber.org

NEW JERSEY

New Jersey Commerce Economic Growth &
  Tourism Commission
20 W State St
PO Box 820
Trenton, NJ 08625
Phone: 609-777-0885; Fax: 609-777-4097
www.state.nj.us/commerce

New Jersey Travel & Tourism Div
PO Box 820
Trenton, NJ 08625
Phone: 609-777-0885; Fax: 609-633-7418
Toll-free: 800-847-4865
www.state.nj.us/travel

New Jersey State Chamber of Commerce
216 W State St

Trenton, NJ 08608
Phone: 609-989-7888; Fax: 609-989-9696
www.njchamber.com

Atlantic City Convention & Visitors
    Authority
2314 Pacific Ave
Atlantic City, NJ 08401
Phone: 609-449-7130; Fax: 609-348-3426
Toll-free: 888-228-4748
www.atlanticcitynj.com

Capital Region Convention & Visitors Bureau
1A Quakerbridge Plaza Dr
Mercerville, NJ 08619
Phone: 609-689-9964; Fax: 609-586-9989
www.visitcapitalregion.org

Atlantic City Regional Chamber of Commerce
1125 Atlantic Ave
Suite 105
Atlantic City, NJ 08401
Phone: 609-345-5600; Fax: 609-345-1666
www.atlanticcitychamber.com

Greater Paterson Chamber of Commerce
100 Hamilton Plaza
Suite 1201
Paterson, NJ 07505
Phone: 973-881-7300; Fax: 973-881-8233
www.greaterpatersoncc.org

Hudson County Chamber of Commerce
660 Newark Ave
Suite 220
Jersey City, NJ 07306
Phone: 201-386-0699; Fax: 201-386-8480
www.hudsonchamber.org

Mercer Regional Chamber of Commerce
1A Quakerbridge Plaza Dr
Mercerville, NJ 08619
Phone: 609-689-9960; Fax: 609-586-9989
www.mercerchamber.org

Newark Regional Business Partnership
744 Broad St
26th Fl
Newark, NJ 07102
Phone: 973-522-0099; Fax: 973-824-6587
www.newarkrbp.org

NEW MEXICO

New Mexico Tourism Dept
491 Old Santa Fe Trail
Santa Fe, NM 87503
Phone: 505-827-7400; Fax: 505-827-7402
Toll-free: 800-545-2070
www.newmexico.org

New Mexico Assn of Commerce & Industry
PO Box 9706
Albuquerque, NM 87119
Phone: 505-842-0644; Fax: 505-842-0734
www.aci.nm.org

Albuquerque Convention & Visitors Bureau
20 First Plaza
Suite 601
Albuquerque, NM 87102
Phone: 505-842-9918; Fax: 505-247-9101
Toll-free: 800-733-9918
www.abqcvb.org

Las Cruces Convention & Visitors Bureau
211 N Water St
Las Cruces, NM 88001
Phone: 505-541-2444; Fax: 505-541-2164
Toll-free: 800-343-7827
www.lascrucescvb.org

Santa Fe Convention & Visitors Bureau
60 E San Francisco St
Santa Fe, NM 87501
Phone: 505-955-6200; Fax: 505-955-6222
Toll-free: 800-777-2489
www.santafe.org

Greater Albuquerque Chamber of
    Commerce
PO Box 25100
Albuquerque, NM 87125
Phone: 505-764-3700; Fax: 505-764-3714
abqchamber.com

Greater Las Cruces Chamber of Commerce
760 W Picacho Ave
Las Cruces, NM 88005
Phone: 505-524-1968; Fax: 505-527-5546
lascruces.org

Santa Fe Chamber of Commerce
8380 Cerrillos Rd
Suite 302
Santa Fe, NM 87507
Phone: 505-988-3279; Fax: 505-984-2205
www.santafechamber.com

NEW YORK

New York (State) Tourism Div
PO Box 2603
Albany, NY 12220
Phone: 518-474-4116; Fax: 518-486-6416
Toll-free: 800-225-5697
www.iloveny.com

Business Council of New York State Inc
152 Washington Ave
Albany, NY 12210
Phone: 518-465-7511; Fax: 518-465-4389
Toll-free: 800-358-1202
www.bcnys.org

Albany County Convention & Visitors
    Bureau
25 Quackenbush Sq
Albany, NY 12207
Phone: 518-434-1217; Fax: 518-434-0887
Toll-free: 800-258-3582
www.albany.org

Greater Buffalo Convention & Visitors
    Bureau
617 Main St
Suite 200
Buffalo, NY 14203
Phone: 716-852-2356; Fax: 716-852-0131
Toll-free: 800-283-3256
www.visitbuffaloniagara.com

Greater Rochester Visitors Assn
45 East Ave
Suite 400
Rochester, NY 14604
Phone: 585-546-3070; Fax: 585-232-4822
Toll-free: 800-677-7282
www.visitrochester.com

NYC & Co
810 7th Ave

3rd Fl
New York, NY 10019
Phone: 212-484-1200; Fax: 212-484-1222
Toll-free: 800-692-8474
www.nycvisit.com

Syracuse Convention & Visitors Bureau
572 S Salina St
Syracuse, NY 13202
Phone: 315-470-1910; Fax: 315-471-8545
Toll-free: 800-234-4797
www.visitsyracuse.org

Westchester County Office of Tourism
222 Mamaroneck Ave
Suite 100
White Plains, NY 10605
Phone: 914-995-8500; Fax: 914-995-8505
Toll-free: 800-833-9282
www.westchestertourism.com

Albany-Colonie Regional Chamber of
    Commerce
107 Washington Ave
Albany, NY 12210
Phone: 518-434-1214; Fax: 518-434-1339
www.ac-chamber.org

Buffalo Niagara Partnership
665 Main St
Suite 200
Buffalo, NY 14203
Phone: 716-852-7100; Fax: 716-852-2761
Toll-free: 800-241-0474
www.thepartnership.org

Greater Syracuse Chamber of Commerce
572 S Salina St
Syracuse, NY 13202
Phone: 315-470-1800; Fax: 315-471-8545
www.syracusechamber.com

New York City Partnership & Chamber of
    Commerce Inc
1 Battery Park Plaza
5th Fl
New York, NY 10004
Phone: 212-493-7500; Fax: 212-344-3344
www.nycp.org

Rochester Business Alliance
150 State St
Rochester, NY 14614
Phone: 585-454-2220; Fax: 585-263-3679
www.rochesterbusinessalliance.com

Yonkers Chamber of Commerce
20 S Broadway
Suite 1205
Yonkers, NY 10701
Phone: 914-963-0332; Fax: 914-963-0455
www.yonkerschamber.com

NORTH CAROLINA

North Carolina Tourism Div
301 N Wilmington St
Raleigh, NC 27601
Phone: 919-733-4171; Fax: 919-733-8582
Toll-free: 800-847-4862
www.visitnc.com

North Carolina Citizens for Business &
   Industry
225 Hillsborough St
Suite 460
Raleigh, NC 27603
Phone: 919-836-1400; Fax: 919-836-1425
www.nccbi.org

Asheville Area Convention & Visitors
   Bureau
36 Montford Ave
PO Box 1010
Asheville, NC 28802
Phone: 828-258-6102; Fax: 828-254-6054
Toll-free: 800-257-5583
www.exploreasheville.com

Charlotte Convention & Visitors Bureau
500 S College St
Suite 300
Charlotte, NC 28202
Phone: 704-334-2282; Fax: 704-342-3972
Toll-free: 800-722-1994
www.charlottecvb.org

Durham Convention & Visitors Bureau
101 E Morgan St
Durham, NC 27701

Phone: 919-687-0288; Fax: 919-683-9555
Toll-free: 800-446-8604
dcvb.durham.nc.us

Greater Raleigh Convention & Visitors
   Bureau
421 Fayetteville St Mall
Suite 1505
Raleigh, NC 27602
Phone: 919-834-5900; Fax: 919-831-2887
Toll-free: 800-849-8499
www.visitraleigh.com

Greensboro Area Convention & Visitors
   Bureau
317 S Greene St
Greensboro, NC 27401
Phone: 336-274-2282; Fax: 336-230-1183
Toll-free: 800-344-2282
www.visitgreensboro.com

Winston-Salem Convention & Visitors
   Bureau
200 Brookstown Ave
Winston-Salem, NC 27101
Phone: 336-728-4200; Fax: 336-728-4220
Toll-free: 800-331-7018
www.wscvb.com

Asheville Area Chamber of Commerce
36 Montford Ave
Asheville, NC 28801
Phone: 828-258-6101; Fax: 828-251-0926
Toll-free: 800-257-1300
www.ashevillechamber.org

Charlotte Chamber of Commerce
PO Box 32785
Charlotte, NC 28232
Phone: 704-378-1300; Fax: 704-374-1903
www.charlottechamber.com

Greater Durham Chamber of Commerce
300 W Morgan St
Suite 1400
Durham, NC 27701
Phone: 919-682-2133; Fax: 919-688-8351
www.durhamchamber.org

Greater Raleigh Chamber of Commerce
PO Box 2978
Raleigh, NC 27602
Phone: 919-664-7000; Fax: 919-664-7099
www.raleighchamber.org

Greater Winston-Salem Chamber of
  Commerce
PO Box 1408
Winston-Salem, NC 27102
Phone: 336-725-2361; Fax: 336-721-2209
www.winstonsalem.com

Greensboro Area Chamber of Commerce
342 N Elm St
Greensboro, NC 27401
Phone: 336-275-8675; Fax: 336-230-1867
www.greensborochamber.com

NORTH DAKOTA

North Dakota Tourism Div
604 E Boulevard Ave
Bismarck, ND 58505
Phone: 701-328-2525; Fax: 701-328-4878
Toll-free: 800-435-5663
www.ndtourism.com

Greater North Dakota Assn
PO Box 2639
Bismarck, ND 58502
Phone: 701-222-0929; Fax: 701-222-1611
Toll-free: 800-382-1405
www.gnda.com

Bismarck-Mandan Convention & Visitors
  Bureau
1600 Burnt Boat Dr
Bismarck, ND 58503
Phone: 701-222-4308; Fax: 701-222-0647
Toll-free: 800-767-3555
www.discoverbismarckmandan.com

Fargo-Moorhead Convention & Visitors
  Bureau
2001 44th St SW
Fargo, ND 58103
Phone: 701-282-3653; Fax: 701-282-7815
Toll-free: 800-235-7654
www.fargomoorhead.org

Greater Grand Forks Convention & Visitors
  Bureau
4251 Gateway Dr
Grand Forks, ND 58203
Phone: 701-746-0444; Fax: 701-746-0775
Toll-free: 800-866-4566
www.grandforkscvb.org

Bismarck Mandan Chamber of Commerce
1640 Burnt Boat Dr
Bismarck, ND 58502
Phone: 701-223-5660; Fax: 701-255-6125
www.bismarckmandan.com

Grand Forks Chamber of Commerce
202 N 3rd St
Grand Forks, ND 58203
Phone: 701-772-7271; Fax: 701-772-9238
www.gfchamber.com

OHIO

Ohio Travel & Tourism Div
PO Box 1001
Columbus, OH 43216
Phone: 614-466-8844; Fax: 614-466-6744
Toll-free: 800-282-5393
www.discoverohio.com

Ohio Chamber of Commerce
230 E Town St
Columbus, OH 43215
Phone: 614-228-4201; Fax: 614-228-6403
Toll-free: 800-622-1893
www.ohiochamber.com

Akron/Summit County Convention &
  Visitors Bureau
77 E Mill St
Akron, OH 44308
Phone: 330-374-7560; Fax: 330-374-7626
Toll-free: 800-245-4254
www.visitakron-summit.org

Convention & Visitors Bureau of Greater
  Cleveland
50 Public Sq
Terminal Tower Suite 3100
Cleveland, OH 44113

Phone: 216-621-4110; Fax: 216-621-5967
Toll-free: 800-321-1001
www.travelcleveland.com

Dayton/Montgomery County Convention &
    Visitors Bureau
1 Chamber Plaza
Suite A
Dayton, OH 45402
Phone: 937-226-8211; Fax: 937-226-8294
Toll-free: 800-221-8235
www.daytoncvb.com

Greater Cincinnati Convention & Visitors
    Bureau
300 W 6th St
Cincinnati, OH 45202
Phone: 513-621-2142; Fax: 513-621-5020
Toll-free: 800-246-2987
www.cincyusa.com

Greater Columbus Convention & Visitors
    Bureau
90 N High St
Columbus, OH 43215
Phone: 614-221-6623; Fax: 614-221-5618
Toll-free: 800-354-2657
www.experiencecolumbus.com

Greater Toledo Convention & Visitors Bureau
401 Jefferson Ave
Toledo, OH 43604
Phone: 419-321-6404; Fax: 419-255-7731
Toll-free: 800-243-4667
www.dotoledo.org

Youngstown/Mahoning County Convention
    & Visitors Bureau
21 W Boardsman St
Youngstown, OH 44503
Phone: 330-740-2130; Fax: 330-286-0093
Toll-free: 800-447-8201
www.youngstowncvb.com

Cincinnati USA Regional Chamber
441 Vine St
Suite 300
Cincinnati, OH 45202
Phone: 513-579-3100; Fax: 513-579-3102
www.cincinnatichamber.com

Dayton Area Chamber of Commerce
1 Chamber Plaza
Suite 200
Dayton, OH 45402
Phone: 937-226-1444; Fax: 937-226-8254
www.daytonchamber.org

Greater Akron Chamber
1 Cascade Plaza
17th Fl
Akron, OH 44308
Phone: 330-376-5550; Fax: 330-379-3164
Toll-free: 800-621-8001
www.greaterakronchamber.org

Greater Cleveland Partnership
50 Public Sq
Suite 200
Cleveland, OH 44113
Phone: 216-621-3300; Fax: 216-621-6013
Toll-free: 800-562-7121
www.gcpartnership.com

Greater Columbus Chamber of Commerce
37 N High St
Columbus, OH 43215
Phone: 614-221-1321; Fax: 614-221-9360
Toll-free: 800-950-1321
www.columbus.org

Toledo Regional Chamber of Commerce
300 Madison Ave
Suite 200
Toledo, OH 43604
Phone: 419-243-8191; Fax: 419-241-8302
www.toledochamber.com

Youngstown Warren Regional Chamber
11 Federal Plaza Center
Suite 1600
Youngstown, OH 44503
Phone: 330-744-2131; Fax: 330-746-0330
www.regionalchamber.com

OKLAHOMA

Oklahoma Tourism & Recreation Dept
15 N Robinson St
Suite 100
Oklahoma City, OK 73105

Phone: 405-521-2406; Fax: 405-521-3992
Toll-free: 800-652-6552
tourism.state.ok.us

Oklahoma State Chamber
330 NE 10th St
Oklahoma City, OK 73104
Phone: 405-235-3669; Fax: 405-235-3670
Toll-free: 800-364-6465
www.okstatechamber.com

Oklahoma City Convention & Visitors Bureau
189 W Sheridan St
Oklahoma City, OK 73102
Phone: 405-297-8912; Fax: 405-297-8888
Toll-free: 800-225-5652
www.visitokc.com

Tulsa Convention & Visitors Bureau
2 W 2nd St Suite 150
Williams Center Tower II
Tulsa, OK 74103
Phone: 918-585-1201; Fax: 918-592-6244
Toll-free: 800-558-3311
www.visittulsa.com

Greater Oklahoma City Chamber of Commerce
123 Park Ave
Oklahoma City, OK 73102
Phone: 405-297-8900; Fax: 405-297-8916
Toll-free: 800-616-1114
www.okcchamber.com

Tulsa Metro Chamber
2 W 2nd St Suite 150
Williams Center Tower II
Tulsa, OK 74103
Phone: 918-585-1201; Fax: 918-585-8016
www.tulsachamber.com

OREGON

Oregon Tourism Commission
670 Hawthorne Ave SE
Suite 240
Salem, OR 97301
Phone: 503-378-8850
Toll-free: 800-547-7842
www.traveloregon.com

Convention & Visitors Assn of Lane County
Oregon
PO Box 10286
Eugene, OR 97440
Phone: 541-484-5307; Fax: 541-343-6335
Toll-free: 800-547-5445
www.visitlanecounty.org

Portland Oregon Visitors Assn
1000 SW Broadway
Suite 2300
Portland, OR 97205
Phone: 503-275-9750; Fax: 503-275-9774
Toll-free: 800-962-3700
www.travelportland.com

Salem Convention & Visitors Assn
1313 Mill St SE
Salem, OR 97301
Phone: 503-581-4325; Fax: 503-581-4540
Toll-free: 800-874-7012
www.travelsalem.com

Eugene Chamber of Commerce
1401 Willamette St
Eugene, OR 97401
Phone: 541-484-1314; Fax: 541-484-4942
www.eugenechamber.com

Portland Business Alliance
200 SW Market St
Suite 1717
Portland, OR 97201
Phone: 503-224-8684; Fax: 503-323-9186
www.portlandalliance.com

Salem Area Chamber of
Commerce
1110 Commercial St NE
Salem, OR 97301
Phone: 503-581-1466; Fax: 503-581-0972
www.salemchamber.org

PENNSYLVANIA

Pennsylvania Tourism Office
404 North St
4th Fl
Harrisburg, PA 17120

Phone: 717-720-1301; Fax: 717-787-0687
Toll-free: 800-847-4872
www.visitpa.com

Pennsylvania Chamber of Business &
    Industry
417 Walnut St
Harrisburg, PA 17101
Phone: 717-255-3252; Fax: 717-255-3298
Toll-free: 800-225-7224
www.pachamber.org

Erie Area Convention & Visitors Bureau
208 E Bayfront Pkwy
Suite 103
Erie, PA 16507
Phone: 814-454-7191; Fax: 814-459-0241
Toll-free: 800-524-3743
www.eriepa.com

Gettysburg Convention & Visitors Bureau
571 Middle St
PO Box 4117
Gettysburg, PA 17325
Phone: 717-334-6274; Fax: 717-334-1166
Toll-free: 800-337-5015
www.gettysburg.com

Greater Pittsburgh Convention & Visitors
    Bureau
425 6th Ave
30th Fl
Pittsburgh, PA 15219
Phone: 412-281-7711; Fax: 412-644-5512
Toll-free: 800-359-0758
www.visitpittsburgh.com

Hershey-Capital Region Visitors Bureau
112 Market St
4th Fl
Harrisburg, PA 17101
Phone: 717-231-7788; Fax: 717-231-2808
Toll-free: 877-727-8573
www.hersheycapitalregion.com

Lehigh Valley Convention & Visitors Bureau
840 Hamilton St
Suite 200
Allentown, PA 18101
Phone: 610-882-9200; Fax: 610-882-0343

Toll-free: 800-747-0561
www.lehighvalleypa.org

Pennsylvania Dutch Convention & Visitors
    Bureau
501 Greenfield Rd
Lancaster, PA 17601
Phone: 717-299-8901; Fax: 717-299-0470
Toll-free: 800-723-8824
www.padutchcountry.com

Philadelphia Convention & Visitors Bureau
1700 Market St
Suite 3000
Philadelphia, PA 19103
Phone: 215-636-3300; Fax: 215-636-3327
Toll-free: 800-225-5745
www.pcvb.org

Erie Regional Chamber & Growth
    Partnership
208 E Bayfront Pkwy
Erie, PA 16507
Phone: 814-454-7191; Fax: 814-459-0241
Toll-free: 800-524-3743
www.eriechamber.com

Gettysburg-Adams County Area Chamber of
    Commerce
18 Carlisle St
Suite 203
Gettysburg, PA 17325
Phone: 717-334-8151; Fax: 717-334-3368
www.gettysburg-chamber.org

Greater Lehigh Valley Chamber of Commerce
462 W Walnut St
Allentown, PA 18102
Phone: 610-841-5800; Fax: 610-437-4907
www.lehighvalleychamber.org

Greater Philadelphia Chamber of Commerce
200 S Broad St
Suite 700
Philadelphia, PA 19102
Phone: 215-545-1234; Fax: 215-790-3600
www.greaterphilachamber.com

Greater Pittsburgh Chamber of Commerce
425 6th Ave

Suite 1100
Pittsburgh, PA 15219
Phone: 412-392-4500; Fax: 412-392-1040
Toll-free: 800-843-8772
www.pittsburghchamber.com

Greater Scranton Chamber of Commerce
222 Mulberry St
Scranton, PA 18503
Phone: 570-342-7711; Fax: 570-347-6262
www.scrantonchamber.com

Harrisburg Regional Chamber
3211 N Front St
Suite 201
Harrisburg, PA 17110
Phone: 717-232-4099; Fax: 717-232-5184
www.harrisburgregionalchamber.org

Lancaster Chamber of Commerce &
    Industry
100 S Queen St
PO Box 1558
Lancaster, PA 17608
Phone: 717-397-3531; Fax: 717-293-3159
www.lcci.com

RHODE ISLAND

Rhode Island Tourism Div
1 W Exchange St
Providence, RI 02903
Phone: 401-222-2601; Fax: 401-273-8270
Toll-free: 800-556-2484
visitrhodeisland.com

Rhode Island Economic Development
    Corp
1 W Exchange St
Providence, RI 02903
Phone: 401-222-2601; Fax: 401-222-2102
www.riedc.com

Newport County Convention & Visitors
    Bureau
23 America's Cup Ave
Newport, RI 02840
Phone: 401-849-8048; Fax: 401-849-0291
Toll-free: 800-326-6030
www.gonewport.com

Providence Warwick Convention & Visitors
    Bureau
1 W Exchange St
Providence, RI 02903
Phone: 401-274-1636; Fax: 401-351-2090
Toll-free: 800-233-1636
www.pwcvb.com

Greater Providence Chamber of
    Commerce
30 Exchange Terr
4th Fl
Providence, RI 02903
Phone: 401-521-5000; Fax: 401-751-2434
www.provchamber.com

Newport County Chamber of Commerce
45 Valley Rd
Middletown, RI 02842
Phone: 401-847-1600; Fax: 401-849-5848
www.newportchamber.com

SOUTH CAROLINA

South Carolina Parks Recreation & Tourism
    Dept
1205 Pendleton St
Columbia, SC 29201
Phone: 803-734-1650; Fax: 803-734-0133
southcarolinaparks.com

South Carolina Chamber of Commerce
1201 Main St
Suite 1700
Columbia, SC 29201
Phone: 803-799-4601; Fax: 803-779-6043
Toll-free: 800-799-4601
www.scchamber.net

Charleston Area Convention & Visitors
    Bureau
423 King St
Charleston, SC 29403
Phone: 843-853-8000; Fax: 843-853-0444
Toll-free: 800-868-8118
www.charlestoncvb.com

Columbia Metropolitan Convention &
    Visitors Bureau
PO Box 15

Columbia, SC 29202
Phone: 803-545-0000; Fax: 803-545-0013
Toll-free: 800-264-4884
www.columbiacvb.com

Greater Greenville Convention & Visitors
    Bureau
631 S Main St
Suite 301
Greenville, SC 29601
Phone: 864-421-0000; Fax: 864-421-0005
Toll-free: 800-351-7180
www.greatergreenville.com

Hilton Head Island Visitors & Convention
    Bureau
1 Chamber Dr
PO Box 5647
Hilton Head Island, SC 29938
Phone: 843-785-3673; Fax: 843-785-7110
Toll-free: 800-523-3373
www.hiltonheadisland.org

Myrtle Beach Area Convention Bureau
1200 N Oak St
Myrtle Beach, SC 29577
Phone: 843-626-7444; Fax: 843-448-3010
Toll-free: 800-356-3016
www.myrtlebeachinfo.com

Charleston Metro Chamber of Commerce
2750 Speissegger Dr
Suite 100
North Charleston, SC 29405
Phone: 843-577-2510; Fax: 843-723-4853
www.charlestonchamber.net

Greater Columbia Chamber of Commerce
930 Richland St
Columbia, SC 29201
Phone: 803-733-1110; Fax: 803-733-1149
www.columbiachamber.com

Greater Greenville Chamber of Commerce
24 Cleveland St
Greenville, SC 29601
Phone: 864-242-1050; Fax: 864-282-8509
www.greenvillechamber.org

Hilton Head Island-Bluffton Chamber of
    Commerce
1 Chamber Dr
Hilton Head Island, SC 29928
Phone: 843-785-3673; Fax: 843-785-7110
Toll-free: 800-523-3373
www.hiltonheadisland.org

Myrtle Beach Area Chamber of Commerce
1200 N Oak St
Myrtle Beach, SC 29577
Phone: 843-626-7444; Fax: 843-626-0009
Toll-free: 800-356-3016
www.myrtlebeachinfo.com/chamber/

SOUTH DAKOTA

South Dakota Tourism Office
711 E Wells Ave
Pierre, SD 57501
Phone: 605-773-3301; Fax: 605-773-3256
Toll-free: 800-732-5682
www.travelsd.com

South Dakota Chamber of Commerce &
    Industry
108 N Euclid Ave
Pierre, SD 57501
Phone: 605-224-6161; Fax: 605-224-7198
www.sdchamber.biz

Rapid City Convention & Visitors Bureau
444 Mt Rushmore Rd N
Rapid City, SD 57701
Phone: 605-343-1744; Fax: 605-348-9217
Toll-free: 800-487-3223
www.rapidcitycvb.com

Sioux Falls Convention & Visitors Bureau
200 N Phillips Ave
Suite 102
Sioux Falls, SD 57104
Phone: 605-336-1620; Fax: 605-336-6499
Toll-free: 800-333-2072
www.siouxfallscvb.com

Pierre Area Chamber of Commerce
800 W Dakota Ave
PO Box 548

Pierre, SD 57501
Phone: 605-224-7361; Fax: 605-224-6485
Toll-free: 800-962-2034
pierre.org

Rapid City Area Chamber of Commerce
444 Mt Rushmore Rd N
Rapid City, SD 57701
Phone: 605-343-1744; Fax: 605-343-6550
www.rapidcitychamber.com

Sioux Falls Area Chamber of Commerce
200 N Phillips Ave
Suite 102
Sioux Falls, SD 57104
Phone: 605-336-1620; Fax: 605-336-6499
www.siouxfalls.com

TENNESSEE

Tennessee Chamber of Commerce & Industry
611 Commerce St
Suite 3030
Nashville, TN 37203
Phone: 615-256-5141; Fax: 615-256-6726
www.tnchamber.org

Chattanooga Area Convention & Visitors
    Bureau
2 Broad St
Chattanooga, TN 37402
Phone: 423-756-8687; Fax: 423-265-1630
Toll-free: 800-322-3344
www.chattanoogafun.com

Johnson City Convention & Visitors Bureau
603 E Market St
Johnson City, TN 37601
Phone: 423-461-8000; Fax: 423-461-8047
Toll-free: 800-852-3392
www.johnsoncitytn.com

Knoxville Tourism & Sports Corp
301 S Gay St
Knoxville, TN 37902
Phone: 865-523-7263; Fax: 865-673-4400
Toll-free: 866-790-5373
www.knoxville.org

Memphis Convention & Visitors Bureau
47 Union Ave
Memphis, TN 38103
Phone: 901-543-5300; Fax: 901-543-5350
Toll-free: 800-873-6282
www.memphistravel.com

Nashville Convention & Visitors Bureau
211 Commerce St
Suite 100
Nashville, TN 37201
Phone: 615-259-4700; Fax: 615-259-4126
Toll-free: 800-657-6910
www.nashvillecvb.com

Chattanooga Area Chamber of Commerce
811 Broad St
Chattanooga, TN 37402
Phone: 423-756-2121; Fax: 423-267-7242
www.chattanoogachamber.com

Johnson City/Jonesborough/Washington
    County Chamber of Commerce
603 E Market St
Johnson City, TN 37601
Phone: 423-461-8000; Fax: 423-461-8047
Toll-free: 800-852-3392
www.johnsoncitytn.com

Knoxville Area Chamber Partnership
17 Market Sq
Suite 201
Knoxville, TN 37902
Phone: 865-637-4550; Fax: 865-523-2071
www.knoxvillechamber.com

Memphis Regional Chamber of Commerce
22 N Front St
Suite 200
Memphis, TN 38103
Phone: 901-543-3500; Fax: 901-543-3510
www.memphischamber.com

Nashville Chamber of Commerce
211 Commerce St
Suite 100
Nashville, TN 37201
Phone: 615-743-3000; Fax: 615-256-3074
www.nashvillechamber.com

TEXAS

Texas Tourism Div
PO Box 12728
Austin, TX 78711
Phone: 512-462-9191; Fax: 512-936-0089
Toll-free: 800-888-8839
www.traveltex.com

Texas Assn of Business
1209 Nueces St
Austin, TX 78701
Phone: 512-477-6721; Fax: 512-477-0836
www.txbiz.org

Abilene Convention & Visitors Bureau
1101 N 1st St
Abilene, TX 79601
Phone: 325-676-2556; Fax: 325-676-1630
Toll-free: 800-727-7704
abilenevisitors.com

Amarillo Convention & Visitor Council
1000 S Polk St
PO Box 9480
Amarillo, TX 79105
Phone: 806-374-1497; Fax: 806-373-3909
Toll-free: 800-692-1338
www.visitamarillotx.com

Arlington Convention & Visitors Bureau
1905 E Randol Mill Rd
Arlington, TX 76011
Phone: 817-265-7721; Fax: 817-265-5640
Toll-free: 800-433-5374
www.acvb.org

Austin Convention & Visitors Bureau
301 Congress Ave
Suite 200
Austin, TX 78701
Phone: 512-474-5171; Fax: 512-583-7282
Toll-free: 800-926-2282
www.austintexas.org

Brownsville Convention & Visitors Bureau
PO Box 4697
Brownsville, TX 78523
Phone: 956-546-3721; Fax: 956-546-3972

Toll-free: 800-626-2639
www.brownsville.org

Corpus Christi Convention & Visitors
  Bureau
1201 N Shoreline Blvd
Corpus Christi, TX 78401
Phone: 361-881-1888; Fax: 361-887-9023
Toll-free: 800-678-6232
www.corpuschristicvb.com

Dallas Convention & Visitors Bureau
325 N Saint Paul St
Suite 700
Dallas, TX 75201
Phone: 214-571-1000; Fax: 214-571-1008
Toll-free: 800-232-5527
www.dallascvb.com

El Paso Convention & Visitors Bureau
1 Civic Center Plaza
El Paso, TX 79901
Phone: 915-534-0600; Fax: 915-534-0687
Toll-free: 800-351-6024
www.elpasocvb.com

Fort Worth Convention & Visitors Bureau
415 Throckmorton St
Fort Worth, TX 76102
Phone: 817-336-8791; Fax: 817-336-3282
Toll-free: 800-433-5747
www.fortworth.com

Greater Houston Convention & Visitors
  Bureau
901 Bagby St
Suite 100
Houston, TX 77002
Phone: 713-437-5200; Fax: 713-227-6336
Toll-free: 800-446-8786
www.visithoustontexas.com

Irving Convention & Visitors Bureau
222 W Las Colinas Blvd
Suite 1550
Irving, TX 75039
Phone: 972-252-7476; Fax: 972-257-3153
Toll-free: 800-247-8464
www.irvingtexas.com

Lubbock Convention & Visitors Bureau
1301 Broadway St
Suite 200
Lubbock, TX 79401
Phone: 806-747-5232; Fax: 806-747-1419
Toll-free: 800-692-4035
www.visitlubbock.org

Plano Convention & Visitors Bureau
2000 E Spring Creek Pkwy
Plano, TX 75074
Phone: 972-422-0296; Fax: 972-424-0002
Toll-free: 800-817-5266
www.planocvb.com

San Antonio Convention & Visitors Bureau
203 S Saint Marys St
2nd Fl
San Antonio, TX 78205
Phone: 210-207-6700; Fax: 210-207-6768
Toll-free: 800-447-3372
www.sanantoniocvb.com

South Padre Island Convention & Visitors
    Bureau
600 Padre Blvd
South Padre Island, TX 78597
Phone: 956-761-6433; Fax: 956-761-9462
Toll-free: 800-767-2373
www.sopadre.com

Abilene Chamber of Commerce
174 Cypress St
Suite 200
Abilene, TX 79601
Phone: 325-677-7241; Fax: 325-677-0622
www.abilene.com/chamber

Amarillo Chamber of Commerce
1000 S Polk St
Amarillo, TX 79101
Phone: 806-373-7800; Fax: 806-373-3909
www.amarillo-chamber.org

Arlington Chamber of Commerce
505 E Border St
Arlington, TX 76010
Phone: 817-275-2613; Fax: 817-261-7535
Toll-free: 800-834-3928
www.arlingtontx.com

Brownsville Chamber of Commerce
1600 University Blvd
Brownsville, TX 78520
Phone: 956-542-4341; Fax: 956-504-3348
www.brownsvillechamber.com

Corpus Christi Chamber of Commerce
1201 N Shoreline Blvd
Corpus Christi, TX 78401
Phone: 361-881-1800; Fax: 361-882-4256
www.corpuschristichamber.org

Fort Worth Chamber of Commerce
777 Taylor St
Suite 900
Fort Worth, TX 76102
Phone: 817-336-2491; Fax: 817-877-4034
www.fortworthcoc.org

Garland Chamber of Commerce
914 S Garland Ave
Garland, TX 75040
Phone: 972-272-7551; Fax: 972-276-9261
www.garlandchamber.com

Greater Austin Chamber of Commerce
210 Barton Springs Rd
Suite 400
Austin, TX 78704
Phone: 512-478-9383; Fax: 512-478-6389
Toll-free: 800-856-5602
www.austinchamber.org

Greater Dallas Chamber of Commerce
700 N Pearl St
Suite 1200
Dallas, TX 75201
Phone: 214-746-6600; Fax: 214-746-6799
www.dallaschamber.org

Greater El Paso Chamber of Commerce
10 Civic Center Plaza
El Paso, TX 79901
Phone: 915-534-0500; Fax: 915-534-0510
Toll-free: 800-651-8065
www.elpaso.org

Greater Houston Partnership
1200 Smith St
Suite 700
Houston, TX 77002

Phone: 713-844-3600; Fax: 713-844-0200
www.houston.org

Greater Irving & Las Colinas Chamber of
   Commerce
5221 N O'Connor Blvd
Suite 100
Irving, TX 75039
Phone: 214-217-8484; Fax: 214-389-2513
www.irvingchamber.com

Greater San Antonio Chamber of Commerce
PO Box 1628
San Antonio, TX 78296
Phone: 210-229-2100; Fax: 210-229-1600
www.sachamber.org

Lubbock Chamber of Commerce
1301 Broadway
Suite 101
Lubbock, TX 79403
Phone: 806-761-7000; Fax: 806-761-7010
Toll-free: 800-321-5822
www.lubbockchamber.com

Plano Chamber of Commerce
1200 E 15th St
Plano, TX 75074
Phone: 972-424-7547; Fax: 972-422-5182
www.planocc.org

UTAH

Utah Travel Development Div
300 N State St
Salt Lake City, UT 84114
Phone: 801-538-1900; Fax: 801-538-1399
Toll-free: 800-200-1160
travel.utah.gov

Mountainland Travel Region Office
586 E 800 North
Orem, UT 84097
Phone: 801-229-3800; Fax: 801-229-3801
www.mountainland.org

Ogden/Weber Convention & Visitors
   Bureau
2501 Wall Ave
Union Stn Suite 201

Ogden, UT 84401
Phone: 801-627-8288; Fax: 801-399-0783
Toll-free: 800-255-8824
www.ogdencvb.org/

Salt Lake Convention & Visitors Bureau
90 S West Temple
Salt Lake City, UT 84101
Phone: 801-521-2822; Fax: 801-355-9323
Toll-free: 800-541-4955
www.visitsaltlake.com

Utah Valley Convention & Visitors Bureau
111 S University Ave
Provo, UT 84601
Phone: 801-851-2100; Fax: 801-851-2109
Toll-free: 800-222-8824
www.utahvalley.org

Ogden/Weber Chamber of Commerce
2484 Washington Blvd
Suite 400
Ogden, UT 84401
Phone: 801-621-8300; Fax: 801-392-7609
Toll-free: 866-990-1299
www.echamber.cc

Provo/Orem Chamber of Commerce
51 S University Ave
Suite 215
Provo, UT 84601
Phone: 801-379-2555; Fax: 801-379-2557
thechamber.org

Salt Lake City Chamber of Commerce
175 E 400 South
Suite 600
Salt Lake City, UT 84111
Phone: 801-364-3631; Fax: 801-328-5098
www.saltlakechamber.org

VERMONT

Vermont Tourism & Marketing Dept
134 State St
Montpelier, VT 05602
Phone: 802-828-3236; Fax: 802-828-3233
Toll-free: 800-837-6668
www.vermontvacation.com

Vermont Convention Bureau
60 Main St
Suite 100
Burlington, VT 05401
Phone: 802-863-3489; Fax: 802-863-1538
Toll-free: 877-264-3503
www.vermontmeetings.org

Vermont Chamber of Commerce
PO Box 37
Montpelier, VT 05601
Phone: 802-223-3443; Fax: 802-223-4257
www.vtchamber.com

Central Vermont Chamber of Commerce
33 Stewart Rd
Berlin, VT 05602
Phone: 802-229-5711; Fax: 802-229-5713
Toll-free: 877-887-3678
www.central-vt.com/chamber

Lake Champlain Regional Chamber of
Commerce
60 Main St
Suite 100
Burlington, VT 05401
Phone: 802-863-3489; Fax: 802-863-1538
Toll-free: 877-686-5253
www.vermont.org

VIRGINIA

Virginia Tourism Corp
901 E Byrd St
Richmond, VA 23219
Phone: 804-786-2051; Fax: 804-786-1919
Toll-free: 800-847-4882
www.vatc.org

Virginia Chamber of Commerce
9 S 5th St
Richmond, VA 23219
Phone: 804-644-1607; Fax: 804-783-6112
Toll-free: 800-477-7682
www.vachamber.com

Alexandria Convention & Visitors Assn
221 King St
Alexandria, VA 22314
Phone: 703-838-4200; Fax: 703-838-4683

Toll-free: 800-388-9119
www.funside.com

Arlington Convention & Visitors Service
1100 N Glebe Rd
Suite 1500
Arlington, VA 22201
Phone: 703-228-0888; Fax: 703-228-0806
Toll-free: 800-296-7996
www.stayarlington.com

Chesapeake Conventions & Tourism Bureau
3815 Bainbridge Blvd
Chesapeake, VA 23324
Phone: 757-502-4898; Fax: 757-502-4883
Toll-free: 888-889-5551
www.visitchesapeake.com

Newport News Tourism Development Office
700 Town Center Dr
Suite 320
Newport News, VA 23606
Phone: 757-926-1400; Fax: 757-926-1441
Toll-free: 888-493-7386
www.newport-news.org

Richmond Metropolitan Convention &
Visitors Bureau
401 N 3rd St
Richmond, VA 23219
Phone: 804-782-2777; Fax: 804-780-2577
Toll-free: 800-370-9004
www.visitrichmond.com

Roanoke Valley Convention & Visitors
Bureau
101 Shenandoah Ave NE
Roanoke, VA 24016
Phone: 540-342-6025; Fax: 540-342-7119
Toll-free: 800-635-5535
www.visitroanokeva.com

Virginia Beach Convention & Visitor Bureau
2101 Parks Ave
Suite 500
Virginia Beach, VA 23451
Phone: 757-437-4700; Fax: 757-437-4747
Toll-free: 800-700-7702
www.vbfun.com

Williamsburg Area Convention & Visitors
Bureau
421 N Boundary St
Williamsburg, VA 23185
Phone: 757-229-6511; Fax: 757-229-2047
Toll-free: 800-368-6511
www.visitwilliamsburg.com

Alexandria Chamber of Commerce
801 N Fairfax St
Suite 402
Alexandria, VA 22314
Phone: 703-549-1000; Fax: 703-739-3805
www.alexchamber.com

Arlington Chamber of Commerce
2009 14th St N
Suite 111
Arlington, VA 22201
Phone: 703-525-2400; Fax: 703-522-5273
www.arlingtonchamber.org

Greater Richmond Chamber of Commerce
600 E Main St
7th Fl
Richmond, VA 23219
Phone: 804-648-1234; Fax: 804-783-9366
www.grcc.com

Hampton Roads Chamber of Commerce
420 Bank St
Norfolk, VA 23510
Phone: 757-622-2312; Fax: 757-622-5563
www.hamptonroadschamber.com

Salem/Roanoke County Chamber of
Commerce
611 E Main St
Salem, VA 24153
Phone: 540-387-0267; Fax: 540-387-4110
www.s-rcchamber.org

Virginia Peninsula Chamber of Commerce
21 Enterprise Pkwy
Suite 100
Hampton, VA 23666
Phone: 757-262-2000; Fax: 757-262-2009
Toll-free: 800-556-1822
www.vpcc.org

Williamsburg Area Chamber of Commerce
PO Box 3495
Williamsburg, VA 23185
Phone: 757-229-6511; Fax: 757-229-2047
Toll-free: 800-368-6511
www.williamsburgcc.com

WASHINGTON

Washington Tourism Div
PO Box 42525
Olympia, WA 98504
Phone: 360-725-4172; Fax: 360-753-4470
www.experiencewashington.com

Association of Washington Business
PO Box 658
Olympia, WA 98507
Phone: 360-943-1600; Fax: 360-943-5811
Toll-free: 800-521-9325
www.awb.org

Olympia/Thurston County Visitor &
Convention Bureau
PO Box 7338
Olympia, WA 98507
Phone: 360-704-7544; Fax: 360-704-7533
Toll-free: 877-704-7500
www.visitolympia.com

Seattle's Convention & Visitors Bureau
1 Convention Pl
701 Pike St Suite 800
Seattle, WA 98101
Phone: 206-461-5800; Fax: 206-461-5855
Toll-free: 866-732-2695
www.seeseattle.org

Southwest Washington Convention &
Visitors Bureau
101 E 8th St
Suite 110
Vancouver, WA 98660
Phone: 360-750-1553; Fax: 360-750-1933
Toll-free: 877-600-0800
www.southwestwashington.com

Spokane Convention & Visitors Bureau
201 W Main
Suite 301

Spokane, WA 99201
Phone: 509-747-3230; Fax: 509-623-1297
Toll-free: 888-776-5263
www.visitspokane.com

Tacoma Regional Convention & Visitor
  Bureau
1119 Pacific Ave
5th Fl
Tacoma, WA 98402
Phone: 253-627-2836; Fax: 253-627-8783
Toll-free: 800-272-2662
www.traveltacoma.com

Greater Seattle Chamber of Commerce
1301 5th Ave
Suite 2500
Seattle, WA 98101
Phone: 206-389-7200; Fax: 206-389-7288
www.seattlechamber.com

Greater Vancouver Chamber of Commerce
1101 Broadway
Suite 100
Vancouver, WA 98660
Phone: 360-694-2588; Fax: 360-693-8279
www.vancouverusa.com

Olympia/Thurston County Chamber of
  Commerce
809 Legion Way
Olympia, WA 98501
Phone: 360-357-3362; Fax: 360-357-3376
www.thurstonchamber.com

Spokane Regional Chamber of Commerce
801 W Riverside Ave
Suite 100
Spokane, WA 99201
Phone: 509-624-1393; Fax: 509-747-0077
www.spokanechamber.org

Tacoma-Pierce County Chamber of
  Commerce
950 Pacific Ave
Suite 300
Tacoma, WA 98402
Phone: 253-627-2175; Fax: 253-597-7305
www.tacomachamber.org

WEST VIRGINIA

West Virginia Tourism Div
2101 Washington St E
Charleston, WV 25305
Phone: 304-558-2200; Fax: 304-558-2956
Toll-free: 800-225-5982
www.state.wv.us/tourism

West Virginia Chamber of Commerce
PO Box 2789
Charleston, WV 25330
Phone: 304-342-1115; Fax: 304-342-1130
www.wvchamber.com

Charleston Convention & Visitors Bureau
200 Civic Center Dr
Charleston, WV 25301
Phone: 304-344-5075; Fax: 304-344-1241
Toll-free: 800-733-5469
www.charlestonwv.com

Greater Morgantown Convention & Visitors
  Bureau
201 High St
Suite 3
Morgantown, WV 26505
Phone: 304-292-5081; Fax: 304-291-1354
Toll-free: 800-458-7373
www.tourmorgantown.com

Wheeling Convention & Visitors Bureau
1401 Main St
Wheeling, WV 26003
Phone: 304-233-7709; Fax: 304-233-1470
Toll-free: 800-828-3097
www.wheelingcvb.com

Charleston Regional Chamber of Commerce
1116 Smith St
Charleston, WV 25301
Phone: 304-340-4253; Fax: 304-340-4275
www.charlestonwvchamber.org

Morgantown Area Chamber of Commerce
1009 University Ave
Morgantown, WV 26507
Phone: 304-292-3311; Fax: 304-296-6619
Toll-free: 800-618-2525
www.morgantownchamber.com

Wheeling Area Chamber of Commerce
1310 Market St
Wheeling, WV 26003
Phone: 304-233-2575; Fax: 304-233-1320
www.wheelingchamber.com

WISCONSIN

Wisconsin Tourism Dept
201 W Washington Ave
2nd Fl
Madison, WI 53707
Phone: 608-266-2161; Fax: 608-266-3403
Toll-free: 800-432-8747
www.travelwisconsin.com

Wisconsin Manufacturers & Commerce
PO Box 352
Madison, WI 53701
Phone: 608-258-3400; Fax: 608-258-3413
www.wmc.org

Greater Madison Convention & Visitors
Bureau
615 E Washington Ave
Madison, WI 53703
Phone: 608-255-2537; Fax: 608-258-4950
Toll-free: 800-373-6376
www.visitmadison.com

Greater Milwaukee Convention & Visitors
Bureau
101 W Wisconsin Ave
Suite 425
Milwaukee, WI 53203
Phone: 414-273-3950; Fax: 414-273-5596
Toll-free: 800-231-0903
www.milwaukee.org

Packer Country Visitor & Convention
Bureau
1901 S Oneida St
Green Bay, WI 54304
Phone: 920-494-9507; Fax: 920-494-9229
Toll-free: 888-867-3342
www.packercountry.com

Greater Madison Chamber of Commerce
PO Box 71
Madison, WI 53701

Phone: 608-256-8348; Fax: 608-256-0333
www.greatermadisonchamber.com

Green Bay Area Chamber of Commerce
400 S Washington St
Green Bay, WI 54301
Phone: 920-437-8704; Fax: 920-437-1024
www.titletown.org

Metropolitan Milwaukee Assn of Commerce
756 N Milwaukee St
Milwaukee, WI 53202
Phone: 414-287-4100; Fax: 414-271-7753
www.mmac.org

WYOMING

Wyoming Tourism Div
214 W 15th St
Cheyenne, WY 82002
Phone: 307-777-2828; Fax: 307-777-2877
Toll-free: 800-225-5996
www.wyomingtourism.org

Casper Area Convention & Visitors Bureau
992 N Poplar St
Casper, WY 82601
Phone: 307-234-5362; Fax: 307-261-9928
Toll-free: 800-852-1889
www.casperwyoming.info

Cheyenne Area Convention & Visitors
Bureau
121 W 15th St
Suite 202
Cheyenne, WY 82001
Phone: 307-778-3133; Fax: 307-778-3190
Toll-free: 800-426-5009
www.cheyenne.org

Casper Area Chamber of Commerce
500 N Center St
Casper, WY 82601
Phone: 307-234-5311; Fax: 307-265-2643
Toll-free: 866-234-5311
www.casperwyoming.org

Greater Cheyenne Chamber of Commerce
121 W 15th St
Suite 204

Cheyenne, WY 82001
Phone: 307-638-3388; Fax: 307-778-1407
www.cheyennechamber.org

Jackson Hole Chamber of Commerce
990 W Broadway St
Jackson, WY 83001
Phone: 307-733-3316; Fax: 307-733-5585
www.jacksonholechamber.com

CANADA

Canadian Tourism Commission
1055 Dunsmuir St Suite 1400
4 Bentall Center Box 49220
Vancouver, BC V7X1L2
Phone: 604-638-8300Toll-free:
www.canadatourisme.com

Canadian Chamber of Commerce
350 Sparks St Delta Office Tower
Suite 501
Ottawa, ON K1R7S8
Phone: 613-238-4000; Fax: 613-238-7643
www.chamber.ca

Canada Consulate General
550 S Hope St
9th Fl
Los Angeles, CA 90071
Phone: 213-346-2700; Fax: 213-620-8827
www.dfait-maeci.gc.ca/los_angeles/

Canada Consulate General
200 S Biscayne Blvd
Suite 1600
Miami, FL 33131
Phone: 305-579-1600; Fax: 305-374-6774
geo.international.gc.ca/can-am/miami/

Canada Consulate General
1175 Peachtree St NE
100 Colony Sq Suite 1700
Atlanta, GA 30361
Phone: 404-532-2000; Fax: 404-532-2050
www.dfait-maeci.gc.ca/atlanta/

Canada Consulate General
180 N Stetson Ave
Suite 2400

Chicago, IL 60601
Phone: 312-616-1860; Fax: 312-616-1877
www.dfait-maeci.gc.ca/chicago

Canada Consulate General
3 Copley Pl
Suite 400
Boston, MA 02116
Phone: 617-262-3760; Fax: 617-262-3415
www.dfait-maeci.gc.ca/boston

Canada Consulate General
600 Renaissance Ctr
Suite 1100
Detroit, MI 48243
Phone: 313-567-2340; Fax: 313-567-2164
www.dfait-maeci.gc.ca/detroit

Canada Consulate General
701 4th Ave S
Suite 900
Minneapolis, MN 55415
Phone: 612-332-7486; Fax: 612-332-4061
www.dfait-maeci.gc.ca/minneapolis

Canada Consulate General
3000 HSBC Ctr
Buffalo, NY 14203
Phone: 716-858-9500; Fax: 716-852-2477
www.dfait-maeci.gc.ca/buffalo/

Canada Consulate General
1251 Ave of the Americas
Concourse Level
New York, NY 10020
Phone: 212-596-1628; Fax: 212-596-1790
geo.international.gc.ca/can-am/new_york/

Canada Consulate General
750 N Saint Paul St
Suite 1700
Dallas, TX 75201
Phone: 214-922-9806; Fax: 214-922-9815
www.dfait-maeci.gc.ca/dallas

Canada Consulate General
1501 4th Ave
Suite 600
Seattle, WA 98101
Phone: 206-443-1777; Fax: 206-443-9662
www.dfait-maeci.gc.ca/seattle/

Canada Embassy
501 Pennsylvania Ave NW
Washington, DC 20001
Phone: 202-682-1740; Fax: 202-682-7726
www.canadianembassy.org

Canada Permanent Mission to the UN
885 2nd Ave
14th Fl
New York, NY 10017
Phone: 212-848-1100; Fax: 212-848-1195
www.un.int/canada

ALBERTA

Travel Alberta
999 8th St SW
Suite 500
Calgary, AB T2R1J5
Phone: 403-297-2700; Fax: 403-297-5068
Toll-free: 800-252-3782
www.travelalberta.com

Alberta Chambers of Commerce
10025 - 102A Ave Suite 1808
Edmonton Ctr
Edmonton, AB T5J2Z2
Phone: 780-425-4180; Fax: 780-429-1061
www.abchamber.ca

Calgary Chamber of Commerce
100 6th Ave SW
Calgary, AB T2P0P5
Phone: 403-750-0400; Fax: 403-266-3413
www.calgarychamber.com

Edmonton Chamber of Commerce
9990 Jasper Ave
Suite 600
Edmonton, AB T5J1P7
Phone: 780-426-4620; Fax: 780-424-7946
www.edmontonchamber.com

BRITISH COLUMBIA

Travel.bc.ca Online Inc.
4708 Beaver Rd
Victoria, BC V9E2J7
Phone: 866-810-6645; Fax: 866-768-1899
travel.bc.ca

British Columbia Chamber of Commerce
750 W Pender St
Suite 1201
Vancouver, BC V6C2T8
Phone: 604-683-0700; Fax: 604-683-0416
www.bcchamber.org

Greater Victoria Chamber of Commerce
852 Fort St
Suite 100
Victoria, BC V8W1H8
Phone: 250-383-7191; Fax: 250-385-3552
www.victoriachamber.ca

North Vancouver Chamber of Commerce
124 W 1st St
Suite 102
North Vancouver, BC V7M3N3
Phone: 604-987-4488; Fax: 604-987-8272
Toll-free: 877-880-4699
www.nvchamber.bc.ca

Vancouver Board of Trade
999 Canada Pl
Suite 400
Vancouver, BC V6C3E1
Phone: 604-681-2111; Fax: 604-681-0437
www.vancouver.boardoftrade.com

West Vancouver Chamber of Commerce
1310 Marine Dr
West Vancouver, BC V7T1B5
Phone: 604-926-6614; Fax: 604-926-6436
Toll-free: 888-471-9996
www.westvanchamber.com

MANITOBA

Travel Manitoba
155 Carlton St
7th Fl
Winnipeg, MB R3C3H8
Phone: 204-927-7800; Fax: 204-927-7828
Toll-free: 800-665-0040
www.travelmanitoba.com

Manitoba Chamber of Commerce
227 Portage Ave

Winnipeg, MB R3B2A6
Phone: 204-948-0100; Fax: 204-948-0110
www.mbchamber.mb.ca

Winnipeg Chamber of Commerce
259 Portage Ave
Suite 100
Winnipeg, MB R3B2A9
Phone: 204-944-8484; Fax: 204-944-8492
www.winnipeg-chamber.com

NEW BRUNSWICK

Tourism New Brunswick
26 Roseberry St
PO Box 12345
Campbellton, NB E3N2G4
Phone: 506-789-4982; Fax: 506-789-2044
Toll-free: 800-561-0123
www.tourismnewbrunswick.ca

Atlantic Provinces Chamber of Commerce
236 Saint George St
Suite 21
Moncton, NB E1C1W1
Phone: 506-857-3980; Fax: 506-859-6131
www.apcc.ca

Enterprise Fredericton
570 Queen St
Suite 102
Fredericton, NB E3B6Z6
Phone: 506-444-4686; Fax: 506-444-4649
Toll-free: 800-200-1180
www.gfedc.nb.ca

Fredericton Chamber of Commerce
270 Rockwood Rd
PO Box 275
Fredericton, NB E3B4Y9
Phone: 506-458-8006; Fax: 506-451-1119
www.frederictonchamber.ca

Saint John Board of Trade
40 King St
PO Box 6037
Saint John, NB E2L4R5
Phone: 506-634-8111; Fax: 506-632-2008
www.sjboardoftrade.com

NEWFOUNDLAND & LABRADOR

Newfoundland & Labrador Tourism
PO Box 8730
Saint John's, NL A1B4K2
Phone: 709-729-2830; Fax: 709-729-0057
Toll-free: 800-563-6353
www.newfoundlandandlabradortourism.
  com

Saint John's Board of Trade
PO Box 5127
Saint John's, NL A1C5V5
Phone: 709-726-2961; Fax: 709-726-2003

NOVA SCOTIA

Nova Scotia Dept of Tourism & Culture
1800 Argyle St
Halifax, NS B3J3N8
Phone: 902-424-5000; Fax: 902-424-2668
Toll-free: 800-565-0000
www.NovaScotia.com

Metropolitan Halifax Chamber of
  Commerce
656 Windmill Rd
Suite 200
Dartmouth, NS B3B1B8
Phone: 902-468-7111; Fax: 902-468-7333
www.halifaxchamber.com

NORTHWEST TERRITORIES

NWT Tourism
Box 610
Yellowknife, NT X1A2N5
Phone: 867-873-7200; Fax: 867-873-4059
Toll-free: 800-661-0788
www.explorenwt.com

Northwest Territories Chamber of
  Commerce
4910 50th St
YK Center PO Box 13
Yellowknife, NT X1A3S5
Phone: 867-920-9505; Fax: 867-873-4174
www.nwtchamber.com

NUNAVUT

Nunavut Tourism
PO Box 1450
Iqaluit, NU X0A0H0
Phone: 867-979-6551; Fax: 867-979-1261
Toll-free: 800-491-7910
www.nunavuttourism.com

ONTARIO

Ontario Tourism Marketing Partnership
  Corp
900 Bay St
Hearst Block 10th Fl
Toronto, ON M7A2E1
Phone: 905-282-1721; Fax: 905-282-7433
Toll-free: 800-668-2746
www.ontariotravel.net

York Region Tourism
17250 Young St
Box 147 4th Fl
Newmarket, ON L3Y6Z1
Phone: 905-883-3442; Fax: 905-895-3482
Toll-free: 888-448-0000
www.yorktourism.com

Canadian Chamber of Commerce Toronto
  Office
55 University Ave
Suite 901
Toronto, ON M5J2H7
Phone: 416-868-6415; Fax: 416-868-0189
www.chamber.ca

Ontario Chamber of Commerce
180 Dundas St W
Suite 505
Toronto, ON M5G1Z8
Phone: 416-482-5222; Fax: 416-482-5879
occ.on.ca

Ottawa Chamber of Commerce
1701 Woodward Dr
Suite LL-20
Ottawa, ON K2C0R4
Phone: 613-236-3631; Fax: 613-236-7498
www.ottawachamber.ca

Toronto Board of Trade
1 First Canadian Pl
PO Box 60
Toronto, ON M5X1C1
Phone: 416-366-6811; Fax: 416-366-6460
www.bot.com

Upper Ottawa Valley Chamber of
  Commerce
2 International Dr
Pembroke, ON K8A6W5
Phone: 613-732-1492; Fax: 613-732-5793
www.upperottawavalleychamber.com

Windsor & District Chamber of Commerce
2575 Ouellette Pl
Windsor, ON N8X1L9
Phone: 519-966-3696; Fax: 519-966-0603
www.windsorchamber.org

PRINCE EDWARD ISLAND

Prince Edward Island Tourism
PO Box 2000
Charlottetown, PE C1A7N8
Phone: 902-368-4441; Fax: 902-368-4438
Toll-free: 888-734-7529
www.gov.pe.ca

QUEBEC

Tourisme Quebec
1255 Peel St
Office 100
Montreal, QC H3B4V4
Phone: 514-873-2015; Fax: 514-864-3838
www.tourisme.gouv.qc.ca/anglais/index.html

Board of Trade of Metropolitan Montreal
380 Saint-Antoine St W
Suite 6000
Montreal, QC H2Y3X7
Phone: 514-871-4000; Fax: 514-871-1255
www.btmm.qc.ca

Canadian Chamber of Commerce Montreal
  Office
1155 University St
Suite 709
Montreal, QC H3B3A7

Phone: 514-866-4334; Fax: 514-866-7296
www.chamber.ca

Chambre de Commerce du Quebec
576 E Saint Catherine St
Suite 200
Montreal, QC H2L2E1
Phone: 514-522-1885; Fax: 514-522-9468
Toll-free: 888-595-8110
www.ccquebec.ca

Chambre de Commerce et d'Industrie du
    Quebec Metropolitain
17 Saint-Louis St
Quebec, QC G1R3Y8
Phone: 418-692-3853; Fax: 418-694-2286
www.ccquebec.ca

SASKATCHEWAN

Tourism Saskatchewan
1922 Park St
Regina, SK S4N7M4
Phone: 306-787-9600; Fax: 306-787-0715
Toll-free: 877-237-2273
www.sasktourism.com

YUKON

Tourism Yukon
PO Box 2703
Whitehorse, YT Y1A2C6
Phone: 867-667-5036; Fax: 867-667-3546
Toll-free: 800-661-0494
www.touryukon.com

Whitehorse Chamber of Commerce
302 Steele St
Suite 101
Whitehorse, YT Y1A2C5
Phone: 867-667-7545; Fax: 867-667-4507
www.whitehorsechamber.com

Yukon Chamber of Commerce
307 Jarvis St
Suite 101
Whitehorse, YT Y1A2H3
Phone: 867-667-2000; Fax: 867-667-2001
www.yukonchamber.com

MEXICO

Mexico Tourism Board
225 N Michigan Ave
Suite 1850
Chicago, IL 60601
Phone: 312-228-0517; Fax: 312-228-0515
Toll-free: 800-446-3942
www.visitmexico.com

Mexico Tourism Board
4507 San Jacinto
Suite 308
Houston, TX 77004
Phone: 713-772-2581; Fax: 713-772-6058
Toll-free: 800-446-3942
www.visitmexico.com

Mexico Tourism Board
5975 Sunset Dr
Suite 305
Miami, FL 33143
Phone: 786-621-2909; Fax: 786-621-2907
Toll-free: 800-446-3942
www.visitmexico.com

Mexico Tourism Board
400 Madison Ave
Suite 11-C
New York, NY 10017
Phone: 212-308-2110; Fax: 212-308-9060
Toll-free: 800-446-3942
www.visitmexico.com

US-Mexico Chamber of Commerce Inter-
    American Chapter
7001 SW 97th Ave
Miami, FL 33173
Phone: 305-275-1536; Fax: 305-275-1480
www.usmcoc.org

US-Mexico Chamber of Commerce
    California Pacific Chapter
2450 Colorado Ave
Suite 400E
Santa Monica, CA 90404
Phone: 310-586-7901; Fax: 310-586-7800
www.usmcocca.org

US-Mexico Chamber of Commerce
1300 Pennsylvania Ave NW
Suite 0003
Washington, DC 20004
Phone: 202-312-1520; Fax: 202-312-1530
www.usmcoc.org

Mexico Consulate General
571 N Grand Ave
Nogales, AZ 85621
Phone: 520-287-2521; Fax: 520-287-3175

Mexico Consulate General
1990 W Camelback Rd
Suite 110
Phoenix, AZ 85015
Phone: 602-242-7398; Fax: 602-242-2957
www.sre.gob.mx/phoenix

Mexico Consulate General
2401 W 6th St
Los Angeles, CA 90057
Phone: 213-351-6800
www.sre.gob.mx/losangeles

Mexico Consulate General
1010 8th St
Sacramento, CA 95814
Phone: 916-441-2987; Fax: 916-441-3176
www.mexico.us/consulate.htm

Mexico Consulate General
1549 India St
San Diego, CA 92101
Phone: 619-231-8414Toll-free:
www.sre.gob.mx/sandiego

Mexico Consulate General
532 Folsom St
San Francisco, CA 94105
Phone: 415-392-5554; Fax: 415-495-3971

Mexico Consulate General
540 N 1st St
San Jose, CA 95112
Phone: 408-294-3414; Fax: 408-294-4506
www.consulmexsj.com

Mexico Consulate General
5350 Leesdale Dr

Denver, CO 80246
Phone: 303-331-1110; Fax: 303-331-1872

Mexico Consulate General
5975 SW 72nd St
Suite 101
Miami, FL 33143
Phone: 786-268-4900; Fax: 786-268-4875
www.sre.gob.mx/miami

Mexico Consulate General
2600 Apple Valley Rd
Atlanta, GA 30319
Phone: 404-266-2233; Fax: 404-266-2302
www.consulmexatlanta.org

Mexico Consulate General
204 S Ashland Ave
Chicago, IL 60607
Phone: 312-855-1380Toll-free:
www.consulmexchicago.com

Mexico Consulate General
20 Park Plaza
Suite 506
Boston, MA 02116
Phone: 617-426-4942; Fax: 617-695-1957
Toll-free: 800-601-1289
www.sre.gob.mx/boston

Mexico Consulate General
27 E 39th St
New York, NY 10016
Phone: 212-217-6400; Fax: 212-217-6493
www.consulmexny.org

Mexico Consulate General
800 Brazos St
Suite 330
Austin, TX 78701
Phone: 512-478-2866; Fax: 512-478-8008
www.sre.gob.mx/austin

Mexico Consulate General
8855 N Stemmons Fwy
Dallas, TX 75247
Phone: 214-252-9250
www.consulmexdallas.com

Mexico Consulate General
910 E San Antonio St

El Paso, TX 79901
Phone: 915-533-3644; Fax: 915-532-7163
www.sre.gob.mx/elpaso

Mexico Consulate General
4506 Carolinas St
Houston, TX 77004
Phone: 713-271-6800; Fax: 713-271-3201
www.sre.gob.mx/houston

Mexico Consulate General
127 Navarro St
San Antonio, TX 78205
Phone: 210-227-9145; Fax: 210-227-9817
www.consulmexsat.org

Mexico Embassy
1911 Pennsylvania Ave NW
Washington, DC 20006
Phone: 202-728-1600; Fax: 202-728-1766
portal.sre.gob.mx/usa

Mexico Permanent Mission to the UN
2 UN Plaza
28th Fl
New York, NY 10017
Phone: 212-752-0220; Fax: 212-688-8862
www.un.int/mexico

Appendix C
Tourism Information Sources
for Countries around the World

The following list includes tourism information sources for countries around the world, except the United States, Canada, and Mexico (see Appendix B). The listings are in alphabetical order by name of the country, with cross references where appropriate to other forms of the countries' names. Within each country section, listings are as follows, although each country may not have all offices:

> *National Tourism Office*
>
> *Chamber of Commerce*
>
> *Consulate General*
>
> *Embassy*
>
> *Permanent Mission to the United Nations*

AFGHANISTAN

Afghanistan Consulate General
360 Lexington Ave
11th Fl
New York, NY 10017
Phone: 212-972-2276; Fax: 212-972-9046

Afghanistan Embassy
2341 Wyoming Ave NW
Washington, DC 20008
Phone: 202-483-6410; Fax: 202-483-6488
www.embassyofafghanistan.org

Afghanistan Permanent Mission to the UN
360 Lexington Ave
11th Fl
New York, NY 10017
Phone: 212-972-1212; Fax: 212-972-1216

ALBANIA

Albania Embassy
2100 'S' St NW
Washington, DC 20008
Phone: 202-223-4942; Fax: 202-628-7342

Albania Permanent Mission to the UN
320 E 79th St
New York, NY 10021
Phone: 212-249-2059; Fax: 212-535-2917

ALGERIA

Algeria Embassy
2118 Kalorama Rd NW
Washington, DC 20008
Phone: 202-265-2800; Fax: 202-667-2174
www.algeria-us.org

Algeria Embassy - Consular Section
2137 Wyoming Ave NW
Washington, DC 20008
Phone: 202-265-2800; Fax: 202-265-1978
www.algeria-us.org

Algeria Permanent Mission to the UN
326 E 48th St
New York, NY 10017
Phone: 212-750-1960; Fax: 212-759-9538
www.algeria-un.org

ANDORRA

Andorra Embassy
2 United Nations Plaza
27th Fl
New York, NY 10017
Phone: 212-750-8064; Fax: 212-750-6630
www.andorra.ad

Andorra Permanent Mission to the UN
2 UN Plaza
27th Fl
New York, NY 10017
Phone: 212-750-8064; Fax: 212-750-6630

ANGOLA

US-Angola Chamber of Commerce
1100 Connecticut Ave NW
Suite 1000
Washington, DC 20036
Phone: 202-223-0540; Fax: 202-223-0551
www.us-angola.org

Angola Embassy
2108 16th St NW
Washington, DC 20009
Phone: 202-785-1156; Fax: 202-822-9049
www.angola.org

Angola Permanent Mission to the UN
125 E 73rd St
New York, NY 10021
Phone: 212-861-5656; Fax: 212-861-9295

ANGUILLA

Anguilla Tourist Marketing Office
246 Central Ave
White Plains, NY 10606
Phone: 914-287-2400; Fax: 914-287-2404
Toll-free: 877-426-4845
www.anguilla-vacation.com

ANTIGUA AND BARBUDA

Antigua & Barbuda Dept of Tourism &
    Trade
25 SE 2nd Ave
Suite 300
Miami, FL 33131
Phone: 305-381-6762; Fax: 305-381-7908
Toll-free: 888-268-4227
www.antigua-barbuda.org

Antigua & Barbuda Dept of Tourism &
    Trade
305 E 47th St
6th Fl
New York, NY 10007
Phone: 212-541-4117; Fax: 212-541-4789
Toll-free: 888-268-4227
www.antigua-barbuda.org

Antigua & Barbuda Consulate General
25 SE 2nd Ave
Suite 300
Miami, FL 33131
Phone: 305-381-6762; Fax: 305-381-7908

Antigua & Barbuda Embassy
3216 New Mexico Ave NW
Washington, DC 20016
Phone: 202-362-5122; Fax: 202-362-5225

Antigua & Barbuda Permanent Mission to
    the UN
305 E 47th St
6th Fl
New York, NY 10017
Phone: 212-541-4117; Fax: 212-757-1607
www.un.int/antigua

ARGENTINA

Argentina National Tourist Office
1101 Brickell Ave Suite 901
South Tower
Miami, FL 33131
Phone: 305-442-1366; Fax: 305-441-7029
www.sectur.gov.ar

Argentina National Tourist Office
12 W 56th St
New York, NY 10019
Phone: 212-603-0443; Fax: 212-586-1786
www.sectur.gov.ar

Argentine-American Chamber of Commerce
     Inc
630 5th Ave
25th Fl
New York, NY 10111
Phone: 212-698-2238; Fax: 212-698-2239
www.argentinechamber.org

Argentina Consulate General
245 Peachtree Center Ave
Suite 2101
Atlanta, GA 30303
Phone: 404-880-0805; Fax: 404-880-0806

Argentina Consulate General
205 N Michigan Ave
Suite 4208
Chicago, IL 60601
Phone: 312-819-2620; Fax: 312-819-2612

Argentina Consulate General
3050 Post Oak Blvd
Suite 1625
Houston, TX 77056
Phone: 713-871-8935; Fax: 713-871-0639

Argentina Consulate General
5055 Wilshire Blvd
Suite 210
Los Angeles, CA 90036
Phone: 323-954-9155; Fax: 323-934-9076

Argentina Consulate General
800 Brickell Ave
PH 1

Miami, FL 33131
Phone: 305-373-7794; Fax: 305-373-1598

Argentina Consulate General
12 W 56th St
New York, NY 10019
Phone: 212-603-0400; Fax: 212-541-7746
www.congenargentinany.com

Argentina Embassy
1600 New Hampshire Ave NW
Washington, DC 20009
Phone: 202-238-6400; Fax: 202-332-3171
www.embassyofargentina.us

Argentina Permanent Mission to the UN
1 UN Plaza
25th Fl
New York, NY 10017
Phone: 212-688-6300; Fax: 212-980-8395
www.un.int/argentina

ARMENIA

Armenia Consulate General
50 N La Cienega Blvd
Suite 210
Beverly Hills, CA 90211
Phone: 310-657-6102; Fax: 310-657-7419

Armenia Embassy
2225 R St NW
Washington, DC 20008
Phone: 202-319-1976; Fax: 202-319-2982
www.armeniaemb.org

Armenia Permanent Mission to the UN
119 E 36th St
New York, NY 10016
Phone: 212-686-9079; Fax: 212-686-3934
www.un.int/armenia

ARUBA

Aruba Tourism Authority
1 Financial Plaza
Suite 2508
Fort Lauderdale, FL 33394
Phone: 954-767-6477; Fax: 954-767-0432

Toll-free: 800-862-7822
www.aruba.com

Aruba Tourism Authority
1144 E State St
Suite A-300
Geneva, IL 60134
Phone: 630-262-5580; Fax: 630-262-5581
Toll-free: 800-862-7822
www.aruba.com

Aruba Tourism Authority
1750 Powder Springs Rd
Suite 190
Marietta, GA 30064
Phone: 404-892-7822; Fax: 404-873-2193
www.aruba.com

Aruba Tourism Authority
10655 Six Pines Dr
Suite 145
The Woodlands, TX 77380
Phone: 281-362-1616; Fax: 281-362-1644
Toll-free: 800-862-7822
www.aruba.com

Aruba Tourism Authority
1200 Harbor Blvd
Weehawken, NJ 07086
Phone: 201-330-0800; Fax: 201-330-8757
Toll-free: 800-862-7822
www.aruba.com

AUSTRALIA

Tourism Australia
6100 Center Dr
Suite 1150
Los Angeles, CA 90045
Phone: 310-695-3200; Fax: 310-695-3201
Toll-free: 800-369-6863
www.australia.com

Australian-American Chamber of Commerce
of Hawaii
1000 Bishop St
Honolulu, HI 96813
Phone: 808-526-2242; Fax: 808-534-0475
aacchawaii.org

Australian American Chamber of Commerce
of Houston
PO Box 130261
Houston, TX 77219
Phone: 713-527-9688; Fax: 713-527-9688
www.aacc-houston.org

Australian-American Chamber of Commerce
of San Francisco
PO Box 210508
San Francisco, CA 94121
Phone: 415-485-6718; Fax: 415-485-6832
www.sfaussies.com

Australian New Zealand American
Chambers of Commerce
c/o Embassy of Australia
1601 Massachusetts Ave NW
Washington, DC 20036
Phone: 202-797-3028; Fax: 202-797-3457
www.anzaccnational.com

Australia Consulate General
123 N Wacker Dr
Suite 1330
Chicago, IL 60606
Phone: 312-419-1480; Fax: 312-419-1499
www.austemb.org/chicago.html

Australia Consulate General
1000 Bishop St
PH
Honolulu, HI 96813
Phone: 808-524-5050; Fax: 808-531-5142
www.austemb.org/honolulu.html

Australia Consulate General
2049 Century Park E
Century Plaza Towers 19th Fl
Los Angeles, CA 90067
Phone: 310-229-4800; Fax: 310-277-3462
www.austemb.org/losangeles.html

Australia Consulate General
150 E 42nd St
34th Fl
New York, NY 10017
Phone: 212-351-6500; Fax: 212-351-6501
www.australianyc.org

Australia Embassy
1601 Massachusetts Ave NW
Washington, DC 20036
Phone: 202-797-3000; Fax: 202-797-3168
www.austemb.org

Australia Permanent Mission to the UN
150 E 42nd St
33rd Fl
New York, NY 10017
Phone: 212-351-6600; Fax: 212-351-6610
www.australiaun.org

AUSTRIA

Austrian Tourist Office
PO Box 1142
New York, NY 10108
Phone: 212-944-6880; Fax: 212-730-4568
www.austria.info/us

US-Austrian Chamber of Commerce
165 W 46th St
New York, NY 10036
Phone: 212-819-0117; Fax: 212-819-0345
www.usatchamber.com

Austria Consulate General
400 N Michigan Ave
Suite 707
Chicago, IL 60611
Phone: 312-222-1515; Fax: 312-222-4113
www.austria.org

Austria Consulate General
11859 Wilshire Blvd
Suite 501
Los Angeles, CA 90025
Phone: 310-444-9310; Fax: 310-477-9897
www.austria.org

Austria Consulate General
31 E 69th St
New York, NY 10021
Phone: 212-737-6400; Fax: 212-772-8926
www.austria-ny.org

Austria Embassy
3524 International Ct NW
Washington, DC 20008

Phone: 202-895-6700; Fax: 202-895-6750
www.austria.org

Austria Permanent Mission to the UN
600 3rd Ave
31st Fl
New York, NY 10016
Phone: 917-542-8400; Fax: 212-949-1840
www.un.int/austria

AZERBAIJAN

Azerbaijan Embassy
2741 34th St NW
Washington, DC 20008
Phone: 202-337-3500; Fax: 202-337-5911
www.azembassy.com

Azerbaijan Permanent Mission to the UN
866 UN Plaza
Suite 560
New York, NY 10017
Phone: 212-371-2559; Fax: 212-371-2784

BAHAMAS

Bahamas Tourism Office
8600 W Bryn Mawr Ave
Suite 580 N
Chicago, IL 60631
Phone: 773-693-1500; Fax: 773-693-1114
www.bahamas.com

Bahamas Tourism Office
11400 W Olympic Blvd
Suite 204
Los Angeles, CA 90064
Phone: 310-312-9544; Fax: 310-445-8800
Toll-free: 800-439-6993
www.bahamas.com

Bahamas Tourism Office
60 E 42nd St
Suite 1850
New York, NY 10165
Phone: 212-758-2777; Fax: 212-753-6531
Toll-free: 800-823-3136
www.bahamas.com

Bahamas Tourism Office
1200 S Pine Island Rd
Suite 750
Plantation, FL 33324
Phone: 954-236-9292; Fax: 954-236-9282
Toll-free: 800-224-3681
www.bahamas.com

Bahamas Consulate General
25 SE 2nd Ave
Miami, FL 33131
Phone: 305-373-6295; Fax: 305-373-6312

Bahamas Consulate General
231 E 46th St
New York, NY 10017
Phone: 212-421-6420; Fax: 212-688-5926

Bahamas Embassy
2220 Massachusetts Ave NW
Washington, DC 20008
Phone: 202-319-2660; Fax: 202-319-2668

Bahamas Permanent Mission to the UN
231 E 46th St
New York, NY 10017
Phone: 212-421-6925; Fax: 212-759-2135

BAHRAIN

Bahrain Consulate General
866 2nd Ave
14th Fl
New York, NY 10017
Phone: 212-223-6200; Fax: 212-223-6206
www.un.int/bahrain/consulate.html

Bahrain Embassy
3502 International Dr NW
Washington, DC 20008
Phone: 202-342-1111; Fax: 202-362-2192
www.bahrainembassy.org

Bahrain Permanent Mission to the UN
866 2nd Ave
14th Fl
New York, NY 10017
Phone: 212-223-6200; Fax: 212-319-0687
www.un.int/bahrain

BANGLADESH

Bangladesh Consulate General
4201 Wilshire Blvd
Suite 605
Los Angeles, CA 90010
Phone: 323-932-0100; Fax: 323-932-9703
www.bangladeshconsulatela.com

Bangladesh Consulate General
211 E 43rd St
Suite 502
New York, NY 10017
Phone: 212-599-6767; Fax: 212-682-9211

Bangladesh Embassy
3510 International Dr NW
Washington, DC 20008
Phone: 202-244-0183; Fax: 202-244-2771
www.bangladoot.org

Bangladesh Permanent Mission to the UN
227 E 45th St
New York, NY 10017
Phone: 212-867-3434; Fax: 212-972-4038
www.un.int/bangladesh

BARBADOS

Barbados Tourism Authority
150 Alhambra Cir
Suite 1000
Coral Gables, FL 33134
Phone: 305-442-7471; Fax: 305-774-9497
Toll-free: 800-221-9831
barbados.org

Barbados Tourism Authority
3440 Wilshire Blvd
Suite 1207
Los Angeles, CA 90010
Phone: 213-380-2198; Fax: 213-384-2763
barbados.org

Barbados Tourism Authority
800 2nd Ave
2nd Fl
New York, NY 10017
Phone: 212-986-6516; Fax: 212-573-9850

Toll-free: 800-221-9831
barbados.org

Barbados Consulate General
150 Alhambra Cir
Suite 1000
Coral Gables, FL 33134
Phone: 305-442-1994; Fax: 305-567-2844

Barbados Vice Consulate
3440 Wilshire Blvd
Suite 1207
Los Angeles, CA 90010
Phone: 213-380-2198; Fax: 213-384-2763

Barbados Consulate General
800 2nd Ave
2nd Fl
New York, NY 10017
Phone: 212-867-8435; Fax: 212-986-1030

Barbados Embassy
2144 Wyoming Ave NW
Washington, DC 20008
Phone: 202-939-9200; Fax: 202-332-7467

Barbados Permanent Mission to the UN
800 2nd Ave
2nd Fl
New York, NY 10017
Phone: 212-867-8431; Fax: 212-986-1030
Toll-free: 800-221-9831

BELARUS

Belarus Consulate General
708 3rd Ave
21st Fl
New York, NY 10017
Phone: 212-682-5392; Fax: 212-682-5491

Belarus Embassy
1619 New Hampshire Ave NW
Washington, DC 20009
Phone: 202-986-1606; Fax: 202-986-1805
www.belarusembassy.org

Belarus Permanent Mission to the UN
136 E 67th St
4th Fl
New York, NY 10021

Phone: 212-535-3420; Fax: 212-734-4810
www.un.int/belarus

BELGIUM

Belgian Tourist Office
220 E 42nd St
Suite 3402
New York, NY 10017
Phone: 212-758-8130; Fax: 212-355-7675
www.visitbelgium.com

Belgian-American Chamber of Commerce in
the US
101 Hudson St
21st Fl
Jersey City, NJ 07302
Phone: 201-631-8065; Fax: 201-631-8067
www.belcham.org

Belgium Consulate General
230 Peachtree St NW
Suite 2710
Atlanta, GA 30303
Phone: 404-659-2150; Fax: 404-659-8474

Belgium Consulate General
6100 Wilshire Blvd
Suite 1200
Los Angeles, CA 90048
Phone: 323-857-1244; Fax: 323-936-2564

Belgium Consulate General
1065 Avenue of the Americas
22nd Fl
New York, NY 10018
Phone: 212-586-5110; Fax: 212-582-9657
www.diplomatie.be/newyork/

Belgium Embassy
3330 Garfield St NW
Washington, DC 20008
Phone: 202-333-6900; Fax: 202-333-3079
www.diplobel.us

Belgium Permanent Mission to the UN
823 UN Plaza
4th Fl
New York, NY 10017
Phone: 212-378-6300; Fax: 212-681-7618
www.un.int/belgium

BELIZE

Belize Consulate General
4801 Wilshire Blvd Suite 250
Park Mile Plaza
Los Angeles, CA 90018
Phone: 323-634-9900; Fax: 323-634-9903

Belize Embassy
2535 Massachusetts Ave NW
Washington, DC 20008
Phone: 202-332-9636; Fax: 202-332-6888
www.embassyofbelize.org

Belize Permanent Mission to the UN
675 3rd Ave
Suite 1911
New York, NY 10017
Phone: 212-593-0999; Fax: 212-593-0932
www.belizemission.com

BENIN

Benin Embassy
2124 Kalorama Rd NW
Washington, DC 20008
Phone: 202-232-6656; Fax: 202-265-1996
www.beninembassy.us

Benin Permanent Mission to the UN
125 E 38th St
New York, NY 10016
Phone: 212-684-1339; Fax: 212-684-2058
www.un.int/benin

BERMUDA

Bermuda Dept of Tourism
675 3rd Ave
20th Fl
New York, NY 10017
Phone: 212-818-9800; Fax: 212-983-5289
Toll-free: 800-223-6106
www.bermudatourism.com

BHUTAN

Bhutan Permanent Mission to the UN
763 UN Plaza
New York, NY 10017
Phone: 212-682-2268; Fax: 212-661-0551

BOLIVIA

Bolivia Consulate General
3701 Wilshire Blvd
Suite 1065
Los Angeles, CA 90010
Phone: 213-388-0475; Fax: 213-384-6272

Bolivia Consulate General
211 E 43rd St
Suite 702
New York, NY 10017
Phone: 212-687-0530; Fax: 212-687-0532

Bolivia Embassy
3014 Massachusetts Ave NW
Washington, DC 20008
Phone: 202-483-4410; Fax: 202-328-3712
www.bolivia-usa.org

Bolivia Permanent Mission to the UN
211 E 43rd St
Rm 802
New York, NY 10017
Phone: 212-682-8132; Fax: 212-687-4642

BONAIRE

Bonaire Government Tourist Office
10 Rockefeller Plaza
Suite 900
New York, NY 10020
Phone: 212-956-5911; Fax: 212-956-5913
Toll-free: 800-266-2473
www.infobonaire.com

BOSNIA AND HERZEGOVINA

Bosnia & Herzegovina Consulate General
2109 E St NW
Washington, DC 20037
Phone: 202-337-6478; Fax: 202-337-2909
www.bhembassy.org

Bosnia & Herzegovina Embassy
2109 'E' St NW
Washington, DC 20037
Phone: 202-337-1500; Fax: 202-337-1502
www.bhembassy.org

Bosnia & Herzegovina Permanent Mission
    to the UN
866 UN Plaza
Suite 585
New York, NY 10017
Phone: 212-751-9015; Fax: 212-751-9019

BOTSWANA

Botswana Embassy
1531 New Hampshire Ave NW
Washington, DC 20036
Phone: 202-244-4990; Fax: 202-244-4164
www.botswanaembassy.org

Botswana Permanent Mission to the UN
154 E 46th St
New York, NY 10017
Phone: 212-889-2277; Fax: 212-725-5061

BRAZIL

Brazilian-American Chamber of Commerce
    of Georgia
PO Box 93411
Atlanta, GA 30377
Phone: 404-880-1551; Fax: 404-880-1555
www.bacc-ga.com

Brazilian-American Chamber of Commerce
    of Florida
PO Box 310038
Miami, FL 33231
Phone: 305-579-9030; Fax: 305-579-9756
www.brazilchamber.org

Brazilian-American Chamber of Commerce
    Inc
509 Madison Ave
Suite 304
New York, NY 10022
Phone: 212-751-4691; Fax: 212-751-7692
www.brazilcham.com

Brazil Consulate General
8484 Wilshire Blvd
Suite 711
Beverly Hills, CA 90211
Phone: 323-651-2664; Fax: 323-651-1274
www.brazilian-consulate.org

Brazil Consulate General
20 Park Plaza
Suite 810
Boston, MA 02116
Phone: 617-542-4000; Fax: 617-542-4318
www.consulatebrazil.org

Brazil Consulate General
401 N Michigan Ave
Suite 3050
Chicago, IL 60611
Phone: 312-464-0244; Fax: 312-464-0299

Brazil Consulate General
1233 West Loop S
Suite 1150
Houston, TX 77027
Phone: 713-961-3063; Fax: 713-961-3070
www.brazilhouston.org

Brazil Consulate General
80 SW 8th St
Suite 2600
Miami, FL 33130
Phone: 305-285-6200; Fax: 305-285-6259
www.brazilmiami.org

Brazil Consulate General
1185 6th Ave
New York, NY 10036
Phone: 917-777-7777; Fax: 212-827-0225
www.brazilny.org

Brazil Consulate General
300 Montgomery St
Suite 900
San Francisco, CA 94104
Phone: 415-981-8170; Fax: 415-981-3628
www.brazilsf.org

Brazil Embassy
3006 Massachusetts Ave NW
Washington, DC 20008
Phone: 202-238-2700; Fax: 202-238-2827
Toll-free: 800-727-2945
www.brasilemb.org

Brazil Embassy - Consular Section
3009 Whitehaven St NW
Washington, DC 20008
Phone: 202-238-2828; Fax: 202-238-2818
www.brasilemb.org

Brazil Permanent Mission to the UN
747 3rd Ave
9th Fl
New York, NY 10017
Phone: 212-372-2600; Fax: 212-371-5716
www.un.int/brazil

BRITISH VIRGIN ISLANDS

British Virgin Islands Tourist Board
3450 Wilshire Blvd
Suite 1202
Los Angeles, CA 90010
Phone: 213-736-8931; Fax: 213-736-8935
Toll-free: 800-835-8530
www.bvitourism.com

British Virgin Islands Tourist Board
1270 Broadway
Suite 705
New York, NY 10001
Phone: 212-696-0400; Fax: 212-563-2263
Toll-free: 800-835-8530
www.bvitourism.com

BRUNEI DARUSSALAM

Brunei Darussalam Embassy
3520 International Ct NW
Washington, DC 20008
Phone: 202-237-1838; Fax: 202-885-0560
www.bruneiembassy.org

Brunei Darussalam Permanent Mission to
the UN
771 1st Ave
New York, NY 10017
Phone: 212-697-3465; Fax: 212-697-9889

BULGARIA

Bulgaria Consulate General
121 E 62nd St
New York, NY 10021
Phone: 212-935-4646; Fax: 212-319-5955
www.consulbulgaria-ny.org

Bulgaria Embassy
1621 22nd St NW

Washington, DC 20008
Phone: 202-387-0174; Fax: 202-234-7973
www.bulgaria-embassy.org

Bulgaria Permanent Mission to the UN
11 E 84th St
New York, NY 10028
Phone: 212-737-4790; Fax: 212-472-9865
www.un.int/bulgaria

BURKINA FASO

Burkina Faso Embassy
2340 Massachusetts Ave NW
Washington, DC 20008
Phone: 202-332-5577; Fax: 202-667-1882
www.burkinaembassy-usa.org

Burkina Faso Permanent Mission to the UN
866 UN Plaza
Suite 326
New York, NY 10017
Phone: 212-308-4720; Fax: 212-308-4690

BURMA
SEE MYANMAR

BURUNDI

Burundi Embassy
2233 Wisconsin Ave NW
Suite 212
Washington, DC 20007
Phone: 202-342-2574; Fax: 202-342-2578
www.burundiembassy-usa.org

Burundi Permanent Mission to the UN
336 E 45th St
12th Fl
New York, NY 10017
Phone: 212-499-0001; Fax: 212-499-0006

CAMBODIA

Cambodia Embassy
4530 16th St NW
Washington, DC 20011
Phone: 202-726-7742; Fax: 202-726-8381
www.embassyofcambodia.org

CAMEROON

Cameroon Embassy
2349 Massachusetts Ave NW
Washington, DC 20008
Phone: 202-265-8790; Fax: 202-387-3826

Cameroon Permanent Mission to the UN
22 E 73rd St
New York, NY 10021
Phone: 212-794-2296; Fax: 212-249-0533

CAPE VERDE

Cape Verde Consulate General
607 Boylston St
4th Fl
Boston, MA 02116
Phone: 617-353-0014; Fax: 617-859-9798

Cape Verde Embassy
3415 Massachusetts Ave NW
Washington, DC 20007
Phone: 202-965-6820; Fax: 202-965-1207

Cape Verde Permanent Mission to the UN
27 E 69th St
New York, NY 10021
Phone: 212-472-0333; Fax: 212-794-1398

CAYMAN ISLANDS

Cayman Islands Dept of Tourism
820 Gessner Rd
Suite 1335
Houston, TX 77024
Phone: 713-461-1317; Fax: 713-461-7409
www.caymanislands.ky

Cayman Islands Dept of Tourism
8300 NW 53rd St
Suite 103
Miami, FL 33166
Phone: 305-599-9033; Fax: 305-599-3766
www.caymanislands.ky

Cayman Islands Dept of Tourism
3 Park Ave
39th Fl
New York, NY 10016
Phone: 212-889-9009; Fax: 212-889-9125

Toll-free: 877-422-9626
www.caymanislands.ky

Cayman Islands Dept of Tourism
18 W 140 Butterfield Rd
Suite 920
Oakbrook Terrace, IL 60181
Phone: 630-705-0650; Fax: 630-705-1383
www.caymanislands.ky

CENTRAL AFRICAN REPUBLIC

Central African Republic Embassy
1618 22nd St NW
Washington, DC 20008
Phone: 202-483-7800; Fax: 202-332-9893

Central African Republic Permanent Mission
to the UN
51 Clifton Ave
Suite 2008
Newark, NJ 07104
Phone: 973-482-9161; Fax: 973-350-1174

CHAD

Chad Embassy
2002 R St NW
Washington, DC 20009
Phone: 202-462-4009; Fax: 202-265-1937
www.chadembassy.org

Chad Permanent Mission to the UN
211 E 43rd St
Suite 1703
New York, NY 10017
Phone: 212-986-0980; Fax: 212-986-0152

CHILE

Chile-US Chamber of Commerce
800 Brickell Ave
Suite 900
Miami, FL 33131
Phone: 786-419-2092; Fax: 305-374-4270
www.chileus.org

Chile Consulate General
875 N Michigan Ave
Suite 3352

Chicago, IL 60611
Phone: 312-654-8780; Fax: 312-654-8948

Chile Consulate General
1300 Post Oak Blvd
Suite 1130
Houston, TX 77056
Phone: 713-621-5853; Fax: 713-621-8672

Chile Consulate General
6100 Wilshire Blvd
Suite 1240
Los Angeles, CA 90048
Phone: 323-933-3697; Fax: 323-933-3842

Chile Consulate General
800 Brickell Ave
Suite 1230
Miami, FL 33131
Phone: 305-373-8623; Fax: 305-379-6613

Chile Consulate General
866 UN Plaza
Suite 601
New York, NY 10017
Phone: 212-980-3366; Fax: 212-888-5288
www.chileny.com

Chile Consulate General
6th & Chestnut St
Public Ledger Bldg Suite 1030
Philadelphia, PA 19106
Phone: 215-829-9520; Fax: 215-829-0594

Chile Consulate General
870 Market St
Suite 1058
San Francisco, CA 94102
Phone: 415-982-7662; Fax: 415-982-2384
www.consuladochilesfo.com

Chile Embassy
1732 Massachusetts Ave NW
Washington, DC 20036
Phone: 202-785-1746; Fax: 202-887-5579
www.chile-usa.org

Chile Permanent Mission to the UN
855 2nd Ave
Suite 44
New York, NY 10017

Phone: 212-832-3323; Fax: 212-832-0236
www.un.int/chile

North American-Chilean Chamber of
  Commerce
30 Vesey St
Suite 506
New York, NY 10007
Phone: 212-233-7776; Fax: 212-233-7779

CHINA

China National Tourist Office
550 N Brand Blvd
Suite 910
Glendale, CA 91203
Phone: 818-545-7507; Fax: 818-545-7506
Toll-free: 800-670-2228
www.cnto.org

China National Tourist Office
350 5th Ave
Suite 6413
New York, NY 10118
Phone: 212-760-8218
www.cnto.org

USA-China Chamber of Commerce
55 W Monroe St
Suite 630
Chicago, IL 60603
Phone: 312-368-9030; Fax: 312-368-9922
www.usccc.org

Chinese Chamber of Commerce of Hawaii
42 N King St
Honolulu, HI 96817
Phone: 808-533-3181; Fax: 808-533-6967
www.ccchi.org

Chinese Chamber of Commerce of Los Angeles
977 N Broadway
Suite E
Los Angeles, CA 90012
Phone: 213-617-0396; Fax: 213-617-2128
www.lachinesechamber.org

Chinese Chamber of Commerce of San
  Francisco
730 Sacramento St

San Francisco, CA 94108
Phone: 415-982-3000; Fax: 415-982-4720

China Consulate General
1 E Erie St
Chicago, IL 60611
Phone: 312-803-0095; Fax: 312-803-0110
www.chinaconsulatechicago.org

China Consulate General
3417 Montrose Blvd
Houston, TX 77006
Phone: 713-520-1462; Fax: 713-524-7656
www.chinahouston.org

China Consulate General
443 Shatto Pl
Los Angeles, CA 90020
Phone: 213-807-8088; Fax: 213-807-8019
www.chinaconsulatela.org

China Consulate General
520 12th Ave
New York, NY 10036
Phone: 212-244-9392
www.nyconsulate.prchina.org

China Consulate General
1450 Laguna St
San Francisco, CA 94115
Phone: 415-674-2900; Fax: 415-563-0494
www.chinaconsulatesf.org

China Embassy
2300 Connecticut Ave NW
Washington, DC 20008
Phone: 202-328-2500; Fax: 202-588-0032
www.china-embassy.org

China Permanent Mission to the UN
350 E 35th St
New York, NY 10016
Phone: 212-655-6100; Fax: 212-634-7626
www.china-un.org

COLOMBIA

Colombian American Chamber of Commerce
250 Catalonia Ave
Suite 407
Coral Gables, FL 33134

Phone: 305-446-2542; Fax: 305-446-2038
www.colombiachamber.com

Colombia Consulate General
8383 Wilshire Blvd
Suite 420
Beverly Hills, CA 90211
Phone: 323-653-9863; Fax: 323-653-2964

Colombia Consulate General
500 N Michigan Ave
Suite 2040
Chicago, IL 60611
Phone: 312-923-1196; Fax: 312-923-1197

Colombia Consulate General
280 Aragon Ave
Coral Gables, FL 33134
Phone: 305-448-5558; Fax: 305-441-9537

Colombia Consulate General
5851 San Felipe
Suite 300
Houston, TX 77057
Phone: 713-527-8919; Fax: 713-529-3395
www.colhouston.org

Colombia Consulate General
10 E 46th St
New York, NY 10017
Phone: 212-370-0004; Fax: 212-972-1725

Colombia Consulate General
595 Market St
Suite 2130
San Francisco, CA 94105
Phone: 415-495-7195; Fax: 415-777-3731

Colombia Embassy
2118 Leroy Pl NW
Washington, DC 20008
Phone: 202-387-8338; Fax: 202-232-8643
www.colombiaemb.org

Colombia Embassy - Consular Section
1101 17th St NW
Suite 1007
Washington, DC 20036
Phone: 202-332-7573; Fax: 202-332-7180
www.colombiaemb.org

Colombia Permanent Mission to the UN
140 E 57th St
5th Fl
New York, NY 10022
Phone: 212-355-7776; Fax: 212-371-2813
www.colombiaun.org

COMOROS

Comoros Embassy
866 United Nations Plaza
Suite 418
New York, NY 10017
Phone: 212-750-1637; Fax: 212-750-1657

Comoros Permanent Mission to the UN
866 UN Plaza
Suite 418
New York, NY 10017
Phone: 212-750-1637; Fax: 212-750-1657
www.un.int/comoros

CONGO, DEMOCRATIC REPUBLIC OF

Congo Democratic Republic of Embassy
1726 M St NW
Washington, DC 20036
Phone: 202-234-7690; Fax: 202-234-2609

Congo Democratic Republic of Permanent
 Mission to the UN
866 UN Plaza
Suite 511
New York, NY 10017
Phone: 212-319-8061; Fax: 212-319-8232
www.un.int/drcongo

CONGO, REPUBLIC OF

Congo Republic of Embassy
4891 Colorado Ave NW
Washington, DC 20011
Phone: 202-726-0825; Fax: 202-726-1860

Congo Republic of Permanent Mission to the
 UN
866 2nd Ave
2nd Fl

New York, NY 10017
Phone: 212-832-6553; Fax: 212-832-6558
www.un.int/congo

COSTA RICA

Costa Rica Consulate General
1870 The Exchange
Suite 100
Atlanta, GA 30339
Phone: 770-951-7025; Fax: 770-951-7073
www.costarica-embassy.org

Costa Rica Consulate General
203 N Wabash Ave
Suite 702
Chicago, IL 60601
Phone: 312-263-2772; Fax: 312-263-5807
www.costarica-embassy.org

Costa Rica Consulate General
3000 Wilcrest Dr
Suite 112
Houston, TX 77042
Phone: 713-266-0484; Fax: 713-266-1527
www.costarica-embassy.org

Costa Rica Consulate General
1605 W Olympic Blvd
Suite 400
Los Angeles, CA 90015
Phone: 213-380-7915; Fax: 213-380-5639
www.costarica-embassy.org

Costa Rica Consulate General
1101 Brickell Ave
Suite 401 North Tower
Miami, FL 33131
Phone: 305-871-7485; Fax: 305-871-0860
www.costarica-embassy.org

Costa Rica Consulate General
225 W 34th St Suite 1203
Penn Plaza Blvd
New York, NY 10122
Phone: 212-509-3066; Fax: 212-509-3068
www.costarica-embassy.org

Costa Rica Consulate General
2112 'S' St NW

Washington, DC 20008
Phone: 202-328-6628; Fax: 202-265-4795
www.costarica-embassy.org

Costa Rica Embassy
2114 'S' St NW
Washington, DC 20008
Phone: 202-234-2945; Fax: 202-265-4795
www.costarica-embassy.org

Costa Rica Permanent Mission to the UN
211 E 43rd St
Rm 903
New York, NY 10017
Phone: 212-986-6373; Fax: 212-986-6842
www2.un.int/public/costarica

COTE D'IVOIRE (IVORY COAST)

Cote d'Ivoire Embassy
2424 Massachusetts Ave
Washington, DC 20008
Phone: 202-797-0300; Fax: 202-462-9444
www.embaci.com

Cote d'Ivoire Permanent Mission to the UN
46 E 74th St
New York, NY 10021
Phone: 212-717-5555; Fax: 212-717-4492
www.un.int/cotedivoire

CROATIA

Croatian National Tourist Office
350 5th Ave
Suite 4003
New York, NY 10118
Phone: 212-279-8672; Fax: 212-279-8683
Toll-free: 800-829-4416
www.croatia.hr

Croatia Consulate General
737 N Michigan Ave
Suite 1030
Chicago, IL 60611
Phone: 312-482-9902; Fax: 312-482-9987
www.croatiaemb.org

Croatia Consulate General
11766 Wilshire Blvd

Suite 1250
Los Angeles, CA 90025
Phone: 310-477-1009; Fax: 310-477-1866
www.croatiaemb.org

Croatia Consulate General
369 Lexington Ave
11th Fl
New York, NY 10017
Phone: 212-599-3066; Fax: 212-599-3106
www.croatiaemb.org

Croatia Embassy
2343 Massachusetts Ave NW
Washington, DC 20008
Phone: 202-588-5899; Fax: 202-588-8936
www.croatiaemb.org

Croatia Permanent Mission to the UN
820 2nd Ave
19th Fl
New York, NY 10017
Phone: 212-986-1585; Fax: 212-986-2011
www.un.int/croatia

CUBA

Cuba Interests Section
Embassy of Switzerland
2630 16th St NW
Washington, DC 20009
Phone: 202-797-8518; Fax: 202-797-8521

Cuba Permanent Mission to the UN
315 Lexington Ave
New York, NY 10016
Phone: 212-689-7215; Fax: 212-689-9073
www.un.int/cuba

CURACAO

Curacao Tourist Board
3361 SW 3rd Ave
Suite 102
Miami, FL 33145
Phone: 305-285-0511; Fax: 305-285-0535
Toll-free: 800-328-7222
www.curacao-tourism.com

CYPRUS

Cyprus Tourism Organization
13 E 40th St
New York, NY 10016
Phone: 212-683-5280; Fax: 212-683-5282
www.cyprustourism.org

Cyprus Consulate General
13 E 40th St
New York, NY 10016
Phone: 212-686-6016; Fax: 212-686-3660

Cyprus Embassy
2211 R St NW
Washington, DC 20008
Phone: 202-462-5772; Fax: 202-483-6710
www.cyprusembassy.net

Cyprus Permanent Mission to the UN
13 E 40th St
New York, NY 10016
Phone: 212-481-6023; Fax: 212-685-7316
www.un.int/cyprus

CZECH REPUBLIC

Czech Center
1109 Madison Ave
New York, NY 10028
Phone: 212-288-0830; Fax: 212-288-0971
www.czechcenter.com

Czech Republic Consulate General
10990 Wilshire Blvd
Suite 1100
Los Angeles, CA 90024
Phone: 310-473-0889; Fax: 310-473-9813
www.mzv.cz/losangeles

Czech Republic Consulate General
1109-1111 Madison Ave
New York, NY 10028
Phone: 646-981-4040; Fax: 212-717-5064
www.mzv.cz/newyork

Czech Republic Embassy
3900 Spring of Freedom St NW
Washington, DC 20008

Phone: 202-274-9100; Fax: 202-966-8540
www.mzv.cz/washington

Czech Republic Permanent Mission to the UN
1109 Madison Ave
New York, NY 10028
Phone: 646-981-4000; Fax: 646-981-4099
www.mzv.cz/un.newyork

DENMARK

Danish Tourist Board
655 3rd Ave
18th Fl
New York, NY 10017
Phone: 212-885-9700; Fax: 212-885-9710
www.visitdenmark.com

Danish-American Chamber of Commerce
885 2nd Ave
18th Fl
New York, NY 10017
Phone: 212-705-4945; Fax: 212-754-1904
www.daccny.com

Denmark Consulate General
211 E Ontario St
Suite 1800
Chicago, IL 60611
Phone: 312-787-8780; Fax: 312-787-8744
www.consulatedk.org

Denmark Consulate General
1 Dag Hammarskjold Plaza 18th Fl
885 2nd Ave
New York, NY 10017
Phone: 212-223-4545; Fax: 212-754-1904
www.denmark.org

Denmark Embassy
3200 Whitehaven St NW
Washington, DC 20008
Phone: 202-234-4300; Fax: 202-328-1470
www.ambwashington.um.dk/en

Denmark Permanent Mission to the UN
885 2nd Ave
18th Fl
New York, NY 10017

Phone: 212-308-7009; Fax: 212-308-3384
www.un.int/denmark

DJIBOUTI

Djibouti Embassy
1156 15th St NW
Suite 515
Washington, DC 20005
Phone: 202-331-0270; Fax: 202-331-0302

Djibouti Permanent Mission to the UN
866 UN Plaza
Suite 4011
New York, NY 10017
Phone: 212-753-3163; Fax: 212-223-1276

DOMINICA

Dominica Consulate General
800 2nd Ave
Suite 400-H
New York, NY 10017
Phone: 212-599-8478; Fax: 212-808-4975

Dominica Embassy
3216 New Mexico Ave NW
Washington, DC 20016
Phone: 202-364-6781; Fax: 202-364-6791

Dominica Permanent Mission to the UN
800 2nd Ave
Suite 400H
New York, NY 10017
Phone: 212-949-0853; Fax: 212-808-4975

DOMINICAN REPUBLIC

Dominican Republic Tourist Board
848 Brickell Ave
Suite 405
Miami, FL 33131
Phone: 305-358-2899; Fax: 305-358-4185
www.dominicanrepublic.com

Dominican Republic Tourist Board
136 E 57th St
Suite 803
New York, NY 10022
Phone: 212-588-1012; Fax: 212-588-1015

Toll-free: 888-374-6361
www.dominicanrepublic.com

Dominican Republic Consulate General
1516 Oak St
Suite 321
Alameda, CA 94501
Phone: 510-864-7777; Fax: 818-504-6617
www.domrep.org

Dominican Republic Consulate General
20 Park Plaza
Statler Bldg Suite 601
Boston, MA 02116
Phone: 617-482-2101; Fax: 617-482-8133
www.domrep.org

Dominican Republic Consulate General
8700 Brynmawr St Suite 818
Presidents Plaza O'Hare Center
Chicago, IL 60631
Phone: 773-714-4924
www.domrep.org

Dominican Republic Consulate General
1038 Brickell Ave
Miami, FL 33131
Phone: 305-358-3220; Fax: 305-358-2318
www.domrep.org

Dominican Republic Consulate General
1501 Broadway
Suite 410
New York, NY 10036
Phone: 212-768-2480; Fax: 212-768-2677
www.domrep.org

Dominican Republic Consulate General
1715 22nd St NW
Washington, DC 20008
Phone: 202-332-6280; Fax: 202-387-2459
www.domrep.org

Dominican Republic Embassy
1715 22nd St NW
Washington, DC 20008
Phone: 202-332-6280; Fax: 202-265-8057
www.domrep.org

Dominican Republic Permanent Mission to
the UN
144 E 44th St
4th Fl
New York, NY 10017
Phone: 212-867-0833; Fax: 212-986-4694
www.un.int/dr

ECUADOR

Ecuadorian-American Chamber of
Commerce of Greater Miami
1390 Brickell Ave
Suite 220
Miami, FL 33131
Phone: 305-539-0010; Fax: 305-539-8001
www.ecuachamber.com

Ecuador Consulate General
8484 Wilshire Blvd
Suite 540
Beverly Hills, CA 90211
Phone: 323-658-6020; Fax: 323-658-1198
www.ecuador.org/consulates.htm

Ecuador Consulate General
30 S Michigan Ave
Suite 204
Chicago, IL 60603
Phone: 312-338-1002; Fax: 312-338-1004
www.ecuador.org/consulates.htm

Ecuador Consulate General
4200 Westheimer Rd
Suite 218
Houston, TX 77027
Phone: 713-572-8731; Fax: 713-572-8732
www.ecuador.org/consulates

Ecuador Consulate General
1101 Brickell Ave
Suite M102
Miami, FL 33131
Phone: 305-539-8214; Fax: 305-539-8313
www.ecuador.org/consulates.htm

Ecuador Consulate General
800 2nd Ave
Suite 600

New York, NY 10017
Phone: 212-808-0170; Fax: 212-808-0188
www.consulecuadornewyork.com

Ecuador Consulate General
400 Market St
4th Fl
Newark, NJ 07105
Phone: 973-344-6900; Fax: 973-344-0008
www.consuladoecuadornj.com

Ecuador Consulate General
235 Montgomery St
Suite 944
San Francisco, CA 94104
Phone: 415-982-1819; Fax: 415-982-1833
www.ecuador.org/consulates.htm

Ecuador Embassy
2535 15th St NW
Washington, DC 20009
Phone: 202-234-7200; Fax: 202-234-3429
www.ecuador.org

Ecuador Permanent Mission to the UN
866 UN Plaza
Suite 516
New York, NY 10017
Phone: 212-935-1680; Fax: 212-935-1835

EGYPT

Egyptian Tourist Authority
630 5th Ave
Suite 2305
New York, NY 10111
Phone: 212-332-2570; Fax: 212-956-6439
Toll-free: 877-773-4978
www.egypttourism.org

American Egyptian Cooperation Foundation
28 E Jackson Blvd
Suite 809
Chicago, IL 60604
Phone: 312-427-9368
www.americanegyptiancoop.org

American Egyptian Cooperation Foundation
1535 West Loop S
Suite 200

Houston, TX 77027
Phone: 713-624-7113
www.americanegyptiancoop.org

American Egyptian Cooperation Foundation
330 E 39th St
Suite 32L
New York, NY 10016
Phone: 212-867-2323; Fax: 212-697-0465
www.americanegyptiancoop.org

American Egyptian Cooperation Foundation
870 Market St
Suite 855
San Francisco, CA 94102
Phone: 415-837-0989; Fax: 415-837-0989
www.americanegyptiancoop.org

Egypt Consulate General
500 N Michigan Ave
Suite 1900
Chicago, IL 60611
Phone: 312-828-9162; Fax: 312-828-9167
www.eg2002.net

Egypt Consulate General
1990 Post Oak Blvd
Suite 2180
Houston, TX 77056
Phone: 713-961-4915; Fax: 713-961-3868

Egypt Consulate General
1110 2nd Ave
Suite 201
New York, NY 10022
Phone: 212-759-7120; Fax: 212-308-7643
www.egyptnyc.net

Egypt Consulate General
3001 Pacific Ave
San Francisco, CA 94115
Phone: 415-346-9700; Fax: 415-346-9480
www.egy2000.com

Egypt Embassy
3521 International Ct NW
Washington, DC 20008
Phone: 202-895-5400; Fax: 202-244-4319
www.egyptembassy.net

Egypt Permanent Mission to the UN
304 E 44th St
New York, NY 10017
Phone: 212-503-0300; Fax: 212-949-5999

EL SALVADOR

El Salvador Consulate General
104 S Michigan Ave
Suite 816
Chicago, IL 60603
Phone: 312-332-1393; Fax: 312-332-4446
www.elsalvador.org

El Salvador Consulate General
2600 Douglas Rd
Suite 104
Coral Gables, FL 33134
Phone: 305-774-0840; Fax: 305-774-0850
www.elsalvador.org

El Salvador Consulate General
1555 W Mockingbird Ln
Suite 216
Dallas, TX 75235
Phone: 214-637-0732; Fax: 214-637-1106
www.elsalvador.org

El Salvador Consulate General
1702 Hillendahl Blvd
Houston, TX 77055
Phone: 713-270-6239; Fax: 713-270-9683
www.elsalvador.org

El Salvador Consulate General
3450 Wilshire Blvd
Suite 250
Los Angeles, CA 90010
Phone: 213-383-8580; Fax: 213-383-8599
www.elsalvador.org

El Salvador Consulate General
46 Park Ave
New York, NY 10016
Phone: 212-889-3608; Fax: 212-679-2835
www.elsalvador.org

El Salvador Consulate General
507 Polk St

Suite 280
San Francisco, CA 94102
Phone: 415-771-8524; Fax: 415-771-8522
www.elsalvador.org

El Salvador Embassy
1400 16th St NW
Suite 100
Washington, DC 20036
Phone: 202-595-7500; Fax: 202-232-3763
www.elsalvador.org

El Salvador Permanent Mission to the UN
46 Park Ave
3rd Fl
New York, NY 10016
Phone: 212-679-1616; Fax: 212-725-3467

EQUATORIAL GUINEA

Equatorial Guinea Embassy
2020 16th St NW
Washington, DC 20009
Phone: 202-518-5700; Fax: 202-518-5252

Equatorial Guinea Permanent Mission to the UN
242 E 51st St
New York, NY 10022
Phone: 212-223-2324; Fax: 212-223-2366

ERITREA

Eritrea Embassy
1708 New Hampshire Ave NW
Washington, DC 20009
Phone: 202-319-1991; Fax: 202-319-1304

Eritrea Permanent Mission to the UN
800 2nd Ave
18th Fl
New York, NY 10017
Phone: 212-687-3390; Fax: 212-687-3138
www.un.int/eritrea

ESTONIA

Estonia Consulate General
600 3rd Ave
26th Fl

New York, NY 10016
Phone: 212-883-0636; Fax: 212-883-0648
www.nyc.estemb.org

Estonia Embassy
2131 Massachusetts Ave NW
Washington, DC 20008
Phone: 202-588-0101; Fax: 202-588-0108
www.estemb.org

Estonia Permanent Mission to the UN
600 3rd Ave
26th Fl
New York, NY 10016
Phone: 212-883-0640; Fax: 212-883-0648

ETHIOPIA

Ethiopia Embassy
3506 International Dr NW
Washington, DC 20008
Phone: 202-364-1200; Fax: 202-587-0195
www.ethiopianembassy.org

Ethiopia Permanent Mission to the UN
866 2nd Ave
3rd Fl
New York, NY 10017
Phone: 212-421-1830; Fax: 212-754-0360
www.un.int/ethiopia

FIJI

Fiji Visitors Bureau
5777 W Century Blvd
Suite 220
Los Angeles, CA 90045
Phone: 310-568-1616; Fax: 310-670-2318
Toll-free: 800-932-3454
www.bulafiji.com

Fiji Embassy
2233 Wisconsin Ave NW
Suite 240
Washington, DC 20007
Phone: 202-337-8320; Fax: 202-337-1996
www.fijiembassy.org

Fiji Permanent Mission to the UN
630 3rd Ave

7th Fl
New York, NY 10017
Phone: 212-687-4130; Fax: 212-687-3963

FINLAND

Finnish Tourist Board
655 3rd Ave
18th Fl
New York, NY 10017
Phone: 212-885-9700; Fax: 212-885-9710
www.gofinland.org

Finnish American Chamber of Commerce Inc
866 United Nations Plaza
New York, NY 10017
Phone: 212-821-0225; Fax: 212-750-4418
www.finlandtrade.com

Finnish-American Chamber of Commerce on
    the Pacific Coast
PO Box 3058
Tustin, CA 92781
Phone: 714-573-0604; Fax: 714-242-9153
www.faccpacific.com

Finland Consulate General
1801 Century Pk E
Suite 2100
Los Angeles, CA 90067
Phone: 310-203-9903; Fax: 310-203-9186
www.finland.org

Finland Consulate General
866 UN Plaza
Suite 250
New York, NY 10017
Phone: 212-750-4400; Fax: 212-750-4418
www.finland.org

Finland Embassy
3301 Massachusetts Ave NW
Washington, DC 20008
Phone: 202-298-5800; Fax: 202-298-6030
www.finland.org

Finland Permanent Mission to the UN
866 UN Plaza
Suite 222
New York, NY 10017

Phone: 212-355-2100; Fax: 212-759-6156
www.un.int/finland

FRANCE

French Government Tourist Office
9454 Wilshire Blvd
Suite 210
Beverly Hills, CA 90212
Phone: 310-271-6665; Fax: 310-276-2835
www.franceguide.com

French Government Tourist Office
205 N Michigan Ave
Suite 3770
Chicago, IL 60601
Phone: 312-327-0290
www.franceguide.com

French Government Tourist Office
444 Madison Ave
16th Fl
New York, NY 10022
Phone: 212-838-7800; Fax: 212-838-7855
us.franceguide.com

French-American Chamber of Commerce of
    Atlanta
321 Pharr Rd
Suite G
Atlanta, GA 30305
Phone: 404-846-2500; Fax: 404-846-2555
www.facc-atlanta.com

French-American Chamber of Commerce of
    Chicago
35 E Wacker Dr
Suite 670
Chicago, IL 60601
Phone: 312-578-0444; Fax: 312-578-0445
www.facc-chicago.com

French-American Chamber of Commerce of
    Dallas
2665 Villa Creek Dr
Suite 214
Dallas, TX 75234
Phone: 972-241-0111; Fax: 972-241-0901
www.faccdallas.com

French-American Chamber of Commerce of
  Houston
5373 W Alabama St
Suite 209
Houston, TX 77056
Phone: 713-960-0575; Fax: 713-960-0495
www.facchouston.com

French-American Chamber of Commerce of
  Los Angeles
8222 Melrose Ave
Suite 203
Los Angeles, CA 90046
Phone: 323-651-4741; Fax: 323-651-2547
www.frenchchamberla.org

French-American Chamber of Commerce of
  Florida
14 NE 1st Ave
Suite 1005
Miami, FL 33132
Phone: 305-374-5000; Fax: 305-358-8203
www.faccmiami.com

French-American Chamber of Commerce of
  Louisiana
2 Canal St
Suite 2426
New Orleans, LA 70130
Phone: 504-561-0070; Fax: 504-592-9999
www.ccife.org/usa/louisiane

French-American Chamber of Commerce of
  New York
122 E 42nd St
Suite 2015
New York, NY 10168
Phone: 212-867-0123; Fax: 212-867-9050
www.ccife.org/usa/new_york

French-American Chamber of Commerce of
  Philadelphia
2000 Market St
Suite 2850
Philadelphia, PA 19103
Phone: 215-419-5559; Fax: 215-419-5533
www.faccphila.org

French-American Chamber of Commerce of
  San Francisco
703 Market St
Suite 450
San Francisco, CA 94103
Phone: 415-442-4717; Fax: 415-442-4621
www.faccsf.com

French-American Chamber of Commerce of
  the Pacific Northwest
2200 Alaskan Way
Suite 490
Seattle, WA 98121
Phone: 206-443-4703; Fax: 206-448-4218
www.ccife.org/usa/seattle

France Consulate General
3475 Piedmont Rd NE
Suite 1840
Atlanta, GA 30305
Phone: 404-495-1660; Fax: 404-495-1661
www.consulfrance-atlanta.org

France Consulate General
31 Saint James Ave
Suite 750
Boston, MA 02116
Phone: 617-832-4400
www.consulfrance-boston.org

France Consulate General
205 N Michigan Ave
Suite 3700
Chicago, IL 60601
Phone: 312-327-5200; Fax: 312-327-5201
www.consulfrance-chicago.org

France Consulate General
777 Post Oak Blvd
Suite 600
Houston, TX 77056
Phone: 713-572-2799; Fax: 713-572-2911
www.consulfrance-houston.org

France Consulate General
10990 Wilshire Blvd
Suite 300
Los Angeles, CA 90024
Phone: 310-235-3200; Fax: 310-312-0704
www.consulfrance-losangeles.org

France Consulate General
1395 Brickell Ave
Suite 1050
Miami, FL 33131
Phone: 305-403-4185; Fax: 305-403-4187
www.consulfrance-miami.org

France Consulate General
1340 Poydras St
Suite 1710
New Orleans, LA 70112
Phone: 504-569-2870; Fax: 504-569-2871
www.consulfrance-nouvelleorleans.org

France Consulate General
934 5th Ave
New York, NY 10021
Phone: 212-606-3680; Fax: 212-606-3614
www.consulfrance-newyork.org

France Consulate General
540 Bush St
San Francisco, CA 94108
Phone: 415-397-4330; Fax: 415-433-8357
www.consulfrance-sanfrancisco.org

France Embassy
4101 Reservoir Rd NW
Washington, DC 20007
Phone: 202-944-6000; Fax: 202-944-6175
www.ambafrance-us.org

France Permanent Mission to the UN
245 E 47th St
44th Fl
New York, NY 10017
Phone: 212-308-5700; Fax: 212-421-6889
www.un.int/france

FRENCH WEST INDIES
SEE MARTINIQUE

GABON

Gabon Tourist Information Office
347 5th Ave
Suite 805
New York, NY 10016
Phone: 212-447-6700; Fax: 212-447-1532

Gabon Consulate
18 E 41st St
9th Fl
New York, NY 10017
Phone: 212-686-9720; Fax: 212-689-5769

Gabon Embassy
2034 20th St NW
Washington, DC 20009
Phone: 202-797-1000; Fax: 202-332-0668

Gabon Permanent Mission to the UN
18 E 41st St
9th Fl
New York, NY 10017
Phone: 212-686-9720; Fax: 212-689-5769
www.un.int/gabon

GAMBIA

Gambia Embassy
1156 15th St NW
Suite 905
Washington, DC 20005
Phone: 202-785-1399; Fax: 202-785-1430
www.gambiaembassy.us

Gambia Permanent Mission to the UN
800 2nd Ave
Rm 400F
New York, NY 10017
Phone: 212-949-6640; Fax: 212-856-9820

GEORGIA

Georgia Embassy
1101 15th St NW
Suite 602
Washington, DC 20005
Phone: 202-387-2390; Fax: 202-393-4537
www.georgiaemb.org

Georgia Permanent Mission to the UN
1 UN Plaza
26th Fl
New York, NY 10017
Phone: 212-759-1949; Fax: 212-759-1823
www.un.int/georgia

GERMANY

German National Tourist Office
122 E 42nd St
20th Fl
New York, NY 10168
Phone: 212-661-7200; Fax: 212-661-7174
www.cometogermany.com

German-American Chamber of Commerce
of the Southern US Inc
530 Means St NW
Suite 120
Atlanta, GA 30318
Phone: 404-586-6800; Fax: 404-586-6820
www.gaccsouth.com

German-American Chamber of Commerce
of the Midwest Inc
401 N Michigan Ave
Suite 3330
Chicago, IL 60611
Phone: 312-644-2662; Fax: 312-644-0738
www.gaccom.org

German-American Chamber of Commerce
Inc
75 Broad St
21st Fl
New York, NY 10004
Phone: 212-974-8830; Fax: 212-974-8867
www.gaccny.com

German-American Chamber of Commerce
Inc - Philadelphia
1600 JFK Blvd Suite 200
4 Penn Center
Philadelphia, PA 19103
Phone: 215-665-1585; Fax: 215-665-0375
www.gaccphiladelphia.com

Representative of German Industry & Trade
1627 'I' St NW
Suite 550
Washington, DC 20006
Phone: 202-659-4777; Fax: 202-659-4779
www.rgit-usa.com

Germany Consulate General
285 Peachtree Center Ave NE

Suite 901
Atlanta, GA 30303
Phone: 404-659-4760; Fax: 404-659-1280
www.germany.info/atlanta

Germany Consulate General
3 Copley Pl
Suite 500
Boston, MA 02116
Phone: 617-536-4414; Fax: 617-536-8573
www.germany.info/boston

Germany Consulate General
676 N Michigan Ave
Suite 3200
Chicago, IL 60611
Phone: 312-202-0480; Fax: 312-202-0466
germany.info/chicago

Germany Consulate General
1330 Post Oak Blvd
Suite 1850
Houston, TX 77056
Phone: 713-627-7770; Fax: 713-627-0506
www.germany.info/houston

Germany Consulate General
6222 Wilshire Blvd
Suite 500
Los Angeles, CA 90048
Phone: 323-930-2703; Fax: 323-930-2805
www.germany.info/losangeles

Germany Consulate General
100 N Biscayne Blvd
Suite 2200
Miami, FL 33132
Phone: 305-358-0290; Fax: 305-358-0307
www.germany.info/miami

Germany Consulate General
871 UN Plaza
New York, NY 10017
Phone: 212-610-9700; Fax: 212-610-9702
www.germany.info/newyork

Germany Consulate General
1960 Jackson St
San Francisco, CA 94109
Phone: 415-775-1061; Fax: 415-775-0187
www.germany.info/sanfrancisco

Germany Embassy
4645 Reservoir Rd NW
Washington, DC 20007
Phone: 202-298-4000; Fax: 202-298-4249
www.germany.info

Germany Permanent Mission to the UN
871 UN Plaza
New York, NY 10017
Phone: 212-940-0400; Fax: 212-940-0402
www.newyork-un.diplo.de

GHANA

Ghana Consulate General
19 E 47th St
New York, NY 10017
Phone: 212-832-1300; Fax: 212-751-6743

Ghana Embassy
3512 International Dr NW
Washington, DC 20008
Phone: 202-686-4520; Fax: 202-686-4527
www.ghanaembassy.org

Ghana Permanent Mission to the UN
19 E 47th St
New York, NY 10017
Phone: 212-832-1300; Fax: 212-751-6743
www.un.int/ghana

GREECE

Greek National Tourist Organization
645 5th Ave
Suite 903
New York, NY 10022
Phone: 212-421-5777; Fax: 212-826-6940
www.gnto.gr

Greece Consulate General
86 Beacon St
Boston, MA 02108
Phone: 617-523-0100; Fax: 617-523-0511
www.greekembassy.org/boston

Greece Consulate General
650 N Saint Clair St
Chicago, IL 60611

Phone: 312-335-3915; Fax: 312-335-3958
www.greekembassy.org/chicago

Greece Consulate General
12424 Wilshire Blvd
Suite 800
Los Angeles, CA 90025
Phone: 310-826-5555; Fax: 310-826-8670
www.greekembassy.org/losangeles

Greece Consulate General
69 E 79th St
New York, NY 10021
Phone: 212-988-5500; Fax: 212-734-8492
www.greekembassy.org/newyork

Greece Consulate General
2441 Gough St
San Francisco, CA 94123
Phone: 415-775-2102; Fax: 415-776-6815
www.greekembassy.org/sanfrancisco

Greece Embassy
2219 Massachusetts Ave NW
Washington, DC 20008
Phone: 202-939-1300; Fax: 202-939-1324
www.greekembassy.org

Greece Embassy - Consular Section
2217 Massachusetts Ave NW
Washington, DC 20008
Phone: 202-939-1306; Fax: 202-234-2803
www.greekembassy.org/dc

Greece Permanent Mission to the UN
866 2nd Ave
13th Fl
New York, NY 10017
Phone: 212-888-6900; Fax: 212-888-4440
www.greeceun.org

GRENADA

Grenada Board of Tourism
PO Box 1668
Lake Worth, FL 33460
Phone: 561-588-8176; Fax: 561-588-7267
Toll-free: 800-927-9554
www.grenadagrenadines.com

Grenada Board of Tourism
305 Madison Ave
Suite 2145
New York, NY 10165
Phone: 212-687-9554; Fax: 212-682-4748
www.grenadagrenadines.com

Grenada Consulate General
800 2nd Ave
Suite 400-K
New York, NY 10017
Phone: 212-599-0301; Fax: 212-599-1540
www.grenadaconsulate.org

Grenada Embassy
1701 New Hampshire Ave NW
Washington, DC 20009
Phone: 202-265-2561; Fax: 202-265-2468
www.grenadaembassyusa.org

Grenada Permanent Mission to the UN
800 2nd Ave
Suite 400-K
New York, NY 10017
Phone: 212-599-0301; Fax: 212-599-1540

GUATEMALA

Guatemala Consulate General
203 N Wabash Ave
Suite 910
Chicago, IL 60601
Phone: 312-332-1587; Fax: 312-332-4256

Guatemala Consulate General
3013 Fountain View Dr
Suite 210
Houston, TX 77057
Phone: 713-953-9531; Fax: 713-953-9383

Guatemala Consulate General
1625 W Olympic Blvd
Suite 1000
Los Angeles, CA 90015
Phone: 213-365-9251; Fax: 213-365-9245

Guatemala Consulate General
1101 Brickell Ave
Suite 1003-S
Miami, FL 33131
Phone: 305-679-9945; Fax: 305-679-9983

Guatemala Consulate General
57 Park Ave
New York, NY 10016
Phone: 212-686-3837; Fax: 212-447-6947

Guatemala Consulate General
870 Market St
Suite 667
San Francisco, CA 94102
Phone: 415-788-5651; Fax: 415-788-5653

Guatemala Embassy
2220 R St NW
Washington, DC 20008
Phone: 202-745-4952; Fax: 202-745-1908
www.guatemala-embassy.org

Guatemala Permanent Mission to the UN
57 Park Ave
New York, NY 10016
Phone: 212-679-4760; Fax: 212-685-8741
www.un.int/guatemala

GUINEA

Guinea Embassy
2112 Leroy Pl NW
Washington, DC 20008
Phone: 202-986-4300; Fax: 202-986-4800

Guinea Permanent Mission to the UN
140 E 39th St
New York, NY 10016
Phone: 212-687-8115; Fax: 212-687-8248
www.un.int/guinea

GUYANA

Guyana Consulate General
370 7th Ave
Suite 402
New York, NY 10001
Phone: 212-947-5110; Fax: 212-947-5163
www.guyana.org/govt/govt_offices.html

Guyana Embassy
2490 Tracy Pl NW
Washington, DC 20008
Phone: 202-265-6900; Fax: 202-232-1297

Guyana Permanent Mission to the UN
801 2nd Ave
5th Fl
New York, NY 10017
Phone: 212-573-5828; Fax: 212-573-6225

HAITI

Haiti Consulate General
545 Boylston St
Rm 201
Boston, MA 02116
Phone: 617-266-3660; Fax: 617-778-6898

Haiti Consulate General
220 S State St
Suite 2110
Chicago, IL 60604
Phone: 312-922-4004; Fax: 312-922-7122
www.haitianconsulate.org

Haiti Consulate General
259 SW 13th St
Miami, FL 33130
Phone: 305-859-2003; Fax: 305-854-7441

Haiti Consulate General
271 Madison Ave
5th Fl
New York, NY 10016
Phone: 212-697-9767; Fax: 212-681-6991
www.haitianconsulate-nyc.org

Haiti Embassy
2311 Massachusetts Ave NW
Washington, DC 20008
Phone: 202-332-4090; Fax: 202-745-7215
www.haiti.org

Haiti Permanent Mission to the UN
801 2nd Ave
Rm 600
New York, NY 10017
Phone: 212-370-4840; Fax: 212-661-8698

HOLY SEE (VATICAN CITY)

Holy See Apostolic Nunciature
3339 Massachusetts Ave NW
Washington, DC 20008
Phone: 202-333-7121; Fax: 202-337-4036

Holy See Permanent Observer Mission to
the UN
25 E 39th St
New York, NY 10016
Phone: 212-370-7885; Fax: 212-370-9622
www.holyseemission.org

HONDURAS

Honduras Tourism Institute
299 Alhambra Cir
Suite 226
Coral Gables, FL 33134
Phone: 305-461-0601; Fax: 305-461-0602
Toll-free: 800-410-9608
www.letsgohonduras.com

Honduras Consulate General
4439 W Fullerton Ave
Chicago, IL 60639
Phone: 773-342-8281; Fax: 773-342-8293

Honduras Consulate General
6161 Savoy Ln
Suite 365
Houston, TX 77036
Phone: 713-785-5932; Fax: 713-785-5625

Honduras Consulate General
3550 Wilshire Blvd
Suite 410
Los Angeles, CA 90010
Phone: 213-383-9244; Fax: 213-383-9309

Honduras Consulate General
7171 Coral Way
Suite 309
Miami, FL 33155
Phone: 305-269-9399; Fax: 305-269-9445

Honduras Consulate General
World Trade Center 2 Canal St
Suite 2340
New Orleans, LA 70130
Phone: 504-522-3118; Fax: 504-523-0544

Honduras Consulate General
35 W 35th St
6th Fl
New York, NY 10001
Phone: 212-714-9451; Fax: 212-714-9453

Honduras Consulate General
6825 Jimmy Carter Blvd
Suite 1490
Bldg 1400
Norcross, GA 30071
Phone: 770-645-8881; Fax: 770-645-8808

Honduras Consulate General
4040 E McDowell Rd
Suite 305
Phoenix, AZ 85008
Phone: 602-273-0173; Fax: 602-273-0547

Honduras Consulate General
870 Market St
Suite 449
San Francisco, CA 94102
Phone: 415-392-0076; Fax: 415-392-6726

Honduras Embassy
3007 Tilden St NW
Suite 4M
Washington, DC 20008
Phone: 202-966-7702; Fax: 202-966-9751
www.hondurasemb.org

Honduras Permanent Mission to the UN
866 UN Plaza
Suite 417
New York, NY 10017
Phone: 212-752-3370; Fax: 212-223-0498
www.un.int/honduras

HONG KONG

Hong Kong Tourism Board
10940 Wilshire Blvd
Suite 2050
Los Angeles, CA 90024
Phone: 310-208-4582; Fax: 310-208-1869
Toll-free: 800-282-4582
www.discoverhongkong.com

Hong Kong Tourism Board
115 E 54th St
2nd Fl
New York, NY 10022
Phone: 212-421-3382; Fax: 212-421-8428
www.discoverhongkong.com

HUNGARY

Hungarian National Tourist Office
350 5th Ave
Suite 7107
New York, NY 10118
Phone: 212-695-1221; Fax: 212-695-0809
www.gotohungary.com

Hungarian-American Chamber of
    Commerce of New England Inc
111 Huntington Ave
26th Fl
Boston, MA 02199
Phone: 508-347-2742; Fax: 508-347-3831
www.hungarianamericanchamber.com

Hungarian-American Chamber of
    Commerce in the US Inc
205 De Anza Blvd
PMB 157
San Mateo, CA 94402
Phone: 650-573-7351

Hungary Consulate General
11766 Wilshire Blvd
Suite 410
Los Angeles, CA 90025
Phone: 310-473-9344; Fax: 310-479-5119

Hungary Consulate General
223 E 52nd St
New York, NY 10022
Phone: 212-752-0661; Fax: 212-755-5986

Hungary Embassy
3910 Shoemaker St NW
Washington, DC 20008
Phone: 202-362-6730; Fax: 202-966-8135
www.huembwas.org

Hungary Permanent Mission to the UN
227 E 52nd St
New York, NY 10022
Phone: 212-752-0209; Fax: 212-755-5395
www.un.int/hungary

ICELAND

Icelandic Tourist Board
PO Box 4649

Grand Central Station, NY 10163
Phone: 212-885-9700; Fax: 212-885-9710
www.icelandtouristboard.com

Icelandic-American Chamber of Commerce
800 3rd Ave
36th Fl
New York, NY 10022
Phone: 212-593-2700; Fax: 212-593-6269
www.iceland.org/us/nyc/consulate-
general/chamber-of-commerce

Iceland Consulate General
800 3rd Ave
36th Fl
New York, NY 10022
Phone: 212-593-2700; Fax: 646-282-9369
www.iceland.org/us/nyc/

Iceland Embassy
1156 15th St NW
Suite 1200
Washington, DC 20005
Phone: 202-265-6653; Fax: 202-265-6656
www.iceland.org/us

Iceland Permanent Mission to the UN
800 3rd Ave
36th Fl
New York, NY 10022
Phone: 212-593-2700; Fax: 212-593-6269
www.iceland.org/un/nyc

INDIA

India Tourist Office
3550 Wilshire Blvd
Suite 204
Los Angeles, CA 90010
Phone: 213-380-8855; Fax: 213-380-6111
Toll-free: 800-422-4634
www.tourismofindia.com

India Tourist Office
1270 Ave of the Americas
Suite 1808
New York, NY 10020
Phone: 212-586-4901; Fax: 212-582-3274
Toll-free: 800-953-9399
www.tourismofindia.com

India Consulate General
455 N Cityfront Plaza Dr
Suite 850
Chicago, IL 60611
Phone: 312-595-0405; Fax: 312-595-0417
www.indianconsulate.com

India Consulate General
1990 Post Oak Blvd
Suite 600
Houston, TX 77056
Phone: 713-626-2148; Fax: 713-626-2450
www.cgihouston.org

India Consulate General
3 E 64th St
New York, NY 10021
Phone: 212-774-0600; Fax: 212-861-3788
www.indiacgny.org

India Consulate General
540 Arguello Blvd
San Francisco, CA 94118
Phone: 415-668-0662; Fax: 415-668-9764
www.cgisf.org

India Embassy
2107 Massachusetts Ave NW
Washington, DC 20008
Phone: 202-939-7000; Fax: 202-265-4351
www.indianembassy.org

India Embassy - Consular Wing
2536 Massachusetts Ave NW
Washington, DC 20008
Phone: 202-939-9806
www.indianembassy.org

India Permanent Mission to the UN
235 E 43rd St
New York, NY 10017
Phone: 212-490-9660; Fax: 212-490-9656
www.un.int/india

INDONESIA

American-Indonesian Chamber of
  Commerce
317 Madison Ave
Suite 1619

New York, NY 10017
Phone: 212-687-4505; Fax: 212-687-5844
www.aiccusa.org

Indonesia Consulate General
211 W Wacker Dr
8th Fl
Chicago, IL 60606
Phone: 312-920-1880; Fax: 312-920-1881
www.indonesiachicago.org

Indonesia Consulate General
10900 Richmond Ave
Houston, TX 77042
Phone: 713-785-1691; Fax: 713-780-9644

Indonesia Consulate General
3457 Wilshire Blvd
Los Angeles, CA 90010
Phone: 213-383-5126; Fax: 213-487-3971

Indonesia Consulate General
5 E 68th St
New York, NY 10021
Phone: 212-879-0600; Fax: 212-570-6206

Indonesia Consulate General
1111 Columbus Ave
San Francisco, CA 94133
Phone: 415-474-9571; Fax: 415-441-4320

Indonesia Embassy
2020 Massachusetts Ave NW
Washington, DC 20036
Phone: 202-775-5200; Fax: 202-775-5365
www.embassyofindonesia.org

Indonesia Permanent Mission to the UN
325 E 38th St
New York, NY 10016
Phone: 212-972-8333; Fax: 212-972-9780
www.indonesiamission-ny.org

IRAN

Iran Interests Section
Embassy of Pakistan
2209 Wisconsin Ave NW
Washington, DC 20007
Phone: 202-965-4990; Fax: 202-965-1073
www.daftar.org

Iran Permanent Mission to the UN
622 3rd Ave
34th Fl
New York, NY 10017
Phone: 212-687-2020; Fax: 212-867-7086
www.un.int/iran

IRAQ

Iraq Permanent Mission to the UN
14 E 79th St
New York, NY 10021
Phone: 212-737-4433; Fax: 212-772-1794

IRELAND

Irish Tourist Board
345 Park Ave
17th Fl
New York, NY 10154
Phone: 212-418-0800; Fax: 212-371-9052
Toll-free: 800-669-9967
www.tourismireland.com

Ireland Chamber of Commerce in the US
556 Central Ave
New Providence, NJ 07974
Phone: 908-286-1300; Fax: 908-286-1200
www.iccusa.org

Ireland-US Council for Commerce &
   Industry
1156 Ave of the Americas
New York, NY 10036
Phone: 212-921-1414; Fax: 212-730-2232

Ireland Consulate General
535 Boylston St
Boston, MA 02116
Phone: 617-267-9330; Fax: 617-267-6375

Ireland Consulate General
400 N Michigan Ave
Suite 911
Chicago, IL 60611
Phone: 312-337-1868; Fax: 312-337-1954

Ireland Consulate General
345 Park Ave
17th Fl

New York, NY 10154
Phone: 212-319-2555; Fax: 212-980-9475

Ireland Consulate General
100 Pine St
33rd Fl
San Francisco, CA 94111
Phone: 415-392-4214; Fax: 415-392-0885

Ireland Embassy
2234 Massachusetts Ave NW
Washington, DC 20008
Phone: 202-462-3939; Fax: 202-232-5993
www.embassyofireland.org

Ireland Permanent Mission to the UN
885 2nd Ave
19th Fl
New York, NY 10017
Phone: 212-421-6934; Fax: 212-752-4726
www.un.int/ireland

ISRAEL

Israel Government Tourist Office
6380 Wilshire Blvd
Suite 1700
Los Angeles, CA 90048
Phone: 323-658-7463; Fax: 323-658-6543
www.goisrael.com

Israel Government Tourist Office
800 2nd Ave
16th Fl
New York, NY 10017
Phone: 212-499-5660; Fax: 212-499-5645
Toll-free: 888-774-7723
www.goisrael.com

American-Israel Chamber of Commerce
Southeast Region
1150 Lake Hearn Dr
Suite 130
Atlanta, GA 30342
Phone: 404-843-9426; Fax: 404-843-1416
www.aiccse.org

America-Israel Chamber of Commerce -
Chicago
247 S State St

15th Fl
Chicago, IL 60604
Phone: 312-235-0586; Fax: 312-641-0724
www.americaisrael.org

American-Israel Chamber of Commerce &
Industry of Minnesota
13100 Wayzata Blvd
Suite 130
Minnetonka, MN 55305
Phone: 952-593-8666; Fax: 952-593-8668
www.aiccmn.org

America-Israel Chamber of Commerce &
Industry
3 New York Plaza
10th Fl
New York, NY 10004
Phone: 212-232-8440; Fax: 646-365-3366
www.aicci.net

Israel Consulate General
1100 Spring St NW
Suite 440
Atlanta, GA 30309
Phone: 404-487-6500; Fax: 404-487-6555
www.israelemb.org

Israel Consulate General
111 E Wacker Dr
Suite 1308
Chicago, IL 60601
Phone: 312-297-4800; Fax: 312-297-4855
www.israelemb.org

Israel Consulate General
24 Greenway Plaza
Suite 1500
Houston, TX 77046
Phone: 713-627-3780; Fax: 713-627-0149
www.israelemb.org

Israel Consulate General
6380 Wilshire Blvd
Suite 1700
Los Angeles, CA 90048
Phone: 323-852-5500; Fax: 323-852-5555
www.israelemb.org

Israel Consulate General
100 N Biscayne Blvd

Suite 1800
Miami, FL 33132
Phone: 305-925-9400; Fax: 305-925-9451
www.israelemb.org

Israel Consulate General
800 2nd Ave
New York, NY 10017
Phone: 212-499-5300; Fax: 212-499-5455
www.israelemb.org

Israel Consulate General
230 S 15th St
Suite 8
Philadelphia, PA 19102
Phone: 215-546-5556; Fax: 215-545-3986
www.israelemb.org

Israel Consulate General
456 Montgomery St
Suite 2100
San Francisco, CA 94104
Phone: 415-844-7500; Fax: 415-844-7555
www.israelemb.org

Israel Embassy
3514 International Dr NW
Washington, DC 20008
Phone: 202-364-5500; Fax: 202-364-5429
www.israelemb.org

Israel Permanent Mission to the UN
800 2nd Ave
New York, NY 10017
Phone: 212-499-5510; Fax: 212-499-5515
www.israel-un.org/

ITALY

Italian Government Tourist Board
500 N Michigan Ave
Suite 2240
Chicago, IL 60611
Phone: 312-644-0996; Fax: 312-644-3019
www.italiantourism.com

Italian Government Tourist Board
12400 Wilshire Blvd
Suite 550
Los Angeles, CA 90025

Phone: 310-820-1898; Fax: 310-820-6357
www.italiantourism.com

Italian Government Tourist Board
630 5th Ave
Suite 1565
New York, NY 10111
Phone: 212-245-5618; Fax: 212-586-9249
www.italiantourism.com

Italian American Chamber of Commerce of
    Chicago
30 S Michigan Ave
Suite 504
Chicago, IL 60603
Phone: 312-553-9137; Fax: 312-553-9142
www.italianchamber.us

Italy-America Chamber of Commerce of
    Texas Inc
1800 W Loop S
Suite 1120
Houston, TX 77027
Phone: 713-626-9303; Fax: 713-626-9309
www.iacctexas.com

Italy-America Chamber of Commerce West Inc
10350 Santa Monica Blvd
Suite 210
Los Angeles, CA 90025
Phone: 310-557-3017; Fax: 310-557-1217
www.italchambers.net/losangeles

Italy-America Chamber of Commerce
    Southeast Inc
270 NE 4th St
Suite 2
Miami, FL 33132
Phone: 305-577-9868; Fax: 305-577-3956
www.iacc-miami.com

Italy-America Chamber of Commerce Inc
730 5th Ave
Suite 600
New York, NY 10019
Phone: 212-459-0044; Fax: 212-459-0090
www.italchamber.org

Italy Consulate General
600 Atlantic Ave
17th Fl

Boston, MA 02210
Phone: 617-722-9201; Fax: 617-722-9407

Italy Consulate General
500 N Michigan Ave
Suite 1850
Chicago, IL 60611
Phone: 312-439-8600; Fax: 312-467-1335
www.conschicago.esteri.it

Italy Consulate General
4000 Ponce de Leon Blvd
Suite 590
Coral Gables, FL 33146
Phone: 305-374-6322; Fax: 305-374-7945
www.consmiami.esteri.it

Italy Consulate General
1300 Post Oak Blvd
Suite 660
Houston, TX 77056
Phone: 713-850-7520; Fax: 713-850-9113
www.conshouston.esteri.it

Italy Consulate General
12400 Wilshire Blvd
Suite 300
Los Angeles, CA 90025
Phone: 310-820-0622; Fax: 310-820-0727
www.conslosangeles.esteri.it

Italy Consulate General
690 Park Ave
New York, NY 10021
Phone: 212-737-9100; Fax: 212-249-4945
www.consnewyork.esteri.it

Italy Vice Consulate
1 Gateway Center
Suite 100
Newark, NJ 07102
Phone: 973-643-1448; Fax: 973-643-3043
www.consnewark.esteri.it

Italy Consulate General
Public Ledger Bldg Suite 1026
100 S 6th St
Philadelphia, PA 19106
Phone: 215-592-7329; Fax: 215-592-9808
www.consfiladelfia.esteri.it

Italy Consulate General
2590 Webster St
San Francisco, CA 94115
Phone: 415-931-4924; Fax: 415-931-7205
www.conssanfrancisco.esteri.it

Italy Embassy
3000 Whitehaven St NW
Washington, DC 20008
Phone: 202-612-4400; Fax: 202-518-2154
www.ambwashingtondc.esteri.it

Italy Permanent Mission to the UN
2 UN Plaza
24th Fl
New York, NY 10017
Phone: 212-486-9191; Fax: 212-486-1036

IVORY COAST
SEE COTE D'IVOIRE

JAMAICA

Jamaica Tourist Board
5201 Blue Lagoon Dr
Suite 1101
Miami, FL 33126
Phone: 305-665-0557; Fax: 305-666-7239
Toll-free: 800-233-4582
www.visitjamaica.com

Jamaica Consulate General
25 SE 2nd Ave
Suite 842
Miami, FL 33131
Phone: 305-374-8431; Fax: 305-577-4970

Jamaica Embassy
1520 New Hampshire Ave NW
Washington, DC 20036
Phone: 202-452-0660; Fax: 202-452-0081
www.jamaicaembassy.org

Jamaica Permanent Mission to the UN
767 3rd Ave
9th Fl
New York, NY 10017
Phone: 212-935-7509; Fax: 212-935-7607
www.un.int/jamaica

JAPAN

Japan National Tourist Organization
515 S Figueroa St
Suite 1470
Los Angeles, CA 90071
Phone: 213-623-1952; Fax: 213-623-6301
www.japantravelinfo.com

Japan National Tourist Organization
1 Rockefeller Plaza
Suite 1250
New York, NY 10020
Phone: 212-757-5640; Fax: 212-307-6754
www.japantravelinfo.com

Japanese Chamber of Commerce & Industry
of Chicago
541 N Fairbanks Ct
Suite 2050
Chicago, IL 60611
Phone: 312-245-8344; Fax: 312-245-8355
www.jccc-chi.org/en

Japanese Chamber of Commerce & Industry
of Hawaii
400 Hualani St
Suite 20B
Hilo, HI 96720
Phone: 808-934-0177; Fax: 808-934-0178

Japanese Chamber of Commerce & Industry
of New York Inc
145 W 57th St
6th Fl
New York, NY 10019
Phone: 212-246-8001; Fax: 212-246-8002
www.jcciny.org

Japanese Chamber of Commerce of
Northern California
1875 S Grant St
Suite 760
San Mateo, CA 94402
Phone: 650-522-8500; Fax: 650-522-8300
www.jccnc.org

Japan Consulate General
3601 C St

Suite 1300
Anchorage, AK 99503
Phone: 907-562-8424; Fax: 907-562-8434
www.anchorage.us.emb-japan.go.jp

Japan Consulate General
1 Alliance Ctr 3500 Lenox Rd
Suite 1600
Atlanta, GA 30326
Phone: 404-240-4300; Fax: 404-240-4311
www.japanatlanta.org

Japan Consulate General
600 Atlantic Ave
Federal Reserve Plaza 14th Fl
Boston, MA 02210
Phone: 617-973-9772; Fax: 617-542-1329
www.boston.us.emb-japan.go.jp

Japan Consulate General
737 N Michigan Ave
Suite 1100
Chicago, IL 60611
Phone: 312-280-0400; Fax: 312-280-9568
www.chicago.us.emb-japan.go.jp

Japan Consulate General
1225 17th St
Suite 3000
Denver, CO 80202
Phone: 303-534-1151; Fax: 303-534-3393
www.denver.us.emb-japan.go.jp

Japan Consulate General
400 Renaissance Ctr
Suite 1600
Detroit, MI 48243
Phone: 313-567-0120; Fax: 313-567-0274
www.detroit.us.emb-japan.go.jp

Japan Consulate General
1742 Nuuanu Ave
Honolulu, HI 96817
Phone: 808-543-3111; Fax: 808-543-3170
www.honolulu.us.emb-japan.go.jp

Japan Consulate General
909 Fannin St Suite 3000
2 Houston Center

Houston, TX 77010
Phone: 713-652-2977; Fax: 713-651-7822
www.houston.us.emb-japan.go.jp

Japan Consulate General
350 S Grand Ave
Suite 1700
Los Angeles, CA 90071
Phone: 213-617-6700; Fax: 213-617-6727
www.la.us.emb-japan.go.jp

Japan Consulate General
80 SW 8th St
Brickell Bay View Ctr Suite 3200
Miami, FL 33130
Phone: 305-530-9090; Fax: 305-530-0950
www.miami.us.emb-japan.go.jp

Japan Consulate General
1801 West End Ave
Suite 900
Nashville, TN 37203
Phone: 615-340-4300; Fax: 615-340-4311
www.nashville.us.emb-japan.go.jp

Japan Consulate General
299 Park Ave
18th Fl
New York, NY 10171
Phone: 212-371-8222; Fax: 212-319-6357
www.ny.us.emb-japan.go.jp

Japan Consulate General
Wells Fargo Ctr 1300 SW 5th Ave
Suite 2700
Portland, OR 97201
Phone: 503-221-1811; Fax: 503-224-8936
www.portland.us.emb-japan.go.jp

Japan Consulate General
50 Fremont St
Suite 2300
San Francisco, CA 94105
Phone: 415-777-3533; Fax: 415-974-3660
www.sf.us.emb-japan.go.jp

Japan Consulate General
601 Union St
Suite 500
Seattle, WA 98101

Phone: 206-682-9107; Fax: 206-624-9097
www.seattle.us.emb-japan.go.jp

Japan Embassy
2520 Massachusetts Ave NW
Washington, DC 20008
Phone: 202-238-6700; Fax: 202-328-2187
www.us.emb-japan.go.jp

Japan Permanent Mission to the UN
866 UN Plaza
2nd Fl
New York, NY 10017
Phone: 212-223-4300; Fax: 212-751-1966
www.un.int/japan

JORDAN

Jordan Tourism Board
6867 Elm St
Suite 102
McLean, VA 22101
Phone: 703-243-7404; Fax: 703-243-7406
Toll-free: 877-733-5673
www.seejordan.org

Jordan Embassy
3504 International Dr NW
Washington, DC 20008
Phone: 202-966-2664; Fax: 202-966-3110
www.jordanembassyus.org

KAZAKHSTAN

Kazakhstan Consulate
305 E. 47th St
3rd Fl
New York, NY 10017
Phone: 212-888-3024; Fax: 212-888-3025
www.kazconsulny.org

Kazakhstan Embassy
1401 16th St NW
Washington, DC 20036
Phone: 202-232-5488; Fax: 202-232-5845
www.kazakhembus.com

Kazakhstan Permanent Mission to the UN
305 E. 47th St
3rd Fl

New York, NY 10017
Phone: 212-230-1900; Fax: 212-230-1172
www.kazakhstanun.org

KENYA

Kenya Tourism Board
c/o Custom Destination Marketing
 Solutions
6442 City West Pkwy
Minneapolis, MN 55344
Phone: 866-445-3692; Fax: 952-914-6946
www.magicalkenya.com

Kenya Embassy
2249 R St NW
Washington, DC 20008
Phone: 202-387-6101; Fax: 202-462-3829
www.kenyaembassy.com

Kenya Permanent Mission to the UN
866 UN Plaza
Rm 486
New York, NY 10017
Phone: 212-421-4740; Fax: 212-486-1985
www.un.int/kenya

KOREA, NORTH
SEE NORTH KOREA
(DEMOCRATIC PEOPLE'S
REPUBLIC OF KOREA)

KOREA, SOUTH
SEE SOUTH KOREA
(REPUBLIC OF KOREA)

KUWAIT

Kuwait Embassy
2940 Tilden St NW
Washington, DC 20008
Phone: 202-966-0702; Fax: 202-966-0517

Kuwait Permanent Mission to the UN
321 E 44th St
New York, NY 10017
Phone: 212-973-4300; Fax: 212-370-1733
www.kuwaitmission.com

KYRGYZSTAN

Kyrgyzstan Embassy
2360 Massachusetts Ave NW
Washington, DC 20008
Phone: 202-449-9822; Fax: 202-386-7550
www.kyrgyzstan.org

Kyrgyzstan Permanent Mission to the UN
866 UN Plaza
Suite 477
New York, NY 10017
Phone: 212-486-4214; Fax: 212-486-5259

LAOS

Lao People's Democratic Republic
 Embassy
2222 'S' St NW
Washington, DC 20008
Phone: 202-332-6416; Fax: 202-332-4923
www.laoembassy.com

Lao People's Democratic Republic
 Permanent Mission to the UN
317 E 51st St
New York, NY 10022
Phone: 212-832-2734; Fax: 212-750-0039
www.un.int/lao

LATVIA

Latvia Embassy
2306 Massachusetts Ave NW
Washington, DC 20008
Phone: 202-328-2840; Fax: 202-328-2860
www.latvia-usa.org

Latvia Permanent Mission to the UN
333 E 50th St
New York, NY 10022
Phone: 212-838-8877; Fax: 212-838-8920

LEBANON

Lebanon Consulate General
3031 W Grand Blvd
Suite 560
Detroit, MI 48202

Phone: 313-758-0753; Fax: 313-758-0756
www.lebconsdet.org

Lebanon Consulate General
660 S Figueroa St
Suite 1050
Los Angeles, CA 90017
Phone: 213-243-0999

Lebanon Consulate General
9 E 76th St
New York, NY 10021
Phone: 212-744-7905; Fax: 212-794-1510
www.lebconsny.org

Lebanon Embassy
2560 28th St NW
Washington, DC 20008
Phone: 202-939-6300; Fax: 202-939-6324
www.lebanonembassyus.org

Lebanon Permanent Mission to the UN
866 UN Plaza
Rm 531-533
New York, NY 10017
Phone: 212-355-5460; Fax: 212-838-2819

LESOTHO

Lesotho Embassy
2511 Massachusetts Ave NW
Washington, DC 20008
Phone: 202-797-5533; Fax: 202-234-6815
www.lesothoemb-usa.gov.ls

Lesotho Permanent Mission to the UN
204 E 39th St
New York, NY 10016
Phone: 212-661-1690; Fax: 212-682-4388
www.un.int/lesotho

LIBERIA

Liberia Consulate General
866 UN Plaza
Suite 478
New York, NY 10017
Phone: 212-687-1025; Fax: 212-599-3189
www.liberiaconsulate.com

Liberia Embassy
5201 16th St NW
Washington, DC 20011
Phone: 202-723-0437; Fax: 202-723-0436
www.embassyofliberia.org

Liberia Permanent Mission to the UN
820 2nd Ave
Suite 1300
New York, NY 10017
Phone: 212-687-1033; Fax: 212-687-1035

LIBYA

Libyan Arab Jamahiriya Permanent Mission
to the UN
309-315 E 48th St
New York, NY 10017
Phone: 212-752-5775; Fax: 212-593-4787
www.libya-un.org

LIECHTENSTEIN

Liechtenstein Embassy
888 17th St NW
Suite 1250
Washington, DC 20006
Phone: 202-331-0590; Fax: 202-331-3221
www.liechtenstein.li

Liechtenstein Permanent Mission to the UN
633 3rd Ave
27th Fl
New York, NY 10017
Phone: 212-599-0220; Fax: 212-599-0064

LITHUANIA

Lithuania Consulate General
211 E Ontario St
Suite 1500
Chicago, IL 60611
Phone: 312-397-0382; Fax: 312-397-0385
www.ltembassyus.org

Lithuania Consulate General
420 5th Ave
3rd Fl
New York, NY 10018

Phone: 212-354-7840; Fax: 212-354-7911
www.ltembassyus.org

Lithuania Embassy
4590 MacArthur Blvd NW
Suite 200
Washington, DC 20009
Phone: 202-234-5860; Fax: 202-328-0466
www.ltembassyus.org

Lithuania Permanent Mission to the UN
420 5th Ave
3rd Fl
New York, NY 10018
Phone: 212-354-7820; Fax: 212-354-7833
www.un.int/lithuania/lithuania.html

LUXEMBOURG

Luxembourg National Tourist Office
17 Beekman Pl
New York, NY 10022
Phone: 212-935-8888; Fax: 212-935-5896
www.ont.lu

Luxembourg-American Chamber of
    Commerce
17 Beekman Pl
New York, NY 10022
Phone: 212-888-6701; Fax: 212-935-5896
www.luxembourgbusiness.org

Luxembourg Consulate General
17 Beekman Pl
New York, NY 10022
Phone: 212-888-6664; Fax: 212-888-6116
www.luxembourgnewyork.com

Luxembourg Consulate General
1 Sansome St
Suite 830
San Francisco, CA 94104
Phone: 415-788-0816; Fax: 415-788-0985
www.luxembourgsf.org

Luxembourg Embassy
2200 Massachusetts Ave NW
Washington, DC 20008
Phone: 202-265-4171; Fax: 202-328-8270
www.luxembourg-usa.org

Luxembourg Permanent Mission to the UN
17 Beekman Pl
New York, NY 10022
Phone: 212-935-3589; Fax: 212-935-5896
www.un.int/luxembourg

MACAU

Macau Government Tourist Office
1334 Parkview Ave
Suite 300
Manhattan Beach, CA 90266
Phone: 310-545-3430; Fax: 310-545-4221
Toll-free: 866-656-2228
www.macautourism.gov.mo

MACEDONIA

Macedonia Consulate General
2000 Town Center
Suite 1130
Southfield, MI 48075
Phone: 248-354-5537; Fax: 248-354-5538

Macedonia Embassy
2129 Wyoming Ave
Washington, DC 20008
Phone: 202-667-0501; Fax: 202-667-2131

Macedonia Permanent Mission to the UN
866 UN Plaza
Suite 517
New York, NY 10017
Phone: 212-308-8504; Fax: 212-308-8724
www.un.int/macedonia

MADAGASCAR

Madagascar Embassy
2374 Massachusetts Ave NW
Washington, DC 20008
Phone: 202-265-5525; Fax: 202-265-3034

Madagascar Permanent Mission to the UN
820 2nd Ave
Suite 800
New York, NY 10017
Phone: 212-986-9491; Fax: 212-986-6271

MALAWI

Malawi Embassy
1156 15th St NW
Suite 320
Washington, DC 20005
Phone: 202-721-0270; Fax: 202-721-0288

Malawi Permanent Mission to the UN
600 3rd Ave
21st Fl
New York, NY 10016
Phone: 212-317-8738; Fax: 212-317-8729

MALAYSIA

Tourism Malaysia
818 W 7th St
Suite 970
Los Angeles, CA 90017
Phone: 213-689-9702; Fax: 213-689-1530
Toll-free: 800-336-6842
www.tourism.gov.my

Tourism Malaysia
120 E 56th St
Suite 810
New York, NY 10022
Phone: 212-754-1113; Fax: 212-754-1116
Toll-free: 800-558-6787
www.tourism.gov.my

Malaysia Consulate General
550 S Hope St
Suite 400
Los Angeles, CA 90071
Phone: 213-892-1238; Fax: 213-892-9031

Malaysia Consulate General
313 E 43rd St
New York, NY 10017
Phone: 212-490-2722; Fax: 212-490-2049

Malaysia Embassy
3516 International Ct NW
Washington, DC 20008
Phone: 202-572-9700; Fax: 202-572-9882

Malaysia Permanent Mission to the UN
313 E 43rd St
New York, NY 10017

Phone: 212-986-6310; Fax: 212-490-8576
www.un.int/malaysia

MALDIVES

Maldives Permanent Mission to the UN
800 2nd Ave
Suite 400-E
New York, NY 10017
Phone: 212-599-6194; Fax: 212-661-6405
www.un.int/maldives

MALI

Mali Embassy
2130 R St NW
Washington, DC 20008
Phone: 202-332-2249; Fax: 202-332-6603
www.maliembassy.us

Mali Permanent Mission to the UN
111 E 69th St
New York, NY 10021
Phone: 212-737-4150; Fax: 212-472-3778
www.un.int/mali

MALTA

Malta Embassy
2017 Connecticut Ave NW
Washington, DC 20008
Phone: 202-462-3611; Fax: 202-387-5470

Malta Permanent Mission to the UN
249 E 35th St
New York, NY 10016
Phone: 212-725-2345; Fax: 212-779-7097

MARSHALL ISLANDS

Marshall Islands Embassy
2433 Massachusetts Ave NW
Washington, DC 20008
Phone: 202-234-5414; Fax: 202-232-3236
www.rmiembassyus.org

Marshall Islands Permanent Mission to the
   UN
800 2nd Ave
18th Fl

New York, NY 10017
Phone: 212-983-3040; Fax: 212-983-3202

MARTINIQUE

Martinique Promotion Bureau
444 Madison Ave
16th Fl
New York, NY 10022
Phone: 800-391-4909
www.martinique.org

French West Indies Tourist Board
444 Madison Ave
16th Fl
New York, NY 10022
Phone: 212-838-7800; Fax: 212-838-7855

MAURITANIA

Mauritania Embassy
2129 Leroy Pl NW
Washington, DC 20008
Phone: 202-232-5700; Fax: 202-319-2623
mauritania-usa.org

Mauritania Permanent Mission to the UN
116 E 38th St
New York, NY 10016
Phone: 212-252-0113; Fax: 212-252-0175

MAURITIUS

Mauritius Embassy
4301 Connecticut Ave NW
Suite 441
Washington, DC 20008
Phone: 202-244-1491; Fax: 202-966-0983
www.maurinet.com/embasydc.html

Mauritius Permanent Mission to the UN
211 E 43rd St
15th Fl
New York, NY 10017
Phone: 212-949-0190; Fax: 212-697-3829

MICRONESIA

Micronesia Consulate
3049 Ualena St

Suite 910
Honolulu, HI 96819
Phone: 808-836-4775; Fax: 808-836-6896

Micronesia Embassy
1725 'N' St NW
Washington, DC 20036
Phone: 202-223-4383; Fax: 202-223-4391

Micronesia Permanent Mission to the UN
820 2nd Ave
Suite 17A
New York, NY 10017
Phone: 212-697-8370; Fax: 212-697-8295
www.fsmgov.org/fsmun

MOLDOVA

Moldova Embassy
2101 'S' St NW
Washington, DC 20008
Phone: 202-667-1130; Fax: 202-667-1204
www.embassyrm.org

Moldova Permanent Mission to the UN
35 E 29th St
New York, NY 10016
Phone: 212-447-1867; Fax: 212-447-4067
www.un.int/moldova

MONACO

Monaco Government Tourist Office
565 5th Ave
23rd Fl
New York, NY 10017
Phone: 212-286-3330; Fax: 212-286-9890
Toll-free: 800-753-9696
www.visitmonaco.com

Monaco Permanent Mission to the UN
866 UN Plaza
Suite 520
New York, NY 10017
Phone: 212-832-0721; Fax: 212-832-5358
www.un.int/monaco

MONGOLIA

Mongolia Embassy
2833 M St NW

Washington, DC 20007
Phone: 202-333-7117; Fax: 202-298-9227
www.mongolianembassy.us

Mongolia Permanent Mission to the UN
6 E 77th St
New York, NY 10021
Phone: 212-861-9460; Fax: 212-861-9464
www.un.int/mongolia

MONTENEGRO

Montenegro Consulate General
801 Second Avenue, 7th Floor
New York, NY 1001
Phone: 212-661-5400; Fax: 212-661-5466

Montenegro Embassy
1610 New Hampshire Avenue NW
Washington, DC 20009
Phone: 202-234-6108; Fax: 202-234-6109
www.vlada.cg.yu/eng/mininos/vijesti.php?
    akcija=rubrika&rubrika=16

MOROCCO

Moroccan National Tourist Office
20 E 46th St
Suite 1201
New York, NY 10017
Phone: 212-557-2520; Fax: 212-949-8148
www.tourism-in-morocco.com

Moroccan National Tourist Office
7208 Sand Lake Rd
Suite 204
Orlando, FL 32819
Phone: 407-264-0133; Fax: 407-264-0134
www.tourism-in-morocco.com

Morocco Consulate General
10 E 40th St
24th Fl
New York, NY 10016
Phone: 212-758-2625; Fax: 212-779-7441
www.moroccanconsulate.com

Morocco Embassy
1601 21st St NW
Washington, DC 20009

Phone: 202-462-7980; Fax: 202-462-7643
www.dcusa.themoroccanembassy.com

Morocco Permanent Mission to the UN
866 2nd Ave
6th & 7th Fl
New York, NY 10017
Phone: 212-421-1580; Fax: 212-980-1512
www.un.int/morocco

MOZAMBIQUE

Mozambique Embassy
1525 New Hampshire Ave NW
Washington, DC 20036
Phone: 202-293-7146; Fax: 202-835-0245
www.embamoc-usa.org

Mozambique Permanent Mission to the UN
420 E 50th St
New York, NY 10022
Phone: 212-644-6800; Fax: 212-644-5972
www.un.int/mozambique

MYANMAR (BURMA)

Myanmar Embassy
2300 'S' St NW
Washington, DC 20008
Phone: 202-332-3344; Fax: 202-332-4351
www.mewashingtondc.com

Myanmar Permanent Mission to the UN
10 E 77th St
New York, NY 10021
Phone: 212-744-1271; Fax: 212-744-1290

NAMIBIA

Namibia Embassy
1605 New Hampshire Ave NW
Washington, DC 20009
Phone: 202-986-0540; Fax: 202-986-0443

Namibia Permanent Mission to the UN
360 Lexington Ave
Suite 1502
New York, NY 10017
Phone: 212-685-2003; Fax: 212-685-1561
www.un.int/namibia

NAURU

Nauru Permanent Mission to the UN
800 2nd Ave
Suite 400-A
New York, NY 10017
Phone: 212-937-0074; Fax: 212-937-0079

NEPAL

Nepal Consulate General
820 2nd Ave
Suite 17B
New York, NY 10017
Phone: 212-370-3988; Fax: 212-953-2038

Nepal Embassy
2131 Leroy Pl NW
Washington, DC 20008
Phone: 202-667-4550; Fax: 202-667-5534
www.nepalembassyusa.org

Nepal Permanent Mission to the UN
820 2nd Ave
Suite 17B
New York, NY 10017
Phone: 212-370-3988; Fax: 212-953-2038
www.un.int/nepal

NETHERLANDS

Netherlands Board of Tourism &
    Conventions
355 Lexington Ave
19th Fl
New York, NY 10017
Phone: 212-370-7360; Fax: 212-370-9507
Toll-free: 888-464-6552
www.holland.com

Netherlands Chamber of Commerce in the
    US Inc
267 5th Ave
Suite 301
New York, NY 10016
Phone: 212-265-6460; Fax: 212-265-6402
www.netherlands.org

Netherlands Consulate General
303 E Wacker Dr

Suite 2600
Chicago, IL 60601
Phone: 312-856-0110; Fax: 312-856-9218
Toll-free: 877-388-2443
www.cgchicago.org

Netherlands Consulate General
11766 Wilshire Blvd
Suite 1150
Los Angeles, CA 90025
Phone: 310-268-1598; Fax: 310-312-0989
www.ncla.org

Netherlands Consulate General
701 Brickell Ave
5th Fl
Miami, FL 33131
Phone: 786-866-0480; Fax: 786-866-0497
www.cgmiami.org

Netherlands Consulate General
1 Rockefeller Plaza
11th Fl
New York, NY 10020
Phone: 212-246-1429; Fax: 212-333-3603
www.cgny.org

Netherlands Embassy
4200 Linnean Ave NW
Washington, DC 20008
Phone: 202-244-5300; Fax: 202-362-3430
www.netherlands-embassy.org

Netherlands Permanent Mission to
    the UN
235 E 45th St
16th Fl
New York, NY 10017
Phone: 212-697-5547; Fax: 212-370-1954
www.pvnewyork.org

NEW ZEALAND

New Zealand Tourism Board
501 Santa Monica Blvd
Suite 300
Santa Monica, CA 90401
Phone: 310-395-7480; Fax: 310-395-5453
Toll-free: 866-639-9325
www.newzealand.com/travel

New Zealand Consulate General
222 E 41st St
Suite 2510
New York, NY 10017
Phone: 212-832-4038; Fax: 212-832-7602

New Zealand Consulate General
2425 Olympic Blvd
Suite 600-E
Santa Monica, CA 90404
Phone: 310-566-6555; Fax: 310-566-6556
www.nzcgla.com

New Zealand Embassy
37 Observatory Cir NW
Washington, DC 20008
Phone: 202-328-4800; Fax: 202-667-5227
www.nzembassy.com

New Zealand Permanent Mission to the UN
1 UN Plaza
25th Fl
New York, NY 10017
Phone: 212-826-1960; Fax: 212-758-0827
nzmissionny.org

NICARAGUA

Nicaraguan-American Chamber of
    Commerce
16161 SW 144th Terrace
Miami, FL 33196
Phone: 305-599-2737; Fax: 305-969-4509
www.naccflorida.com

Nicaragua Consulate General
8989 Westheimer St
Suite 103
Houston, TX 77063
Phone: 713-789-2762; Fax: 713-789-3164

Nicaragua Consulate General
8532 SW 8th St
Suite 270
Miami, FL 33144
Phone: 305-265-1415; Fax: 305-265-1780

Nicaragua Consulate General
820 2nd Ave
Suite 802

New York, NY 10017
Phone: 212-986-6562; Fax: 212-983-2646

Nicaragua Consulate General
870 Market St
Suite 518
San Francisco, CA 94102
Phone: 415-765-6825; Fax: 415-765-6826

Nicaragua Embassy
1627 New Hampshire Ave NW
Washington, DC 20009
Phone: 202-939-6570; Fax: 202-939-6542

Nicaragua Permanent Mission to the UN
820 2nd Ave
Suite 801
New York, NY 10017
Phone: 212-490-7997; Fax: 212-286-0815
www.un.int/nicaragua

NIGER

Niger Embassy
2204 R St NW
Washington, DC 20008
Phone: 202-483-4224; Fax: 202-483-3169

Niger Permanent Mission to the UN
417 E 50th St
New York, NY 10022
Phone: 212-421-3260; Fax: 212-753-6931
www.un.int/niger

NIGERIA

Nigeria Consulate General
828 2nd Ave
New York, NY 10017
Phone: 212-850-2200; Fax: 212-687-1476
www.nigeriahouse.com

Nigeria Embassy
3519 International Ct NW
Washington, DC 20008
Phone: 202-986-8400; Fax: 202-362-6981
www.nigeriaembassyusa.org

Nigeria Permanent Mission to the UN
828 2nd Ave

New York, NY 10017
Phone: 212-953-9130; Fax: 212-697-1970
www.un.int/nigeria

NORTH KOREA (DEMOCRATIC PEOPLE'S REPUBLIC OF KOREA)

North Korea Permanent Mission to the UN
820 2nd Ave
13th Fl
New York, NY 10017
Phone: 212-972-3105; Fax: 212-972-3154

NORWAY

Norwegian Tourist Board
655 3rd Ave
18th Ave
New York, NY 10017
Phone: 212-885-9700; Fax: 212-885-9710
www.visitnorway.com

Norwegian-American Chamber of
    Commerce Southwest Chapter
2777 Allen Pkwy
Suite 1185
Houston, TX 77019
Phone: 713-526-6222; Fax: 713-521-9473
nacchouston.org

Norwegian-American Chamber of
    Commerce Upper Midwest Chapter
821 Marquette Ave
Suite 800
Minneapolis, MN 55402
Phone: 612-332-3338; Fax: 612-332-1386

Norwegian-American Chamber of
    Commerce Inc
835 3rd Ave
38th Fl
New York, NY 10022
Phone: 212-421-1655; Fax: 212-838-0374
www.nacc.no

Norwegian-American Chamber of
    Commerce Northern California Chapter
20 California St
6th Fl

San Francisco, CA 94111
Phone: 415-986-0770; Fax: 415-986-7875
www.nacc.no/sanfrancisco

Norwegian-American Chamber of
    Commerce Southern California Chapter
PO Box 3251
Thousand Oaks, CA 91359
Phone: 818-735-0019; Fax: 818-735-0032
www.naccla.org

Norway Consulate General
2777 Allen Pkwy
Suite 1185
Houston, TX 77019
Phone: 713-521-2900; Fax: 713-521-9648
www.norway.org/embassy

Norway Consulate General
901 Marquette Ave
Suite 2750
Minneapolis, MN 55402
Phone: 612-332-3338; Fax: 612-332-1386
www.norway.org/embassy

Norway Consulate General
825 3rd Ave
38th Fl
New York, NY 10022
Phone: 212-421-7333; Fax: 212-754-0583
www.norway.org/embassy

Norway Consulate General
20 California St
6th Fl
San Francisco, CA 94111
Phone: 415-986-0766; Fax: 415-986-3318
www.norway.org/embassy

Norway Embassy
2720 34th St NW
Washington, DC 20008
Phone: 202-333-6000; Fax: 202-337-0870
www.norway.org/embassy

Norway Permanent Mission to the UN
825 3rd Ave
39th Fl
New York, NY 10022
Phone: 212-421-0280; Fax: 212-688-0554
www.norway-un.org

OMAN

Oman Embassy
2535 Belmont Rd NW
Washington, DC 20008
Phone: 202-387-1980; Fax: 202-745-4933

Oman Permanent Mission to the UN
866 UN Plaza
Suite 540
New York, NY 10017
Phone: 212-355-3505; Fax: 212-644-0070

PAKISTAN

Pakistan Consulate General
10850 Wilshire Blvd
Suite 1250
Los Angeles, CA 90024
Phone: 310-441-5114; Fax: 310-441-9256
www.pakconsulatela.org

Pakistan Consulate General
12 E 65th St
New York, NY 10065
Phone: 212-879-5800; Fax: 212-517-6987
www.pakistanconsulateny.org

Pakistan Embassy
3517 International Ct NW
Washington, DC 20008
Phone: 202-243-6500; Fax: 202-686-1534
www.embassyofpakistanusa.org

Pakistan Permanent Mission to the UN
8 E 65th St
New York, NY 10021
Phone: 212-879-8600; Fax: 212-744-7348
www.un.int/pakistan

PALAU

Palau Embassy
1700 Pennsylvania Ave NW
Suite 400
Washington, DC 20006
Phone: 202-349-8598; Fax: 202-349-8597
www.palauembassy.com

PANAMA

Panama Consulate General
5775 Blue Lagoon Dr
Suite 200
Miami, FL 33126
Phone: 305-447-3700; Fax: 305-447-4142

Panama Consulate General
2424 World Trade Ctr
2 Canal St
New Orleans, LA 70130
Phone: 504-525-3458; Fax: 504-524-8960
www.consulateofpanama.com

Panama Consulate General
1212 Ave of the Americas
6th Fl
New York, NY 10036
Phone: 212-840-2450; Fax: 212-840-2469

Panama Consulate General
124 Chestnut St
Philadelphia, PA 19106
Phone: 215-574-2994; Fax: 215-625-4876

Panama Embassy
2862 McGill Terr NW
Washington, DC 20008
Phone: 202-483-1407; Fax: 202-483-8413
www.embassyofpanama.org

Panama Permanent Mission to the UN
866 UN Plaza
Suite 4030
New York, NY 10017
Phone: 212-421-5420; Fax: 212-421-2694

PAPUA NEW GUINEA

Papua New Guinea Embassy
1779 Massachusetts Ave NW
Suite 805
Washington, DC 20036
Phone: 202-745-3680; Fax: 202-745-3679
www.pngembassy.org

Papua New Guinea Permanent Mission to
the UN
201 E 42nd St

Suite 405
New York, NY 10017
Phone: 212-557-5001; Fax: 212-557-5009

PARAGUAY

Paraguay Consulate General
25 SE 2nd Ave
Suite 705
Miami, FL 33131
Phone: 305-374-9090; Fax: 305-374-5522

Paraguay Consulate General
211 E 43rd St
Suite 1400
New York, NY 10017
Phone: 212-682-9441; Fax: 212-682-9443

Paraguay Embassy
2400 Massachusetts Ave NW
Washington, DC 20008
Phone: 202-483-6960; Fax: 202-234-4508

Paraguay Permanent Mission to the UN
211 E 43rd St
Suite 400
New York, NY 10017
Phone: 212-687-3490; Fax: 212-818-1282
www.un.int/paraguay

PERU

Peru Tourist Office
495 Biltmore Way
Suite 404
Coral Gables, FL 33134
Phone: 305-476-1220
Toll-free: 866-661-7378
www.peru.info/perueng.asp

Peruvian American Chamber of Commerce
9737 NW 41st St
PMB 348
Doral, FL 33178
Phone: 786-221-5890; Fax: 786-221-5834
www.peruvianchamber.org

Peru Consulate General
20 Park Plaza
Suite 511

Boston, MA 02116
Phone: 617-338-2227; Fax: 617-338-2742
www.consuladoperu.com

Peru Consulate General
180 N Michigan Ave
Suite 1830
Chicago, IL 60601
Phone: 312-782-1599; Fax: 312-704-6969
www.consuladoperu.com

Peru Consulate General
1001 S Monaco Pkwy
Suite 210
Denver, CO 80224
Phone: 303-355-8555; Fax: 303-355-8555
www.consuladoperu.com

Peru Consulate General
5177 Richmond Ave
Suite 695
Houston, TX 77056
Phone: 713-355-9517; Fax: 713-355-9377
www.consuladoperu.com

Peru Consulate General
3450 Wilshire Blvd
Suite 800
Los Angeles, CA 90010
Phone: 213-252-5910; Fax: 213-252-8130
www.consuladoperu.com

Peru Consulate General
444 Brickell Ave
Suite M135
Miami, FL 33131
Phone: 305-374-1305; Fax: 305-381-6027
www.consuladoperu.com

Peru Consulate General
241 E 49th St
New York, NY 10017
Phone: 646-735-3828; Fax: 646-735-3866
www.consuladoperu.com

Peru Consulate General
100 Hamilton Plaza
Suite 1221
Paterson, NJ 07505
Phone: 973-278-3324; Fax: 973-278-0254
www.consuladoperu.com

Peru Consulate General
870 Market St
Suite 1067
San Francisco, CA 94102
Phone: 415-362-7136; Fax: 415-362-2836
www.consuladoperu.com

Peru Embassy
1700 Massachusetts Ave NW
Washington, DC 20036
Phone: 202-833-9860; Fax: 202-659-8124
www.peruvianembassy.us

Peru Permanent Mission to the UN
820 2nd Ave
Suite 1600
New York, NY 10017
Phone: 212-687-3336; Fax: 212-972-6975

PHILIPPINES

Philippine Dept of Tourism
556 5th Ave
1st Fl Mezzanine
New York, NY 10036
Phone: 212-575-7915; Fax: 212-302-6759
www.tourism.gov.ph

US Federation of Philippine American
  Chambers of Commerce Inc
2887 College Ave
Suite 1 Box 106
Berkeley, CA 94705
Phone: 510-548-7952; Fax: 510-845-9901
www.fpacc.com

Philippine American Chamber of Commerce
  Inc
317 Madison Ave
Suite 520
New York, NY 10017
Phone: 212-972-9326; Fax: 212-687-5844
www.philamchamber.org

Philippines Consulate General
30 N Michigan Ave
Suite 2100
Chicago, IL 60602
Phone: 312-332-6458; Fax: 312-332-3657
www.chicagopcg.com

Philippines Consulate General
2433 Pali Hwy
Honolulu, HI 96817
Phone: 808-595-6316; Fax: 808-595-2581

Philippines Consulate General
3600 Wilshire Blvd
Suite 500
Los Angeles, CA 90010
Phone: 213-639-0980; Fax: 213-639-0990
www.pcgenla.org

Philippines Consulate General
556 5th Ave
New York, NY 10036
Phone: 212-764-1330; Fax: 212-382-1146
www.pcgny.net

Philippines Consulate General
447 Sutter St
6th Fl
San Francisco, CA 94108
Phone: 415-433-6666; Fax: 415-421-2641
www.philippineconsulate-sf.org

Philippines Embassy
1600 Massachusetts Ave NW
Washington, DC 20036
Phone: 202-467-9300; Fax: 202-328-9417
www.philippineembassy-usa.org

Philippines Permanent Mission to the UN
556 5th Ave
5th Fl
New York, NY 10036
Phone: 212-764-1300; Fax: 212-840-8602
www.un.int/philippines

POLAND

Polish National Tourist Office
5 Marine View Plaza
Suite 208
Hoboken, NJ 07030
Phone: 201-420-9910; Fax: 201-584-9153
www.polandtour.org

Poland Consulate General
820 N Orleans St
Suite 335
Chicago, IL 60610

Phone: 312-337-8166; Fax: 312-337-7841
www.polishconsulatechicago.org

Poland Consulate General
12400 Wilshire Blvd
Suite 555
Los Angeles, CA 90025
Phone: 310-442-8500; Fax: 310-442-8515
www.polishconsulatela.com

Poland Consulate General
233 Madison Ave
New York, NY 10016
Phone: 212-561-8160; Fax: 646-237-2105
www.polandconsulateny.com

Poland Embassy
2224 Wyoming Ave NW
Washington, DC 20008
Phone: 202-234-3800; Fax: 202-328-2152
www.polandembassy.org

Poland Permanent Mission to the UN
9 E 66th St
New York, NY 10021
Phone: 212-744-2506; Fax: 212-517-6771
www.polandun.org

PORTUGAL

Portuguese Trade & Tourism Office
590 5th Ave
4th Fl
New York, NY 10036
Phone: 646-723-0200; Fax: 212-575-4737
Toll-free: 800-767-8842
www.visitportugal.com

Portuguese Trade & Tourist Office
88 Kearny St
Suite 1770
San Francisco, CA 94108
Phone: 415-391-7080; Fax: 415-391-7147
www.visitportugal.com

Portugal-US Chamber of Commerce
590 5th Ave
4th Fl
New York, NY 10036
Phone: 212-354-4627; Fax: 212-575-4737
portugal-us.com

Portugal Consulate General
899 Boylston St
2nd Fl
Boston, MA 02115
Phone: 617-536-8740; Fax: 617-536-2503

Portugal Consulate General
590 5th Ave
3rd FL
New York, NY 10036
Phone: 212-221-3165; Fax: 212-221-3462

Portugal Consulate General
Legal Ctr
1 Riverfront Plaza
Newark, NJ 07102
Phone: 973-643-4200; Fax: 973-643-3900

Portugal Consulate General
3298 Washington St
San Francisco, CA 94115
Phone: 415-346-3400; Fax: 415-346-1440

Portugal Embassy
2125 Kalorama Rd, NW
Washington, DC 20036
Phone: 202-328-8610; Fax: 202-462-3726

Portugal Permanent Mission to the UN
866 2nd Ave
9th Fl
New York, NY 10017
Phone: 212-759-9444; Fax: 212-355-1124
www.un.int/portugal

PUERTO RICO

Puerto Rico Convention Bureau
500 Tanca St
Suite 402
San Juan, PR 00901
Phone: 787-725-2110; Fax: 787-725-2133
Toll-free: 800-875-4765
www.meetpuertorico.com

Puerto Rico Tourism Co
901 Ponce de Leon Blvd
Suite 101
Coral Gables, FL 33134
Phone: 305-445-9112; Fax: 305-445-9450

Toll-free: 800-866-7827
www.gotopuertorico.com

Puerto Rico Tourism Co
3575 W Cahuenga Blvd
Suite 620
Los Angeles, CA 90068
Phone: 323-874-5991; Fax: 323-874-7257
Toll-free: 800-874-1230
www.gotopuertorico.com

Puerto Rico Tourism Co
666 5th Ave
15th Fl
New York, NY 10103
Phone: 212-586-6262; Fax: 212-586-1212
Toll-free: 800-223-6530
www.gotopuertorico.com

Puerto Rico Tourism Co
Paseo La Princesa
PO Box 902-3960
Old San Juan, PR 00902
Phone: 787-721-2400; Fax: 787-722-6238
www.gotopuertorico.com

Puerto Rico Chamber of Commerce
PO Box 9024033
San Juan, PR 00902
Phone: 787-721-6060; Fax: 787-721-6060
camarapr.org

Puerto Rican Chamber of Commerce of
South Florida
3550 Biscayne Blvd
Suite 306
Miami, FL 33137
Phone: 305-571-8006; Fax: 305-571-8007
www.puertoricanchamber.com

QATAR

Qatar Consulate General
11990 Post Oak Blvd
Suite 810
Houston, TX 77056
Phone: 713-355-8221; Fax: 713-355-8184

Qatar Embassy
2555 M St NW
Washington, DC 20037

Phone: 202-274-1600; Fax: 202-237-0061
www.qatarembassy.net

Qatar Permanent Mission to the UN
809 UN Plaza
4th Fl
New York, NY 10017
Phone: 212-486-9335; Fax: 212-758-4952

ROMANIA

Romanian National Tourist Office
355 Lexington Ave
19th Fl
New York, NY 10017
Phone: 212-545-8484
www.romaniatourism.com

Romania Consulate General
11766 Wilshire Blvd
Suite 560
Los Angeles, CA 90025
Phone: 310-444-0043; Fax: 310-445-0043
www.consulateromania.org

Romania Consulate General
200 E 38th St
3rd Fl
New York, NY 10016
Phone: 212-682-9120; Fax: 212-972-8463
www.romconsny.org

Romania Embassy
1607 23rd St NW
Washington, DC 20008
Phone: 202-332-4846; Fax: 202-232-4748
www.roembus.org

Romania Permanent Mission to the UN
573-577 3rd Ave
New York, NY 10016
Phone: 212-682-3274; Fax: 212-682-9746
www.un.int/romania

RUSSIA

Russian National Tourist Office
224 W 30th St6
Suite 701
New York, NY 10001
Phone: 646-473-2233; Fax: 646-473-2205

Toll-free: 877-221-7120
www.russia-travel.com

Russian-American Chamber of Commerce
1552 Pennsylvania St
Denver, CO 80203
Phone: 303-831-0829; Fax: 303-831-0830
www.russianamericanchamber.org

American-Russian Chamber of Commerce &
Industry
1101 Pennsylvania Ave NW
6th Fl
Washington, DC 20004
Phone: 202-756-4943; Fax: 202-362-4634
www.arcci.org

Russia Consulate General
9 E 91st St
New York, NY 10128
Phone: 212-348-0926; Fax: 212-831-9162

Russia Consulate General
2790 Green St
San Francisco, CA 94123
Phone: 415-928-6878; Fax: 415-929-0306
www.consulrussia.org

Russia Consulate General
2001 6th Ave
Westin Bldg Suite 2323
Seattle, WA 98121
Phone: 206-728-1910; Fax: 206-728-1871
www.netconsul.org

Russia Embassy
2650 Wisconsin Ave NW
Washington, DC 20007
Phone: 202-298-5700; Fax: 202-298-5735
www.russianembassy.org

Russia Permanent Mission to the UN
136 E 67th St
New York, NY 10021
Phone: 212-861-4900; Fax: 212-628-0252
www.un.int/russia

RWANDA

Rwanda Embassy
1714 New Hampshire Ave NW

Washington, DC 20009
Phone: 202-232-2882; Fax: 202-232-4544

Rwanda Permanent Mission to the UN
124 E 39th St
New York, NY 10016
Phone: 212-679-9010; Fax: 212-679-9133

SAINT BARTHELEMY

Saint Barthelemy Tourist Office
444 Madison Ave
16th Fl
New York, NY 10022
Phone: 212-838-7800; Fax: 212-838-7855
us.franceguide.com

SAINT KITTS AND NEVIS

Saint Kitts Tourism Authority
414 E 75th St
Suite 5
New York, NY 10021
Phone: 212-535-1234; Fax: 212-734-6511
Toll-free: 800-582-6208
www.stkitts-tourism.com

Saint Kitts & Nevis Embassy
3216 New Mexico Ave NW
Washington, DC 20016
Phone: 202-686-2636; Fax: 202-686-5740

Saint Kitts & Nevis Permanent Mission to
the UN
414 E 75th St
Suite 5
New York, NY 10021
Phone: 212-535-1234; Fax: 212-535-6854
www.stkittsnevis.org

SAINT LUCIA

Saint Lucia Tourist Board
800 2nd Ave
9th Fl
New York, NY 10017
Phone: 212-867-2950; Fax: 212-867-2795
Toll-free: 800-456-3984
www.stlucia.org

Saint Lucia Consulate General
800 2nd Ave
9th Fl
New York, NY 10017
Phone: 212-697-9360; Fax: 212-697-4993
www.un.int/stlucia/consulate.htm

Saint Lucia Embassy
3216 New Mexico Ave NW
Washington, DC 20016
Phone: 202-364-6792; Fax: 202-364-6723

Saint Lucia Permanent Mission to the UN
800 2nd Ave
9th Fl
New York, NY 10017
Phone: 212-697-9360; Fax: 212-697-4993
www.un.int/stlucia

SAINT MARTIN / SAINT MAARTEN

Saint Maarten Tourist Office
675 3rd Ave
Suite 1807
New York, NY 10017
Phone: 212-953-2084; Fax: 212-953-2145
Toll-free: 800-786-2278
www.st-maarten.com

Saint Martin Tourist Office
675 3rd Ave
Suite 1807
New York, NY 10017
Phone: 212-475-8970; Fax: 212-260-8481
Toll-free: 877-956-1234
www.st-martin.org

SAINT VINCENT AND THE GRENADINES

Saint Vincent & the Grenadines Tourist
   Information Office
801 2nd Ave
21st Fl
New York, NY 10017
Phone: 212-687-4981; Fax: 212-949-5946
Toll-free: 800-729-1726
www.svgtourism.com

Saint Vincent & the Grenadines Consulate
   General
801 2nd Ave
21st Fl
New York, NY 10017
Phone: 212-687-4490; Fax: 212-949-5946

Saint Vincent & the Grenadines Embassy
3216 New Mexico Ave NW
Washington, DC 20016
Phone: 202-364-6730; Fax: 202-364-6736

Saint Vincent & the Grenadines Permanent
   Mission to the UN
800 2nd Ave
4th Fl
New York, NY 10017
Phone: 212-599-0950; Fax: 212-599-1020

SAN MARINO

San Marino Permanent Mission to the UN
327 E 50th St
New York, NY 10022
Phone: 212-751-1234; Fax: 212-751-1436

SAO TOME AND PRINCIPE

Sao Tome & Principe Permanent Mission to
   the UN
400 Park Ave
7th Fl
New York, NY 10022
Phone: 212-317-0533; Fax: 212-317-0580

SAUDI ARABIA

Saudi Arabia Consulate General
5718 Westheimer Rd
Suite 1500
Houston, TX 77057
Phone: 713-785-5577; Fax: 713-785-1163

Saudi Arabia Consulate General
2045 Sawtelle Blvd
Los Angeles, CA 90025
Phone: 310-479-6000; Fax: 310-479-2752

Saudi Arabia Consulate General
866 2nd Ave
5th Fl
New York, NY 10017
Phone: 212-752-2740; Fax: 212-688-2719

Saudi Arabia Embassy
601 New Hampshire Ave NW
Washington, DC 20037
Phone: 202-342-3800; Fax: 202-944-5983
www.saudiembassy.net

SENEGAL

Senegal Tourist Office
350 5th Ave
Suite 3118
New York, NY 10118
Phone: 212-279-1953; Fax: 212-279-1958
www.senegal-tourism.com

Senegal Embassy
2112 Wyoming Ave NW
Washington, DC 20008
Phone: 202-234-0540; Fax: 202-332-6315
www.senegalembassy-us.org

Senegal Permanent Mission to the UN
238 E 68th St
New York, NY 10021
Phone: 212-517-9030; Fax: 212-517-3032
www.un.int/senegal

SERBIA

Serbia Consulate General
201 E Ohio St
Suite 200
Chicago, IL 60611
Phone: 312-670-6707; Fax: 312-670-6787
www.scgchicago.org

Serbia Embassy
2134 Kalorama Rd NW
Washington, DC 20008
Phone: 202-332-0333; Fax: 202-332-3933
www.serbiaembusa.org

Serbia Permanent Mission to the UN
854 5th Ave

New York, NY 10021
Phone: 212-879-8700; Fax: 212-879-8705
www.un.int/serbia

SEYCHELLES

Seychelles Embassy
800 2nd Ave
Suite 400C
New York, NY 10017
Phone: 212-972-1785; Fax: 212-972-1786

Seychelles Permanent Mission to the UN
800 2nd Ave
Suite 400C
New York, NY 10017
Phone: 212-972-1785; Fax: 212-972-1786

SIERRA LEONE

Sierra Leone Embassy
1701 19th St NW
Washington, DC 20009
Phone: 202-939-9261; Fax: 202-483-1793
www.embassyofsierraleone.org

Sierra Leone Permanent Mission to the UN
245 E 49th St
New York, NY 10017
Phone: 212-688-1656; Fax: 212-688-4924

SINGAPORE

Singapore Tourism Board
5670 Wilshire Blvd
Suite 1550
Los Angeles, CA 90036
Phone: 323-677-0808; Fax: 323-677-0801
Toll-free: 800-283-9595
www.visitsingapore.com

Singapore Tourism Board
1156 Ave of Americas
Suite 702
New York, NY 10036
Phone: 212-302-4861; Fax: 212-302-4801
www.visitsingapore.com

Singapore Consulate General
595 Market St

Suite 2450
San Francisco, CA 94105
Phone: 415-543-4775; Fax: 415-543-4788
www.mfa.gov.sg/sanfrancisco

Singapore Embassy
3501 International Pl NW
Washington, DC 20008
Phone: 202-537-3100; Fax: 202-537-0876
www.mfa.gov.sg/washington

Singapore Permanent Mission to the UN
231 E 51st St
New York, NY 10022
Phone: 212-826-0840; Fax: 212-826-2964
www.mfa.gov.sg/newyork

SLOVAKIA

Slovakia Embassy
3523 International Ct NW
Washington, DC 20008
Phone: 202-237-1054; Fax: 202-237-6438
www.slovakembassy-us.org

Slovakia Permanent Mission to the UN
801 2nd Ave
12th Fl
New York, NY 10017
Phone: 212-286-8418; Fax: 212-286-8419
www.un.int/slovakia

SLOVENIA

Slovenia Consulate General
55 Public Sq
Suite 945
Cleveland, OH 44113
Phone: 216-589-9220; Fax: 216-589-9210

Slovenia Consulate General
600 3rd Ave
21st Fl
New York, NY 10016
Phone: 212-370-3006; Fax: 212-370-3581

Slovenia Embassy
1525 New Hampshire Ave NW
Washington, DC 20036
Phone: 202-667-5363; Fax: 202-667-4563
washington.embassy.si

Slovenia Permanent Mission to the UN
600 3rd Ave
24th Fl
New York, NY 10016
Phone: 212-370-3007; Fax: 212-370-1824
www.un.int/slovenia

SOLOMON ISLANDS

Solomon Islands Permanent Mission to the
  UN
800 2nd Ave
Suite 400L
New York, NY 10017
Phone: 212-599-6192; Fax: 212-661-8925

SOMALIA

Somalia Permanent Mission to the UN
425 E 61nd St
Suite 702
New York, NY 10021
Phone: 212-688-9410; Fax: 212-759-0651

SOUTH AFRICA

South African Tourism Board
500 5th Ave
20th Fl Suite 2040
New York, NY 10110
Phone: 212-730-2929; Fax: 212-764-1980
Toll-free: 800-593-1318
www.southafrica.net

South Africa Consulate General
200 S Michigan Ave
Suite 600
Chicago, IL 60604
Phone: 312-939-7929; Fax: 312-939-2588

South Africa Consulate General
6300 Wilshire Blvd
Suite 600
Los Angeles, CA 90048
Phone: 323-651-0902; Fax: 323-651-5969
www.link2southafrica.com

South Africa Consulate General
333 E 38th St
9th Fl

New York, NY 10016
Phone: 212-213-4880; Fax: 212-213-0102
www.southafrica-newyork.net

South Africa Embassy
3051 Massachusetts Ave NW
Washington, DC 20008
Phone: 202-232-4400; Fax: 202-265-1607
www.saembassy.org

South Africa Permanent Mission to the UN
333 E 38th St
9th Fl
New York, NY 10016
Phone: 212-213-5583; Fax: 212-692-2498
www.southafrica-newyork.net

SOUTH KOREA
(REPUBLIC OF KOREA)

Korea National Tourism Organization
737 N Michigan Ave
Suite 910
Chicago, IL 60611
Phone: 312-981-1717; Fax: 312-981-1721
Toll-free: 800-868-7567
english.tour2korea.com

Korea National Tourism Organization
2 Executive Dr
Suite 750
Fort Lee, NJ 07024
Phone: 201-585-0909; Fax: 201-585-9041
Toll-free: 800-868-7567
english.tour2korea.com

Korea National Tourism Organization
5509 Wilshire Blvd
Suite 103
Los Angeles, CA 90036
Phone: 323-634-0280; Fax: 323-634-0281
Toll-free: 800-868-7567
english.tour2korea.com

Korean Chamber of Commerce
3440 Wilshire Blvd
Suite 520
Los Angeles, CA 90010
Phone: 213-480-1115; Fax: 213-480-7521

Korean Chamber of Commerce & Industry
in the USA Inc
460 Park Ave
Suite 410
New York, NY 10022
Phone: 212-644-0140; Fax: 212-644-9106
www.kocham.org

South Korea Consulate General
229 Peachtree St
International Tower Suite 500
Atlanta, GA 30303
Phone: 404-522-1611; Fax: 404-521-3169

South Korea Consulate General
455 N City Front Plaza Dr
NBC Tower Suite 2700
Chicago, IL 60611
Phone: 312-822-9485; Fax: 312-822-9849

South Korea Consulate General
2756 Pali Hwy
Honolulu, HI 96817
Phone: 808-595-6109; Fax: 808-595-3046

South Korea Consulate General
1990 Post Oak Blvd
Suite 1250
Houston, TX 77056
Phone: 713-961-0186; Fax: 713-961-3340
www.koreahouston.org

South Korea Consulate General
3243 Wilshire Blvd
Los Angeles, CA 90010
Phone: 213-385-9300; Fax: 213-385-1849
www.koreanconsulatela.org

South Korea Consulate General
335 E 45th St
4th Fl
New York, NY 10017
Phone: 646-674-6000; Fax: 646-674-6023
www.koreanconsulate.org

South Korea Consulate General
1 Gateway Ctr
2nd Fl
Newton, MA 02458

Phone: 617-641-2830; Fax: 617-641-2831
www.kcgboston.org

South Korea Consulate General
3500 Clay St
San Francisco, CA 94118
Phone: 415-921-2251; Fax: 415-921-5946

South Korea Consulate General
2033 6th Ave
Suite 1125
Seattle, WA 98121
Phone: 206-441-1011; Fax: 206-441-7912
www.mofat.go.kr

South Korea Consulate General
2320 Massachusetts Ave NW
Washington, DC 20008
Phone: 202-939-5661; Fax: 202-342-1597

South Korea Embassy
2450 Massachusetts Ave NW
Washington, DC 20008
Phone: 202-939-5600; Fax: 202-797-0595
www.koreaembassyusa.org

South Korea Permanent Mission to the UN
335 E 45th St
New York, NY 10017
Phone: 212-439-4000; Fax: 212-986-1083
www.un.int/korea

SPAIN

Tourist Office of Spain
8383 Wilshire Blvd
Suite 960
Beverly Hills, CA 90211
Phone: 323-658-7188; Fax: 323-658-1061
www.okspain.org

Tourist Office of Spain
845 N Michigan Ave
Suite 915-E
Chicago, IL 60611
Phone: 312-642-1992; Fax: 312-642-9817
www.okspain.org

Tourist Office of Spain
1395 Brickell Ave
Suite 1130

Miami, FL 33131
Phone: 305-358-1992; Fax: 305-358-8223
www.okspain.org

Tourist Office of Spain
666 5th Ave
35th Fl
New York, NY 10103
Phone: 212-265-8822; Fax: 212-265-8864
www.okspain.org

Spain-US Chamber of Commerce
350 5th Ave
Suite 2600
New York, NY 10118
Phone: 212-967-2170; Fax: 212-564-1415
www.spainuscc.org

Spain Consulate General
31 St James Ave
Suite 905
Boston, MA 02116
Phone: 617-536-2506; Fax: 617-536-8512

Spain Consulate General
180 N Michigan Ave
Suite 1500
Chicago, IL 60601
Phone: 312-782-4588; Fax: 312-782-1635
www.consulate-spain-chicago.com

Spain Consulate General
1800 Bering Dr
Suite 660
Houston, TX 77057
Phone: 713-783-6200; Fax: 713-783-6166

Spain Consulate General
5055 Wilshire Blvd
Suite 860
Los Angeles, CA 90036
Phone: 323-938-0158; Fax: 323-938-2502

Spain Consulate General
2655 Le Jeune Rd
Suite 203
Miami, FL 33134
Phone: 305-446-5511; Fax: 305-446-0585
www.conspainmiami.org

Spain Consulate General
2102 World Trade Ctr
2 Canal St
New Orleans, LA 70130
Phone: 504-525-4951; Fax: 504-525-4955

Spain Consulate General
150 E 58th St
30th Fl
New York, NY 10155
Phone: 212-355-4080; Fax: 212-644-3751

Spain Consulate General
1405 Sutter St
San Francisco, CA 94109
Phone: 415-922-2995; Fax: 415-931-9706

Spain Embassy
2375 Pennsylvania Ave NW
Washington, DC 20037
Phone: 202-452-0100; Fax: 202-833-5670
www.spainemb.org

Spain Permanent Mission to the UN
245 E 47th St
36th Fl
New York, NY 10017
Phone: 212-661-1050; Fax: 212-949-7247
www.spainun.org

SRI LANKA

Sri Lanka Consulate General
3250 Wilshire Blvd
Suite 1405
Los Angeles, CA 90010
Phone: 213-387-0210; Fax: 213-387-0216
www.srilankaconsulatela.com

Sri Lanka Embassy
2148 Wyoming Ave NW
Washington, DC 20008
Phone: 202-483-4025; Fax: 202-232-7181
www.slembassyusa.org

Sri Lanka Permanent Mission to the UN
630 3rd Ave
20th Fl
New York, NY 10017
Phone: 212-986-7040; Fax: 212-986-1838

SUDAN

Sudan Embassy
2210 Massachusetts Ave NW
Washington, DC 20008
Phone: 202-338-8565; Fax: 202-667-2406
www.sudanembassy.org

Sudan Permanent Mission to the UN
305 E 47th St
4th Fl
New York, NY 10017
Phone: 212-573-6033; Fax: 212-573-6160

SURINAME

Suriname Consulate General
6303 Blue Lagoon Dr
Suite 325
Miami, FL 33126
Phone: 305-265-4655; Fax: 305-265-4599
www.scgmia.com

Suriname Embassy
4301 Connecticut Ave NW
Suite 460
Washington, DC 20008
Phone: 202-244-7488; Fax: 202-244-5878
www.surinameembassy.org

Suriname Permanent Mission to the UN
866 UN Plaza
Suite 320
New York, NY 10017
Phone: 212-826-0660; Fax: 212-980-7029
www.un.int/suriname

SWAZILAND

Swaziland Embassy
1712 New Hampshire Ave NW
Washington, DC 20009
Phone: 202-234-5002; Fax: 202-234-8254

Swaziland Permanent Mission to the UN
408 E 50th St
New York, NY 10022
Phone: 212-371-8910; Fax: 212-754-2755

SWEDEN

Swedish Travel & Tourism Council
655 3rd Ave
18th Fl
New York, NY 10017
Phone: 212-885-9700; Fax: 212-885-9764
www.visitsweden.com

Swedish-American Chambers of Commerce
USA Inc
1403 King St
Alexandria, VA 22314
Phone: 703-836-6560; Fax: 703-836-6561
www.sacc-usa.org

Swedish-American Chamber of Commerce
Inc Chicago Chapter
150 N Michigan Ave
Suite 2800'
Chicago, IL 60601
Phone: 312-863-8592; Fax: 312-624-7701
www.sacc-usa.org/chicago

Swedish-American Chamber of Commerce
in Colorado
4525 S Decatur St
Englewood, CO 80110
Phone: 720-338-2381; Fax: 720-889-2606
sacc-usa.org/colorado

Swedish-American Chamber of Commerce
of Greater Los Angeles Inc
10940 Wilshire Blvd
Suite 700
Los Angeles, CA 90024
Phone: 310-478-8613; Fax: 310-444-0424
www.sacc-gla.org

Swedish-American Chamber of Commerce
Inc Minnesota Chapter
American Swedish Institute
2600 Park Ave
Minneapolis, MN 55407
Phone: 612-991-3001; Fax: 612-333-3914
www.sacc-minnesota.org

Swedish-American Chamber of Commerce
Inc New York Chapter
570 Lexington Ave

20th Fl
New York, NY 10022
Phone: 212-838-5530; Fax: 212-755-7953
www.saccny.org

Swedish-American Chamber of Commerce
Atlanta Inc
4775 Peachtree Industrial Blvd
Bldg 300 Suite 300
Norcross, GA 30092
Phone: 770-670-2480; Fax: 770-670-2500
sacc-atlanta.org

Swedish-American Chamber of Commerce
San Diego/Tijuana Chapter
1020 Symphony Towers
750 B St
San Diego, CA 92101
Phone: 619-338-4020; Fax: 619-233-9890
www.sacc-sandiego.org

Swedish-American Chamber of Commerce
Inc San Francisco Chapter
564 Market St
Suite 305
San Francisco, CA 94104
Phone: 415-781-4188; Fax: 415-781-4189
www.sacc-usa.org/sf

Swedish-American Chamber of Commerce
Inc Washington DC Chapter
1501 M St NW
9th Fl
Washington, DC 20005
Phone: 202-467-2638; Fax: 202-467-2688
sacc-usa.org

Swedish-American Chamber of Commerce
Inc New England Chapter
49 Walnut St
Bldg 4
Wellesley, MA 02481
Phone: 781-239-3555; Fax: 781-239-3555
www.sacc-ne.org

Sweden Consulate General
10940 Wilshire Blvd
Suite 700
Los Angeles, CA 90024

Phone: 310-445-4008; Fax: 310-473-2229
www.swedenabroad.se

Sweden Consulate General
1 Dag Hammarskjold Plaza
885 2nd Ave 45th Fl
New York, NY 10017
Phone: 212-583-2550; Fax: 212-755-2732
www.swedenabroad.com

Sweden Consulate General
120 Montgomery St
Suite 2175
San Francisco, CA 94104
Phone: 415-788-2631; Fax: 415-788-6841
www.swedenabroad.com

Sweden Embassy
2900 K St NW
Washington, DC 20007
Phone: 202-467-2600; Fax: 202-467-2699
www.swedenabroad.com

Sweden Permanent Mission to the UN
885 2nd Ave
46th Fl
New York, NY 10017
Phone: 212-583-2500; Fax: 212-832-0389
www.un.int/sweden

SWITZERLAND

Switzerland Tourism
608 5th Ave
Suite 202
New York, NY 10020
Phone: 212-757-5944; Fax: 212-262-6116
Toll-free: 800-794-7795
www.myswitzerland.com

Swiss-American Chamber of Commerce
500 5th Ave
Rm 1800
New York, NY 10110
Phone: 212-246-7789; Fax: 212-246-1366

Switzerland Consulate General
1349 W Peachtree St Suite 1000
2 Mid-Town Plaza
Atlanta, GA 30309

Phone: 404-870-2000; Fax: 404-870-2011
www.swissemb.org

Switzerland Consulate General
737 N Michigan Ave
Suite 2301
Chicago, IL 60611
Phone: 312-915-0061; Fax: 312-915-0388
www.swissemb.org

Switzerland Consulate General
11766 Wilshire Blvd
Suite 1400
Los Angeles, CA 90025
Phone: 310-575-1145; Fax: 310-575-1982
www.swissemb.org

Switzerland Consulate General
633 3rd Ave
30th Fl
New York, NY 10017
Phone: 212-599-5700; Fax: 212-599-4266
www.swissemb.org

Switzerland Consulate General
456 Montgomery St
Suite 1500
San Francisco, CA 94104
Phone: 415-788-2272; Fax: 415-788-1402
www.swissemb.org

Switzerland Embassy
2900 Cathedral Ave NW
Washington, DC 20008
Phone: 202-745-7900; Fax: 202-387-2564
www.swissemb.org

Switzerland Permanent Mission to the UN
633 3rd Ave
29th Fl
New York, NY 10011
Phone: 212-286-1540; Fax: 212-286-1555
www.eda.admin.ch/newyork_miss/e

SYRIA

Syria Embassy
2215 Wyoming Ave NW
Washington, DC 20008
Phone: 202-232-6313; Fax: 202-234-9548

Syria Permanent Mission to the UN
820 2nd Ave
15th Fl
New York, NY 10017
Phone: 212-661-1313; Fax: 212-983-4439

TAHITI

Tahiti Tourism
300 Continental Blvd
Suite 160
El Segundo, CA 90245
Phone: 310-414-8484; Fax: 310-414-8490
www.tahiti-tourisme.com

TAIWAN

Taiwan Visitors Assn
3731 Wilshire Blvd
Suite 780
Los Angeles, CA 90010
Phone: 213-389-1158; Fax: 213-389-1094
www.taiwan.net.tw

Taiwan Visitors Assn
405 Lexington Ave
37th Fl
New York, NY 10174
Phone: 212-867-1632; Fax: 212-867-1635
www.taiwan.net.tw

Taiwan Visitors Assn
555 Montgomery St
Suite 505
San Francisco, CA 94111
Phone: 415-989-8677; Fax: 415-989-7242
www.taiwan.net.tw

TAJIKISTAN

Tajikistan Embassy
1005 New Hampshire Ave
Washington, DC 20037
Phone: 202-223-6090; Fax: 202-223-6091
www.tjus.org

Tajikistan Permanent Mission to the UN
136 E 67th St

New York, NY 10021
Phone: 212-744-2196; Fax: 212-472-7645

TANZANIA

Tanzania Embassy
2139 R St NW
Washington, DC 20008
Phone: 202-939-6125; Fax: 202-797-7408
www.tanzaniaembassy-us.org

Tanzania Permanent Mission to the UN
201 E 42nd St
Suite 1700
New York, NY 10017
Phone: 212-972-9160; Fax: 212-682-5232

THAILAND

Tourism Authority of Thailand
611 N Larchmont Blvd
1st Fl
Los Angeles, CA 90004
Phone: 323-461-9814; Fax: 323-461-9834
Toll-free: 800-842-4526
www.tourismthailand.org

Tourism Authority of Thailand
61 Broadway
Suite 2810
New York, NY 10006
Phone: 212-432-0433; Fax: 212-269-2588
Toll-free: 800-842-4526
www.tourismthailand.org

Thailand Consulate General
700 N Rush St
Chicago, IL 60611
Phone: 312-664-3129; Fax: 312-664-3230
www.thaichicago.net

Thailand Consulate General
611 N Larchmont Blvd
2nd Fl
Los Angeles, CA 90004
Phone: 323-962-9574; Fax: 323-962-2128
www.thai-la.net

Thailand Consulate General
351 E 52nd St

New York, NY 10022
Phone: 212-754-1770; Fax: 212-754-1907
www.thaiconsulnewyork.com

Thailand Embassy
1024 Wisconsin Ave NW
Suite 401
Washington, DC 20007
Phone: 202-944-3600; Fax: 202-944-3611
www.thaiembdc.org

Thailand Permanent Mission to the UN
351 E 52nd St
New York, NY 10022
Phone: 212-754-2230; Fax: 212-688-3029

TIMOR-LESTE

Timor-Leste Embassy
4201 Massachusetts Ave NW
Suite 504
Washington, DC 20008
Phone: 202-966-3202; Fax: 202-966-3205

Timor-Leste Permanent Mission to the UN
866 UN Plaza
Suite 1201
New York, NY 10017
Phone: 212-759-3675; Fax: 212-759-4196
www.timor-leste-un.org

TOGO

Togo Embassy
2208 Massachusetts Ave NW
Washington, DC 20008
Phone: 202-234-4212; Fax: 202-232-3190

Togo Permanent Mission to the UN
112 E 40th St
New York, NY 10016
Phone: 212-490-3455; Fax: 212-983-6684

TONGA

Tonga Consulate General
360 Post St
Suite 604

San Francisco, CA 94108
Phone: 415-781-0365; Fax: 415-781-3964

Tonga Embassy
250 E 51st St
New York, NY 10022
Phone: 917-369-1025; Fax: 917-369-1024

Tonga Permanent Mission to the UN
250 E 51st St
New York, NY 10022
Phone: 917-369-1025; Fax: 917-369-1024

TRINIDAD AND TOBAGO

Trinidad & Tobago Consulate General
1000 Brickell Ave
Suite 800
Miami, FL 33131
Phone: 305-374-2199; Fax: 305-374-3199

Trinidad & Tobago Consulate General
475 5th Ave
4th Fl
New York, NY 10017
Phone: 212-682-7272; Fax: 212-986-2146

Trinidad & Tobago Embassy
1708 Massachusetts Ave NW
Washington, DC 20036
Phone: 202-467-6490; Fax: 202-785-3130

Trinidad & Tobago Permanent Mission to
the UN
820 2nd Ave
5th Fl
New York, NY 10017
Phone: 212-697-7620; Fax: 212-682-3580

TUNISIA

Tunisia Embassy
1515 Massachusetts Ave NW
Washington, DC 20005
Phone: 202-862-1850; Fax: 202-862-1858

Tunisia Permanent Mission to the UN
31 Beekman Pl
New York, NY 10022
Phone: 212-751-7503; Fax: 212-751-0569

TURKEY

Turkish Tourist Office
5055 Wilshire Blvd
Suite 850
Los Angeles, CA 90036
Phone: 323-937-8066; Fax: 323-937-1271
www.tourismturkey.org

Turkish Tourist Office
821 UN Plaza
1st Fl
New York, NY 10017
Phone: 212-687-2194; Fax: 212-599-7568
Toll-free: 877-367-8875
www.tourismturkey.org

Turkey Consulate General
360 N Michigan Ave
Suite 1405
Chicago, IL 60601
Phone: 312-263-0644; Fax: 312-263-1449
www.turkishembassy.org

Turkey Consulate General
1990 Post Oak Blvd
Suite 1300
Houston, TX 77056
Phone: 713-622-5849; Fax: 713-623-6639
Toll-free: 888-566-7656
www.turkishembassy.org

Turkey Consulate General
6300 Wilshire Blvd
Suite 2010
Los Angeles, CA 90048
Phone: 323-655-8832
Fax: 323-655-8681
www.turkishembassy.org

Turkey Consulate General
821 UN Plaza
5th Fl
New York, NY 10017
Phone: 212-949-0160; Fax: 212-983-1293
www.turkishconsulateny.org

Turkey Embassy
2525 Massachusetts Ave NW
Washington, DC 20008

Phone: 202-612-6700; Fax: 202-319-1639
www.turkishembassy.org

Turkey Permanent Mission to the UN
821 UN Plaza
10th Fl
New York, NY 10017
Phone: 212-949-0150; Fax: 212-949-0086
www.un.int/turkey

TURKMENISTAN

Turkmenistan Embassy
2207 Massachusetts Ave NW
Washington, DC 20008
Phone: 202-588-1500; Fax: 202-588-0697
www.turkmenistanembassy.org

Turkmenistan Permanent Mission to the UN
866 UN Plaza
Suite 424
New York, NY 10017
Phone: 212-486-8908; Fax: 212-486-2521

TURKS AND CAICOS ISLANDS

Turks & Caicos Islands Tourism Office
60 E 42nd St
Suite 2817
New York, NY 10165
Phone: 646-375-8830; Fax: 646-375-8835
Toll-free: 800-241-0824
www.turksandcaicostourism.com

TUVALU

Tuvalu Permanent Mission to the UN
800 2nd Ave
Suite 400-D
New York, NY 10017
Phone: 212-490-0534; Fax: 212-808-4975

UGANDA

Uganda Embassy
5911 16th St NW
Washington, DC 20011
Phone: 202-726-7100; Fax: 202-726-1727
www.ugandaembassy.com

Uganda Permanent Mission to the UN
336 E 45th St
New York, NY 10017
Phone: 212-949-0110; Fax: 212-687-4517

UKRAINE

Ukraine Consulate General
10 E Huron St
Chicago, IL 60611
Phone: 312-642-4388; Fax: 312-642-4385
www.ukrchicago.com

Ukraine Embassy
3350 M St NW
Washington, DC 20007
Phone: 202-333-0606; Fax: 202-333-0817
Toll-free: 800-779-8347
www.ukremb.com

Ukraine Permanent Mission to the UN
220 E 51st St
New York, NY 10022
Phone: 212-759-7003; Fax: 212-355-9455
www.un.int/ukraine

UNITED ARAB EMIRATES

United Arab Emirates Embassy
3522 International Ct NW
Washington, DC 20008
Phone: 202-243-2400; Fax: 202-243-2432
www.uae-embassy.org

United Arab Emirates Permanent Mission to
the UN
305 E 47th St
7th Fl
New York, NY 10017
Phone: 212-371-0480; Fax: 212-371-4923

UNITED KINGDOM

VisitBritain
551 5th Ave
Suite 701
New York, NY 10176
Phone: 212-986-2266; Fax: 212-986-1188

Toll-free: 800-462-2748
www.visitbritain.com

British-American Chamber of Commerce
Great Lakes Region
1120 Chester Ave
Suite 470
Cleveland, OH 44114
Phone: 216-621-0222; Fax: 216-696-2582
www.baccgl.org

British-American Business Council of Los
Angeles
11766 Wilshire Blvd
Suite 1230
Los Angeles, CA 90025
Phone: 310-312-1962; Fax: 310-312-1914
www.babcla.org

British-American Chamber of Commerce of
Miami
200 S Biscayne Blvd
Suite 4143
Miami, FL 33131
Phone: 305-377-0992; Fax: 305-448-7605

British-American Business Council
52 Vanderbilt Ave
20th Fl
New York, NY 10017
Phone: 212-661-4060; Fax: 212-661-4074
www.babc.org

British-American Chamber of Commerce of
San Francisco
235 Montogmery St
Suite 907
San Francisco, CA 94104
Phone: 415-296-8645; Fax: 415-296-9649
www.baccsf.org

United Kingdom Consulate General
Georgia Pacific Ctr 133 Peachtree St NE
Suite 3400
Atlanta, GA 30303
Phone: 404-954-7700; Fax: 404-954-7702
www.britainusa.com/atlanta

United Kingdom Consulate General
1 Memorial Dr
Suite 1500

Cambridge, MA 02142
Phone: 617-245-4500; Fax: 617-621-0220
www.britainusa.com/boston

United Kingdom Consulate General
400 N Michigan Ave
Suite 1300
Chicago, IL 60611
Phone: 312-970-3800; Fax: 312-970-3854
www.britainusa.com/chicago

United Kingdom Consulate General
1000 Louisiana St
Suite 1900
Houston, TX 77002
Phone: 713-659-6270; Fax: 713-659-7094
www.britainusa.com/houston

United Kingdom Consulate General
11766 Wilshire Blvd
Suite 1200
Los Angeles, CA 90025
Phone: 310-481-0031; Fax: 310-481-2960
www.britainusa.com/la

United Kingdom Consulate General
1001 Brickell Bay Dr
Suite 2800
Miami, FL 33131
Phone: 305-374-1522; Fax: 305-374-8196
www.britainusa.com/miami

United Kingdom Consulate General
845 3rd Ave
New York, NY 10022
Phone: 212-745-0200; Fax: 212-754-3062
www.britainusa.com/ny

United Kingdom Consulate General
1 Sansome St
Suite 850
San Francisco, CA 94104
Phone: 415-617-1300; Fax: 415-434-2018
www.britainusa.com/sf

United Kingdom Embassy
3100 Massachusetts Ave NW
Washington, DC 20008
Phone: 202-588-6500; Fax: 202-588-7870
www.britainusa.com/embassy

United Kingdom Permanent Mission to
the UN
885 2nd Ave
28th Fl
New York, NY 10017
Phone: 212-745-9200; Fax: 212-745-9316
www.ukun.org

URUGUAY

Uruguay Consulate General
1077 Ponce De Leon Blvd
Coral Gables, FL 33134
Phone: 305-443-9764; Fax: 305-443-7802

Uruguay Consulate General
420 Madison Ave
6th Fl
New York, NY 10017
Phone: 212-753-8581; Fax: 212-753-1603
www.conuruyork.org

Uruguay Consulate General
429 Santa Monica Blvd
Suite 400
Santa Monica, CA 90401
Phone: 310-394-5777; Fax: 310-394-5140

Uruguay Embassy
1913 'I' St NW
Washington, DC 20006
Phone: 202-331-1313; Fax: 202-331-8142
www.uruwashi.org

Uruguay Permanent Mission to the UN
866 UN Plaza
Suite 322
New York, NY 10017
Phone: 212-752-8240; Fax: 212-593-0935
www.un.int/uruguay

US VIRGIN ISLANDS

US Virgin Islands Dept of Tourism
245 Peachtree Center Ave
Suite MB-05
Atlanta, GA 30303
Phone: 404-688-0906; Fax: 404-525-1102
www.usvitourism.vi

US Virgin Islands Dept of Tourism
500 N Michigan Ave
Suite 2030
Chicago, IL 60611
Phone: 888-656-87834; Fax: 312-670-8788
www.usvitourism.vi

US Virgin Islands Dept of Tourism
2655 S LeJeune Rd
Suite 907
Coral Gables, FL 33134
Phone: 305-442-7200; Fax: 305-445-9044
Toll-free: 800-372-8784
www.usvitourism.vi

US Virgin Islands Dept of Tourism
3460 Wilshire Blvd
Suite 412
Los Angeles, CA 90010
Phone: 213-739-0138; Fax: 213-739-2005
www.usvitourism.vi

US Virgin Islands Dept of Tourism
1270 Ave of the Americas
Suite 2108
New York, NY 10020
Phone: 212-332-2222; Fax: 212-332-2223
www.usvitourism.vi

US Virgin Islands Dept of Tourism
PO Box 6400
Saint Thomas, VI 00804
Phone: 340-774-8784; Fax: 340-774-4390
Toll-free: 800-372-8784
www.usvitourism.vi

US Virgin Islands Dept of Tourism
444 N Capitol St NW
Suite 305
Washington, DC 20001
Phone: 202-624-3590; Fax: 202-624-3594
Toll-free: 800-372-8784
www.usvitourism.vi

UZBEKISTAN

American-Uzbekistan Chamber of
Commerce
1717 N St NW

Washington, DC 20036
Phone: 202-828-4111
www.aucconline.com

Uzbekistan Consulate General
801 2nd Ave
20th Fl
New York, NY 10017
Phone: 212-754-7403
www.uzbekconsulny.org

Uzbekistan Embassy
1746 Massachusetts Ave NW
Washington, DC 20036
Phone: 202-887-5300; Fax: 202-293-6804
www.uzbekistan.org

Uzbekistan Permanent Mission to the UN
801 2nd Ave
20th Fl
New York, NY 10017
Phone: 212-486-4242; Fax: 212-486-7998

VANUATU

Vanuatu Permanent Mission to the UN
800 E 2nd Ave
New York, NY 10004
Phone: 212-920-5700

VATICAN CITY
SEE HOLY SEE

VENEZUELA

Venezuelan-American Chamber of
Commerce of the US
2332 Galiano St
2nd Fl
Coral Gables, FL 33134
Phone: 305-728-7042; Fax: 305-728-7043
venezuelanchamber.org

Venezuela Consulate General
545 Boylston St
3rd Fl
Boston, MA 02116
Phone: 617-266-9368; Fax: 617-266-2350

Venezuela Consulate General
20 N Wacker Dr
Suite 1925
Chicago, IL 60606
Phone: 312-236-9655; Fax: 312-580-1010

Venezuela Consulate General
2925 Briarpark Dr
Suite 900
Houston, TX 77042
Phone: 713-974-0028; Fax: 713-974-1413
www.consulvenhou.org

Venezuela Consulate General
1101 Brickell Ave
Suite 901
Miami, FL 33131
Phone: 305-577-4214; Fax: 305-372-5167

Venezuela Consulate General
World Trade Ctr
2 Canal St Suite 2300
New Orleans, LA 70130
Phone: 504-522-3284; Fax: 504-522-7092

Venezuela Consulate General
7 E 51st St
New York, NY 10022
Phone: 212-826-1660; Fax: 212-644-7471

Venezuela Consulate General
311 California St
Suite 620
San Francisco, CA 94104
Phone: 415-955-1982; Fax: 415-955-1970

Venezuela Embassy
1099 30th St NW
Washington, DC 20007
Phone: 202-342-2214; Fax: 202-342-6820
www.embavenez-us.org

Venezuela Permanent Mission to the UN
335 E 46th St
New York, NY 10017
Phone: 212-557-2055; Fax: 212-557-3528
www.un.int/venezuela

VIETNAM

Vietnamese-American Chamber of
    Commerce of Hawaii
PO Box 2011
Honolulu, HI 96805
Phone: 808-545-1889; Fax: 808-734-2315
www.vacch.org

Vietnam Consulate General
1700 California St
Suite 430
San Francisco, CA 94109
Phone: 415-922-1707; Fax: 415-922-1848
www.vietnamconsulate-sf.org

Vietnam Embassy
1233 20th St NW
Suite 400
Washington, DC 20036
Phone: 202-861-0737; Fax: 202-861-0917
www.vietnamembassy.us

Vietnam Permanent Mission to the UN
866 UN Plaza
Suite 435
New York, NY 10017
Phone: 212-644-0594; Fax: 212-644-5732
www.un.int/vietnam

YEMEN

Yemen Embassy
2319 Wyoming Ave NW
Washington, DC 20008
Phone: 202-965-4760; Fax: 202-337-2017
www.yemenembassy.org

Yemen Permanent Mission to the UN
413 E 51st St
New York, NY 10022
Phone: 212-355-1730; Fax: 212-750-9613

ZAMBIA

Zambia Embassy
2419 Massachusetts Ave NW
Washington, DC 20008
Phone: 202-265-9717; Fax: 202-332-0826
www.zambiaembassy.org

Zambia Permanent Mission to the UN
237 E 52nd St
New York, NY 10022
Phone: 212-888-5770; Fax: 212-888-5213
www.un.int/zambia

ZIMBABWE

Zimbabwe Embassy
1608 New Hampshire Ave NW
Washington, DC 20009
Phone: 202-332-7100; Fax: 202-483-9326
www.zimbabwe-embassy.us

Zimbabwe Permanent Mission to the UN
128 E 56th St
New York, NY 10022
Phone: 212-980-9511; Fax: 212-308-6705

Appendix D
Tourism Information Sources
for Individual Festivals

The following lists contact information for organizations and groups that are affiliated with the events in this book. These tourism information sources are organized by the name of the entry.

AKWAMBO

Ghana Embassy in the United States
3512 International Dr NW
Washington, DC 20008
Phone: 202-686-4520; Fax: 202-686-4527
www.ghana-embassy.org

ALASITAS FAIR

Bolivia Embassy
3014 Massachusetts Ave NW
Washington, DC 20008
Phone: 202-483-4410; Fax: 202-328-3712
www.bolivia-usa.org

ALASKA DAY

Alaska Day Festival Committee
PO Box 1355
Sitka, AK 99835

Sitka Convention and Visitors Bureau
PO Box 1226
Sitka AK 99835
Phone: 907-747-5940
www.sitka.org

APACHE GIRLS' SUNRISE CEREMONY

Mescalero Apache Tribe
PO Box 227

Mescalero, NM 88340
Phone: 505-464-4494; Fax: 505-464-9191

ARBOR DAY

National Arbor Day Foundation
1100 Arbor Ave
Nebraska City, NE 68410
Phone: 402-474-5655
E-mail: info@arborday. org
www.arborday.org

ARCTIC WINTER GAMES

Arctic Winter Games International
    Committee
c/o 115 Copper Rd
Whitehorse, Yukon Y1A 2Z7
Canada
Phone: 867-668-8094; Fax: 867-667-2458
E-mail: gerry.thick@arcticwintergames.org
www.arcticwintergames.com

BAYOU CLASSIC

Grambling State University
403 Main St
Grambling, LA 71245
Phone: 318-247-3811, 800-569-4714
www.gram.edu

Southern University
J.S. Clark Administration Bldg.
4th Fl, President's Office
Baton Rouge, LA 70813
Phone: 225-771-4500
www.sus.edu

BERBER BRIDE FAIR

Moroccan National Tourist Office
20 E 46th St, Ste 1201
New York, NY 10017
Phone: 212-557-2520; Fax: 212-949-8148

BOSTON MARATHON

Boston Athletic Association
40 Trinity Place, 4th Fl
Boston, MA 02116
Phone: 617-236-1652; Fax: 617-236-4505
E-mail: info@baa.org
www.bostonmarathon.org

BRAEMAR
HIGHLAND GATHERING

Braemar Royal Highland Society
Coilacriech
Ballater, Scotland AB25 5UH
United Kingdom
Phone: 011-44-13397-55377
Fax: 011-44-13397-55377
E-mail: info@braemargathering.org
www.braemargathering.org

CHALMA PILGRIMAGE

Mexico Tourism Board
Viaducto Miguel Alemán No. 105
Col. Escandón
11800 Mexico, D.F. Mexico
Phone: 011-52-55-5278-4200
www.visitmexico.com

Mexico Tourism Board
400 Madison Ave, Ste 11C
New York, NY 10017
Phone: 212-308-2110; Fax: 212-308-9060

CINCO DE MAYO

Mexico Tourism Board
375 Park Ave
New York, NY 10152
Phone: 800-446-3942 or 212-308-2110
Fax: 212-308-9060
www.visitmexico.com

CONFEDERATE
MEMORIAL DAY

United Daughters of the Confederacy
328 North Blvd
Richmond, VA 23220-4009
Phone: 804-355-1636; Fax: 804-353-1396
E-mail:hqudc@rcn.com
www.hqudc.org

Sons of Confederate Veterans
PO Box 59
Columbia, TN 38402
Phone: 800-380-1896; Fax: 931-381-6712
www.scv.org

CROW FAIR

Crow Tribal Council
P. O. Box 159
Crow Agency, MT 59022
Phone: 406-638-2601; Fax: 406-638-7283

DAYTONA 500

Daytona International Speedway
1801 W International Speedway Blvd
Daytona Beach, FL 32114
Phone: 386-254-2700 (info.); 386-253-7223
(tickets)
www.daytonaintlspeedway.com

National Association for Stock Car Auto
Racing
1801 W International Speedway Blvd
Daytona Beach, FL 32114
Phone: 386-253-0611
www.nascar.com

EAGLE DANCE

Pueblo of Tesuque
Route 5, Box 360-T
Santa Fe, NM 87501
Phone: 505-983-2667; Fax: 505-982-2331

Pueblo of Jemez
PO Box 100
Jemez Pueblo, NM 87024
Phone: 505-834-7359; Fax: 505-834-7331

EARTH DAY

Earth Day Network
811 First Ave, Ste 454
Seattle, WA 98104
Phone: 206-876-2000; Fax: 206-876-2015
E-mail: earthday@earthday.net
www.earthday.net

FIESTA DE SANTA FE

Santa Fe Fiesta Council
PO Box 4516
Santa Fe, NM 87502
Phone: 505-988-7575

FLAG DAY

American Flag Foundation
PO Box 435
Riderwood, MD 21139
Phone: 410-563-FLAG (3524)
Fax: 410-821-1252
www.americanflagfoundation.org

Fort McHenry National Monument and
   Historic Shrine
National Park Service
End of South Fort Ave
Baltimore, MD 21230-5393
Phone: 410-962-4290; Fax: 410-962-2500
E-mail: FOMC_Superintendent@nps.gov
www.nps.gov/fomc

National Flag Day Foundation
PO Box 55
Waubeka, WI 53021-0055

Phone: 262-692-9111
www.nationalflagday.com

FLUTE CEREMONY

Hopi Cultural Center
PO Box 67
Second Mesa, AZ 86043
Phone: 520-734-2401; Fax: 520-734-6651
www.hopi.nsn.us

FORGIVENESS SUNDAY

Greek Orthodox Archdiocese of America
8 East 79th St
New York, NY 10075
Phone: 212-570-3500; Fax: 212-570-3569
www.goarch.org

Orthodox Church in America
PO Box 675
Syosset, NY 11791-0675
Phone: 516-922-0550; Fax: 516-922-0954
www.oca.org

FOURTH OF JULY

Fourth of July Celebrations Database
James R. Heintze, Librarian
American University Library
4400 Massachusetts Ave
Washington, DC 20016
Phone: 202-885-3205; Fax: 202-885-3226
E-mail: Jheintz@american.edu
www.american.edu/heintze/fourth.htm

GREAT ELEPHANT MARCH

Department of Tourism
Government of Kerala
Park View
Thiruvananthapuram, Kerala, India 695 033
Phone: 91-471-2321132; 1-800-425-4747
Fax: 91-471-2322279
E-mail: info@keralatourism.org;
   deptour@keralatourism.org
www.keralatourism.org

New York Regional Director, India Tourism
1270 Ave of the Americas, Ste 1808, 18th Fl
New York, NY 10020
Phone: 1-212-586-4901; Fax: 1-212-582-3274
E-mail: goitony@tourindia.com
www.incredibleindia.org

GUY FAWKES DAY

House of Commons Information Office
House of Commons
London SW1A 2T3T
United Kingdom
Phone: 011-44-20-7219-4272
Fax: 011-44-20-7219-5839
E-mail: hcinfo@parliament.uk
www.parliament.uk/documents/upload/
 g08.pdf

Gunpowder Plot Society
E-mail: society@gunpowder-plot.org
www.gunpowder-plot.org

HAJJ

Saudi Arabian Ministry of Pilgrimage
Omar Bin Al-Khatab St
Riyadh 11183
Saudi Arabia
Phone: 011-966-1-402-2200
Fax: 011-966-1-402-2555

HENLEY ROYAL REGATTA

Henley Royal Regatta
Henley-on-Thames
Oxfordshire RG9 2LY
United Kingdom
Phone: 011-44-1491-572-153
Fax: 011-44-1491-575-509
www.hrr.co.uk

HIDRELLEZ

Turkish Tourist Office
2525 Massachusetts Ave
Washington, DC 20008
Phone: 877-367-8875 or 202-612-6800

Fax: 202-319-7446
www.tourismturkey.org

INDIANAPOLIS 500

Indy Racing League, Public Relations
4565 West 16th St
Indianapolis, IN 46222
Phone: 317-484-6526; Fax: 317-484-6526
E-mail: imspr@brickyard.com
www.indy500.com

JUNETEENTH

Juneteenth.com
10001 Lake Forest Blvd, Ste 604
New Orleans, LA 70127
Phone: 504-245-7800
E-mail: mail@juneteenth.com
www.juneteenth.com

KATTESTOET

Toerisme Ieper
Grote Markt 34
Ieper, West Flanders 8900
Belgium
Phone: 011-32-57-22-85-84
Fax: 011-32-57-22-85-89

KENTUCKY DERBY

Churchill Downs
700 Central Ave
Louisville, KY 40208
Phone: 502-636-4400; Fax: 502-636-4430
www.kentuckyderby.com

Kentucky Derby Festival
1001 South Third St
Louisville, KY 40203
Phone: 502-584-6383
www.kdf.org

KERETKUN

Embassy of the Russian Federation
2650 Wisconsin Ave NW
Washington, DC 20007

Phone: 202-298-5700; Fax: 202-298-5735
www.russianembassy.org

KING KAMEHAMEHA DAY

King Kamehameha Celebration Commission
355 North King St
Honolulu, HI 96817
Phone: 808-586-0333; Fax (808) 586-0335

State Council on Hawaiian Heritage
PO Box 25142
Honolulu, HI 96825
Phone: 808-536-6540

KOREA NATIONAL FOUNDATION DAY

Embassy of the Republic of Korea in the
United States
2320 Massachusetts Ave, NW
Washington, DC 20008
Phone: 202-939-5654; Fax: 202-342-1597
www.koreaembassy.org

KWAKIUTL MIDWINTER CEREMONIES

Kwakiutl Nation
99 Tsakis Way
Fort Rupert Reserve, Box 1440
Port Hardy, BC V0N 2P0
Canada
Phone: 250-949-6012; Fax: 250-949-6066

LEIF ERIKSON DAY

Embassy of Iceland
1156 15th St NW, Ste 1200
Washington, DC 20005-1704
Phone: 202-265-6653; Fax: 202-265-6656
E-mail: icemb.wash@utn.stjr.is
www.iceland.org/us

Royal Norwegian Embassy
2720 34th St NW
Washington, DC 20008
Phone: 202-333-6000; Fax: 202-337-0870

E-mail: emb.washington@mfa.no
www.norway.org/Embassy

MARTIN LUTHER KING JR. DAY

The Martin Luther King Jr. Center for
Nonviolent Social Change, Inc.
449 Auburn Ave, NE
Atlanta, GA 30312
Phone: 404-526-8900
E-mail: information@thekingcenter.org
www.thekingcenter.com

MISS AMERICA PAGEANT

The Miss America Organization
Two Ocean Way, Ste 1000
Atlantic City, NJ 08401
Phone: 609-345-7571; Fax: 609-347-6079
E-mail: info@missamerica.org
www.missamerica.org

MIWOK BIG TIME

Federated Indians of the Graton Rancheria
6400 Redwood Dr, Suite 300
Rohnert Park, CA 94928
Phone: 707-566-2288; Fax: 707-566-2291
E-mail: coastmiwok@aol.com
www.gratonrancheria.com

Indian Grinding Rock State Historic Park
14881 Pine Grove-Volcano Rd
Pine Grove, CA 95665
Phone: 209-296-7488
www.parks.ca.gov/?page_id=553

NIMAN KACHINA FESTIVAL

Hopi Cultural Center
PO Box 67
Second Mesa, AZ 86043
Phone: 520-734-2401; Fax: 520-734-6651
www.hopi.nsn.us

ODUNDE FESTIVAL

Odunde, Inc.
PO Box 21748

Philadelphia, PA 19146
Phone: 215-732-8510; Fax: 215-732-8508
E-mail: odundefestival@gmail.com
www.odundeinc.org

OKTOBERFEST

Munich Tourist Office
Sendlinger Str. 1
Munich, Bavaria D-80331
Germany
Phone: 011-49-89-233-96500
Fax: 011-49-89-233-30233
www.oktoberfest.de

OLYMPIC GAMES

International Olympic Committee
Public Affairs
Chateau de Vidy
1007 Lausanne
Switzerland
Phone: 011-41-21-621-6511
Fax: 011-41-21-617-0313
www.olympic.org/

Olympic Museum
1, Quai d'Ouchy
CH-1001 Lausanne
Switzerland
Phone: 011-41-21-621-6511
Fax: 011-41-21-621-6512
E-mail: info@museum.olympic.org
www.museum.olympic.org

PINKSTER

Historic Hudson Valley
150 White Plains Rd
Tarrytown, NY 10591
Phone: 914-631-8200; Fax: 914-631-0089
E-mail: info@hudsonvalley.org
www.hudsonvalley.org

Philipsburg Manor
Route 9
Sleepy Hollow, NY 10591
Phone: 914-631-3992; Fax: 914-631-7740
www.hudsonvalley.org/content/view/14/44

POWAMÛ FESTIVAL

Hopi Cultural Center
PO Box 67
Second Mesa, AZ 86043
Phone: 520-734-2401; Fax: 520-734-6651
www.hopi.nsn.us

RIDVAN

National Spiritual Assembly of the Baha'is
of the U.S.
1233 Central St
Evanston, IL 60201
Phone: 847-733-3559; Fax: 847-733-3578
www.bahai.us

ROYAL ASCOT

Ascot Racecourse
Ascot
Berkshire SL5 7JX
United Kingdom
E-mail: enquiries@ascot.co.uk
www.ascot.co.uk

ROYAL NATIONAL EISTEDDFOD

Eisteddfod Genedlaethol Cymru
40 Parc Ty Glas
Llanisien
Cardiff, Wales CF4 5WU
Phone: 44(0)1222 763 777
Fax: 44(0)1222 763 737
E-mail: info@eisted3dfod.org.uk
www.eisteddfod.org.uk/english

SAN GENNARO FESTIVAL

Figli di San Gennaro, Inc.
Most Precious Blood Church
109 Mulberry St
New York, NY 10002
Phone: 212-226-6427
www.sangennaro.org

SAN JACINTO DAY

San Jacinto Monument and Museum of
    History
1 Monument Circle
La Porte, TX 77571-9585
Phone: 281-479-2421
E-mail: sjm@sanjacinto-museum.org
www.sanjacinto-museum.org

SEVILLE FAIR

Tourism Consortium
Bldg. Laredo Sq
San Francisco, 19 4a
Seville 41004 Spain
Phone: 011-34-954595288
Fax: 011-34-954595295
E-mail: turismo@sevilla.org
www.turismo.sevilla.org/paginas_en/
    portada. asp

Tourist Office of Spain
8383 Wilshire Blvd, Ste 960
Beverly Hills, CA 90211
Phone: 323-658-7188; Fax: 323-658-1061
www.okspain.org

SHALAKO CEREMONY

Pueblo Cultural Center
2401 12th St, NW
Albuquerque, NM 87104
Phone: 505-843-7270 or 800-766-4405
    (outside NM)
E-mail: info@indianpueblo.com
www.indianpueblo.org/ipcc

SOYALUNA

Hopi Cultural Center
PO Box 67
Second Mesa, AZ 86043
Phone: 520-734-2401; Fax: 520-734-6651
www.hopi.nsn.us

ST. CASIMIR'S DAY

Lithuania Embassy
2622 16th St NW

Washington, DC 20009
Phone: 202-234-5860; Fax: 202-328-0466
www.ltembassyus.org

SUPER BOWL SUNDAY

National Football League
410 Park Ave
New York, NY 10022
Phone: 212-758-1500; Fax: 212-758-1742
www.superbowl.com

TENJIN MATSURI

Osaka Convention and Tourism Bureau
5F Resona Semba Bldg
4-4-21, Minamisemba, Chuo-Ku
Osaka 542-0081 Japan
Phone: 011-81-6-6282-5911
Fax: 011-81-6-6282-5914
www.octb.jp/english

TOUR DE FRANCE

Le Société du Tour de France
2, rue Rouget de Lisle
Issy-Les-Moulineau 92135
France
www.letour.fr

URS OF DATA GANJ BAKHSH

Pakistan Embassy
2315 Massachusetts Ave NW
Washington, DC 20006
Phone: 202-452-6814; Fax: 202-452-6281
www.pakistanembassy.com

UTE BEAR DANCE

Southern Ute Tribal Council
PO Box 737
Ignacio, CO 81137
Phone: 970-563-0100
www.southern-ute.nsn.us

Ute Mountain Tribe
General Delivery
Towaoc, CO 81334

Phone: 970-565-3751; Fax: 970-565-7412
www.utemountainute.com

VASALOPPET

Vasaloppet Mora
Vasaloppets Hus
SE-792 32 Mora
Sweden
Phone: 011-46-250-392-00
Fax: 011-46-250-392-50
E-mail: info@vasaloppet.se
www.vasaloppet.se

WAMPANOAG POWWOW

Mashpee Wampanoag Tribal Council
483 Great Neck Rd South
PO Box 1048
Mashpee, MA 02649
Phone: 508-477-0208
www.mashpeewampanoagtribe.com

WATCH NIGHT

African American Odyssey: The Quest for
    Full Citizenship
National Digital Library
Library of Congress
101 Independence Ave, SE
Washington, DC 20540
Phone: 202-707-500
http://rs6.loc.gov/ammem/aaohtml/exhibit
    /aopart4.html

New Georgia Encyclopedia, Georgia
    Humanities Council
Main Library
University of Georgia
Athens, GA 30602
www.georgiaencyclopedia.org/nge/Article.
    jsp?id=h-520&hl=y

WESTMINSTER DOG SHOW

Westminster Kennel Club
149 Madison Ave, Ste 803
New York, NY 10016

Phone: 212-213-3165; Fax: 212-213-3270
www.westminsterkennelclub.org

WIANKI FESTIVAL OF WREATHS

Polish-American Arts Association
PO Box 9442
Washington, DC 20016
Phone: 203-437-9212 or 202-451-7498
www.paaa.us

WILD HORSE FESTIVAL

City of Haramachi
Postcord 975-8686
2-27 Motomachi
Haramachi-shi
Fukushima-ken, Japan
Phone: 011-81-244-22-2111
Fax: 011-81-244-24-5214

WIMBLEDON

The All England Lawn Tennis and Croquet
    Club
Church Rd
Wimbledon, London SW19 5AE
United Kingdom
Phone: 011-44-208-944-1066
Fax: 011-44-208-947-8752
E-mail: internet@aeltc.com
www.wimbledon.org

WORLD AIDS DAY

U.S. Department of Health and Human
    Services
200 Independence Ave SW
Washington, DC 20201
Phone: 202-619-0257; 877-696-6775
www.hhs.gov

World AIDS Campaign
Warmoesstraat 149-151
1012JC Amsterdam
The Netherlands
Phone: 011-31-20-616-9045
E-Mail: info@worldaidscampaign.org
www.worldaidscampaign.info

WORLD CUP SOCCER

Fédération Internationale de Football
    Association
FIFA-Strasse 20
PO Box 8044
Zurich, Switzerland
Phone: 011-41-43-222-7777
Fax: 011-41-43-222-7878
www.fifa.com

WORLD
ESKIMO-INDIAN OLYMPICS

World Eskimo-Indian Olympics, Inc.
PO Box 72433
Fairbanks, AK 99707-2433
Phone: 907-452-6646; Fax: 907-452-2422
E-mail: weio@weio.org
www.weio.org

WORLD SERIES

The Office of the Commissioner of Baseball
245 Park Ave, 31st Fl
New York, NY 10167
Phone: 212-931-7800
www.mlb.com

WUWUCHIM

Hopi Cultural Center
PO Box 67
Second Mesa, AZ 86043
Phone: 520-734-2401; Fax: 520-734-6651
www.hopi.nsn.us

YAQUI EASTER CEREMONY

Pascua Yaqui Tribe
7474 South Camino de Oeste
Tucson, AZ 85757
Phone: 520-883-5000 or 800-572-7282
Fax: 520-883-5014
E-mail: contact@pascuayaqui-nsn.gov
www.pascuayaquitribe.org

YEMANJA FESTIVAL

Brazil Embassy
3006 Massachusetts Ave, NW
Washington, DC 20008
Phone: 202-238-2700; Fax: 202-238-2827
www.brasilemb.org

Appendix E
Entries by Type

This appendix lists the entries in this volume by type of holiday. Some events may be listed under more than one category, as applicable. The holiday types are in this order:

> Ancient
>
> Calendar/Seasonal
>
> Folkloric
>
> Historic
>
> National
>
> Promotional
>
> Religious (organized alphabetically by entry name)
>
> Religious (organized alphabetically by religion)
>
> Sporting

ANCIENT

Beltane
Bouphonia
Compitalia
Dionysia
Floralia
Imbolc
Lemuralia
Lughnasa
Lupercalia
Mabon
October Horse Sacrifice
Parilia
Samhain
Saturnalia
Summer Solstice
Terminalia
Thesmophoria
Vernal Equinox
Winter Solstice

CALENDAR/SEASONAL

April Fools' Day
Autumn Equinox
Aztec New Fire Ceremony
Bella Coola (Nuxalk) Midwinter Rites
Beltane
Chinese New Year

Ching Ming
Chrysanthemum Festival
Chung Yeung
Chusok
Coptic New Year
Distaff Day
Dosmoche
Double Fifth
Galungan
Green Corn Dance
Hanami
Harvest Home Festival
Hidrellez
Higan
Hogmanay
Homowo
Incwala
Inti Raymi Festival
Iroquois Midwinter Ceremony
Kupalo Festival
Kwakiutl Midwinter Ceremonies
Lammas
Lantern Festival
Leap Year Day
Li Ch'un
Losar
Mabon
Martenitza
May Day
Mid-Autumn Festival
Midsummer Day
Miwok Big Time
Navajo Mountain Chant
Nawruz
New Yam Festival
New Year's Day
New Year's Eve
Nyepi
Obzinky
Odwira
Oktoberfest
Oshogatsu

Procession of the Swallow
Rocket Festival
Rosh Hashanah
Setsubun
Shalako Ceremony
Sol
Songkran
Soyaluna
Summer Solstice
Tano Festival
Tet
Tu Bishvat
Vaisakh
Vasant Panchami
Vernal Equinox
Winter Solstice
Wuwuchim

FOLKLORIC

Akwambo
Alasitas Fair
Aoi Matsuri
April Fools' Day
Berber Bride Fair
Candlemas
Chung Yeung
Chusok
Distaff Day
Double Fifth
Halloween
Hidrellez
Hina Matsuri
John Canoe Festival
Kattestoet
Kodomo-No-Hi
Lantern Festival
Luilak
Martenitza
Martinmas
Maslenitsa
Mid-Autumn Festival

Midsummer Day
Procession of the Swallow
Rocket Festival
Royal National Eisteddfod
Setsubun
Seville Fair
St. Urho's Day
Tanabata
Up Helly Aa
Valentine's Day
Walpurgis Night
Wianki Festival of Wreaths
Wind Festival

HISTORIC

Alaska Day
Bastille Day
Cinco de Mayo
Columbus Day
Confederate Memorial Day
Double Fifth
Fiesta de Santa Fe
Flag Day
Fourth of July
Gion Matsuri
Guy Fawkes Day
Hemis Festival
Hiroshima Peace Ceremony
Juneteenth
King Kamehameha Day
Kristallnacht
Leif Erikson Day
Lincoln's Birthday
Martin Luther King Jr. Day
Moors and Christians Fiesta
Oktoberfest
Pinkster
San Jacinto Day
Sennin Gyoretsu
Seville Fair
Shick-Shack Day

Thanksgiving
Veterans Day
Wampanoag Powwow
Washington's Birthday
Watch Night
Wild Horse Festival

NATIONAL

Bastille Day
Columbus Day
Fourth of July
Incwala
Indra Jatra
Korea National Foundation Day
Labor Day
Martin Luther King Jr. Day
Memorial Day
Queen's Birthday
St. George's Day
Thanksgiving
Veterans Day
Washington's Birthday

PROMOTIONAL

Academy Awards
Arbor Day
Earth Day
Father's Day
Kamakura Matsuri
Miss America Pageant
Mother's Day
Pushkar Mela
Sweetest Day
World AIDS Day

RELIGIOUS (ORGANIZED ALPHABETICALLY BY ENTRY NAME, FOLLOWED BY RELIGION)

Aboakyer Festival (Effutu)
Advent (Christian)

All Souls' Day (Christian)

Annunciation of the Blessed Virgin Mary, Feast of the (Christian)

Aoi Matsuri (Shinto)

Apache Girls' Sunrise Ceremony (Apache)

Ascension Day (Christian)

Ash Wednesday (Christian)

Ashura (Muslim)

Assumption of the Blessed Virgin Mary, Feast of the (Christian)

Athabascan Stickdance (Athabascan)

Awoojah (Yoruba)

Awuru Odo Festival (Igbo)

Bella Coola (Nuxalk) Midwinter Rites (Bella Coola)

Beltane (Neopagan)

Blessing of the Waters (Christian)

Burial of the Sardine (Christian)

Candlemas (Christian)

Carnival (Christian)

Chalma Pilgrimage

Christmas (Christian)

Christmas Eve (Christian)

Coptic New Year (Christian)

Corpus Christi, Feast of (Christian)

Dewali (Hindu)

Día de los Muertos (Aztec, Christian)

Dosmoche (Buddhist)

Durga Puja (Hindu)

Eagle Dance (various Native American)

Easter (Christian)

Easter Monday (Christian)

Ebisu Festival (Shinto)

Egungun Festival (Yoruba)

Ember Days (Christian)

Epiphany, Feast of the (Christian)

Esala Perahera (Buddhist, Hindu)

Exaltation of the Cross, Feast of the (Christian)

Feast of Fools (Christian)

Feast of the Dead (various Native American)

Flute Ceremony (Hopi)

Forgiveness Sunday (Christian)

Gai Jatra (Hindu)

Galungan (Hindu)

Ganesh Chaturthi (Hindu)

Ganna (Christian)

Gauri Festival (Hindu)

Gion Matsuri (Shinto)

Good Friday (Christian)

Great Elephant March (Hindu)

Green Corn Dance (various Native American)

Guru Nanak's Birthday (Sikh)

Hajj (Muslim)

Halashashti (Hindu)

Hanukkah (Jewish)

Hari-Kuyo (Shinto)

Hemis Festival (Buddhist)

Hidrellez (Muslim)

Higan (Buddhist)

Hola Mohalla (Sikh)

Holi (Hindu)

Holy Innocents' Day (Christian)

Homowo (Ga)

Hopi Snake Dance (Hopi)

Hungry Ghosts Festival (Buddhist, Taoist)

Id al-Adha (Muslim)

Id al-Fitr (Muslim)

Imbolc (Neopagan)

Indra Jatra (Hindu, Buddhist)

Iroquois Midwinter Ceremony (Iroquois)

Janmashtami (Hindu)

Kartika Snan (Hindu)

Kataklysmos Day (Christian)

Keretkun (Chukchi)

Kumbh Mela (Hindu)

Kwakiutl Midwinter Ceremonies (Kwakiutl)

Lag Ba-Omer (Jewish)
Laylat al-Bara'ah (Muslim)
Laylat al-Miraj (Muslim)
Laylat al-Qadr (Muslim)
Lazarus Saturday (Christian)
Lent (Christian)
Loi Krathong (Buddhist)
Losar (Buddhist)
Lotus, Birthday of the (Buddhist)
Lughnasa (Neopagan)
Mabon (Neopagan)
Magha Puja (Buddhist)
Mahavira Jayanti (Jain)
Martinmas (Christian)
Maskal (Christian)
Maslenitsa (Christian)
Maundy Thursday (Christian)
Mawlid al-Nabi (Muslim)
Michaelmas (Christian)
Mid-Lent Sunday (Christian)
Midsummer Day/St. John's Day
    (Christian)
Nachi No Hi Matsuri (Shinto)
Naga Panchami (Hindu)
Navajo Mountain Chant (Navajo)
Navajo Night Chant (Navajo)
New Yam Festival (Igbo, Yoruba)
Niman Kachina Festival (Hopi)
Obon Festival (Buddhist)
Odunde Festival (Ifa, Santeria, Yoruba)
Ogun Festival (Yoruba)
Onam (Hindu)
Our Lady of Guadalupe, Fiesta of
    (Christian)
Palm Sunday (Christian)
Paro Tsechu (Buddhist)
Paryushana (Jain)
Passover (Jewish)
Pentecost (Christian)
Pitra Paksa Festival (Hindu)
Plough Monday (Christian)
Pongal (Hindu)

Pooram (Hindu)
Posadas, Las (Christian)
Poson (Buddhist)
Powamû Festival (Hopi)
Purim (Jewish)
Pushkar Mela (Hindu)
Raksha Bandhan (Hindu, Buddhist)
Ram Navami (Hindu)
Ramadan (Muslim)
Rath Yatra (Hindu)
Reek Sunday (Christian)
Ridvan (Baha'i)
Rocket Festival (Buddhist)
Rogation Days (Christian)
Rosh Hashanah (Jewish)
Samhain (Neopagan)
San Gennaro Festival (Christian)
Saut d'Eau (Christian, Voodoo)
Shalako Ceremony (Zuni)
Shavuot (Jewish)
Shawnee Death Feast (Shawnee)
Shichi-Go-San (Shinto)
Shivaratri (Hindu)
Shrove Tuesday (Christian)
Simhat Torah (Jewish)
Songkran (Buddhist)
Soyaluna (Hopi)
St. Anthony of Padua, Feast of
    (Christian)
St. Barbara's Day (Christian)
St. Basil's Day (Christian)
St. Blaise's Day (Christian)
St. Bridget's Day (Christian)
St. Casimir's Day (Christian)
St. Catherine's Day (Christian)
St. Christopher's Day (Christian)
St. David's Day (Christian)
St. Elmo's Day (Christian)
St. Francis of Assisi, Feast of (Christian)
St. George's Day (Christian)
St. James the Apostle, Feast of
    (Christian)

St. Joseph's Day (Christian)
St. Lucy's Day (Christian)
St. Mennas's Day (Christian)
St. Patrick's Day (Christian)
St. Stephen's Day (Christian)
St. Swithin's Day (Christian)
St. Sylvester's Day (Christian)
St. Thomas the Apostle's Day (Christian)
Sukkot (Jewish)
Summer Solstice (Neopagan)
Sun Dance (various Native American)
Teej (Hindu)
Tenjin Matsuri (Shinto)
Thaipusam (Hindu)
Tihar (Hindu)
Timkat (Christian)
Tisha be-Av (Jewish)
Tod Kathin (Buddhist)
Tori-no-ichi (Shinto)
Tu Bishvat (Jewish)
Twelfth Night (Christian)
Urs of Data Ganj Bakhsh (Muslim)
Ute Bear Dance (Ute)
Vaisakh (Sikh, Hindu)
Vasant Panchami (Hindu)
Vata Savitri (Hindu)
Vegetarian Festival (Buddhist)
Vernal Equinox (Neopagan)
Vesak (Buddhist)
Waso (Buddhist)
Watch Night (Christian)
Winter Solstice (Neopagan)
Wuwuchim (Hopi)
Yaqui Easter Ceremony (Christian, Yaqui)
Yemanja Festival (Candomblé, Macumba)
Yom Kippur (Jewish)

RELIGIOUS (ORGANIZED ALPHABETICALLY BY RELIGION, FOLLOWED BY ENTRY NAME)

Baha'i
Ridvan

Buddhist
Dosmoche
Esala Perahera
Hemis Festival
Higan
Hungry Ghosts Festival
Indra Jatra
Loi Krathong
Losar
Lotus, Birthday of the
Magha Puja
Obon Festival
Paro Tsechu
Poson
Raksha Bandhan
Rocket Festival
Songkran
Tod Kathin
Vegetarian Festival
Vesak
Waso

Candomblé
Yemanja Festival

Christian
Advent
All Souls' Day
Annunciation of the Blessed Virgin Mary, Feast of the
Ascension Day
Ash Wednesday
Assumption of the Blessed Virgin Mary, Feast of the
Blessing of the Waters
Burial of the Sardine

Candlemas
Carnival
Christmas
Christmas Eve
Coptic New Year
Corpus Christi, Feast of
Día de los Muertos
Easter
Easter Monday
Ember Days
Epiphany, Feast of the
Exaltation of the Cross, Feast of the
Feast of Fools
Forgiveness Sunday
Ganna
Good Friday
Holy Innocents' Day
Kataklysmos Day
Lazarus Saturday
Lent
Martinmas
Maskal
Maslenitsa
Maundy Thursday
Michaelmas
Mid-Lent Sunday
Midsummer Day/St. John's Day
Our Lady of Guadalupe, Fiesta of
Palm Sunday
Pentecost
Plough Monday
Posadas, Las
Reek Sunday
Rogation Days
San Gennaro Festival
Saut d'Eau Pilgrimage
Shrove Tuesday
St. Anthony of Padua, Feast of
St. Barbara's Day
St. Basil's Day
St. Blaise's Day
St. Bridget's Day

St. Casimir's Day
St. Catherine's Day
St. Christopher's Day
St. David's Day
St. Elmo's Day
St. Francis of Assisi, Feast of
St. George's Day
St. James the Apostle, Feast of
St. Joseph's Day
St. Lucy's Day
St. Mennas's Day
St. Patrick's Day
St. Stephen's Day
St. Swithin's Day
St. Sylvester's Day
St. Thomas the Apostle's Day
Timkat
Twelfth Night
Watch Night
Yaqui Easter Ceremony

Chukchi
Keretkun

Effutu
Aboakyer Festival

Ga
Homowo

Hindu
Dewali
Durga Puja
Esala Perahera
Gai Jatra
Galungan
Ganesh Chaturthi
Gauri Festival
Great Elephant March
Halashashti
Holi
Indra Jatra
Janmashtami
Kartika Snan

Kumbh Mela
Naga Panchami
Onam
Pitra Paksa Festival
Pongal
Pooram
Pushkar Mela
Raksha Bandhan
Ram Navami
Rath Yatra
Shivaratri
Teej
Thaipusam
Tihar
Vaisaikh
Vasant Panchami
Vata Savitri

Ifa
Odunde Festival

Igbo
Awuru Odo Festival
New Yam Festival

Jain
Mahavira Jayanti
Paryushana

Jewish
Hanukkah
Lag Ba-Omer
Passover
Purim
Rosh Hashanah
Shavuot
Simhat Torah
Sukkot
Tisha be-Av
Tu Bishvat
Yom Kippur

Macumba
Yemanja Festival

Muslim
Ashura
Hajj
Hidrellez
Id al-Adha
Id al-Fitr
Laylat al-Bara'ah
Laylat al-Miraj
Laylat al-Qadr
Mawlid al-Nabi
Ramadan
Urs of Data Ganj Bakhsh

Native American
Apache Girls' Sunrise Ceremony
    (Apache)
Athabascan Stickdance (Athabascan)
Día de los Muertos (Aztec)
Bella Coola (Nuxalk) Midwinter Rites
    (Bella Coola)
Flute Ceremony (Hopi)
Hopi Snake Dance (Hopi)
Niman Kachina Festival (Hopi)
Powamû Festival (Hopi)
Soyaluna (Hopi)
Wuwuchim (Hopi)
Iroquois Midwinter Ceremony
    (Iroquois)
Kwakiutl Midwinter Ceremonies
    (Kwakiutl)
Navajo Mountain Chant (Navajo)
Navajo Night Chant (Navajo)
Shawnee Death Feast (Shawnee)
Ute Bear Dance (Ute)
Yaqui Easter Ceremony (Yaqui)
Shalako Ceremony (Zuni)
Eagle Dance (various Native American)
Feast of the Dead (various Native
    American)
Green Corn Dance (various Native
    American)
Sun Dance (various Native American)

Neopagan
Beltane
Imbolc
Lughnasa
Mabon
Samhain
Summer Solstice
Vernal Equinox
Winter Solstice

Santeria
Odunde Festival

Shinto
Aoi Matsuri
Ebisu Festival
Gion Matsuri
Hari-Kuyo
Nachi No Hi Matsuri
Shichi-Go-San
Tenjin Matsuri
Tori-no-ichi

Sikh
Guru Nanak's Birthday
Hola Mohalla
Vaisakh

Taoist
Hungry Ghosts Festival

Voodoo
Saut d'Eau

Yaqui
Yaqui Easter Ceremony

Yoruba
Awoojah
Egungun Festival
New Yam Festival
Odunde Festival
Ogun Festival

SPORTING

America's Cup
Arctic Winter Games
Bayou Classic
Boston Marathon
Braemar Highland Gathering
Daytona 500
Henley Royal Regatta
Iditarod
Indianapolis 500
Ironman Triathlon World Championship
Kentucky Derby
Masters Golf Tournament
Naadam
Olympic Games
Palio, Festival of the
Rose Bowl
Royal Ascot
San Fermin Festival
Super Bowl Sunday
Tour de France
Vasaloppet
Westminster Dog Show
Wimbledon
World Cup Soccer
World Eskimo-Indian Olympics
World Series

General Index

General Index

This subject index lists all countries, nationalities, names, symbols, customs, and other terms found in the text. It includes the names of holidays, festivals, and celebrations; people and organizations; place names (U.S. cities and states, as well as other nations); the names of houses of worship; monuments and historic sites; saints and deities; religious groups and denominations; titles of musical, cinematic, theatrical, and literary works; and other subject terms. Bolded page numbers indicate symbol and custom entries in the text.

abalone shell, 33, **34**
Abam Day, 656
Abboud, Joseph, 253
'Abd al-Malik ibn Arwan, Caliph, 490
abhishek, **538**
Aboakyer Festival, 1-3
Aboakyir. *See* Aboakyer Festival
Abraham, 324, 489, 490, 773, 774, 776. *See also* Hanukkah; Id al-Adha
abstaining from work, **763-64**
Academy Awards, 3-7
Academy of Motion Picture Arts and Sciences, 3-4, 6
acorns, 596-98
activism, AIDS, **1057**
Ada, 628
Adam, 323, 324
Adam and Eve, 51, 131, 274
Adams, John, 276, 277
Adams, John Quincy, 277, 280
Adonis, 625
Advent, 7-11, 127
    calendar, **9**

candle, **9,** 136
letters, **9**
plays, **10**
wreath, **10-11,** 136
Afghanistan, 623-27, 835
afikomen, **698-99,** 702
Africa
    Id al-Adha, 391-94
    Id al-Fitr, 394-98
    Laylat al-Miraj, 488-91
    Laylat al-Qadr, 492-95
    Odunde Festival, 652-53
    Ramadan, 752-57
African Americans in baseball, 1066
African-American holidays
    Juneteenth, 428-30
    Kwanzaa, 464
    Pinkster, 708-9
Agricolaus, 855
Ahasuerus, King, 733-34, 736
Ahiajoku, 628, 629
ahimsa, 694
Ahuehuete tree, 113
AIDS, 1056-57
Aillen, 789
airag, **606**

Bolded page numbers indicate symbol and custom entries in the text.

Bolded page numbers indicate symbol and custom entries in the text.

Bolded page numbers indicate symbol and custom entries in the text.

Beltane, 82-86, 1027, 1028
Beltane cake, **83-84,** 85
benching, **1041-42**
Benedict XIV, Pope, 109
Benten, 227
Berber Bride Fair, 86-89
Berkeley Hundred, 952
Berlin, Irving, 216
Berlinale, 5
Bermuda, 219, 743-46
berries, 523
Bessy, The, 715, **716**
best in show, **1042**
Betbeze, Yolande, 594
Bethlehem, 239, 240-41
beverages. *See also* food
  airag, 606
  ama-cha, 1021
  beer, 660-61
  chicha, 411-12
  milk, 408, 529, 818, 991
  mint julep, 442
  o-toso, 669
  Pimm's Cup No. 1, 354
  poteen, 892
  sherry, 811
  tea, 1021
  wassail, 136, 636
  wine, 699-700
Beyond-Being, 491
Bhai Tika, 961
Bhairava, 409, 410, 962
bhangra, **998-99**
Bhutan, 692-93
bicycle race, 975-77
Big Heads, **418**
Big Incwala, 404-5
Big Ten conference, 770
Big Time, 596
bikkurim, **818**
Bikrami calendar, 1110
bilberries, 523
bindhi, 963
birch branches, **506**
Bird Fair. *See* Tori-no-ichi
birds, **47-48,** 209-10, 210-11
Birthday of the Prophet. *See* Mawlid al-Nabi

Birthday of the Twelfth Imam. *See* Laylat al-Bara'ah
Bishamon, 227
Bi-Shevat. *See* Tu Bishvat
bitter herbs, **699**
black cat, **331**
black (color)
  All Souls' Day, 19
  Galungan, 290
  Gauri Festival, 297
  Good Friday, 303
  Hajj, 321
  Halloween, 329
  Kwanzaa, 464, 467
  Li Ch'un, 508, 510
  Shichi-Go-San, 822
  Tisha be-Av, 967
black drink, **312**
Black Hat Dance, 350, 693
black hat dancers, **196-97**
black stone, **323,** 324, 325
blackberries, **576**
blacksmiths, 657-58
blade ladder-climbing, **1015**
Blaise, Saint, 855-57
blanket toss, **444, 1062**
Blessed Sacrament, 167-68, 170, 171
blessing ceremony, **14**
Blessing of the Herbs, 60
Blessing of the Waters, 89-92, **237**
blessings (of)
  animals, **848, 875**
  cars, **868-69**
  draft horses, **856**
  holy images, **112**
  horses, **877-78**
  oils, **557-58**
  plough, **715**
  the sick, 33, **34**
  throat, **856**
blinis, **551-52**
blood, **528,** 650, **651**
blood sacrifice, 71, **72**
Bloomberg, Michael R., 253
blue (color)
  Advent, 7
  Fourth of July, 277

Bolded page numbers indicate symbol and custom entries in the text.

Callistus II, Pope, 868
Cambodia
    Tod Kathin, 970-72
    Waso, 1033-36
Camel Fair, 738-41
camel trading, **740**
camellia, **670**
camels, 738-41
Campbell, Sir Malcolm, 177-78
Canada
    Arctic Winter Games, 42-45
    Bella Coola (Nuxalk) Midwinter Rites, 79-82
    Caribou Carnival, 432
    Corpus Christi, Feast of, 167-72
    Epiphany, Feast of the, 238
    Feast of the Dead, 257-59
    Iroquois Midwinter Ceremony, 416-21
    Kwanzaa, 464-68
    Labor Day, 469-72
    Leif Erikson Day, 500-502
    Martenitza, 539-41
    Oktoberfest, 659-62
    Queen's Birthday, 743-46
    St. Stephen's Day, 896-99
    Thanksgiving, 951-57
    Veterans' Day, 1023-25
candle holder, **465**
candlelight vigils, **455**
Candlemas, 20, 103-6, 135
candles
    Advent, 9
    All Souls' Day, **20**
    Candlemas, **104-5**
    Christmas Eve, **139**
    Easter, 219
    Saturnalia, **798**
    Simhat Torah, **835-36**
    St. Blaise's Day, **857**
    St. Lucy's Day, **887**
    Waso, **1035**
Candomblé, 1078-79
candy, 624, 823, **927-28**
candy cane, **128**
canes, 33, **34**
Cannes Film Festival, 5
Cannibal Society, 462
Canoe, John, **427**

Cape Cod Indians, 1029
Capitanos, **684**
Car Festival. *See* Rath Yatra
carbo-loading party, **415**
cards
    Christmas, 128-29
    New Year's Day, 128-29
    Shanah Tovah, 775
    Sweetest Day, **928**
    Valentine, 1003-4
Caribbean Islands
    Carnival, 106-11
    Kwanzaa, 464-68
Caribou Carnival, 432
carline, 84, **85**
carlings, 584
Carlos III, King, 100
Carman, 522
carnation, **603-4**
Carnival, 99-100, 106-11, 550-51
Carnival king, **108-9**
carols, 127, 128, 129-30, 874
carp, **449-50**
cars, 868-69
casetas, **810**
Casimir Fair, **862-63**
Casimir IV, King, 861
Casimir, Saint, 861-63
Caspar, 239
Castor and Pollux, 873
Catesby, Robert, 317, 318
Catherine bonnet, **865**
Catherine, Saint, 864-66
Catherine wheel, 864, **865-66**
cats, 331, 438-39, **439,** 440, 507, 888
cattail pollen, 33, **34**
Cattern cake, **866**
Cay Neu, **947**
Cayuga Indians, 417
celebrations, Juneteenth, **430**
Celts
    Beltane, 82-83
    cats, 331
    goblins, 333
    Lughnasa, 521-22
    Mabon, 531-34
    Samhain, 330-31

Bolded page numbers indicate symbol and custom entries in the text.

Bolded page numbers indicate symbol and custom entries in the text.

Bolded page numbers indicate symbol and custom entries in the text.

Bolded page numbers indicate symbol and custom entries in the text.

Bolded page numbers indicate symbol and custom entries in the text.

Bolded page numbers indicate symbol and custom entries in the text.

Bolded page numbers indicate symbol and custom entries in the text.

Bolded page numbers indicate symbol and custom entries in the text.

Bolded page numbers indicate symbol and custom entries in the text.

Bolded page numbers indicate symbol and custom entries in the text.

Bolded page numbers indicate symbol and custom entries in the text.

Bolded page numbers indicate symbol and custom entries in the text.

Bolded page numbers indicate symbol and custom entries in the text.

Bolded page numbers indicate symbol and custom entries in the text.

Bolded page numbers indicate symbol and custom entries in the text.

Bolded page numbers indicate symbol and custom entries in the text.

Bolded page numbers indicate symbol and custom entries in the text.

new moon, **756**
New Orleans, Louisiana, 77-79, 108, 109, 110
New Yam Festival, 627-29
New Year. *See* Nawruz
New Year of the Trees. *See* Tu Bishvat
New Year prints, **119**
New Year's Day, 37, 126, 629-34
    baby, **631**
    first-footing, **631-32**
    football games, **632**
    gifts, **632**
    pig, **632**
    resolutions, **632-33**
New Year's Day in Thailand. *See* Songkran
New Year's Eve, 634-37, 1036-37
    "Auld Lang Syne," **635**
    noisemaking, **636**
    old man, **636**
    wassail bowl, **636**
New Year's Eve in Scotland. *See* Hogmanay
New Year's wisp, **368-69**
New York
    Green Corn Dance, 310-13
    Iroquois Midwinter Ceremony, 416-21
    Pinkster, 707-9
    Sweetest Day, 927-28
New York City, 212
    Columbus Day parade, 158-59
    San Gennaro Festival, 792-95
    Westminster Dog Show, 1040-43
New York Giants, 1065
New York Jets, 924
New York Metropolitans, 1065
New York Yacht Club, 23, 24, 25
New Zealand
    America's Cup, 25
    Guy Fawkes Day, 316-19
Newby-Fraser, Paula, 414
Newfoundland, 500
Nguzo Saba, **467**
nian monster, 116, **119-20**
Nicholas, Saint, 134, 140-41, 141-42
Nicklaus, Jack, 554
Nigeria
    Awuru Odo Festival, 69-70
    Egungun Festival, 229-31
    Ogun Festival, 656-59

Night Chant, 619-22
Night in Muzdalifa, 326
Night of Broken Glass. *See* Kristallnacht
Night of Deliverance. *See* Laylat al-Bara'ah
Night of Destiny. *See* Laylat al-Bara'ah; Laylat al-Qadr
Night of Fate. *See* Laylat al-Bara'ah
Night of Forgiveness. *See* Laylat al-Bara'ah
Night of Power. *See* Laylat al-Qadr
Night of Record. *See* Laylat al-Bara'ah
Night of the Dead, 185
Nightway. *See* Navajo Night Chant
Nihangs, **371**
Nike, 127
Nikko, Japan, 803-6
Nila, 244
Nile, 237
Niman Kachina Festival, 637-40
Nine Emperor Gods, 1014-16
Nineteen-day Feast, 1119
Nixon, John, 279
Nixon, Richard, 252
No Ruz. *See* Nawruz
Noah, 36, 239, 436
Noah's ark, 55
Noäkxnim, 80
Noche de los Muertos, 185
noisemakers, **736**
noisemaking, **369, 636, 642**
Norsemen, 142
North Africa, 916-20
North America
    New Year's Day, 629-34
    New Year's Eve, 634-37
    Sun Dance, 920-23
North Korea, 451-53
North Wales, 782-85
Northern Dancer, 441
Northern Ireland, 24, 40. *See also* Britain; British Isles; England; Great Britain; Ireland; Scotland; United Kingdom; Wales
Northwest Territories, 42
Norway
    hanging herbs, 202
    Leif Erikson Day, 500-502
    Michaelmas, 574-77
    Midsummer Day, 588

Bolded page numbers indicate symbol and custom entries in the text.

Bolded page numbers indicate symbol and custom entries in the text.

Bolded page numbers indicate symbol and custom entries in the text.

Bolded page numbers indicate symbol and custom entries in the text.

Bolded page numbers indicate symbol and custom entries in the text.

Bolded page numbers indicate symbol and custom entries in the text.

         Bolded page numbers indicate symbol and custom entries in the text.

    Bolded page numbers indicate symbol and custom entries in the text.

Bolded page numbers indicate symbol and custom entries in the text.

Bolded page numbers indicate symbol and custom entries in the text.

Bolded page numbers indicate symbol and custom entries in the text.

Bolded page numbers indicate symbol and custom entries in the text.